REEDS

Practical Boat Ov

BRITAIN'S BEST-SELLING BOA

SMALL C
ALMAN

2016

EDITORS

Perrin Towler & Mark Fishwick

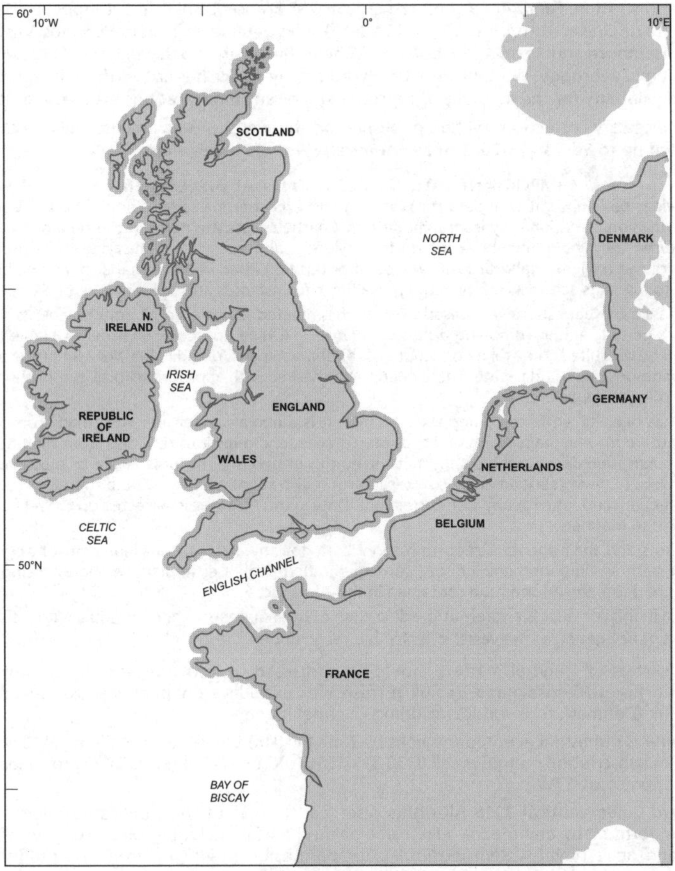

THE UNITED KINGDOM AND IRELAND PLUS DENMARK TO THE GIRONDE

PLEASE SEE IMPORTANT SAFETY NOTE ON PAGE 2

REEDS
Practical Boat Owner
BRITAIN'S BEST-SELLING BOATING MAGAZINE
SMALL CRAFT ALMANAC
2016

Editors: Perrin Towler & Mark Fishwick

The Editors would like to thank the many official bodies who have kindly provided essential information in the preparation of this Almanac. They include the UK Hydrographic Office, Trinity House, Northern Lighthouse Board, Irish Lights, HM Nautical Almanac Office, HM Stationery Office, HM Customs, Meteorological Office and the Maritime and Coastguard Agency.

Information from the Admiralty List of Lights, Admiralty Tide Tables and the Admiralty List of Radio Signals is reproduced with the permission of the UK Hydrographic Office and the Controller of HMSO. Extracts from the following are published by permission of the Controller of HM Stationery Office: International Code of Signals, 1969; Meteorological Office Weather Services for Shipping. Phases of the Moon and Sun/Moon rising and setting times are included by permission of HM Nautical Almanac Office. UK and Foreign tidal predictions are supplied by the UK Hydrographic Office, Taunton TA1 2DN. Acknowledgment is also made to the following authorities for permission to use tidal predictions stated: Danish Safety Administration, Farvandsvæsnet: Esbjerg. SHOM, France: Dunkerque, Dieppe, Le Havre, Cherbourg, St Malo, Brest, Pointe de Grave, Authorisation (No 152/2015). Rijkswaterstaat, The Netherlands: Vlissingen, and Hoek van Holland. BSH, Hamburg and Rostock: Helgoland, Wilhelmshaven and Cuxhaven (BSH 11123/2008-07). Vlaamse Hydrografie, Belgium: Zeebrugge. **Warning**: The UK Hydrographic Office has not verified the reproduced data and does not accept any liability for the accuracy of reproduction or any modifications made thereafter.

Corrections Any necessary corrections will be published on the website www.reedsalmanacs.co.uk. Data in this almanac is corrected up to Edition 25/2015 of the ***Admiralty Notices to Mariners.***

Correspondence Letters on general matters should be addressed to info@reedsalmanacs.co.uk, or on nautical issues to editor.britishisles@reedsalmanacs.co.uk (British Isles excluding Channel Islands) or editor.continental@reedsalmanacs.co.uk (Denmark to Gironde, including Channel Islands).

Practical Boat Owner is published every four weeks by Time Inc (UK) Ltd, Blue Fin Building, 110 Southwark Street, London SE1 0SU. For subscription enquiries call 0330 333 4555 (UK) or +44 (0)330 333 0233 (overseas), quoting code 17W, or visit www.pbo.co.uk/17W.

ISBN 978 1 4729 1944 1. A CIP catalogue record for this book is available from the British Library.

Almanac manager: Chris Stevens
Cartography & production: Chris Stevens

Adlard Coles Nautical
50 Bedford Square, London WC1B 3DP
Tel: +44 (0)207 631 5600 www.reedsalmanacs.co.uk

Foreword

Welcome to the *PBO Small Craft Almanac 2016*. Made using the same trusted data as published in the full-size Reeds Almanac, this handy volume is many leisure boaters' first port of call for tidal data.

Covering all the ports you're likely to visit on a summer cruise from the UK, extending into France, Belgium, Germany, Denmark and the Netherlands, complete with tidal atlases for most areas, the *PBO Small Craft Almanac* contains all you need to get your tides right – including tidal gate advice for major races. But that's not all.

There's waypoint data and pilotage information for major marks, hazards and port entrances, contact details for local harbour authorities and marinas, safety checklists and information on how to obtain and interpret weather forecasts. With all this and more in one compact source, updated monthly via our website www.pbo.co.uk, this is a book no cruiser can afford to be without.

Together with the editors at Reeds, all of us at *Practical Boat Owner* wish you fair winds and sunny skies for the 2016 season.

David Pugh
Editor
Practical Boat Owner
Britain's biggest-selling boating magazine

Contents

ABBREVIATIONS

AC, ACA	Admiralty chart, chart agent
AC	Shore power (electrical)
ACN	Adlard Coles Nautical
Al	Alternating lt
ALL	Admiralty list of lights
ALRS	Admiralty list of radio signals
ASD	Admiralty sailing directions (Pilot)
ATT	Admiralty tide tables
ATT	Atterisage (landfall/SWM) buoy
Bcn, Bn	Beacon
Bkwtr	Breakwater
BST	British summer time (DST)
CD	Chart datum
Cf	Compare, cross-refer to
CG	Coastguard
Ch	Channel (VHF)
chan.	Channel (navigational)
COG	Course over the ground
CROSS	Centre régional opérationnel de surveillance et sauvetage (MRCC)
CRS	Coast radio station(s)
DF	Direction finding
Dia	Diaphone (fog signal)
Dir Lt	Directional light
DSC	Digital selective calling
DST	Daylight saving time
DZ	Danger zone (buoy)
E	East
ECM	East cardinal mark (buoy/beacon)
ED	Existence doubtful, European datum
EPIRB	Emergency pos'n indicating radio bn
F	Fixed light. Beaufort wind force
FFL	Fixed and flashing lt
Fl	Flashing light
FM	Frequency modulation
FV	Fishing vessel
G	Green. Gravel
GMDSS	Global maritime distress & safety system
H, Hrs, h	Hour(s)
H24	Continuous
HAT	Highest astronomical tide
Hbr	Harbour
Hd	Head, headland
HF	High frequency
HJ	Day service, sunrise to sunset
HO	Office hours, Hydrographic office
ht	Height
HW	High water
HX	No fixed hours
Hz	Hertz
IALA	Int'l association of lt ho authorities
IDM	Isolated danger mark (buoy/bcn)
IMO	Int'l maritime organisation
Inmarsat	Int'l maritime satellite system
IPTS	Int'l port traffic signals
Is, I	Island, Islet
Iso	Isophase light
ITZ	Inshore traffic zone
Kn	Knot(s)
Lanby	Large automatic navigational buoy
Lat	Latitude
LB	Lifeboat
Ldg	Leading (lt)
LF	Low frequency
Long	Longitude
LT	Local time
Lt(s)	Light(s)
Lt F	Light float
Lt Ho	Lighthouse
Lt V	Light vessel
LW	Low water
M	Sea mile(s)
m	Metre(s)
MCA	Maritime & Coastguard Agency
Météo	Météorologie/weather
MF	Medium frequency
MHWN	Mean HW neaps
MHWS	Mean HW springs
MHz	Megahertz
MLWN	Mean LW neaps
MLWS	Mean LW springs
MMSI	Maritime mobile service identity
Mo	Morse
MRCC	Maritime rescue co-ordination centre
MRSC	Maritime rescue sub-centre (not in UK)
MSI	Maritime safety information
N	North
NCM	North cardinal mark (buoy/bcn)
Oc	Occulting light
PHM	Port-hand mark (buoy/bcn)
Pt(e), (a)	Point(e), Punta
Q	Quick flashing
R	Red. River
Ra	Coast radar station
Racon	Radar transponder beacon
RG	Emergency RDF station
R/T	Radiotelephony
S	South
s	second(s) of time
SAR	Search and rescue
SCM	South cardinal mark (buoy/bcn)
SHM	Starboard-hand mark (buoy/bcn)
Sig Stn	Signal station
SMS	Short message service (texting)
SNSM	Société nationale de sauvetage en-mer (French LB service)
SOG	Speed over the ground
SOLAS	Safety of life at sea (Convention)
SPM	Special mark (buoy/bcn)
SRR	SAR Region
SSB	Single sideband (radio)
Stn	Station
SWM	Safe water mark, landfall buoy
Tfc	Traffic
TSS	Traffic separation scheme
UQ	Ultra quick flashing lt
UT	Universal time
VHF	Very high frequency
VNF	Voie navigable de France (canals)
VQ	Very quick flashing lt
VTS	Vessel traffic service
W	West, White
WCM	West cardinal mark (buoy/bcn)
WGS	World geodetic system (datum)
WIP	Work in progress
WPT	Waypoint
Y	Yellow, orange, amber

GENERAL VOCABULARY. See also weather vocabulary on page 106

ENGLISH	GERMAN	FRENCH	DUTCH
ASHORE			
Ashore	An Land	A terre	Aan land
Airport	Flughafen	Aéroport	Vliegveld
Bank	Bank	Banque	Bank
Boathoist	Bootskran	Travelift	Botenlift
Boatyard	Bootswerft	Chantier naval	Jachtwerf
Bureau de change	Wechselstelle	Bureau de change	Geldwisselkantoor
Bus	Bus	Autobus	Bus
Chandlery	Yachtausrüster	Shipchandler	Scheepswinkel
Chemist	Apotheke	Pharmacie	Apotheek
Dentist	Zahnarzt	Dentiste	Tandarts
Doctor	Arzt	Médecin	Dokter
Engineer	Motorenservice	Ingénieur/mécanique	Ingenieur
Ferry	Fähre	Ferry/transbordeur	Veer/Pont
Garage	Autowerkstatt	Station service	Garage
Harbour	Hafen	Port	Haven
Hospital	Krankenhaus	Hôpital	Ziekenhuis
Mast crane	Mastenkran	Grue	Masten kraan
Post office	Postamt	Bureau de poste/PTT	Postkantoor
Railway station	Bahnhof	Gare de chemin de fer	Station
Sailmaker	Segelmacher	Voilier	Zeilmaker
Shops	Geschäfte	Boutiques	Winkels
Slip	Slip	Cale	Helling
Supermarket	Supermarkt	Supermarché	Supermarkt
Taxi	Taxi	Taxi	Taxi
Village	Ort	Village	Dorp
Yacht club	Yachtclub	Club nautique	Jacht club
NAVIGATION			
Abeam	Querab	A côté	Naast
Ahead	Voraus	Avant	Voor
Astern	Achteraus	Arrière	Achter
Bearing	Peilung	Cap	Peiling
Buoy	Tonne	Bouée	Boei
Binoculars	Fernglas	Jumelles	Verrekijker
Channel	Kanal	Chenal	Kanaal
Chart	Seekarte	Carte	Zeekaart
Compass	Kompass	Compas	Kompas
Compass course	Kompass Kurs	Cap du compas	Kompas koers
Current	Strömung	Courant	Stroom
Dead reckoning	Koppelnavigation	Estime	Gegist bestek
Degree	Grad	Degré	Graden
Deviation	Deviation	Déviation	Deviatie
Distance	Entfernung	Distance	Afstand
Downstream	Flußabwärts	En aval	Stroom afwaards
East	Ost	Est	Oost
Ebb	Ebbe	Jusant	Eb
Echosounder	Echolot	Sondeur	Dieptemeter
Estimated position	Gegißte Position	Point estimé	Gegiste positie
Fathom	Faden	Une brasse	Vadem
Feet	Fuß	Pieds	Voet
Flood	Flut	Flot	Vloed
Handbearing compass	Handpeilkompass	Compas de relèvement	Handpeil kompas

ENGLISH	GERMAN	FRENCH	DUTCH
Harbour guide	Hafenhandbuch	Guide du port	Havengids
High water	Hochwasser	Pleine mer	Hoog water
Latitude	Geographische Breite	Latitude	Breedte
Leading lights	Feuer in Linie	Alignement	Geleide lichten
Leeway	Abdrift	Dérive	Drift
Lighthouse	Leuchtturm	Phare	Vuurtoren
List of lights	Leuchtfeuer Verzeichnis	Liste des feux	Lichtenlijst
Log	Logge	Loch	Log
Longitude	Geographische Länge	Longitude	Lengte
Low water	Niedrigwasser	Basse mer	Laag water
Metre	Meter	Mètre	Meter
Minute	Minute	Minute	Minuut
Nautical almanac	Nautischer Almanach	Almanach nautique	Almanak
Nautical mile	Seemeile	Mille nautique	Zeemijl
Neap tide	Nipptide	Marée de morte-eau	Dood tij
North	Nord	Nord	Noord
Pilot	Lotse	Pilote	Loods/Gids
Pilotage book	Handbuch	Instructions nautiques	Vaarwijzer
RDF	Funkpeiler	Radio gonio	Radio richtingzoeker
Radar	Radar	Radar	Radar
Radio receiver	Radio, Empfänger	Réceptor radio	Radio ontvanger
Radio transmitter	Sender	Emetteur radio	Radio zender
River outlet	Flußmündung	Embouchure	Riviermond
South	Süd	Sud	Zuid
Spring tide	Springtide	Marée de vive-eau	Springtij/ springvloed
Tide	Tide, Gezeit	Marée	Getijde
Tide tables	Tidenkalender	Annuaire des marées	Getijdetafel
True course	Wahrer Kurs	Vrai cap	Ware Koers
Upstream	Flußaufwärts	En amont	Stroom opwaards
VHF	UKW	VHF	Marifoon
Variation	Mißweisung	Variation	Variatie
Waypoint	Wegpunkt	Point de rapport	Waypoint/Route punt
West	West	Ouest	West
OFFICIALDOM			
Certificate of registry	Schiffszertifikat	Acte de franchisation	Zeebrief
Check in	Einklarieren	Enregistrement	Check-in
Customs	Zoll	Douanes	Douane
Declare	Verzollen	Déclarer	Aangeven
Harbour master	Hafenmeister	Capitaine du port	Havenmeester
Insurance	Versicherung	Assurance	Verzekering
Insurance certificate	Versicherungspolice	Certificat d'assurance	Verzekeringsbewijs
Passport	Paß	Passeport	Paspoort
Police	Polizei	Police	Politie
Pratique	Verkehrserlaubnis	Pratique	Verlof tot ontscheping
Prohibited area	Sperrgebiet	Zone interdite	Verboden gebied
Register	Register	Liste de passagers	Register
Ship's log	Logbuch	Livre de bord	Logboek
Ship's papers	Schiffspapiere	Papiers de bateau	Scheepspapieren
Surveyor	Gutachter	Expert maritime	Opzichter

Chapter 1 – Navigation

PASSAGE PLANNING AND SOLAS V

All passages by any vessel that goes to sea *must* be planned. 'Going to sea' is defined as proceeding beyond sheltered waters. Even in very familiar waters every passage, however short, should be properly planned. Before you set sail you need to determine where you are going, how to get there and what factors may influence the plan.

Full passage planning requirements may be found in Chapter V of the International Convention for Safety of Life at Sea (SOLAS), but more digestible guidance for small craft is in the MCA's Pleasure Craft Information Pack at: **www.dft.gov.uk/mca/pleasure_craft_information_packdec07-2.pdf.**

Although the passage plan does not have to be recorded on paper, in the event of legal action a written plan is clear proof that the required planning has been completed; it can also be referred to during the passage. A suggested passage planning form is overleaf. When completed this would constitute, with due consideration of the points below, a reasonable passage plan. The blank form may be photocopied and modified to suit individual needs.

Although spot checks on small craft are unlikely, the MCA could, following an accident or incident, take action under the Merchant Shipping Act if it could be proved that the skipper did not have a reasonable passage plan.

Passage planning considerations

All passage plans should at least consider the following:

- **Weather.** Before setting out check the weather forecast and know how to get regular updates during the passage.
- **Tides.** Check tidal predictions and determine if there are any limiting depths at your port of departure, during the passage and at the port of arrival (and at alternative ports, if applicable). Tidal streams will almost certainly affect the plan.
- **Vessel.** Confirm she is suitable for the intended trip, is properly equipped, and has sufficient fuel, water and food on board.
- **Crew.** Take into account your crew's experience, expertise and stamina. Cold, tiredness and seasickness can be debilitating – and skippers are not immune.
- **Navigation.** Make sure you are aware of all navigational dangers by consulting up to date charts, pilot books and this Almanac. Never *rely* on GPS for fixing your position.
- **Contingency plan.** Consider bolt holes which can be entered *safely* in an emergency, if the weather deteriorates or mutiny threatens.
- **Information ashore.** Make sure someone ashore knows your plans, when they should become concerned and what action to take if necessary. Be sure to join the Coastguard Voluntary Identification Scheme (Form CG66).

"The winds and waves are always on the side of the ablest navigators." (Edward Gibbon)

Passage planning form

The following notes amplify some of the items on the form:

- The height of tide affects the depth, and tidal streams may hinder sensible progress – off headlands or in narrow passages, for example. On longer passages, which cross main tidal streams, determine the net effect of the streams and calculate a course to steer – more efficient than trying to maintain a track.
- Note which harbours and marinas have restricted times of access due to bars, sills or locks. These may affect your ETA and, probably, your ETD.
- Prepare a detailed pilotage plan for entry/exit of any unfamiliar harbour; a sketch is invaluable.
- Squinting into the setting sun can make pilotage very difficult. At night, light from a full moon can help enormously.
- Know when you expect to see lights at night – a good check on progress. See table of dipping/rising lights.
- Look up and note relevant VHF channels and/or phone numbers for ports of departure and arrival.

PASSAGE PLANNING FORM

DATE: 19/08/16 FROM: Gosport TO: Eastbourne DIST: 55 M

ALTERNATIVE DESTINATION(S): Brighton, Shoreham

WEATHER FORECAST: Wind S-SW, morning 8-13kt,

FORECASTS AVAILABLE DURING PASSAGE:

TIDES

Portsmouth		Selsey Bill		Eastbourne	
DATE:		DATE:		DATE:	
PLACE:		PLACE:		PLACE:	
HW		HW		HW 12:35	7.5
LW 05:58	0.6m	LW 06:11	0.47m	LW 18:13	0.8
HW		HW 12:52	5.5m	HW	
LW		LW		LW	
COEFFICIENT:					
HEIGHT OF TIDE AT:					
hrs	m	hrs	m	hrs	m

DEPTH CONSTRAINTS:

TIDAL STREAMS AT:

TURNS .... AT .... TOTAL SET (FM .... TO ....): ....° .... M

TURNS .... AT .... TOTAL SET (FM .... TO ....): ....° .... M

NET TIDAL STREAM FOR PASSAGE: ....° .... M

ESTIMATED TIME: ....hrs ETD: .... ETA: ....

SUN/MOON SUNRISE: .... SUNSET: ....

MOONRISE: .... MOONSET: .... PHASE: ....

WAYPOINTS

NO	NAME	TRACK/DISTANCE (TO NEXT WAYPOINT)
		/
		/
		/
		/
		/

DANGERS CLEARING BEARINGS/RANGES/DEPTHS

LIGHTS/MARKS EXPECTED

COMMUNICATIONS PORT/MARINA .... VHF .... ☎ ....

PORT/MARINA .... VHF .... ☎ ....

NOTES (CHARTS PREPARED & PAGE NUMBERS OF RELEVANT PILOTS/ALMANACS/ETC):

DISTANCES (M) ACROSS THE ENGLISH CHANNEL

ENGLAND / FRANCE/CI	Longships	Falmouth	Fowey	Plymouth bkwtr	Salcombe	Dartmouth	Torbay	Weymouth	Poole Hbr Ent	Needles Lt Ho	Nab Tower	Littlehampton	Shoreham	Brighton	Newhaven	Eastbourne	Folkestone	Dover
Le Conquet	114	118	134	142	139	152	158	181	199	203	236	256	260	264	269	281	313	318
L'Aberwrac'h	101	103	114	120	122	133	142	171	191	197	197	236	246	247	248	258	297	301
Roscoff	110	97	101	97	91	100	107	130	144	149	165	184	193	197	200	211	246	252
Trébeurden	118	105	107	100	95	103	110	128	148	148	168	186	197	201	206	218	257	262
Tréguier	131	114	112	102	93	99	104	116	132	136	153	170	182	187	192	211	252	253
Lézardrieux	139	124	119	107	97	102	105	117	129	133	150	167	179	184	189	208	249	250
St Q.-Portrieux	151	134	128	120	109	114	115	128	133	136	151	174	180	185	188	200	238	242
St Malo	172	152	145	132	118	121	124	125	130	133	148	170	176	182	185	195	235	240
St Helier	156	133	124	110	95	97	100	103	108	110	125	145	155	160	163	175	211	218
St Peter Port	140	113	105	89	75	71	73	81	87	90	105	126	135	139	142	155	190	196
Braye (Alderney)	149	129	107	90	74	72	71	63	68	71	86	108	115	120	123	135	173	178
Cherbourg	173	144	130	111	98	94	93	67	64	63	72	89	99	102	107	120	153	158
St Vaast	194	165	151	134	119	117	119	86	78	72	69	84	91	94	97	104	140	147
Ouistreham	231	203	190	173	158	155	159	121	111	100	88	93	94	94	93	96	132	133
Deauville	238	210	198	181	164	163	160	127	114	103	89	90	89	87	87	89	124	126
Le Havre	239	210	197	180	164	162	165	125	112	98	84	84	83	82	82	83	119	120
Fécamp	246	218	206	188	173	169	165	127	111	98	81	72	69	66	63	63	98	98
Dieppe	273	243	231	214	200	194	191	151	133	121	97	86	76	72	67	62	78	80
Boulogne	294	264	247	231	216	204	202	161	143	132	101	86	77	73	65	54	28	28
Calais	307	276	261	244	229	218	214	174	155	143	114	99	91	86	78	64	29	24

NOTES

1. This Table applies to Areas 1–3, and 14–16, each of which also contains its own internal Distance Table. Approximate distances in nautical miles are by the most direct route, while avoiding dangers and allowing for Traffic Separation Schemes.
2. For ports within the Solent, add the appropriate distances given in Area 2 to those shown above under either Needles Lighthouse or Nab Tower.

AREA 1 *South West England - Isles of Scilly to Anvil Point*

SELECTED LIGHTS, BUOYS & WAYPOINTS

Positions are referenced to WGS84

ISLES OF SCILLY TO LAND'S END

Bishop Rock ☆ Fl (2) 15s 44m **20M**; part obsc 204°-211°, obsc 211°-233° and 236°-259°; Gy ○ twr with helo platform; ***Racon T, 18M, 254°-215°***; 49°52'·37N 06°26'·74W; 992351137.

Round Rk 49°53'·10N 06°25'·19W.

Old Wreck VQ; 49°54'·26N 06°22'·81W.

ST AGNES and ST MARY'S

Peninnis Hd ☆ Fl 20s 36m 9M; 231°-117° but part obsc 048°-083° within 5M; W ○ twr on B frame, B cupola; 49°54'·28N 06°18'·21W.

Gugh Fl (5) Y 20s; 49°53'·52N 06°18'·73W.

Spanish Ledge Q (3) 10s; *Bell;* 49°53'·94N 06°18'·86W.

Woolpack Q (6) + L Fl 15s; 49°54'·40N 06°19'·37W.

Bartholomew Ledges QR 12m; 49°54'·37N 06°19'·89W.

N Bartholomew Fl R 5s; 49°54'·49N 06°19'·99W.

Bacon Ledge Fl (4) R 5s; 49°55'·22N 06°19'·26W.

Ldg lts 097·3°: Front, Iso RW (vert) 2s; W △, 49°55'·12N 06°18'·50W. Rear, Oc WR (vert) 10s; Or X on W bcn.

St Mary's Pool pier ☆ Fl WRG 2s 5m 4M; 070°-R-100°-W-130°-G-070°; 49°55'·11N 06°19'·00W.

Crow Rock Fl (2) 10s; 49°56'·26N 06°18'·49W.

Hats VQ (6) + L Fl 10s; 49°56'·21N 06°17'·14W.

AROUND TRESCO, BRYHER and ST MARTIN'S

Tresco Flats, Hulman Fl G 4s, 49°56'·29N 06°20'·30W.

Little Rag Ledge Fl (2) R 5s, 49°56'·44N 06°20'·43W.

Bryher, Bar Q (3) 10s, 49°57'·37N 06°20'·84W.

Bryher, Church Quay Q (3) 10s, 49°57'·18N 06°20'·97W.

Spencers Ledge Q (6) + L Fl 15s; 49°54'·78N 06°22'·06W.

Steeple Rock Q (9) 15s; 49°55'·46N 06°24'·24W.

Round Island ☆ Fl 10s 55m **18M**, also shown in reduced vis; 021°-288°; W ○ twr; *Horn (4) 60s*; 49°58'·74N 06°19'·39W.

St Martin's, Higher Town quay ☆ Fl R 5s, 49°57'·45N 06°16'·84W.

SCILLY to LAND'S END

Seven Stones Lt V Fl (3) 30s 12m **15M**; R hull; *Horn (3) 60s*; ***Racon O, 15M***; 50°03'·63N 06°04'·32W; 992351023.

Wolf Rock ☆ Fl 15s 34m **16M**; H24; *Horn 30s*; ***Racon T, 10M***; 49°56'·72N 05°48'·55W; 992351128.

Longships ☆ Fl (2) WR 10s 35m **W15M**, R11M; 189°-R-327°-W- 189°; also shown in reduced vis; Gy ○ twr with helicopter platform; *Horn 10s;* 50°04'·01N 05°44'·81W.

Carn Base Q (9) 15s; 50°01'·48N 05°46'·18W.

Runnel Stone Q (6) + L Fl 15s; *Whis;* 50°01'·18N 05°40'·36W.

LAND'S END TO PLYMOUTH

Tater-du ☆ Fl (3) 15s 34m **20M**; 241°-072°; W ○ twr. FR 31m 13M, 060°-072° over Runnel Stone; 50°03'·14N 05°34'·67W.

NEWLYN

Low Lee Q (3) 10s; 50°05'·56N 05°31'·38W.

S Pier ☆ Fl 5s 10m 9M; W ○ twr; 253°-336°; 50°06'·18N 05°32'·57W.

N Pier ☆ F WG 4m 2M; 238°-G-248°, 50°06'·18N 05°32'·62W.

PENZANCE

S Pier ☆ Fl WR 5s 11m **W17M,** R12M; 159°-R (unintens)-224°-R-268°-W-344·5°-R-shore; 50°07'·06N 05°31'·68W.

Mountamopus Q (6) + L Fl 15s; 50°04'·62N 05°26'·25W.

Lizard ☆ Fl 3s 70m **26M**; 250°-120°, partly visible 235°-250°; W 8-sided twr; *Horn 30s;* 49°57'·61N 05°12'·13W.

Manacle Q (3) 10s; *Bell;* 50°02'·81N 05°01'·91W.

FALMOUTH

St Anthony Head ☆ Iso WR 15s 22m, **W16M,** R14M, H24; 295°-W-004°-R (over Manacles)-022°-W-172°; W 8-sided twr; *Horn 30s;* 50°08'·46N 05°00'·96W.

Black Rock Fl (2) 10s 3M; B IDM bcn twr; 50°08'·72N 05°02'·00W.

Black Rock Fl R 2·5s; 50°08'·68N 05°01'·74W.

Castle Fl G 2·5s; 50°08'·99N 05°01'·62W.

St Mawes Q (6) + L Fl 15s; 50°09'·10N 05°01'·42W.

The Governor VQ (3) 5s; 50°09'·15N 05°02'·40W.

West Narrows Fl (2) R 10s; 50°09'·39N 05°02'·07W.

East Narrows Fl (2) G 10s; 50°09'·43N 05°01'·90W.

The Vilt Fl (4) G 15s; 50°09'·99N 05°02'·28W.

Northbank Fl R 4s; 50°10'·34N 05°02'·26W.

St Just QR; 50°10'·44N 05°01'·72W.

Mylor appr chan Fl G 6s; 50°10'·79N 05°02'·70W. Fl R 5s.

Messack Fl G 15s; 50°11'·31N 05°02'·22W.

Carrick Fl (2) G 10s; 50°11'·59N 05°02'·74W.

Pill Fl (3) G 15s; 50°12'·05N 05°02'·40W.

Turnerware Bar Fl G 5s; 50°12'·40N 05°02'·15W.

Dock Basin Dir ☆ 266°: WRG 2s 15m, 10M; 258°-Iso G-226°-Al WG-264°-Iso W-268°-Al WR-270°-Iso R-274°; 50°09'·38N 05°03'·29W.

N Arm ☆ QR 5m 3M; 50°09'·42N 05°03'·20W.

Inner Hbr Dir ☆ 233°: WRG 3s 5m, 9M; 226°-Iso G-231°-Iso W-236°-Iso R-241°; 50°09'·20N 05°03'·94W.

Falmouth Haven Marina ☆ 2 FR (vert); 50°09'·27N 05°03'·91W.

Falmouth Marina VQ (3) 5s; 50°09'·91N 05°04'·99W.

DODMAN POINT and MEVAGISSEY

Naval gunnery targets SSE of Dodman Point:

'A' Fl Y 10s; 50°08'·53N 04°46'·37W.

'B' Fl Y 5s; 50°10'·30N 04°45'·00W.

'C' Fl Y 2s; 50°10'·40N 04°47'·51W.

Gwineas Q (3) 10s; *Bell;* 50°14'·48N 04°45'·40W.

Mevagissey, Victoria Pier ☆ Fl (2) 10s 9m 12M; *Dia 30s;* 50°16'·15N 04°46'·92W.

FOWEY

Cannis Rock Q (6) + L Fl 15s; *Bell;* 50°18'·38N 04°39'·95W.

Fowey ☆ L Fl WR 5s 28m W11M, R9M; 284°-R-290°-W-028°-R-054°; W 8-sided twr, R lantern; 50°19'·63N 04°38'·83W.

St Catherine's Pt ☆ Fl R 2·5s 15m 2M; vis 150°-295°; 50°19'·69N 04°38'·66W.

Lamp Rock Fl G 5s 3m 2M; vis 357°-214°; 50°19'·70N 04°38'·41W. Whitehouse Pt ☆ Iso WRG 3s 11m W11M, R/G8M; 017°-G-022°- W-032°-R-037°; R col; 50°19'·98N 04°38'·28W.

POLPERRO, LOOE, EDDYSTONE and WHITSAND BAY

Udder Rock VQ (6) + L Fl 10s; *Bell;* 50°18'·93N 04°33'·85W.

POLPERRO, W pier ☆ FW 4m 4M; FR when hbr closed in bad weather; 50°19'·86N 04°30'·96W.

Spy House Pt ☆ Iso WR 6s 30m 7M; W288°-060°, R060°-288°; 50°19'·81N 04°30'·69W.

LOOE, Ranneys Q (6) + L Fl 15s; 50°19'·85N 04°26'·37W.

Mid Main Q (3) 10s 2M; 50°20'·56N 04°26'·94W.

Banjo Pier ☆ Oc WR 3s 8m **W15M,** R12M; 207°-R267°-W-313°-R-332°; 50°21'·06N 04°27'·06W.

White Rock ☆ Fl R 3s 5m 2M; 50°21'·03N 04°27'·09W.

Eddystone ☆ Fl (2) 10s 41m **17M**. Same twr, Iso R 10s 28m 8M; vis 110°-133° over Hand Deeps; Gy twr, helicopter platform; *Horn 30s;* ***Racon T, 10M;*** 50°10'·84N 04°15'·94W; 992351125.

Hand Deeps Q (9) 15s; 50°12'·68N 04°21'·10W.

PLYMOUTH

PLYMOUTH SOUND, WESTERN CHANNEL

Draystone Fl (2) R 5s; 50°18'·85N 04°11'·07W.

Knap Fl G 5s; 50°19'·56N 04°10'·02W.

Plymouth bkwtr W head, ☆ Fl WR 10s 19m W12M, R9M; 262°-W-208°-R-262°; W ○ twr. Same twr, Iso 4s 12m 10M; vis 033°-037°; *Horn 15s;* 50°20'·07N 04°09'·52W.

Maker ☆ Fl (2) WRG 10s 29m, W11M, R/G6M; 270°-G330°-W-004°-R-050°; W twr, R stripe; 50°20'·51N 04°10'·87W.

Queens Ground Fl (2) R 10s; 50°20'·29N 04°10'·08W.

New Ground Fl R 2s; 50°20'·47N 04°09'·43W.

Melampus Fl R 4s; 50°21'·15N 04°08'·72W.

PLYMOUTH SOUND, EASTERN CHANNEL

Wembury Pt ☆ Oc Y 10s 45m; occas; 50°19'·01N 04°06'·63W.

West Tinker VQ (9) 10s; 50°19'·25N 04°08'·64W.

East Tinker Q (3) 10s; 50°19'·20N 04°08'·30W.

Whidbey Oc (2) WRG 10s 29m, W8M, R/G6M, H24; 000°-G-137·5°-W-139·5°-R-159°; Or and W col; 50°19'·53N 04°07'·27W.

The Breakwater, E head L Fl WR 10s 9m W8M, R6M; 190°-R-353°-W-001°-R-018°-W-190°; 50°20'·01N 04°08'·24W.

Staddon Pt Oc WRG 10s 15m W8M, R/G5M; H24. 348°-G-038°-W-050°-R-090°; W structure, R bands; 50°20'·17N 04°07'·54W.

Withyhedge Dir ☆ 070° (for W Chan): WRG 13m W13M, R/G5M; H24; 060°-FG-065°-Al WG (W phase increasing with brg) -069°-FW-071°-Al WR (R phase increasing with brg)-075°-F R-080°; W ▽, orange stripe on col. Same col, Fl (2) Bu 5s; vis 120°-160°; 50°20'·75N 04°07'·44W.

SMEATON PASS (W of Mount Batten and S of The Hoe)

Ldg lts 349°. Front, Mallard Shoal Q WRG 5m W10M, R/G3M; W △, Or bands; 233°-G-043°- R-067°- G-087°-W-099°-R-108° (ldg sector); 50°21'·60N 04°08'·33W. Rear, 396m from front, Hoe Oc G 1·3s 11m 3M, 310°-040°; W ▽, Or bands; 50°21'·81N 04°08'·39W.

S Mallard VQ (6) + L Fl 10s; 50°21'·51N 04°08'·30W.

W Mallard QG; 50°21'·57N 04°08'·36W.

S Winter Q (6) + L Fl 15s; 50°21'·40N 04°08'·55W.

NE Winter QR; 50°21'·54N 04°08'·50W.

NW Winter VQ (9) 10s; 50°21'·55N 04°08'·70W.

ENTRANCE TO THE CATTEWATER

QAB (Queen Anne's Battery) ldg lts ☆ 048·5°. Front, FR; Or/W bcn; 50°21'·84N 04°07'·84W. Rear, Oc R 8s 14m 3M; 139m NE.

Fishers Nose ☆ Fl (3) R 10s 6m 4M; 50°21'·80N 04°08'·01W. Also F Bu ≠ 026·5° with F Bu 50°22'·00N 04°07'·86W, for Cobbler Chan.

DRAKE CHANNEL, THE BRIDGE and THE NARROWS

Ravenness Dir ☆ 225°: WRG 11m, W13M, R/G5M; H24. 217°-FG-221°-Al WG-224° (W phase increasing with brg)-FW-226°-Al WR-229° (R phase increasing with bearing)-FR-237°; W ▽, orange stripe on col. In fog, 160°-FW-305°; power failure QY; 50°21'·14N 04°10'·07W.

Asia Fl (2) R 5s; 50°21'·47N 04°08'·85W.

St Nicholas QR; 50°21'·55N 04°09'·20W.

N Drakes Is Fl R 4s; 50°21'·52N 04°09'·38W.

E Vanguard QG; 50°21'·47N 04°09'·70W.

W Vanguard Fl G 3s; 50°21'·49N 04°09'·98W.

Devils Point QG 5m 3M; Fl 5s in fog; 50°21'·59N 04°10'·04W. Battery Fl R 2s; 50°21'·52N 04°10'·21W.

The Bridge Channel

No 1, QG 4m; 50°21'·03N 04°09'·53W. No 2, QR 4m. No 3, Fl (3) G 10s 4m. No 4, Fl (4) R 10s 4m; 50°21'·09N 04°09'·63W.

Mount Wise, Dir ☆ 343°: WRG 7m, W13M, R/G5M; H24. 331°-FG-338°-Al WG-342° (W phase increasing with brg)-FW-344°-Al WR-348° (R phase increasing with bearing)-FR-351°. In fog, 341·5°-FW-344·5°; 50°21'·96N 04°10'·33W.

Ocean Court Dir Q WRG 15m, W11M, R/G3M; 010°-G-080°-W-090°-R-100°; 50°21'·85N 04°10'·11W.

PLYMOUTH TO START POINT

RIVER YEALM Sand bar Fl R 5s; 50°18'·59N 04°04'·12W.

SALCOMBE

Sandhill Pt Dir ☆ 000°: Fl WRG 2s 27m W/R/G 8M; 337·5°-G-357·5°-W-002·5°-R-012·5°; R/W ◇ on W mast, rear daymark; 50°13'·77N 03°46'·67W. Front daymark, Pound Stone R/W.

Bass Rk Fl R 5s; 50°13'·47N 03°46'·71W.

Wolf Rk Fl G 5s; 50°13'·53N 03°46'·58W.

Blackstone Rk ; 50°13'·61N 03°46'·51W.

Ldg lts 042·5°, front Fl 2s 5m 8M, 50°14'·53N 03°45'·31W; rear Fl 5s 45m 8M.

Start Pt ☆ Fl (3) 10s 62m **25M**; 184°-068°. Same twr: FR 55m 9M; 210°-255° over Skerries Bank; *Horn 60s;* 50°13'·34N 03°38'·54W.

START POINT TO PORTLAND BILL

DARTMOUTH

Kingswear Dir ☆ 328°: Iso WRG 3s 9m 8M; 318°-G-325°-W-331°-R-340°; W ○ twr; 50°20'·82N 03°34'·09W.

Mewstone VQ (6) + L Fl 10s; 50°19'·92N 03°31'·89W.

West Rock Q (6) + L Fl 15s; 50°19'·86N 03°32'·47W.

Homestone QR; 50°19'·61N 03°33'·55W.

Castle Ledge Fl G 5s; 50°19'·99N 03°33'·11W.

Checkstone Fl (2) R 5s; 50°20'·45N 03°33'·81W.

Dir ☆ 104·5°: FW 5m 9M; vis 102°-107°; 50°20'·65N 03°33'·80W.

BRIXHAM

Berry Head ☆ Fl (2) 15s 58m **19M**; vis 100°-023°; W twr; 50°23'·98N 03°29'·01W. R lts on radio mast 5·7M NW, inland of Paignton.

Victoria bkwtr ☆ Oc R 15s 9m 6M; W twr; 50°24'·33N 03°30'·78W.

No. 1 Fl G; 50°24'·30N 03°30'·89W.

No. 2 Fl R; 50°24'·32N 03°30'·83W.

PAIGNTON and TORQUAY

QG (May-Sep); 50°27'·42N 03°31'·80W, 85m off Haldon Pier.

Haldon Pier (E) ☆ QG 9m 6M; 50°27'·43N 03°31'·73W.

Princess Pier (W) ☆ QR 9m 6M; 50°27'·46N 03°31'·73W.

TEIGNMOUTH

Outfall Fl Y 5s; 50°31'·97N 03°27'·77W, 288°/1·3M to hbr ent.

Bar Fl G 2s; 50°32'·44N 03°29'·25W.

Trng wall, middle Oc R 6s 4m 3M; 50°32'·33N 03°29'·93W.

The Point Oc G 6s 3M & FG (vert); 50°32'·42N 03°30'·05W.

RIVER EXE to SIDMOUTH and AXMOUTH

Exe Mo(A) 10s; 50°35'·86N 03°23'·79W.

No. 1 50°36'·05N 03°23'·84W.

No. 2 50°36'·02N 03°23'·94W.

Exmouth Dir ☆ 305°: WRG 6m, 6M; 299°-Iso G-304°-Iso W-306°-Iso R-311°; W col, 50°36'·99N 03°25'·34W.

No. 10 Fl R 3s; 50°36'·73N 03°24'·77W.

No. 12 Warren Pt 50°36'·91N 03°25'·41W.

Sidmouth ☆ Fl R 5s 5m 2M; 50°40'·48'N 03°14'·43W.

Axmouth jetty ☆ Fl G 4s 7m 2M; 50°42'·12N 03°03'·29W.

LYME REGIS

Outfall Q (6) + L Fl 15s; 50°43'·17N 02°55'·66W.

Ldg lts 284°: Front, Victoria Pier ☆ Oc WR 8s 6m, W9M, R7M; 284°-R-104°-W-284°; Bu col; 50°43'·19N 02°56'·17W. Rear, FG 8m 9M.

WEST BAY (BRIDPORT)

W pier root, Dir ☆ 336°: F WRG 5m 4M; 165°-G-331°-W-341°-R-165°; 50°42'·62N 02°45'·89W.

W pier outer limit ☆ Iso R 2s 5m 4M; 50°42'·51N 02°45'·83W.

E pier outer limit ☆ Iso G 2s 5m 4M; 50°42'·53N 02°45'·80W.

PORTLAND BILL TO ANVIL POINT

Portland Bill lt ho ☆ Fl (4) 20s 43m **25M**. vis 221°-244° (gradual change from 1 Fl to 4 Fl); 244°-117° (shows 4 Fl); 117°-141° (gradual change from 4 Fl to 1 Fl). W ○ twr; *Dia 30s*; 50°30'·85N 02°27'·39W. Same twr, FR 19m 13M; 265°-291° over Shambles.

W Shambles Q (9) 15s; *Bell;* 50°29'·78N 02°24'·41W.

E Shambles Q (3) 10s; *Bell;* 50°31'·26N 02°20'·08W.

PORTLAND HARBOUR

Outer Bkwtr Fort Head (N end) ☆ QR 14m 5M; 013°-268°; 50°35'·11N 02°24'·87W.

NE Bkwtr (A Hd) ☆ Fl 2·5s 22m 10M; 50°35'·16N 02°25'·07W.

NE Bkwtr (B Hd) ☆ Oc R 15s 11m 5M; 50°35'·65N 02°25'·88W.

N Arm (C Hd) ☆ Oc G 10s 11m 5M; 50°35'·78N 02°25'·95W.

WEYMOUTH

Ldg lts 239·6°: both FR 5/7m 7M; Front 50°36'·46N 02°26'·87W, S Pier hd ☆ Q 10m 9M; 50°36'·58N 02°26'·49W. IPTS 190m SW.

LULWORTH RANGE TO ANVIL POINT

Targets off St Alban's Hd:

DZ 'A', Fl Y 2s, 50°33'·34N 02°06'·52W.

DZ 'B', Fl Y 10s, 50°32'·11N02°05'·92W.

DZ 'C', Fl Y 5s, 50°32'·76N 02°04'·56W.

Anvil Pt ☆ Fl 10s 45m 9M; vis 237°-076° (H24); W ○ twr and dwelling; 50°35'·51N 01°57'·60W. Measured mile close west.

DISTANCE TABLES

Approx distances in nautical miles are by the most direct route allowing for dangers and TSS.

		1	2	3	4	5	6	7	8	9	10	11	12	13	14	15	16	17
1	Longships	1																
2	Scilly (Crow Rock)	22	2															
3	Penzance	15	35	3														
4	Lizard Point	23	42	16	4													
5	Falmouth	39	60	32	16	5												
6	Mevagissey	52	69	46	28	17	6											
7	Fowey	57	76	49	34	22	7	7										
8	Looe	63	80	57	39	29	16	11	8									
9	Plymouth (bkwtr)	70	92	64	49	39	25	22	11	9								
10	River Yealm (ent)	72	94	66	51	41	27	24	13	4	10							
11	Salcombe	81	102	74	59	50	40	36	29	22	19	11						
12	Start Point	86	103	80	63	55	45	40	33	24	21	7	12					
13	Dartmouth	95	116	88	72	63	54	48	42	35	32	14	9	13				
14	Torbay	101	118	96	78	70	62	55	50	39	36	24	15	11	14			
15	Exmouth	113	131	107	90	82	73	67	61	51	48	33	27	24	12	15		
16	Lyme Regis	126	144	120	104	96	86	81	74	63	60	48	41	35	30	21	16	
17	Portland Bill	135	151	128	112	104	93	89	81	73	70	55	49	45	42	36	22	17

AREA 2 *South Central England – Anvil Point to Selsey Bill*

SELECTED LIGHTS, BUOYS & WAYPOINTS

SWANAGE TO ISLE OF WIGHT

SWANAGE

Pier Hd ☆ 2 FR (vert) 6m 3M; 50°36′·56N 01°56′·95W.
Peveril Ledge QR; 50°36′·41N 01°56′·10W.

POOLE BAR and SWASH CHANNEL

Poole Bar (No. 1) QG; *Bell*; 50°39·29N 01°55′·14W.
(Historic wreck) Fl Y 5s; 50°39′·70N 01°54′·86W.
South Hook (No. 11) 50°39′·70N 01°55′·20W.
No. 2 Fl R 2s; 50°39′·23N 01°55′·24W.
No. 3 Fl G 3s; 50°39′·76N 01°55′·49W.
No. 4 Fl R 2s; 50°39′·72N 01°55′·60W.
Training Bank 2 FR (vert); 50°39′·82N 01°55′·86W.
No. 6 Fl R 4s; 50°40′·14N 01°55′·91W.
No. 5 Fl G 5s; 50°40′·19N 01°55′·81W.
Hook Sands (No. 7) Fl G 3s; 50°40′·50N 01°56′·16W.
Channel (No. 8) Fl R 2s; 50°40′·45N 01°56′·27W.
No. 10 Fl R 4s; 50°40′·84N 01°56′·86W.
Swash (No. 9) Q (9) 15s; 50°40′·88N 01°56′·70W.

EAST LOOE CHANNEL

East Hook 50°40′·58W 01°55′·23W.
East Looe 1 Fl G 5s; 50°41′·09N 01°55′·82W.
East Looe 2 Fl R 4s; 50°41′·07N 01°55′·83W.
East Looe 3 (Limit 10 kn) Fl G 3s; 50°41′·11N 01°56′·16W.
East Looe 4 (Limit 10 kn) Fl R 2s; 50°41′·09N 01°56′·17W.
North Hook Fl (2) R 5s; 50°41′·01N 01°56′·44W.

BROWNSEA ROADS

No. 12 Q R; 50°40′·94N 01°57′·17W.
No.14 Fl R 2s; 50°41′·03N 01°57′·32W.
N Haven Q (9) 15s 5m; 50°41′·15N 01°57′·17W.
Brownsea Q (3) 10s; 50°41′·14N 01°57′·39W.
Brownsea Island Dir lt 299°F WRG; 296·5°-G-297·8°-AltWG-298·8°-W-299·2°-AltWR-300·2°-R-301·5°; 50°41′·16N 01°57′·67W (only shown for commercial vessels); 2FR(vert); 301·5°-296·5° (H24).

MIDDLE SHIP CHANNEL

Bell (No. 15) Q (6) + L Fl 15s; 50°41′·36N 01°57′·12W.
No. 16 VQ R; 50°41′·43N 01°57′·25W.
No. 17 Fl G 3s; 50°41′·68N 01°57′·02W.
Aunt Betty (No. 22) Q (3)10s; 50°41′·97N 01°57′·25W.
Diver (No. 25) Q (9) 15s; 50°42′·29N 01°58′·32W.

NORTH CHANNEL

Salterns Marina Outer Bkwtr Hd ☆ 2 FR (vert) 2M; Tfc sigs; 50°42′·23N 01°57′·10W.
Parkstone YC platform ☆ Q 8m 1M; hut on dolphin; 50°42′·37N 01°58′·08W.
Stakes (No. 29) Q (6) + L Fl 15s; 50°42′·43N 01°59′·00W.

POOLE BAY

Bournemouth Rocks 50°42′·32N 01°53′·40W.
Lightwave 50°41′·50N 01°51′·68W.
Christchurch Ledge 50°41′·57N 01°41′·55W (Apr-Oct).
(x2) Fl (5) Y 20s; 50°37′·98N 01°43′·02W; (265° 2.6M from Needles F'wy).

WESTERN APPROACHES TO THE SOLENT

NEEDLES CHANNEL

Needles Fairway L Fl 10s; *Whis*; 50°38′·24N 01°38′·98W.
SW Shingles Fl R 2·5s; 50°39′·29N 01°37′·52W.
Bridge VQ (9) 10s; ***Racon (T) 10M***; 50°39′·63N 01°36′·88W.
NEEDLES ☆ 50°39′·73N 01°35′·50W; Oc (2) WRG 20s 24m **W17M,** R14M, R13M G14M; ○ Twr, R band and lantern; vis: shore-R-300°-W-083°-R (unintens)-212°-W-217°-G-224° (H24). *Horn (2) 30s*.
Shingles Elbow Fl (2) R 5s; 50°40′·37N 01°36′·05W.
Mid Shingles Fl (3) R 10s; 50°41′·21N 01°34′·66W.
Warden Fl G 2·5s; *Bell*; 50°41′·48N 01°33′·55W.
NE Shingles Q (3) 10s; 50°41′·96N 01°33′·41W.
Hurst Point ☆ 50°42′·48N 01°33′·03W; FL (4) WR 15s 23m W13M, R11M; W ○ Twr; vis:080°-W(unintens)-104°, 234°-W-244°-R-250°- W-053°. Same structure, Iso WRG 4s 19m **W21M, R18M, G17M**; vis: 038·8°-G-040·8°-W-041·8°-R-043·8°; By day W7M, R5M, G5M.

NORTH CHANNEL

North Head Fl (3) G 10s; 50°42′·69N 01°35′·52W.

THE WESTERN SOLENT

Note: Numerous yellow yacht racing buoys are laid throughout the Solent (seasonal, Mar-Dec). Most, but not all, are lit Fl Y 4s.

SOLENT MARKS

Sconce Q; *Bell*; 50°42′·53N 01°31′·43W.
Black Rock Fl G 5s; 50°42′·57N 01°30′·59W.
Lymington Bank Fl (2) R 5s; *Bell*; 50°43′·10N 01°30′·85W.
Solent Bank Fl (3) R 10s; 50°44′·23N 01°27′·37W.
Hamstead Ledge Fl (2) G 5s; 50°43′·87N 01°26′18W.
Newtown River Q (9) 15s; 50°43′·75N 01°24′·96W.
W Lepe Fl R 5s; 50°45′·24N 01°24′·09W.
Salt Mead Fl (3) G 10s; 50°44′·51N 01°23′·04W.
Gurnard Ledge Fl (4) G 15s; 50°45′·51N 01°20′·59W.
E Lepe Fl (2) R 5s; *Bell*; 50°45′·93N 01°21′·07W.
Lepe Spit Q (6) + L Fl 15s; 50°46′·78N 01°20′·64W.
Gurnard Q; 50°46′·22N 01°18′·84W.

YARMOUTH

East Fairway Fl R 2s; 50°42′·62N 01°29′·95W.
Poole Belle Fl Y 5s; 50°42′·54N 01°30′·17W.
Pier Head, centre, ☆ 2 FR (vert) 2M; G col. High intensity FW (occas); 50°42′·51N 01°29′·97W.
Ldg Lts 187·6° Front FG 5m 2M; 50°42′·36N 01°30′·06 W. Rear, 63m from front, FG 9m 2M; both W ◇.

LYMINGTON

Ldg Lts 319·5°, Or posts. Front, FR 12m 8M; 50°45′·19N 01°31′·65W. vis: 309·5°-329·5°. Rear, FR 17m 8M.
Jack in the Basket Fl R 2s 9m; 50°44′·27N 01°30′·57W.
No. 1 Fl G 2s 2m 3M; G △ on pile; 50°44′·41N 01°30′·48W.
No. 2 (Cross Boom) Fl R 2s 4m 3M; 50°44′·36N 01°30′·58W.
Yacht Haven ldg lts 244°. Front FY 4m; R △; 50°45′·09N 01°31′·53W. Rear, 22m from front, FY 6m; R ▽.

BEAULIEU RIVER

Millennium Dir lt 334°. ☆ Oc WRG 4s 13m W4M, R3M, G3M; vis: 318°-G-330°-W-337°-R-348°; 50°47′·12N 01°21′·90W.

Beaulieu Spit, E end Fl R 5s 3M; R dolphin, W band; 50°46'·85N 01°21'·76W.
No. 1 50°46'·91N 01°21'·70W.
No 2 50°46'·92N 01°21'·78W.

COWES
Prince Consort VQ; 50°46'·41N 01°17'·56W.
Trinity House Fl Y 5s; 50°46'·31N 01°17'·75W.
No. 1 Fl G 3s; 50°46'·07N 01°18'·03W.
No. 2 Q R; 50°46'·07N 01°17'·87W.
No 2A LFl R 10s; 50°45'·92N 01°17'·70W.
Tide gauge L Fl R 5s; 50°45'·78N 01°17'·66W.
E. Cowes Bkwtr Hd ☆ 2F R; 50°45'·88N 01°17'·52W.
Fl G 3s; 50°45'·91N 01°17'·55W.
Fl R 3s; 50°45'·89N 01°17'·53W.
Shrape Mud Fl G 5s; 50°46'·02N 01°17'·38W.
Fl R 5s; 50°46'·00N 01°17'·37W.
Boat Chan Ent Fl G 2s; 50°46'·08N 01°17'·05W.
Q R; 50°46'·06N 01°17'·04W.
Shrape Bn LFl R 10S 3m 3M; 50°46'·09N 01°16'·90W.

CENTRAL SOLENT AND SOUTHAMPTON WATER

Note: Numerous yellow yacht racing buoys are laid throughout the Solent (seasonal, Mar-Dec). Most, but not all, are lit Fl Y 4s.

SOLENT MARKS
Lepe Spit Q (6) + L Fl 15s; 50°46'·78N 01°20'·64W.
NE Gurnard Fl (3) R 10s; 50°47'·06N 01°19'·42W.
South Bramble Fl G 2·5s; 50°46'·98N 01°17'·72W.
W Bramble VQ (9) 10s; *Bell*; ***Racon (T) 3M***; 50°47'·20N 01°18'·65W.
Thorn Knoll Fl G 5s; 50°47'·50N 01°18'·44W.
Bourne Gap Fl R 3s; 50°47'·83N 01°18'·34W.
West Knoll Fl Y 2·5s; 50°47'·43N 01°17'·84W.
North Thorn QG; 50°47'·91N 01°17'·84W.
Stanswood Outfall Iso R 10s 6m 5M; 4 FR Lts; 50°48'·26N 01°18'·82W.

CALSHOT REACH
East Knoll 50°47'·96N 01°16'·83W.
CALSHOT SPIT Fl 5s 5m 10M; R hull, Lt Twr amidships; *Horn (2) 60s*; 50°48'·35N 01°17'·64W.
Calshot VQ; *Bell*; 50°48'·44N 01°17'·03W.
Castle Point IQ R 10s; 50°48'·71N 01°17'·67W.
Reach Fl (3) G 10s; 50°49'·05N 01°17'·65W .
Black Jack Fl (2) R 4s; 50°49'·13N 01°18'·09W.
Hook QG; *Horn (1) 15s*; 50°49'·52N 01°18'·30W.
Coronation Fl Y 5s; 50°49'·55N 01°17'·62W.
Bald Head Fl G 2·5s; 50°49'·80N 01°18'·06W.

RIVER HAMBLE
Hamble Pt Q (6) + L Fl 15s; 50°50'·15N 01°18'·66W.
Hamble Common Dir lt 351·7°, Oc (2) WRG 12s 5m W4M; R4M; G4M; vis: 348·7°-G-350·7°-W-352·7°-R-354·7°; 50°51'·00N 01°18'·84W.
Sailing Club Dir lt 028·9° ☆ Iso WRG 6s 5m W4M, R4M, G4M: vis: 025·9°-G-027·9°-W-029·9°-R-031·9°; 50°51'·10N 01°18'·34W.

SOUTHAMPTON WATER
Fawley Marine Terminal. SE end ☆ 2 FR (vert) 9m 10M; 50°50'·06N 01°19'·42W.
Greenland Iso G 2s; 50°51'·11N 01°20'·38W.
Cadland Fl R 3s; 50°51'·02N 01°20'·54W.
Lains Lake Fl (2) R 4s; 50°51'·59N 01°21'·65W.
Hound Fl (3) G 10s; 50°51'·68N 01°21'·52W.
Netley Fl G 3s; 50°52'·03N 01°21'·81W.
Deans Elbow Oc R 4s; 50°52'·16N 01°22'·76W.
NW Netley Fl G 7s; 50°52'·31N 01°22'·73W.
Weston Shelf Fl (3) G 15s; 50°52'·71N 01°23'·26W.

HYTHE
Hythe Pier Hd ☆ 2 FR (vert) 12m 5M; 50°52'·49N 01°23'·61W.
Hythe Marina Ent Q (3) 10s; 50°52'·63N 01°23'·88W.
Hythe Knock Fl R 3s; 50°52'·83N 01°23'·81W.

SOUTHAMPTON and RIVER ITCHEN
Swinging Ground No. 1 Oc G 4s; 50°53'·00N 01°23'·44W.
E side. No. 1 QG; 50°53'·15N 01°23'·40W.
No. 2 Fl G 5s 2M; 50°53'·29N 01°23'·38W.
No. 3 Fl G 7s; 50°53'·48N 01°23'·28W.
No. 4 QG 4m 2M; 50°53'·62N 01°23'·16W.

SOUTHAMPTON and RIVER TEST
Queen Elizabeth II Terminal, S end ☆ 4 FG (vert) 16m 3M; 50°53'·00N 01°23'·71W.
Gymp QR; 50°53'·17N 01°24'·30W.
Town Quay Ldg Lts 329°, both F 12/22m 3/2M.
Gymp Elbow Oc R 4s; 50°53'·50N 01°24'·68W.
Dibden Bay Q; 50°53'·70N 01°24'·92W.

THE EASTERN SOLENT

Note: Numerous yellow yacht racing buoys are laid throughout the Solent (seasonal, Mar-Dec). Most, but not all, are lit Fl Y 4s.

SOLENT MARKS
West Ryde Middle Q (9) 15s; 50°46'·48N 01°15'·79W.
Norris Fl (3) R 10s; 50°45'·97N 01°15'·51W.
North Ryde Middle Fl (4) R 20s; 50°46'·61N 01°14'·31W.
South Ryde Middle Fl G 5s; 50°46'·13N 01°14'·16W.
Peel Bank Fl (2) R 5s; 50°45'·49N 01°13'·35W.
SE Ryde Middle VQ (6)+L Fl 10s; 50°45'·93N 01°12'·10W.
NE Ryde Middle Fl (2) R 10s; 50°46'·21N 01°11'·88W.
Mother Bank Fl R 3s; 50°45'·49N 01°11'·21W.
Browndown Fl G 15s; 50°46'·57N 01°10'·95W.
Fort Gilkicker ☆ Oc G 10s 7M; 50°46'·43N 01°08'·47W.
N Sturbridge VQ; 50°45'·33N 01°08'·23W.
Ryde Sands Fl R 10s; 50°44'·56N 01°07'·26W.
Ryde Sands L Fl R 12s; 50°44'·16N 01°05'·99W.
No Man's Land Fort ☆ Iso R 2s 21m 8M; 50°44'·40N 01°05'·70W.
Horse Sand Fort ☆ Iso G 2s 21m 8M; 50°45'·01N 01°04'·34W.
Saddle VQ (3) G 10s; 50°45'·20N 01°04'·98W.

NORTH CHANNEL and HILLHEAD
Calshot VQ; *Bell (1) 30s*; 50°48'·44N 01°17'·03W.
Hillhead Fl R 2·5s; 50°48'·07N 01°16'·00W.
E Bramble VQ (3) 5s; 50°47'·23N 01°13'·64W.

WOOTTON CREEK
Wootton Beacon Q 1M; (NB); 50°44'·53N 01°12'·13W.
Dir lt. Oc WRG 10s vis: 220·8°-G-224·3°-W-225·8°-R-230·8°; 50°44'·03N 01°12'·86W.

RYDE
Ryde Pier ☆, NW corner, N and E corner marked by 2 FR (vert). In fog FY from N corner, vis: 045°-165°, 200°-320°; 50°44'·34N 01°09'·72W.

Leisure Hbr E side ☆ 2 FR (vert) 7m 1M. FY 6m shown when depth of water in Hbr greater than 1m; 2 FY 6m when depth exceeds 1·5m; 50°43′·99N 01°09′·29W.

PORTSMOUTH APPROACHES

Horse Sand Fl G 2·5s; 50°45′·53N 01°05′·27W.
Outer Spit Q (6) + L Fl 15s; 50°45′·58N 01°05′·50W.
Mary Rose Fl Y 5s; 50°45′·80N 01°06′·20W.
Boyne Fl G 5s; 50°46′·15N 01°05′·26W.
Spit Refuge Fl R 5s; 50°46′·15N 01°05′·46W.
Spit Sand Fort ☆ Fl R 5s; 18m 7M. 50°46′·24N 01°05′·94W.
Castle (NB) Fl (2) G 6s; 50°46′·45N 01°05′·38W.
Southsea Castle N corner ☆ Iso 2s 16m 11M, W stone Twr, B band; vis: 337°-071°; 50°46′·69N 01°05′·33W.
Southsea Castle Dir lt 001·5° WRG 11m W13M, R5M, G5M; same structure; vis: 351·5°-FG-357·5°-Al WG (W phase incr with brg), 000°-FW-003°-AlWR(R phase incr with brg), 005·5°-FR-011·5°; 50°46′·69N 01°05′·33W.
Ridge Fl (2) R 6s; 50°46′·44N 01°05′·65W.
No. 1 Bar (NB) Fl (3) G 10s; 50°46′·77N 01°05′·81W.
No. 2 Fl (3) R 10s; 50°46′·69N 01°05′·97W.
No. 3 QG; 50°47′·08N 01°06′·24W.
No. 4 QR; 50°47′·01N 01°06′·36W.
BC Outer Oc R 15s; 50°47′·32N 01°06′·68W.

PORTSMOUTH HARBOUR

Fort Blockhouse ☆ Dir lt 320°; WRG 6m W13M, R5M, G5M; vis: 310°- Oc G-316°-Al WG(W phase incr with brg), 318·5°-Oc-321·5°- Al WR (R phase incr with brg), 324°-Oc R-330°. 2 FR (vert) 20m E; 50°47′·37N 01°06′·74W.
Ballast Fl R 2·5s; 50°47′·62N 01°06′·83W.
Hbr Ent Dir lt (NB) (Fuel Jetty) ☆ WRG 2m 1M; vis: 322·5°-Iso G 2s -330°-Al WG-332·5°-Iso 2s(main chan) -335°-Al WR-337·5°-Iso R 2s-345° (Small Boat Chan) H24; 50°47′·85N 01°06′·98W.

EASTERN APPROACHES to THE SOLENT

Outer Nab 1 VQ (9) 10s; 50°38′·18N 00°56′·88W.
Outer Nab 2 VQ (3) 5s; 50°38′·43N 00°57′·70W.
Nab Tower ☆ Fl 10s 17m 12M; *Horn (2) 30s; RACON T;* 50°40′·08N 00°57′·15W; 992351136.
N 2 Fl Y 2·5s. 6M; 50°41′·03N 00°56′·74W.
N 1 Fl Y (4)10s; 50°41′·26N 00°56′·52W.
N 4 Fl Y 7·5s; 50°41′·86N 00°57′·24W.
N 3 Fl (3) Y 15s; 50°41′·63N 00°56′·74W.
N 5 Fl Y 5s; 50°41′·99N 00°56′·97W.
N 7 Fl Y 2·5s; 50°42′·35N 00°57′·20W.
New Grounds VQ (3) 5s; 50°41′·84N 00°58′·49W.
Nab End Fl R 5s; *Whis*; 50°42′·63N 00°59′·49W.
Dean Tail Fl G 5s; 50°42′·99N 00°59′·17W.
Dean Tail S Q (6) + L Fl 10s; 50°43′·04N 00°59′·57W.
Dean Tail N Q; 50°43′·13N 00°59′·57W.
Horse Tail Fl (2) G 10s; 50°43′·23N 01°00′·23W.
Nab East Fl (2) R 10s; 50°42′·86N 01°00′·80W.
Dean Elbow Fl (3) G 15s; 50°43′·69N 01°01′·88W.
St Helens Fl (3) R 15s; 50°43′·36N 01°02′·41W.
Horse Elbow QG; 50°44′·26N 01°03′·88W.
Cambrian Wreck 50°44′·43N 01°03′·43W.
Warner QR; *Whis*; 50°43′·87N 01°03′·99W.

BEMBRIDGE

St Helen's Fort ☆ (IOW) Fl (3) 10s 16m 8M; large ○ stone structure; 50°42′·30N 01°05′·05W.
Bembridge Tide Gauge Fl Y 2s 1M; 50°42′·46N 01°05′·02W.

SOUTH EAST COAST of the ISLE OF WIGHT

St Catherine's Point ☆ 50°34′·54N 01°17′·87W; Fl 5s 41m **25M**; vis: 257°-117°; FR 35m 13M (same Twr) vis: 099°-116°.
Ventnor Haven W Bwtr ☆ 2 FR (vert) 3M; 50°35′·50N 01°12′·30W.
Sandown Pier Hd ☆ 2 FR (vert) 7m 2M; 50°39′·05N 01°09′·18W.
W Princessa Q (9) 15s; 50°40′·16N 01°03′·65W.
Bembridge Ledge Q (3) 10s; 50°41′·15N 01°02′·81W

LANGSTONE and APPROACHES

Eastney Pt Fraser Trials Range ☆ FR, Oc (2) Y 10s, and FY Lts (occas) when firing taking place; 50°47′·19N 01°02′·22W.
Winner ; 50°45′·10N 01°00′·10W.
Roway Wk Fl (2) 5s; 50°46′·11N 01°02′·28W.
Langstone Fairway L Fl 10s; 50°46′·32N 01°01′·36W.

DISTANCE TABLES

Approx distances in nautical miles are by the most direct route allowing for dangers and TSS.

1	Portland Bill	1																	
2	Weymouth	8	2																
3	Swanage	23	22	3															
4	Poole Hbr ent	28	26	6	4														
5	Needles Lt Ho	35	34	14	14	5													
6	Lymington	42	40	21	21	7	6												
7	Yarmouth (IOW)	40	39	19	19	6	2	7											
8	Beaulieu River ent	46	45	25	25	12	7	7	8										
9	Cowes	49	46	28	28	15	15	9	5	9									
10	Southampton	55	54	34	34	24	15	15	9	9	10								
11	R. Hamble (ent)	53	51	32	32	19	12	12	6	6	4	11							
12	Portsmouth	58	57	37	37	24	18	18	11	15	18	15	12						
13	Langstone Hbr	61	59	40	40	25	22	24	15	12	16	13	5	13					
14	Chichester Bar	63	62	42	42	29	29	24	17	15	20	17	8	5	14				
15	Bembridge	59	58	38	38	24	15	19	12	10	19	14	6	6	8	15			
16	Nab Tower	60	63	39	39	30	25	25	18	16	21	18	10	7	6	6	16		
17	St Catherine's Pt	45	44	25	25	14	15	18	27	25	30	27	19	20	19	17	15	17	
18	Littlehampton	79	79	60	61	46	44	45	38	36	45	42	31	28	25	28	22	35	18

Eastney Pt Outfall QR 2m 2M; 50°47'·23N 01°01'·68W.
East Milton Fl (4) R 10s; 50°48'·16N 01°01'·76W.
NW Sinah Fl G 5s; 50°48'·14N 01°01'·58W.

CHICHESTER ENTRANCE

West Pole (tripod) Fl R 5s 14m 7M; 50°45'·45N 00°56'·59W.
Bar Fl(2) R 10s 10m 4M; 50°45'·92N 00°56'·46W.
Eastoke QR; 50°46'·68N 00°56'·11W.
West Winner QG; Tide gauge. 50°46'·88N 00°55'·98W.

EMSWORTH CHANNEL

Fishery Q (6) + L Fl 15s; 50°47'·38N 00°56'·07W.
NW Pilsey Fl G 5s; 50°47'·50N 00°56'·20W.
Verner Fl R 10s; 50°48'·20N 00°56'·63W.
Marker Pt Fl (2) G 10s 8m; 50°48'·91N 00°56'·72W.
Emsworth Q (6) + L Fl 15s; tide gauge; 50°49'·66N 00°56'·76W.

THORNEY CHANNEL

Camber Q (6) + L Fl 15s; 50°47'·87N 00°54'·06W.
Pilsey Fl (2) R 10s ; 50°47'·98N 00°54'·24W.
Thorney Fl G 5s; 50°48'·20N 00°54'·28W.

CHICHESTER CHANNEL

NW Winner Fl G 10s; 50°47'·19N 00°55'·92W.
N Winner Fl (2) G 10s; 50°47'·31N 00°55'·83W.
Mid Winner Fl (3) G 10s; 50°47'·38N 00°55'·69W.
Stocker Fl (3) R 10s; 50°47'·45N 00°55'·52W.
Copyhold Fl (4) R 10s; 50°47'·50N 00°54'·93W.
East Head Spit Fl (4) G 10s; 50°47'·45N 00°54'·82W.
Snowhill Fl G 5s; 50°47'·52N 00°54'·34W.
Sandhead Fl R 10s; 50°47'·67N 00°54'·25W.
Chalkdock Fl (2) G 10s; 50°48'·49N 00°53'·30W.

AREA 3 *South East England – Selsey Bill to North Foreland*

SELECTED LIGHTS, BUOYS & WAYPOINTS

OWERS TO BEACHY HEAD

SELSEY BILL and THE OWERS

S Pullar VQ (6) + L Fl 10s; 50°38'·84N 00°49'·29W.
Pullar Q (9) 15s; 50°40'·47N 00°50'·09W.
Boulder Fl G 2·5s; 50°41'·56N 00°49'·09W.
Street QR; 50°41'·69N 00°48'·89W.
Mixon Bn Q(6) + L Fl 15s; 50°42'·38N 00°46'·32E.
Owers Q (6) + L Fl 15s; *Bell*; ***Racon (O) 10M***; 50°38'·59N 00°41'·09W.
E Borough Hd Q (3) 10s *Bell;* 50°41'·54N 00°39'·09W.

LITTLEHAMPTON

West Pier Hd QR 7m 6M; 50°47'·88N 00°32'·46W.
Training Wall Hd QG 10m 2M; 50°47'·87N 00°32'·38W.
Ldg lts 346°. Front, E Pier Hd FG 6m 7M; B col. Rear, 64m from front, Oc W 7·5s 9m10M; W twr; vis: 290°-W-042°; 50°48'·09N 00°32'·51W.
Outfall Fl Y 5s; 50°46'·27N 00°30'·53W.
Littlehampton Fl (5) Y 20s 9m 5M; 50°46'·19N 00°29'·54W.

WORTHING and SHOREHAM

Met Mast Mo(U) 15s 16m 10M*;* Aero FR (103m), *Horn Mo(U) 15s;* 50°41'·29N 00°20'·59W.
Outfall Fl R 2·5s 3m; 50°48'·38N 00°20'·34W.
Express Fl Y 5s; (Apr-Oct); 50°47'·28N 00°17'·09W.
W Bkwtr Head Fl R 5s 7m 7M; 50°49'·49N 00°14'·89W.
Ldg Lts 355°. Middle Pier Front, Oc 5s 8m 10M; W watch-house, R base; tidal Lts, tfc sigs; *Horn 20s*. **Rear**, 192m from front, Fl 10s 13m **15M**; Gy twr vis: 283°-103°; 50°49'·75N 00°14'·88W.
Outfall 50°49'·47N 00°14'·39W.
Shoreham Outfall Q (6) + L Fl 15s; 50°47'·88N 00°13'·72W.

BRIGHTON and BRIGHTON MARINA

Black Rk Ledge Fl Y 4s; 50°48'·07N 00°06'·46W.
W Bkwtr Hd QR 10m 7M; W ○ structure, R bands; *Horn (2) 30s*; 50°48'·50N 00°06'·38W.
E Bkwtr Hd QG 8m 7M and Fl (4) WR 20s 16m W10M, R8M; W pillar, G bands; vis: 260°-R-295°-W-100°; 50°48'·47N 00°06'·37W.
Saltdean Outfall Fl Y 5s; 50°46'·72N 00°02'·13W.

NEWHAVEN

Bkwtr Hd Oc (2) 10s 17m 12M; 50°46'·56N 00°03'·50E.
E Pier Hd Iso G 10s 12m 6M; W twr; 50°46'·81N 00°03'·59E.

OFFSHORE MARKS

CS 1 Fl Y 2·5s; *Whis*; 50°33'·69N 00°03'·92W.
GREENWICH 50°24'·54N 00°00'·10E; Fl 5s 12m **15M**; Riding light FW; R hull; ***Racon (M) 10M***; *Horn 30s* .
CS 2 Fl Y 5s; 50°39'·14N 00°32'·60E.
CS 3 Fl Y 10s; 50°52'·04N 01°02'·18E.

BEACHY HEAD TO DUNGENESS

Beachy Head 50°44'·03N 00°14'·49E; Fl (2) 20s 31m 8M; W round twr, R band and lantern; vis: 248°-101°; (H24).
Royal Sovereign Fl 20s 28m 12M; W ○ twr, R band on W cabin on col; *Horn (2) 30s*; 50°43'·45N 00°26'·09E.
Royal Sovereign QR; 50°44'·23N 00°25'·84E.

EASTBOURNE and SOVEREIGN HARBOUR

SH L Fl 10s; 50°47'·40N 00°20'·71E.
Martello Tower Fl (3) 15s 12m 7M.; 50°47'·24N 00°19'·83E.
Dir lt 258°Fl WRG 5s 4m 1M; vis: 252·5°-G-256·5°-W-259·5°-R-262·5°; 50°47'·28N 00°19'·71E.
S Bkwtr Hd Fl (4) R 12s 3m 6M; 50°47'·30N 00°20'·03E.
St Leonard's Outfall Fl Y 5s; 50°49'·31N 00°31'·95E.

HASTINGS

Ldg Lts 356·3°. Front, FR 14m 4M; 50°51'·29N 00°35'·38E. Rear, West Hill, 357m from front, FR 55m 4M; W twr.

RYE

Rye Fairway, L Fl 10s; 50°54'·04N 00°48'·04E.
W Groyne Hd No. 2 Fl R 5s 7m 6M; 50°55'·58N 00°46'·55E.
E Arm Hd No. 1 Q (9) 15s 7m 5M; G △; *Horn 7s*; 50°55'·73N 00°46'·46E.
Dungeness Outfall Q (6) + L Fl 15s; 50°54'·45N 00°58'·21E.
Dungeness ☆ 50°54'·81N 00°58'·56E; Fl 10s 40m **21M**; B ○ twr, W bands and lantern, floodlit; Part obsc 078°-shore; (H24). F RG 37m 10M (same twr); vis: 057°-R-073°-G-078°-196°-R-216°; *Horn (3) 60s*; FR Lts shown between 2·4M and 5·2M WNW when firing taking place. QR on radio mast 1·2M NW.

DUNGENESS TO NORTH FORELAND

FOLKESTONE

Hythe Flats Outfall Fl Y 5s; 51°02′·52N 01°05′·32E.

Breakwater Head ☆ Fl (2) 10s 14m **22M**; 51°04′·56N 01°11′·69E.

DOVER

Admiralty Pier Extension Head ☆ 51°06′·69N 01°19′·66E; Fl 7·5s 21m **20M**; W twr; vis: 096°-090°, obsc in The Downs by S Foreland inshore of 226°; *Horn 10s;* Int Port Tfc sigs.

S Bkwtr W Hd ☆ 51°06′·78N 01°19′·80E;Oc R 30s 21m **18M**; W twr.

Knuckle ☆ 51°07′·04N 01°20′·49E; Fl (4) WR 10s 15m **W15M**, R13M; W twr; vis: 059°-R-239°-W-059°.

N Head ☆ Fl R 2·5s 11m 5M; 51°07′·20N 01°20′·61E.

Eastern Arm Hd ☆ Fl G 5s 12m 5M; *Horn (2) 30s*; Int port tfc sigs; 51°07′·31N 01°20′·59E.

DOVER STRAIT

Bullock Bank VQ; 50°46′·94N 01°07′·60E.

Ridens SE VQ (3) 5s; 50°43′·47N 01°18′·87E.

Colbart SW VQ (6) + L Fl 10s; 50°48′·86N 01°16′·30E.

South Varne Q (6) + L Fl 15s; 50°55′·64N 01°17′·30E.

Mid Varne VQ(9)10s; 50°58′·94N 01°19′·88E.

East Varne VQ(3)5s; 50°58′·22N 01°20′·90E.

Colbart N VQ; 50°57′·45N 01°23′·29E.

Varne NW Q; 51°00′·80N 01°22′·70E.

Varne NE Q (3) 10s; 50°59′·80N 01°22′·70E.

VARNE 51°01′·29N 01°23′·90E; Fl R 5s 12m **15M**; ***Racon (T) 10M***; *Horn 30s*; 992351038.

CS 4 Fl (4) Y 15s; 51°08′·62N 01°33′·92E.

MPC Fl Y 2·5s; ***Racon (O) 10M***; 51°06′·12N 01°38′·20E; 992351122.

SW Goodwin Q (6) + L Fl 15s; 51°08′·50N 01°28′·88E; 992351036.

S Goodwin Fl (4) R 15s; 51°10′·60N 01°32′·26E.

SE Goodwin Fl (3) R 10s; 51°12′·99N 01°34′·45E.

E GOODWIN 51°13′·26N 01°36′·37E; Fl 15s 12m **23M**; R hull with lt twr amidships; ***Racon (T) 10M***; *Horn 30s*; 992351035.

E Goodwin Q (3) 10s; 51°15′·67N 01°35′·69E.

NE Goodwin Q (3) 10s; ***Racon (M) 10M***. 51°20′·31N 01°34′·16E.

DEAL and THE DOWNS

Trinity Bay VQ (9) 10s; 51°11′·60N 01°29′·00E.

Deal Bank QR; 51°12′·92N 01°25′·57E.

Goodwin Fork Q (6) + L Fl 15s; *Bell;* 51°14′·38N 01°26′·70E.

Downs Fl (2) R 5s; *Bell;* 51°14′·50N 01°26′·22E.

GULL STREAM

W Goodwin Fl G 5s; 51°15′·61N 01°27′·38E.

S Brake Fl (3) R 10s; 51°15′·77N 01°26′·82E.

NW Goodwin Q (9) 15s; 51°16′·73N 01°28′·60E.

Brake Fl (4) R 15s; 51°16′·98N 01°28′·19E.

N Goodwin Fl G 2·5s; 51°18′·12N 01°30′·35E.

Gull Stream QR; 51°18′·26N 01°29′·69E.

Gull VQ (3) 5s; 51°19′·57N 01°31′·30E.

Goodwin Knoll Fl (2) G 5s; 51°19′·57N 01°32′·20E.

RAMSGATE CHANNEL

B2 Fl (2) G 5s; 51°18′·26N 01°23′·93E.

W Quern Q (9) 15s; 51°18′·98N 01°25′·39E.

RAMSGATE

RA Q(6) + L Fl 15s; 51°19′·60N 01°30′·13E.

E Brake Fl R 5s; 51°19′·47N 01°29′·20E.

No. 1 QG; 51°19′·56N 01°27′·29E.

No. 2 Fl (4) R 10s; 51°19′·46N 01°27′·28E.

No. 3 Fl G 2·5s; 51°19′·56N 01°26′·61E.

No. 4 QR; 51°19′·46N 01°26′·60E.

N Quern Q; 51°19′·41N 01°26′·11E.

No. 5 Q (6) + L Fl 15s; 51°19′·56N 01°25′·91E.

No. 6 Fl (2) R 5s; 51°19′·46N 01°25′·91E.

South Bkwtr Hd VQ R 10m 5M; 51°19′·46N 01°25′·41E.

N Bkwtr Hd QG 10m 5M; 51°19′·56N 01°25′·47E.

Western Marine terminal Dir lt 270°, Oc WRG 10s 10m 5M; B △, Or stripe; vis: 259°-G-269°-W- 271°-R-281°; 51°19′·51N 01°24′·85E. Rear 493m from front Oc 5s 17m 5M; B ▽, Or stripe; vis: 263°-278°.

BROADSTAIRS and NORTH FORELAND

Broadstairs Knoll Fl R 2·5s; 51°20′·88N 01°29′·48E.

Pier SE End ☆ 2 FR (vert) 7m 4M; 51°21′·50N 01°26′·74E.

Elbow Q; 51°23′·23N 01°31′·59E.

North Foreland ☆ 51°22′·49N 01°26′·70E; Fl (5) WR 20s 57m **W19M, R16M, R15M**; W 8-sided twr; vis: shore-W-150°-R(**16M**)-181°-R(**15M**)-200°-W-011°; H24; 992351020.

1	Nab Tower	**1**																
2	Boulder Lt Buoy	5	**2**															
3	Owers Lt Buoy	10	6	**3**														
4	Littlehampton	19	13	12	**4**													
5	Shoreham	32	24	21	13	**5**												
6	Brighton	35	28	24	17	5	**6**											
7	Newhaven	40	34	29	24	12	7	**7**										
8	Beachy Head Lt	46	41	36	30	20	14	8	**8**									
9	Eastbourne	51	45	40	34	24	19	12	7	**9**								
10	Rye	72	67	62	56	46	41	34	25	23	**10**							
11	Dungeness Lt	76	71	66	60	50	44	38	30	26	9	**11**						
12	Folkestone	92	84	81	76	65	60	53	43	40	23	13	**12**					
13	Dover	97	89	86	81	70	65	58	48	45	28	18	5	**13**				
14	Ramsgate	112	104	101	96	85	80	73	63	60	43	33	20	15	**14**			
15	N Foreland Lt	115	107	104	99	88	83	76	66	63	46	36	23	18	3	**15**		
16	Sheerness	146	139	135	132	119	114	107	97	96	79	67	54	49	34	31	**16**	
17	London Bridge	188	184	177	177	161	156	149	139	141	124	109	96	91	76	73	45	**17**

DISTANCE TABLES

Approx distances in nautical miles are by the most direct route allowing for dangers and TSS.

OFFSHORE MARKS

SANDETTIE 51°09′·36N 01°47′·12E; Fl 5s 12m **15M**; R hull with lt twr amidships; *Racon*; *Horn 30s*; 992351029.
F1 Fl (4) Y 15s; 51°11′·21N 01°44′·91E.
South Falls Q (6) + L Fl 15s; 51°13′·84N 01°43′·93E.
Sandettie W Fl (3) G 12s; 51°15′·09N 01°54′·47E.
Mid Falls Fl (3) R 10s; 51°18′·63N 01°46′·99E.
Inter Bank Fl Y 5s; *Bell*; ***Racon (M) 10M***; 51°16′·47N 01°52′·23E. F2 Fl (4) Y 15s; 51°20′·41N 01°56′·19E.

AREA 4 *East England – North Foreland to Berwick-upon-Tweed*

SELECTED LIGHTS, BUOYS & WAYPOINTS

THAMES ESTUARY – SOUTHERN

(Direction of buoyage generally East to West)

APPROACHES to THAMES ESTUARY

Foxtrot 3 51°24′·15N 02°00′·38E; Fl 10s 12m **15M**; ***Racon (T) 10M***; *Horn 10s;* 992351033.
Falls Hd Q; 51°28′·23N 01°49′·89E.
Drill Stone Q (3) 10s; 51°25′·88N 01°42′·89E.
Thanet N VQ 15s; 51°28′·28N 01°38′·06E.
NE Spit VQ (3) ***Racon (T) 10M;*** 51°27′·93N 01°29′·89E; 992351037
East Margate Fl R 2·5s; 51°27′·03N 01°26′·40E.
Elbow Q; 51°23′·23N 01°31′·59E.
Foreness Pt Outfall Fl R 5s; 51°24′·61N 01°26′·02E.
Longnose 51°24′·15N 01°26′·08E.
Longnose Spit Fl R 2·5s 5m 2M; 51°23′·93N 01°25′·68E.

MARGATE and GORE CHANNEL

SE Margate Q (3) 10s; 51°24′·05N 01°20′·40E.
S Margate Fl G 2·5s; 51°23′·83N 01°16′·65E.
Copperas QG; 51°23′·81N 01°11′·18E.
Reculver QR; 51°23′·63N 01°12′·56E.

HERNE BAY

Beltinge Bay Bn Fl Y 5s; 51°22′·73N 01°08′·63E.
Landing Stage ☆ Q 18m 4M, (isolated); 51°22′·91N 01°06′·89E.
N Pier Hd ☆ 2 FR (vert); 51°22′·43N 01°07′·27E.

WHITSTABLE

Whitstable Street ; 51°24′·00N 01°01′·54E. (See Swale.)
Oyster Fl (2) R 10s; 51°22′·14N 01°01′·16E.
W Quay Dn ☆ Fl G 5s 2m.

THE SWALE

Whitstable Street Fl R 2s; 51°24′·00N 01°01′·54E.
Columbine Fl G 2s; 51°24′·26N 01°01′·34E.
Columbine Spit Fl (3) G 10s; 51°23′·86N 01°00′·03E.
Ham Gat Q G; 51°23′·08N 00°58′·32E.
Pollard Spit Q R; 51°22′·98N 00°58′·57E.
Sand End Fl G 5s; 51°21′·43N 00°55′·90E.
Receptive Point Fl G 10s; 51°20′·86N 00°54′·41E.
Queenborough Spit Q (3) 10s; 51°25′·81N 00°43′·93E.
South Oaze Fl R 2s; 51°21′·34N 00°56′·01E.

QUEENS CHANNEL and FOUR FATHOMS CHANNEL

E Margate Fl R 2·5s; 51°27′·03N 01°26′·40E.
Spaniard Q (3) 10s; 51°26′·23N 01°04′·00E.
Spile Fl G 2·5s; 51°26′·43N 00°55′·70E.

PRINCES CHANNEL

Tongue Sand E VQ (3) 5s; 51°29′·48N 01°22′·21E.
Tongue Sand N Q; 51°29′·68N 01°22′·03E.
Princes Outer VQ (6) + L Fl 10s; 51°28′·89N 01°20′·43E.
Princes North Q G; 51°29′·25N 01°18′·35E.
Princes South Q R; 51°28′·74N 01°18′·26E.
Princes No.1 Fl (4) G 15s; 51°29′·23N 01°16′·02E.
Princes No.2 Fl (2) R 5s; 51°28′·81N 01°13′·08E.
Princes No.3 Fl (2) G 5s; 51°29′·33N 01°13′·10E.
Princes No.4 Fl (3) R 10s; 51°28′·83N 01°09′·90E.
Princes No.5 Fl (3) G 10s; 51°29′·39N 01°10′·00E.
Princes Mid Fl Y 5s; 51°29′·19N 01°09′·00E.
Shivering Sand Twr N Q; 51°30′·01N 01°04′·76E.
Shivering Sand Twr S Q (6)+L Fl 15s; *Bell*; 51°29′·75N 01°04′·83E.
Princes No.8 Fl (2) R 5s; 51°29′·14N 01°03′·00E.
Princes Inner Fl Y 2·5s; 51°29′·59N 01°03′·47E.

FOULGER'S GAT and KNOB CHANNEL

N Edinburgh Channel is not buoyed. Foulger's Gat, lies within the boundary of the London Array Wind Farm.
Long Sand Outer Iso 2s; 51°34′·61N 01°28′·34E.
Long Sand Middle Iso 5s; 51°35′·60N 01°26′·45E.
Long Sand Inner Iso 2s; 51°38′·78N 01°25′·44E.
SE Knob Fl G 5s; 51°30′·89N 01°06′·41E.
Knob Iso 5s; *Whis*; 51°30′·69N 01°04′·28E.

OAZE DEEP

Oaze Deep Fl (2) G 5s; 51°29′·18N 00°56′·77E.
Red Sand Trs N Fl (3) R 10s; *Bell*; 51°28′·73N 00°59′·32E.
N Oaze QR; 51°30′·03N 00°57′·65E.
Oaze Fl (4) Y 10s; 51°29′·06N 00°56′·93E.
W Oaze Iso 5s; 51°29′·06N 00°55′·43E.
Oaze Bank Q G 5s; 51°33′·24N 00°46′·32E.
Cant (unlit); 51°27′·77N 00°53′·36E.
East Cant QR; 51°28′·53N 00°55′·60E.

MEDWAY, SHEERNESS

Medway Mo (A) 6s; 51°28′·83N 00°52′·81E.
No. 1 Fl G 2·5s; 51°28′·55N 00°50′·50E.
No. 2 Q; 51°28′·33N 00°50′·52E.
No. 7 Fl G 10s; 51°27′·91N 00°47′·52E.
No. 9 Fl G 5s; 51°27′·74N 00°46′·61E.
No. 11 Fl (3) G 10s; 51°27′·51N 00°45′·80E.
Grain Hard Fl G 5s; 51°26′·98N 00°44′·17E.
Isle of Grain ☆ Q 20m 13M; RW ◇ on R twr; 51°26′·70N 00°43′·38E.
Queenborough Spit Q (3) 10s; 51°25′·81N 00°43′·93E.

RIVER THAMES

SEA REACH, NORE and YANTLET

Sea Reach 1 (N) Fl Y 2·5s; ***Racon (T) 10M***; 51°29′·59N 00°52′·71E.
Sea Reach 1 (S) Fl R 2·5s; 51°29′·39N 00°52′·45E.
Sea Reach 2 (N) Fl R 2·5s; 51°29′·49N 00°49′·73E.

Sea Reach 2 (S) Fl R 2·5s; 51°29'·30N 00°49'·75E.
Sea Reach 3 (N) Q G (sync); 51°29'·41N 00°46'·80E.
Sea Reach 3 (S) Q R (sync); 51°29'·22N 00°46'·71E.
Sea Reach 4 (N) Fl (2) G 5s; 51°29'·69N 00°44'·19E.
Sea Reach 4 (S) Fl (2) R 5s; 51°29'·50N 00°44'·12E.
Sea Reach 5 (N) VQ G; 51°30'·04N 00°41'·47E.
Sea Reach 5 (S) VQ R; 51°29'·85N 00°41'·43E.
Sea Reach 6 (N) Fl G 5s; 51°30'·13N 00°39'·87E.
Sea Reach 6 (S) Fl R 5s; 51°29'·93N 00°39'·84E.
Sea Reach 7 (N) Fl Y 2·5s; 51°30'·21N 00°36'·94E.
Sea Reach 7 (S) Fl R 2·5s; ***Racon (T) 10M***; 51°30'·01N 00°36'·91E.
Nore Swatch Fl (4) R 15s; 51°28'·28N 00°45'·55E.
Mid Swatch Fl G 5s; 51°28'·68N 00°44'·16E.
W Nore Sand Fl (3) R 10s; 51°29'·48N 00°40'·87E.
East Blyth Q; 51°29'·73N 00°37'·81E.
Mid Blyth Q; 51°30'·08N 00°32'·38E.

LEIGH-ON-SEA and SOUTHEND-ON-SEA
Leigh ; 51°31'·07N 00°42'·56E.
Southend Pier E End ☆ 2 FG (vert) 7m; *Horn Mo (N) 30s, Bell (1)*

LOWER HOPE REACH
West Blyth Q R; 51°29'·57N 00°28'·39E.
Mucking 1 Q G; 51°29'·70N 00°37'·28E.
Lower Hope Fl R 5s; 51°29'·32N 00°28'·02E.
Mucking 3 Fl G 2·5s; 51°29'·33N 00°27'·68E.
Mucking 5 Fl (3) G 10s; 51°28'·76N 00°27'·19E.
Mucking 7 Fl G 5s; 51°28'·03N 00°26'·77E.
Bell Ovens Q G; 51°27'·50N 00°26'·35E.
Higham Fl (2) R 5s; 51°27'·40N 00°26'·85E.
Tilbury Q(6) + L Fl 15s; 51°27'·16N 00°25'·50E.

GRAVESEND
Shornmead ☆ Fl (2) WR 10s 12m, W11/7M, R11M; vis 070°-W-084°-R(Intens)-089°-W(Intens)-094°-W-250°; 51°26'·92N 00°26'·24E.
Northfleet Upper ☆ Oc WRG 10s 30m **W16M**, R12M, G12M; vis:126°-R-149°-W-159°-G-268°-W-279°; 51°26'·93N 00°20'·06E.

THAMES TIDAL BARRIER
Spans B, C, D, E, F, G are navigable. Spans C–F are for large ships. E-bound small craft/yachts use Span B (51°29'·73N 00°02'·23E). W-bound small craft/yachts use Span G (51°29'·91N 00°02'·21E). **Red X** indicates span closed **Green →** indicates span open. W lights show either side of open spans in poor visibility.

KENTISH KNOCK
Kentish Knock Q (3) 10s; 51°38'·08N 01°40·43E.
S Knock Q (6) + L Fl 15s; *Bell*; 51°34'·13N 01°34'·29E.

KNOCK JOHN CHANNEL
No. 7 Fl (4) G 15s; 51°32'·03N 01°06'·40E.
No. 5 Fl (3) G 10s; 51°32'·49N 01°07'·75E.
No. 4 QR 10s; 51°32'·40 N 01°08'·08E.
No. 2 Fl (3) R 10s; 51°33'·03N 01°09'·63E.
No. 3 Q (6) + L Fl 15s; 51°33'·29N 01°09'·83E.
No. 1 Fl G 5s; 51°33'·75N 01°10'·72E.
Knock John Fl (2) R 5s; 51°33'·61N 01°11'·37E.

BLACK DEEP
No. 12 Fl (4) R 15s; 51°33'·83N 01°13'·50E.
No. 11 Fl (3) G 10s; 51°34'·33N 01°13'·40E.
No. 10 Fl (3) R 10s; 51°34'·74N 01°15'·60E.
No. 9 Q (6) + L Fl 15s; 51°35'·13N 01°15'·09E.
No. 8 Q (9) 15s; 51°36'·36N 01°20'·43E.
No. 7 QG. 51°37'·08N 01°17'·69E.
No. 6 Fl R 2·5s; 51°38'·53N 01°24'·41E.
No. 5 VQ (3) 5s; 51°39'·53N 01°23'·00E.
No. 4 Fl (2) R 5s; 51°41'·42N 01°28'·49E.
Long Sand Bcn ; 51°41'·48N 01°29'·49E.
No. 3 Fl (3) G 15s; 51°42'·39N 01°26'·66E.
No. 1 Fl G 5s, 51°44'·03N 01°28'·09E.
No. 2 Fl (4) R 15s; 51°45'·63N 01°32'·20E.
SHM Fl Y 2·5s; ***Racon (T) 10M***; 51°29'·59N 00°52'·71E.

SUNK
Sunk Head Tower Q; *Whis*; 51°46'·63N 01°30'·51E.
Black Deep QR; 51°48'·10N 01°36'·60E.
Long Sand Head VQ; *Whis*; 51°47'·90N 01°39'·42E.
SUNK CENTRE 51°50'·11N 01°46'·02E; Fl (2) 20s 12m **16M**; ***Racon (C) 10M***; *Horn (2) 60s*; 992351094.
Dynamo Fl Y 2·5s; 51°29'·59N 00°52'·71E.
Trinity Q (6) + L Fl 15s; 51°49'·03N 01°36'·39E.
SUNK INNER 51°51'·17N 01°34'·40E; Iso 3s 11m 12M; ***Racon (C) 10M***; *Horn 30s*; 992351027.

FISHERMANS GAT
Outer Fisherman Q (3) 10s; 51°34'·02N 01°25'·10E.
Fisherman No. 1 Fl G 2·5s (sync); 51°34'·50N 01°23'·52E.
Fisherman No. 2 Fl R 2·5s (sync); 51°34'·30N 01°23'·50E.
Fisherman No. 3 Fl G 5s; 51°34'·78N 01°22'·65E.
Fisherman No. 4 Fl (2) R 5s; 51°34'·77N 01°22'·08E.
Fisherman No. 5 Fl (2) G 5s; 51°35'·25N 01°21'·84E.
Fisherman No. 6 Fl (3) R 10s; 51°35'·08N 01°21'·56E.
Inner Fisherman Q R; 51°36'·10N 01°19'·97E.

BARROW DEEP
SW Barrow Q(6) + L Fl 15s; *Bell*; 51°32'·29N 01°00'·31E.
Alice Wk Fl (2) 5s; 51°32'·33N 01°04'·22E.
Barrow No. 14 Fl R 2·5s; 51°31'·83N 01°00'·43E.
Barrow No. 13 Fl (2) G 5s; 51°32'·82N 01°03'·07E.
Barrow No. 12 Fl (2) R 5s; 51°33'·24N 01°05'·94E.
Barrow No.11 Fl (3) G 10s; 51°34'·08N 01°06'·70E.
Barrow No. 9 VQ (3) 5s; 51°35'·34N 01°10'·30E.
Barrow No. 8 Fl (2) R 5s; 51°35'·03N 01°11'·40E.
Barrow No. 6 Fl (4) R 15s; 51°37'·30N 01°14'·69E.
Barrow No. 5 Fl G 10s; 51°40'·03N 01°16'·20E.
Barrow No. 4 VQ (9) 10s; 51°39'·88N 01°17'·48E.
Barrow No. 3 Q (3) 10s; ***Racon (M)10M***; 51°42'·02N 01°20'·24E.
Barrow No. 2 Fl (2) R 5s; 51°41'·98N 01°22'·89E.

WEST SWIN and MIDDLE DEEP
Blacktail (W) ; 51°31'·46N 00°55'·19E.
Maplin Q G (sync W Swin); *Bell*; 51°33'·66N 01°01'·40E.
W Swin Q R (sync Maplin); 51°33'·40N 01°01'·97E.
Maplin Edge Fl G 2.5s; 51°35'·33N 01°03'·64E.
Maplin Bank Fl (3) R 10s; 51°35'·50N 01°04'·70E.

EAST SWIN and KING'S CHANNEL
NE Maplin Fl G 5s; *Bell*; 51°37'·43N 01°04'·90E.
W Hook Middle 51°39'·18N 01°07'·97E.
S Whitaker Fl (2) G 10s; 51°40'·17N 01°09'·11E.
N Middle Q; 51°41'·35N 01°12'·61E.
W Sunk Q (9) 15s; 51°44'·33N 01°25'·80E.
Gunfleet Spit Q (6) + L Fl 15s; *Bell*; 51°45'·33N 01°21'·70E.

WHITAKER CHANNEL and RIVER CROUCH
Whitaker Q (3) 10s; *Bell*; 51°41'·43N 01°10'·51E.

Inner Whitaker VQ (6) + L Fl 10s; 51°40'·76N 01°08'·40E.
Swin Spitway Iso 10s; *Bell;* 51°41'·95N 01°08'·35E.
Whitaker 1 FlG 5s (sync Whit 2), 51° 40'.69N 01° 06'.67E.
Whitaker 2 FlR 5s (sync Whit 1), 51° 40'.41N 01° 06'.78E.
Whitaker 3 Fl(2) G 5s (sync Whit 4) 51° 40'.41N 01° 04'.74E.
Whitaker 4 Fl(2) R 5s (sync Whit 4) 51° 40'.16N 01° 04'.91E.
Whitaker 5 Fl(3) G 10s (sync Whit 6) 51° 40'.03N 01° 03'.22E.
Whitaker 6 Fl(3) R 10s (sync Whit 5) 51° 39'.77N 01° 03'.43E.
Whitaker 7 Fl(4) G 10s (sync Whit 8) 51° 39'.54N 01° 02'.00E.
Whitaker 8 Fl(4) R 10s (sync Whit 7) 51° 39'.35N 01° 02'.00E.
Swallowtail 1 Fl Y 5s, 51° 41'.38N 01° 08'.20E.
Swallowtail 2 Fl Y 10s, 51° 41'.19N 01° 06'.28E.
Swallowtail 3 Fl Y 15s, 51° 40.84N 01° 04.39E.
Swallowtail 4 (2) Y 10s, 51° 40'.52N 01° 03'.47E.
Buxey Edge Fl G 10s, 51° 40'.65N 01° 03'.48E.
Swallowtail VQ (9) 10s, 51° 40'.04N 01° 02'.65E.
Sunken Buxey VQ; 51°39'·59N 01°00'·77E.
Buxey No. 1 VQ (6) + L Fl 10s; 51°39'·18N 01°01'·13E.
Buxey No. 2 Q; 51°39'·08N 01°00'·23E.
Outer Crouch 1 Fl G 5s (sync Cr 2) 51° 38'.71N 00° 59'.00E.
Outer Crouch 2 Fl R 5s (sync Cr 1) 51° 38'.62N 00° 59'.20E.
Outer Crouch 3 Fl G 10s (sync Cr 4) 51° 38'.10N 00° 57'.83E.
Outer Crouch 4 Fl R 10s (sync Cr 3) 51° 37'.95N 00° 58'.00E.
Crouch Q.Fl, 51° 37.650N 00° 56.582E.
Inner Crouch L Fl 10s, 51° 37'.19N 00° 55'.09E.
Branklet (RGR) **Pref Chan to Stbd,** Comp grp Fl (R) 2+1 10s, 51° 36'.99N 00° 52'.10E.

GOLDMER GAT and WALLET

NE Gunfleet Q (3) 10s; 51°49'·93N 01°27'·79E.
Wallet No. 2 Fl R 5s; 51°48'·88N 01°22'·99E.
Wallet No. 4 Fl (4) R 10s; 51°46'·53N 01°17'·23E.
Wallet Spitway L Fl 10s; *Bell*; 51°42'·86N 01°07'·30E.
Knoll Q; 51°43'·88N 01°05'·07E.
Eagle QG; 51°44'·13N 01°03'·82E.
N Eagle Q; 51°44'·71N 01°04'·32E.
NW Knoll Fl (2) R 5s; 51°44'·35N 01°02'·17E.
Colne Bar Fl (2) G 5s; 51°44'·61N 01°02'·57E.
Bench Head Fl (3) G 10s; 51°44'·69N 01°01'·10E.

RIVER BLACKWATER

The Nass VQ (3) 5s 6m 2M; 51°45'·83N 00°54'·83E.
Thirslet Fl (3) G 10s; 51°43'·73N 00°50'·39E.
No. 1 ; 51°43'·44N 00°48'·02E.

RIVER COLNE and BRIGHTLINGSEA

Inner Bench Head No. 2 Fl (2) R 5s; 51°45'·96N 01°01'·74E.
Colne Pt No. 1 Fl G 3s; 51°46'·01N 01°01'·92E.
No. 8 Fl R 3s; 51°46'·90N 01°01'·30E.
No. 9 Fl G 3s; 51°47'·36N 01°01'·07E.
Ldg lts 041°. Front, FR 7m 4M; W □, R stripe on post; vis: 020°-080°; 51°48'·39N 01°01'·20E. Rear, 50m from front, FR 10m 4M; W □, R stripe on post. FR lts are shown on 7 masts between 1·5M and 3M NW when firing occurs.

WALTON BACKWATERS

Pye End L Fl 10s; 51°55'·03N 01°17'·90E.
No. 2 Fl (2) 5s; 51°54'·62N 01°16'·80E.
Crab Knoll No. 3 Fl G 5s; 51°54'·41N 01°16'·41E.
No. 16 51°53'·17N 01°15'·52E.

HARWICH APPROACHES

(Direction of buoyage is North to South)

MEDUSA CHANNEL

Medusa Fl G 5s; 51°51'·23N 01°20'·35E.
Stone Banks FlR 5s; 51°53'·19N 01°19'·23E.
Pennyhole ; 51°53'·55N 01°18'·00E (Mar–Sep).

CORK SAND and ROUGH SHOALS

S Cork Q (6) + L Fl 15s; 51°51'·33N 01°24'·09E.
SE Roughs Tower Q (3) 10s; 51°53'·64N 01°28'·94E.
NW Roughs Tower VQ (9) 10s; 51°53'·81N 01°28'·77E.
Cork Sand Fl (3) R 10s; 51°55'·51N 01°25'·42E.

HARWICH CHANNEL

S Threshold Fl (4) Y 10s; 51°52'·20N 01°33'·14E.
S Shipwash 2 By(s) Q (6) + L Fl 15s; 51°52'·71N 01°33'·97E.
Outer Tidal Bn Mo (U) 15s 2m 3M; 51°52'·85N 01°32'·34E.
E Fort Massac VQ (3) 5s; 51°53'·36N 01°32'·79E.
W Fort Massac VQ (9) 10s; 51°53'·36N 01°32'·49E.
Walker Q (9)15s; 51°53'·79N 01°33'·90E.
N Threshold Fl Y 5s; 51°54'·49N 01°33'·47E.
SW Shipwash Fl Y 2·5s; 51°54'·75N 01°34'·21E.
Haven Mo (A) 5s; 51°55'·76N 01°32'·56E.
W Shipwash Fl (2) R 10s; 51°57'·13N 01°35'·89E.
NW Shipwash Fl R 5s; 51°58'·98N 01°37'·01E.
Harwich App (HA) Iso 5s; 51°56'·75N 01°30'·66E.
Cross Fl (3) Y 10s; 51°56'·23N 01°30'·48E.
Harwich Chan No. 1 Fl Y 2·5s; ***Racon (T) 10M***; 51°56'·13N 01°27'·06E.
Harwich Chan No. 3 Fl (3) Y 10s; 51°56'·04N 01°25'·54E.
Harwich Chan No. 5 Fl (5) Y 10s; 51°55'·96N 01°24'·01E.
Harwich Chan No. 7 Fl (3) Y 10s; 51°55'·87N 01°22'·49E.
S Bawdsey Q (6) + L Fl 15s; *Whis*; 51°57'·23N 01°30'·19E.
Washington QG; 51°56'·52N 01°26'·59E.
Felixstowe Ledge Fl (3) G 10s; 51°56'·30N 01°23'·72E.
Wadgate Ledge Fl (4) G 15s; 51°56'·16N 01°21'·99E.
Platters Q (6) + L Fl 15s; 51°55'·64N 01°20'·97E.
Rolling Ground QG; 51°55'·55N 01°19'·75E.
Beach End Fl (2) G 5s; 51°55'·62N 01°19'·21E.
Cork Sand Yacht Bn VQ 2M; 51°55'·21N 01°25'·20E.
Rough VQ; 51°55'·19N 01°31'·00E.
Pitching Ground Fl (4) R 15s; 51°55'·43N 01°21'·05E.
Inner Ridge QR; 51°55'·38N 01°20'·20E.
Deane L Fl R 6s; 51°55'·36N 01°19'·28E.
Landguard Q; 51°55'·45N 01°18'·84E.

RIVERS STOUR AND ORWELL

RIVER STOUR and HARWICH

Shotley Spit Q (6) + L Fl 15s; 51°57'·21N 01°17'·69E.
Shotley Marina Lock E side Dir lt 339·5° 3m 1M (uses Moiré pattern); Or structure; 51°57'·46N 01°16'·60E.
Guard Fl R 5s; *Bell*; 51°57'·07N 01°17'·86E.

RIVER ORWELL and IPSWICH

Suffolk Yacht Harbour. Ldg lts Front Iso Y 1M; 51°59'·73N 01°16'·09E. Rear Oc Y 4s 1M.

HARWICH TO ORFORD NESS

FELIXSTOWE, R DEBEN and WOODBRIDGE HAVEN

Woodbridge Haven Mo(A)15s; 51°58'·20N 01°23'·85E.
Deben ; 51°59'·30N 01°23'·53E.

RIVERS ORE and ALDE

Orford Haven L Fl 10s; *Bell*. 52°01'·85N 01°28'·20E.

OFFSHORE MARKS

S Galloper Q (6) L Fl 15s; ***Racon (T) 10M***; 51°43'·98N 01°56'·43E.

N Galloper Q; 51°49′·84N 01°59′·99E.
S Inner Gabbard Q (6) + L Fl 15s. 51°49′·92N 01°51′·89E.
N Inner Gabbard Q; 51°59′·20N 01°56′·00E.
Outer Gabbard Q (3) 10s; ***Racon (O) 10M***; 51°57′·83N 02°04′·19E.
NHR-SE Fl G 5s; 51°45′·39N 02°39′·89E.

SHIPWASH and BAWDSEY BANK
E Shipwash VQ (3) 5s; 51°57′·08N 01°37′·89E.
NW Shipwash Fl R 5s; 51°58′·98N 01°37′·01E.
N Shipwash Q 7M; ***Racon (M) 10M***; *Whis*; 52°01′·73N 01°38′·27E; 992351069.
S Bawdsey Q (6) + L Fl 15s; *Whis*; 51°57′·23N 01°30′·22E.
Mid Bawdsey Fl (3) G 10s; 51°58′·88N 01°33′·59E.
NE Bawdsey Fl G 10s; 52°01′·73N 01°36′·09E.

CUTLER and WHITING BANKS
Cutler QG; 51°58′·51N 01°27′·48E.
SW Whiting Q (6) + L Fl 10s; 52°00′·96N 01°30′·69E.
Whiting Hook Fl R 10s; 52°02′·98N 01°31′·82E.
NE Whiting Q (3) 10s; 52°03′·61N 01°33′·32E.

ORFORD NESS TO WINTERTON

(Direction of buoyage is South to North)
Orford Ness Lt Ho (dis) 52°05′·04N 01°34′·45E; W ○ twr, R bands.
Aldeburgh Ridge QR; 52°06′·49N 01°36′·95E.

SOUTHWOLD
Southwold ☆ 52°19′·63N 01°40′·89E; Fl 10s 37m **W24M**; vis 204°-W-032·5°, 992351019.

LOWESTOFT and APPR VIA STANFORD CHANNEL
E Barnard Q (3) 10s; 52°25′·14N 01°46′·38E.
Newcome Sand QR; 52°26′·28N 01°46′·97E.
S Holm VQ (6) + L Fl 10s; 52°26′·85N 01°47′·15E.
Stanford Fl R 2·5s; 52°27′·35N 01°46′·67E.
SW Holm Fl (2) G 5s; 52°27′·87N 01°46′·99E.
Kirkley ☆ Oc WRG 10s 17m, W8M, R6M, G6M, vis: 210°-G-224°-W-229°-R-313°; 52°27′·71N 01°44′·54E.
Outer Hbr S Pier Hd ☆ Oc R 5s 12m 6M; *Horn (4) 60s*; Tfc sigs; 52°28′·29N 01°45′·36E.
N Newcome Fl (4) R 15s; 52°28′·39N 01°46′·37E.
Lowestoft ☆ 52°29′·22N 01°45′·35; Fl 15s 37m **23M**; W twr; part obscd 347°- shore.

LOWESTOFT NORTH ROAD and CORTON ROAD
Lowestoft Ness SE Q (6) + L Fl 15s; 52°28′·84N 01°46′·25E.
Lowestoft Ness N VQ (3) 5s; *Bell*; 52°28′·89N 01°46′·23E.
W Holm Fl (3) G 10s; 52°29′·80N 01°47′·09E.
NW Holm Fl (4) G 15s; 52°31′·93N 01°46′·70E.

GREAT YARMOUTH APPROACH via HOLM CHANNEL
E Newcome Fl (2) R 5s; 52°28′·51N 01°49′·21E.
Holm Approach Q (3) 10s; 52°30′·88N 01°50′·22E.
Holm Sand Q (9) 15s; 52°33′·18N 01°46′·54E.
S Corton Q (6) + L Fl 15s; *Bell*; 52°32′·94N 01°49′·12E.
NE Holm Fl R 2·5s; 52°32′·69N 01°48′·48E.
Mid Corton Fl G 2·5s; 52°33′·62N 01°48′·01E.
N Holm Q. 52°33′·93N 01°47′·23E.
W Corton Fl (3) G 10s; 52°34′·12N 01°47′·50E.

GREAT YARMOUTH and GORLESTON
Gorleston South Pier Hd ☆ Fl R 3s 11m 11M; vis: 235°-340°; 52°34′·33N 01°44′·28E.
N Pier Hd ☆ QG 8m 6M; vis: 176°-078°; *Horn(3) 60s*; 52°34′·38N 01°44′·38E.
Outer Hbr S Pier ☆ Q R 17m 3M; 52°34′·61N 01°44′·73E.
Outer Hbr N Pier ☆ Q G 17m 3M; 52°34′·70N 01°44′·74E.

GREAT YARMOUTH TO THE WASH

(Direction of buoyage South to North)

YARMOUTH and CAISTER ROADS/COCKLE GATEWAY
SW Scroby Fl G 2·5s; 52°35′·13N 01°46′·69E.
Scroby Elbow Fl (2) G 5s; *Bell*; 52°36′·55N 01°46′·26E.
Yarmouth Outfall Q R; 52°37′·58N 01°45′·70E.
Mid Caister Fl (2) R 5s; *Bell*; 52°38′·99N 01°45′·66E.
NW Scroby Fl (3) G 10s; 52°40′·36N 01°46′·31E.
N Caister Fl (3) R 10s; 52°40′·77N 01°45′·65E.
Hemsby Fl R 2·5s; 52°41′·80N 01°46′·00E.
N Scroby VQ; 52°41′·39N 01°46′·47E.
Cockle VQ (3) 5s; *Bell*; 52°44′·03N 01°43′·59E.

OFFSHORE ROUTE
Cross Sand L Fl 10s 6m 5M; ***Racon (T) 10M***; 52°37′·03N 01°59′·14E.
E Cross Sand Fl (4) R 15s; 52°38′·55N 01°53′·55E.
NE Cross Sand VQ (3) 5s; 52°44′·22N 01° 53′·80E.
Smith's Knoll Q (6) + L Fl 15s 7M; ***Racon (T) 10M***; 52°43′·52N 02°17′·89E.
S Winterton Ridge Q (6) + L Fl 15s; 52°47′·21N 02°03′·44E.
E Hammond Knoll Q (3) 10s; 52°52′·32N 01°58′·64E.
Hammond Knoll Q (9) 15s; 52°49′·68N 01°57′·54E.
Newarp L Fl 10s 7M; ***Racon (O) 10M***; 52°48′·37N 01°55′·69E; 992351118.
S Haisbro Q (6) + L Fl 15s; *Bell*; 52°50′·82N 01°48′·29E.
Mid Haisbro Fl (2) G 5s; 52°54′·22N 01°41′·59E.
N Haisbro Q; ***Racon (T) 10M***; 53°00′·22N 01°32′·29E; 992351031.
Happisburgh ☆ Fl (3) 30s 41m 14M; 52°49′·21N 01°32′·18E.

(Direction of buoyage East to West)

CROMER
Cromer ☆ 52°55′·45N 01°19′·01E; Fl 5s 84m **21M**; W 8-sided twr; vis: 102°-307° H24; ***Racon (O) 25M***; 992351015.
Tayjack Wk Fl R 2·5s; 52°57′·61N 01°15′·37E.
E Sheringham Q (3) 10s; 53°02′·21N 01°14′·84E.
W Sheringham Q (9) 15s; 53°02′·95N 01°06′·72E.

BLAKENEY
Blakeney Fairway (SWM); 52°59′·31N 00°57′·83E (approx).
Blakeney Overfalls Fl (2) R 5s; *Bell*; 53°03′·01N 01°01′·37E.

WELLS-NEXT-THE-SEA/BRANCASTER STAITHE
Wells WCM Q(9) 15s; 52°59′·64N 00°51′·00E.
Bridgirdle Fl R 2·5s; 53°01′·73N 00°43′·95E.

APPROACHES TO THE WASH
S Race Q (6) + L Fl 15s; *Bell*; 53°07′·81N 00°57′·34E.
E Docking Fl R 2·5s; 53°09′·82N 00°50′·39E.
N Race Fl G 5s; *Bell*; 53°14′·98N 00°43′·87E.
N Docking Q; 53°14′·82N 00°41′·49E.
Scott Patch VQ (3) 5s; 53°11′·12N 00°36′·39E.
S Inner Dowsing Q (6) + L Fl 15s; *Bell*; 53°12′·12N 00°33′·69E.
Boygrift Tower Fl (2) 10s 12m 5M; 53°17′·63N 00°19′·24E.
Burnham Flats Q (9) 15s; *Bell*; 53°07′·53N 00°34′·89E.
Lincs WF E Q (3) 10s; 53°07′·61N 00°31′·06E.

THE WASH
Met Mast Mo(U) 15s 12m 10M Mast (87); *Horn Mo(U) 30s*; 53°18′·82N 00°44′·85E.

West Ridge Q (9) 15s; 53°19′·06N 00°44′·47E.
N Well L Fl 10s; *Whistle*; ***Racon (T) 10M***; 53°03′·02N 00°27′·87E.
Roaring Middle L Fl 10s 7m 8M; 52°58′·64N 00°21′·08E.

CORK HOLE/KING'S LYNN

Sunk Q (9) 15s; 52°56′·29N 00°23′·40E.
Seal Sand Q; *Bell*; 52°56′·00N 00°20′·00E.

WISBECH CHANNEL/RIVER NENE

Beacons are moved as required.

FREEMAN CHANNEL

Boston Roads L Fl 10s; 52°57′·69N 00°16′·96E.
Boston No. 1 Fl G 3s; 52°57′·88N 00°15′·16E.
Alpha Fl R 3s; 52°57′·65N 00°14′·99E.
No. 3 Fl G 6s; 52°57′·93N 00°15′·42E.
No. 5 Fl G 3s; 52°58′·51N 00°12′·72E.
Freeman Inner Q (9) 15s; 52°58′·59N 00°11′·36E.
Delta Fl R 6s; 52°58′·38N 00°11′·25E.

BOSTON LOWER ROAD

Echo Fl R 3s; 52°58′·38N 00°10′·13E.
Foxtrot Fl R 3s; 52°57′·60N 00°08′·94E.
Boston No. 9 Fl G 3s; 52°57′·58N 00°08′·36E.
Black Buoy Fl (2) R 6s; 52°56′·82N 00°07′·74E.
Tabs Head Q WG 4m 1M; R □ on W mast; vis: W shore - 251°- G - shore; 52°56'·00N 00°04'·91E.

BOSTON, NEW CUT AND RIVER WITHAM

Ent N side, Dollypeg QG 4m 1M; B △ on Bn; 52°56′·13N 00°05′·03E.
New Cut Fl G 3s; △ on pile; 52°55′·98N 00°04′·67E.
New Cut Ldg Lts 240°. Front, No. 1, F 5m 5M; 52°55′·85N 00°04′·40E. Rear, 90m from front, F 8m 5M.

WELLAND CUT/RIVER WELLAND

SE side ☆ Iso R 2s; NW side Iso G 2s. Lts QR (to port) and QG (to stbd) mark the chan upstream; 52°55′·72E 00°04′·68E.

(Direction of buoyage North to South)

BOSTON DEEP/WAINFLEET ROADS

Scullridge ; 52°59′·76N 00°13′·86E.
Off Ingoldmells Point ☆ Fl Y 5s 22m 5M; Mast; *Mo (U) 30s*; 53°12′·49N 00°25′·85E.

THE WASH TO THE RIVER HUMBER

(Direction of buoyage South to North)

Dudgeon Q (9) 15s 7M; ***Racon (O) 10M;*** 53°16′·62N 01°16′·90E.
E Dudgeon Q (3) 10s; 53°19′·72N 00°58′·69E.
W Ridge Q (9) 15s; 53°19′·04N 00°44′·50E.
Inner Dowsing Q (3) 10s 7M, ***Racon (T) 10M***; Horn 60s; 53°19′·10N 00°34′·80E.
Mid Outer Dowsing Fl (3) G 10s; 53°24′·82N 01°07′·79E.
N Outer Dowsing Q; 53°33′·52N 00°59′·59E; ***Racon (T) 10M***; 992351031.
B.1D Platform Dowsing 53°33′·68N 00°52′·63E; Fl (2) 10s 28m **22M**; Morse (U) R 15s 28m 3M; *Horn (2) 60s*.

RIVER HUMBER APPROACHES

Protector Fl R 2·5s; 53°24′·84N 00°25′·12E.
DZ No. 4 Fl Y 5s; 53°27′·15N 00°19′·06E.
DZ No. 3 Fl Y 2·5s 53°29′·30N 00°19′·21E.
Rosse Spit Fl (2) R 5s 53°30′·56N 00°16′·60E.
Outer Sand Q (3) 10s; 53°36′·41N 00°29′·39E; 992351119.
Haile Sand No. 2 Fl (3) R 10s; 53°32′·42N 00°13′·18E.
Humber lt float L Fl G 10s 5M; ***Racon (T) 7M***; 53°38′·70N 00°21′·24E.
Humber Gateway Met Mast Mo(U) 15s 12m 10M; 53°38′·24N 00°15′·73E; *Horn Mo(U) 30s*; Y framework mast.
N Binks Fl G 4s; 53°36′·01N 00°18′·28E.
S Binks Fl G 2s 53°34′·74N 00°16′·55E.
SPURN Q (3) 10s 10m 8M; ***Racon (M) 5M***; 53°33′·49N 00°14′·20E.
SE CHEQUER VQ (6)+L Fl 10s 6m 6M; 53°33′·27N 00°12′·33E.
Chequer No. 3 Q (6) + L Fl 15s; 53°33′·07N 00°10′·63E.
No 2B Fl R 4s; 53°32′·33N 00°09′·10E.
TETNEY 2 VQ Y (vert); *Horn Mo (A)60s*; QY on 290m floating hose; 53°32′·35N 00°06′·76E.

RIVER HUMBER/GRIMSBY/HULL

Binks No. 3A Fl G 4s; 53°33′·92N 00°07′·43E.
Spurn Pt Fl G 3s 11m 5M; 53°34′·37N 00°06′·47E.
BULL VQ 8m 6M; 53°33′·54N 00°05′·70E.
Bull Sand Q R ; 53°34′·45N 00°03′·69E.
North Fort Q; 53°33′·80N 00°04′·19E.
South Fort Q (6) + L Fl 15s; 53°33′·65N 00°03′·96E.
Haile Sand Fort ☆ Fl R 5s 21m 3M; 53°32′·07N 00°01′·99E.
Haile Chan No. 4 Fl R 4s; 53°33′·64N 00°02′·84E.
Middle No. 7 VQ (6) + L Fl 10s; 53°35′·80N 00°01′·50E.
Grimsby Royal Dock ent E side ☆ Fl (2) R 6s 10m 8M; Dn; 53°35′·08N 00°04′·04W.
Killingholme Lts in line 292°. Front, Iso R 2s 10m 14M. 53°38′·78N 00°12′·96W. Rear, 215m from front, F WRG 22m 3M; vis: 289·5°-G-290·5°-G/W-291·5°-W-292·5°-R/W-293·5° -R-294·5° (H24).

RIVER HUMBER TO WHITBY

Canada & Giorgios Wreck VQ (3) 5s; 53°42′·37N 00°07′·16E.
Albrough intake ☆ Q R 17m 2M; 53°49′·01N 00°03′·38W.

BRIDLINGTON

SW Smithic Q (9) 15s; 54°02′·41N 00°09′·21W.
N Pier Hd ☆ Fl 2s 12m 9M; *Horn 60s;* (Tidal Lts) Fl R or Fl G; 54°04′·77N 00°11′·19W.
N Smithic VQ; *Bell*; 54°06′·22N 00°03′·90W.
Flamborough Hd ☆ 54°06′·98N 00°04′·96W; Fl (4) 15s 65m **24M**; W ○ twr; *Horn (2) 90s*.

FILEY/SCARBOROUGH/WHITBY

Filey Brigg Q (3) 10s; *Bell*; 54°12′·74N 00°14′·60W.
Scarborough E Pier Hd ☆ QG 8m 3M; 54°16′·88N 00°23′·36W.
Scarborough Pier ☆ Iso 5s 17m 9M; W ○ twr; vis: 219°-039° (tide sigs); *Dia 60s*; 54°16′·91N 00°23′·40W.
Whitby Q; *Bell*; 54°30′·33N 00°36′·58W.
Whitby High ☆ 54°28′·67N 00°34′·10W; Fl WR 5s 73m **18M**,R16M; W 8-sided twr & dwellings; vis:128°-R-143°-W- 319°.
Whitby E Pier ☆ Fl(2) R 4s 16m 5M; 54°29′·57N 00°36′·71W; Masonry Twr.

Whitby E Pier Ext Hd Q R 12m 5M; 54°29′·65N 00°36′·74W.
Whitby W Pier Fl(2) G 4s 24m 5M; 54°29′·57N 00°36′·78W; Masonry Twr.
Whitby W Pier Ext Hd Q G 12m 5M; 54°29′·65N 00°36′·80W.

WHITBY TO THE RIVER TYNE

RUNSWICK/REDCAR

Salt Scar 54°38′·12N 01°00′·12W VQ; *Bell*.
Luff Way Ldg Lts 197°. Front, on Esplanade, FR 8m 7M; vis: 182°-212°; 54°37′·10N 01°03′·71W. Rear, 115m from front, FR 12m 7M; vis: 182°-212°.
High Stone. Lade Way Ldg Lts 247°. Front, Oc R 2·5s 9m 7M; 54°37′·15N 01°03′·92W. Rear, 43m from front, Oc R 2·5s 11m 7M; vis: 232°-262°.

TEES APPROACHES/HARTLEPOOL

Tees Approach L FL 10s 8M; ***Racon (B)***; *Horn*; 54°40′·60N 01°04′·00W; AIS.
Bkwtr Hd S Gare ☆ 54°38′·85N 01°08′·25W; Fl WR 12s 16m **W20M, R17M**; W ○ twr; vis: 020°-W-240°-R-357°; Sig Stn.
Ldg Lts 210·1° Front, FR 18m 13M; 54°37′·22N 01°10′·20W. **Rear**, 560m from front, FR 20m **16M**.
Longscar Q (3) 10s; *Bell*; 54°40′·86N 01°09′·89W.
The Heugh ☆ 54°41′·79N 01°10′·56W; Fl (2) 10s 19m **19M**; W twr.
Hartlepool Marina Lock Dir Lt 308° Dir Fl WRG2s 6m 3M; vis: 305·5°-G-307°-W-309°-R-310·5°; 54°41′·45N 01°11′·92W.

SEAHAM/SUNDERLAND

Seaham N Pier Hd Fl G 10s 12m 5M; W col, B bands; 54°50′·26N 01°19′·26W.
Sunderland Roker Pier Hd ☆ 54°55′·28N 01°21′·15W; Fl 5s 25m **18M**; W □ twr, 3 R bands and cupola: vis: 211°-357°; *Siren 20s*.
Old N Pier Hd QG 12m 8M; metal column; 54°55′·13N 01°21′·61W.
DZ 54°57′·04N 01°18′·90W and 54°58′·61N 01°19′·90W; both Fl Y 2·5s.

TYNE ENTRANCE/NORTH SHIELDS

Ent North Pier Hd ☆ 55°00′·88N 01°24′·18W; Fl (3) 10s 26m **26M**; Gy □ twr, W lantern; *Horn 10s*.
Herd Groyne Hd Dir Ldg Lt 249°, Oc 10s 14m **19M**; vis: 246·5°-W-251·5°; R pile structure, R&W lantern. Same structure Oc RG 10s 13m, 11M; vis: 224°-G-246·5°, 251·5°-R-277°; sync with Dir lt FR (unintens) 080°-224°. *Bell (1) 5s*; 55°00′·49N 01°25′·44W.

RIVER TYNE TO BERWICK-UPON-TWEED

CULLERCOATS and BLYTH

Cullercoats Ldg Lts 256°. Front, FR 27m 3M; 55°02′·06N 01°25′·91W. Rear, 38m from front, FR 35m 3M.
Blyth Ldg Lts 324°. Front, F Bu 11m 10M; 55°07′·42N 01°29′·82W. Rear, 180m from front, F Bu 17m 10M. Both Or on twr.
Blyth E Pier Hd ☆ 55°06′·98N 01°29′·21W; Fl (4) 10s 19m **21M**, W twr; same structure FR 13m 13M, vis:152°-249°; Horn (3) 30s.
Met Mast; Mo(U)15s 17m 10M; 55°08′·78N 01°25′·25W; Aero 3 FR (107m), *Horn 30s*.

COQUET ISLAND, AMBLE and WARKWORTH

Coquet ☆ 55°20′·03N 01°32′·39W; Fl (3) WR 20s 25m **W19M, R15M;** W □ twr, turreted parapet, lower half Gy; vis: 330° - R - 140° - W - 163° - R - 180° - W-330°; sector boundaries are indeterminate and may appear as Alt WR; *Horn 30s*.
Amble N Pier Head Fl G 6s 12m 6M; 55°20′·39N 01°34′·25W.

SEAHOUSES, BAMBURGH and FARNE ISLANDS

N Sunderland Fl R 2·5s; 55°34′·62N 01°37′·12W.
Bamburgh Black Rocks Point ☆ 55°36′·99N 01°43′·45W; Oc(2) WRG 8s 12m **W14M**, R11M, G11M; W bldg; vis: 122°-G-165°-W- 175°-R-191°-W- 238°-R- 275°-W- 289°-G-300°.
Inner Farne Fl (2) WR 15s 27m W10M, R7M; W ○ twr; vis: 119°- R - 280° - W -119°; 55°36′·92N 01°39′·35W.
Longstone ☆ **W side** 55°38′·63N 01°36′·66W; Fl 20s 23m **24M** (H24); R twr, W band; 992351127.
Swedman Fl G 2·5s; 55°37′·65N 01°41′·63W.

HOLY ISLAND

Ridge Q (3) 10s; 55°39′·70N 01°45′·97W.
Plough Rock Q (9) 15s; 55°40′·24N 01°46′·00W.
Old Law E Bn (Guile Pt) Oc WRG 6s 9m 4M; vis: 180·5°-G-258·5°-W-261·5°-R-300°, 55°39′·49N 01°47′·59W; stone obelisk.
Heugh Oc WRG 6s 24m 5M; vis: 135°-G-308°-W-311-R-shore; 55°40′·09N 01°47′·99W.
Plough Seat QR; 55°40′·37N 01°44′·97W.
Goldstone QG; 55°40′·25N 01°43′·64W.

BERWICK-UPON-TWEED

Bkwtr Hd Fl 5s 15m 6M; vis: 201°-009°, (obscured 155°-201°); W ○ twr, R cupola and base; FG (same twr) 8m 1M; vis 009°-G-155°; 55°45′·88N 01°59′·06W.

1	Ramsgate	1											11	31	61	78	91	107	126	189	205	205	232	Berwick-upon-Tweed	11
2	Sheerness	34	2											10	27	42	65	81	102	157	176	185	203	Amble	10
3	Gravesend	56	22	3											9	16	36	51	70	138	149	156	180	Sunderland	9
4	London Bridge	76	45	23	4											8	24	39	58	122	137	140	169	Hartlepool	8
5	Burnham-on-Crouch	44	34	54	77	5											7	16	35	88	114	121	143	Whitby	7
6	Brightlingsea	41	28	48	71	21	6											6	20	81	98	105	130	Scarborough	6
7	Harwich	40	50	66	93	31	20	7											5	58	83	87	114	Bridlington	5
8	River Deben (ent)	45	55	75	98	36	25	6	8											4	79	75	113	Hull	4
9	Southwold	62	72	92	115	53	42	25	23	9											3	34	83	Boston	3
10	Lowestoft	72	82	102	125	63	52	35	33	10	10											2	85	King's Lynn	2
11	Great Yarmouth	79	87	105	132	70	59	42	40	18	7	11											1	Great Yarmouth	1

AREA 5 *E Scotland – Berwick-upon-Tweed to C Wrath & N Isles*

SELECTED LIGHTS, BUOYS & WAYPOINTS

BERWICK-UPON-TWEED TO BASS ROCK

BURNMOUTH

Ldg lts 241°. Front, FR 29m 4M; 55°50'·53N 02°04'·25W. Rear, 45m from front, FR 35m 4M. Both on W posts (unclear by day).

EYEMOUTH

Blind Buss Q; 55°52'·80N 02°05'·25E.

Ldg Lts 174°. Front, W Bkwtr Hd ☆, FG 9m 6M; 55°52'·47N 02°05'·29W. Rear, elbow 55m from front, FG 10m 6M.

ST ABBS to DUNBAR and BASS ROCK

St Abbs Hd ☆ 55°54'·96N 02°08'·29W; Fl 10s 68m **26M**; W twr; ***Racon (T) 18M***.

Barns Ness Twr (Lt ho disused 36m); 55°59'·22N 02°26'·76W.

Torness Pwr Stn Ldg Lts 215°. Front, Iso G 4s 6m 6M; W □ with B vert stripe on plinth; 55°58'·27N 02°24'·86W. Rear, Iso G 4s 22m 3M; W □ with B vert stripe on post; sync with front.

Dunbar Hbr Ldg Lts (Bayswell Hill) 198°. Front, Oc G 6s 15m 3M; 3 Or △ on col; 56°00'·26N 02°31'·21W. Rear, Oc G 6s 22m 3M; 3 Or ▽; sync with front; both lts 188°-G(intens)-208°.

Bass Rock, S side, ☆ Fl (3) 20s 46m 10M; W twr; vis: 241°-107°; 56°04'·61N 02°38'·48W.

FIRTH OF FORTH AND SOUTH SHORE

(Direction of buoyage East to West)

NORTH BERWICK

Outfall Fl Y; 56°04'·29N 02°40'·89W.

Fidra ☆ 56°04'·39N 02°47'·13W; Fl (4) 30s 34m **15M**; W twr; obsc by Bass Rock, Craig Leith and Lamb Island.

PORT SETON, COCKENZIE, FISHERROW and S CHANNEL

Port Seton, E Pier Hd ☆ Iso WR 4s 10m W9M, R6M; vis: shore - R - 105°- W - 225°- R - shore; *Bell (occas)*; 55°58'·40N 02°57'·23W.

Fisherrow E Pier Hd ☆ Oc 6s 5m 6M; 55°56'·79N 03°04'·11W.

Narrow Deep Fl (2) R 10s; 56°01'·46N 03°04'·59W.

Herwit Fl (3) G 10s; 56°01'·05N 03°06'·52W.

North Craig Q (3) 10s 56°01'·02N 03°03'·52W.

Craigh Waugh Fl (2) 10s;56°00'·26N 03°04'·47W.

Diffuser Hds (Outer) 55°59'·81N 03°07'·84W.

LEITH and GRANTON

Leith Approach Fl R 3s; 55°59'·95N 03°11'·51W.

East Bkwtr Hd ☆ Iso R 4s 7m 9M; 55°59'·48N 03°10'·94W.

Granton E Pier Hd ☆ Fl R 2s 5m 6M; 55°59'·28N 03°13'·27W.

NORTH CHANNEL and MIDDLE BANK

Inchkeith Fairway Iso 2s; ***Racon (T) 5M***; 56°03'·49N 03°00'·10W.

No. 1 Fl G 9s; 56°03'·22N 03°03'·71W.

No. 2 Fl R 9s; 56°02'·90N 03°03'·72W.

No. 3 Fl G 6s; 56°03'·22N 03°06'·10W.

No. 4 Fl R 6s; 56°02'·89N 03°06'·11W.

No. 5 Fl G 3s; 56°03'·18N 03°07'·88W.

No. 6 Fl R 3s; 56°03'·05N 03°08'·44W.

No. 8 Fl R 9s 56°02'·95N 03°09'·62W.

Inchkeith ☆ 56°02'·01N 03°08'·17W; Fl 15s 67m 14M; stone twr.

Pallas Rock VQ (9) 10s 56°01'·50N 03°09'·30W.

East Gunnet Q (3) 10s; 56°01'·41N 03°10'·38W.

West Gunnet Q (9) 15s 56°01'·34N 03°11'·06W.

No. 7 QG; ***Racon (T) 5M***; 56°02'·80N 03°10'·97W.

No. 9 Fl G 6s; 56°02'·32N 03°13'·48W.

No. 10 Fl R 6s; 56°02'·07N 03°13'·32W.

No. 11 Fl G 3s 56°02'·08N 03°15'·26W.

No. 12 Fl R 3s; 56°01'·78N 03°15'·15W.

No. 13 Fl G 9s; 56°01'·77N 03°16'·94W.

No. 14 Q R; 56°01'·51N 03°16'·90W.

Oxcars ☆ Fl (2) WR 7s 16m W13M, R12M; W twr, R band; vis: 072°-W-087°- R-196°-W-313°-R-072°; 56°01'·36N 03°16'·84W.

Inchcolm E Pt ☆ Fl (3) 15s 20m 10M; Gy twr; part obsc by land 075°-145·5°; 56°01'·72N 03°17'·83W.

No. 15 Fl G 6s; 56°01'·39N 03°18'·95W.

MORTIMER'S DEEP

Hawkcraig Point Ldg Lts 292°. Front, Iso 5s 12m 14M; W twr; vis: 282°-302°; 56°03'·03N 03°17'·07W. Rear, 96m from front, Iso 5s 16m 14M; W twr; vis: 282°-302°.

Inchcolm S Lts in line 066°. Front, 84m from rear, Q 7m 7M; W twr; vis: 062·5°-082·5°; 56°01'·78N 03°18'·28W. Common Rear, Iso 5s 11m 7M; W twr; vis: 062·5°-082·5°; 56°01'·80N 03°18'·13W. N Lts in line 076·7°. Front, 80m from rear, Q 7m 7M; W twr; vis: 062·5°-082·5°.

APPROACHES TO FORTH BRIDGES

No. 17 Fl G 3s; 56°01'·23N 03°19'·84W.

No. 16 Fl R 3s; 56°00'·87N 03°19'·60W.

No. 19 Fl G 9s; 56°00'·71N 03°22'·47W.

Beamer Rk W ☆ Fl 3s 5m 9M; W post; vis: 050°-230°; 56°00'·30N 03°24'·79W.

Beamer Rk E ☆ Fl 3s 5m 9M; W post; vis: 230°-050°; 56°00'·27N 03°24'·72W.

PORT EDGAR

W Bkwtr Hd ☆ Fl R 4s 4m 8M; 55°59'·86N 03°24'·78W. W blockhouse.

FIRTH OF FORTH – NORTH SHORE (INWARD)

BURNTISLAND

W Pier Outer Hd ☆ Fl (2) R 6s 7m; W twr; 56°03'·22N 03°14'·26W.

E Pier Outer Hd ☆ Fl (2) G 6s 7m 5M; 56°03'·24N 03°14'·17W.

ABERDOUR, BRAEFOOT BAY and INCHCOLM

Hawkcraig Pt ☆ (see **MORTIMER'S DEEP** above).

Braefoot Bay Terminal, W Jetty. Ldg Lts 247·3°. **Front**, Fl 3s 6m **15M**; W △ on E dolphin; vis: 237·2°-257·2°; 56°02'·16N 03°18'·71W; 4 dolphins with 2 FG (vert). **Rear**, 88m from front, Fl 3s 12m **15M**; W ▽ on appr gangway; vis: 237·2°-257·2°; sync with front.

INVERKEITHING BAY

St David's Fl G 5s 3m 7M; Or □, on pile; 56°01'·37N 03°22'·29W.

Channel QG; 56°01'·43N 03°23'·02W.

ROSYTH

Main Chan Dir lt 323·5°. Bn 'A' Oc WRG 7m 4M; R □ on W post with R bands; vis: 318°-G-321°-321°-W-326°-R-328° (H24); 56°01'·19N 03°25'·61W.

Dir lt 115°, Bn 'C' Oc WRG 6s 7m 4M; W ▽ on W Bn; vis: 110°-R -113° W -116·5° - G -120°; 56°00'·61N 03°24'·25W.

S Arm Jetty Hd ☆ L Fl (2) WR 12s 5m W9M; R6M; vis: 010°-W-280°-R-010°; 56°01'·09N 03°26'·58W.

RIVER FORTH

ROSYTH to GRANGEMOUTH

Dhu Craig Fl G 5s; 56°00'·74N 03°27'·23W.

Blackness QR; 56°01'·06N 03°30'·30W.

Tancred Bank Fl (2) R 10s; 56°01'·58N 03°31'·91W.

Dods Bank Fl R 3s; 56°02'·03N 03°34'·07W.

Bo'ness Fl R 10s; 56°02'·23N 03°35'·38W.

Torry ☆ Fl G 10s 5m 7M; G ○ structure; 56°02'·46N 03°35'·28W.

Bo'ness Bcns 2 QR 3m 2M; 56°01'·85N 03°36'·22W.

Bo'ness Hbr ; 56°01'·26N 03°36'·46W.

GRANGEMOUTH

Grangemouth App No. 1 Fl (3) 10s 4m 6M;56°02'·12N 03°38'·10W.

Hen & Chickens Fl (3) G 10s; 56°02'·35N 03°38'·08W.

FIRTH OF FORTH – NORTH SHORE (OUTWARD)

KIRKCALDY and METHIL

Kirkcaldy W Pier Hd ☆ Fl R 5s 7m 3M; 56°06'·80N 03°08'·97W.

Kirkcaldy E Pier Hd ☆ Fl G 5s 12m 3M; 56°06'·78N 03°08'·90W.

Methil Outer Pier Hd ☆ Oc G 6s 8m 5M; W twr; vis: 280°-100°; 56°10'·76N 03°00'·48W.

ELIE and ST MONANS

Elie Ness ☆ 56°11'·04N 02°48'·77W; Fl 6s 15m **17M**; W twr.

St Monans Bkwtr Hd ☆ Oc WRG 6s 5m W7M, R4M, G4M; vis: 282°-G-355°-W-026°-R-038°; 56°12'·20N 02°45'·94W.

PITTENWEEM and ANSTRUTHER EASTER

Pittenweem, Ldg Lts 037° Middle Pier Hd. Front, FR 4m 5M. Rear, FR 8m 5M. Both Gy Cols, Or stripes; 56°12'·69N 02°43'·69W.

Pittenweem, E Bkwtr Hd ☆ Fl (2) RG 5s 9m R9M, G6M; vis: 265°-R-345°-G-055°; *Horn 90s (occas);* 56°12'·63N 02°43'·74W.

Anstruther, Ldg Lts 019°. Front FG 7m 4M; 56°13'·28N 02°41'·76W. Rear, 38m from front, FG 11m 4M, (both W masts).

MAY I, CRAIL, ST ANDREWS and FIFE NESS to MONTROSE

Isle of May ☆ 56°11'·12N 02°33'·46W(Summit); Fl (2) 15s 73m **22M**; □ twr on stone dwelling.

Crail, Ldg Lts 295°. Front, FR 24m 6M (not lit when hbr closed); 56°15'·46N 02°37'·84W. Rear, 30m from front, FR 30m 6M.

Fife Ness ☆ 56°16'·74N 02°35'·19W; Iso WR 10s 12m **W15M,** R12M; W bldg; vis: 143°-W-197°-R-217°-W-023°; 002320798.

N Carr Q (3) 10s 3m 5M; 56°18'·05N 02°32'·94W.

St Andrews ☆ 56°20'·38N 02°47'·07W; Dir lt 277·7; Iso WRG 2s 17m 9M; vis: 272°-G-276°-AlWG-277°-W-278°-AlWR-279°-R-283°.St Andrews N Bkwtr Bn ☆ Fl G 3M 56°20'·36N 02°46'·77W.

Bell Rk ☆ 56°26'·08N 02°23'·21W; Fl 5s 28m **18M**; ***Racon (M) 18M***.

Met Mast ☆ Mo(U) 15s 22m 10M; Aero FR (116m), *Horn Mo(U) 30s;* 56°26'·40N 02°14'·49W; 992351153.

RIVER TAY, TAYPORT, DUNDEE and PERTH

Tay Fairway L Fl 10s; *Bell;* 56°28'·30N 02°36'·60W.

Middle Fl G 3s; 56°28'·08N 02°38'·24W.

Middle Fl (2) R 6s 56°27'·82N 02°37'·97W.

Abertay N Q (3) 10s; ***Racon (T) 8M***; 56°27'·39N 02°40'·36W.

Abertay S (Elbow) Fl R 6s 56°27'·13N 02°39'·83W.

Tayport High Lt ☆ 56°27'·17N 02°53'·95W; Dir lt 269°; Iso WRG 3s 4m W14M, R14M, G14M; W twr vis: 267°-G-268°-W-270°-R-271°.

ARBROATH

Ldg lts 299·2°. Front , FR 7m 5M; W col; 56°33'·29N 02°35'·16W. Rear, 50m from front, FR 13m 5M; W col.

MONTROSE

Scurdie Ness ☆ 56°42'·10N 02°26'·24W; Fl (3) 20s 38m **23M**; W twr; ***Racon (T) 14-16M***.

Outer Ldg Lts 271·5°; Front, FR 11m 5M; W twin pillars, R bands; 56°42'·21N 02°27'·41W; Rear, 272m from front, FR 18m 5M; W twr, R cupola.

Inner Ldg Lts 265°; Front FG 21m 5M; Rear FG 33m 5M.

MONTROSE TO RATTRAY HEAD

JOHNSHAVEN and GOURDON HARBOUR

Johnshaven, Ldg Lts 316°. Front, FR 5m; 56°47'·62N 02°20'·26W. Rear, 85m from front, FG 20m; shows R when unsafe to ent hbr.Gourdon Hbr, Ldg Lts 358°. Front, FR 5m 5M; W twr; shows G when unsafe to enter; *Siren (2) 60s* (occas); 56°49'·69N 02°17'·24W. Rear, 120m from front, FR 30m 5M; W twr.

Gourdon E B'water ☆ Q 3m 3M; 49°57'·60N 02°17'·19W.

Todhead Lighthouse (disused), white tower, 13m.

STONEHAVEN to GIRDLE NESS

Outer Pier Hd ☆ Iso WRG 4s 7m 5M; vis: 214°-G-246°-W-268°-R-280°; 56°57'·59N 02°12'·00W.

Girdle Ness ☆ Fl (2) 20s 56m **22M**; obsc by Greg Ness when brg more than about 020°; ***Racon (G) 25M***; 57°08'·34N 02°02'·91W.

ABERDEEN

Fairway Mo (A) 5s; ***Racon (T) 7M***; 57°09'·31N 02°01'·95W.

Torry Ldg lts 237·2°, Front FR or G 14m 5M; R when ent safe, FG when dangerous to navigate; W twr; 57°08'·38N 02°04'·50W.

Rear, 220m from front, FR or G 19m 5M; R when ent safe, FG when dangerous to navigate; W twr; 57°08'·31N 02°04'·68W.

Aberdeen Harbour Ent ☆ 57°08'·38N 02°04'·48W; Dir lt 237·2° Fl WRG 1s 7m 9M; metal post; vis: 235·2°-QG-236·2°-AlQGW-236·7°-QW-237·7°-AlQRW-238·2°-QR-239·2°.

S Bkwtr Hd ☆ Fl (3) R 8s 23m 7M; 57°08'·69N 02°03'·34W.

N Pier Hd ☆ Iso G 4s 11m 10M; W twr; 57°08'·74N 02°03'·69W. In fog FY 10m (same twr) vis: 136°-336°; *Bell (3) 12s.*

S Skates Nose Jetty Hd ☆ Q R 4m 4M; 57°08'·49N 02°04'·06W.

Abercrombie Jetty Hd ☆ Oc G 4s 5m 4M; 57°08'·53N 02°04'·15W.

BUCHAN NESS TO INVERNESS

PETERHEAD and RATTRAY HEAD

Buchan Ness ☆ Fl 5s 40m **18M**; W twr, R bands; ***Racon (O) 14-16M;*** 57°28'·23N 01°46'·51W.

Kirktown Ldg lts 314°. Front, Oc R 6s 14m 10M; Or △ on lattice mast; 57°30′·22N 01°47′·21W. Rear, Oc R 6s 21m 10M (sync with front); Or ▽ on lattice mast.

S Bkwtr Hd ☆ Fl (2) R 12s 24m 7M; 57°29′·79N 01°46′·54W.

N Bkwtr Hd ☆ Iso RG 6s 19m 11M; W tripod; vis: 171°-R-236°-G-171°; *Horn 30s;* 57°29′·84N 01°46′·32W.

Rattray Hd ☆ 57°36′·61N 01°49′·03W Fl (3) 30s 28m **18M**; W twr; ***Racon (M) 15M***; *Horn (2) 45s*.

Smith Bank Met Mast Mo(U) 15s 17m 10M Mast (101); Horn Mo(U) 30s; 58°10′·93N 02°49′·22W.

FRASERBURGH

Fraserburgh Ldg lt 291°; Iso R 2s 12m 9M; 57°41′·57N 02°00′·13W. Rear, 75m from front, Iso R 2s 17m 9M.

Fraserburgh, Balaclava Bkwtr Head ☆ Fl (2) G 8s 26m 6M; dome on W twr; vis: 178°-326°; 57°41′·51N 01°59′·70W.

Kinnaird Hd ☆ 57°41′·87N 02°00′·26W Fl 5s 25m **22M**; vis: 092°-297°.

MACDUFF, BANFF and WHITEHILLS

Macduff Pier Hd ☆ Fl (2) WRG 6s 12m W9M, R7M; W twr; vis: shore-G-115°-W-174°-R-210°; 57°40′·26N 02°30′·01W.

Macduff Ldg Lts 130°, Front FR 28m 3M; 57°40′·18N 02°29′·85W. Rear, 220m from front, FR 55m 3M; both Or △ on mast.

Banff Ldg Lts 295°, Front Fl R 4s; 57°40·30N 02°31·36W. Rear, QR; both vis: 210°-345°.

Whitehills Pier Hd ☆ 57°40′·80N 02°34′·88W Fl WR 3s 7m W9M, R6M; W twr; vis: 132°-R-212°-W-245°.

PORTSOY and FINDOCHTY

Portsoy Pier Ldg Lts 173°, Front Fl G 4s 20m 3M; post; 57°41′·09N 02°41′·40W; Rear Q G 22m 3M; R △ on BW post.

Findochty Middle Pier Ldg Lts 166°, Front FR 6m 3M; 57°41′·90N 02°54′·20W. Rear FR 10m 3M.

BUCKIE

West Muck ☆ QR 5m 7M; tripod; 57°41′·06N 02°58′·01W.

N Pier 60m from Hd ☆ 57°40′·9N 02°57′·5W Oc R 10s 15m **15M** W twr.

LOSSIEMOUTH, HOPEMAN and BURGHEAD

Lossiemouth S Pier Hd ☆ Fl R 6s 11m 5M; 57°43′·42N 03°16′·69W.

Halliman Skerries Q; ***Racon M,*** 57°44′·33N 03°18′·57W.

Hopeman Ldg Lts 081°, Front,FR 3m; 57°42′·71N 03°26′·18W. Rear, 10m from front, FR 4m.

Burghead N Bkwtr Hd ☆ Oc 8s 7m 5M; 57°42′·09N 03°30′·03W.

FINDHORN, NAIRN and INVERNESS FIRTH

Findhorn Landfall LF 10s 57°40′·34N 03°38′·77W.

Nairn E Pier Hd ☆ Oc WRG 4s 6m 5M; 8-sided twr; vis: shore-G-100°-W-207°-R-shore; 57°35′·62N 03°51′·65W.

Riff Bank E Fl Y 10s 3m 5M 57°38′·38N 03°58′·18W; AIS.

SOUTH CHANNEL

Riff Bank S Q (6) + L Fl 15s; 57°36′·73N 04°00′·97W.

Chanonry ☆ 57°34′·45N 04°05′·56W Oc 6s 12m 12M; W twr; vis: 148°-073°.

Munlochy L Fl 10s; 57°32′·91N 04°07′·65W .

Petty Bank Fl R 5s 57°31′·58N 04°08′·98W.

Meikle Mee Fl G 3s 57°30′·26N 04°12′·02W.

Longman Pt Fl WR 2s 7m W5M, R4M; vis: 078°-W-258°-R-078°; 57°29′·99N 04°13′·31W.

Craigton Point ☆ Fl WRG 4s 6m W11M, R7M, G7M; vis: 312° - W - 048° - R - 064° - W - 085°- G - shore; 57°30′·05N 04°14′·09W.

Bridge Centre, Or △; ***Racon (K) 6M***; 57°29′·97N 04°13′·79W.

INVERNESS and CALEDONIAN CANAL

R. Ness Outer QR 3m 4M; 57°29′·83N 04°13′·93W.

Carnarc Pt ☆ Fl G 2s 8m 4M; G lattice twr; 57°29′·72N 04°14′·25W.

Clachnaharry, S Tr'ng Wall Hd Iso G 4s 5m 2M; tfc sigs; 57°29′·43N 04°15′·86W.

INVERNESS TO DUNCANSBY HEAD

CROMARTY FIRTH and INVERGORDON

Fairway L Fl 10s; ***Racon (M) 5M***; 57°39′·96N 03°54′·19W.

Cromarty Bank Fl (2) G 10s; 57°40′·66N 03°56′·78W.

Buss Bank Fl R 3s 57°40′·97N 03°59′·54W.

Cromarty - The Ness (Lt ho disused W tr 13m); 57°40′·98N 04°02′·20W

Nigg Oil Terminal Pier Hd ☆ Oc G 5s 31m 5M; Gy twr, floodlit; 57°41′·54N 04°02′·60W.

DORNOCH FIRTH to LYBSTER

Tarbat Ness ☆ 57°51′·88N 03°46′·76W Fl (4) 30s 53m **24M**; W twr, R bands; ***Racon (T) 14-16M***.

Lybster, S Pier Hd ☆ Oc R 6s 10m 3M; 58°17′·79N 03°17′·41W.

Clyth Ness Lt Ho (unlit); W twr, R band; 58°18′·64N 03°12′·74W.

WICK

S Pier Hd ☆ Fl WRG 3s 12m W12M, R9M, G9M; W 8-sided twr; vis: 253°-G-270°-W-286°-R-329°; *Bell (2) 10s* (occas); 58°26′·34N 03°04′·73W.

Dir lt 288·5° F WRG 9m W10M, R7M, G7M; col, N end of bridge; vis: 283·5°-G-287·2°-W-289·7°-R-293·5°; 58°26′·54N 03°05′·34W

Noss Hd ☆ 58°28′·71N 03°03′·09W Fl WR 20s 53m **W25M, R21M**; W twr; vis: shore-R-191°-W-shore.

DUNCANSBY HEAD TO CAPE WRATH

Duncansby Hd ☆ 58°38′·65N 03°01′·58W Fl 12s 67m **22M**; W twr; **Racon (T)**.

Muckle Skerry ☆ 58°41′·41N 02°55′·49W Fl (3) 30s 52m **23M**; W twr; 992351086.

Lother Rock ☆ Fl 2s 13m 6M; ***Racon (M) 10M***; 58°43′·79N 02°58′·69W.

Swona ☆ Fl 8s 17m 9M; vis: 261°-210°; 58°44′·25N 03°04′·24W.

Swona N Hd ☆ Fl (3) 10s 16m 10M; 58°45′·11N 03°03′·10W.

Stroma ☆, Swilkie Point 58°41′·75N 03°07′·01W Fl (2) 20s 32m **20M**; W twr; 992351092.

Dunnet Hd ☆ 58°40′·28N 03°22′·60W Fl (4) 30s 105m **23M**.

THURSO, SCRABSTER and CAPE WRATH

Thurso Ldg Lts 195°. Front, FG 5m 4M; Gy post; 58°35′·96N 03°30′·76W. Rear, FG 6m 4M; Gy mast.

Scrabster Q. E. Pier Hd ☆ Fl (2) 4s 8m 8M 58°36′·66N 03°32′·31W.

Strathy Pt Lt Ho (disused) W twr on W dwelling; 58°36'·04N 04°01'·12W.

Sule Skerry ☆ 59°05'·09N 04°24'·38W Fl (2) 15s 34m **21M**; W twr; ***Racon (T)***.

North Rona ☆ 59°07'·27N 05°48'·91W Fl (3) 20s 114m **22M**.

Sula Sgeir ☆ Fl 15s 74m 11M; □ structure; 59°05'·61N 06°09'·57W.

Loch Eriboll, White Hd ☆ Fl WR10s 18m W13M, R12M; W twr and bldg; vis: 030°-W-172°-R-191°-W-212°; 58°31'·01N 04°38'·90W.

Cape Wrath ☆ 58°37'·54N 04°59'·99W Fl (4) 30s 122m **22M**; W twr.

ORKNEY ISLANDS

Tor Ness ☆ 58°46'·78N 03°17'·86W Fl 5s 21m **17M**; W twr.

Cantick Hd (S Walls, SE end) ☆ 58°47'·23N 03°07'·88W Fl 20s 35m 13M; W twr.

SCAPA FLOW and APPROACHES

Long Hope, S Ness Pier Hd ☆ Fl WRG 3s 6m W7M, R5M, G5M; vis: 082°-G- 242°-W- 252°-R-082°; 58°48'·05N 03°12'·35W.

Hoxa Head ☆ Fl WR 3s 15m W9M, R6M; W twr; vis: 026°-W-163°-R-201°-W-215°; 58°49'·31N 03°02'·09W.

Nevi Skerry ⚓ Fl (2) 6s 7m 6M; 58°50'·67N 03°02'·70W.

Flotta Grinds ⚓ Fl (2) R; 58°50'·97N 03°00'·77W; 992351083.

Rose Ness ☆ 58°52'·33N 02°49'·97W Fl 6s 24m 8M; W twr.

Barrel of Butter ☆ Fl (2) 10s 6m 7M; 58 53'·40N 03°07'·62W.

Cava ☆ Fl WR 3s 11m W10M, R8M; W ○ twr; vis: 351°-W-143°-196°-W-251°-R-271°-R-298°; 58°53'·21N 03°10'·70W.

Holm of Houton ☆ 58°54'·62N 03°10'·97W; Fl R 3s 7m 5M.

Houton Bay Ldg Lts 316°. Front ⚓ Fl G 3s 8m. Rear ⚓, 200m from front, FG 16m; vis: 312°- 320°; 58°54'·97N 03°11'·56W.

CLESTRAN SOUND and HOY SOUND

Graemsay Is Hoy Sound ☆ Ldg Lts 104°. Front Low, Iso 3s 17m 12M; W twr; vis: 070°-255°, 58°56'·42N 03°18'·60W. **High Rear**, 1·2M from front, Oc WR 8s 35m **W20M, R16M**; W twr; vis: 097°-R-112°-W-163°-R-178°-W-332°; obsc on Ldg line within 0·5M.

Skerry of Ness ☆ Fl WG 4s 7m W7M, G4M; vis: shore -W-090°- G-shore; 58°56'·95N 03°17'·83W.

STROMNESS

Ldg Lts 317°. Front FR 29m 11M; W twr; 58°57'·61N 03°18'·15W. Rear, 55m from front, FR 39m 11M; vis: 307°-327°; H24.

AUSKERRY

Copinsay ☆ Fl (5) 30s 79m 14M; W twr; 58°53'·77N 02°40'·35W.

Auskerry ☆ 59°01'·51N 02°34'·34W Fl 20s 34m **20M**; W twr.

Helliar Holm, S end ☆ Fl WRG 10s 18m W14M, R11M, G11M; W twr; vis: 256°-G-276°-W-292°-R-098°-W-116°-G-154°; 59°01'·13N 02°54'·09W.

Balfour Pier Shapinsay ☆ Fl (2) WRG 5s 5m W3M, R2M, G2M; vis: 270°-G-010°-W-020°-R-090°; 59°01'·86N 02°54'·49W.

KIRKWALL

Thieves Holm, ☆ Q R 8M; 59°01'·09N 02°56'·21W.

Pier N end ☆ 58°59'·29N 02°57'·72W Iso WRG 5s 8m **W15M**, R13M, G13M; W twr; vis: 153°-G-183°-W-192°-R-210°.

WIDE FIRTH

Linga Skerry ⚓ Q (3) 10s; 59°02'·39N 02°57'·56W.

Boray Skerries ⚓ Q (6) + L Fl 15s; 59°03'·65N 02°57'·66W.

Skertours ⚓ Q; 59°04'·11N 02°56'·72W.

Galt Skerry ⚓ Q; 59°05'·21N 02°54'·20W.

Seal Skerry ☆ Fl R 3s 5m 3M; platform; 59°05'·21N 02°54'·20W.

Brough of Birsay ☆ 59°08'·19N 03°20'·41W Fl (3) 25s 52m **18M**.

Papa Stronsay NE end, The Ness ☆ Fl(4)20s 8m 9M; W twr; 59°09'·34N 02°34'·93W.

SANDAY ISLAND and NORTH RONALDSAY

Quiabow ⚓ Fl (2) G 12s; 59°09'·82N 02°36'·30W.

Start Pt ☆ 59°16'·69N 02°22'·71W Fl (2) 20s 24m **18M**.

Kettletoft Pier Hd ☆ Fl WRG 3s 7m W7M, R5M, G5M; vis: 351°-W- 011°-R-180°-G-351°; 59°13'·80N 02°35'·86W.

N Ronaldsay ☆ NE end, 59°23'·34N 02°22'·91W Fl 10s 43m **24M**; R twr, W bands; ***Racon (T) 14-17M***.

EDAY and EGILSAY

Calf Sound ☆ Fl (3) WRG 10s 6m W8M, R6M, G6M; W twr; vis: shore-R-215°-W-222°-G-301°-W-305°; 59°14'·21N 02°45'·82W.

Backaland Pier ☆ 59°09'·43N 02°44'·88W Fl R 3s 5m 4M; vis: 192°-250°.

Egilsay Graand ⚓ Q (6) + L Fl 15s; 59°06'·86N 02°54'·42W.

WESTRAY and PIEROWALL

Noup Head ☆ 59°19'·86N 03°04'·23W Fl 30s 79m **20M**; W twr; vis: about 335°-282° but partially obsc 240°-275°.

Pierowall E Pier Head ☆ Fl WRG 3s 7m W11M, R7M, G7M; vis: 254°-G-276°-W-291°-R-308°-G-215°; 59°19'·35N 02°58'·53W.

Papa Westray, Moclett Bay Pier Head ☆ Fl WRG 5s 7m W5M, R3M, G3M; vis: 306°-G-341°-W-040°-R-074°; 59°19'·60N 02°53'·52W.

SHETLAND ISLES

FAIR ISLE

Skadan South ☆, 59°30'·84N 01°39'·16W Fl (4) 30s 32m **22M**; W twr; vis: 260°-146°, obsc inshore 260°-282°.

Skroo ☆ N end 59°33'·13N 01°36'·58W Fl (2) 30s 80m **22M**; W twr; vis: 086·7°-358°.

MAINLAND, SOUTH

Sumburgh Head ☆ 59°51'·21N 01°16'·58W Fl (3) 30s 91m **23M**.

Lt Ho disused 59°51'·48N 01°16'·28W; W twr.

Mousa, Perie Bard ☆ Fl 3s 20m 10M; 59°59'·84N 01°09'·51W.

BRESSAY and LERWICK

Bressay, Kirkabister Ness ☆ 60°07'·20N 01°07'·31W; Fl (2) 10s 18m 10M. Adjacent Lt Ho disused.

Maryfield Ferry Terminal ☆ Oc WRG 6s 5m 5M; vis: W008°-R013°-G-111°-008°; 60°09'·43N 01°07'·45W.

North Ness ☆ Iso WG 4s 4m 5M; vis: shore-W-158°-G-216°-W-301°; 60°09′·57N 01°08′·77W

Loofa Baa Q (6) + L Fl 15s 4m 5M; 60°09′·72N 01°08′·79W.

Soldian Rock Q (6) + L Fl 15s 60°12′·51N 01°04′·73W.

N ent Dir lt 215°, Oc WRG 6s 27m 8M; Y △, Or stripe; vis: 211°-R-214°-W-216°-G-221°; 60°10′·47N 01°09′·53W.

Rova Hd ☆ 60°11′·46N 01°08′·60W Fl (3) WRG 18s 12m W12M, R9M, G9M; W twr; vis: 090°-R-182°-W-191°-G-213°-R-241°-W-261·5°-G-009°-R-040°. Same structure and synchronised: Fl (3) WRG 18s 14m **W16M**, R13M, G13M; vis: 176·5°-R-182°-W-191°-G-196·5°.

Dales Voe ☆ Fl (2) WRG 8s 5m W4M, R3M, G3M; vis: 220°-G-227°-W-233°-R-240°; 60°11′·79N 01°11′·23W.

Hoo Stack ☆ Fl (4) WRG 12s 40m W7M, R5M, G5M; W pylon; vis: 169°-R-180°-W-184°-G-193°-W-169°. Same structure, Dir lt 182°. Fl (4) WRG 12s 33m W9M, R6M, G6M; vis: 177°- R-180°-W-184°-W-187°; synch with upper lt; 60°14′·96N 01°05′·38W.

Mull (Moul) of Eswick ☆ Fl WRG 3s 50m W9M, R6M, G6M; W twr; vis: 028°-R-200°-W-207°-G-018°-W-028°; 60°15′·74N 01°05′·90W.

Inner Voder Q (9) 15s; 60°16′·44N 01°05′·18W; AIS.

WHALSAY and SKERRIES

Symbister Ness ☆ Fl (2) WG 12s 11m W8M, G6M; W twr; vis: shore-W-203°-G-shore; 60°20′·43N 01°02′·29W.

Suther Ness ☆ Fl WRG 3s 10m W10M, R8M, G7M; vis: shore-W-038°-R-173°-W-206°-G-shore; 60°22′·12N 01°00′·20W.

Bound Skerry ☆ 60°25′·47N 00°43′·72W Fl 20s 44m **20M**; W twr.

South Mouth. Ldg Lts 014°. Front, FY3m 2M; 60°25′·33N 00°45′·01W. Rear, FY 12m 2M.

Muckle Skerry ☆ Fl (2) WRG 10s 15m W7M, R5M, G5M; W twr; vis: 046°-W-192°-R-272°-G-348°-W-353°-R-046°; 60°26′·41N 00°51′·84W.

YELL SOUND

S ent, Lunna Holm ☆ Fl (3) WRG 15s 19m W10M,R7M,G7M; W ○twr; vis: shore-R-090°-W-094°-G-209°-W-275°-R-shore; 60°27′·34N 01°02′·52W.

Firths Voe ☆, N shore 60°27′·21N 01°10′·63W Oc WRG 8s 9m **W15M**, R10M, G10M; W twr; vis: 189°-W-194°-G-257°-W-261°-R-339°-W-066°.

Linga Is. Dir lt 150° ☆ Q (4) WRG 8s 10m W9M, R9M, G9M; vis: 145°-R-148°-W-152°-G-155°. Q (4) WRG 8s 10m W7M, R4M, G4M; same structure; vis: 052°-R-146°, 154°-G-196°-W-312°; synch; 60°26′·80N 01°09′·13W.

The Rumble Bn ☆ R Bn; Fl 10s 8m 4M; ***Racon (O)***; 60°28′·16N 01°07′·26W.

Yell, Ulsta Ferry Term. Bkwtr Hd ☆ Oc RG 4s 7m R5M, G5M; vis: shore-G-354°, 044°-R-shore. Same structure; Oc WRG 4s 5m W8M, R5M, G5M; vis: shore-G-008°-W-036°-R-shore; 60°29′·74N 01°09′·52W.

Toft Ferry Terminal ☆,Dir lt 241° (H24); Dir Oc WRG 10s 8m **W16M,** R10M, G10M; vis: 236° -G-240°-W-242°-R-246°; by day W2M, R1M, G1M. 60°27′·96N 01°12′·34W.

Ness of Sound, W side ☆ Fl (3) WRG 12s 18m W9M, R6M, G6M; vis: shore-G-345°-W-350°-R-160°-W-165°-G-shore; 60°31′·34N 01°11′·28W.

Brother Is. Dir lt 329°, Fl (4) WRG 8s 16m W10M, R7M, G7M; vis: 323·5°-G-328°-W-330°-R-333·5°; 60°30′·95N 01°14′·11W.

Mio Ness ☆ Q (2) WR 10s 12m W7M, R4M; W ○ twr; vis: 282° - W - 238° - R - 282°; 60°29′·66N 01°13′·68W.

Tinga Skerry ☆ Q(2)G 10s 9m 5M. W ○ twr; 60°30′·48N 01°14′·86W.

YELL SOUND, NORTH ENTRANCE

Bagi Stack ☆ Fl (4) 20s 45m 10M; 60°43′·53N 01°07′·54W.

Gruney Is ☆ Fl WR 5s 53m W8M, R6M; W twr; vis: 064°-R-180°-W-012°; ***Racon (T) 14M***; 60°39′·15N 01°18′·17W.

Pt of Fethaland ☆ 60°38′·05N 01°18′·70W Fl (3) WR 15s 65m **W24M, R20M**; vis 080°-R-103°-W-160°-206°-W-340°.

Muckle Holm ☆ Fl (4) 10s 32m 10M 60°34′·83N 01°16′·01W.

Little Holm ☆ Iso 4s 12m 6M; W twr; 60°33′·42N 01°15′·88W.

Outer Skerry ☆ Fl 6s 12m 8M; 60°33′·04N 01°18′·32W.

Quey Firth ☆ Oc WRG 6s 22m W12M, R8M, G8M; W twr; vis: shore (through S & W)-W-290°-G-327°-W-334°-W-shore; 60°31′·43N 01°19′·58W.

Lamba, S side ☆Fl WRG 3s 30m W8M, R5M, G5M; W twr; vis: shore-G-288°-W-293°-R-327°-W-044°-R-140°-W-shore. Dir lt 290·5° Fl WRG 3s 24m W10M, R7M, G7M; vis: 285·5°-G-288°-W-293°-W-295·5°; 60°30′·73N 01°17′·84W.

SULLOM VOE

Gluss Is ☆ Ldg Lts 194·7° (H24). **Front,** 60°29′·77N 01°19′·44W F 39m **19M;** □ on Gy twr; **Rear,** 0·75M from front, F 69m **19M;** □ on Gy twr; both Lts 9M by day.

Little Roe ☆ Fl (3) WR 10s 16m W5M, R4M; W structure, Or band; vis: 036°-R-095·5°-W-036°; 60°29′·99N 01°16′·46W.

Skaw Taing ☆ Ldg Lts 150·5°. Front, Oc WRG 5s 21m W8M, R5M, G5M; Or and W structure; vis: 049°-W-078°-G-147°-W-154°-R-169°-W-288°; 60°29′·10N 01°16′·86W. Rear, 195m from front, Oc 5s 35m 8M; vis: W145°-156°.

Ness of Bardister ☆ Oc WRG 8s 20m W9M, R6M, G6M; Or &W structure; vis: 180·5°- W-240°- R-310·5°- W-314·5°-G-030·5°; 60°28′·19N 01°19′·63W.

Fugla Ness. Lts in line 212·3°. Rear, 60°27′·25N 01°19′·74W Iso 4s 45m 14M. Common front 60°27′·45N 01°19′·57W Iso 4s 27m 14M; synch with rear Lts. Lts in line 203°. Rear, 60°27′·26N 01°19′·81W Iso 4s 45m 14M.

Sella Ness ☆ Dir lt 133·5°; 60°26′·76N 01°16′·66W Oc WRG 10s 19m **W16M,** R3M, G3M; vis: 123·5° -G- 130·5°-Al WG (white phase increasing with brg)-132·5°-W-134·5°-Al WR(R phase inc with brg)-136·5°-R-143·5°; H24. By day Oc WRG 10s 19m W2M, R1M,G1M as above.

EAST YELL, UNST and BALTA SOUND

Whitehill ☆ Fl WR 3s 24m W9M, R6M; W clad metal frame twr; vis: 147°-W-163°-R-211°-W-352°-R-003°; 60°34′·80N 01°00′·22W.Fetlar. Hamars Ness ☆ Iso G 6s 5m 3M; 60°37′·78N 00°55′·73W.

Balta Sound ☆Fl WR 10s 17m 10M, R7M; vis: 249°-W-008°-R-058°-W-154°; 60°44′·43N 00°47′·68W.

Holme of Skaw ☆ Fl 5s 8m 8M; white metal framework twr; 60°49′·87N 00°46′·30W.

Muckle Flugga ☆ 60°51′·32N 00°53′·13W Fl (2) 20s 66m **22M.**

Yell. Cullivoe Bkwtr Hd ☆ Fl (2) WRG 10s 3m 4M; vis: 080°-G- 294°-W-355°-R-080°; 60°41′·86N 00°59′·70W.

Unst. Head of Mula ☆ Fl WRG 5s 48m W10M, G7M, R7M; metal framework twr; vis: 292°-G-357°-W-002°-R-157°-W-161·5; 60°40′·76N 00°57′·58W.

MAINLAND, WEST

Esha Ness ☆ 60°29′·34N 01°37′·65W Fl 12s 61m **25M.**

Ness of Hillswick ☆ Fl (4) WR 15s 34m W9M, R6M; vis: 217°-W-093°-R-114°; 60°27′·21N 01°29′·80W.

Muckle Roe, Swarbacks Minn ☆ Fl WR 3s 30m W9M, R6M; vis: 314°-W-041°-R-075°-W-137°; 60°20′·98N 01°27′·07W.

W Burra Firth Outer ☆ Oc WRG 8s 27m W9M, R7M, G7M; vis: 136°-G-142°-W-150°-R-156°. H24; 60°17′·79N 01°33′·56W.

W Burra Firth Inner ☆ 60°17′·78N 01°32′·17W F WRG 9m **W15M**, R9M, G9M; vis: 095°-G-098°-W-102°-105°; H24.

Ve Skerries ☆ Fl (2) 20s 17m 11M; W twr; ***Racon (T) 15M***; 60°22′·36N 01°48′·78W.

Papa Stour Housa Voe Dir lt 228° ☆ F WRG 2m W9M, R7M, G7M; vis: 219°- G-226°- W-230°-R-239°; 60°19′·58N 01°40′·47W.

Rams Head ☆ Fl WRG 8s 16m W9M, R6M; G6M; W house; vis: 265°-G-355°-W-012°-R-090°-W-136°, obsc by Vaila I when brg more than 030°; 60°11′·96N 01°33′·47W.

North Havra ☆ Fl(3) WRG 12s 24m W11M, R8M, G8M; W twr; vis: 001°-G-053·5°-W-060·5°-R-144°, 274°- G-334°-W-337·5°-R -001°; 60°09′·85N 01°20′·29W.

SCALLOWAY

Bullia Skerry ☆ Fl 5s 5m 5M; stainless steel pillar & platform 60°06′·55N 01°21′·57W.

Point of the Pund ☆ Fl WRG 5s 20m W7M, R5M, G5M; W GRP twr; vis: 267°-W-350°-R-090°-G-111°-R-135°-W-140°-G-177°; 60°07′·99N 01°18′·31W.

Whaleback Skerry Q; 60°07′·95N 01°18′·90W.

Blacks Ness Pier SW corner ☆ Oc WRG 10s 10m W11M, G8M, R8M; vis: 052°-G-063·5°-W-065·5°-R-077°; 60°08′·02N 01°16′·59W.

Fugla Ness ☆ Fl (2) WRG 10s 20m W10M, R7M, G7M; W twr; vis: 014°-G-032°-W-082°-R-134°-W-shore; 60°06′·38N 01°20′·85W.

FOULA

South Ness ☆ 60°06′·75N 02°03′·86W Fl WR (3) 15s 36m **W18M** R14M; W twr; vis: 221°-W-255°-R-277°-W-123°-obscured-221°.

		1	2	3	4	5	6	7	8	9	10	11
1	Berwick-upon-Tweed	**1**										
2	Eyemouth	10	**2**									
3	Dunbar	26	17	**3**								
4	Port Edgar	58	50	34	**4**							
5	Methil	45	36	20	20	**5**						
6	Fife Ness	38	29	17	34	16	**6**					
7	Dundee	58	49	37	54	36	20	**7**				
8	Montrose	59	51	43	61	43	27	27	**8**			
9	Stonehaven	72	66	60	78	60	44	45	20	**9**		
10	Aberdeen	82	78	73	90	72	56	57	32	13	**10**	
11	Peterhead	105	98	93	108	94	78	80	54	35	25	**11**

11	10	9	8	7	6	5	4	3	2	1		
11	155	79	47	76	104	144	126	120	125	145	Cape Wrath	**11**
	10	95	124	120	148	190	170	162	156	160	Lerwick	**10**
		9	50	46	74	114	104	90	95	115	Kirkwall	**9**
			8	31	59	99	89	75	80	100	Scrabster	**8**
				7	29	69	58	44	50	72	Wick	**7**
					6	43	32	26	44	74	Helmsdale	**6**
						5	13	34	59	90	Inverness	**5**
							4	23	48	79	Nairn	**4**
								3	25	56	Lossiemouth	**3**
									2	33	Banff/Macduff	**2**
										1	Peterhead	**1**

AREA 6 *NW Scotland – C Wrath to Oban including The Western Isles*

SELECTED LIGHTS, BUOYS & WAYPOINTS

CAPE WRATH TO LOCH TORRIDON

Cape Wrath ☆ 58°37′·54N 04°59′·99W Fl (4) 30s 122m **22M**; W twr.

LOCH INCHARD and LOCH LAXFORD

Kinlochbervie Dir lt 327° ☆ 58°27′·49N 05°03′·08W WRG 15m **16M** vis: 326°-FG-326·5°-AlGW-326·8°-FW-327·3°-AlRW-327·5°-FR-328°.

Creag Mhòr Dir lt 147°; Iso WRG 2s 16m 4M; vis: 136·5°-R -146·5°-W-147·5°-G-157·5°; 58°26′·99N 05°02′·45W.

Stoer Head ☆ 58°14′·43N 05°24′·07W Fl 15s 59m **24M**; W twr.

LOCH INVER, SUMMER ISLES and ULLAPOOL

Soyea I ☆ Fl (2) 10s 34m 6M; 58°08′·56N 05°19′·67W.

Glas Leac ☆ Fl WRG 3s 7m 5M; vis: 071°- W-078°-R-090°-G-103°-W-111°, 243°-W-247°-G-071°; 58°08′·68N 05°16′·36W.

Rubha Cadail ☆ Fl WRG 6s 11m W9M, R6M, G6M; W twr; vis: 311°-G-320°-W-325°-R-103°-W-111°-G-118°-W-127°-R-157°-W-199°;57°55′·51N 05°13′·40W.

Ullapool Pt ☆ Iso R 4s 8m 6M; W twr; vis: 258°-108°; 57°53′·59N 05°09′·93W.

Cailleach Head ☆ Fl (2) 12s 60m 9M; W twr; vis: 015°-236°; 57°55′·81N 05°24′·23W.

LOCH EWE and LOCH GAIRLOCH

Fairway L Fl 10s; 57°51′·98N 05°40′·09W.

Rubha Reidh ☆ 57°51′·52N 05°48′·72W Fl (4) 15s 37m **24M.**

Glas Eilean ☆ Fl WRG 6s 9m W6M, R4M; vis: 080°-W-102°-R-296°-W-333°-G-080°; 57°42′·79N 05°42′·42W.

Sgeir Dhubh Mhór ; 57°42′·02N 05°42′·72W

OUTER HEBRIDES – EAST SIDE

LEWIS

Butt of Lewis ☆ 58°30′·89N 06°15′·84W Fl 5s 52m **25M**; R twr; vis: 056°-320°.

Tiumpan Head ☆ 58°15′·66N 06°08′·29W Fl (2) 15s 55m **25M**; W twr.

Broad Bay Tong ⚓ Ldg Lts 320°, Oc R 8s 8m 4M; 58°14′·48N 06°19′·98W. Rear, 70m from front, Oc R 8s 9m 4M.

STORNOWAY

Arnish Point ☆ Fl WR 10s 17m W9M, R7M; W ○ twr; vis: 088°-W-198°-R-302°-W-013°; 58°11′·50N 06°22′·16W.

Sandwick Bay, NW side ☆ Oc WRG 6s 10m 9M; vis: 334°-G-341°-W-347°-R-354°; 58°12′·20N 06°22′·11W.

No. 1 Pier SW corner ☆ Q WRG 5m 11M; vis: shore-G-335°-W-352°-R-shore; 58°12′·36N 06°23′·43W.

Creed Estuary ☆ Iso WRG 10s 24m 5M; vis: 277°-G-282°-W-290°-R-295°; 58°12′·03N 06°23′·47W.
No. 3 Pier ☆ Q (2) G 10s 7m 2M 58°12′·31N 06°23′·28W.
Glumaig Hbr ☆ Iso WRG 3s 8m 3M; 58°11′·27N 06°22′·9W; grey framework twr; vis: 150°-G-174°-W-180°-R-205°.

LOCH ERISORT, LOCH SHELL and EAST LOCH TARBERT

Shiants QG; 57°54′·57N 06°25′·70W.
Sgeir Inoe Fl G 6s; ***Racon (M) 5M***; 57°50′·93N 06°33′·93W.
Eilean Glas (Scalpay) ☆ 57°51′·41N 06°38′·55W Fl (3) 20s 43m **23M**; W twr, R bands; ***Racon (T) 16-18M***; 992356014.
Sgeir Graidach Q (6) + L Fl 15s; 57°50′·36N 06°41′·37W.
Sgeir Ghlas ☆ Iso WRG 4s 9m W9M, R6M, G6M; W ○ twr; vis: 282°-G-319°-W-329°-R-153°-W-164°-G-171°; 57°52′·36N 06°45′·24W.
Tarbert ☆ Dir Iso WRG 4s 9m 4M; vis : 290°-Iso G-297°-Al WG-300°-Iso W-303°-Al WR-306°-Iso R306°-313°; 57°53′·82N 06°47′·93W.

SOUND OF HARRIS, LEVERBURGH and BERNERAY

No.1 QG; 57°41′·20N 07°02′·67W.
No. 3 Fl G 5s; 57°41′·86N 07°03′·44W.
No. 4 Fl R 5s; 57°41′·76N 07°03′·63W.
Suilven Fl (3)R 10s; 57°41′·68N 07°04′·36W.
Cabbage Fl (2) R 6s; ***Racon (T) 5M (3cm)***; 57°42′·13N 07°03′·96W.
Leverburgh Ldg Lts 014·7°. Front, Q 10m 4M 57°46′·23N 07°02′·04W. Rear, Oc 3s 12m 4M.
Jane's Tower Q (2) G 5s 6m 4M; vis: obscured 273°-318°; 57°45′·76N 07°02′·12W.
Leverburgh Reef Fl R 2s 4m 57°45′·97N 07°01′·86W.
Laimhrig Mhor ☆ Q G; 57°45′·92N 07°01′·65W.
Leverburgh Pier Ldg Lts 063°. Front, Iso Bu 4s 8s 6m 4M; 57°46′·00N 07°01′·61W, metal col. Rear, Iso Bu 4s 8s 7m 4M.

NORTH UIST

Fairway L Fl 10s; 57°40′·23N 07°01′·39W.
Vallay Island ☆ Fl WRG 3s 4m 8M; vis: 206°-W-085°-G-140°-W-145°-R-206°; 57°39′·69N 07°26′·42W.
Griminish Hbr Ldg Lts 183°. Front, QG 6m 4M; 57°39′·38N 07°26′·75W. Rear, 110m from front, QG 7m 4M.

LOCH MADDY and GRIMSAY

Weaver's Pt ☆ Fl 3s 24m 7M; W hut; 57°36′·49N 07°06′·00W.
Glas Eilean Mòr ☆ Fl (2) G 4s 8m 5M; 57°35′·95N 07°06′·70W.
Vallaquie Is Dir lt 207·5°/255·5° ☆ 57°35′·50N 07°09′·40W; W pillar; vis:Fl (3) WRG 8s 11m W5M, R5M, G5M; shore - G -205°-W-210°-R-240°; Fl (3) WRG 8s 11m W8M, R8M, G8M; 249°-G-254°-W-257°-R-262°.
Lochmaddy Ldg Lts 298°. Front, Ro-Ro Pier 2 FG (vert) 8m 4M. Rear, 110m from front, Oc G 8s 10m 4M; vis: 284°-304°; 57°35′·76N 07°09′·36W.
Grimsay No. 1 Fl (2) R 8s; 57°28′·26N 07°11′·82W.

SOUTH UIST and LOCH CARNAN

Landfall L Fl 10s; 57°22′·27N 07°11′·52W.
Ldg Lts 222°. Front Fl R 2s 7m 5M; W ◊ on post; 57°22′·00N 07°16′·34W. Rear, 58m from front, Iso R 10s 11m 5M; W ◊ on post.
Ushenish ☆ (S Uist) 57°17′·90N 07°11′·57W Fl W 20s 54m **W19M**; W twr; vis: 193°- 018°.

LOCH BOISDALE

MacKenzie Rk Fl (3) R 15s 3m 4M; 57°08′·24N 07°13′·71W.
Calvay E End ☆ Fl (2) WRG 10s 16m W7M, R7M, G7M; W twr; vis: 111°-W-190°-G-202°-W-286°-R-111°; 57°08′·53N 07°15′·38W; 992351139.
Gasay I ☆ Fl WR 5s 10m W7M, R7M; W twr; vis: 120°-W-284°-R-120°; 57°08′·93N 07°17′·39W.
LochBoisdaleDirlt☆,292·5°;WRG4s4m5M;vis:287·5°-IsoG-290·5°-AlWG-292°-IsoW-293°-AlW-294·5°-IsoR-298·5°; 57°09′·19N 07°18′·24W.
2 FG 8m 3M on dn; 57°09′·13N 07°18′·18W.

LUDAIG and ERISKAY

Ludaig Bwtr ☆ 2 FR (vert) 6m 3M; 57°06′·17N 07°19′·49W.
Acairseid Mhor Ldg Lts 285°. Front, Oc R 6s 9m 4M; 57°03′·89N 07°17′·25W. Rear, 24m from front, Oc R 6s 10m 4M.

BARRA, CASTLEBAY and VATERSAY SOUND

Drover Rocks Q (6) + L Fl 15s; 57°04′·08N 07°23′·54W.
Binch Rock Q (6) + L Fl 15s; 57°01′·60N 07°17′·12W.
Curachan Q (3) 10s; 56°58′·56N 07°20′·51W.
Ardveenish ☆ Oc WRG 6m 9/6M; vis: 300°-G-304°-W-306°-R-310°; 57°00′·21N 07°24′·43W.
Bo Vich Chuan Q(6)+L Fl 15s; ***Racon (M) 5M***; 56°56′·15N 07°23′·31W.
Channel Rk ☆ Fl WR 6s 4m W6M, R4M; vis: 121·5°-W-277°-R-121·5°; 56°56′·24N 07°28′·94W.
Sgeir a Scape Fl (2) G 8s; 56°56′·25N 07°27′·21W.
Rubha Glas. Ldg Lts 295°. Front FBu 9m 6M; Or △ on W twr; 56°56′·77N 07°30′·64W. Rear , 457m from front, FBu 15m 6M; Or ▽ on W twr; vis: 15° and 8° respectively either side of ldg line.
Barra Hd ☆ 56°47′·12N 07°39′·21W Fl 15s 208m **18M**; W twr; obsc by islands to NE; 992351095.

OUTER HEBRIDES – WEST SIDE

Flannan I ☆, Eilean Mór Fl (2) 30s 101m **20M**; W twr; 58°17′·29N 07°35′·29W, obsc in places by Is to W of Eilean Mór.
Rockall ☆ Fl 15s 19m 8M (unreliable); 57°35′·76N 13°41′·27W.
Gasker Lt ☆ Fl (3) 10s 38m 10M; 57°59′·05N 07°17′·20W.
Whale Rock Q (3) 10s 5m 5M; ***Racon (T)***; 57°54′·40N 07°59·91W.
Haskeir I ☆ 57°41′·96N 07°41·31W Fl 20s 44m **24M**; W twr; ***Racon (M) 17–15M***; 992351140.
Monach Isles ☆ Fl (2) 15s 47m **18M**; R brick twr; 57°31′·55N 07°41′·68W.

EAST LOCH ROAG

Aird Laimishader Carloway ☆ Fl 6s 63m 8M; W hut; obsc on some brgs; 58°17′·06N 06°49′·50W.
Ardvanich Pt ☆ Fl G 3s 4m 2M; 58°13′·48N 06°47′·68W.
Tidal Rk ☆ Fl R 3s 2m 2M (sync with Ardvanich Pt above); 58°13′·45N 06°47′·57W.
Grèinam ☆ Fl WR 6s 8m W8M, R7M; W bn; vis: R143°-169°, W169°-143°; 58°13′·30N 06°46′·16W.

LOCH ROAG

Rubha Domhain ☆ Fl G 5s 9m 1M; post; 58°12′·96N 06°45′·40W.
Bogha na Muilne Fl (2) 10s; 58°12′·70N 06°54′·23W.
Mia Vaig Bay Fl G 2s 2m 1M; bn; 58°11′·83N 06°56′·60W.

NORTH UIST and SOUTH UIST

Vallay I ☆ Fl WRG 3s 8M; vis: 206°-W-085°-G-140°-W-145°-R-206°; 57°39′·70N 07°26′·34W.

Falconet twr ☆ FR 25m 8M (3M by day); shown 1hr before firing, changes to Iso R 2s 15 min before firing until completion; 57°22′·04N 07°23′·58W.

ST KILDA

Ldg Lts 270°. Front, Oc 5s 26m 3M; 57°48′·32N 08°34′·31W. Rear, 100m from front, Oc 5s 38m 3M; sync.

LOCH TORRIDON TO MALLAIG

LITTLE MINCH and W SKYE

Eugenie Rock Q 6 + LF 15s; 57°46′·47N 06°27′·28W.
Eilean Trodday ☆ Fl (2) WRG 10s 52m W12M, R9M, G9M; W Bn; vis: W062°-R088°-130°-W-322°-G-062°; 57°43′·63N 06°17′·93W; 992351084.
Uig, Edward Pier Hd ☆ 57°35′·09N 06°22′·29W Iso WRG 4s 9m W7M, R4M, G4M; vis: 180-W-006°-G-050°-W-073°-R-180°.
Waternish Pt ☆ Fl 20s 21m 8M; W twr; 57°36′·48N 06°37′·99W.
Loch Dunvegan, Uiginish Pt ☆ Fl WRG 3s 16m W7M,R5M,G5M; W lattice twr; vis: 041°-G-132°-W-145°-R-148°-W-253°-R- 263°-W-273°-G-306°, (>148° obsc by Fiadhairt Pt); 57°26′·84N 06°36′·53W.
Neist Point ☆ 57°25′·41N 06°47′·30W Fl 5s 43m **16M**; W twr.
Loch Harport, Ardtreck Pt ☆ 57°20′·38N 06°25′·80W Fl 6s 18m 9M; small W twr.

RONA, LOCH A'BHRAIGE and INNER SOUND

Na Gamhnachain Q; 57°35′·89N 05°57′·71W.
Rona NE Point ☆ 57°34′·69N 05°57′·54W Fl 12s 69m **19M**; W twr; vis: 050°-358°; 992351045.
Loch A'Bhraige, Sgeir Shuas ☆ Fl R 2s 6m 3M; vis: 070°-199°; 57°35′·02N 05°58′·61W.
Ldg Lts 136·5°. Front, Q WRG 3m W4M, R3M; vis: 135°-W- 138°-R-318°-G-135°; 57°34′·41N 05°58′·09W. Rear, Iso 6s 28m 5M.
Ru Na Lachan ☆ Oc WR 8s 21m 10M; twr; vis: 337°-W-022°- R-117°-W-162°; 57°29′·02N 05°52′·15W.

SOUND OF RAASAY, PORTREE and CROWLIN ISLANDS

Sgeir Mhór Fl G 5s; 57°24′·57N 06°10′·53W.
Eilean Beag ☆ Fl 6s 32m 6M; W Bn; 57°21′·21N 05°51′·42W.
Eyre Pt ☆ Fl WR 3s 6m W9M R6M; W clad framework twr; vis: 215°-W-267°-R-288°-W-063°; 57°20′·01N 06°01′·28W.
Sgeir Thraid ☆ Q 12m 3M; metal twr; 57°19′·82N 05°56′·51W.
Sgeir Ghobhlach ☆ Fl(3)10s 10m 3M; metal twr; 57°15′·69N 05°52′·25W.

LOCH CARRON

Sgeir Golach ☆ Fl 10s 5m 3M; 57°21′·20N 05°39′·01W.
Eilean a Chait Lt ho (dis) 13M; 57°20′·96N 05°38′·87W.
Bogha Dubh Sgeir Fl (2)R 6s 4m 2M; 57°20′·92N 05°37′·85W.

RAASAY and LOCH SLIGACHAN

Suisnish ☆ 2 FG (vert) 8m 2M; 57°19′·87N 06°03′·91W.
Eyre Point ☆ Fl WR 3s 6m W9M, R6M; W twr; vis: 215°-W-266°-R- 288°-W-063°; 57°20′·01N 06°01′·29W.

KYLEAKIN and KYLE OF LOCH ALSH

Carragh Rk Fl (2) G 12s; ***Racon (T) 5M***; 57°17′·18N 05°45′·36W.
Bow Rk Fl (2) R 12s; 57°16′·71N 05°45′·85W.
Fork Rks Fl G 6s; 57°16′·85N 05°44′·93W.
Black Eye Rk Fl R 6s; 57°16′·72N 05°45′·31W.
Eileanan Dubha East ☆ Fl (2) 10s 9m 8M; vis: obscured 104°-146°; 57°16′·56N 05°42′·32W.
8 Metre Rock ☆ Fl G 6s 5m 4M; 57°16′·60N 05°42′·69W.
String Rock Fl R 6s; 57°16′·50N 05°42′·89W.
Sgeir-na-Caillich ☆ Fl (2) R 6s 3m 4M; 57°15′·59N 05°38′·90W.

SOUND OF SLEAT

Kyle Rhea ☆ Fl WRG 3s 7m W8M, R5M, G5M; W Bn; vis: shore-R-219°-W-228°-G-338°-W-346°-R-shore; 57°14′·22N 05°39′·93W.
Sandaig I, NW point ☆ Fl 6s 13m 8M; W twr; 57°10′·05N 05°42′·29W.
Ornsay, SE end ☆ Oc 8s 18m 12M; W twr; vis: 157°-030°; 57°08′·60N 05°46′·85W.
Pt. of Sleat ☆ Fl 3s 20m 9M; W twr; 57°01′·08N 06°01′·08W.

MALLAIG and LOCH NEVIS ENTRANCE

Sgeir Dhearg QG; 57°00′·74N 05°49′·50W.
Northern Pier E end ☆ Iso WRG 4s 6m W9M, R6M, G6M; Gy twr; vis: 181°-G-185°-W-197°-R-201°. Fl G 3s 14m 6M; same structure; 57°00′·47N 05°49′·50W.
Sgeir Dhearg ☆ 57°00′·63N 05°49′·61W Fl (2) WG 8s 6m 5M; Gy Bn; vis: 190°-G-055°-W-190°.

SMALL ISLES AND WEST OF MULL

CANNA and RUM

Canna, E end Sanday Is ☆ Fl 10s 32m 9M; W twr; vis: 152°-061°; 57°02′·82N 06°28′·02W.
Loch Scresort Q; 57°00′·79N 06°14′·61W.

HYSKEIR, EIGG, MUCK and ARISAIG

Humla Fl G 6s 3m 4M 57°00′·46N 06°37′·39W.
Hyskeir ☆ 56°58′·16N 06°40′·83W Fl (3) 30s 41m **24M**; W twr. ***Racon (T) 14-17M***; 992351094.
SE point Eigg (Eilean Chathastail) ☆ Fl 6s 24m 8M; W twr; vis: 181°-shore; 56°52′·25N 06°07′·28W.
Eigg, Sgeir nam Bagh (Ferry Terminal) ☆ Dir 245°; Fl WRG 3s 9m W14, R11, G11; H24; steel pole; vis: 242·5°-G-244°-W-246°-R-247·5°. 2FR(vert) on same structure; 56°52′·79N 06°07′·56W.
Isle of Muck (Port Mor) ☆ Dir Fl WRG 3s 7m W14, R11, G11, by day W1, R1, G1; steel twr; vis: 319·5°-G-321°-W-323°-R-324·5°; 56°49′·96N 06°13′·64W.
Bogha Ruadh ☆ Fl G 5s 4m 3M; 56°49′·56N 06°13′·05W.
Bo Faskadale Fl (3) G 18s; 56°48′·18N 06°06′·37W.
Ardnamurchan ☆ 56°43′·63N 06°13′·58W Fl (2) 20s 55m **22M**; Gy twr; vis: 002°-217°.
Cairns of Coll, Suil Ghorm ☆ Fl 12s 23m 10M; W twr; 56°42′·26N 06°26′·75W.

TIREE, COLL and ARINAGOUR

Loch Eatharna, Pier Head ☆ Dir 325°; Oc WRG 7s 6m 2M; vis: 316°-G-322°-W-328°-R-334°; 56°36′·86N 06°31′·29W.
Loch Eatharna, Bogha Mór Fl G 6s; 56°36′·65N 06°30′·90W.
Roan Bogha Q (6) + L Fl 15s 3m 5M; 56°32′·23N 06°40′·18W.
Placaid Bogha Fl G 4s; 56°33′·22N 06°44′·06W.
Scarinish ☆ Fl 3s 11m 12M; W □ twr; vis: 210°-030°; S side of ent, 56°30′·02N 06°48′·26W.
Cairn na Burgh More (Treshnish Is), Fl (3) 15s 36m 8M; solar panels on framework tr; 56°31′·05N 06°22′·95W.
Gott Bay Ldg Lts 286·5°. Front FR 8m; 56°30′·61N 06°47′·82W. Rear 30m from front FR 11m.

Skerryvore ☆ Fl 10s 46m **23M**; Gy twr; ***Racon (M) 18M***. 56°19′·36N 07°06′·88W; 992351091.

LOCH NA KEAL and LOCH NA LÀTHAICH

Sgeir a Charraigein Q(6) + LFl 15s; 56°28′·29N 06°07′·71W.
Eileanan na Liathanaich, SE end ☆ Fl WR 6s 12m W8M, R6M; vis: R088°- W108°-088°; 56°20′·56N 06°16′·38W.

DUBH ARTACH

Dubh Artach ☆ 56°07′·94N 06°38′·08W Fl (2) 30s 44m **20M**; Gy twr, R band; 992351088.

SOUND OF MULL

LOCH SUNART, TOBERMORY and LOCH ALINE

Ardmore Pt ☆ Fl (2) 10s 18m 13M; 56°39′·37N 06°07′·70W.
New Rks Fl G 6s 56°39′·05N 06°03′·30W.
Rubha nan Gall ☆ 56°38′·33N 06°04′·00W Fl 3s 17m **15M**; W twr.
Tobermory Slip ☆ Iso WRG 3s 5m 4M; vis: 220°-G-232°-W-244°-R-256°; metal column; 56°37′·41N 06°03′·77W.
Eileanan Glasa (Dearg Sgeir) ☆ 56°32′·25N 05°54′·80W Fl 6s 7m 8M; W ○ twr.
Fiunary Spit Fl G 6s; 56°32′·66N 05°53′·17W.
Fishnish Ferry Slip ☆ Iso WRG 3s 5m 4M; vis: 158°-G-170°-W-195°-R-230°; metal column; 56°30′·89N 05°48′·61W.
Loch Aline, ☆ Dir 357°; Oc WRG 6s 2m 4M; vis: 353°-G-356°-W-358°-R-002°; Or concrete plinth; 56°32′·38N 05°46′·47W.
Ardtornish Pt ☆ Fl (2) WRG 10s 8m W8M, R6M, G6M; W twr; vis: G shore- 301°-W-308°-R-342°-W-057°-R-095°-W-108°-G-shore; 56°31′·09N 05°45′·21W.
Craignure Ldg Lts 240·9°. Front, FR 10m; 56°28′·26N 05°42′·28W. Rear, 150m from front, FR 12m; vis: 225·8°-255·8°.

MULL TO CALEDONIAN CANAL AND OBAN

Lismore ☆, SW end 56°27′·34N 05°36′·45W Fl 10s 31m **17M**; W twr; vis: 237°-208°.
Lady's Rk Fl 6s 12m 5M; Red clad lattice tower on W base 56°26′·92N 05°37′·05W; 992351093.
Duart Pt ☆ Fl (3) WR 18s 14m W5M, R3M; vis: 162°-W-261°-R- 275°-W-353°-R-shore; 56°26′·84N 05°38′·77W.

LOCH LINNHE

Corran Shoal QR 56°43′·69N 05°14′·39W.
Corran Pt ☆ Iso WRG 4s 12m W10M, R7M, G7M; W twr; vis: shore-R-195°-W-215°-G-020-W-030°-R-shore; 56°43′·25N 05°14′·54W.
Corran Narrows NE ☆ Fl 5s 4m 4M; W twr; vis: S shore-214°; 56°43′·62N 05°13′·90W.
Clovullin Spit Fl (2) R 15s; 56°42′·29N 05°15′·56W.
Cuil-cheanna Spit Fl G 6s; 56°41′·17N 05°15′·72W.
Mc Lean Rk QR 56°49′·80N 05°07′·04W.
Eilean na Creiche Fl (2) 5s; 56°50′·25N 05°07′·02W.
Eilean na Craobh Fl (2) R 6s 4m 2M; 56°50′·43N 05°07′·95W.

FORT WILLIAM and CALEDONIAN CANAL

Corpach, Caledonian Canal Lock ent ☆ Iso WRG 4s 6m 5M; W twr; vis: G287°- W310°- R335°-030°; 56°50′·52N 05°07′·44W.

LYNN OF LORN

Sgeir Bhuidhe Appin Fl (2) WR 7s 8m W9M R6M; W Bn; vis: W013·5°- R184°-220°; 56°33′·63N 05°24′·65W.
Appin Point Fl G 6s; 56°32′·69N 05°25′·97W.
Dearg Sgeir, off Aird's Point Fl WRG 2s 2m W3M, R1M, G1M; vis: 196°-R-246°-W-258°-G-041°-W-058°-R-093°-W-139°; 56°32′·20N 05°25′·22W.
Rubha nam Faoileann (Eriska) QG 2m 2M; G col; vis 128°-329°; 56°32′·20N 05°24′·11W.
Branra Rk ☆ Fl(2) 10s 4m 5M; metal frame on W twr; 56°32′·02N 05°26′·60W.

OBAN

N spit of Kerrera ☆ Fl R 3m 4M; W post; 56°25′·32N 05°29′·29W.
Dunollie ☆ Fl (2) WRG 6s 6m W8M, R6M, G6M; vis: 351°-G- 020°- W-047°-R-120°-W-138°-G-143°; 56°25′·37N 05°29′·05W.
Rubh'a'Chruidh ☆ Q R 3m 2M; W col, R bands; 56°25′·49N 05°29′·56W.
Kerrera QR; 56°24′·15N 05°30′·81W.
Corran Ledge VQ (9) 10s; 56°25′·19N 05°29′·11W.
Oban Bay Q; 56°24′·92N 05°29′·23W.
Sgeir Rathaid Q(6)+L Fl 15s; 56°24′·75N 05°29′·37W.
North Pier 2 F G (vert); metal post; 56°24′·89N 05°28′·49W.
Ro-Ro Jetty 2 F G (vert); post on dn; 56°24′·69N 05°28′·65W.
Northern Lt Pier 2 F G (vert); metal post; 56°24′·71N 05°28′·91W.

DISTANCE TABLES

Approx distances in nautical miles are by the most direct route allowing for dangers and TSS.

		1	2	3	4	5	6	7	8	9	10	11	12	13	14	15	16	17
1	Cape Wrath	1																
2	Ullapool	54	2															
3	Stornoway	53	45	3														
4	East Loch Tarbert	75	56	33	4													
5	Portree	83	57	53	42	5												
6	Kyle of Lochalsh	91	63	62	63	21	6											
7	Mallaig	112	82	83	84	42	21	7										
8	Eigg	123	98	97	75	54	35	14	8									
9	Castlebay (Barra)	133	105	92	69	97	76	59	46	9								
10	Tobermory	144	114	115	87	74	53	32	20	53	10							
11	Loch Aline	157	127	128	100	87	66	45	33	66	13	11						
12	Fort William	198	161	162	134	121	98	75	63	96	43	34	12					
13	Oban	169	138	139	111	100	77	56	44	77	24	13	29	13				
14	Loch Melfort	184	154	155	117	114	93	69	61	92	40	27	45	18	14			
15	Craobh Haven	184	155	155	117	114	92	70	60	93	40	27	50	21	5	15		
16	Crinan	187	157	158	129	112	95	74	63	97	42	30	54	25	14	9	16	
17	Mull of Kintyre	232	203	189	175	159	143	121	105	120	89	87	98	72	62	57	51	17

OBAN TO LOCH CRAIGNISH

Heather Is ☆ Fl R 2·5s 11m 2M; 56°24′·41N 05°30′·24W.

Ferry Rks SE Q (3) 10s; 56°23′·99N 05°30′·53W.

Sgeirean Dubha ☆ Fl (2) 12s 7m 5M; W ○ twr; 56°22′·81N 05°32′·27W.

Sgeir an Fheuran Fl G 3s; 56°22′·80N 05°31′·94W.

Bogha Nuadh Q (6) + LFl 15s; 56°21′·69N 05°37′·87W; 992351090.

Bogha Ghair Q (3) 10s; 56°16′·50N 05°40′·44W.

Bono Rock Q (9) 15s; 56°16′·21N 05°41′·22W.

Fladda ☆ Fl (2) WRG 9s 13m W11M, R9M, G9M; W twr; vis: 169°-R-186°-W-337°-G-344°-W-356°-R-026°; 56°14′·89N 05°40′·83W.

Dubh Sgeir (Luing) ☆ Fl WRG 6s 9m W6M, R4M. G4M; W twr; vis: W000°- R010°- W025°- G199°-000°; ***Racon (M) 5M***; 56°14′·76N 05°40′·20W.

The Garvellachs, Eileach an Naoimh, SW end ☆ Fl 6s 21m 9M; W Bn; vis: 240°-215°; 56°13′·04N 05°49′·06W.

LOCH MELFORT and CRAOBH HAVEN

Melfort Pier ☆ Dir FR 6m 3M; (Apr -Nov); 56°16′·14N 05°30′·19W.

56°12′·88N 05°33′·59W.

Craobh Marina Bkwtr Hd ☆ Iso WRG 5s 10m, W5M, R3M, G3M; vis:114°-G-162°-W-183°-R-200°; 56°12′·78N 05°33′·52W.

AREA 7 *SW Scotland – Colonsay to Kirkcudbright*

SELECTED LIGHTS, BUOYS & WAYPOINTS

COLONSAY TO ISLAY

COLONSAY

Scalasaig, Rubha Dubh ☆ Fl (2) WR 10s 8m W8M, R6M; W bldg; vis: shore-R- 230°-W-337°-R-354°; 56°04′·01N 06°10′·90W.

SOUND OF ISLAY

Rhubh' a Mhàil (Ruvaal) ☆ 55°56′·18N 06°07′·46W Fl (3) 15s 45m **19M**; W twr.

Carragh an t'Struith ☆ Fl 3s 8m 9M; W twr; vis: 354°-180°; 55°52′·30N 06°05′·78W.

Carraig Mòr ☆ Fl (2) WR 6s 7m W8M, R6M; W twr; vis: shore-R- 175°-W-347°-R-shore; 55°50′·42N 06°06′·13W.

McArthur's Hd ☆ Fl (2) WR 10s 39m W13M, R10M; W twr; W in Sound of Islay from NE coast,159°-R-244°-W-E coast of Islay; 55°45′·84N 06°02′·90W.

Orsay Is, **Rhinns of Islay** ☆ 55°40′·40N 06°30′·84W Fl 5s 46m **24M**; W twr; vis: 256°-184°.

PORT ELLEN and LOCH INDAAL

Carraig Fhada ☆ Fl WRG 3s 20m W8M, R6M, G6M; W □ twr; vis: W shore- 248°-G-311°-W-340°-R-shore; 55°37′·22N 06°12′·71W.

Otter Gander VQ (3) 5s; 55°36′·60N 06°12′·34W.

Fhada Q (3) 10s; 55°37′·21N 06°12′·41W.

Sgeir nan Ron Q R; 55°45′·53N 06°17′·32W.

Hbr entrance Q G; 55°37′·55N 06°11′·45W.

Rubh'an Dùin ☆ Fl (2) WR 7s 15m W11M, R8M; W twr; vis: shore-R-218°-W-249°-R-350°-W-shore; 55°44′·70N 06°22′·28 W.

JURA TO MULL OF KINTYRE

SOUND OF JURA, CRAIGHOUSE, L SWEEN and GIGHA

Skervuile ☆ Fl 15s 22m 9M; 55°36′·60N 06°12′·34W; W twr.

Nine Foot Rk Q (3) 10s; 55°52′·44N 05°52′·91W.

Goat Rock VQ (3) 5s; 55°50′·12N 05°55′·67W.

Eilean nan Gabhar ☆ Fl 5s 9m 8M; 55°50′·01N 05°56′·25W.

Craighouse ☆ Fl R 6s 3m 5M; 55°49′·98N 05°56′·43W.

Na Cùiltean ☆ Fl 10s 9m 9M; 55°48′·64N 05°54′·90W.

Gamhna Gigha ☆ Fl (2) 6s 7m 5M; 55°43′·78N 05°41′·08W.

WEST LOCH TARBERT

Dunskeig Bay ☆ Q (2) 10s 11m 8M; 55°45′·22N 05°35′·00W.

Eileen Tràighe (off S side) Fl (2) R 5s 5m 3M; R post; 55°45′·37N 05°35′·75W.

MULL OF KINTYRE

Mull of Kintyre ☆ 55°18′·64N 05°48′·25W Fl (2) 20s 91m **24M**; W twr on W bldg; vis: 347°-178°.

CRINAN CANAL and ARDRISHAIG

Crinan, E of lock ent ☆ Fl WG 3s 8m 4M; W twr, R band; vis: shore-W-146°-G-shore; 56°05′·48N 05°33′·37W.

Ardrishaig Bkwtr Hd ☆ L Fl WRG 6s 9m 4M; vis: 287°-G-339°-W- 350°-R-035°; 56°00′·76N 05°26′·59W.

LOCH FYNE TO SANDA ISLAND

EAST LOCH TARBERT

Eilean na Beithe ☆ Fl WRG 3s 7m 5M; vis: G036°- W065°-R078°-106°; 55°52′·68N 05°19′·62W.

KILBRANNAN SOUND, CRANNAICH and CARRADALE BAY

Port Crannaich Bkwtr Hd ☆ Fl R 10s 5m 6M; vis: 099°-279°; 55°35′·60N 05°27′·84W.

CAMPBELTOWN LOCH to SANDA ISLAND

Davaar N Pt ☆ 55°25′·69N 05°32′·42W Fl (2) 10s 37m **23M**; W twr; vis: 073°-330°.

Sanda Island ☆ 55°16′·50N 05°35′·01W Fl 10s 50m **15M**; W twr; vis: 242°-121°; 992351116.

Patersons Rock Fl (3) R 18s; 55°16′·90N 05°32′·48W.

KYLES OF BUTE TO RIVER CLYDE

WEST KYLE

Ardlamont Point No. 47 Fl R 4s; 55°49′·59N 05°11′·76.

Carry Rk No 46 Fl R 4s; 55°51′·40N 05°12′·14W.

BURNT ISLAND CHANNEL

Fl R 4s; 55°55′·80N 05°10′·46W.

Fl G 3s; 55°55′·79N 05°10′·48W.

Fl R 2s; 55°55′·76N 05°10′·39W.

Fl G 5s; 55°55′·74N 05°10′·38W.

Creyke Rk No 45 ; 55°55′·68N 05°10′·89W.

Beere Rk No 44 ; 55°55′·10N 05°10′·63W.

Wood Fm Rk ; 55°55′·42N 05°10′·31W.

EAST KYLE

Colintrave Pt ☆ Fl R 3s 7m 2M; metal post; 55°55′·39N 05°09′·22W.

Ardmaleish Point No. 41 Q; 55°53′·02N 05°04′·70W.

ROTHESAY SOUND

Ardyne Fl G 3s; 55°52′·10N 05°03′·20W.

Bogany Point No. 36 Fl R 4s; 55°50′·78N 05°01′·41W.

FIRTH OF CLYDE

Toward Pt ☆ Fl 10s 21m **22M**; W twr; 55°51′·73N 04°58′·79W.

No. 34 Q (3) 10s; 55°51′·44N 04°59′·11W.

Skelmorlie Iso 5s; 55°51′·65N 04°56′·34W.

WEMYSS and INVERKIP

Cowal L Fl 10s; 55°56′·00N 04°54′·83W.

The Gantocks Fl R 6s 12m 6M; ○ twr; 55°56′·45N 04°55′·08W.

The Gantocks No. 31 Q; 55°56′·56N 04°55′·13W.

DUNOON

Cloch Point ☆ Fl 3s 24m 8M; W ○ twr, B band, W dwellings; 55°56′·55N 04°52′·74W.

LOCH LONG and LOCH GOIL

Loch Long Oc 6s; 55°59′·15N 04°52′·42W.

Baron's Pt No. 3 ☆ Oc (2) Y 10s 5m 3M; 55°59′·18N 04°51′·12W.

Ravenrock Pt ☆ Fl 4s 12m 10M; W twr on W col. Dir lt 204°, WRG 9m (same twr); vis: 201·5°-F R-203°-Al WR(W phase incr with brg)-203·5°-FW-204·5°-Al WG(G phase incr with brg)-205°-FG-206·5°; 56°02′·14N 04°54′·39W.

Port Dornaige ☆ Fl 6s 8m 11M; W col; vis: 026°-206°; 56°03·75N 04°53′·65W.

Rubha Ardnahein ☆ Fl R 5s 3m 3M; vis: 132°-312°; 56°06′·15N 04°53′·60W.

The Perch, Ldg Lts 318° Front, F WRG 3m 5M; vis: 311°-G-317°-W- 320°-R-322°. Same structure, Fl R 3s 3m 3M; vis: 187°-322°; 56°06′·90N 04°54′·31W. Rear, 700m from front, F 7m 5M; vis: 312°-322·5°.

Cnap Pt ☆ Ldg Lts 031°. Front, Q 8m 10M; W col; 56°07′·40N 04°49′·96W. Rear, 87m from front F 13m; R line on W twr.

GOUROCK

Ashton Iso 5s; 55°58′·10N 04°50′·65W.

Rosneath Patch Fl (2) 10s 5m 10M; 55°58′·52N 04°47′·45W.

ROSNEATH, RHU NARROWS and GARELOCH

Ldg Lts 356°. **Front, No. 7N** 56°00′·05N 04°45′·36W Dir lt 356°. WRG 5m **W16M,** R13M, G13M; vis: 353°-Al WG- 355°- FW-357°-Al WR-000°-FR-002°.

Dir lt 115° WRG 5m **W16M,** R13M, G13M; vis: 111°-Al WG-114°-FW- 116°-Al WR-119°-FR-121°. Passing lt Oc G 6s 6m 3M; G △ on G pile . Rear, Ardencaple Castle Centre ☆ 56°00′·54N 04°45′·43W 2 FG (vert) 26m 12M; twr on Castle NW corner; vis: 335°-020°.

No. 8N Lt Bn 55°59′·09N 04°44′·21W Dir lt 080° WRG 4m; **W16M,** R13M,G13M;vis: 075°-FG-077·5°-Al WG-079·5°-FW-080·5°-AltWR-082·5°-FR-085°. **Dir lt 138°** WRG 4m **W16M,** R13M, G13M; vis: 132°-FG-134°-Al WG-FW137°-139°-Al WR-142°. Passing lt Fl Y 3s 6m 3M.

Gareloch No. 1 Lt Bn ☆ VQ (4) Y 5s 9m; Y 'X' on Y structure; 55°59′·12N 04°43′·89W.

No. 3N Lt Bn 56°00′·07N 04°46′·72W Dir lt 149° WRG 9m **W16M,** R13M, G13M F & Al; vis: 144°-FG-145°-Al WG-148°-FW-150°-Al WR-153°-FR-154°. Passing lt Oc R 8s 9m 3M.

Rosneath DG Jetty ☆ 2 FR (vert) 5M; W col; vis: 150°-330°; 56°00′·39N 04°47′·51W.

Rhu Pt Dir lt 318° WRG **W16M,** R13M, G13M; vis: 315°-Al WG-317°-F-319°-Al WR-321°-FR-325°; Dir W; vis: 325°-QW-340°-FW-345°-OcW-350°; 56°00′·95N 04°47′·20W.

Limekiln No. 2N Lt Bn 56°00′·67N 04°47′·64W Dir lt 295° WRG 5m **W16M,** R13M, G13M F & Al; R □ on R Bn; vis: 291°-Al WG- 294°-FW- 296°-Al WR-299°-FR-301°.

Mambeg Dir lt 331°, Q (4) WRG 8s 10m 14M; vis: 328·5°-G-330°-W- 332°-R-333°; H24; 56°03′·74N 04°50′·47W.

GREENOCK and PORT GLASGOW

Anchorage Lts in line 196°. Front, FG 7m 12M; Y col; 55°57′·62N 04°46′·58W. Rear, 32m from front, FG 9m 12M. Y col.

Lts in line 194·5°. Front, FG 18m; 55°57′·45N 04°45′·91W. Rear, 360m from front, FG 33m.

Steamboat Quay, W end ☆ FG 12m 12M; B&W chequered col; vis 210°-290°; 55°56′·25N 04°41′·44W. From here to Glasgow Lts on S bank are Fl G and Lts on N bank are Fl R.

CLYDE TO MULL OF GALLOWAY

HUNTERSTON CHANNEL

'C' Fl G 5s; 55°48′·10N 05°55′·30W.

Hun 1 (Y) Fl (4) Y 15s; 55°48′·10N 04°54′·21W.

Hun 3 Fl R 2s; 55°47′·60N 04°53′·52W.

LARGS and FAIRLIE

Approach L Fl 10s; 55°46′·40N 04°51′·85W.

Fairlie Patch Fl G 1·5s; 55°45′·38N 04°52′·34W.

MILLPORT and GREAT CUMBRAE

Tomont End Daymark 55°47′·56N 04°54′·10W.

Tattie Pier ☆ WRG 3s 5m 4M; vis: 222°-G-234°-W-246°-R-258°; metal column; 55°47′·20N 04°53′·89W.

Ldg Lts 333°. Pier Head front, 55°45′·04N 04°55′·85W FR 7m 5M. Rear, 137m from front, FR 9m 5M.

Mountstuart L Fl 10s; 55°48′·00N 04°57′·57W.

Runnaneun Pt (Rubha'n Eun) ☆ Fl R 6s 8m 12M; W twr; 55°43′·79N 05°00′·23W.

Little Cumbrae Is, Cumbrae Elbow ☆ Fl 6s 28m 14M; W twr; vis: 334°-193°; 55°43′·22N 04°58′·06W.

DISTANCE TABLES

Approx distances in nautical miles are by the most direct route allowing for dangers and TSS.

1	Loch Craignish	1													
2	Crinan	5	2												
3	Ardrishaig	14	9	3											
6	East Loch Tarbert	24	19	10	4										
5	Campbeltown	55	50	39	31	5									
6	Lamlash	48	43	34	25	24	6								
7	Largs	48	43	34	24	39	17	7							
8	Kip Marina	53	48	39	28	50	25	10	8						
9	Greenock	59	54	45	36	53	31	16	6	9					
10	Rhu (Helensburgh)	62	57	48	37	59	33	19	9	4	10				
11	Troon	54	49	40	33	33	16	20	29	34	38	11			
12	Girvan	67	62	53	43	29	20	33	46	49	51	21	12		
13	Stranraer	89	84	75	65	34	39	56	69	65	74	44	23	13	
14	Kirkcudbright	136	131	122	114	88	92	110	116	124	125	97	94	71	14

ARDROSSAN

Approach Dir lt 055°, WRG 15m W14M, R11M, G11M; vis: 050°-F G-051·2°-Alt WG(W phase inc with Brg)- 053·8°-FW-056·2°-Alt WR(R phase inc with brg)-058·8°-FR-060°; 55°38'·66N 04°49'·22W. Same structure FR 13m 6M; vis: 325°-145°.

Lt ho Pier Hd ☆ Iso WG 4s 11m 9M; W twr; vis: 035°-W-317°-G-035°; 55°38'·47N 04°49'·57W.

IRVINE

Ldg Lts 051°. Front, FG 10m 5M; 55°36'·40N 04°41'·57W. Rear, 101m from front, FR 15m 5M; G masts, both vis: 019°-120°.

TROON

Troon Approach ▲ Fl G 4s; 55°33'·06N 04°41'·34W.

W Pier Hd ☆ Fl (2) WG 5s 11m 9M; W twr; vis: 036°-G-090°-W-036°; 55°33'·07N 04°41'·02W.

Lady I ☆ Fl 2s 19m 11M; W Tr R vert stripes; ***Racon (T) 13-11M***; 55°31'·63N 04°44'·05W.

ARRAN, RANZA, LAMLASH and BRODICK

Pillar Rk Pt ☆ (Holy Island), 55°31'·04N 05°03'·65W Fl (2) 20s 38m **18M**; W □ twr.

Holy Is SW end ☆ Fl G 3s 14m 6M; W twr; vis: 282°-147°; 55°30'·73N 05°04'·21W.

Pladda ☆ 55°25'·50N 05°07'·12W Fl (3) 30s 40m **17M**; W twr.

AYR and AILSA CRAIG

S Pier Hd ☆ Q 7m 7M; R twr; vis: 012°-161°. Also FG 5m 5M; vis: 012°-082°; 55°28'·17N 04°38'·74W.

Ldg Lts 098°. Front, FR 10m 5M; Tfc sigs; 55°28'·15N 04°38'·38W. Rear, 130m from front Oc R 10s 18m 9M.

Maidens Hbr, E side ☆ Fl G 5s 4m 3M; 55°20'·24N 04°49'·20W.

Maidens Hbr, W side ☆ Fl R 3s 4m 2M; 55°20'·23N 04°49'·19W.

Turnberry Point ☆, near castle ruins 55°19'·57N 04°50'·69W Fl 15s 29m 12M; W twr.

Ailsa Craig ☆ 55°15'·12N 05°06'·52W Fl 4s 18m **17M**; W twr; vis: 145°-028°.

GIRVAN

S Pier Hd ☆2 FG (vert) 8m 4M; W twr; 55°14'·72N 04°51'·90W.

LOCH RYAN and STRANRAER

Milleur Point ⊥ Q; 55°01'·28N 05°05'·66W.

Fairway ⊕ Iso 4s; 54°59'·77N 05°03'·82W.

Forbes Shoal ⊖ QR; 54°59'·47N 05°02'·96W.

Loch Ryan W ▲QG;54°59'·23N 05°03'·24W .

Cairn Pt ☆ Fl (2) R 10s 14m 12M; W twr; 54°58'·46N 05°01'·85W.

Cairnryan ☆ Fl R 5s 5m 5M; 54°57'·77N 05°00'·99W.

Stranraer No.1 ⊥ Oc G 6s; 54°56'·67N 05°01'·32W.

No. 3 ⊥ QG; 54°55'·87N 05°01'·60W.

No. 5 ⊥ Fl G 3s; 54°55'·08N 05°01'·86W.

E Pier Hd ☆ 2 FR (vert) 9m; 54°54'·61N 05°01'·60W.

Corsewall Point ☆ 55°00'·41N 05°09'·58W Fl (5) 30s 34m **22M**; W twr; vis: 027°-257°.

Black Head Old Lighthouse (disused); W tower, 22m; 54°51'·70N 05°08'·80W.

PORTPATRICK

Ldg Lts 050·5°. Front, FG (occas); 54°50'·50N 05°07'·02W. Rear, 68m from front, FG 8m (occas).

Crammag Hd ☆ 54°39'·90N 04°57'·92W Fl 10s 35m **18M**; W twr.

Mull of Galloway ☆, SE end 54°38'·08N 04°51'·45W Fl 20s 99m **28M**; W twr; vis: 182°-105°.

MULL OF GALLOWAY and WIGTOWN BAY

Port William Ldg Lts 105°. Front, Pier Hd Fl G 3s 7m 3M; 54°45'·66N 04°35'·28W. Rear, 130m from front, FG 10m 2M.

Isle of Whithorn ☆ Fl WR 3s 20m 6/4M; vis: 310°-W-005°-R-040°; 54°41'·79N 04°21'·54W.

Whithorn Ldg Lts 335°. Front, Oc R 8s 7m 7M; Or ♦; 54°42'·01N 04°22'·05W. Rear, 35m from front, Oc R 8s 9m 7M; Or ♦, synch.

Little Ross ☆ Fl 5s 50m 12M; W twr; obsc in Wigtown B when brg more than 103°; 54°45'·93N 04°05'·10W.

KIRKCUDBRIGHT BAY and KIPPFORD

Little Ross NNE end of Is ☆ Fl (2) 5s 21m 5M; Stone bcn; 54°46'·06N 04°05'·02W.

Hestan I, E end ☆ Fl (2) 10s 42m 9M; 54°49'·95N 03°48'·53W.

AREA 8 *NW England, Isle of Man & N Wales – Solway Firth to Bardsey I*

SELECTED LIGHTS, BUOYS & WAYPOINTS

FURNESS

SILLOTH and MARYPORT

Lees Scar ☆ Fl G 5s 11m 4M; W piles; 54°51'·78N 03°24'·79W.

Groyne Hd ☆ 2 FG (vert) 4m 4M; Fl Bu tfc signals close by; 54°52'·14N 03°23'·93W.

Maryport S Pier Hd ☆.Fl 1·5s 10m 6M; 54°43'·07N 03°30'·64W.

WORKINGTON and HARRINGTON

N Workington ⊥ Q; 54°40'·10N 03°38'·18W.

S Workington ⊥ VQ (6) + L Fl 10s; 54°37'·01N 03°38'·58W.

South Pier ☆ Fl 5s 11m 5M; R bldg; 54°39'·12N 03°34'·67W.

Ldg Lts 131·8°. Front, FR 10m 3M; 54°38'·92N 03°34'·19W. Rear, 134m from front, FR 12m 3M.

WHITEHAVEN

W Pier Hd ☆ Fl G 5s 16m 8M; W ○ twr; 54°33'·17N 03°35'·92W.

N Pier Hd ☆ Fl R 5s 8m 10M; W ○ twr; 54°33'·17N 03°35'·75W.

Saint Bees Hd ☆ 54°30'·81N 03°38'·23W Fl (2) 20s 102m **18M**; W○ twr; obsc shore-340°.

RAVENGLASS

Blockhouse ☆ FG; (Eskdale Range); 54°20'·16N 03°25'·34W.

Selker ▲ Fl (3) G 10s; *Bell;* 54°16'·14N 03°29'·58W.

BARROW-IN-FURNESS

Lightning Knoll ⊕ L Fl 10s; 53°59'·83N 03°14'·28W.

Halfway Shoal ⊥ QR 19m 10s; R&W chequer Bn; 54°01'·46N 03°11'·88W.

Isle of Walney ☆ 54°02'·92N 03°10'·64W Fl 15s 21m **23M**; stone twr; obsc 122°-127° within 3M of shore.

Walney Chan Ldg Lts 040·7°. No.1 Front ⊥, Q 7m 10M; B Pile; 54°03'·19N 03°09'·22W. No. 2 Rear ⊥, 0·61M from front, Iso 2s 13m 10M; Pile.

Rampside Sands Ldg Lts 005·1°. No. 3 Front, Q 9m10M; W ○ twr; 54°04′·41N 03°09′·79W. No. 4 Rear, 0·77M from front, Iso 2s 14m 6M; R col, W face.

ISLE OF MAN

Whitestone Bank Q (9) 15s; 54°24′·58N 04°20′·41W.
Point of Ayre ☆ 54°24′·94N 04°22′·13W Fl (4) 20s 32m **19M**; W twr, two R bands, ***Racon (M) 13-15M***.
Low Lt Ho (unlit), RW twr, B base, 54°25′·03N 04°21′·86W.

PEEL

Peel Bkwtr Hd ☆ Oc 7s 11m 6M; W twr; 54°13′·67N 04°41′·69W.

PORT ERIN and PORT ST MARY

Ldg Lts 099·1°. Front, 54°05′·23N 04°45′·57W FR 10m 5M; W twr, R band. Rear, 39m from front, FR 19m 5M; W col, R band.
Calf of Man Lighthouse (disused), white 8-sided tower.
Chicken Rk ☆ Fl 5s 38m **20M**; ***Racon (C)*** 54°02′·27N 04°50′·32W
Alfred Pier Hd ☆ Oc R 10s 8m 6M; 54°04′·33N 04°43′·82W.

CASTLETOWN and DERBY HAVEN

Dreswick Pt ☆ Fl (2) 30s 23m 12M; W twr; 54°03′·29N 04°37′·45W.
New Pier Hd ☆ Oc R 15s 8m 5M; 54°04′·33N 04°38′·97W.
Derby Haven, Bkwtr SW end ☆Iso G 2s 5m 5M; W twr, G band; 54°04′·58N 04°37′·06W.

DOUGLAS

Douglas Head ☆ 54°08′·60N 04°27′·95W Fl 10s 32m **24M**; W twr; obsc brg more than 037°. FR Lts on radio masts 1 and 3M West.
No. 1 Q (3) G 5s; 54°09′·04N 04°27′·68W.
Princess Alexandra Pier Hd ☆ Fl R 5s 16m 8M; R mast; *Whis (2) 40s;* 54°08′·84N 04°27′·85W.
Ldg Lts 229·3°, Front, Oc Bu 10s 9m 5M; W △ R border on mast; 54°08′·72N 04°28′·25W. Rear, 62m from front, Oc Bu 10s 12m 5M; W ▽ on R border; synch with front.
Victoria Pier Hd ☆ Iso G 10s 10m 3M; W col; vis: 225°-327°; Intnl Port Tfc Signals; 54°08′·84N 04°28′·08W.
Conister Rk Refuge Q 3M; vis: 234°-312°; 54°09′·03N 04°28′·12W.

LAXEY to RAMSEY

Laxey Pier Hd ☆ Oc R 3s 7m 5M; W twr, R band; obsc when brg less than 318°; 54°13′·50N 04°23′·43W.

Maughold Head ☆ 54°17′·72N 04°18′·58W Fl (3) 30s 65m **21M**.
Bahama VQ (6) + L Fl 10s; 54°20′·01N 04°08′·57W.
Queens Pier Dn ☆ Fl R 5s; 54°19′·28N 04°21′·95W.
King William Bank Q (3) 10s; 54°26′·01N 04°00′·08W.

BARROW TO RIVERS MERSEY AND DEE

MORECAMBE

Met Mast ☆ Fl Y 5s 20m 5M; 54°00′·13N 03°33′·38W; Aero FR (80m), *Horn 30s*.
Lightning Knoll L Fl 10s; 53°59′·84N 03°14′·28W.
Morecambe Q (9) 15s; 53°52′·00N 03°22′·00W.
Lune Deep Q (6) + L Fl 15s; ***Racon (T)***; 53°56′·07N 03°12·90W.
Lts in line about 090°. Front, FR 10m 2M; G mast; 54°04′·41N 02°52′·63W. Rear, 140m from front, FR 14m 2M; G mast.

HEYSHAM

SW Quay Ldg Lts 102·2°. Front, both F Bu 11/14m 2M; Or & B ♦ on masts; 54°01′·91N 02°55′·22W.

RIVER LUNE, GLASSON DOCK and FLEETWOOD

R Lune Q (9) 15s; 53°58′·63N 03°00′·03W.
Fairway No. 1(Fleetwood) 53°57′·67N 03°02′·03W Q; *Bell*.
Fleetwood Esplanade Ldg Lts 156°. Front, Iso G 2s 14m 9M; 53°55′·71N 03°00′·56W. Rear, 320m from front, Iso G 4s 28m 9M. Both vis on Ldg line only. (H24) (chan liable to change).

RIVER RIBBLE

Gut L Fl 10s; 53°41′·74N 03°08′·98W.
Perches show Fl R on N side, and Fl G on S side of chan. S side, 14¼M Perch ☆ Fl G 5s 6m 3M; 53°42′·75N 03°04′·90W.
Jordan's Spit Q (9) 15s; 53°35′·76N 03°19′·28W.
FT Q; 53°34′·56N 03°13′·20W.

RIVER MERSEY and LIVERPOOL

Bar Fl.5s 12M; ***Racon (T) 10M***; 53°32′·01N 03°20′·98W.
Q1 VQ; 53°31′·00N 03°16′·72W.
Q2 VQ R; 53°31′·47N 03°14′·95W.
Q3 Fl G 3s; 53°30′·95N 03°15′·10W.
Formby Iso 4s; 53°31′·13N 03°13′·48W.
C4 Fl R 3s; 53°31′·82N 03°08′·51W.
Crosby Oc 5s; 53°30′·72N 03°06′·29W.
C14 Fl R 3s; R hull; 53°29′·91N 03°05′·34W.
Brazil QG; 53°26′·85N 03°02′·23W.

RIVER DEE, MOSTYN and CONNAH'S QUAY

HE1 Q (9) 15s; 53°26′·33N 03°18′·08W.
HE2 Fl G 2·5s; 53°24′·90N 03°12′·88W.
HE3 Q G; 53°24′·55N 03°12′·74W.

DISTANCE TABLES

Approx distances in nautical miles are by the most direct route allowing for dangers and TSS.

1. Portpatrick	**1**																
2. Mull of Galloway	16	**2**															
3. Kirkcudbright	48	32	**3**														
4. Maryport	65	49	26	**4**													
5. Workington	63	47	25	6	**5**												
6. Ravenglass	70	54	40	30	23	**6**											
7. Point of Ayre	38	22	28	37	31	34	**7**										
8. Peel	41	26	46	55	49	52	18	**8**									
9. Douglas	60	42	46	50	44	39	19	30	**9**								
10. Glasson Dock	101	85	74	66	60	37	64	85	63	**10**							
11. Fleetwood	95	79	68	59	53	30	58	80	57	10	**11**						
12. Liverpool	118	102	97	89	83	60	80	86	70	52	46	**12**					
13. Conwy	111	95	95	92	86	58	72	72	59	62	56	46	**13**				
14. Beaumaris	109	93	94	95	89	72	71	73	58	66	60	49	12	**14**			
15. Caernarfon	117	103	104	105	99	82	81	73	68	76	70	59	22	10	**15**		
16. Holyhead	93	81	94	96	90	69	68	62	50	79	73	68	36	32	26	**16**	
17. Fishguard	171	158	175	175	169	160	153	140	134	153	147	136	100	88	78	89	**17**

West Hoyle Spit (Earwig) Dir Lt 090. 53°21′·21N 03°24′·07W; Iso WRG 2s W10M, R7M, G7M (day W3M, R2M, G2M).
vis: 087·5°-G-089·5°-W-090·5°-R-092·5°; occasional.
Mostyn Dir Lt ☆ 177·5°. 53°19′·23N 03°16′·38W Iso WRG 2s 11m W 10M R,G 7M, by day W 3M R,G 2M; vis: 175°-G-177°-W-178°-R-180°; H24.

WALES – NORTH COAST AND INNER PASSAGE

South Hoyle Outer Fl R 2·5s; 53°21′·47N 03°24′·70W.
Prestatyn QG; 53°21′·51N 03°28′·51W.
Inner Passage Fl R 5s; 53°21′·91N 03°31′·95W.
Mid Patch Spit QR; 53°22′·25N 03°32′·67W.
Mast ☆ Mo (U) 15s 12m 10M & 2FR (vert); Horn Mo (U) 30s; Mast (80); 53°28′·84N 03°30′·50W.
W Constable Q (9) 15s; ***Racon (M) 10M***; 53°23′·14N 03°49′·26W.
N Constable VQ; 53°23′·76N 03°41′·42W.

RHYL, LLANDUDNO and CONWY

River Clwyd Outfall Q R 7m 2M; 53°19′·45N 03°30′·34W.
Rhyll SWM Mo(A) 10s; 53°19′·60N 03°32′·00W.
Llandudno Pier Hd ☆ 2 FG (vert) 8m 4M; 53°19′·90N 03°49′·51W.
Great Ormes Hd Lt Ho, (unlit); 53°20′·56N 03°52′·17W.
Conwy Fairway L Fl 10s; 53°17′·95N 03°55′·58W.
C1 Fl G 10s; 53°17′·83N 03°54′·58W.
C2 Fl (2) R 10s; 53°17′·94N 03°54′·52W.
River Conwy ent, ☆ L Fl G 15s 5m 2M; 53°18′·03N 03°50′·86W.

ANGLESEY

Point Lynas ☆ 53°24′·98N 04°17′·35W Oc 10s 39m **18M**; W castellated twr; vis: 109°-315°; H24.

AMLWCH to HOLYHEAD BAY

Main Bkwtr ☆ Fl G 15s 11m 3M; W mast; vis: 141°-271°; 53°25′·02N 04°19′·91W.
Furlong Fl G 2·5s; 53°25′·41N 04°30′·47W.
Archdeacon Rock Q; 53°26′·71N 04°30′·87W.
Victoria Bank VQ; 53°25′·61N 04°31′·37W.
Coal Rk Q (6) + L Fl 15s; 53°25′·91N 04°32′·79W.
Ethel Rk VQ; 53°26′·64N 04°33′·67W.
The Skerries ☆ 53°25′·27N 04°36′·50W Fl (2) 15s 36m **20M**; W ○ twr, R band; ***Racon (T) 25M***. Iso R 4s 26m 10M; same twr; vis: 233°-252°, sector unreliable > 4M; *Horn (2) 60s*. H24 in periods of reduced visibility; 992351084.
Langdon Q (9) 15s; 53°22′·74N 04°38′·74W.
Bolivar FL G 2·5s; 53°21′·51N 04°35′·33W.
Wk Fl (2) R 10s; 53°20′·43N 04°36′·60W.

HOLYHEAD to SOUTH STACK

Bkwtr Head ☆ Fl (3) G 10s 21m 14M; W □ twr, B band; Fl Y vis: 174°-226°; *Siren 20s;* 53°19′·86N 04°37′·16W.
Spit Fl G 3s; 53°19′·79N 04°37′·15W.
South Stack ☆ 53°18′·41N 04°41′·98W Fl 10s 60m **24M**; (H24); W ○ twr; obsc to N by N Stack and part obsc in Penrhos bay; *Horn 30s*. Fog Det lt vis: 145°-325°.

MENAI STRAIT TO BARDSEY ISLAND

Ten Feet Bank QR; 53°19′·47N 04°02′·82W.
Dinmor QG; 53°19′·34N 04°03′·32W.
Trwyn-Du ☆ Fl 5s 19m 12M; W ○ castellated twr, B bands; vis: 101°-023°; *Bell (1) 30s*, sounded continuously; 53°18′·77N 04°02′·44W. FR on radio mast 2M SW.

APPROACHES to BEAUMARIS and BANGOR
(Direction of buoyage NE to SW)

Perch Rock Fl R 5s; 53°18′·73N 04°02′·09W.

PORT DINORWIC and CAERNARFON

Port Dinorwic Pier Hd ☆ 53°11′·21N 04°12′·60W F WR 5m 2M; vis: 225°-R- 357°-W-225°.

(Direction of buoyage SW to NE)

Caernarfon N Pier Hd ☆ 2 FG (vert) 5m 2M; 53°08′·72N 04°16′·56W.
Abermenai Point ☆ Fl WR 3·5s 6m 3M; W mast; vis: 065°-R-245°-W-065°; 53°07′·62N 04°19′·72W.
C1 Fl G 5s; 53°06′·85N 04°24′·35W.
C2 Fl R 10s; 53°06′·95N 04°24′·46W.
Caernarfon Bar L Fl 10s; 53°06′·45N 04°25′·00W.
Llanddwyn I ☆Fl WR 2·5s 12m W7M, R4M; W twr; vis: 280°-R- 015°-W-120°; 53°08′·05N 04°24′·79W.

PORTH DINLLÄEN

CG Stn ☆ FR when firing 10M N; 52°56′·82N 04°33′·89W.
Careg y Chwislen Fl(2) 10s 2M 52°56′·99N 04°33′·51W.
Bardsey I ☆ 52°44′·97N 04°48′·02W Fl (5) 15s 39m **26M**; W □ twr, R bands; obsc by Bardsey Is 198°-250° and in Tremadoc B when brg < 260°.

AREA 9 *S Wales & SW England – Cardigan Bay to St Ives*

SELECTED LIGHTS, BUOYS & WAYPOINTS

CARDIGAN BAY

Bardsey I ☆ 52°44′·98N 04°48′·01W Fl R 10s 39m **18M**; W □ twr, R bands; obsc by Bardsey I 198°-250° and in Tremadoc B when brg less than 260°.
St Tudwal's ☆ Fl WR 15s 46m W14, R10M; vis: 349°-W-169°-R- 221°-W-243°-R-259°-W-293°-R-349°; obsc by East I 211°-231°; 52°47′·92N 04°28′·30W.

PWLLHELI and PORTHMADOG

Pwllheli App Iso 2s; 52°53′·03N 04°22′·90W.
Porthmadog Fairway L Fl 10s; 52°53′·01N 04°11′·10W.

BARMOUTH and ABERDOVEY

Diffuser Fl Y 5s; 52°43′·19N 04°05′·38W.
Barmouth Outer L Fl 10s; 52°42′·62N 04°04′·83W.
Aberdovey Outer Iso 4s; 52°32′·00N 04°05′·56W.
Patches Q (9) 15s; 52°25′·83N 04°16′·41W.

ABERYSTWYTH, ABERAERON and NEW QUAY

Aberystwyth S Bkwtr Hd ☆ Fl (2) WG 10s 12m 10M; vis: 030°-G- 053°-W-210°; 52°24′·40N 04°05′·52W.
Ldg Lts 133°. Front, FR 4m 5M; 52°24′·37N 04°05′·39W. Rear, 52m from front, FR 7m 6M.
Aberaeron N Pier ☆ Fl (4) WRG 15s 10m 6M; vis: 050°-G-104°-W-178°-R-232°; 52°14′·61N 04°15′·87W.
Carreg Ina Q; 52°13′·25N 04°20′·75W.
New Quay Pier Hd ☆ Fl WG 3s 12m W8M, G5M; G △; vis: 135°-W- 252°-G-295; 52°12′·95N 04°21′·35W.

CARDIGAN and FISHGUARD
Cardigan Channel Fl (2) 5s; 52°06′·44N 04°41′·43W.
Cardigan Cliff Base Bn 1 ☆ Fl R 4s 3M; 52°07′·05N 04°41′·39W.
Cardigan Cliff Base Bn 2 ☆ Fl R 2s 3M; 52°06′·91N 04°41′·34W.
Fishguard N Bkwtr Hd ☆ Fl G 4·5s 18m 13M; *Bell (1) 8s;* 52°00′·76N 04°58′·23W.
Strumble Head ☆ 52°01′·79N 05°04′·43W Fl (4) 15s 45m **26M**; vis: 038°-257°; (H24).

BISHOPS and SMALLS
South Bishop ☆ 51°51′·14N 05°24′·74W Fl 5s 44m **16M**; W ○ twr; *Horn (3) 45s;* ***Racon (O)10M***; (H24).
The Smalls ☆ 51°43′·27N 05°40′·19W Fl (3) 15s 36m **18M**; ***Racon (T)***; *Horn (2) 60s*. Same twr, Iso R 4s 33m 13M; vis: 253°-285° over Hats & Barrels Rk; both Lts shown H24 in periods of reduced visibility; 992351123.
Skokholm I ☆, 51°41′·64N 05°17′·22W Fl WR 10s 54m W8M, R8M; vis: 301°-W-154°-R-301°; partially obsc 226°-258°.

WALES – SOUTH COAST – BRISTOL CHANNEL

MILFORD HAVEN
St Ann's Head ☆ 51°40′·87N 05°10′·42W Fl WR 5s 48m **W18M, R17M**, R14M; W 8-sided twr; vis: 233°-W-247°-R-332°-W131°, partially obscured 124°-129°; *Horn (2) 60s*.
W Blockhouse Point Ldg Lts 022·5°. Front, F 54m 13M (day 10M); B stripe on W twr; vis: 004·5°-040·5°; intens on lead line. vis: 004·5°-040·5°; ***Racon (Q)***; 51°41′·31N 05°09′·56W.
Watwick Point Common Rear ☆, 0·5M from front, F 80m **15M** (day 10M); vis: 013·5°-031·5°; ***Racon (Y)***.
W Blockhouse Point Q WR 21m W9M, R7M; R lantern on W base: vis: 220°-W-250°-R-020°-W-036°-R-049°; 51°41′·31N 05°09′·56W.
Dale Fort ☆ Fl (2) WR 5s 20m W5M, R3M; vis: 222°-R-276°-W-019°; 51°42′·16N 05°09′·01W.
Gt Castle Hd F WRG 27m W5M, R3M, G3M; vis: 243°-R-281°-G- 299°-W-029°; 51°42′·68N 05°07′·06W. Co-located Dir WRG (040°); vis: 038·25°-G-039°-AlWG-039·5°-W-040·5°-AlWR-041°-R-041·75° (**not** used in conjunction with the front ldg light below) **Ldg Lts ≠ 039·7° Front,** Oc 4s 27m **15M**; vis: 031·2°-048·2°. **Rear**, 890m from front. Oc 8s 53m **15M** (day 10M); vis: 031·2°-048·2°.
St Ann's Fl R 2·5s; 51°40′·25N 05°10′·51W.
Mid Channel Rks Q (9) 15s; 51°40′·18N 05°10′·14W.
Mid Channel Rk ☆ Fl (3) G 7s 18m 8M; 51°40′·31N 05°09′·83W.
Rows Rks Q R; 51°40′·22N 05°09′·02W.
Sheep QG; 51°40′·06N 05°08′·31W.
Millbay Fl (2) R 5s; 51°41′·05N 05°09′·45W.
W Chapel Fl G 10s; 51°40′·98N 05°08′·67W.
E Chapel Fl R 5s; 51°40′·87N 05°08′·15W.
Rat Fl G 5s; 51°40′·80N 05°07′·86W.
Angle VQ; 51°41′·63N 05°08′·27W.
Thorn Rock Q (9) 15s; 51°41′·53N 05°07′·76W.
Turbot Bank VQ (9) 10s; 51°37′·41N 05°10′·08W.
ODAS Fl(5) Y 20s; 51°36′·70N 05°08′·70W.
St Gowan Q (6) + L Fl 15s, ***Racon (T) 10M***; 51°31′·93N 04°59′·77W; 992351126.

TENBY to SWANSEA BAY
Caldey I ☆ Fl (3) WR 20s 65m W13M, R9M; vis: R173°-W212°- R088°-102°; 51°37′·90N 04°41′·08W.
Woolhouse Q (6) + L Fl 15s; 51°39′·35N 04°39′·69W.
Burry Port Inlet ☆ Fl 5s 7m 6½M; 51°40′·62N 04°15′·06W.
W. Helwick (9) 15s; ***Racon (T) 10M***; 51°31′·40N 04°23′·65W.
E. Helwick VQ (3) 5s; *Bell;* 51°31′·80N 04°12′·68W.

SWANSEA BAY and SWANSEA
Ledge VQ (6) + L Fl 10s; 51°29′·93N 03°58′·77W.
Mixon Fl (2) R 5s; *Bell;* 51°33′·12N 03°58′·78W.
Outer Spoil Gnd Fl Y 2·5s; 51°32′·11N 03°55′·73W.
Grounds VQ (3) 5s; 51°32′·81N 03°53′·47W.
Mumbles ☆ 51°34′·01N 03°58′·27W Fl (4) 20s 35m **15M**; W twr; *Horn (3) 60s*.
SW Inner Green Grounds Q(6)+L Fl 15s; *Bell;* 51°34′·06N 03°57′·03W.
Swansea Lts in line 020°. Front: E Breakwater head, Oc G 4s 5m 2M & 2FG(vert) 10m 6M; 51°36′·38N 03°55′·62W. Rear, 3·1ca from front: FG 6M.

SWANSEA BAY, RIVER NEATH and PORT TALBOT
Neath App Chan Fl G 5s; 51°35′·71N 03°52′·83W.
Cabenda VQ (6) + L Fl 10s; ***Racon (Q)***; 51°33′·36N 03°52′·23W.
Ldg Lts 059·8° (occas). Front, Oc R 3s 12m 6M; 51°34′·92N 03°48′·10W. Rear, 400m from front, Oc R 6s 32m 6M.

BRISTOL CHANNEL – N SHORE (EASTERN PART)

W Scar Q (9) 15s, *Bell*, ***Racon (T) 10M***; 51°28′·31N 03°55′·57W.
South Scar (S SCAR) Q (6) + L Fl 15s; 51°27′·61N 03°51′·58W.
Hugo Q R; 51°28′·55N 03°48′·03W.
E. Scarweather Q (3) 10s; *Bell;* 51°27′·98N 03°46′·76W.

PORTHCAWL
Fairy Q (9) 15s; *Bell;* 51°27′·86N 03°42′·07W.
Porthcawl Bkwtr Hd ☆ 51°28′·39N 03°41′·98W F WRG 10m W6M, R4M, G4M; vis: 302°-G-036°-W-082°-R-122°.
W Nash VQ (9) 10s ; *Bell;* 51°25′·99N 03°45′·95W.
Nash ☆ 51°24′·03N 03°33′·06W Fl (2) WR 15s 56m **W21M, R16M**; vis: 280°-R-290°-W-100°-R-120°-W-128°.
Breaksea L Fl 10s; ***Racon (T) 10M***; 51°19′·88N 03°19′·08W; 992351124.

BARRY
W Bkwtr Hd ☆ Fl 2·5s 12m 10M; 51°23′·46N 03°15′·52W.
N. One Fathom Q; 51°20′·94N 03°12′·17W.
Mackenzie QR; 51°21′·75N 03°08′·24W.

CARDIFF and PENARTH ROADS
Lavernock Outfall Fl Y 5s; 51°23′·95N 03°09′·50W.
Ranie Fl (2) R 5s; 51°24′·23N 03°09′·39W.
S Cardiff Q (6) + L Fl 15s; *Bell;* 51°24′·18N 03°08′·57W.
Mid Cardiff Fl (3) G 10s; 51°25′·60N 03°08′·09W.
Cardiff Spit QR; 51°24′·57N 03°07′·12W.
N Cardiff QG; 51°26′·52N 03°07′·19W.
Wrach Chan Dir lt 348·5°. Oc WRG 10s 5m; W3M, R3M, G3M; vis: 344·5°-G-347°-W-350°-R-352°; H24; 51°27′·16N 03°09′·75W.
Outer Wrach Q (9) 15s; 51°26′·20N 03°09′·46W.

FLATHOLM to THE BRIDGE

Flat Holm ☆, SE Pt 51°22′·54N 03°07′·14W Fl (3) WR 10s 50m **W15M**, R12M; W ○ twr; vis: 106°-R-140°-W-151°-R-203°-W-106°; (H24).

Monkstone ☆ Fl 5s 13m 12M; R column on W ○ twr; 51°24′·89N 03°06′·01W.

Tail Patch QG; 51°23′·53N 03°03′·65W.

Hope Q (3) 10s; 51°24′·84N 03°02′·68W.

NW Elbow VQ (9) 10s; *Bell;* 51°26′·28N 02°59′·93W.

EW Grounds L Fl 10s 7M; *Whis;* ***Racon (T) 7M***; 51°27′·12N 02°59′·95W.

NEWPORT DEEP, RIVER USK and NEWPORT

Newport Deep Fl (3) G 10s; *Bell;*51°29′·36N 02°59′·12W.

East Usk ☆ 51°32′·40N 02°58′·01W; Fl (2) WRG 10s 11m W11M, R10M, G10M; vis: 284°-W-290° -obscured shore-324°-R- 017°-W-037°-G-115°-W-120°. Also Oc WRG 10s 10m W11M, R9M, G9M; vis: 013°-G-017°-W- 019°-R-023°.

Julians Pill Ldg Lts 062°. Front, FG 5m 4M; 51°33′·30N 02°57′·94W. Rear, 61m from front, FG 8m 4M.

BRISTOL CHANNEL – S SHORE (EASTERN PART)

BRISTOL DEEP

N Elbow QG; *Bell;* 51°26′·97N 02°58′·65W.

S Mid Grounds VQ (6) + L Fl 10s; 51°27′·62N 02°58′·68W.

E Mid Grounds Fl R 5s; 51°27′·75N 02°54′·98W.

Clevedon VQ; 51°27′·39N 02°54′·93W.

Welsh Hook Q (6) + L Fl 15s; 51°28′·53N 02°51′·86W.

Avon Fl G 2·5s; 51°27′·92N 02°51′·73W.

Black Nore Pt Lt Ho; W ○ twr on frame; 51°29′·09N 02°48′·05W.

Newcome 51°30′·01N 02°46′·71W Fl (3) R 10s.

Denny Shoal VQ (6) + L Fl 10s; 51°30′·15N 02°45′·45W.

Cockburn 51°30′·45N 02°44′·10W Fl R 2·5s.

W Dock Middle 51°29.95′·01N 02°44′·20W Q G.

W Dock Outer 51°30′·00N 02°44′·85W Fl G 5s.

Firefly Fl (2) G 5s; 51°29′·96N 02°45′·35W.

Portishead Point ☆ 51°29′·68N 02°46′·42W Q (3) 10s 9m **16M**; B twr, W base; vis: 060°-262°; *Horn 20s*.

PORTISHEAD

Pier Hd ☆ Iso G 2s 5m 3M; 51°29′·69N 02°45′·27W.

Seabank. Dir WG 6m 5M; vis: 085·8°-FG-086·7°-AltWG-086·9°-FW-089·7°. 5M; vis: 070·3°-103·3°; by day 1M, vis: 076·8°-096·8°.

Lts in line 086·8°. Q(8) 5M 10/16m; vis: 070·3°-103·3°; day 1M vis: 076·8°-096·8° Front 51°30′·07N 02°43′·80W; Rear, 500m behind.

Knuckle Lts in line 099·6°, Oc G 5s 6m 6M; 51°29′·94N 02°43′·67W. Rear, 165m from front, FG 13m 6M; vis: 044°-134°.

AVONMOUTH

Royal Edward Dock N Pier Hd ☆ Fl 4s 15m 10M; vis: 060°-228·5°; 51°30′·49N 02°43′·09W.

King Road Ldg Lts 072·4°. N Pier Hd ☆ Front, Oc R 5s 5m 9M; W obelisk, R bands; vis: 062°-082°; 51°30′·49N 02°43′·09W. Rear ☆, 546m from front, QR 15m 10M; vis: 066°- 078°.

RIVER AVON, CUMBERLAND BASIN and AVON BRIDGE

S Pier Hd ☆ Oc RG 30s 9m 10M and FBu 4m 1M; vis: 294°-R-036°-G-194°; 51°30′·37N 02°43′·10W. *Bell(1) 10s.*

Ldg Lts 127·2°. Front, Iso R 2s 6m 3M, vis: 010°-160°; 51°30′·10N 02°42′·59W. Rear , Iso R 2s10m 3M, vis: 048°-138°.

BRISTOL CHANNEL (SOUTH SHORE)

WESTON-SUPER-MARE

Pier Hd ☆ 2 FG (vert) 6m; 51°20′·88N 02°59′·26W.

E Culver Q (3) 10s; 51°18′·00N 03°15′·44W.

W Culver VQ (9) 10s; 51°17′·47N 03°19′·00W.

Gore Iso 5s; *Bell;* 51°13′·94N 03°09′·79W.

BURNHAM-ON-SEA and RIVER PARRETT

Ent ☆ Fl 7·5s 7m 12M; vis: 074°-164°; 51°14′·89N 03°00′·36W; Dir lt 076°. F WRG 4m W12M, R10M, G10M; vis: 071°-G-075°-W-077°- R-081°.

DZ No. 1 Fl Y 2·5s; 51°15′·28N 03°09′·49W.

DZ No. 2 Fl Y 10s; 51°13′·77N 03°19′·86W.

DZ No. 3 Fl Y 5s; 51°16′·34N 03°14′·98W.

WATCHET, MINEHEAD and PORLOCK WEIR

Watchet W Bkwtr Hd ☆ Oc G 3s 9m 9M; 51°11′·03N 03°19′·74W.

Watchet E Pier ☆ 2 FR (vert) 3M; 51°11′·01N 03°19′·72W.

Minehead Bkwtr Hd ☆ Fl (2) G 5s 4M; vis: 127°-262°; 51°12′·81N 03°28′·36W.

Lynmouth Foreland ☆ 51°14′·73N 03°47′·21W Fl (4) 15s 67m **18M**; W ○ twr; vis: 083°-275°; (H24).

LYNMOUTH and WATERMOUTH

River Training Arm ☆ 2 FR (vert) 6m 5M; 51°13′·90N 03°49′·83W.

Harbour Arm ☆ 2 FG (vert) 6m 5M; 51°13′·92N 03°49′·84W.

Sand Ridge Q G; 51°15′·01N 03°49′·77W.

Copperas Rock Fl G 2·5s; 51°13′·78N 04°00′·60W.

Watermouth ☆ Oc WRG 5s 1m 3M; W △; vis: 149·5°-G-151·5°-W- 154·5°-R-156·5°; 51°12′·93N 04°04′·60W.

ILFRACOMBE to BAGGY POINT

Ldg Lts 188°. Front, Oc 10s 8m 3M; 51°12′·53N 04°06′·65W. Rear, Oc 10s 6m 3M.

Horseshoe Q; 51°15′·02N 04°12′·96W.

1	Aberystwyth	**1**											
2	Fishguard	40	**2**										
3	Milford Haven	84	48	**3**									
4	Tenby	107	71	28	**4**								
5	Swansea	130	94	55	36	**5**							
6	Cardiff	161	125	86	66	46	**6**						
7	Sharpness	192	156	117	106	75	33	**7**					
8	Avonmouth	175	139	100	89	58	20	18	**8**				
9	Burnham-on-Sea	169	133	94	70	48	53	50	33	**9**			
10	Ilfracombe	128	92	53	35	25	44	74	57	45	**10**		
11	Padstow	142	106	70	70	76	97	127	110	98	55	**11**	
12	Longships	169	133	105	110	120	139	169	152	140	95	50	**12**

12	64	66	122	164	192	224	254	286	299	318	361	Kilrush	12
	11	13	69	111	139	171	201	233	246	265	308	Dingle	11
		10	56	102	131	165	188	227	242	252	295	Valentia	10
			9	42	70	102	132	164	177	196	239	Baltimore	9
				8	35	69	95	135	150	168	202	Kinsale	8
					7	34	65	100	115	133	172	Youghal	7
						6	32	69	84	102	139	Dunmore East	6
							5	34	47	66	108	Rosslare	5
								4	15	36	75	Arklow	4
									3	21	63	Wicklow	3
										2	48	Dun Laoghaire	2
											1	Carlingford Lough	1

Bull Point ☆ 51°11'·94N 04°12'·09W Fl (3) 10s 54m **20M**; W ○ twr, obscd shore-056°. Same twr; FR 48m 12M; vis: 058°-096°.
Morte Stone Fl G 5s; 51°11'·30N 04°14'·95W.
Baggy Leap Fl (2) G 10s; 51°08'·92N 04°16'·97W.

BIDEFORD, RIVERS TAW and TORRIDGE
Bideford Fairway L Fl 10s; *Bell;* 51°05'·25N 04°16'·25W.
Bideford Bar Q G; 51°04'·89N 04°14'·62W.
Instow ☆ Ldg Lts 118°. **Front,** 51°03'·62N 04°10'·66W Oc 6s 22m **15M**; vis: 103·5°-132°. **Rear,** 427m from front, Oc 10s 38m **15M**; vis: 103°-132·5°; (H24).
Crow Pt ☆ Fl WR 2. 5s 8m W6M R5M; vis: 225°-R-232°-W-237°-R-358°-W- 015°-R-045°; 51°03'·96N 04°11'·39W.

LUNDY
Near North Point ☆ 51°12'·10N 04°40'·65W Fl 15s 48m **17M**; vis: 009°-285°.
South East Point ☆ 51°09'·72N 04°39'·37W Fl 5s 53m **15M**; vis: 170°-073°.
Hartland Point ☆ 51°01'·3N 04°31'·6W Fl (6) 15s 30m 8M; adjacent to Hartland Point Light House (disused).

NORTH CORNWALL

BUDE, PADSTOW and NEWQUAY
Compass Point twr 50°49'·71N 04°33'·42W.
Stepper Point (Padstow) ☆ L Fl 10s 12m 4M; 50°34'·12N 04°56'·72W.
Trevose Head ☆ 50°32'·94N 05°02'·13W Fl 7·5s 62m **21M**.
North Pier Hd (Newquay) ☆ 2 FG (vert) 5m 2M; 50°25'·07N 05°05'·19W.

HAYLE and ST IVES
The Stones Q; 50°15'·64N 05°25'·51W.
Godrevy I ☆ Fl WR 10s 28m 8M; metal post; vis: 022°-W-101°-R-145°-W-272°; 50°14'·56N 05°24'·01W; adjacent to Godrevy Light House (disused).
Hayle App QR; 50°12'·26N 05°26'·30W.
St Ives App 50°12'·85N 05°28'·42W.
Bann Shoal Fl G 2.5s; ***Racon (B) 10M***; 50°20'·03N 05°51'·11W; 992351053.
Pendeen ☆ 50°09'·90N 05°40'·30W Fl (4) 15s 59m **16M**; vis: 042°-240°; between Gurnard Hd and Pendeen it shows to coast.

AREA 10 *Ireland – Clockwise from Lambay Island*

SELECTED LIGHTS, BUOYS & WAYPOINTS

LAMBAY ISLAND TO TUSKAR ROCK

MALAHIDE and LAMBAY ISLAND
Taylor Rks Q; 53°30'·21N 06°01'·87W.
Burren Rocks Fl G 5s; 53°29'·35N 06°02'·35W.
Malahide approach L Fl 10s; 53°27'·12N 06°06'·87W.

HOWTH
Rowan Rocks Q (3) 10s; 53°23'·88N 06°03'·27W.
Howth 53°23.727'N 006°03.593'W; 992501250.
E Pier Hd ☆ Fl (2) WR 7·5s 13m W12M, R9M; W twr; vis: W256°- R295°-256°; 53°23'·64N 06°04'·02W.
Baily ☆ 53°21'·69N 06°03'·16W Fl 15s 41m **20M**; twr. Fog Det Lt VQ; 992501010.
Rosbeg E Q (3) 10s; 53°21'·02N 06°03'·45W.
Rosbeg S Q (6) + L Fl 15s; 53°20'·22N 06°04'·17W.

PORT OF DUBLIN
Dublin Bay Mo (A) 10s; ***Racon (M)***; 53°19'·92N 06°04'·65W; 992351301.
No. 1 Fl (3) G 5s; 53°20'·30N 06°05'·56W.
No. 3 IQ G; 53°20'·57N 06°06'·76W.
No. 4 IQ R; 53°20'·48N 06°06'·93W.
No. 5 Fl G 2s; 53°20'·64N 06°08'·60W.
No. 6 Fl R 2s; 53°20'·56N 06°08'·75W.
Great S Wall Hd Poolbeg ☆ Fl R 4s 20m 10M *(sync with N.Bull)*; R ○ twr; 53°20'·52N 06°09'·08W.
N Bull ☆ Fl G 4s 15m 10M; G ○ twr; 53°20'·70N 06°08'·98W.
N Bank ☆ 53°20'·69N 06°10'·59W Oc G 8s 10m **16M**; G □ twr.

DUN LAOGHAIRE
E Bkwtr Hd ☆ Fl (2) R 8s 16m **17M**; granite twr, R lantern 7M; 53°18'·14N 06°07'·62W. Fog Det Lt VQ.
Outfall Fl Y 5s; 53°18'·41N 06°08'·35W.
Muglins ☆ Fl R 5s 14m 11M; 53°16'·52N 06°04'·58W.

OFFSHORE MARKS
Bennett Bank Q(6)+ L Fl 15s; 53°20'·17N 05°55'·11W; 992501012.
Kish Bank ☆ 53°18'·65N 05°55'·54W Fl (2) 20s 29m **21M** (H24); W twr, R band; ***Racon (T) 15M***; 992501017.
N Kish VQ; 53°18'·56N 05°56'·44W.
E Kish Fl (2) R 10s; 53°14'·35N 05°53'·56W; 992501020.
N Burford Q 53°20.51'N 006° 01.49'W; 992501016.
S Burford VQ(6)+L Fl 10s; 53°18.06'N 006° 01.30'W; 992501018.
E Codling Fl (4) R 10s; 53°08'·54N 05°46'·07W; 992501024.
W Codling Fl G 10s; 53°06'·97N 05°54'·51W.
Moulditch Fl R 10s; 53°08'·43N 06°01'·23W; 992501022.
S Codling VQ (6) + L Fl 10s; 53°04'·74N 05°49'·76W.
Codling Q(3) 10s; 53°03.020'N 005°40.815'W, ***Racon (G) 10M***, 992501028.
Breaches Shoal Fl (2) R 6s; 53°05'·67N 05°59'·81W.
North India Q; 53°03'·12N 05°53'·46W.
South India Q (6) + L Fl 15s; 53°00'·36N 05°53'·31W; 992501030.

WICKLOW to ARKLOW
Wicklow Fl (4) Y 10s; 52°59'·54N 06°01'·29W.
E Pier Hd ☆ Fl WR 5s 11m 6M; W twr, R base and cupola; vis: 136°-R-293°-W-136°; 52°58'·99N 06°02'·07W.
W Packet Quay Hd ☆ Fl WG 10s 5m 6M; vis: 076°-G-256°-W-076°; 52°58'·88N 06°02'·08W.
Wicklow Hd ☆ 52°57'·95N 05°59'·89W Fl (3) 15s 37m **23M**; W twr; 992501031.
Horseshoe Fl R 3s; 52°56'·84N 05°58'·47W; 992501032.
N Arklow Q; 52°53'·86N 05°55'·21W; 992501034.
Arklow Bank Wind Farm from 52°48'·47N 05°56'·57W to 52°46'·47N 05°57'·11W, N and S Turbines Fl Y 5s14m 10M. No 7 Turbine 992501302. Other turbines Fl Y 5s.

ARKLOW to WEXFORD
S Pier Hd ☆ Fl WR 6s 11m 13M; twr; vis: R shore- W223°-R350°-shore; 52°47'·61N 06°08'·22W.
Roadstone Bkwtr Hd ☆ QY; 52°46'·65N 06°08'·23W.
S Arklow Q (6) + LFl 15s; ***Racon (O) 10M;*** 52°40'·20N 05°58'·89W; 992501040.
No. 2 Glassgorman Fl (4) R 10s; 52°45'·35N 06°05'·34W; 992501038.
No. 1 Glassgorman Fl (2) R 6s; 52°37'·69N 06°07'·34W.
N Blackwater Q; 52°32'·22N 06°09'·51W; 992501046.
No. 6 Rusk Fl R 3s; 52°32'·65N 06°10'·41W.
No. 4 Rusk Fl (2) R 5s; 52°31'·07N 06°10'·86W.
No. 2 Rusk Fl (2) R 5s; 52°28'·64N 06°12'·61W.
No. 1 Rusk Fl (2) G 5s; 52°28'·54N 06°11'·80W; 992501048.
W Blackwater Fl G 6s; 52°25'·87N 06°13'·56W.
SE Blackwater Q (3) 10s, 52°25'·62N 06°08'·42W; ***Racon (M) 10M***; 992501050.
S Blackwater Q (6) + L Fl 15s; 52°22'·76N 06°12'·87W.
North Long Q; 52°21'·44N 06°17'·04W.
West Long QG; 52°18'·18N 06°17'·96W.
Lucifer VQ (3) 5s; 52°17'·02N 06°12'·67W; 992501054.

ROSSLARE
S Long Fl (2) G 6s (sync with Splaugh); 52°14'·74N 06°15'·80W.
Splaugh Fl (2) R 6s (sync with S Long); 52°14'·37N 06°16'·76W; 992501062.
South Holdens Fl G 3s; 52°15'·14N 06°17'·24W. (sync Calmines).
Calmines Fl R 3s; 52°15'·01N 06°17'·77W. (sync S Holdens).
W Holdens Fl (3) G 10s; 52°15'·77N 06°18'·74W.
Rosslare Pier Hd ☆ Oc WRG 5s 15m W13M, R10M, G10M; R twr; vis:098°-G-188°-W-208°-R-246°-G-283°-W-286°-R-320°; 52°15'·43N 06°20'·29W.
Ballygeary ☆ Oc WR 1·7s 7m 4M vis: shore-R-152°-W-200°- W(unintens)-205°; 52°15'·25N 06°20'·48W.

TUSKAR ROCK TO OLD HEAD OF KINSALE

Tuskar ☆ 52°12'·17N 06°12'·44W Q (2) 7·5s 33m **24M**; W twr; ***Racon (T) 18M;*** 992501065.
S Rock Q (6)+L Fl 15s; 52°10'·80N 06°12'·84W; 992501068.
Fundale Fl (2) R 10s; 52°11'·04N 06°19'·78W.
Barrels Q (3) 10s; 52°08'·32N 06°22'·05W; 992501070.

KILMORE
Kilmore Quay SWM Iso 10s; (Apr-Sep); 52°09'·20N 06°35'·30W.
Kilmore Bkwtr Hd ☆ Q RG 7m 5M; vis: 269°-R-354°-G-003°-R-077°; 52°10'·20N 06°35'·15W.
Ldg lts 007·9°, Front 52°10'·37N 06°35'·08W Oc 4s 3m 6M. Rear, 100m from front, Oc 4s 6m 6M; sync with front.
Bore Rks Q (3) 10s; 52°06.07'N 006°31.87'W; 992501072.
Coningbeg Q(6)+LFl 15s; 52°03'·20N 06°38'·57W; ***Racon (T) 7M***; 992501074.
Red Bank W ; 52°04.499'N 006°41.652'W; 992501076.
'M5' ODAS 35 51°41'·40N 06°42'·24W; Fl (5) Y 20s.

WATERFORD
Hook Hd ☆ 52°07'·42N 06°55'·77W Fl 3s 46m **23M**; W twr, two B bands; ***Racon (K) 10M***. Fog Det Lt VQ. 992501079.
Waterford Fl R 3s. Fl (3) R 10s; 52°08'·95N 06°57'·00W.
Duncannon Dir lt ☆ F WRG 13m 10M, white tower on fort, 359·5°-FG-001·2°-Alt GW-001·7°-FW-002·4°-Alt WR-002·9°-FR-004·5°; 52°13'·23N 06°56'·25W; Oc WR 4s 13m W 9M R 7M on same tower, 119°-R-149°-W-172°.
Passage Pt ☆ Fl WR 5s 7m W6M, R5M; R pile structure; vis: W shore- R127°-302°; 52°14'·26N 06°57'·77W.
Cheek Pt ☆ Q WR 6m 5M; W mast; vis: W007°-R289°-007°; 52°16'·12N 06°59'·38W.
Sheagh ☆ Fl R 3s 29m 3M; Gy twr; vis: 090°-318°; 52°16'·29N 06°59'·34W.
Snowhill Point Ldg lts 255°. Front, Fl WR 2·5s 5m 3M; vis: W222°- R020°- W057°-107°; 52°16'·39N 07°00'·91W. Rear, Flour Mill, 750m from front, Q 12m 5M.
Queen's Chan Ldg lts 098°. Front, QR 8m 5M; B twr, W band; vis: 030°-210°;52°15'·32N 07°02'·38W. Rear, 550m from front, Q 15m 5M; W mast.
Beacon Quay ☆ Fl G 3s 9m; vis: 255°-086°; 52°15'·50N 07°04'·21W.
Cove ☆ Fl WRG 6s 6m 2M; W twr; vis: R111°- G161°-W234°-111°; 52°15'·05N 07°05'·16W.
Smelting Ho Pt ☆ Q 8m 3M; W mast; 52°15'·15N 07°05'·27W.
Ballycar ☆ Fl RG 3s 5m; vis: G127°- R212°-284°; 52°15'·06N 07°05'·51W.

DUNMORE EAST
East Pier Head ☆ 52°08'·93N 06°59'·34W Fl WR 8s 13m **W17M**, R13M; Gy twr, vis: W225°- R310°-004°.
Dunmore East 1 Q G; 52°09'·06N 06°59'·38W.
Dunmore East 2 Fl G 2s; 52°09'·00N 06°59'·47W.
W Wharf ☆ Fl G 2s 6m 4M; vis: 165°-246°; 52°08'·97N 06°59'·45W.

DUNGARVAN
Ballinacourty Pt ☆ Fl (2) WRG 10s 16m W10M, R8M, G8M; W twr; vis: G245°- W274°- R302°- W325°-117°; 52°04'·69N 07°33'·18W.
Helvick Q (3) 10s; 52°03'·61N 07°32'·25W.
Mine Head ☆ 51°59'·56N 07°35'·23W Fl (4) 30s 87m 12M; W twr, B band; vis: 228°-052°; 992501085.

YOUGHAL
Bar Rocks Q (6) + L Fl 15s; 51°54'·85N 07°50'·05W.
Blackball Ledge 51°55'·34N 07°48'·53W Q (3) 10s.
W side of ent ☆ 51°56'·57N 07°50'·53W Fl WR 2·5s 24m **W17M**, R13M; W twr; vis: W183°- R273°- W295°- R307°-W351°-003°.

BALLYCOTTON
Ballycotton ☆ 51°49'·50N 07° 59'·13W Fl WR 10s 59m **W18M, R14M**; B twr, within W walls, B lantern; vis: 238°-W-048°-R-238°; 992501093.
The Smiths Fl (3) R 10s; 51°48'·62N 08°00'·71W.
Power Q (6) + L Fl 15s; 51°45'·59N 08°06'·67W; 992501098.

CORK
Cork L Fl 10s; 51°42'·92N 08°15'·60W; ***Racon (T) 7M***; 992501100.
Daunt Rock Fl (2) R 6s; 51°43'·52N 08°17'·66W; 992501102.
Fort Davis Ldg lts 354·1°. Front, 51°48'·82N 08°15'·80W Dir WRG 29m **17M**; vis: FG351·5°-AlWG352·25°-FW353°-

AlWR355°-FR355·75°-356·5°. Rear, Dognose Quay, 203m from front, Oc 5s 37m 10M; Or 3, synch with front.

Roche's Pt ☆ 51°47'·59N 08°15'·29W Fl WR 3s 30m **W20M, R16M**; vis: shore-R-292°-W-016°-R-033°, 033°- W (unintens)-159°-R-shore; 992501099.

Outer Hbr Rk E2 Fl R 2·5s; 51°47'·52N 08°15'·67W.

Chicago Knoll E1 Fl G 5s; 51°47'·66N 08°15'·54W.

W1 Fl G 10s; 51°47'·69N 08°16'·05W.

W2 Fl R 10s; 51°47'·69N 08°16'·34W.

White Bay Ldg lts 034·6°. Front, Oc R 5s 11m 5M; W hut; 51°48'·53N 08°15'·22W. Rear, 113m from front, Oc R 5s 21m 5M; W hut; synch with front.

Spit Bank Pile ☆ Iso WR 4s 10m W10M, R7M; W house on R piles; vis: R087°- W196°- R221°- 358°; 51°50'·72N 08°16'·45W.

KINSALE and OYSTER HAVEN

Bulman Q (6) + L Fl 15s; 51°40'·14N 08°29'·74W; 992501104.

Charlesfort ☆ Fl WRG 5s 18m W9M, R6M, G7M; vis: G348°- W358°- R004°-168°; H24; 51°41'·75N 08°29'·84W.

OLD HEAD OF KINSALE TO MIZEN HEAD

Old Head of Kinsale ☆, S point 51°36'·29N 08°32'·02W Fl (2) 10s 72m **20M**; B twr, two W bands; 992501107.

COURTMACSHERRY

Barrel Rock 51°37'·01N 08°37'·30W.

Black Tom Fl G 5s; 51°36'·41N 08°37'·95W; 992501110.

Wood Pt (Land Pt) ☆ Fl (2) WR 5s 15m 5M; vis: W315°- R332°-315°; 51°38'·16N 08°41'·00W.

Galley Head ☆ summit 51°31'·80N 08°57'·21W Fl (5) 20s 53m **23M**; W twr; vis: 256°-065°.

GLANDORE and CASTLETOWNSHEND

Reen Point ☆ Fl WRG 10s 9m W5M, R3M, G3M; W twr; vis: shore-G-338°-W-001°-R-shore; 51°30'·98N 09°10'·50W.

Kowloon Bridge Q (6) + L Fl 15s; 51°27'·58N 09°13'·75W; 992501118.

BALTIMORE and FASTNET

Barrack Pt ☆ Fl (2) WR 6s 40m W6M, R3M; vis: R168°- W294°-038°; 51°28'·33N 09°23'·65W.

Loo Rock Fl G 3s; 51°28'·44N 09°23'·46W; 992501119.

Lousy Rks ; 51°28'·93N 09°23'·39W.

Wallis Rk Fl (3) R 10s; 51°28'·93N 09°22'·99W.

Lettuce Pt VQ (3) 5s; 51°29'·32N 09°23'·81W.

Mealbeg Q (6) + L Fl 15s; 51°29'·68N 09°24'·69W.

Inane Pt Q (6) + L Fl 15s; 51°30'·02N 09°23'·66W.

Hare Is Q; 51°30'·17N 09°25'·38W.

Fastnet ☆, W end 51°23'·35N 09°36'·19W Fl 5s 49m **27M**; Gy twr, ***Racon (G) 18M***. Fog Det Lt VQ; 992501123.

SCHULL and LONG ISLAND CHANNEL

Amelia ; 51°29.979'N 009°31.461'W; 992501120.

Copper Point ☆ 51°30'·25N 09°32'·06W Q (3) 10s 16m 8M. Ldg lts 346° Front, Oc 5s 5m 11M, W mast; 51°31'·68N 09°32'·43W. Rear, 91m from front, Oc 5s 8m11M; W mast.

CROOKHAVEN

Rock Is Pt ☆ L Fl WR 8s 20m W13M, R11M; W twr; vis: W over Long Is B to 281°-R-340°; inside harbour 281°-R-348°- towards N shore; 51°28'·59N 09°42'·27W; 992501124.

MIZEN HEAD TO DINGLE BAY

Mizen Head ☆ Iso 4s 55m 12M; vis: 313°-133°; 51°26'·99N 09°49'·23W; 992501127.

Sheep's Hd ☆ 51°32'·59N 09°50'·92W Fl (3) WR 15s 83m **W15M** R9M; W bldg; vis: 011·3°-R-016·6°-W-212·5°- (partially obs) 233° (shore); 992501129.

BANTRY BAY, CASTLETOWN BEARHAVEN, WHIDDY ISLE, BANTRY and GLENGARIFF

Roancarrigmore ☆ Fl WR 5s 13m W11M, R9M, R(unintens) 5M; s/steel twr; vis: 312°-W-050°-R-122°-R(unintens)- 207°-obsc-246°-R-312°; 51°39'·18N 09°44'·82W. Old Lt ho W twr, B band; 992501130.

Ardnakinna Pt ☆ 51°37'·10N 09°55'·09W Fl (2) WR 10s 62m W14M, R9M; W ○ twr; vis: 319°-R- 348°-W- 066°-R- shore; 992501131.

Walter Scott Rk Q (6) + L Fl 15s; 51°38'·52N 09°54'·20W; 992501128.

Castletown (Dinish Is) Dir lt 023·25° ☆ Oc WRG 5s 7m W15M, R12M, G12M; W hut, R stripe; vis: 019·5°-G-023°- W-023·5°-R-027°; 51°38'·78N 09°54'·32W; 992501125.

Castletown Ldg lts 008°. Front, Oc Bu 6s 4m 6M; W col, R stripe; vis: 005°-013°; 51°39'·16N 09°54'·40W. Rear, 80m from front, Oc Bu 6s 7m 6M; W with R stripe; vis: 005°-013°.

Bull Rock ☆ 51°35'·52N 10°18'·07W Fl 15s 91m **18M;** W twr; 992501131.

KENMARE RIVER, DARRYNANE and BALLYCROVANE

Illaunnameanla (Ballycrovane) ☆ Fl R 3s; 51°42'·60N 09°57'·50W.

Book Rks Fl(2) R 10s; 51°46'·54N 09°49'·74W.

Cuskeal Fl R 5s; 51°46'·45N 09°48'·85W.

Bunaw Ldg Lts 041°. Front, Oc R 3s 9m 2M; B col, Y bands; 51°46'·80N 09°48'·40W. Rear, 200m from front Iso R 2s 11m 2M.

Maiden Rk Fl G 5s; 51°48'·98N 09°47'·98W; 992501134.

Bat Rk Fl G 5s; 51°50'·89N 09°40'·89W.

Carrignaronebeg Fl R 5s; 51°50'·99N 09°41'·39W.

No1 Fl G 5s; 51°52'·09N 09°36'·35W.

Carrignarone (Seal Rk) Fl 5s 2m 2M; 51°48'·58N 09°52'·65W.

Castlecove Ldg Lts 045°. Front, Oc 2s 5m 6M; concrete post W front; 51°46'·29N 10°02'·04W. Rear, 400m from front Oc 2s 18m 6M.

West Cove Hbr ☆ Fl R 3s; post W front; 51°46'·00N 10°02'·93W.

West Cove Hbr Ldg Lts 312°. Front, Fl 2s 2m 6M; concrete post; 51°46'·11N 10°03'·08W. Rear, 200m from front Fl 2s 4m 6M.

Darrynane Ldg lts 034°. Front, Oc 3s 10m 4M; 51°45'·90N 10°09'·20W. Rear, Oc 3s 16m 4M.

SKELLIG ISLANDS

Skelligs Rock ☆ Fl (3) 15s 53m 12M; W twr; vis: 262°-115°; part obsc within 6M 110°-115°; 51°46'·11N 10°32'·52W; 992501137.

VALENTIA and PORTMAGEE

Fort (Cromwell) Point ☆ 51°56'·02N 10°19'·28W Fl WR 2s 16m **W17M, R15M**; W twr; vis: 304°-R-351°,102°-W-304°; obsc from seaward by Doulus Head when brg more than 180°; 992501141.

Dir lt 141° ☆ Oc WRG 4s 25m W11M, R8M, G8M (by day: W3M, R2M, G2M); W twr, R stripe; vis:136°-G-140°-W-142°-R-146°; 51°55′·51N 10°18′·42W.
The Foot ⫫ VQ (3) 5s; 51°55′·72N 10°17′·07W; 992501140.

DINGLE BAY TO LOOP HEAD

DINGLE BAY, VENTRY and DINGLE

Ldg lts 182° Oc 3s. Front 52°07′·41N 10°16′·59W, rear 100m behind.
Inishtearaght ☆, W end Blasket Islands 52°04′·54N 10°39′·67W Fl (2) 20s 84m **19M**; W twr; vis: 318°-221°; ***Racon (O);*** 992501143.

BRANDON BAY, TRALEE BAY and FENIT HARBOUR

Little Samphire Is ☆ 52°16′·26N 09°52′·91W Fl WRG 5s 17m **W16M**, R13M; G13M; Bu ◯ twr; vis: 262°-R-275°, 280-R-090°-G-140°-W-152°-R-172°.
Great Samphire I ☆ QR 15m 3M; vis: 242°-097°; 52°16′·15N 09°51′·81W.
Fenit Hbr Pier Hd ☆ 2 FR (vert) 12m 3M; vis: 148°-058°; 52°16′·24N 09°51′·55W.

SHANNON ESTUARY

Ballybunnion ⫫ VQ; ***Racon (M) 6M***; 52°32′·52N 09°46′·93W; 992501146.
Kilstiffin ⌂ Fl R 3s; 52°33′·80N 09°43′·83W; 992501148.
Kilcredaun ⌂ Q R (sync); 52°34′·42N 09°41′·16W.
Tail of Beal ▲ Q G (sync); 52°34′·37N 09°40′·71W; 992501150.
Kilcredaun Head ⌂, W twr; 52°34′·78N 09°42′·58W.
Carrigaholt ⌂ Fl (2) R 6s (sync); 52°34′·90N 09°40′·47W.
Beal Spit ▲ Fl (2) G 6s (sync); 52°34′·80N 09°39′·94W.
Beal Bar ▲ Fl G 3s (sync); 52°35′·18N 09°39′·05W.
Doonaha ⌂ Fl R 3s (sync); 52°35′·54N 09°39′·01W; 992501154.
Letter Point ⌂ Fl R 7s; 52°35′·44N 09°35′·89W.
Asdee ⌂ Fl R 5s; 52°35′·09N 09°34′·55W.
Rineanna ⌂ QR; 52°35′·59N 09°31′·24W.
North Carraig ⫫ Q; 52°35′·60N 09°29′·76W.
Scattery Is, Rineanna Pt ☆ Fl (2) 8s 15m 10M; W twr; vis: 208°-092°; 52°36′·35N 09°31′·07W.

KILRUSH

Marina Ent Chan Ldg lts 355°. Front, Oc 3s; 52°37′·99N 09°30′·27W. Rear, 75m from front, Oc 3s.
Tarbert Is N Point ☆ Q WR 4s 18m W14M, R10M; W ◯ twr; vis: W069°- R277°- W287°-339°; 52°35′·52N 09°21′·83W.
Tarbert (Ballyhoolahan Pt) Ldg lts 128·2° ⫫. Front, Iso 3s 13m 3M; △ on W twr; vis: 123·2°-133·2°; 52°34′·35N 09°18′·80W. Rear, 400m from front, Iso 5s 18m 3M; G stripe on W Bn.
Garraunbaun Pt ☆ Fl (3) WR 10s 16m W8M, R5M; W ☐ col, vis: R shore - W072°- R242°- shore; 52°35′·62N 09°13′·94W.
Rinealon Pt ☆ Fl 2·5s 4m 7M; B col, W bands; vis: 234°-088°; 52°37′·12N 09°09′·82W.

FOYNES

W Chan Ldg lts 107·9° (may be moved for changes in chan). Front, Oc 4s 34m 12M; 52°36′·91N 09°06′·59W . Rear, Oc 4s 39m 12M.

RIVER SHANNON

Beeves Rock ☆ Fl WR 5s 12m W12M, R9M; vis: 064·5°-W-091°-R- 238°-W-265°-W(unintens)-064·5°; 52°39′·01N 09°01′·35W .
North Channel Ldg lts 093°. Front, Tradree Rock Fl R 2s 6m 5M; W Trs; vis: 246°-110°; 52°41′·00N 08°49′·87W. Rear 0·65M from front, Iso 6s 14m 5M; W twr, R bands; vis: 327°-190°.
N side, Ldg lts 061°. Front, 52°40′·72N 08°45′·27W, Crawford Rock 490m from rear, Fl R 3s 6m 5M. Crawford No. 2, Common Rear, Iso 6s 10m 5M; 52°40′·85N 08°44′·88W.
Ldg lts 302·1°, Flagstaff Rock, 670m from rear, Fl R 7s 7m 5M; 52°40′·66N 08°44′·40W.
Ldg lts 106·5°. Meelick Rk, Front Iso R 4s 6m 5M; 52°40′·24N 08°42′·32W. Meelick No. 2, rear 275m from front Iso R 4s 9m 5M; both W beacons.

LOOP HEAD

Loop Head ☆ 52°33′·67N 09°55′·94W Fl (4) 20s 84m **23M**; vis: 280°-218°; 992501161.
Mal Bay ⌂ Fl(5) Y 20s 52°46.42′N 009°35.15′W; *AIS.*

LISCANNOR BAY TO SLYNE HEAD

GALWAY BAY and INISHMORE

Eeragh, Rock Is ☆ 53°08′·91N 09°51′·40W Fl 15s 35m **18M**; W twr, two B bands; vis: 297°-262°; 992501172.
Straw Is ☆ Fl (2) 5s 11m 12M; W twr; 53°07′·08N 09°37′·82W.
Killeany Ldg lts 192°. Front, Oc 5s 6m 3M; W col on W ☐ base; vis: 142°-197°, 53°06′·25N 09°39′·74W. Rear, 43m from front, Oc 5s 8m 2M; W col on W ☐ base; vis: 142°-197°.
Inishmaan, Ldg lts 199°, Oc 6s 8M; 53°06′·08N 09°34′·77W.
Killeaney ▲ Fl G 3s; 53°07.33′N 009°38.37′W; 992501166.
Inisheer ☆ 53°02′·76N 09°31′·61W Iso WR 12s 34m **W18M**, R11M; vis: 225°-W(partially vis >7M)-231°, 231°-W-245°-R-269°-W-115°; ***Racon (K) 13M;*** 992501165.
Finnis ⫫ Q (3) 10s; 53°02′·82N 09°29′·14W, 992501164.
Black Hd ☆ Fl WR 5s 20m W11M, R8M, W ☐ twr; vis: 045°- R268°-276°; 53°09′·25N 09°15′·83W.

GALWAY

Margaretta Shoal ▲ Fl G 3s; *Whis;* 53°13′·68N 09°05′·99W, 992501170.
Leverets ☆ Q WRG 9m 10M; B ☐ twr, W bands; vis: 015°-G-058°-W-065°-R-103°-G-143·5°-W-146·5°-R-015°; 53°15′·33N 09°01′·90W.
Rinmore ☆ Iso WRG 4s 7m 5M; W ☐ twr; vis: 359°-G-008°-W-018°-R-027°; 53°16′·12N 09°01′·97W.
Appr Chan Dir lt 325°, WRG 7m 3M; vis: 322·25°-FG-323·75°-AlGW-324·75°-FW-325·25°-AlRW-326·25°-FR-331·25°-FlR-332·25°; 53°16′·12N 09°02′·83W.

GALWAY to SLYNE HEAD

Barna Quay Hd ☆ Fl 2 WRG 5s 6m W8M, R5M, G5M; vis:250°-G-344·5°-W-355·5°-R-090°; 53°14′·93N 09°08′·90W.
Spiddle Pier Hd ☆ Fl WRG 3·5s 11m W8M, R8M, G8M; Y col; vis: 265°-G-308°-W-024°-R-066°; 53°14′·42N 09°18′·54W.
Cashla Bay Ent, W side ☆ Fl (3) WR 10s 8m W6M, R3M; W col on concrete twr; vis: 216°-W-000°-R-069°; 53°14′·23N 09°35′·20W.
Cannon Rk ▲ Fl G 5s; 53°14′·08N 09°34′·35W, 992501173.
Lion Pt Dir lt 010°, Iso WRG 5s 6m (H24), G6M, W8M, R6M,(night), G2M, W3M, R2M(day); vis: 005°-G- 008·5°-

W-011·5°-R-015°; 53°15'·83N 09°33'·98W; 992501171.
Rossaveel Pier Ldg lts 116°. Front, 53°16'·02N 09°33'·38W Oc 3s 7m 3M; W mast. Rear, 90m from front, Oc 3s 8m 3M.
Kiggaul Bay ☆ Fl WRG 3s 5m W5M, R3M, G3M; vis: 310°-G-329°-W-349°-R-059°; 53°14'·03N 09°43'·02W.
Croaghnakeela Is ☆ Fl 3·7s 7m 5M; W col; vis: 034°-045°, 218°-286°, 311°-325°; 53°19'·40N 09°58'·21W.
Inishnee ☆ Fl (2) WRG 10s 9m W5M, R3M, G3M; W col on W □ base; vis: 314°-G-017°-W-030°-R-080°-W-194°; 53°22'·75N 09°54'·53W.
Slyne Head, North twr, Illaunamid ☆ 53°23'·99N 10°14'·05W Fl (2) 15s 35m **19M**; B twr; 992501175.

SLYNE HEAD TO EAGLE ISLAND

CLIFDEN BAY and INISHBOFIN

Carrickrana Rocks Bn, large W Bn; 53°29'·24N 10°09'·48W.
Cleggan Point ☆ Fl (3) WRG 15s 20m W6M, R3M, G3M; W col on W hut; vis: shore-G-091°-W-124°-R-221°; 53°34'·48N 10°07'·69W.
Inishlyon Lyon Head ☆ Fl WR 7·5s 13m W7M, R4M; W post; vis: 036°-W-058°-R-184°-W-325°-R-036°; 53°36'·74N 10°09'·56W.
Gun Rock ☆ Fl (2) 6s 8m 4M; W col; vis: 296°-253°; 53°36'·59N 10°13'·23W.
Inishbofin Dir lt 021°, Oc WRG 6s 10m 11M; W pole; vis: 015·75°-G-020·75°-W-021·25°-R-026·25°; 53°36'·78N 10°13'·16W.

CLEW BAY and WESTPORT

Roonagh Quay Ldg lts 144°. Front 53°45'·75N 09°54'·23W. Rear, 54m from front, both Iso Bu 10s 9/15m.
Inishgort ☆ L Fl 10s 10M; 53°49.59'N 009°40.25'W; 992501179.
Cloughcormick Q (9) 15s; 53°50'·56N 09°43'·20W.
Achillbeg I, S Point ☆ 53°51'·51N 09°56'·84W Fl WR 5s 56m **W16M, R18M**, R11M; W ○ twr on □ building; vis: 262°-R-281°-W-342°-R-060°-W-092°-R(intens)-099°-W-118°; 992501181.

ACHILL SOUND

Ldg lts 330°, 53°52'·50N 09°56'·91W Whitestone Point. Front and rear both Oc 4s 5/6m; W ◇, B stripe.
Achill I Ldg lts 310°, Purteen, Oc 8s 5m; 53°57'·83N 10°05'·93W (PA). Rear, 46m from front Oc 8s 6m.

BLACKSOD BAY

Blacksod Q (3) 10s; 54°05'·89N 10°03'·01W.
Blacksod Pier Root ☆ Fl (2) WR 7·5s 13m W12M, R9M; W twr on bldg; vis: 189°-R-210°-W-018°; 54°05'·92N 10°03'·63W; 992501186.
Carrigeenmore VQ(3) 5s 3M; 54°06'·56N 10°03'·4W.
Black Rock ☆ 54°04'·06N 10°19'·23W Fl WR 12s 86m **W20M, R16M**; W twr; vis: 276°-W-212°-R-276°; 992501183.
Eagle Is, W end ☆ 54°17'·02N 10°05'·56W Fl (3) 20s 67m **18M**; W twr; 992501189.

EAGLE ISLAND TO RATHLIN O'BIRNE

BROAD HAVEN BAY

Rinroe Pt ☆ Fl (2) 10s 5m 3M; 54°17'·83N 09°50'·59W.
Gubacashel Point ☆ Iso WR 4s 27m **W17M**, R12M; 110°-R-133°-W-355°-R-021° W twr; 54°16'·06N 09°53'·33W.

KILLALA

Carrickpatrick Q (3) 10s; 54°15'·56N 09°09'·14W; 992501192.
Inishcrone Pier Root ☆ Fl WRG 1·5s 8m 2M; vis: 098°-W-116°-G- 136°-R-187°; 54°13'·21N 09°05'·79W.
Ldg lts 230°. Rinnaun Point. Front No. 1, Oc 10s 7m 5M; □ twr; 54°13'·21N 09°05'·79W. Rear, 150m from front, No. 2 Oc 10s 12m 5M; □ twr.
Inch Is Dir lt 215°, Fl WRG 2s 6m 3M; □ twr; vis: 205°-G-213°-W- 217°-R-225°; 54°13'·29N 09°12'·30W.
Ldg lts 196°. Kilroe. Front, 54°12'·63N 09°12'·33W Oc 4s 5m 2M; □ twr. Rear,120m from front, Oc 4s 10m 2M; □ twr.
Ldg lts 236°. Pier. Front, Iso 2s 5m 2M; W ◇ on twr; 54°13'·02N 09°12'·84W. Rear, 200m from front, Iso 2s 7m 2M; W ◇ on pole.

SLIGO

Black Rock ☆ Fl WR 5s 24m 10/8M; vis: 130°-W-107°-R-130° (R sector covers Wheat and Seal rks); W twr, B band; 54°18'·46N 08°37'·06W Fl G 3s; *Whis;* 53°13'·68N 09°05'·99W, 992501195.
Lower Rosses, (N of Cullaun Bwee) ☆ Fl (2) WRG 10s 8m 10M; W hut on piles; vis: 061°-G-066°-W-070°-R-075°; shown H24; 54°19'·73N 08°34'·41W.
Ldg lts 125° Fl (3) 6s 7M (sync). Front, Metal Man; 54°18'·24N 08°34'·55W, 3m. Rear, Oyster Is, 365m from front, 13m; H24.
Wheat Rock Q (6) + LFl 15s; 54°18'·84N 08°39'·10W; 992501196.

DONEGAL BAY and KILLYBEGS

St John's Pt ☆ Fl 6s 30m 14M; W twr; 54°34'·16N 08°27'·66W; 992501197.
Bullockmore Q (9) 15s; 54°33'·98N 08°30'·14W; 992501198.
Rotten I ☆ 54°36'·97N 08°26'·41W Fl WR 4s 20m **W15M**, R11M; W twr; vis: W255°- R008°- W039°-208°.
New Landing Dir lt 338°, Oc WRG 8s 17m; vis: 328°-G-334°-Al WG-336°-W-340°-Al WR-342°-R-348°; 54°38'·14N 08°26'·38W.
Killybegs Outer VQ (6) + L Fl 10s; 54°37'·92N 08°29'·15W.

RATHLIN O'BIRNE TO BLOODY FORELAND

S of ARAN and RUTLAND S CHANNEL

Rathlin O'Birne ☆ Fl WR 15s 35m W12M, R10M; W twr; vis: 195°-R-307°-W-195°; ***Racon (O) 13M***, vis 284°-203°. 54°39'·82N 08°49'·95W; 992501203.
Dawros Head ☆ L Fl 10s 39m 4M; 54°49'·63N 08°33'·64W.
Wyon Point ☆ Fl (2) WRG 10s 8m W6M, R3M; W □ twr; vis: shore-G-021°-W-042°-R-121°-W-150°-R-shore; 54°56'·51N 08°27'·54W.

BURTONPORT

Ldg lts 068·1°. Front , FG 17m 1M; Gy Bn, W band; 54°58'·95N 08°26'·40W. Rear, 355m from front, FG 23m 1M; Gy Bn, Y band.

N SOUND OF ARAN and RUTLAND N CHANNEL

Rutland I Ldg lts 137·6°. Front, 54°58'·97N 08°27'·68W Oc 6s 8m 1M; W Bn, B band. Rear, 330m from front, Oc 6s 14m 1M.
Inishcoo Ldg lts 119·3°. Front, Iso 6s 6m 1M; W Bn, B band; 54°59'·43N 08°29'·63W. Rear, 248m from front, Iso 6s 11m 1M.

Ldg lts 186°. Front, Oc 8s 8m 3M; B Bn, W band; 54°58'·94N 08°29'·27W. Rear, 395m from front, Oc 8s 17m 3M; B Bn.

Aranmore, Rinrawros Pt ☆ 55°00'·90N 08°33'·67W Fl (2) 20s 71m **27M**; W twr; obsc by land about 234°-007° and about 013°. Auxiliary lt Fl R 3s 61m 13M, same twr; vis: 203°-234°; 992501205.

OWEY SOUND to INISHSIRRER

Cruit Is. Owey Sound Ldg lts 068·3°. Oc 10s. Front, 55°03'·06N 08°25'·85W. Rear, 107m from front.

Rinnalea Point ☆ 55°02'·59N 08°23'·72W Fl 7·5s 19m 9M; □ twr; vis: 132°-167°.

Gola Is Ldg lts 171·2°. Oc 3s 2M (sync). Front, 9m; W Bn, B band; 55°05'·11N 08°21'·07W. Rear, 86m from front, 13m; B Bn, W band.

Glassagh. Ldg lts 137·4°. Front, Oc 8s 12m 3M; 55°06'·83N 08°18'·97W. Rear, 46m from front, Oc 8s 17m 3M; synch.

Inishsirrer, NW end ☆ Fl 3·7s 20m 4M; W □ twr vis: 083°-263°; 55°07'·40N 08°20'·93W.

BLOODY FORELAND TO INISHTRAHULL

BLOODY FORELAND to SHEEPHAVEN

Bloody Foreland ☆ Fl WG 7·5s 14m W6M, G4M; vis: 062°-W-232°-G-062°; 55°09'·51N 08°17'·03W.

Tory Island ☆ 55°16'·36N 08°14'·96W Fl (4) 30s 40m **18M**; B twr, W band; vis: 302°-277°; ***Racon (M) 12-23M;*** 992501211.

West Town Ldg lts 001° ☆ Iso 2s 9m 7M △ on Y structure R stripe; 55°15'·79N 08°13'·50W. Rear Iso 2s 11m 7M ▽ ditto (sync).

Inishbofin Pier ☆ Fl 8s 3m 3M; 55°10'·14N 08°10'·01W.

Ballyness Hbr. Ldg lts 119·5°. Front, Iso 4s 25m 1M; 55°09'·06N 08°06'·98W. Rear, 61m from front, Iso 4s 26m 1M.

Portnablahy Ldg lts 125·3°. Front Oc 6s 7m 2M; B col, W bands; 55°10'·79N 07°55'·65W. Rear, 81m from front, Oc 6s 12m 2M; B col, W bands.

MULROY BAY

Limeburner Q Fl; 55°18'·54N 07°48'·40W; 992501214.

Ravedy Is ☆ Fl 3s 9m 3M; vis 177°-357°; 55°15'·14N 07°46'·90W

LOUGH SWILLY, BUNCRANA and RATHMULLAN

Fanad Head ☆ 55°16'·57N 07°37'·92W Fl (5) WR 20s 39m **W18M**, R14M; W twr; vis 100°-R-110°-W-313°-R-345°-W-100°; 992501215.

Swillymore Fl G 3s; 55°15'·12N 07°35'·79W; 992501216.

Dunree ☆ Fl (2) WR 5s 49m W12M, R9M; vis: 320°-R-328°-W-183°-R-196°; 55°11'·89N 07°33'·25W.

Buncrana Pier near Hd ☆ Iso WR 4s 11m W13M, R10M; R twr, W band; vis: R shore- over Inch spit, 052°-W-139°-R-shore over White Strand Rock; 55°07'·60N 07°27'·88W.

Rathmullan Pier Hd ☆ Fl G 3s 5M; vis: 206°-345°; 55°05'·70N 07°31'·66W.

Inishtrahull ☆ 55°25'·89N 07°14'·63W Fl (3) 15s 59m **19M**; W twr; obscd 256°-261° within 3M; ***Racon (T) 24M 060°-310°***. Fog Det Lt VQ; 992501229.

INISHTRAHULL TO RATHLIN ISLAND

LOUGH FOYLE

Foyle L Fl 10s; 55°15'·32N 06°52'·62W; ***Racon (M)***; 992501230.

Tuns Fl R 3s; 55°14'·00N 06°53'·46W; 992501232.

Inishowen Dunagree ☆ 55°13'·60N 06°55'·70W Fl (2) WRG 10s 28m **W18M**, R14M, G14M; W twr, 2 B bands; vis: 197°-G-211°-W-249°-R-000°. Fog Det lt VQ 16m vis: 270°.

Greencastle S Bkwtr Dir lt 042·5°. Fl (2) WRG 3s 4m W11M, R9M, G9M; vis 307°-G- 040°-W-045°-R-055°; 55°12'·17N 06°59'·13W.

McKinney's Fl R 5s; 55°10'·9N 07°00'·5W.

Moville Fl WR 2·5s 11m 4M; W house on G piles vis: 240°-W-064°-R-240°; 55°10'·98N 07°02'·13W.

RIVER BANN, COLERAINE and PORTRUSH

River Bann Ldg lts 165°. Front, Oc 5s 6m 2M; W twr; 55°09'·96N 06°46'·23W. Rear, 245m from front, Oc 5s 14m 2M; W □ twr.

W Mole ☆ Fl G 5s 4m 2M; vis: 170°-000°; 55°10'·25N 06°46'·45W.

Portstewart Point ☆ Oc R 10s 21m 5M; R □ hut; vis: 040°-220°; 55°11'·33N 06°43'·26W.

N Pier Hd ☆ Fl R 3s 6m 3M; vis: 220°-160°; 55°12'·34N 06°39'·58W.

Skerries Fl R 5s; 53°13'·90N 06°36'·90W; 992351096.

RATHLIN ISLAND

Rathlin W 0·5M NE of Bull Pt ☆ 55°18'·05N 06°16'·82W Fl R 5s 62m **22M**; W twr, lantern at base; vis: 015°-225°; H24. Fog Det Lt VQ; 992351000.

Drake Wreck 55°17'·00N 06°12'·48W Q (6) + L Fl 15s.

Manor House ☆ Oc WRG 4s 5M; vis: 020°-G-023°-W-026°-R-029°; 55°17'·52N 06°11'·73W.

Rue Pt ☆ Fl(2) 5s 16m 14M; W twr B bands; 55°15'·53N 06°11'·47W; 992351131.

Altacarry Head ☆ 55°18'·11N 06°10'·31W Fl (4) 20s 74m **26M**; W twr, B band; vis: 110°-006° and 036°-058°; ***Racon (G) 15-27M;*** 992320707.

FAIR HEAD TO LAMBAY ISLAND

RED BAY, CARNLOUGH and LARNE

Red Bay Pier ☆ Fl 3s 10m 5M; 55°03'·93N 06°03'·21W.

Carnlough Hbr N Pier ☆ Fl G 3s 4m 5M; 54°59'·59N 05°59'·29W.

East Maiden ☆ Fl (3) 15s 29m **23M**; W twr, B band; ***Racon (M) 11-21M.*** Auxiliary lt Fl R 5s 15m 8M; 54°55'·75N 05°43'·71W; same twr; vis:142°-182° over Russel and Highland Rks; 992351110.

N Hunter Rock Q; 54°53'·04N 05°45'·13W.

S Hunter Rock VQ(6) + LFl 10s; 54°52'·69N 05°45'·22W; 992351007.

Larne No. 1 QG; 54°51'·68N 05°47'·67W; *AIS*.

Chaine Twr ☆ Iso WR 5s 23m **W16M,** R12M; Gy twr; vis: 232°-W-240°-R-000° (shore); 54°51'·27N 05°47'·90W.

Larne Ldg lts 184°, No. 11 Front, 54°49'·60N 05°47'·81W Oc 4s 6m 12M; W 2 with R stripe on R pile structure; vis: 179°-189°. No. 12 Rear, 610m from front, Oc 4s 14m 12M; W 2 with R stripe on R □ twr; synch with front, vis: 5° either side of Ldg line.

CARRICKFERGUS

Black Hd ☆ 54°46'·02N 05°41'·34W Fl 3s 45m **27M**; W 8-sided twr; 992351002.

Cloghan Jetty 54°44'·10N 05°41'·58W QG. Marina Ent Appr ☆ Dir Oc WRG 3s 5m 3M; vis: G308°- W317·5°-R322·5°-332°; 54°42'·58N 05°48'·78W.

BELFAST LOUGH and BANGOR

Mew Is ☆ NE end 54°41′·92N 05°30′·82W Fl (4) 30s 35m **18M**; B twr, W band; ***Racon (O) 14M***. Fog Det Lt VQ; 992351109.

Belfast Fairway Iso 4s; 54°42′·32N 05°42′·30W; ***Racon (G)***; *AIS*.

Kilroot Fl QG (sync); 54°42′·85N 05°42′·85W.

Helen's Bay QR (sync); 54°41′·86N 05°42′·85W.

No 1 Fl G 2s (sync); 54°41′·67N 05°46′·51W.

No 2 Fl R 2s (sync); 54°41′·55N 05°46′·43W.

Briggs Fl (2)R 10s; 54°41′·52N 05°53′·70W; 992351133.

DONAGHADEE

Merandoragh Fl (2) G 6s (sync); 54°39′·84N 05°32′·24W.

Foreland Spit Fl (2) R 6s (sync); 54°39′·64N 05°32′·31W.

Governor's Fl G 3s (sync); 54°39′·36N 05°31′·99W; 992351134.

Riggs Bank ⊙ V–AIS PHM; 54°38′·63N 05°27′·10W; 992356011.

Donaghadee ☆, S Pier Hd 54°38′·71N 05°31′·86W Iso WR 4s 17m **W18M**, R14M; twr; vis: shore-W-326°-R-shore; 002320792.

BALLYWATER and PORTAVOGIE

Ballywalter, Bkwtr Hd Fl WRG 3s 4m 9M; vis: 240°-G-267°-W-277°-R-314°; 54°32′·68N 05°28′·83W.

Skulmartin L Fl 10s; 54°31′·82N 05°24′·80W; 992351022.

Portavogie Bkwtr Hd ☆ Iso WRG 5s 9m W10M, R8M, G8M; □ twr; vis: shore-G-258°-W-275°-R-348°; 54°27′·44N 05°26′·14W.

Plough Rock 54°27′·40N 05°25′·12W Fl R 3s.

South Rock Fl (3) R 30s 7M 54°24′·49N 05°22′·02W; 992351004.

STRANGFORD LOUGH

Strangford L Fl 10s; 54°18′·63N 05°28′·69W; 992351028.

Bar Pladdy Q (6) + L Fl 15s; 54°19′·34N 05°30′·51W; 992351135.

Dogtail Pt Ldg lts 341°. Front, Iso 4s 2m 5M; G Bn; 54°20′·79N 05°31′·84W. Rear, Gowlands Rk, 0·8M fm front, Iso 4s 6m 5M; W twr, G top, B base.

Swan Is Q (3) 5m; BYB brick twr; 54°22′·38N 05°33′·16W.

Strangford East Ldg lts 256°. Front, Oc WRG 5s 6m W9M, R6M, G6M: vis: 190°-R-244°-G-252°-W- 260°-R-294°; 54°22′·29N 05°33′·27W. Rear, 46m from front, Oc R 5s 10m 6M; vis: 250°-264°.

Portaferry Pier Hd ☆ Oc WR 10s 9m W9M, R6M; Or mast; vis: W335°- R005°- W017°-128°; 54°22′·82N 05°33′·03W.

ARDGLASS

Inner Pier Hd ☆ Iso WRG 4s 10m W8M, R7M, G5M; twr; vis: shore-G-308°-W-314°-R-shore; 54°15′·79N 05°36′·33W.

DUNDRUM BAY

St John's Point ☆ 54°13′·61N 05°39′·61W Q (2) 7·5s 37m **25M**; B twr, Y bands. **Auxiliary Light** ☆ Fl WR 3s 14m **W15M**, R11M; same twr, vis: 064°-W-078°-R-shore; Fog Det lt VQ 14m vis: 270°; 992351005.

DZ East Fl (2) Y 10s; 54°12′·05N 05°45′·30W.

DZ West Fl Y 5s; 54°11′·84N 05°50′·82W.

ANNALONG

E Bkwtr Hd ☆ Oc WRG 5s 8m 9M; twr; vis: 204°-G-249°-W-309°-R-024°; 54°06′·51N 05°53′·73W.

KILKEEL

Pier Hd ☆ Fl WR 2s 8m 8M; vis: R296°-W313°-017°; 54°03′·46N 05°59′·30W; 992356010 [emergency AIS 992356008].

CARLINGFORD LOUGH and NEWRY RIVER

Hellyhunter Q(6) + LFl 15s; 54°00′·35N 06°02′·10W; 992351009.

Haulbowline ☆ 54°01′·19N 06°04′·74W Fl (3) 10s 32m 10M; Grey twr; 992501235.

Ldg lts 310·4° Front, Oc 3s 7m 11M; R △ on twr; vis: 295°-325°; 54°01′·80N 06°05′·43W; 992501237. Rear, 457m from front, Oc 3s 12m 11M; R ▽ on twr; vis: 295°-325°; both H24.

Newry River Ldg lts 310·4°. Front, 54°06′·37N 06°16′·51W. Rear, 274m from front. Both Iso 4s 5/15m 2M; stone cols.

DUNDALK

Imogene Fl (2) R 10s; 53°57′·41N 06°07′·02W; 992501238.

Pile Light ☆ 53°58′·56N 06°17′·71W Fl WR 15s 10m 10M; W Ho.

Dunany Fl R 3s; 53°53′·56N 06°09′·47W; 992501243.

SKERRIES BAY

Skerries Pier Hd ☆ Oc R 6s 7m 7M; W col; vis: 103°-R-154°; 53°35′·09N 06°06′·49W

DROGHEDA to LAMBAY ISLAND

Port Approach Dir lt 53°43′·30N 06°14′·73W WRG 10m **W19M, R15M**, G15M; vis: 268°-FG-269°-Al WG-269·5°-FW-270·5°-Al WR-271°-FR-272°; H24.

Balbriggan ☆ Fl (3) WRG 10s 12m W13M, R10M, G10M; W twr; vis: 159°-G-193°-W-288°-R-305°; 53°36′·76N 06°10′·80W.

Rockabill ☆ 53°35′·81N 06°00′·30W Fl WR 12s 45m **W17M, R13M;** W twr, B band; vis: 178°-W-329°-R-178°; 992501246.

Skerries Bay Pier Hd ☆ Oc R 6s 7m 7M; W col; vis: 103°-154°; 53°35′·09N 06°06′·49W.

DISTANCE TABLES

Approx distances in nautical miles are by the most direct route allowing for dangers and TSS.

1	Strangford Lough	1														
2	Bangor	34	2													
3	Carrickfergus	39	6	3												
4	Larne	45	16	16	4											
5	Carnlough	50	25	26	11	5										
6	Portrush	87	58	60	48	35	6									
7	Lough Foyle	92	72	73	55	47	11	7								
8	L Swilly (Fahan)	138	109	104	96	81	48	42	8							
9	Burtonport	153	130	130	116	108	74	68	49	9						
10	Killybegs	204	175	171	163	148	115	109	93	43	10					
11	Sligo	218	189	179	177	156	123	117	107	51	30	11				
12	Eagle Island	234	205	198	193	175	147	136	123	72	62	59	12			
13	Westport	295	266	249	240	226	193	187	168	120	108	100	57	13		
14	Galway	338	309	307	297	284	253	245	227	178	166	163	104	94	14	
15	Kilrush	364	335	332	323	309	276	270	251	203	191	183	142	119	76	15

AREA 11 *West Denmark – Skagen to Rømø*

SELECTED LIGHTS, BUOYS & WAYPOINTS

SKAGEN TO THYBORØN

SKAGEN

Skagen W ☆ Fl (3) WR 10s 31m **W17M**/R12M; 053°-W-248°-R-323°; W ○ twr; 57°44'·94N 10°35·70E.

Skagen ☆ Fl 4s 44m **23M**; Gy ○ twr; ***Racon G, 20M***; 57°44'·14N 10°37'·81E.

Skagen No 1A L Fl 10s; ***Racon N***; 57°43'·46N 10°53'·55E. (Route T)

Skagen No. 2 L Fl 10s; 57°37'·61N 11°05'·51E. (Route T)

Skagens Rev Q; 57°45'·97N 10°43'·74E.

Q (3) 10s; 57°43'·87N 10°42'·31E.

Skagen Harbour, Fl(4)Y10s, 57°42'·55N 10°35'·80E.

E bkwtr ☆ FG 8m 5M; G twr; *Horn (2) 30s*; 57°42'·88N 10°35'·66E.

HIRTSHALS

Hirtshals ☆ F Fl 30s 57m **F 18M**; **Fl 25M**; W ○ twr, approx 1M SSW of hbr ent; 57°35'·10N 09°56'·55E.

Ldg lts 166°, both 156°-176°. Front, Iso R 2s 10m 11M; R △ on twr; 57°35'·69N 09°57'·64E; marina ent is close N of this lt. Rear, Iso R 4s 18m 11M; R ▽ on twr; 330m from front.

Approach chan Fl (3) G 10s; 57°36'·18N 09°56·94E.

Fl R 3s; 57°36'·44N 09°57'·67E.

Fl (5) Y 20s; 57°36'·43N 09°57'·72E.

Fl G 5s; 57°36'·11N 09°57·14E.

Outer W mole ☆ Fl G 3s 14m 6M; G mast; *Horn 15s*; 57°35'·97N 09°57'·37E.

W mole spur ☆ Fl G 5s 9m 4M; G mast; 57°35'·77N 09°57'·51E.

E mole ☆ Fl R 5s 9m 6M; G mast; 57°35'·85N 09°57'·61E.

LØKKEN

Lee bkwtr ☆ Fl 5s 5m 5M; 57°22'·39N 09°42'·11E.

TRANUM STRAND (Firing ranges)

Tranum No. 1 ☆ Al Fl WR 4s 19m W7M, R7M; twr; by day Q 4M; shown when firing in progress; 57°12'·43N 09°30'·34E.

Tranum No. 2 ☆ light as per No.1; 57°10'·57N 09°26'·22E.

LILD STRAND

Bragerne Fl G 5s; 57°10'·67N 08°56'·35E.

Ldg lts 138°, three ☆: F 12/22m 7/8M; 127°-149°; 3 masts. Front 57°09'·22N 08°57'·75E.

HANSTHOLM

Hanstholm ☆ Fl (3) 20s 65m **26M**; shown by day in poor vis; W 8-sided twr; 57°06'·77N 08°35'·92E, approx 1M S of the hbr ent.

Hanstholm LFl 10s; 57°08'·06N 08°34'·87E.

Ldg lts 142·6°, both Iso 2s 37/45m 13M; synch; 127·6°-157·6°; R △ on mast. Front, 57°07'·12N 08°36'·15E. Rear, 170m from front, R ▽ on mast.

Note: The 4 outer/inner mole heads are floodlit.

W outer mole ☆ Fl G 3s 11m 9M; G pillar; 57°07'·56N 08°35'·45E. E outer mole ☆ Fl R 3s 11m 9M; R pillar; 57°07'·61N 08°35'·57E.

Roshage ☆ Fl 5s 7m 5M; 57°07'·75N 08°37'·25E (1M E of hbr).

NØRRE VORUPØR

Mole ☆ Fl G 5s 6m 5M; 56°57'·75N 08°21'·679E.

Ldg lts, both Iso R 4s 20/30m 9M, indicate safest landing place for FVs; vis 22·5° either side of ldg line; synch. Front 57°57'·46N 08°22'·10E. Rear, 80m from front.

Lodbjerg ☆ Fl (2) 20s 48m **23M**; ○ twr; 56°49'·40N 08°15'·76E.

THYBORØN

Landfall L Fl 10s; ***Racon T, 10m***; 56°42'·54N 08°08'·69E.

Agger Tange ldg lts 082°: Front, Iso WRG 4s 8m W11M, R/G8M; 074·5°-G-079·5°-W-084·5°-R-089·5°; R △ on bcn; 56°42'·97N 08°14'·14E. Rear, Iso 4s 17m 11M; 075°-089°; synch; R ▽ on Gy twr; 804m from front.

Off Havmolen 56°43'·25N 08°12'·52E.

Approach ☆ Fl (3) 10s 24m 12M; intens 023·5°-203·5°; also lit by day in poor vis; lattice twr; 56°42'·49N 08°12'·91E (S side of ent).

Langholm ldg lts 120°, both Iso 2s 7/13m 11M; synch; 113°-127°. Front, R △ on R hut, 56°42'·45N 08°14'·54E. Rear, R ▽ on Gy twr.

Thyborøn Havn ☆ Oc (2) WRG 12s 6m W11M, R/G8M; 122·5°-G-146·5°- W-150°- R-211·3°-G-337·5°- W-340°-R-344°; W twr R band; 56°42'·35N 08°13'·39E (680m N of ent to Yderhavn and Basins).

Yderhavn approach ☆ Dir Iso WRG 2s 21m 5M (0.5M by day); 213°-G-218°-W-223°-R-228°; 56°41'·85N 08°13'·32E

N mole ☆ Fl G 3s 6m 4M; G pedestal; 56°42'·02N 08°13'·52E.

S mole ☆ Fl R 3s 6m 4M; R pedestal; 56°41'·97N 08°13'·53E.

LIMFJORD (Limited coverage E, only to 08°42'E)

Sælhundeholm Løb, into Nissum Bredning ('Broad').

No. 1 Fl (2) G 5s; 56°41'·14N 08°14'·17E.

No. 3 Fl G 3s; 56°40'·75N 08°13'·79E.

No. 7 Fl G 3s; 56°40'·31N 08°13'·52E.

No. 11 Fl G 3s; 56°39'·83N 08°13'·59E.

No. 16 Fl R 3s; 56°38'·51N 08°13'·89E.

No. 18 Fl (2) R 5s; 56°38'·20N 08°14'·34E.

No. 21 Fl G 3s; 56°38'·98N 08°14'·71E.

No. 26 Fl R 3s; 56°38'·71N 08°15'·38E.

No. 29 Fl G 3s; 56°38'·40N 08°15'·94E.

APPROACHES TO LEMVIG (Marina and Havn)

Toftum Dir ☆ 120°, Iso WRG 4s 24m, W12M, R/G 8M; 110°-G-120°-W-137°-R-144°; hut; 56°33'·09N 08°18'·33E.

Rønnen Fl G 3s; 56°36'·71N 08°21'·74E.

Rønnen L Fl 10s; 56°35'·58N 08°21'·62E.

Søgard Mark ldg lts 243·5°: both FR 20/30m 5M; vis 90° either side of ldg line. Front, R △ on W bcn; 56°34'·39N 08°17'·29E. Rear, R ▽ on W post; 235m from front.

Chan 56°33'·27N 08°18'·31E.

Ldg lts, W of hbr 177·7°, both FR 8/20m 5M; 153°-203°. Front R △ on twr; 56°33'·04N 08°18'·16E. Rear, R ▽ on W post; 184m from front.

Vinkel Hage Marina, N mole ☆ FG 3m 5M; 56°33'·09N 08°18'·33E.

S mole, FR 3m 4M. Marina is 9ca N of the Havn on the W side.

Ostre Havn ⸸ 56°33'·17N 08°18'·40E. Havn ent, FG/FR 4m 5M.

THISTED HAVN (Marina)

Outer W mole ☆ Fl R 3s 4m 2M; 56°57'·10N 08°41'·90E.

Outer E mole ☆ Fl G 3s 4m 2M; 56°57'·10N 08°41'·95E.

Thisted Bredning ☆ Aero 3 Fl R 1·5s (vert; 45m apart) 183m 10M; TV mast; 56°58'·52N 08°41'·15E, 1·55M NNW of hbr ent.

THYBORØN TO BLÅVANDS HUK

Bovbjerg ☆ Fl (2) 15s 62m 16M; 56°30'·79N 08°07'·18E.

Wave recorder buoy Fl (5) Y 20s; 56°28'·49N 08°03'·35E.

THORSMINDE HAVN

(All Lat/Longs for this harbour are approximate)

Lt ho ☆ F 30m 13M; Gy twr; 56°22'·34N 08°06'·99E.

Groyne, N ☆ Fl 5s 8m 5M; Gy hut; 56°22'·46N 08°06'·82E.

N mole ☆ Iso R 2s 9m 4M; R hut; 56°22'·36N 08°06'·62E.

S mole ☆ Iso G 2s 9m 4M; G hut; 56°22'·26N 08°06'·92E.

West hbr, W mole ☆ FG 5m 2M; Gy post; 56°22'·36N 08°07'·12E.

E mole ☆ FR 5m 2M; Gy post; 56°22'·26N 08°07'·18E.

NW dolphin ☆ FG 5m 4M; Gy post; 56°22'·26N 08°07'·22E.

SE dolphin ☆ FG 5m 4M; Gy post; 56°22' 26N 08°07' 26E.

Lock, E side ☆ Iso 4s 12m 4M; Gy mast; 020°-160°; 56°22'·36N 08°07'·22E.

Road bridge ☆ Iso 4s 5m 4M; 200°-340°; 56°22'·36N 08°07'·26E.

HVIDE SANDE

Lyngvig ☆ Fl 5s 53m **23M** (may have Y tint); W ○ twr; 56°02'·99N 08°06'·22E.

N outer bkwtr ☆ Fl R 3s 7m 8M; R hut; 55°59'·94N 08°06'·55E.

N mole ☆ Fl R 5s 10m 6·5M; R floodlit edifice; 55°59'·98N 08°06'· 84E.

S mole ☆ Fl G 5s 10m 6M; 55°59'·96N 08°06'·98E.

Lt ho ☆ F 27m 14M; Gy twr; 56°00'·00N 08°07'·35E.

Nordhavn, E pier ☆ FG 4m 4M; 56°00'·16N 08°07'·42E.

W pier ☆ 2 FR 3m 2M; W posts; 060°-035°; 56°00'·07N 08°07'·12E.

Sydhavn, W pier ☆ FG 4m 2M; 56°00'·06N 08°07'·52E.

E Pier ☆ FR 4m 2M; Gy post; 56°00'·06N 08°07'·53E.

Lock entrance ldg lts 293·5°: both FR 11/14m 2M; 201·6°-021·6°. Front, R △ on Gy tr, 56°00'·0N 08°07'·8E. Rear, R ▽ on Gy twr, 72m from front.

Fjordhavn ldg lts 246·6° (both vis 7·5° either side of ldg line): Front, Iso G 2s 4m 4M; Or △ on mast; 56°00'·5N 08°07'·9E. Rear, Iso G 4s 6m 4M, Or ▽ on mast, 128m from front.

HORNS REV (marks westward from coast)

Oskbøl firing range. Two lights (4M apart) both AlFl WR 4s 35m **16M**, R13M, (by day Q 10M) are shown when firing is in progress: North ☆ 55°37'·24N 08°07'·04E. South ☆ 55°33'·53N 08°04'·67E.

Range safety buoys: Fl Y 5s; 55°42'·32N 08°06'·92E. Fl Y 3s; 55°38'·63N 07°50'·91E. Fl Y 3s; 55°37'·35N 07°56'·98E. 55°36'·02N 08°02'·49E.

Blåvands Huk ☆ Fl (3) 20s 55m **23M;** W □ twr; 55°33'·46N 08°04'·95E.

Horns Rev is encircled by:

Tuxen Q; 55°34'·22N 07°41'·92E on the N side.

Vyl Q (6) + L Fl 15s; 55°26'·22N 07°49'·99E on the S side.

No. 2 L Fl 10s; 55°28'·74N 07°36'·49E on the SW side.

Horns Rev W Q (9) 15s; 55°34'·47N 07°26'·05E, off the W end.

Slugen Channel (crosses Horns Rev ESE/WNW)

L Fl G 10s; 55°33'·99N 07°49'·38E.

Fl G 3s; 55°32'·26N 07°53'·65E.

Fl (2) R 5s; 55°31'·46N 07°52'·88E.

Fl (2) G 5s; 55°30'·52N 07°59'·20E.

Fl (3) R 10s; 55°29'·42N 08°02'·56E.

Søren Bovbjergs Dyb (unlit N/S side channel off Slugen Chan)

55°33'·57N 07°55'·55E.

55°32'·80N 07°55'·30E.

55°32'·19N 07°56'·29E.

55°31'·24N 07°57'·46E.

Horns Rev 1 wind farm, 2.7M x 2.5M, centred on 55°29'·22N 07° 50'·21E: 80 turbines all R lts, 12 perimeter turbines Fl (3) Y 10s. NE turbine, ***Racon (U);*** 55°30'·28N 07°52'·63E. Platform 2 x Mo (U) 15s 15m 5M; 55°30'·52N 07°52'·52E. SW turbine ***Racon (U)***, 55° 28'·11N 07°48'·26E.

Horns Rev 2 wind farm, 2M x 6M, centred on 55° 36 08N 07° 34 78E: 91 turbines, all R lts, 14 perimeter turbines Fl (3) Y 10s. NW turbine ***Racon (U)***; 55° 38 88N 07° 35 55E. Platform 2 x Mo (U) 15s 5M; 55° 35 99N 07° 37 37E.

BLÅVANDS HUK TO RØMØ

APPROACHES TO ESBJERG

Grådyb L Fl 10s; ***Racon G, 10M***; 55°24'·63N 08°11'·59E.

Sædding Strand 053·8° triple ldg lts: valid up to Nos 7/8 buoys; H24: **Front** Iso 2s 13m **21M**; 052°-056°; R bldg; 55°29'·74N 08°23'·87E.

Middle Iso 4s 26m **21M**; 051°-057°; R twr, W bands; 55°29'·94N 08°24'·33E, 630m from front.

Rear F 37m **18M**; 052°-056°; R twr; 55°30'·18N 08°24'·92E, 0·75M from front.

No. 1 Q; 55°25'·49N 08°13'·89E.

No. 2 Fl (3) R 10s; 55°25'·62N 08°13'·73E.

No. 3 Fl G 3s; 55°25'·93N 08°14'·84E.

No. 4 Fl R 3s; 55°26'·02N 08°14'·72E.

Tide Gauge ☆ Fl (5) Y 20s 8m 4M; 55°26'·05N 08°15'·93E.

No. 5 Fl G 5s; 55°26'·32N 08°15'·83E.

No. 6 Fl R 5s; 55°26'·44N 08°15'·70E.

No. 7 Q; 55°26'·76N 08°16'·91E.

No. 8 Fl (2) R 5s; 55°26'·89N 08°16'·81E.

Ldg lts 067°, valid up to Nos 9/10 buoys. Both FG 10/25m **16M**, H24. Front, Gy tripod; rear, Gy twr, 55°28'·76N 08°24'·70E.

No. 9 Fl (2) G 10s; 55°27'·04N 08°18'·21E.

No.10 Fl (2) R 10s; 55°27'·20N 08°18'·04E.

Ldg lts 049°, valid up to No 16 buoy/Jerg. Both FR 16/27m **16M**, H24. Front, W twr; rear, Gy twr, 55°29'·92N 08°23'·75E.

No. 11 Fl G 3s; 55°27'·71N 08°19'·59E.

No. 12 Fl R 3s; 55°27'·88N 08°19'·39E.

No. 13 Fl G 5s; 55°28'·40N 08°20'·99E.

No. 14 Fl R 5s; 55°28'·57N 08°20'·73E.

Jerg ☆ Fl G 3s 7m 5M; G twr, Y base; 55°28'·88N 08°22'·00E.

No. 16 Q (6) + L Fl 15s; 55°29′·04N 08°21′·80E.
No. 15A Fl (2) G 5s; 55°29′·01N 08°22′·47E.
No 18 Fl (2) R 5s; 55°29′·19N 08°22′·71E.
Fovrfelt N ☆ Oc (2) WRG 6s 7m W6M, R/G4M; 066·5°-G-073°-W-077°-R-085·5°; 327°-G-331°- W-333·5°-R-342°; Y twr; 55°29′·29N 08°23′·79E.
Fovrfelt ☆ Fl (2) R 10s 11m 6M; R twr; 55°29′·03N 08°23′·75E.
No 15B Fl (2) G 10s; 55°28′·83N 08°23′·65E.

ESBJERG HAVN

Strandby, shelter mole, NW corner ☆ Oc WRG 5s 6m W13M, R/G9M; 101·7°-G-105·5°-W-109·5°-R-111·7°; W bldg, R band; 55°28′·76N 08°24′·63E.
Industrifiskerihavn, W mole ☆ Fl R 5s 6m 4M; R structure; 55°28′·57N 08°24′·89E.
E mole ☆ Fl G 5s 7m 4M; G structure; 55°28′·52N 08°25′·03E.
Nordsøkai Q (9) 15s 5m; Y twr, B band; 55°28′·45N 08°25′·04E.
Konsumfiskerihavn, W mole ☆ FlR 3s 6m; 203°-119°; R twr; 55°28′·31N 08°25′·33E. Yacht hbr in SSE part of Basin II.
E mole ☆ Fl G 3s 6m; 023°-256°; G tr; 55°28·31N 08°25·40E.
Trafikhavn, NW corner, ☆ Oc (2) WRG 12s 6m W11M, R/G8M; 118°-G-124·5°-W-129°-R-131°; W bldg, R band; 55°28·22N 08°25·43E.
N mole ☆ FR 8m 5M; 232°-135°; R bldg; 55°28′·13N 08°25′·46E.
S mole ☆ FG 8m 4M; 045°-276°; G bldg; 55°28′·08N 08°25′·51E.
No. 22 Fl (2) R 5s; 55°27′·62N 08°25′·50E.
Sønderhavn (industrial) W mole ☆ FR 9m 4M; 55°27′·49N 08°26′·12E. E mole ☆ FG 9m 4M; 55°27′·43N 08°26′·31E.
Aero ☆ 3 x Fl 1·5s (vert, 82m apart) 251m 12M, H24; on chimney; 55°27′·27N 08°27′·32E (1200m ESE of Sønderhavn ent).

FANØ

Slunden outer ldg lts 242°, both Iso 2s 5/8m 3M; 227°-257°. Front, twr; 55°27′·20N 08°24′·53E. Rear, twr, 106m from front.
E shore, reciprocal ldg lts 062°, both FR 10/13m 3M; 047°-077°. Front, twr; 55°27′·65N 08°26′·01E. Rear, twr, 140m from front.
No. 1 ☆ Fl (2) G l0s 5m 2M; G pile; 55°27′·45N 08°25′·28E.
No. 2 ☆ Fl (2+1) Y 5s 5m 2M; Y pile; 55°27′·42N 08°25′·32E.
No. 3 ☆ Fl G 3s 5m 2M; G pile; 55°27′·39N 08°25′·07E.
No. 4 ☆ Fl R 3s 5m 2M; R pile; 55°27′·35N 08°25′·10E.
Nordby ldg lts 214°, both FR 7/9m 4M; 123·7°-303·7°. Front, W mast;55°26′·94N 08°24′·44E. Rear, Gy twr, 84m from front.-Kremer Sand ☆ FG 5m 3M; G dolphin; 55°27′·3N 08°24′·9E.
Næs Søjord ☆ FR 5m 3M; R pile; 55°27′·27N 08°24′·86E.
Nordby marina 55°26′·65N 08°24′·53E.

KNUDEDYB

G 55°20′·50N 08°24′·28E.
K 55°18′·92N 08°20′·06E.
No. 2 55°18′·82N 08°21′·33E.
No. 4 55°18′·81N 08°22′·21E.
No. 6 55°18′·38N 08°24′·63E.
No. 10 55°18′·68N 08°28′·50E.
Knoben 55°18′·71N 08°30′·60E.

JUVRE DYB

No. 4 55°13′·76N 08°24′·73E.
No. 6 55°13′·41N 08°26′·60E.
No. 8 55°12′·69N 08°26′·83E.
No. 10 55°12′·55N 08°28′·72E.
Rejsby Stjært 55°13′·15N 08°30′·55E.

OUTER APPROACH (Lister Tief) TO RØMØ

See also Area 15 for details of lights on Sylt.
Rode Klit Sand, Recording stn Fl (3) Y 15s, 55°08′·40N 08°07′·25E.
Lister Tief Iso 8s, *Whis;* 55°05′·32N 08°16′·80E.
No. 1 55°05′·48N 08°18′·50E.
No. 3 Fl G 4s; 55°05′·36E 08°20′·14E.
No. 2 Fl (3) R 10s; 55°04′·23N 08°22′·32E.
No. 9 Fl (2) G 9s; 55°03′·76N 08°23′·05E.
Lister Landtief No 5 55°03′·68N 08°24′·73E.
No. 4 FL (2) R 5s; 55°03′·84N 08°25′·29E.
G1 Fl Y 4s; 55°03′·27N 08°28′·32E.

RØMØ DYB and HAVN

No. 1 Fl (2) G 10s; 55°03′·23N 08°30′·30E.
No. 10 ☆ Fl (2) R 10s 5m 3M; R pole; 55°03′·50N 08°31′·10E.
No. 14 ☆ Fl R 3s 6m 2M; R pole; 55°03′·85N 08°32′·55E.
No. 20 ☆ Fl R 5s 5m 2M; R pole; 55°04′·79N 08°34′·13E.
No. 9 55°04′·79N 08°34′·63E.
No. 11 55°05′·17N 08°34′·69E.
Rømø Hbr:
S mole ☆ Fl R 3s 7m 2M; Gy twr; 55°05′·19N 08°34′·31E.
N mole ☆ Fl G 3s 7m 2M; Gy twr; 55°05′·23N 08°34′·30E.
Inner S mole ☆ FR 4m 1M; 55°05′·2N 08°34′·2E.

1	Skagen	**1**																	
2	Hirtshals	33	**2**																
3	Hanstholm	85	52	**3**															
4	Thyborłn	114	84	32	**4**														
5	Torsminde	141	108	56	24	**5**													
6	Hvide Sande	162	179	77	45	24	**6**												
7	Esbjerg	200	174	122	90	76	54	**7**											
8	Fanł	210	177	125	93	79	57	3	**8**										
9	Rłmł	233	200	148	116	94	73	30	33	**9**									
10	H rnum	248	215	163	131	108	86	70	73	29	**10**								
11	Husum	275	247	195	163	152	131	95	98	68	45	**11**							
12	Kiel/Holtenau	261	233	281	249	232	208	180	183	189	126	129	**12**						
13	Bremerhaven	306	285	233	201	185	163	127	129	107	83	82	123	**13**					
14	Wilhelmshaven	414	296	242	310	184	162	125	128	106	82	82	123	45	**14**				
15	Helgoland	259	238	186	154	141	119	83	85	63	39	47	104	44	43	**15**			
16	Cuxhaven	304	284	232	200	162	138	110	113	85	56	66	70	58	56	38	**16**		
17	Wangerooge	283	262	210	178	168	147	109	112	94	68	52	108	38	27	24	42	**17**	
18	Hamburg	338	317	265	233	216	192	163	167	139	99	113	90	81	110	88	54	61	**18**

DISTANCE TABLES

Approx distances in nautical miles are by the most direct route allowing for dangers and TSS.

AREA 12 *Germany (North Sea coast) – List to Emden*

SELECTED LIGHTS, BUOYS & WAYPOINTS

DANISH BORDER TO BÜSUM

SYLT

Lister Tief Iso 8s; *Whis;* 55°05'·33N 08°16'·79E.
List West (Ellenbogen) ☆ Oc WRG 6s 19m W14M, R11M, G10M; 040°-R-133°-W-227°-R-266·4°-W-268°-G-285°-W-310°- W(unintens)-040°; W twr, R lantern; 55°03'·15N 08°24'·00E.
List Hafen, S mole ☆ FR 5m 4M; 218°-353°; R mast; 55°01'·01N 08°26'·51E.
Hörnum ☆ Fl (2) 9s 48m **20M**; 54°45'·23N 08°17'·47E.
Vortrapptief Iso 4s; 54°34'·80N 08°14'·36E, toward Hörnum.
S mole ☆ FR 7m 4M; 54°45'·57N 08°17'·97E.

AMRUM ISLAND

Rütergat Iso 8s; 54°30'·08N 08°12'·32E.
Amrum ☆ Fl 7·5s 63m **23M**; R twr, W bands; 54°37'·84N 08°21'·23E.
Wriakhorn Cross ☆ L Fl (2) WR 15s 26m W9M, R7M; 297·5°-W-319·5°-R-330°-W-005·5°-R-034°; 54°37'·62N 08°21'·22E.

FÖHR ISLAND

Nieblum Dir lt showing over Rütergat. ☆ Oc (2) WRG 10s 11m **W19M, R/G15M**; 028°-G-031°-W-032·5°-R-035·5°; R twr, W band; 54°41'·10N 08°29'·20E.
Ohlörn ☆ Oc (4) WR 15s 10m 13/10M, 208°-W-237·5°-R-298°- W-353°- R-080°; R twr, Gy lantern; 54°40'·85N 08°34'·00E (SE Föhr).
Wyk Hbr outer ent, FR 54°41'·55N 08°34'·69E; and FG.

DAGEBÜLL

Dagebüll Iso WRG 8s 23m **W18M, R/G15M**; 042°-G-043°-W-044·5°- R-047°; 54°43'·82N 08°41'·43E. FW lts on ent moles.

LANGENESS ISLAND

Nordmarsch ☆ L Fl (3) WR 20s 13m W14M, R11M; 268°-W-279°-R-306°-W-045°-R-070°-W-218°; dark brown twr; 54°37'·58N 08°31'·85E.

SCHLÜTTSIEL

No. 2/SA 26 54°36'·84N 08°38'·95E. Hbr ent ▲ 54°40'·89N 08°45'·10E.

RIVER HEVER

Hever Iso 4s; *Whis;* 54°20'·41N 08°18'·82E.
Westerheversand ☆ Oc (3) WRG 15s 41m **W21M, R17M, G16M**; 012·2°-W-069°-G-079·5°-W-080·5° (ldg sector for Hever)-R-107°-W-233°-R-248°; R twr, W bands; 54°22'·37N 08°38'·36E.
Norderhever No. 1 Fl (2+1) R 15s; 54°22'·46N 08°30'·83E.

PELLWORM ISLAND

Pellworm ☆ Oc WRG 5s 38m **20M, R 16M, G 15M**; 037·5°-G-040°-W-042·5°-R-045°; R twr, W band; 54°29'·78N 08°39'·98E.

NORDSTRAND

Suderhafen, S mole 54°28'·07N 08°55'·62E.

HUSUM

Fl G 4s, 54°28'·80N 08°58'·60E, start of access chan. Ldg lts 090°, both Iso G 8s 7/9m 3M.

RIVER EIDER

Eider Iso 4s; 54°15'·70N 08° 29'·20E.
St Peter ☆ L Fl (2) WR 15s 23m **W15M**, R12M; 271°-R-280·5°-W-035°-R-055°-W-068°-R-091°-W-120°; 54°17'·24N 08°39'·10E.
Eiderdamm lock, N mole, W end ☆ Oc (2) R 12s 8m 5M; W twr.

BÜSUM

Süderpiep Iso 8s; *Whis;* 54°05'·82N 08°25'·70E.
Büsum ☆ Iso WR 6s 22m **W19M**, R12M; 248°-W-317°-R-024°-W-148°; 54°07'·60N 08°51'·48E.
E mole ☆ Oc (3) G 12s 10m 4M; vis 260°-168°; G twr; 54°07'·19N 08°51'·65E.

GERMAN BIGHT TO RIVER ELBE

GB Light V Iso 8s 12m **17M**; R hull marked G-B; *Horn Mo (R) 30s*; 54°09'·89N 06°20'·84E.

HELGOLAND

Helgoland ☆ Fl 5s 82m **28M**; brown □ twr, B lantern, W balcony; 54°10'·91N 07°52'·93E.
Vorhafen. Ostmole, S elbow ☆ Oc WG 6s 5m W6M, G3M; 203°-W-250°-G-109°; G post; fog det lt; 54°10'·31N 07°53'·94E.

RIVER ELBE (LOWER)

APPROACHES

Nordergründe N VQ; 53°57'·06N 08°00'·12E.
Elbe Iso 10s; ***Racon T, 8M;*** 53°59'·95N 08°06'·49E.
No.1 QG; 53°59'·21N 08°13'·20E.
No.25 QG; 53°56'·62N 08°38'·25E.
Neuwerk ☆, S side, L Fl (3) WRG 20s 38m **W16M**, R12M, G11M; 165·3°-G-215·3°-W-238·8°-R-321°; 343°-R-100°; 53°54'·92N 08°29'·73E.

CUXHAVEN

No. 31 Fl G 4s; 53°53'·93N 08°41'·21E.
Yacht hbr ent, F WR and F WG lts; 53°52'·43N 08°42'·49E.

OTTERNDORF

No. 43 Oc (2) G 9s; 53°50'·23N 08°52'·24E.
Otterndorf 3 Fl (3) G 12s; 53°50'·22N 08°53'·94E.

BRUNSBÜTTEL

No. 57a Fl G 4s; 53°52'·62N 09°07'·93E, 030°/ 8 cables to lock.
Alter Vorhafen ent, mole 1 ☆ F WG 14m W10M, G6M; 266·3°-W-273·9°-G-088·8°, floodlit; 53°53'·27N 09°08'·59E.

RIVER ELBE (BRUNSBÜTTEL TO HAMBURG)

Some of the more accessible yacht hbrs are listed below, but not the many ldg lts and dir lts which define the main river fairway.

FREIBURG

Reede 1 Oc (2) Y 9s; 53°50'·41N 09°19'·45E, off ent.

STÖRLOCH

Stör ldg lts 093·8°, both Fl 3s 7/12m 6M; synch. Front, 53°49'·29N 09°23'·91E; △ on R ○ twr. Rear, 200m east; ▽ on white mast.

GLÜCKSTADT

Glückstadt ldg lts 131·8°, both Iso 8s 15/30m **19/21M**; intens on ldg line; W twrs, R bands. **Front** ☆, 53°48′·31N 09°24′·24E. **Rear** ☆, 0·68M from front.

Rhinplatte Nord ☆ Oc WRG 6s 11m W6M, R4M, G3M; 122°-G-144°-W-150°-R-177°- W-122°; 53°48′·09N 09°23′·36E.

N mole ☆ Dir Oc WRG 6s 9m W9M R7M, G6M; 330°-R-343°-W-346°-G-008°; 123°-G-145°-W-150°-R-170°; W twr with gallery; 53°47′·12N 09°24′·53E.

N pier hd ☆ FR 5m 5M; 53°47′·10N 09°24′·50E. (S mole hd, FG).

KRUCKAU

S mole Oc WRG 6s 8m, W6M, R4M, G3M; 116·3°-W-120·7° (ldg sector)-R-225°-G-315°-R-331·9°-W-335·4° (ldg sector)-335·4°-G-116·3°; B dolphin; 53°42′·85N 09°30′·72E.

PINNAU

Ldg lts 112·7°, both Iso 4s8/13m 6M. Front, 53°40′·08N 09°34′·02E.

STADE

Stadersand ☆ Iso 8s 20m 14M; 53°37′·69N 09°31′·64E (ent).

HAMBURG YACHT HARBOUR, WEDEL

Both entrances show FR & FG, May to Oct; 53°34′·25N 09°40′·77E.

CITY SPORTHAFEN

Brandenburger Hafen Ent ☆ Iso Or 2s; 53°32′·52N 09°58′·81E.

WESER ESTUARY

ALTE WESER

Schlüsseltonne Iso 8s; 53°56′·25N 07°54′·76E.

Alte Weser ☆ F WRG 33m **W23M, R19M, G18M**; 288°-W-352°-R-003°-W-017° (ldg sector for Alte Weser)- G-045°-W-074°-G-118°- W-123° (ldg sector for Alte Weser)- R-140°-G-175°-W-183°-R-196°-W-238°; R ○ twr, 2 W bands, B base; Fog det lt; *Horn Mo (AL) 60s;* 53°51′·79N 08°07′·65E.

16/A15 Fl (2+1) R 15s; 53°49′·66N 08°06′·44E (junction with Neuwe Weser).

NEUE WESER

Tegeler Plate, N end ☆ Oc (3) WRG 12s 21m **W21M, R17M, G16M**; 329°-W-340°-R-014°-W-100°-G-116°- W-119° (ldg sector for Neue Weser)-R-123°-G-144°-W-147° (ldg sector for Alte Weser)-R-264°; R ○ twr, gallery, W lantern, R roof; Fog det lt; 53°47′·87N 08°11′·45E.

BREMERHAVEN

No. 61 QG; 53°32′·26N 08°33′·93E (Km 66·0).

Vorhafen N pier ☆ FR 15m 5M; 245°-166°; F in fog; 53°32′·15N 08°34′·50E.

RIVER JADE

1b/Jade1 Oc G 4s; 53°52′·40N 07°44′·02E.

Mellumplate ☆ FW 28m **24M**; 116·1°-116·4° (ldg sector for outer part of Wangerooger Fahrwasser); R □ twr, W band; 53°46′·28N 08°05′·51E.

No.19 QG; 53°47′·10N 08°01′·83E.

No. 31/P-Reede/W Siel 1 Oc (3) G 12s; 53°41′·59N 08°04′·51E.

HOOKSIEL

No. 37/Hooksiel 1 IQ G 13s; 53°39′·37N 08°06′·58E.

Vorhafen ent ☆ L Fl R 6s 9m 3M; 53°38′·63N 08°05′·25E.

WILHELMSHAVEN

Fluthafen N mole ☆ F WG 9m,W6M, G3M; 216°-W-280°-G-010°-W-020°-G-130°; G twr; 53°30′·86N 08°09′·32E.

EAST FRISIAN ISLANDS

NORTH EDGE OF INSHORE TRAFFIC ZONE

TG9/Weser 2 Fl (2+1) G 15s; 53°55′·0N 07°44′·60E.

TG13 Oc (3) G 12s; 53°50′·85N 07°15′·43E.

TG7 Fl (2) G 9s; 53°47′·24N 06°49′·65E.

TG1 Oc (3) G 12s; 53°44′·90N 06°33′·20E.

WANGEROOGE

Harle Iso 8s; 53°49′·25N 07°50′·47E.

Wangerooge, W end ☆ Fl R 5s 60m **23M**; R ○ twr, 2 W bands; 53°47′·40N 07°51′·37E.

Dir lt 145·5°, Dir WRG 24m W22M G18M R17M; 119·4°-G-138·8°-W-152·2°-R-159·9°.

Buhne H VQ (9) 10s; 53°46′·86N 07°49′·65E.

W2 ; 53°46′·25N 07°51′·89E, off hbr ent.

SPIEKEROOG

Otzumer Balje Iso 4s; 53°48′·29N 07°38′·00E (often moved).

Spiekeroog ☆ FR 6m 4M; 197°-114°; R mast; 53°45′·0N 07°41′·3E.

LANGEOOG

Accumer Ee Iso 8s; 53°46·92N 07°25·92E (often moved).

W mole head ☆ Oc WRG 6s 8m W7M, R5M, G4M; 064°-G-070°-W-074°-R-326°-W-330°-G-335°-R-064°; R basket on R mast; *Horn Mo (L) 30s* (0730-1800LT); 53°43′·42N 07°30′·13E.

BALTRUM

Groyne hd ☆ Oc WRG 6s 6m; W6M, R4M, G3M; 074·5°-G-090°-W-095°-R-074·5°; 53°43′·3N 07°21′·7E.

DISTANCE TABLES

Approx distances in nautical miles are by the most direct route allowing for dangers and TSS.

1	Esbjerg	1																
2	H rnum Lt (Sylt)	47	2															
3	Husum	95	48	3														
4	Hamburg	163	112	113	4													
5	Kiel/Holtenau	179	128	129	90	5												
6	Brunsb ttel	126	75	76	37	53	6											
7	Cuxhaven	110	63	66	54	70	17	7										
8	Bremerhaven	127	80	82	81	131	78	58	8									
9	Wilhelmshaven	125	78	82	110	123	70	56	45	9								
10	Hooksiel	116	69	73	101	117	64	47	36	9	10							
11	Helgoland	83	38	47	88	104	51	38	44	43	35	11						
12	Wangerooge	109	60	52	61	108	55	42	38	27	19	24	12					
13	Langeoog	119	72	77	114	130	77	60	47	43	34	35	21	13				
14	Norderney	123	77	85	81	137	84	69	62	53	44	44	29	18	14			
15	Emden	165	129	137	174	190	137	120	115	106	97	85	80	63	47	15		
16	Borkum	133	97	105	104	163	110	95	88	80	71	67	55	46	31	32	16	
17	Delfzijl	155	119	127	159	173	120	105	100	89	83	81	65	56	41	10	22	17
18	Den Helder	187	192	198	229	245	192	175	180	159	150	153	148	130	115	125	95	115	18

NORDERNEY

Norderney ☆ Fl (3) 12s 59m **23M**; unintens 067°-077° and 270°-280°; R 8-sided twr; 53°42'·54N 07°13'·79E.
Dovetief Iso 4s; 53°45'·47N 07°12'·70E.
Schluchter Iso 8s; 53°44'·80N 07°06'·00E.
W mole head ☆ Oc (2) R 9s 13m 4M; 53°41'·9N 07°09'·9E.

JUIST

Juist-N VQ; 53°43'·82N 06°55'·42E.
Training wall, S end ☆ Oc (2) R 9s 7m 3M; 53°39'·65N 06°59'·81E.

MAINLAND HARBOURS: R. JADE TO R. EMS

HARLESIEL

Carolinensieler Balje, Leitdamm ☆ L Fl 8s 7m 6M; G mast; 53°44'·13N 07°50'·10E.
Ldg lts 138°, both Iso 6s 12/18m 9M, intens on ldg line; Front 53°40'·70N 07°34'·50E. Rear 167m from front.
N mole head ☆ Iso R 4s 6m 7M; 53°42'·58N 07°48'·64E.

NEUHARLINGERSIEL

Training wall head ☆ Oc 6s 6m 5M; 53°43'·22N 07°42'·30E.

BENSERSIEL

E training wall head ☆ Oc WRG 6s 6m W5M, R3M, G2M; 110°-G-119°-W-121°-R-110°; R post & platform; 53° 41'·80N 07°32'·84E.

DORNUMER-ACCUMERSIEL

W bkwtr head, approx 53°41'·04N 07°29'·30E.

NESSMERSIEL

N mole head ☆ Oc 4s 6m 5M; G mast; 53°41'·9N 07°21'·7E.

NORDDEICH

W trng wall head ☆ FG 8m 4M, 021°-327°; G framework twr; 53°38'·62N 07°09'·0E.

GREETSIEL

Meßstation lt bcn, Fl Y 4s 15m 3M; 53°32'·94N 07°02'·18E.

RIVER EMS

APPROACHES

GW/EMS Iso 8s 14m **17M** (H24); Emergency Lt, FR, occas. 2 FR vert; R Lt vessel, floodlit; *Horn Mo (R) 30s (H24);* 54°09'·98N 06°20'· 85E.
Borkumriff Oc 4s; 53°47'·48N 06°22'·27E.
Osterems Iso 4s; 53°41'·91N 06°36'·17E.
Riffgat Iso 8s; 53°38'·96N 06°27'·10E.
Westerems Iso 4s; 53°36'·93N 06°19'·39E.
H1 53°34'·91N 06°17'·97E.

BORKUM

Borkum Grosser ☆ Fl (2) 12s 63m **24M**; brown ○ twr; 53°35'·32N 06°39'·64E. Same twr, ☆ F WRG 46m **W19M, R/G15M;** 107·4°-G-109°-W-111·2°- R-112·6°.
Fischerbalje ☆ Oc (2) 16s 15m 3M; 260°-W-123°. Fog det lt; R/W ○ twr on tripod; 53°33'·18N 06°42'·90E.
Schutzhafen, E mole hd ☆ FG10m 4M; 53°33'·48N 06°45'·02E. W mole hd, FR 8m 4M.

RIVER EMS (LOWER)

No. 27 Fl G 4s; 53°30'·24N 06°47'·52E.
No. 35 Fl G 4s; 53°27'·03N 06°52'·80E.
No. 37 QG; 53°26'·01N 06°54'·85E.
No. 41 Fl (2) G 9s; 53°24'·25N 06°56'·68E.
No. 49 Oc (2) G 9s; 53°19'·95N 06°59'·71E.

KNOCK

Knock ☆ F WRG 28m W12M,R9M, G8M; 270°-W-299°-R-008·3°-G-023°-W-026·8°-R-039°-W-073°-R-119°-W-154°; fog det lt; Gy twr, white conical radar antenna; 53°20'·32N 07°01'·40E.

EMDEN

No. 59 Oc (2) G 9s; 53°19'·41N 07°03'·86E.
No. 65 Fl (2) G 9s; 53°19'·82N 07°06'·56E.
Outer hbr, W pier ☆ FR 10m 4M; R 8-sided twr; *Horn Mo (ED) 30s;* 53°20'·06N 07°10'·49E.
E pier ☆ FG 7m 5M; G mast on pedestal; 53°20'·05N 07°10'·84E.

AREA 13 *Netherlands & Belgium – Delfzijl to Nieuwpoort*

SELECTED LIGHTS, BUOYS & WAYPOINTS

TSS OFF NORTHERN NETHERLANDS

TERSCHELLING-GERMAN BIGHT TSS

TG1/Ems IQ G 13s; 53°43'·33N 06°22'·24E.
TE5 Fl (3) G 10s; 53°37'·79N 05°53'·69E.
TE1 Fl (3) G 10s; 53°29'·58N 05°11'·31E.

OFF VLIELAND TSS

VL-CENTER Fl 5s 12M*; **Racon C, 12–15M;*** 53°26'·93N 04°39'·88E. VL7 L Fl G 10s; 53°26'·40N 04°57'·60E.
VL1 Fl (2) G 10s; 53°10'·96N 04°35'·31E.

DELFZIJL TO HARLINGEN

DELFZIJL

PS3/BW26 Fl (2+1) G 12s; 53°19'·25N 07°00'·32E.
W mole ☆ FG; 53°19'·01N 07°00'·27E.
Ldg lts 203° both Iso 4s. Front, 53°18'·63N 07°00'·17E.

SCHIERMONNIKOOG AND LAUWERSOOG

WG (Westgat) Iso 8s; ***Racon N;*** 53°32'·55N 06°00'·70E.
WRG Q; 53°32'·87N 06°03'·24E.
AM VQ; 53°30'·95N 05°44'·72E.
Schiermonnikoog ☆ Fl (4) 20s 43m **28M**; dark R ○ twr. Same twr: F WR 29m **W15M,** R12M; 210°-W-221°-R-230°. 53°29'·20N 06°08'·79E.
Lauwersoog W mole ☆ FG; *Horn (2) 30s;* 53°24'·68N 06°12'·00E.

ZEEGAT VAN AMELAND

BR Q; 53°30'·66N 05°33'·52E.
TS VQ; 53°28'·15N 05°21'·53E.
WA 53°28'·35N 05°28'·64E. (Westgat buoys all unlit)
Ameland, W end ☆ Fl (3) 15s 57m **30M;** 53°26'·89N 05°37'·42E.

NES

VA2-R1 VQ(6) + L Fl 10s; 53°25'·71N 05°45'·88E.
Reegeul R3 ☆ Iso G 4s; 53°25'·80N 05°45'·93E.
R7 ☆ QG; 53°25'·91N 05°46'·21E.

HET VLIE (ZEEGAT VAN TERSCHELLING)

ZS Iso 4s; ***Racon T;*** 53°19'·56N 04°55'·80E.

ZS1 ▲ VQ G; 53°19′·29N 04°57′·19E.
ZS3 ▲ Fl G 5s; 53° 19′·38N 04° 57′·19E
ZS5 ▲ L Fl G 8s; 53°18′·55N 05°00′·86E.
ZS11-VS2 ⟂ Q (9) 15s; 53°18′·66N 05°05′·95E.

NOORD MEEP/SLENK TO WEST TERSCHELLING
WM3 ▲ Iso G 2s; 53°17′·45N 05°12′·28E.
NM 4-S 21 ⟂ VQ (3) 5s; 53°19′·02N 05°15′·47E.
SG 15-S 2 ⟂ Q (9) 15s; 53°20′·44N 05°11′·70E.
Brandaris Twr ☆ Fl 5s 54m **29M**; Y □ twr partly obscured by dunes; 53°21′·62N 05°12′·86E.
W Terschelling W hbr mole ☆ FR 5m 5M; R post, W bands; *Horn 15s;* 53°21′·26N 05°13′·09E. E pier hd ☆ FG 4m 4M.

VLIELAND
VS3 (Vliesloot) ▲ VQ G; 53°18′·27N 05°06′·25E.
VS14 ▲ Iso R 4s; 53°17′·58N 05°05′62E.
VS16-VB1 ▲ Fl (2+1) R 10s; 53°17′·62N 05°05′·19E.
E/W mole hds ☆ FG and ☆ FR; 53°17′·68N 05°05′·51E.
Ldg lts 282° ☆ Iso 4s 10/16m 1M, synch; 53°17′·75N 05°04′·47W (100m apart); mainly for the ferry terminal at E Vlieland.
E Vlieland (Vuurduin) ☆ Iso 4s 54m **20M;** 53°17′·75N 05°03′·49E.

APPROACHES TO HARLINGEN (selected marks):
VLIESTROOM buoys are frequently moved.
VL1 ▲ QG; 53°18′·99N 05°08′·82E. VL 2 ▲ QR; 53°19′·40N 05°09′·19E.
VL 11 ▲ Iso G 8s; 53°16′·42N 05°09′·70E.

BLAUWE SLENK
BS1-IN2 ⟂ VQ (3) 5s; 53°15′·41N 05°09′·41E.
BS13 ▲ QG; 53°13′·31N 05°17′·13E. BS19 ▲ VQ G; 53°11′·90N 05°18′·28E.
BS23 ▲ L Fl G 8s; 53°11′·42N 05°19′·60E.

POLLENDAM
Ldg lts 112°, both Iso 6s 8/19m 13M (H24); B masts, W bands. Front, 53°10′·52N 05°24′·19E. Use only between P2 and P6.
P2 ⟂; 53°11′·47N 05°20′·38E on the training wall.
P4, Iso R 8s; P6, Iso R 4s; P8, Iso R 8s; and P10, Iso R 2s.
Yachts should keep outboard of P1 thru 7 SHM buoys. P1 ▲ Iso G 2s; 53°11′·39N 05°20′·32E. P7 ▲ VQ G; 53°10′·68N 05°23′·45E.

HARLINGEN
S mole hd ☆ FG 9m; *Horn (3) 30s;* 53°10′·56N 05°24′·18E.
N mole hd ☆ FR 9m 4M; R/W pedestal; 53°10′·59N 05°24′·32E.

TEXEL AND THE WADDENZEE

TEXEL (from NW and W)
Eierland ☆ Fl (2) 10s 52m **29M;** R ○ twr; 53°10′·93N 04°51′·31E.
TX ⟂ Q(9) 15s; 53°06′·81N 04°41′·19E

MOLENGAT (from the N)
MG-A,Y ▲; 53°02′·54N 04°41′·88E.
MG-B, Y ⟂; 53°02′·00N 04°42′·11E
MG-D, Y ⟂; 53°00′·90N 04°42′·04E;
MG-G, Y ⟂; 52°59′·30N 04°42′·56E;
MG-H, Y ▲; 52°58′·91N 04°43′·10E.

OUDESCHILD
T12 ▲ Iso R 8s; 53°02′·23N 04°51′·52E.
Oudeschild Dir ☆ Oc 6s; intens 291°; 53°02′·40N 04°50′·94E; leads 291° into hbr between N mole head FG 6m; and S mole head ☆ FR 6m; 53°02′·33N 04°51′·17E.

APPROACHES TO KORNWERDERZAND SEALOCK

DOOVE BALG (From Texelstroom eastward)
T23 ▲ VQ G; 53°03′·60N 04°55′·85E, 066°/3M from Oudeschild.
T29 ▲ 53°03′·25N 05°00′·05E.
D1 ▲ Iso G 4s; 53°02′·18N 05°03′·42E.
D21 ▲ Iso G 8s; 53°03′·55N 05°15′·71E.
BO2-WG1 ⟂ Q (6) + L Fl 10s; 53°05′·00N 05°17′·91E.

KORNWERDERZAND SEALOCK
W mole ☆ FG 9m 7M; *Horn Mo(N) 30s;* 53°04′·78N 05°20′·03E.
E mole ☆ FR 9m 7M; 53°04′·70N 05°20′·08E.
W mole elbow ☆ Iso G 6s 6m 7M; 53°04′·61N 05°19′·90E.

APPROACHES TO DEN OEVER SEALOCK

MALZWIN and VISJAGERSGAATJE CHANS TO DEN OEVER
MH4-M1 ⟂ VQ (9) 10s; 52°58′·14N 04°47′·49E, close N Den Helder.
M15 ▲ QG; 52°59′·39N 04°55′·48E (hence use DYC 1811.3).
VG1-W2 ▲ Fl (2+1) G 10s; 52°59′·00N 04°56′·85E.
O9 ▲ Iso G 8s; 52°56′·63N 05°02′·38E.

DEN OEVER SEALOCK
Ldg lts 131°, both Oc 10s 6m 7M; 127°-137°. Front, 52°56′·32N 05°02′·98E. Rear, 280m from front.
E end of swing bridge, ☆ Iso WRG 5s 14m 10/7M; 226°-G-231°-W-235°-R-290°-G-327°-W-335°-R-345°; 52°56′·12N 05°02′·52E.

ZEEGAT VAN TEXEL AND DEN HELDER

OFFSHORE MARKS W and SW OF DEN HELDER
NH (Noorderhaaks) ⟂ VQ; 53°00′·24N 04°35′·37E.
MR ⟂ Q (9) 15s; 52°56′·77N 04°33′·82E.
ZH (Zuiderhaaks) ⟂ VQ (6) + L Fl 10s; 52°54′·65N 04°34′·72E.
Vinca G wreck ⟂ Q (9) 15s; ***Racon D***; 52°45′·93N 04°12′·31E.

SCHULPENGAT (from the SSW)
Schulpengat Dir ☆ 026·5°, Dir WRG, Al WR, Al WG, **W22M R/G18M**, church spire; 025.1°–FG–025.6°–AlWG–026.3°–FW–026.7°–Al WR–027.4°–F R–027.9°; shown H24.
Schilbolsnol ☆ F WRG 27m W8-3M, R8M, G5M; 333°-W-026°-G-033°-W (Ldg sector for Schulpengat)- 038°-R-070°; Obsc 070°-333°; Post; 53°00′·50N 04°45′·70E (on Texel).
SG ⟂ Mo (A) 8s; ***Racon Z;*** 52°52′·90N 04°37′·90E.
S1 ▲ Iso G 4s; 52°53′·53N 04°38′·82E.
S7 ▲ QG; 52°56′·25N 04°40′·92E. S6A ▲ QR; 52°56′·52N 04°40′·51E.
S10 ▲ Iso R 8s; 52°57′·59N 04°41′·57E. S14-MG17 ⟂, see Molengat.
S11 ▲ Iso G 8s; 52°57′·55N 04°43′·25E.
Huisduinen ☆ F WR 26m W14M, R11M; 070°-W-113°-R-

158°-W-208°; □ twr; 52°57′·14N 04°43′·30E (abeam S10 PHM buoy).

Kijkduin ☆ Fl (4) 20s 56m **30M**; vis 360°, except where obsc'd by dunes on Texel; brown twr; 52°57′·33N 04°43′·58E (mainland).

MARSDIEP and DEN HELDER

T1 Fl (3) G 10s; 52°57′·99N 04°44′·62E.
T3 Iso G 8s; 52°58′·07N 04°46′·42E.
Den Helder ldg lts 191°, both Oc G 5s 16/25m 3M, synch. Front, vis 183·5°-198·5°; B ▽ on bldg; 52°57′·37N 04°47′·08E.
Marinehaven, W bkwtr head ☆ QG 11m 8M; *Horn 20s;* 52°57′·95N 04°47′·07E (Harssens Island).
W side, ☆ Fl G 5s 9m 4M (H24); 180°-067°; 52°57′·78N 04°47′·08E.
Yacht hbr (KMYC) ent ☆ FR & FG; 165m SW of ☆ Fl G 5s, above.
E side, MH6 Iso R 4s; 52°57′·99N 04°47′·41E.
Ent E side, ☆ QR 9m 4M (H24); 52°57′·77N 04°47′·37E.

DEN HELDER TO AMSTERDAM

Zanddijk Grote Kaap ☆ Oc WRG 10s 30m 8M; 041°-G-088°-W-094°-R-120°; brown twr; 52°52′·86N 04°42′·88E.
Petten VQ (9) 10s; 52°47′·33N 04°36′·78E (Power stn outfall).
Egmond-aan-Zee ☆ Iso WR 10s 36m **W18M**, R14M; 010°-W-175°-R-188°; W ○ twr; 52°36′·99N 04°37′·16E.
Wind farm approx 6·4M W of Egmond-aan-Zee is marked by: a Meteomast, Mo (U) 15s 11m 10M; 52°36′·36N 04°23′·41E; and by L Fl Y 15s; Horn Mo (U) 30s on 5 of the peripheral wind turbines.

IJMUIDEN

Baloeran Q (9) 15s; 52°29′·21N 04°32′·00E.
IJmuiden Mo (A) 8s; ***Racon Y, 10M;*** 52°28′·45N 04°23′·92E.
Ldg lts 100·5° (FW 5M by day; 090·5°-110·5°). **Front** ☆ F WR 30m **W16M**, R13M; 050°-W-122°-R-145°-W-160°; (Tidal and traffic sigs); dark R ○ twrs; 52°27′·70N 04°34′·47E. **Rear** ☆ Fl 5s 52m **29M**; 019°-199° (FW 5M by day; 090·5°-110·5°); 560m from front.
S bkwtr hd ☆ FG 14m 10M (in fog Fl 3s); W twr, G bands; 52°27′·82N 04°31′·93E.
N bkwtr hd ☆ FR 15m 10M; 52°28′·05N 04°32′·55E.
IJM 1 Iso G 4s; 52°27′·75N 04°33′·59E.
S outer chan ☆ Iso G 6s, 52°27′·75N 04°33′·81E. ☆ Iso R 6s, 52°27′·84N 04°34′·39E (Forteiland). Kleine Sluis 52°27′·84N 04°35′·43E.

AMSTERDAM

IJ8 Iso R 8s (for Sixhaven marina); 52°22′·86N 04°54′·37E.
Oranjesluizen, N lock 52°22′·93N 04°57′·60E (for IJsselmeer).

AMSTERDAM TO ROTTERDAM

Noordwijk-aan-Zee ☆ Oc (3) 20s 32m **18M**; W □ twr; 52°14′·88N 04°26′·02E.

SCHEVENINGEN

Lighthouse ☆ Fl (2) 10s 48m **29M**; 014°-244°; brown twr; 52°06′·23N 04°16′·13E, 5ca E of hbr ent.
Ldg lts 156°, both Iso 4s 14M, H24; synch; Gy masts. Front 52°05′·99N 04°15′·44E; rear 250m from front. Intens at night.
SCH Iso 4s; 52°07′·76N 04°14′·12E.
KNS Q (9)15s; 52°06′·41N 04°15′·32E.
W mole ☆ FG 12m 9M; G twr, W bands; 52°06′·23N 04°15′·16E.
E mole ☆ , FR 12m 9M; R twr, W bands; 52°06′·24N 04°15′·37E.
Inner ldg lts 131°: both Iso G 4s synch; Gy posts. Front 52°05′·81N 04°15′·89E. Rear, 34m from front.

NOORD HINDER N & S TSS and JUNCTION

NHR-N L Fl 8s; ***Racon K, 10M;*** 52°10′·91N 03°04′·76E.
Noord Hinder Fl (2) 10s; *Horn (2) 30s*; ***Racon T, 12-15M;*** 52°00′·10N 02° 51′·11E.
NHR-S Fl Y 10s; 51°51′·37N 02°28′·72E.
NHR-SE Fl G 5s; 51°45′·42N 02°39′·96E.
Birkenfels Q (9) 15s; 51°38′·96N 02°32′·03E.
Twin Fl (3) Y 9s; 51°32′·05N 02°22′·62E.
Garden City Q (9) 15s; 51°29′·12N 02°17′·92E.

APPROACHES TO HOEK VAN HOLLAND

Europlatform Mo (U) 15s; W structure, R bands; helicopter platform; *Horn Mo(U) 30s;* 51°59′·89N 03°16′·46E.
Goeree ☆ Fl (4) 20s 32m **28M**; R/W chequered twr on platform; helicopter platform; *Horn (4) 30s*; ***Racon T, 12-15M;*** 51°55′·42N 03°40′·03E.
Maasvlakte ☆ Fl (5) 20s 67m **28M**, H24; 340°-267°; W twr, B bands; 51°58′·20N 04°00′·84E, 1·5M SSW of Maas ent.
Maas Center Iso 4s; ***Racon M, 10M;*** 52°00′·92N 03°48′·79E.
MO Mo (A) 8s; 52°01′·10N 03°58′·19E.
MN3 Fl (3) G 10s; 52°07′·04N 04°00′·00E.
MN1 Fl G 5s; 52°02′·23N 04°01′·91E.

HOEK VAN HOLLAND

Maasmond ldg lts 112° (for deep draught vessels): both Iso 4s 30/46m **21M**; 101°-123°, synch; W twr, B bands. **Front**, 51°58′·88N 04°04′·88E (NW end of Splitsingsdam). **Rear**, 0·6M from front.
Indusbank N VQ; 52°02′·89N 04°03′·57E.
MVN VQ; 51°59′·61N 04°00′·23E.
MV Q (9) 15s; 51°58′·40N 03°56′·58E.
Maas 1 L Fl G 5s; 51°59′·35N 04°01′·68E.
Nieuwe Waterweg ldg lts 107°: both Iso R 6s 29/43m **18M**; 099.5°-114.5°; R twr, W bands. Front, 51°58′·55N 04°07′·52E. Rear, 450m from front.
Noorderdam Head ☆ FR 25m 10M (In fog Al Fl WR 6s; 278°-255°); R twr, W bands; 51°59′·67N 04°02′·80E.
Nieuwe Zuiderdam ☆ FG 25m 10M, 330°-307°; (In fog Al Fl WG 6s); G twr, W bands; 51°59′·14N 04°02′·49E.

ROTTERDAM

Maassluis ☆ FG 6m; 51°54′·94N 04°14′·81E; and FR.
Vlaardingen ☆ FG; 51°53′·99N 04°20′·95E; and FR.
Spuihaven, W ent ☆ FR; 51°53′·98N 04°23′·97E.
Veerhaven, E ent ☆ FG; 51°54′·42N 04°28′·75E; and FR.
City marina ent, 51°54′·64N 04°29′·76E.

APPROACHES TO HARINGVLIET

Buitenbank , Iso 4s; 51°51′·16N 03°25′·71E.
Hinder Q (9) 15s; 51°54′·55N 03°55′·42E.
SH VQ (9) 10s; 51°49′·49N 03°45′·79E.
Westhoofd ☆ Fl (3) 15s 55m **30M**; R □ tr; 51°48′·79N 03°51′·85E.
Ooster Q (9) 15s; 51°47′·90N 03°41′·27E.

SLIJKGAT

SG Iso 4s; 51°51′·95N 03°51′·42E.
SG 2 Iso R 4s; 51°51′·71N 03°53′·45E.
SG 5 Iso G 4s; 51°50′·00N 03°55′·56E.
SG 11 Iso G 4s; 51°50′·81N 03°58′·52E.
P1 Iso G 4s; 51°51′·30N 04°01′·12E.
P3 Iso G 8s; 51°51′·12N 04°01′·45E.
P9 Iso G 8s; 51°49′·98N 04°02′·15E.

STELLENDAM

N mole ☆ FG; *Horn (2) 15s;* 51°49′·88N 04°02′·03E.
Buitenhaven ☆ Oc 6s; 51°49′·73N 04°01′·75E.

APPROACHES TO OOSTERSCHELDE

OUTER APPROACHES

Schouwenbank Mo (A) 8s; ***Racon O, 10M;*** 51°44′·94N 03°14′·32E.
Middelbank Iso 8s; 51°40′·86N 03°18′·20E.
MW Q (9) 15s; 51°44′·55N 03°24′·04E (Schouwendiep).
MD 3 Fl G 5s; 51°42′·70N 03°26′·98E.
SW Thornton Iso 8s; 51°30′·98N 02°50′·90E.
Wind farm, Thornton Bank in □ 5.5M x 2.7M centred on 51°32′·58N 2°57′·56E: 54 turbines all R lts, the 11 perimeter turbines are lit Mo U Y 15s, Horn Mo U 30s.
Rabsbank Iso 4s; 51°38′·25N 03°09′·93E.
Westpit Iso 8s; 51°33′·65N 03°09′·92E.
ZSB VQ (9) 10s; 51°36′·57N 03°15′·62E.
OG1 QG; 51°36′·14N 03°20′·08E.

WESTGAT, OUDE ROOMPOT and ROOMPOTSLUIS

West Schouwen ☆ Fl (2+1)15s 57m **30M**; Gy twr, R diagonals on upper part; 51°42′·52N 03°41′·50E, 5·8M N of Roompotsluis.
OG-WG VQ (9) 10s; 51°37′·18N 03°23′·82E.
WG1 Iso G 8s; 51°38′·00N 03°26′·24E.
WG4 ☆ L Fl R 8s; 51°38′·62N 03°28′·78E.
WG7 Iso G 4s 51°39′·40N 03°32′·67E.
WG-GB (Geul van de Banjaard) 51°39′·72N 03°32′·69E.
OR1 51°39′·15N 03°33′·59E.
OR5 Iso G 8s; 51°38′·71N 03°35′·53E.
OR11 Iso G 4s; 51°36′·98N 03°38′·40E.
OR12 Iso R 4s; 51°37′·27N 03°39′·25E.
OR-R VQ (3) 5s; 51°36′·41N 03°38′·96E.
Roompotsluis ldg lts 073·5°, both Oc G 5s; synch. Front, 51°37′·33N 03°40′·75E. Rear, 280m from front.
N bkwtr ☆ FR 7m; 51°37′·31N 03°40′·09E.

WESTKAPELLE TO VLISSINGEN

OOSTGAT

Ldg lts 149·5°: Front, Noorderhoofd Oc WRG 10s 20m; W13M, R/G10M; 353°-R-008°-G-029°-W-169°; R ○ twr, W band; 51°32′·40N 03°26′·21E, 0·73M from rear (Westkapelle).
Westkapelle ☆, rear, Fl 3s 50m **28M**; obsc'd by land on certain brgs; □ twr, R top; 51°31′·75N 03°26′·83E.
Kaloo Iso 8s; 51°35′·55N 03°23′·24E. Chan is well buoyed/lit.
OG5 Iso G 8s; 51°33′·95N 03°25′·92E.
OG-GR VQ (3) 5s; 51°32′·74N 03°24′·71E.
Molenhoofd ☆ Oc WRG 6s 10m; 306°-R-329°-W-349°-R-008°-G-034·5°-W-036·5°-G-144°-W-169°-R-198°; W mast R bands; 51°31′·58N 03°26′·05E.
Zoutelande FR 21m 12M; 321°-352°; R □ twr; 51°30′·28N 03°28′·41E.
Kaapduinen, ldg lts 130°: both Oc 5s 25/34m 13M; synch; Y □ twrs, R bands. Front, 115°-145°; 51°28′·47N 03°30′·99E. Rear, 107·5°-152·5°; 220m from front.
Fort de Nolle ☆ Oc WRG 9s 11m W6M, R/G4M; 293°-R-309°-W-324·5°-G-336·5°-R-014°-G-064°-R-099·5°-W-110·5°-G-117°-R-130°; W col, R bands; 51°26′·94N 03°33′·12E.
Ldg lts 117°: Front, Leugenaar, Oc R 5s 6m 7M; intens 108°-126°; W&R pile; 51°26′·43N 03°34′·14E.
Rear, Sardijngeul Oc WR 5s 8m W12M, R9M, synch; 245°-R-272°-W-123.5°-R-147°; R △, W bands on R & W mast; 550m from front; 51°26′·30N 03°34′·56E.

OFFSHORE: W HINDER TSS TO SCHEUR CHANNEL

West Hinder ☆ Fl (4) 30s 23m 13M; *Horn Mo (U) 30s;* ***Racon W;*** 51°23′·30N 02°26′·27E.
WH Zuid Q (6) + L Fl 15s; 51°22′·78N 02°26′·25E.
OostdyckBk Q; 51°21′·38N 02°31′·12E.
BerguesBk-N Q; 51°19′·95N 02°24′·50E.
Oost-Dyck West Q (9) 15s; 51°17′·15N 02°26′·32E.
Oostdyck radar twr; ☆ Mo (U) 15s 15m 12M on 4 corners; *Horn Mo (U) 30s;* ***Racon O.*** R twr, 3 W bands, with adjacent red twr/helipad; 51°16′·49N 02°26′·85E.
A-N Fl (4) R 20s; 51°23′·45N 02°36′·90E.
AS Fl (3) G 10s; 51°21′·15N 02°36′·92E.
KB2 VQ; 51°21′·04N 02°42′·22E.
KB Q; ***Racon K;*** 51°21′·03N 02°42′·83E.
MBN Q; 51°20′·82N 02°46′·29E.
Akkaert-SW Q (9) 15s; 51°22′·28N 02°46′·34E.
VG Q ; 51°23′·38N 02°46′·21E, Vaargeul 1.
VG1 VQ G; 51°25′·03N 02°49′·04E.
VG2 Q (6) + L Fl R 15s; ***Racon V;*** 51°25′·96N 02°48′·16E.
VG3 QG; 51°25′·05N 02°52′·92E.
VG5 Fl G 5s; 51°24′·63N 02°57′·92E.
SVG Q ; 51°24′·53N 02°59′·92E.
Goote Bank Q (3) 10s; 51°26′·95N 02°52′·72E.
A1 Iso 8s; 51°22′·36N 02°53′·33E.
A1bis L Fl 10s; 51°21′·68N 02°58′·02E.

WESTERSCHELDE APPROACHES

SCHEUR CHANNEL

S1 Fl G 5s; 51°23′·14N 03°00′·12E.
S3 Q; 51°24′·30N 03°02′·92E.
MOW 0 Fl (5) Y 20s; ***Racon S, 10M;*** 51°23′·67N 03°02′·75E.
S5 Fl G 5s; 51°23′·70N 03°06′·30E.
S7 Fl G 5s; 51°23′·98N 03°10′·42E.
S9 QG; 51°24′·42N 03°14′·99E.
S12 Fl (4) R 10s; 51°24′·67N 03°18′·22E.
S-W Q; 51°24′·13N 03°18′·22E, here Wielingen chan merges.
S14 Fl R 5s; 51°24′·58N 03°19′·67E.

WIELINGEN CHANNEL

BVH Q (6) + L Fl R 15s; 51°23′·15N 03°12′·04E.
MOW3 tide gauge ☆ Fl (5) Y 20s; ***Racon H, 10M;*** 51°23′·38N 03°11′·92E.
W Fl (3) G 15s; 51°23′·27N 03°14′·92E.
W1 Fl G 5s; 51°23′·48N 03°18′·22E.
Fort Maisonneuve VQ (9) 10s; wreck; 51°24′·20N 03°21′·50E.

W3 Iso G 8s; 51°23′·96N 03°21′·49E.
W5 Iso G 4s; 51°24′·31N 03°24′·50E.
W7 Iso G 8s; 51°24′·60N 03°27′·27E.
W9 Iso G 4s; 51°24′·96N 03°30′·43E.
Nieuwe Sluis ☆ Oc WRG 10s 26m W14M, R11M, G10M; 055°-R-089°-W-093°-G-105°-R-134°-W-136·5°-G-156·5°-W-236·5°-G-243°-W-254°-R-292°-W-055°; B 8-sided twr, W bands; 51°24′·41N 03°31′·29E.
Songa QG; 51°25′·26N 03°33′·66E.
W10 QR; 51°25′·85N 03°33′·28E.

VLISSINGEN

Koopmanshaven, W mole root, ☆ Iso WRG 3s 15m W12M, R10M, G9M; 253°-R-277°-W-284°-R-297°- W-306·5°-G-013°-W-024°-G-033°-W-035°-G-039°-W-055°-G-084·5°-R-092°-G-111°-W-114°; R pylon; 51°26′·37N 03°34′·52E.
Sardijngeul Oc WR 5s; 51°26′·30N 03°34′·56E: see OOSTGAT last 3 lines. E mole head, ☆ FG 7m; W mast; 51°26′·32N 03°34′·67E.
Buitenhaven ent, W side ☆ FR 10m 5M; also Iso WRG 4s: W073°-324°, G324°-352°, W352°-017°, G017°-042°, W042°-056°, R056°-073°; W post, R bands; tfc sigs; 51°26′·38N 03°36′·06E.
Buitenhaven ent, E side ☆ FG 7m 4M; 51°26′·41N 03°36′·38E.
Schone Waardin ☆ Oc WRG 9s 10m W13M, R10M, G9M; 235°-R-271°-W-288°-G-335°-R-341°-G-026°-W-079°-R-091°; R mast, W bands; 51°26′·54N 03°37′·91E (1M E of Buitenhaven ent).

BRESKENS

ARV-VH Q; 51°24′·71N 03°33′·89E.
VH2 (Vaarwaterlangs Hoofdplaat) 51°24′·34N 03°33′·90E.
Yacht hbr, W mole ☆ FG 7m; in fog FY; Gy post; 51°24′·03N 03°34′·06E. E mole ☆ FR 6m; Gy mast; 51°23′·95N 03°34′·09E.

WESTERSCHELDE: TERNEUZEN TO PAAL

TERNEUZEN

Nieuw Neuzenpolder ldg lts 125°, both Oc 5s 6/16m 9/13M; intens 117°-133°; synch. Front, W col, B bands; 51°20′·97N 03°47′·24E. Rear, B & W twr; 365m from front.
Oost Buitenhaven E mole ☆ FR 5M; 51°20′·56N 03°49′·19E.
Former ferry hbr (W part) & marinas (E part) W mole head ☆ FG, Gy mast; 51°20′·57N 03°49′·64E. E mole, FR.
W mole ☆ Oc WRG 5s 15m W9M, R7M, G6M; 090°-R-115°-W-120°-G-130°-W-245°-G-249°-W-279°-R-004°; B & W post; 51°20′·54N 03°49′·58E, close SW of ☆ FG.

HANSWEERT

W mole ☆ Oc WRG 10s 9m W6M, R6M, G6M; (in fog FY); 288°-R-311°-G-320°-W-332·5°-G-348·5°-W-042·5°-R-061·5°-W-078°-G-099°-W-114·5°-R-127·5°-W-288°; R twr, W bands; 51°26′·42N 04°00′·53E.

BELGIUM
ZANDVLIET TO ANTWERPEN

ZANDVLIET

Dir ☆ 118·3°,WRG 20m W4M, R/ G3M; 116·63°-Oc G-117·17°- FG-117·58°-Alt GW-118·63°-F-118·63°-Alt RW-119·18°-FR-119·58°- Oc R-120·13°; 51°20′·61N 04°16′·47E, near Zandvliet locks.

ANTWERPEN

No 107 Iso G 8s, 51°14′·12N 04°23′·80E (Kattendijksluis for Willemdok).
Royerssluis, ldg lts 091°, both FR. Ent FR/FG.
No. 109 Iso G 8s; 51°13′·88N 04°23′·87E, (off Linkeroever).
Linkeroever marina F WR 9m W3M, R2M; shore-W-283°- R-shore; B ⊙, R lantern; 51°13′·91N 04°23′·70E. Marina ent, FR/FG.

COASTAL MARKS

AW2 Fl (4) R 20s; 51°21′·95N 03°00′·94E; Wandelaar.
AW1 QG; 51°21′·50N 03°02′·59E; Wandelaar.
Oostende Bank N Q; 51°21′·20N 02°52′·93E.
Wenduine Bank E QR; 51°18′·83N 03°01′·64E.
Wenduine Bank W Q (9) 15s; 51°17′·23N 02°52′·76E.
Nautica Ena wreck Q; 51°18′·08N 02°52′·79E.
Oostendebank E Fl (4) R 20s; 51°17′·35N 02°51′·91E.
Oostendebank W Q (9)15s; 51°16′·20N 02°44′·74E.
LST 420 Q (9)15s; 51°15′·45N 02°40′·67E.
MBN Q; 51°20′·82N 02°46′·29E.
Middelkerke Bank Fl G 5s; 51°18′·19N 02°42′·75E.
Middelkerke Bank S Q (9) R 15s; 51°14′·73N 02°41′·89E.
D1 Q (3) 10s; 51°13′·95N 02°38′·59E.
BT Ratel Fl (4) R 15s; 51°11′·63N 02°27′·92E; Buiten Ratel.

ZEEBRUGGE TO THE FRENCH BORDER

ZEEBRUGGE

AW Iso 8s; 51°22′·41N 03°07′·05E.
Ldg lts 136°, both Oc 5s 22/45m 8M; 131°-141°; H24, synch; W cols, R bands. Front, 51°20′·71N 03°13′·11E. Rear, 890m SE.
SZ Q (3) 10s; 51°23′·30N 03°08′·65E (Scheur Channel).
Z QG; 51°22′·48N 03°09′·95E.
WZ Q (9) 15s; 51°22′·57N 03°10′·72E.
W outer mole ☆ Oc G 7s 31m 7M; G vert strip lts visible from seaward; 057°-267°; *Horn (3) 30s;* IPTS; 51°21′·74N 03°11′·17E.
E outer mole ☆ Oc R 7s 31m 7M; R vert strip lts visible from seaward; 087°-281°; *Bell 25s;* 51°21′·78N 03°11′·86E.
Ldg lts 154°: Front, Oc WR 6s 20m 3M, 135°-W-160°-R-169°; W pylon, R bands; 51°20′·33N 03°12′·89E. Rear, Oc 6s 38m 3M, H24, synch; 520m from front.
Leopold II mole ☆ Oc WR 15s 22m, **W20M, R18M**; 068°-W-145°-R-212°-W-296°; IPTS; *Horn (3+1) 90s;* 51°20′·85N 03°12′·17E.
Entrance to Marina and FV hbr 51°19′·88N 03°11′·85E.

BLANKENBERGE

Promenade pier Fl (3) Y 20s, 8m 4M; 51°19′·28N 03°08′·18E.
Lt ho ☆ Fl (2) 8s 30m **20M**; 065°-245°; W twr, B top; 51°18′·75N 03°06′·85E.
Ldg lts 134°, both FR 5/9m 3/10M, R cross (X) topmarks on masts; front 51°18′·70N 03°08′·82E; rear 81m from front.
E pier ☆ FR 12m 11M; R290°-245°(315°); W ○ twr; 51°18′·91N 03°06′·56E.
W pier ☆ FG 14m 11M; intens 065°-290°, unintens 290°-335°; W ○ twr; 51°18′·89N 03°06′·42E.
OBST 4 – OBST 14 are eleven s Q approx 3ca offshore, marking Spoil Ground between Blankenberge and Oostende.

OOSTENDE
Oostendebank East Fl (4) R 20s; 51°17′·35N 02°51′·91E.
Wenduinebank West Q (9) 15s; 51°17′·23N 02°52′·76E.
Buitenstroombank Q; 51°15′·17N 02°51′·71E.
Binnenstroombank Q (3) 10s; 51°14′·47N 02°53′·65E.
Ldg lts 143°: both Iso 4s (triple vert) 36/46m 4M, 068°-218°; X on metal mast, R/W bands. Front, 51°13′·80N 02°55′·89E.
Oostende lt ho ☆ Fl (3) 10s 65m **27M**; obsc 069·5°-071°; Gy twr, 2 sinusoidal Bu bands; 51°14′·18N 02°55′·84E.
IPTS at E bkwtr Hd, Radar tr, G,R top, 51° 14′·51 02° 55′·19E, plus QY when chan closed.
Inner W pier ☆ FG 12m 10M, G057°-327°(270°); W ○ twr 51°14′·31N 02°55′·03E.

NIEUWPOORT
Zuidstroombank Fl R 5s; 51°12′·28N 02°47′·37E.
Weststroombank Fl (4) R 20s; 51°11′·34N 02°43′·03E.
Wreck 4 Q (6) + L Fl 15s; 51°10′·98N 02°40′·10E.
Nieuwpoort Bank Q (9) 15s; 51°10′·16N 02°36′·09E.
Whitley Q; 51°09′·15N 02°39′·44E.
Lt ho ☆ Fl (2) R 14s 28m **16M**; R/W twr; 51°09′·27N 02°43′·79E.
E pier ☆ FR 10m 10M; R025°-250°(225°) R307°-347°(40°); W ○ twr; 51°09′·41N 02°43′·08E.
W pier ☆ FG 10m 9M; G025°-250°(225°) G284°-324°(40°); W ○ twr; 51°09′·35N 02°43′·00E.
☆ QG 51°08′·65N 02°44′·31E marks the Y-junction where the channel forks stbd for KYCN and port for WSKLM and VVW-N.

WESTDIEP and PASSE DE ZUYDCOOTE
Den Oever wreck 2 Q; 51°08′·11N 02°37′·43E.
Wreck 1 Q; 51°08′·32N 02°35′·03E (adjacent to next line).
Wave recorder Fl (5) Y 20s; 51°08′·25N 02°34′·98E.
Trapegeer Fl G 10s; 51°08′·41N 02°34′·36E.
E12 VQ (6) + L Fl 10s; 51°07′·92N 02°30′·61E.
French waters, for continuity (see also Area 17):
CME Q (3) 10s; 51°07′·30N 02°30′·00E.
E11 Fl G 4s; 51°06′·85N 02°30′·83E.
E10 Fl (2) R 6s; 51°06′·26N 02°30′·40E.
E9 Fl (2) G 6s; 51°05′·61N 02°29′·60E.
E8 Fl (3) R 12s; 51°05′·12N 02°28′·60E.

1	Delfzijl	1																
2	Terschelling	85	2															
3	Harlingen	102	19	3														
4	Den Oever	110	34	21	4													
5	Den Helder	115	39	30	11	5												
6	Amsterdam	159	83	81	62	51	6											
7	IJmuiden	146	70	68	49	38	13	7										
8	Scheveningen	171	95	93	74	63	38	25	8									
9	Rotterdam	205	129	127	108	97	72	59	34	9								
10	Hook of Holland	185	109	107	88	77	52	39	14	20	10							
11	Stellendam	201	125	123	104	93	68	55	30	36	16	11						
12	Roompotsluis	233	157	155	136	125	100	87	50	68	48	32	12					
13	Vlissingen	228	152	150	131	120	99	86	61	67	47	45	24	13				
14	Zeebrugge	239	163	161	142	131	106	93	68	74	54	50	28	16	14			
15	Blankenberge	244	168	166	147	136	111	98	73	79	59	55	33	21	5	15		
16	Oostende	239	163	161	142	131	110	106	81	87	67	72	40	29	13	9	16	
17	Nieuwpoort	262	186	184	165	154	129	116	91	97	77	83	51	39	23	18	9	17

DISTANCE TABLES
Approx distances in nautical miles are by the most direct route allowing for dangers and TSS.

AREA 14 *North France – Dunkerque to Cap de la Hague*

SELECTED LIGHTS, BUOYS & WAYPOINTS

OFFSHORE MARKS: W Hinder to Dover Strait
Fairy South VQ (6) + L Fl 10s; 51°21′·20N 02°17′·31E.
Fairy West VQ (9) 10s 6M; 51°23′·89N 02°09′·27E.
Hinder 1 Fl (2) 6s; 51°20′·80N 02°10′·93E.
Bergues Fl G 4s 7m 4M; 51°17′·14N 02°18′·63E.
Bergues S Q (6) + L Fl 15s; 51°15′·09N 02°19′·42E.
Ruytingen E VQ; 51°14′·55N 02°17′·93E.
Ruytingen N VQ 4M; 51°13′·16N 02°10′·28E.
Ruytingen SE VQ (3) 15s; 51°09′·20N 02°08′·94E.
Ruytingen NW Fl G 4s 3M; 51°09′·11N 01°57′·30E.
Ruytingen W VQ 4M; 51°06′·93N 01°50′·45E.
Ruytingen SW Fl (3) G 12s 3M; 51°04′·33N 01°45′·84E.
Sandettié N VQ 6M; 51°18′·35N 02°04′·73E.
Sandettié E Fl R 4s 7m 3M; 51°14′·88N 02°02′·65E.

DUNKERQUE TO BOULOGNE

PASSE DE ZUYDCOOTE
E12 VQ (6) + L Fl 10s; 51°07′·92N 02°30′·61E.(Belgium).
CME Q (3) 10s; 51°07′·30N 02°30′·00E.
E11 Fl G 4s; 51°06′·85N 02°30′·83E.
E10 Fl (2) R 6s; 51°06′·26N 02°30′·40E.
E9 Fl (2) G 6s; 51°05′·61N 02°29′·60E.
E8 Fl (3) R 12s; 51°05′·12N 02°28′·60E. (E7 does not exist)

PASSE DE L'EST
E6 QR; 51°04′·86N 02°27′·08E.
E4 Fl R 4s; 51°04′·58N 02°24′·52E.
E1 Fl (2) G 6s; 51°04′·12N 02°23′·04E.
E2 Fl (2) R 6s; 51°04′·35N 02°22′·31E.
Q (6) + L Fl 15s; 51°04′·28N 02°21′·73E.

DUNKERQUE PORT EST
E jetty ☆ Fl (2) R 6s 12m 10M; R □, W pylon; 51°03′·59N 02°21′·20E.
W jetty ☆ Fl (2) G 6s 35m 11M; W twr, brown top; 51°03′·63N 02°20′·95E.
Ldg lts 137·5°, front Q7m11M 51°02′·98N 02°22′·05E, rear, Q10m11M, 114m from front, both W cols, R tops, synched.

Inner W jetty ⍊ Q 11m 9M; 51°03′·33N 02°21′·43E.
Dunkerque lt ho ☆ Fl (2) 10s 59m **26M;** 51°02′·93N 02°21′·86E.

DUNKERQUE INTERMEDIATE CHANNEL
DW30 ⍊ QR; 51°04′·14N 02°20′·16E.
DW29 ⍊ QG; 51°03′·85N 02°20′·21E.
DW16 ⍊ Fl (2) R 6s; 51°03′·52N 02°08′·62E.
DKB ⍊ VQ (9) 10s; 51°02′·95N 02°09′·26E.
DW12 ⍊ Fl (3) R 12s; 51°03′·38N 02°05′·36E.
DW11 ⍊ Fl (3) G 12s; 51°02′·79N 02°05′·53E. (DW10-7 omitted)

GRAVELINES
W jetty ☆ Fl (2) WG 6s 9m W/G4M; 085°-W-224°-G-085°; Y ○ twr, G top; 51°00′·94N 02°05′·49E.

PASSE DE L'OUEST
DW6 ⍊ VQ R; 51°02′·60N 02°01′·01E.
DW5 ⍊ QG; 51°02′·20N 02°00′·92E.
DKA ⍊ L Fl 10s; 51°02′·55N 01°56′·96E.
RCE (Ridens de Calais E) ⍊ Iso G 4s; 51°02′·44N 01°53′·24E.
Dyck ⍊ Fl 3s; ***Racon B***; 51°02′·99N 01°51′·79E.
RCA (Ridens de Calais Approach) ⍊ Q; 51°01′·00N 01°48′·53E. 992271117.

CALAIS
E jetty ☆ Fl (2) R 6s 12m **17M**; (in fog two Fl (2) 6s (vert) on request); Gy twr, R top; *Horn (2) 40s;* 50°58′·39N 01°50′·45E.
W jetty ☆ Iso G 3s 12m 9M; (in fog Fl 5s on request); W twr, G top; *Bell 5s;* 50°58′·24N 01°50′·40E.
Calais ☆ Fl (4) 15s 59m **22M**; vis 073°-260°; W 8-sided twr, B top; 50°57′·68N 01°51′·21E (440m E of marina entry gate).

CALAIS, WESTERN APPROACH
CA6 ⍊ Fl (3) R 12s; 50°58′·63N 01°49′·92E.
CA4 ⍊ Fl (2)R 6s; 50°58′·38N 01°48′·65E.
CA1 ⍊ Fl G 4s; 50°57′·64N 01°46′·14E (0·5M NNW of Sangatte). Sangatte ☆ Oc WG 4s 13m W8M, G5M; 065°-G-089°-W-152°-G-245°; W pylon, B top; 50°57′·19N 01°46′·50E.
Les Quénocs ⍊ VQ; 50°56′·85N 01°41′·12E.
Abbeville wreck ⍊ VQ (9) 10s; 50°56′·08N 01°37′·58E.
Cap Gris-Nez ☆ Fl 5s 72m **29M**; 005°-232°; W twr, B top; 50°52′·09N 01°34′·96E.

OFFSHORE MARKS: DOVER STRAIT TSS, French side
Colbart N ⍊ Q 6M; 50°57′·46N 01°23′·29E.
Colbart SW ⍊ VQ (6) + L Fl 10s 8m; 50°48′·87N 01°16′·32E.
ZC2 (Zone Cotière) ⍊ Fl (2+1) Y 15s 5M; 50°53′·54N 01°30′·89E.
ZC1 ⍊ Fl (4) Y 15s 4MN; 50°44′·99N 01°27′·21E.
Ridens SE ⍊ VQ (3) 5s 6M; 50°43′·48N 01°18′·87E.
Bassurelle ⍊ Fl (4) R 15s 6M; ***Racon B, 5-8M;*** 50°32′·74N 00°57′·69E.
Vergoyer N ⍊ VQ 5M; 50°39′·67N 01°22′·21E.
Vergoyer NW ⍊ Fl (2) G 6s 4M; 50°37′·16N 01°17′·85E.
Vergoyer E ⍊ VQ (3) 5s 6M; 50°35′·76N 01°19′·70E.
Vergoyer W ⍊ Fl G 4s 4M; 50°34′·66N 01°13′·57E.
Vergoyer SW ⍊ VQ (9) 10s 6M; 50°27′·01N 01°00′·03E.

BOULOGNE TO DIEPPE

BOULOGNE
Bassure de Baas ⍊ VQ; 50°48′·53N 01°33′·05E.
Approches Boulogne ⍊ VQ (6) + L Fl 10s 8m 6M; 50°45′·31N 01°31′·07E.
Digue N (detached) ☆ Fl (2) R 6s 10m 7M; 50°44′·71N 01°34′·18E.
Digue S (Carnot) ☆ Fl (2+1) 15s 25m **19M**; W twr, G top; 50°44′·44N 01°34′·05E.
Clearing brg 122·4° : Front, FG in a neon ▽ 4m 5M; 50°43′·71N 01°35′·66E. Rear, FR 44m 11M; intens 113°-133°; 560m from front.
Inner NE jetty ☆ FR 11m 7M; 50°43′·91N 01°35′·24E.
Inner SW jetty ☆ FG 17m 5M; W col, G top; *Horn 30s;* 50°43′·90N 01°35′·11E.
Cap d'Alprech ☆ Fl (3) 15s 62m **23M**; W twr, B top; 50°41′·91N 01°33′·75E, 2·5M S of hbr ent.

LE TOUQUET/ÉTAPLES
Pointe de Lornel ⍊ VQ (9) 10s 6m 3M; 50°33′·24N 01°35′·12E.
Mérida wreck ⍊ 50°32′·85N 01°33′·44E.
Camiers lt ho ☆ Oc (2) WRG 6s 17m W10M, R/G7M; 015°-G-090°-W-105°-R-141°; R pylon; 50°32′·86N 01°36′·28E.
Canche Est groyne ⍊ Fl R 4s 8m; 50°32′·57N 01°35′·66E.
Le Touquet ☆ Fl (2) 10s 54m **25M**; Or twr, brown band, W&G top; 50°31′·43N 01°35′·52E.
Pointe du Haut-Blanc ☆ Fl 5s 44m **23M**; W twr, R bands, G top; 50°23′·90N 01°33′·67E (Berck).

BAIE DE LA SOMME
ATSO ⍊ Mo (A) 12s; 50°14′·00N 01°28′·08E (often moved).
Pte du Hourdel ☆ Oc (3) WG 12s 19m, W12M, G9M; 053°-W-248°-G-323°; tidal sigs; *Horn (3) 30s*; W twr, G top; 50°12′·90N 01°33′·98E.
Cayeux-sur-Mer ☆ Fl R 5s 32m **22M**; W twr, R top; 50°11′·65N 01°30′·72E.
Le Crotoy ☆ Oc (2) R 6s 19m 8M; 285°-135°; W pylon; 50°12′·91N 01°37′·40E. Marina ☆ Fl R & Fl G 2s 4m 2M; 50°12′·98N 01°38′·20E.

ST VALÉRY-SUR-SOMME
Trng wall head, ⍊ Fl G 2.5s 2m 1M; 50°12′·25N 01°35′·85E.
Embankment head ☆ Iso G 4s 9m 9M; 347°-222°; W pylon, G top; 50°12′·25N 01°36′·02E.
La Ferté môle ☆ Fl R 4s 9m 9M; 000°-250°; W pylon, R top; 50°11′·18N 01°38′·14E (ent to marina inlet).

LE TRÉPORT
Ault ☆ Oc (3) WR 12s 95m **W15M**, R11M; 040°-W-175°-R-220°; W twr, R top; 50°06′·28N 01°27′·23E (4M NE of Le Tréport).
W jetty ☆ Fl (2) G 10s 15m **20M**; W twr, G top; *Horn (2) 30s*; 50°03′·88N 01°22′·14E.

DIEPPE
W jetty ☆ Iso G 4s 11m 8M; W twr, G top; *Horn 30s;* 49°56′·27N 01°04′·97E.
Quai de la Marne ⍊ QR 12m 3M; 49°55′·93N 01°05′·20E, E quay.
Pointe d'Ailly ☆ Fl (3) 20s 95m **31M**; W □ twr, G top; *Horn (3) 60s;* 49°54′·96N 00°57′·50E.

DIEPPE TO LE HAVRE

SAINT VALÉRY-EN-CAUX
W jetty ☆ Fl (2) G 6s 13m 11M; W twr, G top; 49°52′·40N 00°42′·54E. Paluel power station ⍊ Q; 49°52′·22N 00°38′·03E.

FÉCAMP

N jetty ☆ Fl (2) 10s 15m **16M**; Gy twr, R top; 49°45'·94N 00°21'·80E.

Fécamp NW, Met Mast FECO1-YO2 ☆ Mo(U) W 15s 13m 10M, Aero F R 36m, Aero UQ R 60m, Aero UQ W 60m(day) Gy pylon,Y platform; Horn Mo(U) 30s; 49°50'·85N 00°13'·14E. 992271122.

PORT D'ANTIFER

Cap d'Antifer ☆ Fl 20s 128m **29M**; 021°-222°; Gy 8-sided twr, G top, on 90m cliffs; 49°41'·01N 00°09'·93E.

A17 Iso G 4s; 49°41'·53N 00°01·75E.

A18 QR; 49°42'·02N 00°02'·18E. Cross the chan W of A17/18.

Ldg lts 127·5°, both Dir Oc 4s 113/135m **22M**; 127°-128°; by day F **33M** 126·5°-128·5° occas. **Front** ☆, 49°38'·32N 00°09'·12E.

LE HAVRE, APPROACH CHANNEL

Cap de la Hève ☆ Fl 5s 123m **24M**; 225°-196°; W 8-sided twr, R top; 49°30'·74N 00°04'·16E.

LHA Mo (A) 12s 10m 6M; R&W; ***Racon, 8-10M*** (a series of 8 dots, or 8 groups of dots; distance between each dot or group represents 0·3M); 49°31'·38N 00°09'·86W. Reserve lt Mo (A).

Ldg lts 106·8°, both Dir F 36/78m **25M** (H24); intens 106°-108°; Gy twrs, G tops. Front, 49°28'·91N 00°06'·50E; rear, 0·73M from front.

LH3 QG; 49°30'·84N 00°04'·02W. (LH1 & 2 buoys do not exist).

LH4 QR; 49°31'·11N 00°03'·90W.

FVs and yachts <19.8m LOA may cross the appr chan west of LH 7/8 buoys, keeping clear of all other shipping, even if under sail:

LH7 Iso G 4s; 49°30'·25N 00°00'·82W.

LH8 Fl (2) R 6s; 49°30'·44N 00°00'·70W.

Note the W-E longitude change. (LH9 buoy does not exist).

LH13 Fl G 4s; 49°29'·32N 00°03'·62E (Ent to Port 2000).

LH14 Fl R 4s; 49°29'·67N 00°03'·43E; 1m shoal depth close W.

LH16 Fl (2) R 6s; 49°29'·45N 00°04'·28E.

LH 2000 VQ (9) 10s; 49°29'·14N 00°04'·78E (Ent to Port 2000).

LE HAVRE

Digue N ☆ Fl R 5s 15m **21M**; IPTS; W ○ twr, R top; *Horn 15s;* 49°29'·19N 00°05'·44E.

Digue S ☆ VQ (3) G 2s 15m 11M; W twr, G top; 49°29'·05N 00°05'·38E.

Marina ent, W spur ☆ Fl (2) R 6s 3M; 49°29'·22N 00°05'·53E.

THE SEINE ESTUARY UP TO HONFLEUR

CHENAL DE ROUEN

Nord du Mouillage Fl (4) Y 15s; 49°28'·80N 00°00'·22E.

No. 2 QR; ***Racon T***; 49°27'·70N 00°00'·60E.

No. 4 Fl R 2·5s; 49°27'·19N 00°01'·97E. Yachts keep N of chan.

Amfard SW QR; 49°26'·30N 00°04'·82E.

No. 10 Fl R 4s; 49°26'·10N 00°06'·39E.

Digue du Ratier VQ 10m 4M; 49°25'·94N 00°06'·59E.

Falaise des Fonds ☆ Fl (3) WRG 12s 15m, **W17M**, R/G13M; 040°-G-080°-R-084°-G-100°- W-109°-R-162°-G-260°; W twr, G top; 49°25'·47N 00°12'·85E.

No. 20 QR; 49°25'·85N 00°13'·71E. (Cross here to Honfleur)

HONFLEUR

Digue Ouest ☆ QG 10m 6M; 49°25'·67N 00°13'·83E.

Digue Est ☆ Q 9m 8M; *Horn (5) 40s;* 49°25'·67N 00°13'·95E.

Inner E jetty, Oc (2) R 6s 12m 6M; W twr, R top; 49°25'·38N 00°14'·12E.

No. 22 Fl R 4s; 49°25'·85N 00°15'·37E.

TROUVILLE TO COURSEULLES

CHENAL DE ROUEN TO DEAUVILLE and TROUVILLE

Ratelets Q (9) 15s; 49°25'·29N 00°01'·71E.

Semoy VQ (3) 5s; 49°24'·15N 00°02'·35E, close to 148° ldg line.

Trouville SW VQ (9) 10s; 49°22'·54N 00°02'·56E.

DEAUVILLE and TROUVILLE

Ldg lts 148°, both Oc R 4s 11/17m 12/10M: Front, East inner jetty (*estacade*); 330°-150°; W twr, R top; 49°22'·03N 00°04'·48E.

Rear, Pte de la Cahotte; synch; 120°-170°; 49°21'·93N 00°04'·58E.

W trng wall ☆ Fl WG 4s 10m W9M, G6M; 005°-W-176°-G-005°; B pylon, G top; 49°22'·37N 00°04'·11E. Also 4 unlit SHM bcns.

E trng wall ☆ Fl (4) WR 12s 8m W7M, R4M; 131°-W-175°-R-131°; W pylon, R top; 49°22'·22N 00°04'·33E. Also 3 unlit PHM bcns.

W outer bkwtr ☆ Iso G 4s 9m 5M; 49°22'·11N 00°04'·33E.

West inner jetty (*estacade*) ☆ QG 11m 9M; 49°22'·03N 00°04'·43E.

DIVES-SUR-MER *Note the E-W longitude change.*

DI Iso 4s; 49°19'·17N 00°05'·86W.

No. 1 VQ G; 49°18'·50N 00°05'·67W. Ch bys freq moved.

No. 2 VQ R; 49°18'·51N 00°05'·56W.

No. 3 QG 7m 4M; W pylon, G top; 49°18'·30N 00°05'·55W.

No. 5 Fl G 4s 8m 4M; W pylon, G top; 49°18'·09N 00°05'·50W.

Bcns 3 & 5, if damaged, may be temporarily replaced by buoys.

No. 7 Fl G 4s; 49°17'·65N 00°05'·31W.

OUISTREHAM and CAEN

Merville VQ; 49°19'·65N 00°13'·39W; spoil ground buoy.

Ouistreham VQ (3) 5s; wreck buoy; 49°20'·42N 00°14'·81W.

Ldg lts 185°, both Dir Oc (3+1) R 12s 10/30m **17M**; intens 183·5°-186·5°, synch. **Front** ☆, E jetty, W mast, R top, 49°16'·99N 00°14'·81W. **Rear** ☆, 610m from front, tripod, R top.

No. 1 QG; 49°19'·19N 00°14'·67W.

No. 2 QR; 49°19'·17N 00°14'·43W.

Barnabé ☆ QG 7m 5M; W pylon, G top; 49°18'·02N 00°14'·76W.

St-Médard ☆ QR 7m 5M; 49°18'·02N 00°14'·62W.

Riva ☆ Fl G 4s 9m 3M; W pylon, G top; 49°17'·73N 00°14'·79W.

Quilbé ☆ Fl R 4s 9m 3M; W pylon, R top; 49°17'·72N 00°14'·67W.

Ouistreham lt ho ☆ Oc WR 4s 37m **W17M**, R13M; 115°-R-151°-W-115°; W twr, R top; 49°16'·79N 00°14'·87W.

COURSEULLES-SUR-MER

Courseulles Iso 4s; 49°21'·28N 00°27'·68W.

W jetty ☆ Iso WG 4s 7m; W9M, G6M; 135°-W-235°-G-135°; brown pylon on dolphin, G top; 49°20'·41N 00°27'·37W.

E jetty ☆ Oc (2) R 6s 9m 7M; 49°20'·26N 00°27'·39W.

COURSEULLES TO ST VAAST

Ver ☆ Fl (3)15s 42m **26M;** obsc'd by cliffs of St Aubin when brg >275°; conspic lt ho, W twr, Gy top; 49°20'·41N 00°31'·13W.

ARROMANCHES

Ent buoys: 49°21'·35N 00°37'·26W; 49°21'·25N 00°37'·30W.

Bombardons wreck buoys; 49°21'·66N 00°38'·97W.

PORT-EN-BESSIN

Ldg lts 204°, both Oc (3) 12s 25/42m 10/11M; synch. Front, 069°-339°, W pylon, G top; 49°20'·96N 00°45'·53W. Rear; 114°-294°, W and Gy ho; 93m from front.

E mole ☆ Oc R 4s 14m 7M, R pylon; 49°21'·12N 00°45'·38W.

W mole ☆ Fl WG 4s 14m, W10M, G7M; G065°-114·5°, W114·5°-065°; G pylon; 49°21'·17N 00°45'·43W.

COASTAL MARKS

Omaha Beach, 1M off : 49°22'·66N 00°50'·28W; 49°23'·17N 00°51'·93W; 49°23'·66N 00°53'·74W.

Broadsword Q (3) 10s, wreck buoy; 49°25'·34N 00°52'·96W.

Est du Cardonnet VQ (3) 5s; 49°26'·83N 01°01'·10W.

GRANDCAMP

Les Roches de Grandcamp: No. 1 49°24'·72N 01°01'·75W; No. 3 49°24'·92N 01°03'·70W; No. 5 49°24'·78N 01°04'·98W.

Ldg lts 146°, both Dir Q 9/12m **15M**, 144·5°-147·5°. **Front** ☆, 49°23'·42N 01°02'·90W. **Rear** ☆,102m from front.

Jetée Est ☆ Oc (2) R 6s 9m 9M; *Horn Mo(N) 30s;* 49°23'·53N 01°02'·96W.

Jetée Ouest ☆ Fl G 4s 9m 6M; 49°23'·47N 01°02'·96W.

ISIGNY-SUR-MER

IS, small B/Y, no topmark (on AC 2135); 49°24'·28N 01°06'·37W.

No 1 , Fl R 4s; 49°23'·60N 01°07·27W

Dir lts 173°, both Dir Q WRG 7m 9M; 49°19'·57N 01°06·78W.

Training wall heads Fl G 4s; 49°21'·40N 01°07'·20W; Fl R 4s, 49°21'·40N 01°07'·10W, off Pte du Grouin.

CARENTAN

C-I Iso 4s; 49°25'·44N 01°07'·08W; 210°/1·76M to 1 & 2 bys.

No. 1 Fl G 2·5s; 49°23'·93N 01°08'·52W.

No. 2 Fl R 2·5s; 49°23'·88N 01°08'·37W.

Trng wall Fl (4) G 15s; G △ on G bcn;49°21'·96N 01°09'·95W.

Trng wall Fl (4) R 15s; R □ on R bcn;49°21'·93N 01°09'·878W.

Ldg lts 209·5°. **Front** ☆ Dir Oc (3) R 12s 6m **18M**; intens 208·2°-210·7°; W mast, R top; 49°20'·47N 01°11'·17W. Rear, Dir Oc (3) 12s 14m 10M; vis 120°-005°; W gantry, G top; 723m from front.

ÎLES SAINT-MARCOUF

Iles St-Marcouf ☆ VQ (3) 5s 18m 8M; □ Gy twr, G top; 49°29'·86N 01°08'·81W.

Ouest-Saint-Marcouf Q (9) 15s; 49°29'·73N 01°11'·97W.

Saint Floxel 49°30'·64N 01°13'·94W.

Quineville Q (9) 10s, wreck buoy; 49°31'·79N 01°12'·38W.

ST VAAST TO POINTE DE BARFLEUR

ST VAAST-LA-HOUGUE

Ldg lts 267°: Front, La Hougue Oc 4s 9m 10M; W pylon, G top; 49°34'·25N 01°16'·37W. Rear, Morsalines Oc (4) WRG 12s 90m, W11M, R/G8M; 171°-W-316°-G-321°-R-342°-W-355°; W 8-sided twr, G top; 49°34'·16N 01°19'·10W, 1·8M from front.

Le Manquet 49°34'·26N 01°15'·56W.

Le Bout du Roc 49°34'·68N 01°15'·27W.

La Dent 49°34'·57N 01°14'·20W.

Le Gavendest Q (6) + L Fl 15s; 49°34'·36N 01°13'·89W.

Jetty ☆ Dir Oc (2) WRG 6s 12m W10M, R/G7M; 219°-R-237°-G-310°-W-350°-R-040°; W 8-sided twr, R top; *Siren Mo(N) 30s;* 49°35'·17N 01°15'·41W.

Pte de Saire ☆ Oc (2+1) 10s 11m 10M; squat W twr, G top; 49°36'·36N 01°13'·78W.

BARFLEUR

Ldg lts 219·5°, both Oc (3) 12s 7/13m 10M; synch. Front, W□ twr;49°40'·18N 01°15'·61W. Rear, 085°-355°; Gy and W□ twr, G top; 288m from front.

La Grotte 49°41'·06N 01°14'·86W.

Roche-à-l'Anglais 49°40'·78N 01°14'·93W.

La Vimberge 49°40'·54N 01°15'·25W.

W jetty ☆ Fl G 4s 8m 6M; 49°40'·32N 01°15'·57W.

E jetty ☆ Oc R 4s 5m 6M; 49°40'·31N 01°15'·47W.

La Jamette 49°41'·87N 01°15'·59W.

Pte de Barfleur ☆ Fl (2) 10s 72m **25M**; obsc when brg less than 088°; Gy twr, B top; 49°41'·78N 01°15'·96W.

POINTE DE BARFLEUR TO CAP DE LA HAGUE

Les Équets Q 8m 3M; 49°43'·62N 01°18'·36W.

Basse du Rénier VQ 8m 4M; 49°44'·84N 01°22'·09W.

Les Trois Pierres 49°42'·90N 01°21'·80W.

Anse de Vicq, 158° ldg lts; both Iso R 4s 8/14m 6M; front 49°42'·20N 01°23'·95W.

La Pierre Noire Q (9) 15s 8m 4M;49°43'·54N 01°29'·07W.

PORT DU LÉVI

Cap Lévi ☆ Fl R 5s 36m **17M**; Gy □ twr; 49°41'·75N 01°28'·38W.

Port Lévi ☆ Oc (2) WRG 6s 7m 7M; 055°-G-083°-W-105°-R-163°; W & Gy hut, W lantern; 49°41'·24N 01°28'·34W.

PORT DU BECQUET

Ldg lts 186·3°, both intens 183°-190°; synch. Front, Dir Oc (3) 12s 8m 10M; W 8-sided twr; 49°39'·23N 01°32'·84W. Rear, Dir Oc (3) R 12s 13m 7M. W 8-sided twr, R top; 49m from front.

CHERBOURG, EASTERN ENTRANCES

Passe Collignon ☆ Fl (2) R 6s 5m 4M; 49°39'·59N 01°34'·24W.

Passe de l'Est, Jetée des Flamands ldg lts 189°, both Q 9/16m 13M. Front, 49°39'·33N 01°35'·94W . Rear, 516m from front.

Roches du Nord-Ouest Fl R 2·5s; 49°40'·64N 01°35'·28W.

La Truite Fl (4) R 15s; 49°40'·33N 01°35'·49W.

Fort d'Île Pelée ☆ Oc (2) WR 6s 19m; W10M, R7M; 055°-W-120°-R-055°; W & R pedestal; 49°40'·21N 01°35'·08W.

Fort de l'Est ☆ 49°40'·28N 01°35'·92W, Iso G 4s 19m 9M.

Fort Central ☆ VQ (6) + L Fl 10s 5m 4M; 322°-032°; 49°40'·40N 01°37'·04W.

CHERBOURG, PASSE DE L'OUEST

CH1 ⊙; V-AIS; 49°43'·24N 01°42'·09W.

Passe de l'Ouest outer ldg lts 141·2°. **Front,** Dir Q (2 horiz, 63m apart) 5m **17M**; intens 137·3°-143·3° & 139·2°-145·2°; W △ on bcn; 49°39'·55N 01°37'·95W. **Rear,** Dir Q 35m **19M**; intens 140°-142·5°; W △ on Gy pylon.

Fort de l'Ouest ☆ Fl (3) WR 15s 19m **W24M, R20M**; 122°-W-355°-R-122°; Gy twr, R top; 49°40'·45N 01°38'·87W.

Fort de l'Ouest Fl R 4s; 49°40'·39N 01°38'·89W.

Q (6) + L Fl 15s; 49°40'·34N 01°38'·65W.

Digue de Querqueville ☆ Fl (2) G 6s 8m 6M; W col, G top; 49°40'·30N 01°39'·80W.

Inner ldg lts 124·3°; both intens 114·3°-134·3°: Front, Digue du Homet head, QG 10m 6M; 49°39'·48N 01°36'·96W. Rear, Dir Iso G 4s 16m 13M; W col, B bands, 397m from front.

La Ténarde VQ 8m 4M; 49°39'·74N 01°37'·75W.

CHERBOURG, PETITE RADE and MARINA

Entrance, W side, Digue du Homet ☆ QG 10m 8M; intens 114·3°-134·3°; W pylon, G top; 49°39'·48N 01°36'·96W.

E side, Q R, off Jetée des Flamands; 49°39'·44N 01°36'·60W.

Marina ent, E side, ☆ Fl (3) R 12s 6m 6M; W col, R lantern; 49°38'·91N 01°37'·08W.

W mole ☆ Fl (3) G 12s 7m 6M; G pylon; 49°38'·87N 01°37'·15W.

E quay☆ Fl (4) R 15s 3m 3M; R bcn; 49°38'·79N 01°37'·12W.

Wavescreen pontoon, N end ☆ Fl (4) G 15s 4m 2M; W post, G top.

CHERBOURG TO CAP DE LA HAGUE

Raz de Bannes 49°41'·32N 01°44'·53W.

Omonville Dir lt 257°: Iso WRG 4s13m; W10M, R/G7M; 180°-G-252°-W-262°-R-287°; W pylon, G top; 49°42'·24N 01°50'·15W.

L'Étonnard 49°42'·33N 01°49'·84W.

Basse Bréfort VQ 8m 4M; 49°43'·90N 01°51'·15W.

Jobourg Nuclear plant chimney, R lts; 49°40'·80N 01°52'·91W.

La Plate Fl (2+1) WR 10s 11m; W9M, R6M; 115°-W-272°-R-115°; Y 8-sided twr, with B top; 49°43'·97N 01°55'·74W.

Cap de la Hague (Gros du Raz) ☆ Fl 5s 48m **23M**; Gy twr, W top; *Horn 30s;* 49°43'·31N 01° 57'·26W.

La Foraine VQ (9) 10s, 12m 6M; 49°42'·90N 01°58'·31W.

DISTANCE TABLES

Approx distances in nautical miles are by the most direct route allowing for dangers and TSS.

1. Dunkerque-Est	**1**																		
2. Calais	28	**2**																	
3. Boulogne	49	21	**3**																
4. St Valéry-sur-Somme	86	58	37	**4**															
5. Le Tréport	90	62	41	16	**5**														
6. Dieppe	100	74	53	30	15	**6**													
7. St Valéry-en-Caux	109	81	62	42	28	16	**7**												
8. Fécamp	121	93	76	57	44	32	17	**8**											
9. Le Havre	148	121	103	84	71	61	47	27	**9**										
10. Honfleur	157	129	108	92	80	67	51	35	13	**10**									
11. Deauville/Trouville	152	125	108	91	79	61	53	34	9	13	**11**								
12. Dives-sur-Mer	155	129	110	94	83	66	55	38	16	19	9	**12**							
13. Ouistreham	160	138	115	97	85	73	59	41	20	24	15	9	**13**						
14. Courseulles	162	136	115	100	87	75	60	44	24	30	23	18	14	**14**					
15. Grandcamp	177	150	130	118	104	94	80	62	47	52	45	41	37	27	**15**				
16. Carentan	187	159	139	126	112	100	85	69	56	61	55	50	45	36	13	**16**			
17. St Vaast	179	151	131	120	107	96	80	65	54	61	54	50	46	35	16	20	**17**		
18. Barfleur	175	147	128	118	105	94	78	64	56	62	57	53	48	39	21	26	10	**18**	
19. Cherbourg	188	160	142	131	120	108	94	80	71	77	73	69	66	57	40	44	28	21	**19**

AREA 15 *N Central France (Cap de la Hague to St Quay) & Channel Is*

SELECTED LIGHTS, BUOYS & WAYPOINTS

CAP DE LA HAGUE TO ST MALO

GOURY

La Foraine VQ (9) 10s 12m 6M; 49°42'·90 N 01°58'·32W.

Ldg lts 065·2°: Front, QR 5m 7M; R □ in W □ on pier, 49°42'·89N 01°56'·70W. Rear, 116m from front, Q 11m 7M; W pylon/hut.

Hervieu 49°42'·77N 01°56'·92W.

DIELETTE

W bkwtr Dir lt 140°, Iso WRG 4s 12m W10M, R/G7M; 070°-G-135°-W-145°-R-180°; W twr, G top ;49°33'·18N 01°51'·81W.

E bkwtr ☆ Fl R 4s 6m 2M; 49°33'·21N 01°51'·78W.

Inner N jetty, Fl (2) R 6s. Inner S jetty, Fl (2) G 6s; bth 6m 1M.

Banc des Dious Q (9) 15s; 49°32'·58N 01°54'·02W.

CARTERET

Cap de Carteret ☆ Fl (2+1) 15s 81m **26M**; Gy twr, G top; 49°22'·40N 01°48'·41W.

W bkwtr ☆ Oc R 4s 7m 7M; W post, R top; 49°22'·07N 01°47'·32W.

E training wall ☆ Fl G 2·5s 4m 2M; W post, G top; 49°22'·17N 01°47'·30W.

Channel bend ☆ Fl (2) R 6s 5m 1M; R pylon; 49°22'·58N 01°47'·23W. Inside the bend: ☆ Fl (2) G 6s 5m 1M; G pylon; 49°22'·55N 01°47'·20W.

Marina entry sill: ☆ Fl (3) R 12s and Fl (3) G 12s; R & G pylons.

PORTBAIL
PB 49°18'·37N 01°44'·75W.
Ldg lts 042°: Front, Q 14m 10M; W pylon, R top, 49°19'·75N 01°42'·50W. Rear, 870m frm front, Oc 4s 20m 10M; ch belfry.
49°19'·32N 01°43'·16W.
49°19'·20N 01°43'·00W.
Training wall head Fl (2) R 5s 5m 4M; W mast, R top; 49°19'·43N 01°42'·99W.

REGNÉVILLE
La Catheue Q (6) + L Fl 15s, 48°57'·67N 01°42'·23W.
Le Ronquet Fl (2) WR 6s, W6M, R4M; 100°-R-293°-W-100°; 49°00'·11N 01°38'·07W.
Pte d'Agon ☆ Oc (2) WR 6s 12m, W10M, R7M; 063°-R-110°-W-063°; W twr, R top, W dwelling; 49°00'·18N 01°34'·63W.
Dir lt 028°, Oc WRG 4s 9m, W12M, R/G9M; 024°-G-027°-W-029°-R-033°; house; 49°00'·63N 01°33'·36W.

PASSAGE DE LA DÉROUTE
Les Trois-Grunes Q (9) 15s, 49°21'·84N 01°55'·21W.
Écrévière Q (6) + L Fl 15s; *Bell;* 49°15'·27N 01°52'·16W.
Basse Jourdan Q (3) 10s; 49°06'·85N 01°43'·96W.
Le Boeuf 49°06'·56N 01°47'·17W.
Les Boeuftins 49°07'·03N 01°45'·96W.
La Basse du Sénéquet 49°05'·96N 01°41'·11W.
Le Sénéquet ☆ Fl (3) WR 12s 18m W13M, R10M; 083·5°-R-116·5°-W-083·5°; W twr; 49°05'·48N 01°39'·73W.
Les Nattes 49°03'·46N 01°41'·81W.
International F 49°02'·16N 01°42'·98W.
International E 49°02'·08N 01°47'·21W.
Basse le Marié Q (9) 15s; 49°01'·79N 01°48'·57W.
NE Minquiers VQ (3) 5s; *Bell;* 49°00'·85N 01°55'·30W.
Les Ardentes Q (3) 10s; 48°57'·89N 01°51'·53W.
SE Minquiers Q (3) 10s; *Bell;* 48°53'·42N 02°00'·09W.
S Minquiers Q (6) + L Fl 15s; 48°53'·09N 02°10'·10W.

ÎLES CHAUSEY
La Pointue 48°54'·44N 01°50'·92W.
L'Enseigne, W twr, B top; 48°53'·67N 01°50'·37W.
L'Etat, BW, 48°54'·67N 01°46'·21W.
Anvers wreck 48°53'·91N 01°41'·07W.
Le Founet Q (3) 10s; 48°53'·25N 01°42'·34W.
Le Pignon ☆ Fl (2) WR 6s 10m, W9M, R6M; 005°-R-150°-W-005°; B twr, W band; 48°53'·49N 01°43'·36 W.
La Haute Foraine 48°52'·89N 01°43'·66W.
Grande Île ☆ Fl 5s 39m **23M**; Gy □ twr, G top; *Horn 30s;* 48°52'·17N 01°49'·34W.
Channel Fl G 2s; 48°52'·07N 01°49'·08W.
La Crabière Est Dir Oc(3)WRG 12s 5m, W9M, R/G6M;079°-W-291°-G-329°-W-335°-R-079°; B beacon, Y top; 48°52'·46N 01°49'·39W.
La Cancalaise 48°51'·90N 01°51'·11W.

GRANVILLE
Le Videcoq VQ (9) 10s; 48°49'·66N 01°42'·06W.
La Fourchie 48°50'·15N 01°37'·00W.
Pointe du Roc ☆ Fl (4) 15s 49m **23M;** 48°50'·06N 01°36'·78W.
Le Loup Fl (2) 6s 8m 11M; 48°49'·57N 01°36'·24W.
Avant Port, E jetty ☆ Fl G 2·5s 11m 4M; 48°49'·93N 01°36'·19W.
W jetty ☆ Fl R 2·5s 12m 4M; 48°49'·86N 01°36'·23W.
Marina S bkwtr ☆ Fl (2) R 6s 12m 5M; W post, R top; *Horn (2) 40s;* 48°49'·89N 01°35'·90W.
N bkwtr ☆ Fl (2) G 6s 4m 5M; 48°49'·93N 01°35'·90W.
Sill, W side, QR 2M, E side QG 2M; Gy pylons topped R (W) and G (E).

CANCALE
La Fille 48°44'·16N 01°48'·46W.
Pierre-de-Herpin ☆ Oc (2) 6s 20m 13M; W twr, B top and base; 48°43'·77N 01°48'·92W.
Ruet *Bell;* 48°43'·44N 01°50'·11W.
Grande Bunouze 48°43'·17N 01°50'·95W.
Barbe Brûlée 48°42'·11N 01°50'·57W.
Jetty hd ☆ Oc (3) G 12s 9m 3M; W pylon B top; 48°40'·10N 01°51'·11W.

ST MALO AND RIVER RANCE

CHENAL DE LA BIGNE
Basse Rochefort (aka Basse aux Chiens) 48°42'·69N 01°57'·31W.
La Petite Bigne 48°41'·66N 01°58'·72W.
La Crolante; 48°41'·01N 01°59'·51W, off Pte de la Varde.
Les Létruns; *Bell;* 48°40'·71N 02°00'·61W.
Roches-aux-Anglais Fl G 4s; 48°39'·65N 02°02'·27W.
Les Crapauds-du-Bey Fl R 4s; 48°39'·37N 02°02'·57W.

CHENAL DES PETITS POINTUS
Dinard ch spire (74m) brg 203° to right of Le Petit Bé rocks.
La Saint-Servantine Fl G 2·5s; *Bell;* 48°41'·93N 02°00'·94W.
Les Petits Pontus 48°41'·30N 02°00'·86W.

CHENAL DE LA GRANDE CONCHÉE
Villa Brisemoulin 181·5°, on with LH edge of Le Petit Bé rocks.
La Plate Q WRG 11m, W10M, R/G7M; 140°-W-203°-R-210°-W-225°-G-140°; 48°40'·78N 02°01'·91W.
Le Bouton 48°40'·59N 02°01'·85W.

CHENAL DU BUNEL
Dinard water twr lt 158·2° on with St Énogat lts.
St Énogat ldg lts 158·2°; both Iso 4s 3/85m 6/8M, synch. Front 48°38'·29N 02°04'·11W, vis 126°-236°. Rear, 1.4M from front, on water twr; vis 143°-210°.
Bunel Q (9) 15s; 48°40'·84N 02°05'·38W.

CHENAL DE LA PETITE PORTE
Outer ldg lts 129·7°: **Front, Le Grand Jardin** ☆ Fl (2) R 10s 24m **15M**, 48°40'·20N 02°04'·97W. 992271314. Rear, **La Balue** ☆ FG 20m **22M;** 3·1M from front; intens 128°-129·5°; Gy □ twr; 48°38'·16N 02°01'·30W.
Vieux-Banc E Q; 48°42'·38N 02°09'·12W.
Vieux-Banc W VQ (9) 10s; 48°41'·84N 02°10'·20W.
St Malo Atterrisage (Fairway) Iso 4s; 48°41'·39N 02°07'·28W.
Les Courtis Fl G 4s 14m 7M; 48°40'·46N 02°05'·80W.

Nearing Le Grand Jardin, move stbd briefly onto Ch du Bunel 152·8° ldg lts to pick up: Inner ldg lts 128·6°, both Dir FG 20/69m **22/25M**; H24. Front, **Les Bas Sablons** ☆, intens 127·2°-130·2°; W □ twr, B top; 48°38'·16N 02°01'·30W. 992271312. Rear, **La Balue** ☆, 0·9M from front; intens 128°-129·5°; Gy □ twr; 48°37'·60N 02°00'·24W. 992271313.

Basse du Nord No. 5 48°39′·98N 02°05′·04W.
Les Pierres-Garnier No. 8 48°39′·98N 02°04′·41W.
Les Patouillets Fl (3) G 12s, 48°39′·68N 02°04′·30W.
Clef d'Aval No. 10 48°39′·72N 02°03′·91W.
Basse du Buron No. 12 Fl (4) R 15s, 48°39′·42N 02°03′·51W.
Le Buron Fl (4) G 15s 15m 7M; G twr, 48°39′·32N 02°03′·66W.
Les Grelots VQ (6) + L Fl 10s, 48°39′·16N 02°03′·03W.

CHENAL DE LA GRANDE PORTE
Banchenou VQ, 48°40′·44N 02°11′·48W.
Outer ldg lts 089·1°: **Front, Le Grand Jardin** ☆ Fl (2) R 10s 24m **15M,** 48°40′·20N 02°04′·97W.
Rear, **Rochebonne** ☆ Dir FR 40m **24M**; intens 088·2°-089·7°; Gy □ twr, R top, 4·2M from front; 48°40'·26N 01°58'·71W. 992271311.
Buharats W No. 2 Fl R 2·5s, 48°40′·22N 02°07′·50W.
Buharats E No. 4 *Bell;* 48°40′·24N 02°07′·20W.
Bas du Boujaron No. 1 Fl (2) G 6s, 48°40'·17N 02°05'·97W.
Le Sou VQ (3) 5s; 48°40′·11N 02°05′·30W.
Continue on inner 128·6° ldg line: see Chenal de la Petite Porte.

RADE DE ST MALO
Plateau Rance Nord VQ, 48°38′·64N 02°02′·35W.
Plateau Rance Sud Q (6) + L Fl 15s, 48°38′·43N 02°02′·28W.
Crapaud de la Cité QG, 48°38′·34N 02°02′·01W.

ST MALO
Môle des Noires hd ☆ VQ R 11m 6M; W twr, R top; *Horn (2) 20s*; 48°38′·52N 02°01′·91W.
Écluse du Naye ldg lts 070·4°, both FR 7/23m 3/7M. Front, 48°38′·58N 02°01′·48W. Rear, 030°-120°.
Ferry jetty hd, ☆ VQ G 6M; 48°38′·44N 02°01′·82W (128·6° ldg line). Ferry jetty, ☆ Fl R 4s 3m 1M; 260°-080°; 48°38′·44N 02°01′·76W.
Bas-Sablons marina, mole head ☆ Fl G 4s 7m 5M; Gy mast; 48°38′·42N 02°01′·70W.

LA RANCE BARRAGE
La Jument Fl G 4s 6m 4M; G twr, 48°37′·44N 02°01′·76W.
ZI 12 Fl R 4s, 48°37′·47N 02°01′·62W.
NE dolphin ☆ Fl (2) R 6s 6m 5M; 040°-200°, 48°37′·09N 02°01′·71W.
Barrage lock, NW wall ☆ Fl (2) G 6s 6m 5M,191°-291°; G pylon, 48°37′·06N 02°01′·73W.
Barrage lock, SW wall, ☆ Fl (3) G 12s, 48°37′·00N 02°01′·70W.
SE dolphin ☆ Fl (3) R 12s, 48°36′·97N 02°01′·66W.
ZI 24 Fl (2) R 6s, 48°36′·63N 02°01′·33W.

ST MALO TO ST QUAY-PORTRIEUX

ST BRIAC
R. Frémur mouth. Dir lt 125° Iso WRG 4s 10m, W13M, R/G 11M; 121·5°-G-124·5°-W-125·5°-R-129·5°; W mast on hut, 48°37′·07N 02°08′·20W.

ST CAST
Les Bourdinots 48°39′·01N 02°13′·48W.
St Cast môle ☆ Iso WG 4s 12m, W9M, G6M; 180°-G-206°-W-217°-G-235°-W-245°-G-340°; G&W structure; 48°38′·41N 02°14′·61W.

Laplace , 48°39′·73N 2°16′·45W; 5ca SE of Pte de la Latte.
Cap Fréhel ☆ Fl (2) 10s 85m **29M**; Gy □ twr, G lantern; 48°41′·05N 02°19′·13W. Reserve lt range **15M**.

CHENAL and PORT D'ERQUY
Les Justières Q (6) + L Fl 15s; 48°40′·56N 02°26′·48W.
Basses du Courant VQ (6) + L Fl 10s; 48°39′·21N 02°29′·16W.
L'Evette 48°38′·51N 02°31′·45W.
S môle ☆ Fl (2) WRG 6s 11m W10M, R/G7M; 055°-R-081°-W-094°-G-111°-W-120°-R-134°; W twr; 48°38′·06N 02°28′·68W.
Inner jetty ☆ Fl (3) R 12s 10m 3M; R/W twr; 48°38′·09N 02°28′·39W.

DAHOUET
Petit Bignon 48°36′·82N 02°35′·06W.
Le Dahouet 48°35′·15N 02°35′·43W.
La Petite Muette Fl WRG 4s 10m W9M, R/G6M; 055°-G-114°-W-146°-R-196°; W twr, G band; 48°34′·82N 02°34′·30W.
Entry chan, Fl (2) G 6s 5m 1M; 156°-286°; 48°34′·71N 02°34′·19W.

BAIE DE ST BRIEUC
Grand Léjon ☆ Fl (5) WR 20s 17m **W18M**, R14M; 015°-R-058°-W-283°-R-350°-W-015°; R twr, W bands; 48°44′·91N 02°39′·87W. 992271325.
Petit Léjon ; 48°41′·80N 02°37′·55W.
Les Landas Q, 48°41′·43N 02°31′·29W.
Le Rohein Q (9) WRG 15s 13m, W8M, R/G5M; 072°-R-105°-W-180°-G-193°-W-237°-G-282°-W-301°-G-330°-W-072°; Y twr, B band; 48°38′·80N 02°37′·77W.

SAINT-BRIEUC LE LÉGUÉ
Tra-Hillion 48°33′·38N 02°38′·50W.
Le Légué Mo (A)10s; 48°34′·32N 02°41′·15W.
No. 1 Fl G 2·5s; 48°32′·42N 02°42′·51W.
No. 2 Fl R 2·5s; 48°32′·37N 02°42′·40W.
No. 3 Fl (2) G 6s; 48°32′·27N 02°42′·78W.
No. 4 Fl (2) R 6s; 48°32′·23N 02°42′·70W.
No. 5 Fl (3) G 12s; 48°32′·18N 02°42′·92W.
No. 6 Fl (3) R 12s; 48°32′·14N 02°42′·90W.
NE jetty ☆ VQ R 4M; 48°32′·12N 02°42′·88W.
Pte à l'Aigle jetty ☆ VQ G 13m 8M; 160°-070°; W twr, G top; 48°32′·12N 02°43′·11W.
No. 7 Fl (4) G 15s; 48°32′·11N 02°43′·08W.
No. 8 Fl R 2·5s; 48°32′·01N 02°43′·16W.
No. 9 Fl (2) G 6s; 48°31′·96N 02°43′·29W.
No. 10 Fl (2) R 6s; 48°31′·91N 02°43′·31W.
Jetty☆ Iso G 4s 6m 2M; W cols, G top; 48°31′·90N 02°43′·43W.
No. 11 Fl (3) G 12s; 48°31′·90N 02°43′·43W.
No. 13 Fl (4) G 15s; 48°31′·76N 02°43′·56W.
No. 14 Fl (4) R 15s; 48°31′·70N 02°43′·61W.

BINIC
N môle ☆ Oc (3) 12s 12m 11M; unintens 020°-110°; W twr, G lantern; 48°36′·07N 02°48′·92W.

ST QUAY-PORTRIEUX
Les Hors 48°39′·60N 02°44′·04W.
Caffa Q (3) 10s; 48°37′·82N 02°43′·08W.

La Longue ♁ 48°37′·88N 02°44′·68W.
La Roselière ⚓ VQ (6) + L Fl 10s; 48°37′·31N 02°46′·19W.
Herflux Dir ☆ 130°, Fl (2) WRG 6s 10m, W 8M, R/G 6M; 115°-G-125°-W-135°-R-145°; 48°39′·07N 02°47′·95W.
Île Harbour (Roches de Saint-Quay) ☆ Fl WRG 4s 16m, W9M, R/G 6M; 011°-R-133°-G-270°-R-306°-G-358°-W-011°; W twr & dwelling, R top; 48°39′·99N 02°48′·49W. 992271321.
Madeux 48°40′·41N 02°48′·81W.
Grandes Moulières de St Quay 48°39′·76N 02°49′·91W.
Moulières de Portrieux 48°39′·26N 02°49′·21W.
Les Noirs 48°39′·09N 02°48·46W.
Marina, **NE mole elbow**, Dir lt 318·2°: Iso WRG 4s 16m **W15M**, R/G11M; W159°-179°, G179°-316°, W316°-320·5°, R320·5° -159°; Reserve lt ranges 11/8M; 48°38′·99N 02°49′·09W. 992271322.
NE môle hd ☆ Fl (3) G 12s 10m 2M; 48°38′·84N 02°48′·91W.
S môle hd ☆ Fl (3) R 12s 10m 2M; 48°38′·83N 02°49′·03W.
Old hbr ent: N side, Fl G 2.5s 11m 2M; 48°38′·71N 02°49′·36W.
S side, Fl R 2.5s 8m 2M; 48°38′·67N 02°49′·35W.

MID-CHANNEL MARKS

CHANNEL LT VESSEL Fl 15s 12m **15M**; R hull with lt twr amidships; *Horn (20s)*; ***Racon O, 15M;*** 49°54′·46N 02°53′·74W; 992351028.
E Channel Fl Y 5s 6M; ***Racon T, 10M;*** 49°58′·67N 02°29′·01W.

COTENTIN PENINSULA (NW COAST)

La Plate Fl (2+1) WR 10s 11m; W9M, R6M; 115°-W-272°-R-115°; Y 8-sided twr, with B top; 49°43′·98N 01°55′·76W.
Cap de la Hague (Gros du Raz) ☆ Fl 5s 48m **23M**; Gy twr, W top; *Horn 30s;* 49°43′·31N 01° 57′·27W.
La Foraine VQ (9) 10s 12m 6M; 49°42′·90 N 01°58'·32W.
Cap de Carteret ☆ Fl (2+1) 15s 81m **26M**; Gy twr, G top; 49°22′·41N 01°48′·41W.

THE CASQUETS AND ALDERNEY

Casquets ☆ Fl (5) 30s 37m **18M**, H24; W twr, 2 R bands; NW'most of three; ***Racon T, 25M;*** 49°43′·32N 02°22′·63W. 992351121.
Ortac rock, unlit; 49°43′·40N 02°17′·44W.
Pierre au Vraic, unmarked rk 1·2m ✻; 49°41′·61N 02°16′·94W.
Quenard Pt (Alderney) ☆ Fl (4) 15s 37m 12M; 085°-027°; W ○ twr, B band; 49°43′·75N 02°09′·86W.
Château à L'Étoc Pt ☆ Iso WR 4s 20m W10M, R7M; 071·1°-R- 111·1°-W-151·1°; 49°43′·94N 02°10′·63W.

BRAYE

Ldg bns 142° (to clear the submerged Adm'ty bkwtr). Front, W, 49°43′·90N 02°10′·97W. Rear, BW; 720m from front.
Ldg lts 215°: both Q 8/17m 9/12M, synch; 210°-220°; orange △s. Front, old pier elbow, 49°43′·40N 02°11′·91W. Rear, 215°/335m.
Admiralty bkwtr head ☆ L Fl 10s 7m 5M; 49°43′·82N 02°11′·67W.
FairwayNo. 1 QG; 49°43′·72N 02°11′·72W.
No. 2 QR; 49°43′·60N 02°11′·75W.
Inner fairway Q (2) G 5s; 49°43′·58N 02°11′·98W.
Braye quay ☆ 2 FR (vert) 8m 5M; 49°43′·53N 02°12′·00W.
Little Crabby hbr ent ☆ FG & FR 5m 2M; 49°43′·45N 02°12′·12W.

GUERNSEY, NORTHERN APPROACHES

LITTLE RUSSEL CHANNEL

Grande Amfroque, two unlit bcn twrs: larger, BW-banded; smaller, white; 49°30′·57N 02°24′·62W.
Tautenay ☆ Q (3) WR 6s 7m W7M, R6M; 050°-W-215°-R-050°; B & W striped bcn 49°30′·11N 02°26′·84W.
Platte Fougère ☆ Fl WR 10s 15m **16M**; 155°-W-085°-R-155°; W 8-sided twr, B band; *Horn 45s*; ***Racon P;*** 49°30′·83N 02°29′·14W.
Corbette d'Amont Y bcn twr, topmark; 49°29′·64N 02°29′·38W.
Roustel ☆ Q 8m 7M; BW chequered base, W framework col; 49°29′·23N 02°28′·79W.
Rousse, Y bcn twr, topmark ✠; 49°28′·98N 02°28′·36W.
Platte ☆, Fl WR 3s 6m, W7M, R5M; 024°-R-219°-W-024°; G conical twr; 49°29′·08N 02°29′·57W.
Vivian bcn twr, BW bands, 49°28′·45N 02°30′·66W.
Brehon ☆ Iso 4s 19m 9M; bcn on ○ twr, 49°28'·28N 02°29′·28W.
Demie Flieroque, Y bcn twr, topmark F; 49°28′·13N 02°31′·38W.

BIG RUSSEL

Noire Pute ☆ Fl (2) WR 15s 8m 6M; 220°-W-040°-R-220°; on 2m high rock; 49°28′·21N 02°25′·02W; unreliable.
Fourquies Q; 49°27′·34N 02°26′·47W.
Lower Heads Q (6) + L Fl 15s; *Bell;* 49°25′·85N 02°28′·55W.

GUERNSEY, HERM AND SARK

BEAUCETTE MARINA

Petite Canupe Q (6) + L Fl 15s; 49°30′·20N 02°29′·14W.
Ldg lts 277°: Both FR. Front, W □, R stripe; 49°30′·19N 02°30′·23W. Rear, R □, W stripe; 185m from front.
Appr chan buoys: SWM L Fl 10s 49°30′·15N 02°29′·66W. SHM Fl G 5s, PHM Fl R 5s & Fl (3) R 5s. NCM perch Q 49°30′·165N 02°30′·06W. SHM perch Q (3) G 5s at ent; 49°30′·18N 02°30′·24W.

ST SAMPSON

Ldg lts 286°: Front, FR 3m 5M; 230°-340°; tfc sigs; 49°28′·90N 02°30′·74W. Rear, FG 13m; clock twr, 390m from front.
N Pier ☆ FG 3m 5M; 230°-340°; 49°28′·92N 02°30′·71W.
Crocq pier ☆ FR 11m 5M; 250°-340°; 49°28′·98N 02°31′·00W.

ST PETER PORT

Outer ldg lts 220°: **Front**, Castle bkwtr, Al WR 10s 14m **16M**; 187°-007°; dark ○ twr, W on NE side; *Horn 15s;* 49°27′·31N 02°31′·45W.
Rear 220° ldg lt, Belvedere, Oc 10s 61m 14M; 179°-269°; intens 217°-223°; W □ on W twr; 980m from front. The lts are synchronised so that the rear lt is on when the front is W, and the off when the front is R.
Queen Elizabeth II marina, 270° Dir Oc ☆ WRG 3s 5m 6M; 258°-G-268°-W-272°-R-282°; 49°27′·73N 02°31′·87W.
Reffée Q (6) + L Fl 15s; 49°27′·74N 02°31′·27W.

Appr buoys: outer pair QG; 49°27'·83N 02°31'·54W. QR; 49°27'·71N 02°31'·52W. Inner pair: QG; 49°27'·76N 02°31'·74W. QR; 49°27'·72N 02°31'·74W.

The Pool ldg lts 265° (*not* into moorings): Front, Victoria marina, S Pier, Oc R 5s 10m 14M; 49°27'·32N 02°32'·03W. Rear, Iso R 2s 22m 3M; 260°-270°; on Creasey's bldg, 160m from front.

White Rock pier Oc G 5s 11m 14M; intens 174°-354°; ○ twr; tfc sigs; 49°27'·38N 02°31'·59W.

S Fairway QG; 49°27'·30N 02°31'·76W; pontoon W of buoy.

Fl R; 49°27'·28N 02°31'·74W. 49°27'·27N 02°31'·80W. 49°27'·27N 02°31'·86W.

HAVELET BAY

Oyster Rock Y bcn, topmark 'O'; 49°27'·09N 02°31'·46W.

Oyster Rock QG; 49°27'·04N 02°31'·47W.

Moulinet QR; 49°26'·97N 02°31'·54W.

Moulinet Y bcn, topmark 'M'; 49°26'·95N 02°31'·58W.

GUERNSEY, SOUTH-EAST and SOUTH COASTS

Anfré, Y bcn, topmark 'A'; 49°26'·45N 02°31'·48W.

Longue Pierre, Y bcn, topmark 'LP'; 49°25'·36N 02°31'·48W.

St Martin's Pt Fl (3) WR 10s 15m 14M; 185°-R-191°-W-011°-R-061·5°; flat-topped, W bldg. *Horn (3) 30s;* 49°25'·30N 02°31'·70W.

GUERNSEY, NORTH-WEST COAST

Les Hanois Fl (2) 13s 33m **20M**; 294°-237°; Gy ○ twr, B lantern, helicopter platform; *Horn (2) 60s.* 49°26'·10N 02°42'·15W.

4 FR on mast 1·3M ESE of Les Hanois lt ho.

Portelet Hbr, bkwtr bcn, 49°26'·16N 02°39'·84W.

Cobo Bay, Grosse Rock, B bcn 11m; 49°29'·02N 02°36'·19W.

Grand Havre, Rousse Point bkwtr, B bcn; 49°29'·92N 02°33'·05W.

HERM

Corbette de la Mare, Wh disc (W side) and R disc (E side) on Y pole, 49°28'·48N 02°28'·72W.

Petit Creux QR; red 'C' on red pole; 49°28'·09N 02°28'·72W.

Alligande Fl (3) G 5s; B pole, Or 'A'; 49°27'·86N 02°28'·78W.

Épec Fl G 3s; black 'E' on G mast; 49°27'·98N 02°27'·89W.

Vermerette Fl (2) Y 5s; Or 'V' on bcn; 49°28'·12N 02°27'·75W.

Gate Rock (Percée Pass) Q (9) 15s; 49°27'·88N 02°27'·54W.

Hbr ldg lts 078°: White drums. 2F occas; 49°28'·25N 02°27'·11W.

Hbr pier, N end 2 FG; G □ on G bcn; 49°28'·21N 02°27'·26W.

SARK

Courbée du Nez Fl (4) WR 15s 14m 8M; 057°-W-230°-R-057°; W structure on rock; 49°27'·09N 02°22'·17W.

Point Robert Fl 15s 65m **20M**; vis 138°-353°; W 8-sided twr; *Horn (2) 30s;* 49°26'·19N 02°20'·75W.

Founiais, topmark 'F'; 49°26'·02N 02°20'·36W.

Blanchard Q (3) 10s; *Bell;* 49°25'·36N 02°17'·42W.

Pilcher monument (070° appr brg); 49°25'·71N 02°22'·44W.

JERSEY, WEST AND SOUTH COASTS

Desormes Q (9) 15s; 49°18'·94N 02°17'·98W.

Grosnez Point Fl (2) WR 15s 50m **W19M, R17M**; 081°-W-188°-R-241°; W hut; 49°15'·50N 02°14'·80W.

L a Rocco twr (conspic) 15m; 49°11'·90N 02°14'·05W.

La Frouquie (seasonal); 49°11'·30N 02°15'·38W.

La Corbière Iso WR 10s 36m **W18M, R16M**; shore-W-294°-R-328°-W-148°-R-shore; W ○ twr; *Horn Mo (C) 60s;* 49°10'·79N 02°15'·01W.

Pt Corbière FR; R □, W stripe; 49°10'·87N 02°14'·38W.

WESTERN PASSAGE

Ldg lts 082°. Front, La Gréve d'Azette Oc 5s 23m 14M; 034°-129°; 49°10'·16N 02°05'·09W. Rear, Mont Ubé, Oc R 5s 46m 12M; 250°-095°; 1M from front.

Passage Rock VQ; 49°09'·54N 02°12'·26W.

Les Fours Q; 49°09'·59N 02°10'·16W.

Noirmont Pt Fl (4) 12s 18m 10M; B twr, W band; 49°09'·91N 02°10'·08W.

Pignonet 49°09'·88N 02°09'·70W.

Ruaudière Rock Fl G 3s; *Bell;* 49°09'·74N 02°08'·62W.

ST AUBIN'S BAY and HARBOUR

Les Grunes du Port 49°10'·02N 02°09'·14W.

Diamond Rock Fl (2) R 6s; 49°10'·12N 02°08'·64W.

Castle pier Fl R 4s 8m 1M; 49°11'·13N 02°09'·634W.

North pier, Dir lt 254° F WRG 5m, 248°-G-253°-W-255°-R-260°; 49°11'·22N 02°10'·03W. Same col, Iso R 4s 12m 10M.

Beach Rock 49°11'·29N 02°08'·42W, (Apr-Oct).

Rocquemin 49°10'·64N 02°07'·95W.

Baleine 49°10'·41N 02°08'·23W.

ST HELIER

Elizabeth marina, west appr: Dir 106°: F WRG 4m 1M; 096°-G-104°-W-108°-R-119°; R dayglo □, B stripe; 49°10'·76N 02°07'·12W.

La Vrachiére 49°10'·90N 02°07'·59W, Fl (2) 5s 1M.

Fort Charles North 49°10'·81N 02°07'·50W.

Marina ent Oc G & Oc R, both 4s 2M; 49°10'·83N 02°07'·13W.

Red & Green Passage, ldg lts 022·7° on dayglo R dolphins: Front, Elizabeth E berth Dn Oc G 5s 10m 11M; 49°10'·63N 02°06'·94W. Rear, Albert Pier root Oc R 5s 18m 12M; synch; 230m SSW.

East Rock QG; 49°09'·96N 02°07'·28W.

Dog's Nest Rk Fl Y 3s 3M; Y cross on bcn; 49°09'·99N 02°06'·95W.

Oyster Rocks, R/W bcn, topmark 'O'; 49°10'·10N 02°07'·49W.

Platte Rock Fl R 1·5s 6m 5M; R col; 49°10'·16N 02°07'·34W.

Small Road No. 2 QR; 49°10'·39N 02°07'·24W.

No. 4 QR; 49°10'·53N 02°07'·12W.

Elizabeth marina, S appr: E1 Fl G 3s; 49°10'·59N 02°07'·09W.

E2 Fl R 2s; 49°10'·58N 02°07'·13W.

E5 Fl G 5s; 49°10'·70N 02°07'·17W.

E6 Fl R 2s; 49°10'·69N 02°07'·21W.

Fort Charles East Q (3) 5s 2m 1M; 49°10′·74N 02°07′·26W.
La Collette basin QR; 49°10′·54N 02°06′·91W. 49°10′·52N 02°06′·90W.
St Helier Hbr, ldg lts 078°, both FG on W cols. Front, 49°10′·62N 02°06′·66W. Rear, 80m from front.
Victoria pier hd, Port control twr; IPTS; 49°10′·57N 02°06′·88W.

JERSEY, SOUTH-EAST AND EAST COASTS

Hinguette QR; 49°09′·33N 02°07′·32W.
Hettich Fl Y 5s; 49°08′·10N 02°09′·00W.
South Pier Marine Fl Y 5s; 49°09′·10N 02°06′·30W.
Demie de Pas Mo (D) WR 12s 11m, W14M, R10M; 130°-R-303°-W-130°; *Horn (3) 60s*; ***Racon T, 10M***; B bn twr, Y top; 49°09′·01N 02°06′·15W. Icho Tower (conspic, 14m) 49°08′·89N 02°02′·90W.
Canger Rock Q (9) 15s; 49°07′·35N 02°00′·38W.
La Conchière Q (6) + L Fl 15s 2M; 49°08′·22N 02°00′·17W.
Frouquier Aubert Q (6) + L Fl 15s; 49°06′·08N 01°58′·84W.
Violet L Fl 10s; 49°07′·81N 01°57′·14W.
Petite Anquette; SCM ; 49°08′·47N 01°56′·29W.
Grande Anquette VQ(9) 10s; 49°08′·32N 01°55′·20W.
Le Cochon 49°09′·77N 01°58′·80W.
La Noire 49°10′·13N 01°59′·23W. Le Giffard 49°10′·59N 01°59′·00W.

GOREY

Pier Hd Dir lt 298°, ☆ WRG, 6m 8M; 293·5°-G-296·5°-W-299·5°-R-302·5°; ☆ Oc RG 5s 6m 8M; 304°-R-353°-G-304°; W twr on pierhead; 49°11′·80N 02°01′·34W.
Horn Rock , topmark 'H'; 49°10′·96N 01°59′·85W.
Les Burons, R bcn, topmark 'B'; 49°11′·33N 02°00′·81W.
Fairway QG; 49°11′·50N 02°00′·34W.
Écureuil Rock 49°11′·67N 02°00′·78W.
Equerrière Rk, bcn 'fishtail' topmark; 49°11′·80N 02°00′·67W.
Les Arch , BW bcn, 'A' topmark; 49°12′·02N 02°00′·60W.

ST CATHERINE BAY

St Catherine Bay, Le Fara Q (3) 10s 3M; 49°12′·85N 02°00′·48W.
Archirondel Tower (conspic, 16m) 49°12′·72N 02°01′·42W.
Verclut bkwtr ☆ Fl 1·5s 18m 13M; 49°13′·34N 02°00′·64W. In line 315° with unlit turret, 49°13′·96N 02°01′·57W, on La Coupe Pt.

JERSEY, NORTH COAST

Rozel Bay Dir lt 245°, F WRG 11m 5M; 240°-G-244°-W-246°-R-250°; W col; 49°14′·21N 02°02′·76W.
Bonne Nuit Bay ldg lts 223°: both FG 7/34m 6M. Front, Pier 49°15′·10N 02°07′·17W. Rear, 170m from front.
Demie Rock 49°15′·56N 02°07′·36W.
Sorel Point ☆ L Fl WR 7·5s 50m **15M**; 095°-W-112°-R-173°-W-230°-R-269°-W-273°; W ○ twr, only 3m high; 49°15'·60N 02°09'·54W.

OFFLYING ISLANDS

LES ÉCREHOU

Écrevière Q (6) + L Fl 15s; 49°15′·26N 01°52′·15W.
Mâitre Ile 49°17′·08N 01°55′·60W.

PLATEAU DES MINQUIERS

N Minquiers Q; 49°01′·64N 02°00′·58W.
NE Minquiers VQ (3) 5s; *Bell;* 49°00′·85N 01°55′·30W.
SE Minquiers Q (3) 10s; *Bell;* 48°53′·42N 02°00′·09W.
S Minquiers Q (6) + L Fl 15s; 48°53′·09N 02°10′·10W.
SW Minquiers Q (9) 15s 5M; *Whis;* 48°54′·35N 02°19′·41W.
NW Minquiers Q 5M; *Whis;* 48°59′·63N 02°20′·59W.
Refuge ; B/W bcn; 49°00′·13N 02°10′·16W.
Demie de Vascelin 49°00′·81N 02°05′·17W.
Grand Vascelin, BW bcn 48°59′·97N 02°07′·26W.
Maitresse Ile, Puffin B&W bcn twr 48°58′·33N 02°03′·65W.
Le Coq Reef, Q (3) 10s 6m 3M; 48°57′·88N 02°01′·29W.

FRENCH MARKS NORTH OF ILE DE BRÉHAT

Roches Douvres ☆ Fl 5s 60m **24M**; pink twr on dwelling with G roof; 49°06′·30N 02°48′·87W. 992271319. (16M NNE of Ile de Bréhat).
Barnouic VQ (3) 5s 15m 7M; 49°01′·64N 02°48′·41W.
Roche Gautier VQ (9) 10s; 49°02′·013N 02°54′·36W.
Les Héaux de Bréhat ☆ Fl (4) WRG 15s 48m, **W15M**, R/G11M; 227°-R-247°-W-270°-G-302°-W-227°; Gy twr; 48°54′·50N 03°05′·18W (4·7M WNW of Ile de Bréhat).

DISTANCE TABLES

Approx distances in nautical miles are by the most direct route allowing for dangers and TSS.

1	Cherbourg	**1**																
2	Omonville	10	**2**															
3	Braye (Alderney)	25	15	**3**														
4	St Peter Port	44	34	23	**4**													
5	Creux (Sark)	37	29	22	10	**5**												
6	St Helier	64	51	46	29	24	**6**											
7	Carteret	41	29	28	31	23	26	**7**										
8	Portbail	49	33	32	35	27	25	5	**8**									
9	Iles Chausey	69	61	58	48	43	25	33	30	**9**								
10	Granville	75	67	66	55	50	30	38	35	9	**10**							
11	Dinan	102	91	85	66	64	50	62	59	29	35	**11**						
12	St Malo	90	79	73	54	52	38	50	47	17	23	12	**12**					
13	Dahouet	88	80	72	54	52	41	60	59	37	45	41	29	**13**				
14	Le Légué/St Brieuc	96	86	76	57	56	46	69	69	41	49	45	33	8	**14**			
15	Binic	95	84	75	56	55	46	70	70	43	51	45	33	10	8	**15**		
16	St Quay-Portrieux	88	80	73	56	51	46	64	64	47	54	47	35	11	7	4	**16**	
17	Lézardrieux	88	80	68	48	38	47	68	71	53	54	61	49	33	32	30	21	**17**

AREA 16 *N & S Brittany – Paimpol to Lesconil*

SELECTED LIGHTS, BUOYS & WAYPOINTS

OFFSHORE MARKS

Roches Douvres ☆ Fl 5s 60m **24M**; pink twr on dwelling with G roof; 49°06'·30N 02°48'·87W. 992271319.
Barnouic VQ (3) 5s 15m 7M; 49°01'·63N 02°48'·41W.
Roche Gautier VQ (9) 10s; 49°02'·013N 02°54'·36W.

PAIMPOL TO ÎLE DE BRÉHAT

PAIMPOL

Les Calemarguiers 48°46'·98N 02°54'·84W.
L'Ost Pic Fl(4)WR 15s 20m, W9M, R6M; 105°-W-116°-R-221°-W-253°- R-291°-W-329°; obsc by islets near Bréhat when brg < 162°; W twr/turret, R top; 48°46'·77N 02°56'·42W.
Les Charpentiers 48°47'·89N 02°56'·01W.
Pte de Porz-Don ☆ Oc (2) WR 6s 13m **W15M**, R11M; 269°-W-272°-R-279°; W house; 48°47'·48N 03°01'·55W. 992271327.
El Bras Fl G 2·5s; 48°47'·21N 03°01'·50W.
Fl R 2·5s; 48°47'·17N 03°01'·49W.
Ldg lts 262·2°, both QR 5/12m 7/10M. Front, Kernoa jetty; W & R hut; 48°47'·09N 03°02'·44W. Rear, Dir QR, intens 260·2°-264·2°; W pylon, R top; 360m from front. QG 48°47'·12N 03°02'·47W.

CHENAL DU FERLAS (277°-257°-271°)

Lel Ar Serive 48°49'·98N 02°58'·76W.
Loguivy Dir lt 257°: Q WRG 12m 10/8M; 254°-G-257°-W-257·7°- R-260·7°; Gy twr; 48°49'·37N 03°03'·67W.
Les Piliers 48°49'·77N 02°59'·99W.
Kermouster Dir 271°: Fl WRG 2s 16m, W 10M, R/G 8M; 267°-G-270°-W-272°- R-274°; W col; 48°49'·55N 03°05'·19W (R. Trieux).

ÎLE DE BRÉHAT

Le Paon Oc WRG 4s 22m W11M, R/G8M; 033°-W-078°-G-181°-W-196°- R-307°-W-316°-R-348°; Y twr; 48°51'·92N 02°59'·15W.
Roche Guarine 48°51'·63N 02°57'·63W, Chenal de Bréhat.
Rosédo ☆ Fl 5s 29m **20M**; W twr; vis 006°-340° (334°); 48°51'·45N 03°00'·29W.
La Chambre 48°50'·16N 02°59'·58W.
Men-Joliguet Fl (2) WRG 4s 6m W11M, R/G8M; 255°-R-279°-W-283°-G-175°; 48°50'·12N 03°00'·20W.

LÉZARDRIEUX TO TRÉGUIER

LE TRIEUX RIVER to LÉZARDRIEUX

Nord Horaine 48°54'·54N 02°55'·23W.
La Horaine Fl (3) 12s 13m 7M; Gy 8-sided twr on B hut; 48°53'·50N 02°55'·22W.
Men-Marc'h 48°53'·17N 02°51'·82W.
Ldg lts 224·8°: Front, **La Croix** ☆ Q 15m **18M**; intens 215°-235°; two Gy ○ twrs joined, W on NE side, R tops; 48°50'·23N 03°03'·25W. Rear **Bodic** ☆ Dir Q 55m **22M**; intens 221°-229°; W ho with G gable; 2·1M from front.
Les Sirlots *Whis;* 48°52'·95N 02°59'·58W.
Men-Grenn Q (9) 15s 7m 7M; 48°51'·22N 03°03'·89W.
Coatmer ldg lts 218·7°. Front, Q RG 16m R/G7M; 200°-R-250°-G-053°; W gable; 48°48'·26N 03°05'·75W. Rear, QR 50m 7M; vis 197°-242°; W gable; 660m from front.

Les Perdrix Fl (2) WG 6s 5m, W6M, G3M; 165°-G-197°-W-202·5°-G-040°; G twr; 48°47'·74N 03°05'·79W.

CH DE LA MOISIE (339·4°); PASSE DE LA GAINE (241·5°)

La Vieille du Tréou 48°52'·00N 03°01'·09W.
An Ogejou Bihan 48°53'·37N 03°01'·91W.
La Moisie 48°53'·83N 03°02'·22W.
Les Héaux de Bréhat ☆ Fl (4) WRG 15s 48m, **W15M**, R/G11M; 227°-R-247°-W-270°-G-302°-W-227°; Gy ○ twr; 48°54'·50N 03°05'·17W. 992271320.
Basse des Héaux 48°54'·07N 03°05'·28W.
Pont de la Gaine 48°53'·12N 03°07'·40W.

JAUDY RIVER TO TRÉGUIER

La Jument des Héaux VQ; 48°55'·36N 03°08'·04W.
Grande Passe ldg lts 137°. Front, Port de la Chaine, Oc 4s 12m 11M; 042°-232°; W house; 48°51'·55N 03°07'·89W.
Rear, **St Antoine** ☆ Dir Oc R 4s 34m **15M**; intens 134°-140°; R & W house; 0·75M from front. (Both marks are hard to see by day.)
Basse Crublent QR; *Whis;* 48°54'·29N 03°11'·16W.
Le Corbeau Fl R 4s; 48°53'·35N 03°10'·26W.
Pierre à l'Anglais Fl G 4s; 48°53'·21N 03°10'·46W.
Petit Pen ar Guézec Fl (2) G 6s; 48°52'·52N 03°09'·44W.
La Corne Fl (3) WRG 12s 14m W8M, R/G6M; 052°-W-059°-R-173°-G-213°-W-220°-R-052°; W twr, R base; 48°51'·35N 03°10'·62W.

TRÉGUIER TO TRÉBEURDEN

PORT BLANC

Le Voleur Dir ☆ 150°: Fl WRG 4s 17m, W14M, R/G 11M; 140°-G-148°-W-152°-R-160°; W twr; 48°50'·20N 03°18'·52W.
Basse Guazer ; 48°51'·58N 03°20'·96W.

PERROS-GUIREC

Passe de l'Est, ldg lts 224·8°. Front, Le Colombier Dir Q 28m 14M; intens 214·5°-234·5°; W house; 48°47'·87N 03°26'·66W. Rear, **Kerprigent** ☆, Dir Q 79m **21M**; intens 221°-228°; W twr, 1·5M from front.
Pierre du Chenal 48°49'·29N 03°24'·67W.
Passe de l'Ouest. Kerjean ☆ Dir lt 143·6°, Oc (2+1) WRG 12s 78m, **W15M**, R/G12M; 133·7°-G-143·2°-W-144·8°-R-154·3°; W twr, B top; 48°47'·79N 03°23'·39W.
Les Couillons de Tomé 48°50'·88N 03°25'·68W.
La Horaine 48°49'·89N 03°27'·26W.
Roche Bernard 48°49'·43N 03°25'·46W.
Gommonénou VQ R 1M; 48°48'·27N 03°25'·83W.
Jetée du Linkin Fl (2) G 6s 4m 6M; W pile, G top; 48°48'·20N 03°26'·31W.

PLOUMANAC'H

Mean-Ruz Oc WR 4s 26m W12M, R9M; 226°-W-242°-R-226°; obsc by Pte de Trégastel when brg <080°; partly obsc by Les Sept-Îles 156°-207° and partly by Île Tomé 264°-278°; pink □ twr; 48°50'·25N 03°29'·00W.

LES SEPT ÎLES

Île-aux-Moines ☆ Fl (3) 20s 59m **24M**; obsc by Îliot Rouzic and E end of Île Bono 237°-241°, and in Baie de Lannion when brg <039°; Gy twr/dwelling; 48°52'·72N 03°29'·40W. 992271326.
Les Dervinis 48°52'·35N 03°27'·32W.

TRÉGASTEL-PLAGE

Île Dhu 48°50′·37N 03°31′·24W.

Les Triagoz ☆ Fl (2) WR 6s 31m W14M, R11M; 010°-W-339°-R-010°; obsc in places 258°-268° by Les Sept-Îles; Gy □ twr, R lantern; 48°52′·28N 03°38′·80W. 992271324.

Bar-ar-Gall VQ (9) 10s; 48°49′·79N 03°36′·22W.

Le Crapaud Q (9) 15s; 48°46′·67N 03°40′·59W.

TRÉBEURDEN

Pte de Lan Kerellec ☆ Iso WRG 4s; W8M, R/G5M; 058°-G-064°-W-069°-R-130°; Gy twr; 48°46′·74N 03°35′·06W.

Ar Gouredec VQ (6) + L Fl 10s; 48°46′·41N 03°36′·59W.

An Ervennou Fl (2) R 6s; 48°46′·48N 03°35′·96W.

NW bkwtr ☆ Fl G 2·5s 8m 2M; IPTS; 48°46′·33N 03°35′·21W.

TRÉBEURDEN TO MORLAIX

LÉGUER RIVER

Beg-Léguer ☆ Oc (4) WRG 12s 60m W12M, R/G9M; 007°-G-084°-W-098°-R-129°; west face of W house, R lantern; 48°44′·31N 03°32′·91W.

Kinierbel ; *Bell;* 48°44′·15N 03°35′·18W.

LOCQUÉMEAU

Ldg lts 121°: Front, ☆ QR 21m 7M; 068°-228°; W pylon, R top; 48°43′·41N 03°34′·44W. Rear, ☆ QR 39m 7M; 016°-232°; W gabled house; 484m from front.

Locquémeau *Whis;* 48°43′·86N 03°35′·93W.

LOCQUIREC

Gouliat 48°42′·57N 03°38′·97W.

PRIMEL-TRÉGASTEL

Méloine 48°45′·56N 03°50′·68W.

Ldg lts 152°, both ☆ QR 35/56m 7M. Front, 134°-168°; W □, R stripe, on pylon; 48°42′·45N 03°49′·19W. Rear, R vert stripe on W wall; 172m from front.

W bkwtr ☆ Fl G 4s 6m 7M; 48°42′·77N 03°49′·52W.

BAIE DE MORLAIX

Chenal de Tréguier ldg lts 190·5°: Front, ☆ Île Noire Oc (2) WRG 6s 15m, W11M, R/G8M; 051°-G-135°-R-211°-W-051°; obsc in places; W □ twr, R top; 48°40′·35N 03°52′·54W. Common Rear, **La Lande** ☆ Fl 5s 85m **23M**; obsc by Pte Annelouesten when brg >204°; W □ twr, B top; 48°38′·20N 03°53′·14W.

La Pierre Noire 48°42′·56N 03°52′·20W.

La Chambre 48°40′·74N 03°52′·51W.

Grande Chenal ldg lts 176·4°: Front, **Île Louet** ☆ Oc (3) WG 12s 17m **W15M**,G10M; 305°-W (except where obsc by islands)-244°-G-305°; W □ twr, B top; 48°40′·41N 03°53′·34W. Common Rear, **La Lande** as above.

Pot de Fer *Bell;* 48°44′·23N 03°54′·02W.

Stolvezen 48°42′·64N 03°53′·41W.

Ricard 48°41′·54N 03°53′·51W.

Vieille 48°42′·60N 03°54′·11W. (Chenal Ouest de Ricard 188·8°)

La Noire 48°41′·65N 03°54′·06W.

Corbeau 48°40′·63N 03°53′·33W.

MORLAIX RIVER

Barre de-Flot No. 1 48°40′·18N 03°52′·95W.

No. 2 Fl R 2s; 48°39′·88N 03°52′·53W.

No. 3 Fl G 2s; 48°39′·25N 03°52′·32W.

No. 4 Fl R 2s; 48°38′·62N 03°51′·62W.

No. 5 Fl G 2s; 48°38′·04N 03°51′·34W.

No. 7 48°37′·68N 03°51′·03W.

PENZÉ RIVER

Cordonnier 48°42′·93N 03°56′·59W.

Guerhéon 48°42′·73N 03°57′·18W.

Trousken 48°42′·26N 03°56′·54W.

Pte Fourche 48°42′·14N 03°56′·76W.

Ar Tourtu 48°41′·99N 03°56′·57W.

An Nehou (Caspari) 48°41′·56N 03°56′·45W.

Le Figuier 48°40′·46N 03°56′·16W.

ROSCOFF TO ÎLE VIERGE

BLOSCON/ROSCOFF

Astan VQ (3) 5s 9m 6M; 48°44′·91N 03°57′·66W.

Le Menk Q (9) WR 15s 6m W5M, R3M; 160°-W-188°-R-160°; 48°43′·28N 03°56′·71W.

Basse de Bloscon VQ; 48°43′·71N 03°57′·55W.

Bloscon pier ☆ Fl WG 4s 9m W10M, G7M (in fog Fl 2s); 200°-W-210°-G-200°; W twr, G top; 48°43′·21N 03°57′·69W.

Roscoff Marina ent, E side, ☆ Fl (2) R 6s 4M; 48°43′·10N 03°57′·90W.

Ar Pourven Q; 48°43′·04N 03°57′·70W.

Ar-Chaden Q (6) + L Fl WR 15s 14m, W8M, R6M; 262°-R-289·5°-W-293°-R-326°- W-110°; YB twr; 48°43′·94N 03°58′·26W.

Men-Guen-Bras Q WRG 14m, W9M, R/ G6M; 068°-W-073°-R-197°-W-257°-G-068°; BY twr; 48°43′·76N 03°58′·07W.

Roscoff ldg lts 209°: Front, N môle ☆ Oc (3) G 12s 7m 7M; synch; 078°-318°; W col, G top; 48°43′·56N 03°58′·67W. **Rear** ☆ Oc (3) 12s 24m **15M**; 062°-242°; Gy □ twr, W on NE side; 430m from front.

CANAL DE L'ÎLE DE BATZ

Roc'h Zu 48°43′·88N 03°58′·59W.

Jetty hd (LW landing) ☆ Q 5m 1M; BY col; 48°43′·92N 03°58′·97W.

Run Oan 48°44′·10N 03°59′·30W.

Perroch 48°44′·10N 03°59′·71W.

Tec'hit Bihan 48°44′·02N 04°00′·88W.

La Croix 48°44′·19N 04°01′·30W.

L'Oignon 48°44′·04N 04°01′·35W.

Basse Plate 48°44′·25N 04°02′·53W.

ÎLE DE BATZ

Île aux Moutons VQ (6)+ L Fl 10s 3m 7M; 48°44′·25N 04°00′·52W; landing stage, S end and ent to hbr.

Malvoch 48°44′·26N 04°00′·67W, W side of ent.

Lt ho ☆ Fl (4) 25s 69m **23M**; Gy twr; 48°44′·71N 04°01′·62W. Same twr, auxiliary lt, FR 65m 7M; 024°-059°. 992271315.

MOGUÉRIEC

Ldg lts 162°: Front ☆ Iso WG 4s 9m W11M, G6M; 158°-W-166°-G-158°; W twr, G top; jetty 48°41′·34N 04°04′·47W. Rear ☆ Iso G 4s 22m 7M, synch; 142°-182°; W col, G top; 440m from front.

PONTUSVAL

Pointe de Pontusval 48°41′·42N 04°19′·32W.

Ar Peich 48°40′·90N 04°19′·16W.

Pte de Beg-Pol ☆ Oc (3) WR 12s 16m W10M, R7M; Shore-W-056°-R-096°-W-shore; W twr, B top, W dwelling; 48°40′·67N 04°20′·76W. QY and FR lts on towers 2·4M S.

Aman-ar-Ross Q 7M; 48°41′·88N 04°27′·03W.
Lizen Ven Ouest VQ (9) 10s 5M; 48°40′·53N 04°33′·63W.
Île-Vierge ☆ Fl 5s 77m **27M**; 337°-325°; Gy twr; *Horn 60s*; 48°38′·33N 04°34′·05W. 992271317.

ÎLE VIERGE TO L'ABER-ILDUT

L'ABER WRAC'H

Libenter Q (9) 15s 6M; 48°37′·45N 04°38′·46W.
Outer ldg lts 100·1°: Front, Île Wrac'h ☆ QR 20m 7M; W □ twr, Or top; 48°36′·88N 04°34′·56W. Rear, Lanvaon ☆ Q 55m 12M; intens 090°-110°; W □ twr, Or △ on top; 1·63M from front.
Grand Pot de Beurre 48°37′·21N 04°36′·48W.
Petit Pot de Beurre 48°37′·12N 04°36′·23W.
Basse de la Croix Fl G 2·5s; 48°36′·92N 04°35′·99W.
Breac'h Ver Fl (2) G 6s 6m 3M; △ on twr; 48°36′·63N 04°35′·38W.
Dir ☆ 128°, Oc (2) WRG 6s 5m W13M, R/G11M; 125·7°-G-127·2°-W-128·7°-R-130·2°; 48°35′·89N 04°33′·82W, root of W bkwtr .
Marina ent: QG 3m 2M; vis 186°-167° (341°); 48°35′·97N 04°33′·64W. QR 3m 2M; vis 244°-226° (342°).

L'ABER BENOÎT

Petite Fourche 48°36′·99N 04°38′·75W.
Rusven Est 48°36′·30N 04°38′·63W.
Rusven Ouest *Bell;* 48°36′·07N 04°39′·43W.
Basse du Chenal 48°35′·81N 04°38′·53W.
Poul Orvil 48°35′·52N 04°38′·29W.
La Jument 48°35′·10N 04°37′·41W.
Ar Gazel 48°34′·90N 04°37′·27W.
Le Chien 48°34′·67N 04°36′·88W.

ROCHES DE PORTSALL

Le Relec 48°35′·99N 04°40′·84W.
Corn-Carhai ☆ Fl (3) 12s 19m 9M; W 8-sided twr, B top; 48°35′·19N 04°43′·94W.
Grande Basse de Portsall VQ (9) 10s 9m 4M; 48°36′·70N 04°46′·13W.
Basse Paupian 48°35′·31N 04°46′·27W.
Bosven Aval 48°33′·82N 04°44′·27W.
Men ar Pic 48°33′·65N 04°44′·03W.
Portsall ☆ Oc (4) WRG 12s 9m W13M, R/G10M; 058°-G-084°-W- 088°-R-058°; W col, R top; 48°33′·84N 04°42′·26W.

ARGENTON to L'ABER-ILDUT

Le Taureau 48°31′·46N 04°47′·34W.
Argenton, Île Dolvez, front ldg bcn 086° 48°31′·25N 04°46′·23W.
Le Four ☆ Fl (5) 15s 28m **22M**; Gy ○ twr; 48°31′·38N 04°48′·32W.
L'Aber-Ildut ☆ Dir Oc (2) WR 6s 12m **W25M, R20M**; 081°-W-085°-R-087°; W bldg; 48°28′·26N 04°45′·56W.
Le Lieu Fl R 2.5s 4M; 48°28′·25N 04°46′·66W.

CHENAL DU FOUR AND CHENAL DE LA HELLE

Ldg lts 158·5°. Front, **Kermorvan** ☆ Fl 5s 20m **22M**; obsc'd by Pte de St Mathieu when brg <341°; W □ twr; *Horn 60s*; 48°21′·72N 04°47′·40W. 992271316.
Rear, **Pte de St Mathieu** ☆ Fl 15s 56m **24M**; W twr, R top; 48°19′·79N 04°46′·26W. 992271318. Same twr: Dir F 54m **28M**; intens 157·5°-159·5°.
☆ Q WRG 26m, W12M, R/G 8M; 085°-G-107°-W-116°-R-134°; W twr 54 m WNW of previous entry; 48°19′·80N 04°46′·30W.
Plâtresses N Fl G 2·5s; 48°26′·46N 04°50′·71W.
Valbelle Fl R 2·5s; 48°26′·43N 04°50′·03W.
Plâtresses SE Fl (2) G 6s; 48°25′·96N 04°50′·52W.
Saint Paul Fl (2) R 6s; 48°24′·82N 04°49′·16W.
Pte de Corsen ☆ Dir Q WRG 33m W12M, R/G8M; 008°-R-012°-W-015° (ldg sector)-G-021°; W hut; 48°24′·89N 04°47′·61W.

CHENAL DE LA HELLE

Ldg lts 137·9°: Front, **Kermorvan** ☆ see above. Rear, **Lochrist** ☆ Dir Oc (3) 12s 49m **22M**; intens 135°-140°; W 8-sided twr, R top; 48°20′·55N 04°45′·82W. 992271310.
Luronne ; 48°26′·61N 04°53′·78W.
Ldg lts 293·5° astern (to join Ch du Four S of St Paul): Front, Le Faix VQ 16m 8M; 48°25′·73N 04°53′·91W. Rear, **Le Stiff** ☆ (below at Ouessant); 6·9M from front.
Ldg line 142·5°, optional day only (to join Ch du Four SE of St Pierre): Front, **Kermorvan** ☆ see above. Rear, two W gables (Les Pignons de Kéravel, 48m) 48°20′·10N 04°45′·55W
Pourceaux Q; 48°24′·00N 04°51′·31W.
Saint-Pierre 48°23′·09N 04°49′·09W.
Rouget Fl G 4s; 48°22′·04N 04°48′·88W (Ch du Four).
Grande Vinotière Fl R 4s 12m 5M; R 8-sided twr; 48°21′·94N 04°48′·42W.
Le Conquet, Môle Ste Barbe ☆ Fl G 2·5s 5m 6M; 48°21′·57N 04°46′·98W.
Les Renards 48°21′·00N 04°47′·48W.
Tournant et Lochrist Fl (2) R 6s; 48°20′·64N 04°48′·12W.
Ar Christian Braz 48°20′·68N 04°50′·14W, E of Ile de Béniguet.
Ldg line 325°: Front, Grand Courleau ; rear, La Faix (above).
Ldg lts 007°: Front, **Kermorvan** ☆ above. Rear, **Trézien** ☆ Dir Oc (2) 6s 84m **20M**; intens 003°-011°; Gy twr, W on S side; 48°25′·41N 04°46′·74W. 992271309.
Les Vieux-Moines Fl R 4s 16m 5M; 280°-133°; R 8-sided twr; 48°19′·33N 04°46′·63W, 5ca SSW of Pte de St Mathieu.
La Fourmi Fl G 4s; 48°19′·25N 04°47′·96W.

OUESSANT AND ÎLE MOLÉNE

OFF USHANT TSS

Ouessant NE ⊙; V-AIS; 48°59′·51N 05°24′·00W.
Ouessant SW ⊙; V-AIS 48°30′·00N 05°45′·00W.

ÎLE D'OUESSANT

Le Stiff ☆ Fl (2) R 20s 85m **24M**; two adjoining W twrs; 48°28′·47N 05°03′·41W. Radar twr, conspic, 340m NE, ☆ Q (day); ☆ FR (night).
Port du Stiff, E môle ☆ Dir Q WRG 11m W10M, R/G7M; 251°-G-254°-W-264°-R-267°; W twr, G top; 48°28′·12N 05°03′·25W.
Baie du Stiff: Gorle Vihan 48°28′·32N 05°02′·60W.
Men-Korn VQ (3) WR 5s 21m 8M; 145°-W-040°-R-145°; BYB twr; 48°27′·96N 05°01′·32W.
Men ar Froud 48°26′·62N 05°03′·67W.
La Jument ☆ Fl (3) R 15s 36m 10M; 241°-199°; Gy 8-sided twr, R top; 48°25′·33N 05°08′·03W.

Nividic ☆ VQ (9) 10s 28m 10M; 290°-225°; Gy 8-sided twr, helicopter platform; 48°26'·74N 05°09'·06W.
Créac'h ☆ Fl (2) 10s 70m **32M**; obsc 247°-255°; *Horn (2) 120s*; W twr, B bands; 48°27'·55N 05°07'·76W.

ÎLE MOLÈNE and ARCHIPELAGO

Kéréon ☆ Oc (2+1) WR 24s 38m **W18M,** R14M; 019°-W-248°-R-019°; Gy twr; 48°26'·24N 05°01'·54W; unreliable.
Les Trois-Pierres ☆ Iso WRG 4s 15m W9M, R/G6M; 070°-G-147°-W-185°-R-191°-G-197°-W-213°-R-070°; W col; 48°24'·70N 04°56'·84W.
Molène, Old môle Dir ☆ 191°, Fl (3) WRG 12s 6m W9M, R/G7M; 183°-G-190°-W-192°-R-203°; 48°23'·85N 04°57'·29W.
Same structure: Chenal des Laz , Dir ☆ 261°: Fl (2) WRG 6s 9m W9M, R/G7M ; 252·5°-G-259·5°-W-262·5°-R-269·5°.
Pierres-Vertes VQ (9) 10s 9m 5M; 48°22'·19N 05°04'·76W.
Pierres Noires ; 48°18'·47N 04°58'·15W.
Les Pierres Noires ☆ Fl R 5s 27m **19M**; W twr, R top; 48°18'·67N 04°54'·88W.

BREST AND APPROACHES

Basse Royale Q (6) + L Fl 15s; 48°17'·45N 04°49'·61W.
Vandrée VQ (9) 10s; *Whis;* 48°15'·21N 04°48'·24W.
Goëmant ; 48°15'·12N 04°46'·34W.
La Parquette Fl RG 4s 17m R6M, G6M; 244°-R-285°-G-244°; W 8-sided twr, B diagonal stripes; 48°15'·90N 04°44'·29W.
Coq Iroise 48°19'·07N 04°43'·99W.
Charles Martel Fl (4) R 15s; 48°18'·95N 04°41'·92W.
Trépied 48°16'·73N 04°41'·50W.
Swansea Vale Fl (2) 6s; *Whis;* 48°18'·27N 04°38'·85W.

GOULET DE BREST

Le Chat 48°20'·29N 04°41'·72W (Anse de Bertheaume).
Le Trez Hir 48°20'·78N 04°41'·96W.
Pte du Petit-Minou ☆ Fl (2) WR 6s 32m **W19M, R15M**; Shore-R-252°-W-260°-R-307°-W(unintens)-015°-W-065·5°; 036·5°-R(intens)- 039·5°; 70·5°-W-shore; Gy twr, R top; 48°20'·19N 04°36'·86W. 992271300.
Ldg lts 068°, both Dir Q 30/54m **23/22M. Front, Pte du Petit-Minou**, intens 067·3°-068·8°. **Rear, Pte du Portzic** ☆, Aux Dir Q 54m **22M**; intens 065°-071° (see below).
Fillettes VQ (9) 10s; 48°19'·75N 04°35'·66W.
Kerviniou Fl R 2·5s; 48°19'·77N 04°35'·25W.
Basse Goudron Fl (2) R 6s; 48°20'·03N 04°34'·86W.
Mengam Fl (3) WR 12s 10m W11M, R8M; 034°-R-054°-W-034°; R twr, B bands; 48°20'·32N 04°34'·56W.
Pte du Portzic ☆ Oc (2) WR 12s 56m **W19M, R15M**; 219°-R-259°-W-338°-R-000°-W-065·5° (vis 041°-069° when west of Goulet)-W-219°; Gy twr; 48°21'·49N 04°32'·05W. Same lt ho, Aux Dir Q, rear 068° ldg lt. Aux ☆ Dir Q (6) + L Fl 15s 54m **23M**; intens 045°-050°.

BREST

Pénoupèle Fl R 2·5s; 48°21'·45N 04°30'·53W.
S jetty ☆ QR 10m 7M; 094°-048°; W/R twr; 48°22'·10N 04°29'·46W.
E jetty ☆ QG 10m 7M; W/G twr; 48°22'·15N 04°29'·22W.
Ldg lts 343.5°: Front ☆ Dir Q WRG 24m W9M, R/G6M; 334°-G-342°-W-346°-R-024°; 48°22'·80N 04°29'·62W. Rear ☆ Dir Q 32m 9M; intens 342°-346°; 115m from front.
Le Château Marina, S Jetty hd, ☆ Fl G 2·5s 8m 4M; 48°22'·66N 04°29'·49W.
Le Château Marina, N Jetty hd, ☆ Fl R 2·5s 8m 4M; 48°22'·67N 04°29'·45W.
Port de Commerce, E ent: N jetty ☆ Oc (2) G 6s 8m 7M; W/G pylon; 48°22'·76N 04°28'·53W. S jetty ☆ Oc (2) R 6s 8m 5M; W pylon, R top; 48°22'·69N 04°28'·48W.
R2 Fl (2) R 6s; 48°22'·01N 04°28'·75W.
R1 Fl G 6s; 48°21'·83N 04°28'·29W.
R4 Fl (3) R 12s; 48°22'·22N 04°28'·06W.
R3 Q (6) + L Fl 15s; 48°22'·48N 04°27'·36W.

LE MOULIN BLANC MARINA

Moulin Blanc Fl (2) R 6s; 48°22'·80N 04°25'·91W
MBA Q(3) 10s 3m 2M; pontoon elbow; 48°23'·54N 04°25'·74W.

CAMARET

N môle ☆ Iso WG 4s 7m W12M, G9M; 135°-W-182°-G-027°; W pylon, G top; 48°16'·85N 04°35'·31W.
Port Vauban wavebreak, S end, ☆ Fl (2) G 6s 2m 2M; 48°16'·74N 04° 35'·33W.
S môle ☆ Fl (2) R 6s 9m 5M; R pylon; 48°16'·63N 04°35'·33W.

POINTE DU TOULINGUET TO RAZ DE SEIN

Pte du Toulinguet ☆ Oc (3) WR 12s 49m **W15M,** R11M; Shore-W-028°-R-090°-W-shore; W □ twr; 48°16'·81N 04°37'·72W.
La Louve 48°16'·76N 04°38'·03W.
Mendufa 48°16'·05N 04°39'·43W.
Basse du Lis Q (6) + L Fl 15s 9m 6M; 48°12'·99N 04°44'·53W.
Le Chevreau 48°13'·30N 04°36'·98W.
Le Bouc Q (9) 15s; 48°11'·51N 04°37'·37W.
Basse Vieille Fl (2) 6s 8m 7M; 48°08'·22N 04°35'·75W.

DISTANCE TABLES

Approx distances in nautical miles are by the most direct route allowing for dangers and TSS.

1	Lézardrieux	**1**		**12**	16	18	24	42	43	45	72	97	100	105	124	Pornic	**12**
2	Tréguier	22	**2**		**11**	12	24	39	40	41	66	87	90	95	113	St Nazaire	**11**
3	Perros-Guirec	28	21	**3**		**10**	13	30	30	34	55	78	80	85	106	La Baule/Pornichet	**10**
4	Trébeurden	40	32	17	**4**		**9**	18	22	27	48	73	75	79	100	Le Croisic	**9**
5	Morlaix	60	46	36	23	**5**		**8**	28	36	57	78	80	84	105	Arzal/Camöel	**8**
6	Roscoff	54	41	28	17	12	**6**		**7**	16	37	58	60	64	85	Crouesty	**7**
7	L'Aberwrac'h	84	72	60	49	48	32	**7**		**6**	26	47	48	54	74	Le Palais (Belle Ile)	**6**
8	Le Conquet	106	98	83	72	68	55	29	**8**		**5**	32	33	38	61	Lorient	**5**
9	Brest (marina)	114	107	92	83	79	67	42	18	**9**		**4**	4	12	37	Concarneau	**4**
10	Morgat	126	118	103	92	88	75	49	20	24	**10**		**3**	12	36	Port-la-Forêt	**3**
11	Douarnenez	131	123	108	97	93	80	54	25	29	11	**11**		**2**	30	Loctudy	**2**
12	Audierne	135	128	113	102	98	86	55	30	34	27	30	**12**		**1**	Audierne	**1**

MORGAT

Pointe de Morgat ☆ Oc (4) WRG 12s 77m **W15M**, R11M, G10M; Shore-W-281°-G-301°-W-021°-R-043°; W □ twr, R top, W dwelling; 48°13′·17N 04°29′·80W. Fl R 4s; 48°13′·60N 04°29′·55W.

DOUARNENEZ to RAZ DE SEIN

Île Tristan ☆ Fl (3) WR 12s 35m, W6M, R6M; Shore-W-138°-R-153°-W-shore; Gy twr, W band, B top; 48°06′·14N 04°20′·24W.

Pointe du Millier ☆ Oc (2) WRG 6s 34m **W16M**, R12M, G11M; 080°-G-087°-W-113°-R-120°-W-129°-G-148°-W-251°-R-258°; W house; 48°05′·92N 04°27′·93W. 992271015.

Basse Jaune 48°04′·70N 04°42′·45W.

RAZ DE SEIN

Tévennec ☆ Q WR 28m W9M R6M; 090°-W-345°-R-090°; W □ twr and dwelling; 48°04′·28N 04°47′·73W. Same twr, Dir ☆ Fl 4s 24m 12M; intens 324°-332° (through Raz de Sein).

La Vieille ☆ Oc (2+1) WRG 12s 33m **W18M**, R13M, G14M; 290°-W-298°-R-325°-W-355°-G-017°-W-035°-G-105°-W-123°-R-158°-W-205°; Gy □ twr; 48°02′·44N 04°45′·40W.

La Plate Q (9) 15s 19m 6M; 48°02′·37N 04°45′·58W.

Le Chat Fl (2) WRG 6s 27m, W9M, R/ G6M; 096°-G-215°-W-230°-R-271°-G-286°-R-096°; YB twr; 48°01′·43N 04°48′·86W.

CHAUSSÉE DE SEIN and ÎLE DE SEIN

Cornoc-An-Ar-Braden Fl G 4s; 48°03′·23N 04°50′·84W.

Men-Brial ☆ Oc (2) WRG 6s 16m, W12M, R9M, G7M; 149°-G-186°-W-192°-R-221°-W-227°-G-254°; G&W twr; 48°02′·28N 04°50′·97W.

Île de Sein Fl (4) 25s 49m **29M**; W twr, B top; 48°02′·62N 04°52′·02W. Same twr, Dir Q WRG, W8M, R/G 6M; 267°-G-269°-W-271°-R-275°.

Ar-Men Fl (3) 20s 29m **23M**; W twr, B top; 48°03′·01N 04°59′·87W.

Chaussée de Sein VQ (9) 10s 9m 6M; *Whis*; ***Racon O (3cm), 10M;*** 48°03′·74N 05°07′·75W.

AUDIERNE

Pointe de Lervily ☆ Fl WR 4s 20m W14M, R11M; 236°-W-269°-R-294°-W-087°-R-109°; W twr, R top; 48°00′·04N 04°33′·94W. Gamelle W, VQ (9) 10s; 47°59′·46N 04°32′·85W.

Jetée de Ste-Évette ☆ Fl (2) R 6s 2m 7M; R lantern; 090°-000° (270°); 48°00′·31N 04°33′·07W.

Passe de l'Est ldg lts 331°: Front, Jetée de Raoulic ☆ Fl (3) RG 12s 11m, R/G6M; 085°-R-034°-G-085°-R-085°; 48°00′·55N 04°32′·46W.

Kergadec ☆ 006°: Dir Q WRG 43m W12M, R/G9M; 000°-G-005·3°-W-006·7°-R-017°; W 8-sided twr, R top; 48°00′·96N 04°32′·78W.

Gamelle E; 47°59′·46N 04°32′·05W.

POINTE DE PENMARC'H

Eckmühl ☆ Fl 5s 60m **23M**; Gy 8-sided twr; 47°47′·89N 04°22′·36W.

Men-Hir ☆ Fl (2) WG 6s 19m, W7M, G4M; G135°-315°, W315°-135°; W twr, B band; 47°47′·74N 04°23′·99W.

Cap Caval Q (9) 15s; 47°46′·47N 04°22′·68W.

Locarec ☆ Iso WRG 4s 11m, W9M, R/G6M; 063°-G-068°-R-271°-W-285°-R-298°-G-340°-R-063°; iron col on rk; 47°47′·29N 04°20′·31W.

LE GUILVINEC

Névez Fl G 2·5s; 47°45′·84N 04°20′·08W.

Ldg lts (triple Q) 053°, all synch: **Front**, ☆ Q 7m 8M; 233°-066°; W pylon; Môle de Léchiagat, spur; 47°47′·43N 04°17′·07W. Middle, ☆ Q WG 12m W14M, G11M; 006°-W-293°-G-006°; synch; R □ on R col; Rocher Le Faoutés, 210m from front. Rear, ☆ Q 26m 8M, 051·5°-054·5°, R □ on W twr; 0·58M from front.

Spineg Q (6) + L Fl 15s; 47°45′·19N 04°18′·90W.

LESCONIL

Karek Greis Q (3) 10s; 47°46′·03N 04°11′·36W.

Q (6) + LFl 15s; 47°46′·53N 04°10′·63W

Men-ar-Groas ☆ Fl (3) WRG 12s 14m, W10M, R/G7M; 268°-G-313°-W-333°-R-050°; W lt ho, G top; 47°47′·79N 04°12′·68W.

AREA 17 *South Biscay – River Loire to Bordeaux*

SELECTED LIGHTS, BUOYS & WAYPOINTS

LOCTUDY TO CONCARNEAU

Rostolou 47°46′·64N 04°07′·29W.

Boulanger VQ (6) + L Fl 10s;47°47′·38N 04°09′·13W.

Chenal de Bénodet 47°48′·53N 04°07′·04W.

Bilien VQ (3) 5s; 47°49′·10N 04°08′·09W.

LOCTUDY

Pte de Langoz ☆ Fl (4) WRG 12s 12m, **W15M**, R/G11M; 115°-W-257°-G-284°-W-295°-R-318°-W-328°-R-025°; W twr, R top; 47°49′·88N 04°09′·55W.

Karek-Saoz Fl R 2·5s 3m 1M; R twr; 47°50′·02N 04°09′·38W.

Men Audierne 47°50′·34N 04°08′·94W.

No. 2 (Karek-Croisic) Fl (2) R 6s; 47°50′·19N 04°09′·49W.

No. 1 Fl (2) G 6s; 47°50′·22N 04°09′·73W.

No. 3 Fl (3) G 12s; 47°50′·22N 04°09′·99W.

Groyne head ☆ Q 3m 10M; 47°50′·21N 04°10′·34W.

Le Blas Fl (4) G 15s 5m 1M; truncated col; 47°50′·28N 04°10′·23W.

BENODET

Ldg lts 345·5°: Front, Pte du Coq ☆ Dir Oc (3) G 12s 11m 10M; intens 345°-347°; W ○ twr, G stripe; 47°52′·31N 04°06′·70W. Pyramide ☆ Oc (3) 12s 48m 14M; 338°-016°, synch; W twr, G top; common rear, 348m from front.

Lts in line 000·5°: Front, Pte de Combrit ☆ Oc (2) WR 6s 19m, W12M, R9M; 325°-W-017°-R-325°; W □ twr, Gy corners 47°51′·86N 04°06′·78W. Common rear, Pyramide; see above.

Rousse 47°51′·55N 04°06′·47W. La Potée 47°51′·78N 04°06′·55W.

Pte du Toulgoët ☆ Fl R 2·5s 2m 1M; 47°52′·30N 04°06′·86W.

Le Taro 47°50′·51N 04°04′·83W.

La Voleuse Q (6) + L Fl 15s; 47°48′·76N 04°02′·49W.

ILE AUX MOUTONS and LES POURCEAUX

Île-aux-Moutons ☆ Iso WRG 2s 18m, **W15M**, R/G11M; 035°-W-050°-G-063°-W-081°-R-141°-W-292°-R-035°; W □ twr and dwelling; 47°46′·48N 04°01′·66W. 992271013.
Rouge de Glénan VQ (9) 10s 8m 8M; 47°45′·48N 04°03′·95W.
Grand Pourceaux Q; 47°45′·98N 04°00′·80W.

ÎLES DE GLÉNAN

Penfret ☆ Fl R 5s 36m **21M**; W □ twr, R top; 47°43′·26N 03°57′·18W. Same twr: auxiliary ☆ Dir Q 34m 12M; 295°-315°.
La Pie Fl (2) 6s 9m 3M; 47°43′·75N 03°59′·76W.
Pte de la Baleine VQ (3) 5s 2M; 47°43′·26N 03°59′·20W.
Les Bluiniers 47°43′·35N 04°03′·81W.
Offlying marks, anticlockwise from the west:
Basse Pérennès Q (9) 15s 8m 5M; 47°41′·06N 04°06′·14W.
Jument de Glénan Q (6) + L Fl 15s 10m 4M; 47°38′·76N 04°01′·41W.
Laoennou 47°39′·65N 03°54′·70W.
Jaune de Glénan Q (3) 10s; 47°42′·56N 03°49′·83W.

PORT-LA-FORÊT

Linuen Q (3) 10s; 47°50′·76N 03°57′·31W.
Laouen Pod 47°51′·23N 03°58′·00W.
Cap Coz mole ☆ Fl (2) WRG 6s 5m, W7M, R/G5M; Shore-R-335°-G-340°-W-346°-R-shore; 47°53′·49N 03°58′·28W.
Le Scoré 47°52′·75N 03°57′·56W.
Les Ormeaux 47°53′·27N 03°58′·34W.
Entry channel Fl G 2·5s; 47°53′·39N 03°58′·12W.
Fl R 2·5s; 47°53′·39N 03°58′·22W.
Kerleven mole ☆ Fl G 4s 8m 6M; 47°53′·60N 03°58′·37W.

CONCARNEAU

Ldg lts 028·5°: Front, La Croix ☆ Q 14m 13M; 006·5°-093°; R&W twr; 47°52′·16N 03°55′·08W. **Rear, Beuzec** ☆ Dir Q 87m **23M**; synch, intens 026·5°-030·5°; spire, 1·34M from front.
QR; 47°51′·40N 03°55′·75W.
Le Cochon Fl (3) WRG 12s 5m W9M, R/G6M; 230°-R-352°-W-048°-G-207°-Obsc'd-230°; G twr; 47°51′·47N 03°55′·55W.
Basse du Chenal Fl R 4s; 47°51′·54N 03°55′·66W.
Men Fall Fl (2) G 6s; 47°51′·76N 03°55′·28W.
Kersos 47°51′·80N 03°54′·93W (Anse de Kersos).
Lanriec ☆ QG 13m 8M; 063°-078°; G window on W gable end; 47°52′·01N 03°54′·64W.
La Medée Fl (3) R 12s 9m 4M; 47°52′·07N 03°54′·80W.
Ville-Close ☆ Q WR, W9M, R6M; 209°-R-354°-W-007°-R-018°; R turret; 47°52′·27N 03°54′·76W.
No. 1 ☆ Fl (4) G 15s 4m 5M; G turret; 47°52′·16N 03°54′·72W.
Marina wavescreen ☆ Fl (4) R 15s 3m 1M; 47°52′·23N 03°54′·79W. No. 2 ☆ Fl R 4s 4m 5M; G turret; 47°52′·31N 03°54′·71W.
Ville-Close (NE end) ☆ Fl (2) R 6s; R twr; 47°52′·37N 03°54′·68W.
Ent to FV basin ☆ Fl (2) G 6s; G twr; 47°52′·36N 03°54′·63W.
Pouldohan ☆ Fl G 4s 6m 8M; 053°-065°; W □ twr, G top; 47°50′·97N 03°53′·69W.
Roché Tudy 47°50′·52N 03°54′·49W.

CONCARNEAU TO ÎLE DE GROIX

PTE DE TRÉVIGNON TO PORT MANEC'H

Les Soldats VQ (9) 10s; 47°47′·86N 03°53′·42W.
Trévignon mole ☆ Fl G 4s 5m 6M; 47°47′·69N 03°51′·30W.
Trévignon bkwtr root ☆ Fl (2) WRG 6s 11m, W10/7M, R/G7M; 004°-W-051°-G-085°-W-092°-R-127°; 322°-R-351°; W □ twr, G top; 47°47′·59N 03°51′·33W.
Men Du 47°46′·41N 03°50′·50W.
Men an Tréas 47°45′·77N 03°49′·66W.

PORT MANEC'H (Aven and Bélon rivers)

Port Manech ☆ Oc (4) WRG 12s 38m, W10M, R/G7M; obscd by Pte de Beg-Morg when brg <299°; 050°-W (unintens)-140°-W-296°-G-303°-W-311°-R (over Les Verrès)-328°-W-050°; W & R twr; 47°47′·99N 03°44′·34W.
Les Verrès 47°46′·65N 03°42′·71W.

BRIGNEAU

Brigneau 47°46′·11N 03°40′·10W.
W mole, ☆ Oc (2) WRG 6s 7m, W12M, R/G9M; R col, W top; 280°-G-329°-W-339°-R-034°; 47°46′·86N 03°40′·18W. In line 331° with W □ daymark behind, Hard to see, rear beacon unlit.

MERRIEN

☆ Dir QR 26m 7M; 004°-009°; W □ twr, R top; 47°47′·04N 03°38′·97W.
Ent, W side . E side 47°46′·45N 03°38′·89W.

DOËLAN

Ldg lts 013·8°: Front ☆ Oc (3) WG 12s 20m, W13M, G10M; W shore-305°, G305°-314°, W314°-shore; W lt ho, G band and top; 47°46′·32N 03°36′·51W. Rear ☆ Oc (3)R 12s 27m 9M; W lt ho, R band & top; 326m from front.

LE POULDU

Ent 47°45′·74N 03°32′·25W.
Grand Cochon 47°43′·03N 03°30′·81W.
Pte de Kerroc'h ☆ Oc (2) WRG 6s 22m W11M, R/G8M; 096·5°-R-112°·5-G-132°-R-302°-W-096·5°; W twr, R top; 47°41′·97N 03°27′·66W. 992271009.

ÎLE DE GROIX

Pen Men ☆ Fl (4) 25s 60m **29M**; 309°-275°; W □ twr, B top; 47°38′·84N 03°30′·56W.
Speerbrecker, 47°39′·10N 03°26′·33W.
Port Tudy, N môle ☆ Iso G 4s 12m 6M; W twr, G top; 47°38′·72N 03°26′·74W.
E môle ☆ Fl (2) R 6s 11m 6M; 112°-226°; W twr R top; 47°38′·68N 03°26′·78W.
Basse Melité 47°38′·84N 03°25′·54W.
Pte de la Croix ☆ Oc WR 4s 16m, W12M, R9M; 169°-W-336°-R-345°-W-353°; W pedestal, R lantern; 47°38′·05N 03°25′·02W.
Edouard de Cougy 47°37′·93N 03°23′·90W.
Pointe des Chats ☆ Fl R 5s 16m **19M**; W □ twr and dwelling; 47°37′·24N 03°25′·30W.
Les Chats Q (6) + L Fl 15s; 47°35′·70N 03°23′·57W.

LORIENT AND RIVER ÉTEL

LORIENT, PASSE DE L'OUEST

Passe de l'Ouest ldg lts 057°: both Dir Q 11/22m 13/**18M**. Front, Les Sœurs; intens 042·5°-058·5°, 058·5°-042·5°, 4M range only; R twr, W bands; 47°42′·13N 03°21′·84W. Rear **Port Louis** ☆, 740m from front (see below).

Banc des Truies Q (9) 15s; 47°40′·76N 03°24′·48W.
Loméner, Anse de Stole, Dir ☆ 357·2°: Q WRG 13m, W10M, R/G8M; 349·2°-G-355·2°-W-359·2°-R-005·2°; W twr, R top; 47°42′·30N 03°25′·54W.
A2 Fl R 2·5s; 47°40′·94N 03°24′·98W.
Les Trois Pierres Q RG 11m R/G6M; 060°-G-196°-R-002°; B twr, W bands; 47°41′·53N 03°22′·47W.
A8 Fl R 2·5s; 47°41′·90N 03°22′·52W.

PASSE DU SUD
Bastresses Sud QG; 47°40′·77N 03°22′·09W.
Les Errants Fl (2) R 6s; 47°41′·10N 03°22′·38W.
Bastresses Nord Fl (2) G 6s; 47°41′·11N 03°22′·20W.
Locmalo Fl (3) G 12s; 47°41′·67N 03°22′·13W.

SOUTH OF PORT LOUIS
La Paix; 47°41′·97N 03°21′·84W.
Île aux Souris ☆ Dir Q WG 6m, W3M, G2M; 041·5°-W-043·5°-G-041·5°; G twr; 47°42′·15N 03°21′·52W.
Fl G 2·5s; 47°42′·13N 03°21′·21W.
Ban-Gâvres FV/yacht hbr, W jetty ☆ Fl (2) G 6s 3M; 47°42′·06N 03°21′·11W. E jetty ☆ Fl (2) R 6s 3M; 47°42′·06N 03°21′·06W.

ENTRANCE CHANNEL
Ldg lts 016·5°, both Dir QG 8/14m 13M; intens 014·5°-017·5°; synch; W twrs, G tops. Front ☆, 47°43′·47N 03°21′·63W (Île St Michel). Rear ☆, 306m from front.
La Citadelle Oc G 4s 6m 6M; 012°-192°; 47°42′·59N 03°21′·94W.
Secondary yacht chan, RGR, 47°42′·49N 03°22′·12W.
La Petite Jument Oc R 4s 5m 6M; 182°-024°; R twr; 47°42′·58N 03°22′·07W.
Le Cochon Fl R 4s 5m 5M; RGR twr; 47°42′·80N 03°22′·00W.
No. 1 47°42′·80N 03°21′·84W.

PORT LOUIS (Port de la Pointe)
D 1 47°42′·76N 03°21′·52W.
Jetty ☆ Fl G 2·5s 7m 6M; W twr, G top; 47°42′·71N 03°21′·37W.
Anse du Driasker Stage Head Fl R 2·5s 2M, metal mast.

KERNEVEL
Kéroman ldg lts 350°, both Dir Oc (2) R 6s 25/31m **15M**; synch; intens 349°-351°: **Front** ☆, 47°43′·60N 03°22′·02W, R ho, W bands. **Rear** ☆ R&W topmark on Gy pylon, R top; 91m from front.
Banc du Turc Fl G 2·5s; 47°43′·33N 03°21′·85W.
Kernével marina, entrance: ☆ QR 1M; 47°43′·39N 03°22′·10W.
Ldg lts 217°, both Dir QR 10/18m **15M**; intens 215°-219°; synch**: Front, Kernével** ☆ R&W twr; 47°43′·02N 03°22′·32W. **Rear** ☆ W □ twr, R top; 290m from front.
Q (3) 10s; marks wreck; 47°43′·49N 03°22′·05W.

NORTHERN PART OF LORIENT HARBOUR
Grand Bassin (FV hbr) E side of ent, ☆ Fl RG 4s 7m 6M; 000°-G-235°-R-000°; W twr, G top; 47°43′·63N 03°21′·87W.
Ste Catherine marina ent ☆ QG 5m 3M; 47°43′·52N 03°21′·12W.
N side of marina ent ☆ QR 2m 2M 47°43′·53N 03°21′·10W.
Pengarne Fl G 2·5s 3m 3M; G twr; 47°43′·88N 03°21′·23W.
No. 9 Fl (2) G 6s; 47°43′·95N 03°21′·16W.
No. 11 Fl (3) G 12s; 47°44′·04N 03°21′·01W.
Pen-Mané marina, bkwtr elbow ☆ Fl (2) G 6s 4M; 47°44′·11N 03°20′·86W.
Blavet River, No. 1 Fl (2+1)G 10s; 47°44′·20N 03°20′·78W.
No. 2 Fl R 2·5s; 47°44′·26N 03°20′·74W.
Pointe de l'Espérance, Dir ☆ 037°, Q WRG 8m W10M, R/G8M; 034·2°-G-036·7°-W-037·2°-R-047·2°; W twr, G top; 47°44′·51N 03°20′·66W.
Ro-Ro jetty ☆ QR 7m 2M; 47°44′·42N 03°20′·96W.
No. 8 Fl R 2·5s; 47°44′·56N 03°20′·98W, ent to Lorient marina.

RIVIÈRE D'ÉTEL
Roheu 47°38′·54N 03°14′·70W.
Épi de Plouhinec ☆ Fl R 2·5s 7m 2M; 47°38′·59N 03°12′·86W.
W side ent ☆ Oc (2) WRG 6s 13m W9M, R/G6M; 022°-W-064°-R-123°-W-330°-G-022°; R twr; 47°38′·69N 03°12′·83W.
Conspic R/W radio mast (CROSS Étel) 47°39′·73N 03°12′·11W.
Les Pierres Noires 47°35′·53N 03°13′·29W.

BELLE ÎLE and QUIBERON BAY (W of 2° 50′W)

PLATEAU DES BIRVIDEAUX (6M NNW of Belle Île)
Fl (2) 6s 24m 10M; BRB twr; 47°29′·15N 03°17′·46W.

BELLE ÎLE
Pte des Poulains ☆ Fl 5s 34m **23M**; 023°-291°; W □ twr and dwelling; 47°23′·31N 03°15′·11W.
Les Poulains 47°23′·44N 03°16′·68W.
N Poulains 47°23′·68N 03°14′·88W.
Sauzon, NW jetty ☆ Fl G 4s 8m 8M; 47°22′·49N 03°13′·04W.
SE jetty ☆ Fl R 4s 8m 8M; 315°-272°; W twr, R top; 47°22′·45N 03°13′·00W. Inner hbr, W jetty ☆, QG 9m 5M; 194°-045°; W twr, G top; 47°22′·37N 03°13′·13W.
Le Palais, N jetty ☆ QG 11m 7M; obsc 298°-170° by Ptes de Kerdonis and Taillefer; W twr, G top; 47°20′·84N 03°09′·04W.
No 1 Fl (2) G 6s; 47°20′·82N 03°08′·96W;
No 2 Fl R 4s; 47°20′·71N 03°08′·89W;
No 4 Fl (2) R 6s; 47°20′·78N 03°09′·01W.
S jetty ☆ QR 11m 7M; obsc'd 298°-170° (see N jetty); W twr, R lantern; 47°20′·82N 03°09′·07W.
Pointe de Kerdonis ☆ Fl (3) R 15s 49m **15M**; obsc'd 225°-320°
(095°) by vegetation, 004°-155° (151°) by land. W □ twr, R top and W dwelling; 47°18′·60N 03°03′·58W.
Les Galères 47°18′·77N 03°02′·76W.
SW coast of Belle Île: La Truie 47°17′·11N 03°11′·79W.
Goulphar ☆ Fl (2) 10s 87m **27M**; Gy twr; 47°18′·65N 03°13′·63W.

PORT MARIA (Quiberon ferry port)
Light ho ☆ Q WRG 28m W14M, R/ G10M; 246°-W-252°-W-297°-G-340°-W-017°-R-051°-W-081°-G-098°-W-143°; W twr, G lantern; 47°28′·78N 03°07′·45W.
Le Pouilloux 47°27′·88N 03°08′·01W.
Ldg lts 006·5°, both Dir QG 5/13m **16/17M**; intens 005°-008°; W twrs, B bands: **Front**, 47°28′·63N 03°07′·18W. **Rear**, 230m north; 992271030.

Les Deux Frères Fl R 2·5s; 175°-047°;47°28'·34N 03°07'·29W.

S bkwtr ☆ Oc (2) R 6s 9m 7M; W twr, R top; 47°28'·54N 03°07'·31W.

CHAUSSÉE and PASSAGE DE LA TEIGNOUSE

Le Four 47°27'·78N 03°06'·54W.

Les Trois Pierres 47°27'·46N 03°05'·24W.

Roc er Vy 47°27'·70N 03°04'·40W; Chenal en Toull Bras.

Roc er Vy 47°27'·86N 03°04'·35W.

Basse Cariou 47°26'·94N 03°06'·38W.

Basse du Chenal 47°26'·66N 03°05'·77W.

Goué Vaz S Q (6) + L Fl 15s; 47°25'·76N 03°04'·93W.

La Teignouse ☆ Fl WR 4s 20m **W15M**, R11M; 033°-W-039°-R-033°; W ○ twr, R top; 47°27'·44N 03°02'·75W. 992271007.

Basse du Milieu Fl (2) G 6s 9m 2M; 47°25'·91N 03°04'·12W.

Goué Vaz E Fl (3) R 12s; 47°26'·23N 03°04'·28W.

NE Teignouse Fl (3) G 12s; 47°26'·55N 03°01'·87W.

Basse Nouvelle Fl R 2·5s; 47°26'·98N 03°01'·99W.

CHAUSSÉE and PASSAGE DU BÉNIGUET

Les Esclassiers 47°25'·68N 03°03'·05W.

Le Grand Coin 47°24'·45N 03°00'·26W.

Bonen Bras 47°24'·26N 02°59'·88W.

ÎLE DE HOUAT

Le Rouleau 47°23'·67N 03°00'·31W.

Port St-Gildas N môle ☆ Fl (2) WG 6s 8m W9M, G6M; 168°-W-198°-G-210°-W-240°-G-168°; W twr, G top; 47°23'·57N 02°57'·34W.

Mussel beds, 1 -1.5M NNE of above ☆ and in its G sector (198°-210°) marked by 2 at S end, and VQ (3) 5s & VQ at N end.

Bcns SE and S of Houat: Men Groise 47°22'·77N 02°55'·00W.

Er Spernec Bras 47°22'·09N 02°55'·23W.

Men er Houteliguet 47°22'·54N 02°56'·38W.

ÎLE DE HOËDIC

Les Sœurs 47°21'·14N 02°54'·74W.

La Chèvre 47°21'·08N 02°52'·55W.

Port de l'Argol bkwtr ☆ Fl WG 4s 10m W9M, G6M; 143°-W-163°-G-183°-W-194°-G-143°; W twr, G top; 47°20'·66N 02°52'·48W.

Er Gurranic'h 47°20'·51N 02°50'·44W.

Cohfournik 47°19'·49N 02°49'·69W.

Grands Cardinaux ☆ Fl (4) 15s 28m 13M; R and W twr; 47°19'·27N 02°50'·10W. 992271025; 2·1M SE of Argol.

Le Chariot 47°18'·87N 02°52'·95W.

Er Palaire 47°20'·16N 02°55'·01W.

PORT HALIGUEN

Banc de Quiberon S Q (6) + L Fl 15s; 47°28'·04N 03°02'·34W.

Banc de Quiberon N 47°29'·65N 03°02'·58W.

E bkwtr hd ☆ Oc (2) WR 6s 10m, W11M, R8M; 233°-W-240·5°-R-299°-W-306°-R-233°; W twr, R top; 47°29'·36N 03°05'·94W.

Port Haliguen 47°29'·38N 03°05'·55W; marks 1·7m patch.

NW bkwtr hd ☆ Fl G 2·5s 9m 6M; 47°29'·34N 03°06'·02W.

Bugalet wreck 47°31'·19N 03°05'·45W.

Men er Roué 47°32'·25N 03°06'·06W.

LA TRINITÉ-SUR-MER

Rivière de Crac'h ☆ Q WRG 11m W10M, R/G7M; 321°-G-345°-W-013·5°-R-080°; W twr, G top; 47°34'·09N 03°00'·37W.

Buissons de Méaban 47°31'·66N 02°58'·49W.

Le Petit Buisson 47°32'·14N 02°58'·57W.

Roche Révision 47°32'·63N 02°59'·36W.

Petit Trého Fl R 2·5s; 47°33'·47N 03°00'·71W.

R. de Crac'h Dir ☆ 347°: Oc WRG 4s 9m W13M, R/G 11M; 345°-G-346°-W-348°-R-349°; W twr; 47°35'·03N 03°00'·98W.

S pier ☆ Q WR 6s 6m, W9M, R6M; 090°-R-293·5°-W-300·5°-R-329°; W twr, R top; 47°35'·09N 03°01'·50W.

Marina wavebreak/pier ☆ Iso R 4s 8m 5M; 47°35'·28N 03°01'·46W.

GOLFE DU MORBIHAN

Méaban 47°30'·77N 02°56'·23W.

Outer ldg marks 001°: Front, Petit Vezid ; W obelisk; 47°34'·17N 02°55'·23W. Rear, Baden ch spire (83m) 47°37'·20N 02°55'·14W.

Pointe de Port-Navalo ☆ Oc (3) WRG 12s 32m, **W15M**, R/G11M; 155°-W-220°; 317°-G-359°-W-015°-R-105°; W twr and dwelling; 47°32'·87N 02°55'·11W.

Ldg marks 359°: Front, Grégan Q (6) + L Fl 15s 3m 8M; 47°33'·91N 02°55'·05W. Rear, Baden ch spire (5 lines above).

Auray river: Catis 47°36'·14N 02°57'·23W.

César 47°38'·36N 02°58'·22W.

No. 13 47°39'·48N 02°58'·64W (last bcn before 14m bridge).

Morbihan: Grand Mouton QG; 47°33'·71N 02°54'·85W.

Gavrinis 47°34'·21N 02°54'·05W.

Jument 47°34'·29N 02°53'·43W.

Creizic S 47°34'·63N 02°52'·84W.

Creizic N 47°34'·93N 02°52'·20W.

Les Rechauds, two 47°36'·18N 02°51'·30W.

Truie d'Arradon 47°36'·58N 02°50'·27W.

Logoden 47°36'·70N 02°49'·91W.

Drenec 47°36'·84N 02°48'·39W.

Bœdic 47°36'·85N 02°47'·59W.

Roguédas Fl G 2·5s 4m 4M; G twr; 47°37'·12N 02°47'·28W.

CROUESTY

Ldg lts 058°, both Dir Q 10/27m 8M; intens 056·5°-059·5°: Front ☆ R panel, W stripe; 47°32'·53N 02°53'·95W. Rear ☆, W twr; 315m from front.

No. 1 QG; 47°32'·26N 02°54'·76W.

No. 2 47°32'·26N 02°54'·76W.

N jetty ☆ Fl R 4s 9m 7M; R&W □ twr; 47°32'·47N 02°54'·14W.

S jetty ☆ Fl G 4s 9m 7M; G&W □ twr; 47°32'·45N 02°54'·10W.

PLATEAU DU GRAND MONT

Chimère 47°28'·83N 02°53'·98W.

L'Epieu 47°29'·51N 02°52'·91W.

St Gildas 47°29'·78N 02°52'·87W.

Grand Mont 47°28'·98N 02°51'·12W.

QUIBERON BAY (E of 2° 50'W) to PTE DU CROISIC

PLATEAU DE SAINT JACQUES

Le Bauzec 47°28'·89N 02°49'·40W.

St Jacques 47°28'·17N 02°47'·52W.
Port St Jacques, jetty Oc (2) R 6s 5m 6M; W 8-sided twr, R top; 47°29'·24N 02°47'·41W.

PLATEAU DE LA RECHERCHE

Recherche Q (9) 15s; 47°25'·56N 02°50'·39W.
Locmariaquer 47°25'·82N 02°47'·36W.

PÉNERF

Fl (5) Y 20s; 47°27'·58N 02°39'·56W.
Penvins 47°28'·93N 02°40'·09W. Borenis 47°29'·21N 02°38'·35W.
Tour des Anglais W bcn; 47°30'·21N 02°37'·94W; appr brg 031·4°.
Pignon Fl (3) WR 12s 6m W9M, R6M; 028·5°-R-167°-W-175°-R-349·5°-W-028·5°; R twr; 47°30'·03N 02°38'·89W.

VILAINE RIVER

Pte de Penlan Oc (2) WRG 6s 26m, **W15M**, R/G11M; 292·5°-R-025°-G-052°-W-060°-R-138°-G-180°; W sector defines Passe de la Grande Accroche; W twr, R bands; 47°30'·97N 02°30'·11W.
Bertrand Iso WG 4s 6m, W9M, G6M; 040°-W-054°-G-227°-W-234°-G-040°; G twr; 47°31'·06N 02°30'·72W.
Basse de Kervoyal Dir Q WR W8M, R5M; 269°-W-271°-R-269°; W sector leads to/from Nos 1 & 2 buoys; 47°30'·37N 02°32'·62W.
No. 1 Fl G 2·5s; 47°30'·32N 02°28'·73W.
No. 2 Fl R 2·5s; 47°30'·41N 02°28'·71W.
Pointe du Scal QG 8m 4M; 47°29'·67N 02°26'·87W.

ÎLE DUMET

Fort Fl (3) WRG 15s 14m, W7M, R/G4M; 090°-G-272°-W-285°-R-335°-W-090°; W col, G top; 47°24'·69N 02°37'·21W.
Basse-Est Île Dumet Q (3) 10s; 47°25'·20N 02°34'·93W.
Île Dumet Q; 47°25'·90N 02°36'·05W.

MESQUER

Laronesse 47°25'·96N 02°29'·50W.
Basse Normande 47°25'·47N 02°29'·80W.
Jetty Oc WRG 4s 7m W10M, R/G7M; 067°-W-072°-R-102°-W-118°-R-293°-W-325°-G-067°; W col & bldg; 47°25'·31N 02°28'·05W.

PIRIAC-SUR-MER

Grand Norven Q; 47°23'·55N 02°32'·89W.
Inner mole Oc (2) WRG 6s 8m, W10M, R/G7M; 066°-R-148°-G-194°-W-201°-R-221°; W col; 47°22'·93N 02°32'·71W. *Siren 120s (occas), 35m SW.* E bkwtr Fl R 4s 4m 5M; W pylon, R top; 47°23'·00N 02°32'·67W.
Les Bayonnelles Q (9) 15s;47°22'·56N 02°35'·23W.

LA TURBALLE

Ldg lts 006·5°, both Dir Iso R 4s 11/19m 3M; intens 004°-009°: Front, 47°20'·70N 02°30'·87W. Rear, 275m N of the front lt.
Ouest Jetée de Garlahy Fl (4) WR 12s 13m, W10M, R7M; 060°-R-315°-W-060°; W pylon, R top; 47°20'·70N 02°30'·93W.
Digue Tourlandroux Fl G 4s 4m 2M; G post, E side of access chan; 47°20'·75N 02°30'·88W.

LE CROISIC

Basse Hergo Fl G 2·5s 5m 3M; 47°18'·62N 02°31'·69W.
Jetée du Tréhic Iso WG 4s 12m W14M, G11M; 042°-G-093°-W-137°-G-345°; Gy twr, G top; 47°18'·49N 02°31'·42W. F Bu fog det lt, 100m SE.
Outer ldg lts 155·5°, both Dir Q 10/14m 13M; intens 154°-158°: Front 47°17'·96N 02°30'·99W . Rear , 116m from front.
Middle ldg lts 174°, both QG 5/8m 11M; 170·5°-177·5°: Front 47°18'·06N 02°31'·07W. Rear, 48m from front.
Le Grand Mabon Fl (3) R 12s 6m 2M; 47°18'·05N 02°31'·03W.
Inner ldg lts 134·7°, both QR 6/10m 8M; intens 132·5°-143·5°; synch.
Basse Castouillet Q (9) 15s; 47°18'·12N 02°34'·37W.
Basse Lovre 47°15'·87N 02°29'·58W, Chenal du Nord.

PLATEAU DU FOUR/BANC DE GUÉRANDE

Bonen du Four Q; 47°18'·53N 02°39'·29W.
Le Four Fl 5s 23m **18M**; W twr, B diagonal stripes; 47°17'·87N 02°38'·05W. 992271016.
Ouest Basse Capella Q (9) 15s; *Whis;* 47°15'·66N 02°42'·78W.
Goué-Vas-du-Four Q (6) + L Fl 15s; 47°14'·91N 02°38'·20W.
Sud Banc Guérande VQ (6) + L Fl 10s; 47°08'·80N 02°42'·81W. Restricted Area centred on 47°14'·37N 2°46'·65W, limits marked by 4 Fl Y 4s, enclosing 2 Fl (5) Y 20s ODAS bys.

POINTE DU CROISIC TO POINTE DE ST GILDAS

PLATEAU DE LA BANCHE

NW Banche Q 8m 4M; 47°12'·86N 02°31'·02W.
W Banche VQ (9) 10s; 47°11'·64N 02°32'·41W.
La Banche Fl (2) WR 6s 22m **W15M**, R11M; 266°-R-280°-W-266°; B twr, W bands; 47°10'·62N 02°28'·08W. 992271020.
SE Banche 47°10'·40N 02°26'·10W.

PLATEAU DE LA LAMBARDE

NW Lambarde 47°10'·84N 02°22'·93W.
SE Lambarde Q (6) + L Fl 15s; 47°10'·04N 02°20·80W.

BAIE DU POULIGUEN (or Baie de la Baule)

Penchateau Fl R 2·5s; 47°15'·24N 02°24'·35W.
Les Guérandaises Fl G 2·5s; 47°15'·03N 02°24'·29W.
47°15'·24N 02°23'·50W.
Les Evens 47°14'·32N 02°22'·55W.
Les Troves 47°14'·23N 02°22'·41W.
NNW Pierre Percée 47°13'·63N 02°20'·63W.
La Vieille 47°14'·03N 02°19'·51W.
Sud de la Vieille 47°13'·75N 02°19'·54W.
Le Caillou 47°13'·65N 02°19'·18W.
Le Petit Charpentier 47°13'·34N 02°18'·95W.
Le Grand Charpentier Q WRG 22m, W14M, R/G10M; 020°-G-054°-W-062°-R-092°-W-111°-R-310°-W-020°; Gy lt ho, G lantern; 47°12'·83N 02°19'·13W. 992271026.

LE POULIGUEN

Basse Martineau 47°15'·54N 02°24'·34W.
Petits Impairs Fl (2) G 6s 6m 2M; 47°15'·99N 02°24'·61W.
SW jetty QR 13m 9M; 171°-081°; W col; 47°16'·39N 02°25'·39W.

PORNICHET (La Baule)

S bkwtr Iso WRG 4s 11m, W10M, R/G7M; 303°-G-081°-

W-084°-R-180°; W twr, G top; 47°15'·49N 02°21'·14W.
Ent,W side ☆ QG 3m 1M; B perch, G top; 47°15'·51N 02°21'·12W.
E side ☆ QR 4m 1M; B perch, R top; 47°15'·50N 02°21'·10W.

ST NAZAIRE APPROACH (Chenal du Sud)

S-N1 L Fl 10s 8m 5M; ***Racon Z (3cm), 3–8M;*** 47°00'·07N 02°39'·84W.
S-N2 Iso 4s 8m 5M; 47°02'·08N 02°33'·47W.
Les Chevaux Fl G 2·5s; 47°03'·53N 02°26'·37W.
Thérèsia Fl R 2·5s; 47°04'·84N 02°27'·27W.
La Couronnée Fl (2) G 6s; ***Racon T, 3–5M;*** 47°07'·60N 02°20'·05W.
Lancastria Fl (2) R 6s;47°08'·88N 02°20'·37W.

PASSE DES CHARPENTIERS

Portcé ☆ ldg lts 025·5°, both Dir Q 6/36m **22/24M**: **Front**, intens 024·7°-026·2°; synch; W col; 47°14'·57N 02°15'·44W. 992271021. **Rear** ☆ (H24); intens 024°-027°; W twr; 0·75M from front.
Wreck (Y) Fl (3) R 12s; 47°09'·87N 02°19'·46W.
No. 1 VQ G; 47°09'·94N 02°18'·40W.
No. 2 VQ R; 47°10'·06N 02°18'·72W.
No. 6 Fl (3) R 12s; 47°12'·05N 02°17'·31W.
No. 5 Fl (4) G 15s; 47°12'·65N 02°16'·57W.
No. 8 Fl (4) R 15s; 47°12'·75N 02°16'·86W.
No. 7 VQ G; 47°13'·30N 02°16'·11W.
No. 10 VQ R; 47°13'·62N 02°16'·16W. (Buoys 9 - 18 not listed).
Pointe d'Aiguillon ☆ Oc (3) WR 12s 27m, W13M, R10M; 207°-R-233°-W-293°; 297°-W-300°-R-327°-W-023°; 027°-R-089°; W lt ho, conspic; 47°14'·54N 02°15'·79W. 992271018.
Ville-ès-Martin jetty ☆ Fl (2) 6s 10m 10M; W twr, R top; 47°15'·33N 02°13'·65W.
Morées Fl (3) WR 12s 12m, W6M, R4M; W058°-224°, R300°-058°; G twr; 47°15'·00N 02°13'·02W.

SAINT NAZAIRE

W jetty ☆ Oc (4) R 12s 11m 8M; W twr, R top; 47°15'·97N 02°12'·25W.
E jetty ☆ Oc (4) G 12s 11m 11M; W twr, G top; 47°15'·99N 02°12'·14W. (Ent lock for big ships into Bassin St Nazaire)
No. 20 QR; 47°16'·19N 02°11'·37W.
Sud Basse Nazaire Q (6) + L Fl 15s; 47°16'·21N 02°11'·51W.
Basse Nazaire Fl G 2·5s; 47°16'·24N 02°11'·63W.
SE Old mole Fl R 2·5s; 47°16'·24N 02°11'·73W.
Old Môle ☆ Q (3) 10s 18m 11M; 153·5°-063·5°; W twr, R top; weather signals; 47°16'·27N 02°11'·82W.
Fl (2) R 6s 5m 1M; R dolphin ; 47°16'·37N 02°11'·80W.
Entrée Est ☆ Fl (3) R 12s 9m 9M; R pylon; 47°16'·47N 02°11'·85W.
Ldg lts 280° (into E lock) 2 VQ Vi; front 47°16'·49N 02°11'·92W.

EAST SIDE OF RIVER, SOUTH TO PTE DE ST GILDAS

Le Pointeau, Digue S ☆ Fl WG 4s 4m, W10M, G7M; 050°-G-074°-W-149°-G-345°-W-050°; G&W ○ hut; 47°14'·02N 02°10'·96W.
Port de Comberge La Truie 47°12'·06N 00°13'·36W.
S jetty ☆ Oc WG 4s 7m W9M, G6M; 123°-W-140°-G-123°; W twr, G top; 47°10'·70N 02°09'·90W.
Port de la Gravette La Gravette 47°09'·81N 02°13'·06W.
Bkwtr hd ☆ Fl (3) WG 12s 7m, W8M, G5M; 183°-W-188°-G-124°-W-138°-G-183°; W structure, G top; 47°09'·64N 02°12'·70W.
Anse du Boucau bkwtr ☆ Fl (2) G 6s 3M; 47°08'·41N 02°14'·80W.
Pte de Saint Gildas ☆ Q WRG 20m, W14M, R/G10M; 264°-R-308°-G-078°-W-088°-R-174°-W-180°-G-264°; col on W house, G top; 47°08'·02N 02°14'·74W.
Nord Couronnée Q; 47°07'·34N 02°17'·78W.

RIVER LOIRE TO NANTES

Well buoyed/lit to Île de Bois, thence G lts, S side; R lts N side.
No. 21 VQ G; 47°16'·96N 02°10'·25W.
Suspension bridge, mid-span ☆ Iso 4s 55m, vis up/down stream; 47°17'·10N 02°10'·24W; between 2 conspic R/W twrs.
MA Fl (2) G 6s; 47°17'·50N 02°09'·22W.
MB Fl (3) G 12s; 47°17'·95N 02°07'·53W.
Fernais-25 Fl (4) G 15s; 47°18'·10N 02°06'·60W.
Paimboeuf, môle root ☆ Oc (3) WG 12s 9m, W10M, G7M; Shore-G-123°-W-shore; W twr, G top; 47°17'·42N 02°01'·95W.
Île de Bois (upstream) Fl (2) G 6s; 47°12'·79N 01°48'·27W.
Ldg lts 064° Rear Dir VQ R; 47°12'·00N 01°34'·35W, Y-junction with Bras de la Madeleine.

POINTE DE SAINT GILDAS TO FROMENTINE

Pte de Saint Gildas ☆ Q WRG 20m, W14M, R/G10M; 264°-R-308°-G-078°-W-088°-R-174°-W-180°-G-264°; 47°08'·02N 02°14'·75W. 992271017.
Notre Dame VQ (9) 10s 7m 3M; 47°05'·42N 02°08'·26W.

PORNIC

Approaches Fl G 4s; 47°06'·39N 02°06'·60W; Fl R 4s; 47°06'·40N 02°06'·64W
Marina ent, S side ☆ Fl (2) R 6s 4m 2M; 47°06'·47N 02°06'·67W.
Pte de Noëveillard ☆ Oc (4) WRG 12s 22m W13M, R/G9M; Shore-G-051°-W-079°-R-shore; W □ twr, G top, W house; 47°06'·62N 02°06'·92W.

ÎLE DE NOIRMOUTIER anti-clockwise from the East

Pte des Dames ☆ Oc (3) WRG 12s 34m, **W19M, R/G15M**; 016·5°-G-057°-R-124°-G-165°-W-191°-R191°-267°-W-357°-R-016·5°; W □ twr; 47°00'·67N 02°13'·26W. La Chaise 47°01'·21N 02°12'·64W.
L'Herbaudière, ldg lts 187·5°, both Q 5/21m 7M, Gy masts. Front, 47°01'·59N 02°17'·84W. Rear, 310m from front.
Martroger Q WRG 11m W9M, R/G6M; 033°-G-055°-W-060°-R-095°-G-124°-W-153°-R-201°-W-240°-R-033°; 47°02'·61N 02°17'·11W.
W jetty ☆ Oc (2+1) WG 12s 9m W10M, G7M; 187·5°-W-190°-G-187·5°; W col and hut, G top; 47°01'·63N 02°17'·84W.
E jetty ☆ Fl (2) R 6s 8m 4M; 47°01'·61N 02°17'·81W.
Île du Pilier ☆ Fl (3) 20s 33m **29M**; Gy twr; 47°02'·55N 02°21'·60W. 992271019. Same twr, aux ☆ QR 10m 11M, 321°-034°.

Passe de la Grise Q (6) + L Fl 15s; 47°01'·66N 02°19'·97W.
Les Boeufs VQ (9) 10s; 46°55'·04N 02°27'·99W.
Réaumur Q (9) 15s; 46°57'·46N 02°24'·22W.
Le Bavard VQ (6) + L Fl 10s; 46°56'·79N 02°23'·34W.
Pte du Devin (Morin) ☆ Oc (4) WRG 12s 10m W11M, R/G8M; 314°-G-028°-W-035°-R-134°; W col & hut, G top; 46°59'·15N 02°17'·60W.

GOULET DE FROMENTINE
Fromentine L Fl (3) 10s 3m 6M; 46°53'·10N 02°11'·40W
Milieu Fl (4) R 15 s 6m 5M; 46°53'·59N 02°09'·63W.
Pte de Notre Dame-de-Monts ☆ Dir Oc (2) WRG 6s 21m, W13M, R/G10M; 000°-G-043°-W-063°-R-073°-W-094°-G-113°-W-116°-R-175°-G-196°-R-230°; W twr, B top; 46°53'·33N 02°08'·54W.

ÎLE D'YEU TO BOURGENAY

ÎLE D'YEU
Petite Foule (main lt) ☆ Fl 5s 56m **24M**; W □ twr, G lantern; 46°43'·04N 02°22'·91W. 992271031.
Les Chiens Perrins Q (9) WG 15s 16m W7M, G4M; 330°-G-350°-W-200°; 46°43'·60N 02°24'·58W.
Pont d'Yeu 46°45'·81N 02°13'·81W.
La Sablaire Q (6) + L Fl 15s; 46°43'·62N 02°19'·49W.
Port Joinville ldg lts 219°, both QR 11/16m 6M, 169°-269°: Front, Quai du Canada 46°43'·61N 02°20'·94W. Rear, 85m from front.
NW jetty ☆ Oc (3) WG 12s 7m, W11M, G8M; Shore-G-150°-W-232°-G-279°-W-285°-G-shore; W 8-sided twr, G top; 46°43'·77N 02°20'·82W. La Galiote 46°43'·73N 02°20'·71W.
Pte des Corbeaux ☆ Fl (2+1) R 15s 25m **20M**; 083°-143° obsc by Île de Yeu; W □ twr, R top; 46°41'·41N 02°17'·08W.
Port de la Meule ☆ Oc WRG 4s 9m, W9M, R/G6M; 007·5°-G-018°-W-027·5°-R-041·5°; Gy twr, R top; 46°41'·62N 02°20'·72W.

SAINT GILLES-CROIX-DE-VIE
Pte de Grosse Terre ☆ Fl (4) WR 12s 25m, **W18M, R15M**; 290°- R-339°-W-125°-R-145°; W truncated twr; 46°41'·54N 01°57'·92W.
Ldg lts 043·7°, both Q 7/28m **15M**; 033·5°-053·5°; synch; W □ twrs, R tops: Front, 46°41'·86N 01°56'·75W. 992271027. Rear, 260m NE.
Pilours Q (6) + L Fl 15s; *Bell;* 46°40'·99N 01°58'·09W.
Jetée de la Garenne ☆ Fl G 4s 8m 6M; 46°41'·46N 01°57'·25W.
Jetée de Boisvinet ☆ Fl R 4s 8m 6M; 46°41'·62N 01°57'·16W.

LES SABLES D'OLONNE
Les Barges ☆ Fl (2) R 10s 25m 13M; Gy twr; 46°29'·70N 01°50'·50W.
Petite Barge Q (6) + L Fl 15s 3M; *Whis;* 46°28'·90N 01°50'·61W.
L'Armandèche ☆ Fl (2+1) 15s 42m **24M**; 295°-130°; W 6-sided twr, R top; 46°29'·39N 01°48'·29W. 992271035.
Nouch Sud Q (6) + L Fl 15s; 46°28'·55N 01°47'·41W.
Nouch Nord 46°28'·88N 01°47'·36W.
SW Pass, ldg lts 032·5°, both Iso 4s 12/33m **16M**, H24: **Front** ☆, 46°29'·42N 01°46'·37W. 992271024. Mast. **Rear** ☆, **La Potence**, W □ twr.
SE Pass, ldg lts 320°: Front, E jetty ☆ QG 11m 8M; W twr, G top; 46°29'·44N 01°47'·51W. 992271032. Rear, Tour d'Arundel ☆ Q 33m 13M, synch; large Gy □ twr; 46°29'·63N 01°47'·74W. 992271022.
Jetée St Nicolas (W jetty) ☆ QR 1·2s 16m 8M; 143°-094°; W twr, R top; 46°29'·23N 01°47'·52W.

BOURGENAY
Ldg lts 040°, both QG 9/19m 7M. Front, 020°-060°; on S bkwtr; 46°26'·34N 01°40'·62W. Rear, 010°-070°; 162m from front.
Landfall L Fl 10s; 46°25'·26N 01°41'·93W.
Ent ☆ Fl R 4s 8m 9M & ☆ Iso G 4s 6m 5M; 46°26'·29N 01°40'·75W.

PLATEAU DE ROCHEBONNE (Shoal 32M offshore)
NW Q (9) 15s; *Whis;* 46°12'·92N 02°31'·58W.
NE Iso G 4s; 46°12'·73N 02°24'·83W.
SE Q (3) 10s; *Bell;* 46°09'·20N 02°21'·13W.
SW Fl (2) R 6s; 46°10'·11N 02°27'·04W.

PERTUIS BRETON

JARD-SUR-MER and LA TRANCHE-SUR-MER
Ldg marks 036°, two unlit W bcns; 46°24'·47N 01°34'·16W.
Pte du Grouin du Cou ☆ Fl WRG 5s 29m, **W20M, R/G16M**; 034°-R-061°-W-117°-G-138°-W-034°; W 8-sided twr, B top; 46°20'·67N 01°27'·83W.
La Tranche pier ☆ Fl (2) R 6s 6m 6M; R col; 46°20'·55N 01°25'·63W.
Mussel farm, No entry, marked by: Q, 46°17'·17N 01°22'·19W. Q (3) 10s, 46°15'·73N 01°18'·42W. Q (6) + L Fl 15s, 46°15'·16N 01°19'·98W. Q (9) 15s, 46°16'·28N 01°22'·88W.

L'AIGUILLON and LA FAUTE-SUR-MER
Le Lay Q (6) + L Fl 15s; 46°16'·10N 01°16'·53W.
No. 1 46°16'·65N 01°16'·25W. Many mussel beds.

ANSE DE L'AIGUILLON (for La Sèvre Niortaise & Marans)
ATT de L'Aiguillon L Fl 10s; 46°15'·33N 01°11'·50W.
Inner fairway 46°17'·19N 01°09'·65W.
Port du Pavé ☆ Fl G 4s 9m 7M; W col, G top; 46°18'·15N 01°08'·01W.

ÎLE DE RÉ

Les Baleineaux ☆ VQ 23m 7M; pink twr, R top; 46°15'·81N 01°35'·22W.
Les Baleines ☆ Fl (4) 15s 53m **27M**; conspic Gy 8-sided twr, R lantern; 46°14'·64N 01°33'·69W.

ARS-EN-RÉ
Dir ☆ 268° Oc WRG 4s, W10M, R/G 7M, 275·5°-G-267·5°-W-268·5°-R-274·5°; W hut with W □ topmark; 46°14'·05N 01°28'·60W.
Les Islattes Q 13m 3M; NCM bcn twr 46°14'·03N 01°23'·32W.
Bûcheron No 1 Fl G 2·5s; 46°14'·21N 01°25'·98W.
Bûcheron No 3 Fl (2) G 6s; 46°14'·14N 01°26'·94W.
Le Fier d'Ars, inner ldg lts 232·5°, both Q 5/13m 9/11M: Front ☆ R/W frame on W col; 46°12'·75N 01°30'·59W. Rear ☆ 142°-322°; B vert rectangle on W mast, 370m from front.

ST MARTIN DE RÉ

Lt ho, E of ent ☆ Oc (2) WR 6s 18m W10M, R7M; Shore-W-245°-R-281°-W-shore; W twr, R top; 46°12'·44N 01°21'·89W.

W mole ☆ Fl G 2·5s 10m 5M; obsc'd by Pte du Grouin when brg <124°; W post, G top; 46°12'·49N 01°21'·91W.

LA FLOTTE

N bkwtr ☆ Fl WG 4s 10m W12M, G9M; 130°-G-205°-W-220°-G-257°; W ○ twr, G top; 46°11'·33N 01°19'·30W.

Dir lt 212·5°, Moiré effect, is next to the main lt twr.

ÎLE DE RÉ (South coast, from the W, inc bridge)

Chanchardon ☆ Fl WR 4s 15m W11M, R8M; 118°-R-290°-W-118°; B 8-sided twr, W base; 46°09'·71N 01°28'·41W.

Chauveau ☆ Oc (3) WR 12s 27m **W15M**, R11M; 057°-W-094°-R-104°-W-342°-R-057°; W ○ twr, R top; 46°08'·03N 01°16'·42W.

Bridge span (30m cl'nce) for SE-bound vessels, ☆ Iso 4s 34m 8M; 46°10'·18N 01°14'·75W . Span (30m cl'nce) for NW-bound vessels, ☆ Iso 4s 34m 8M; 46°10'·26N 01°14'·52W.

La Pallice, W mole, ☆ Fl G 4s 5m 6M; 46°09'·78N 01°14'·45W. S end, ☆ Q (6) + L Fl 15s 6m 9M; 46°09'·36N 01°14'·52W.

LA ROCHELLE and LA CHARENTE TO ROCHEFORT

LA ROCHELLE

Chauveau VQ (6) + L Fl 10s; 46°06'·56N 01°16'·06W.

Roche du Sud Q (9) 15s; 46°06'·37N 01°15'·22W.

La Rochelle ldg lts 059°, both Dir Q 15/25m 13/14M; synch; by day Fl 4s. Front; intens 056°-062°; R ○ twr, W bands; 46°09'·35N 01°09'·16W. Rear, 044°-074°, obsc'd 061°-065°; W 8-sided twr, G top, 235m from front.

Lavardin Fl (2) 6s 14m 7M; BRB IDM twr; 46°08'·09N 01°14'·52W.

Les Minimes Q (9) 15s; 46°08'·01N 01°11'·60W.

Pte des Minimes ☆ Fl (3) WG 12s 8m; W8M, G5M; 059°-W-213°; 313°-G-059°; 8-sided twr on piles; 46°08'·27N 01°10'·76W.

Chan buoy QG; 46°08'·53N 01°10'·87W; marking hbr limit.

Tour Richelieu Fl R 4s 10m 9M; R twr; 46°08'·90N 01°10'·34W.

Port des Minimes, W bkwtr ☆ Fl (2) G 6s 9m 7M; 46°08'·82N 01°10'·15W.

LA CHARENTE

Fort Boyard twr ☆ Q (9) 15s; 45°59'·96N 01°12'·85W.

Ldg lts 115°, both Dir QR 8/21m **19/20M**; intens 113°-117°; W □ twr, R top: **Front** ☆, 45°57'·96N 01°04'·38W. **Rear, Soumard** ☆, 600m from front. Same twr: ☆ QR 21m 8M; vis 322°-067°.

Île d'Aix ☆ Fl WR 5s 24m **W24M, R20M**; 103°-R-118°-W-103°; two conspic W ○ twrs, R top; 46°00'·60N 01°10'·67W.

Pte Ste Catherine, jetty hd Q (6) + L Fl 15s 5m 4M; 45°59'·05N 01°07'·85W. Les Palles Q; 45°59'·54N 01°09'·56W.

Fouras, Port Sud bkwtr ☆ Fl WR 4s 6m 9/6M; 115°-R-177°-W-115°; 45°58'·97N 01°05'·72W. Rear 75m from front.

ROCHEFORT

Night passage by yachts is not advised.

☆ Fl (2) G 6s; bcn 45°55'·21N 00°56'·98W, 1·4M S of Rochefort.

ÎLE D'OLÉRON

Pte de Chassiron ☆ Fl 10s 50m, **28M**; conspic W twr, B bands; 46°02'·80N 01°24'·62W, NW tip of island.

Antioche Q 20m 11M; 46°03'·94N 01°23'·71W.

ST DENIS

Dir ☆ 205°, Iso WRG 4s 14m, W11M, R/G8M; 190°-G-204°-W-206°-R-220°; 46°01'·61N 01°21'·92W.

E jetty ☆ Fl (2) WG 6s 6m, W9M, G6M; 205°-G-277°-W-292°-G-165°; □ hut; 46°02'·10N 01°22'·06W.

PORT DU DOUHET and PASSAGE DE L'OUEST

Seaweed farm VQ; 46°00'·65N 01°17'·38W.

N ent 46°00'·10N 01°19'·20W.

Fishfarm Q; 46°00'·24N 01°15'·34W. Q (3) 10s; 45°59'·84N 01°14'·79W.

BOYARDVILLE

Mole ☆ Fl (2) R 6s 8m 5M; obsc'd by Pte des Saumonards when brg <150°; W twr, R top; 45°58'·24N 01°13'·83W.

COUREAU D'OLÉRON and LE CHÂTEAU D'OLÉRON

Juliar Q (3) WG 10s 12m, W11M; G8M; 147°-W-336°-G-147°; 45°54'·11N 01°09'·48W.

Chateau d'Oléron, ldg lts 318·5°, both QR 11/24m 7M; synch. Front, 191°-087°; R line on W twr; 45°53'·03N 01°11'·45W. Rear, W twr, R top; 240m from front.

LA SEUDRE RIVER

Pte du Mus de Loup ☆ Oc G 4s 8m 6M; 118°-147°; 45°47'·70N 01°08'·60W.

Pertuis de Maumusson. Depths & buoys subject to change.

ATT Maumusson L Fl 10s; 45°46'·46N 01°18'·13W.

La Barre 45°46'·59N 01°16'·25W.

Tabouret 45°46'·93N 01°16'·15W.

Mattes 45°46'·93N 01°15'·29W.

Gatseau 45°47'·36N 01°14'·70W.

LA COTINIÈRE (SW side of island)

Ent ldg lts 339°, both ☆ Dir Oc (2) 6s 6/14m 13/12M; synch: Front, 329°-349°; W twr, R top; 45°54'·72N 01°19'·79W. Rear, intens 329°-349°; W twr, R bands; 425m from front on W bkwtr.

W bkwtr head, Fl R 4s 10m; 45°54'·63N 01°19'·70W.

GIRONDE APPROACHES and to BORDEAUX

GRANDE PASSE DE L'OUEST

Pte de la Coubre ☆ Fl (2) 10s 64m **28M**; W twr, R top; 45°41'·78N 01°13'·99W. Same twr, Q R 42m10M; 030°-R-110°.

BXA Iso 4s 8m 7M; ***Racon B***; 45°34'·10N 01°26'·63W. 992271005.

La Palmyre Wtr Twr Dir ☆ 056·7°, WRG 54m **W25M R/G20M**; 055·25°-FG-055·95°-AlWG-056·58°-FW-057·42°-AlWR-058·02-FR-058·72°; Gy Wtr Twr; 45°41'·65N 01°10'·18W.

Duc d'Albe ☆ Fl(2) 6s 10m 2M; W pylon on dolphin; 45°39'·56N 01°08'·77W.
No. 1 QG; 45°36'·17N 01°21'·70W; 992271036 .
No. 6 VQ (6) + L Fl 10s; 45°38'·27N 01°17'·91W.
No. 7a Fl G 4s; 45°38'·96N 01°14'·85W.
No. 9 Q; 45°39'·43N 01°12'·79W.
No. 11 Iso G 4s; 45°39'·06N 01°10'·60W.
No. 11A Fl G 2·5s; 45°38'·37N 01°07'·90W.
No. 13 Fl (2) G 6s; 45°37'·34N 01°06'·41W.
No. 13A Fl (3) G 12s; 45°35'·68N 01°04'·19W.
No. 13B QG; 45°34'·65N 01°02'·99W.

Ldg lts 327° (down-river): Front, Terre-Nègre ☆, Oc (3) WRG 12s 39m W14M, R/G11M; 304°-R-319°-W-327°-G-000°-W-004°-G-097°-W-104°-R-116°; W twr, R top on W side; 45°38'·77N 01°06'·39W. Rear, **La Palmyre** Oc (3) R 12s 57m 17M; W radar Twr; 45°39'·72N 01° 07'·25W. 1.1M from front (Terre Nègre) above.

Cordouan ☆ Oc (2+1) WRG 12s 60m, **W19M, R16M, G15M**; 014°-W-126°-G-178·5°-W-250°-W (unintens) -267°-R (unintens)-294·5°-R-014°; obsc'd in estuary when brg >285°; W twr, Gy band; 45°35'·18N 01°10'·40W.

PASSE SUD (or DE GRAVE)

Ldg lts 063°: **Front, St Nicolas** ☆ Dir QG 22m **16M**; intens 061·5°-064·5°; W □ twr; 45°33'·73N 01°05'·01W.
Rear, Pte de Grave ☆ Oc WRG 4s 26m, **W17M, R/G13M**; 033°-W(unintens)-054°-W-233·5°-R-303°-W-312°-G-330°-W-341°- W(unintens)-025°; W □ twr, B corners and top, 0·84M from front.
G 45°30'·33N 01°15'·55W. G3 45°32'·79N 01°07'·72W.
Ldg lts 041°, both Dir QR 33/61m **18M. Front, Le Chay** ☆ 45°37'·31N 01°02'·43W. **Rear, St Pierre** ☆, 0·97M from front.
G4 45°34'·70N 01°05'·80W. G6 45°34'·88N 01°04'·80W.

ROYAN

R1 Iso G 4s; 45°36'·56N 01°01'·96W.
S jetty ☆ Fl (2) R 10s 11m 12M; 199°-116°; 45°37'·00N 01°01'·81W.
Hbr ent, W jetty ☆ Fl (3) R 12s 8m 6M; 45°37'·12N 01°01'·53W.

PORT BLOC and PORT-MÉDOC

Pte de Grave, jetty Q 6m 2M; 45°34'·42N 01°03'·68W.
Port Bloc, ent N side ☆ Fl G 4s 9m 3M; 45°34'·14N 01°03'·74W.
Port-Médoc, N bkwtr head ☆ QG 4M; 45°33'·40N 01°03'·39W.

MESCHERS, MORTAGNE, PORT MAUBERT, PAUILLAC and BLAYE

Meschers ldg lts 354·4°: QG (privately maintained). Front 45°33'·20N 00°56'·63W, on E bkwtr head. Rear, 130m from front.
Mortagne ent VQ (9) 10s; 45°28'·24N 00°49'·02W.
Port Maubert, ldg lts 024·5°, both QR 5/9m 5M; 45°25'·56N 00°45'·47W.
Pauillac, No. 43 Fl (2) G 6s; 45°12'·44N 00°44'·27W.
NE elbow ☆ Fl G 4s 7m 5M; 45°11'·95N 00°44'·59W.
Ent E side ☆ QG 7m 4M; 45°11'·83N 00°44'·59W.
Blaye, No. S9 ▲ 45°09'·35N 00°40'·27W; 1·8M N of Blaye.
N quay ☆ Q (3) R 5s 6m 3M; 45°07'·49N 00°39'·99W.
D6 Fl (2) R 6s; 45°06'·91N 00°39'·93W, 0.6M S of Blaye.
Bec d'Ambés QG 5m 5M; 45°02'·53N 00°36'·47W (here Rivers Dordogne and Garonne flow into River Gironde).

BORDEAUX

Pont d'Aquitaine ☆ 4 F Vi; 44°52'·82N 00°32'·28W.
No 73 Iso G 4s; 44°52'·72N 00°32'·24W.
Lormont Iso R 4s, S end of Ⓥ pontoon; 44°52'·62N 00°32'·12W.
Lock ent to Bassins Nos 1 and 2, 44°51'·72N 00°33'·07W.
Pont de Pierre, 44°50'·30N 00°33'·78W, Km 0.

1	Port Joinville	**1**															
2	St Gilles-C-de-Vie	18	**2**														
3	Sables d'Olonne	31	16	**3**													
4	Bourgenay	40	25	9	**4**												
5	St Martin (I de Ré)	55	44	27	20	**5**											
6	La Rochelle	66	51	36	29	12	**6**										
7	Rochefort	84	75	61	54	36	26	**7**									
8	R La Seudre	89	71	58	52	33	24	30	**8**								
9	Port St Denis	59	48	33	30	21	13	26	22	**9**							
10	Port Bloc/Royan	97	85	71	60	56	52	68	27	42	**10**						
11	Bordeaux	152	140	126	115	111	107	123	82	97	55	**11**					
12	Cap Ferret	138	130	113	110	102	98	114	75	88	68	123	**12**				
13	Capbreton	192	186	169	166	165	156	172	131	145	124	179	58	**13**			
14	Anglet/Bayonne	200	195	181	178	177	168	184	143	157	132	187	70	12	**14**		
15	Santander	212	210	204	204	206	202	218	184	192	180	235	133	106	103	**15**	
16	Cabo Finisterre	377	395	393	394	406	407	423	399	397	401	456	376	370	373	274	**16**

DISTANCE TABLES

Approx distances in nautical miles are by the most direct route allowing for dangers and TSS.

Times are UT - add 1 hour in non-shaded months to convert to Summer Time

SUN RISE/SET LATITUDE 56°N – 2016

	JANUARY Rise	JANUARY Set	FEBRUARY Rise	FEBRUARY Set	MARCH Rise	MARCH Set	APRIL Rise	APRIL Set	MAY Rise	MAY Set	JUNE Rise	JUNE Set
1	0831	1536	0756	1632	0651	1735	0530	1839	0415	1940	0322	2035
4	0830	1539	0750	1638	0643	1741	0522	1845	0409	1946	0319	2039
7	0829	1544	0744	1645	0635	1748	0514	1851	0402	1952	0316	2042
10	0827	1548	0738	1652	0628	1754	0506	1857	0356	1958	0315	2045
13	0824	1553	0731	1658	0620	1800	0459	1904	0350	2004	0314	2047
16	0821	1559	0724	1705	0612	1806	0451	1910	0345	2009	0313	2049
19	0817	1605	0717	1711	0604	1813	0444	1916	0340	2015	0313	2050
22	0813	1611	0710	1718	0556	1819	0436	1922	0335	2020	0313	2051
25	0808	1617	0703	1724	0548	1825	0429	1928	0330	2025	0315	2051
28	0803	1623	0656	1731	0540	1831	0422	1934	0326	2029	0316	2050
31	0758	1630			0532	1837			0323	2034		

	JULY Rise	JULY Set	AUGUST Rise	AUGUST Set	SEPTEMBER Rise	SEPTEMBER Set	OCTOBER Rise	OCTOBER Set	NOVEMBER Rise	NOVEMBER Set	DECEMBER Rise	DECEMBER Set
1	0319	2049	0405	2007	0505	1853	0604	1734	0708	1619	0807	1531
4	0321	2047	0410	2001	0511	1846	0610	1726	0714	1612	0812	1528
7	0325	2045	0416	1954	0517	1838	0616	1719	0720	1606	0816	1527
10	0328	2042	0422	1947	0522	1830	0622	1711	0727	1600	0820	1525
13	0332	2038	0428	1941	0528	1822	0628	1703	0733	1555	0824	1525
16	0337	2034	0434	1933	0534	1814	0634	1656	0739	1550	0826	1525
19	0342	2030	0439	1926	0540	1806	0640	1649	0745	1545	0829	1526
22	0347	2025	0445	1919	0546	1758	0647	1641	0751	1541	0830	1527
25	0352	2020	0451	1911	0552	1750	0653	1634	0757	1537	0831	1529
28	0357	2015	0457	1904	0558	1742	0659	1627	0802	1533	0832	1532
31	0403	2009	0503	1856			0706	1621			0831	1535

SUN RISE/SET LATITUDE 48°N – 2016

	JANUARY Rise	JANUARY Set	FEBRUARY Rise	FEBRUARY Set	MARCH Rise	MARCH Set	APRIL Rise	APRIL Set	MAY Rise	MAY Set	JUNE Rise	JUNE Set
1	0750	1617	0729	1659	0640	1745	0538	1831	0441	1914	0405	1952
4	0750	1620	0724	1704	0635	1749	0532	1835	0437	1918	0403	1954
7	0749	1623	0720	1709	0629	1754	0526	1839	0432	1922	0401	1957
10	0748	1627	0716	1713	0623	1759	0520	1844	0428	1926	0401	1959
13	0747	1631	0711	1718	0617	1803	0514	1848	0424	1930	0400	2001
16	0745	1635	0706	1723	0611	1807	0508	1852	0420	1934	0400	2002
19	0742	1639	0701	1728	0604	1812	0502	1857	0416	1938	0400	2003
22	0740	1644	0655	1733	0558	1816	0457	1901	0413	1941	0401	2003
25	0737	1648	0650	1737	0552	1821	0452	1905	0410	1945	0402	2004
28	0733	1653	0644	1742	0546	1825	0446	1909	0407	1948	0403	2003
31	0730	1657			0540	1829			0405	1951		

	JULY Rise	JULY Set	AUGUST Rise	AUGUST Set	SEPTEMBER Rise	SEPTEMBER Set	OCTOBER Rise	OCTOBER Set	NOVEMBER Rise	NOVEMBER Set	DECEMBER Rise	DECEMBER Set
1	0405	2003	0437	1935	0518	1840	0600	1739	0645	1641	0729	1609
4	0407	2002	0440	1931	0522	1834	0604	1733	0650	1637	0733	1608
7	0409	2000	0444	1926	0527	1828	0608	1726	0655	1632	0736	1607
10	0412	1959	0448	1921	0531	1822	0612	1721	0659	1628	0739	1607
13	0414	1957	0452	1916	0535	1816	0617	1715	0704	1624	0742	1607
16	0418	1954	0457	1911	0539	1810	0621	1709	0708	1621	0744	1607
19	0421	1951	0501	1905	0543	1803	0626	1703	0713	1618	0746	1608
22	0424	1948	0505	1900	0547	1757	0630	1658	0717	1615	0748	1610
25	0428	1944	0509	1854	0551	1751	0635	1653	0721	1613	0749	1612
28	0431	1941	0513	1848	0555	1745	0639	1648	0725	1611	0750	1614
31	0435	1937	0517	1842			0644	1643			0750	1617

SUN RISE/SET LATITUDE 40°N – 2016

	JANUARY Rise	JANUARY Set	FEBRUARY Rise	FEBRUARY Set	MARCH Rise	MARCH Set	APRIL Rise	APRIL Set	MAY Rise	MAY Set	JUNE Rise	JUNE Set
1	0722	1645	0709	1718	0633	1752	0544	1825	0500	1855	0433	1923
4	0722	1648	0706	1722	0628	1755	0539	1828	0456	1858	0432	1925
7	0722	1650	0703	1726	0624	1759	0534	1831	0453	1901	0431	1927
10	0722	1653	0700	1729	0619	1802	0529	1834	0449	1904	0431	1928
13	0721	1656	0656	1733	0614	1805	0525	1837	0446	1907	0431	1930
16	0720	1700	0652	1736	0609	1808	0520	1840	0444	1910	0431	1931
19	0718	1703	0649	1740	0605	1811	0516	1843	0441	1912	0431	1932
22	0717	1706	0644	1743	0600	1814	0512	1846	0439	1915	0432	1933
25	0715	1710	0640	1747	0555	1817	0507	1849	0437	1918	0432	1933
28	0713	1714	0636	1750	0550	1821	0504	1852	0435	1920	0434	1933
31	0710	1717			0545	1824			0434	1922		

	JULY Rise	JULY Set	AUGUST Rise	AUGUST Set	SEPTEMBER Rise	SEPTEMBER Set	OCTOBER Rise	OCTOBER Set	NOVEMBER Rise	NOVEMBER Set	DECEMBER Rise	DECEMBER Set
1	0435	1933	0459	1913	0528	1831	0557	1742	0629	1657	0703	1635
4	0437	1932	0501	1910	0531	1826	0559	1737	0633	1654	0706	1635
7	0438	1931	0504	1907	0534	1821	0603	1732	0636	1651	0709	1635
10	0440	1930	0507	1903	0536	1816	0606	1728	0640	1648	0711	1635
13	0443	1929	0510	1859	0539	1812	0609	1723	0643	1645	0713	1635
16	0445	1927	0513	1855	0542	1807	0612	1719	0647	1643	0716	1636
19	0447	1925	0516	1851	0545	1802	0615	1714	0650	1641	0717	1637
22	0450	1923	0519	1846	0548	1757	0618	1710	0653	1639	0719	1639
25	0452	1920	0521	1842	0551	1752	0622	1706	0657	1637	0720	1640
28	0455	1917	0524	1837	0554	1747	0625	1702	0700	1636	0721	1642
31	0458	1914	0527	1833			0628	1658			0722	1645

MOON RISE/SET LATITUDE 56°N – 2016

	JANUARY Rise	JANUARY Set	FEBRUARY Rise	FEBRUARY Set	MARCH Rise	MARCH Set	APRIL Rise	APRIL Set	MAY Rise	MAY Set	JUNE Rise	JUNE Set
1	****	1125	0046	1115	0032	1023	0155	1131	0153	1235	0203	1514
4	0200	1244	0342	1311	0315	1246	0356	1456	0331	1620	0355	1900
7	0500	1433	0614	1610	0526	1609	0537	1850	0521	2013	0639	2157
10	0739	1722	0807	1951	0709	2001	0733	2237	0756	2319	0954	2346
13	0935	2055	0945	2336	0857	2345	1011	0038	1105	0042	1301	0039
16	1109	****	1143	0156	1122	0151	1315	0241	1411	0209	1601	0156
19	1258	0257	1424	0444	1421	0404	1618	0404	1711	0325	1855	0337
22	1533	0600	1731	0635	1725	0534	1918	0521	2007	0459	2120	0607
25	1840	0804	2035	0756	2026	0651	2211	0659	2238	0717	2305	0924
28	2146	0928	2333	0916	2321	0822	****	0922	****	1024	0006	1259
31	****	1046			0107	1034			0131	1358		

	JULY Rise	JULY Set	AUGUST Rise	AUGUST Set	SEPTEMBER Rise	SEPTEMBER Set	OCTOBER Rise	OCTOBER Set	NOVEMBER Rise	NOVEMBER Set	DECEMBER Rise	DECEMBER Set
1	0126	1707	0237	1855	0502	1854	0617	1800	0831	1738	0921	1732
4	0348	2018	0607	2029	0830	1955	0936	1907	1123	1936	1125	2029
7	0716	2202	0938	2131	1147	2106	1235	2053	1321	2241	1245	****
10	1047	2306	1256	2237	1443	2301	1447	2348	1440	0111	1355	0251
13	1406	****	1600	****	1651	0100	1615	0219	1557	0523	1542	0702
16	1716	0105	1821	0213	1816	0449	1732	0632	1759	0931	1852	1007
19	1947	0325	1950	0555	1934	0902	1922	1042	2116	1212	2234	1140
22	2122	0656	2105	1000	2130	1257	2221	1335	****	1334	0053	1240
25	2234	1053	2245	1356	****	1533	0041	1505	0305	1433	0412	1345
28	****	1452	0028	1652	0250	1659	0408	1606	0623	1540	0715	1528
31	0137	1809	0351	1831			0727	1710			0929	1819

MOON RISE/SET LATITUDE 48°N – 2016

	Rise	Set	Rise	Set	Rise	Set	Rise	Set	Rise	Set	Rise	Set
	JANUARY		FEBRUARY		MARCH		APRIL		MAY		JUNE	
1	****	1125	0046	1115	0032	1023	0155	1131	0153	1235	0203	1514
4	0200	1244	0342	1311	0315	1246	0356	1456	0331	1620	0355	1900
7	0500	1433	0614	1610	0526	1609	0537	1850	0521	2013	0639	2157
10	0739	1722	0807	1951	0709	2001	0733	2237	0756	2319	0954	2346
13	0935	2055	0945	2336	0857	2345	1011	0038	1105	0042	1301	0039
16	1109	****	1143	0156	1122	0151	1315	0241	1411	0209	1601	0156
19	1258	0257	1424	0444	1421	0404	1618	0404	1711	0325	1855	0337
22	1533	0600	1731	0635	1725	0534	1918	0521	2007	0459	2120	0607
25	1840	0804	2035	0756	2026	0651	2211	0659	2238	0717	2305	0924
28	2146	0928	2333	0916	2321	0822	****	0922	****	1024	0006	1259
31	****	1046			0107	1034			0131	1358		

	JULY		AUGUST		SEPTEMBER		OCTOBER		NOVEMBER		DECEMBER	
1	0149	1640	0309	1826	0515	1845	0614	1806	0806	1804	0847	1805
4	0421	1947	0624	2015	0824	2003	0915	1930	1049	2009	1058	2054
7	0736	2146	0935	2136	1124	2130	1202	2126	1256	2304	1236	****
10	1048	2308	1236	2258	1410	2334	1420	****	1434	0121	1407	0242
13	1349	****	1528	0010	1626	0128	1606	0232	1613	0509	1613	0632
16	1645	0134	1753	0243	1810	0459	1744	0622	1832	0859	1921	0936
19	1917	0357	1941	0608	1950	0849	1953	1012	2142	1145	2244	1127
22	2109	0713	2116	0951	2201	1226	2250	1305	****	1325	0050	1246
25	2241	1049	2314	1328	****	1505	0058	1452	0300	1441	0351	1407
28	****	1427	0101	1622	0306	1647	0406	1610	0600	1605	0642	1602
31	0209	1737	0410	1816			0707	1731			0900	1847

MOON RISE/SET LATITUDE 40°N – 2016

	Rise	Set	Rise	Set	Rise	Set	Rise	Set	Rise	Set	Rise	Set
	JANUARY		FEBRUARY		MARCH		APRIL		MAY		JUNE	
1	2357	1126	0032	1130	0013	1042	0134	1152	0140	1247	0207	1507
4	0148	1257	0320	1334	0253	1308	0344	1506	0333	1616	0413	1839
7	0439	1455	0555	1628	0512	1620	0541	1843	0538	1954	0701	2137
10	0718	1742	0801	1955	0711	1956	0751	2216	0819	2258	1006	2336
13	0926	2102	0954	2324	0914	2327	1033	0015	1120	0026	1300	0038
16	1115	****	1203	0136	1144	0128	1328	0226	1412	0206	1547	0208
19	1317	0239	1445	0423	1436	0348	1618	0402	1659	0334	1833	0358
22	1554	0538	1741	0624	1728	0529	1905	0532	1945	0518	2100	0629
25	1853	0750	2032	0757	2015	0659	2149	0719	2216	0739	2258	0934
28	2145	0927	2318	0929	2300	0840	****	0944	****	1037	0008	1254
31	****	1057			0045	1057			0130	1357		

	JULY		AUGUST		SEPTEMBER		OCTOBER		NOVEMBER		DECEMBER	
1	0205	1621	0331	1805	0525	1838	0611	1811	0749	1822	0823	1829
4	0444	1925	0636	2006	0820	2009	0900	1946	1026	2032	1039	2112
7	0750	2134	0934	2139	1107	2147	1140	2149	1239	2320	1229	****
10	1049	2309	1222	2314	1347	2357	1401	****	1430	0128	1416	0236
13	1337	0009	1506	0031	1608	0148	1559	0242	1624	0500	1635	0611
16	1623	0154	1734	0304	1806	0506	1754	0615	1855	0837	1941	0915
19	1856	0420	1935	0618	2002	0839	2015	0951	2200	1126	2251	1118
22	2059	0725	2125	0945	2223	1204	2310	1244	0003	1317	0048	1250
25	2247	1046	2335	1308	0017	1446	0111	1442	0256	1447	0336	1424
28	0004	1409	0123	1600	0317	1639	0405	1613	0543	1623	0619	1625
31	0232	1714	0424	1804			0654	1747			0840	1906

SPEED, TIME AND DISTANCE (NAUTICAL MILES)

Time in minutes	Speed in knots 1	2	3	4	5	6	7	8	9	10	15	20
1	0·0	0·0	0·1	0·1	0·1	0·1	0·1	0·1	0·2	0·2	0·3	0·3
2	0·0	0·1	0·1	0·1	0·2	0·2	0·2	0·3	0·3	0·3	0·5	0·7
3	0·1	0·1	0·2	0·2	0·3	0·3	0·4	0·4	0·5	0·5	0·8	1·0
4	0·1	0·1	0·2	0·3	0·3	0·4	0·5	0·5	0·6	0·7	1·0	1·3
5	0·1	0·2	0·3	0·3	0·4	0·5	0·6	0·7	0·8	0·8	1·3	1·7
6	0·1	0·2	0·3	0·4	0·5	0·6	0·7	0·8	0·9	1·0	1·5	2·0
7	0·1	0·2	0·4	0·5	0·6	0·7	0·8	0·9	1·1	1·2	1·8	2·3
8	0·1	0·3	0·4	0·5	0·7	0·8	0·9	1·1	1·2	1·3	2·0	2·7
9	0·2	0·3	0·5	0·6	0·8	0·9	1·1	1·2	1·4	1·5	2·3	3·0
10	0·2	0·3	0·5	0·7	0·8	1·0	1·2	1·3	1·5	1·7	2·5	3·3
11	0·2	0·4	0·6	0·7	0·9	1·1	1·3	1·5	1·7	1·8	2·8	3·7
12	0·2	0·4	0·6	0·8	1·0	1·2	1·4	1·6	1·8	2·0	3·0	4·0
13	0·2	0·4	0·7	0·9	1·1	1·3	1·5	1·7	2·0	2·2	3·3	4·3
14	0·2	0·5	0·7	0·9	1·2	1·4	1·6	1·9	2·1	2·3	3·5	4·7
15	0·3	0·5	0·8	1·0	1·3	1·5	1·8	2·0	2·3	2·5	3·8	5·0
16	0·3	0·5	0·8	1·1	1·3	1·6	1·9	2·1	2·4	2·7	4·0	5·3
17	0·3	0·6	0·9	1·1	1·4	1·7	2·0	2·3	2·6	2·8	4·3	5·7
18	0·3	0·6	0·9	1·2	1·5	1·8	2·1	2·4	2·7	3·0	4·5	6·0
19	0·3	0·6	1·0	1·3	1·6	1·9	2·2	2·5	2·9	3·2	4·8	6·3
20	0·3	0·7	1·0	1·3	1·7	2·0	2·3	2·7	3·0	3·3	5·0	6·7
21	0·4	0·7	1·1	1·4	1·8	2·1	2·5	2·8	3·2	3·5	5·3	7·0
22	0·4	0·7	1·1	1·5	1·8	2·2	2·6	2·9	3·3	3·7	5·5	7·3
23	0·4	0·8	1·2	1·5	1·9	2·3	2·7	3·1	3·5	3·8	5·8	7·7
24	0·4	0·8	1·2	1·6	2·0	2·4	2·8	3·2	3·6	4·0	6·0	8·0
25	0·4	0·8	1·3	1·7	2·1	2·5	2·9	3·3	3·8	4·2	6·3	8·3
30	0·5	1·0	1·5	2·0	2·5	3·0	3·5	4·0	4·5	5·0	7·5	10·0
35	0·6	1·2	1·8	2·3	2·9	3·5	4·1	4·7	5·3	5·8	8·8	11·7
40	0·7	1·3	2·0	2·7	3·3	4·0	4·7	5·3	6·0	6·7	10·0	13·3
45	0·8	1·5	2·3	3·0	3·8	4·5	5·3	6·0	6·8	7·5	11·3	15·0
50	0·8	1·7	2·5	3·3	4·2	5·0	5·8	6·7	7·5	8·3	12·5	16·7

DISTANCE (NAUTICAL MILES) OFF RISING/DIPPING LIGHTS

Height of light in metres	Height of eye in feet 2	3	4	5	6	7	8	9	10	20	30	40	50
2	4·6	4·9	5·2	5·5	5·7	6·0	6·2	6·4	6·6	8·1	9·2	10·2	11·0
3	5·2	5·6	5·9	6·2	6·4	6·6	6·8	7·0	7·2	8·7	9·9	10·8	11·7
4	5·8	6·1	6·4	6·7	6·9	7·2	7·4	7·6	7·8	9·3	10·4	11·4	12·2
5	6·3	6·6	6·9	7·2	7·4	7·7	7·9	8·1	8·3	9·8	10·9	11·9	12·7
6	6·7	7·1	7·4	7·6	7·9	8·1	8·3	8·5	8·7	10·2	11·3	12·3	13·2
7	7·1	7·5	7·8	8·0	8·3	8·5	8·7	8·9	9·1	10·6	11·8	12·7	13·6
8	7·5	7·8	8·2	8·4	8·7	8·9	9·1	9·3	9·5	11·0	12·1	13·1	14·0
9	7·8	8·2	8·5	8·8	9·0	9·2	9·5	9·7	9·8	11·3	12·5	13·5	14·3
10	8·2	8·5	8·8	9·1	9·4	9·6	9·8	10·0	10·2	11·7	12·8	13·8	14·6
11	8·5	8·9	9·2	9·4	9·7	9·9	10·1	10·3	10·5	12·0	13·1	14·1	15·0
12	8·8	9·2	9·5	9·7	10·0	10·2	10·4	10·6	10·8	12·3	13·4	14·4	15·3
13	9·1	9·5	9·8	10·0	10·3	10·5	10·7	10·9	11·1	12·6	13·7	14·7	15·6
14	9·4	9·7	10·0	10·3	10·6	10·8	11·0	11·2	11·4	12·9	14·0	15·0	15·8
15	9·6	10·0	10·3	10·6	10·8	11·1	11·3	11·5	11·6	13·1	14·3	15·3	16·1
16	9·9	10·3	10·6	10·8	11·1	11·3	11·5	11·7	11·9	13·4	14·6	15·5	16·4
17	10·2	10·5	10·8	11·1	11·3	11·6	11·8	12·0	12·2	13·7	14·8	15·8	16·6
18	10·4	10·8	11·1	11·4	11·6	11·8	12·0	12·2	12·4	13·9	15·1	16·0	16·9
19	10·7	11·0	11·3	11·6	11·8	12·1	12·3	12·5	12·7	14·2	15·3	16·3	17·1
20	10·9	11·3	11·6	11·8	12·1	12·3	12·5	12·7	12·9	14·4	15·5	16·5	17·3
25	12·0	12·3	12·6	12·9	13·2	13·4	13·6	13·8	14·0	15·5	16·6	17·6	18·4
30	13·0	13·3	13·6	13·9	14·1	14·4	14·6	14·8	15·0	16·5	17·6	18·6	19·4
40	14·7	15·1	15·4	15·7	15·9	16·1	16·3	16·5	16·7	18·2	19·4	20·3	21·2
50	16·3	16·6	16·9	17·2	17·4	17·7	17·9	18·1	18·3	19·8	20·9	21·9	22·7
60	17·7	18·0	18·3	18·6	18·8	19·1	19·3	19·5	19·7	21·2	22·3	23·3	24·1

CONVERSION TABLE

Sq inches to sq millimetres *multiply by* **645.20**	**Sq millimetres to sq inches** *multiply by* **0.0016**
Inches to millimetres *multiply by* **25.40**	**Millimetres to inches** *multiply by* **0.0394**
Sq feet to square metres *multiply by* **0.093**	**Sq metres to sq feet** *multiply by* **10.7640**
Inches to centimetres *multiply by* **2.54**	**Centimetres to inches** *multiply by* **0.3937**
Feet to metres *multiply by* **0.305**	**Metres to feet** *multiply by* **3.2810**
Nautical miles to kilometres *multiply by* **1.852**	**Kilometres to nautical miles** *multiply by* **0.5400**
Statute miles to kilometres *multiply by* **1.609**	**Kilometres to statute miles** *multiply by* **0.6214**
Statute miles to nautical miles *multiply by* **0.8684**	**Nautical miles to statute miles** *multiply by* **1.1515**
HP to metric HP *multiply by* **1.014**	**Metric HP to HP** *multiply by* **0.9862**
Pounds per sq inch to kg per sq centimetre *multiply by* **0.0703**	**Kg per sq centimetre to pounds per sq inch** *multiply by* **14.2200**
HP to kilowatts *multiply by* **0.746**	**Kilowatts to HP** *multiply by* **1.341**
Cu inches to cu centimetres *multiply by* **16.39**	**Cu centimetres to cu inches** *multiply by* **0.0610**
Imperial gallons to litres *multiply by* **4.540**	**Litres to imperial gallons** *multiply by* **0.2200**
Pints to litres *multiply by* **0.5680**	**Litres to pints** *multiply by* **1.7600**
Pounds to kilogrammes *multiply by* **0.4536**	**Kilogrammes to pounds** *multiply by* **2.2050**

LIGHT CHARACTERISTICS

CLASS OF LIGHT		International abbreviations	National abbreviations
FIXED		F	
OCCULTING *(total duration of light longer than dark)*			
Single-occulting			Oc Occ
Group-occulting	eg	Oc(2)	Gp Occ(2)
Composite group-occulting	eg	Oc(2+3)	Gp Occ(2+3)
ISOPHASE *(light and dark equal)*			Iso
FLASHING *(total duration of light shorter than dark)*			
Single-flashing		Fl	
Long-flashing *(flash 2s or longer)*			L Fl
Group-flashing	eg	Fl(3)	Gp Fl(3)
Composite group-flashing	eg	Fl(2+1)	Gp Fl(2+1)
QUICK *(50 to 79, usually either 50 or 60, flashes per min.)*			
Continuous quick		Q	Qk Fl
Group quick	eg	Q(3)	Qk Fl(3)
Interrupted quick		IQ	Int Qk Fl
VERY QUICK *(80 to 159, usually either 100 or 120, flashes per min.)*			
Continuous very quick		VQ	V Qk Fl
Group very quick	eg	VQ(3)	V Qk Fl(3)
Interrupted very quick		IVQ	Int V Qk Fl
ULTRA QUICK *(160 or more, usually 240 to 300, flashes per min.)*			
Continuous ultra quick		UQ	
Interrupted ultra quick		IUQ	
MORSE CODE	eg	Mo(K)	
FIXED AND FLASHING		F Fl	
ALTERNATING	eg	Al. WR	Alt. WR

Illustration
Period shown

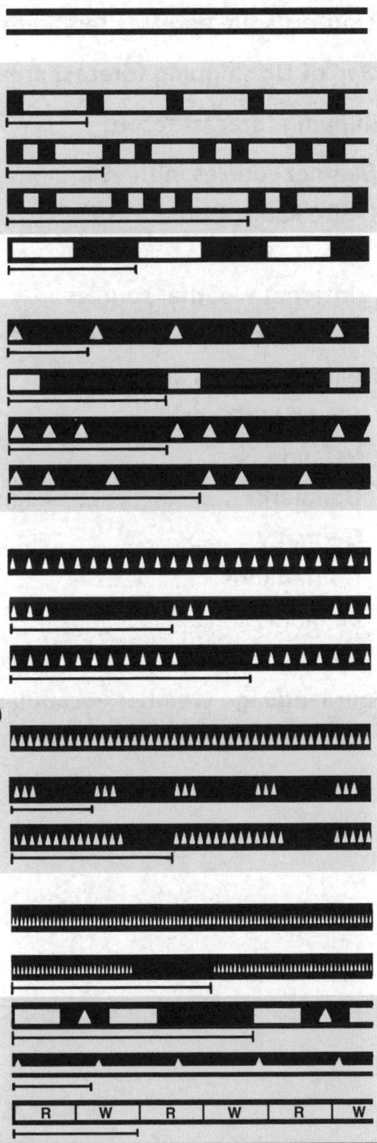

COLOUR	International abbreviations
White	W *(may be omitted)*
Red	R
Green	G
Blue	Bu
Violet	Vi
Yellow	Y
Orange	Y
Amber	Y

NOMINAL RANGE in miles		International abbreviations
Light with single range	eg	15M
Light with two different ranges	eg	15/10M
Light with three or more ranges	eg	15-7M
PERIOD is given in seconds	eg	90s
DISPOSITION horizontally disposed		(hor)
VERTICALLY DISPOSED		(vert)
SYNCHRONISED with (an)other light(s)		(sync)
ELEVATION is given in metres (m) or feet (ft) above MHWS		

Chapter 2 – Weather

Beaufort scale

Force	Wind speed (knots)	(km/h)	(m/sec)	Description	State of sea	Probable wave ht(m)
0	0–1	0–2	0–0·5	Calm	Like a mirror	0
1	1–3	2–6	0·5–1·5	Light airs	Ripples like scales are formed	0
2	4–6	7–11	2–3	Light breeze	Small wavelets, still short but more pronounced, not breaking	0·1
3	7–10	13–19	4–5	Gentle breeze	Large wavelets, crests begin to break; a few white horses	0·4
4	11–16	20–30	6–8	Moderate breeze	Small waves growing longer; fairly frequent white horses	1
5	17–21	31–39	8–11	Fresh breeze	Moderate waves, taking more pronounced form; many white horses, perhaps some spray	2
6	22–27	41–50	11–14	Strong breeze	Large waves forming; white foam crests more extensive; probably some spray	3
7	28–33	52–61	14–17	Near gale	Sea heaps up; white foam from breaking waves begins to blow in streaks	4
8	34–40	63–74	17–21	Gale	Moderately high waves of greater length; edge of crests break into spindrift; foam blown in well-marked streaks	5·5

Terminology used in forecasts

Pressure systems' speed of movement

Slowly	< 15 knots
Steadily	15–25 knots
Rather quickly	25–35 knots
Rapidly	35–45 knots
Very rapidly	> 45 knots

Visibility

Good	> 5 miles
Moderate	2–5 miles
Poor	1000 metres–2 miles
Fog	< 1000 metres

Barometric pressure tendency

Rising/falling slowly: Change of 0·1 to 1·5 hPa/mb in the preceding 3 hours.

Rising/falling: Change of 1·6 to 3·5 hPa/mb in the preceding 3 hours.

Rising/falling quickly: Change of 3·6 to 6 hPa/mb in the preceding 3 hours.

Rising/falling very rapidly: Change of > 6 hPa/mb in the preceding 3 hours.

Now rising/falling: Pressure has been falling (rising) or steady in the preceding 3 hours, but was definitely rising (falling) at the time of observation.

Gale warnings

A ***Gale*** warning means that winds of at least F8 (34-40kn) or gusts up to 43-51kn are expected somewhere within the area, but not necessarily over the whole area

Severe Gale means winds of at least F9 (41-47kn) or gusts reaching 52-60kn

Storm means winds of F10 (48-55kn) or gusts of 61-68kn

Violent Storm means winds of F11 (56-63kn) or gusts of 69+ kn

Hurricane Force means winds of F12 (64+ kn)

Gale warnings remain in force until amended or cancelled. If a gale persists for >24 hours the warning is re-issued.

Timing of gale warnings from time of issue

Imminent	<6 hrs
Soon	6–12 hrs
Later	>12 hrs

Strong wind warnings

Issued, if possible 6 hrs in advance, when winds F6 or more are expected up to 5M offshore; valid for 12 hrs.

MAP OF UK SHIPPING FORECAST AREAS

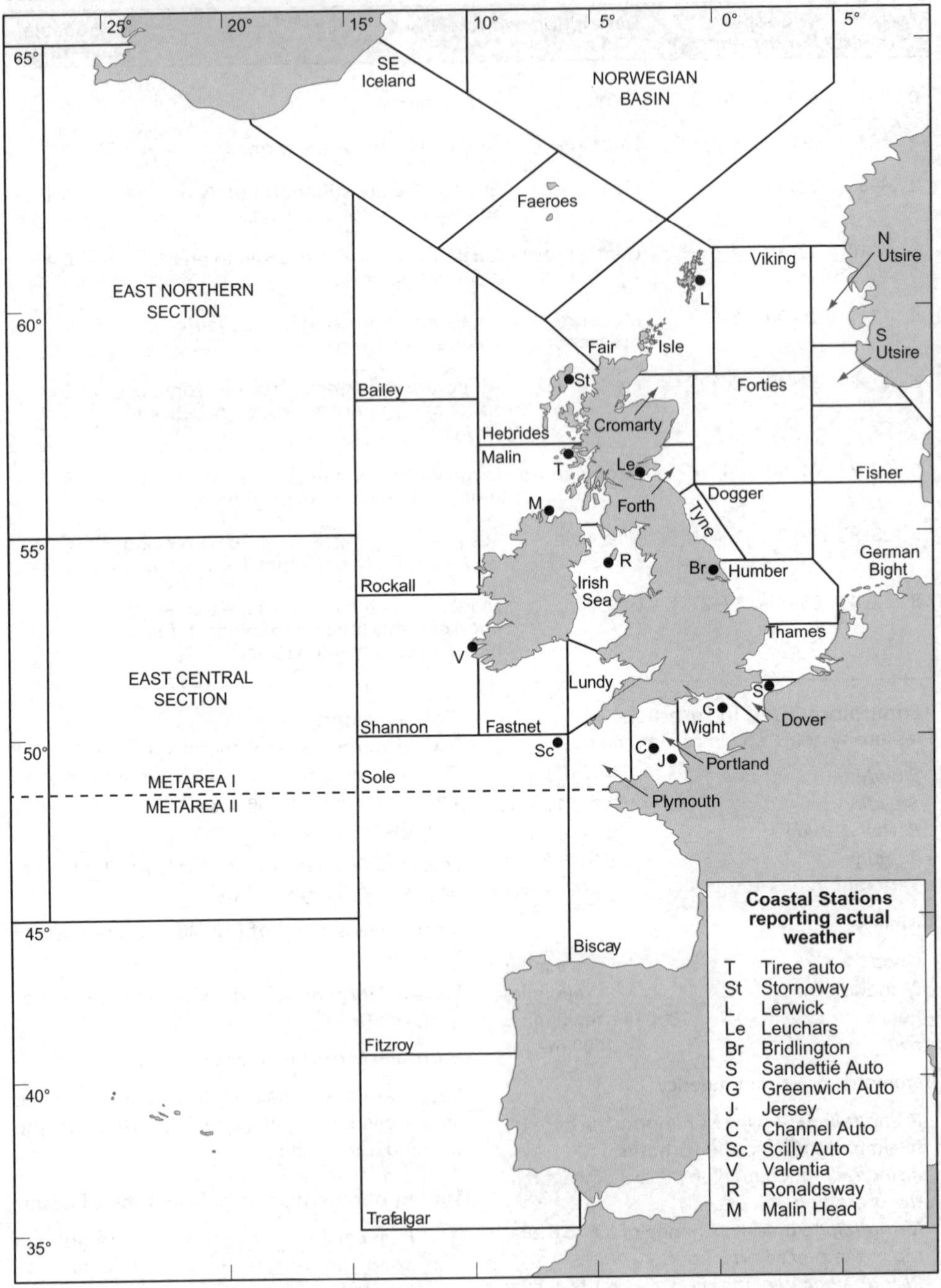

SHIPPING FORECAST RECORD TIME/DAY/DATE ....

GENERAL SYNOPSIS	At 0048, 0520, 1201, 1754 UT/BST			
System	Present position	Movement	Forecast position	At

Gales	SEA AREA FORECAST	Wind (At first)	Wind (Later)	Weather	Visibility
	VIKING				
	NORTH UTSIRE				
	SOUTH UTSIRE				
	FORTIES				
	CROMARTY				
	FORTH				
	TYNE				
	DOGGER				
	FISHER				
	GERMAN BIGHT				
	HUMBER				
	THAMES				
	DOVER				
	WIGHT				
	PORTLAND				
	PLYMOUTH				
	BISCAY				
	TRAFALGAR (0048)				
	FITZROY				
	SOLE				
	LUNDY				
	FASTNET				
	IRISH SEA				
	SHANNON				
	ROCKALL				
	MALIN				
	HEBRIDES				
	BAILEY				
	FAIR ISLE				
	FAEROES				
	S E ICELAND				

COASTAL REPORTS at .... UT BST	Wind Direction	Wind Force	Weather	Visibility	Pressure	Change
Tiree auto (T)						
Stornoway (St)						
Lerwick (L)						
Leuchars (Le)						
Bridlington (Br)						
Sandettié auto (S)						

COASTAL REPORTS	Wind Direction	Wind Force	Weather	Visibility	Pressure	Change
Greenwich auto (G)						
Jersey (J)						
Channel auto (C)						
Scilly auto (Sc)						
Valentia (V)						
Ronaldsway (R)						
Malin Head (M)						

SOURCES OF WEATHER INFORMATION IN THE UK

BBC Radio 4 Shipping forecasts

are broadcast at:

0048 LT[1]	LW, MW, FM
0520 LT[1]	LW, MW, FM
1201 LT	LW only
1754 LT	LW, FM (Sat/Sun)

[1] Includes weather reports from coastal stations

Frequencies

LW		198 kHz
MW	**Tyneside**	603 kHz
	London & N Ireland	720 kHz
	Redruth	756 kHz
	Plymouth & Enniskillen	774 kHz
	Aberdeen	1449 kHz
	Carlisle	1485 kHz
FM	**England**	92·4–94·6 MHz
	Scotland	91·3–96·1 MHz
		103·5–104·9 MHz
	Wales	92·8–96·1 MHz
		103·5–104·9 MHz
	N Ireland	93·2–96·0 MHz
		103·5–104·6 MHz
	Channel Islands	94·8 MHz

The Shipping forecast contains:

Time of issue; summary of gale warnings in force at that time; a general synopsis of weather systems and their expected development and movement over the next 24 hours; sea area forecasts for the same 24 hours, including wind direction/force, weather and visibility in each; and an outlook for the following 24 hours.

Gale warnings for all affected areas are broadcast at the earliest break in Radio 4 programmes after receipt, as well as after the next news bulletin.

Shipping forecasts cover large sea areas, and rarely include the detailed variations that may occur near land. The inshore waters forecast can be more helpful on coastal passages.

Weather reports from coastal stations follow the 0048 and 0520 shipping forecasts. They include wind direction and force, present weather, visibility, and sea-level pressure and tendency, if available. The stations are shown on the previous page.

BBC Radio 4 Inshore waters forecast

A forecast for inshore waters (up to 12M offshore) in 17 areas around the UK and N Ireland, valid for 24 hrs, is broadcast after the 0048 and 0520 coastal station reports.

It includes forecasts of wind direction and force, weather, visibility and sea state. The 17 inshore areas are defined by the following well-known places and headlands, clockwise around the UK: Cape Wrath, Orkney, Rattray Hd, Berwick-upon-Tweed, Whitby, Gibraltar Point, N Foreland, Selsey Bill, Lyme Regis, Land's End, St David's Head, Great Ormes Head, Isle of Man, Mull of Galloway, Carlingford Lough, Lough Foyle, Mull of Kintyre, Ardnamurchan Pt and Shetland.

Strong wind warnings are issued by the Met Office whenever winds of Force 6 or more are expected over coastal waters up to 5M offshore.

Reports of actual weather are broadcast from all the coastal stations below after the 0048 inshore waters forecast and also after the 0520 forecast, except those in italics: Tiree*, Stornoway, Lerwick, *Wick*, Aberdeen,* Leuchars, *Boulmer*, Bridlington, Sandettie LV*, Greenwich LV*, *St Catherines Point**, Jersey, Channel LV*, Scilly*, *Milford Haven, Aberporth, Valley, Liverpool (Crosby),* Valentia, Ronaldsway, Malin Head, *Macrihanish**. An asterix* denotes an automatic station.

BBC general (land) forecasts

Land area forecasts may include an outlook up to 48 hours beyond the shipping forecast, plus more details of frontal systems and weather along the coasts. The most comprehensive land area forecasts are broadcast by Radio 4 on the frequencies above.

Land area forecasts – Wind strength

Wind descriptions used in land forecasts, with their Beaufort scale equivalents, are:

Calm	0	Fresh	5
Light	1–3	Strong	6–7
Moderate	4	Gale	8

Land area forecasts – Visibility

The following visibility definitions are used in land forecasts:

Mist	2000m–1000m
Fog	<1000m
Dense fog	< 50m

NAVTEX

NAVTEX is the prime method of disseminating MSI to at least 200 miles offshore. A dedicated aerial and receiver with an LCD screen (or integrated printer) are required. The user selects which stations and message categories are recorded for automatic display or printing.

Two frequencies are used. On the international frequency, 518kHz, messages are always available in English with excellent coverage of Europe. Interference between stations is minimised by scheduling time slots and and by limiting transmission power; see Fig 6(3). NAVTEX information applies only to the geographical area for which each station is responsible.

490 kHz (for clarity shown in italics throughout this chapter) is used abroad for transmissions in the national language. In the UK it is used for inshore waters forecasts in English. Identification letters for 490 kHz stations differ from 518 kHz stations.

NAVTEX is convenient and particularly useful when preoccupied handling your vessel as you will not miss potentially important information.

Messages

Each message is prefixed by a four-character group:

The first character is the code letter of the transmitting station (eg **E** for Niton).

The second character is the message category, see below.

The third and fourth are message serial numbers, running from 01 to 99 and then re-starting at 01.

The serial number 00 denotes urgent messages which are always printed.

Messages which are corrupt or have already been printed are rejected. Weather messages, and certain other message types, are dated and timed.

Message categories

A*	Navigational warnings
B*	Meteorological warnings
C	Ice reports
D*	SAR info and piracy warnings
E	Weather forecasts
F	Pilot service
H	Loran-C
J	Satellite navigation
K	Other electronic navaids
L	Subfacts and Gunfacts (UK)
V	Amplifies Navwarnings initially sent under A; plus weekly oil/gas rig moves.
W-Y	Special service, trials
Z	No messages on hand at scheduled time

Missing category letters are unallocated.

*The receiver cannot reject these categories.

NAVTEX stations/areas – UK & W Europe

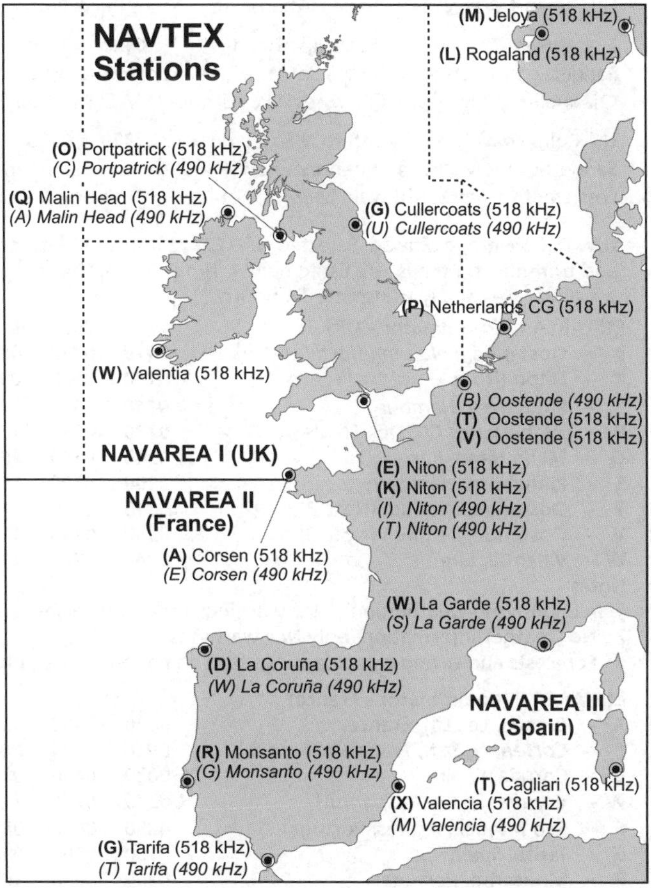
NAVTEX Stations
(M) Jeloya (518 kHz)
(L) Rogaland (518 kHz)
(O) Portpatrick (518 kHz)
(C) Portpatrick (490 kHz)
(Q) Malin Head (518 kHz)
(A) Malin Head (490 kHz)
(G) Cullercoats (518 kHz)
(U) Cullercoats (490 kHz)
(P) Netherlands CG (518 kHz)
(W) Valentia (518 kHz)
(B) Oostende (490 kHz)
(T) Oostende (518 kHz)
(V) Oostende (518 kHz)
NAVAREA I (UK)
(E) Niton (518 kHz)
(K) Niton (518 kHz)
(I) Niton (490 kHz)
(T) Niton (490 kHz)
NAVAREA II (France)
(A) Corsen (518 kHz)
(E) Corsen (490 kHz)
(W) La Garde (518 kHz)
(S) La Garde (490 kHz)
(D) La Coruña (518 kHz)
(W) La Coruña (490 kHz)
NAVAREA III (Spain)
(R) Monsanto (518 kHz)
(G) Monsanto (490 kHz)
(T) Cagliari (518 kHz)
(X) Valencia (518 kHz)
(M) Valencia (490 kHz)
(G) Tarifa (518 kHz)
(T) Tarifa (490 kHz)

UK/ROI 518 kHz stations

The times (UT) of weather messages are in bold; the times of an extended outlook (a further 2 or 3 days beyond the shipping forecast period) are in italics.

G –	**Cullercoats**	*0100*	0500	**0900**	1300	1700	**2100**
	Fair Isle clockwise to Thames, excluding N & S Utsire, Fisher and German Bight.						
O –	**Portpatrick**	*0220*	**0620**	1020	1420	**1820**	2220
	Lundy clockwise to SE Iceland.						
E –	**Niton**	*0040*	0440	**0840**	1240	1640	**2040**
	Thames clockwise to Fastnet, excluding Trafalgar.						
Q –	**Malin Head** sea areas Shannon,Rockall, Malin, Hebrides			**0640**	**1840**		

UK/ROI 490 kHz broadcasts (in italic) provide forecasts for UK inshore waters, a national 3 day outlook for inshore waters and, at times in bold, reports of actual weather at some or all of the places listed below. To receive these reports select message category 'V' on the receiver. Times (UT) are listed in chronological order. Reports include some or all of: Sea level pressure (hPa/mb), wind direction and speed (kn), weather, visibility (M), air and sea temperatures (°C), dewpoint temperature (°C) and mean wave height (m).

A – **Malin Head**	**0000**	**0400**	0800	**1200**	**1600**	2000
C – **Portpatrick** Land's End to Shetland	**0020**	**0420**	0820	**1220**	**1620**	2020
I – **Niton** The Wash to St David's Head	**0120**	0520	**0920**	**1320**	1720	**2120**
U – **Cullercoats** Cape Wrath to N Foreland	**0320**	0720	**1120**	**1520**	1920	**2320**

A – Malin Head: Lough Foyle to Carlingford Lough, Mull of Galloway to Cape Wrath, the Minch.

Note times of forecasts and actuals not known at time of going to press.

C – Portpatrick: N Rona, Stornoway, S Uist, Lusa (Skye), Tiree, Macrihanish, Belfast, Malin Hd, Belmullet, St Bees Hd, Ronaldsway, Crosby, Valley, Aberporth, Roches Pt, Valentia, St Mawgan.

I – Niton: Sandettie Lt V, Greenwich Lt V, Solent, Hurn airport, Guernsey airport, Jersey airport, Portland, Channel Lt V, Plymouth, Culdrose, Seven Stones Lt V, St Mawgan & Roches Pt.

U – Cullercoats: Sandettie Lt V, Manston, Shoeburyness, Weybourne, Donna Nook, Boulmer, Leuchars, Aberdeen, Lossiemouth, Wick, Kirkwall, Lerwick, Foula, K7 Met buoy, Sule Skerry.

NAVTEX coverage abroad: Selected NAVTEX stations in Metareas I and II, with identity codes and transmission times, are listed below. Times of weather messages are shown in **bold**. Gale warnings are usually transmitted 4 hourly.

METAREA I (Co-ordinator – UK)	**Transmission times (UT)**					
B – **Oostende**, *Belgium (mostly Dutch)*	***0010***	***0410***	*0810*	*1210*	***1610***	***2010***
K – **Niton** (Note 1)	0140	0540	0940	1340	1740	2140
L – **Pinneberg**, *Hamburg*	***0150***	***0550***	*0950*	*1350*	***1750***	***2150***
P – **Netherlands CG**, Den Helder	**0230**	0630	1030	**1430**	1830	2230
Q – **Malin Head**, Eire	0240	**0640**	**1040**	1440	**1840**	**2240**
S – **Pinneberg**, Hamburg	**0300**	**0700**	**1100**	**1500**	**1900**	**2300**
T – **Oostende**, Belgium (Note 3)	0310	**0710**	1110	1510	**1910**	2310
V – **Oostende**, Belgium (Note 2)	0330	0730	1130	1530	1930	2330
W – **Valentia**, Eire	0340	**0740**	**1140**	1540	**1940**	**2340**

Notes:

1 In English, no weather; only Nav warnings for waters from Cap Gris Nez to Île de Bréhat.
2 No weather information, only Nav warnings.
3 Forecasts and strong wind warnings for Thames and Dover, plus Nav info for Belgium.

METAREA II (Co-ordinator – France)						
A – **Corsen**, Le Stiff, France	**0000**	0400	0800	**1200**	1600	2000
E – ***Corsen**, Le Stiff, France (In French)*	*0040*	*0440*	***0840***	*1240*	*1640*	***2040***
D – **Coruña**, Spain	0030	0430	**0830**	1230	1630	**2030**
W – ***Coruña**, Spain (in Spanish)*	*0340*	*0740*	***1140***	*1540*	***1940***	*2340*
F – **São Miguel** , Açores, Portugal	**0050**	**0450**	**0850**	**1250**	**1650**	**2050**
G – **Tarifa**, Spain	0100	0500	**0900**	1300	1700	**2100**
R – **Monsanto**, Portugal	**0250**	**0650**	**1050**	**1450**	**1850**	**2250**

INTERNET WEATHER SOURCES

The Internet provides a useful back-up for GMDSS services as well as information not available by conventional means.

www.metoffice.gov.uk/weather/marine/ has texts of all marine forecasts, warnings and weather actuals from coastal stations, light vessels and data buoys. www.bbc.co.uk/weather/coast/ has texts of NAVTEX broadcasts.

National meteorological services provide the most reliable forecasts for their own waters.

Other useful websites include:

www.weather.mailasail.com/Franks-Weather/Home

www.weatheronline.com/ www.saildocs.com/

www.mailasail.com/ www.grib.us/

www.passageweather.com/

www.windfinder.com/ www.xcweather.co.uk/

www.windguru.com/ www.theyr.com /

www.wetterzentrale.de/topkarten/tknf.html

www.weatherweb.net/marine

Broadcasts of shipping and inshore waters forecasts by HM Coastguard

HM CGOC routinely broadcast MSI every 3 hours at the times shown below,UTC).

Each broadcast contains one of 3 different Groups of MSI:

Group A, the full broadcast, contains the Shipping forecast, a new Inshore waters forecast and 24 hrs outlook, Gale warnings, a 3 day forecast for Fishermen in the winter months*, Navigational (WZ) warnings and Subfacts & Gunfacts where relevant ‡. '**A**' broadcast times are in bold type.

Group B contains a new Inshore waters forecast, plus the previous outlook, and Gale warnings. '**B**' broadcast times are in plain type.

Group C is a repeat of the Inshore forecast and Gale warnings (as per the previous Group A or B) plus new Strong wind warnings. '**C**' broadcast times are italicised.

Note: ‡ indicates Subfacts & Gunfacts.

Coastguard	Shipping forecast areas	Inshore areas	Broadcast times, UTC							
South Coast			B	*C*	**A**	*C*	B	*C*	**A**	*C*
Falmouth‡ CGOC	Portland, Plymouth, Sole, Shannon, Lundy, Fastnet, Biscay, Fitzroy.	8,9	0110	*0410*	**0710**	*1010*	1310	*1610*	**1910**	*2210*
Fareham NMOC	Wight, Portland	6,7	0130	*0430*	**0730**	*1030*	1330	*1630*	**1930**	*2230*
Dover CGOC	Thames, Dover, Wight	5,6	0110	*0410*	**0710**	*1010*	1310	*1610*	**1910**	*2210*
East Coast			B	*C*	**A**	*C*	B	*C*	**A**	
Fareham NMOC	Thames, Humber, German Bight	5,6	0110	*0410*	**0710**	*1010*	1310	*1610*	**1910**	*2210*
Humber CGOC	Forties, Forth, Tyne Dogger Fisher, Humber, German Bight	3,4	0150	*0450*	**0750**	*1050*	1350	*1650*	**1950**	*2250*
Aberdeen‡ CGOC	Cromarty, Forties, Forth, Fair Isle, Viking, S Utsire, Fisher	1,2	0130	*0430*	**0730**	*1030*	1330	*1630*	**1930**	*2230*
Shetland CGOC	Viking, Fair Isle,Faroes, N Utsire	18	0110	*0410*	**0710**	*1010*	1310	*1610*	**1910**	*2210*
West Coast			B	*C*	**A**	*C*	B	*C*	**A**	*C*
Stornoway‡ CGOC	Rockall, Malin, Hebrides, Bailey, Fair Is, Faeroes, SE Iceland	15,16,17	0110	*0410*	**0710**	*1010*	1310	*1610*	**1910**	*2210*
Belfast‡ CGOC	Irish Sea, Rockall, Malin	13,14	0210	*0510*	**0810**	*1110*	1410	*1710*	**2010**	*2310*
Holyhead CGOC	Irish Sea	11,12	0130	*0450*	**0730**	*1050*	1330	*1650*	**1930**	*2250*
Milford Haven CGOC	Shannon,Lundy, Fastnet, Irish Sea	9, 10	0150	*0450*	**0750**	*1050*	1350	*1650*	**1950**	*2250*

CAUTION: HM Coastguard modernisation was due to be completed by the end of 2015. However, information on this and the next two pages might still change and readers are advised to check the free monthly updates from January 2016 to June 2016 at www.reedsalmanacs.co.uk.

Remote CG transmitters and their VHF working channels

MSI broadcasts are transmitted every 3 hours from the start times (UTC) shown via remote aerial sites selected to give optimum coverage. The table below lists their positions and the VHF broadcast channel to be used, either channel 10, 23, 84 or 86 usually specified in a prior announcement on Ch 16.

To avoid of missing a broadcast, pre-select Ch 16 on Dual watch with the relevant (clearest channel; and/or monitor the prior announcemen to verify the working channel.

MF frequencies (*kHz*), as quoted below, are als used for the broadcasts, primarily for fishermen

INSHORE WATER FORECAST AREAS, MSI TRANSMITTERS, WORKING CHANNELS AND START TIMES

1 Cape Wrath to Rattray Head inc Orkney, 0130

Durness (Loch Eriboll)	23	58°34'N 04°44'W
Wideford Hill (Kirkwall)	86	58°59'N 03°01'W
Noss Head (Wick)	84	58°29'N 03°03'W
Rosemarkie (Cromarty)	86	57°38'N 04°05'W
Windyheads Hill	23	57°39'N 02°14'W

2 Rattray Head to Berwick-upon-Tweed, 0130

Gregness *2226kHz*,	86	57°08'N 02°03'W
Inverbervie	23	56°51'N 02°16'W
Fife Ness	84	56°17'N 02°35'W
Craigkelly (Burntisland)	23	56°04'N 03°14'W
St Abbs Head/Cross Law	86	55°54'N 02°12'W

3 Berwick-upon-Tweed to Whitby, 0150

Newton	23	55°31'N 01°37'W
Cullercoats(Blyth) *1925kHz*,	86	55°04'N 01°28'W
Boulby	23	54°34'N 00°51'W

4 Whitby to Gibraltar Point, 0150

Ravenscar	86	54°24'N 00°30'W
Flamborough	23	54°07'N 00°05'W
Easington (Spurn Hd)	86	53°39'N 00°06'E
Skegness	84	53°09'N 00°20'E

5 Gibraltar Point to North Foreland, 0110

Guy's Head (Wisbech)	23	52°48'N 00°13'E
Langham (Blakeney)	86	52°57'N 00°58'E
Trimingham (Cromer)	23	52°54'N 01°21'E
Great Yarmouth	86	52°36'N 01°43'E
Lowestoft	23	52°29'N 01°46'E
Bawdsey (R Deben)	84	52°00'N 01°25'E
Walton-on-the-Naze	23	51°51'N 01°17'E
Bradwell (R Blackwater)	86	51°44'N 00°53'E
Shoeburyness	23	51°31'N 00°47'E

6 North Foreland to Selsey Bill, 0110

North Foreland	86	51°22'N 01° 26'E
Langdon (Dover)	86	51°08'N 01°21'E
Fairlight (Hastings)	84	50°52'N 00°39'E
Newhaven	86	50°47'N 00°03'E

7 Selsey Bill to Lyme Regis, 0130

Boniface (Ventnor, IoW)	23	50°36'N 01°12'W
Needles	86	50°39'N 01°35'W
St Alban's Head	23	50°34N 02°03W
Grove Pt (Portland Bill)	84	50°33'N 02°25'W
Beer Head (Lyme Bay)	86	50°41'N 03°05'W

8 Lyme Regis to Land's End inc Isles of Scilly, 0110

Berry Head	23	50°24'N 03°29'W
Dartmouth	10	50°21'N 03°35'W
East Prawle	84	50°13'N 03°42'W
Rame Head	86	50°19'N 04°13'W
Fowey	10	50°20'N 04°38'W
Falmouth	84	50°09'N 05°03'W
Lizard	23	49°58'N 05°12'W
St Marys, Scilly *1880kHz*,	86	49°56'N 06°18'W

9 Land's End to St David's Head inc the Bristol Channel, 0150

Trevose Head	84	50°33'N 05°02'W
Hartland Point	86	51°01'N 04°31'W
Combe Martin	23	51°12'N 04°03'W
Severn Bridges	86	51°36'N 02°38'W
St Hilary (Barry)	23	51°27'N 03°25'W
Monkstone (Tenby)	84	51°42'N 04°41'W
St Ann's Head	84	51°40'N 05°11'W

10 St David's Head to Great Orme Head, inc St George's Channel, 0150

Dinas Hd (Fishguard)	86	52°00'N 04°54'W
Blaenplwyf (Aberystwyth)	84	52°22'N 04°06'W
South Stack (Holyhead)	23	53°19'N 04°41'W
Great Orme Head	86	53°20'N 03°51'W

11 Great Orme Head to the Mull of Galloway, 0130

Moel-y-Parc (Anglesey)	23	53°13'N 04°28'W
Langthwaite (Lancaster)	84	54°02'N 02°46'W
Caldbeck (Carlisle)	23	54°46'N 03°07'W

12 Isle of Man, 0130

Snaefell (Isle of Man)	86	54°16'N 04°28'W

13 Lough Foyle to Carlingford Lough, 0210

Slievemartin (Rostrevor)	86	54°06'N 06°10'W
Orlock Head (Bangor)	84	54°40'N 05°35'W
Black Mountain (Belfast)	23	54°35'N 06°01'W
West Torr (Fair Head)	86	55°12'N 06°06'W
Limvady (Lough Foyle)	84	55°06'N 06°53'W
Navar (Lower L Erne)	86	54°28'N 07°54'W

14 Mull of Galloway to Mull of Kintyre inc the Firth of Clydeand North Channel, 0210

Rhu Staffnish (Kintyre)	10	55°22'N 05°32'W
Lawhill (Ardrossan)	86	55°42'N 04°50'W
Clyde (Greenock)	84	55°58'N 04°48'W

15 Mull of Kintyre to Ardnamurchan Point, 0210

Kilchiaran (W Islay)	84	55°46'N 06°27'W
S Knapdale (Loch Fyne)	23	55°55'N 05°28'W
Torosay (E Mull)	10	56°27'N 05°43'W
Glengorm (N Mull)	84	56°38'N 06°08'W
Tiree *1883kHz*,	23	56°31'N 06°57'W

16 The Minch, 0110

Arisaig (S of Mallaig)	86	56°55'N 06°50'W
Drumfearn (SE Skye)	23	57°12'N 05°48'W
Skriag (Portree, Skye)	10	57°23'N 06°15'W
Rodel (S Harris)	84	57°45'N 06°57'W
Melvaig (Loch Ewe)	86	57°50'N 05°47'W
Portnaguran (Stornoway)	23	58°15'N 06°10'W

Continued opposite, top

17 Ardnamurchan Point to Cape Wrath, 0110

Barra	10	57°01'N 07°30'W
Clettreval (N Uist)	23	57°37'N 07°26'W
Forsnaval (W Lewis)	84	58°13'N 07°00'W
Butt of Lewis *1743kHz*,	10	58°28'N 06°14'W

18 Shetland Isles and 60 nautical mile radius, 0110

Fitful Head (Sumburgh)	23	59°54'N 01°23'W
Lerwick (Shetland)	84	60°10'N 01°08'W
Collafirth *2226kHz*,	86	60°32'N 01°23'W
Saxa Vord (Unst)	23	60°42'N 00°51'W

Inshore waters forecasts: Area boundaries used by the Coastguard

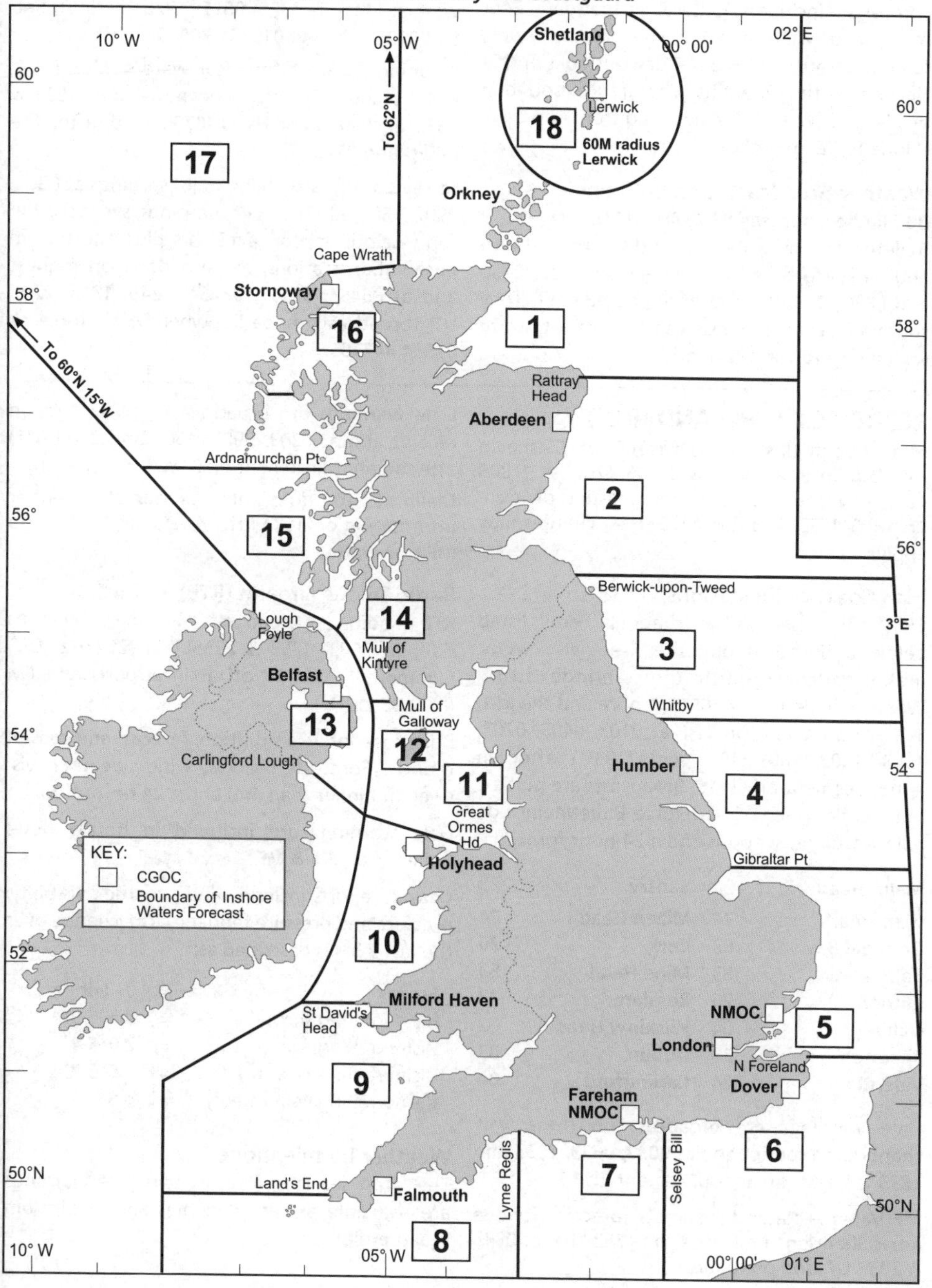

WEATHER

CHANNEL ISLANDS

Jersey Meteorological department

From the CI and UK call ☎ 0900 669 0022 (60p per min) for the Channel Islands recorded shipping forecast. For Guernsey only, call ☎ 06969 8800; it is chargeable. For more detailed info call ☎ +44 1534 448770, 📠 448778.

Forecasts include: general situation, 24hr forecast for wind, weather, vis, sea state, swell, sea temperature, plus 2 & 4 day outlooks and St Helier tide times/heights. The area is bounded by 50°N, 03°W and the mainland from Cap de la Hague to Ile de Bréhat.

Weather broadcasts and bulletins

BBC Radio Guernsey 93·2 MHz, 1116 kHz
Bulletins for the waters around Guernsey, Herm and Sark are broadcast Mon-Fri at 0630, 0730 and 0830 LT; Sat/Sun at 0730 and 0830 LT. They contain forecast, synopsis, coastal forecast, storm warnings and wind strength.

In the summer coastal reports are included from: Portland, Chan It V, Alderney, Guernsey, Jersey, Cherbourg, Cap de la Hague and Dinard. ☎ 01481 200600

BBC Radio Jersey 1026 kHz, 88·8 MHz.
Storm warnings on receipt. Wind info for Jersey waters: Mon-Fri 0725, 0825, 1325, 1725 LT; Sat/Sun 0725, 0825. ☎ 01534 870000

Shipping forecast for local waters: Mon-Fri @ H+00 (0600-1900, after the news) and 0625 & 1625 LT; Sat/Sun @ H+00 (0700-1300, after the news) and 0725 LT.

Jersey Coastguard Ch 82. Gale warnings at 0307, 0907, 1507, 2107UT. Gale warnings, synopsis, 24h forecast, outlook for next 24 hrs, plus reports from observation stations, are broadcast on request and at 0645*, 0745*, 0845*, 1245, 1845, 2245 UT; *broadcast 1 hr earlier when DST in force. ☎ 01534 447705.

REPUBLIC OF IRELAND (ROI)

Met Éireann (Irish Met Office) is at Glasnevin Hill, Dublin 9, Ireland. ☎ 1 806 4200, 📠 1 806 4247, www.met.ie. General forecasting division: ☎ 1 806 4255, 📠 1 806 4275 (H24, charges may apply).

Irish Coast radio stations

CRS and their VHF channels are listed below and shown opposite, (see: also www.malinheadcoastguardradio.com/index.htm). Weather bulletins for 30M offshore and the Irish Sea are broadcast on VHF at 0103, 0403, 0703, 1003, 1303, 1603, 1903 and 2203UT after an announcement on Ch 16. Broadcasts are made 1 hour earlier when DST is in force. Bulletins include gale warnings, synopsis and a 24-hour forecast.

Malin Head	23	**Bantry**	23
Glen Head	24	**Mizen Head**	04
Donegal Bay	02	**Cork**	26
Belmullet	83	**Mine Head**	83
Clifden	26	**Rosslare**	23
Galway	04	**Wicklow Head**	02
Shannon	28	**Dublin**	83
Valentia	24	**Carlingford**	04

Gale warnings are broadcast on these VHF channels on receipt and at 0033, 0633, 1233 and 1833 UT, after an announcement Ch 16.

MF Valentia Radio broadcasts forecasts for sea areas Shannon and Fastnet on 1752 kHz at 0833 & 2033 UT, and on request.

Gale warnings are broadcast on 1752 kHz on receipt and at 0303, 0903, 1503 and 2103 (UT) after an announcement on 2182 kHz.

Malin Head does not broadcast weather information on 1677 kHz. At Dublin there is no MF transmitter.

Radio Telefís Éireann (RTE) Radio 1

RTE Radio 1 broadcasts weather bulletins daily at 0602, 1253 & 2355LT on 252kHz (LW) Summerhill (15M W ofDublin airport) and FM (88·2-95·2MHz).

Bulletins contain a situation, forecast and coastal reports. Forecasts include: wind, weather, vis, swell (if higher than 4m) and a 24 hrs outlook.

Gale warnings are included in hourly news bulletins on FM & MF.

Coastal reports include wind, weather, visibility, pressure and pressure tendency. The change over the last 3 hrs is described as:

Steady	=	0–0·4hPa
Rising/falling slowly	=	0·5–1·9
Rising/falling	=	2·0–3·4
Rising/falling rapidly	=	3·5–5·9
Rising/falling very rapidly	=	> 6·0

Weather by telephone

The latest sea area forecast and gale warnings are available as recorded messages H24 from Weatherdial.

Dial ☎ 1550 123 plus the suffixes below:

850	Munster
851	Leinster
852	Connaught
853	Ulster
854	Dublin (plus winds in Dublin Bay and HW times)
855	Coastal waters and Irish Sea.

Weather by fax

Similar information, plus isobaric, swell and wave charts and any small craft warnings (>F6 up to 10M offshore; Apr-Sep inc) is available H24 by Weatherdial Fax.

Dial 📠 1550 131 838 (from within ROI only). From the menu below select the required 4-digit product code (see 0400 for full listing):

0015: Latest analysis chart
0016: Forecast valid for next 24 hrs
0017: Forecast valid for next 36 hrs
0018: Forecast valid for next 48 hrs
0021: Forecasts for coastal waters and Irish Sea
0031, 0032, 0033, 0034: Forecast (days 1-4) for sea/swell wave hts/periods

5-day forecasts (plain language, farming/national) 0001: Munster. 0002: Leinster. 0003: Connaught. 0004: Ulster. 0005: Dublin.

Sea Planners provide graphic forecasts for up to 5 days (updated at 0430 daily) of expected winds and waves at the following seven offshore positions:

0041:	53°N 05°30'W
0042:	51°N 06°W
0043:	51°N 10°30'W
0044:	53°N 11°W
0045:	54°N 11°W
0046:	55°N 10°W
0047:	56°N 08°W

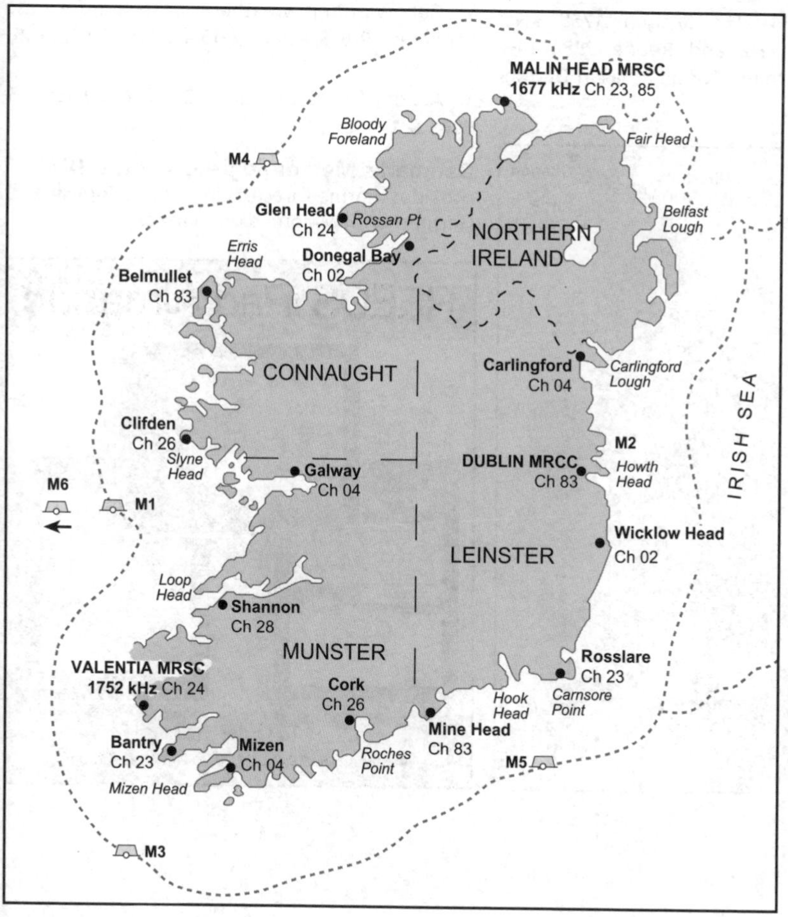

Provinces, headlands, sea areas and coastal stations referred to in weather broadcasts are shown here. Forecasts for coastal waters cover areas within 30M of the shore.

DENMARK

Gale warnings and forecasts are broadcast on receipt, on request and at 0133, 0533, 0933, 1333, 1733, 2133 UT in Danish/English by remote CRS, callsign *Lyngby Radio:*

Areas	VHF Channels
2 South Baltic	02, 04,
3 West Baltic	01, 02, 03, 04, 61, 85
4 The Belts & Sound	01, 02, 03, 04, 05, 07, 28, 65, 83, 85
5 Kattegat	03, 04, 05, 07, 64, 65, 66, 83
6 Skagerrack	01, 02, 04, 64, 66
8 Fisher	01, 02, 23, 26
9 German Bight	02, 23

Forecast areas: see above. Skagen and Blåvand CRS broadcast on MF gale warnings for all areas on receipt.

Areas 2–5 are north of the Kiel Canal and east of 10°E.

MF: Blåvand 1734 kHz, Skagen 1758 kHz, Skamlebæk 1704 kHz and Rønne 2586 kHz broadcast gale warnings for all areas in Danish/ **English** on receipt.

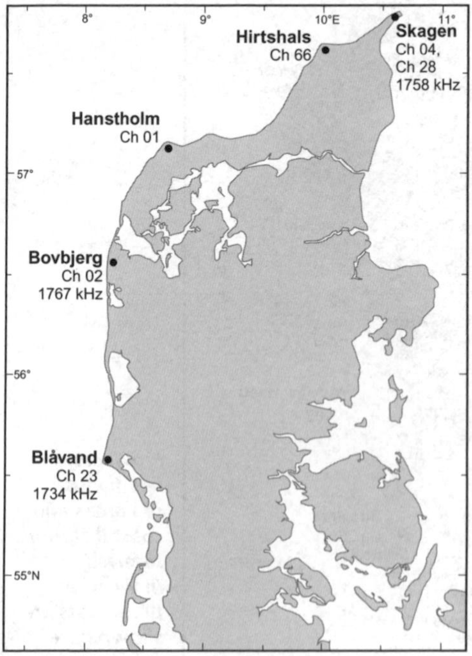

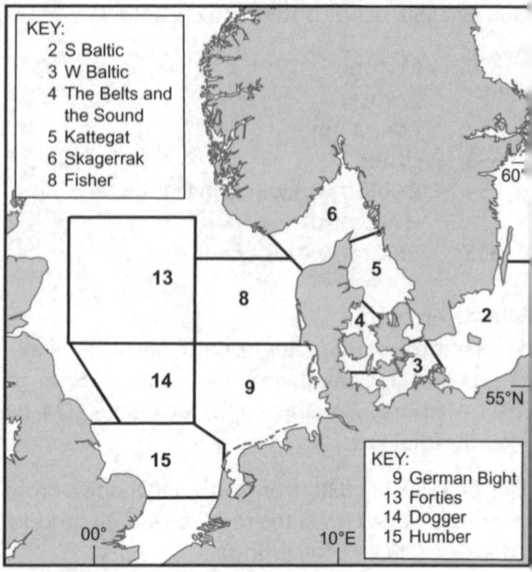

Danmarks Radio, Programme 1

Kalundborg (55°44'N 11°E) broadcasts on LW 243 kHz:

- Gale warnings, weather reports and forecast for areas 2-6, 8, 9 and 13-15 at 0545, 0845, 1145, 1745LT.
- A 5 day forecast for areas 2-6, 8 and 9 at 0545 0845 & 1745LT.

Danmarks Meteorologiske Institut (DM) provides marine forecasts in Danish, **English** and German on www.dmi.dk/dmi/index/

GERMANY

Deutsche Wetterdienst (DWD)

DWD (German weather service) provides Met info through a databank which is updated twice daily; more often for weather reports and text forecasts.

DWD ☎ +49 (0) 69 8062 6201. 📠 +49 (0) 69 8062 6193. www.dwd.de
seeschifffahrt@dwd.de.

Traffic Centres

Traffic Centres, below, broadcast local storm warnings, weather bulletins, visibility (and when appropriate ice reports) in German or **English** on request.

Traffic Centre	VHF Ch	Every
German Bight Traffic	**80**	**H+00**
Cuxhaven-Elbe Traffic	**71 (outer Elbe)**	**H+35**
Brunsbüttel-Elbe Traffic	**68 (lower Elbe)**	**H+05**
Kiel Kanal II (E-bound)	**02**	**H+15 & H+45**
Kiel Kanal III (W-bound)	**03**	**H+20 & H+50**
Bremerhaven-Weser Traffic	**02, 04, 05, 07, 21, 22, 82**	**H+20**
Bremen-Weser Traffic	**19, 78, 81**	**H+30**
Hunte Traffic	**63**	**H+30**
Jade Traffic	**20, 63**	**H+10**
Ems Traffic	**15, 18, 20, 21**	**H+50**

Coast Radio Stations

DP07 (Seefunk) has commercial CRS, below, at:

Nordfriesland (Sylt) Ch 26. **Elbe-Weser** Ch 01, 24. **Hamburg** (Control centre) Ch 83. **Bremen** Ch 25. **Borkum** Ch 28.

DP07 broadcasts (only in German): gale and strong wind warnings on receipt. At 0745®, 0945, 1245, 1645 and 1945® UT for Fisher, German Bight and Humber, DP07 broadcasts: a synopsis, 12hr forecast, 24hrs outlook and coastal station reports. ®summer only. Also a 4–5 day outlook for the North Sea (and Baltic) at 0945 and 1645.

Radio broadcasting: Nord Deutscher Rundfunk (NDR)

NDR 1 Welle Nord (FM)

A summary, outlook and wind forecast for the German Bight are broadcast after the news (1006,1300,1906LT) by **Sylt** 92.7MHz; **Helgoland** 92.5MHz; **Hamburg** 92.3MHz; **Flensburg** 87.7MHz;

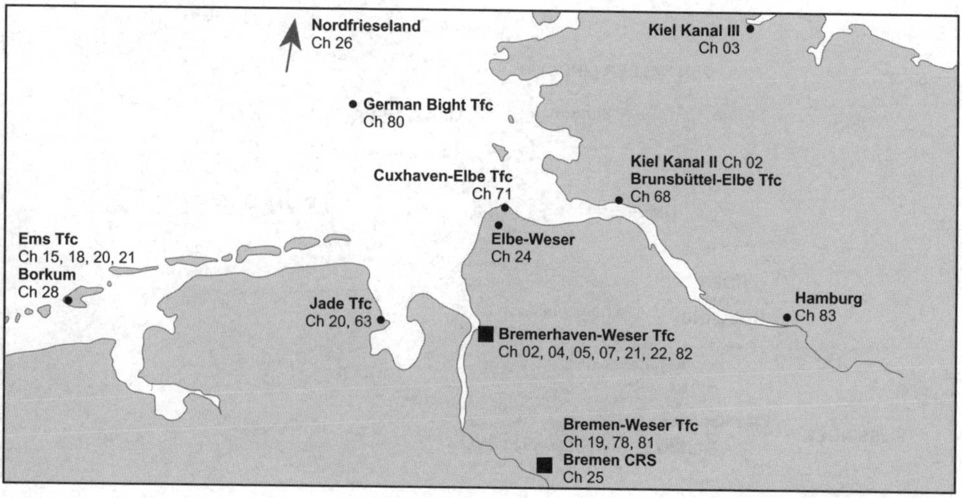

WEATHER

Heide, 87.9MHz; **Keil** 99.7MHz.

NDR Info (AM)

Synopsis, forecast and coastal station reports for the North Sea (and Baltic) are broadcast at 0005, 0830 and 2205 UT on 972 (Hamburg) & 702 (Flensburg) kHz.

Radio Bremen (MW and FM)

Warnings of extreme weather conditions in German Bight, with associated hazards, are broadcast after the news by: **Bremerhaven** 936 kHz; 89·3, 92·1, 95·4 & 100·8 MHz; and by **Bremen** 88·3, 93·8, 96·7 & 101·2 MHz.

Telephone forecasts (Marineweather)

For wind forecast and outlook (1 April – 30 Sept) call 0190 1160 (only within Germany) plus two digits for the following areas:

45	North Frisian Islands and Helgoland
46	R Elbe, Cuxhaven to Hamburg
47	Weser , Jade Bay and Helgoland
48	East Frisians and Ems Estuary
53	For pleasure craft

For year-round weather synopsis, forecast and outlook, call 0190 1169 plus two digits:

20	General information
21	North Sea and Baltic
22	German Bight, Fisher and SW North Sea
31	Reports for North Sea and Baltic

For the latest wind warnings (greater than F6) and storm warnings for individual areas of the North Sea coasts, call +49 (0) 69 8062 6101 (H24). If no warning is in force, a wind forecast for the German Bight, west and southern Baltic is given.

NETHERLANDS

VHF MSI broadcasts

Forecasts for 7 areas to 30M offshore and 3 inland waterways (IJsselmeer, Marken and Zierikzee) are broadcast in **English** and Dutch at 0805, 1305, 1905, 2305 LT on VHF as shown below, **without** prior announcement on Ch 16 or 70.

VHF Ch 23: Schiermonnikoog, Kornwerderzand, Wezep, Huisduinen (Den Helder), IJmuiden, Renesse, Woensdrecht.
VHF Ch 83: Appingedam, West Terschelling, Hoorn, Schoorl, Scheveningen, Westkapelle.
All stations monitor Ch 16.

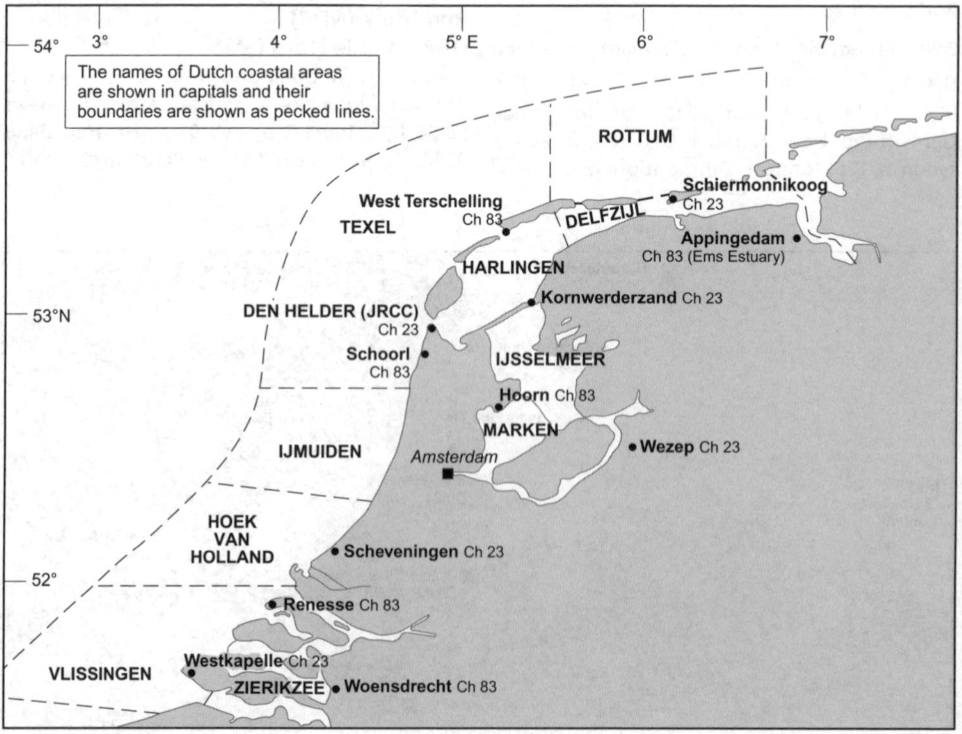

MF weather broadcasts

Forecasts for areas Dover, Thames, Humber, German Bight, Dogger, Fisher, Forties and Viking are broadcast by Scheveningen in **English** at 0940 & 2140 UT on 3673 kHz. Gale warnings for these areas are broadcast in **English** on receipt and at 0333, 0733, 1133, 1533, 1933 and 2333 UT.

Radio Noord-Holland (FM)

Coastal forecasts for northern areas, gale warnings and wind strength are broadcast in Dutch, Mon-Fri at 0730, 0838, 1005, 1230 and 1705LT; Sat/Sun 1005, by: **Haarlem** 97.6 MHz and **Wieringermeer** 93.9 MHz.

Omroep Zeeland (FM)

Coastal forecasts for southern areas, synopsis, gale warnings and wind strength are broadcast in Dutch, Mon-Fri at 0715, 0915, 1215 and 1715LT; Sat/Sun 1015, by:

Philippine 97.8 MHz and **Goes** 101.9 MHz.

BELGIUM, Coast radio stations

Oostende Radio, after prior notice on VHF 16, 24, DSC 70 and 2182kHz, broadcasts in **English** and Dutch on VHF 27, MF 2256, 2376 and 2761 kHz: Strong wind warnings on receipt and after the next 2 silent periods. Forecasts for Thames, Dover and the Belgian coast at 0720 LT and 0820, 1720 UT.

Antwerpen Radio broadcasts in **English** and Dutch on VHF Ch 24 for the Schelde estuary: Gale warnings on receipt and at every H+55. Also strong wind warnings (F6+) on receipt and at every H+55.

FRANCE

Le Guide Marine is a useful, free annual booklet which summarises the various means by which weather forecasts and warnings are broadcast or otherwise disseminated. It is usually available from marinas or from www.meteofrance.fr/publications/nos-collections/guides-pratiques/guide-marine.

CROSS VHF and MF broadcasts

CROSS broadcasts Met bulletins in French, after an announcement on Ch 16. In the English Channel broadcasts can be given in English, on request Ch 16. Broadcasts include: Any gale warnings, general situation, 24 hrs forecast (actual weather, wind, sea state and vis) and further trends for coastal waters, which extend 20M offshore. VHF channels, remote stations and local times are shown below.

French forecast areas

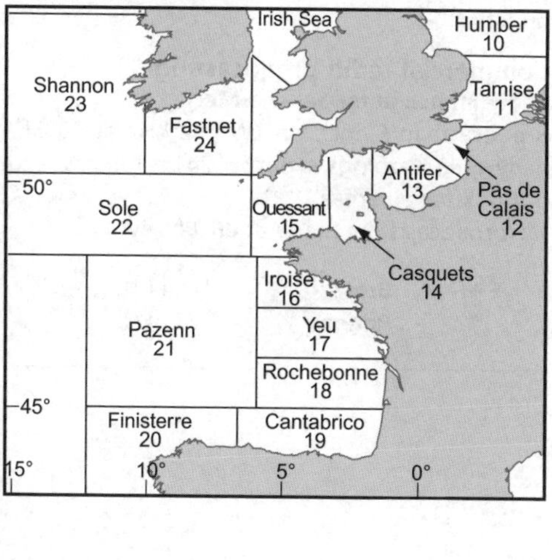

Gale warnings feature in Special Met Bulletins (*Bulletins Météorologique Spéciaux* or BMS). They are broadcast in French by all CROSS on VHF at H+03 and at other times on MF frequencies as shown below.

CROSS GRIS-NEZ Ch 79

Belgian border to Baie de la Somme

Dunkerque	0720, 1603, 1920
St Frieux	0710, 1545, 1910

Baie de la Somme to Cap de la Hague

St Valéry-en-Caux

0703, 1533, 1903

Gale warnings for areas 12-13 are broadcast in French on MF 1650 & 2677 kHz at 0833 & 2033LT

CROSS JOBOURG Ch 80

Baie de la Somme to Cap de la Hague

Antifer	0803, 1633, 2003
Port-en-Bessin	0745, 1615, 1945
Jobourg	0733, 1603, 1933

Cap de la Hague to Pointe de Penmarc'h

Jobourg	0715, 1545, 1915
Granville	0703, 1533, 1903

Gale warnings for areas 13-14 in **English** on receipt and at H+20 and H+50. No gale warnings on MF.

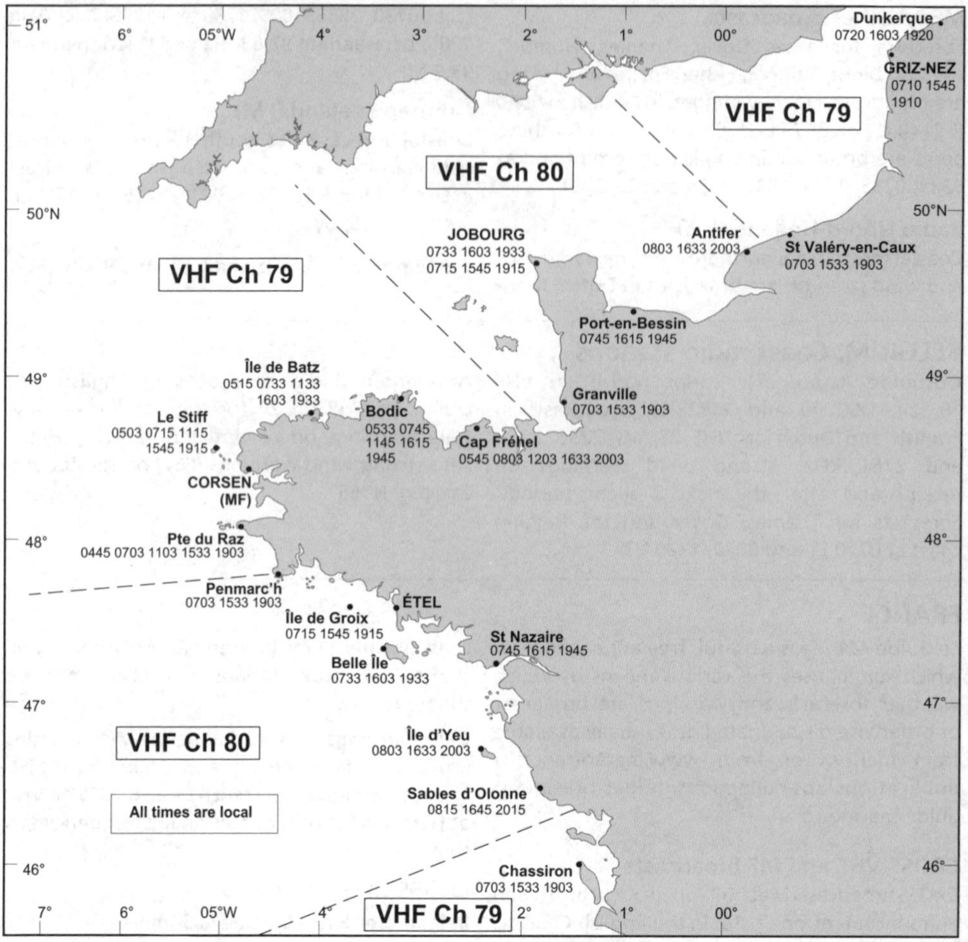

CROSS CORSEN Ch 79

Cap de la Hague to Pte de Penmarc'h (Times in bold = 1 May to 30 Sep only).

Cap Fréhel 0545, 0803, **1203**, 1633, 2003 **Bodic** 0533, 0745, **1145**, 1615, 1945

Ile de Batz	0515, 0733, **1133**, 1603, 1933
Le Stiff	0503, 0715, **1115**, 1545, 1915
Pte du Raz	0445, 0703, **1103**, 1533, 1903

Corsen broadcasts gale warnings for areas 13-22 in French at 0815 and 2015LT on MF 1650 & 2677 kHz.

CROSS ÉTEL Ch 80

Pte de Penmarc'h to l'Anse de l'Aiguillon
(46° 15'N 01°10'W). Étel has no MF freqs

Penmarc'h	0703, 1533, 1903
Ile de Groix	0715, 1545, 1915
Belle Ile	0733, 1603, 1933
Saint-Nazaire	0745, 1615, 1945
Ile d'Yeu	0803, 1633, 2003
Les Sables d'Olonne	0815, 1645, 2015

CROSS ÉTEL Ch 79 **L'Anse de l'Aiguillon to Spanish border**

Chassiron	0703, 1533, 1903

Ch 63 Pointe de Penmarc'h to the Spanish border (A continuously transmitted weather bulletin).

Commercial radio broadcasting

Radio France (Inter-Service-Mer)

Broadcasts in French on LW 162 kHz at 2003LT daily: gale warnings, synopsis, 24 hrs forecast and outlook for all areas.

MF broadcasts are made at 0640LT by:

Brest	1404 kHz
Rennes	711 kHz

Local radio (FM)

France Blue Cotentin broadcasts daily at 0834 LT:

Coastal forecast, gale warnings, visibility, wind strength, tidal information, small craft warnings, in French, for the Cherbourg peninsula on the following frequencies:

St Vaast-la-Hougue	95·0 MHz
Cherbourg	95·0, 100·7 MHz
Cap de la Hague	99·8 MHz
Carteret	99·9 MHz

Forecasts by telephone

For recorded Inshore and Coastal forecasts. Dial 08·92·68·02·dd (dd is the number, as given, for the *département*); press the * key then 1 to access the main menu. Follow instructions:

For Inshore (*rivage*) or Coastal (*côte*) bulletins, say 'STOP' as your choice is spoken.

Inshore bulletins contain 7 day forecasts, tide times, actual reports, sea temperature, surf conditions, etc.

Coastal bulletins contain strong wind/gale warnings, general synopsis, 24 hrs forecast and outlook. Five bulletins cover the N & W coasts, out to 20M offshore.

For Offshore bulletins (*large*), out to 200M offshore, dial ☎ 08·92·68·08·77. Select one of three offshore areas (English Channel & southern North Sea, Bay of Biscay or the N part of the western Mediterranean) by saying 'STOP' as it is named. Offshore bulletins contain strong wind/gale warnings, the general synopsis and forecast, and the outlook for up to 7 days.

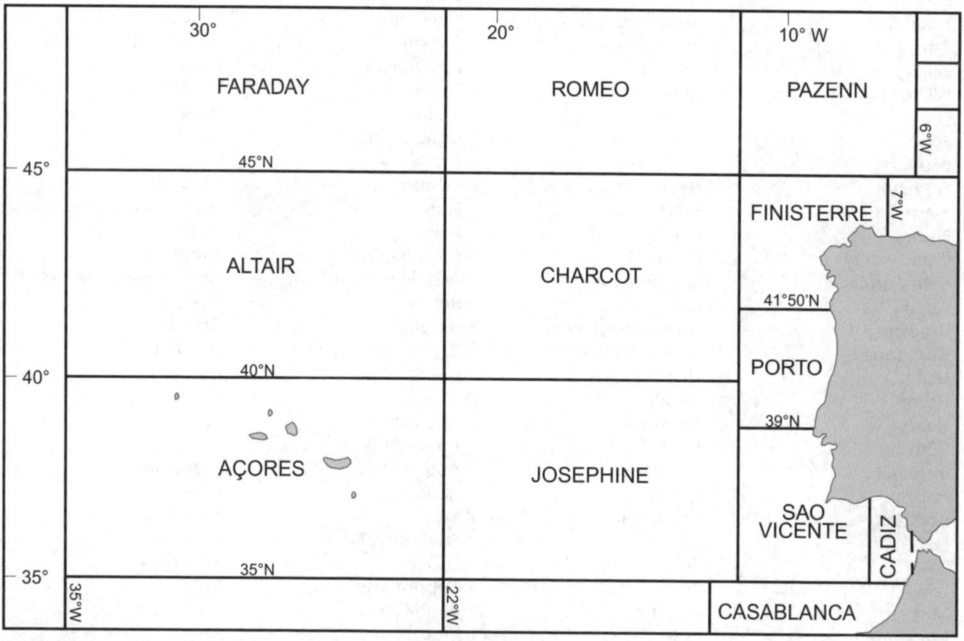

Forecast areas for the Eastern Atlantic and Coastal/Offshore Areas off France, Spain, Portugal and North West Africa

WEATHER VOCABULARY

ENGLISH	GERMAN	FRENCH	DUTCH
Air mass	Luftmasse	Masse d'air	Luchtmassa
Anticyclone	Antizyklonisch	Anticyclone	Hogedrukgebied
Area	Gebiet	Zone	Gebied
Backing wind	Rückdrehender Wind	Vent reculant	Krimpende wind
Barometer	Barometer	Baromètre	Barometer
Breeze	Brise	Brise	Bries
Calm	Flaute	Calme	Kalmte
Centre	Zentrum	Centre	Centum
Clouds	Wolken	Nuages	Wolken
Cold	Kalt	Froid	Koud
Cold front	Kaltfront	Front froid	Kou front
Cyclonic	Zyklonisch	Cyclonique	Cycloonachtig
Decrease	Abnahme	Affaiblissement	Afnemen
Deep	Tief	Profond	Diep
Deepening	Vertiefend	Approfondissant	Verdiepend
Depression	Sturmtief	Dépression	Depressie
Direction	Richtung	Direction	Richting
Dispersing	Auflösend	Se dispersant	Oplossend
Disturbance	Störung	Perturbation	Verstoving
Drizzle	Niesel	Bruine	Motregen
East	Ost	Est	Oosten
Extending	Ausdehnung	S'étendant	Uitstrekkend
Extensive	Ausgedehnt	Etendu	Uitgebreid
Falling	Fallend	Descendant	Dalen
Filling	Auffüllend	Secomblant	Vullend
Fog	Nebel	Brouillard	Nevel
Fog bank	Nebelbank	Ligne de brouillard	Mist bank
Forecast	Vorhersage	Prévision	Vooruitzicht
Frequent	Häufig	Fréquent	Veelvuldig
Fresh	Frisch	Frais	Fris
Front	Front	Front	Front
Gale	Sturm	Coup de vent	Storm
Gale warning	Sturmwarnung	Avis de coup de vent	Stormwaarschuwing
Good	Gut	Bon	Goed
Gradient	Druckunterschied	Gradient	Gradiatie
Gust, squall	Bö	Rafalle	Windvlaag
Hail	Hagel	Grêle	Hagel
Haze	Diesig	Brume	Nevel
Heavy	Schwer	Abondant	Zwaar
High	Hoch	Anticyclone	Hoog
Increasing	Zunehmend	Augmentant	Toenemend
Isobar	Isobar	Isobare	Isobar
Isolated	Vereinzelt	Isolé	Verspreid
Lightning	Blitze	Eclair de foudre	Bliksem
Local	Örtlich	Locale	Plaatselijk
Low	Tief	Dépression	Laag
Mist	Dunst	Brume légere	Mist
Moderate	Mäßig	Modéré	Matig
Moderating	Abnehmend	Se modérant	Matigend
Moving	Bewegend	Se déplacant	Bewegend
North	Nord	Nord	Noorden
Occluded	Okklusion	Couvert	Bewolkt
Poor	Schlecht	Mauvais	Slecht
Precipitation	Niederschlag	Précipitation	Neerslag
Pressure	Druck	Pression	Druk
Rain	Regen	Pluie	Regen
Ridge	Hochdruckbrücke	Crête	Rug
Rising	Ansteigend	Montant	Stijgen
Rough	Rauh	Agitée	Ruw
Sea	See	Mer	Zee
Seaway	Seegang	Haute mer	Zee

ENGLISH	GERMAN	FRENCH	DUTCH
Scattered	Vereinzelt	Sporadiques	Verspreid
Shower	Schauer	Averse	Bui
Slight	Leicht	Un peu	Licht
Slow	Langsam	Lent	Langzaam
Snow	Schnee	Neige	Sneeuw
South	Süd	Sud	Zuiden
Storm	Sturm	Tempête	Storm
Sun	Sonne	Soleil	Zon
Swell	Schwell	Houle	Deining
Thunder	Donner	Tonnerre	Donder
Thunderstorm	Gewitter	Orage	Onweer
Trough	Trog, Tiefausläufer	Creux	Trog
Variable	Umlaufend	Variable	Veranderlijk
Veering	Rechtdrehend	Virement de vent	Ruimende wind
Warm front	Warmfront	Front chaud	Warm front
Weather	Wetter	Temps	Weer
Wind	Wind	Vent	Wind
Weather report	Wetterbericht	Météo	Weer bericht meteorologica

Chapter 3 – Communications

RADIO OPERATION

Avoiding interference

Before transmitting, first listen on the VHF channel. If occupied, wait for a break before transmitting, or choose another channel. If you cause interference you must comply immediately with any request from a Coastguard or Coast radio station to stop transmitting.

Control of communications

Ship-to-Shore: Communications between ship and shore stations are controlled by the latter, except in distress, urgency or safety cases.

Intership: The ship *called* controls communication. If you call another ship, then it has control. If you are called by a ship, you assume control. If a shore-based station breaks in, both ships must comply with instructions given.

Radio confidentiality

Private conversations heard on the radio must not be reproduced, passed on or otherwise used.

Making yourself understood

Clear R/T speech is vital. If a message cannot be understood by the receiver it is useless. Messages which have to be written down at the receiving station should be spoken slowly. This gives time for it to be written down by the receiving operator. If the transmitting operator himself writes it down all should be well. The average reading speed is 250 words a minute, whilst average writing speed is only 20.

When speaking, consider the following:

- **What** to say, ie *voice Procedure*
- **How** to say it, ie *voice Technique*

Voice Procedure is discussed below and overleaf. It includes procedural words, callsigns, making contact etc.

Voice Technique depends on a few simple rules:

Hold the microphone a few inches in front of the mouth and speak directly into it at a normal level. Speak clearly so that there can be no confusion. The voice should be pitched up at a higher level than normal. Do not drop the voice pitch at the end of a phrase or sentence. Emphasise words with weak syllables; 'Tower', if badly pronounced, could sound like 'tar'. Non Anglophones, or people with strong regional accents must try to pronounce words as clearly as possible.

Difficult words may be spelled phonetically, preceded with 'I spell'. If the word can be pronounced, include it before and after it has been spelt. For example, the message 'I will berth on the yacht *Coila*' would be sent as: 'I will berth on the yacht *Coila* – I spell – Charlie Oscar India Lima Alfa – *Coila*'.

The phonetic alphabet (ITU)

The syllables to emphasise are underlined

Letter	*Morse*	*Phonetic*	*Spoken as*
A	•–	Alfa	AL-fah
B	–•••	Bravo	BRAH-voh
C	–•–•	Charlie	CHAR-lee
D	–••	Delta	DELL-tah
E	•	Echo	ECK-oh
F	••–•	Foxtrot	FOKS-trot
G	––•	Golf	GOLF
H	••••	Hotel	hoh-TELL
I	••	India	IN-dee-ah
J	•–––	Juliett	JEW-lee-ett
K	–•–	Kilo	KEY-loh
L	•–••	Lima	LEE-mah
M	––	Mike	MIKE
N	–•	November	no-VEM-ber
O	–––	Oscar	OSS-car
P	•––•	Papa	pa-PAH
Q	––•–	Quebec	keh-BECK
R	•–•	Romeo	ROW-me-oh
S	•••	Sierra	see-AIR-rah
T	–	Tango	TANG-go
U	••–	Uniform	OO-nee-form
V	•••–	Victor	VIK-tah
W	•––	Whiskey	WISS-key
X	–••–	X-ray	ECKS-ray
Y	–•––	Yankee	YANG-key
Z	––••	Zulu	ZOO-loo

Phonetic numerals

When numerals are transmitted, the following pronunciations make them easier to understand.

No	*Morse*	*Spoken*	*No*	*Morse*	*Spoken*
1	•––––	WUN	6	–••••	SIX
2	••–––	TOO	7	––•••	SEV-EN
3	•••––	TREE	8	–––••	AIT
4	••••–	FOW-ER	9	––––•	NIN-ER
5	•••••	FIFE	0	–––––	ZERO

Numerals are transmitted digit by digit except that multiples of thousands may be spoken as follows:

Numeral	*Spoken as*
44	FOW-ER FOW-ER
90	NIN-ER ZERO
136	WUN TREE SIX
500	FIFE ZERO ZERO
1478	WUN FOW-ER SEV-EN AIT
7000	SEV-EN THOU-SAND

Punctuation
Punctuation marks should be used only where their omission would cause confusion.

Mark	*Word*	*Spoken as*
.	Decimal	DAY-SEE-MAL
,	Comma	COMMA
.	Stop	STOP

Procedural words or 'prowords'

These are used to shorten transmissions

All after and **All before.** Used after proword *'say again'* to request repetition of a part of a message

Correct Reply to repeat of message that was preceded by prowords *'read back for check'* when it has been correctly repeated. Often said twice

Correction Cancel the last word or group of words. The correct word or group follows. Spoken when an error has been made in a transmission.

I say again I repeat the transmission or the part indicated (see 'All after' and 'All before').

I spell I shall spell the next word or group of letters phonetically

Out This is the end of working to you

Over Invitation to reply

Read back If the receiver is doubtful about accuracy of all or part of message he may repeat it back to the sending station, preceding the repetition with prowords *'I read back'*

Station calling Used when a station is uncertain of the calling station's identification/callsign

This is This transmission is from the station whose callsign or name immediately follows

Wait If a called station cannot accept traffic immediately, it will reply **'WAIT.......MINUTES'**, with reason if delay may exceed 10 minutes

Word after or Word before Used after the proword *'say again'* to request repetition

Wrong Reply to repetition of message preceded by prowords *'read back'* when it has been incorrectly repeated

Calls, calling and callsigns
Shore stations normally use a callsign of their geographic name followed by Coastguard or Radio, eg Solent Coastguard, Dublin Radio etc. Vessels usually identify themselves by the ship's name but the International callsign may be used in certain cases. If two yachts have the same or confusingly similar names, give your International callsign when starting communications, and thereafter use your ship's name as callsign.

'All ships' broadcast
Address used by Coastguard Radio where broadcast information is to be received or used by all who intercept it, eg gale warnings etc. No reply is needed.

Communicating with a coast radio station
Call initially on a working channel or very briefly on channel 16 to establish a working channel.

- Pause to check the working channel is clear before transmitting
- Use low power *(1 watt)* if close enough , ie up to 10 miles away. High power *(25 watts)* drains more from the battery
- The callsign of calling station up to three times only, and prowords 'This is'
- Say how many R/T calls you have to make
- Proword 'Over'

Using high power decreases battery state and the range your VHF will achieve. Continued calling also clutters up the channel and denies access to other users.

Aerial faults commonly reduce your transmitting range. Possibly the station aerial for the channel chosen is directionally orientated and you are on the wrong side. Try another channel or station. Call again when closer.

RADIO DATA

SHORT, MEDIUM and LONG RANGE RADIO COMMUNICATIONS

A suitable radio receiver on board will provide weather forecasts and time signals at scheduled times on a number of frequencies in various wavebands. With a maritime receiver you are not limited to the familiar BBC and commercial broadcasts. HM Coastguard transmit navigation warnings, storm warnings and weather messages for shipping in their respective sea areas.

Short range radiotelephony (RT) transmits and receives on VHF channels in the marine VHF (Very High Frequency) band. The equipment and procedures are simple, but range is normally limited to about 20 miles from ship to shore, rather less from ship to ship. Interconnection with national telephone systems is possible on certain VHF/RT channels when a yacht is within range of a Coast Radio Station, although there are now no such stations on the mainland of the UK, France or the Netherlands. Mobile telephones are now by far the most common form of ship to shore communication.

Medium range two-way communication operate in the marine MF (medium frequency) RT band, the 2MHz 'trawler band'. Single sideband techniques are employed on these medium frequencies and SSB equipment is essential. The effective range depends on the power of the transmitter and the sensitivity of the associated receiver; in general this might be up to 200 miles from certain (but not all) Coast Radio Stations.

THE MARINE VHF BAND

VHF is used by most vessels, Coast Radio Stations, CG centres and other rescue services. Its range is slightly better than the line of sight between the transmitting and receiving aerials. A good aerial, as high as possible, is most important.

In the Marine VHF band (156·00–174·00 MHz) the individual frequencies are separated from their neighbours by exactly 25kHz 'elbow-room' to eliminate mutual interference. Each frequency is given a channel number, not necessarily consecutive. Thus 55 channels are available, plus some with special purposes (see below).

VHF Channel Grouping

Channels are grouped for three main purposes, but some can be used for more than one purpose. They are listed below in their preferred order of usage:

- **Public correspondence** (ie link calls via CRS into the shore telephone system): Ch 26, 27, 25, 24, 23, 28, 04, 01, 03, 02, 07, 05, 84, 87, 86, 83, 85, 88, 61, 64, 65, 62, 66, 63, 60, 82, 78, 81.

- **Inter-ship:** Ch 06, 08, 10, 13, 09, 72, 73, 67, 69, 77, 15, 17. Remember these, so that if another vessel calls you, you can swiftly nominate a working channel from within this group.

- **Port Operations:**
Ch 12, 14, 11, 13, 09, 68, 71, 74, 69, 73, 17, 15, 20, 22, 18, 19, 21, 05, 07, 02, 03, 01, 04, 78, 82, 79, 81, 80, 60, 63, 66, 62, 65, 64, 61, 84.

Special purposes. The following channels have one specific purpose only:

Ch 0 (156·00 MHz): SAR ops, not available to yachts.

Ch's 10 (156·500 MHz), **23** (161·750 MHz) **84** (161·825 MHz) and **86** (161·925 MHz): for MSI broadcasts by HMCG.

Ch 13 (156·650 MHz): Intership safety of navigation (sometimes referred to as bridge-to-bridge); a possible channel for calling a merchant ship if no contact on Ch 16.

Ch 16 (156·80 MHz): Distress, Safety and calling. *See Chapter 4 for Distress and Safety.* Ch 16 will be monitored by ships, CG centres (and, in some areas, any remaining Coast Radio Stations) for Distress and Safety until at least 2005, in parallel with DSC Ch 70. Yachts should monitor Ch 16. After an initial call, the stations concerned **must** switch to a working channel, except for Safety matters.

Ch 67 (156·375 MHz): the Small Craft Safety channel in the UK, accessed via Ch 16.

Ch 70 (156·525 MHz): exclusively for digital selective calling for Distress and Safety purposes.

Ch 80 (157·025 MHz): the primary working channel between yachts and UK marinas.

Ch M (157·85 MHz): the secondary working channel between yachts and UK marinas; previously known as Ch 37.

Ch M2 (161·425 MHz): for race control, with Ch M as stand-by. YCs may apply to use Ch M2.

SILENCE PERIODS

The periods are the 3 minutes immediately after the whole and half hours, ie H to H+03 and H+30 to H+33, when no transmissions should be made.

MEDIUM RANGE MF RADIO

Single sideband MF/RT provides communications in the offshore waters of the UK and Western Europe where small craft may be out of VHF contact. A receiver alone gives the ability to hear weather bulletins, storm and navigation warnings for local sea areas broadcast from CRS in the 1.6 to 4.0MHz maritime band, ie on frequencies from 1605 to 4200 kHz.

MF transmissions tend to follow the curvature of the earth, which makes them suitable for direction-finding. For this reason, and because of their good range, the marine Distress R/T frequency (2182 kHz) is in the MF band.

TRAFFIC LISTS

If a Coast Radio station has messages for a vessel, but is unable to contact her, that vessel's name will be added to the Traffic List broadcast at (usually) two hour intervals. This is not a system much used by yachts and small craft.

LONG RANGE HF RADIO

HF radios use short wave frequencies in the 4, 8, 12, 16 and 22 MHz bands, as chosen to suit propagation conditions. HF is more expensive than MF and requires more power, but can provide worldwide coverage. A good installation and skilled operating techniques are essential for satisfactory results.

GLOBAL COMMUNICATIONS

Once out of range of VHF/MF or wireless telephony/broadband service, the yachtsman's communications options are limited to MF/HF radio and satellite systems (Satcoms).

A yachtsman embarking on an extended offshore venture would usually choose a mix of equipment for sensible reasons of redundancy, this will allow a choice of listening and transmitting, via terrestrial and satellite radio systems, to meet his needs at various times and in different circumstances. A typical setup might include a fixed or handheld satcoms transceiver, a HF SSB transceiver and receiver. For data capability, these would be interfaced to an on-board PC.

HF/single sideband radio (HF-SSB)

HF SSB radios use frequencies in the 4, 8, 12, 16 and 22 MHz bands (short wave), provide worldwide coverage and usually include MF frequencies as well.

Despite rapid growth in marine satellite communications, HF SSB remains a popular choice amongst long-distance cruisers, providing a cost-free voice (and limited email) capability for cruisers, sometimes operating over vast distances. Operators have the Long Range Certificate (LRC) or General Operators Certificate (GOC). To use Amateur (ham) bands (giving more frequencies and higher power, therefore range) operators must take the ham examination.

Using HF SSB radio for email requires a radio modem, often proprietary to the supplier. Though slow and requiring some skill to operate effectively, the almost-nil operating costs appeal to many and SSB radio has a strong following amongst blue-water cruisers. Established suppliers include Sailmail and Globe Wireless.

HF SSB radio is also extensively used for receipt of weatherfax images, although a receive-only SSB radio (with an adequate, grounded antenna installation) may be used rather than a full transceiver. Though declining in popularity, several useful weatherfax transmitting stations remain, including Northwood, UK and Offenbach, Germany.

Satellite Communications (Satcoms)

Satellite communications systems operate over **Ultra High Frequency (UHF)** radio using digital technology that makes them simpler-to-operate and more reliable for voice (and data) communications than HF SSB radio; they operate with either a dedicated ship installation or a standalone handheld terminal. Apart from the equipment purchase (and installation if necessary), ongoing costs usually include a monthly service fee and usage charges that will be related to either the amount of satellite time used, or the volume of data transmitted and received.

For two-way voice communications, the 'Ship Station' (aka 'Mobile Earth Station') transmits to a visible satellite that is simultaneously in sight of a 'Land Earth Station', eg Goonhilly, Cornwall. From there, the call is routed to its destination through the normal terrestrial telephone network.

The satellite 'constellations' have different architectures. Inmarsat for example has four geostationary (GEO) satellites, one each positioned over the Pacific and Indian oceans and two over the Atlantic. Because they are comparatively high up 19,400M (36,000km), each satellite has a large signal 'footprint', overlapping the next one and thus world-wide coverage is provided (although not in the polar regions above about 70°N and 70°S).

Other systems employ many more Low Earth Orbit (LEO) satellites orbiting the Earth about 540M (1,000km) above the surface.

The smaller, low-data rate, handheld voice terminals incorporate an omni-directional antenna that works best with an unobstructed view of the satellite. Fixed installations use an external gyro-stabilised antenna (to keep it pointing at the satellite as the boat moves); more powerful systems that support higher data rates employ antenna radomes that are really too large for installation aboard a 10–15m yacht.

The GMDSS provides automatic distress, urgency and safety communications, with some satcom systems (eg Inmarsat C) providing a red button that alerts a Maritime Rescue Coordination Centre (MRCC) when pressed.

There are several service providers, each offering an array of capabilities. The table opposite provides a useful summary of systems that might be used aboard a 10–20m yacht.

This is a fast moving market place and you should check with manufacturers/retailers for up-to-date specifications and prices.

[1] typical, if in coverage area
[2] using VOIP
[3] Likely to be expensive

	Wired Broadband	Wi-Fi	Cellular GSM	Cellular GPRS	Cellular 3G	Wi-Max
Range offshore[1] (NM)	0	0-1	0-15	0-15	0-15	0-30
Voice communication	Y [2]	Y [2]	Y	Y	Y	Y [2]
Text messages	Y	Y	Y	Y	Y	Y
Light email traffic	Y	Y	Y [3]	Y	Y	Y
Text weather forecasts	Y	Y	Y [3]	Y	Y	Y
Heavy email traffic	Y	Y	×	Y [3]	Y	Y
Graphical weather forecasts	Y	Y	×	Y [3]	Y	Y
Full web browsing	Y	Y	×	Y [3]	Y	Y

SATELLITE COMMUNICATION SERVICES

System	Antenna	Satellites	Coverage	GMDSS	Phone (voice)	Fax	SMS text	Position tracking	Data rate
INMARSAT C	Omni-directional	4 GEO	Global excepting polar regions	Yes	No	Yes	Yes	Yes (GPS)	Very low, uneconomic for email
INMARSAT Mini-M	Gyro-stabilised 40cms diameter	4 GEO	Global excepting polar regions	No	Yes	Yes	No	No	2.4kbps
INMARSAT D+	Omni-directional	4 GEO	Global excepting polar regions	No	No	No	No	Yes (GPS)	Very low, uneconomic for email
Fleet 33	Gyro-stabilised 40cms diameter	4 GEO	Global excepting polar regions	No	Yes	Yes	Yes	No	9.6kbps uncom-pressed
Iridium	Omni-directional	66 LEO	Global	No	Yes	Out only	Yes	No	Data kit required 2.4kbps, higher with compression
Globalstar	Omni-directional	40 LEO	Global excepting polar regions	No	Yes	Yes	Yes	To 10km	9.6kbps uncom-pressed, 38.6kbps compressed, 56k with data kit
Thuraya	Omni-directional	1 GEO	Europe, N Africa & Middle East, India	No	Yes	Yes	Yes	Yes (GPS)	9.6kbps (144kbps possible with land *DSL receiver)

*DSL (Digital Subscriber Line) allows broadband Internet access via normal copper telephone lines. It is used in the wireless/Satcoms arena to denote broadband-like speeds over the wireless link. This usually means data transfer speeds of 5 to 24mbps which is fast for Satcoms.

PORT and/or MARINA VHF channels and telephone details

In larger ports it is sensible to monitor the VTS channel (if any) or the primary port channel (in bold) before changing to a marina channel. Times are local, unless marked UT. Abbreviations are at the front of the book. Telephone codes are shown only once unless more than one applies.

ENGLAND – SOUTH COAST

ISLES OF SCILLY, St Mary's HM Ch 14 (0800-1700); ☎ 01720 422768. *Falmouth CG* covers Scilly and the TSS off Land's End on Ch 23.
Tresco HM ☎ 07778 601237.

NEWLYN HM Ch 09, **12** (M-F: 0800-1700, Sat: 0800-1200). ☎ 01736 362523.

PENZANCE HM Ch 09, **12** (M-F: 0830-1730 and HW –2 to +1). ☎ 01736 366113.

FALMOUTH *Falmouth Hbr Radio* Ch 11, **12**, 14 (M-F 0800-1700). ☎ 01326 310991.
Ch 80: Falmouth ☎ 316620 and Port Pendennis marinas ☎ 311113. **Ch 12**: Falmouth Haven ☎ 310991; St Mawes HM ☎ 270553. **Ch M** (HO): Mylor Yacht Hbr ☎ 372121.

TRURO HM *Carrick One* Ch 12. ☎ 01872 272130. **Ch M** (HO): Malpas Marine ☎ 271260.

MEVAGISSEY HM Ch 14 (Summer: 0900-2100, Winter: 0900-1700). ☎ 01726 842496.

CHARLESTOWN HM Ch 14, HW –2 to +1, only when a vessel is expected. ☎ 01726 70241.

FOWEY HM Ch 12 (0900-1700); also Hbr Patrol (0900-2000). ☎ 01726 832471. Water taxi: Ch 06.

LOOE. HM Ch 16, occas. ☎ 01503 262839.

PLYMOUTH *Long Room Port Control* Ch 14 H24, ☎ 01752 836528. **QAB** Ch 80, ☎ 671142. **Sutton Hbr lock**: Ch 12 H24, ☎ 204702. **Cattewater HM** Ch 14 (M-F 0900-1700), ☎ 836528. **Plymouth Yacht Haven**, Ch 80, M; ☎ 404231. **King Point Marina** ☎ 424297. **Mayflower Marina**, Ch 80; ☎ 556633.

SALCOMBE HM & launch: Ch 14, May to mid-Sep: 7/7, 0600-2100; otherwise: M-F 0900-1600; ☎ 01548 843791. *Hbr Taxi* Ch 12. Fuel barge Ch 06, ☎ 07801 798862. *Egremont* (ICC) Ch M.

DARTMOUTH HM *Dartnav* Ch 11, 7/7 0730-dusk; ☎ 01803 832337. Darthaven marina Ch 80, ☎ 752242. Dart marina Ch 80, ☎ 837161. Noss marina ☎ 839087. Fuel barge Ch 06. Water taxi Ch 08.

TORBAY HBRS Brixham Marina Ch 80, ☎ 01803 882929; YC, ☎ 853332, & Water taxi *Shuttle* Ch M. Torquay Marina Ch 80, ☎ 200210. Fuel Ch M.

EXETER Exmouth Marina Ch 14, ☎ 01395 269314. **Retreat BY**: Ch M, ☎ 01392 874720. **Port of Exeter** HM Ch 12, M-F: 0730-1730 and when vessel due; ☎ 274306.

LYME REGIS HM Ch 14. Summer 0800-2000, winter 1000-1500. ☎ 01297 442137.

BRIDPORT HM Ch 11. ☎ 01308 423222.

PORTLAND PORT Port Control Ch 74 (H24). ☎ 01305 824044. **Sailing Academy** ☎ 866000.

WEYMOUTH HM & Town Bridge: Ch 12, M-F 0800-2000 summer & when vessel due; ☎ 01305 838423. **Marina** Ch 80, ☎ 767576. **Fuel** Ch 60.

POOLE
HM Ch 14 (H24); Code 01202 ☎ 440233.
Poole Bridge Ch12.
Marinas Ch 80 M: Salterns ☎ 709971. Parkstone YC ☎ 743610. Poole Quay ☎ 649488. Cobbs Quay ☎ 674299.

YARMOUTH (IoW)
HM & Yar bridge **Ch 68** H24. ☎ 01983 760321. Water taxi **Ch 15.**

LYMINGTON
Marinas Ch 80, M: Yacht Haven ☎ 01590 677071. Berthon Marina ☎ 01590 673312.

COWES
Harbour Radio, Chain Ferry & Folly Inn Ch 69 Mon-Fri: 0800-1700. Marinas **Ch 80, M.** Tel code 01983: Yacht Haven ☎ 299975. Shepards ☎ 297821. East Cowes ☎ 293983. Island Hbr **Ch 80,** ☎ 822999. Water Taxi **Ch 06.**

NEWPORT HM & Yacht Hbr Ch 69 0800-1600. ☎ 01983 525994.

RYDE HM Ch 80. Summer 0900-2000, Winter HX. ☎ 01983 613879. Access HW±2.

BEMBRIDGE Marina **Ch 80,** ☎ 01983 872828. Water Taxi **Ch 80.**

SOUTHAMPTON
Port Ops and VTS Ch 12 14. Marinas **Ch 80, M.** Tel code 02380: Hythe ☎ 207073. Ocean Village ☎ 229385. Shamrock Quay ☎ 229461. Kemp's ☎ 632323. Town Quay ☎ 234397.

HAMBLE
Hbr Radio Ch 68 Apr-Sep daily 0600-2200; Oct-Mar 0700-1830. Marinas **Ch 80, M.** Tel code 02380: Hamble Pt ☎ 452464. Port Hamble ☎ 452741. Mercury ☎ 455994. Water Taxi **Ch 77,** ☎ 454512. Tel code 01489: Universal ☎ 574272. Swanwick ☎ 884081.

PORTSMOUTH
VTS **Ch 11** (& *QHM* if essential). Marinas **80.** Tel code 02392: Haslar ☎ 601201. Gosport ☎ 524811. Royal Clarence ☎ 523810. Port Solent ☎ 210765. THE CAMBER (Commercial Hbr): *Portsmouth Hbr Radio* **Ch 11** 14 (H24).

LANGSTONE HBR
HM **Ch 12**. Summer, daily 0830-1700; Winter, M-F 0830-1700; Sat/Sun 0830-1300. Southsea Marina **Ch 80, M,** ☎ 02392 822719.

CHICHESTER
HM *Chichester Hbr Radio* **Ch 14**. 1 Apr-Sep: M-Fri: 0830-1700. Sat: 0900-1300. 1 Oct - 31 Mar: 0900-1300, 1400-1700. Marinas **Ch 80, M**. Sparkes ☎ 02392 463572. Tel code 01243: Northney ☎ 466321. Emsworth Yacht Hbr ☎ 377727. Thornham ☎ 375335. Birdham Pool ☎ 512310. Chichester ☎ 512731. Water taxi **Ch 08** 0900-1800, mobile 07970 378350

LITTLEHAMPTON HM/Bridge **Ch 71** 0900-1700. Marina **Ch 80, M;** ☎ 01903 241663.

SHOREHAM HM & lock *Shoreham Hbr Radio* **Ch 14** (H24). Marina ☎ 01273 593801.

BRIGHTON
Marina *Brighton Control* **Ch M 80**; ☎ 01273 819919.

NEWHAVEN HM & Bridge *Newhaven Radio* **Ch 12**. HM / Port Control 612926 (H24). Marina **Ch 80, M**; ☎ 01273 513881.

EASTBOURNE
Sovereign Hbr, inc lock/berthing: **Ch 17.** ☎ 01323 470099.

RYE *Hbr Radio,* **Ch 14** 0900-1700 or when ship due. ☎ 01797 225225.

FOLKESTONE
Port Control **Ch 15** for entry; ☎ 01303 254597.

DOVER
Port Control **Ch 74** for entry. Marina Ch 80; ☎ 01304 241663.

RAMSGATE
Port Control **Ch 14**. Marina **Ch 80**; ☎ 01843 572110.

ENGLAND – EAST COAST

WHITSTABLE
Hbr Radio Ch 09 12, Mon-Fri: 0830-1700 and –3HW+1. ☎ 01227 274086.

MEDWAY
Medway VTS **Ch 74**. Kingsferry Bridge (W Swale) **Ch 10** H24. Marinas **Ch 80, M**. Tel code 01634: Gillingham ☎ 280022. Hoo ☎ 250311. Chatham ☎ 899200.

PORT OF LONDON
LONDON VTS: Ch 69 from sea to Sea Reach No 4 buoy. **Ch 68** Sea Reach No 4 to Crayford Ness. **Ch 14**, 22, W of Crayford Ness.
Thames Barrier Ch 14. ☎ 020 8855 0315.

RIVER THAMES
Patrol Launches *Thames Patrol* **Ch 06, 13, 14, 68**
King George V Dock lock *KG Control* **Ch 13.**
West India Dock lock **Ch 13**
Greenwich Yacht Club **Ch M**
Thames lock (Brentford) **Ch 74** Summer 0800-1800; Winter 0800-1630.
Cadogan Pier **Ch 14** 0900-1700.
Marinas Ch 80, M; Tel code 0207: Gallions Point ☎ 4767054. Poplar Dock ☎ 5151046. South Dock ☎ 2522244. Limehouse Basin ☎ 3089930. St Katherine Haven ☎ 2645312. Chelsea Hbr ☎ 2259100. Brentford Dock ☎ 0208 2328941.

RIVER ROACH Havengore Bridge **Ch 72** *Shoe Bridge* HW±2. ☎ 01702 383436.

BURNHAM-ON-CROUCH
Ch 80: HM Launch 0900-1700. Yacht Hbr ☎ 01621 782150. Essex Marina ☎ 01702 258531.

RIVER BLACKWATER
Marinas **Ch 80, M**; Tel code 01621: Tollesbury ☎ 869202. Bradwell ☎ 776235. **Ch M**: Blackwater ☎ 740264. Heybridge Lock, **Ch 80** ☎ 853506.

RIVER COLNE
Brightlingsea Hbr **Ch 68** 0800-2000. Tel code 01206 ☎ 302200. Waterside Marina ☎ 308709.

WALTON BACKWATERS
Titchmarsh Marina **Ch 80,** ☎ 01255 672185.

RIVERS STOUR AND ORWELL
HARWICH VTS **Ch 71,** 11, 20, H24
SUNK VTS **Ch 14,** H24
Orwell Navigation Service **Ch 68,** H24, ☎ 211066.
Marinas **Ch 80, M**. Tel code 01473: Shotley ☎ 788982. Suffolk Hbr ☎ 659240. Woolverstone ☎ 780206. Fox's ☎ 689111. Neptune ☎ 215204. Ipswich Haven ☎ 236644.

RIVER DEBEN HM ☎ 07803 476621.
Tidemill Yacht Hbr ☎ 01394 385745.

SOUTHWOLD *Port Radio* **Ch** 09 **12**. HM ☎ 01502 724712.

LOWESTOFT
Hbr Control **Ch** 11, **14.** HM ☎ 01502 572286.
Royal Norfolk & Suffolk YC **Ch 80.** ☎ 566726.
Haven Marina **Ch 80** ☎ 580300. **Mutford Bridge & Lock Ch 73** ☎ 531778.

GREAT YARMOUTH
Yarmouth Radio **Ch 12**. HM ☎ 01493 335511.
Haven & Breydon bridges **Ch 12.**

WELLS-NEXT-THE-SEA
Wells Hbr **Ch 12**, HJ, HW±2 and when vessel expected. HM ☎ 01328 711646.

WISBECH Ch 09 HW–3 when vessel expected. HM 01945 588059. Sutton Bridge **Ch 09**

KING'S LYNN
Harbour Radio **Ch 14** 11 Mon-Fri: 0800-1700 and –3HW+1. HM ☎ 01553 773411.

BOSTON
Port Control **Ch 12** Mon-Fri 0800-1700 and HW HW -2½ to HW + 1½. HM ☎ 01205 362328.
Grand Sluice **Ch 74** only when lock operates.
Marina ☎ 364420.

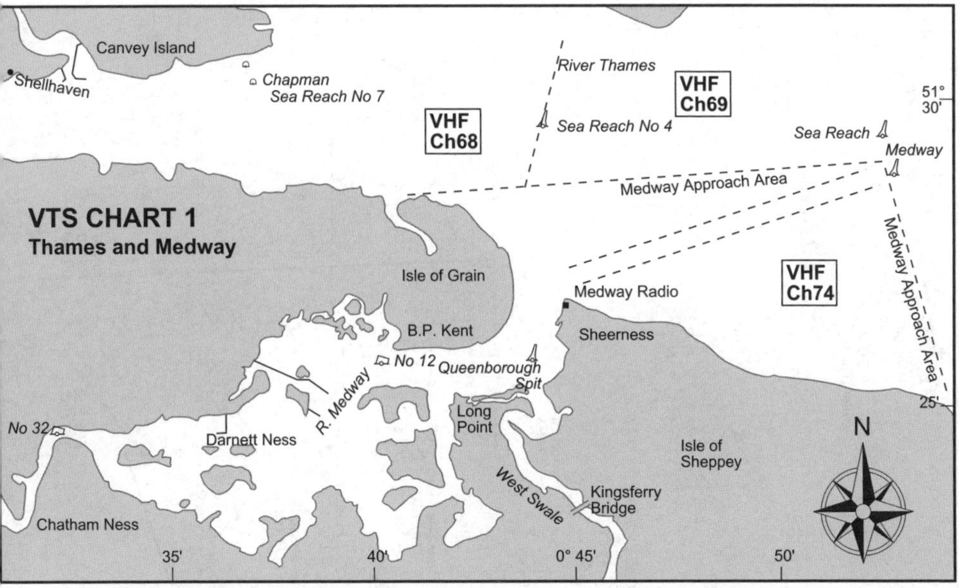
Canvey Island
Shellhaven
Chapman
Sea Reach No 7
River Thames
VHF Ch69
VHF Ch68
Sea Reach No 4
51° 30'
Sea Reach
Medway
Medway Approach Area
Isle of Grain
Medway Radio
VHF Ch74
B.P. Kent
Sheerness
Medway Approach Area
No 12
Queenborough Spit
R. Medway
Long Point
25'
No 32
Darnett Ness
Isle of Sheppey
N
West Swale
Kingsferry Bridge
Chatham Ness
35'
40'
0° 45'
50'

VTS CHART 1
Thames and Medway

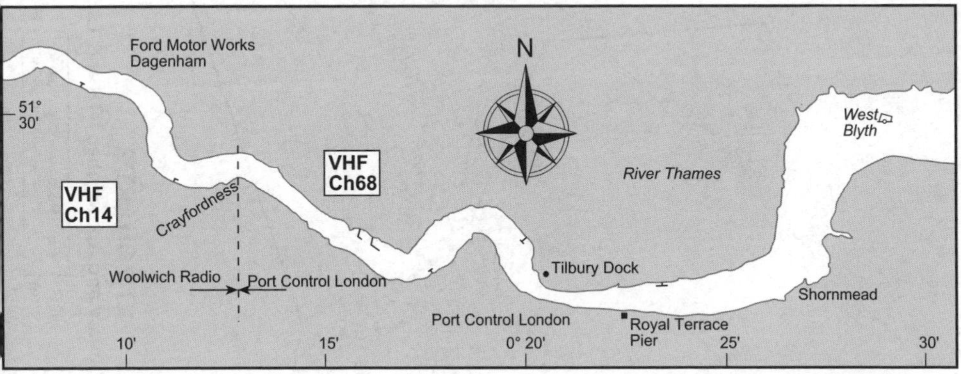
Ford Motor Works Dagenham
N
51° 30'
West Blyth
VHF Ch68
River Thames
VHF Ch14
Crayfordness
Tilbury Dock
Woolwich Radio
Port Control London
Shornmead
Port Control London
Royal Terrace Pier
10'
15'
0° 20'
25'
30'

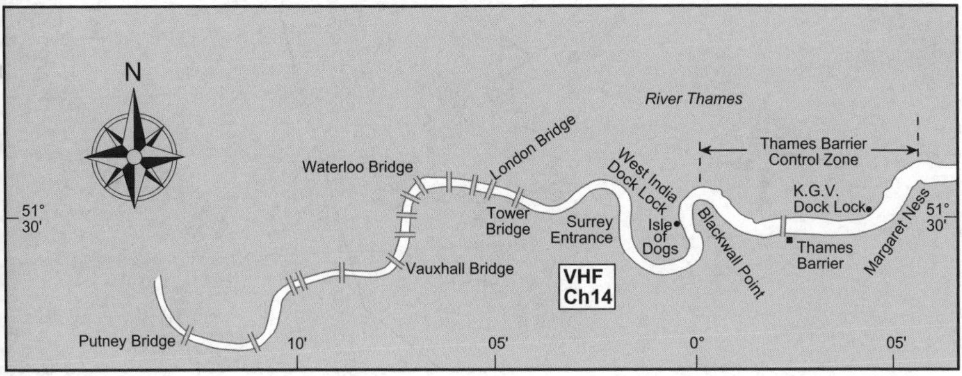
N
River Thames
Thames Barrier Control Zone
London Bridge
Waterloo Bridge
West India Dock Lock
K.G.V. Dock Lock
51° 30'
Tower Bridge
Surrey Entrance
Isle of Dogs
Blackwall Point
Thames Barrier
Margaret Ness
51° 30'
Vauxhall Bridge
VHF Ch14
Putney Bridge
10'
05'
0°
05'

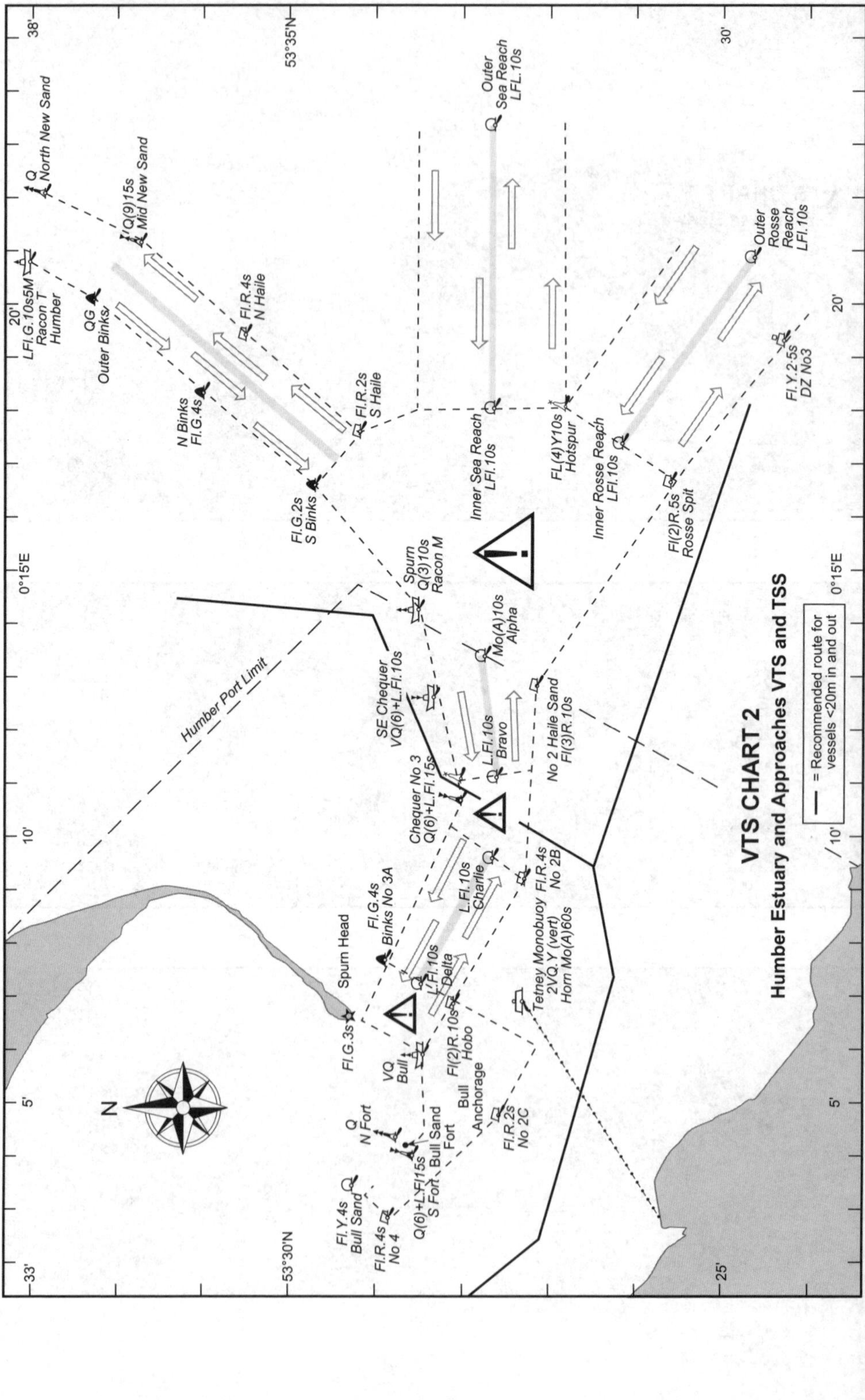
VTS CHART 2
Humber Estuary and Approaches VTS and TSS
— = Recommended route for vessels <20m in and out
N
53°35'N
53°30'N
0°15'E
38'
33'
30'
25'
20'
10'
5'
Q North New Sand
Q(9)15s Mid New Sand
LFl.G.10s5M Racon T Humber
QG Outer Binks
Fl.R.4s N Haile
N Binks Fl.G.4s
Fl.R.2s S Haile
Fl.G.2s S Binks
Outer Sea Reach LFL.10s
Inner Sea Reach LFl.10s
FL(4)Y10s Hotspur
Inner Rosse Reach LFl.10s
Outer Rosse Reach LFl.10s
Fl(2)R.5s Rosse Spit
Fl.Y.2·5s DZ No3
Spurn Q(3)10s Racon M
Mo(A)10s Alpha
SE Chequer VQ(6)+L.Fl.10s
Humber Port Limit
Chequer No 3 Q(6)+L.Fl.15s
L.Fl.10s Bravo
No 2 Haile Sand Fl(3)R.10s
L.Fl.10s Charlie
Fl.R.4s No 2B
Fl.G.4s Binks No 3A
Spurn Head
Fl.G.3s
L.Fl.10s Delta
Tetney Monobuoy 2VQ.Y (vert) Horn Mo(A)60s
VQ Bull
Fl(2)R.10s Hobo
Bull Anchorage
Fl.R.2s No 2C
Q N Fort
Bull Sand Fort
Q(6)+LFl15s S Fort
Fl.Y.4s Bull Sand
Fl.R.4s No 4

RIVER HUMBER
VTS 1, Ch 14 to seaward of Clee Ness Lt F
VTS 2, Ch 12 Clee Ness–Gainsborough (R Trent) & Goole (R Ouse). MSI broadcasts Ch 12 & 14 every 2 hrs from 0103LT.
Grimsby Docks Radio **Ch 74**; 18 79 H24
Marinas: Grimsby, Meridian Quay **Ch 74**, ☎ 01472 268424. **Hull, Ch 80**, ☎ 01482 330508.
South Ferriby, Sluice **Ch 74. Brough**, Humber Yawl club ☎ 01482 667224. **Goole** Boathouse ☎ 01405 763985.

BRIDLINGTON
HM, call Ch 16; work **Ch 12**. ☎ 01262 670148.

SCARBOROUGH
HM *Scarborough Port Control* **Ch 12** H24. ☎ 01723 373530.

WHITBY HM, Bridge & Marina **Ch 11,** 12 H24. ☎ 01947 602354.

RIVER TEES and HARTLEPOOL
Monitor *Tees Port control* **Ch 14**, 08, 11, 12, 22.
Hartlepool Marina **Ch 80, M** H24. ☎ 01429 865744.

SEAHAM
HM **Ch 12**, M-F 0800-1700. ☎ 0191 5161700.

SUNDERLAND
Hbr Radio **Ch 14** (H24). Marina **Ch 80, M.** ☎ 0191 5144721.

RIVER TYNE
Tyne VTS **Ch 12**, 08, 11, inc Info service.
Royal Quays Marina **Ch 80** ☎ 0191 2728282.
St Peter's Marina **Ch 80** ☎ 0191 2654472.
Newcastle City Marina ☎ 0191 2211348.

BLYTH
Port control **Ch 12**, 11. ☎ 01670 352066. Marina ☎ 01670 353636 (R Northumberland YC).

WARKWORTH HARBOUR (Amble)
HM Ch 16, work **Ch 14.** ☎ 01665 710306. Marina **Ch 80,** ☎ 01665 712168.

BERWICK-UPON-TWEED
HM **Ch 12**, M-F 0800-1700. ☎ 01289 307404.

SCOTLAND

EYEMOUTH HM **Ch 12**, 06 HO. ☎ 01890 750223.

FIRTH OF FORTH
Forth and Tay Navigation **Ch 71**; may work 12, 20.

PORT EDGAR Marina **Ch 80, M.** ☎ 0131 313330.

GRANTON, Royal Forth YC, Call *Boswell* **Ch M.** ☎ 0131 5523006.

GRANGEMOUTH Docks **Ch 14.** ☎ 01324 498566.

FORTH & CLYDE CANAL *Carron Sea Lock* **Ch 74.** ☎ 01324 483034.

METHIL Docks **Ch 14.** ☎ 01324 4426725.

ANSTRUTHER Ch 11. ☎ 01333 310836.

DUNDEE *Harbour Radio* **Ch 12.** ☎ 01382 224121.
Royal Tay YC Ch M. ☎ 01382 477516.

PERTH *Perth Harbour* **Ch 09.** ☎ 01738 624056.

ARBROATH *Port Control* **Ch 11.** ☎ 01241 872166.

MONTROSE *Port Control* **Ch 12.** ☎ 01674 672302.

STONEHAVEN HM **Ch 11.** ☎ 01569 762741.

ABERDEEN VTS **Ch 12,** ☎ 01224 597000.

PETERHEAD *Peterhead Hbrs* **Ch 14** for cl'nce to enter/exit. Marina ☎ 01779 477868.

FRASERBURGH Ch 12 H24, ☎ 01346 515858.

MACDUFF Ch 12 H24, ☎ 01261 832236.

BANFF Ch 12, ☎ 01261 815544.

WHITEHILLS *Whitehills Hbr Radio* **Ch 14,** ☎ 01261 861291.

BUCKIE Ch 12, 16 (H24), ☎ 01542 831700.

LOSSIEMOUTH
HM **Ch 12** 0700-1700. Marina, ☎ 01343 813066.

HOPEMAN and BURGHEAD
Same HM: *Burghead Radio* **Ch 14** HX, ☎ 01343 835337.

NAIRN HM/Marina ☎ 01667 454330. No VHF.

INVERNESS
HM **Ch 12**, M-Fri 0900-1700; Tel code 01463: ☎ 715715.
Clachnaharry Sealock **Ch 74,** ☎ 713896. HW ±4.
Inverness Marina **Ch 12**.
Seaport Marina ☎ 239745.
Caley Marina ☎ 236539.

HELMSDALE Ch 13, ☎ 01431 821692.

WICK Ch 14 HM, ☎ 01955 602030.

SCRABSTER HM **Ch 12** H24, Call on arr/dep. ☎ 01847 892779.

ORKNEY HARBOURS NAVIGATION SERVICE
Orkney Harbour Radio **Ch** 09 **11** 12
Stromness HM **Ch 14** M-Fri 0900-1700; ☎ 07810 465825. Marina, ☎ 465825.
Kirkwall *Hbr Radio* **Ch 14,** ☎ 872292. M-Fri, 0800-1700.
Westray Pier, *Pierowall Hbr* **Ch 14** when vessel expected. ☎ 01857 677216.

SHETLAND
Lerwick Hbr Radio **Ch 12** ☎ 01595 692991.
Scalloway Hbr Radio **Ch** 09, **12,** M-F 0700-1800, Sat 0900-1230. Piermaster ☎ 01595 744221.
Sullom Voe VTS **Ch 14** for tfc info, weather & radar assistance on request. ☎ 01806 242551.
Balta Sound Harbour **Ch 16, 20** HO

OUTER HEBRIDES
STORNOWAY HM **Ch 12** H24, ☎ 01851 702688.
Loch Maddy, N Uist Ch 12, ☎ 01876 500337.
St Kilda, *Kilda Radio* **Ch 16,** ☎ 01870 604406.

MAINLAND
Kinlochbervie Ch 14 HX, ☎ 01971 521235.
Loch Inver Ch 09 HX, ☎ 01571 844247.

ULLAPOOL Ch 14, ☎ 01854 612724.

Loch Gairloch Hbr Ch 16, ☎ 01445 712140.

ISLE OF SKYE
Portree Ch 12 (occas), ☎ 01478 612926.

Kyle Akin Ch 11, ☎ 01599 534167.

KYLE OF LOCH ALSH Ch 11, ☎ 01599 534589.

Mallaig Ch 09 HO, ☎ 01687 462154.

Tiree, Gott Bay Pier, **Ch 31,** ☎ 01879 230337.

Coll, Arinagour Pier, **Ch 31,** ☎ 01879 230347.

L Sunart, Salen Bay, **Ch 16,** ☎ 01967 431510.

ISLAND OF MULL
Tobermory, Ch 12, M HJ, ☎ 01688 302876.

Loch Lathaich; Sound of Iona; Craignure Pier.

Corpach basin & lock/Caledonian Canal Ch 74, ☎ 01397 772249.

DUNSTAFFNAGE Marina, Ch M, ☎ 01631 566555.

Oban *North Bay* **Ch 12. Marina,** ☎ 01631 565333.

L Melfort, Kilmelford Haven, **Ch M,** ☎ 01852 200248.

L Shuna, Craobh Marina, **Ch M,** ☎ 01852 500222.

L Craignish, Ardfern **Ch 80, M,** ☎ 01852 500247.

CRINAN CANAL, Ch 74. BWB, ☎ 01546 603210.

Islay, Port Ellen, ☎ 01496 300301; no VHF.

Tarbert, Loch Fyne Ch 14, ☎ 01880 820344.

Portavadie Marina Ch 80, ☎ 01700 811075.

CAMPBELTOWN Ch 12, 13, ☎ 01586 552552.

ROTHESAY, Bute Ch 12, ☎ 07799 724225.

LARGS Yacht Haven **Ch 80, M,** ☎ 01475 675333.

KIP Marina **Ch 80, M,** ☎ 01475 521485.

HOLY LOCH Marina **Ch 80, M,** ☎ 01369 701800.

RHU Marina **Ch 80, M,** ☎ 01436 820238.

ARDROSSAN Marina **Ch 80, M,** ☎ 01294 607077.

IRVINE HM/Bridge **Ch 12,** ☎ 01292 487286.

TROON Ch 14. Marina **Ch 80, M,** ☎ 01294 315553.

GIRVAN HM **Ch 12,** ☎ 01465 713648.

STRANRAER Ch 14, ☎ 01776 707500.

KIRKCUDBRIGHT HM **Ch 12,** ☎ 01557 331135.

ENGLAND W COAST AND WALES

MARYPORT Marina **Ch 80,** ☎ 01900 814431.

WORKINGTON HM **Ch 14,** ☎ 01900 602301.

WHITEHAVEN Marina **Ch 12,** ☎ 01946 692435.

ISLE OF MAN (Tel code 01624) If unable to contact IoM hbrs below, call Douglas.

Douglas *Hbr Control* **Ch 12** H24.

Port St Mary HM **Ch 12** HJ, ☎ 833205.

Peel HM **Ch 12** HJ, ☎ 842338.

Ramsey HM **Ch 12** 0800-1600. HO, ☎ 812245.

MAINLAND
GLASSON DOCK Marina **Ch 69,** ☎ 01524 751491.

FLEETWOOD *Fleetwood Dock Radio* (HW±2) **Ch 12** for Marina, ☎ 01253 879062.

PRESTON Lock *Riversway* **Ch 14**. Marina **Ch 80,** ☎ 01772 733595.

LIVERPOOL *Mersey Radio* **Ch 12.** Info **Ch 09**. Radar **Ch 18**. Liverpool Marina (Brunswick Dock) **Ch M,** ☎ 0151 7076777. Albert Dock **Ch M,** ☎ 0151 7096558; access via Canning Dock lock.

CONWY HM **Ch 14.** Marinas, both **Ch 80:** Conwy, ☎ 01492 593000. Deganwy 576888.

MENAI STRAIT and ANGLESEY
Beaumaris/Menai HM **Ch 69,** ☎ 01248 712312.

Caernarfon, HM & Victoria Dock **Ch 80,** ☎ 01286 672118. Mon-Fri: 0900-1700 Sat: 0900-1200

HOLYHEAD *Port Control* **Ch 14,** ☎ 01407 606700. Marina 764242.

MAINLAND
PWLLHELI, HM **Ch 12,** ☎ 701219 . Marina **Ch 80, M,** ☎ 01758 704081.

PORTHMADOG *Hbr* **Ch 12,** ☎ 01766 512927.

BARMOUTH HM *Barmouth Hbr* **Ch 12,** ☎ 01341 280671.

ABERDOVEY *Aberdovey Hbr* **Ch 12,** ☎ 01654 767626.

ABERYSTWYTH HM **Ch 14**. Marina **Ch 80,** ☎ 01970 611422.

FISHGUARD HM **Ch 14**.

MILFORD HAVEN Monitor *Port Control* (and *Patrol launch*) **Ch 12,** whilst under way. **Milford Docks** *Pierhead* **Ch 18.** Milford Dock Marina **Ch 14,** ☎ 01646 696312. Neyland Yacht Haven **Ch 80, M,** ☎ 01646 601601.

Tenby Ch 80, ☎ 01834 842717.

Saundersfoot Ch 11

SWANSEA Tawe Lock Ch 18. Marina **Ch 80,** ☎ 01792 470310.

BARRY *Barry Radio* **Ch 11.** HM ☎ 01446 732665.

CARDIFF *Cardiff Radio* **Ch 14.** Barrage control **Ch 18.** Penarth Marina **Ch 80,** ☎ 02920 705021.

NEWPORT HM **Ch 71,** ☎ 0870 6096699.

SHARPNESS *Sharpness Radio* **Ch 13** for lock. Marina, ☎ 01453 811476. Canal **Ch 74**

BRISTOL *Bristol VTS* **Ch 12** ☎ 0117 980 2638. *City Docks Radio* **Ch 14** (low power) to confirm. *Bristol Floating Hbr* **Ch 73**. Bristol Marina **Ch 80,** ☎ 0117 9213198.

PORTISHEAD Marina **Ch 80,** ☎ 0198 4631264.

BURNHAM-ON-SEA HM **Ch 08,** ☎ 01938 822666.

WATCHET Marina **Ch 80,** ☎ 01984 631264.

ILFRACOMBE HM **Ch 80,** ☎ 01271 862108.

APPLEDORE-BIDEFORD HM *Two Rivers* **Ch 12,** Appledore ☎ 01237 428700.

BUDE HM **Ch 12,** ☎ 01288 353111.

PADSTOW HM **Ch 12,** ☎ 01841 532239.

ST IVES HM **Ch 12,** ☎ 07793 515460.

IRELAND

ROSSAVEEL Ch 12, ☎ 091 572108.

GALWAY, HM **Ch 12,** ☎ 091 561874.

SHANNON ESTUARY *Shannon Ports Radio* **Ch 11** (HO), ☎ 087 2560427.

KILRUSH Marina Ch 80, ☎ 06590 52072.

LIMERICK HBR Ch 12 13, ☎ 061 315377.

MFENIT HM **Ch 14, M,** ☎ 066 7136231.

DINGLE HM **Ch 14** (no calls req'd), ☎ 087 9254115.

CAHERSIVEEN (Valentia) Marina Ch 80, ☎ 066 9472777.

BANTRY BAY, Lawrence Cove Marina **Ch M,** ☎ 027 75044.

CASTLETOWN BEARHAVEN ⚓, ☎ 027 70220.

CROOKHAVEN ⚓, ☎ 028 35319.

SCHULL ⚓, mobile ☎ 086 1039105.

BALTIMORE Ch 09, mobile 087 2351485.

GLANDORE HM **Ch 06,** ☎ 028 34737.

COURTMACSHERRY HM ☎ 08610 40812.

KINSALE HM **Ch 14** ☎ 021 4772503. Marinas **Ch M:** KYC ☎ 4772196. Castlepark ☎ 4774959.

CORK *Cork Hbr Radio* **Ch 12,** 14 H24. HM ☎ 021 4273125. Marinas **Ch M**: Crosshaven ☎ 4831161. Salve ☎ 4831145. Royal Cork YC ☎ 4831023. East Ferry ☎ 4813390. Cork Hbr ☎ (087) 3669009.

YOUGHAL HM/Pilots **Ch 14** Mon-Fri 0900-1700 and when ships expected. ☎ 024 92577.

DUNMORE EAST HM/Pilots **Ch 14** ☎ 051 383166.

WATERFORD & **NEW ROSS Ch** 12, **14.** ☎ 051 873501.

KILMORE QUAY Ch 09. Marina, ☎ 053 29955.

ROSSLARE HM **Ch 12** H24, ☎ 053 33114.

WEXFORD Hbr Boat club. **Ch 16,** ☎ 053 22039.

ARKLOW HM **Ch 12,** ☎ 0402 32466. Marina 39901.

WICKLOW HM **Ch 14** 12, ☎ 0404 67455.

DUN LAOGHAIRE HM **Ch 14,** ☎ 01 2801130. Marina **Ch M,** ☎ 2020040. YCs: National 2805725; R. St George 2801811; R. Irish 2809452; DL Motor 2801371.

Greystones Marina, ☎ 353 (086) 2718161

DUBLIN HM and VTS *Dublin VTS* **Ch 12,** 13. Poolbeg Marina **Ch M,** ☎ 01 6689983. Lifting bridge *Eastlink* **Ch 12, 13.** City moorings, ☎ 01 8183300.

HOWTH HM **Ch 11.** Marina Ch M, 80, ☎ 01 8392777.

MALAHIDE Marina **Ch 80, M,** ☎ 01 8454129.

CARLINGFORDFORD LOUGH
Carlingford Marina Ch M, ☎ 042 9373072.

Warrenpoint Ch 12, ☎ 028 41752878.

Kilkeel Ch 12, ☎ 028 41762287.

ARDGLASS (Phennick Cove) HM **Ch 12.** Marina **Ch M, 80,** ☎ 028 44842332.

STRANGFORD LOUGH
HM **Ch 12 14,** ☎ 028 44881637.

Portaferry Marina Ch 80, M, ☎ 07703 209780.

Donaghadee Copelands Marina, ☎ 028 91882184.

BELFAST VTS *Belfast Hbr Radio* **Ch 12. Marinas Ch 80, M:** Carrickfergus, ☎ 028 93366666. Bangor, ☎ 028 91453217.

LARNE *Port Control* **Ch 14,** 11.

Glenarm HM/Marina, mobile ☎ 07703 606763.

Ballycastle HM/Marina, mob ☎ 07803 505084.

PORTRUSH HM **Ch 12,** ☎ 028 70822307.

COLERAINE HM **Ch 12.** Marina, ☎ 028 70832086.

LONDONDERRY *Hbr radio* **Ch 14,** ☎ 028 71860313.

L SWILLY Fahan Marina, ☎ 074 9360008.

KILLYBEGS HM **Ch 14,** ☎ 07497 31032.

Burton Port HM **Ch** 06, 12, **14,** ☎ 075 42155.

SLIGO HM **Ch 12,** 14, ☎ 071 9153819.

DENMARK

Skagen HM **Ch 12** 13 HX, ☎ 98 941346.

Hirtshals HM **Ch 12** 13 HX, ☎ 98 941422.

Torup Strand HM **Ch 12** 13 HX.

Hanstholm HM **Ch 12** 13 HX, ☎ 97 961833/ 96550710.

THYBORØN HM **Ch 12** 13 H24, ☎ 97 831188.

Thisted (Limfjord) Ch 12 13 HX, ☎ 97 911400.

Torsminde HM **Ch 12** 13, ☎ 24 233345.

Hvide Sande HM **Ch 12** (0700-1700), ☎ 97 311633 H24.

ESBJERG *Hbr Control* **Ch 12** 13 14 H24, ☎ 75 124000. **Fanø** HM, ☎ 75 163100.

Rømø HM **Ch 10, 12, 13** HX, ☎ 74 755245.

GERMANY

HELGOLAND HM **Ch 67,** ☎ 04725 81593583.
May-Aug Mon-Thu 0700-1200, 1300-2000. Fri-Sun 0700-1200.
Sep-Apr Mon-Thu 0700-1200, 1300-1600. Fri 0700-1200.

COMMUNICATIONS

List HM **Ch 11,** ☎ 046 51870374.
Hörnum HM **67,** ☎ 046 51881027.
Wyk HM **Ch 11,** ☎ 046 81500430.
Pellworm HM **Ch 11,** ☎ 048 44726.
Husum HM **Ch 11,** ☎ 048 16670.
R. Eider sealock **Ch 14,** ☎ 04833 4535211.
Büsum HM **Ch 11,** ☎ 048 413607.

INNER DEUTSCHE BUCHT (GERMAN BIGHT)
VTS, Eastern part **Ch 80,** ☎ 04421 489282.
VTS, Western part **Ch 79**

BRUNSBÜTTEL WSA (hbr info) ☎ 04852 8850.

NORD-OSTSEE KANAL (KIEL CANAL)

VTS Canal I	**Ch 13,** ☎ 04852 885371.
VTS Canal II	**Ch 02,** ☎ 04852 885369.
VTS Canal III	**Ch 03,** ☎ 0431 3603456.
VTS Canal IV	**Ch 12,** ☎ 0431 3603465.

Brieholz, Ch 73. Ostermoor, Ch 73.
Kiel-Holtenau, HM ☎ 0431 363830.

RIVER ELBE
CUXHAVEN HM **Ch 69** HX, ☎ 04721 500150. **Lock Ch 69,** ☎ 500120. **Cuxhaven** Marina, ☎ 175 90 20015. **YC** Marina, ☎ 34111. **R. Stör Lock Ch 09** Bridge opens on request. **Glückstadt** HM **Ch 08,** ☎ 04124 913200.

HAMBURG Port HM **Ch 12,** ☎ 040 7411540. **VTS** *Hamburg Port Traffic* **Ch** 13, **14, 74**. Wedel Yacht Hbr, ☎ 040 1034438. City Sporthafen, ☎ 040 364297.Lloyd & R Geeste Marinas ☎

BREMERHAVEN *Weser VTS* **Ch 22. Port Ch 12,** ☎ 0471 59613401. **HM,** ☎ 59613416. **Locks Ch 69, 10. Marinas** Weser YC, ☎ 23531. NYC, ☎ 77555. WVW, ☎ 73268.Lloyds/Geeste ☎1428690

BREMEN *Port Radio* **Ch 03,** ☎ 0421 3618504.

JADE VTS *Jade Traffic* **Ch 63, 20.**

WILHEMSHAVEN
Port Ch 11, ☎ 04421 154580. **Sealock Ch 13. Bridges Ch 11. Marinas** Nassauhafen, ☎ 41439. Wiking Sportsboothafen, ☎ 41301.

HOOKSIEL Ch 63. Alterhafen Marina.

WANGEROOGE HM **Ch 17,** ☎ 04469 1322.

SPIEKEROOG HM No VHF, ☎ 04976 9193133.

DORNUMER-ACCUMERSIEL HM No VHF, ☎ 04933 2510. YC ☎ 2240.

LANGEOOG HM **Ch 17,** ☎ 04972 301.

NORDERNEY HM **Ch 17,** ☎ 04932 82826.

NORDDEICH HM **Ch 17,** ☎ 04931 81317.

BORKUM HM **Ch 14,** ☎ 04922 81317.

EMS VTS *Ems Traffic* **Ch** 15, 18, 20, 21

EMDEN HM & locks **Ch 13,** ☎ 04921 897260. YC Marina, ☎ 997147. Mariners' Club, ☎ 953795. City Marina, ☎ 8907211.

NETHERLANDS

DELFZIJL/EEMSHAVEN VTS is not compulsor for leisure craft. **Delfzijl Radar** Ch 03 gives rada assistance when visibility falls below 2000m **Eemshaven Radar** Ch 01. **Port Control** Ch 6 broadcasts info every even H+10.

DELFZIJL HBR. HM Ch 14; ☎ 0596 640400. **Lock** Ch 26, M-Sat H24, Sun & hols on request; ☎ 693293. **Bridges:** Weiwerder Ch 11. Heemskes & Handelshaven Ch 14. **Farmsumerhaven,** Ch 66 ☎ 640494.

EEMSHAVEN HM Ch 14; ☎ 516142. Radar Ch 19.

LAUWERSOOG. HM, *Havendienst*, Ch 09; ☎ 051 39023. Mon 0000-1700; Tu-Wed 0800-1700; Th-Sa 0700-1500.

TERSCHELLING VTS Call/monitor *Brandaris* Ch 02, ☎ 0562 443100. **Marina,** Ch 31; ☎ 443337.

VLIELAND. HM Ch 12. **Marina,** Ch 31; ☎ 0562 451729.

HARLINGEN HM Ch 11 (not on Sun); ☎ 0517 413423. **Locks** Ch 22.

OUDESCHILD HM Ch 12; ☎ 0222 312710. **Marina,** Ch 31; ☎ 0222 321227. See Den Helder VTS.

DEN HELDER VTS. Monitor *Tfc Centre* Ch 62, H24; broadcasts info and gives radar surveillance. **PORT CONTROL** Ch 14; ☎ 0223 62770. **Marina** ☎ 652645. **Bridge**: Moormanbrug Ch 18. **Lock**: Koopvaarders Ch 22.

IJSSELMEER Den Oever lock Ch 20, ☎ 0227 511383. **Port** Ch 11, ☎ 511303. Marina ☎ 511789. **Kornwerderzand lock** Ch 18, ☎ 0517 57441.

ENKHUIZEN Naviduct (also Krabbersgat) Ch 22.

IJMUIDEN VTS. Traffic Centre Ch 07, Roads (W of IJmuiden buoy). Thence **Port Control** Ch 61 to Noordzeesluizen (locks).

Seaport Marina Ch 75, ☎ 0255 560300.

NORDZEEKANAAL VTS
Noordzeesluizen. *Sluis IJmuiden* Ch 22. **Noordzeekanaal.** Ch 03, from locks to km 11·2.

AMSTERDAM Port Control Ch 68 (Km 11·2 to Oranjesluizen). **Port Info** Ch 14. Access to Standing Mast route: **Westerkeersluis** Ch 22. **Haarlem hbr** Ch 18. **Westerdoksbrug** ☎ 6241457, Ch 22, 69. **Marinas: Amsterdam Marina** ☎ 6310767. **Marina Het Realeneiland,** ☎ 6238855. **Sixhaven,** ☎ 020 6329429. **WV Aeolus,** ☎ 6360791. **Aquadam,** ☎ 6320616. Access to Markermeer: **Oranjesluisen** Ch 18.

SCHEVENINGEN. Traffic Centre & Port Ch 21; ☎ 070 3527711. **Marina** Ch 31; ☎ 070 3520017.

HOEK VAN HOLLAND ROADSTEAD
To cross the mouth of the Maas, call *Maas Entrance* **Ch 03**, with vessel's name, position and course. Follow a track close W of a line joining buoys MV, MVN and Indusbank N. See VTS Chart No 4. Whilst

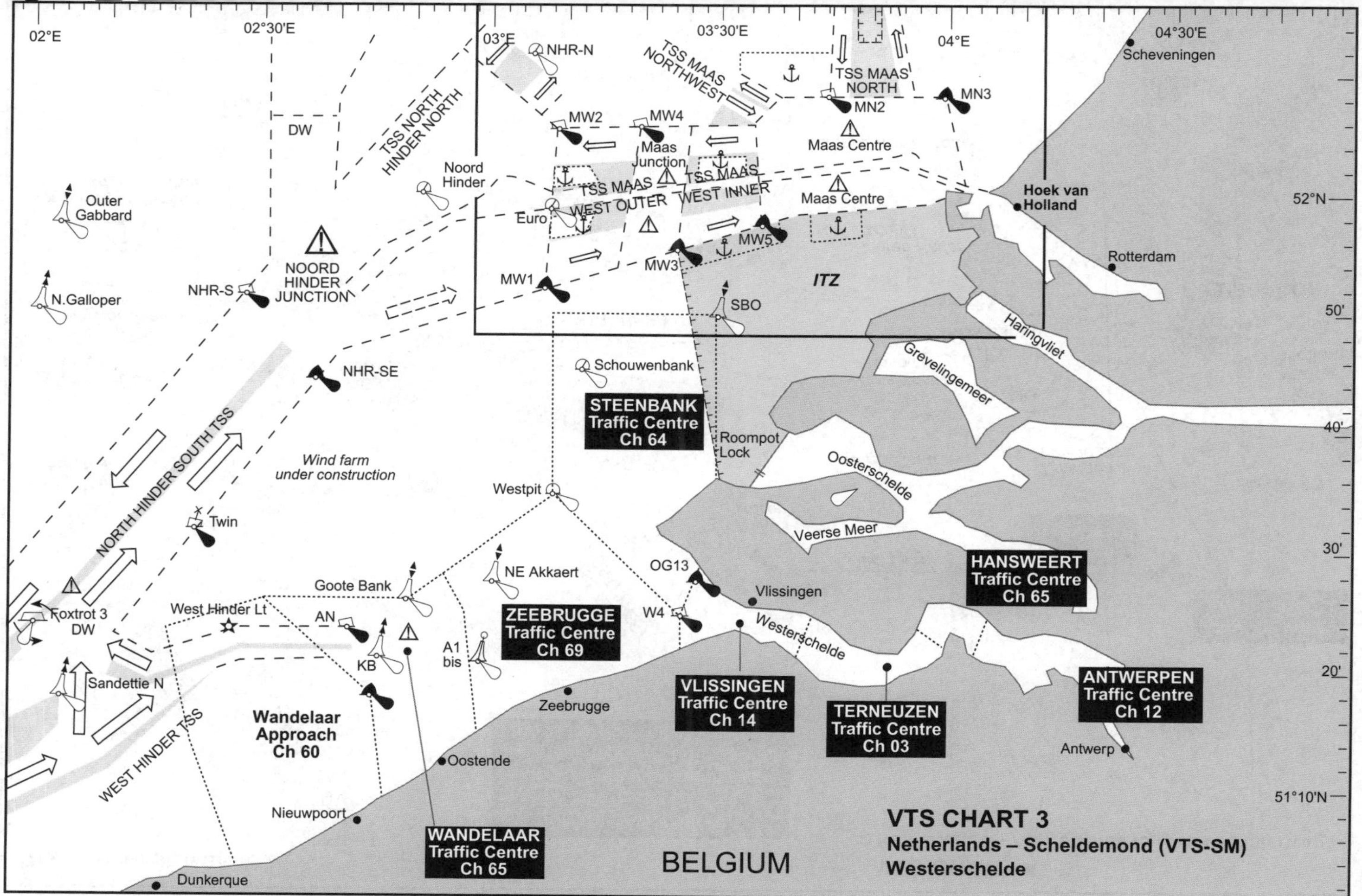
02°E
02°30'E
03°E
03°30'E
04°E
04°30'E
52°N
50'
40'
30'
20'
51°10'N
Scheveningen
Hoek van Holland
Rotterdam
Haringvliet
Grevelingemeer
Oosterschelde
Veerse Meer
Roompot Lock
ITZ
TSS MAAS NORTHWEST
TSS MAAS NORTH
TSS MAAS WEST OUTER
TSS MAAS WEST INNER
TSS NORTH HINDER NORTH
NORTH HINDER SOUTH TSS
WEST HINDER TSS
NHR-N
MW2
MW4
MN2
MN3
Maas Centre
Maas Junction
Maas Centre
Noord Hinder
Euro
MW1
MW3
MW5
SBO
DW
NOORD HINDER JUNCTION
NHR-S
NHR-SE
Outer Gabbard
N.Galloper
Wind farm under construction
Schouwenbank
STEENBANK Traffic Centre Ch 64
Westpit
Twin
Goote Bank
NE Akkaert
OG13
Vlissingen
W4
Westerschelde
HANSWEERT Traffic Centre Ch 65
West Hinder Lt
AN
Foxtrot 3 DW
ZEEBRUGGE Traffic Centre Ch 69
A1 bis
KB
Sandettie N
Zeebrugge
VLISSINGEN Traffic Centre Ch 14
TERNEUZEN Traffic Centre Ch 03
ANTWERPEN Traffic Centre Ch 12
Antwerp
Wandelaar Approach Ch 60
Oostende
Nieuwpoort
Dunkerque
WANDELAAR Traffic Centre Ch 65
BELGIUM
VTS CHART 3
Netherlands – Scheldemond (VTS-SM)
Westerschelde

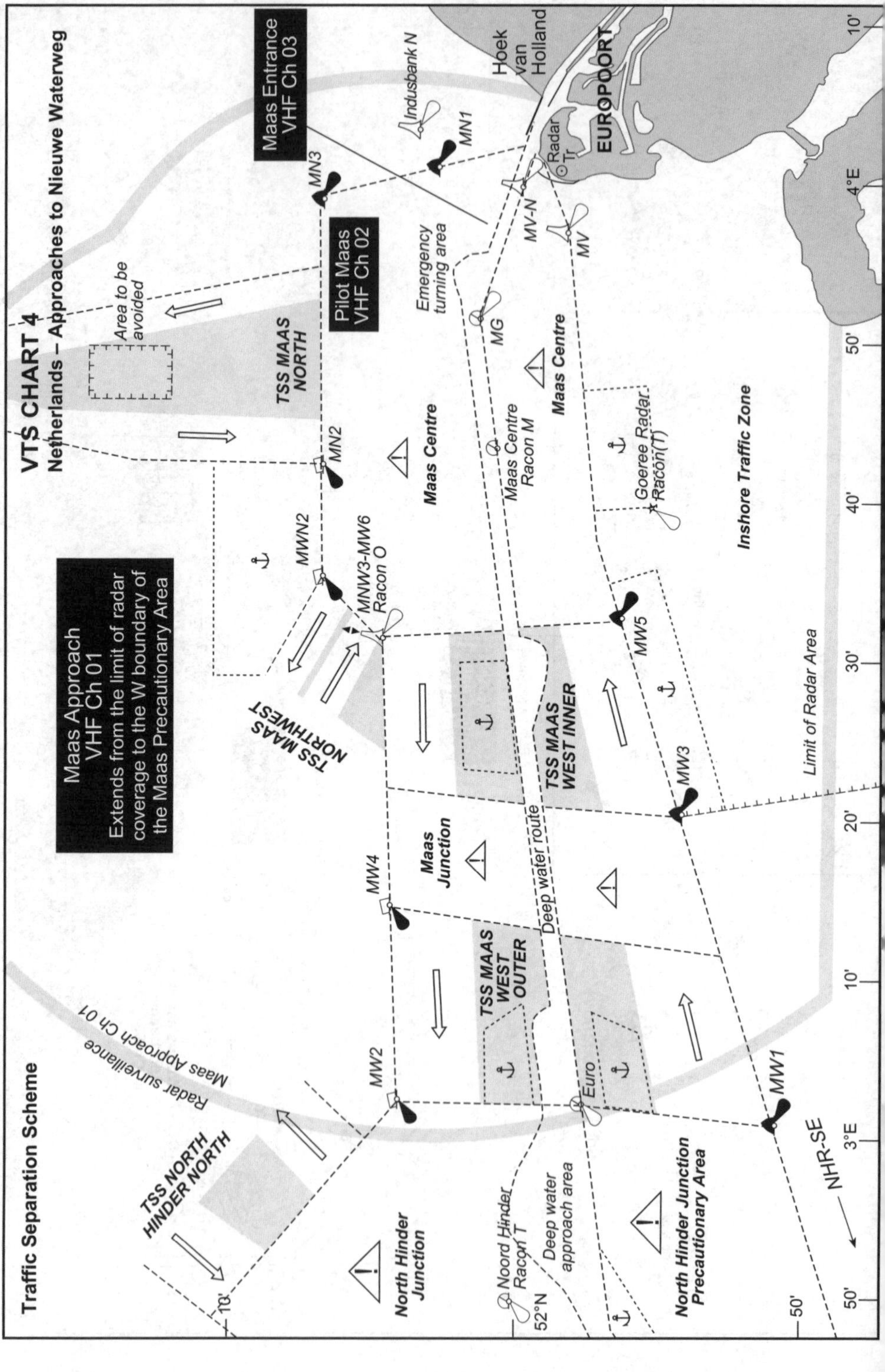
Traffic Separation Scheme
VTS CHART 4
Netherlands – Approaches to Nieuwe Waterweg
Maas Approach
VHF Ch 01
Extends from the limit of radar coverage to the W boundary of the Maas Precautionary Area
Maas Entrance
VHF Ch 03
Pilot Maas
VHF Ch 02
Area to be avoided
TSS MAAS NORTH
TSS MAAS NORTHWEST
TSS MAAS WEST INNER
TSS MAAS WEST OUTER
TSS NORTH HINDER NORTH
Radar surveillance
Maas Approach Ch 01
Maas Centre
Maas Centre
Racon M
Maas Junction
North Hinder Junction
North Hinder Junction Precautionary Area
Inshore Traffic Zone
Limit of Radar Area
Deep water route
Deep water approach area
Emergency turning area
Goeree Radar Racon (T)
Noord Hinder Racon T
MNW3-MW6
Racon O
MN1
MN2
MN3
MWN2
MW1
MW2
MW3
MW4
MW5
MG
MV
MV-N
Euro
Indusbank N
Radar Tr
Hoek van Holland
EUROPOORT
NHR-SE
52°N
3°E
4°E
50'
10'
20'
30'
40'
50'
10'

crossing, maintain continuous listening watch and keep a very sharp lookout.

NIEUWE WATERWEG VTS. Outer areas as shown on VTS Charts 3 & 4: **Maas Approach** Ch 01. **Pilot Maas** Ch 02. **Maas Entrance** Ch 03.

HCC *Central Traffic Control* Ch 14 19. Report to/ monitor continuously the relevant Tfc Centre, as listed from seaward to City Marina: Rozenburg Ch 65; Maassluis Ch 80; Botlek Ch 61; Eemhaven Ch 63; Waalhaven Ch 60; Maasbruggen Ch 81.

ROTTERDAM Rotterdam Tfc Centre Ch 11. **Hbr Coordination Centre** (HCC) Ch 19. **Marinas/ Yacht hbrs: Vlaardingen** ☎ 010 2484333; Lock Ch 20. **Spuihaven** ☎ 4667765, mob 0644326722. Coolhaven ☎ 4764146. **Veerhaven** ☎ 4365446, mob 0653536107. **City Marina** ☎ 48540986, via Erasmus bridge Ch 18.

STELLENDAM Haringvliet lock & lifting bridge: *Goereese Sluis* Ch 20, ☎ 0187 497350. Opening hrs: M-F 0000-2200. 1 Nov - 1 Apr: Sat 0800-2200; Sun 0800-1000, 1600-1800. 1 Apr - 1 Nov: Sat & Sun 0800-2000. **Marina** Ch 31, ☎ 493769.

OOSTERSCHELDE Lock *Roompotsluis* Ch 18, ☎ 0111 659265. Opening hours: Mon & Thu, 0000-2200; Tue & Sun, 0600-0000; Wed H24; Fri & Sat: 0600-2200.

Roompot Marina Ch 31.

WESTERSCHELDE VTS See VTS Chart No 3. Reporting is not compulsory for leisure craft, but they should monitor the VHF channel for the appropriate Traffic Area. Each Traffic Area is controlled by a Traffic Centre and bounded by buoys. *In emergency call the relevant Traffic Centre: Ch 67*.

Tfc Centre Steenbank & Radar Ch 64.

Tfc Centre Vlissingen Ch 14. **Radar** Ch 21. **Info broadcast** Ch 14 H+55.

Tfc Centre Terneuzen & Radar Ch 03. **Info broadcast** Ch 11 H+00.

Tfc Centre Hansweert Ch 65.

Antwerpen, Zeebrugge and Wandelaar Traffic Areas are listed under Belgium.

VLISSINGEN De Ruyter Marina no VHF, ☎ 0118 414498, mobile 06 5353 7181. *Flushing Port Control* Ch 09. **Sealocks & canal bridge** Ch 22. **VVW Schelde Marina** Ch 14, ☎ 465912 / 0615538515.

BRESKENS Marina, Ch 31, ☎ 0117 381902.

TERNEUZEN Port control Ch 11. **Marina**, ☎ 0115 697089. **Oostsluis** (E lock, small craft) Ch 18.

BELGIUM

ANTWERPEN, Tfc Centre Zandvliet Ch 12. **Info broadcast** Ch 12 H+35.

ANTWERPEN PORT Calling and safety Ch 74. **Royerssluis** Ch 22. **Siberia & Londen bridges** Ch 62. **Willemdok Marina** Ch 23, ☎ 03 2315066. **Linkeroever Marina** Ch 09, ☎ 03 2190895.

ZEEBRUGGE Tfc Centre Zeebrugge Ch 69. **Info broadcasts** Ch 69 H+15.

ZEEBRUGGE Port Control Ch 71 H24, ☎ 050 546867/550801. **Marina** ☎ 544903. **E lock** Ch 68.

BLANKENBERGE Marinas: VNZ, ☎ 050 429150, **& SYCB**, ☎ 411420, Ch 31. **VVW** ☎ 417536, Ch 23.

WANDELAAR Tfc Centre Wandelaar Ch 65. **Wandelaar Approach** Ch 60.

OOSTENDE Port Control Ch 09 H24, ☎ 059 566313. **Mercator lock**, ☎ 321669, **& marina**, ☎ 705762: Ch 14 H24. **Marinas**: RNSYC, ☎ 505912. RYCO, ☎ 321452.

NIEUWPOORT Port HM Ch 60 H24, ☎ 058 233000. **Marinas: KYCN**, Ch 23, ☎ 234413. **WSKLM**, Ch 23, ☎ 5233641. **VVW-N**, Ch 08, ☎ 235232.

NORTH FRANCE

DUNKERQUE Port & VTS Ch 73, H24. The VTS does not affect leisure craft, but monitor Ch 73. **Marinas** Ch 09: Grande Large ☎ 03.28.63.23.00. YCMN ☎ 03.28.66.79.90. **Trystram lock** Ch 14.

GRAVELINES HM/Marina, Ch 09, ☎ 03·59·73·42·42.

CALAIS VTS, Port Control & Marina Ch 17 H24, ☎ 03.21.34.55.23.

BOULOGNE Boulogne Port, ☎ 03.21.31.52.43, Ch 12, H24. **Marina** Ch 09, ☎ 06.76.98.74.98 / 03.21.99.66.50.

LE TOUQUET/ÉTAPLES-SUR-MER Ch 09, 77. **Étaples Marina**, ☎ 03.21.84.54.03.

LE TRÉPORT Marina/lock Ch 12, 72, ☎ 02.35.50.63.06

DIEPPE Port HM Ch 12, HO. **Marina** Ch 09, ☎ 02.35.40.19.79.

ST VALÉRY-EN-CAUX Entry gate & marina Ch 09, ☎ 02.35.97.01.30.

FÉCAMP Port HM, Ch 10, **12**, ☎ 02.35.28.25.53. **Marina & Bérigny lock**, Ch 09, ☎ 02.35.28.13.58.

LE HAVRE Control Tower Ch **12**, 20. **Port Ops** Ch 67, 69. **Marina**, Ch 09, ☎ 02.35.21.23.95.

LA SEINE VTS Rouen Port Control Ch 73 (Estuary), 68 (River). **Honfleur radar** Ch 15, 19, **73**.

HONFLEUR HM Ch **17,** 73 HX, ☎ 02.31.14.61.09. **Lock**, ☎ 02.31.98.72.82, **& Bridge** Ch 17 H24.

ROUEN Port HM Ch **73,** 68 H24. **Halte Nautique**, ☎ 02.35.07.33.94. **Marina** ☎ 02.35.08.30.59.

ROUEN – PARIS, LOCKS Amfreville Ch 18. **Notre-Dame-de-la-Garenne** Ch 22. **Mericourt** Ch 18. **Andrésy** Ch 22. **Bougival** Ch 22. **Chatou** Ch 18. **Suresnes** Ch 22. **PARIS-ARSENAL Marina** Ch 09, ☎ 01.43.41.39.32.

DEAUVILLE Port Deauville lock, ☎ 02.31.88.95.66; Marina ☎ 02.31.98.30.01, Ch 09 0800-1730. **Port Morny** gate ☎ 02.31.88.57.89; Marina, Ch 09, ☎ 02.31.98.50.40.

DIVES-SUR-MER. Marina Ch 09, ☎ 02.31.24.48.00.

OUISTREHAM Port 74; lock Ch 12, ☎ 02.31.36.22.00.

Marina Ch 09, ☎ 02.31.96.91.37. **Canal** Ch 68. **CAEN HM/Marina** Ch 74, ☎ 02.31.95.24.47.

COURSEULLES-SUR-MER Marina Ch 09, ☎ 02.31.37.51.69.

PORT-EN-BESSIN HM, ☎ 02.31.21.70.49. **Gate/bridge** Ch 18, ☎ 02.31.21.71.77.

GRANDCAMP Marina Ch 09, ☎ 02.31.22.63.16.

CARENTAN Lock Ch 09, ☎ 02.33.71.10.85. **Marina** Ch 09, ☎ 02.33.42.24.44.

ST VAAST-LA-HOUGUE Marina Ch 09, ☎ 02.33.21.61.00.

BARFLEUR HM, ☎ 02.33.54.08.29. No VHF.

CHERBOURG VTS (yachts to monitor) *Vigie du Homet* Ch 12 H24. **Marina** *Chantereyne* Ch 09, ☎ 02.33.87.65.70. **Gate** (B du Commerce) Ch 06.

OMONVILLE-LA-ROGUE No VHF/Tel. 6 W ⚓s.

DIÉLETTE Marina Ch 09, ☎ 02.33.53.68.78.

CARTERET Marina Ch 09, ☎ 02.33.04.70.84.

PORTBAIL Yacht hbr Ch 09, ☎ 02.33.04.83.48.

GRANVILLE Port HM Ch 12. **Marina** Ch 09, ☎ 02.33.50.20.06.

ST MALO Port HM Ch 12 H24. **Marinas** Ch 09: **Bas Sablons**, ☎ 02.99.81.71.34. **Bassin Vauban**, ☎ 02.99.56.51.91. **DINARD**, ☎ 02.99.46.65.55.

R RANCE barrage lock Ch 13, ☎ 02.99.46.21.87. **Chatelier lock** Ch 14, ☎ 02.99.39.55.66.

ST CAST-LE-GUILDO Marina ☎ 02 96 81 04 43

DAHOUËT Marina Ch 09, ☎ 02.96.72.82.85.

LE LÉGUÉ HM/Marina Ch 12, ☎ 02.96.77.49.85.

BINIC Marina Ch 09, ☎ 02.96.73.61.86.

ST QUAY-PORTRIEUX Marina ☎ 02.96.70.81.30. Ch 09.

PAIMPOL Lock/Marina Ch 09, ☎ 02.96.20.47.65.

LÉZARDRIEUX Marina Ch 09, ☎ 02.96.20.14.22.

PONTRIEUX Lock/Marina Ch 12, ☎ 02.96.95.34.87.

TRÉGUIER Marina Ch 09, ☎ 02.96.92.42.37.

PERROS-GUIREC Marina Ch 09, ☎ 02.96.49.80.50.

PLOUMANAC'H Marina Ch 09, ☎ 02.96.91.44.31.

TRÉBEURDEN Marina Ch 09, ☎ 02.96.23.64.00.

MORLAIX Lock, ☎ 06.77.50.15.90 / 02.98.88.15.10. **Marina** Ch 09, ☎ 02.98.62.13.14.

ROSCOFF HM/S Basin Ch 09, ☎ 02.98.69.76.37.

ROSCOFF Marina Ch 09, ☎ 02.98.79.79.49. **Ferry Port** Ch 12, ☎ 02.98.61.27.84.

L'ABERWRACH Marina Ch 09, ☎ 02.98.04.91.62.

CHANNEL ISLANDS

ALDERNEY, Braye Hbr, *Alderney Coastguard* Ch 67, ☎ 01481 822620. Otherwise, try *Guernsey Coastguard*. *Alderney Port Control* Ch 74.

GUERNSEY Beaucette Marina, Ch 80, ☎ 01481 245000. **St Sampson** Ch 12 H24 via **St Peter Port** Control Ch 12 H24, ☎ 720229. **Victoria Marina** Ch 80 HO, ☎ 725987. *Guernsey Coastguard* Ch 20 H24 (Ch 62 for emergecy link calls).

JERSEY St Helier Port Control Ch 14 H24; 8M max range. **St Helier Marina,** ☎ 01534 447730/447708, has no VHF; call Ch 14 only if essential. **Gorey** Ch 74, ☎ 853616.

WEST FRANCE

BREST VTS *Brest Port* Ch 08 H24. **Marinas** Ch 09. **Marina du Chateau,** ☎ 02·98·33·12·50. **Port du Moulin Blanc,** ☎ 02·98·33·12·50.

CAMARET Marina Ch 09, ☎ 02.98.27.95.99.

MORGAT Marina Ch 09, ☎ 02.98.27.01.97.

DOUARNENEZ HM Ch 12. **Marinas** Ch 09: Tréboul ☎ 02.98.74.02.56; Port Rhu ☎ 02.98.92.00.67.

AUDIERNE HM Ch 09. **Marina** ☎ 02.98.74.04.93. **Ste Evette** ☎ 02.98.70.00.28.

LOCTUDY Marina Ch 09, ☎ 02.98.87.51.36.

BENODÉT Marinas Ch 09: Penfoul ☎ 02.98.57.05.78. **Ste Marine** ☎ 02.98.56.38.72.

PORT-LA-FORÊT Marina Ch 09, ☎ 02.98.56.98.45.

CONCARNEAU Marina Ch 09, ☎ 02.98.97.57.96.

LORIENT Port Ch 12. **Marinas** Ch 09: Ban-Gâvres ☎ 02.97.65.48.25. Kernével ☎ 02.97.65.48.25. Port Louis ☎ 02.97.83.59.55. Locmiquélic ☎ 02.97.33.59.51. Lorient ☎ 02.97.21.10.14.

PORT TUDY Marina Ch 09, ☎ 02.97.86.54.62.

RIVER ÉTEL Marina Ch 13, ☎ 02.97.55.46.62.

BELLE ILE Sauzon HM Ch 09, ☎ 02.97.31.63.40. **Le Palais** HM Ch 09, ☎ 02.97.31.42.90.

PORT HALIGUEN Marina Ch 09, ☎ 02.97.50.20.56.

LA TRINITÉ Marina Ch 09, ☎ 02.97.55.71.49.

VANNES Marina Ch 09 (0800-1200, 1500-1900 July-Aug), ☎ 02.97.01.55.20.

CROUESTY Marina Ch 09, ☎ 02.97.53.73.33.

LA VILAINE Arzal Marina Ch 09, ☎ 02.97.45.02.97.

PIRIAC Marina Ch 09, ☎ 02.40.23.52.32.

LA TURBALLE Marina Ch 09, ☎ 02.40.23.41.65.

LE CROISIC Marina Ch 09, ☎ 09.81.12.75.92.

LE POULIGUEN Marina Ch 09, ☎ 02.40.11.97.97.

PORNICHET Marina Ch 09, ☎ 02.40.61.03.20.

ST-NAZAIRE VTS *Loire Ports Control* Ch 14. **Port HM** Ch 14, ☎ 02.40.00.45.89.

PORNIC Marina Ch 09, ☎ 02.40.82.05.40.

L'HERBAUDIÈRE Marina Ch 09, ☎ 02.51.39.05.05.

PORT JOINVILLE Marina Ch 09, ☎ 02.51.58.38.11.

ST GILLES CROIX DE VIE Marina Ch 09, ☎ 02.51.55.30.83.

LES SABLES D'OLONNE Port HM Ch 12, ☎ 02.51.95.11.79. **Marina** Ch 09, ☎ 02.51.32.51.16.

BOURGENAY Marina Ch 09, ☎ 02.51.22.20.36.

ILE DE RÉ Ars-en-Ré Ch 09, ☎ 05.46.29.08.52. **St Martin** Ch 09, ☎ 05.46.09.26.69.

LA ROCHELLE Marinas Ch 09: **Port des Minimes** ☎ 05.46.44.41.20. **Vieux Port** ☎ 05.46.41.32.05.

ROCHEFORT Marina Ch 09, ☎ 05.46.83.99.06.

ILE D'OLÉRON St Denis Ch 09, ☎ 05.46.47.97.97. **Boyardville** Ch 09, ☎ 05.46.76.48.56.

LA GIRONDE VTS Ch 12 (yachts to monitor). **Radar** *Bordeaux Port Control* Ch 12 on request. Depths in Gironde broadcast Ch 17 every 5 mins.

ROYAN Marina Ch 09, ☎ 05.46.38.72.22.

COAST RADIO STATIONS

Coast Radio Stations (CRS) deal with public correspondence (and a few other things). They enable a yachtsman to be linked by radio into the public telephone system in order to converse with a subscriber ashore, ie he can make or receive a Link call.

However the mobile 'phone has to a great extent rendered Link calls obsolescent. Thus there are no longer any CRS in the UK, France and Netherlands. In Germany a limited service is provided by a commercial company (see below).

CRS still operate in the Channel Islands, Ireland*, Denmark, Belgium, Spain and Portugal; see below. But they too may gradually be withdrawn. *In Ireland CRS no longer handle commercial link calls, but Medico link calls are still available on both VHF and MF.

The CG does **not** handle Link calls, except in Denmark and Belgium where the functions of CG and CRS have always been co-located.

CHANNEL ISLANDS

GUERNSEY COASTGUARD 49°27'·00N 02°32'00W ☎ 01481 720672 📠 01534 714177
Emergency link calls on **Ch 62** only. Ch 20 is used for navigation, pilotage and ships' business

JERSEY COAST GUARD 49°10'·85N 02°14'30W ☎ 01534 447705 📠 01534 499089
Link calls on **Ch 25** only

REPUBLIC OF IRELAND

A Coast Radio service is provided by the Dept of the Marine, Leeson Lane, Dublin 2, Eire. ☎ +353 (0)1 662 0922; ext 670 for enquiries. Broadcasts are made on a working channel/frequency following a prior announcement on Ch 16 and 2182 kHz. Ch 67 is used for Safety messages only.
VHF calls to an Irish Coast Radio Station should be made on a working channel. Only use Ch 16 in case of difficulty or in emergency.

NW and SE Ireland

Weather broadcasts at 0103, 0403, 0703, 1003, 1303, 1603, 1903, 2203 UT and at 0033, 0633, 1233, 1833 UT on the VHF Channels below. Nav warnings are broadcast at 0033, 0433, 0833, 1233, 1633 and 2033 UT.

Clifden Radio	53°30'N 09°56'W	Ch 26
Belmullet Radio	54°16'N 10°03'W	Ch 83
Donegal Bay	54°22'N 08°31'W	Ch 02
Glen Head Radio	54°44'N 08°43'W	Ch 24
MALIN HD RADIO	55°22'N 07°21'W	Ch 23
MF 1677 kHz, ☎ +353 (0) 77 70103		
MMSI 002500100 DSC: 2187·5 kHz		
Carlingford Radio	54°05'N 06°19'W	Ch 04
DUBLIN RADIO	53°23'N 06°04'W	Ch 83
Wicklow Hd Radio	52°58'N 06°00'W	Ch 02
Rosslare Radio	52°15'N 06°20'W	Ch 23
Mine Hd Radio	52°00'N 07°35'W	Ch 83

SW Ireland

Weather is broadcast at 0103, 0403, 0703, 1003, 1303, 1603, 1903, 2203 and at 0033, 0633, 1233, 1833 UT on the VHF Channels listed.
Navwarnings are broadcast every 4 hrs from 0233.

Cork Radio	51°51'N 08°29'W	Ch 26
Mizen Radio	51°34'N 09°33'W	Ch 04
Bantry Radio	51°38'N 10°00'W	Ch 23
VALENTIA RADIO	51°56'N 10°21'W	Ch 24
MF 1752 kHz, ☎ + 353 (0) 66947 6109		
MMSI 002500200, DSC: 2187·5 kHz		
Shannon Radio	52°31'N 09°36'W	Ch 28
Galway Bay Radio	53°18'N 09°07'W	Ch 04

DENMARK

All VHF/MF CRS are remotely controlled from Lyngby Radio (55°50N 11°25'E) (MMSI 002191000). The callsign for all stations is Lyngby Radio. Call on working frequencies to help keep Ch 16 clear. The stations listed below monitor Ch 16 H24 and Ch 70 DSC. Traffic lists are broadcast on all VHF channels every odd H+05. All MF stations, except Skagen, keep watch H24 on 2182 kHz. Blåvand, Skagen and Lyngby also monitor MF 2187·5 kHz DSC. MF DSC Public correspondence facilities are available from Blåvand and Skagen on 1624·5 and 2177 kHz.

VHF & MF CRS		
Skagen	57°44'N 10°35'E	Ch 04, Ch 28
	MF: Tx 1758, Rx 2102	
Hirtshals	57°31'N 09°57'E	Ch 66
Hanstholm	57°07'N 08°39'E	Ch 01
Bovbjerg	56°32'N 08°10'E	Ch 02
	MF: Tx 1767, Rx 2111	
Blåvand	55°33'N 08°07'E	Ch 23
	MF: Tx 1734, Rx 2078	

GERMANY

CRS: DPO7 – Seefunk (Hamburg) *(MMSI 002113100).* All stns monitor DSC Ch 70 and 16. Traffic lists are broadcast (LT): 0745, 0945, 1245, 1645, 1945 and H & H+30 on request Ch 16.

Nordfriesland	54°31'N 08°41'E	Ch 26
Elbe-Weser	53°50'N 08°39'E	Ch 24
Hamburg	53°33'N 09°58'E	Ch 83
Bremen	53°05'N 08°48'E	Ch 25
Accumersiel	53°40'N 07°29'E	Ch 28
Borkum	53°35'N 06°40'E	Ch 61

SHAPES

♦	Towing vessel - length of tow > 200m	**Rule 24**
▼	Yacht under sail *and* power	**Rule 25**
⧗	Vessel fishing or trawling	**Rule 26**
⧗+▲	Vessel fishing with outlying gear >150m long	**Rule 26**
● ♦ ●	Vessel restricted in her ability to manoeuvre	**Rule 27**
● ●	Vessel not under command	**Rule 27**
▮	Vessel constrained by her draught	**Rule 28**
●	Vessel at anchor	**Rule 30**

SOUND SIGNALS

MANOEUVRING AND WARNING Rule 34

•	A short blast = about 1 second.
–	A prolonged blast = 4 – 6 seconds.
•	I am altering course to **Starboard**
••	I am altering course to **Port**
•••	My engines are going **Astern**
•••••	I do not understand your intentions/ actions

Note: The above sound signals may be supplemented by light signals flashed on an all-round white light with least range of 5 miles.

In a narrow channel

– – •	I intend to overtake on your starboard side.
– – ••	I intend to overtake on your port side.
– • – •	I agree with your overtaking signal
–	Warning by vessel nearing a bend where other vessels may not be seen
–	Approaching vessel acknowledges.

VESSELS IN RESTRICTED VISIBILITY Rule 35

–	Power-driven vessel making way.
– –	Power-driven vessel underway, but stopped and not making way.
– ••	**A sailing vessel**; vessels not under command; restricted in ability to manoeuvre; constrained by draught; engaged in fishing, towing or pushing.
– •••	Vessel being towed or, if more than one vessel is towed, the last vessel in the tow.

VESSELS AT ANCHOR

🔔	Bell, ring for 5 seconds every minute
🔔	Vessel >100m: Bell forward, ring for 5 seconds every minute; plus
⊙	Gong aft, for 5 seconds every minute.
• – •	Optional extra to warn any approaching vessel

Sailing vessels < 12m at ⚓ do not have to sound the above fog signals. But if they do not, they *must* make an efficient noise every 2 minutes.

INTERNATIONAL PORT TRAFFIC SIGNALS (IPTS)

IPTS are widely used on the Continent, but less so around the UK. They may also be used to control traffic at locks and bridges.

No	Lights		Main message
1	(R) (R) (R) (flashing)	Flashing	Serious emergency – all vessels to stop or divert according to instructions
2	(R) (R) (R)	Fixed or Slow Occulting	Vessels shall not proceed (*Note:* Some ports may use an exemption signal, as in 2a below)
3	(G) (G) (G)	Fixed or Slow Occulting	Vessels may proceed. One-way traffic
4	(G) (G) (W)	Fixed or Slow Occulting	Vessels may proceed. Two-way traffic
5	(G) (W) (G)	Fixed or Slow Occulting	A vessel may proceed only when she has received specific orders to do so. (*Note:* Some ports may use an exemption signal, as in 5a below)
			Exemption signals and messages
2a	(Y) (R) (R) (R)	Fixed or Slow Occulting	Vessels shall not proceed, except that vessels which navigate outside the main channel need not comply with the main message
5a	(Y) (G) (W) (G)	Fixed or Slow Occulting	A vessel may proceed when she has received specific orders to do so, except that vessels which navigate outside the main channel need not comply with the main message
			Auxiliary signals and messages
White and/or yellow lights, displayed with the main lights			

- The main movement signal is always 3 lights in a vertical column, to which no extra light shall be added. Thus it is always recognisable as IPTS, as distinct from some kind of navigational lights.
- Red lights Ⓡ indicate ***Do not proceed.***
- Green lights Ⓖ indicate ***Proceed, subject to the conditions stipulated***. To avoid confusion Ⓡ and Ⓖ lights are never displayed together.
- Signals may be omni-directional ie seen by all vessels simultaneously; or directional, ie seen only from outside or from inside the harbour.
- Some ports may only use signals 2 and 4, or only Signal 1 when necessary
- Signal 1 ***Serious Emergency*** must show at least 60 flashes/minute.
- All other signals may be fixed or slow occulting, eg every 10s (helpful when background glare poses a problem), but never a mixture of both.
- Signal 5 assumes that VHF, signal lamp, loud-hailer, auxiliary signal or other means of communication will specifically inform a vessel that she may proceed.
- Exemption signals. A single Ⓨ light, shown to the left of signals 2 or 5 and level with the upper light, means ***Vessels which can safely navigate outside the main channel need not comply with the main message.*** This signal is obviously important to small craft, which nevertheless have a clear duty to keep clear of manoeuvring vessels.
- Auxiliary signals (only Ⓦ and/or Ⓨ lights) may be locally authorised and displayed to the right of the main signal. Their meanings must be promulgated.

COMMUNICATIONS

Chapter 4 – Safety

ANCHORING

Much is written in Skippers' handbooks and the boating press about anchoring. It is a simple concept – securing a boat to the seabed using an anchor or weight or combination of the two.

Many pages have been devoted to the advantages and capabilities of different designs of anchors. The Bruce, CQR and Danforth have largely given way to modern variants which claim greater holding power and better 'burial' characteristics. Guidance is also available on calculating the length of cable needed for a given depth of water and the approach to the anchorage position. Less has been written on anchoring safely among other boats and exercising due consideration.

In the vicinity of larger yacht harbours and along the south coast of the UK in particular, some spots are greatly favoured as anchorages. Often these are frequented for lunchtime stops, swimming or entertaining children. In settled weather boats enjoy the freedom to anchor in these bays for several days away from the bustle of busy marinas. Increasingly boats can be seen huddled in anchorages, too close for comfort or good seamanship and with little room for manoeuvre.

In planning an overnight anchorage, it is normal to lay out a length of chain/warp equal to up to five times the depth of water at the top of the tide. Typically this may equate to 4 boat lengths. However in busy anchorages it is common to see boats anchoring within 2-3 boat lengths of one another. This is barely acceptable if the conditions are good, the position of anchors known, the boats manned, and their characteristics similar.

Different boats lie at varying angles to the wind; a high sided power boat or catamaran will 'sail' more on its anchor than a deep keeled yacht of equal size owing to their greater windage. The latter will be much more influenced by the prevailing current or tidal stream. The combination of wind on the bow and current on the keel may result in such a yacht lying across the stream. If boats are alike they are more likely to lie to an anchor at about the same angle to wind and current. More importantly they have a better chance of swinging to a new direction at about the same time. Even so it is difficult to know how much ground tackle has been deployed, and how close another boat may be to its anchor. It may have 10m of warp deployed, but be sitting close to or over the 'hook'. The scope of the cable will increase as the tide ebbs. If insufficient room is left the swinging circles of boats may well overlap – and often does. *Leave adequate space*!

Worse still a boat may inadvertently drop its own anchor closer to another's than intended. Modern practice often avoids the use of anchor marking buoys and without them the position of other anchors is a matter of guesswork.

There are three types of anchor 'rode' or cable; chain, warp or a combination. The length and weight of the cable is important. It damps the motion of the boat through the action of the catenary delivering the pull to the anchor at a suitable angle – preferably along the seabed. Frequently boats rely on short 'rodes' and are susceptible to changes in weather, tidal height and even wakes. Any of these may cause the anchor to drag if insufficient cable is deployed.

Many Skippers seem to seek the security of being amongst other boats for the night. In reality more hazards are created in anchorages by boat users than by the weather. Not only do boats anchor too closely often with too little cable, but frequently pay scant attention to the position of the anchor. Few take bearings of the anchor's position or calculate a swinging circle. Many do not hoist an anchor ball and some do not have an anchor light at night. Almost none keep an anchor watch. *Boats do drag*! Room is invaluable; especially if rudely awoken and disorientated at night.

When weighing anchor there is a period as the anchor is recovered when the boat is neither made fast to the ground nor free to manoeuvre. In poor conditions it is easy to get set down rapidly onto an adjacent boat. This can be exacerbated if the anchor is fouled or there is a tangle on deck.

It is easy to misjudge the forces exerted as a boat rides to its anchor in a moderate breeze. Weight on the cable can change suddenly as the bow pays off. Pitching adds to the difficulty. Fingers are nipped and sometimes lost on the foredeck. Keep hands clear of capstan, fittings and roller. Use a sail tie or rope tail to move chain or a judicious boot to free any stoppage when slipping.

DISTRESS, URGENCY, SAFETY

MAYDAY (Distress) must only be used if a ship or person is in ***grave and imminent danger and requires immediate assistance.*** It is appropriate for a man overboard if not quickly recovered.

PAN-PAN (Urgency) is appropriate for ***a very urgent message concerning the safety of a vessel or person.***

SÉCURITÉ (Safety) is used typically by coast stations to announce navigational or weather warnings. May also be used by vessels to report a hazard.

DISTRESS CALL BY RADIO

A distress call may only be made with the skipper's authority, and only if the ***boat or a person*** is in ***grave and imminent danger***. The initial call may be made by DSC or voice.

Distress alert by DSC

Depending on the particular layout of your radio, a distress alert is typically sent as follows:

> Briefly press the red, guarded Distress button. The set will automatically switch to Ch 70. Press ***again*** for 5 seconds to transmit a basic distress alert* with position and time. The set then reverts to Ch 16.
>
> *If time permits, select the nature of the distress from the menu (eg Collision, Fire, Flooding) then press the Distress button for 5 seconds to send a full distress alert.

A CG/CRS should automatically send a distress acknowledgement on Ch 70 before replying on Ch 16. Ships in range should reply directly on Ch 16. If a distress acknowledgement is not received from a CG/CRS, the distress alert will automatically be repeated by the radio every four minutes.

> When a DSC distress acknowledgement has been received, or after about 15 seconds, the vessel in distress should transmit a MAYDAY message by voice on Ch 16 (see below), including its MMSI and callsign.

False alerts

If a distress alert is inadvertently transmitted, an All Stations voice message on VHF Ch 16 cancelling the false alert must be sent at once: 'Cancel my Distress Alert of (date/time (GMT/UT)'.

MAYDAY call by voice

The MAYDAY message format below should be displayed near the radio. A MAYDAY call by voice should usually be sent on VHF Ch 16. A distress call has priority over all other transmissions. If you hear a MAYDAY call, immediately cease all transmissions that may interfere with the call, listen on the frequency concerned and note down the details.

Before making the call check that the radio is ON, and that HIGH POWER (25 watts) and Ch 16 are selected.

Press and hold down the transmit button, and say slowly and distinctly:

> **MAYDAY MAYDAY MAYDAY**
>
> **THIS IS** ....
> (name of boat, spoken three times)
>
> **MAYDAY** ....
> (name of boat spoken once & MMSI No)
>
> **MY POSITION IS** ....
> (latitude and longitude or true bearing and distance *from* a known point)
>
> **Nature of distress** ....
> (sinking, on fire etc)
>
> **Help required** ....
> (immediate assistance)
>
> **Number of persons on board** ....
> **Any other important, helpful information** ..
> (you are taking to the liferaft; distress rockets are being fired etc)
>
> **OVER**

Release the transmit button and listen.

MAYDAY acknowledgement

An acknowledgement should be expected:

> **MAYDAY** ....
> (name of vessel sending the distress message, spoken three times)
>
> **THIS IS** ....
> (name of station acknowledging, spoken three times)
>
> **RECEIVED MAYDAY**

If an acknowledgement is not received, check the set and repeat the distress call.

If you hear a distress message, write down the details and, if you can help, acknowledge accordingly but only after giving an opportunity for the nearest Coastguard station or more suitable vessel to do so.

MAYDAY relay

If you hear a distress message from a vessel which is not acknowledged, you should pass on the message as follows:

> **MAYDAY RELAY** ....
> (spoken three times)
>
> **THIS IS** ....
> (name of vessel re-transmitting the distress message, spoken three times), followed by the intercepted message.

HELICOPTER RESCUE

- **COMMUNICATE ON CHANNEL 16**
- Use flares or smoke when helicopter is seen or heard
- Helicopter may ask you to drop sails and motor on a specific course
- You may be asked to stream the casualty astern in the dinghy
- Brief your crew early (too noisy when helicopter is close)
- **MAINTAIN YOUR COURSE** and do not get distracted
- Weighted line lowered
- Let it touch boat or water first (to earth any static charge)
- Take in slack line only
- **PULL LINE IN AS DIRECTED**
- **DO NOT SECURE IT TO THE BOAT**
- **DO EXACTLY AS YOU ARE TOLD**

Note: The text and sketch relate to a Hi-line transfer, one of several techniques which may be used

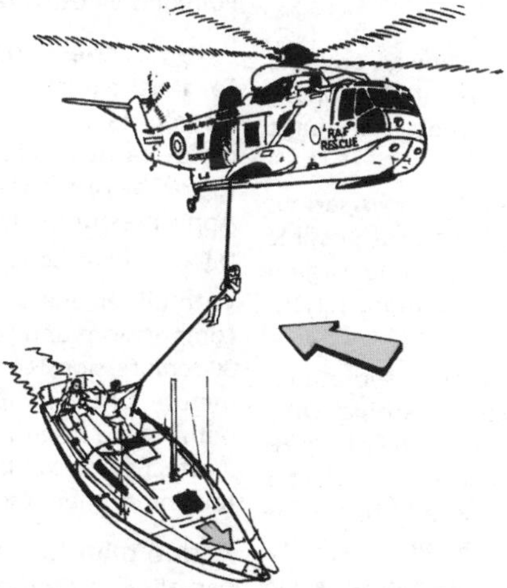

URGENT MEDICAL HELP - PAN PAN

- **Send an URGENCY call by DSC**, if possible, and/or...
- **Make a PAN PAN voice call:**
- **CHANNEL 16, HIGH POWER (25W)** (if necessary, turn off dual watch)
- **PAN PAN** .... (repeat 3 times)
- **ALL STATIONS** .... (repeat 3 times)
- **THIS IS** .... (vessel's name; repeat 3 times)
- **OVER**

Next message should include:

Yacht's name, callsign, nationality
Yacht's position and nearest harbour
Patient's details, symptoms and advice wanted
The medication you have on board

SAFETY

FIRST AID

The objectives of First Aid at sea are to:

- **Preserve life** • **Prevent further damage**
- **Relieve pain and distress**
- **Deliver a live casualty ashore**

With any casualty be calm, reassuring and methodical. First ensure your own safety and that of the vessel. If in doubt call for advice and assistance.

Completion of a First Aid Course is strongly recommended. In the UK, RYA approved, one-day, basic training is available through sailing clubs and schools. The St Johns Ambulance and British Red Cross provide a variety of recognised courses.

MEDICAL ADVICE can be obtained almost anywhere in European waters by making an All Stations 'PAN PAN' call or a DSC Urgency Alert to the Coastguard or to a Coast Radio Station. You will then be connected to a doctor or to the nearest hospital.

The Urgency signal 'PAN PAN' is always advised, especially abroad, because it is internationally understood and eliminates most language problems; it is also free.

If you are not qualified to judge how serious the casualty's condition is, get the best possible advice and/or help as quickly as possible. **Urgent help needed** is shown against the more serious medical problems.

Be ready to describe the patient's symptoms, eg consciousness, pulse rate, breathing rate, temperature, skin colour, site and type of injury, any pain, amount of blood lost etc. If a doctor needs to come aboard, or a casualty has to be landed, the Coastguard will arrange.

If non-urgent, wait until in harbour. Consider calling the port authority before arrival so that a doctor or paramedic can meet you on arrival.

MEDICAL CARE ABROAD It is advisable for each person on board to carry the European Health Insurance Card (EHIC) which entitles you to medical treatment on a reciprocal basis, although it may not cover the full charge. See *www.dh.gov.uk* for full details.

EMERGENCY RESUSCITATION (ABC)

The immediate procedure for any collapsed or apparently unconscious person is: Assess whether or not the casualty is conscious. Carefully shake his/her shoulders and ask loudly 'What's happened?' or 'Are you all right?' or give a command such as 'Open your eyes'. An unconscious casualty will not respond.

A = Airway

Remove any visible obstruction from the casualty's mouth (leave well-fitting dentures in place). Listen at the mouth for breathing. Tilt the head backwards, using head tilt and chin lift to maintain a clear airway.

Look, listen and feel for ***no more than 10 seconds*** to determine if the casualty is breathing normally. If in any doubt, act as if it is ***not*** normal.

If breathing, place casualty in recovery position. Check the area is clear of danger.

B = Breathing and C = Circulation

If not breathing and the airway is clear, start chest compressions. This situation is called **cardiac arrest**. The casualty will be unconscious and may appear very pale, grey or bluish in colour. An artificial circulation will have to be provided by chest compression. If the circulation stops, the breathing will also stop. Casualties with cardiac arrest will need both rescue breathing and chest compression, a combination known as Cardio Pulmonary Resuscitation (**CPR**).

External chest compression

To start external chest compression, lay the casualty face up on a hard, flat surface. Kneel beside casualty. Place the heel of your hand on top of the other hand and interlock your fingers. Apply pressure at the centre of the chest.

Depress breastbone 5–6cm (2-2½in) then release.

With either one or two operators give 30 chest compressions and continue cycles of 2 breaths to 30 compressions. Use a compression rate of 100 per minute. Chest compression should be combined with rescue breaths; after 30 compressions, give 2 effective rescue breaths (2 breaths should not take more than 5 seconds). *Do not stop.*

Action plan for the resuscitation of adults

Casualty unconscious but is breathing normally:

- ***Urgent help needed***
- Turn casualty into the recovery position
- Check for continued breathing

Casualty is unconscious and not breathing:

- ***Urgent help needed***
- Start chest compressions
- After 30 compressions, give 2 rescue breaths

Continue with chest compressions and rescue breaths in a ratio of 30:2. If you are untrained, or are unwilling to give rescue breaths, give chest compressions only. Stop to re-check casualty only if he/she starts to show signs of regaining consciousness; coughing, opening eyes, speaking or moving purposefully ***and*** starts to breath normally. If so place the casualty in the recovery position. Otherwise, ***do not interrupt resuscitation***.

BITES AND STINGS Injected poison from bites and stings usually only causes local swelling and discomfort, but some people may react severely. For insect stings, resuscitate if collapse occurs; otherwise give rest, painkillers, antihistamines (eg chlorpheniramine).

BLEEDING – OPEN WOUND Bleeding is often very dramatic, but is virtually always controllable.

- Apply firm continuous direct pressure; bandage on a large pad. If bleeding continues, bandage more pads on top of initial pads; then press directly over wound for at least 10 minutes (blood takes this long to clot).
- Elevate if wound is on a limb.
- Do *not* apply a tourniquet. This practice is out of date due to the danger of losing a limb.

BLEEDING – INTERNAL (CLOSED INJURY)
Follows fractured bones, crush injuries, or rupture of organs such as the liver or spleen. Treat for shock which may appear rapidly. ***Urgent help needed***.

BURNS AND SCALDS Move the victim into fresh air to avoid inhaling smoke.

ABC – Airway, Breathing, Circulation

- Stop further injury: dip the whole of the burnt part into cold water for 10–15 minutes. Seawater is excellent but may be very painful.
- Remove only loose clothing. Do not pull off clothing stuck to the skin.
- Cover with sterile dressing. If skin is broken or blistered, use sterile paraffin gauze beneath the dressing. Separate burnt fingers with paraffin gauze. Never use adhesive dressings.
- Do not prick blisters or apply ointments.
- Elevate burnt limb and immobilise.
- Give strong painkillers.
- Treat for shock: give frequent and copious drinks of water.
- Start giving antibiotics for major burns. If burns extensive or deep, ***urgent help needed***.

CHOKING If blockage by some object (eg a peanut) is suspected, turn the casualty on his side and give up to 5 sharp back slaps with the flat of the hand between the shoulder blades. Check mouth and remove any obstruction.

If unsuccessful, wrap both arms around the victim's waist from behind, and give 5 sharp upward thrusts with both fists into the abdomen above the navel but below the ribs so as to cause coughing. Clear object from mouth.

CUTS AND WOUNDS Often dramatic but only potentially serious if nerves, tendons or blood vessels are severed.

Clean thoroughly with antiseptic. Remove dirt or other foreign bodies. Small clean cuts can be closed using as many Steristrips as necessary to keep the skin edges together. Skin must be dry. Leave for 5 days at least. Larger deep cuts may require stitches; apply a dressing and seek help. Do not try amateur surgery at sea.

Ragged lacerations or very dirty wounds – do not attempt to close these. Clean as well as possible, sprinkle antibiotic powder in wound and apply a dressing. Seek help. If in doubt a wound is best left open and lightly covered to keep it clean and dry.

Fingers and toes Blood may collect under the nail following an injury. Release the blood by piercing the nail with a red hot needle or paper clip. It will not hurt!

DENTAL PAIN seems worse at sea; prevention is better than cure. Dentanurse is an emergency treatment pack which enables an amateur to make temporary repairs, eg replacing crowns, lost fillings. It contains zinc oxide and Eugenol.

Throbbing toothache made worse by hot or cold or when bitten on. Clean out any cavity and apply temporary filling. Take painkiller.

Dull toothache tender to bite on; gum swollen or red with possible discharge. Treat as above but also take an antibiotic.

Broken tooth or filling Cover exposed surfaces with zinc oxide paste. Teeth knocked out should be put in a clean container with milk or moist gauze for a dentist to re-implant asap. This can be attempted onboard - ideally within 1 hour

Bleeding gums Clean teeth more thoroughly. Use regular hot salt water rinses and antibiotics.

Pain round wisdom tooth Clean area with toothbrush; use hot salt water rinses; take antibiotics and painkillers.

Mouth ulcers Hot salt water rinses.

DIARRHOEA Can become serious, especially in young children if much fluid is lost. Stop food, give plenty of fluid. Plain water is usually sufficient, or add salt (1 teaspoonful/litre) and sugar (4–5 teaspoons/litre). Lomotil or Imodium tablets are very effective in adults.

DROWNING ABC Clear seaweed, dentures. If not breathing start mouth to mouth ventilation as soon as possible and in the water if practicable. If no pulse, start chest compression as soon as on board. Keep the head low so that vomit is not inhaled and water can drain.

If stomach is bulging, turn casualty on to side to empty water and avoid inhaling it. Prevent cooling. Remove wet clothes; wrap casualty in blankets to warm him/her.

Continue resuscitation until the casualty revives or death is certain. Hypothermia may mimic death. Do not abandon resuscitation until the casualty has been warmed or signs of death persist despite attempts at warming.

Once revived, put in the recovery position.

Any person rescued from drowning may collapse in the next 24 hours as the lungs react to inhaled water. ***Urgent help needed***.

EYE INJURIES are potentially serious. Never put old or previously opened ointment or drops into an eye; serious infection could result.

Foreign object Flush with clean water, pull the lower lid out to inspect, remove object with a clean tissue. For objects under upper eyelid, ask casualty to grasp lashes and pull the upper lid over the lower lid. An eye-bath is very effective. Blinking under water may help. After removal of object, insert sterile antibiotic ointment inside pulled out lower lid. Cover with pad.

Corrosive fluid Flush continuously with water for 15 minutes. Give painkillers and chloramphenicol ointment; cover with pad. ***Seek help asap***.

Conjunctivitis Sticky, weeping eye with yellow discharge. Chloramphenicol 4 times a day.

FISH HOOKS Push the hook round until the point and barb can be cut off; withdraw the hook. Dress the holes and give an antibiotic.

FRACTURES AND DISLOCATIONS Fracture is a broken bone. Dislocation is a displaced joint. Both produce pain (aggravated by attempted movement), localised swelling, abnormal shape, and a grating feeling on movement (if it is a fracture). Blood vessels or nerves around the fracture or dislocation may also be damaged causing a cold, pale, or numb limb below the site of the injury.

Fractures of large bones such as the femur (upper leg) will result in major internal bleeding and may cause shock. When complications occur ***urgent help is needed***.

Early application of a splint and raising the injured limb where possible will reduce pain and complications. Treat for shock and pain.

Specific fractures and dislocations

Cheek Caused by a direct blow. Rarely serious but requires specialist care.

Jaw Beware of associated brain or spinal injury. Remove blood and teeth fragments; leave loose teeth in place; protect broken teeth. Ensure airway is clear. Start regular antiseptic mouth washes and antibiotics. Support jaw with bandage over top of the head. Give only fluids by mouth.

Neck May result from a direct blow, a fall or a whiplash type injury. If conscious, casualty may complain of pain, tingling, numbness or weakness in limbs below the injury. ***Mishandling may damage the spinal cord, causing paralysis or death***. Avoid movement and support the head. Immobilise by wrapping a folded towel around the neck. If movement is necessary then lift the victim as one rigid piece, never allowing the neck to bend. ***Urgent help needed.***

Nose Control bleeding by pinching.

Ribs Very painful. Strapping is not advised.

Spine Fracture of the spine below the neck, may cause ***paralysis or death***. Mishandling of the victim may greatly worsen the damage. Avoid movement if possible. Lift the casualty without allowing the spine to sag. ***Urgent help needed.***

Collar bone Support arm in sling.

Dislocated shoulder If this has happened before, the casualty may remedy the dislocation himself; otherwise do not attempt to remedy it in case a fracture exists.

Upper arm Support the arm with a collar and cuff inside the shirt, ie tie a clove hitch around the wrist and loop the ends behind the neck.

Forearm and wrist Splint (eg with battens or wood). Do not bandage tightly. Elevate or support in a sling.

Fingers Elevate hand and, unless badly crushed, leave unbandaged; keep moving. If very wobbly, bandage to adjacent finger.

Lower limb

Thigh Shock may be considerable. Strap to other leg with padding between. Gently straighten the lower leg. If necessary apply traction at the ankle to help straighten the leg. Do not bandage too tightly.

Knee Twisting injuries or falls damage the ligaments and cartilages of the knee. Very painful and swollen. Treat as for fracture.

Lower leg Pad very well. Splint using oar, broom handle or similar pieces of wood.

Ankle Fracture or severe sprain may be indistinguishable. Immobilise in neutral position with foot at right angles. Raise the limb.

HEART ATTACK Severe 'crushing' chest pain; may spread to shoulders, neck or arms. Sweating, then bluish lips, then collapse. Breathing and heart may stop. Give one 300mg aspirin tablet (to chew) ***Urgent help needed***.

Rest, reassure. If unconscious: recovery position; observe breathing and pulse. If breathing stops or no pulse, start mouth to mouth ventilation and chest compression immediately; do not stop.

STROKE Symptoms: if a person develops **sudden** onset weakness on one side of the body, problems with speech &/or visual problems: ***think of stroke***.

Recognise a stroke using the FAST test:

- Face – Has side of face fallen; can they smile?
- Arms – Can both arms be raised and kept up?
- Speech – Is it slurred or muddled?
- Time – To call for help.

Place in recovery position and check airway. ***Urgent help needed*** – specialist treatment within 4½ hours can reverse the effects of a stroke. If you are more than 4½ hours from help, and the casualty is conscious and able to swallow, give 300mg of asprin even if he/she is improving.

HEAT STROKE Cool casualty by spraying with cold water or wrap the casualty in a cold wet sheet until their temperature under the tongue falls to 38°C. Encourage drinking (1 teaspoon of salt/half litre of water). If casualty stops sweating, has a rapid pounding pulse and is becoming unconscious: ***Urgent help needed***.

HYPOTHERMIA Symptoms: unreasonable behaviour, apathy and confusion; unsteady gait, stumbling; slurring of speech; pale, cold skin; slow, weak pulse; slow breathing; shivering. It leads to collapse, unconsciousness and ultimately death.

ABC Put in recovery position. If not breathing, start mouth to mouth ventilation. Be prepared to use chest compressions.

Remove wet clothing. Avoid wind chill. Dry and wrap in blankets or sleeping bag plus warm hat and cover, if available, in foil survival bag. ***Urgent help needed***.

Give hot sweet drinks if conscious. Do not give alcohol, rub or place very hot objects against skin.

SEASICKNESS is aggravated by anxiety, fatigue and boredom. Symptoms: lethargy, dizziness, headache and nausea/vomiting. Help prevent with anti-seasickness pills, avoiding rich foods and alcohol. Take frequent small amounts of fluid and food. Keep warm; keep busy. Prolonged seasickness may cause serious loss of fluid – seek advice.

SHOCK can result from almost any accident or medical emergency; it can lead to collapse.

Signs and symptoms Thirst, apathy, nausea, restlessness. Pale, cold, clammy skin, sweating. Rapid, weak pulse. Rapid, shallow breathing. Dull, sunken eyes, bluish lips.

ABC Control any bleeding. Lay the casualty flat or in recovery position; raise legs 20°. Splint any fractures; avoid movement. Avoid chilling, keep warm. Give pain killers. Reassure the casualty. Do not let the casualty eat, drink, smoke or move unnecessarily. If complaining of thirst, moisten the lips with a little water. Note: Fluids may be life saving in cases of dehydration (eg diarrhoea, vomiting, severe burns).

FIRST AID KIT

Stow the following items in a waterproof container, readily accessible and clearly marked:

Triangular bandage x 2 (doubles as a sling)

Crepe bandage 75mm x 2

Gauze bandage 50mm x 2

Elastoplast 75mm x 1

Band Aids (or similar) various shapes and sizes

Wound dressings, 1 large, 1 medium

Sterile non-adhesive dressing (Melolin) x 5

Steristrips x 5 packs

Cotton wool. Safety pins. Thermometer.

Scissors and forceps, good quality stainless steel

Disposable gloves

Antiseptic solution (eg Savlon)

Sunscreen with high protection factor

Antifungal powder or cream (athlete's foot)

Insect repellent (DEET, diethyltoluamide)

Individual choice of anti-seasick tablets

Antibiotic eye ointment (prescription only)

Additional items for extended cruising

Vaccinations – a course may need to start as much as 6 months before departure.

Syringes 2ml x 2 (if carrying injections)

Dental kit – see Dental pain.

DRUGS AND MEDICATION

Paracetamol, painkiller. 1-2 500mg tablets 4 hrly.

Asprin, blood thiner. 300mg single dose for heart attack or stroke.

Ibuprofen, anti-inflammatory. 400mg every 8 hours (avoid if history of asthma or stomach ulcer).

**Dihydrocodeine*, strong painkiller. 1-2 30mg tablets 4 hourly.

Certirizine, antihistamine. 10mg once a day.

Aludrox, indigestion. 1-2 before meals.

Loperamide, diarrhoea. 2 x 2mg capsules initially, then 1 after each loose stool; max 8 day.

Senokot, constipation. 2-4 tablets per day.

**Amoxycillin*, antibiotic. 2 x 250mg capsules 8 hourly (beware penicillin allergy)

**Erythromycin*, antibiotic for penicillin-allergic adults. 4 x 250mg tablets daily.

Cinnarizine, seasickness. 2 x 15mg tablets before sailing, then 1 every 8 hours.

**Scopolamine patches*, seasickness. 1 patch behind ear 5-6 hours before voyage; replace after 72 hrs if necessary.

Chloramphenicol ointment 1%, eye infection, apply 3-4 times/day

* Only available on prescription.

OBSERVATION FORM

The information recorded by you on this form will be invaluable in helping doctors and/or paramedics ashore to diagnose the problem and arrange the best possible treatment for your casualty.

This is particularly important if there may be a considerable time lapse between requesting medical help and the casualty reaching hospital.

- Keep photocopies of this form in your First Aid kit so as to preserve the original.
  Whilst awaiting help, record your careful observations by ticking or annotating the various boxes at 10 minute intervals. This will help doctors detect any improvement or deterioration in the casualty's condition.
- If within radio range of shore attempt to pass the observations via the Coastguard to a medical authority; or ask a ship to relay.
- Before the casualty is taken off the yacht ensure that this form and personal documents (money, passport, EHIC and mobile 'phone) are securely tied to him/her.

DATE .... CASUALTY'S NAME .... AGE .... M/F ....

Times of observations @ 10 minute intervals:		**10**	**20**	**30**	**40**	**50**	**60**
EYES Observe for reactions whilst testing other responses	Open spontaneously						
	Open when spoken to						
	Open to painful stimulus						
	Nil response						
MOVEMENT Apply painful stimulus: Pinch ear lobe or skin on back of hand	Obeys commands						
	Responds						
	Nil response						
SPEECH Speak clearly and directly, close to the casualty's ear	Responds sensibly to queries						
	Seems confused						
	Uses inappropriate words						
	Incomprehensible sounds						
	Nil response						
PULSE (Beats per minute) Take adult's pulse at wrist or neck. Note rate and whether beats are: weak (w); strong (s); regular (reg) or irregular (irreg)	Over 110						
	101-110						
	91-100						
	81-90						
	71-80						
	61-70						
	Below 61						
BREATHING (Breaths per minute) Note rate and whether breathing is: quiet (q); noisy (n); easy (e); or difficult (d)	Over 40						
	31-40						
	21-30						
	11-20						
	Below 11						

GMDSS

The Global Maritime Distress and Safety System (GMDSS) is a sophisticated, but complex, semi-automatic, third-generation communications system. Although not compulsory for yachts, its potential for saving life, particularly when far offshore and out of VHF range, is so great that every yachtsman should seriously consider it. Equipment costs continue to fall. Training courses, leading to the award of the Short Range Certificate (SRC) of Competence, are widely available. The Long Range Certificate covers MF, HF, SatCom, EPIRBs and SART.

Recommended reading:

- *ALRS, Vol 5* (UK Hydrographic Office)
- *GMDSS: a User's Handbook* (Bréhaut/ACN)
- *GMDSS for small craft* (Clemmetsen/Fernhurst)
- *Reeds VHF/DSC Handbook* (Fletcher/ACN)

Purpose

GMDSS enables a coordinated SAR operation to be mounted rapidly and reliably anywhere at sea. To this end, terrestrial and satellite communications and navigation equipment is used to alert SAR authorities ashore and ships in the vicinity to a Distress incident or Urgency situation. GMDSS also promulgates Maritime Safety Information.

Sea areas

For the purposes of GMDSS, the world's sea areas are divided into 4 categories (A1-4), defined mainly by the range of radio communications. These are:

A1 An area within R/T coverage of at least one VHF Coastguard or Coast radio station in which continuous VHF alerting is available via DSC. Range: 20–50M from the CG/CRS.

A2 An area, excluding sea area A1, within R/T coverage of at least one MF CG/CRS in which continuous DSC alerting is available. Range: approx 50–250M from the CG/CRS.

A3 An area between 76°N and 76°S, excluding sea areas A1 and A2, within coverage of HF or an Inmarsat satellite in which continuous alerting is available.

A4 An area outside sea areas A1, A2 and A3, ie the polar regions, within coverage of HF.

In each category of sea area certain types of radio equipment must be carried by GMDSS vessels: in A1 areas VHF DSC; A2 areas VHF and MF DSC; A3 areas VHF, MF and HF or SatCom; A4 VHF, MF and HF.

Most UK yachtsmen will operate in A1 areas (the English Channel, for example, is an A1 area) where a simple VHF radio and a NAVTEX receiver will initially meet GMDSS requirements. As equipment becomes more affordable, yachtsmen may decide to fit GMDSS. This will become increasingly necessary as the present system for sending and receiving Distress calls is run down. The CG will continue a loudspeaker watch on VHF Ch 16 until further notice.

Functions

Regardless of the sea areas in which they operate, vessels complying with GMDSS must be able to perform certain functions:

- transmit ship-to-shore Distress alerts by two independent means
- receive shore-to-ship Distress alerts
- transmit & receive ship-to-ship Distress alerts
- transmit signals for locating incidents
- transmit and receive communications for SAR co-ordination
- transmit/receive maritime safety info, eg navigation and weather warnings

Distress alerts

A Distress alert is simply a Distress call using DSC. It is transmitted on Ch 70 and is automatically repeated five times. Whenever possible, a Distress alert should always include the last known position and time in UT. The position is normally entered automatically from an interfaced GPS, but can be entered manually if required. The nature of the distress can also be selected from the receiver's menu. The vessel's identity (MMSI number) is automatically included.

GMDSS requires participating ships to be able to send Distress alerts by two out of three independent means. These are:

- Digital Selective Calling (DSC) using terrestrial communications, ie VHF Ch 70, MF 2187·5 kHz, or HF distress and alerting frequencies in the 4, 6, 8,12 and 16 MHz bands.
- Emergency Position Indicating Radio Beacons (EPIRBs). See below.
- Inmarsat, via ship terminals.

Digital Selective Calling

DSC is an essential component of GMDSS. It is so called because information is sent by a burst of digital code; selective because it can be addressed to a specific DSC-equipped vessel or to a selected group of vessels.

In all DSC messages every vessel and relevant shore station has a 9-digit identification number, or MMSI (Maritime Mobile Service Identity), which is in effect an automatic, electronic callsign.

DSC is used to transmit Distress alerts from ships, to receive Distress acknowledgements from ships or shore stations; to send Urgency and Safety alerts; to relay Distress alerts; and for routine calling & answering. A thorough working knowledge is needed.

Maritime Safety Information (MSI)

MSI consists of the vital navigational, weather and safety messages which traditionally were sent to vessels at sea by CRS in Morse, but by R/T on VHF and MF in more recent years – and now by GMDSS. For navigation and weather warnings see this and chapter 2 respectively.

GMDSS transmits MSI in English by two independent but complementary means, NAVTEX and SafetyNet.

- NAVTEX on MF (518 kHz and 490 kHz) which can be received out to about 300 miles offshore, see Chapter 2.
- SafetyNet uses Inmarsat-C satellites to cover beyond MF range, except Area A4. Enhanced Group Calling (EGC) is a part of SafetyNet which enables MSI to be sent to selected groups of users in any of the four oceans.

Emergency Position Indicating Radio Beacons (EPIRB) may be hand-held or float-free, they transmit on 406 MHz. (Note that 121·5 MHz, 243·0 MHz and L-band EPIRBS are no longer used.) Most EPIRBs have a built in GPS and about 48 hours of battery life. They communicate via the Cospas-Sarsat (C/S) network of geostationary and polar orbit satellites. Although C/S will relay an EPIRB signal to earth with no delay, the position of a non-GPS EPIRB may take several hours to determine. The cost of an EPIRB ranges from less than £300 to more than £1000 for float-free, GPS models.

An EPIRB transmits data which is uniquely coded to identify the individual beacon and, because it may be transmitting from anywhere in the world, it must be registered. The UK registration centre is:

The EPIRB Registry, The Maritime and Coastguard Agency, CGOC Falmouth, Pendennis Point, Castle Drive, Falmouth, Cornwall TR11 4WZ; ☎ 01326 211569; email: epirb@mcga.gov.uk.

It is just as important that any changes are immediately notified. False alerts caused by inadvertent or incorrect use of EPIRBs put a significant burden on SAR Centres and may coincide with an actual distress situation.

All crew members should be aware of the proper use of the particular EPIRB onboard. Make sure that testing is adequately supervised; that the EPIRB is correctly installed and maintained; and that it is not activated if assistance is already available. If an EPIRB is activated accidentally, make every effort to advise the nearest MRCC of the false alert as soon as possible.

Personal Locator Beacons (PLB) operate on the same principle. They must also be registered but they do not have a vessel-specific MMSI. A PLB with GPS costs about £200.

Search And Rescue Transponders (SART) are radar transceivers which operate on 9 GHz and respond to 3 cm (X-band) radars, like a small portable Racon (see Chapter 3). They are primarily intended for use in liferafts to help searching ships and aircraft find survivors. The transmitted signal shows on a radar screen as 12 dots radiating out from the SART's position. A SART costs about £500.

HM COASTGUARD – CONTACT DETAILS

EASTERN REGION

NATIONAL MARITIME OPERATIONS CENTRE FAREHAM, (NMOC)

50°51′·50N 01°14′·90W DSC MMSI, 002320011 ☎ 02392 552100 📠 02392 554131/01305 760451. Kites Croft, Fareham PO14 4LW. Area: South Coast: Topsham (River Exe) to Beachy Head (Note: in this area make initial contact using call sign *Solent Coastguard* on Ch 67 (H24) to avoid congestion on Ch 16). East Coast: Reculver Towers to Southwold.

The new NMOC in Fareham is supported by the 10 networked Coast Guard Operations Centres (CGOC). listed on this page. These still accept calls on the ☎ numbers and VHF call signs of the former stations closed during 2015. Fareham and Aberdeen are the main hubs supported by these CGOC's.

DOVER COASTGUARD

50°08′N 01°20′E DSC MMSI 002320010 ☎ 01304 210008 📠 01304 225762
Langdon Battery, Swingate, Dover CT15 5NA. Area: Beachy Head to Reculver Towers Operates Channel Navigation Information Service (CNIS).

LONDON COASTGUARD

51°30′N 00°03′E MMSI 002320063 ☎ 0208 3127380 📠 0208 3098196. Thames Barrier Navigation Centre, Unit 28, 34 Bowater Road, Woolwich, London SE18 5TF.
Area: River Thames from Shell Haven Pt (N bank) and Egypt Bay (S bank), up-river to Teddington Lock

†HUMBER COASTGUARD

54°06′N 00°11′W. MMSI 002320007
Lime Kiln Lane, Bridlington,
N Humberside YO15 2LX.
☎ 01262 672317. 📠 01262 606915.
Area: Southwold to the Scottish border.

SCOTLAND & NORTHERN IRELAND

†ABERDEEN COASTGUARD

57°08′N 02°05′W. MMSI 002320004
Marine House, Blaikies Quay, Aberdeen AB11 5PB.
☎ 01224 592334. 📠 01224 212862.
Area: English border to Cape Wrath, incl Pentland Firth.

†SHETLAND COASTGUARD

60°09′N 01°08′W. MMSI 002320001
Knab Road, Lerwick ZE1 0AX.
☎ 01595 692976. 📠 01595 694810.
Area: Orkney, Fair Isle and Shetland and mainland from C Wrath to S of Brora, incl Pentland Firth.

†*STORNOWAY COASTGUARD

58°12′N 06°22′W. MMSI 002320024
Battery Pt, Stornoway, Isle of Lewis H51 2RT.
☎ 01851 702013. 📠 01851 704387.
Area: Cape Wrath to Mull, Western Isles and St Kilda.

†*BELFAST COASTGUARD

54°40′N 05°40′W. MMSI 002320021
Bregenz House, Quay St, Bangor, Co Down BT20 5ED.
☎ 02891 463933. 📠 02891 465886.
Area: Carlingford Lough to Lough Foyle and Firth of Clyde, incl islands.

WESTERN REGION

†HOLYHEAD COASTGUARD

53°19′N 04°38′W. MMSI 002320018
Prince of Wales Rd, Holyhead,
Anglesey LL65 1ET.
☎ 01407 762051. 📠 01407 764373.
Area: Area: Mull of Galloway to Friog (1·6M S of Barmouth) inc Isle of Man.

†MILFORD HAVEN COASTGUARD

51°42′N 05°03′W. MMSI 002320017
Gorsewood Drive, Hakin,
Milford Haven, SA73 2HD.
☎ 01646 690909. 📠 01646 692176.
Area: Friog to Marsland Mouth (nr Bude).

†*FALMOUTH COASTGUARD

50°09′N 05°03′W. MMSI 002320014
Pendennis Point, Castle Drive,
Falmouth TR11 4WZ.
☎ 01326 317575. 📠 01326 318342.
Area: Marsland Mouth to Topsham (R. Exe).

NOTES: †Monitors DSC MF 2187.5 kHz.
*Broadcasts Gunfacts/Subfacts.

CAUTION: The HM Coastguard modernisation programme was due to be completed by the end of 2015. However, information on this page still remains subject to potential change and readers are advised to check the free monthly updates from January 2016 to June 2016 available for download at www.reedsnauticalalmanacs.co.uk.

THE NATIONAL COASTWATCH INSTITUTION (NCI) operates on dedicated **VHF Ch 65**. There are 50 operational stations (2015) around the English and Welsh coast. Manned by volunteers, most keep a visual watch during daylight hours throughout the year, (see specific times for each station at www.nci.org.uk) and they can provide, on request, details of actual weather conditions and sea state at their locations, radio checks, and invaluable local knowledge, from visitors' moorings to hazards. They all monitor VHF Ch 16, as well as AIS (A), DSC (D) and radar (R) as shown below.

South West and South Coast

St Mary's, Scilly	Under review 2015
Gwennap Head ⒶⒹⓇ	01736 871351
Penzance ⒶⒹ	01736 367063
Bass Point (Lizard) ⒶⒹⓇ	01326 290212
Nare Point (Helford)ⒶⒹⓇ	01326 231113
Portscatho (w/ends only)	01872 580180
Charlestown Ⓡ	01726 817068
Polruan (Fowey) ⒶⓇ	01726 870291
Rame Head (Plymouth) ⒶⒹⓇ	01752 823706
Prawle Point (Salcombe) ⒶⒹⓇ	01548 511259
Froward Pt (Dartmouth) ⒶⒹⓇ	07976 505649
Torbay ⒶⒹⓇ	01803 411145
Teignmouth ⒶⒹⓇ	01626 772377
Exmouth Ⓓ	01395 222492
West Bay Ⓓ	07745 756872
Portland Bill ⒶⒹⓇ	01305 860178
St Alban's Head ⒶⒹⓇ	01929 439220

South East

Peveril Pt (Swanage) ⒶⒹⓇ	01929 422596
Needles Ⓐ	01983 754321
Calshot ⒶⒹⓇ	02380 893562
Lee on Solent ⒶⒹ	02392 556758
Gosport	02392 765194
Shoreham ⒶⒹⓇ	01273 463292
Newhaven ⒶⓇ	01273 516464
Folkestone (Copt Pt) ⒶⒹ	01303 227132
Herne Bay (w/ends only) ⒶⒹⓇ	01227 744454
Whitstable (w/ends only) Ⓓ	07864 646209

East Anglia

Holehaven (Canvey Is) ⒶⒹ	01268 696971
Southend (w/ends only)	0781 5945210
Felixstowe Ⓓ	01394 670808
Gorleston (Gt Yarmouth) ⒶⒹⓇ	01493 440384
Caister ⒶⒹ	07527 977613
Mundesley ⒶⒹⓇ	01263 722399
Runton ⒶⒹⓇ	01263 513725
Wells-next-the-Sea ⒶⒹⓇ	01328 710587

East Coast

Mablethorpe ⒶⒹ	07958 038564

North East Coast

Sunderland Life Brigade ⒶⓇ	01915 672579

North West Coast

Rossall Point (Fleetwood) ⒶⒹⓇ	01253 681378

Wales

Point Lynas (being established 2015)	
Porth Dinllean Ⓓ	07773 362005
Rhoscolyn Ⓐ	07887 955496
Morfa Bychan (Porthmadog) Ⓓ	07521 446050
Wooltack Point (St Brides) Ⓓ	01646 636802
Worms Head (Gower) Ⓓ	01792 390167
Nells Point (Barry) ⒶⒹ	01446 420746

South West, North Coast

Boscastle ⒶⒹⓇ	01840 250965
Stepper Point (Padstow) ⒶⒹⓇ	01841 530039
St Agnes Head ⒶⓇ	01872 552073
St Ives ⒶⓇ	01736 799398
Cape Cornwall ⒶⒹⓇ	01736 787890

Royal National Lifeboat Institution

The RNLI is a registered charity which saves life at sea. It provides, on call H24, a lifeboat service up to 50M off the UK and Irish coasts.

There are over 230 lifeboat stations, 130 all-weather and 191 inshore LBs from 4·9 to 17·0m LOA, plus 3 hovercraft. There are 131 LBs in the reserve fleet. All new LBs are capable of at least 25 knots.

When launched on service, lifeboats >10m keep watch on VHF and MF DSC as well as VHF Ch 16. They can also use alternative frequencies to contact other vessels, SAR aircraft, HM CG, Coast radio stations or other SAR agencies. All lifeboats show a quick-flashing blue light when on operational service.

The RNLI also actively promotes safety at sea by providing a free comprehensive safety service to members and the general public including advice, publications and demonstrations. The RNLI aims to save lives and prevent accidents by helping people be prepared through water safety awareness.

A useful A5 size, ring-bound RNLI Handbook covers emergencies, first aid, seamanship, weather, navigation and engines. It is recommended.

For more details of how the RNLI can help you to be safer at sea, to support the work of the RNLI by becoming a Shoreline Member, Offshore Member or a Governor call the RNLI on 0845 122 6999, or visit www.rnli.org.uk.

The headquarters are at: RNLI, West Quay Road, Poole, Dorset BH15 1HZ.

THE CHANNEL ISLANDS

Guernsey and Jersey Coastguard stations direct SAR operations in the North and South of the CI area respectively, they also provide communications on VHF and DSC.

Close liaison is maintained with adjacent French SAR authorities. A distress situation may be controlled by the Channel Islands or France, whichever is more appropriate. For example a British yacht in difficulty in French waters may be handled by St Peter Port or Jersey so as to avoid language problems; and vice versa for a French yacht.

GUERNSEY CG 49°27'·00N 02°32'00W. DSC MMSI 002320064. ☎ 01481 720672. 📠 714177. Area: Channel Islands North.

JERSEY CG 49°10'·85N 02°14'30W. DSC MMSI 002320060. ☎: 01534 447705/04. 📠: 499089. Area: Channel Islands South.

SEARCH AND RESCUE ABROAD

THE IRISH REPUBLIC

The Irish CG co-ordinates SAR operations around the coast of Ireland via Dublin MRCC, Malin Head and Valentia MRSCs and remote sites. It may liaise with the UK and France during any rescue operation within 100M of the Irish coast.

It is part of the Dept of Marine, Leeson Lane, Dublin 2. ☎ (01) 6620922; 📠 (01) 6620795. The Irish EPIRB Registry is co-located; ☎ (01) 6199280; 📠 (01) 6621571.

The MRCC/MRSCs are co-located with the Coast radio stations of the same name and manned by the same staff. All stations keep watch H24 on VHF Ch 16 and DSC Ch 70. If ashore dial 999 or 112 in an emergency and ask for Marine Rescue.

Details of the MRCC/MRSCs are as follows:

DUBLIN (MRCC)

53°20'N 06°15W. DSC MMSI 002500300 (+2187·5 kHz).

☎ +353 1 662 0922/3; 📠 +353 1 662 0795.

Area: Carlingford Lough to Youghal.

VALENTIA (MRSC)

51°56'N 10°21'W.DSC MMSI 002500200 (+2187·5 kHz).

☎ +353 669 476 109; 📠 +353 669 476 289.

Area: Youghal to Slyne Head.

MALIN HEAD (MRSC)

55°22'N 07°20W. DSC MMSI 002500100 (+2187·5 kHz).

☎ +353 749 370103; 📠 +353 749 370221.

Area: Slyne Head to Lough Foyle.

SAR resources

The Irish CG provides some 50 units around the coast and is on call H24. The RNLI maintains 4 stations around the coast and operates 42 lifeboats; six community-run inshore rescue boats are also available.

Sikorsky S-61 helicopters, based at Dublin, Waterford, Shannon and Sligo, can respond within 15 to 45 minutes and operate to a radius of 200M. They are equipped with infrared search equipment and can uplift 30 survivors.

Military and civilian aircraft and vessels, together with the Garda and lighthouse service, can also be called upon.

Some stations provide specialist cliff climbing services. They are manned by volunteers, who are trained in first aid and equipped with inflatables, breeches buoys, cliff ladders, etc. Their ☎ numbers (the Leader's residence) are given, where appropriate, under each port.

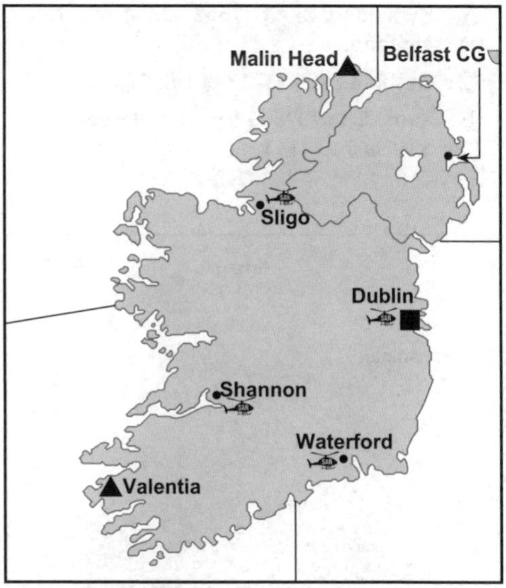

Irish Coastguard centres

DENMARK

The national SAR agency is: JRCC Admiral Danish Fleet, PO Box 1483, DK-8220 Brabrand, Denmark. ☎ +45 894 33099; 📠 +45 728 50384.

The SAR coordinator for Denmark is: **JRCC Denmark**, ☎ +45 728 50000 switchboard; 📠 +45 728 50384; jrcc@sok.dk MMSI 002191000

JRCC Denmark has no direct communications with vessels in distress, but operates via two Maritime Operations Centres (MOC's) and Coast Radio Station

SAFETY

(CRS) Lyngby Radio. **MOC North** (MRSC) ☎ +45 992 21520; 📠 +45 992 21538, mocn-orum@mil.dk, covers the W coast of Denmark.

Lyngby Radio

This is the main Danish CRS and is DSC VHF/MF/HF equipped (☎ +45 452 89800; 📠 +45 458 82485, lyngby-radio@tdc.dk MMSI 002191000).

Its remote sites at Skagen, Hirtshals, Hantsholm, Bovbjerg and Blavand, all monitor Ch 16 H24 and use callsign *Lyngby Radio*. Their VHF and MF frequencies are shown in the chartlet below.

Firing practice areas

There are 4 such areas on the W coast as in the chartlet and listed below. Firing times are broadcast daily by Danmarks Radio 1 after the weather at 1645UT. Times can also be obtained from the Range office Ch 16 or ☎.

Ⓐ Tranum & Blokhus ☎ 982 35088 or call *Tranum.*

Ⓑ Nymindegab ☎ 7652 3334 or call *Nymindegab.*

Ⓒ Oksbøl ☎ 765 41213 or call *Oksbøl.*

Ⓓ Rømø E ☎ 7375 5219 – or call *Fly Rømø;* Rømø W ☎ 745 41340 .

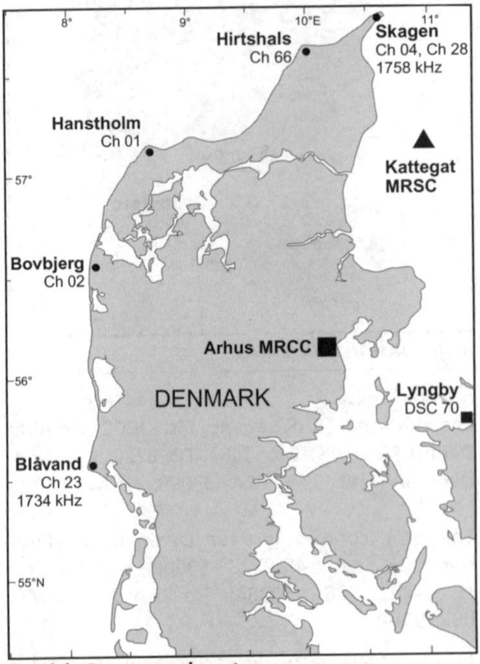

Danish Coastguard centres

GERMANY

The national SAR agency is: *Deutsche Gesellschaft zur Rettung Schiffbrüchiger* (DGzRS), the German Sea Rescue Service. Werderstrasse 2, Hermann-Helms-Haus, D-28199 Bremen. info@seenotretter.de. ☎ +49 421 536870 (emergency), 421 53707-0 (ops); 📠 421 537 07690.

DGzRS is responsible for coordinating SAR operations, supported by ships and SAR helicopters of the German Navy.

Bremen MRCC (☎ +49421536870; MMSI 002111240), using callsign *Bremen Rescue*, maintains an H24 watch on Ch 16 and DSC Ch 70 via remote Coast radio stations at:

Blumenthal / Borkum / Cuxhaven / Helgoland / kampen / Norderney / Stade / Wangerooge / Westerhever.

There are 21 offshore lifeboats, LOA 23–44m, and 21 smaller <10m lifeboats, based at List, Amrum, Helgoland, Cuxhaven, Bremerhaven, Wilhelmshaven, Langeoog, Norderney and Borkum. There are also many inshore lifeboats.

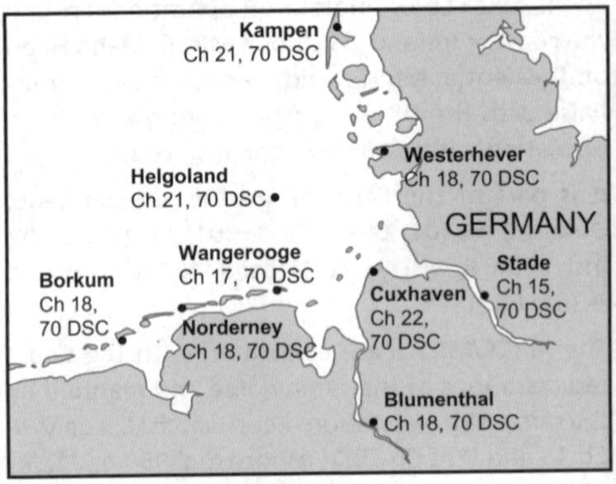

German Coastguard stations

THE NETHERLANDS

The national SAR agency is: SAR Commission, Directorate Transport Safety (DGG), PO Box 20904, 2500 EX The Hague, Netherlands.

The Netherlands CG at Den Helder, co-located with the Navy HQ, coordinates SAR operations as the Dutch JRCC for A1 and A2 Sea Areas. (JRCC = Joint Rescue Coordination Centre – marine & aeronautical.) Callsign is *Netherlands Coastguard*, but *Den Helder Rescue* during SAR operations.

The JRCC keeps a listening watch H24 on DSC Ch 70, and MF DSC 2187·5 kHz (but not on 2182 kHz); MMSI 002442000.

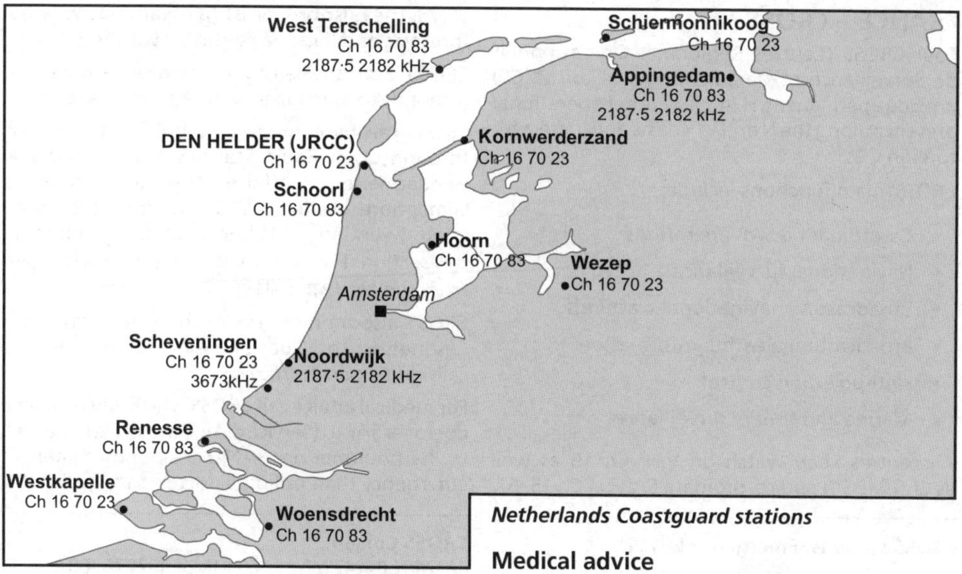
West Terschelling
Ch 16 70 83
2187·5 2182 kHz
Schiermonnikoog
Ch 16 70 23
Appingedam
Ch 16 70 83
2187·5 2182 kHz
DEN HELDER (JRCC)
Ch 16 70 23
Kornwerderzand
Ch 16 70 23
Schoorl
Ch 16 70 83
Hoorn
Ch 16 70 83
Wezep
Ch 16 70 23
Amsterdam
Scheveningen
Ch 16 70 23
3673kHz
Noordwijk
2187·5 2182 kHz
Renesse
Ch 16 70 83
Westkapelle
Ch 16 70 23
Woensdrecht
Ch 16 70 83

Netherlands Coastguard stations

Coastguard Operations can be contacted H24 via:

In emergency:

☎ + 31 9000 111 or dial 112.

Operational telephone number:

☎ + 31 223 542300. 📠 + 31 223 658358; ccc@kustwacht.nl If using a mobile phone, call 9000 111, especially if the International emergency number 112 is subject to delays.

Admin/info (HO)

☎+ 31 223 658300. 📠+31 223 658303. info@kustwacht.nl PO Box 10000, 1780 CA Den Helder.

Remote CG stations are shown above. Working channels are VHF 23 and 83.

Medical advice

Call initially on Ch 16, DSC Ch 70 or 2187·5 kHz (MMSI 002442000). Working chans are VHF Ch 23 & 83 or MF 2824 kHz (transmit), 2520 kHz (receive).

Resources

The Dutch Lifeboat Ass'n (KNRM) manages 26 lifeboat stations and 13 inshore lifeboat stations along the coast. The 60 lifeboats include 13m LOA water-jet, rigid inflatables capable of 36 kn. Helicopters, fixed wing aircraft and ships of the RNLN can be called upon; also Air Force helos at Leeuwarden. The area of activity extends across the Dutch Continental Shelf and into the Waddenzee, IJsselmeer and estuaries of Zuid Holland and Zeeland.

BELGIUM

The Belgian CG coordinates SAR operations from Oostende MRCC, callsign *Coastguard Oostende*. The MRCC and *Oostende Radio* (Coast radio station) both keep listening watch H24 on Ch 16, 67, 2182 kHz and DSC Ch 70 and 2187·5 kHz.

Coast Radio stations

OOSTENDE Radio

☎ 50 558241; 📠 50 558748.
Ch 16, DSC Ch 70 and MF DSC 2187·5 kHz.
MMSI 002050480.

Antwerpen Radio (remotely controlled by Oostende CRS) MMSI 002050485. Ch 16, DSC Ch 70.

Coastguard stations

MRCC OOSTENDE

☎ +32 59 701000; 📠 +32 59 703605.
MMSI 002059981.

RCC Brussels (COSPAS/SARSAT agency)

☎ +32 2 751 4615; 📠 +32 2 7524201.

Resources

Offshore and inshore lifeboats are based at Nieuwpoort, Oostende and Zeebrugge.

The Belgian Air Force provides helicopters from Koksijde near the French border. The Belgian Navy also participates in SAR operations as required.

FRANCE – CROSS

Four CROSS (Centres Régionaux Opérationnels de Surveillance et de Sauvetage, ie an MRCC) provide a permanent, H24, all weather operational presence along the N and W coasts and liaise with foreign CGs.

CROSS' main functions include:

- Co-ordinating SAR operations.
- Navigational surveillance.
- Broadcasting navigational warnings.
- Broadcasting weather information.
- Anti-pollution control.
- Marine and fishery surveillance.

All centres keep watch on VHF Ch 16 as well as Ch 70 (DSC) and co-ordinate SAR on Ch 15, 67, 68, 73. They also broadcast gale warnings, weather forecasts and local navigational warnings.

CROSS Étel specialises in medical advice and responds to alerts from Cospas/Sarsat satellites.

CROSS can be contacted by R/T, by ☎ dial 112, through Coast Radio Stations, via the National Gendarmerie or Affaires Maritimes, or via a Semaphore station. Call *Semaphore* stations on Ch 16 (working Ch 10) or by ☎ as listed later in this section. If a nautical emergency *is witnessed from the land*, ☎ dial196.

CROSS also monitor TSS in the Dover Strait, off Casquets and off Ouessant using, for example, the callsign *Corsen Traffic*.

For medical advice call CROSS which will contact a doctor or SAMU (Service d'Aide Médicale Urgente). In harbour/marina SAMU responds faster in emergency than calling a doctor. Simply dial 15.

CROSS stations (Emergency ☎ 112).

CROSS Gris-Nez
50°52'N 01°35'E MMSI 002275100
☎ 03 21 87 21 87; 📠 03 21 87 78 55
Belgian border to Cap d'Antifer.

NavWarnings Ch 79 at every H+10 via Dunkerque, Saint-Frieux and L'Ailly. CROSS Gris-Nez responds to COSPAS/SARSAT alerts.

CROSS Jobourg
49°41'N 01°54'W MMSI 002275200
☎ 02 33 52 16 16; 📠 02 33 52 71 72
Cap de la Hague to Mont St Michel

NavWarnings Ch 80 every H+20 and H+50 via Antifer, Ver-sur-Mer, Gatteville, Jobourg, Granville and Roche Douvres.

CROSS Corsen
48°24'N 04°47'W MMSI 002275300
☎ 02 98 89 31 31; 📠 02 98 89 65 75
Mont St Michel to Pointe de Penmarc'h.

NavWarnings Ch 79 every H+10 and H+40 via Cap Fréhel, Bodic, Ile de Batz, Le Stiff and Pte du Raz.

CROSS Étel
47°39'N 03°12'W MMSI 002275000
☎ 02 97 55 35 35; 📠 02 97 55 49 34
Pte de Penmarc'h to the Spanish border

NavWarnings Ch 79 for Landes range activity via Chassiron 1903.

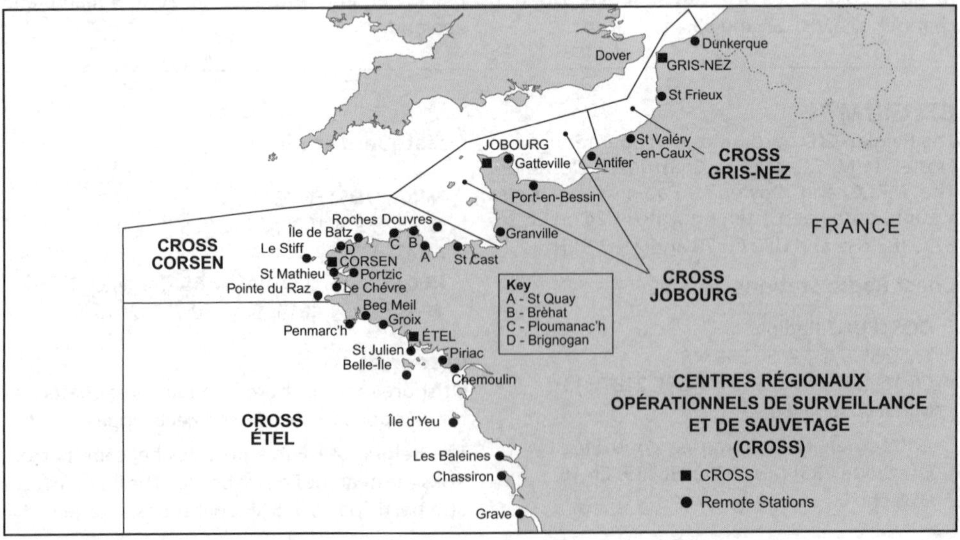

CROSS locations and areas of responsibility

Semaphore stations keep visual, radar and radio watch (Ch 16); are equipped with VHF DF; relay emergency calls to CROSS; show gale warning signals, repeat forecasts and offer local weather reports. Hours sunrise-sunset, but * H24.

* Dunkerque	03·28·66·86·18
* Boulogne	03·21·31·32·10
* Ault	03·22·60·47·33
* Dieppe	02·35·84·23·82
* Fécamp	02·35·28·00·91
* La Hève	02·35·46·07·81
* Villerville	02·31·88·11·13
* Port-en-Bessin	02·31·21·81·51
* St-Vaast	02·33·54·44·50
* Barfleur	02·33·54·04·37
* Le Homet	02·33·92·60·08
* La Hague	02·33·52·71·07
* Barneville-Carteret	02·33·53·85·08
* Granville Le Roc	02·33·50·05·85
St-Cast	02·96·41·85·30
* St Quay-Portrieux	02·96.70.42.18
Bréhat	02·96·20·00·12
* Ploumanac'h	02·96·91·46·51
Batz	02·98·61·76·06
* Brignogan	02·98·83·50·84
* Ouessant Stiff	02·98·48·81·50
* St-Mathieu	02·98·89·01·59
* Portzic (Ch 08)	02·98·22·21·47
Toulinguet	02·98·27·90·02
Cap-de-la-Chèvre	02·98·27·09·55
* Pointe-du-Raz	02·98·70·66·57
* Penmarc'h	02·98·58·61·00
Beg Meil	02·98·94·98·92
Étel Mât Fenoux	02·97·55·35·39
* Beg Melen (Groix)	02·97·86·80·13
Talut (Belle-Île)	02·97·31·85·07
* St-Julien	02·97·50·09·35
Piriac-sur-Mer	02·40·23·59·87
* Chemoulin	02·40·91·99·00
* St-Sauveur (Yeu)	02·51·58·31·01
Les Baleines (Ré)	05·46·29·42·06
* Chassiron (Oléron)	05·46·47·85·43

Lifeboats

The lifeboat service Société National de Sauvetage en Mer (SNSM) comes under CROSS, At sea all vessels must call CROSS to call upon the services of SNSM, they should not be contacted directly in an emergency. A hefty charge may be levied if a SNSM lifeboat attends a vessel not in distress.

Navigation warnings

Long-range warnings are broadcast by SafetyNet for Navarea II, which includes the W coast of France. The N coast is in Navarea I.

Avurnavs (AVis URgents aux NAVigateurs) are regional, coastal and local warnings issued by Cherbourg and Brest and broadcast by Niton and Brest Navtex and on MF. Warnings are prefixed by '*Sécurité Avurnav*'.

EMERGENCY VHF DF SERVICE

A yacht in emergency can call CROSS on VHF Ch 16, 11 or 67 to obtain a true bearing of the yacht *from* the DF station. These monitor Ch 16 and other continuously scanned frequencies, which include Ch 1-29, 36, 39, 48, 50, 52, 55, 56 and 60-88. The Semaphore stations overleaf are also equipped with VHF DF.

HJ = Day service only.

VHF DF stations, are listed below geographically from NE to W then S:

Station	Lat/Long	Hrs
Dunkerque	51°03'.40N 02°20'.40E	H24
*Gris-Nez	50°52'.20N 01°35'.01E	H24
Boulogne	50°44'.00N 01°36'.00E	H24
Ault	50°06'.50N 01°27'.50E	H24
Dieppe	49°56'.00N 01°05'.20E	H24
Fécamp	49°46'.10N 00°22'.20E	H24
La Hève	49°30'.60N 00°04'.20E	H24
Villerville	49°23'.20N 00°06'.50E	H24
Port-en-Bessin	49°21'.10N 00°46'.30W	H24
Saint-Vaast	49°34'.50N 01°16'.50W	H24
Barfleur	49°41'.90N 01°15'.90W	H24
Levy	49°41'.70N 01°28'.20W	H24
†Homet	49°39'.50N 01°37'.90W	H24
*Jobourg	49°41'.50N 01°54'.50W	H24
La Hague	49°43'.60N 01°56'.30W	H24
Carteret	49°22'.40N 01°48'.30W	H24
Le Roc	48°50'.10N 01°36'.90W	H24
Grouin/Cancale	48°42'.60N 01°50'.60W	**HJ**
Saint-Cast	48°38'.60N 02°14'.70W	H24
St-Quay-Port'x	48°39'.30N 02°49'.50W	**HJ**
Bréhat	48°51'.30N 03°00'.10W	H24
Ploumanac'h	48°49'.50N 03°28'.20W	**HJ**
Batz	48°44'.80N 04°00'.60W	H24
Brignogan	48°40'.60N 04°19'.70W	**HJ**
Creac'h (Ushant)	48°27'.60N 05°07'.70W	H24
*Creac'h	48°27'.60N 05°07'.80W	H24
†Saint-Mathieu	48°19'.80N 04°46'.20W	H24
Toulinguet	48°16'.80N 04°37'.50W	**HJ**
Cap de la Chèvre	48°10'.20N 04°33'.00W	**HJ**
Pointe du Raz	48°02'.30N 04°43'.80W	H24
Penmarc'h	47°47'.90N 04°22'.40W	H24
Beg-Meil	47°51'.30N 03°58'.40W	**HJ**
Beg Melen	47°39'.20N 03°30'.10W	H24
*Etel	47°39'.80N 03°12'.00W	H24
Saint-Julien	47°29'.70N 03°07'.50W	**HJ**
Taillefer	47°21'.80N 03°09'.00W	H24
Le Talut	47°17'.70N 03°13'.00W	H24
Piriac	47°22'.50N 02°33'.40W	H24
Chemoulin	47°14'.10N 02°17'.80W	H24
Saint-Sauveur	46°41'.70N 02°18'.80W	H24
Les Baleines	46°14'.60N 01°33'.70W	**HJ**
Chassiron	46°02'.80N 01°24'.50W	H24

Chapter 5 – Tides

2016 TIDAL COEFFICIENTS

Date	Jan		Feb		Mar		Apr		May		June		July		Aug		Sept		Oct		Nov		Dec	
	am	pm	am	pm	am	pm	am	pm	am	pm	am	pm	am	pm	am	pm	am	pm	am	pm	am	pm	am	pm
1	57	52	46	41	53	47	39	36	43	46	63	69	68	73	78	82	90	92	90	90	84	82	80	79
2	47	43	37	35	42	37	37	40	50	56	75	81	77	82	86	90	93	93	90	89	81	78	78	76
3	40	37	34	36	34	33	46	53	63	71	87	92	86	90	92	93	92	90	87	85	76	72	74	71
4	37	38	39	44	35	40	61	70	78	86	96	100	93	95	94	93	88	85	82	78	69	64	68	64
5	40	43	50	57	46	53	79	88	93	100	102	103	96	96	92	90	82		75		60	55	61	
6	48	53	64	71	61	70	96	103	105	109	103	102	96	94	87		77	73	70	65	51		57	54
7	58	63	78	84	78	87	109	114	112	113	100	97	92		83	79	68	62	60	55	46	42	51	49
8	68	74	90	96	94	101	117	118	112	110	92		88	84	75	70	57	51	49	44	39	38	48	49
9	78	83	100	104	107	112	117	115	106	101	87	82	80	75	64	59	45	40	39	35	40	43	52	55
10	87	90	107	108	115	116	111		95		76	70	70	65	53	48	35	32	32	32	48	55	61	67
11	93	95	108	106	116	114	105	99	88	81	64	59	59	54	43	39	31	32	35	40	63	71	73	80
12	95	96	103	99	111	105	91	82	74	66	54	49	49	45	35	34	36	41	47	55	79	86	86	92
13	95	93	94		99		73	65	59	53	46	44	42	39	34	36	48	56	64	72	94	100	97	101
14	91		88	81	91	83	57	50	48	45	43	43	38	39	40	46	64	72	81	88	105	109	104	106
15	87	83	73	66	74	66	45	43	43	44	45	47	41	44	52	58	79	87	96	102	111	112	106	105
16	78	74	59	53	57	50	43	45	46	48	50	53	48	52	64	71	93	99	108	111	111	109	103	99
17	68	64	50	49	46	44	49	54	52	56	57	61	57	62	77	83	104	108	114	114	105	100	95	90
18	60	57	50	53	45	48	59	64	60	63	64	68	67	71	88	93	110	111	113	111	94	87	84	
19	56	56	58	64	53	58	68	72	67	70	71	74	75	79	97	100	111	108	106		79		78	71
20	59	62	69	74	64	69	76	79	73	75	77	79	83	86	102	103	105		101	94	72	64	65	59
21	67	72	79	83	75	79	81	83	77	79	80	82	88	90	102		100	93	86	77	58	52	53	49
22	76	81	87	89	82	85	84	85	80	81	82	83	91	91	101	98	86	78	69	61	48	46	45	43
23	85	88	91	92	87	89	85	85	81	81	82	81	91		94	89	70	61	54	48	45	46	42	43
24	90	92	92	91	89	89	84	82	80	79	80		90	87	83	77	54	49	45	45	49	52	45	47
25	92	92	90	87	89	87	80	78	77		78	75	85	81	70	63	46	46	47	51	56	60	51	55
26	91	89	85	81	86	83	75		75	72	73	70	77	73	58	53	49	54	55	60	63	67	58	62
27	87	84	78	73	80		71	67	69	65	67	64	68	64	50	50	59	65	65	70	70	73	66	69
28	80	76	68		77	73	63	58	62	58	62	60	60	58	53	57	70	76	74	77	75	77	72	75
29	71		63	58	68	63	53	49	56	54	60	60	57	57	62	68	80	84	80	82	78	79	77	79
30	67	61			58	52	46	44	53	53	62	65	60	63	73	79	86	88	84	84	80	80	81	82
31	56	51			47	42			55	59			68	73	83	87			85	85			82	82

Tidal coefficients indicate the magnitude of the tide on any particular day without having to look up and calculate the range, and thus determine whether it is springs, neaps or somewhere in between. This table, which is based on Cherbourg, is valid for all areas covered by this Almanac. Typical values are:

120	Very big spring tide
95	**Mean spring tide**
70	Average tide
45	**Mean neap tide**
20	Very small neap tide

TIDAL CALCULATIONS

Find the height at a given time (STANDARD PORT)

1. On Standard Curve diagram, plot heights of HW and LW occuring either side of required time and join by sloping line.
2. Enter HW Time and sufficient others to bracket required time.
3. From required time, proceed vertically to curves, using heights plotted in (1) to help interpolation between Spring and Neaps. Do NOT extrapolate.
4. Proceed horizontally to sloping line, thence vertically to Height scale.
5. Read off height.

EXAMPLE:

Find the height of tide at ULLAPOOL at 1900 on 6th January

Find the time for a given height (STANDARD PORT)

From tables	JANUARY	
ULLAPOOL	**6** 0420	4.6
	1033	1.6
	1641	4.6
	F 2308	1.2

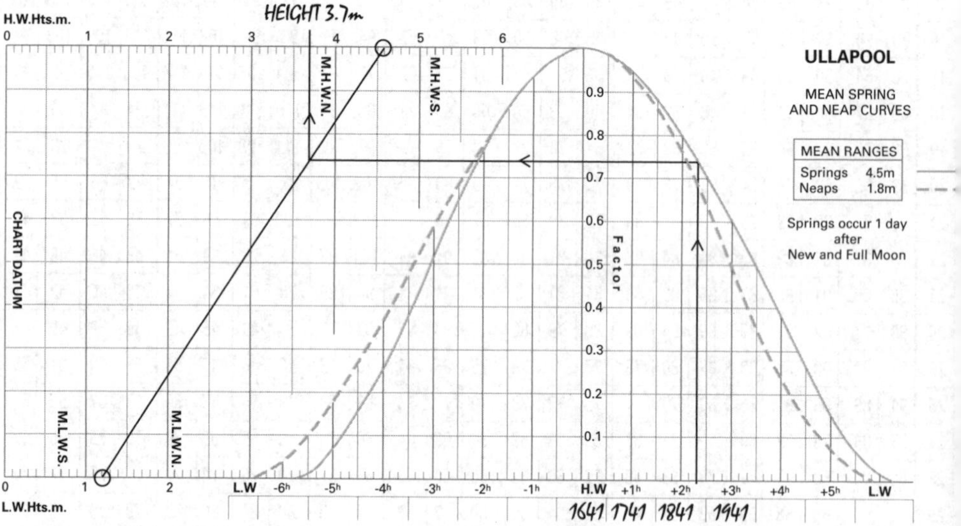

1. On Standard Curve diagram, plot heights of HW and LW occurring either side of required event and join by sloping line.
2. Enter HW time and those for half-tidal cycle covering required event.
3. From required height, proceed vertically to sloping line, thence horizontally to curves, using heights plotted in (1) to assist interpolation between Spring and Neaps. Do NOT extrapolate.
4. Proceed vertically to Time scale.
5. Read off time.

XAMPLE:

ind the time at which the afternoon tide at ULLAPOOL falls to 3.7m on 6 January

From tables		JANUARY	
ULLAPOOL	6	0420	4.6
		1033	1.6
		1641	4.6
		F 2308	1.2

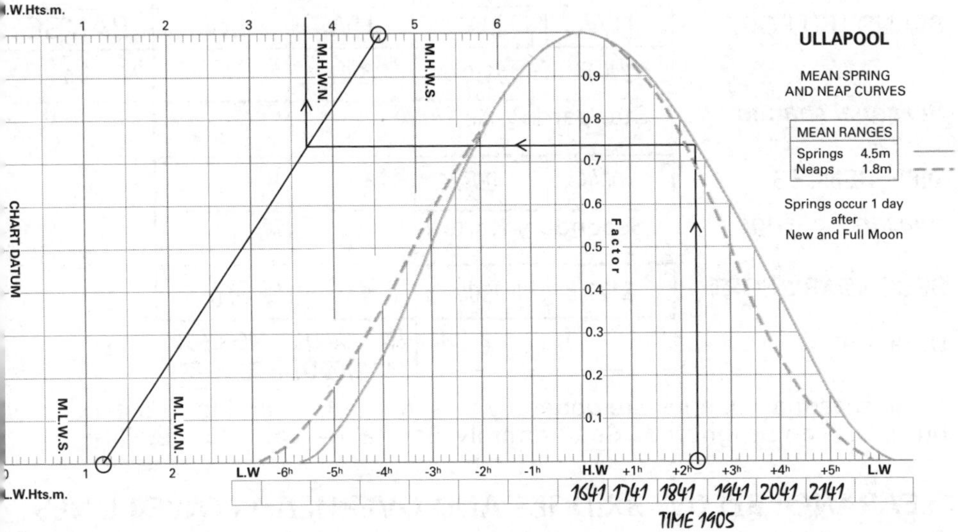

Find the time and height of HW and LW at a Secondary Port

EXAMPLE:

Find the time and height of the afternoon HW and LW at ST MARY's (Isles of Scilly) on 14th July (BST)

Note: *The data used in this example do not refer to the year of these tables.*

From tables		JULY	
PLYMOUTH (DEVONPORT)	14	0309	1.0
		0927	5.3
		1532	1.1
		SA 2149	5.0

From tables

Location	Lat Long	High Water		Low Water		MHWS	MHWN	MLWN	MLWS
DEVONPORT *Standard port*	50°22′N 4°11′W	**0000 and 1200**	**0600 and 1800**	**0000 and 1200**	**0600 and 1800**	**5.5**	**4.4**	**2.2**	**0.8**
St Mary's, *Scilly*	49° 55′N 6°19′W	–0035	–0100	–0040	–0025	+0.2	–0.1	–0.2	–0.1

TIDES

TIDAL PREDICTION FORM (NP 204)

STANDARD PORT *Devonport* TIME/HEIGHT REQUIRED *pm*

SECONDARY PORT *St Mary's* DATE *14 July* TIME ZONE *B.S.T*

	TIME		HEIGHT		
STANDARD PORT	HW	LW	HW	LW	RANGE
	1 2149	2 1532	3 5·0	4 1·1	5 3·9
Seasonal change	Standard Ports -		6 0·0	6 0·0	
DIFFERENCES	7* -0044	8 -0032	9 0·1	10 -0·1	
*Seasonal change **	Secondary Ports +		11 0·0	11 0·0	
SECONDARY PORT	12 2105	13 1500	14 5·1	15 1·0	
Duration	16 0605		LW 1500 UT = 1600 BST HW 2105 UT = 2205 BST		

* The seasonal changes are generally less than – 0.1m and for most purposes can be ignored. See Admiraly Tide Tables Vol 1. for details

CLEARANCE BELOW BRIDGES AND OVERHEAD POWER LINES

Vertical clearance heights are above the level of HAT (Highest Astronomical Tide) instead of MHWS as in the past. HAT is always a higher level than MHWS, as shown in the diagram on the back cover flap. It helps to draw such a diagram and insert the relevant dimensions when calculating overhead clearances. The Height of HAT above Chart Datum is stated at the foot of each page of Standard port tide tables. New editions of Admiralty charts are referenced to HAT; earlier editions to MHWS. Check the title block under **Heights**.

INTERMEDIATE TIMES/HEIGHTS (SECONDARY PORT)

These are the same as the appropriate calculations for a Standard Port except that the Standard Curve diagram for the Standard Port must be entered with HW and LW heights and times for the Secondary Port obtained on Form N.P. 204. When interpolating between the Spring and Neap curves the Range at the Standard Port must be used.

EXAMPLE:

Find the height of the tide at PADSTOW at 1100 on 28th February. Find the time at which the morning tide at PADSTOW falls to 4.9m on 28th February.

Note: The data in these examples do not refer to the year of these tables.

From tables

MILFORD HAVEN — **FEBRUARY**

Day	Time	Height
28 TU	0315	1.1
	0922	6.6
	1538	1.3
	2145	6.3

From tables

Location	Lat	Long	High Water		Low Water		MHWS	MHWN	MLWN	MLWS
MILFORD HAVEN *Standard port*	51°42′N	5°03′W	0100 and 1300	0700 and 1900	0100 and 1300	0700 and 1900	7.0	5.2	2.5	0.7
River Camel										
Padstow	50°33′N	4°56′W	–0055	–0050	–0040	–0050	+0.3	+0.4	+0.1	+0.1
Wadebridge	50°31′N	4°50′W	–0052	–0052	+0235	+0245	–3.8	–3.8	–2.5	–0.4

TIDAL PREDICTION FORM (NP 204)

STANDARD PORT *Milford Haven* TIME/HEIGHT REQUIRED *1100 : 4.9*

SECONDARY PORT *Padstow* DATE *28 Feb* TIME ZONE *UT*

	TIME		HEIGHT		
	HW	LW	HW	LW	RANGE
STANDARD PORT	1 *0922*	2 *1538*	3 *6.6*	4 *1.3*	5 *5.3*
Seasonal change	Standard Ports +		6 *0.0*	6 *0.0*	
DIFFERENCES	7* *-0052*	8 *–*	9 *+0.3*	10 *+0.1*	
Seasonal change *	Secondary Ports -		11 *0.0*	11 *0.0*	
SECONDARY PORT	12 *0830*	13 *–*	14 *6.9*	15 *1.4*	
Duration	16 *–*				

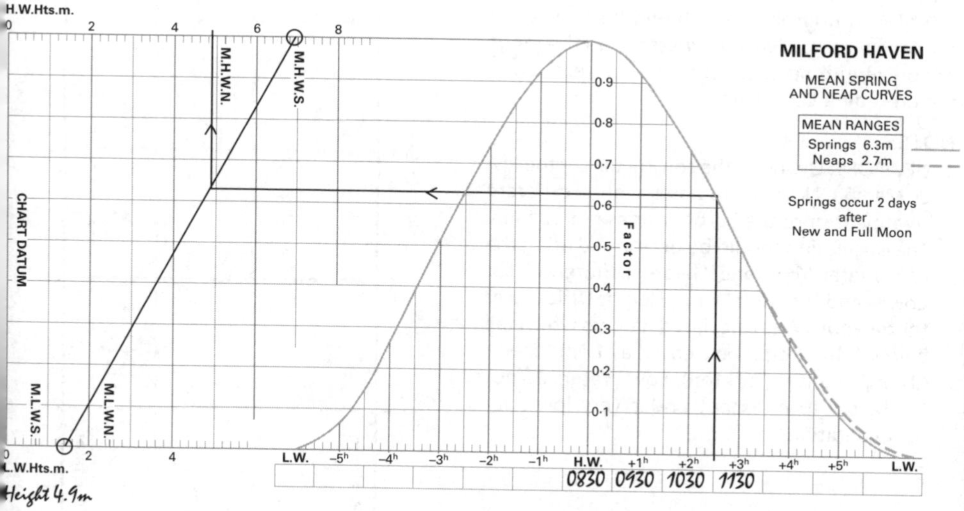

H.W.Hts.m.
0
2
4
6
8
M.H.W.N.
M.H.W.S.
CHART DATUM
M.L.W.S.
M.L.W.N.
0
2
4
L.W.Hts.m.
Height 4.9m
0·9
0·8
0·7
0·6
0·5
0·4
0·3
0·2
0·1
Factor
L.W.
–5h
–4h
–3h
–2h
–1h
H.W.
+1h
+2h
+3h
+4h
+5h
L.W.
0830
0930
1030
1130
MILFORD HAVEN
MEAN SPRING AND NEAP CURVES
MEAN RANGES
Springs 6.3m
Neaps 2.7m
Springs occur 2 days after New and Full Moon

TIDES

SPECIAL INSTRUCTIONS FOR PLACES BETWEEN BOURNEMOUTH AND SELSEY BILL

• Owing to the rapid change of tidal characteristics and distortion of the tidal curve in this area, curves are shown for individual ports. It is a characteristic of the tide here that Low Water is more sharply defined than High Water and these curves have therefore been drawn with their times relative to that of Low Water.

• Apart from differences caused by referring the times to Low Water the procedure for obtaining intermediate heights at places whose curves are shown is identical to that used for normal Secondary Ports.

• The **height** differences for ports between Bournemouth and Yarmouth always refer to the higher High Water, i.e. that which is shown as reaching a factor of 1.0 on the curves. Note that the **time** differences, which are not required for this calculation, also refer to the higher High Water.

• The tide at ports between Bournemouth and Christchurch shows considerable change of shape and duration between Springs and Neaps and it is not practical to define the tide with only two curves. A third curve has therefore been drawn for the range at Portsmouth at which the two High Waters are equal at the port concerned – this range being marked on the body of the graph. Interpolation here should be between this 'critical' curve and either the Spring or Neap curve as appropriate. Note that while the critical curve extends throughout the tidal cycle the Spring and Neap curves stop at the higher High Water. Thus for a range at Portsmouth of 3.5m the factor for 7 hours after LW at Bournemouth should be referred to the following Low Water, whereas had the range at Portsmouth been 2.5, it should be referred to the preceding Low Water.

NOTES

1. NEWPORT. Owing to the constriction of the River Medina, Newport requires slightly different treatment since the harbour dries out at 1.4m. The calculation should be performed using the Low Water Time and Height Differences for Cowes and the High Water Height Differences for Newport. Any calculated heights which fall below 1.4m should be treated as 1.4m
2. CHRISTCHURCH (Tuckton). Low Waters do not fall below 0.7m except under very low river flow conditions.

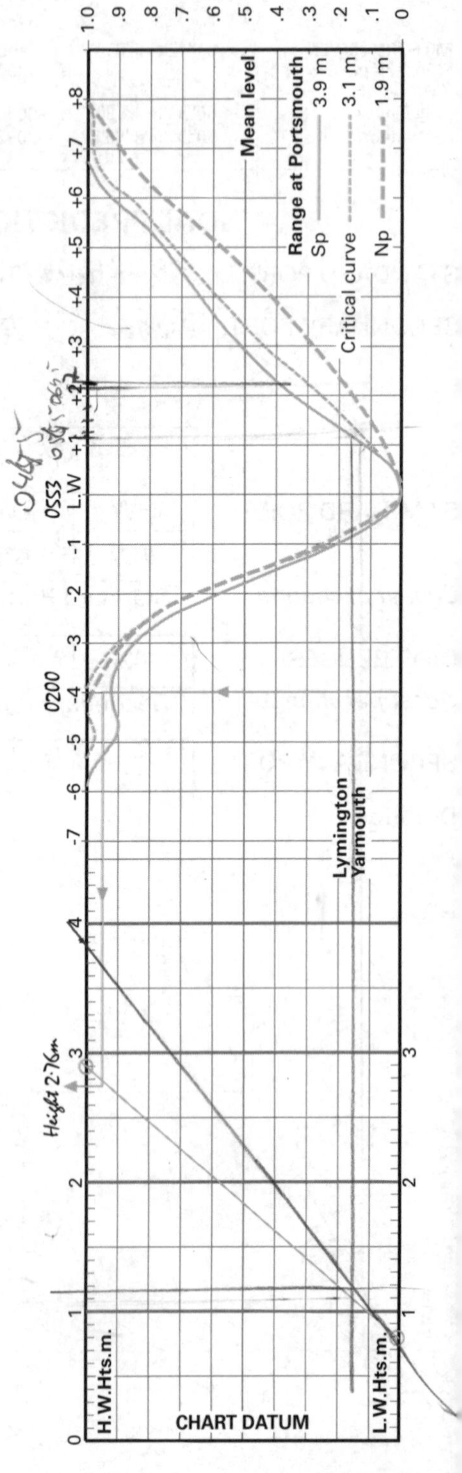

To find the Height of tide at a given time at any Secondary Port between Bournemouth and Selsey Bill

1. Complete top section of N.P. 204 (as below). Omit HW time column (Boxes 1,7,12)
2. On Standard Curve diagram (previous page), plot Secondary Port HW and LW heights and join by sloping line.
3. From the time required, using Secondary Port LW time, proceed vertically to curve, interpolating as necessary using Range at Portsmouth. Do NOT extrapolate.
4. Proceed horizontally to sloping line, thence vertically to Height Scale.
5. Read off height.

EXAMPLE:

Find the height of tide at LYMINGTON at 0200 UT on 18th November

From tables	NOVEMBER		
		0110	4.6
PORTSMOUTH	**18**	0613	1.1
		1318	4.6
	SA	1833	1.0

From tables Location	Lat	Long	High Water		Low Water		MHWS	MHWN	MLWN	MLWS
			0000 and **1200**	**0600** and **1800**	**0500** and **1700**	**1100** and **2300**				
PORTSMOUTH *Standard port*	50°48′N	1°07′W					**4.7**	**3.8**	**1.9**	**0.8**
Lymington	50°46′N	1°32′W	−0110	+0005	−0020	−0020	−1.7	−1.2	−0.5	−0.1

STANDARD PORT Portsmouth TIME/~~HEIGHT~~ REQUIRED 0200

SECONDARY PORT Lymington DATE 18 Nov TIME ZONE UT

	TIME HW	TIME LW	HEIGHT HW	HEIGHT LW	RANGE
STANDARD PORT	1 –	2 0613	3 4.6	4 1.1	5 3.5
Seasonal change	Standard Ports -		6 0.0	6 0.0	
DIFFERENCES	7* –	8 −0020	9 −1.7	10 −0.2	
Seasonal change *	Secondary Ports +		11 0.0	11 0.0	
SECONDARY PORT	12 –	13 0553	14 2.9	15 0.9	
Duration	16 –				

* *The Seasonal changes are generally less than ± 0.1m and for most purposes can be ignored. See Admiralty Tide Tables Vol 1 for full details.*

TIDAL CURVES - BOURNEMOUTH TO FRESHWATER

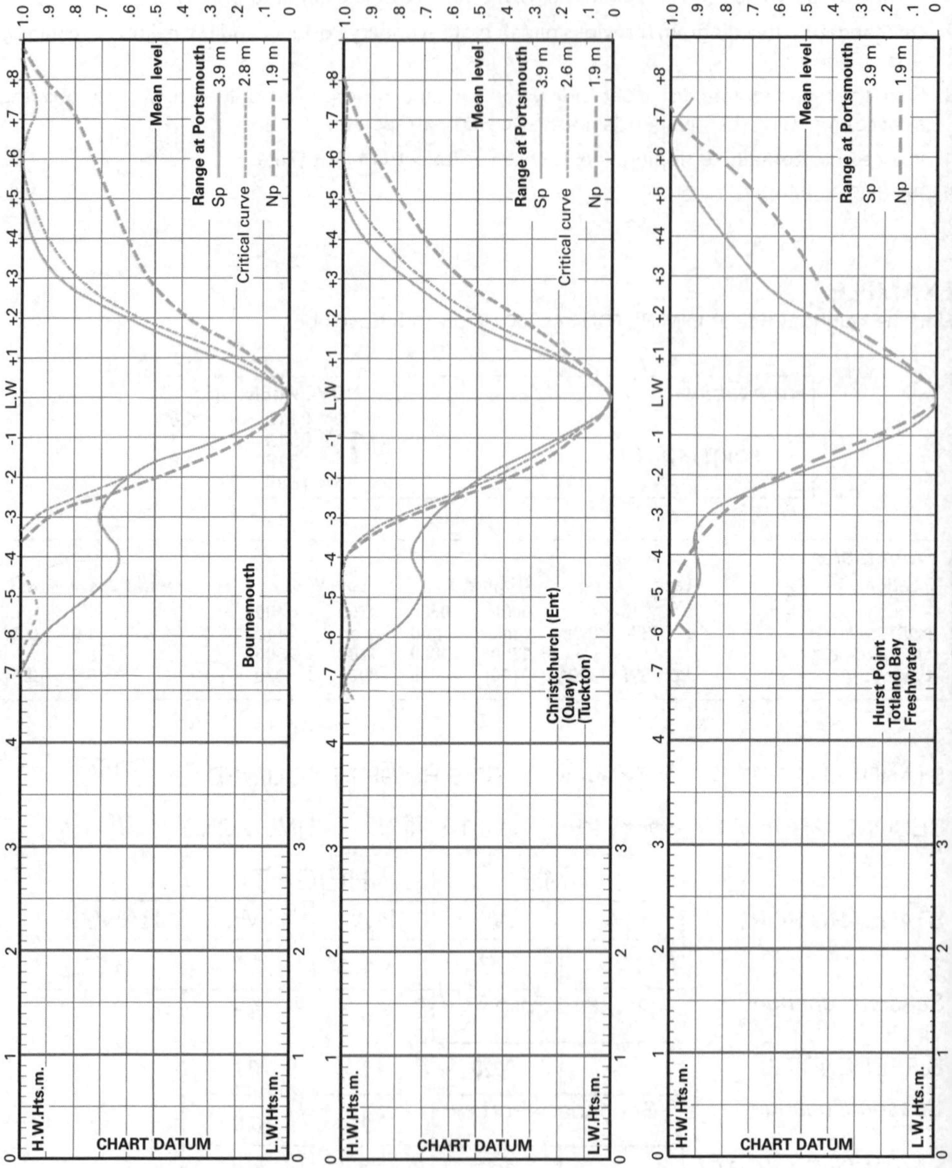

Note: The curves for Lymington and Yarmouth are on page 154, together with a worked example.

TIDAL CURVES - BUCKLERS HARD TO SELSEY BILL

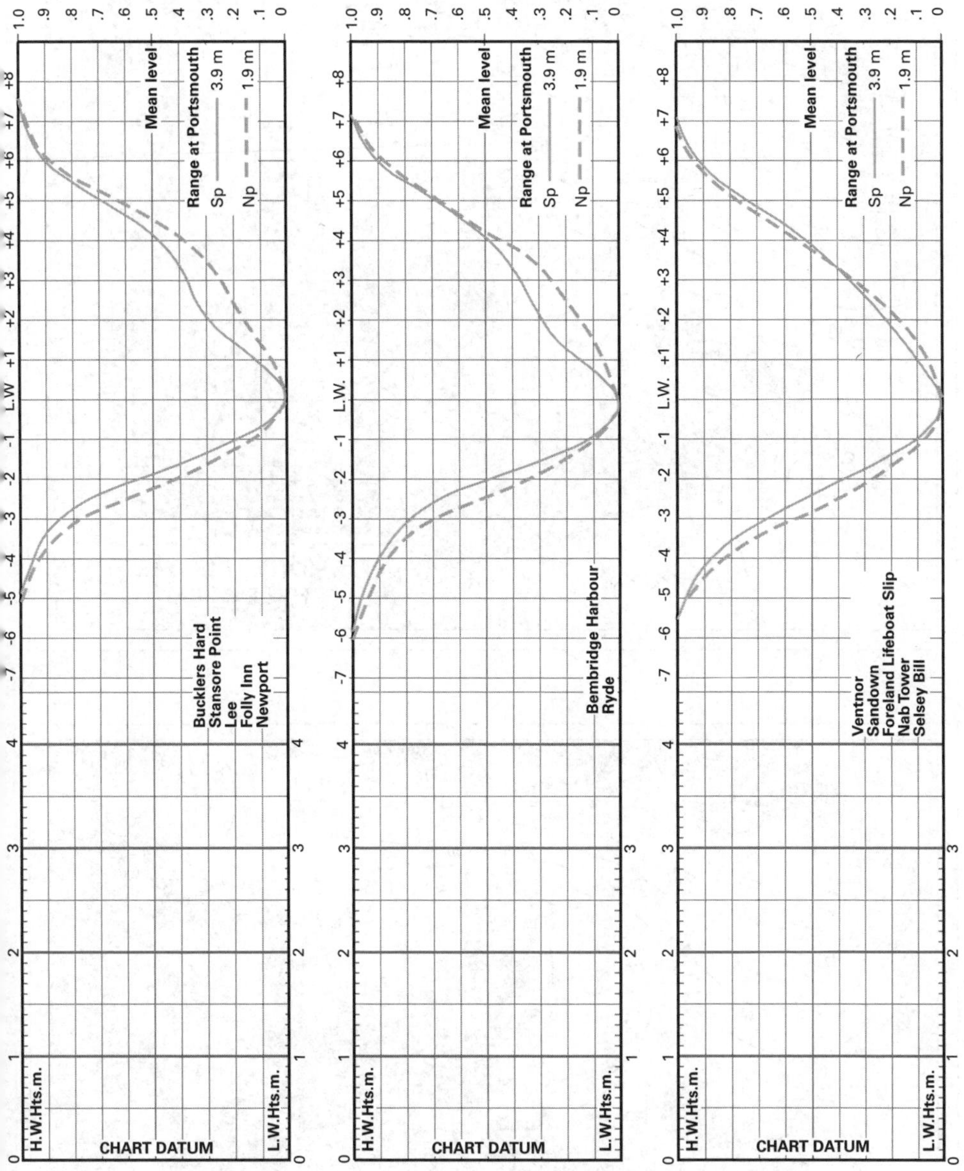

TIDES

19 Aug HW 1225 DST

ENGLISH CHANNEL AND SOUTH BRITTANY

0655 0755

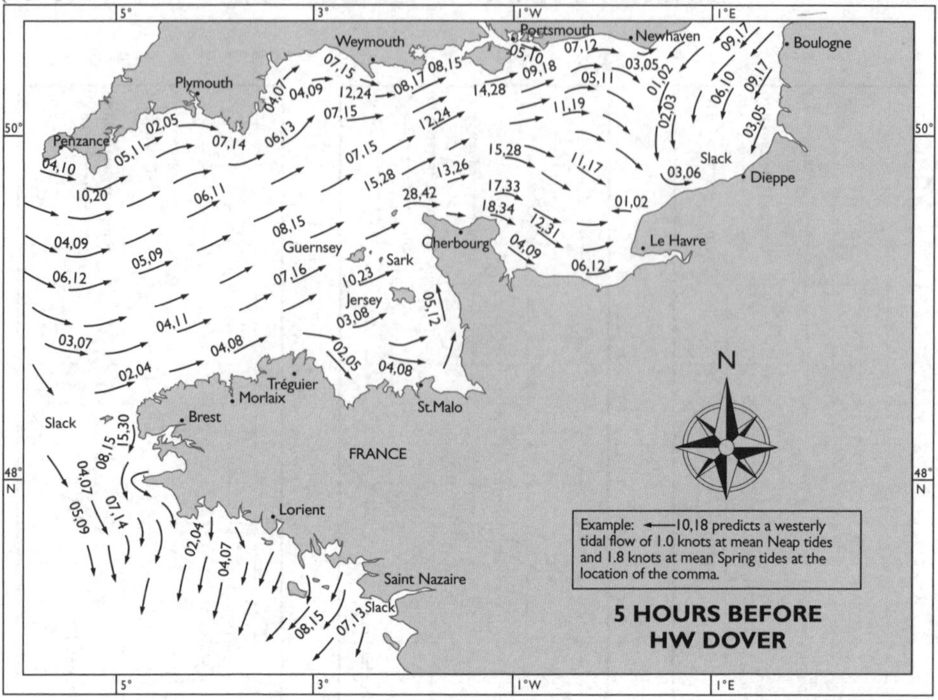

0755 0855

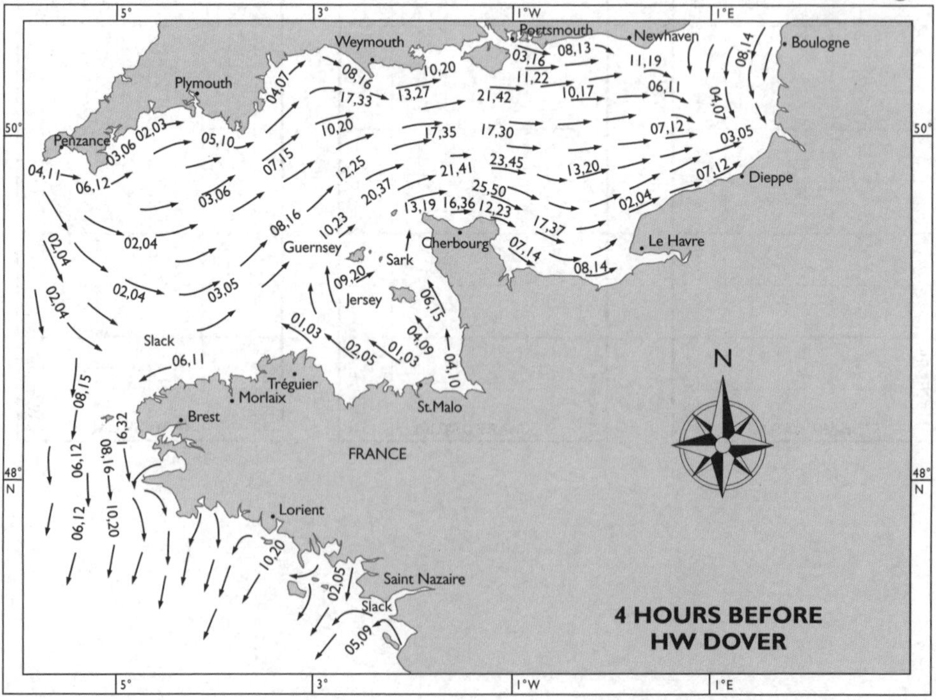

19 Aug

ENGLISH CHANNEL AND SOUTH BRITTANY

0855 0955

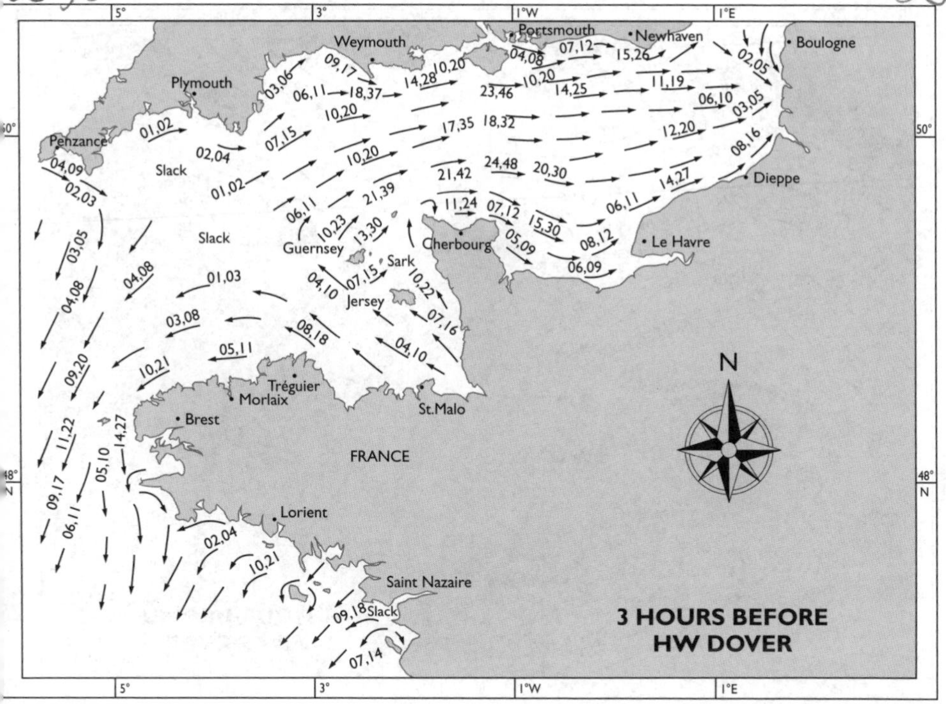

0955 1055

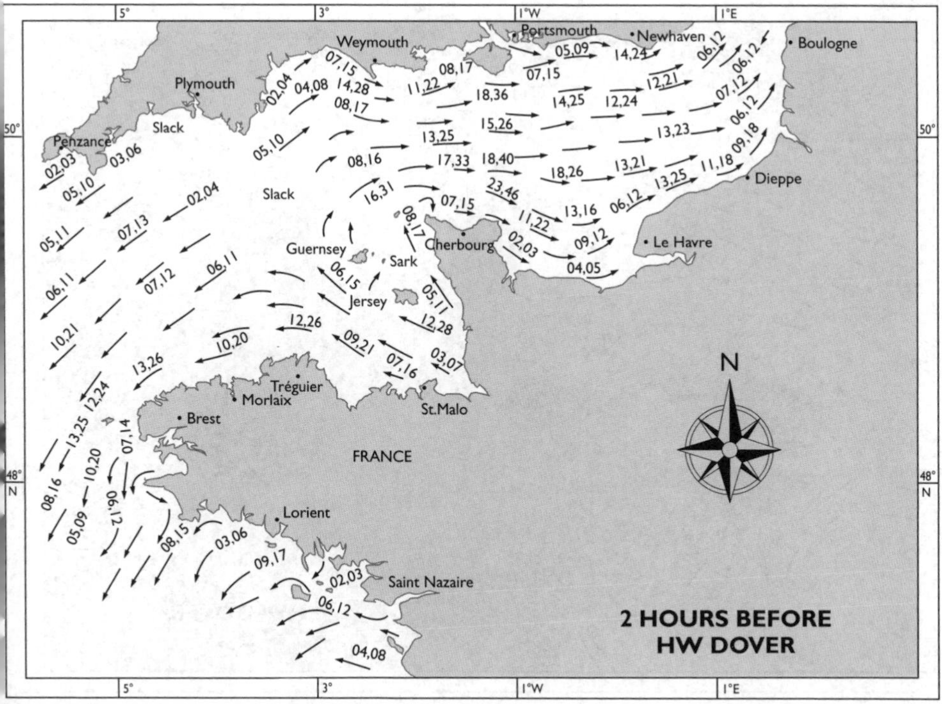

TIDES

ENGLISH CHANNEL AND SOUTH BRITTANY

1055 1155

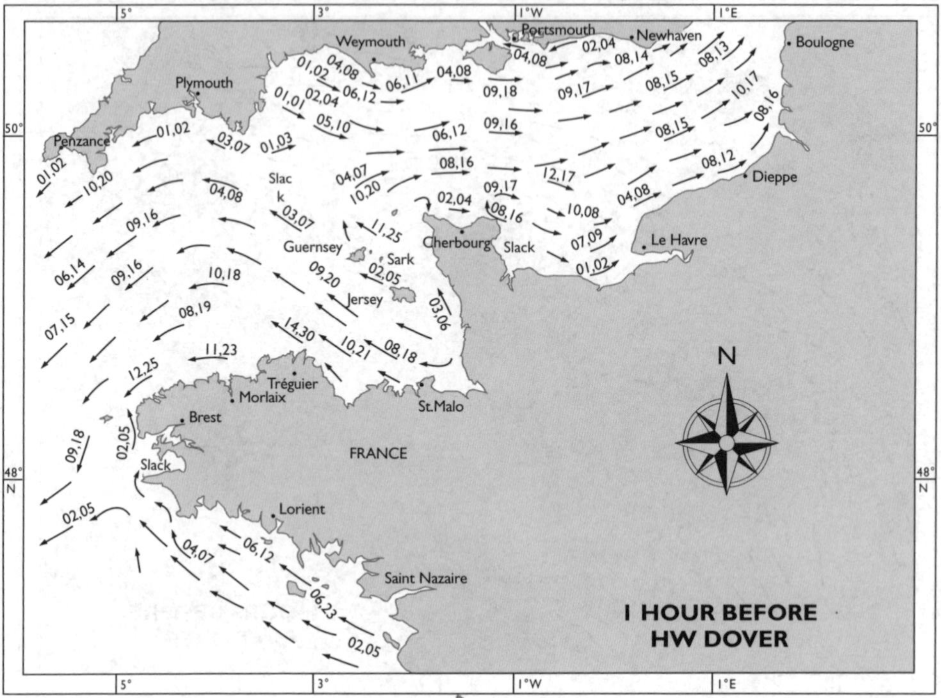

19 Aug 1225 DST

1155 1255

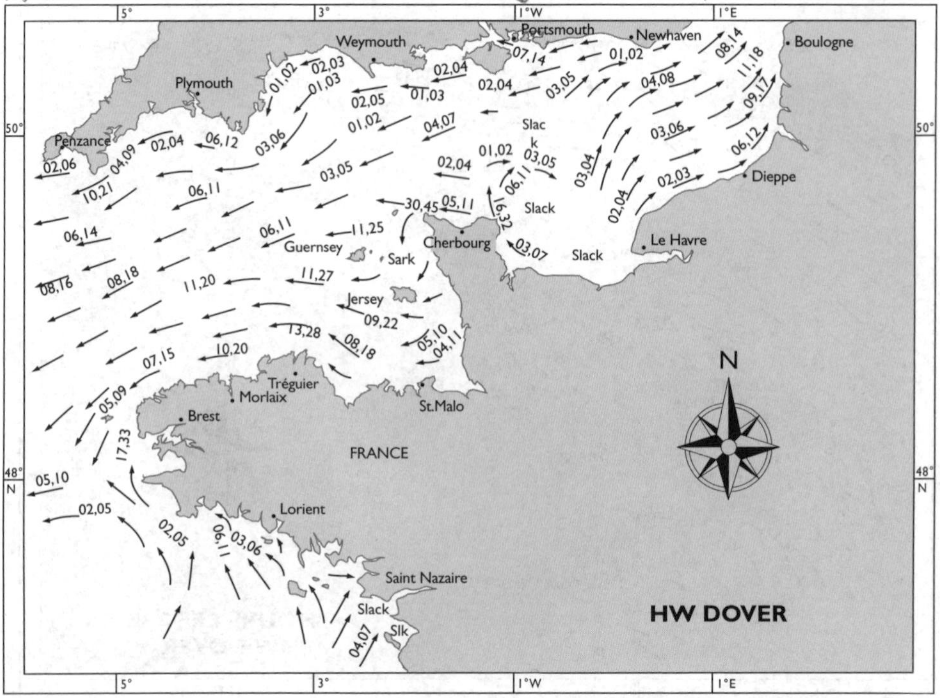

ENGLISH CHANNEL AND SOUTH BRITTANY

1255 — 1355

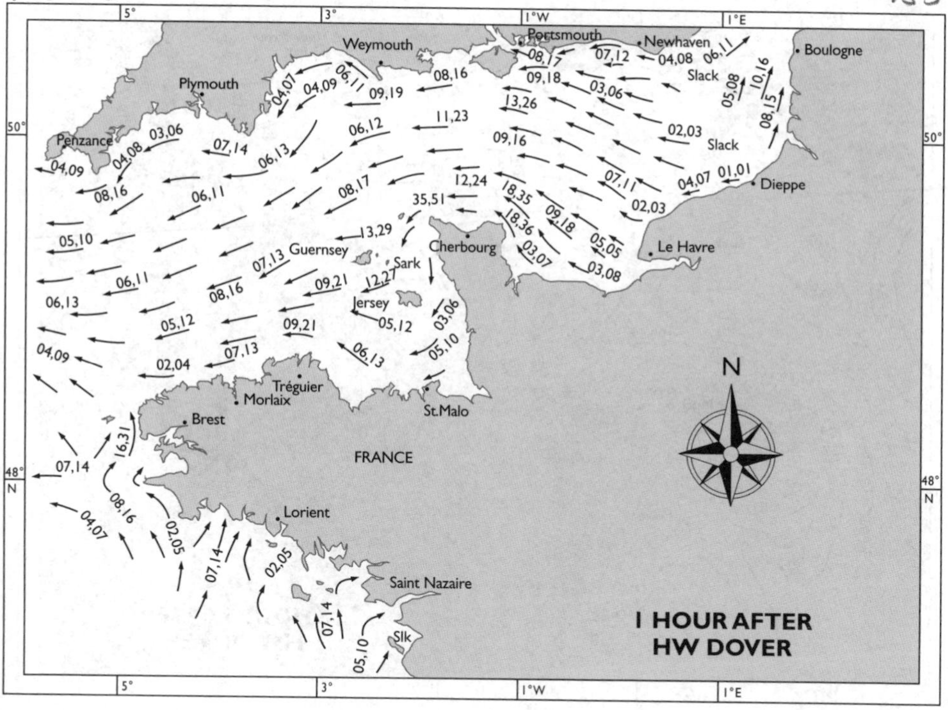

1355 — 1455

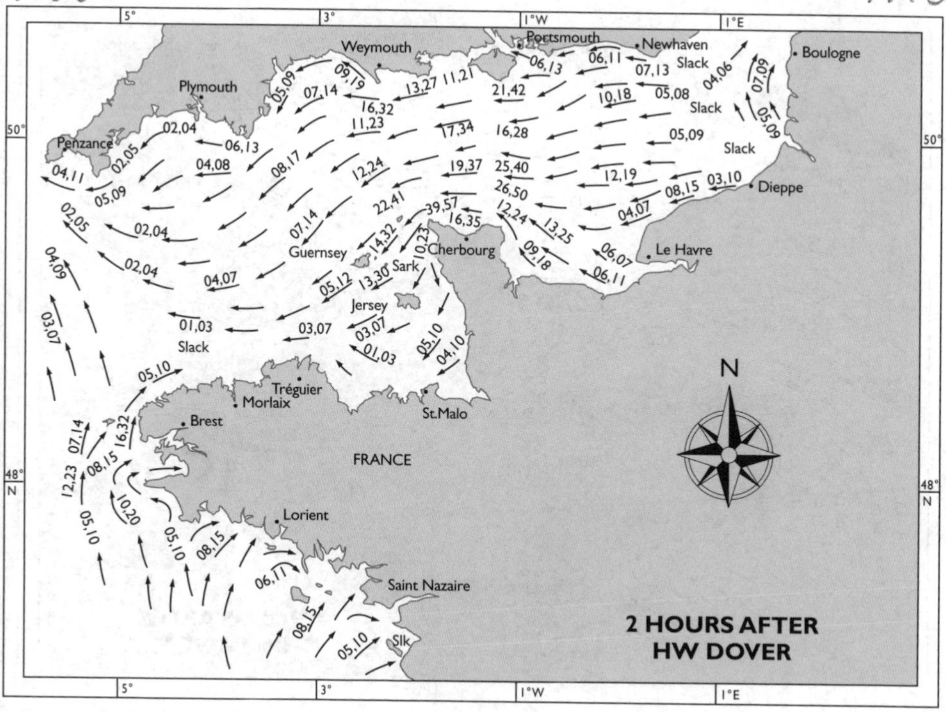

TIDES

19 Aug

ENGLISH CHANNEL AND SOUTH BRITTANY

1455 1555

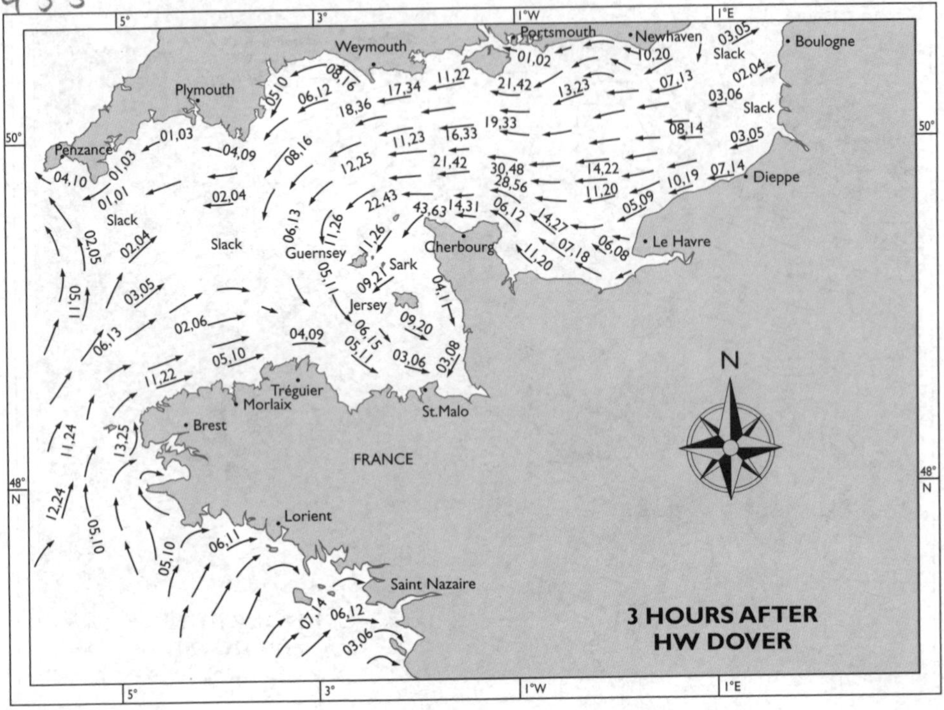

1555 19 Aug 1655

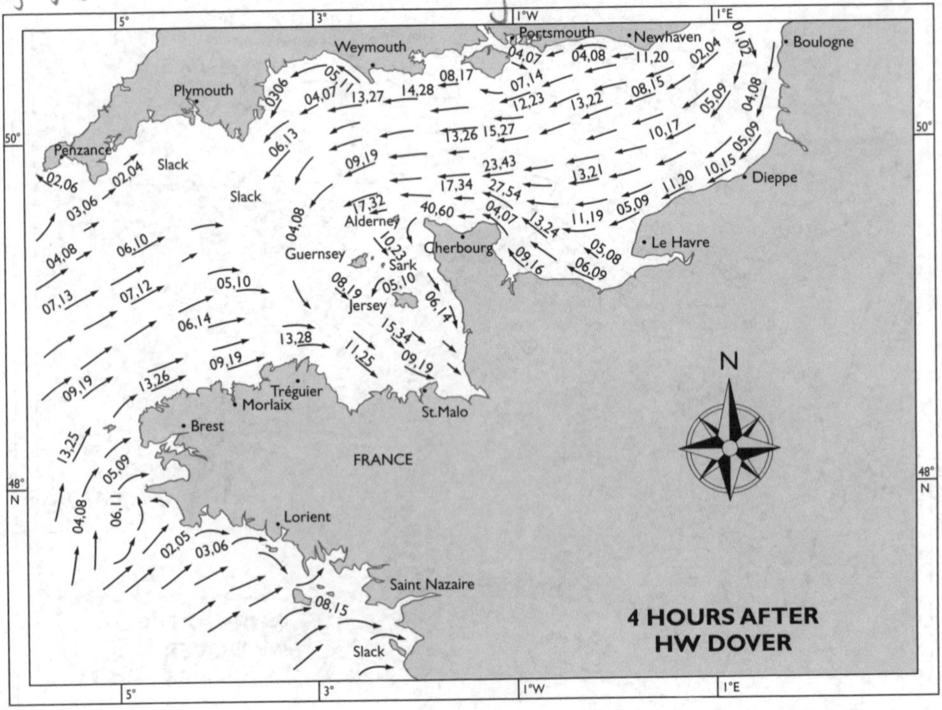

19 Aug

1655 1755

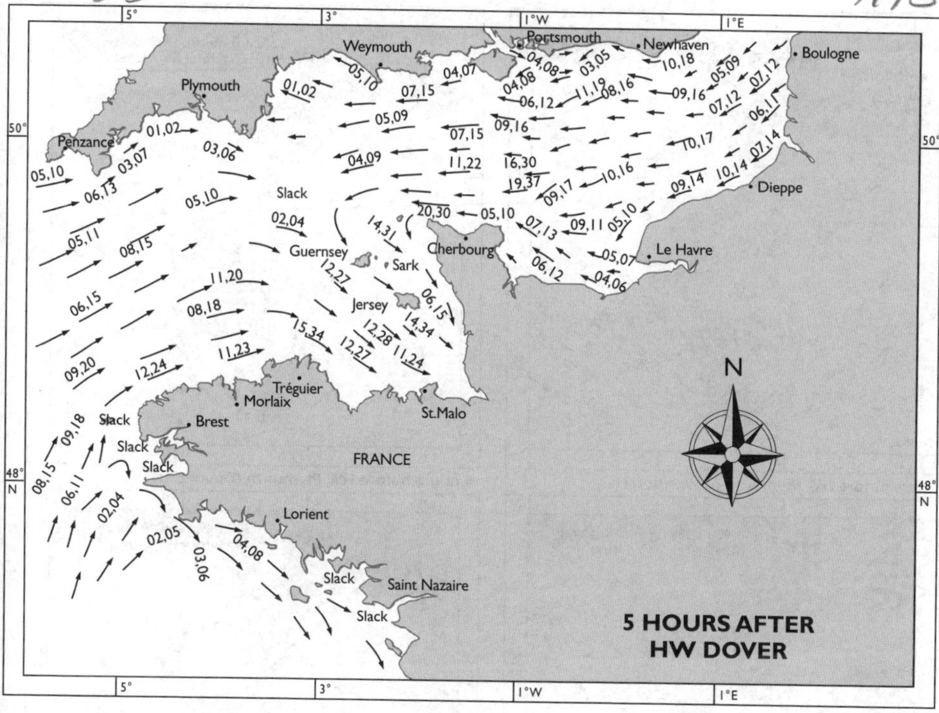

5 HOURS AFTER HW DOVER

1755 19 Aug 1855

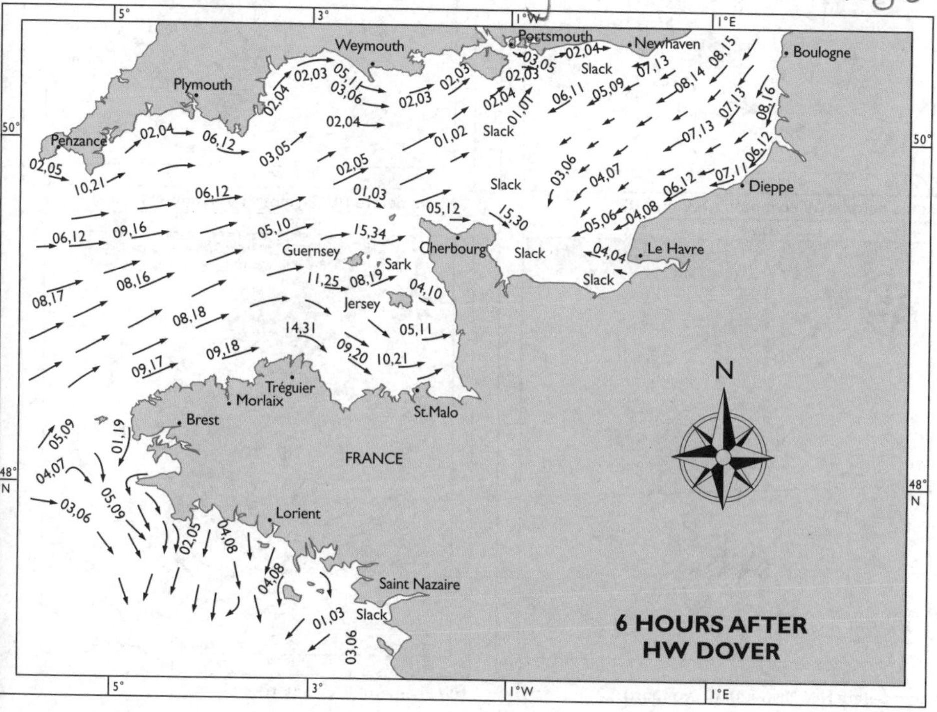

6 HOURS AFTER HW DOVER

PORTLAND

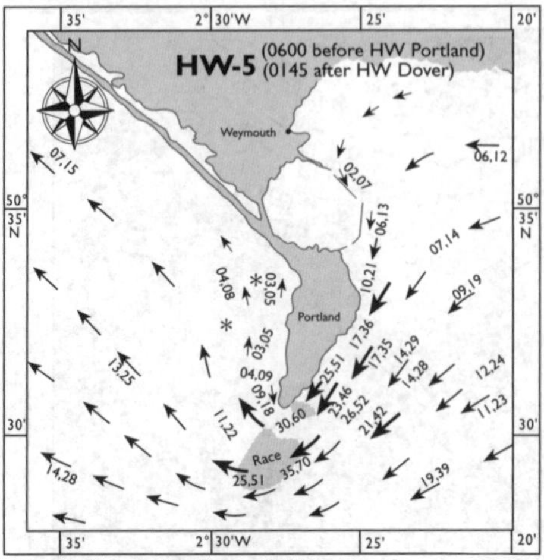

5 hours before HW Plymouth (Devonport)

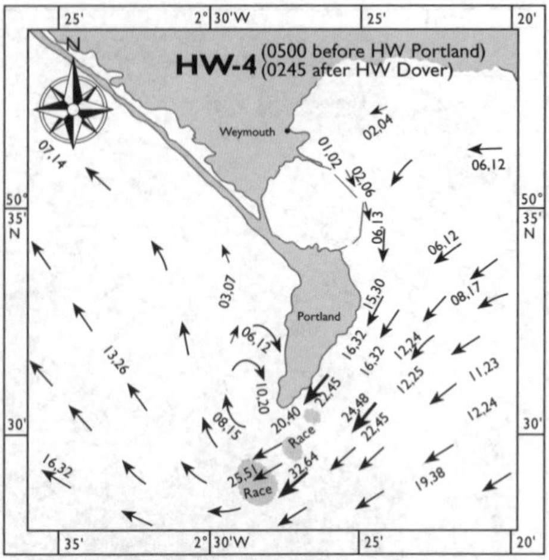

4 hours before HW Plymouth (Devonport)

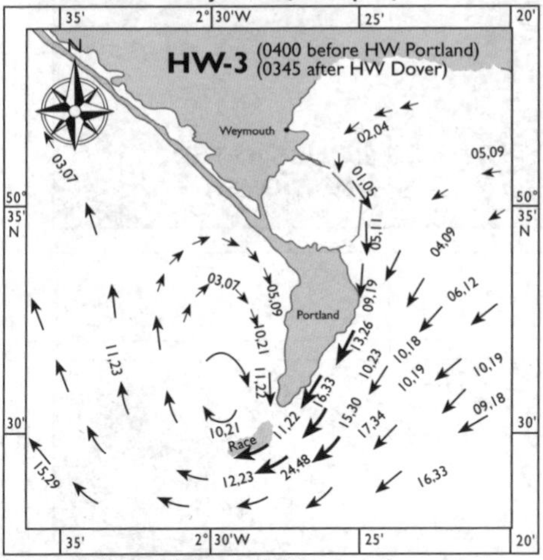

3 hours before HW Plymouth (Devonport)

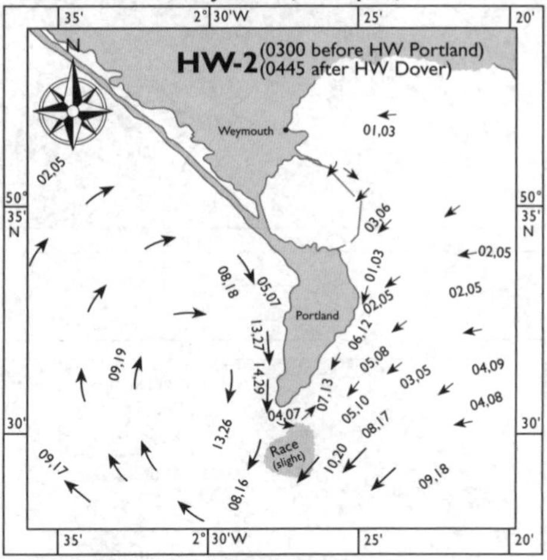

2 hours before HW Plymouth (Devonport)

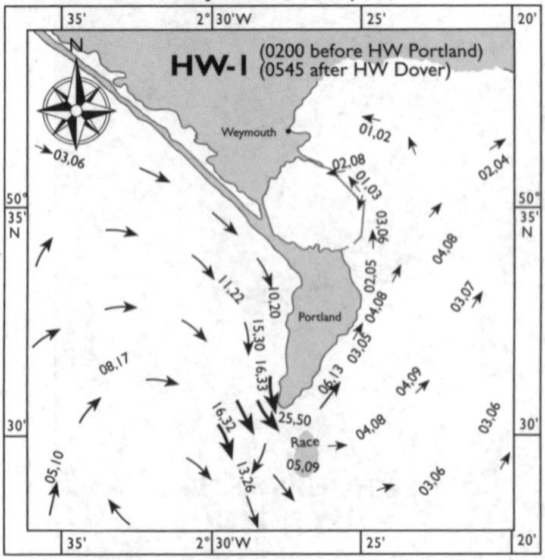

1 hour before HW Plymouth (Devonport)

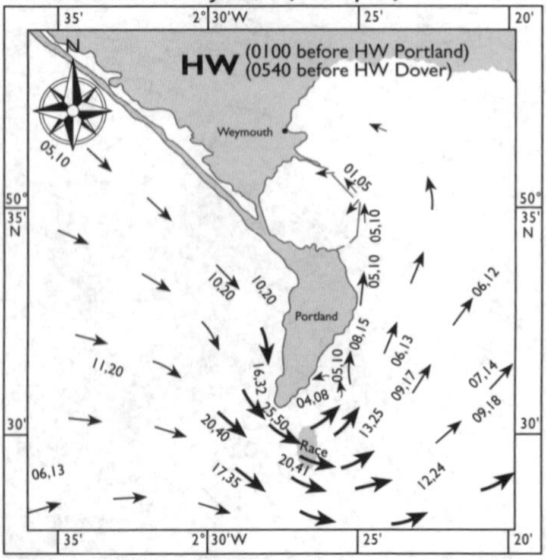

HW Plymouth (Devonport)

PORTLAND

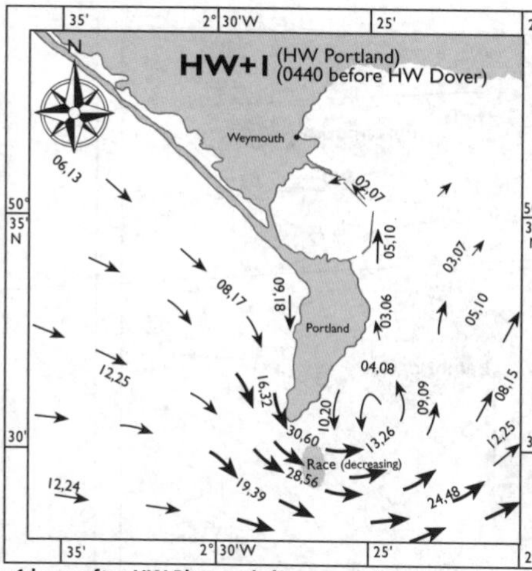

1 hour after HW Plymouth (Devonport)

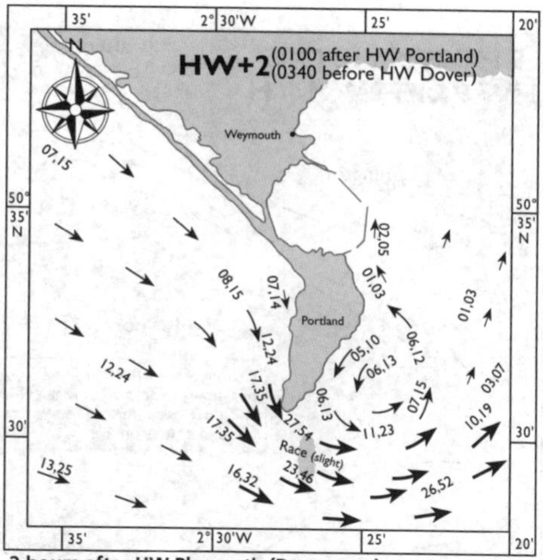

2 hours after HW Plymouth (Devonport)

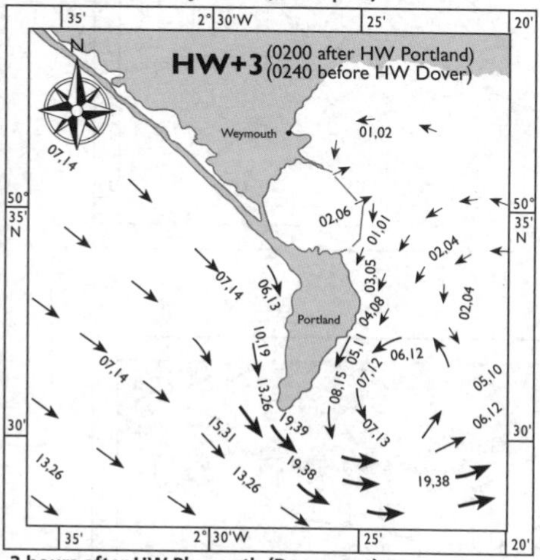

3 hours after HW Plymouth (Devonport)

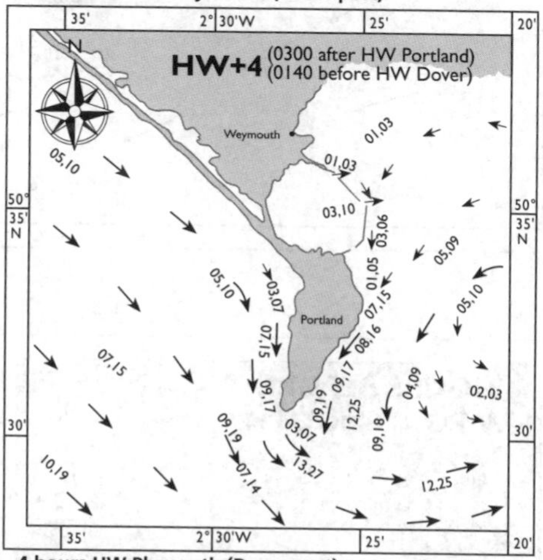

4 hours HW Plymouth (Devonport)

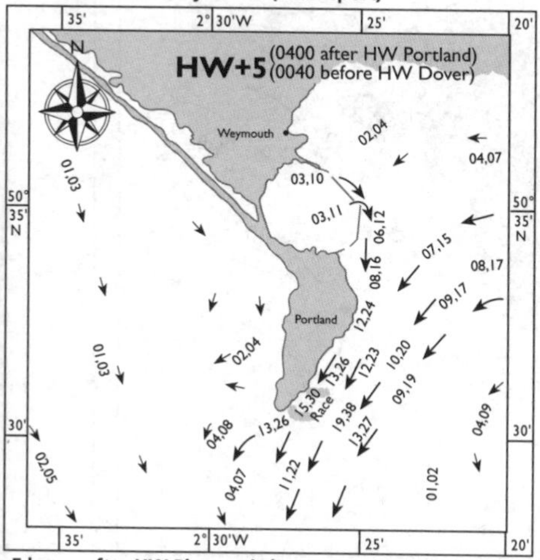

5 hours after HW Plymouth (Devonport)

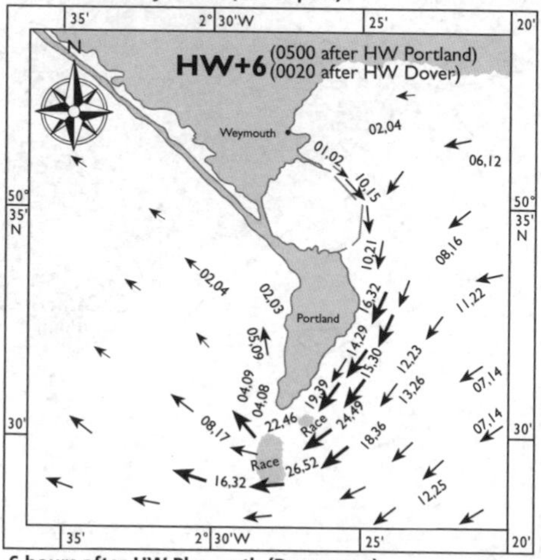

6 hours after HW Plymouth (Devonport)

TIDES

LW 0.8m

ISLE OF WIGHT

0657 0757

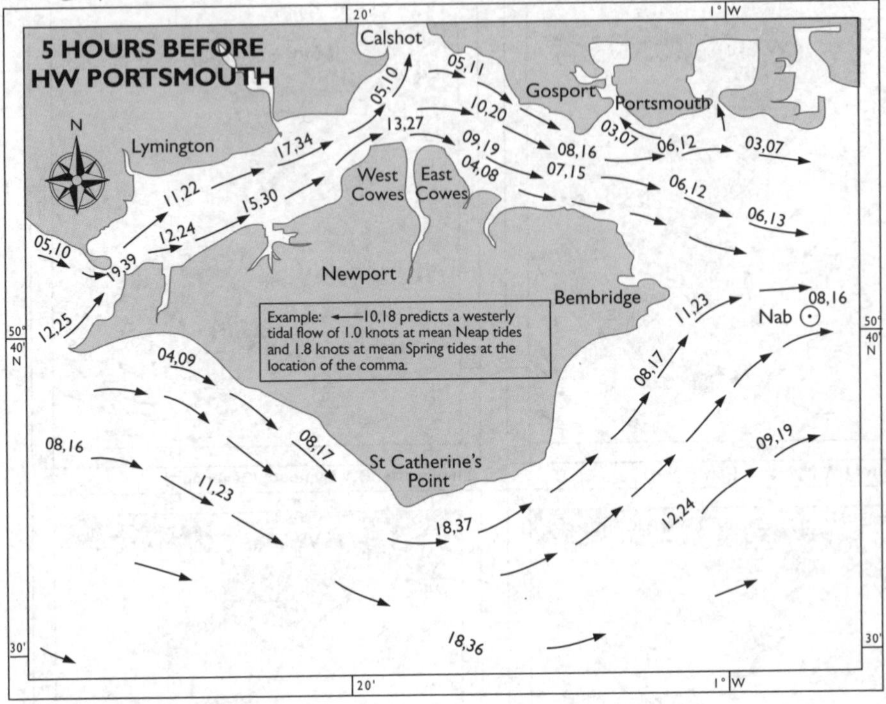

0751 0851

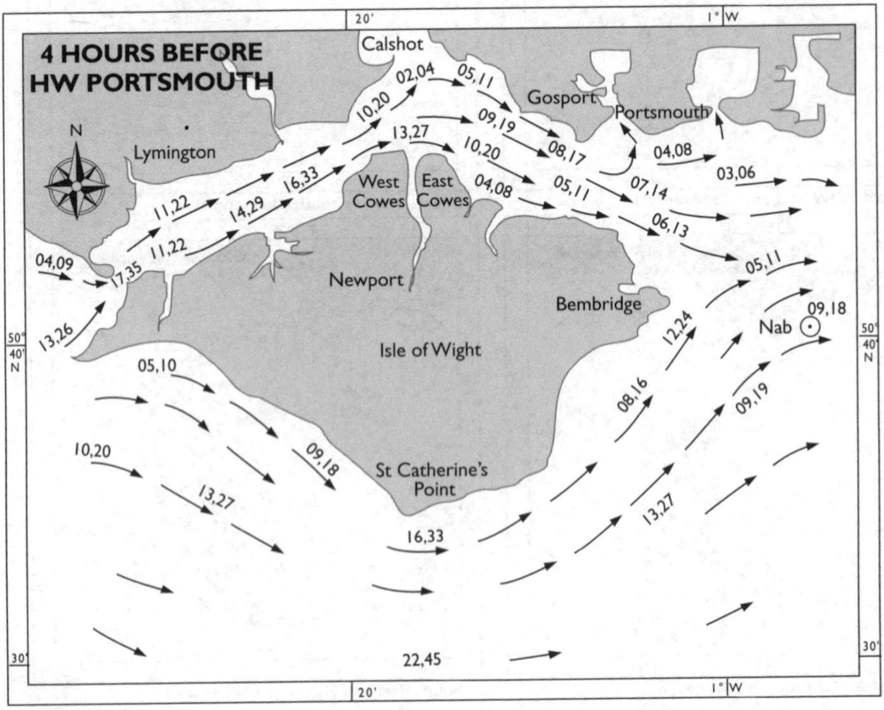

ISLE OF WIGHT

0851 0951

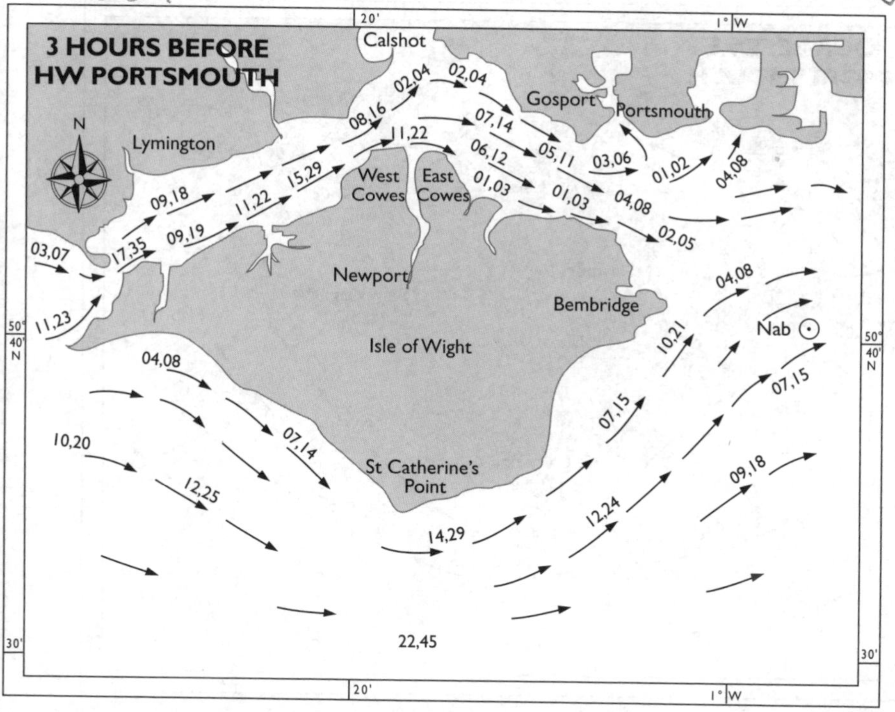

3 HOURS BEFORE HW PORTSMOUTH
20'
1° W
50° 40' N
30'
Calshot
Lymington
Gosport
Portsmouth
West Cowes
East Cowes
Newport
Bembridge
Nab
Isle of Wight
St Catherine's Point
N
02,04
02,04
08,16
07,14
11,22
06,12
05,11
03,06
01,02
04,08
15,29
11,22
09,18
01,03
01,03
04,08
09,19
17,35
02,05
03,07
11,23
04,08
10,21
04,08
07,15
07,15
07,14
10,20
12,25
14,29
12,24
09,18
22,45

0951 1051

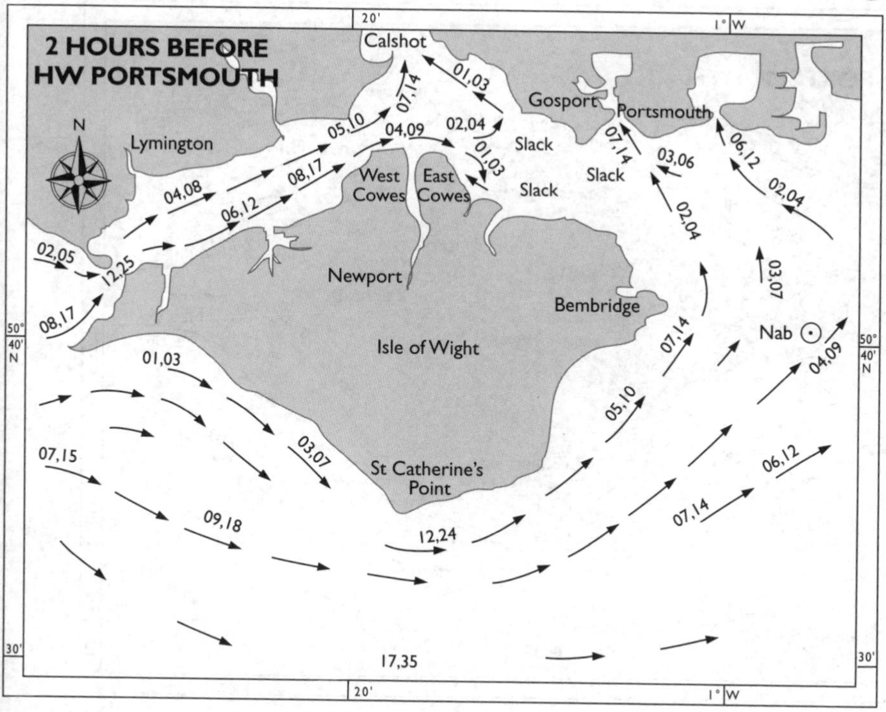

2 HOURS BEFORE HW PORTSMOUTH
20'
1° W
50° 40' N
30'
Calshot
Lymington
Gosport
Portsmouth
West Cowes
East Cowes
Newport
Bembridge
Nab
Isle of Wight
St Catherine's Point
N
Slack
Slack
Slack
07,14
01,03
05,10
04,09
02,04
01,03
07,14
03,06
06,12
08,17
04,08
06,12
02,04
02,04
02,05
12,25
08,17
03,07
07,14
01,03
05,10
04,09
03,07
07,15
09,18
12,24
07,14
06,12
17,35

ISLE OF WIGHT

1051 1151

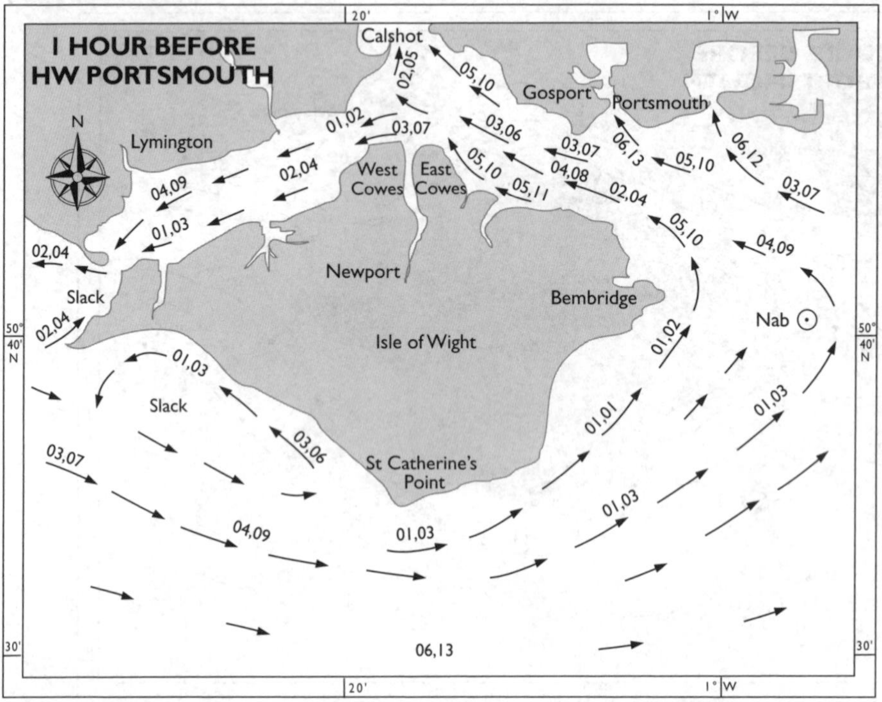

1151 1221 1253

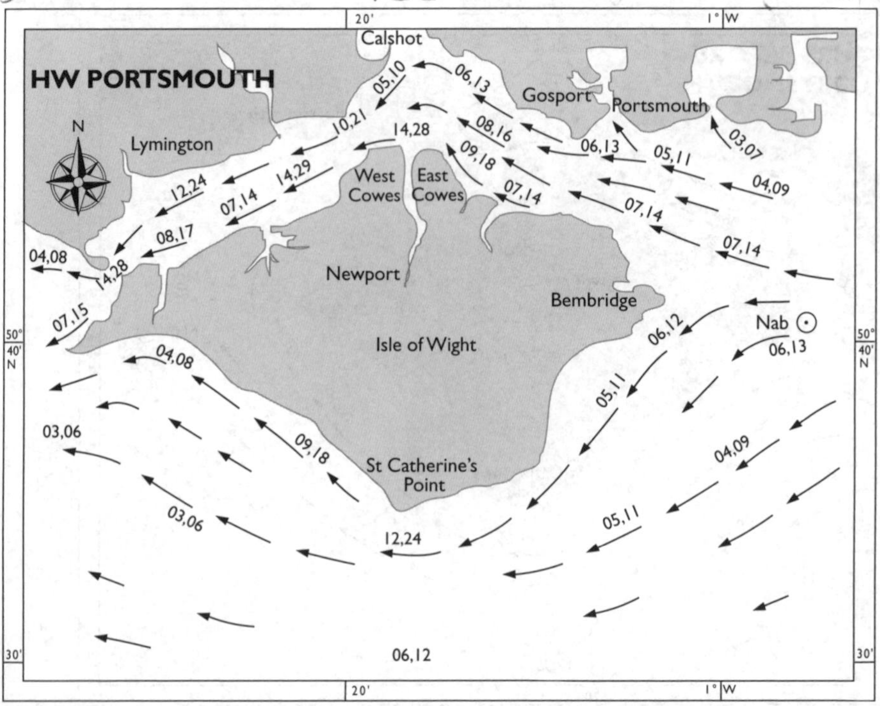

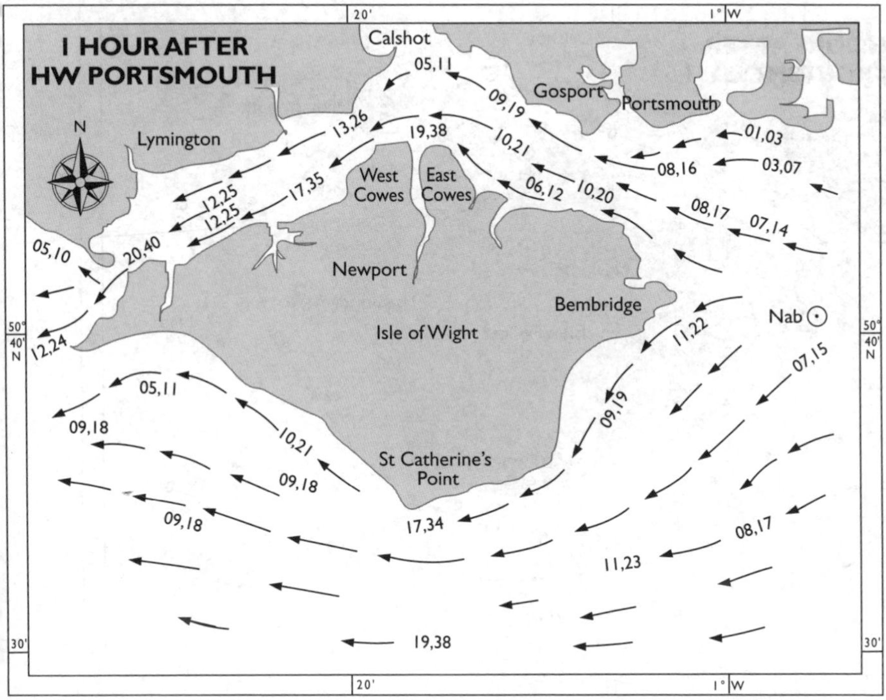
1 HOUR AFTER HW PORTSMOUTH
20'
1° W
N
Calshot
Lymington
Gosport
Portsmouth
West Cowes
East Cowes
Newport
Bembridge
Nab
Isle of Wight
St Catherine's Point
50° 40' N
30'
05,11
09,19
13,26
19,38
10,21
01,03
08,16
03,07
06,12
10,20
08,17
07,14
12,25
12,25
17,35
20,40
05,10
11,22
07,15
12,24
05,11
09,18
10,21
09,19
09,18
09,18
17,34
08,17
11,23
19,38

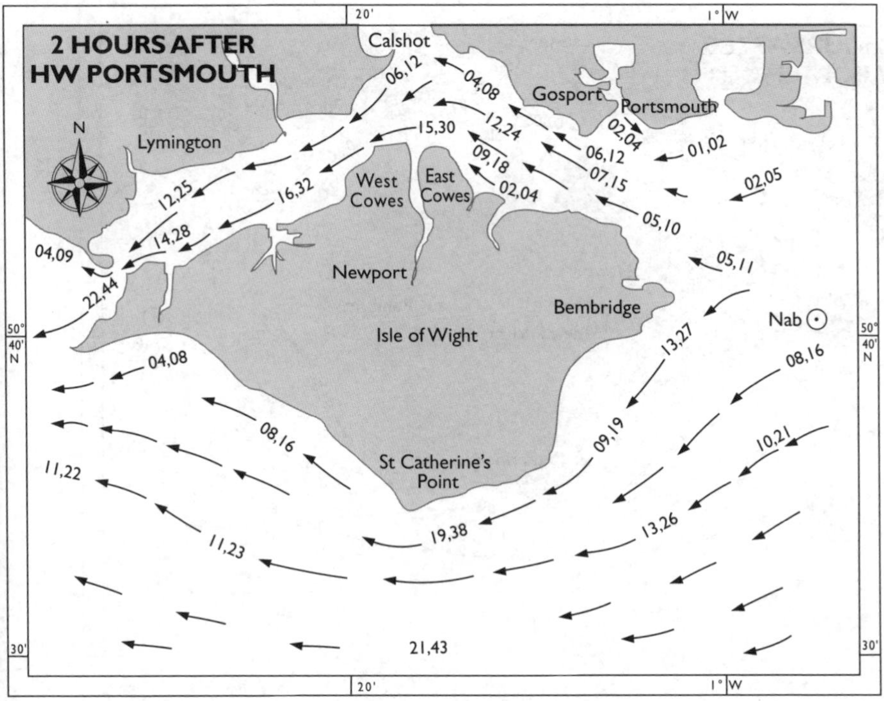
2 HOURS AFTER HW PORTSMOUTH
20'
1° W
N
Calshot
Lymington
Gosport
Portsmouth
West Cowes
East Cowes
Newport
Bembridge
Nab
Isle of Wight
St Catherine's Point
50° 40' N
30'
06,12
04,08
12,24
15,30
02,04
06,12
01,02
09,18
02,04
07,15
02,05
16,32
12,25
05,10
14,28
04,09
05,11
22,44
13,27
04,08
08,16
08,16
09,19
11,22
10,21
19,38
13,26
11,23
21,43

ISLE OF WIGHT

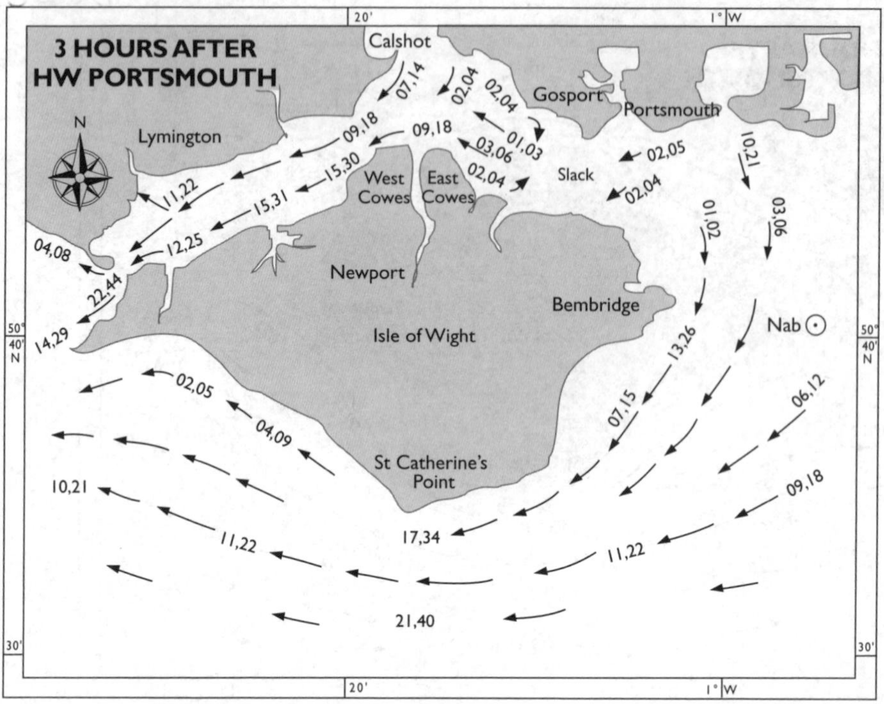

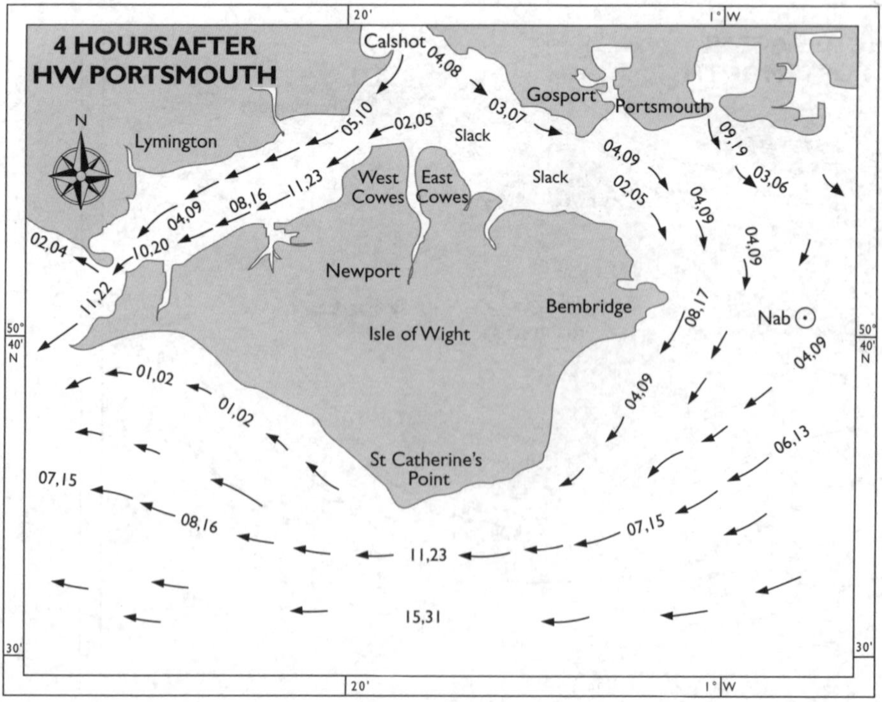

1 Aug

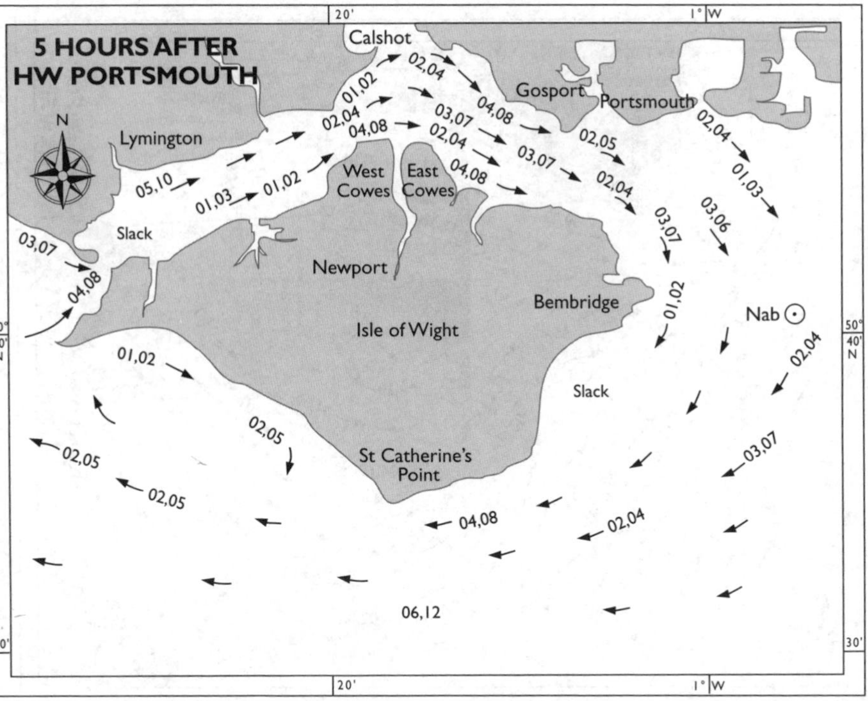
5 HOURS AFTER HW PORTSMOUTH
20'
1° W
Calshot
Gosport
Portsmouth
Lymington
N
West Cowes
East Cowes
Slack
Newport
Bembridge
Nab
Isle of Wight
Slack
St Catherine's Point
50° 40' N
30'
02,04
01,02
02,04
04,08
03,07
04,08
02,04
02,05
03,07
02,04
02,04
01,03
05,10
01,03
01,02
04,08
03,07
03,06
03,07
04,08
01,02
02,04
01,02
02,05
02,05
02,05
03,07
04,08
02,04
06,12

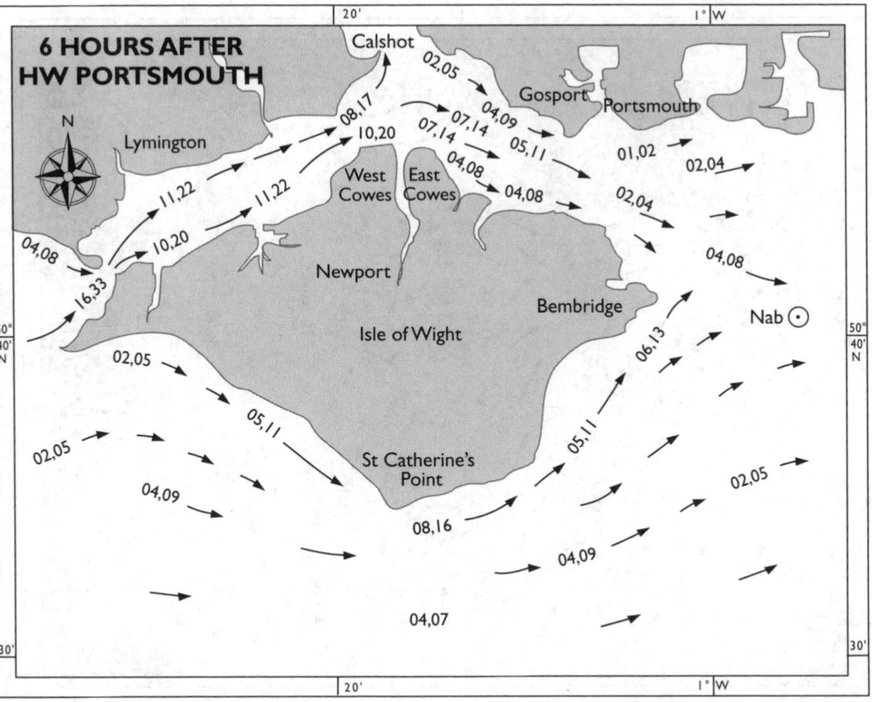
6 HOURS AFTER HW PORTSMOUTH
20'
1° W
Calshot
Gosport
Portsmouth
Lymington
N
West Cowes
East Cowes
Newport
Bembridge
Nab
Isle of Wight
St Catherine's Point
50° 40' N
30'
02,05
08,17
04,09
07,14
10,20
07,14
05,11
01,02
02,04
04,08
11,22
11,22
04,08
02,04
04,08
10,20
16,33
04,08
06,13
02,05
05,11
02,05
05,11
04,09
08,16
02,05
04,09
04,07

TIDES

CHANNEL ISLANDS

Example: ⟵10,18 predicts a westerly tidal flow of 1.0 knots at mean Neap tides and 1.8 knots at mean Spring tides at the location of the comma.

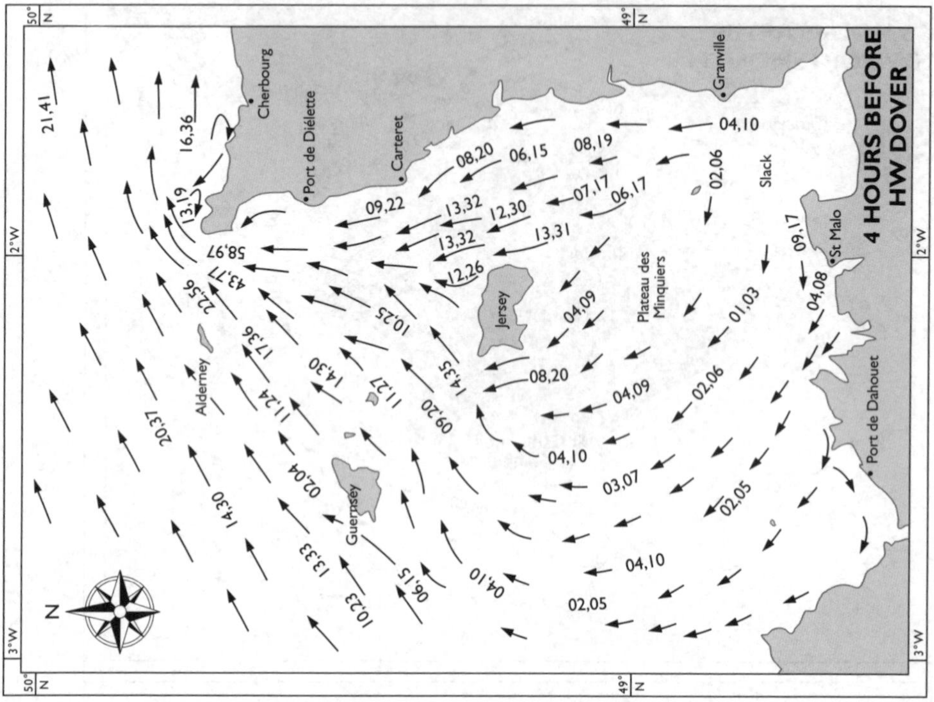

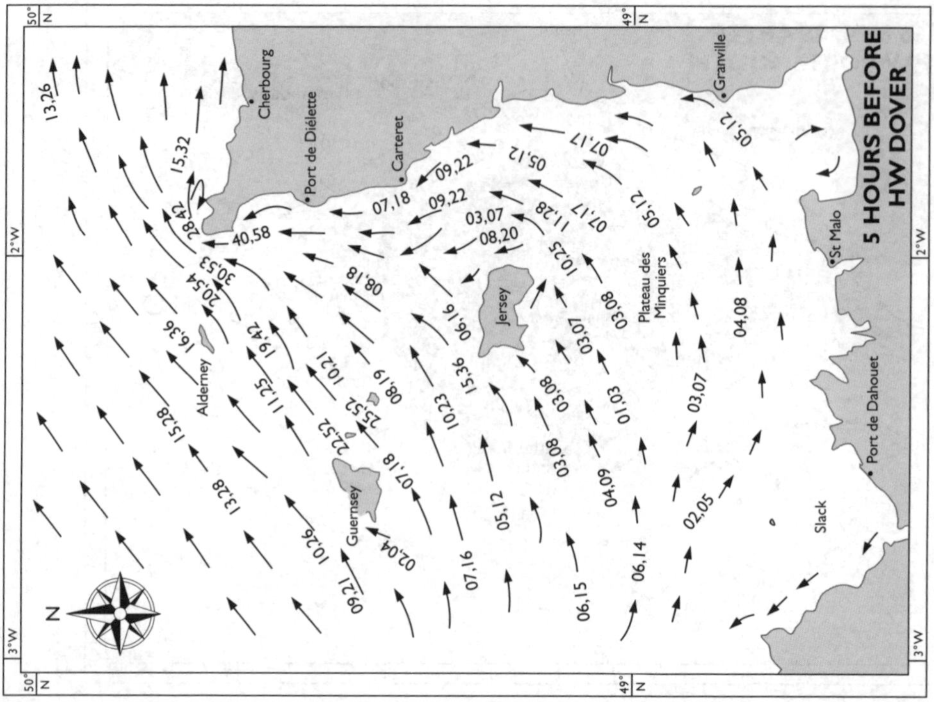

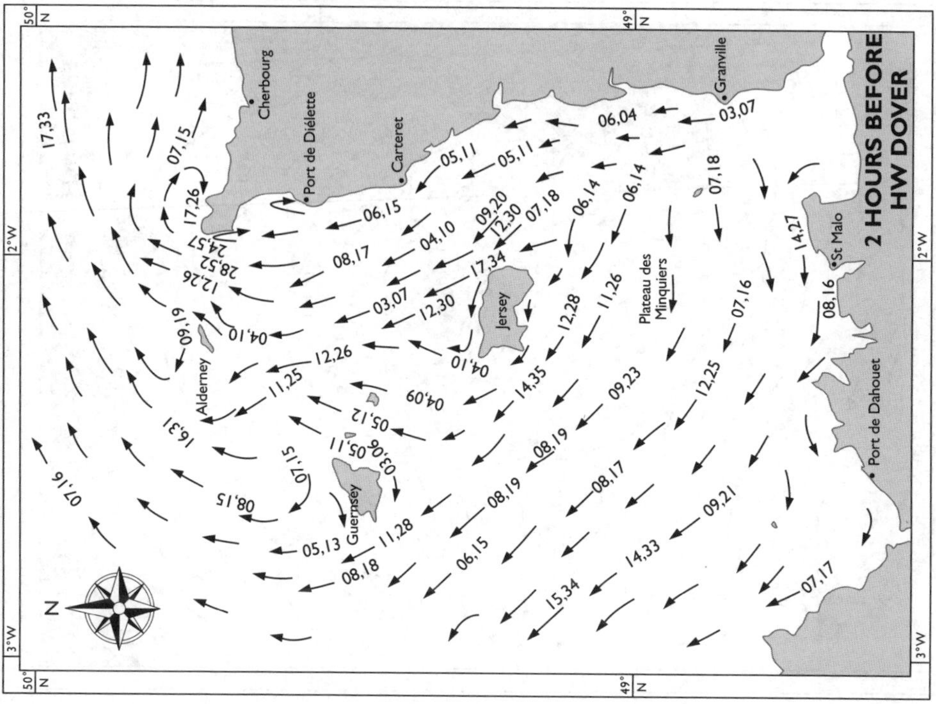

2 HOURS BEFORE HW DOVER
Cherbourg
Port de Diélette
Carteret
Granville
St Malo
Port de Dahouet
Jersey
Guernsey
Alderney
Plateau des Minquiers
N
50° N
49° N
2°W
3°W

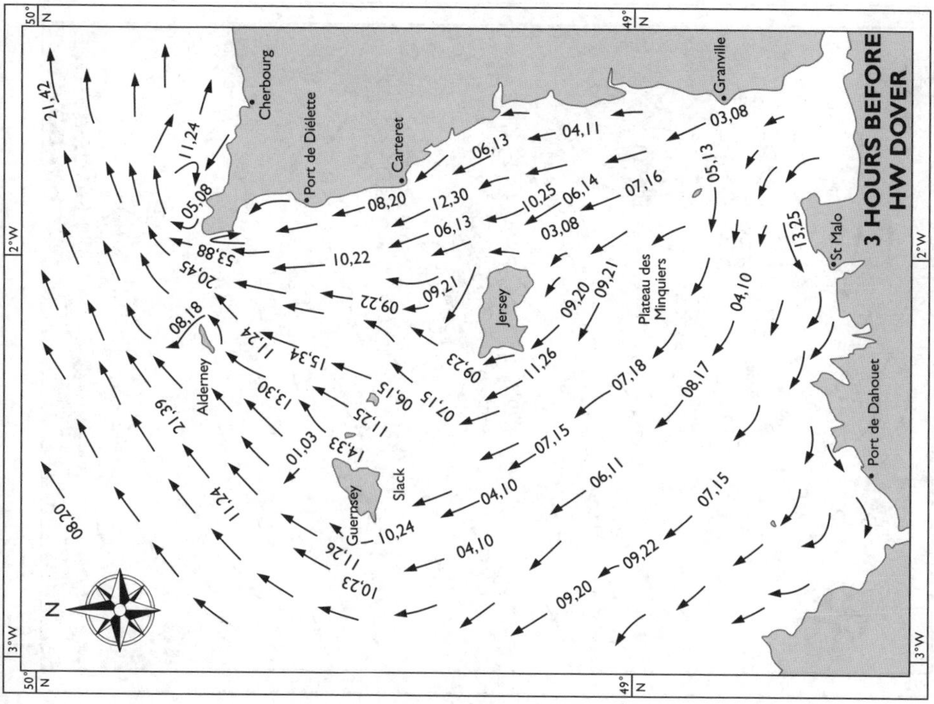

3 HOURS BEFORE HW DOVER
Cherbourg
Port de Diélette
Carteret
Granville
St Malo
Port de Dahouet
Jersey
Guernsey
Alderney
Plateau des Minquiers
Slack
N
50° N
49° N
2°W
3°W

TIDES

CHANNEL ISLANDS

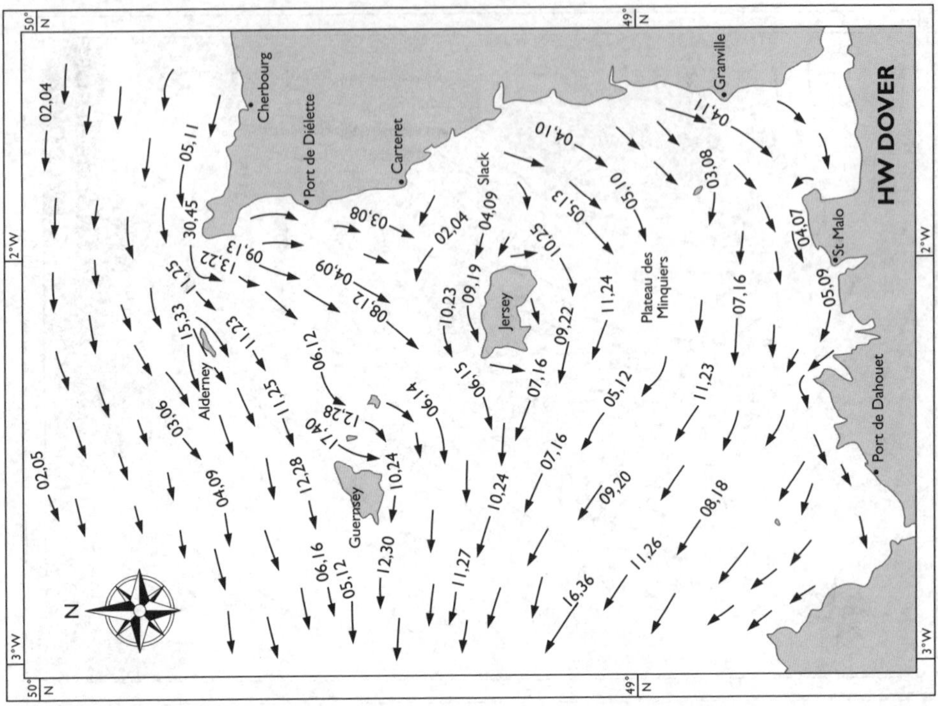

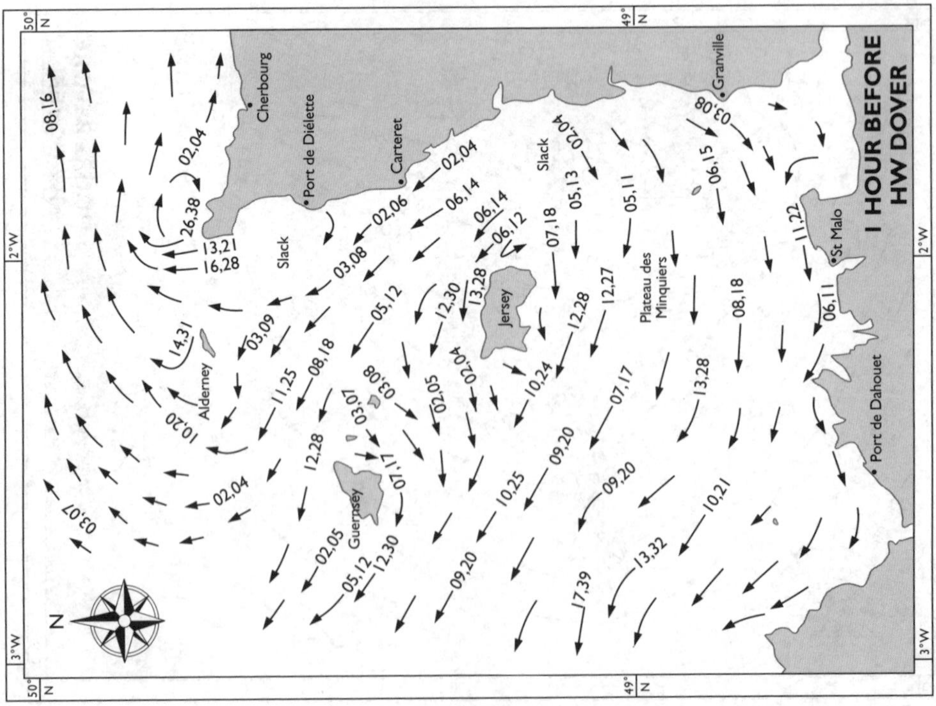

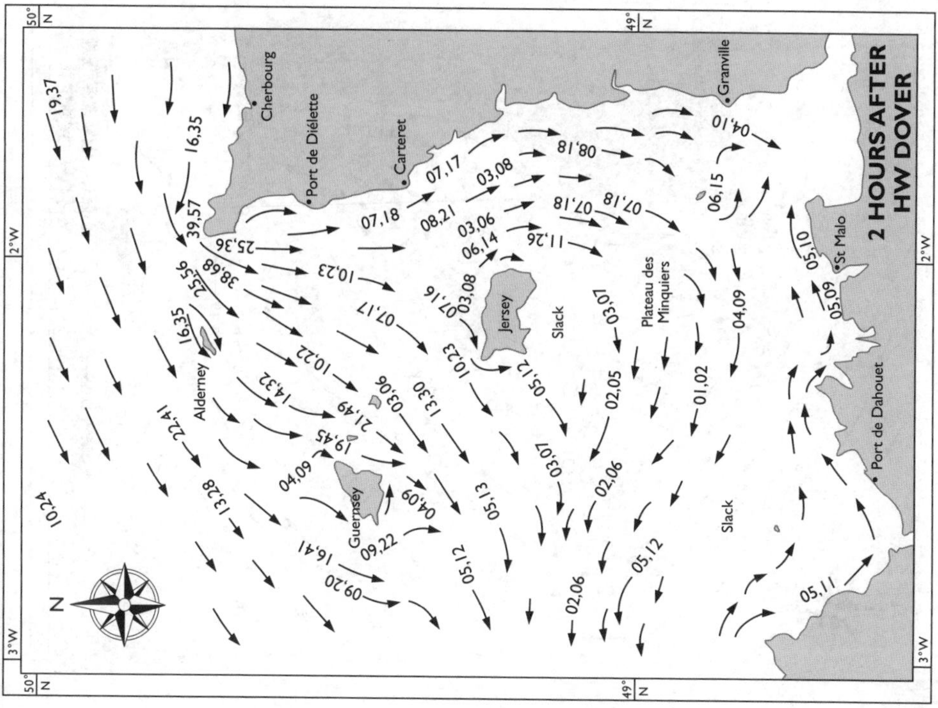
2 HOURS AFTER HW DOVER
Cherbourg
Port de Diélette
Carteret
Granville
Alderney
Guernsey
Jersey
Plateau des Minquiers
St Malo
Port de Dahouet
Slack
Slack
N

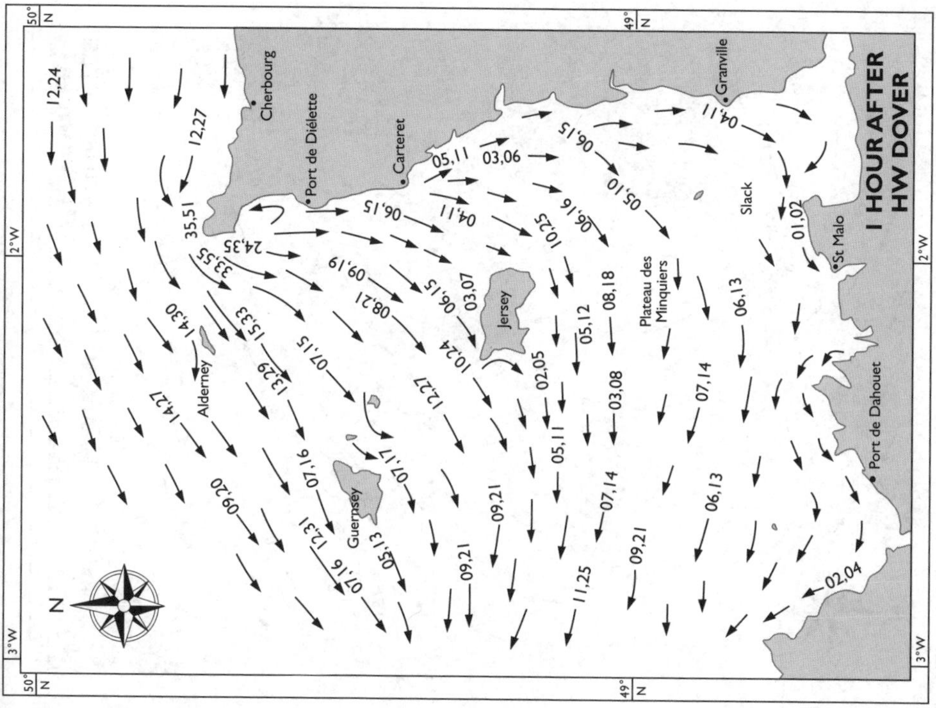
1 HOUR AFTER HW DOVER
Cherbourg
Port de Diélette
Carteret
Granville
Alderney
Guernsey
Jersey
Plateau des Minquiers
St Malo
Port de Dahouet
Slack
N

CHANNEL ISLANDS

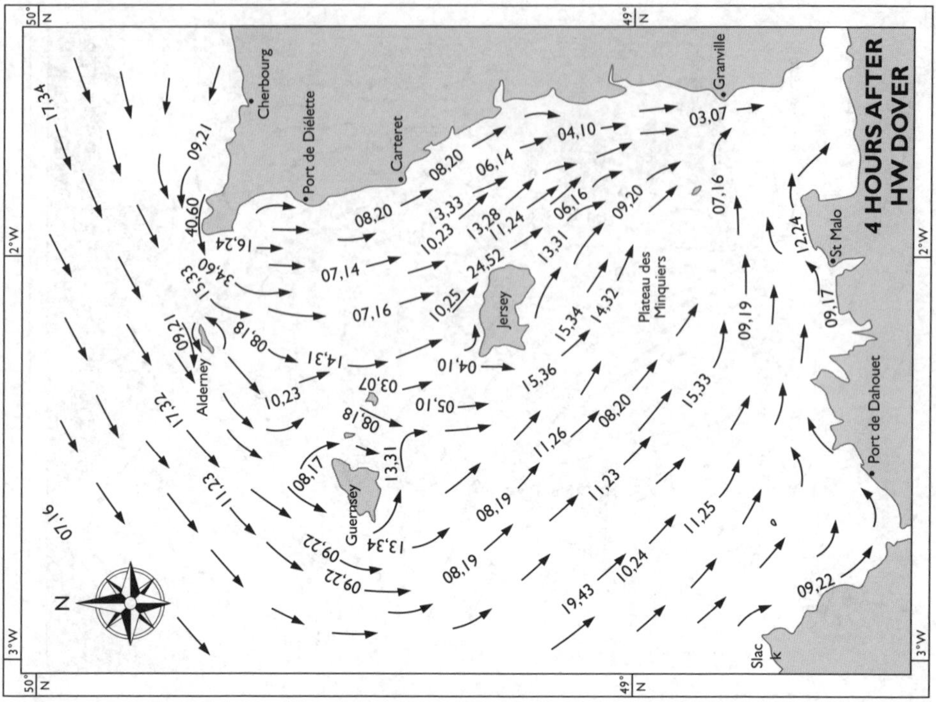

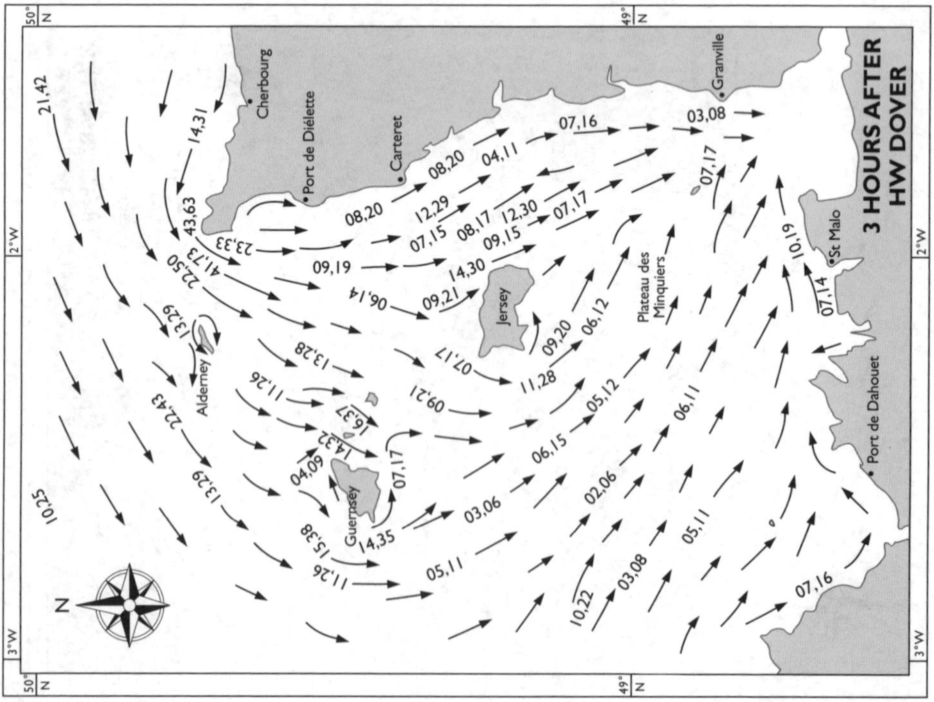

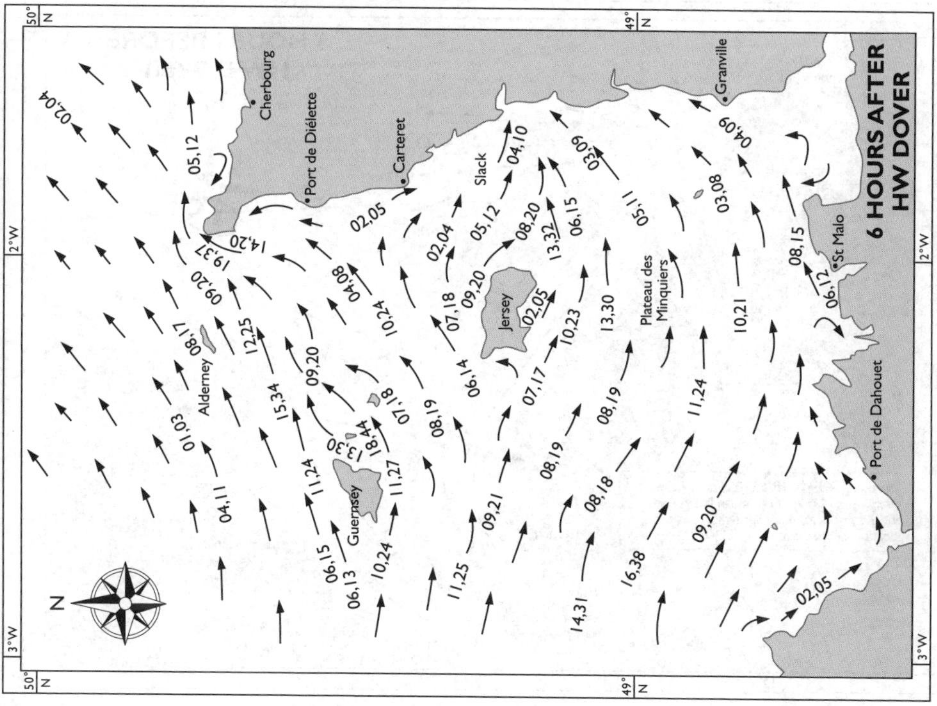
6 HOURS AFTER HW DOVER
Cherbourg
Port de Diélette
Carteret
Granville
Slack
Alderney
Guernsey
Jersey
Plateau des Minquiers
St Malo
Port de Dahouet
50° N
49° N
3°W
2°W

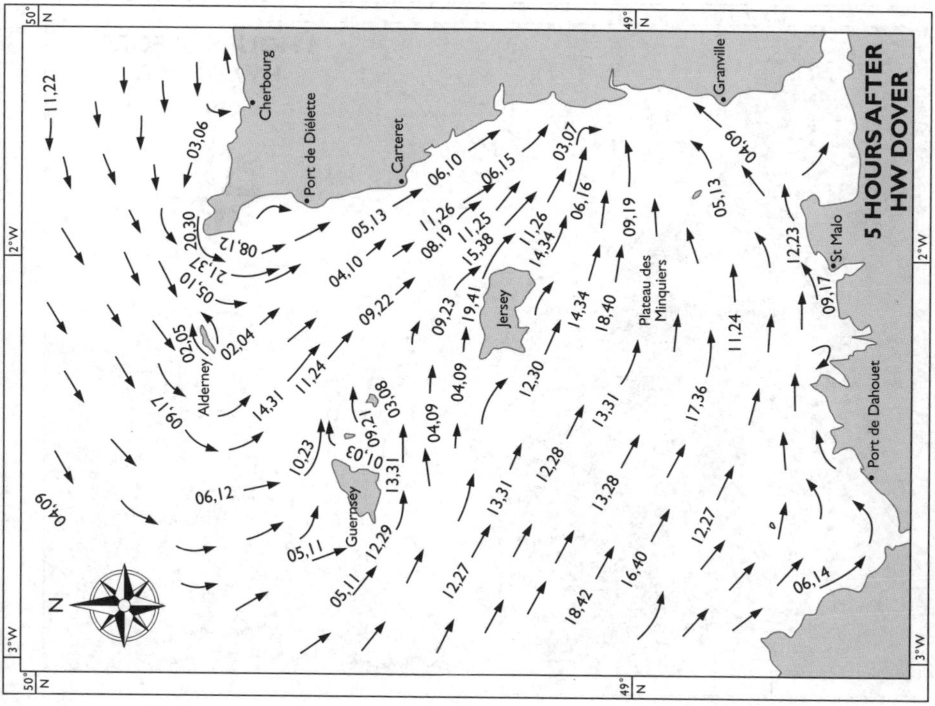
5 HOURS AFTER HW DOVER
Cherbourg
Port de Diélette
Carteret
Granville
Alderney
Guernsey
Jersey
Plateau des Minquiers
St Malo
Port de Dahouet
50° N
49° N
3°W
2°W

TIDES

NORTH SEA

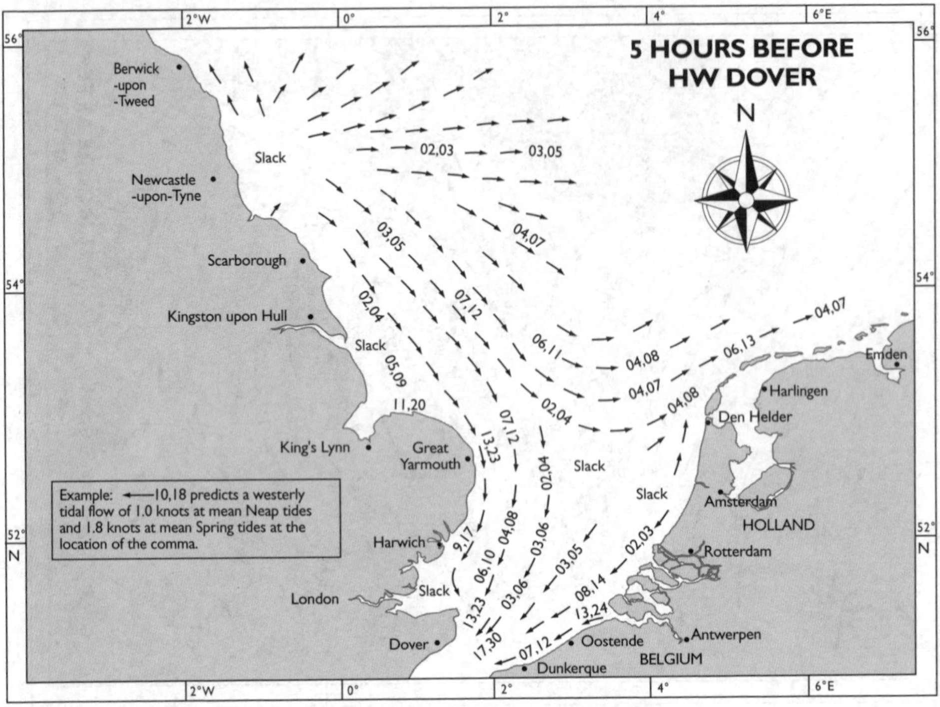
5 HOURS BEFORE HW DOVER
N
2°W
0°
2°
4°
6°E
56°
54°
52° N
Berwick -upon -Tweed
Newcastle -upon-Tyne
Scarborough
Kingston upon Hull
King's Lynn
Great Yarmouth
Harwich
London
Dover
Dunkerque
Oostende
BELGIUM
Antwerpen
Rotterdam
HOLLAND
Amsterdam
Den Helder
Harlingen
Emden
Slack
02,03
03,05
03,05
04,07
02,04
07,12
Slack
05,09
06,11
04,08
06,13
04,07
04,07
04,08
11,20
02,04
07,12
13,23
02,04
Slack
Slack
9,17
04,08
03,06
03,05
02,03
06,10
03,06
08,14
Slack
13,23
13,24
17,30
07,12
Example: ←10,18 predicts a westerly tidal flow of 1.0 knots at mean Neap tides and 1.8 knots at mean Spring tides at the location of the comma.

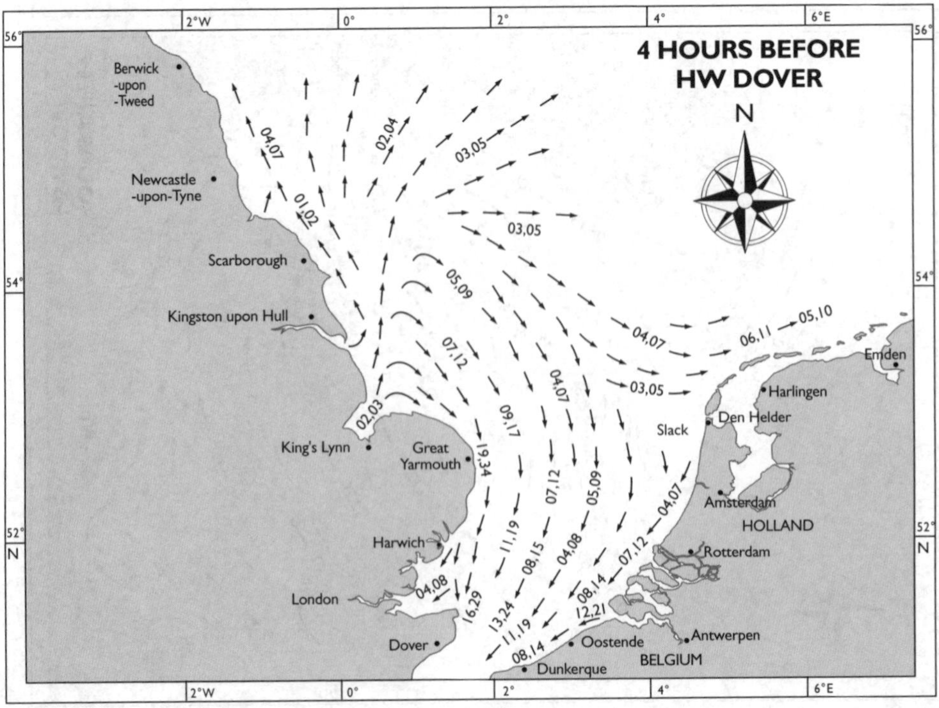
4 HOURS BEFORE HW DOVER
N
2°W
0°
2°
4°
6°E
56°
54°
52° N
Berwick -upon -Tweed
Newcastle -upon-Tyne
Scarborough
Kingston upon Hull
King's Lynn
Great Yarmouth
Harwich
London
Dover
Dunkerque
Oostende
BELGIUM
Antwerpen
Rotterdam
HOLLAND
Amsterdam
Den Helder
Harlingen
Emden
04,07
02,04
03,05
01,02
03,05
05,09
04,07
06,11
05,10
07,12
03,05
02,03
09,17
04,07
Slack
19,34
07,12
05,09
04,07
11,19
08,15
04,08
07,12
04,08
16,29
13,24
08,14
12,21
11,19
08,14

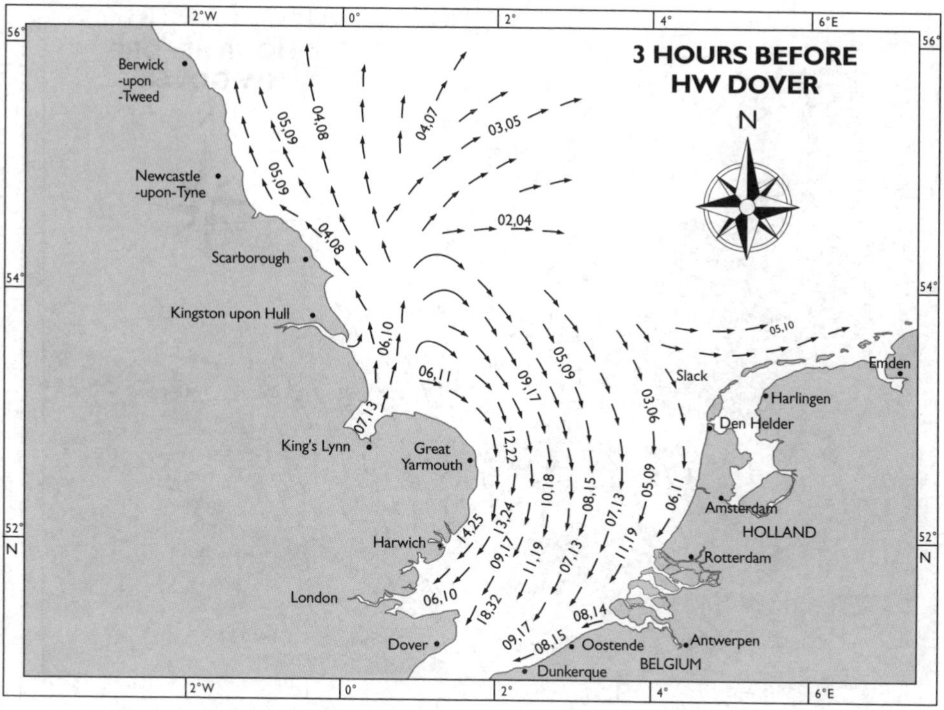
3 HOURS BEFORE HW DOVER
N
2°W
0°
2°
4°
6°E
56°
54°
52° N
Berwick -upon -Tweed
Newcastle -upon-Tyne
Scarborough
Kingston upon Hull
King's Lynn
Great Yarmouth
Harwich
London
Dover
Dunkerque
Oostende
BELGIUM
Antwerpen
Rotterdam
HOLLAND
Amsterdam
Den Helder
Harlingen
Emden
Slack
05,09
04,08
05,09
04,08
04,07
03,05
02,04
06,10
06,11
07,13
09,17
05,09
03,06
05,10
12,22
10,18
08,15
07,13
05,09
06,11
14,25
13,24
09,17
11,19
07,13
11,19
06,10
18,32
09,17
08,15
08,14

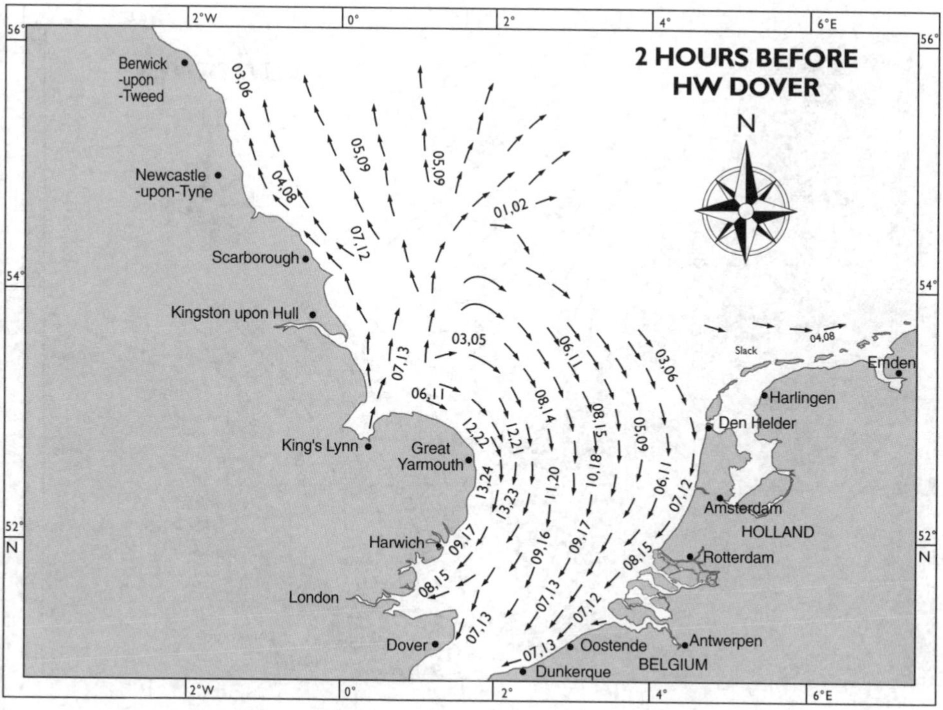
2 HOURS BEFORE HW DOVER
N
2°W
0°
2°
4°
6°E
56°
54°
52° N
Berwick -upon -Tweed
Newcastle -upon-Tyne
Scarborough
Kingston upon Hull
King's Lynn
Great Yarmouth
Harwich
London
Dover
Dunkerque
Oostende
BELGIUM
Antwerpen
Rotterdam
HOLLAND
Amsterdam
Den Helder
Harlingen
Emden
Slack
03,06
05,09
05,09
04,08
01,02
07,12
07,13
03,05
06,11
03,06
04,08
06,11
12,22
12,21
08,14
08,15
05,09
13,24
13,23
11,20
10,18
06,11
07,12
09,17
09,16
09,17
08,15
08,15
07,13
07,13
07,12
07,13

TIDES

NORTH SEA

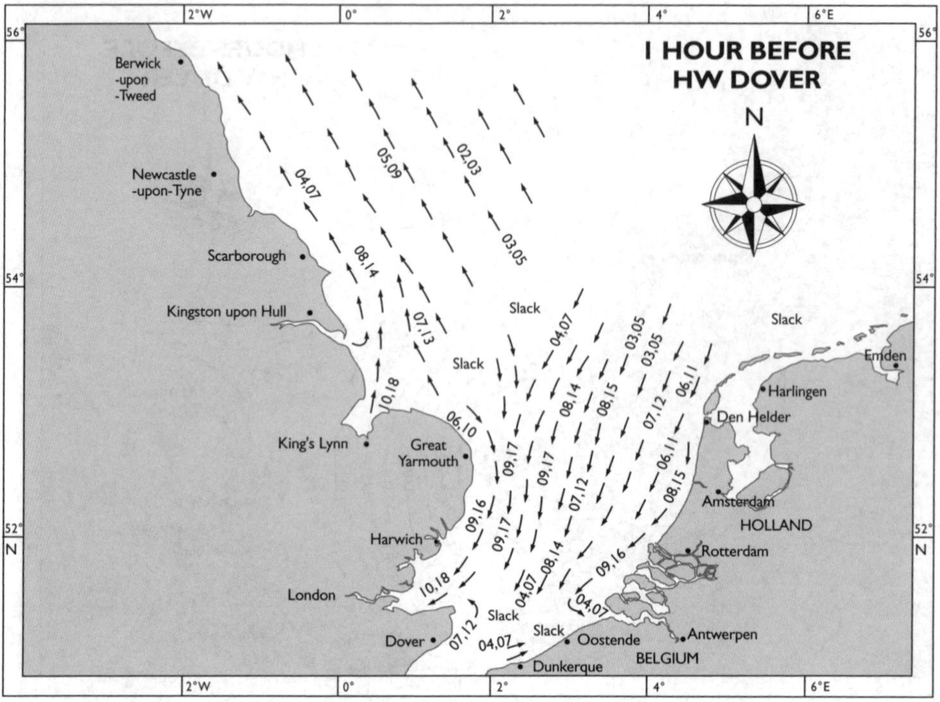
1 HOUR BEFORE HW DOVER
N
2°W
0°
2°
4°
6°E
56°
54°
52° N
Berwick -upon -Tweed
Newcastle -upon-Tyne
Scarborough
Kingston upon Hull
King's Lynn
Great Yarmouth
Harwich
London
Dover
Dunkerque
Oostende
BELGIUM
Antwerpen
Rotterdam
HOLLAND
Amsterdam
Den Helder
Harlingen
Emden
Slack
04,07
05,09
02,03
08,14
03,05
07,13
10,18
06,10
09,17
09,16
10,18
07,12
04,07
08,14
07,12
08,15
06,11
09,16
08,15

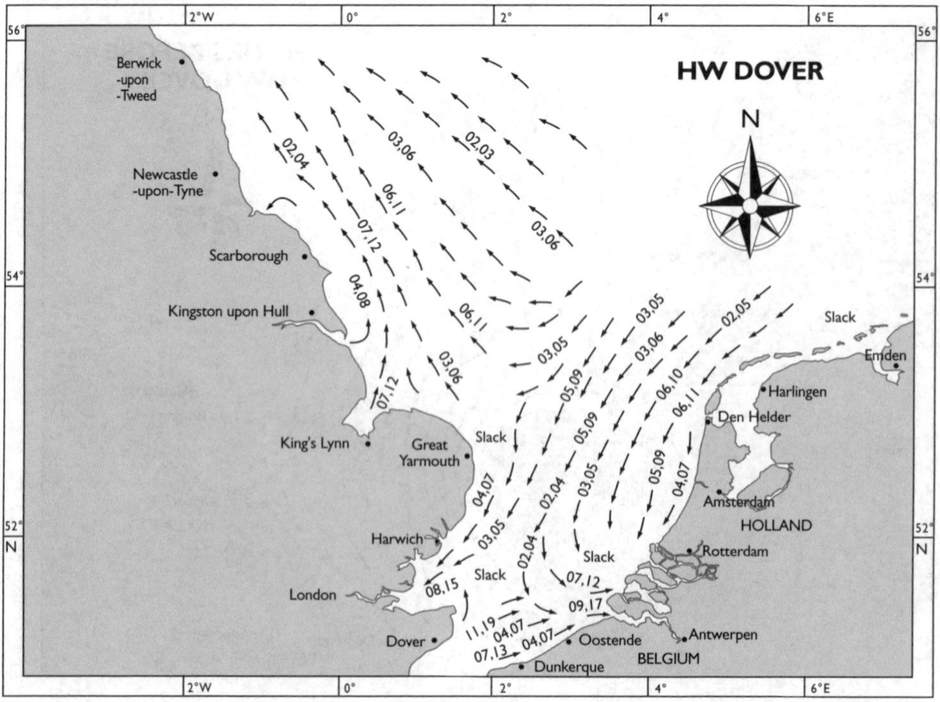
HW DOVER
N
2°W
0°
2°
4°
6°E
56°
54°
52° N
Berwick -upon -Tweed
Newcastle -upon-Tyne
Scarborough
Kingston upon Hull
King's Lynn
Great Yarmouth
Harwich
London
Dover
Dunkerque
Oostende
BELGIUM
Antwerpen
Rotterdam
HOLLAND
Amsterdam
Den Helder
Harlingen
Emden
Slack
02,04
03,06
02,03
06,11
07,12
03,06
04,08
06,11
03,06
07,12
03,05
05,09
03,05
03,06
02,05
06,10
06,11
05,09
04,07
02,04
08,15
07,12
09,17
11,19
04,07
07,13

NORTH SEA

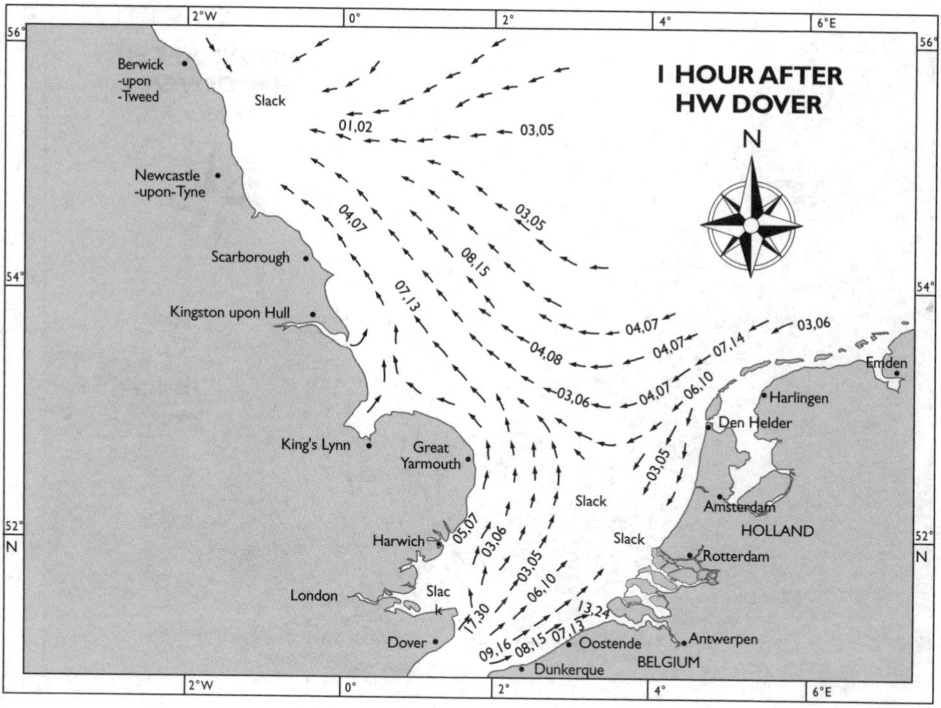

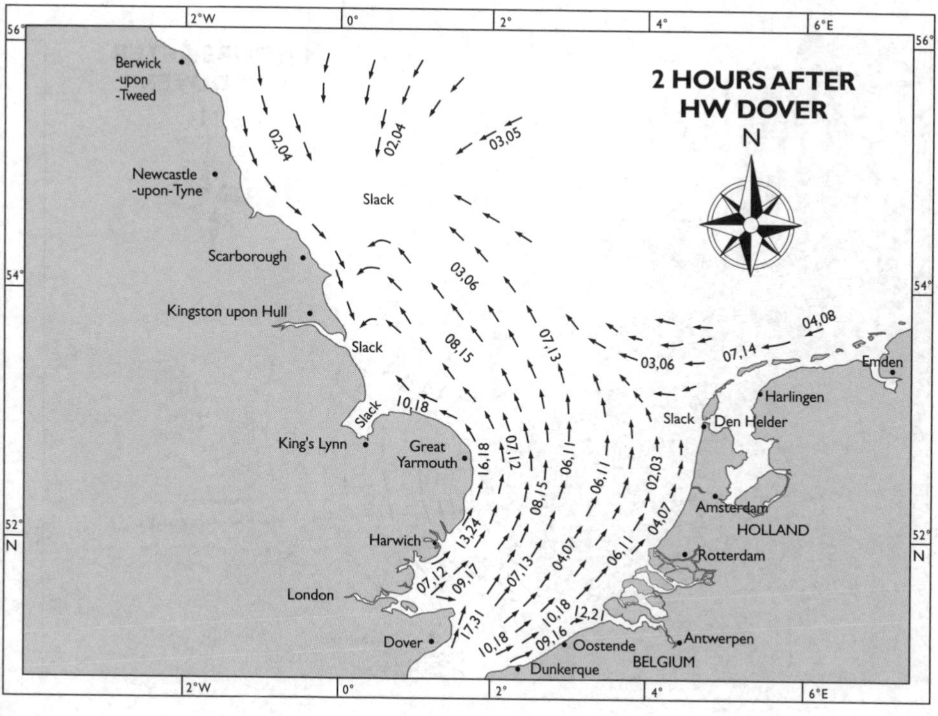

TIDES

NORTH SEA

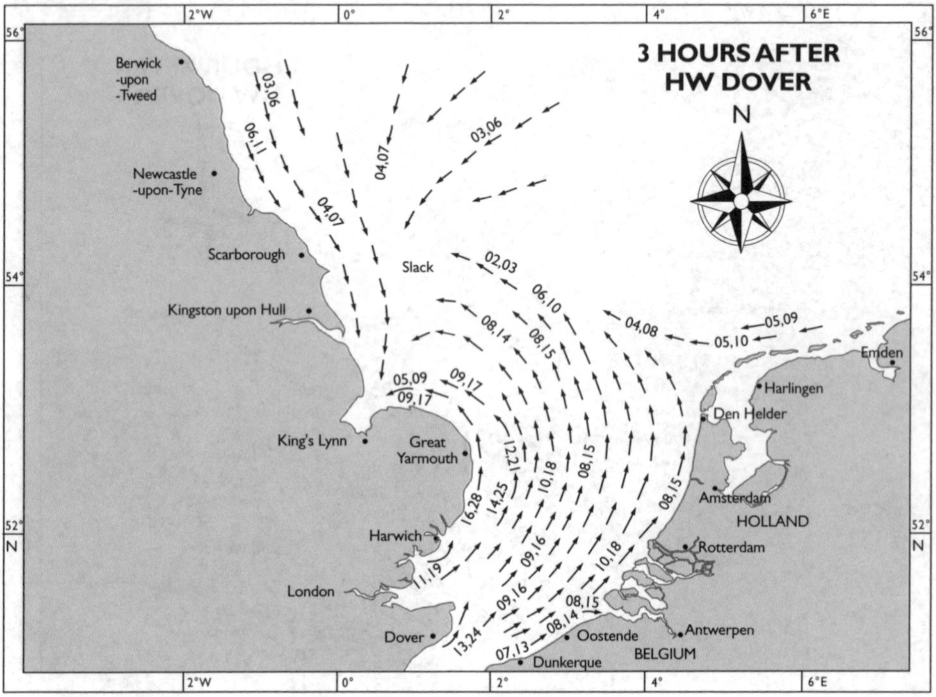
3 HOURS AFTER HW DOVER
N
Berwick -upon -Tweed
Newcastle -upon-Tyne
Scarborough
Kingston upon Hull
King's Lynn
Great Yarmouth
Harwich
London
Dover
Dunkerque
Oostende
BELGIUM
Antwerpen
Rotterdam
HOLLAND
Amsterdam
Den Helder
Harlingen
Emden
Slack
2°W
0°
2°
4°
6°E
56°
54°
52° N

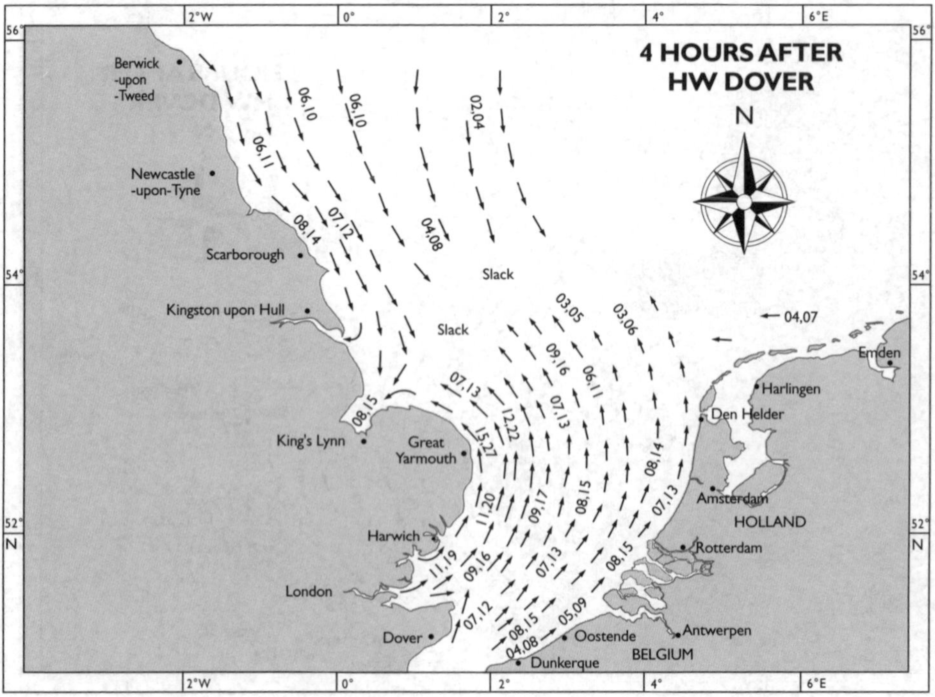
4 HOURS AFTER HW DOVER
N
Berwick -upon -Tweed
Newcastle -upon-Tyne
Scarborough
Kingston upon Hull
King's Lynn
Great Yarmouth
Harwich
London
Dover
Dunkerque
Oostende
BELGIUM
Antwerpen
Rotterdam
HOLLAND
Amsterdam
Den Helder
Harlingen
Emden
Slack
Slack
2°W
0°
2°
4°
6°E
56°
54°
52° N

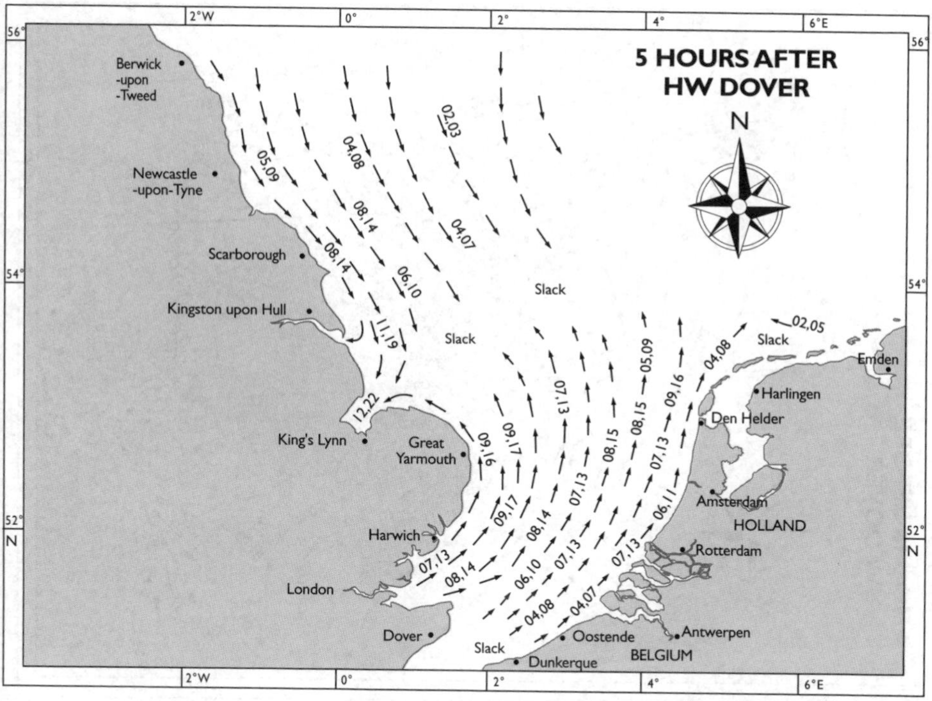
5 HOURS AFTER HW DOVER
N
Berwick -upon -Tweed
Newcastle -upon-Tyne
Scarborough
Kingston upon Hull
King's Lynn
Great Yarmouth
Harwich
London
Dover
Dunkerque
Oostende
Antwerpen
BELGIUM
Rotterdam
HOLLAND
Amsterdam
Den Helder
Harlingen
Emden
Slack
02,03
04,08
05,09
08,14
04,07
08,14
06,10
11,19
12,22
09,16
09,17
07,13
08,15
05,09
09,16
04,08
02,05
07,13
08,14
06,10
04,08
04,07
06,11
2°W
0°
2°
4°
6°E
56°
54°
52° N

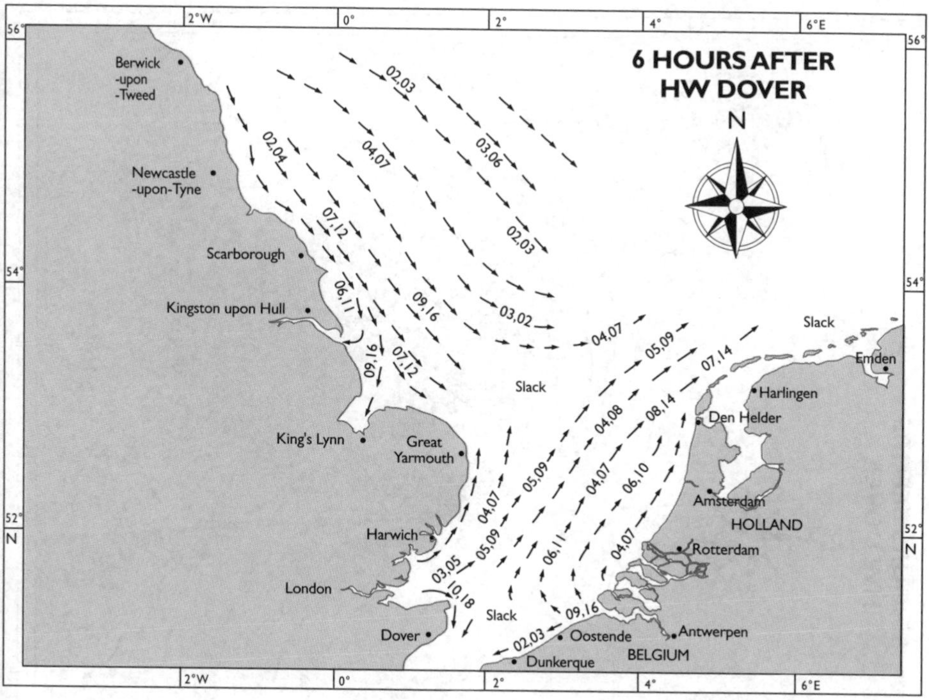
6 HOURS AFTER HW DOVER
N
Berwick -upon -Tweed
Newcastle -upon-Tyne
Scarborough
Kingston upon Hull
King's Lynn
Great Yarmouth
Harwich
London
Dover
Dunkerque
Oostende
Antwerpen
BELGIUM
Rotterdam
HOLLAND
Amsterdam
Den Helder
Harlingen
Emden
Slack
02,03
02,04
04,07
03,06
07,12
02,03
06,11
09,16
03,02
04,07
05,09
07,14
09,16
07,12
04,08
08,14
04,07
05,09
04,07
06,10
05,09
06,11
03,05
10,18
09,16
02,03
2°W
0°
2°
4°
6°E
56°
54°
52° N

TIDES

SCOTLAND

Example: ⟵10,18 predicts a westerly tidal flow of 1.0 knots at mean Neap tides and 1.8 knots at mean Spring tides at the location of the comma.

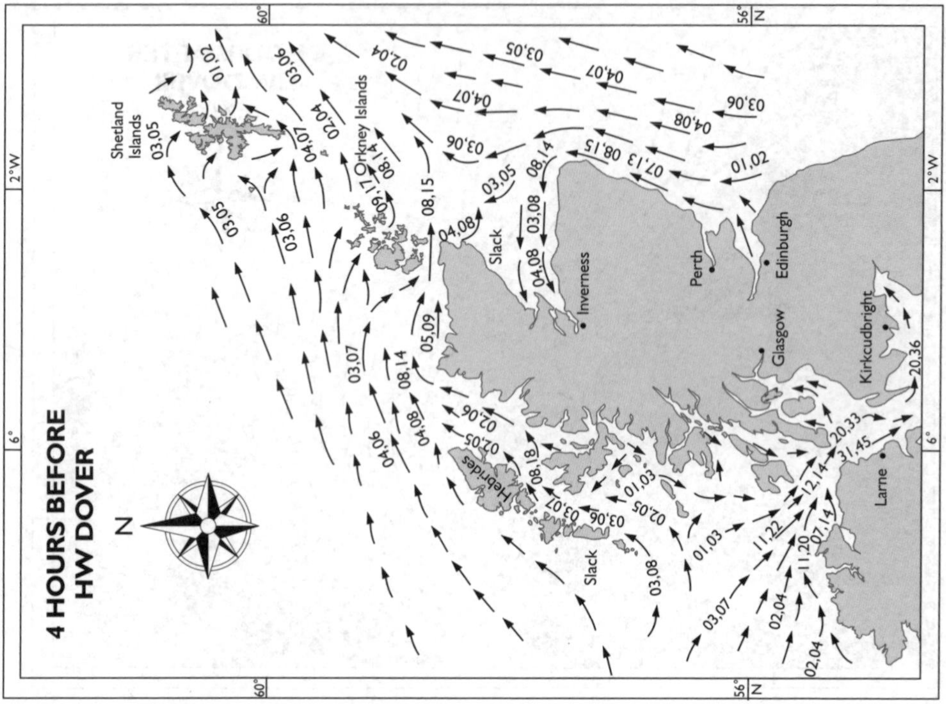

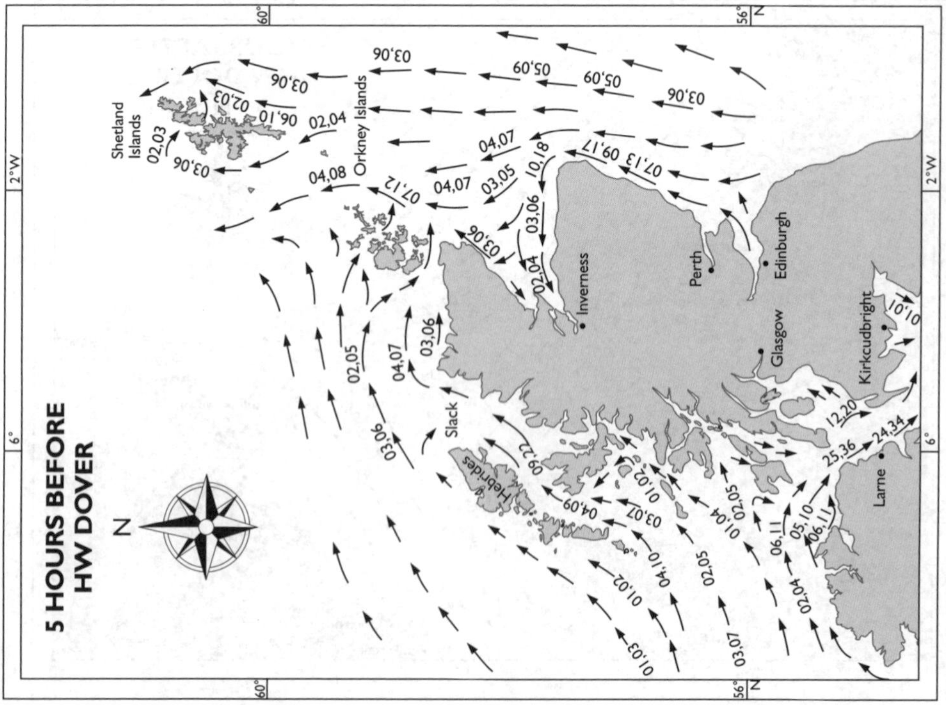

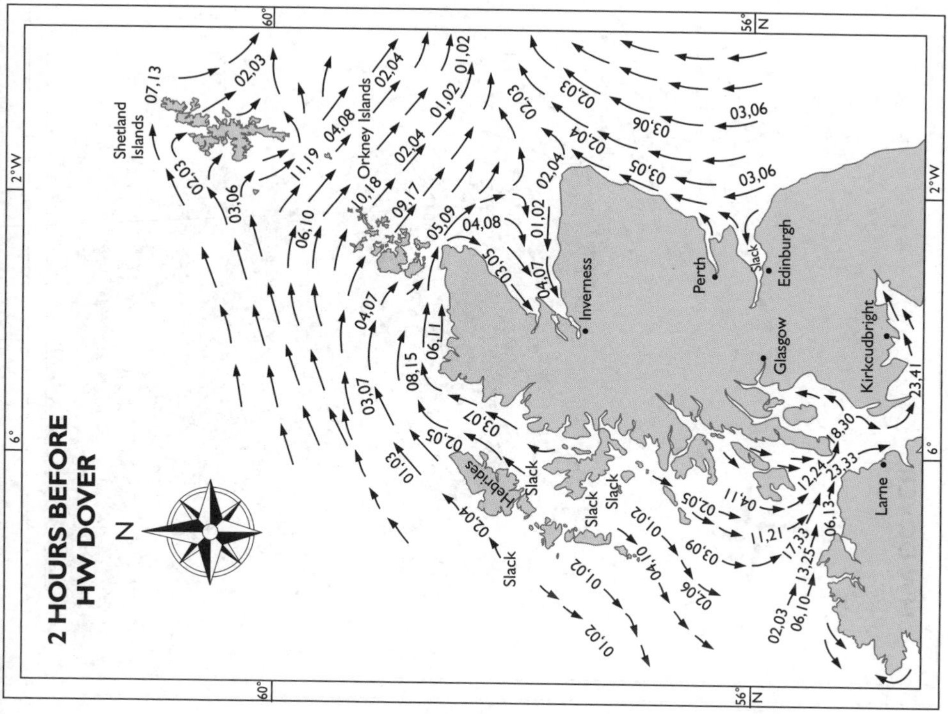
2 HOURS BEFORE
HW DOVER
N
Shetland Islands
Orkney Islands
Hebrides
Inverness
Perth
Edinburgh
Glasgow
Kirkcudbright
Larne
Slack
60°
56° N
2° W
6°

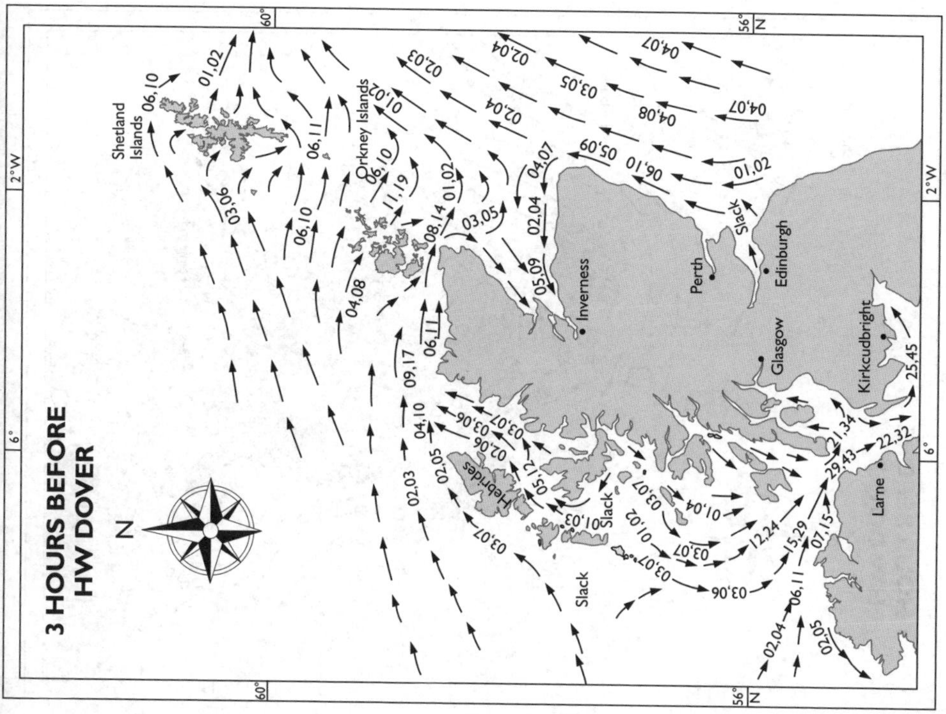
3 HOURS BEFORE
HW DOVER
N
Shetland Islands
Orkney Islands
Hebrides
Inverness
Perth
Edinburgh
Glasgow
Kirkcudbright
Larne
Slack
60°
56° N
2° W
6°

SCOTLAND

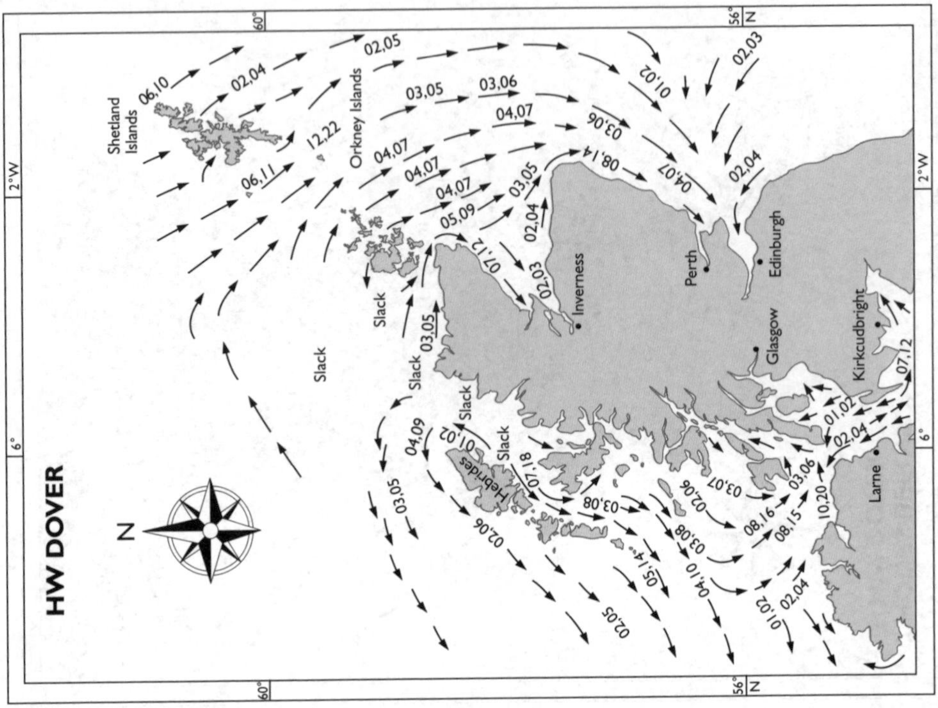
HW DOVER
Shetland Islands
Orkney Islands
Hebrides
Inverness
Perth
Edinburgh
Glasgow
Kirkcudbright
Larne
Slack

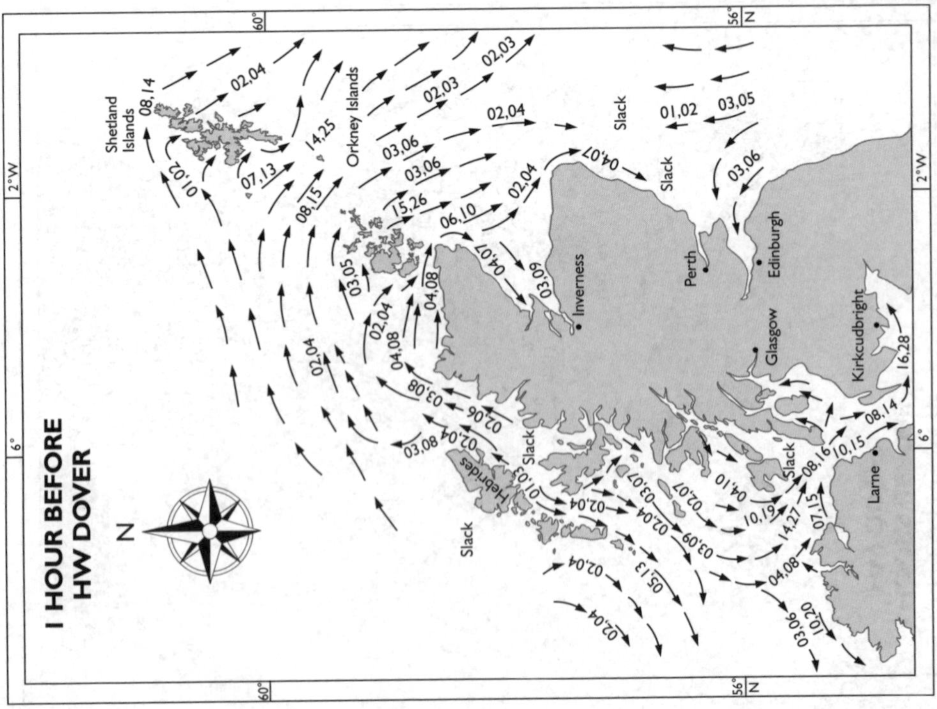
1 HOUR BEFORE HW DOVER
Shetland Islands
Orkney Islands
Hebrides
Inverness
Perth
Edinburgh
Glasgow
Kirkcudbright
Larne
Slack

SCOTLAND

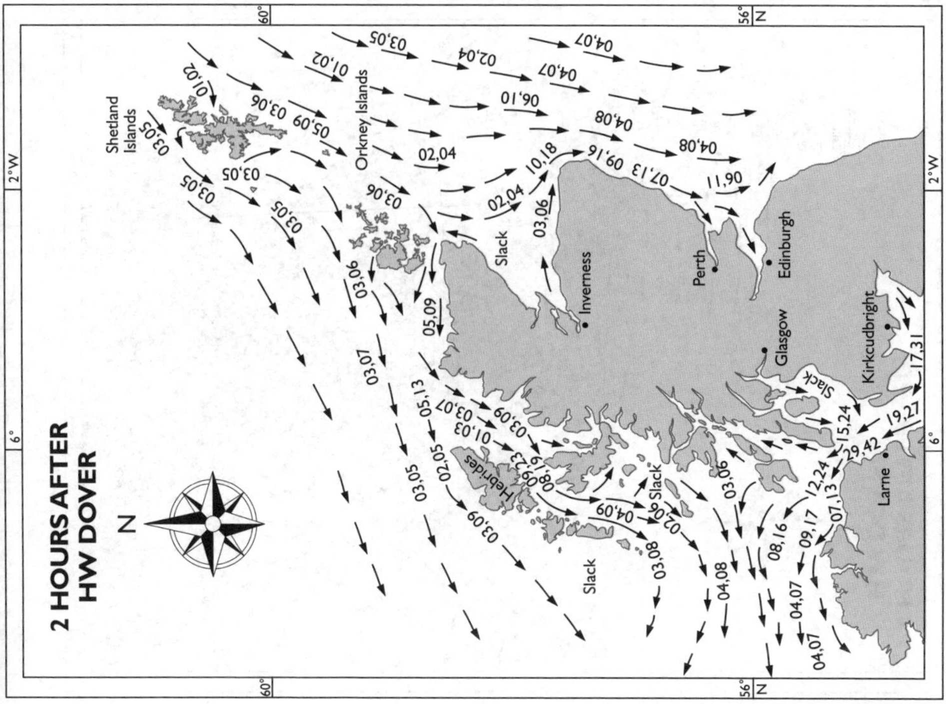

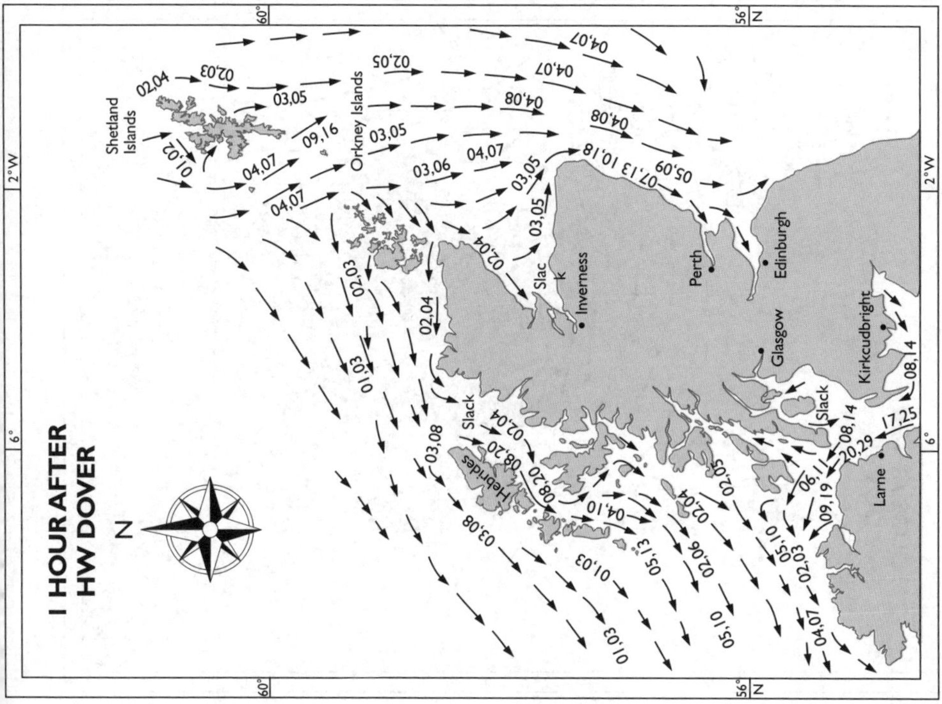

TIDES

SCOTLAND

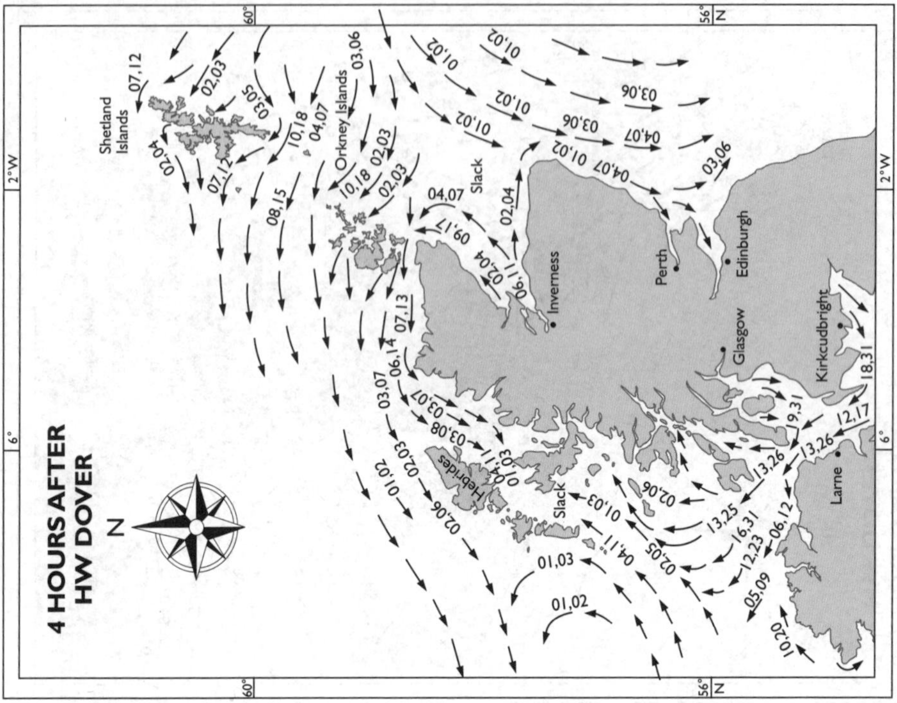
4 HOURS AFTER HW DOVER
N
60°
56°N
2°W
6°
Shetland Islands
Orkney Islands
Hebrides
Slack
Inverness
Perth
Edinburgh
Glasgow
Kirkcudbright
Larne

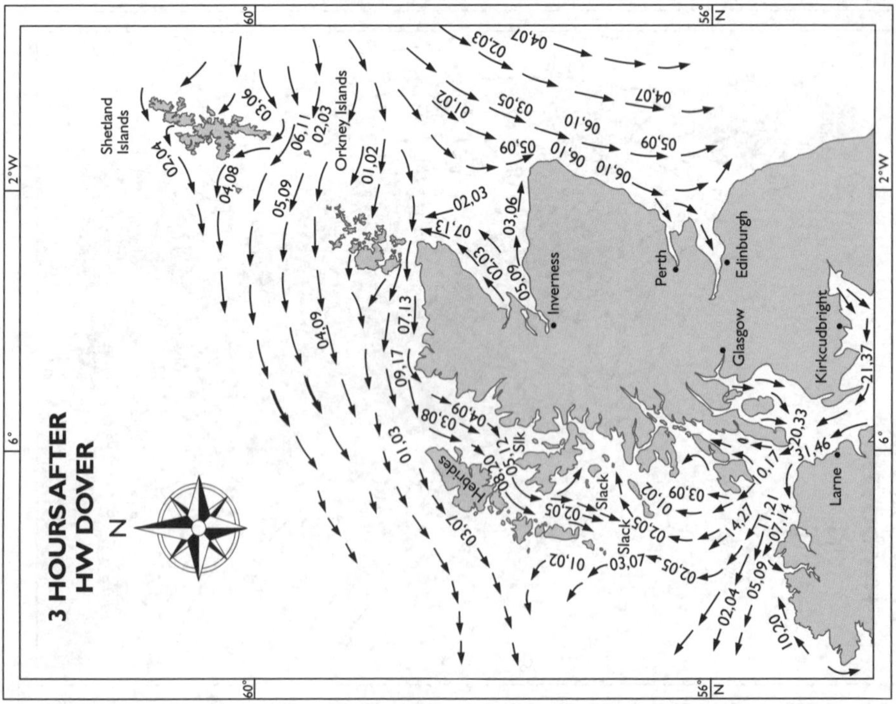
3 HOURS AFTER HW DOVER
N
60°
56°N
2°W
6°
Shetland Islands
Orkney Islands
Hebrides
Slk
Slack
Inverness
Perth
Edinburgh
Glasgow
Kirkcudbright
Larne

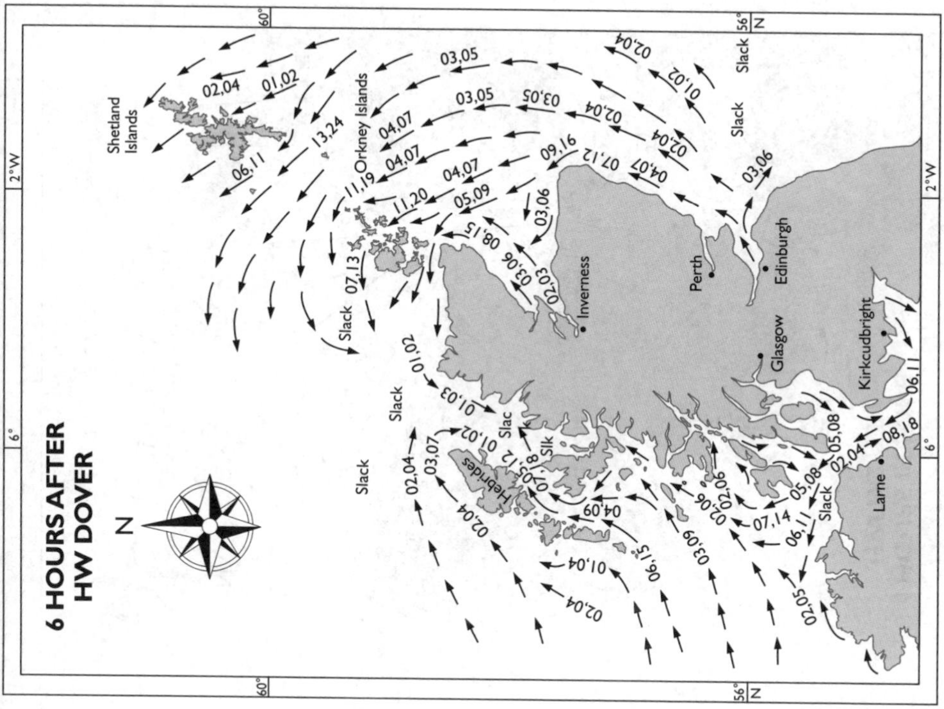
6 HOURS AFTER HW DOVER
N
Shetland Islands
Orkney Islands
Hebrides
Inverness
Perth
Edinburgh
Glasgow
Kirkcudbright
Larne
Slack
60°
56° N
2° W
6°

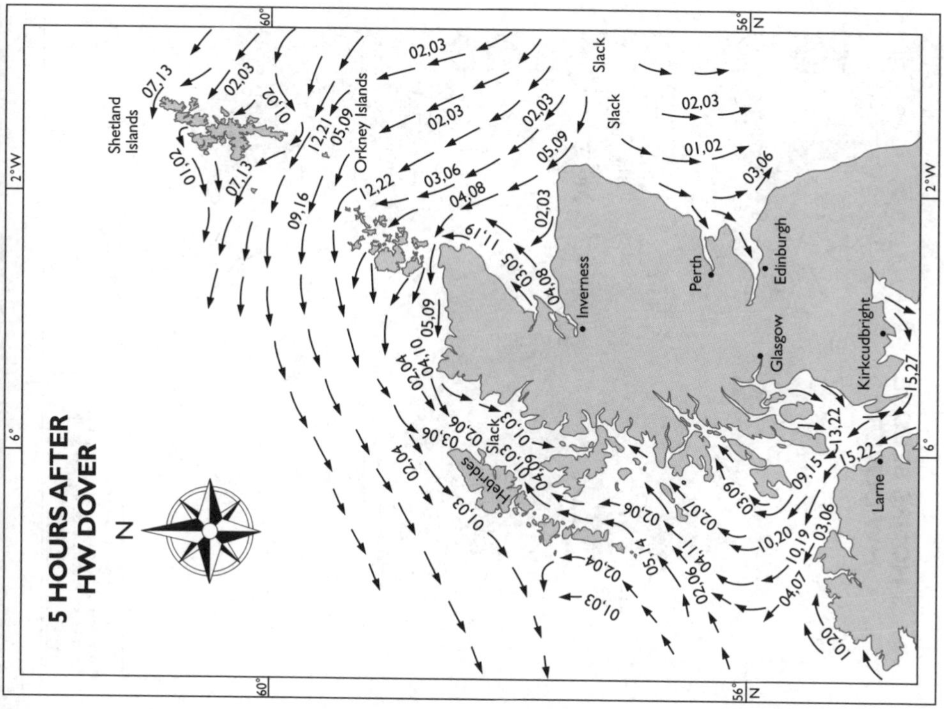
5 HOURS AFTER HW DOVER
N
Shetland Islands
Orkney Islands
Hebrides
Inverness
Perth
Edinburgh
Glasgow
Kirkcudbright
Larne
Slack
60°
56° N
2° W
6°

WEST UK AND IRELAND

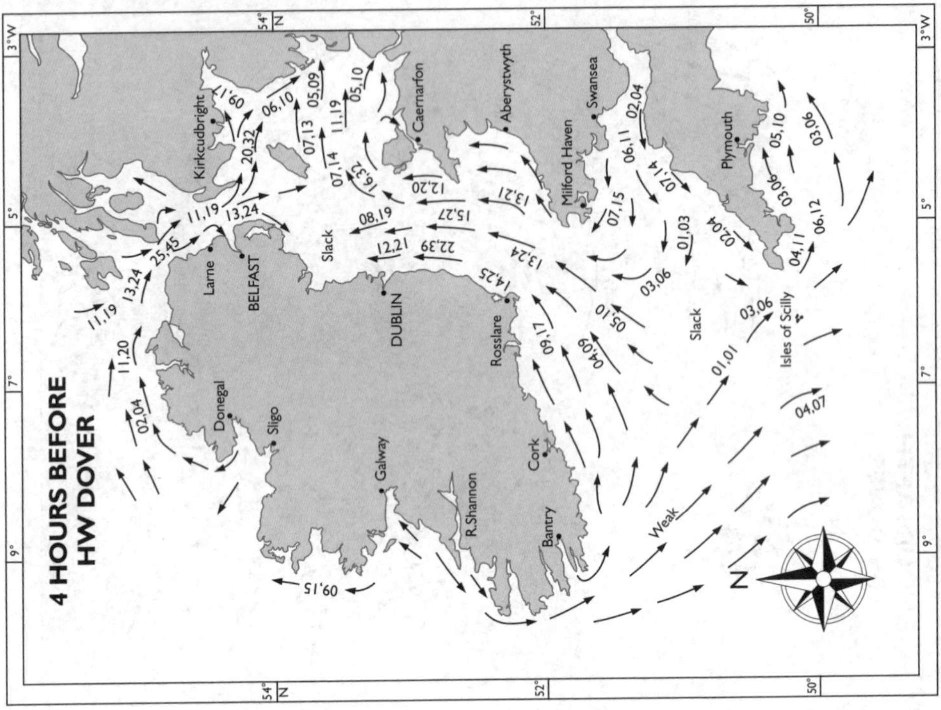

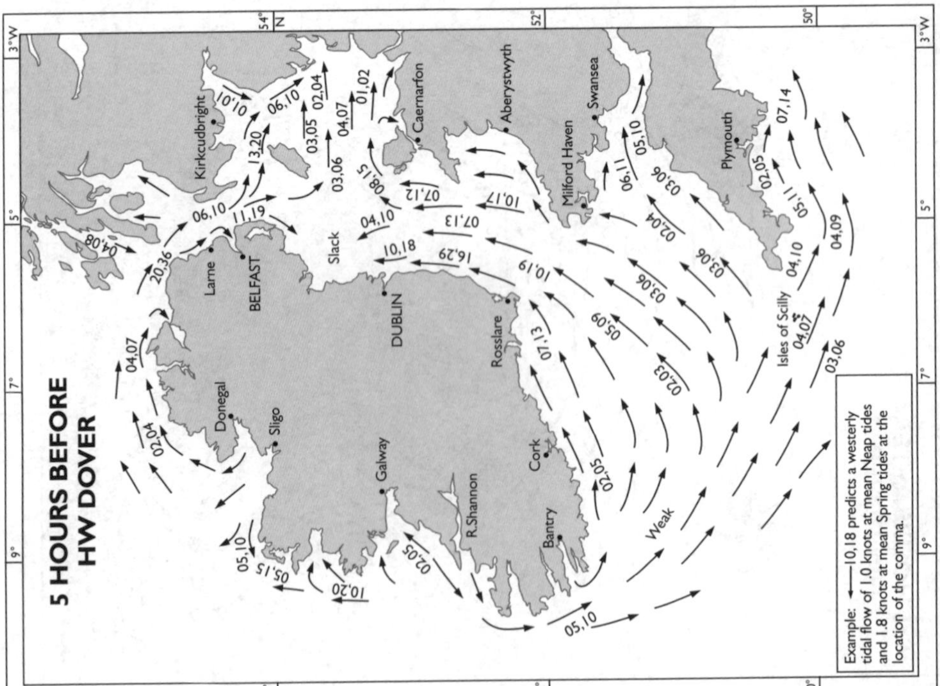

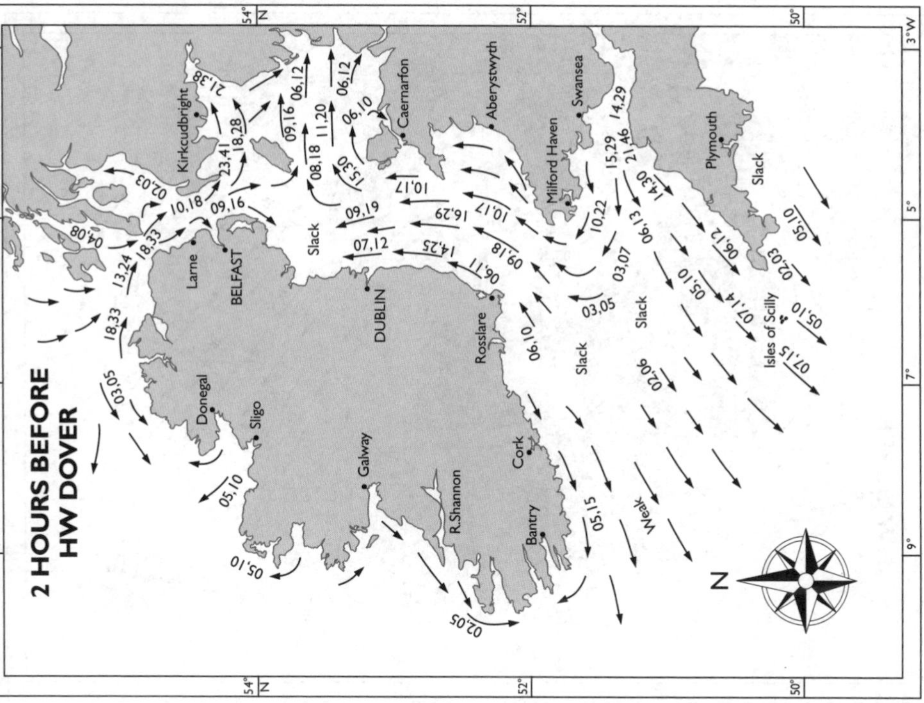
2 HOURS BEFORE HW DOVER
Kirkcudbright
Larne
BELFAST
DUBLIN
Caernarfon
Aberystwyth
Milford Haven
Swansea
Plymouth
Rosslare
Donegal
Sligo
Galway
R.Shannon
Cork
Bantry
Isles of Scilly
Slack
Weak
N

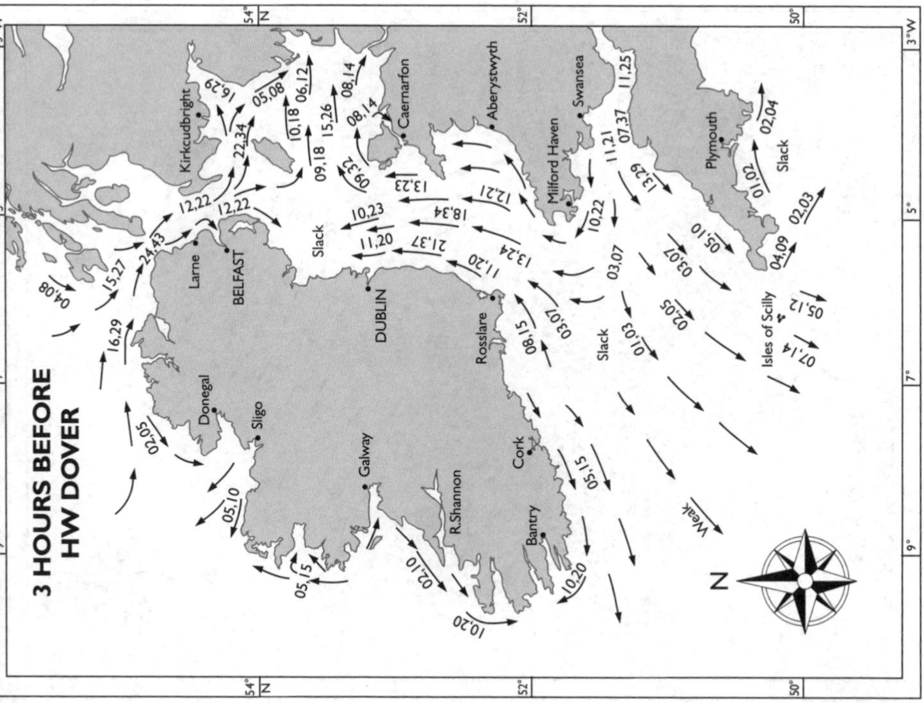
3 HOURS BEFORE HW DOVER
Kirkcudbright
Larne
BELFAST
DUBLIN
Caernarfon
Aberystwyth
Milford Haven
Swansea
Plymouth
Rosslare
Donegal
Sligo
Galway
R.Shannon
Cork
Bantry
Isles of Scilly
Slack
Weak
N

TIDES

WEST UK AND IRELAND

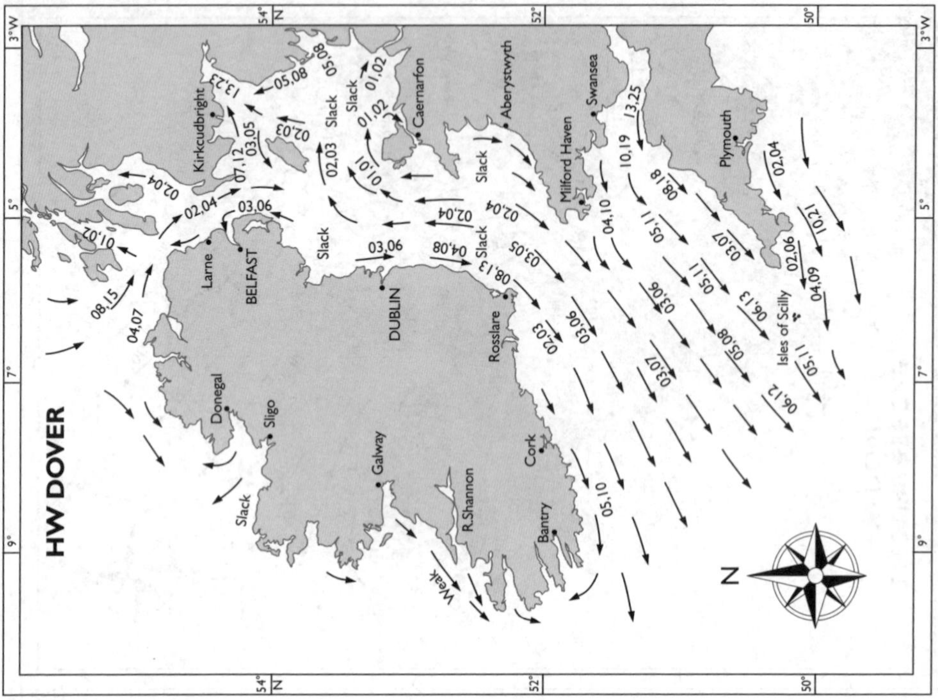

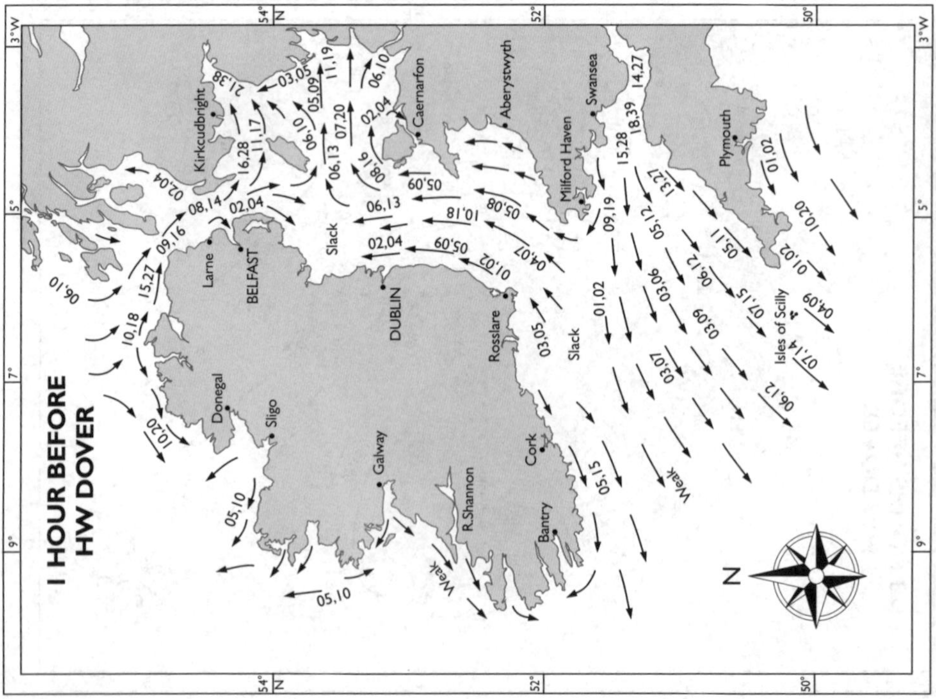

WEST UK AND IRELAND

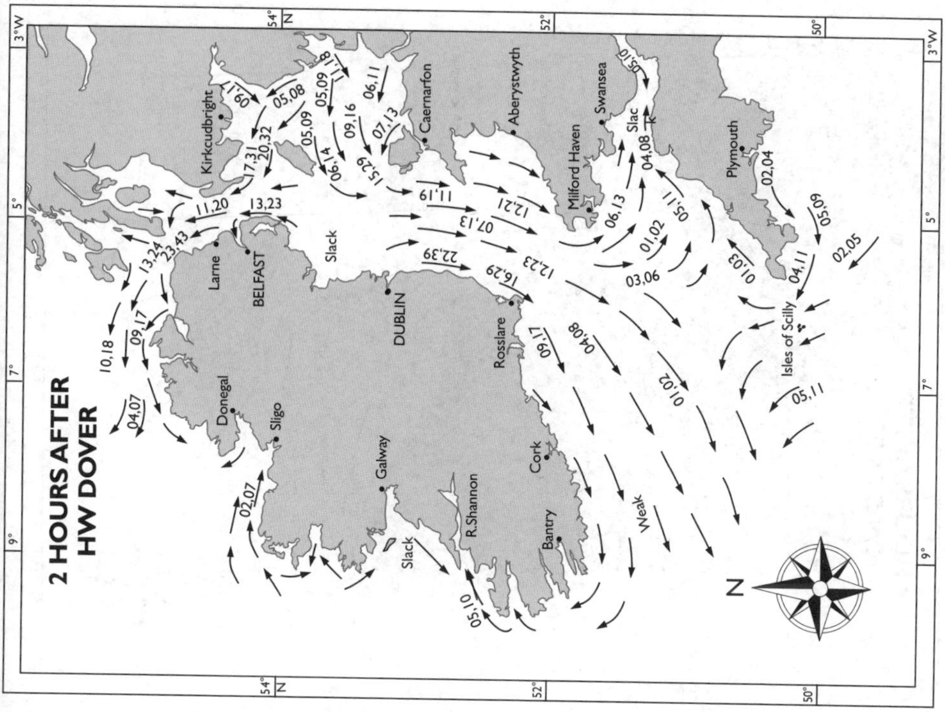

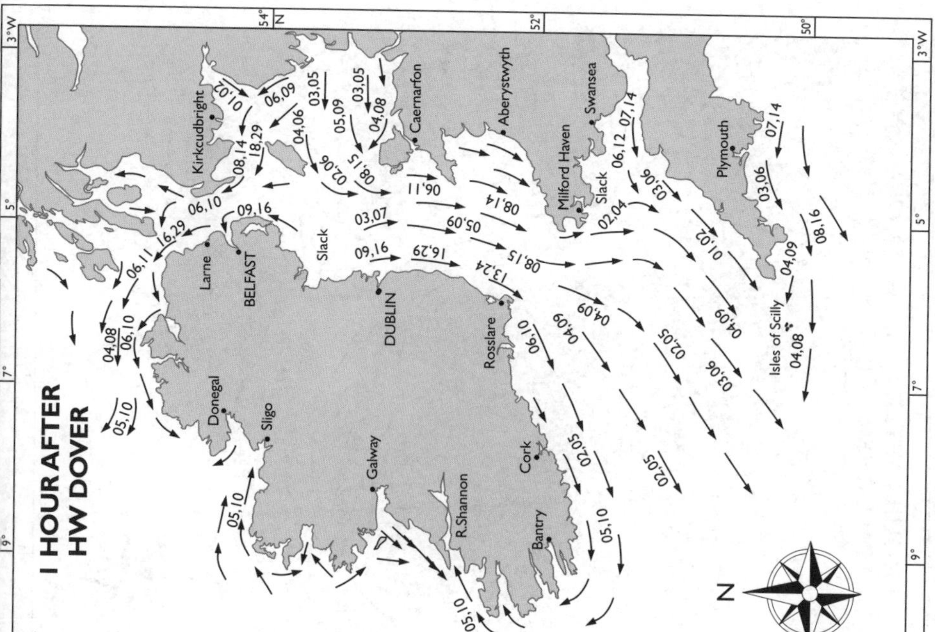

WEST UK AND IRELAND

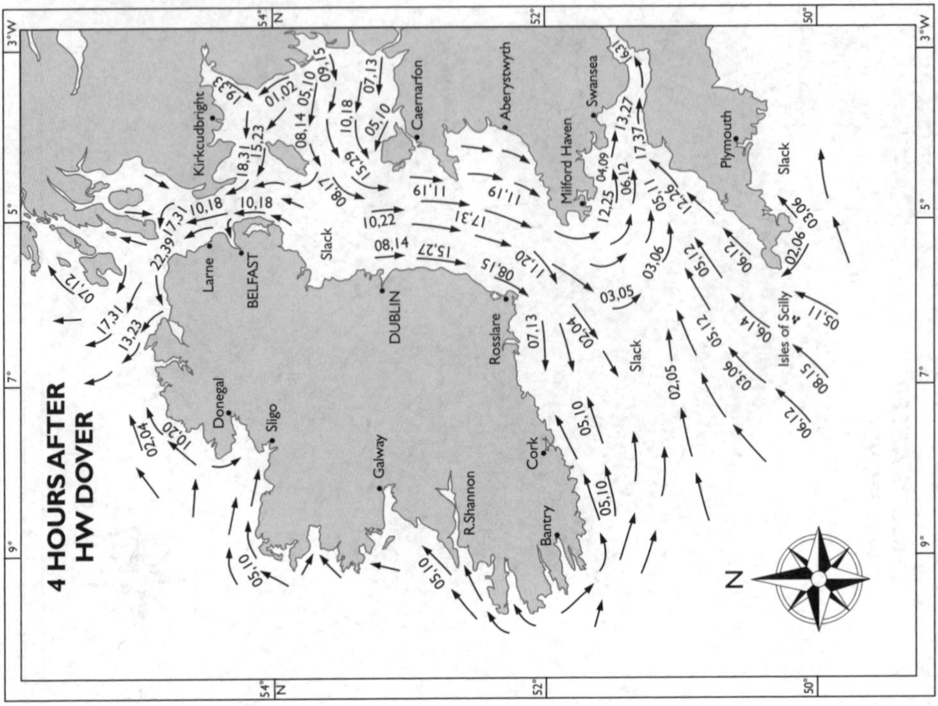

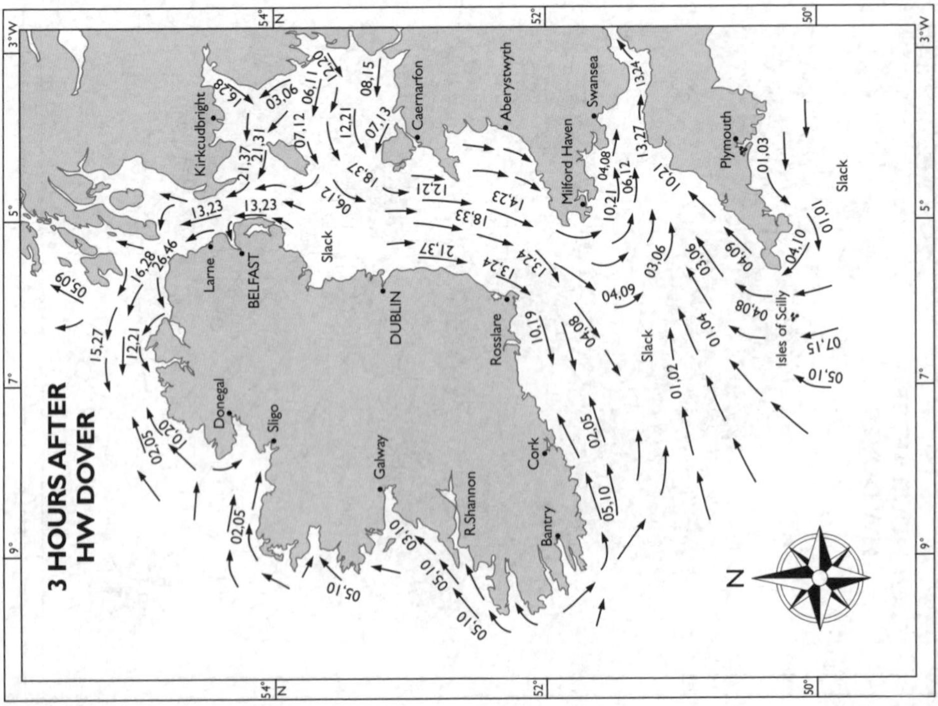

WEST UK AND IRELAND

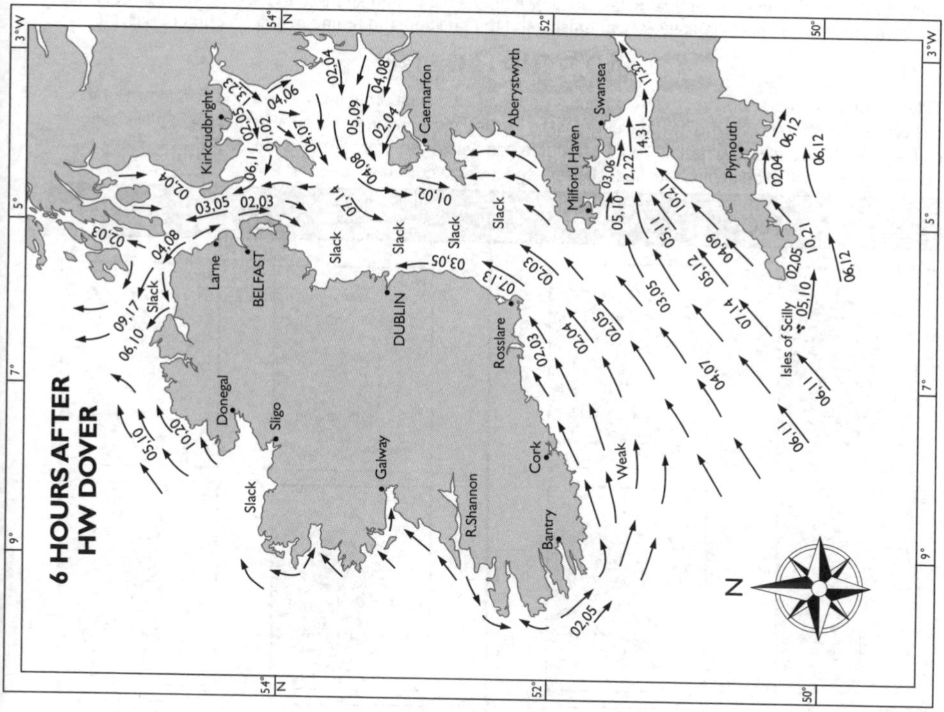

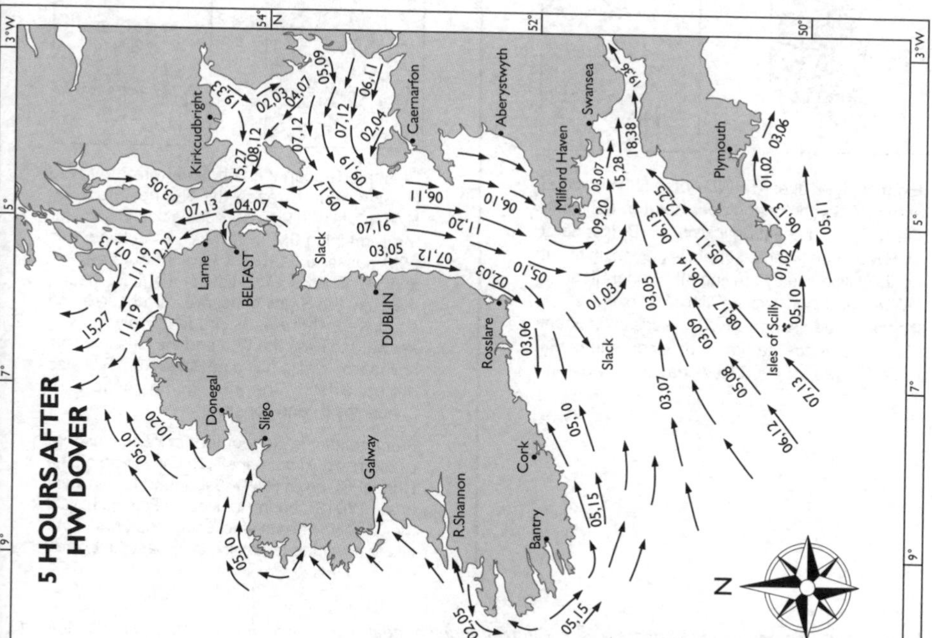

TIDES

TIDAL GATES – SOUTHERN ENGLAND

A guide to the time of tide turn at tidal gates, the approximate maximum strength of the tidal flow (spring rates shown - neaps are approximately 60% of these), and the position and timing of races, counter tides, etc.

LAND'S END (AC 1148)

Tidal streams set hard north/south round Land's End, and east/west around Gwennap and Pendeen. But the inshore currents run counter to the tidal streams. By staying close inshore, this tidal gate favours a N-bound passage. With careful timing nearly 9½hrs of fair tide can be carried, from HWD–3 to HWD+5. The chartlets, referenced to HW Dover, depict both tidal streams and inshore currents.

FLOOD

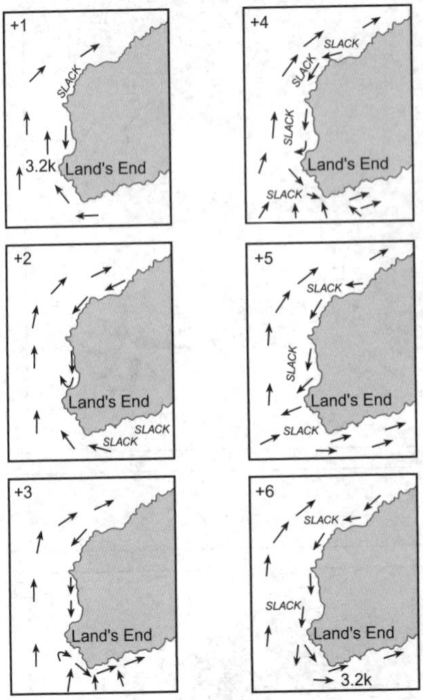

Example N-bound: At HWD+1 the N-going flood starts off Gwennap and does not turn NE along the N Cornish coast until HWD+3. But as early as HWD–3 an inshore current is beginning to set north. Utilise this by arriving off Runnel Stone at HWD–2 and then keeping within ¼M of the shore. If abeam the Brisons at HWD, the tide and current should serve for the next 6 or 7 hours to make good St Ives, or even Newquay and Padstow.

EBB

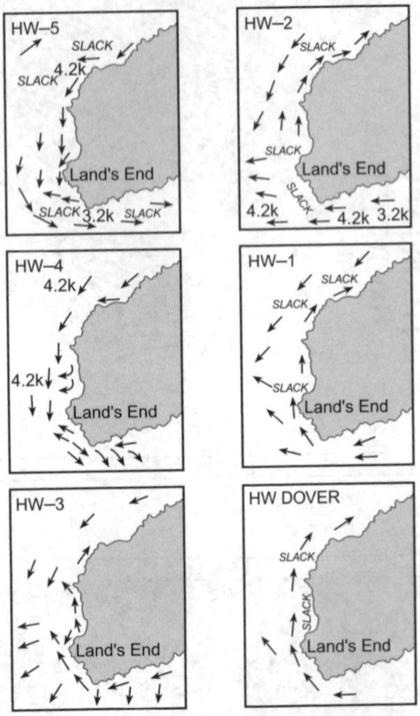

Example S-bound: If S-bound from St Ives to Newlyn, aim to reach the Runnel Stone by HWD+5, ie with 2hrs of E-going tide in hand for the remaining 9M to Newlyn. To achieve this 20M passage, leave St Ives 5 hours earlier, ie at HWD. Buck a foul tide for the first 3 hours, then use the S-going inshore current, keeping as close inshore as is prudent, only moving seaward to clear the Wra and the Brisons. This timing would also suit a passage from S Wales or the Bristol Channel, going inshore of Longships if conditions allow.

From Ireland, ie Cork or further W, the inshore passage would not benefit. But aim to be off the Runnel Stone at HWD+5 if bound for Newlyn; or at HWD+3 if bound for Helford/Falmouth, with the W-going stream slackening and 5hrs of fair tide to cover the remaining 20M past the Lizard.

With acknowledgements to the Royal Cruising Club Pilotage Foundation for their kind permission to use the tid[al] stream chartlets and text written by Hugh Davies, as first published in Yachting Monthly *magazine.*

TIDAL GATES – SOUTHERN ENGLAND

A guide to the time of tide turn at tidal gates, the approximate maximum strength of the tidal flow (spring rates shown - neaps are approximately 60% of these), and the position and timing of races, counter tides, etc.

FLOOD	EBB

THE LIZARD (AC 777, 2345)

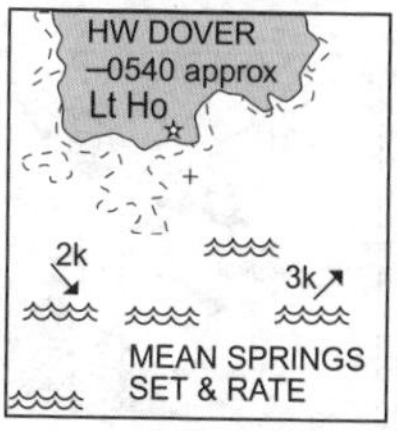

HW DOVER
–0540 approx
Lt Ho
2k
3k
MEAN SPRINGS
SET & RATE

Drying rocks lie approx 5 cables S of the Lizard lt ho and extend westwards. 49°57'N is about as far N as yachts may safely pass inshore of the Race, which extends 2-3M to seaward of these rocks. Race conditions may also exist SE of the Lizard with short, heavy seas in westerlies. If passing S of the Race, route via 49°55'N 05°13'W to clear the worst of the Race.

Inshore the E-going Channel flood, 2kn max @ springs, begins at HW Dover +0145; and outside the Race at approx HWD +0300.

Inshore the W-going Channel ebb, 3kn max @ springs, begins at HW Dover –0345; and outside the Race at HWD –0240.

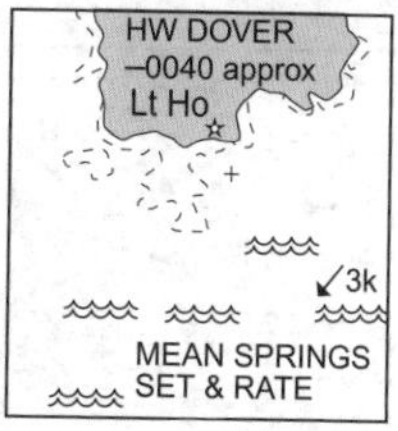

HW DOVER
–0040 approx
Lt Ho
3k
MEAN SPRINGS
SET & RATE

START POINT (AC 1634)

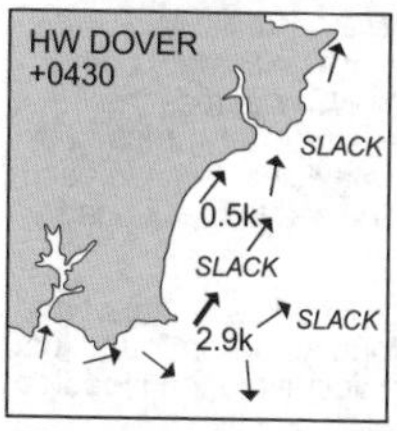

HW DOVER
+0430
SLACK
0.5k
SLACK
2.9k
SLACK

Start Pt, and to a lesser extent Prawle Pt (3.3M WSW), can be slow to round when W-bound with a fair tide against a W'ly wind raising a bad sea. Drying rocks extend 3 cables SSE of the lt ho and a Race may extend up to 1.7M ESE and 1.0M S of the lt ho. It is safe to pass between the Race and the rocks, but in bad weather wiser to go outside the Race. The Skerries Bank (least depth 2.1m) lies 8 cables NE of Start Pt. On both the flood and the ebb back eddies form between Start Pt and Hallsands, 1M NW.

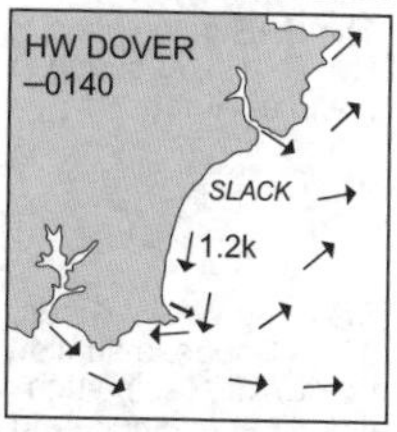

HW DOVER
–0140
SLACK
1.2k

The NE-going Channel flood, 3.1kn max @ springs, begins at HW Dover +0430.

The SW-going Channel ebb, 2.2kn max @ springs, begins at HW Dover –0140, but an hour earlier it is possible to round Start Pt close inshore using the back eddy.

PORTLAND (AC 2255)

Tidal streams off Portland Bill run very strongly. The notorious Portland Race is caused by the almost constant strong southerly flow down both sides of the Bill meeting the main E and W-going streams in the English Channel. The violence of the race is increased by the sudden decrease in depth on Portland Ledge. The tidal stream chartlets on Pages 158–159 show that the race shifts to the E on the flood, and to the W on the ebb. Even in calm weather the race can be dangerous for small craft; in heavy weather or with wind against tide the whole area should be given a wide berth. In such conditions, pass at least 3 miles S of the Bill and do not pass between Portland and The Shambles bank.

In settled weather, with winds <F4/5, but not at springs nor with wind against tide, passage may be made very close S of the Bill in the narrow stretch of relatively smooth water N of the race. Night passage should not be attempted due to numerous fishing floats which may be semi-submerged.

Seaward of the race the Channel flood sets east from HW Plymouth -1 to HW +5; the ebb sets west from HW Plymouth +5 to HW -1.

Inshore passage

E-bound across Lyme Bay timing is critical to be close inshore about 2M north of the Bill by HW Plymouth –2 to achieve passage around the Bill between HW Plymouth –2 to HW+1.

W-bound timing is easier if starting from Portland Hbr, Weymouth or Lulworth Cove. Aim to be close inshore about 2M north of the Bill at HW Plymouth +4, and make the passage between HW Plymouth +5 and HW–5.

When using the inshore passage be particularly wary of being set S into the race itself.

ST ALBAN'S HEAD (AC 2610)

A sometimes vicious Race forms over St Alban's Ledge, a rocky dorsal ridge (least depth 8.5m) which extends approx 4M SW from St Alban's Head. Three yellow naval target buoys (DZ A, B and C) straddle the middle and outer sections, but are only occasionally used. In settled weather and at neaps the Race may be barely perceptible in which case it can be crossed with impunity. Avoid it either by keeping to seaward via 50°31'.40N 02°07'.80W; or by using the narrow inshore passage at the foot of St Alban's Head.

Based on a position 1M S of St Alban's Head, the tidal stream windows are:

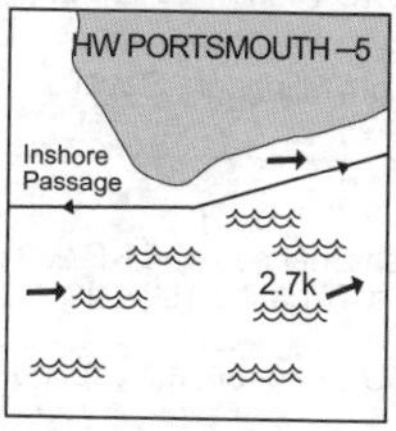

HW PORTSMOUTH –5
Inshore
Passage
2.7k

ESE-going stream starts at HW Portsmouth +0530. Spring rates are the same, max 4kn. Along the W side of St Alban's Head the stream runs almost continuously SE due to a back eddy.

WNW-going stream starts at HW Portsmouth. Overfalls extend 2.5M further SW than on the E-going stream and are more dangerous to small craft. Slack water lasts barely half an hour.

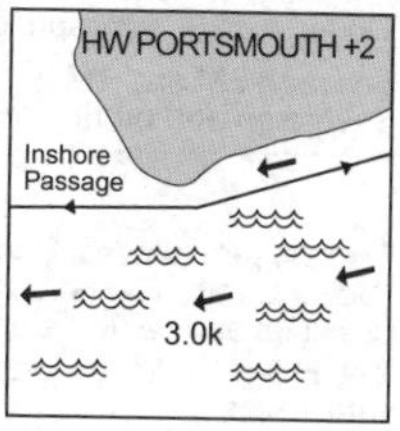

HW PORTSMOUTH +2
Inshore
Passage
3.0k

The inshore passage lies as close to the foot of St Alban's Head as feels comfortable. It may be hard to see the width of clear water in the inshore passage until committed to it, but except in onshore gales when it is better to stay offshore, the passage will be swiftly made with only a few, if any, overfalls. The NCI station on the Head (☎ 01929 439220) may advise on conditions.

TIDAL GATES – SOUTHERN ENGLAND

A guide to the time of tide turn at tidal gates, the approximate maximum strength of the tidal flow (spring rates shown - neaps are approximately 60% of these), and the position and timing of races, counter tides, etc.

FLOOD	EBB

THE NEEDLES CHANNEL (AC 2035)

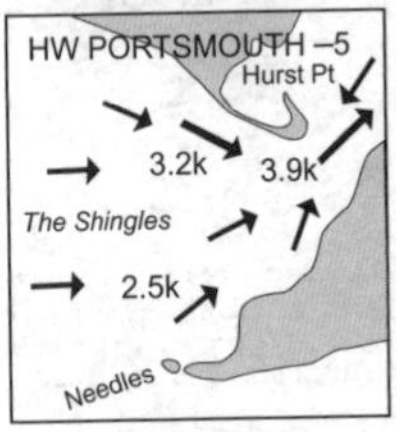

The Needles Channel lies between the SW Shingles PHM buoy and the Bridge WCM buoy. Once through this narrow section the channel widens with the Island shore to starboard and the long, drying 1.2m, Shingles bank to port. Abeam Hurst Castle the channel again narrows (assisted by The Trap, a shoal spit south of Hurst Castle) before opening out into the west Solent.

Study carefully the hourly tidal stream chartlets for the Isle of Wight on pp.186-191 and the values shown on AC 2035 at tidal diamonds B, C, D and E.

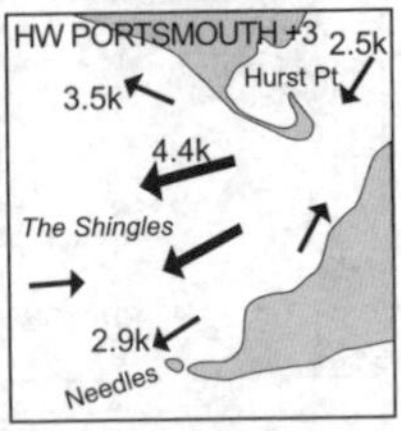

The ENE-going flood runs from HW Portsmouth +5 until HW P –1½, at springs reaching 3.1kn at The Bridge and 3.9kn at Hurst.

The WSW-going ebb runs from HW P –1 until HW P +4½, reaching 4.4kn at Hurst and 3.4kn at The Bridge, both spring rates. The ebb sets strongly WSW across the Shingles which with adequate rise is routinely crossed by racing yachts; but cruisers should stay clear even in calm conditions when any swell causes the sea to break heavily.

Prevailing W/SW winds, even if only F4, against the ebb raise dangerous breaking seas in the Needles Channel and at The Bridge, a shallow ridge extending 9 cables west from the Needles light. Worst conditions are often found just after LW slack. In such conditions it is safer to go via the North Channel to Hurst. In W/SW gales avoid the Needles altogether by sheltering at Poole or going east-about via Nab Tower.

ON PASSAGE UP CHANNEL

The following 3 tidal gates (Looe Channel, Beachy Head and Dungeness) are components in the tidal conveyor belt which, if stepped onto at the outset, can enable a fastish yacht to carry a fair tide for 88M from Selsey Bill to Dover. Go through the Looe at slackish water, HW Portsmouth +4½ (HW Dover +5). Based on a mean SOG of 7 knots, Beachy Head will be passed at HW D –1, Dungeness at HW D +3 and Dover at HW +5½, only bucking the first of the ebb in the last hour. A faster boat could make Ramsgate. The down-Channel passage is less rewarding and many yachts will pause at Brighton.

LOOE CHANNEL (AC 2045, 1652)

This channel is little shorter than the detour south of the Owers, but is much used by yachts on passage from/to points east of the Solent. Although adequately lit, it is best not attempted at night due to many lobster floats; nor in onshore gales as searoom is limited by extensive shoals on which the sea breaks.

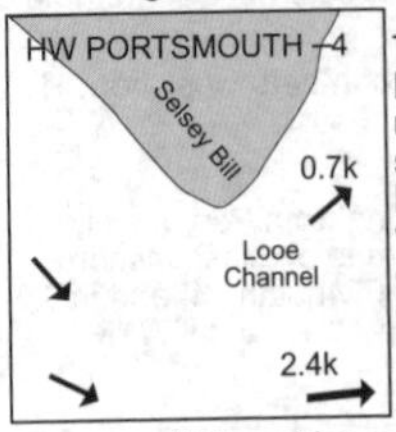

The E-going flood runs from HW Portsmouth +4½ (HW Dover +5) until HW P –1½ (HW D –1), at springs reaching 2.4kn near the Boulder and Street light buoys which mark its narrow western end; they may be hard to see in other than good visibility. Max neap rate is 1.2kn.

The W-going ebb runs from HW P –1½ (HW D –1) until HW P +4½ (HW D +5), at springs reaching 2.6kn near Boulder and Street. Max neap rate is 1.3kn.

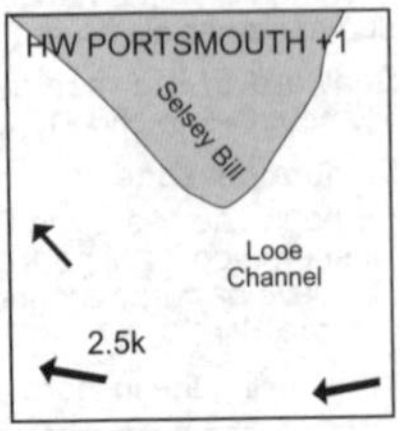

At the wider eastern end of the channel (near E Borough Head buoy) rates are greatly reduced.

BEACHY HEAD (AC 1652, 536)

Stay at least 5 cables to seaward of the towering chalk cliffs to avoid isolated boulders and rocky, part-drying ridges such as Head Ledge. The lt ho stands on a drying rock ledge. Close inshore many fishing floats are a trap for the unwary. In bad weather stay 2M offshore to avoid overfalls caused by a ridge of uneven ground which extends 1M SSE from Beachy Head.

2M south of Beachy Head the E-going flood starts at HW Dover +0530, max spring rate 2.6kn.

The W-going ebb starts at HW Dover +0030, max spring rate 2.0kn.

Between 5M and 7M east of Beachy Head avoid breakers and eddies caused by the Horse of Willingdon, Royal Sovereign and other shoals.

DUNGENESS (AC 536, 1892)

Tidal stream atlases: Dungeness is on the east and west edges respectively of NP 250 (English Channel) and NP 233 (Dover Strait). The nearest tidal stream diamond (2.2M SE of Dungeness) is 'H' on AC 536 and 'B' on AC 1892; their positions and values are the same.

The NE-going flood starts at HW Dover –0100, max spring rate 1.9kn.

The SW-going ebb starts at HW Dover +0430, max spring rate 2.1kn.

TIDAL GATES – NORTH EAST SCOTLAND

A guide to the time of tide turn at tidal gates, and in straits and estuaries, showing the approximate strength of the tidal flow (spring rates shown - neaps are approximately 60% of these), and the position and timing of races, counter tides etc.

FLOOD	EBB

FIRTHS of FORTH (AC 175) & TAY (AC 1481)

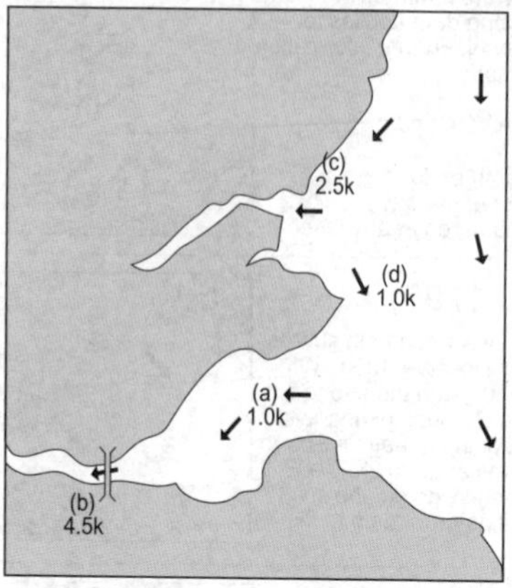

Tidal streams are quite weak in the outer part of the Firth, increasing as the narrows at islands and the bridges are approached.
Apart from the stream of the Tay, which attains 5 knots in most places, the coastwise tidal streams between Fife Ness and Arbroath are weak.

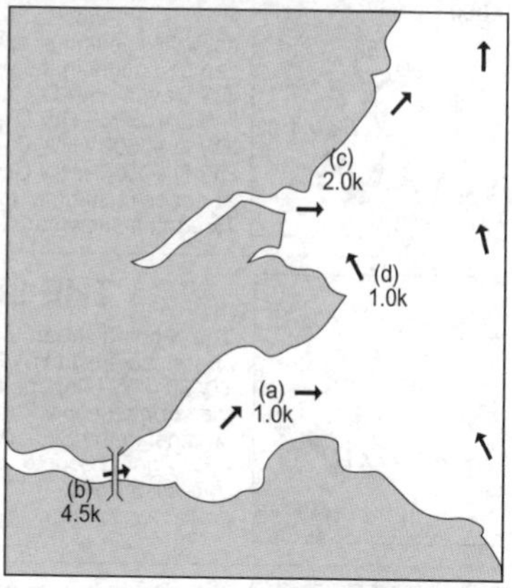

Flood:
(a) Dover –0225 to Dover +0330
(b) Dover –0200 to Dover +0400
(c) Dover –0210 to Dover +0420
(d) Dover –0110 to Dover +0520

Ebb:
(a) Dover +0330 to Dover –0225
(b) Dover +0400 to Dover –0200
(c) Dover +0420 to Dover –0210
(d) Dover +0520 to Dover –0110

PASSAGES FROM FORTH & TAY

Northbound. Leave before HW (Dover +0400) to be at N Carr at Dover +0600. Bound from Forth to Tay aim to arrive at Abertay By at LW slack (Dover –0200).

Southbound. Leave before LW (Dover -0200) to be at Bass Rk at HW Dover. Similar timings if bound from Tay to Forth, leave late in ebb to pick up early flood off St Andrews to N Carr and into Forth.

INVERNESS & CROMARTY FIRTHS (AC 1077)

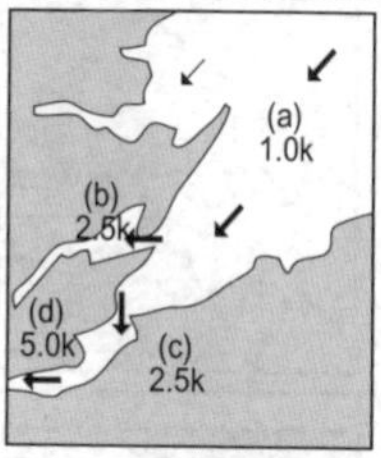

Tidal streams in the Inverness Firth and approaches are not strong, except in the Cromarty Firth Narrows, the Fort George Narrows and the Kessock Road, including off the entrance to the Caledonian Canal.

Flood	Ebb
(a) Dover –0555 to Dover +0030	(a) Dover +0030 to Dover –0555
(b) Dover –0400 to Dover +0115	(b) Dover +0115 to Dover –0400
(c) Dover –0400 to Dover –0220	(c) Dover +0115 to Dover –0440
(d) Dover –0430 to Dover +0100	(d) Dover –0130 to Dover +0545

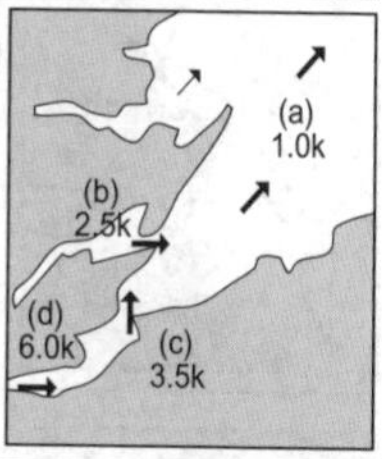

PENTLAND FIRTH & ORKNEYS (AC 1954)

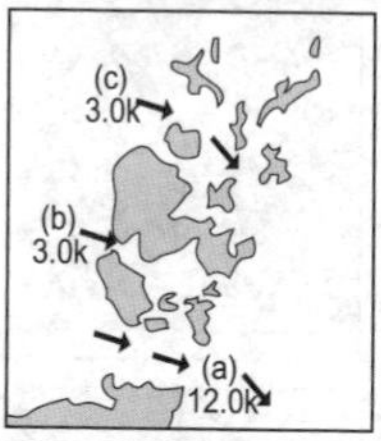

The tide flows strongly around and through the Orkney Islands. The Pentland Firth is a dangerous area for all craft, tidal flows reach 12 knots between Duncansby Head and S Ronaldsay. W of Dunnet Hd & Hoy is less violent. There is little tide within Scapa Flow.

Flood	Ebb
(a) Dover –0500 to Dover +0100	(a) Dover +0115 to Dover –0535
(b) Dover +0530 to Dover –0110	(b) Dover –0110 to Dover +0530
(c) Dover –0530 to Dover +0040	(c) Dover +0040 to Dover –0530

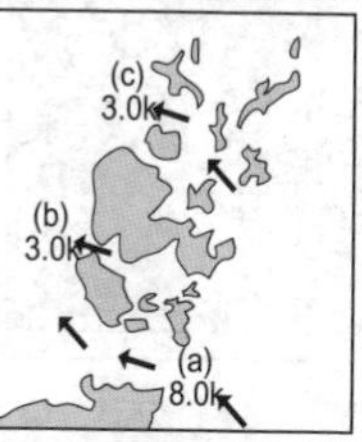

SHETLAND ISLANDS (AC 219)

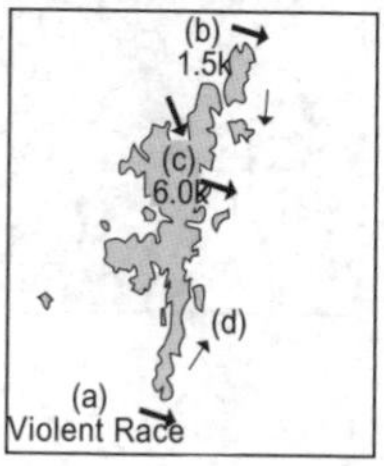

The tidal flow around the Shetland Islands rotates as the cycle progresses. When the flood begins, at –0400 HW Dover, the tidal flow is to the E, at HW Dover it is S, at Dover +0300 it is W, and at –0600 Dover it is N.

Flood	Ebb
(a) Dover –0410 to Dover +0020	(a) Dover +0050 to Dover –0410
(b) Dover –0400 to Dover +0030	(b) Dover +0130 to Dover –0500
(c) Dover –0530 to Dover +0100	(c) Dover +0100 to Dover –0530
(d) Dover –0400 to Dover –0200	(d) Dover +0200 to Dover +0500

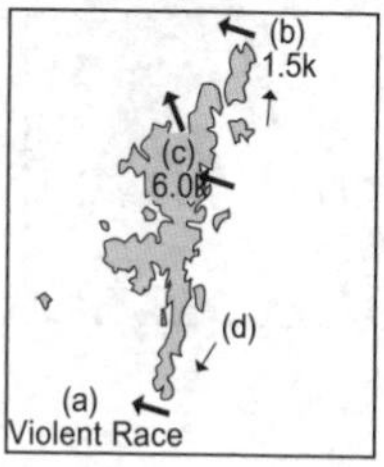

TIDAL GATES – NORTH WEST SCOTLAND

A guide to the time of tide turn at tidal gates, the approximate maximum strength of the tidal flow (spring rates shown – neaps are approximately 60% of these), and the position and timing of races, counter tides, etc.

FLOOD	EBB

SOUND OF HARRIS (AC 2802)

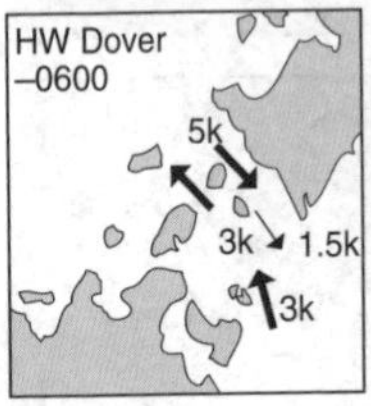

The behaviour of tidal streams in the Sd of Harris varies from day to night, springs to neaps, and winter to summer. The following data applies to daylight, in summer at spring tides in the Cope Channel. Further information can be sought in the Admiralty West of Scotland Pilot.

HW Dover - HW D +0200: SE stream.
HW D +0300 - HW D +0600: Incoming stream from both ends.
HW D –0600 - HW D –0500: NW stream.
HW D –0500 - HW Dover: Outgoing stream from both ends.
At neaps in summer the stream will run SE for most of the day.
Tide rates shown are the maxima likely to be encountered at any time.

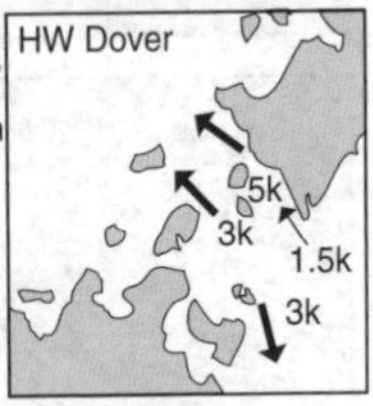

THE LITTLE MINCH (AC 1795)

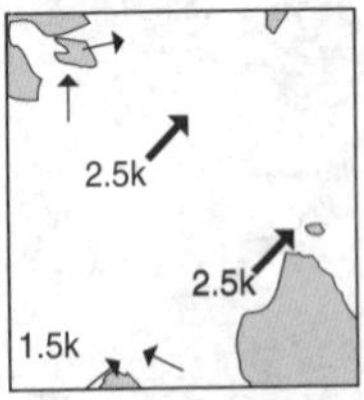

The N going stream on both shores begins at HW Dover +0430 (HW Ullapool -0345), with the strongest flow from mid channel to the Skye coast. There is a W going counter tide E of Vaternish Point.

The S going stream on both shores begins at HW Dover –0130 (HW Ullapool +0240), with the strongest flow from mid channel to the Skye coast. The E going stream in Sound of Scalpay runs at up to 2k.The E going flood and W going ebb in Sound of Scalpay run at up to 2k.

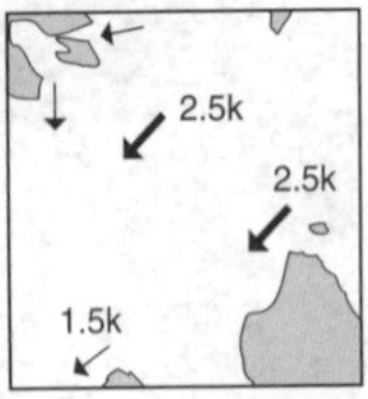

KYLE OF LOCHALSH & KYLERHEA (AC 2540)

NOTE: THESE STREAMS ARE SUBJECT TO VARIATION

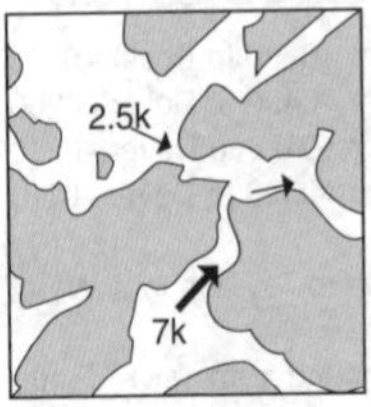

N going stream in Kyle Rhea begins HW Dover +0140 (HW Ullapool +0555) and runs for 6 hours. The E going stream in Kyle Akin begins (Sp) HW Dover +0350 (HW Ullapool –0415). (Nps) HW Dover –0415 (HW Ullapool).

S going stream in Kyle Rhea begins HW Dover -0415 (HW Ullapool) and runs for 6 hours. The W going stream in Kyle Akin begins (Sp) HW Dover –0015 (HW Ullapool +0400). (Nps) HW Dover +0140 (HW Ullapool +0555).

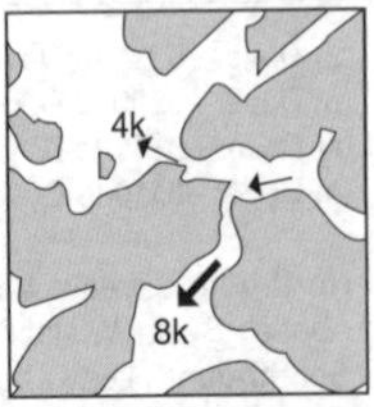

ARDNAMURCHAN POINT (AC 2171)

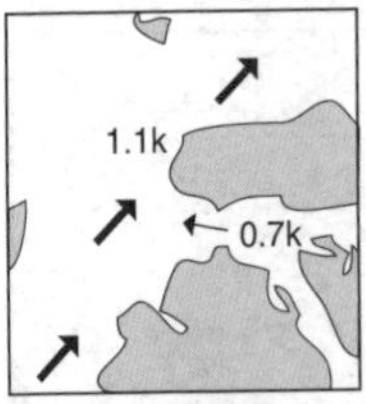

The N going stream off Ardnamurchan begins at HW Dover +0130 (HW Oban –0525). The E going stream in the Sound of Mull begins at HW Dover +0555 (HW Oban –0100).

The S going stream off Ardnamurchan begins at HW Dover –0430 (HW Oban +0100). The W going stream in the Sound of Mull begins at HW Dover –0130 (HW Oban +0400).

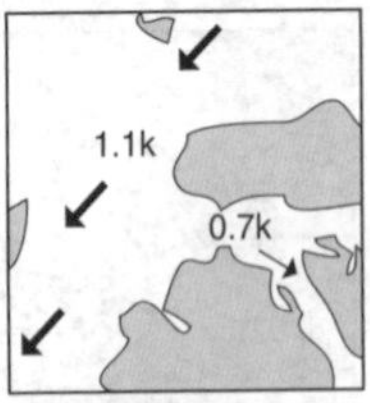

SOUND OF MULL – EAST (AC 2171)

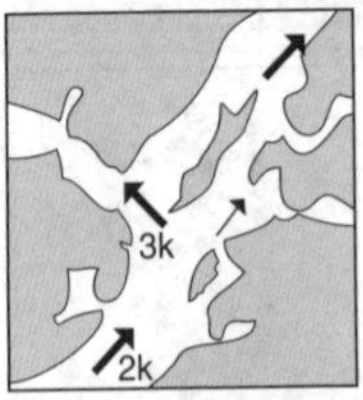

The N going stream in the Firth of Lorne begins at HW Dover –0100 (HW Oban +0430). The W going stream in the Sound of Mull begins at HW Dover +0105 (HW Oban –0550). The ingoing tides at Lochs Feochan, Etive and Creran begin at HW Dover +0300, –0100 & +0030.

The S going stream in the Firth of Lorne begins at HW Dover +0500 (HW Oban –0155). The E going stream in the Sound of Mull begins at HW Dover +0555 (HW Oban –0025). The outgoing tides at Lochs Feochan, Etive and Creran begin at HW Dover –0500, –0520 & –0505.

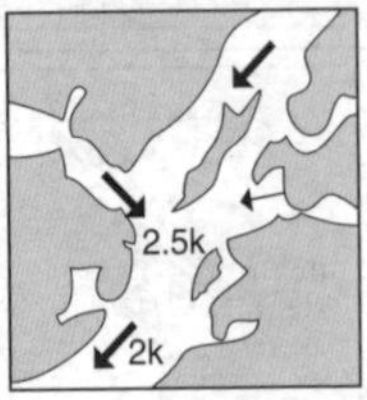

SOUND OF LUING & DORUS MOR (AC 2343)

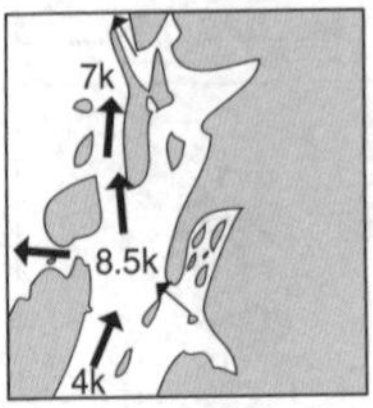

The N or W going stream begins as follows:

Dorus Mor:	HW Dover –0200 (HW Oban +0330). Springs: 8 knots.
Corryvreckan:	HW D –0120 (HW O +0410). Sp: 8.5 knots.
Cuan Sound:	HW D –0110 (HW O +0420). Sp: 6 knots.
Sound of Jura:	HW D –0130 (HW O +0400). Sp: 4 knots.
Sound of Luing:	HW D –0100 (HW O +0430). Sp: 7 knots.

The S or E going stream begins as follows:

Dorus Mor:	HW Dover +0440 (HW Oban –0215). Springs: 8 knots.
Corryvreckan:	HW D +0445 (HW O –0210). Sp: 8.5 knots.
Cuan Sound:	HW D +0455 (HW O –0200). Sp: 6 knots.
Sound of Jura:	HW D +0450 (HW O –0205). Sp: 4 knots.
Sound of Luing:	HW D +0500 (HW O –0155). Sp: 7 knots.

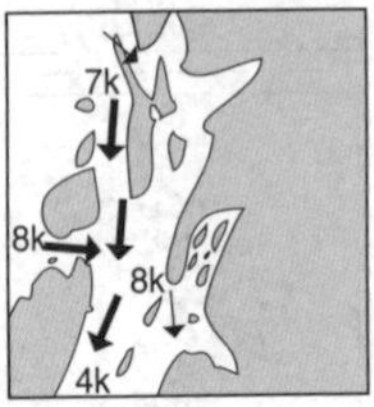

TIDAL GATES – SOUTH WEST SCOTLAND

A guide to the time of tide turn at tidal gates, the approximate maximum strength of the tidal flow (spring rates shown - neaps are approximately 60% of these), and the position and timing of races, counter tides, etc.

FLOOD	EBB

SOUNDS OF ISLAY AND GIGHA (AC 2168)

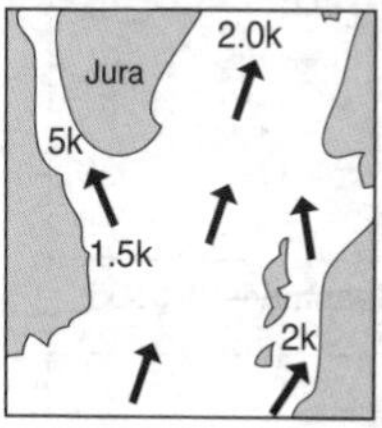

Flood: Main flood begins +0015 HW Dover (HW Oban +0545). Streams turn approx 1 hr earlier in Gigha Sd & at Kintyre & Jura shores. S going stream for 9hrs close inshore between Gigha and Machrihanish starting HW Dover (HW Oban –0530).

Ebb: Main ebb begins HW Dover –0545 (HW Oban –0015). Streams turn 1 hr earlier in Gigha Sd, Kintyre & Jura shores. Overfalls off McArthur's Hd.

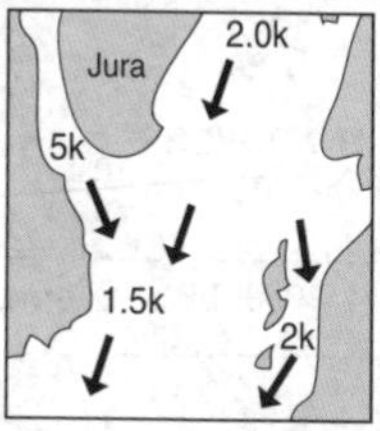

NORTH CHANNEL – NORTH (AC 2798)

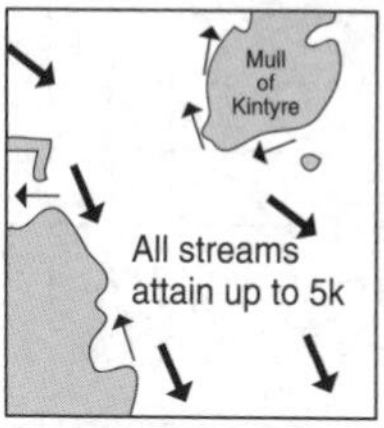

Flood: Main flood begins HW Dover –0600 (HW Greenock +0505). Races off Mull of Kintyre, Altacarry Hd & Fair Hd. Counter tides in bays of Antrim coast. W-going streams in Rathlin Sd, counter tide from Sanda Sd to Machrihanish last 1h30 - 2 hrs.

Ebb: Main ebb begins HW Dover (HW Greenock –0120). Races off Mull of Kintyre & Altacarry Hd. Counter tides in bays of Antrim coast, counter tide from Macrihanish to Sanda Sd last 1h30 - 2 hrs.

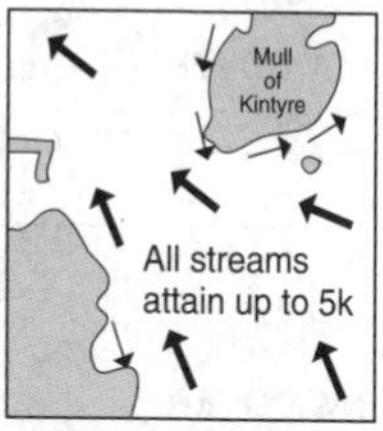

NORTH CHANNEL – SOUTH (AC 2198)

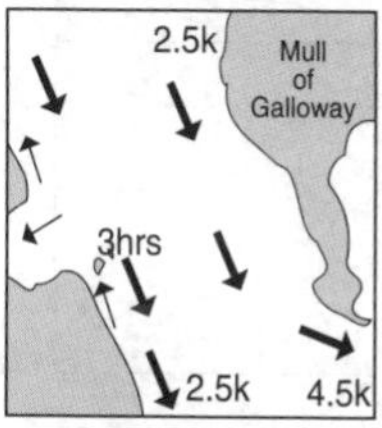

Flood: Irish coast - flood begins HW Dover +0610 (HW Belfast –0600). Scottish coast - HW Dover +0430 (HW Greenock +0310). Races off Copeland Is. & Mull of Galloway. Counter tide off Donaghadee and Island Magee last 3 hrs of flood.

Ebb: Irish coast - ebb begins HW Dover –0015 (HW Belfast). Scottish coast - HW Dover –0130 (HW Greenock –0250). Races off Copeland Is. & Mull of Galloway. Flood begins 2 hrs early close inshore N of Mull of Galloway.

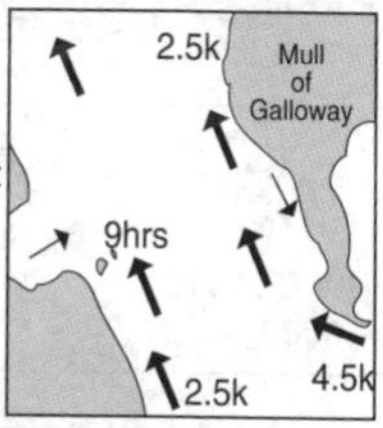

APPROACHES TO STRANGFORD LOUGH (AC 2156)

The tide cycle is approx 3 hours later than in the N Channel

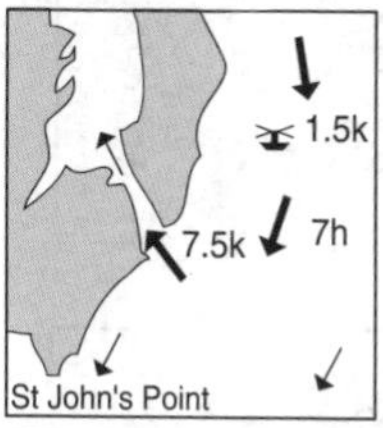

Flood: Flood runs for 6 hours from HW Dover –0345 (HW Belfast –0330), with a maximum rate of 7.5 knots at Rue Point. The strong flow flattens the sea in onshore winds and entrance can be made in strong winds.

Ebb: Ebb runs for 6 hours from HW Dover +0215 (HW Belfast +0230), max rate 7.5k, E of Angus Rk. If entering against ebb use West Channel with care. Smoothest water near Bar Pladdy Buoy when leaving.

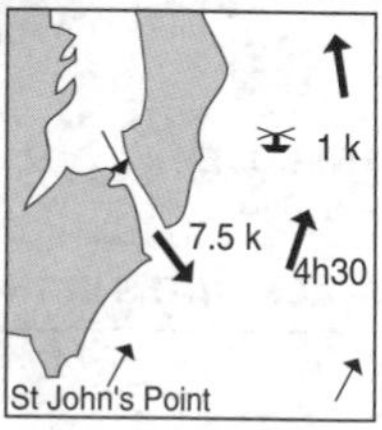

ISLE OF MAN – NORTH (AC 2094)

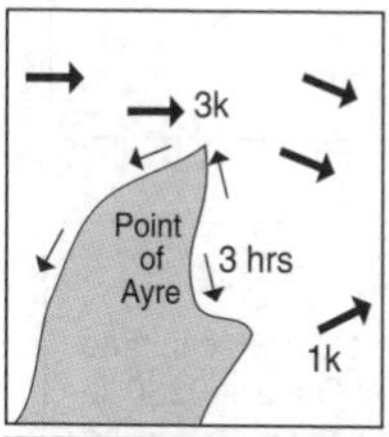

Flood: E going stream at Point of Ayre begins HW Dover –0545 (HW Liverpool –0600). Counter tide inside banks E of Point.
In Ramsey Bay the S Going tide runs for 3h from +0530 Dover (+0515 Liverpool).

Ebb: W going stream at Point of Ayre begins HW Dover +0015 (HW Liverpool). Counter tide inside banks W of Point.
In Ramsey Bay the N going tide runs for 9h from –0330 Dover (–0345 Liverpool).

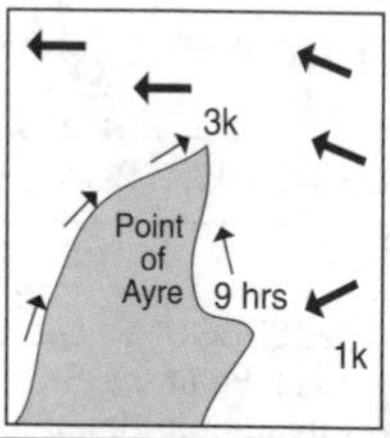

ISLE OF MAN – SOUTH (AC 2094)

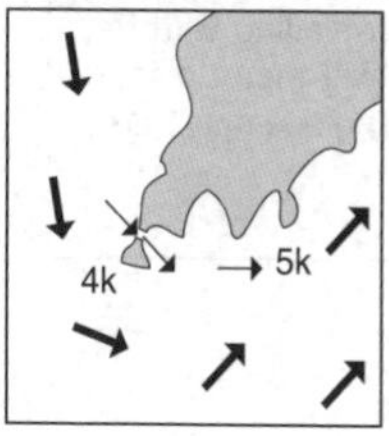

Flood: E going stream begins –0600 Dover (Liverpool +0610). Overfalls and race E of Chicken Rock.
Calf Sound: The E going stream begins earlier, at approximately Dover +0400 (Liverpool +0345).

Ebb: W going stream begins +0015 Dover (HW Liverpool). Overfalls and race N of Chicken Rock.
Calf Sound: The W going stream begins earlier, at approximately –0130 Dover (–0145 Liverpool).
Note: all times may vary due to weather conditions.

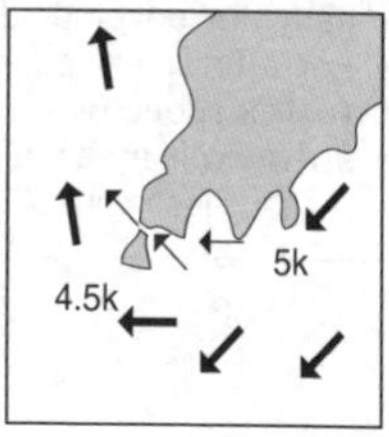

MENAI STRAIT (AC 1464) – TIDAL GATES

FLOOD

(T): turning → : < 2k ➟ : 2-4k ➡ : 4k +

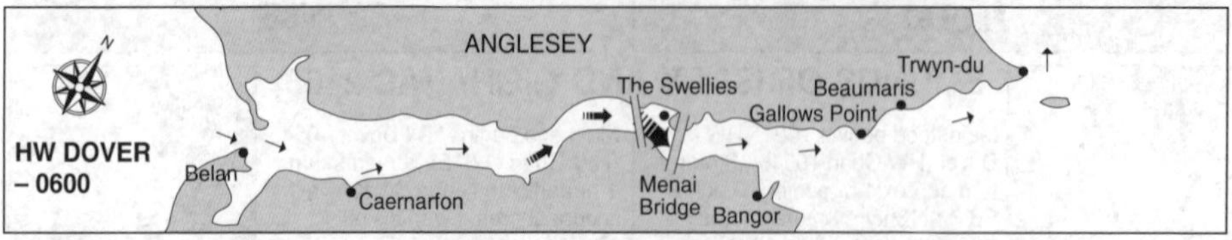

LOCAL LW: Caernarfon: HW Dover –0555. Port Dinorwic: –0620. Menai: –0540. Beaumaris: –0605.

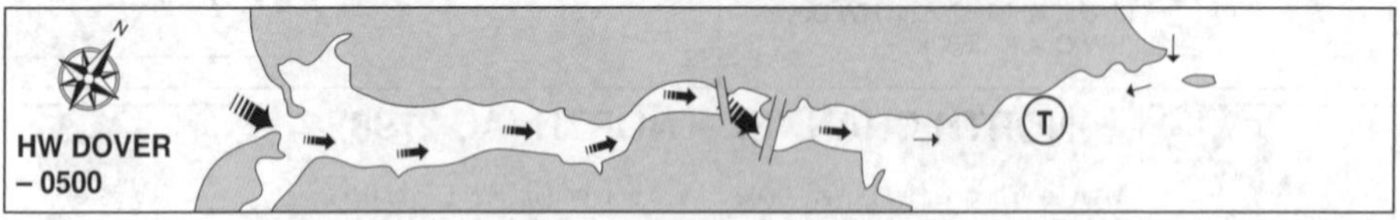

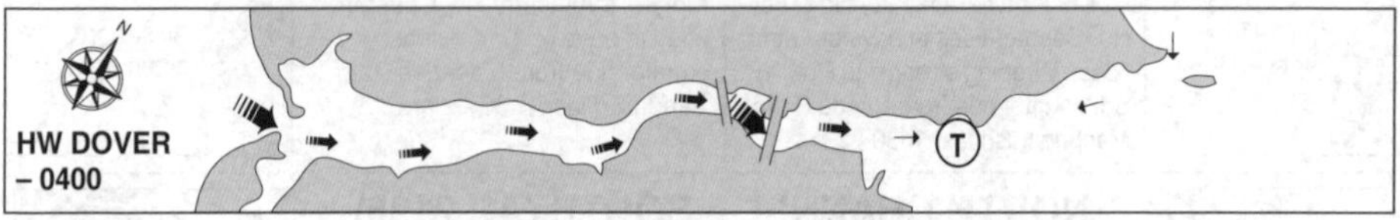

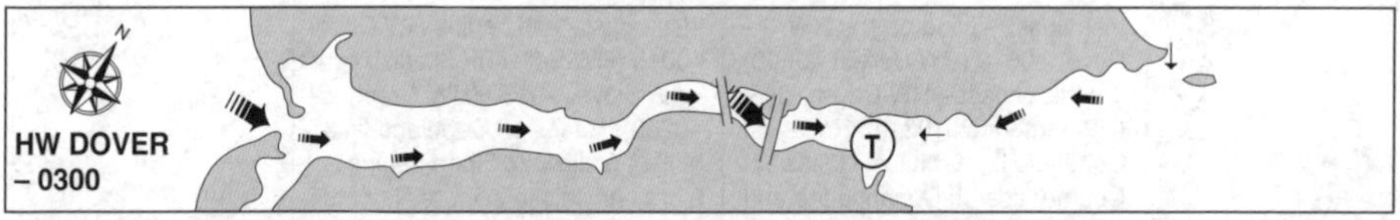

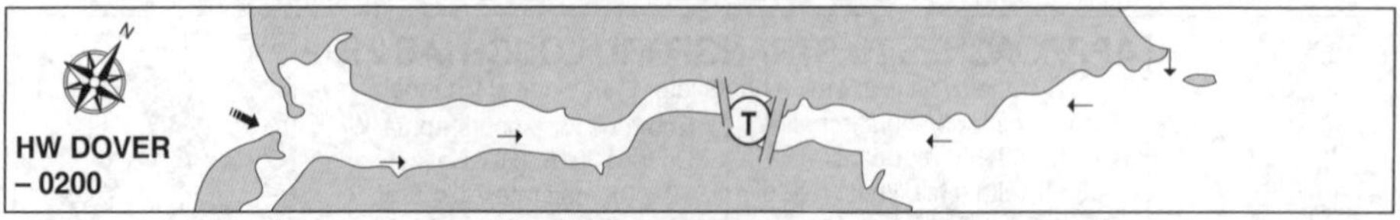

SLACK WATER IN THE SWELLIES: HW Dover –0200 to –0230.

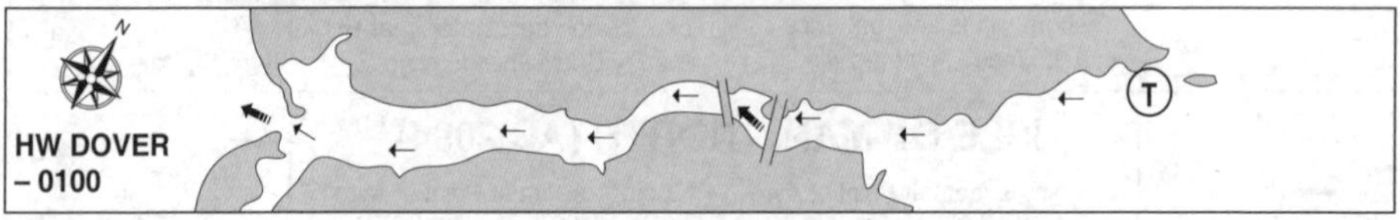

LOCAL HW: Belan: HW Dover –0115. Caernarfon: –0105. Port Dinorwic: –0050.

THE SWELLIES

WESTBOUND: Leave or pass Beaumaris in time to arrive at the Swellies by HW Dover –0230 to –0200. If in doubt about passage speed, leave early; the adverse tide will check your progress. For a first time passage this is useful, as the yacht's speed over the ground is reduced. Late arrival will mean a faster passage, but with perhaps less control.

EASTBOUND: Leave or pass Port Dinorwic in time to arrive at Menai Bridge by HW Dover –0230 to –0200. Progress towards the Swellies should be closely monitored, as you are travelling with the last of the flood. Early arrival will mean a fast, perhaps dangerous passage, being late may make it impossible.

MENAI STRAIT (AC 1464) – TIDAL GATES *contd*

EBB

(T): turning → : < 2k ➡ : 2-4k ➡ : 4k +

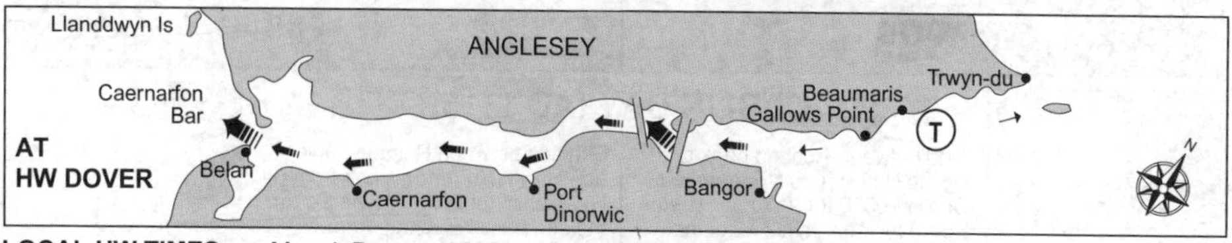

LOCAL HW TIMES: Menai: Dover – 0005. Beaumaris: Dover – 0010

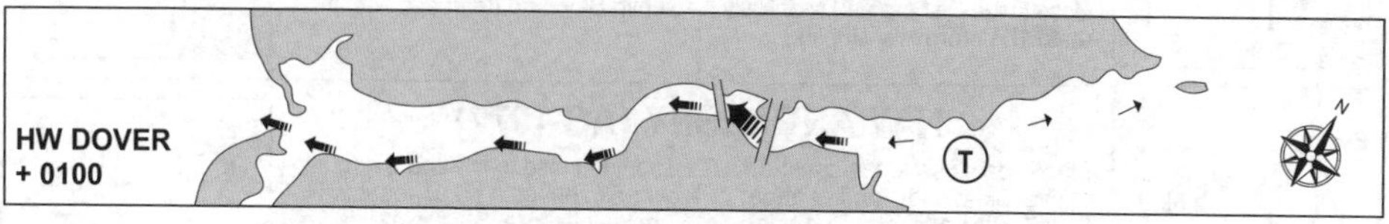

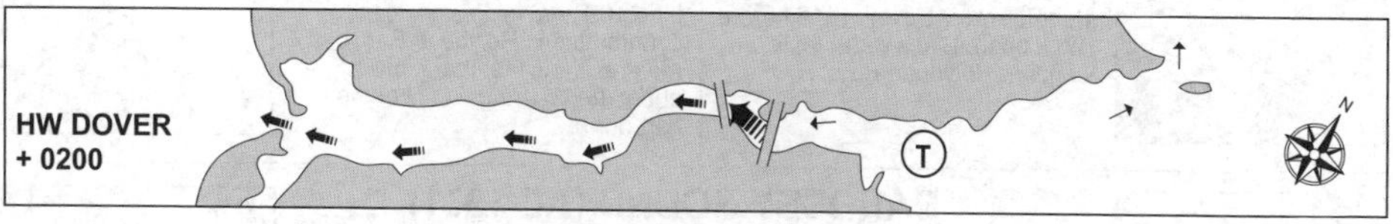

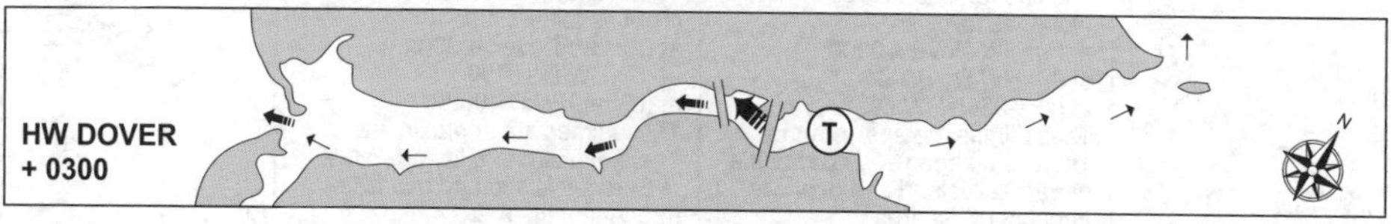

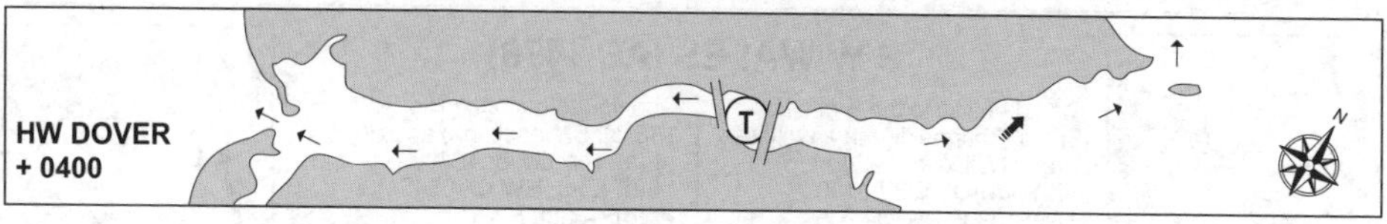

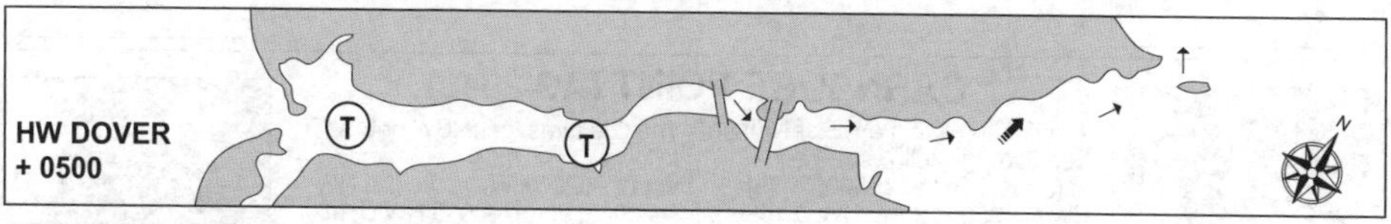

LOCAL LW TIMES: Belan: Dover + 0520.

CAERNARFON BAR

CAERNARFON BAR is without question highly dangerous in certain conditions. Buoys are located to suit changing channel; positions obtainable from Caernarfon Port Radio - VHF Ch 16; 06, 12: 2h–HW, or when vessel expected. Beware cross track tides near high water. Bar impassable during or after fresh or strong onshore weather. Keep strictly in channel.

OUTWARD BOUND: Do not leave Belan Narrows after half tide, better as soon as possible after the ebb commences, which gives maximum depth and duration of fair tide if bound S & W.

INWARD BOUND: Locating the bar buoys may be difficult; head for Llanddwyn I. until they are located. Only cross after half tide (HW Dover –0400), which inevitably limits onward passage to max of 3 hours.

TIDAL GATES – IRISH SEA

A guide to the time of tide turn at tidal gates, the approximate strength of the tidal flow (spring rates shown – neaps are approximately 60% of these), and the position and timing of races, counter tides, etc.

FLOOD	EBB

DUBLIN BAY (AC 1415)

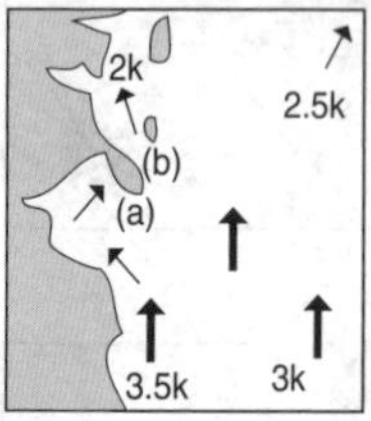

Flood: Tide between Rosbeg bank and Howth Hd (a) runs NE from HW Dublin +0300 for 9h30. In Howth Sd (b) the stream is NW going from +0430 to –0130.
New flood and ebb tides begin close to the S shore and N of Baily up to 1h before HW Dublin .

Ebb: The tide between Rosbeg bank and Howth Hd (a) runs SW from HW Dublin for 3h. In Howth Sd (b) the stream is SE going from –0130 to +0430.
Strengths of streams increase S of Dublin Bay, and decrease N of it.

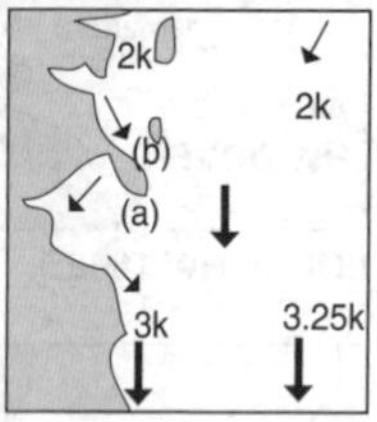

N W ANGLESEY (AC 1977)

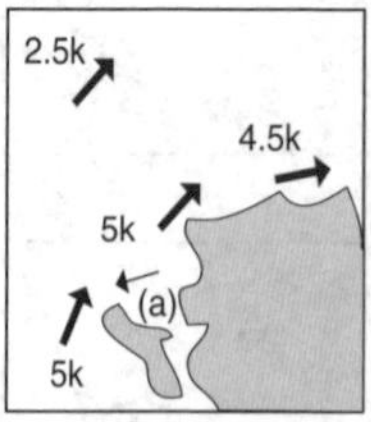

Flood: Flood tide close to the coast runs at over 5k springs, and at about 2.5k 7 miles offshore. The brief period of slack water offshore is 1h before HW Dover (1h15 before HW L'pool). Slack water lasts longer in Holyhead Bay.

Ebb: Ebb tide close to the coast runs at over 5k springs, and at about 2.5k 7 miles offshore. Slack water is 5h after HW Dover (4h45 after HW L'pool). There is no significant counter tide in Holyhead Bay, but the ebb starts first there, giving about 9h W-going tide N of the harbour (a).

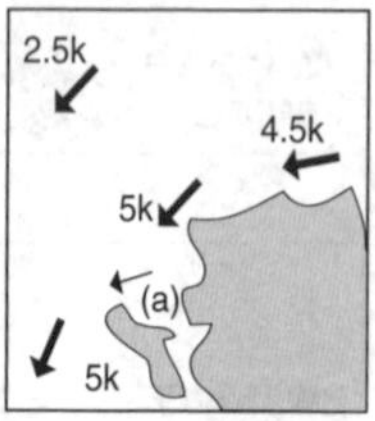

BARDSEY SOUND (AC 1971)

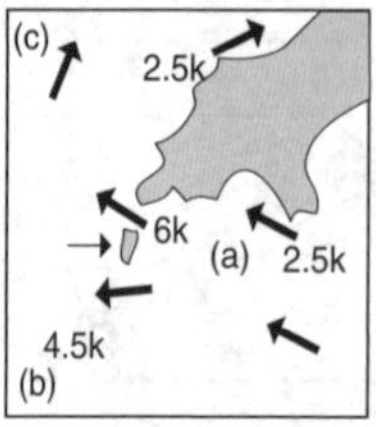

Flood: The tide turns to the NW or NE (flood) as follows:
at (a): HW Dover +0300;
at (b): HW D +0500;
at (c): –0545 HW D.
These times are approximate.
There is a strong eddy down tide of Bardsey Island and overfalls throughout the area.

Ebb: The tide turns to the SW or SE (ebb) as follows:
at (a): HW Dover –0300;
at (b): HW D –0100 ;
at (c): at HW D –0030.
These times are approximate.
There is a strong eddy down tide of Bardsey Island and overfalls throughout the area.

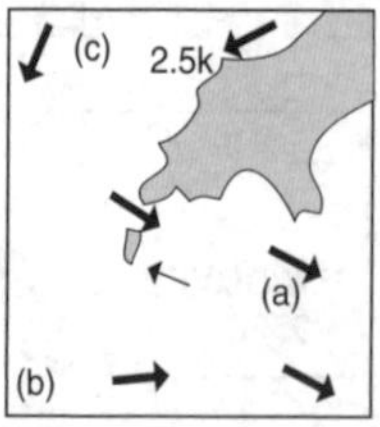

S W WALES (AC 1478)

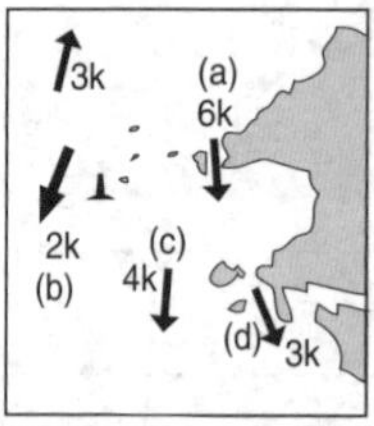

Flood: The tide turns to the S or SE (Bristol Channel flood) as follows:
at (a): HW Dover –0200;
at (b) & (c): HW D –0100 ;
at (d): –0300 HW D

Ebb: The tide turns to the N or NW (Bristol Channel ebb) as follows:
at (a): HW Dover +0400;
at (b) & (c): HW D +0500 ;
at (d): +0300 HW D

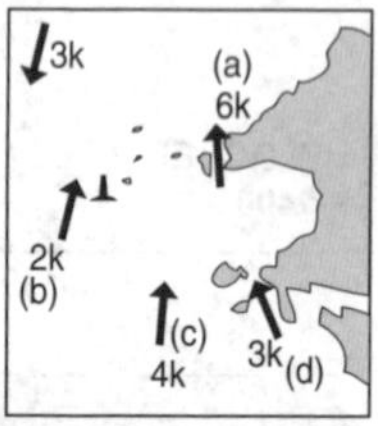

CARNSORE POINT (AC 2049)

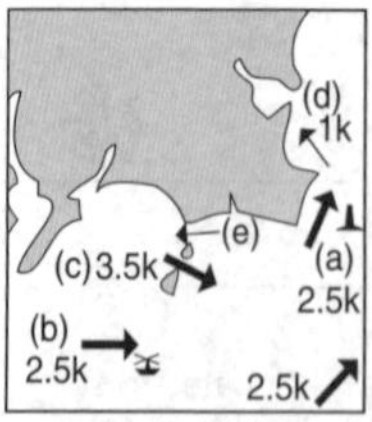

Flood: The tide turns to the NE or N (Irish Sea flood) as follows:
at (a): HW Dover +0500; at (b): HW D +0520; at (c): HW D +0600; at (d): –0600 HW D. NE going streams are shorter in duration and weaker than SE going - careful passage planning is essential.

Ebb: The tide turns to the SW or S as follows:
at (a): –0200 HW D ; at (b): HW D –0020; at (c): –0015 HW D; at (d): –0300 HW Dover. Leaving Rosslare at –0300 HW D a yacht can carry a fair tide for about 8h until HW D +0515 off Hook Head.

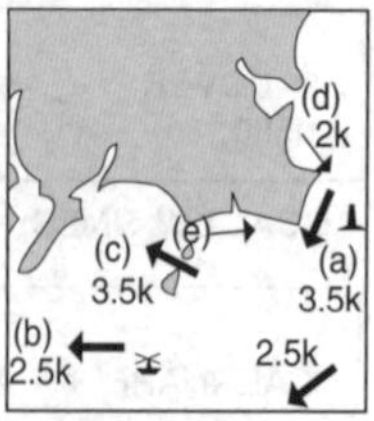

NOTE: The tide turns on St Patrick's Bridge (e) up to 2 hours earlier than in Saltee Sound

CORK COAST (AC 2049)

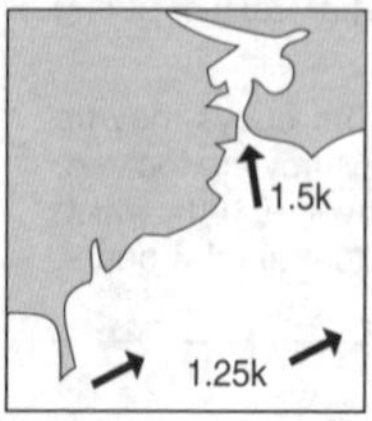

Flood: The tide, which flows coastwise, turns to the NE at HW Dover +0045. There is an eddy 5 miles ESE of Old Head of Kinsale at HW Dover +0400. The ingoing Cork Harbour tide begins at HW Dover +0055.

Ebb: The tide turns SW at HW Dover +0500. The outgoing Cork Harbour tide begins at HW Dover –0540.

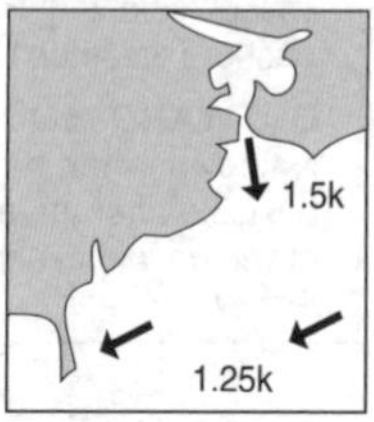

SECONDARY PORTS: TIME & HEIGHT DIFFERENCES

SOUTH COAST OF ENGLAND *Time zone UT*

Location	Lat	Long	High Water		Low Water		MHWS	MHWN	MLWN	MLWS
			0000	0600	0000	0600				
PLYMOUTH (DEVONPORT)	50 22N	4 11W	and	and	and	and	**5.5**	**4.4**	**2.2**	**0.8**
Standard port			**1200**	**1800**	**1200**	**1800**				
Isles of Scilly, St Mary's	49 55N	6 19W	–0052	–0103	–0048	–0045	+0.2	–0.1	–0.2	–0.1
Penzance & Newlyn	50 06N	5 33W	–0053	–0108	–0035	–0036	0.0	–0.1	–0.2	0.0
Porthleven	50 05N	5 19W	–0045	–0105	–0030	–0025	0.0	–0.1	–0.2	0.0
Lizard Point	49 57N	5 12W	–0045	–0100	–0030	–0030	–0.2	–0.2	–0.3	–0.2
Coverack	50 01N	5 05W	–0030	–0050	–0020	–0015	–0.2	–0.2	–0.3	–0.2
Helford River Entrance	50 05N	5 05W	–0030	–0035	–0015	–0010	–0.2	–0.2	–0.3	–0.2
FALMOUTH	50 09N	5 03W	*Standard port (no Secondaries)*							
River Fal, Truro	50 16N	5 03W	–0020	–0025	*Dries*	*Dries*	–2.0	–2.0	*Dries*	
Mevagissey	50 16N	4 47W	–0015	–0020	–0010	–0005	–0.1	–0.1	–0.2	–0.1
Par	50 21N	4 42W	–0010	–0015	–0010	–0005	–0.4	–0.4	–0.4	–0.2
River Fowey, Fowey	50 20N	4 38W	–0010	–0015	–0010	–0005	–0.1	–0.1	–0.2	–0.2
Lostwithiel	50 24N	4 40W	+0005	–0010	*Dries*	*Dries*	–4.1	–4.1	*Dries*	
Looe	50 21N	4 27W	–0010	–0010	–0005	–0005	–0.1	–0.2	–0.2	–0.2
Whitsand Bay	50 20N	4 15W	0000	0000	0000	0000	0.0	+0.1	–0.1	+0.2
River Tamar										
Saltash	50 24N	4 12W	0000	+0010	0000	–0005	+0.1	+0.1	+0.1	+0.1
Cargreen	50 26N	4 12W	0000	+0010	+0020	+0020	0.0	0.0	–0.1	0.0
Cotehele Quay	50 29N	4 13W	0000	+0020	+0045	+0045	–0.9	–0.9	–0.8	–0.4
River Tavy, Lopwell	50 28N	4 09W	*No data*	*No data*	*Dries*	*Dries*	–2.6	–2.7	*Dries*	
River Lynher, Jupiter Point	50 23N	4 14W	+0010	+0005	0000	–0005	0.0	0.0	+0.1	0.0
St Germans	50 23N	4 18W	0000	0000	+0020	+0020	–0.3	–0.1	0.0	+0.2
Turnchapel	50 22N	4 07W	0000	0000	+0010	–0015	0.0	+0.1	+0.2	+0.1
Bovisand Pier	50 20N	4 08W	–0010	–0010	–0008	–0009	–0.1	0.0	+0.2	+0.2
River Yealm, Entrance	50 18N	4 04W	+0006	+0006	+0002	+0002	–0.1	–0.1	–0.1	–0.1
			0100	0600	0100	0600				
PLYMOUTH (DEVONPORT)	50 22N	4 11W	and	and	and	and	**5.5**	**4.4**	**2.2**	**0.8**
Standard port			**1300**	**1800**	**1300**	**1800**				
Salcombe	50 13N	3 47W	0000	+0010	+0005	–0005	–0.2	–0.3	–0.1	–0.1
Start Point	50 13N	3 39W	+0015	+0015	+0005	+0010	–0.1	–0.2	+0.1	+0.2
River Dart										
DARTMOUTH	50 21N	3 34W	*Standard port (no Secondaries)*							
Greenway Quay	50 23N	3 35W	+0030	+0045	+0025	+0005	–0.6	–0.6	–0.2	–0.2
Totnes	50 26N	3 41W	+0030	+0040	+0115	+0030	–2.0	–2.1	*Dries*	
Torquay	50 28N	3 31W	+0025	+0045	+0010	0000	–0.6	–0.7	–0.2	–0.1
Teignmouth, Approaches	50 33N	3 29W	+0020	+0050	+0025	0000	–0.9	–0.8	–0.2	–0.1
Teignmouth, New Quay	50 33N	3 30W	+0025	+0055	+0040	+0005	–0.8	–0.8	–0.2	+0.1
Exmouth Approaches	50 36N	3 23W	+0030	+0050	+0015	+0005	–0.9	–1.0	–0.5	–0.3
River Exe										
Exmouth Dock	50 37N	3 25W	+0035	+0055	+0050	+0020	–1.5	–1.6	–0.9	–0.5
Starcross	50 38N	3 27W	+0040	+0100	+0055	+0025	–1.4	–1.5	–0.8	–0.1
Turf Lock	50 40N	3 28W	+0045	+0100	+0034	*No data*	– 1.6	–1.6	–1.2	*No data*
Topsham	50 41N	3 28W	+0045	+0105	*No data*	*No data*	– 1.5	–1.6	*No data*	
Lyme Regis	50 43N	2 56W	+0040	+0100	+0005	–0005	–1.2	–1.3	–0.5	–0.2
Bridport (West Bay)	50 42N	2 45W	+0025	+0040	0000	0000	–1.4	–1.4	–0.6	–0.1
Chesil Beach	50 37N	2 33W	+0040	+0055	–0005	+0010	–1.6	–1.5	–0.5	0.0
Chesil Cove	50 34N	2 28W	+0035	+0050	–0010	+0005	–1.5	–1.6	–0.5	–0.2
			0100	0700	0100	0700				
PORTLAND	50 34N	2 26W	and	and	and	and	**2.1**	**1.4**	**0.8**	**0.1**
Standard port			**1300**	**1900**	**1300**	**1900**				
Lulworth Cove, Mupe Bay	50 37N	2 14W	+0005	+0015	–0005	0000	+0.1	+0.1	+0.2	+0.1
			—	—	0500	1100				
POOLE HARBOUR	50 42N	1 59W			and	and	**2.2**	**1.7**	**1.2**	**0.6**
Standard port			—	—	**1700**	**2300**				
Swanage	50 37N	1 57W	—	—	–0045	+0050	–0.1	+0.1	+0.2	+0.2
Poole Harbour Entrance	50 41N	1 57W	—	—	–0025	–0010	0.0	0.0	0.0	0.0
Ro-Ro terminal	50 42N	1 59W	*Standard port*							
Pottery Pier	50 42N	1 59W	—	—	+0010	+0010	–0.2	0.0	+0.1	+0.2
Wareham, River Frome	50 41N	2 06W	—	—	+0130	+0045	0.0	0.0	0.0	+0.3
Cleavel Point	50 40N	2 00W	—	—	–0005	–0005	–0.1	–0.2	0.0	–0.1
			0000	0600	0500	1100				
PORTSMOUTH	50 48N	1 07W	and	and	and	and	**4.7**	**3.8**	**1.9**	**0.8**
Standard port			**1200**	**1800**	**1700**	**2300**				
Bournemouth	50 43N	1 52W	–0240	+0055	–0050	–0030	–2.6	–2.0	–0.6	–0.2
Christchurch Entrance	50 43N	1 45W	–0230	+0030	–0035	–0035	–2.9	–2.4	–1.2	–0.2

Location	Lat	Long	High Water		Low Water		MHWS	MHWN	MLWN	MLWS
Christchurch Quay	50 44N	1 47W	–0210	+0100	+0105	+0055	–2.9	–2.4	–1.0	0.0
Christchurch, Tuckton	50 44N	1 47W	–0205	+0110	+0110	+0105	–3.0	–2.5	–1.0	+0.1
Hurst Point	50 42N	1 33W	–0115	–0005	–0030	–0025	–2.0	–1.5	–0.5	–0.1
Lymington	50 46N	1 32W	–0110	+0005	–0020	–0020	–1.6	–1.2	–0.4	–0.1
Bucklers Hard	50 48N	1 25W	–0040	–0010	+0010	–0010	–1.0	–0.8	–0.2	–0.3
Stansore Point	50 47N	1 20W	–0030	–0010	–0005	–0015	–0.8	–0.5	–0.3	–0.3
Isle of Wight										
Yarmouth	50 42N	1 30W	–0105	+0005	–0025	–0030	–1.7	–1.2	–0.3	0.0
Totland Bay	50 41N	1 33W	–0130	–0045	–0035	–0045	–2.2	–1.7	–0.4	–0.1
Freshwater	50 40N	1 31W	–0210	+0025	–0040	–0020	–2.1	–1.5	–0.4	0.0
Ventnor	50 36N	1 12W	–0025	–0030	–0025	–0030	–0.8	–0.6	–0.2	+0.2
Sandown	50 39N	1 09W	0000	+0005	+0010	+0025	–0.6	–0.5	–0.2	0.0
Foreland Lifeboat Slip	50 41N	1 04W	–0005	0000	+0005	+0010	+0.1	+0.1	0.0	+0.1
Bembridge Harbour	50 42N	1 07W	+0020	0000	+0100	+0020	–1.5	–1.4	–1.3	–1.0
Ryde	50 44N	1 10W	–0010	–0010	–0005	–0005	–0.1	0.0	0.0	0.0
Medina River										
Cowes	50 46N	1 18W	–0015	+0015	0000	–0020	–0.5	–0.3	–0.1	0.0
Folly Inn	50 44N	1 17W	–0015	+0015	0000	–0020	–0.6	–0.4	–0.1	+0.2
Newport	50 42N	1 17W	*No data*	*No data*	*No data*	*No data*	–0.6	–0.4	+0.1	+0.8
SOUTHAMPTON	50 53N	1 24W	**0400** and **1600**	**1100** and **2300**	**0000** and **1200**	**0600** and **1800**	**4.5**	**3.7**	**1.8**	**0.5**
Standard port										
Calshot Castle	50 49N	1 18W	0000	+0025	0000	0000	0.0	0.0	+0.2	+0.3
Redbridge	50 55N	1 28W	–0020	+0005	0000	–0005	–0.1	–0.1	–0.1	–0.1
River Hamble										
Warsash	50 51N	1 18W	+0020	+0010	+0010	0000	0.0	+0.1	+0.1	+0.3
Bursledon	50 53N	1 18W	+0020	+0020	+0010	+0010	+0.1	+0.1	+0.2	+0.2
PORTSMOUTH	50 48N	1 07W	**0500** and **1700**	**1000** and **2200**	**0000** and **1200**	**0600** and **1800**	**4.7**	**3.8**	**1.9**	**0.8**
Standard port										
Lee-on-the-Solent	50 48N	1 12W	–0005	+0005	–0015	–0010	–0.2	–0.1	+0.1	+0.2
Chichester Harbour Entrance	50 47N	0 56W	–0010	+0005	+0015	+0020	+0.2	+0.2	0.0	+0.1
Northney	50 50N	0 58W	+0020	+0010	0000	+0005	0.0	–0.2	–0.2	–0.4
Bosham	50 50N	0 52W	+0010	+0005	*No data*	*No data*	0.0	–0.1	*No data*	
Itchenor	50 48N	0 52W	+0005	0000	–0010	+0005	–0.1	–0.2	–0.2	–0.3
Dell Quay	50 49N	0 49W	+0015	+0010	*no data*	*No data*	0.0	–0.1	*No data*	
Selsey Bill	50 43N	0 47W	+0010	–0010	+0035	+0020	+0.5	+0.3	–0.1	–0.2
Nab Tower	50 40N	0 57W	+0015	0000	+0015	+0015	–0.2	0.0	+0.2	0.0
SHOREHAM	50 50N	0 15W	**0500** and **1700**	**1000** and **2200**	**0000** and **1200**	**0600** and **1800**	**6.3**	**4.8**	**1.9**	**0.6**
Standard port										
Pagham	50 46N	0 43W	+0015	0000	–0015	–0025	–0.7	–0.5	–0.1	–0.1
Bognor Regis	50 47N	0 40W	+0010	–0005	–0005	–0020	–0.6	–0.5	–0.2	–0.1
River Arun										
Littlehampton Entrance	50 48N	0 33W	+0010	0000	–0005	–0010	–0.4	–0.4	–0.2	–0.2
Littlehampton UMA wharf	50 49N	0 33W	+0015	+0005	0000	+0045	–0.7	–0.7	–0.3	+0.2
Arundel	50 51N	0 33W	*No data*	+0120	*No data*	*No data*	–3.1	–2.8	*No data*	
Worthing	50 48N	0 22W	+0010	0000	–0005	–0010	–0.1	–0.2	0.0	0.0
Brighton	50 49N	0 08W	–0002	–0002	0000	0000	+0.2	+0.2	+0.1	+0.1
Newhaven	50 47N	0 04E	–0003	–0005	0000	+0005	+0.5	+0.4	+0.2	+0.2
Eastbourne	50 46N	0 17E	–0010	–0005	+0015	+0020	+1.1	+0.6	+0.2	+0.1
DOVER	51 07N	1 19E	**0000** and **1200**	**0600** and **1800**	**0100** and **1300**	**0700** and **1900**	**6.8**	**5.3**	**2.1**	**0.8**
Standard port										
Hastings	50 51N	0 36E	0000	–0010	–0030	–0030	+0.8	+0.5	+0.1	–0.1
Rye Approaches	50 55N	0 47E	+0005	–0010	*No data*	*No data*	+1.0	+0.7	*No data*	
Rye Harbour	50 56N	0 48E	+0005	–0010	*Dries*	*Dries*	–1.4	–1.7	*Dries*	
Dungeness	50 55N	0 58E	–0010	–0015	–0020	–0010	+1.0	+0.6	+0.4	+0.1
Folkestone	51 05N	1 12E	–0020	–0005	–0010	–0010	+0.4	+0.4	0.0	–0.1
Deal	51 13N	1 25E	+0012	+0010	+0004	+0002	–0.5	–0.3	0.0	+0.1
Richborough	51 18N	1 21E	+0015	+0015	+0030	+0030	–3.4	–2.6	–1.7	–0.7
Ramsgate	51 20N	1 25E	+0030	+0030	+0017	+0007	–1.6	–1.3	–0.7	–0.2
EAST COAST ENGLAND *Time Zone UT*										
MARGATE	51 23N	1 23E	**0100** and **1300**	**0700** and **1900**	**0100** and **1300**	**0700** and **1900**	**4.8**	**3.9**	**1.4**	**0.5**
Standard port										
Herne Bay	51 23N	1 07E	+0022	+0020	+0019	+0017	+0.6	+0.3	+0.2	+0.1
Whitstable approaches	51 22N	1 02E	+0042	+0029	+0025	+0050	+0.6	+0.6	+0.1	0.0

Location	Lat	Long	High Water		Low Water		MHWS	MHWN	MLWN	MLWS
			0200 and **1400**	**0800** and **2000**	**0200** and **1400**	**0700** and **1900**				
SHEERNESS	51 27N	0 45E					**5.8**	**4.7**	**1.5**	**0.6**
Standard port										
River Swale										
Grovehurst Jetty	51 22N	0 46E	–0007	0000	0000	+0016	0.0	0.0	0.0	–0.1
Faversham	51 19N	0 54E	*No data*	*No data*	*No data*	*No data*	–0.2	–0.2	*No data*	
River Medway										
Bee Ness	51 25N	0 39E	+0002	+0002	0000	+0005	+0.2	+0.1	0.0	0.0
Bartlett Creek	51 23N	0 38E	+0016	+0008	*No data*	*No data*	+0.1	0.0	*No data*	
Darnett Ness	51 24N	0 36E	+0004	+0004	0000	+0010	+0.2	+0.1	0.0	–0.1
Chatham, Lock approaches	51 24N	0 33E	+0010	+0012	+0012	+0018	+0.3	+0.1	–0.1	–0.2
Upnor	51 25N	0 32E	+0015	+0015	+0015	+0025	+0.2	+0.2	–0.1	–0.1
Rochester, Strood Pier	51 24N	0 30E	+0018	+0018	+0018	+0028	+0.2	+0.2	–0.2	–0.3
Wouldham	51 21N	0 27E	+0030	+0025	+0035	+0120	–0.2	–0.3	–1.0	–0.3
New Hythe	51 19N	0 28E	+0035	+0035	+0220	+0240	–1.6	–1.7	–1.2	–0.3
Allington Lock	51 17N	0 30E	+0050	+0035	*No data*	*No data*	–2.1	–2.2	–1.3	–0.4
River Thames										
Southend–on–Sea	51 31N	0 43E	–0005	–0005	–0005	–0005	+0.1	0.0	–0.1	–0.1
Coryton	51 30N	0 31E	+0005	+0010	+0010	+0010	+0.4	+0.3	0.0	0.0
			0300 and **1500**	**0900** and **2100**	**0400** and **1600**	**1100** and **2300**				
LONDON BRIDGE	51 30N	0 05W					**7.1**	**5.9**	**1.3**	**0.5**
Standard port										
Tilbury	51 27N	0 22E	–0055	–0040	–0050	–0115	–0.7	–0.5	+0.1	0.0
North Woolwich	51 30N	0 05E	–0020	–0020	–0035	–0045	–0.1	0.0	+0.2	0.0
Albert bridge	51 29N	0 10W	+0025	+0020	+0105	+0110	–0.9	–0.8	–0.7	–0.4
Hammersmith bridge	51 29N	0 14W	+0040	+0035	+0205	+0155	–1.4	–1.3	–1.0	–0.5
Kew bridge	51 29N	0 17W	+0055	+0050	+0255	+0235	–1.8	–1.8	–1.2	–0.5
Richmond lock	51 28N	0 19W	+0105	+0055	+0325	+0305	–2.2	–2.7	–0.9	–0.5
			0200 and **1400**	**0700** and **1900**	**0100** and **1300**	**0700** and **1900**				
SHEERNESS	51 27N	0 45E					**5.8**	**4.7**	**1.5**	**0.6**
Standard port										
Thames Estuary Shivering Sand	51 30N	1 05E	–0025	–0019	–0008	–0026	–0.6	–0.6	–0.1	–0.1
			0000 and **1200**	**0600** and **1800**	**0500** and **1700**	**1100** and **2300**				
WALTON-ON-THE-NAZE	51 51N	1 17E					**4.2**	**3.4**	**1.1**	**0.4**
Standard port										
Whitaker Beacon	51 40N	1 06E	+0022	+0024	+0033	+0027	+0.6	+0.5	+0.2	+0.1
Holliwell Point	51 38N	0 56E	+0034	+0037	+0100	+0037	+1.1	+0.9	+0.3	+0.1
River Roach Rochford	51 35N	0 43E	+0050	+0040	*Dries*	*Dries*	–0.8	–1.1	*Dries*	
River Crouch										
Burnham-on-Crouch	51 37N	0 48E	+0050	+0035	+0115	+0050	+1.0	+0.8	–0.1	–0.2
North Fambridge	51 38N	0 41E	+0115	+0050	+0130	+0100	+1.1	+0.8	0.0	–0.1
Hullbridge	51 38N	0 38E	+0115	+0050	+0135	+0105	+1.1	+0.8	0.0	–0.1
Battlesbridge	51 37N	0 34E	+0120	+0110	*Dries*	*Dries*	–1.8	–2.0	*Dries*	
River Blackwater										
Bradwell Waterside	51 45N	0 54E	+0035	+0023	+0047	+0004	+1.0	+0.8	+0.2	0.0
Osea Island	51 43N	0 46E	+0057	+0045	+0050	+0007	+1.1	+0.9	+0.1	0.0
Maldon	51 44N	0 42E	+0107	+0055	*No data*	*No data*	–1.3	–1.1	*No data*	
West Mersea	51 47N	0 54E	+0035	+0015	+0055	+0010	+0.9	+0.4	+0.1	+0.1
River Colne										
Brightlingsea	51 48N	1 00E	+0025	+0021	+0046	+0004	+0.8	+0.4	+0.1	0.0
Colchester	51 53N	0 56E	+0035	+0025	*Dries*	*Dries*	0.0	–0.3	*Dries*	
Clacton–on–Sea	51 47N	1 10E	+0012	+0010	+0025	+0008	+0.3	+0.1	+0.1	+0.1
Bramble Creek	51 53N	1 14E	+0010	–0007	–0005	+0010	+0.3	+0.3	+0.3	+0.3
Sunk Head	51 47N	1 30E	0000	+0002	–0002	+0002	–0.3	–0.3	–0.1	–0.1
Harwich	51 57N	1 17E	+0007	+0002	–0010	–0012	–0.2	0.0	0.0	0.0
Mistley	51 57N	1 05E	+0032	+0027	–0010	–0012	0.0	0.0	–0.1	–0.1
Ipswich	52 03N	1 10E	+0022	+0027	0000	–0012	0.0	0.0	–0.1	–0.1
			0100 and **1300**	**0700** and **1900**	**0100** and **1300**	**0700** and **1900**				
WALTON–ON–THE–NAZE	51 51N	1 17E					**4.2**	**3.4**	**1.1**	**0.4**
Standard port										
Felixstowe Pier	51 57N	1 21E	–0005	–0007	–0018	–0020	–0.5	–0.4	0.0	0.0
River Deben										
Woodbridge Haven	51 59N	1 24E	0000	–0005	–0020	–0025	–0.5	–0.5	–0.1	+0.1
Woodbridge	52 05N	1 19E	+0045	+0025	+0025	–0020	–0.2	–0.3	–0.2	0.0
Bawdsey	52 01N	1 26E	–0016	–0020	–0030	–0032	–0.8	–0.6	–0.1	–0.1
Orford Haven										
Bar	52 02N	1 28E	–0026	–0030	–0036	–0038	–1.0	–0.8	–0.1	0.0
Orford Quay	52 05N	1 32E	+0040	+0040	+0055	+0055	–1.4	–1.1	0.0	+0.2
Slaughden Quay	52 08N	1 36E	+0105	+0105	+0125	+0125	–1.3	–0.8	–0.1	+0.2
Iken Cliffs	52 09N	1 31E	+0130	+0130	+0155	+0155	–1.3	–1.0	0.0	+0.2

Location	Lat	Long	High Water		Low Water		MHWS	MHWN	MLWN	MLWS
LOWESTOFT *Standard port*	52 28N	1 45E	**0300** and **1500**	**0900** and **2100**	**0200** and **1400**	**0800** and **2000**	**2.4**	**2.1**	**1.0**	**0.5**
Orford Ness	52 05N	1 35E	+0135	+0135	+0135	+0125	+0.4	+0.6	–0.1	0.0
Aldeburgh	52 09N	1 36E	+0130	+0130	+0115	+0120	+0.3	+0.2	–0.1	–0.2
Minsmere Sluice	52 14N	1 38E	+0110	+0110	+0110	+0110	0.0	–0.1	–0.2	–0.2
Southwold	52 19N	1 40E	+0105	+0105	+0055	+0055	0.0	0.0	–0.1	0.0
Great Yarmouth										
Gorleston-on-Sea	52 34N	1 44E	–0035	–0035	–0030	–0030	0.0	0.0	0.0	0.0
Britannia Pier	52 36N	1 45E	–0105	–0100	–0040	–0055	+0.1	+0.1	0.0	0.0
Caister-on-Sea	52 39N	1 44E	–0120	–0120	–0100	–0100	0.0	–0.1	0.0	0.0
Winterton-on-Sea	52 43N	1 42E	–0225	–0215	–0135	–0135	+0.8	+0.5	+0.2	+0.1
IMMINGHAM *Standard port*	53 38N	0 11W	**0100** and **1300**	**0700** and **1900**	**0100** and **1300**	**0700** and **1900**	**7.3**	**5.8**	**2.6**	**0.9**
Cromer	52 56N	1 18E	+0044	+0032	+0108	+0059	–2.3	–1.8	–0.7	0.0
Blakeney Bar	52 59N	0 59E	+0035	+0025	+0030	+0040	–1.6	–1.3	*No data*	
Blakeney	52 57N	1 01E	+0115	+0055	*No data*	*No data*	–3.9	–3.8	*No data*	
Wells Bar	52 59N	0 49E	+0020	+0020	+0020	+0020	–1.3	–1.0	*No data*	
Wells	52 57N	0 51E	+0035	+0045	+0340	+0310	–3.8	–3.8	*Not below CD*	
Burnham Overy Staithe	52 58N	0 48E	+0045	+0055	*No data*	*No data*	–5.0	–4.9	*No data*	
The Wash										
Hunstanton	52 56N	0 29E	+0010	+0020	+0105	+0025	+0.1	–0.2	–0.1	0.0
West Stones	52 50N	0 21E	+0025	+0025	+0115	+0040	–0.3	–0.4	–0.3	+0.2
King's Lynn	52 45N	0 24E	+0030	+0030	+0305	+0140	–0.5	–0.8	–0.8	+0.1
Outer Westmark Knock	52 53N	0 13E	+0010	+0015	+0040	+0020	–0.2	–0.5	–0.6	–0.4
Wisbech Cut	52 48N	0 13E	+0020	+0010	+0120	+0055	–0.3	–0.7	–0.4	*No data*
Port Sutton bridge	52 46N	0 12E	+0030	+0020	+0130	+0105	–0.3	–0.6	–0.6	+0.3
Wisbech	52 40N	0 09E	+0055	+0040	*Dries*	*Dries*	–0.2	–0.6	*Dries*	*Dries*
Lawyer's Creek	52 53N	0 05E	+0010	+0020	*No data*	*No data*	–0.3	–0.6	*No data*	
Tabs Head	52 56N	0 05E	0000	+0005	+0125	+0020	+0.2	–0.2	–0.2	–0.2
Boston	52 58N	0 01W	0000	+0010	+0140	+0050	–0.5	–1.0	–0.9	–0.5
Skegness	53 09N	0 21E	+0010	+0015	+0030	+0020	–0.4	–0.5	–0.1	0.0
Inner Dowsing Light Tower	53 19N	0 35E	0000	0000	+0010	+0010	–0.9	–0.7	–0.1	+0.3
River Humber										
Bull Sand Fort	53 34N	0 04E	–0020	–0030	–0035	–0015	–0.4	–0.3	+0.1	+0.2
Grimsby	53 35N	0 04W	–0012	–0012	–0015	–0013	–0.3	–0.2	+0.1	+0.4
Hull, King George Dock	53 44N	0 16W	+0010	+0010	+0021	+0017	+0.3	+0.2	–0.1	–0.2
Hull, Albert Dock	53 44N	0 21W	+0019	+0019	+0033	+0027	+0.3	+0.1	–0.1	–0.2
Humber Bridge	53 43N	0 27W	+0027	+0022	+0049	+0039	–0.1	–0.4	–0.7	–0.6
River Trent										
Burton Stather	53 39N	0 42W	+0105	+0050	+0240	+0205	–2.0	–2.7	–2.2	–1.1
Flixborough Wharf	53 37N	0 42W	+0100	+0115	+0305	+0220	–2.1	–2.8	–2.2	–0.9
Keadby	53 36N	0 44W	+0130	+0115	+0320	+0235	–2.8	–3.3	–2.3	–0.9
Owston Ferry	53 29N	0 46W	+0155	+0145	*Dries*	*Dries*	–3.5	–3.9	*Dries*	
River Ouse										
Blacktoft	53 42N	0 43W	+0100	+0055	+0325	+0255	–1.6	–1.8	–2.2	–1.1
Goole	53 42N	0 52W	+0130	+0115	+0355	+0350	–1.6	–2.1	–1.9	–0.6
R TEES ENTRANCE *Standard port*	54 38N	1 09W	**0000** and **1200**	**0600** and **1800**	**0000** and **1200**	**0600** and **1800**	**5. 5**	**4.3**	**2.0**	**0.9**
Bridlington	54 05N	0 11W	+0100	+0050	+0055	+0050	+0.6	+0.4	+0.3	+0.2
Filey Bay	54 13N	0 16W	+0042	+0042	+0047	+0034	+0.3	+0.6	+0.4	+0.1
Scarborough	54 17N	0 23W	+0040	+0040	+0030	+0030	+0.2	+0.3	+0.3	0.0
Whitby	54 29N	0 37W	+0020	+0020	+0018	+0017	+0.1	+0.1	+0.2	+0.1
Middlesborough Dock ent	54 35N	1 13W	0000	+0002	0000	–0003	+0.1	+0.2	+0.1	–0.1
Tees (Newport) Bridge	54 34N	1 16W	–0002	+0004	+0005	–0003	+0.1	+0.2	0.0	–0.1
Hartlepool	54 42N	1 12W	–0004	–0004	–0006	–0006	–0.1	–0.1	–0.2	–0.1
Seaham	54 50N	1 19W	–0015	–0015	–0015	–0015	–0.3	–0.2	0.0	–0.2
Sunderland	54 55N	1 22W	–0017	–0017	–0016	–0016	–0.2	–0.1	0.0	0.0
R TYNE, NORTH SHIELDS *Standard port*	55 00N	1 26W	**0200** and **1400**	**0800** and **2000**	**0100** and **1300**	**0800** and **2000**	**5. 0**	**3.9**	**1.8**	**0.7**
Newcastle-upon-Tyne	54 58N	1 36W	+0003	+0003	+0008	+0008	+0.3	+0.2	+0.1	+0.1
Blyth	55 07N	1 29W	+0005	–0007	–0001	+0009	0.0	0.0	–0.1	+0.1
Coquet Island	55 20N	1 32W	–0010	–0010	–0020	–0020	+0.1	+0.1	0.0	+0.1
Amble	55 20N	1 34W	–0013	–0013	–0016	–0020	0.0	0.0	+0.1	+0.1

Location	Lat	Long	High Water		Low Water		MHWS	MHWN	MLWN	MLWS
North Sunderland	55 35N	1 39W	–0048	–0044	–0058	–0102	–0.2	–0.2	–0.2	0.0
Holy Island	55 40N	1 48W	–0043	–0039	–0105	–0110	–0.2	–0.2	–0.3	–0.1
Berwick	55 46N	1 59W	–0053	–0053	–0109	–0109	–0.3	–0.1	–0.5	–0.1
SCOTLAND *Time Zone UT*										
LEITH *Standard port*	55 59N	3 11W	**0300** and **1500**	**0900** and **2100**	**0300** and **1500**	**0900** and **2100**	**5.6**	**4.4**	**2.0**	**0.8**
Eyemouth	55 52N	2 05W	–0005	+0007	+0012	+0008	–0.4	–0.3	0.0	+0.1
Dunbar	56 00N	2 31W	–0005	+0003	+0003	–0003	–0.3	–0.3	0.0	+0.1
Fidra	56 04N	2 47W	–0001	0000	–0002	+0001	–0.2	–0.2	0.0	0.0
Cockenzie	55 58N	2 57W	–0007	–0015	–0013	–0005	–0.2	0.0	*No data*	
Granton	55 59N	3 13W	0000	0000	0000	0000	0.0	0.0	0.0	0.0
River Forth Grangemouth	56 02N	3 41W	+0015	+0010	–0050	–0045	0.0	–0.1	–0.2	–0.2
Kincardine	56 04N	3 43W	+0015	+0030	–0030	–0030	0.0	–0.2	–0.5	–0.3
Alloa	56 06N	3 48W	+0040	+0040	+0025	+0025	–0.2	–0.5	*No data*	–0.7
Stirling	56 07N	3 56W	+0100	+0100	*No data*		–2.9	–3.1	–2.3	–0.7
Firth of Forth										
Burntisland	56 03N	3 14W	+0013	+0004	–0002	+0007	+0.1	0.0	+0.1	+0.2
Kirkcaldy	56 09N	3 09W	+0005	0000	–0004	–0001	–0.3	–0.3	–0.2	–0.2
Methil	56 11N	3 00W	–0005	–0001	–0001	–0001	–0.1	–0.1	–0.1	–0.1
Anstruther Easter	56 13N	2 42W	–0018	–0012	–0006	–0008	–0.3	–0.2	0.0	0.0
ABERDEEN *Standard port*	57 09N	2 04W	**0000** and **1200**	**0600** and **1800**	**0100** and **1300**	**0700** and **1900**	**4.3**	**3.4**	**1.6**	**0.6**
River Tay										
Bar	56 28N	2 38W	+0100	+0100	+0050	+0110	+0.9	+0.8	+0.3	+0.1
Dundee	56 27N	2 58W	+0140	+0120	+0055	+0145	+1.2	+1.0	+0.5	+0.4
Newburgh	56 21N	3 14W	+0215	+0200	+0250	+0335	–0.2	–0.4	–1.1	–0.5
Perth	56 24N	3 25W	+0220	+0225	+0510	+0530	–0.9	–1.4	–1.2	–0.3
Arbroath	56 33N	2 35W	+0056	+0037	+0034	+0055	+1.0	+0.8	+0.4	+0.2
Montrose	56 42N	2 28W	+0050	+0045	+0035	+0030	+0.6	+0.4	+0.3	+0.2
Stonehaven	56 58N	2 12W	+0013	+0008	+0013	+0009	+0.2	+0.2	+0.1	0.0
Peterhead	57 30N	1 46W	–0035	–0045	–0035	–0040	–0.3	–0.2	0.0	+0.1
Fraserburgh	57 41N	2 00W	–0122	–0118	–0115	–0115	–0.5	–0.4	–0.1	+0.2
ABERDEEN *Standard port*	57 09N	2 04W	**0200** and **1400**	**0900** and **2100**	**0400** and **1600**	**0900** and **2100**	**4.3**	**3.4**	**1.6**	**0.6**
Banff	57 40N	2 31W	–0100	–0150	–0150	–0050	–0.4	–0.2	–0.1	+0.2
Whitehills	57 41N	2 35W	–0122	–0137	–0117	–0127	–0.4	–0.3	+0.1	+0.1
Buckie	57 41N	2 57W	–0130	–0145	–0125	–0140	–0.2	–0.2	0.0	+0.1
Lossiemouth	57 43N	3 18W	–0125	–0200	–0130	–0130	–0.2	–0.2	0.0	0.0
Burghead	57 42N	3 29W	–0120	–0150	–0135	–0120	–0.2	–0.2	0.0	0.0
Nairn	57 36N	3 52W	–0120	–0150	–0135	–0130	0.0	–0.1	0.0	+0.1
McDermott Base	57 36N	3 59W	–0110	–0140	–0120	–0115	–0.1	–0.1	+0.1	+0.3
ABERDEEN *Standard port*	57 09N	2 04W	**0300** and **1500**	**1000** and **2200**	**0000** and **1200**	**0700** and **1900**	**4.3**	**3.4**	**1.6**	**0.6**
Inverness Firth										
Fortrose	57 35N	4 08W	–0125	–0125	–0125	–0125	0.0	0.0	*No data*	
Inverness	57 30N	4 15W	–0050	–0150	–0200	–0150	+0.5	+0.3	+0.2	+0.1
Cromarty Firth										
Cromarty	57 42N	4 03W	–0120	–0155	–0155	–0120	0.0	0.0	+0.1	+0.2
Invergordon	57 41N	4 10W	–0105	–0200	–0200	–0110	+0.1	+0.1	+0.1	+0.1
Dingwall	57 36N	4 25W	–0045	–0145	*No data*	*No data*	+0.1	+0.2	*No data*	
ABERDEEN *Standard port*	57 09N	2 04W	**0300** and **1500**	**0800** and **2000**	**0200** and **1400**	**0800** and **2000**	**4.3**	**3.4**	**1.6**	**0.6**
Dornoch Firth										
Portmahomack	57 50N	3 50W	–0120	–0210	–0140	–0110	–0.2	–0.1	+0.1	+0.1
Meikle Ferry	57 51N	4 08W	–0100	–0140	–0120	–0055	+0.1	0.0	–0.1	0.0
Golspie	57 58N	3 59W	–0130	–0215	–0155	–0130	–0.3	–0.3	–0.1	0.0
WICK *Standard port*	58 26N	3 05W	**0000** and **1200**	**0700** and **1900**	**0200** and **1400**	**0700** and **1900**	**3.5**	**2.8**	**1.4**	**0 .7**
Helmsdale	58 07N	3 39W	+0025	+0015	+0035	+0030	+0.5	+0.3	+0.1	–0.1
Duncansby Head	58 39N	3 02W	–0115	–0115	–0110	–0110	–0.4	–0.4	*No data*	
Orkney Islands										
Muckle Skerry	58 41N	2 55W	–0025	–0025	–0020	–0020	–0.9	–0.8	–0.4	–0.3

Location	Lat	Long	High Water		Low Water		MHWS	MHWN	MLWN	MLWS
Burray Ness	58 51N	2 52W	+0005	+0005	+0015	+0015	–0.2	–0.3	–0.1	–0.1
Deer Sound	58 58N	2 50W	–0040	–0040	–0035	–0035	–0.3	–0.3	–0.1	–0.1
Kirkwall	58 59N	2 58W	–0042	–0042	–0041	–0041	–0.5	–0.4	–0.1	–0.1
Egilsay	59 09N	2 57W	–0125	–0125	–0125	–0125	–0.1	0.0	+0.2	+0.1
Whitehall	58 09N	2 36W	–0030	–0030	–0025	–0030	–0.1	0.0	+0.2	+0.2
Loth	59 11N	2 42W	–0045	–0045	–0055	–0105	–0.4	–0.3	+0.1	+0.2
Kettletoft Pier	59 14N	2 36W	–0030	–0025	–0025	–0025	0.0	0.0	+0.2	+0.2
Rapness	59 15N	2 52W	–0205	–0205	–0205	–0200	+0.1	+0.1	+0.2	0.0
Pierowall	59 19N	2 59W	–0150	–0150	–0145	–0145	+0.2	0.0	0.0	–0.1
Tingwall	59 05N	3 03W	–0200	–0125	–0145	–0125	–0.4	–0.4	–0.1	–0.1
Stromness	58 58N	3 18W	–0225	–0135	–0205	–0205	+0.1	–0.1	0.0	0.0
St Mary's	58 54N	2 55W	–0140	–0140	–0140	–0140	–0.2	–0.2	0.0	–0.1
Widewall Bay	58 49N	3 01W	–0155	–0155	–0150	–0150	+0.1	–0.1	–0.1	–0.3
Bur Wick	58 44N	2 58W	–0100	–0100	–0150	–0150	–0.1	–0.1	+0.2	+0.1
LERWICK	60 09N	1 08W	**0000 and 1200**	**0600 and 1800**	**0100 and 1300**	**0800 and 2000**	**2.1**	**1.7**	**0.9**	**0.5**
Standard port										
Fair Isle	59 32N	1 36W	–0006	–0015	–0031	–0037	+0.1	0.0	+0.1	+0.1
Shetland Islands										
Sumburgh (Grutness Voe)	59 53N	1 17W	+0006	+0008	+0004	–0002	–0.3	–0.3	–0.2	–0.1
Dury Voe	60 21N	1 10W	–0015	–0015	–0010	–0010	0.0	–0.1	0.0	–0.2
Out Skerries	60 25N	0 45W	–0025	–0025	–0010	–0010	+0.1	0.0	0.0	–0.1
Toft Pier	60 28N	1 12W	–0105	–0100	–0125	–0115	+0.2	+0.1	–0.1	–0.1
Burra Voe (Yell Sound)	60 30N	1 03W	–0025	–0025	–0025	–0025	+0.2	+0.1	0.0	–0.1
Mid Yell	60 36N	1 03W	–0030	–0020	–0035	–0025	+0.3	+0.2	+0.2	+0.1
Balta Sound	60 46N	0 50W	–0040	–0045	–0040	–0045	+0.3	+0.2	+0.1	0.0
Burra Firth	60 48N	0 52W	–0110	–0110	–0115	–0115	+0.4	+0.2	0.0	0.0
Bluemull Sound	60 42N	1 00W	–0135	–0135	–0155	–0155	+0.5	+0.2	+0.1	0.0
Sullom Voe	60 27N	1 18W	–0135	–0125	–0135	–0120	0.0	0.0	–0.2	–0.2
Hillswick	60 29N	1 29W	–0220	–0220	–0200	–0200	–0.1	–0.1	–0.1	–0.1
Scalloway	60 08N	1 16W	–0150	–0150	–0150	–0150	–0.5	–0.4	–0.3	0.0
Bay of Quendale	59 54N	1 21W	–0025	–0025	–0030	–0030	–0.4	–0.3	0.0	+0.1
Foula	60 07N	2 03W	–0140	–0140	–0130	–0130	–0.1	–0.1	0.0	0.0
WICK	58 26N	3 05W	**0200 and 1400**	**0700 and 1900**	**0100 and 1300**	**0700 and 1900**	**3.5**	**2.8**	**1.4**	**0.7**
Standard port										
Stroma	58 40N	3 08W	–0115	–0115	–0110	–0110	–0.4	–0.5	–0.1	–0.2
Gills Bay	58 38N	3 10W	–0150	–0150	–0202	–0202	+0.7	+0.7	+0.6	+0.3
Scrabster	58 37N	3 33W	–0255	–0225	–0240	–0230	+1.5	+1.2	+0.8	+0.3
Sule Skerry	59 05N	4 24W	–0320	–0255	–0315	–0250	+0.4	+0.3	+0.2	+0.1
Loch Eriboll Portnancon	58 30N	4 42W	–0340	–0255	–0315	–0255	+1.6	+1.3	+0.8	+0.4
Kyle of Durness	58 36N	4 47W	–0350	–0350	–0315	–0315	+1.1	+0.7	+0.4	–0.1
Rona	59 08N	5 49W	–0350	–0350	–0350	–0340	–0.3	–0.4	–0.2	–0.4
STORNOWAY	58 12N	6 23W	**0100 and 1300**	**0700 and 1900**	**0300 and 1500**	**0900 and 2100**	**4.8**	**3.7**	**2.0**	**0.7**
Standard port										
Outer Hebrides										
Loch Shell	58 00N	6 25W	–0013	0000	0000	–0017	0.0	–0.1	–0.1	0.0
E Loch Tarbert	57 54N	6 48W	–0025	–0010	–0010	–0020	+0.2	0.0	+0.1	+0.1
Leverburgh	57 46N	7 02W	–0041	–0020	–0015	–0025	–0.2	–0.2	–0.2	–0.1
Bays Loch	57 43N	7 10W	–0038	–0013	–0014	–0027	–0.1	–0.2	–0.2	–0.1
Loch Maddy	57 36N	7 09W	–0044	–0014	–0016	–0030	0.0	–0.1	–0.1	0.0
Loch Carnan	57 22N	7 16W	–0050	–0010	–0020	–0040	–0.3	–0.5	–0.1	–0.1
Loch Skiport	57 20N	7 16W	–0100	–0025	–0024	–0024	–0.2	–0.4	–0.3	–0.2
Loch Boisdale	57 09N	7 16W	–0055	–0030	–0020	–0040	–0.7	–0.7	–0.3	–0.2
Barra (North Bay)	57 00N	7 24W	–0103	–0031	–0034	–0048	–0.6	–0.5	–0.2	–0.1
Castle Bay	56 57N	7 29W	–0115	–0040	–0045	–0100	–0.5	–0.6	–0.3	–0.1
Barra Head	56 47N	7 38W	–0115	–0040	–0045	–0055	–0.8	–0.7	–0.2	+0.1
Shillay	57 32N	7 42W	–0103	–0043	–0047	–0107	–0.6	–0.7	–0.7	–0.3
Balivanich	57 29N	7 23W	–0103	–0017	–0031	–0045	–0.7	–0.6	–0.5	–0.2
Scolpaig	57 39N	7 29W	–0033	–0033	–0040	–0040	–1.0	–0.9	–0.5	0.0
W Loch Tarbert	57 55N	6 55W	–0015	–0015	–0046	–0046	–1.1	–0.9	–0.5	0.0
Little Bernera	58 16N	6 52W	–0021	–0011	–0017	–0027	–0.5	–0.6	–0.4	–0.2
Carloway	58 17N	6 47W	–0040	+0020	–0035	–0015	–0.7	–0.5	–0.3	0.0
St Kilda Village Bay	57 48N	8 34W	–0040	–0040	–0045	–0045	–1.4	–1.1	–0.8	–0.3
Flannan Isles	58 17N	7 35W	–0026	–0016	–0016	–0026	–0.9	–0.7	–0.6	–0.2
Rockall	57 36N	13 41W	–0055	–0055	–0105	–0105	–1.8	–1.5	–0.9	–0.2

Location	Lat	Long	High Water		Low Water		MHWS	MHWN	MLWN	MLWS
ULLAPOOL *Standard port*	57 54N	5 09W	**0000** and **1200**	**0600** and **1800**	**0300** and **1500**	**0900** and **2100**	**5.2**	**3.9**	**2.1**	**0.7**
Loch Bervie	58 27N	5 03W	+0017	+0020	+0015	+0015	–0.4	–0.2	–0.1	+0.1
Loch Laxford	58 24N	5 05W	+0015	+0015	+0005	+0005	–0.3	–0.4	–0.2	0.0
Eddrachillis Bay										
Badcall Bay	58 19N	5 08W	+0005	+0005	+0005	+0005	–0.7	–0.5	–0.5	+0.2
Loch Nedd	58 14N	5 10W	0000	0000	0000	0000	–0.3	–0.2	–0.2	0.0
Loch Inver	58 09N	5 18W	–0005	–0005	–0005	–0005	–0.2	0.0	0.0	+0.1
Summer Isles Tanera Mor	58 01N	5 24W	–0005	–0005	–0010	–0010	–0.1	+0.1	0.0	+0.1
Loch Ewe Mellon Charles	57 51N	5 38W	–0005	–0010	–0005	–0005	–0.1	–0.1	–0.1	+0.1
Loch Gairloch Gairloch	57 43N	5 41W	–0012	–0011	–0011	–0011	–0.2	+0.1	–0.2	+0.2
Loch Torridon Shieldaig	57 31N	5 39W	–0020	–0020	–0015	–0015	+0.4	+0.3	+0.1	0.0
Inner Sound Applecross	57 26N	5 49W	–0010	–0015	–0010	–0010	0.0	0.0	0.0	+0.1
Loch Carron Plockton	57 21N	5 39W	+0005	–0025	–0005	–0010	+0.5	+0.5	+0.5	+0.2
Rona Loch a' Bhraige	57 35N	5 58W	–0020	0000	–0010	0000	–0.1	–0.1	–0.1	–0.2
Skye										
Broadford Bay	57 15N	5 54W	–0015	–0015	–0010	–0015	+0.2	+0.1	+0.1	0.0
Portree	57 24N	6 11W	–0025	–0025	–0025	–0025	+0.1	–0.2	–0.2	0.0
Loch Snizort (Uig Bay)	57 35N	6 22W	–0045	–0020	–0005	–0025	+0.1	–0.4	–0.2	0.0
Loch Dunvegan	57 27N	6 38W	–0105	–0030	–0020	–0040	0.0	–0.1	0.0	0.0
Loch Harport	57 20N	6 25W	–0115	–0035	–0020	–0100	–0.1	–0.1	0.0	+0.1
Soay Camus nan Gall	57 09N	6 13W	–0055	–0025	–0025	–0045	–0.4	–0.2	*No data*	
Loch Alsh										
Kyle of Lochalsh	57 17N	5 43W	–0040	–0020	–0005	–0025	+0.1	0.0	0.0	–0.1
Dornie Bridge	57 17N	5 31W	–0040	–0010	–0005	–0020	+0.1	–0.1	0.0	0.0
Kyle Rhea Glenelg Bay	57 13N	5 38W	–0105	–0035	–0035	–0055	–0.4	–0.4	–0.9	–0.1
Loch Hourn	57 06N	5 34W	–0125	–0050	–0040	–0110	–0.2	–0.1	–0.1	+0.1
OBAN *Standard port*	56 25N	5 29W	**0000** and **1200**	**0600** and **1800**	**0100** and **1300**	**0700** and **1900**	**4.0**	**2.9**	**1.8**	**0.7**
Loch Nevis										
Inverie Bay	57 02N	5 41W	+0030	+0020	+0035	+0020	+1.0	+0.9	+0.2	0.0
Mallaig	57 00N	5 50W	+0017	+0017	+0030	+0024	+1.0	+0.7	+0.3	+0.1
Eigg Bay of Laig	56 55N	6 10W	+0015	+0030	+0040	+0005	+0.7	+0.6	–0.2	– 0.2
Loch Moidart	56 47N	5 53W	+0015	+0015	+0040	+0020	+0.8	+0.6	– 0.2	–0.2
Coll Loch Eatharna	56 37N	6 31W	+0025	+0010	+0015	+0025	+0.4	+0.3	*No data*	
Tiree Gott Bay	56 31N	6 48W	0000	+0010	+0005	+0010	0.0	+0.1	0.0	0.0
OBAN *Standard port*	56 25N	5 29W	**0100** and **1300**	**0700** and **1900**	**0100** and **1300**	**0800** and **2000**	**4.0**	**2.9**	**1.8**	**0.7**
Mull										
Carsaig Bay	56 19N	5 58W	–0015	–0005	–0030	+0020	+0.1	+0.2	0.0	–0.1
Iona	56 20N	6 23W	–0010	–0005	–0020	+0015	0.0	+0.1	–0.3	–0.2
Bunessan	56 19N	6 14W	–0015	–0015	–0010	–0015	+0.3	+0.1	0.0	–0.1
Ulva Sound	56 29N	6 08W	–0010	–0015	0000	–0005	+0.4	+0.3	0.0	–0.1
Loch Sunart Salen	56 43N	5 47W	–0015	+0015	+0010	+0005	+0.6	+0.5	–0.1	–0.1
Sound of Mull										
Tobermory	56 37N	6 04W	+0025	+0010	+0015	+0025	+0.5	+0.6	+0.1	+0.2
Salen	56 31N	5 57W	+0045	+0015	+0020	+0030	+0.2	+0.2	–0.1	0.0
Loch Aline	56 32N	5 46W	+0012	+0012	*No data*	*No data*	+0.5	+0.3	*No data*	
Craignure	56 28N	5 42W	+0030	+0005	+0010	+0015	0.0	+0.1	–0.1	–0.1
Loch Linnhe										
Corran	56 43N	5 14W	+0007	+0007	+0004	+0004	+0.4	+0.4	–0.1	0.0
Corpach	56 51N	5 07W	0000	+0020	+0040	0000	0.0	0.0	–0.2	–0.2
Loch Eil Head	56 51N	5 20W	+0025	+0045	+0105	+0025	*No data*		*No data*	
Loch Leven Head	56 43N	5 00W	+0045	+0045	+0045	+0045	*No data*		*No data*	
Loch Linnhe Port Appin	56 33N	5 25W	–0005	–0005	–0030	0000	+0.2	+0.2	+0.1	+0.1
Loch Creran										
Barcaldine Pier	56 32N	5 19W	+0010	+0020	+0040	+0015	+0.1	+0.1	0.0	+0.1
Loch Creran Head	56 33N	5 16W	+0015	+0025	+0120	+0020	–0.3	–0.3	–0.4	–0.3
Loch Etive										
Dunstaffnage Bay	56 27N	5 26W	+0005	0000	0000	+0005	+0.1	+0.1	+0.1	+0.1
Connel	56 27N	5 24W	+0020	+0005	+0010	+0015	–0.3	–0.2	–0.1	+0.1
Bonawe	56 27N	5 13W	+0150	+0205	+0240	+0210	–2.0	–1.7	–1.3	–0.5
Seil Sound	56 18N	5 35W	–0035	–0015	–0040	–0015	–1.3	–0.9	–0.7	–0.3
Colonsay Scalasaig	56 04N	6 11W	–0020	–0005	–0015	+0005	–0.3	–0.2	–0.3	0.0
Jura Glengarrisdale Bay	56 07N	5 47W	–0020	0000	–0010	0000	–0.4	–0.2	0.0	–0.2

Location	Lat	Long	High Water		Low Water		MHWS	MHWN	MLWN	MLWS
Islay										
Rubha A'Mhail	55 56N	6 07W	–0020	0000	+0005	–0015	–0.3	–0.1	–0.3	–0.1
Ardnave Point	55 52N	6 20W	–0035	+0010	0000	–0025	–0.4	–0.2	–0.3	–0.1
Orsay	55 41N	6 31W	–0110	–0110	–0040	–0040	–1.4	–0.6	–0.5	–0.2
Bruichladdich	55 46N	6 22W	–0105	–0035	–0110	–0110	–1.8	–1.3	–0.4	+0.3
Port Ellen	55 38N	6 11W	–0530	–0050	–0045	–0530	–3.1	–2.1	–1.3	–0.4
Port Askaig	55 51N	6 06W	–0030	–0035	–0015	–0025	–1.8	–1.3	–0.7	–0.2
Sound of Jura										
Craighouse	55 50N	5 57W	–0230	–0250	–0150	–0230	–3.0	–2.4	–1.3	–0.6
Loch Melfort	56 15N	5 29W	–0055	–0025	–0040	–0035	–1.2	–0.8	–0.5	–0.1
Loch Beag	56 09N	5 36W	–0110	–0045	–0035	–0045	–1.6	–1.2	–0.8	–0.4
Carsaig Bay	56 02N	5 38W	–0105	–0040	–0050	–0050	–2.1	–1.6	–1.0	–0.4
Sound of Gigha	55 41N	5 44W	–0450	–0210	–0130	–0410	–2.5	–1.6	–1.0	–0.1
Machrihanish	55 25N	5 45W	–0520	–0350	–0340	–0540	*Mean range 0.5 metres*			
GREENOCK	55 57N	4 46W	**0000 and 1200**	**0600 and 1800**	**0000 and 1200**	**0600 and 1800**	**3.4**	**2.8**	**1.0**	**0.3**
Standard port										
Firth of Clyde										
Southend, Kintyre	55 19N	5 38W	–0030	–0010	+0005	+0035	–1.3	–1.2	–0.5	–0.2
Campbeltown	55 25N	5 36W	–0025	–0005	–0015	+0005	–0.5	–0.3	+0.1	+0.2
Carradale	55 36N	5 28W	–0015	–0005	–0005	+0005	–0.3	–0.2	+0.1	+0.1
Loch Ranza	55 43N	5 18W	–0015	–0005	–0010	–0005	–0.4	–0.3	–0.1	0.0
Loch Fyne										
East Loch Tarbert	55 52N	5 24W	–0005	–0005	0000	–0005	+0.2	+0.1	0.0	0.0
Inveraray	56 14N	5 04W	+0011	+0011	+0034	+0034	–0.1	+0.1	–0.5	–0.2
Kyles of Bute										
Rubha a'Bhodaich	55 55N	5 09W	–0020	–0010	–0007	–0007	–0.2	–0.1	+0.2	+0.2
Tighnabruich	55 55N	5 13W	+0007	–0010	–0002	–0015	0.0	+0.2	+0.4	+0.5
Firth of Clyde – continued										
Millport	55 45N	4 56W	–0005	–0025	–0025	–0005	0.0	–0.1	0.0	+0.1
Rothesay Bay	55 50N	5 03W	–0020	–0015	–0010	–0002	+0.2	+0.2	+0.2	+0.2
Wemyss Bay	55 53N	4 53W	–0005	–0005	–0005	–0005	0.0	0.0	+0.1	+0.1
Loch Long										
Coulport	56 03N	4 53W	–0011	–0011	–0008	–0008	0.0	0.0	0.0	0.0
Lochgoilhead	56 10N	4 54W	+0015	0000	–0005	–0005	–0.2	–0.3	–0.3	–0.3
Arrochar	56 12N	4 45W	–0005	–0005	–0005	–0005	0.0	0.0	–0.1	–0.1
Gare Loch										
Rhu Marina	56 01N	4 46W	–0007	–0007	–0007	–0007	–0.1	–0.1	–0.1	–0.2
Faslane	56 04N	4 49W	+0003	+0003	+0003	+0003	+0.1	+0.1	+0.1	0.0
Garelochhead	56 05N	4 50W	0000	0000	0000	0000	0.0	0.0	0.0	–0.1
River Clyde										
Helensburgh	56 00N	4 44W	0000	0000	0000	0000	0.0	0.0	0.0	0.0
Port Glasgow	55 56N	4 41W	+0010	+0005	+0010	+0020	+0.2	+0.1	0.0	0.0
Bowling	55 56N	4 29W	+0020	+0010	+0030	+0055	+0.6	+0.5	+0.3	+0.1
Clydebank (Rothesay Dock)	55 54N	4 24W	+0025	+0015	+0035	+0100	+1.1	+0.9	+0.6	+0.3
Glasgow	55 51N	4 16W	+0025	+0015	+0035	+0105	+1.4	+1.1	+0.8	+0.4
Firth of Clyde – continued										
Brodick Bay	55 35N	5 08W	–0013	–0013	–0008	–0008	–0.2	–0.1	0.0	+0.1
Lamlash	55 32N	5 07W	–0016	–0036	–0024	–0004	–0.2	–0.2	*No data*	
Ardrossan	55 38N	4 49W	–0020	–0010	–0010	–0010	–0.2	–0.2	+0.1	+0.1
Irvine	55 36N	4 42W	–0020	–0020	–0030	–0010	–0.3	–0.3	–0.1	0.0
Troon	55 33N	4 41W	–0025	–0025	–0020	–0020	–0.2	–0.2	0.0	0.0
Ayr	55 28N	4 39W	–0025	–0025	–0030	–0015	–0.4	–0.3	+0.1	+0.1
Girvan	55 15N	4 52W	–0025	–0040	–0035	–0010	–0.3	–0.3	–0.1	0.0
Loch Ryan Stranraer	54 55N	5 02W	–0030	–0025	–0010	–0010	–0.2	–0.1	0.0	+0.1
LIVERPOOL	53 27N	3 01W	**0000 and 1200**	**0600 and 1800**	**0200 and 1400**	**0800 and 2000**	**9.4**	**7.5**	**3.2**	**1.1**
Standard port										
Portpatrick	54 51N	5 07W	+0038	+0032	+0009	–0008	–5.5	–4.4	–2.0	–0.6
Luce Bay										
Drummore	54 42N	4 53W	+0035	+0045	+0010	+0015	–3.5	–2.6	–1.2	–0.5
Port William	54 46N	4 35W	+0035	+0035	+0020	–0005	–3.0	–2.3	–1.1	*Nodata*
Wigtown Bay										
Isle of Whithorn	54 42N	4 22W	+0025	+0030	+0020	0000	–2.5	–2.1	–1.1	–0.4
Garlieston	54 47N	4 22W	+0030	+0040	+0025	0000	–2.4	–1.8	–0.8	*Nodata*
Solway Firth										
Kirkcudbright Bay	54 48N	4 04W	+0020	+0020	+0005	–0005	–1.9	–1.6	–0.8	–0.3
Hestan Islet	54 50N	3 48W	+0030	+0030	+0015	+0020	–1.1	–1.2	–0.8	–0.2
Southerness Point	54 52N	3 36W	+0035	+0035	+0025	+0005	–0.8	–0.8	*No data*	

Location	Lat	Long	High Water		Low Water		MHWS	MHWN	MLWN	MLWS
Annan Waterfoot	54 58N	3 16W	+0055	+0110	+0215	+0305	–2.3	–2.7	–3.0	
Torduff Point	54 58N	3 09W	+0110	+0145	+0515	+0405	–4.2	–5.0	*Not below CD*	
Redkirk	54 59N	3 06W	+0115	+0220	+0710	+0440	–5.6	–6.3	*Not below CD*	
WEST COAST OF ENGLAND										
Silloth	54 52N	3 24W	+0035	+0045	+0040	+0050	–0.2	–0.4	–0.9	–0.3
Maryport	54 43N	3 30W	+0021	+0036	+0017	+0002	–0.8	–0.9	–0.7	–0.2
Workington	54 39N	3 34W	+0029	+0027	+0014	+0004	–1.1	–1.1	–0.5	–0.1
Whitehaven	54 33N	3 36W	+0010	+0020	+0005	0000	–1.4	–1.2	–0.8	–0.1
Tarn Point	54 17N	3 25W	+0010	+0010	+0005	–0005	–1.1	–1.1	–0.7	–0.2
Duddon Bar	54 09N	3 20W	+0007	+0007	+0005	–0001	–0.9	–0.9	–0.6	–0.2
LIVERPOOL *Standard port*	53 27N	3 01W	**0000** and **1200**	**0600** and **1800**	**0200** and **1400**	**0700** and **1900**	**9.4**	**7.5**	**3.2**	**1.1**
Barrow-in-Furness	54 06N	3 12W	+0020	+0020	+0010	+0010	+0.1	–0.2	–0.2	0.0
Ulverston	54 11N	3 04W	+0025	+0045	*No data*	*no data*	–0.1	–0.2	*No data*	
Arnside	54 12N	2 51W	+0105	+0140	*No data*	*no data*	+0.4	+0.1	*No data*	
Morecambe	54 04N	2 53W	+0010	+0015	+0025	+0010	+0.1	–0.1	–0.3	0.0
Heysham	54 02N	2 55W	+0014	+0012	+0002	–0003	+0.2	–0.1	–0.2	0.0
River Lune Glasson Dock	54 00N	2 51W	+0025	+0035	+0215	+0235	–2.8	–3.1	*No data*	
Lancaster	54 03N	2 49W	+0115	+0035	*Dries*	*Dries*	–5.1	–5.0	*Dries*	
River Wyre										
Wyre Lighthouse	53 57N	3 02W	–0005	–0005	0000	–0005	–0.2	–0.2	*No data*	
Fleetwood	53 56N	3 00W	–0004	–0004	–0006	–0006	–0.2	–0.2	–0.1	+0.1
Blackpool	53 49N	3 04W	–0010	0000	–0010	–0020	–0.5	–0.5	–0.4	–0.1
River Ribble Preston	53 45N	2 45W	+0015	+0015	+0330	+0305	–4.1	–4.2	–3.1	–1.0
Liverpool Bay										
Southport	53 39N	3 01W	–0015	–0005	*No data*	*No data*	–0.4	–0.4	*No data*	
Formby	53 32N	3 07W	–0010	–0005	–0025	–0025	–0.4	–0.2	–0.3	–0.1
River Mersey										
Alfred Dock	53 24N	3 01W	+0007	+0007	0000	0000	–0.1	–0.1	–0.3	–0.2
Eastham	53 19N	2 57W	+0014	+0014	+0006	+0006	+0.2	0.0	–0.4	–0.5
Hale Head	53 19N	2 48W	+0035	+0030	*No data*	*No data*	–2.5	–2.6	*No data*	
Widnes	53 21N	2 44W	+0045	+0050	+0355	+0340	–4.3	–4.5	–2.8	–0.6
Fiddler's Ferry	53 22N	2 40W	+0105	+0120	+0535	+0445	–6.0	–6.4	–2.7	–0.6
River Dee										
Hilbre Island	53 23N	3 14W	–0011	–0008	–0013	–0018	–0.4	–0.3	–0.1	+0.2
Chester	53 12N	2 54W	+0110	+0110	+0455	+0455	–5.4	–5.5	*Dries*	
Connah's Quay (Wales)	53 13N	3 03W	+0005	+0020	+0350	+0335	–4.7	–4.5	*Dries*	
Mostyn Docks (Wales)	53 19N	3 16W	–0015	–0010	–0025	–0025	–0.9	–0.8	*No data*	
Isle of Man Peel	54 14N	4 42W	+0010	+0010	–0020	–0030	–4.2	–3.2	–1.7	–0.7
Ramsey	54 19N	4 22W	+0010	+0020	–0010	–0020	–2.0	–1.6	–0.9	–0.2
Douglas	54 09N	4 28W	+0010	+0020	–0020	–0030	–2.5	–2.1	–0.8	–0.3
Port St Mary	54 04N	4 44W	+0010	+0020	–0015	–0035	–3.5	–2.7	–1.6	–0.6
Calf Sound	54 04N	4 48W	+0010	+0010	–0020	–0030	–3.3	–2.7	–1.2	–0.5
Port Erin	54 05N	4 46W	+0018	+0010	–0013	–0028	–4.1	–3.3	–1.6	–0.6
WALES										
Colwyn Bay	53 18N	3 43W	–0015	–0015	*No data*	*No data*	–1.6	–1.4	*No data*	
Llandudno	53 20N	3 50W	–0019	–0021	–0031	–0038	–1.7	–1.6	–0.9	–0.6
HOLYHEAD *Standard port*	53 19N	4 37W	**0000** and **1200**	**0600** and **1800**	**0500** and **1700**	**1100** and **2300**	**5.6**	**4.4**	**2.0**	**0.7**
Conwy	53 17N	3 50W	+0025	+0035	+0120	+0105	+2.3	+1.8	+0.6	+0.4
Menai Strait										
Beaumaris	53 16N	4 05W	+0025	+0010	+0055	+0035	+2.0	+1.6	+0.5	+0.1
Menai Bridge	53 13N	4 10W	+0030	+0010	+0100	+0035	+1.7	+1.4	+0.3	0.0
Port Dinorwic	53 11N	4 13W	–0015	–0025	+0030	0000	0.0	0.0	0.0	+0.1
Caernarfon	53 09N	4 16W	–0030	–0030	+0015	–0005	–0.4	–0.4	–0.1	–0.1
Fort Belan	53 07N	4 20W	–0040	–0015	–0025	–0005	–1.0	–0.9	–0.2	–0.1
Trwyn Dinmor	53 19N	4 03W	+0025	+0015	+0050	+0035	+1.9	+1.5	+0.5	+0.2
Moelfre	53 20N	4 14W	+0025	+0020	+0050	+0035	+1.9	+1.4	+0.5	+0.2
Amlwch	53 25N	4 20W	+0020	+0010	+0035	+0025	+1.6	+ 1.3	+0.5	+0.2
Cemaes Bay	53 25N	4 27W	+0020	+0025	+0040	+0035	+1.0	+0.7	+0.3	+0.1
Trearddur Bay	53 16N	4 37W	–0045	–0025	–0015	–0015	–0.4	–0.4	0.0	+0.1
Porth Trecastell	53 12N	4 30W	–0045	–0025	–0005	–0015	–0.6	–0.6	0.0	0.0
Llanddwyn Island	53 08N	4 25W	–0115	–0055	–0030	–0020	–0.7	–0.5	–0.1	0.0
Trefor	53 00N	4 25W	–0115	–0100	–0030	–0020	–0.8	–0.9	–0.2	–0.1
Porth Dinllaen	52 57N	4 34W	–0120	–0105	–0035	–0025	–1.0	–1.0	–0.2	–0.2
Porth Ysgaden	52 54N	4 39W	–0125	–0110	–0040	–0035	–1.1	–1.0	–0.1	–0.1
Bardsey Island	52 46N	4 47W	–0220	–0240	–0145	–0140	–1.2	–1.2	–0.5	–0.1

Location	Lat	Long	High Water		Low Water		MHWS	MHWN	MLWN	MLWS
MILFORD HAVEN *Standard port*	51 42N	5 03W	**0100** and **1300**	**0800** and **2000**	**0100** and **1300**	**0700** and **1900**	**7.0**	**5.2**	**2.5**	**0.7**
Cardigan Bay										
Aberdaron	52 48N	4 43W	+0210	+0200	+0240	+0310	–2.4	–1.9	–0.6	–0.2
St Tudwal's Roads	52 49N	4 29W	+0155	+0145	+0240	+0310	–2.2	–1.9	–0.7	–0.2
Pwllheli	52 53N	4 24W	+0210	+0150	+0245	+0320	–1.9	–1.6	–0.6	–0.1
Criccieth	52 55N	4 14W	+0210	+0155	+0255	+0320	–2.0	–1.8	–0.7	–0.3
Porthmadog	52 55N	4 08W	+0235	+0210	*No data*	*No data*	–1.9	–1.8	*No data*	
Barmouth	52 43N	4 03W	+0207	+0200	+0300	+0233	–2.0	–1.5	–0.6	0.0
Aberdovey	52 33N	4 03W	+0215	+0200	+0230	+0305	–2.0	–1.7	–0.5	0.0
Aberystwyth	52 24N	4 05W	+0145	+0130	+0210	+0245	–2.0	–1.7	–0.7	0.0
New Quay	52 13N	4 21W	+0150	+0125	+0155	+0230	–2.1	–1.8	–0.6	–0.1
Aberporth	52 08N	4 33W	+0135	+0120	+0150	+0220	–2.1	–1.8	–0.6	–0.1
Port Cardigan	52 07N	4 41W	+0140	+0120	+0220	+0130	–2.3	–1.8	–0.5	0.0
Cardigan (Town)	52 05N	4 40W	+0220	+0150	*No data*	*No data*	–2.2	–1.6	*No data*	
Fishguard	52 01N	4 59W	+0115	+0100	+0110	+0135	–2.2	–1.8	–0.5	+0.1
Porthgain	51 57N	5 11W	+0055	+0045	+0045	+0100	–2.5	–1.8	–0.6	0.0
Ramsey Sound	51 53N	5 19W	+0030	+0030	+0030	+0030	–1.9	–1.3	–0.3	0.0
Solva	51 52N	5 12W	+0015	+0010	+0035	+0015	–1.5	–1.0	–0.2	0.0
Little Haven	51 46N	5 07W	+0010	+0010	+0025	+0015	–1.1	–0.8	–0.2	0.0
Martin's Haven	51 44N	5 15W	+0010	+0010	+0015	+0015	–0.8	–0.5	+0.1	+0.1
Skomer Island	51 44N	5 17W	–0005	–0005	+0005	+0005	–0.4	–0.1	0.0	0.0
Dale Roads	51 42N	5 09W	–0005	–0005	–0008	–0008	0.0	0.0	0.0	–0.1
Cleddau River										
Neyland	51 42N	4 57W	+0002	+0010	0000	0000	0.0	0.0	0.0	0.0
Black Tar	51 45N	4 54W	+0010	+0020	+0005	0000	+0.1	+0.1	0.0	–0.1
Haverfordwest	51 48N	4 58W	+0010	+0025	*Dries*	*Dries*	–4.8	–4.9	*Dries*	
Stackpole Quay	51 37N	4 54W	–0005	+0025	–0010	–0010	+0.9	+0.7	+0.2	+0.3
Tenby	51 40N	4 42W	–0015	–0010	–0015	–0020	+1.4	+1.1	+0.5	+0.2
Towy River										
Ferryside	51 46N	4 22W	0000	–0010	+0220	0000	–0.3	–0.7	–1.7	–0.6
Carmarthen	51 51N	4 18W	+0010	0000	*Dries*	*Dries*	–4.4	–4.8	*Dries*	
Burry Inlet										
Burry Port	51 41N	4 15W	+0003	+0003	+0007	+0007	+1.6	+1.4	+0.5	+0.4
Llanelli	51 40N	4 10W	–0003	–0003	+0150	+0020	+0.8	+0.6	*No data*	
Mumbles	51 34N	3 58W	+0001	+0003	–0012	–0005	+2.5	+2.0	+0.8	+0.4
River Neath Entrance	51 37N	3 51W	+0002	+0011	*Dries*	*Dries*	+2.7	+2.2	*Dries*	
Port Talbot	51 35N	3 49W	0000	+0005	–0010	–0005	+2.7	+2.1	+1.0	+0.4
Porthcawl	51 28N	3 42W	+0005	+0010	–0010	–0005	+2.9	+2.3	+0.8	+0.3
BRISTOL, AVONMOUTH *Standard port*	51 30N	2 44W	**0600** and **1800**	**1100** and **2300**	**0300** and **1500**	**0800** and **2000**	**13.2**	**9.8**	**3.8**	**1.0**
Barry	51 23N	3 16W	–0025	–0025	–0130	–0045	–1.5	–1.1	0.0	+0.2
Flat Holm	51 23N	3 07W	–0015	–0015	–0035	–0035	–1.4	–1.0	–0.5	0.0
Steep Holm	51 20N	3 06W	–0020	–0020	–0040	–0040	–1.7	–1.1	–0.5	–0.4
Cardiff	51 27N	3 10W	–0015	–0015	–0035	–0030	–0.9	–0.7	+0.2	+0.2
Newport	51 33N	2 59W	–0005	–0010	–0015	–0015	–0.9	–0.9	–0.2	–0.2
River Wye Chepstow	51 39N	2 40W	+0020	+0020	*No data*	*No data*	*No data*		*No data*	
BRISTOL, AVONMOUTH *Standard port*	51 30N	2 44W	**0000** and **1200**	**0600** and **1800**	**0000** and **1200**	**0700** and **1900**	**13.2**	**9.8**	**3.8**	**1.0**
WEST COAST OF ENGLAND										
River Severn										
Sudbrook	51 35N	2 43W	+0010	+0010	+0025	+0015	+0.2	+0.1	–0.1	+0.1
Beachley (Aust)	51 36N	2 38W	+0010	+0015	+0040	+0025	–0.2	–0.2	–0.5	–0.3
Inward Rocks	51 39N	2 37W	+0020	+0020	+0105	+0045	–1.0	–1.1	–1.4	–0.6
Narlwood Rocks	51 39N	2 36W	+0025	+0025	+0120	+0100	–1.9	–2.0	–2.3	–0.8
White House	51 40N	2 33W	+0025	+0025	+0145	+0120	–3.0	–3.1	–3.6	–1.0
Berkeley	51 42N	2 30W	+0030	+0045	+0245	+0220	–3.8	–3.9	–3.4	–0.5
Sharpness Dock	51 43N	2 29W	+0035	+0050	+0305	+0245	–3.9	–4.2	–3.3	–0.4
Wellhouse Rock	51 44N	2 29W	+0040	+0055	+0320	+0305	–4.1	–4.4	–3.1	–0.2
Epney	51 42N	2 24W	+0130	*No data*	*No data*	*No data*	–9.4	*No data*	*No data*	
Minsterworth	51 50N	2 23W	+0140	*No data*	*No data*	*No data*	–10.1	*No data*	*No data*	
Llanthony	51 51N	2 21W	+0215	*No data*	*No data*	*No data*	–10.7	*No data*	*No data*	
BRISTOL, AVONMOUTH *Standard port*	51 30N	2 44W	**0200** and **1400**	**0800** and **2000**	**0300** and **1500**	**0800** and **2000**	**13.2**	**9.8**	**3.8**	**1.0**
River Avon										
Shirehampton	51 29N	2 41W	0000	0000	+0035	+0010	–0.7	–0.7	–0.8	0.0
Sea Mills	51 29N	2 39W	+0005	+0005	+0105	+0030	–1.4	–1.5	–1.7	–0.1
Cumberland Basin Entrance	51 27N	2 37W	+0010	+0010	*Dries*	*Dries*	–2.9	–3.0	*Dries*	
Portishead	51 30N	2 45W	–0002	0000	*No data*	*No data*	–0.1	–0.1	*No data*	

Location	Lat	Long	High Water		Low Water		MHWS	MHWN	MLWN	MLWS
levedon	51 27N	2 52W	–0010	–0020	–0025	–0015	–0.4	–0.2	+0.2	0.0
t Thomas Head	51 24N	2 56W	0000	0000	–0030	–0030	–0.4	–0.2	+0.1	+0.1
nglish & Welsh Grounds	51 28N	2 59W	–0008	–0008	–0030	–0030	–0.5	–0.8	–0.3	0.0
Veston-super-Mare	51 21N	2 59W	–0020	–0030	–0130	–0030	–1.2	–1.0	–0.8	–0.2
iver Parrett										
Burnham-on-Sea	51 14N	3 00W	–0020	–0025	–0030	0000	–2.3	–1.9	–1.4	–1.1
Bridgwater	51 08N	3 00W	–0015	–0030	+0305	+0455	–8.6	–8.1	*Dries*	
Iinkley Point	51 13N	3 08W	–0032	–0028	–0055	–0049	–1.4	–1.1	–0.1	0.0
Minehead	51 13N	3 28W	–0037	–0052	–0155	–0045	–2.6	–1.9	–0.2	0.0
orlock Bay	51 13N	3 38W	–0045	–0055	–0205	–0050	–3.0	–2.2	–0.1	–0.1
ynmouth	51 14N	3 50W	–0055	–0115	*No data*	*No data*	–3.6	–2.7	*No data*	
			0100	**0700**	**0100**	**0700**				
MILFORD HAVEN	51 42N	5 03W	and	and	and	and	**7.0**	**5.2**	**2.5**	**0.7**
tandard port			**1300**	**1900**	**1300**	**1900**				
fracombe	51 13N	4 07W	–0016	–0016	–0041	–0031	+2.3	+1.8	+0.6	+0.3
ivers Taw & Torridge										
Appledore	51 03N	4 12W	–0020	–0025	+0015	–0045	+0.5	0.0	–0.9	–0.5
Yelland Marsh	51 04N	4 10W	–0010	–0015	+0100	–0015	+0.1	–0.4	–1.2	–0.6
Fremington	51 05N	4 07W	–0010	–0015	+0030	–0030	–1.1	–1.8	–2.2	–0.5
Barnstaple	51 05N	4 04W	0000	–0015	–0155	–0245	–2.9	–3.8	–2.2	–0.4
Bideford	51 01N	4 12W	–0020	–0025	0000	0000	–1.1	–1.6	–2.5	–0.7
lovelly	51 00N	4 24W	–0030	–0030	–0020	–0040	+1.3	+1.1	+0.2	+0.2
undy	51 10N	4 39W	–0025	–0025	–0035	–0030	+1.0	+0.8	+0.2	+0.1
ude	50 50N	4 33W	–0040	–0040	–0035	–0045	+0.7	+0.6	*No data*	
oscastle	50 41N	4 42W	–0045	–0010	–0110	–0100	+0.3	+0.4	+0.2	+0.2
ort Isaac	50 35N	4 50W	–0100	–0100	–0100	–0100	+0.5	+0.6	0.0	+0.2
iver Camel										
Padstow	50 33N	4 56W	–0055	–0050	–0040	–0050	+0.3	+0.4	+0.1	+0.1
Wadebridge	50 31N	4 50W	–0052	–0052	+0235	+0245	–3.8	–3.8	–2.5	–0.4
lewquay	50 25N	5 05W	–0100	–0110	–0105	–0050	0.0	+0.1	0.0	–0.1
erranporth	50 21N	5 09W	–0100	–0110	–0110	–0050	–0.1	0.0	0.0	+0.1
t Ives	50 13N	5 29W	–0050	–0115	–0105	–0040	–0.4	–0.3	–0.1	+0.1
ape Cornwall	50 08N	5 42 W	–0130	–0145	–0120	–0120	–1.0	–0.9	–0.5	–0.1
ennen Cove	50 05N	5 42W	–0130	–0145	–0125	–0125	–0.9	–0.4	*No data*	
RELAND			**0000**	**0700**	**0000**	**0500**				
DUBLIN, NORTH WALL	53 21N	6 13W	and	and	and	and	**4.1**	**3.4**	**1.5**	**0.7**
tandard port			**1200**	**1900**	**1200**	**1700**				
ourtown	52 39N	6 13W	–0328	–0242	–0158	–0138	–2.8	–2.4	–0.5	0.0
rklow	52 48N	6 08W	–0315	–0201	–0140	–0134	–2.7	–2.2	–0.6	–0.1
Vicklow	52 59N	6 02W	–0019	–0019	–0024	–0026	–1.4	–1.1	–0.4	0.0
ireystones	53 09N	6 04W	–0008	–0008	–0008	–0008	–0.5	–0.4	*No data*	
un Laoghaire	53 18N	6 08W	0000	0000	+0002	+0003	0.0	+0.1	0.0	0.0
ublin Bar	53 21N	6 09W	–0006	–0001	–0002	–0003	0.0	0.0	0.0	0.0
lowth	53 23N	6 04W	–0007	–0005	+0001	+0005	0.0	–0.1	–0.2	–0.2
Malahide	53 27N	6 09W	+0002	+0003	+0009	+0009	+0.1	–0.2	–0.4	–0.2
albriggan	53 37N	6 11W	–0021	–0015	+0010	+0002	+0.3	+0.2	*No data*	
iver Boyne Bar	53 43N	6 14W	–0005	0000	+0020	+0030	+0.4	+0.3	–0.1	–0.2
unany Point	53 52N	6 14W	–0028	–0018	–0008	–0006	+0.7	+0.9	*No data*	
undalk Soldiers Point	54 00N	6 21W	–0010	–0010	0000	+0045	+1.0	+0.8	+0.1	–0.1
NORTHERN IRELAND										
arlingford Lough										
Cranfield Point	54 01N	6 04W	–0027	–0011	+0005	–0010	+0.7	+0.9	+0.3	+0.2
Warrenpoint	54 06N	6 15W	–0020	–0010	+0025	+0035	+1.0	+0.7	+0.2	+0.0
Newry (Victoria Lock)	54 09N	6 19W	+0005	+0015	+0045	*Dries*	+1.2	+0.9	+0.1	*Dries*
			0100	**0700**	**0000**	**0600**				
BELFAST	54 36N	5 55W	and	and	and	and	**3.5**	**3.0**	**1.1**	**0.4**
tandard port			**1300**	**1900**	**1200**	**1800**				
ilkeel	54 03N	5 59W	+0040	+0030	+0010	+0010	+1.2	+1.1	+0.4	+0.4
lewcastle	54 12N	5 53W	+0025	+0035	+0020	+0040	+1.6	+1.1	+0.4	+0.1
illough Harbour	54 15N	5 38W	0000	+0020	*No data*	*No data*	+1.8	+1.6	*No data*	
rdglass	54 16N	5 36W	+0010	+0015	+0005	+0010	+1.7	+1.2	+0.6	+0.3
trangford Lough										
Killard Point	54 19N	5 31W	+0011	+0021	+0005	+0025	+1.0	+0.8	+0.1	+0.1
Strangford	54 22N	5 33W	+0147	+0157	+0148	+0208	+0.1	+0.1	–0.2	0.0
Quoile Barrier	54 22N	5 41W	+0150	+0200	+0150	+0300	+0.2	+0.2	–0.3	–0.1
Killyleagh	54 24N	5 39W	+0157	+0207	+0211	+0231	+0.3	+0.3	*No data*	
outh Rock	54 24N	5 25W	+0023	+0023	+0025	+0025	+1.0	+0.8	+0.1	+0.1
ortavogie	54 27N	5 26W	+0010	+0020	+0010	+0020	+1.2	+0.9	+0.3	+0.2
onaghadee	54 39N	5 32W	+0020	+0020	+0023	+0023	+0.5	+0.4	0.0	+0.1
arrickfergus	54 43N	5 48W	+0005	+0005	+0005	+0005	–0.3	–0.3	–0.2	–0.1
arne	54 51N	5 48W	+0005	0000	+0010	–0005	–0.7	–0.5	–0.3	0.0
Red Bay	55 04N	6 03W	+0022	–0010	+0007	–0017	–1.9	–1.5	–0.8	–0.2

TIDES

Location	Lat	Long	High Water		Low Water		MHWS	MHWN	MLWN	MLWS
Cushendun	55 08N	6 02W	+0010	–0030	0000	–0025	–1.7	–1.5	–0.6	–0.2
Portrush	55 12N	6 40W	–0433	–0433	–0433	–0433	–1.6	–1.6	–0.3	0.0
Coleraine	55 08N	6 40W	–0403	–0403	–0403	–0403	–1.3	–1.2	–0.2	0.0
GALWAY	53 16N	9 03W	**0200** and **1400**	**0900** and **2100**	**0200** and **1400**	**0800** and **2000**	**5.1**	**3.9**	**2.0**	**0.8**
Standard port										
Londonderry	55 00N	7 19W	+0254	+0319	+0322	+0321	–2.4	–1.8	–0.8	–0.1
IRELAND										
Inishtrahull	55 26N	7 14W	+0100	+0100	+0115	+0200	–1.8	–1.4	–0.4	–0.4
Bulbinbeg	55 22N	7 20W	+0120	+0120	+0135	+0135	–1.3	–1.1	–0.4	–0.3
Trawbreaga Bay	55 19N	7 23W	+0115	+0059	+0109	+0125	–1.1	–0.8	*No data*	
Lough Swilly										
Rathmullan	55 06N	7 32W	+0125	+0050	+0126	+0118	–0.8	–0.7	–0.1	–0.3
Fanad Head	55 17N	7 38W	+0115	+0040	+0125	+0120	–1.1	–0.9	–0.5	–0.3
Mulroy Bay Bar	55 15N	7 46W	+0108	+0052	+0102	+0118	–1.2	–1.0	*No data*	
Fanny's Bay	55 12N	7 49W	+0145	+0129	+0151	+0207	–2.2	–1.7	*No data*	
Seamount Bay	55 11N	7 44W	+0210	+0154	+0226	+0242	–3.1	–2.3	*No data*	
Cranford Bay	55 09N	7 42W	+0329	+0313	+0351	+0407	–3.7	–2.8		
No data										
Sheephaven Downies Bay	55 11N	7 50W	+0057	+0043	+0053	+0107	–1.1	–0.9	*No data*	
Inishbofin Bay	55 10N	8 10W	+0040	+0026	+0032	+0046	–1.2	–0.9	*No data*	
GALWAY	53 16N	9 03W	**0600** and **1800**	**1100** and **2300**	**0000** and **1200**	**0700** and **1900**	**5.1**	**3.9**	**2.0**	**0.8**
Standard port										
Gweedore Harbour	55 04N	8 19W	+0048	+0100	+0055	+0107	–1.3	–1.0	–0.5	–0.3
Burtonport	54 59N	8 26W	+0042	+0055	+0115	+0055	–1.2	–1.0	–0.6	–0.3
Loughros More Bay	54 47N	8 30W	+0042	+0054	+0046	+0058	–1.1	–0.9	*No data*	
Donegal Bay										
Killybegs	54 38N	8 26W	+0040	+0050	+0055	+0035	–1.0	–0.9	–0.5	–0.2
Donegal Hbr, Salt Hill Quay	54 38N	8 12W	+0038	+0050	+0052	+0104	–1.2	–0.9	*No data*	
Mullaghmore	54 28N	8 27W	+0036	+0048	+0047	+0059	–1.4	–1.0	–0.4	–0.4
Sligo Hbr (Oyster Island)	54 18N	8 34W	+0043	+0055	+0042	+0054	–1.0	–0.9	–0.5	–0.3
Ballysadare Bay, Culleenamore	54 16N	8 36W	+0059	+0111	+0111	+0123	–1.2	–0.9	*No data*	
Killala Bay (Inishcrone)	54 13N	9 06W	+0035	+0055	+0030	+0050	–1.3	–1.2	–0.7	–0.4
Broadhaven	54 16N	9 53W	+0035	+0035	+0040	+0040	–1.4	–1.0	–0.6	–0.2
Blacksod Bay										
Blacksod Quay	54 06N	10 04W	+0025	+0035	+0040	+0040	–1.2	–1.0	–0.6	–0.4
Inishbiggle	54 00N	9 53W	+0055	+0100	+0125	+0110	–1.3	– 0.9	–0.5	–0.2
Clare Island	53 48N	9 57W	+0015	+0021	+0039	+0027	–0.6	–0.4	–0.1	0.0
Clew Bay Inishgort	53 50N	9 40W	+0035	+0045	+0115	+0100	–0.7	–0.5	–0.2	0.0
Killary Harbour	53 38N	9 53W	+0021	+0015	+0035	+0029	–1.0	–0.8	–0.4	–0.3
Inishbofin Bofin Harbour	53 37N	10 12W	+0013	+0009	+0021	+0017	–1.0	–0.8	–0.4	–0.3
Clifden Bay	53 29N	10 04W	+0005	+0005	+0016	+0016	–0.7	–0.5	*No data*	
Slyne Head	53 24N	10 14W	+0002	+0002	+0010	+0010	–0.7	–0.5	*No data*	
Roundstone Bay	53 23N	9 55W	+0003	+0003	+0008	+0008	–0.7	–0.5	–0.3	–0.3
Kilkieran Cove	53 19N	9 44W	+0005	+0005	+0016	+0016	–0.3	–0.2	–0.1	–0.2
Aran Islands Killeany Bay	53 07N	9 40W	0000	0000	+0001	–0001	–0.1	+0.1	+0.1	+0.2
Liscannor	52 56N	9 23W	–0003	–0007	+0006	+0002	–0.4	–0.3	*No data*	
Seafield Point	52 48N	9 30W	–0006	–0014	+0004	–0004	–0.5	–0.4	*No data*	
Kilrush	52 38N	9 30W	–0006	+0027	+0057	–0016	–0.1	–0.2	–0.3	–0.1
Limerick Dock	52 40N	8 38W	+0135	+0141	+0141	+0219	+1.0	+0.7	–0.8	–0.2
COBH	51 51N	8 18 W	**0500** and **1700**	**1100** and **2300**	**0500** and **1700**	**1100** and **2300**	**4.1**	**3.2**	**1.3**	**0.4**
Standard port										
Tralee Bay Fenit Pier	52 16N	9 52W	–0057	–0017	–0029	–0109	+0.5	+0.2	+0.3	+0.1
Smerwick Harbour	52 12N	10 24W	–0107	–0027	–0041	–0121	–0.3	–0.4	*No data*	
Dingle Harbour	52 07N	10 15W	–0111	–0041	–0049	–0119	–0.1	0.0	+0.3	+0.4
Castlemaine Hbr Cromane Pt	52 08N	9 54W	–0026	–0006	–0017	–0037	+0.4	+0.2	+0.4	+0.2
Valentia Harbour										
Knights Town	51 56N	10 18W	–0118	–0038	–0056	–0136	–0.6	–0.4	–0.1	0.0
Ballinskelligs Bay Castle	51 49N	10 16W	–0119	–0039	–0054	–0134	–0.5	–0.5	–0.1	0.0
Kenmare River										
West Cove	51 46N	10 03W	–0113	–0033	–0049	–0129	–0.6	–0.5	–0.1	0.0
Dunkerron Harbour	51 52N	9 39W	–0117	–0027	–0050	–0140	–0.2	–0.3	+0.1	0.0
Coulagh Bay										
Ballycrovane Hbr	51 43N	9 57W	–0116	–0036	–0053	–0133	–0.6	–0.5	–0.1	0.0
Black Ball Harbour	51 36N	10 02W	–0115	–0035	–0047	–0127	–0.7	–0.6	–0.1	+0.1
Bantry Bay										
Castletown Bearhaven	51 39N	9 54W	–0048	–0012	–0025	–0101	–0.8	–0.6	–0.2	0.0
Bantry	51 41N	9 28W	–0045	–0025	–0040	–0105	–0.7	–0.6	–0.2	+0.1

Location	Lat	Long	High Water		Low Water		MHWS	MHWN	MLWN	MLWS
unmanus Bay										
Dunbeacon Harbour	51 37N	9 33W	–0057	–0025	–0032	–0104	–0.8	–0.7	–0.3	–0.1
Dunmanus Harbour	51 32N	9 40W	–0107	–0031	–0044	–0120	–0.7	–0.6	–0.2	0.0
rookhaven	51 28N	9 44W	–0057	–0033	–0048	–0112	–0.8	–0.6	–0.4	–0.1
kull	51 31N	9 32W	–0040	–0015	–0015	–0110	–0.9	–0.6	–0.2	0.0
altimore	51 29N	9 23W	–0025	–0005	–0010	–0050	–0.6	–0.3	+0.1	+0.2
astletownshend	51 32N	9 10W	–0020	–0030	–0020	–0050	–0.4	–0.2	+0.1	+0.3
lonakilty Bay	51 35N	8 50W	–0033	–0011	–0019	–0041	–0.3	–0.2	*No data*	
ourtmacsherry	51 38N	8 43W	–0025	–0008	–0008	–0015	–0.1	–0.1	–0.0	+0.1
insale	51 42N	8 31W	–0019	–0005	–0009	–0023	–0.2	0.0	+0.1	+0.2
oberts Cove	51 45N	8 19W	–0005	–0005	–0005	–0005	–0.1	0.0	0.0	+0.1
ork Harbour										
Ringaskiddy	51 50N	8 19W	+0005	+0020	+0007	+0013	+0.1	+0.1	+0.1	+0.1
Marino Point	51 53N	8 20W	0000	+0010	0000	+0010	+0.1	+0.1	0.0	0.0
Cork City	51 54N	8 27W	+0005	+0010	+0020	+0010	+0.4	+0.4	+0.3	+0.2
allycotton	51 50N	8 01W	–0011	+0001	+0003	–0009	0.0	0.0	–0.1	0.0
oughal	51 57N	7 51W	0000	+0010	+0010	0000	–0.2	–0.1	–0.1	–0.1
ungarvan Harbour	52 05N	7 34W	+0004	+0012	+0007	–0001	0.0	+0.1	–0.2	0.0
Vaterford Harbour										
Dunmore East	52 09N	6 59W	+0008	+0003	0000	0000	+0.1	0.0	+0.1	+0.2
Cheekpoint	52 16N	7 00W	+0026	+0021	+0019	+0022	+0.5	+0.4	+0.3	+0.2
Kilmokea Point	52 17N	7 00W	+0026	+0022	+0020	+0020	+0.2	+0.1	+0.1	+0.1
Waterford	52 16N	7 07W	+0053	+0032	+0015	+0100	+0.6	+0.6	+0.4	+0.2
New Ross	52 24N	6 57W	+0100	+0030	+0055	+0130	+0.3	+0.4	+0.3	+0.4
aginbun Head	52 10N	6 50W	+0003	+0003	–0008	–0008	–0.2	–0.1	+0.2	+0.2
ireat Saltee	52 07N	6 37W	+0019	+0009	–0004	+0006	–0.3	–0.4	*No data*	
arnsore Point	52 10N	6 22W	+0029	+0019	–0002	+0008	–1.1	–1.0	*No data*	
osslare Europort	52 15N	6 21W	+0045	+0035	+0015	–0005	–2.2	–1.8	–0.5	–0.1
Vexford Harbour	52 20N	6 27W	+0126	+0126	+0118	+0108	–2.1	–1.7	–0.3	+0.1
ENMARK *Time zone –0100*										
			0300	**0700**	**0100**	**0800**				
SBJERG	55 28N	8 27E	and	and	and	and	**2.0**	**1.6**	**0.6**	**0.2**
tandard port			**1500**	**1900**	**1300**	**2000**				
irtshals	57 36N	9 58E	+0055	+0320	+0340	+0100	–1.7	–1.4	–0.5	–0.2
anstholm	57 07N	8 36E	+0100	+0340	+0340	+0130	–1.7	–1.3	–0.5	–0.2
hyborøn	56 42N	8 13E	+0120	+0230	+0410	+0210	–1.6	–1.3	–0.5	–0.2
horsminde	56 22N	8 07E	+0045	+0050	+0040	+0010	–1.4	–1.1	–0.5	–0.2
vide Sande	56 00N	8 08E	0000	+0010	–0015	–0025	–1.2	–0.9	–0.4	–0.2
lavands Huk	55 33N	8 05E	–0120	–0110	–0050	–0100	–0.2	–0.2	–0.3	–0.2
sbjerg, Gradyb Bar	55 26N	8 15E	–0130	–0115	*No data*	*No data*	–0.5	–0.4	–0.3	–0.2
avneby (Rømø)	55 05N	8 34E	–0040	–0005	0000	–0020	–0.1	0.0	–0.3	–0.3
ojer	54 58N	8 40E	–0020	+0015	*No data*	*No data*	+0.4	+0.5	–0.2	–0.2
GERMANY *Time zone –0100*										
			0100	**0600**	**0100**	**0800**				
HELGOLAND	54 11N	7 53E	and	and	and	and	**3.1**	**2.8**	**0.8**	**0.4**
Standard port			**1300**	**1800**	**1300**	**2000**				
ister Tief, List	55 01N	8 26E	+0252	+0240	+0201	+0210	–0.7	–0.6	–0.3	0.0
Hörnum	54 45N	8 18E	+0223	+0218	+0131	+0137	–0.4	–0.3	–0.1	0.0
Amrum - Hafen	54 38N	8 23E	+0138	+0137	+0128	+0134	+0.3	+0.3	+0.1	+0.1
Dagebüll	54 44N	8 41E	+0226	+0217	+0211	+0225	+0.8	+0.7	+0.2	+0.2
Suderoogsand	54 25N	8 30E	+0116	+0102	+0038	+0122	+0.6	+0.5	+0.2	+0.2
River Hever, Husum	54 28N	9 01E	+0205	+0152	+0118	+0200	+1.2	+1.1	+0.2	+0.1
Suederhoeft	54 16N	8 42E	+0103	+0056	+0051	+0112	+0.7	+0.6	–0.2	0.0
Eidersperrwerk	54 16N	8 51E	+0120	+0115	+0130	+0155	+0.7	+0.5	0.0	0.0
Linnenplate	54 13N	8 40E	+0047	+0046	+0034	+0046	+0.7	+0.5	–0.1	0.0
Büsum	54 07N	8 52E	+0054	+0049	–0001	+0027	+0.9	+0.8	–0.1	0.0
			0200	**0800**	**0200**	**0900**				
CUXHAVEN	53 52N	8 43E	and	and	and	and	**3.7**	**3.3**	**0.8**	**0.4**
Standard port			**1400**	**2000**	**1400**	**2100**				
River Elbe Großer Vogelsand	54 00N	8 29E	–0044	–0046	–0101	–0103	+0.1	0.0	+0.1	+0.1
Scharhörn	53 58N	8 28E	–0045	–0047	–0101	–0103	0.0	0.0	+0.1	0.0
Otterndorf	53 50N	8 52E	+0029	+0029	+0027	+0027	0.0	–0.1	0.0	+0.1
Brunsbüttel	53 53N	9 08E	+0057	+0105	+0121	+0112	–0.1	–0.2	–0.1	+0.1
Glückstadt	53 47N	9 25E	+0205	+0214	+0220	+0213	–0.1	0.0	0.0	+0.1
Stadersand	53 38N	9 32E	+0241	+0245	+0300	+0254	+0.1	+0.2	–0.1	+0.1
Schulau	53 34N	9 42E	+0304	+0315	+0337	+0321	+0.3	+0.3	–0.2	0.0
Seemannshoeft	53 32N	9 53E	+0324	+0332	+0403	+0347	+0.4	+0.4	–0.3	–0.1
Hamburg	53 33N	9 58E	+0338	+0346	+0422	+0406	+0.5	+0.5	–0.3	–0.2

Location	Lat	Long	High Water		Low Water		MHWS	MHWN	MLWN	MLWS
			0200	**0800**	**0200**	**0900**				
WILHELMSHAVEN	53 31N	8 09E	and	and	and	and	**4.7**	**4.2**	**1.1**	**0.5**
Standard port			**1400**	**2000**	**1400**	**2100**				
River Weser										
Alter Weser lt ho	53 32N	8 08E	–0055	–0048	–0015	–0029	–1.0	–0.9	–0.1	0.0
Dwarsgat	53 43N	8 18E	–0015	+0002	–0006	–0001	–0.5	–0.5	–0.1	–0.1
Bremerhaven	53 33N	8 34E	+0029	+0046	+0033	+0038	–0.1	0.0	–0.1	0.0
Nordenham	53 28N	8 29E	+0051	+0109	+0055	+0058	0.0	+0.1	–0.2	–0.1
Brake	53 19N	8 29E	+0120	+0119	+0143	+0155	–0.2	–0.1	–0.5	–0.3
Elsfleth	53 16N	8 29E	+0137	+0137	+0206	+0216	–0.2	–0.2	–0.5	–0.2
Vegesack	53 10N	8 37E	+0208	+0204	+0250	+0254	–0.1	–0.1	–0.5	–0.2
Bremen	53 07N	8 43E	+0216	+0211	+0311	+0314	0.0	0.0	–0.6	–0.3
River Jade										
Wangerooge East	53 46N	7 59E	–0058	–0053	–0024	–0034	–0.9	–0.9	–0.2	–0.1
Wangerooge West	53 47N	7 52E	–0101	–0058	–0035	–0045	–1.0	–1.0	–0.2	0.0
Schillig	53 42N	8 03E	–0031	–0025	–0006	–0014	–0.6	–0.6	–0.1	0.0
Hooksiel	53 39N	8 05E	–0023	–0022	–0008	–0012	–0.5	–0.4	–0.1	0.0
			0200	**0700**	**0200**	**0800**				
HELGOLAND	54 11N	7 53E	and	and	and	and	**3.1**	**2.8**	**0.8**	**0.4**
Standard port			**1400**	**1900**	**1400**	**2000**				
East Frisian Islands and coast										
Spiekeroog	53 45N	7 41E	+0003	–0003	–0031	–0012	+0.4	+0.3	+0.1	0.0
Neuharlingersiel	53 42N	7 42E	+0014	+0008	–0024	–0013	+0.5	+0.4	+0.1	0.0
Langeoog	53 43N	7 30E	+0003	–0001	–0034	–0018	+0.3	+0.2	+0.1	0.0
Norderney (Riffgat)	53 42N	7 09E	–0024	–0030	–0056	–0045	+0.1	0.0	0.0	0.0
Norddeich Hafen	53 39N	7 09E	–0018	–0017	–0029	–0012	+0.2	+0.1	+0.1	+0.1
Juist	53 40N	7 00E	–0026	–0032	–0019	–0008	+0.2	+0.1	+0.1	0.0
River Ems										
Memmert	53 38N	6 54E	–0032	–0038	–0114	–0103	+0.1	+0.1	+0.1	0.0
Borkum (Fischerbalje)	53 33N	6 45E	–0048	–0052	–0124	–0105	–0.1	0.0	–0.1	–0.1
Emshorn	53 30N	6 50E	–0037	–0041	–0108	–0047	+0.2	+0.1	0.0	0.0
Knock	53 20N	7 02E	+0018	+0005	–0028	+0004	+0.6	+0.6	0.0	0.0
Emden	53 20N	7 11E	+0041	+0028	–0011	+0022	+0.8	+0.8	–0.1	–0.1

NETHERLANDS *Time zone –0100*

Location	Lat	Long	High Water		Low Water		MHWS	MHWN	MLWN	MLWS
			0200	**0700**	**0200**	**0800**				
HELGOLAND	54 11N	7 53E	and	and	and	and	**3.2**	**2.8**	**0.9**	**0.5**
Standard port			**1400**	**1900**	**1400**	**2000**				
Delfzijl	53 20N	6 56E	+0020	–0005	–0040	0000	+0.5	+0.6	–0.1	–0.1
Eemshaven	53 27N	6 50E	–0025	–0045	–0115	–0045	0.0	+0.1	–0.1	–0.1
Huibertgat	53 35N	6 24E	–0150	–0150	–0210	–0210	–0.5	–0.4	–0.2	–0.2
Schiermonnikoog	53 28N	6 12E	–0120	–0130	–0240	–0220	–0.3	–0.2	–0.2	–0.2
Waddenzee										
Lauwersoog	53 25N	6 12E	–0130	–0145	–0235	–0220	–0.3	–0.2	–0.2	0.0
Nes	53 26N	5 47E	–0135	–0150	–0245	–0225	–0.3	–0.2	–0.2	0.0
West Terschelling	53 22N	5 13E	–0220	–0250	–0335	–0310	–0.8	–0.7	–0.3	–0.2
Vlieland-Haven	53 18N	5 06E	–0250	–0320	–0355	–0330	–0.8	–0.6	–0.3	–0.1
Harlingen	53 10N	5 25E	–0155	–0245	–0210	–0130	–0.8	–0.7	–0.4	–0.2
Kornwerderzand	53 04N	5 20E	–0210	–0315	–0300	–0215	–1.0	–0.8	–0.4	–0.2
Den Oever	52 56N	5 02E	–0245	–0410	–0400	–0305	–1.2	–1.0	–0.5	–0.2
Oudeschild	53 02N	4 51E	–0310	–0420	–0445	–0400	–1.4	–1.1	–0.4	–0.2
Den Helder	52 58N	4 45E	–0410	–0520	–0520	–0430	–1.3	–1.1	–0.4	–0.2
Noordwinning (Platform K13–A)	53 13N	3 13E	–0420	–0430	–0520	–0530	–1.4	–1.4	–0.3	–0.3
			0300	**0900**	**0400**	**1000**				
VLISSINGEN	51 27N	3 36E	and	and	and	and	**4.9**	**4.1**	**1.0**	**0.5**
Standard port			**1500**	**2100**	**1600**	**2200**				
IJmuiden	52 28N	4 33E	+0145	+0140	+0305	+0325	–2.8	–2.4	–0.7	–0.3
Scheveningen	52 06N	4 16E	+0105	+0100	+0220	+0245	–2.7	–2.3	–0.7	–0.2
Europlatform	52 00N	3 17E	+0005	–0005	–0030	–0055	–2.7	–2.3	–0.5	–0.1
Nieuwe Waterweg										
HOEK VAN HOLLAND		*Standard port, no Secondaries*								
Maassluis	51 55N	4 15E	+0155	+0115	+0100	+0310	–2.9	–2.4	–0.8	–0.3
Nieuwe Maas, Vlaardingen	51 54N	4 21E	+0150	+0120	+0130	+0330	–2.8	–2.3	–0.7	–0.2
Haringvlietsluizen	51 50N	4 03E	+0015	+0015	+0015	–0020	–1.9	–1.9	–0.6	–0.2
Ooster Schelde										
Roompot Buiten	51 37N	3 40E	–0015	+0005	+0005	–0020	–1.2	–1.1	–0.3	–0.1
Walcheren, Westkapelle	51 32N	3 26E	–0025	–0015	–0010	–0025	–0.6	–0.6	–0.1	–0.1
Westerschelde										
Terneuzen	51 20N	3 50E	+0020	+0020	+0020	+0030	+0.4	+0.3	+0.1	0.0
Hansweert	51 27N	4 00E	+0100	+0050	+0040	+0100	+0.7	+0.6	+0.1	0.0
Bath	51 24N	4 13E	+0125	+0115	+0115	+0140	+1.2	+1.0	+0.2	+0.1

Location	Lat	Long	High Water		Low Water		MHWS	MHWN	MLWN	MLWS
ELGIUM *Time zone –0100*										
ntwerpen	51 21N	4 14E	+0128	+0116	+0121	+0144	+1.2	+1.0	+0.1	+0.1
lankenberge	51 19N	3 07E		–0007		–0002	+0.1	+0.1	–0.1	–0.1
			0300	**0900**	**0300**	**0900**				
EEBRUGGE	51 21N	3 12E	and	and	and	and	**4.8**	**4.0**	**1.1**	**0.5**
tandard port			**1500**	**2100**	**1500**	**2100**				
ostende	51 14N	2 56E	–0019	–0019	–0008	–0008	+0.4	+0.2	+0.2	+0.1
ieuwpoort	51 09N	2 43E	–0031	–0031	–0010	–0010	+0.7	+0.5	+0.3	+0.1
RANCE *Time zone –0100*										
			0200	**0800**	**0200**	**0900**				
UNKERQUE	51 03N	2 22E	and	and	and	and	**6.0**	**5.0**	**1.5**	**0.6**
tandard port			**1400**	**2000**	**1400**	**2100**				
ravelines	51 01N	2 06E	–0010	–0015	–0010	–0005	+0.5	+0.3	+0.1	0.0
andettie Bank	51 15N	2 03E	–0010	–0015	–0015	–0010	–0.6	–0.6	–0.2	–0.1
alais	50 58N	1 51E	–0020	–0030	–0015	–0005	+1.2	+0.9	+0.6	+0.3
Vissant	50 53N	1 40E	–0035	–0050	–0030	–0010	+2.0	+1.5	+0.9	+0.4
oulogne	50 44N	1 35E	–0045	–0100	–0045	–0025	+2.8	+2.2	+1.1	+0.5
			0100	**0600**	**0100**	**0700**				
IEPPE	49 56N	1 05E	and	and	and	and	**9.3**	**7.4**	**2.5**	**0.8**
tandard port			**1300**	**1800**	**1300**	**1900**				
e Touquet, Étaples	50 31N	1 35E	+0010	+0015	+0030	+0030	+0.2	+0.2	+0.3	+0.4
erck	50 24N	1 34E	+0005	+0015	+0025	+0030	+0.4	+0.5	+0.3	+0.4
a Somme										
Le Hourdel	50 13N	1 34E	+0020	+0020	*No data*	*No data*	+0.8	+0.6	*No data*	
St Valéry	50 11N	1 37E	+0035	+0035	*No data*	*No data*	+0.9	+0.7	*No data*	
ayeux	50 11N	1 29E	0000	+0005	+0015	+0010	+0.5	+0.6	+0.4	+0.4
e Tréport	50 04N	1 22E	+0005	0000	+0005	+0015	+0.3	+0.2	+0.1	+0.1
t Valéry–en–Caux	49 52N	0 42E	–0005	–0005	–0015	–0015	–0.5	–0.4	–0.1	–0.1
écamp	49 46N	0 22E	–0015	–0010	–0030	–0040	–0.8	–0.5	+0.3	+0.4
tretat	49 42N	0 12E	–0020	–0015	–0050	–0050	–1.1	–0.8	+0.3	+0.4
			0000	**0500**	**0000**	**0700**				
E HAVRE	49 29N	0 07E	and	and	and	and	**8.0**	**6.7**	**2.9**	**1.2**
tandard port			**1200**	**1700**	**1200**	**1900**				
ntifer (Le Havre)	49 39N	0 09E	+0025	+0015	+0005	–0005	+0.1	0.0	0.0	0.0
a Seine										
Chenal du Rouen	49 26N	0 07E	0000	0000	0000	+0015	0.0	–0.1	0.0	–0.1
Honfleur	49 25N	0 14E	–0150	–0135	+0025	+0040	0.0	0.0	+0.1	+0.4
Tancarville	49 28N	0 28E	–0135	–0120	+0030	+0145	+0.1	+0.1	+0.3	+1.0
Quilleboeuf	49 28N	0 32E	–0055	–0110	+0105	+0210	+0.1	+0.1	+0.5	+1.4
Vatteville	49 29N	0 40E	+0015	–0040	+0205	+0240	–0.1	–0.1	+0.9	+2.2
Caudebec	49 32N	0 44E	–0005	–0030	+0220	+0300	–0.1	–0.1	+1.0	+2.3
Heurteauville	49 27N	0 49E	+0055	+0005	+0250	+0330	–0.2	–0.1	+1.2	+2.6
Duclair	49 29N	0 53E	+0210	+0145	+0350	+0410	–0.2	0.0	+1.5	+3.2
Rouen	49 27N	1 06E	+0305	+0240	+0505	+0515	–0.1	+0.2	+1.6	+3.3
rouville	49 22N	0 05E	–0100	–0010	0000	+0005	+0.4	+0.3	+0.3	+0.1
ives	49 18N	0 05W	–0100	–0010	0000	0000	+0.3	+0.2	+0.2	+0.1
uistreham	49 17N	0 15W	–0045	–0010	–0005	0000	–0.3	–0.3	–0.2	–0.3
ourseulles-sur-Mer	49 20N	0 27W	–0100	–0005	–0015	–0025	–0.6	–0.6	–0.3	–0.1
rromanches	49 21N	0 37W	–0055	–0025	–0025	–0035	–0.6	–0.6	–0.2	–0.2
ort-en-Bessin	49 21N	0 45W	–0055	–0030	–0030	–0035	–0.7	–0.7	–0.2	–0.1
lpha-Baie de Seine	49 49N	0 20W	+0030	+0020	–0005	–0020	–1.0	–0.9	–0.4	–0.2
			0300	**1000**	**0400**	**1000**				
HERBOURG	49 39N	1 38W	and	and	and	and	**6.4**	**5.1**	**2.6**	**1.1**
tandard port			**1500**	**2200**	**1600**	**2200**				
ade de la Capelle	49 25N	1 05W	+0125	+0055	+0125	+0110	+0.7	+0.7	0.0	+0.1
les Saint Marcouf	49 30N	1 08W	+0130	+0055	+0120	+0110	+0.5	+0.5	0.0	0.0
t Vaast-la-Hougue	49 34N	1 16W	+0115	+0045	+0120	+0110	+0.3	+0.3	–0.2	–0.1
arfleur	49 40N	1 15W	+0115	+0050	+0045	+0050	+0.2	+0.1	0.0	+0.1
monville	49 42N	1 50W	–0015	–0010	–0015	–0015	–0.1	–0.1	0.0	0.0
oury	49 43N	1 57W	–0100	–0040	–0105	–0120	+1.2	+1.3	+0.7	0.0
CHANNEL ISLANDS *Time zone UT*										
			0300	**0900**	**0200**	**0900**				
ST HELIER	49 11N	2 07W	and	and	and	and	**11.0**	**8.1**	**4.0**	**1.4**
Standard port			**1500**	**2100**	**1400**	**2100**				
Alderney, Braye	49 43N	2 12W	+0050	+0040	+0025	+0105	–4.8	–3.4	–1.5	–0.5
Sark, Maseline Pier	49 26N	2 21W	+0005	+0015	+0005	+0010	–2.1	–1.5	–0.6	–0.3
Guernsey, ST PETER PORT	49 27N	2 31W	*Standard port (no Secondaries)*							

Location	Lat	Long	High Water		Low Water		MHWS	MHWN	MLWN	MLWS
Jersey										
St Catherine Bay	49 13N	2 01W	0000	+0010	+0010	+0010	0.0	–0.1	0.0	+0.1
Bouley Bay	49 15N	2 05W	+0002	+0002	+0004	+0004	–0.3	–0.3	–0.1	–0.1
Les Ecrehou	49 17N	1 56W	+0005	+0009	+0011	+0009	–0.2	+0.1	–0.2	0.0
Les Minquiers	48 57N	2 08W	–0014	–0018	–0001	–0008	+0.5	+0.6	+0.1	+0.1
FRANCE *Time zone –0100*										
ST MALO	48 38N	2 02W	**0100** and **1300**	**0800** and **2000**	**0300** and **1500**	**0800** and **2000**	**12.2**	**9.3**	**4.2**	**1.5**
Standard port										
Les Ardentes	48 58N	1 52W	+0010	+0010	+0020	+0010	0.0	–0.1	0.0	–0.1
Iles Chausey	48 52N	1 49W	+0005	+0005	+0015	+0015	+0.8	+0.7	+0.6	+0.4
Diélette	49 33N	1 52W	+0045	+0035	+0020	+0035	–2.5	–1.9	–0.7	–0.3
Carteret	49 22N	1 47W	+0030	+0020	+0015	+0030	–1.6	–1.2	–0.7	–0.3
Portbail	49 18N	1 45W	+0030	+0025	+0025	+0030	–0.8	–0.6	–0.2	–0.1
St Germain sur Ay	49 14N	1 36W	+0025	+0025	+0035	+0035	–0.7	–0.5	0.0	+0.1
Le Sénéquet	49 05N	1 40W	+0015	+0015	+0025	+0025	–0.3	–0.3	+0.1	+0.1
Regnéville sur Mer	49 01N	1 33W	+0010	+0010	+0030	+0020	+0.5	+0.4	+0.2	0.0
Granville	48 50N	1 36W	+0010	+0005	+0025	+0015	+0.7	+0.4	+0.3	0.0
Cancale	48 40N	1 51W	0000	0000	+0010	+0010	+0.8	+0.6	+0.3	+0.1
Ile des Hebihens	48 37N	2 11W	0000	0000	–0005	–0005	–0.2	–0.2	–0.1	–0.1
St Cast	48 38N	2 15W	0000	0000	–0005	–0005	–0.2	–0.2	–0.1	–0.1
Erquy	48 38N	2 28W	0000	–0005	–0020	–0010	–0.8	–0.6	–0.2	–0.2
Dahouët	48 35N	2 34W	–0005	0000	–0025	–0010	–0.8	–0.7	–0.2	–0.1
Le Légué (Buoy)	48 34N	2 41W	–0010	–0005	–0020	–0015	–0.8	–0.5	–0.2	–0.1
Binic	48 36N	2 49W	–0005	–0005	–0025	–0015	–0.8	–0.6	–0.2	–0.1
St Quay-Portrieux	48 38N	2 49W	–0010	–0010	–0030	–0010	–0.9	–0.7	–0.2	–0.1
Paimpol	48 47N	3 02W	–0010	–0005	–0035	–0025	–1.4	–0.9	–0.4	–0.1
Ile de Bréhat	48 50N	3 00W	–0015	–0005	–0040	–0030	–1.6	–1.2	–0.5	0.0
Les Héaux de Bréhat	48 55N	3 05W	–0015	–0010	–0010	–0045	–2.3	–1.6	–0.6	–0.1
Lézardrieux	48 47N	3 06W	–0020	–0015	–0055	–0045	–1.7	–1.3	–0.5	–0.2
Port-Béni	48 51N	3 10W	–0020	–0020	–0105	–0050	–2.4	–1.7	–0.6	–0.2
Tréguier	48 47N	3 13W	–0020	–0020	–0100	–0045	–2.3	–1.6	–0.6	–0.2
Perros-Guirec	48 49N	3 28W	–0035	–0035	–0115	–0100	–2.8	–2.0	–0.7	–0.1
Ploumanac'h	48 50N	3 29W	–0035	–0040	–0120	–0100	–2.9	–2.0	–0.7	–0.2
BREST	48 23N	4 30W	**0000** and **1200**	**0600** and **1800**	**0000** and **1200**	**0600** and **1800**	**7.0**	**5.5**	**2.7**	**1.1**
Standard port										
Trébeurden	48 46N	3 35W	+0100	+0110	+0120	+0100	+2.2	+1.8	+0.8	+0.3
Locquirec	48 42N	3 38W	+0100	+0110	+0125	+0100	+2.2	+1.8	+0.8	+0.4
Anse de Primel	48 43N	3 50W	+0100	+0110	+0120	+0100	+2.0	+1.6	+0.7	+0.2
Chateau du Taureau (Morlaix)	48 41N	3 53W	+0055	+0105	+0115	+0055	+1.9	+1.6	+0.7	+0.2
Roscoff	48 43N	3 58W	+0055	+0105	+0115	+0055	+1.9	+1.6	+0.7	+0.2
Ile de Batz	48 44N	4 00W	+0045	+0100	+0105	+0055	+1.9	+1.5	+0.8	+0.3
Brignogan	48 40N	4 19W	+0040	+0045	+0100	+0040	+1.4	+1.1	+0.5	+0.1
L'Aber Wrac'h	48 36N	4 34W	+0030	+0030	+0040	+0035	+0.7	+0.6	+0.1	–0.1
Aber Benoit	48 35N	4 37W	+0022	+0025	+0035	+0020	+0.9	+0.8	+0.3	+0.1
Portsall	48 34N	4 43W	+0015	+0020	+0025	+0015	+0.5	+0.4	0.0	–0.1
L'Aber-Ildut	48 28N	4 45W	+0010	+0010	+0020	+0010	+0.3	+0.2	–0.1	–0.1
Ouessant, Baie de Lampaul	48 27N	5 06W	+0010	+0010	–0005	+0005	–0.1	–0.1	–0.1	–0.1
Molene	48 24N	4 58W	+0015	+0010	+0020	+0020	+0.3	+0.3	+0.1	+0.1
Le Conquet	48 22N	4 47W	0000	0000	+0005	+0005	–0.2	–0.2	–0.1	0.0
Le Trez Hir	48 21N	4 42W	–0005	–0005	–0015	–0010	–0.4	–0.4	–0.2	–0.1
Camaret	48 17N	4 35W	–0010	–0010	–0015	–0010	–0.4	–0.4	–0.3	–0.1
Morgat	48 13N	4 30W	–0005	–0010	–0020	–0005	–0.5	–0.4	–0.2	0.0
Douarnenez	48 06N	4 19W	–0010	–0010	–0020	–0010	–0.4	–0.4	–0.2	–0.1
Ile de Sein	48 02N	4 51W	–0005	–0005	–0015	–0010	–0.9	–0.7	–0.4	–0.2
Anse de Feunteun Aod	48 02N	4 42W	–0030	–0040	–0035	–0025	–1.4	–1.2	–0.6	–0.2
Audierne	48 01N	4 33W	–0035	–0030	–0035	–0030	–1.8	–1.4	–0.7	–0.3
Le Guilvinec	47 48N	4 17W	–0010	–0025	–0025	–0015	–1.9	–1.5	–0.7	–0.2
Lesconil	47 48N	4 13W	–0010	–0030	–0030	–0020	–2.0	–1.5	–0.7	–0.2
Pont l'Abbe River, Loctudy	47 50N	4 10W	–0010	–0030	–0035	–0020	–2.1	–1.7	–0.9	–0.4
Odet River										
Bénodet	47 53N	4 07W	–0010	–0025	–0030	–0020	–1.7	–1.4	–0.6	–0.1
Corniguel	47 58N	4 06W	+0015	+0010	–0015	–0010	–2.1	–1.7	–1.1	–0.8

Location	Lat	Long	High Water		Low Water		MHWS	MHWN	MLWN	MLWS
Concarneau	47 52N	3 55W	−0010	−0030	−0030	−0020	−1.9	−1.5	−0.7	−0.2
Iles de Glenan, Ile de Penfret	47 44N	3 57W	−0005	−0030	−0030	−0020	−2.0	−1.6	−0.8	−0.3
Port Louis	47 42N	3 21W	+0005	−0020	−0020	−0010	−1.9	−1.5	−0.7	−0.2
Lorient	47 45N	3 21W	+0005	−0020	−0020	−0010	−1.9	−1.5	−0.7	−0.3
Hennebont	47 48N	3 17W	+0015	−0015	+0005	+0005	−2.0	−1.6	−0.9	−0.3
Ile de Groix, Port Tudy	47 39N	3 27W	0000	−0025	−0025	−0015	−1.8	−1.4	−0.6	−0.2
Port d'Etel	47 39N	3 12W	+0020	−0010	+0030	+0010	−2.1	−1.4	−0.5	+0.4
Port Haliguen	47 29N	3 06W	+0010	−0020	−0015	−0010	−1.7	−1.3	−0.7	−0.3
Port Maria	47 29N	3 08W	+0010	−0025	−0025	−0015	−1.7	−1.4	−0.7	−0.2
Belle Ile, Le Palais	47 21N	3 09W	−0005	−0025	−0025	−0010	−1.9	−1.4	−0.8	−0.3
Crac'h River, La Trinité	47 35N	3 01W	+0025	−0020	−0015	−0010	−1.7	−1.2	−0.6	−0.3
Golfe du Morbihan										
Port Navalo	47 33N	2 55W	+0030	−0005	−0010	−0005	−2.1	−1.6	−0.9	−0.4
Auray	47 40N	2 59W	+0035	0000	+0015	−0005	−2.3	−1.9	−1.2	−0.5
Arradon	47 37N	2 50W	+0135	+0145	+0140	+0115	−3.9	−3.1	−1.9	−0.8
Vannes	47 39N	2 46W	+0200	+0150	+0140	+0120	−3.8	−3.0	−2.1	−0.9
St Armel (Le Passage)	47 36N	2 43W	+0200	+0200	+0210	+0135	−3.8	−3.0	−2.0	−0.9
Le Logeo	47 33N	2 51W	+0140	+0140	+0145	+0115	−4.1	−3.2	−2.1	−0.9
Port du Crouesty	47 32N	2 54W	+0010	−0025	−0015	−0010	−1.6	−1.2	−0.7	−0.3
Ile de Houat	47 24N	2 57W	+0005	−0025	−0025	−0010	−1.8	−1.4	−0.7	−0.4
Ile de Hoëdic	47 20N	2 52W	+0010	−0035	−0025	−0020	−1.9	−1.5	−0.8	−0.4
Pénerf	47 31N	2 37W	+0015	−0025	−0015	−0015	−1.6	−1.2	−0.7	−0.4
Tréhiguier	47 30N	2 27W	+0035	−0020	−0005	−0010	−1.5	−1.1	−0.6	−0.4
Le Croisic	47 18N	2 31W	+0015	−0040	−0020	−0015	−1.6	−1.2	−0.7	−0.4
Le Pouliguen	47 17N	2 25W	+0020	−0025	−0020	−0025	−1.6	−1.2	−0.7	−0.4
Le Grand-Charpentier	47 13N	2 19W	+0015	−0045	−0025	−0020	−1.6	−1.2	−0.7	−0.4
Pornichet	47 16N	2 21W	+0020	−0045	−0022	−0022	−1.5	−1.1	−0.6	−0.3
La Loire										
St Nazaire	47 16N	2 12W	+0030	−0040	−0010	−0010	−1.2	−0.9	−0.5	−0.3
Donges	47 18N	2 05W	+0035	−0040	+0005	+0005	−1.1	−0.8	−0.6	−0.5
Cordemais	47 17N	1 54W	+0055	−0005	+0105	+0030	−0.8	−0.6	−0.8	−0.5
Le Pellerin	47 12N	1 46W	+0110	+0010	+0145	+0100	−0.8	−0.6	−1.0	−0.5
Nantes (Chantenay)	47 12N	1 35W	+0135	+0055	+0215	+0125	−0.7	−0.4	−0.9	−0.2
BREST *Standard port*	48 23N	4 30W	**0500** and **1700**	**1100** and **2300**	**0500** and **1700**	**1100** and **2300**	**7.0**	**5.5**	**2.7**	**1.1**
Pointe de Saint–Gildas	47 08N	2 15W	−0030	+0025	−0005	−0020	−1.4	−1.0	−0.6	−0.3
Pornic	47 06N	2 07W	−0050	+0030	−0010	−0010	−1.2	−0.9	−0.5	−0.3
Ile de Noirmoutier, L'Herbaudière	47 02N	2 18W	−0045	+0025	−0020	−0020	−1.5	−1.1	−0.6	−0.3
Fromentine	46 54N	2 10W	−0045	+0020	−0015	+0005	−1.8	−1.4	−0.9	−0.2
Ile de Yeu, Port Joinville	46 44N	2 21W	−0040	+0015	−0030	−0035	−2.0	−1.5	−0.8	−0.4
St Gilles-Croix-de-Vie	46 41N	1 56W	−0030	+0015	−0030	−0030	−1.9	−1.4	−0.7	−0.4
Les Sables d'Olonne	46 30N	1 48W	−0030	+0015	−0035	−0035	−1.8	−1.3	−0.7	−0.4
POINTE DE GRAVE *Standard port*	45 34N	1 04W	**0000** and **1200**	**0600** and **1800**	**0000** and **1200**	**0500** and **1700**	**5.3**	**4.4**	**2.1**	**1.0**
Ile de Ré, St Martin	46 12N	1 22W	+0005	−0030	−0025	−0030	+0.7	+0.5	+0.3	−0.1
La Pallice	46 10N	1 13W	+0015	−0030	−0020	−0025	+0.7	+0.5	+0.3	−0.1
La Rochelle	46 09N	1 09W	+0015	−0030	−0020	−0025	+0.7	+0.5	+0.3	−0.1
Ile d'Aix	46 01N	1 10W	+0015	−0040	−0025	−0030	+0.8	+0.5	+0.3	−0.1
La Charente, Rochefort	45 57N	0 58W	+0035	−0015	+0125	+0030	+1.2	+0.9	+0.1	−0.2
Le Chapus	45 51N	1 11W	+0015	−0040	−0015	−0025	+0.7	+0.6	+0.4	+0.2
La Cayenne	45 47N	1 08W	+0030	−0015	−0005	−0010	+0.3	+0.2	+0.3	0.0
Pointe de Gatseau	45 48N	1 14W	+0015	0000	−0020	−0015	0.0	−0.1	+0.2	+0.1
Cordouan	45 35N	1 10W	−0010	−0010	−0025	−0015	−0.4	−0.4	−0.1	−0.2
La Gironde										
Royan	45 37N	1 01W	0000	−0005	0000	0000	−0.1	−0.1	0.0	0.0
Richard	45 27N	0 56W	+0020	+0020	+0035	+0030	0.0	−0.1	−0.4	−0.5
Lamena	45 20N	0 48W	+0035	+0045	+0125	+0100	+0.3	+0.1	−0.5	−0.3
Pauillac	45 12N	0 45W	+0100	+0100	+0205	+0135	+0.2	0.0	−1.0	−0.5
La Reuille	45 03N	0 36W	+0135	+0145	+0305	+0230	−0.1	−0.3	−1.3	−0.7
La Garonne										
Le Marquis	45 00N	0 33W	+0145	+0150	+0320	+0245	−0.2	−0.4	− 1.5	−0.9
Bordeaux	44 52N	0 33W	+0200	+0225	+0405	+0330	0.0	−0.2	−1.7	−1.0

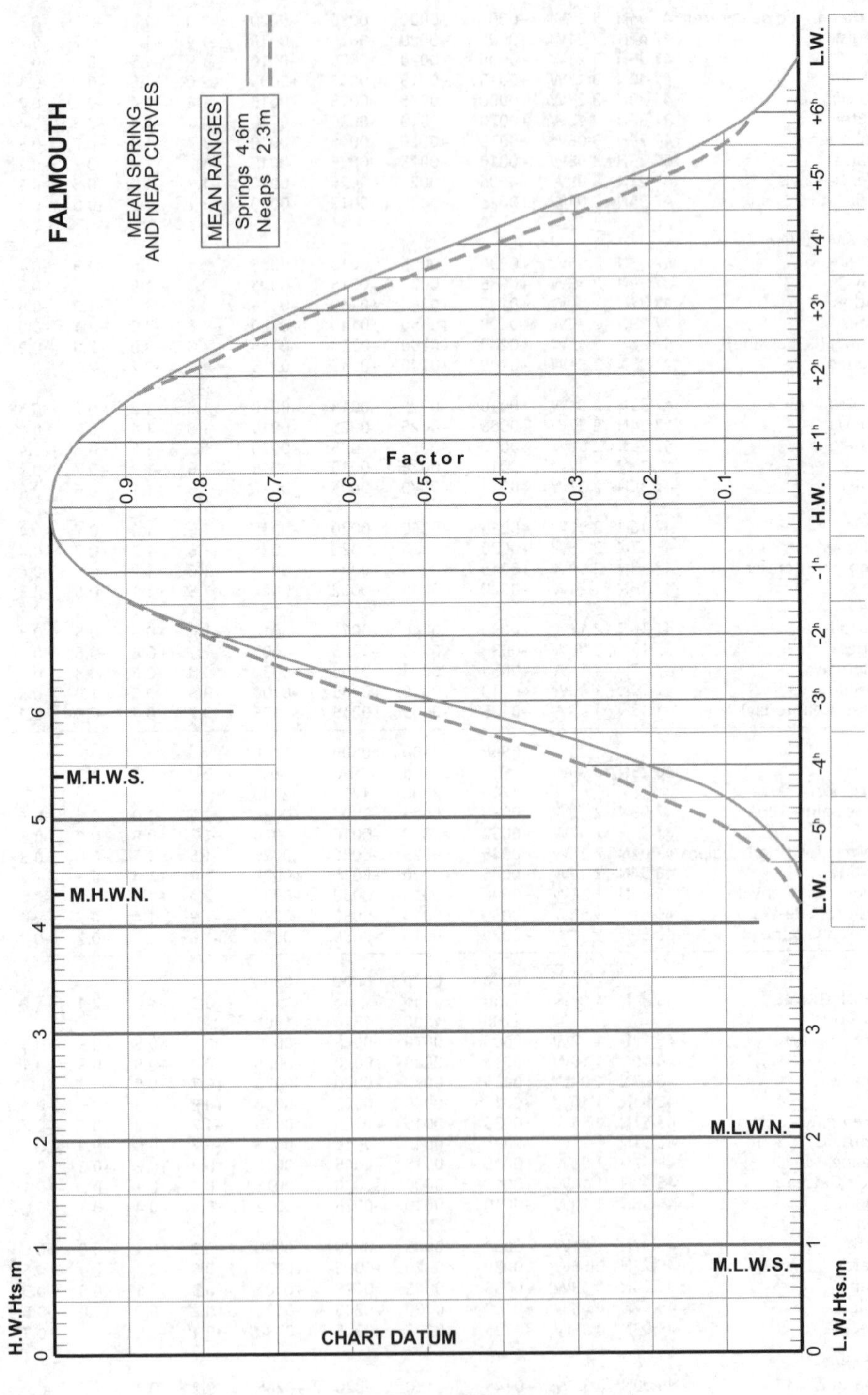
FALMOUTH
MEAN SPRING
AND NEAP CURVES
MEAN RANGES
Springs 4.6m
Neaps 2.3m
Factor
0.9
0.8
0.7
0.6
0.5
0.4
0.3
0.2
0.1
L.W.
-5h
-4h
-3h
-2h
-1h
H.W.
+1h
+2h
+3h
+4h
+5h
+6h
L.W.
H.W.Hts.m
0
1
2
3
4
5
6
M.H.W.S.
M.H.W.N.
CHART DATUM
L.W.Hts.m
M.L.W.S.
M.L.W.N.

TIME ZONE (UT)
For Summer Time add ONE hour in **non-shaded areas**

FALMOUTH

LAT 50°09′N LONG 5°03′W

TIMES AND HEIGHTS OF HIGH AND LOW WATERS

Dates in amber are **SPRINGS**
Dates in grey are **NEAPS**

2016

JANUARY

Date	Day	Time	m	Time	m	Time	m	Time	m
1	F	0334	1.4	0919	4.6	1602	1.5	2149	4.2
2	SA ◑	0415	1.7	1007	4.3	1649	1.7	2244	4.0
3	SU	0510	1.9	1104	4.2	1751	1.8	2349	4.0
4	M	0620	1.9	1210	4.1	1901	1.8		
5	TU	0104	4.0	0731	1.8	1325	4.1	2006	1.6
6	W	0215	4.2	0834	1.6	1433	4.3	2103	1.4
7	TH	0309	4.5	0929	1.3	1525	4.5	2152	1.1
8	F	0352	4.7	1017	1.1	1610	4.7	2239	0.9
9	SA	0433	4.9	1104	0.8	1652	4.9	2323	0.7
10	SU ●	0513	5.1	1148	0.6	1735	4.9		
11	M	0007	0.6	0553	5.2	1231	0.5	1817	5.0
12	TU	0049	0.5	0635	5.3	1313	0.4	1900	5.0
13	W	0129	0.5	0718	5.3	1354	0.5	1942	4.9
14	TH	0210	0.6	0800	5.2	1435	0.6	2024	4.8
15	F	0251	0.7	0844	5.0	1519	0.7	2110	4.6
16	SA ◐	0337	0.9	0933	4.8	1608	1.0	2204	4.4
17	SU	0430	1.2	1030	4.6	1705	1.2	2309	4.3
18	M	0534	1.4	1138	4.4	1814	1.4		
19	TU	0025	4.2	0648	1.5	1257	4.3	1934	1.4
20	W	0145	4.3	0814	1.4	1413	4.3	2054	1.2
21	TH	0251	4.5	0930	1.1	1516	4.5	2159	1.0
22	F	0345	4.7	1030	0.8	1608	4.7	2253	0.7
23	SA	0431	4.9	1121	0.6	1654	4.8	2341	0.5
24	SU ○	0514	5.1	1207	0.4	1736	4.9		
25	M	0024	0.5	0553	5.2	1247	0.4	1814	4.9
26	TU	0102	0.5	0631	5.2	1323	0.4	1851	4.9
27	W	0135	0.6	0707	5.2	1355	0.6	1927	4.9
28	TH	0204	0.7	0741	5.1	1423	0.8	2001	4.8
29	F	0230	1.0	0814	4.9	1448	1.0	2034	4.6
30	SA	0254	1.2	0847	4.7	1512	1.3	2109	4.4
31	SU	0321	1.4	0924	4.5	1544	1.5	2152	4.2

FEBRUARY

Date	Day	Time	m	Time	m	Time	m	Time	m
1	M ◑	0401	1.7	1012	4.2	1632	1.7	2248	4.0
2	TU	0500	1.9	1113	4.1	1745	1.9	2355	4.0
3	W	0626	2.0	1222	4.0	1911	1.8		
4	TH	0108	4.1	0747	1.8	1338	4.1	2022	1.6
5	F	0222	4.3	0853	1.5	1447	4.3	2121	1.3
6	SA	0318	4.6	0950	1.1	1541	4.6	2215	1.0
7	SU	0404	4.9	1042	0.8	1628	4.8	2304	0.7
8	M ●	0449	5.1	1131	0.5	1714	5.0	2352	0.4
9	TU	0534	5.3	1217	0.3	1800	5.1		
10	W	0036	0.3	0618	5.4	1301	0.2	1844	5.2
11	TH	0119	0.2	0702	5.4	1342	0.1	1926	5.1
12	F	0158	0.2	0745	5.4	1422	0.2	2007	5.0
13	SA	0237	0.4	0827	5.2	1502	0.5	2047	4.8
14	SU	0319	0.6	0910	4.9	1544	0.8	2132	4.6
15	M ◐	0406	1.0	1000	4.6	1635	1.2	2230	4.3
16	TU	0504	1.3	1105	4.2	1739	1.5	2351	4.1
17	W	0617	1.6	1235	4.0	1901	1.6		
18	TH	0123	4.1	0754	1.6	1400	4.1	2039	1.5
19	F	0235	4.3	0920	1.3	1504	4.3	2148	1.1
20	SA	0329	4.6	1018	0.9	1554	4.5	2240	0.8
21	SU	0414	4.8	1107	0.6	1637	4.7	2326	0.6
22	M ○	0454	5.0	1149	0.5	1716	4.9		
23	TU	0006	0.5	0532	5.1	1228	0.4	1753	5.0
24	W	0041	0.5	0609	5.2	1301	0.4	1829	5.0
25	TH	0112	0.5	0645	5.1	1329	0.5	1904	5.0
26	F	0138	0.6	0718	5.1	1352	0.7	1936	4.9
27	SA	0159	0.8	0748	4.9	1412	0.9	2005	4.7
28	SU	0219	1.0	0816	4.7	1434	1.1	2031	4.5
29	M	0245	1.2	0844	4.5	1503	1.3	2101	4.3

MARCH

Date	Day	Time	m	Time	m	Time	m	Time	m
1	TU ◑	0320	1.4	0922	4.3	1541	1.6	2152	4.1
2	W	0408	1.7	1025	4.1	1639	1.8	2303	4.0
3	TH	0523	1.9	1138	3.9	1812	1.9		
4	F	0017	4.0	0701	1.9	1255	4.0	1942	1.8
5	SA	0133	4.2	0819	1.5	1410	4.2	2051	1.4
6	SU	0240	4.5	0923	1.1	1512	4.6	2150	1.0
7	M	0334	4.9	1019	0.7	1603	4.8	2244	0.6
8	TU	0423	5.2	1111	0.4	1651	5.1	2334	0.3
9	W ●	0511	5.4	1159	0.1	1738	5.2		
10	TH	0020	0.1	0558	5.5	1244	0.0	1824	5.3
11	F	0103	0.0	0644	5.5	1326	-0.1	1907	5.3
12	SA	0143	0.0	0728	5.4	1405	0.1	1947	5.2
13	SU	0222	0.2	0809	5.2	1443	0.3	2025	5.0
14	M	0301	0.5	0849	4.9	1523	0.7	2106	4.7
15	TU ◐	0346	0.9	0934	4.5	1610	1.2	2158	4.4
16	W	0441	1.3	1037	4.1	1711	1.5	2317	4.1
17	TH	0552	1.6	1217	3.9	1831	1.7		
18	F	0101	4.0	0734	1.6	1345	3.9	2021	1.6
19	SA	0214	4.2	0904	1.3	1447	4.2	2130	1.3
20	SU	0308	4.5	0959	1.0	1535	4.4	2220	0.9
21	M	0352	4.7	1044	0.7	1614	4.7	2303	0.7
22	TU	0431	4.9	1125	0.5	1652	4.9	2341	0.6
23	W ○	0509	5.0	1201	0.4	1728	5.0		
24	TH	0015	0.5	0545	5.1	1233	0.5	1804	5.0
25	F	0045	0.5	0621	5.1	1300	0.6	1839	5.0
26	SA	0110	0.6	0654	5.0	1321	0.7	1910	4.9
27	SU	0130	0.8	0723	4.9	1341	0.8	1936	4.8
28	M	0151	0.9	0747	4.7	1405	1.0	1957	4.6
29	TU	0218	1.1	0809	4.5	1434	1.2	2016	4.5
30	W	0252	1.3	0832	4.3	1510	1.4	2058	4.3
31	TH ◑	0337	1.5	0944	4.1	1601	1.7	2221	4.1

APRIL

Date	Day	Time	m	Time	m	Time	m	Time	m
1	F	0444	1.8	1105	4.0	1726	1.9	2339	4.1
2	SA	0622	1.8	1221	4.0	1904	1.8		
3	SU	0053	4.2	0745	1.5	1336	4.2	2020	1.4
4	M	0204	4.5	0854	1.1	1442	4.6	2123	1.0
5	TU	0304	4.9	0953	0.7	1536	4.9	2220	0.6
6	W	0357	5.2	1047	0.3	1626	5.1	2312	0.3
7	TH ●	0448	5.4	1137	0.1	1715	5.3		
8	F	0000	0.0	0537	5.5	1224	-0.1	1801	5.4
9	SA	0045	-0.1	0624	5.5	1307	-0.1	1846	5.4
10	SU	0127	-0.1	0710	5.4	1347	0.1	1927	5.3
11	M	0206	0.1	0752	5.2	1426	0.4	2006	5.1
12	TU	0246	0.5	0832	4.8	1506	0.7	2046	4.8
13	W	0330	0.9	0916	4.5	1552	1.2	2135	4.4
14	TH ◐	0423	1.3	1015	4.1	1650	1.6	2244	4.1
15	F	0530	1.6	1154	3.8	1803	1.8		
16	SA	0030	4.0	0656	1.6	1320	3.9	1937	1.7
17	SU	0145	4.1	0830	1.4	1420	4.1	2057	1.4
18	M	0239	4.4	0927	1.1	1507	4.4	2148	1.1
19	TU	0324	4.6	1012	0.9	1547	4.6	2231	0.9
20	W	0404	4.8	1052	0.7	1624	4.8	2309	0.7
21	TH	0442	4.9	1128	0.6	1702	4.9	2343	0.7
22	F ○	0520	4.9	1200	0.6	1738	5.0		
23	SA	0014	0.7	0556	4.9	1228	0.7	1813	5.0
24	SU	0041	0.7	0629	4.9	1253	0.7	1844	4.9
25	M	0105	0.8	0659	4.8	1317	0.8	1910	4.8
26	TU	0130	0.9	0725	4.7	1344	1.0	1934	4.7
27	W	0200	1.0	0750	4.5	1415	1.1	2000	4.6
28	TH	0236	1.2	0821	4.4	1453	1.3	2044	4.4
29	F	0320	1.4	0923	4.2	1543	1.6	2155	4.3
30	SA ◑	0424	1.6	1039	4.1	1659	1.7	2309	4.3

Chart Datum: 2·91 metres below Ordnance Datum (Newlyn)
HAT is 5·7 metres above Chart Datum

TIME ZONE (UT)
For Summer Time add ONE hour in **non-shaded areas**

FALMOUTH

LAT 50°09'N LONG 5°03'W

TIMES AND HEIGHTS OF HIGH AND LOW WATERS

Dates in amber are **SPRINGS**
Dates in grey are **NEAPS**

2016

MAY

Date	Day	Time	m	Time	m	Time	m	Time	m
1	SU	0550	1.6	1152	4.1	1828	1.7		
2	M	0022	4.4	0711	1.4	1305	4.3	1945	1.4
3	TU	0132	4.6	0822	1.1	1412	4.6	2053	1.0
4	W	0236	4.9	0925	0.7	1510	4.9	2153	0.7
5	TH	0332	5.1	1022	0.4	1602	5.1	2248	0.3
6	F	0425	5.3	1114	0.2	1652	5.3	● 2339	0.1
7	SA	0516	5.4	1203	0.0	1740	5.4		
8	SU	0027	0.0	0606	5.4	1249	0.0	1826	5.4
9	M	0111	0.0	0653	5.3	1332	0.2	1910	5.3
10	TU	0153	0.2	0736	5.1	1412	0.4	1950	5.1
11	W	0235	0.5	0818	4.8	1453	0.8	2031	4.9
12	TH	0318	0.8	0901	4.5	1538	1.1	2115	4.6
13	F	0408	1.2	0953	4.2	1630	1.5	◐ 2212	4.3
14	SA	0506	1.5	1110	3.9	1732	1.7	2336	4.1
15	SU	0613	1.6	1237	3.9	1841	1.7		
16	M	0100	4.1	0727	1.5	1341	4.0	1955	1.6
17	TU	0201	4.2	0835	1.3	1432	4.3	2057	1.4
18	W	0250	4.4	0926	1.1	1515	4.5	2146	1.1
19	TH	0333	4.6	1010	1.0	1555	4.7	2229	1.0
20	F	0414	4.7	1049	0.8	1634	4.8	2307	0.9
21	SA	0453	4.8	1125	0.8	1711	4.9	○ 2342	0.8
22	SU	0530	4.8	1157	0.8	1747	4.9		
23	M	0014	0.8	0604	4.8	1228	0.8	1818	4.9
24	TU	0044	0.8	0637	4.8	1258	0.9	1849	4.9
25	W	0115	0.8	0709	4.7	1330	0.9	1919	4.8
26	TH	0150	0.9	0742	4.6	1405	1.1	1954	4.7
27	F	0228	1.0	0820	4.5	1446	1.2	2039	4.6
28	SA	0314	1.2	0912	4.3	1536	1.4	2137	4.5
29	SU	0413	1.3	1016	4.3	1642	1.5	◑ 2244	4.5
30	M	0524	1.4	1126	4.2	1756	1.5	2353	4.5
31	TU	0638	1.3	1236	4.4	1910	1.3		

JUNE

Date	Day	Time	m	Time	m	Time	m	Time	m
1	W	0103	4.6	0749	1.1	1344	4.6	2020	1.1
2	TH	0210	4.8	0855	0.8	1446	4.8	2125	0.8
3	F	0311	5.0	0956	0.6	1541	5.0	2225	0.5
4	SA	0406	5.1	1053	0.4	1633	5.2	2320	0.3
5	SU	0459	5.2	1145	0.3	1722	5.3	●	
6	M	0011	0.2	0550	5.2	1234	0.2	1810	5.3
7	TU	0059	0.2	0638	5.1	1319	0.3	1854	5.3
8	W	0142	0.3	0722	5.0	1400	0.5	1935	5.1
9	TH	0224	0.5	0803	4.8	1440	0.7	2014	5.0
10	F	0305	0.8	0843	4.6	1521	1.0	2055	4.7
11	SA	0348	1.1	0926	4.3	1606	1.3	2141	4.5
12	SU	0436	1.3	1018	4.1	1657	1.6	◐ 2236	4.2
13	M	0530	1.5	1125	4.0	1754	1.7	2345	4.1
14	TU	0629	1.6	1240	4.0	1856	1.7		
15	W	0103	4.1	0731	1.6	1345	4.1	1958	1.6
16	TH	0207	4.2	0831	1.4	1438	4.3	2055	1.4
17	F	0258	4.4	0922	1.2	1524	4.5	2145	1.2
18	SA	0343	4.6	1008	1.1	1605	4.7	2230	1.1
19	SU	0424	4.7	1050	1.0	1644	4.8	2311	0.9
20	M	0503	4.8	1129	0.9	1720	4.9	○ 2350	0.9
21	TU	0541	4.8	1207	0.8	1756	5.0		
22	W	0027	0.8	0618	4.8	1244	0.8	1831	5.0
23	TH	0105	0.8	0656	4.8	1321	0.8	1908	5.0
24	F	0143	0.8	0734	4.7	1400	0.9	1947	4.9
25	SA	0224	0.8	0814	4.7	1441	1.0	2030	4.9
26	SU	0308	0.9	0900	4.6	1528	1.1	2121	4.8
27	M	0400	1.1	0955	4.4	1623	1.2	◑ 2220	4.6
28	TU	0500	1.2	1059	4.4	1728	1.3	2326	4.6
29	W	0606	1.2	1208	4.4	1837	1.3		
30	TH	0037	4.5	0716	1.2	1321	4.5	1950	1.2

JULY

Date	Day	Time	m	Time	m	Time	m	Time	m
1	F	0149	4.6	0828	1.0	1428	4.7	2102	1.0
2	SA	0255	4.7	0936	0.8	1526	4.9	2208	0.8
3	SU	0353	4.9	1037	0.6	1619	5.1	2307	0.5
4	M	0446	5.0	1132	0.5	1708	5.2	●	
5	TU	0000	0.4	0535	5.0	1222	0.4	1754	5.2
6	W	0048	0.3	0622	5.0	1307	0.4	1837	5.3
7	TH	0130	0.3	0704	5.0	1347	0.5	1917	5.2
8	F	0209	0.5	0743	4.9	1424	0.7	1954	5.1
9	SA	0246	0.7	0819	4.7	1459	0.9	2031	4.9
10	SU	0322	1.0	0856	4.5	1535	1.2	2108	4.7
11	M	0359	1.3	0937	4.3	1615	1.5	2151	4.4
12	TU	0442	1.5	1025	4.2	1702	1.7	◐ 2242	4.2
13	W	0534	1.7	1124	4.1	1801	1.9	2343	4.1
14	TH	0635	1.8	1234	4.0	1905	1.9		
15	F	0057	4.1	0738	1.7	1350	4.2	2008	1.7
16	SA	0214	4.2	0838	1.5	1449	4.4	2106	1.5
17	SU	0310	4.4	0931	1.3	1536	4.6	2157	1.2
18	M	0356	4.6	1019	1.1	1617	4.8	2244	1.0
19	TU	0438	4.7	1105	0.9	1655	5.0	○ 2329	0.8
20	W	0519	4.9	1149	0.8	1734	5.1		
21	TH	0012	0.7	0600	4.9	1231	0.7	1814	5.2
22	F	0054	0.6	0642	5.0	1312	0.6	1855	5.2
23	SA	0135	0.5	0723	4.9	1352	0.6	1936	5.2
24	SU	0215	0.6	0803	4.9	1432	0.7	2018	5.1
25	M	0257	0.7	0845	4.8	1514	0.9	2104	5.0
26	TU	0342	0.9	0934	4.6	1603	1.1	◑ 2157	4.7
27	W	0435	1.1	1032	4.5	1701	1.3	2300	4.5
28	TH	0537	1.3	1143	4.4	1809	1.4		
29	F	0015	4.4	0648	1.4	1303	4.4	1927	1.4
30	SA	0136	4.4	0809	1.3	1417	4.5	2050	1.2
31	SU	0247	4.5	0925	1.1	1517	4.8	2200	1.0

AUGUST

Date	Day	Time	m	Time	m	Time	m	Time	m
1	M	0345	4.7	1028	0.9	1608	5.0	2258	0.7
2	TU	0435	4.9	1121	0.6	1655	5.1	● 2349	0.5
3	W	0521	5.0	1209	0.5	1738	5.2		
4	TH	0034	0.4	0603	5.0	1251	0.5	1817	5.3
5	F	0114	0.4	0642	5.0	1328	0.5	1855	5.2
6	SA	0149	0.5	0718	5.0	1401	0.7	1930	5.1
7	SU	0220	0.7	0752	4.9	1431	0.9	2003	5.0
8	M	0249	1.0	0826	4.7	1458	1.2	2036	4.8
9	TU	0316	1.2	0900	4.5	1525	1.4	2111	4.6
10	W	0345	1.5	0939	4.3	1557	1.7	◐ 2155	4.3
11	TH	0425	1.8	1029	4.2	1649	1.9	2251	4.1
12	F	0529	1.9	1131	4.1	1807	2.0	2358	4.0
13	SA	0647	2.0	1244	4.1	1925	1.9		
14	SU	0115	4.1	0758	1.8	1405	4.3	2031	1.7
15	M	0234	4.3	0859	1.5	1504	4.6	2128	1.4
16	TU	0328	4.6	0953	1.2	1548	4.9	2220	1.0
17	W	0413	4.8	1043	0.9	1629	5.1	2309	0.8
18	TH	0456	5.0	1131	0.7	1711	5.3	○ 2355	0.5
19	F	0540	5.1	1216	0.5	1755	5.4		
20	SA	0039	0.4	0624	5.2	1259	0.4	1838	5.4
21	SU	0121	0.3	0707	5.2	1339	0.4	1921	5.4
22	M	0201	0.3	0748	5.1	1418	0.5	2003	5.3
23	TU	0241	0.5	0828	5.0	1458	0.7	2046	5.1
24	W	0322	0.8	0912	4.8	1543	1.0	2135	4.8
25	TH	0411	1.1	1006	4.5	1637	1.3	◑ 2237	4.4
26	F	0510	1.4	1119	4.3	1746	1.6		
27	SA	0001	4.2	0624	1.6	1250	4.3	1914	1.6
28	SU	0131	4.2	0759	1.6	1407	4.4	2049	1.4
29	M	0241	4.4	0920	1.3	1507	4.7	2154	1.1
30	TU	0336	4.6	1018	1.0	1555	4.9	2247	0.7
31	W	0421	4.8	1107	0.7	1638	5.1	2333	0.5

Chart Datum: 2·91 metres below Ordnance Datum (Newlyn)
HAT is 5·7 metres above Chart Datum

TIME ZONE (UT)
For Summer Time add ONE hour in **non-shaded areas**

FALMOUTH

LAT 50°09′N LONG 5°03′W

TIMES AND HEIGHTS OF HIGH AND LOW WATERS

Dates in amber are **SPRINGS**
Dates in grey are **NEAPS**

2016

SEPTEMBER

Date	Day	Time	m	Time	m	Time	m	Time	m
1	TH ●	0502	5.0	1151	0.5	1717	5.2		
2	F	0014	0.4	0539	5.1	1230	0.5	1754	5.3
3	SA	0051	0.4	0616	5.1	1304	0.6	1830	5.3
4	SU	0122	0.6	0651	5.1	1334	0.7	1904	5.2
5	M	0149	0.7	0724	5.0	1359	0.9	1935	5.0
6	TU	0212	1.0	0756	4.9	1420	1.1	2005	4.8
7	W	0232	1.2	0825	4.7	1440	1.4	2036	4.6
8	TH	0255	1.4	0859	4.5	1508	1.6	2115	4.4
9	F	0328	1.7	0944	4.3	1550	1.9	◐ 2211	4.1
10	SA	0420	2.0	1046	4.1	1702	2.1	2319	4.0
11	SU	0551	2.1	1157	4.1	1842	2.1		
12	M	0034	4.0	0721	2.0	1313	4.3	1959	1.8
13	TU	0155	4.3	0830	1.6	1424	4.6	2102	1.4
14	W	0258	4.6	0928	1.3	1517	4.9	2156	1.0
15	TH	0346	4.9	1021	0.9	1603	5.2	2247	0.7
16	F	0431	5.1	1111	0.6	1648	5.4	○ 2335	0.4
17	SA	0517	5.3	1157	0.4	1734	5.5		
18	SU	0020	0.2	0602	5.4	1241	0.2	1819	5.6
19	M	0103	0.1	0646	5.4	1322	0.2	1904	5.5
20	TU	0143	0.2	0728	5.3	1402	0.3	1947	5.4
21	W	0222	0.4	0809	5.2	1441	0.6	2029	5.1
22	TH	0303	0.8	0851	4.9	1525	1.0	2116	4.7
23	F	0349	1.2	0942	4.6	1618	1.4	◑ 2219	4.3
24	SA	0448	1.6	1056	4.3	1728	1.7	2353	4.1
25	SU	0605	1.8	1234	4.2	1906	1.7		
26	M	0123	4.1	0750	1.7	1352	4.4	2040	1.5
27	TU	0230	4.3	0907	1.4	1450	4.6	2139	1.1
28	W	0320	4.6	1001	1.1	1536	4.9	2227	0.8
29	TH	0401	4.8	1046	0.8	1616	5.1	2309	0.6
30	F	0438	5.0	1126	0.6	1653	5.2	2347	0.5

OCTOBER

Date	Day	Time	m	Time	m	Time	m	Time	m
1	SA ●	0513	5.1	1203	0.6	1729	5.2		
2	SU	0021	0.5	0548	5.1	1235	0.6	1804	5.2
3	M	0051	0.6	0623	5.1	1304	0.7	1837	5.1
4	TU	0116	0.8	0656	5.1	1327	0.9	1908	5.0
5	W	0137	1.0	0727	5.0	1347	1.1	1937	4.8
6	TH	0157	1.2	0754	4.8	1408	1.3	2006	4.6
7	F	0222	1.4	0824	4.6	1437	1.5	2041	4.4
8	SA	0255	1.6	0906	4.4	1517	1.7	2137	4.2
9	SU	0340	1.9	1009	4.2	1617	2.0	◐ 2248	4.0
10	M	0459	2.1	1120	4.2	1759	2.0		
11	TU	0002	4.0	0641	2.0	1233	4.3	1925	1.8
12	W	0118	4.3	0758	1.7	1344	4.6	2032	1.4
13	TH	0225	4.6	0901	1.3	1444	4.9	2130	1.0
14	F	0318	4.9	0956	0.9	1535	5.2	2222	0.6
15	SA	0405	5.2	1047	0.5	1623	5.4	2312	0.3
16	SU	0452	5.4	1136	0.3	1712	5.6	○ 2359	0.1
17	M	0539	5.5	1221	0.1	1800	5.6		
18	TU	0043	0.1	0625	5.5	1305	0.1	1846	5.5
19	W	0125	0.2	0709	5.4	1346	0.2	1930	5.3
20	TH	0205	0.4	0750	5.3	1427	0.5	2014	5.0
21	F	0246	0.8	0833	5.0	1511	0.9	2101	4.6
22	SA	0332	1.2	0922	4.7	1603	1.3	◑ 2201	4.3
23	SU	0428	1.6	1030	4.3	1710	1.6	2335	4.0
24	M	0541	1.8	1206	4.2	1839	1.7		
25	TU	0101	4.0	0716	1.8	1325	4.3	2011	1.5
26	W	0206	4.2	0838	1.5	1423	4.5	2111	1.2
27	TH	0255	4.5	0932	1.2	1509	4.7	2157	0.9
28	F	0335	4.7	1016	1.0	1549	4.9	2238	0.8
29	SA	0411	4.9	1055	0.8	1626	5.0	2314	0.7
30	SU	0446	5.0	1131	0.7	1703	5.1	● 2348	0.7
31	M	0522	5.1	1204	0.7	1739	5.1		

NOVEMBER

Date	Day	Time	m	Time	m	Time	m	Time	m
1	TU	0018	0.7	0557	5.1	1234	0.8	1812	5.0
2	W	0045	0.8	0631	5.1	1259	0.9	1844	4.9
3	TH	0108	1.0	0701	5.0	1322	1.0	1914	4.8
4	F	0133	1.1	0730	4.9	1348	1.1	1945	4.6
5	SA	0201	1.3	0800	4.7	1419	1.3	2020	4.4
6	SU	0235	1.5	0840	4.5	1459	1.5	2111	4.2
7	M	0319	1.7	0939	4.4	1554	1.8	◐ 2219	4.1
8	TU	0426	1.9	1047	4.3	1719	1.9	2330	4.1
9	W	0559	1.9	1157	4.4	1846	1.7		
10	TH	0042	4.3	0720	1.7	1307	4.6	1958	1.4
11	F	0150	4.5	0828	1.3	1411	4.8	2100	1.0
12	SA	0248	4.8	0928	0.9	1508	5.1	2156	0.6
13	SU	0340	5.1	1022	0.6	1600	5.3	2248	0.4
14	M	0429	5.3	1114	0.3	1651	5.4	○ 2338	0.2
15	TU	0518	5.4	1203	0.2	1741	5.5		
16	W	0024	0.2	0605	5.5	1249	0.1	1829	5.4
17	TH	0109	0.2	0651	5.4	1333	0.2	1915	5.2
18	F	0151	0.4	0734	5.3	1415	0.5	2000	5.0
19	SA	0233	0.7	0817	5.1	1459	0.8	2045	4.6
20	SU	0317	1.1	0902	4.8	1548	1.2	2137	4.3
21	M	0409	1.5	0957	4.5	1646	1.5	◑ 2250	4.1
22	TU	0510	1.7	1113	4.2	1754	1.7		
23	W	0018	4.0	0620	1.8	1238	4.2	1912	1.6
24	TH	0126	4.1	0738	1.7	1343	4.3	2023	1.5
25	F	0219	4.3	0845	1.5	1435	4.5	2116	1.2
26	SA	0303	4.5	0935	1.2	1519	4.7	2159	1.0
27	SU	0342	4.7	1017	1.0	1559	4.8	2237	0.9
28	M	0420	4.9	1056	0.9	1637	4.9	2314	0.8
29	TU	0457	5.0	1133	0.8	1715	4.9	● 2347	0.8
30	W	0534	5.1	1206	0.8	1751	4.9		

DECEMBER

Date	Day	Time	m	Time	m	Time	m	Time	m
1	TH	0018	0.8	0609	5.1	1236	0.9	1824	4.9
2	F	0047	0.9	0641	5.0	1305	0.9	1857	4.8
3	SA	0116	1.0	0712	4.9	1335	1.0	1930	4.7
4	SU	0148	1.1	0745	4.8	1409	1.1	2005	4.5
5	M	0224	1.3	0823	4.7	1449	1.3	2050	4.4
6	TU	0307	1.5	0913	4.6	1539	1.4	2149	4.2
7	W	0404	1.6	1016	4.5	1646	1.6	◐ 2257	4.2
8	TH	0518	1.7	1122	4.4	1804	1.5		
9	F	0006	4.2	0637	1.6	1231	4.5	1918	1.4
10	SA	0115	4.4	0751	1.4	1339	4.7	2027	1.1
11	SU	0219	4.7	0858	1.1	1442	4.9	2129	0.8
12	M	0317	4.9	0959	0.7	1540	5.1	2226	0.5
13	TU	0410	5.2	1054	0.5	1634	5.2	2319	0.4
14	W ○	0500	5.3	1147	0.3	1725	5.3		
15	TH	0009	0.3	0549	5.4	1236	0.2	1814	5.2
16	F	0056	0.3	0635	5.4	1322	0.2	1901	5.1
17	SA	0140	0.4	0718	5.3	1405	0.4	1943	4.9
18	SU	0221	0.6	0800	5.2	1447	0.6	2025	4.7
19	M	0301	0.9	0840	4.9	1529	0.9	2108	4.5
20	TU	0344	1.2	0924	4.7	1615	1.3	2157	4.2
21	W	0433	1.5	1016	4.4	1708	1.5	◑ 2258	4.0
22	TH	0530	1.7	1119	4.2	1808	1.7		
23	F	0013	4.0	0633	1.8	1236	4.1	1914	1.7
24	SA	0127	4.1	0740	1.7	1348	4.2	2018	1.5
25	SU	0224	4.3	0843	1.6	1444	4.3	2113	1.3
26	M	0312	4.5	0936	1.3	1531	4.5	2159	1.1
27	TU	0355	4.7	1022	1.1	1613	4.7	2241	1.0
28	W	0435	4.9	1103	1.0	1653	4.8	2319	0.9
29	TH	0513	5.0	1141	0.9	1731	4.8	● 2355	0.8
30	F	0549	5.0	1216	0.8	1807	4.8		
31	SA	0030	0.8	0623	5.0	1251	0.8	1842	4.8

Chart Datum: 2·91 metres below Ordnance Datum (Newlyn)
HAT is 5·7 metres above Chart Datum

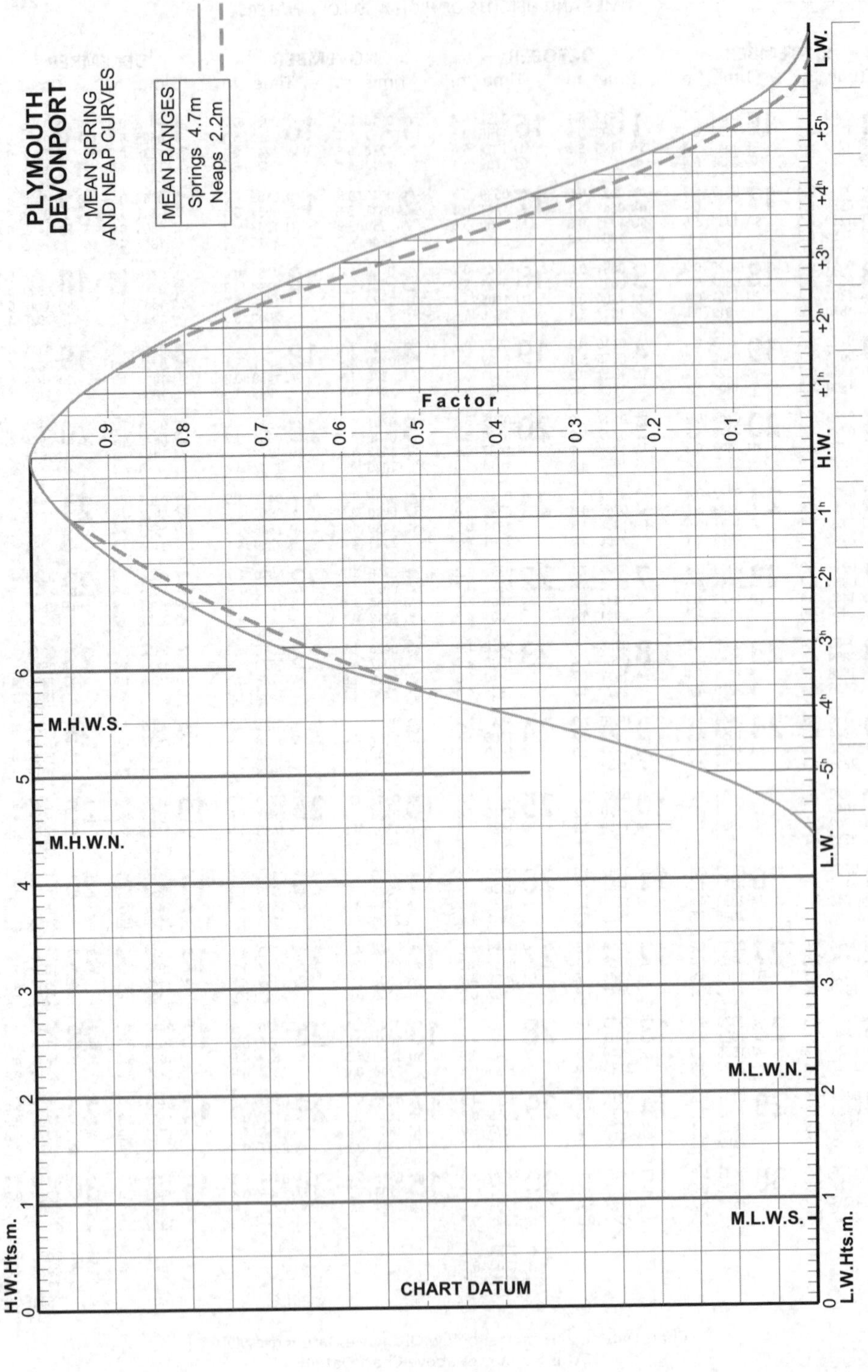

PLYMOUTH
DEVONPORT
MEAN SPRING
AND NEAP CURVES
MEAN RANGES
Springs 4.7m
Neaps 2.2m
Factor
0.9
0.8
0.7
0.6
0.5
0.4
0.3
0.2
0.1
L.W.
-5h
-4h
-3h
-2h
-1h
H.W.
+1h
+2h
+3h
+4h
+5h
L.W.
H.W.Hts.m.
0
1
2
3
4
5
6
M.H.W.S.
M.H.W.N.
M.L.W.N.
M.L.W.S.
CHART DATUM
L.W.Hts.m.

TIME ZONE (UT)
For Summer Time add ONE hour in **non-shaded areas**

PLYMOUTH (DEVONPORT)

LAT 50°22′N LONG 4°11′W

TIMES AND HEIGHTS OF HIGH AND LOW WATERS

Dates in amber are **SPRINGS**
Dates in grey are **NEAPS**

2016

JANUARY

Date	Day	Time	m	Time	m	Time	m	Time	m	Moon
1	F	0346	1.8	0943	4.9	1612	1.9	2211	4.6	
2	SA	0427	2.1	1028	4.7	1658	2.1	2302	4.4	◑
3	SU	0520	2.3	1122	4.5	1756	2.2			
4	M	0007	4.4	0626	2.4	1232	4.5	1902	2.2	
5	TU	0124	4.4	0735	2.3	1351	4.5	2007	2.1	
6	W	0234	4.6	0839	2.1	1458	4.7	2107	1.9	
7	TH	0331	4.8	0936	1.8	1554	4.9	2200	1.6	
8	F	0421	5.1	1027	1.5	1643	5.0	2249	1.3	
9	SA	0506	5.3	1115	1.2	1729	5.2	2334	1.1	
10	SU	0549	5.4	1200	1.0	1813	5.3			●
11	M	0018	1.0	0630	5.5	1244	0.9	1854	5.3	
12	TU	0101	0.9	0712	5.6	1327	0.8	1936	5.4	
13	W	0142	0.9	0753	5.6	1408	0.8	2017	5.3	
14	TH	0223	1.0	0835	5.5	1450	0.9	2059	5.2	
15	F	0304	1.1	0918	5.4	1532	1.1	2143	5.1	
16	SA	0348	1.3	1005	5.2	1619	1.4	2233	4.9	◐
17	SU	0438	1.6	1059	5.0	1714	1.6	2333	4.7	
18	M	0541	1.8	1206	4.8	1824	1.9			
19	TU	0048	4.6	0702	2.0	1324	4.7	1948	1.9	
20	W	0206	4.7	0830	1.9	1439	4.7	2106	1.7	
21	TH	0314	4.9	0941	1.6	1544	4.9	2208	1.4	
22	F	0412	5.1	1038	1.3	1640	5.1	2301	1.1	
23	SA	0503	5.3	1128	1.0	1729	5.2	2348	0.9	
24	SU	0548	5.5	1213	0.8	1813	5.3			○
25	M	0030	0.8	0628	5.5	1255	0.7	1852	5.3	
26	TU	0109	0.8	0705	5.5	1332	0.8	1927	5.3	
27	W	0144	0.9	0738	5.5	1406	0.9	1958	5.2	
28	TH	0215	1.1	0809	5.4	1435	1.1	2028	5.1	
29	F	0243	1.3	0841	5.2	1503	1.4	2100	4.9	
30	SA	0310	1.5	0914	5.0	1529	1.6	2135	4.7	
31	SU	0337	1.8	0950	4.8	1558	1.9	2215	4.6	

FEBRUARY

Date	Day	Time	m	Time	m	Time	m	Time	m	Moon
1	M	0412	2.0	1033	4.6	1640	2.1	2304	4.4	◑
2	TU	0511	2.3	1129	4.4	1753	2.3			
3	W	0010	4.3	0638	2.3	1242	4.3	1915	2.3	
4	TH	0134	4.4	0754	2.2	1411	4.4	2026	2.0	
5	F	0252	4.6	0901	1.9	1523	4.6	2129	1.7	
6	SA	0351	4.9	1000	1.5	1619	4.9	2225	1.4	
7	SU	0441	5.2	1054	1.2	1708	5.1	2317	1.1	
8	M	0528	5.4	1144	0.8	1755	5.3			●
9	TU	0005	0.8	0612	5.6	1232	0.6	1839	5.4	
10	W	0050	0.6	0657	5.7	1316	0.5	1922	5.5	
11	TH	0133	0.5	0741	5.7	1358	0.4	2005	5.5	
12	F	0213	0.5	0823	5.7	1438	0.5	2045	5.4	
13	SA	0253	0.7	0905	5.5	1518	0.8	2126	5.3	
14	SU	0333	1.0	0949	5.3	1559	1.1	2210	5.0	
15	M	0417	1.3	1037	4.9	1647	1.5	2303	4.7	◐
16	TU	0512	1.7	1140	4.6	1748	1.9			
17	W	0018	4.5	0626	2.0	1304	4.4	1914	2.1	
18	TH	0143	4.5	0810	2.0	1424	4.5	2049	1.9	
19	F	0256	4.7	0930	1.7	1531	4.6	2156	1.6	
20	SA	0356	4.9	1026	1.3	1627	4.9	2248	1.2	
21	SU	0446	5.2	1114	1.0	1713	5.1	2332	0.9	
22	M	0529	5.4	1157	0.8	1754	5.2			○
23	TU	0013	0.8	0607	5.5	1236	0.7	1829	5.3	
24	W	0050	0.7	0642	5.5	1311	0.7	1902	5.3	
25	TH	0123	0.8	0714	5.4	1342	0.8	1932	5.2	
26	F	0150	0.9	0745	5.3	1408	1.0	2002	5.2	
27	SA	0215	1.1	0815	5.2	1429	1.2	2032	5.0	
28	SU	0236	1.3	0846	5.0	1449	1.4	2102	4.9	
29	M	0258	1.5	0917	4.8	1513	1.6	2134	4.7	

MARCH

Date	Day	Time	m	Time	m	Time	m	Time	m	Moon
1	TU	0327	1.8	0953	4.6	1547	1.9	2216	4.5	◑
2	W	0410	2.0	1044	4.4	1640	2.2	2315	4.3	
3	TH	0530	2.3	1151	4.2	1821	2.3			
4	F	0032	4.3	0713	2.2	1319	4.3	1949	2.1	
5	SA	0204	4.5	0828	1.9	1449	4.5	2100	1.8	
6	SU	0317	4.8	0934	1.5	1552	4.8	2202	1.4	
7	M	0413	5.1	1032	1.0	1644	5.1	2257	0.9	
8	TU	0503	5.4	1125	0.7	1732	5.4	2347	0.6	
9	W	0551	5.6	1213	0.4	1819	5.5			●
10	TH	0033	0.3	0638	5.8	1258	0.2	1903	5.6	
11	F	0117	0.2	0723	5.8	1341	0.2	1946	5.7	
12	SA	0158	0.3	0807	5.8	1421	0.3	2027	5.6	
13	SU	0237	0.5	0849	5.6	1500	0.6	2107	5.4	
14	M	0317	0.8	0931	5.2	1540	1.0	2147	5.1	
15	TU	0359	1.2	1017	4.9	1625	1.5	2235	4.7	◐
16	W	0450	1.7	1119	4.5	1721	1.9	2349	4.4	
17	TH	0559	2.0	1247	4.3	1842	2.2			
18	F	0121	4.4	0748	2.1	1407	4.3	2029	2.1	
19	SA	0235	4.5	0911	1.8	1513	4.5	2136	1.7	
20	SU	0334	4.8	1007	1.4	1606	4.8	2227	1.3	
21	M	0422	5.1	1052	1.0	1650	5.0	2310	1.0	
22	TU	0504	5.2	1134	0.8	1728	5.2	2350	0.8	
23	W	0542	5.3	1211	0.7	1802	5.3			○
24	TH	0025	0.7	0616	5.4	1245	0.7	1834	5.3	
25	F	0056	0.8	0648	5.4	1314	0.8	1905	5.3	
26	SA	0123	0.9	0720	5.3	1338	1.0	1935	5.2	
27	SU	0146	1.0	0751	5.2	1358	1.1	2005	5.1	
28	M	0207	1.2	0820	5.0	1419	1.3	2033	5.0	
29	TU	0230	1.4	0849	4.8	1443	1.5	2102	4.8	
30	W	0259	1.6	0924	4.6	1517	1.8	2141	4.6	
31	TH	0341	1.8	1013	4.4	1605	2.0	2238	4.4	◑

APRIL

Date	Day	Time	m	Time	m	Time	m	Time	m	Moon
1	F	0447	2.1	1119	4.2	1730	2.2	2350	4.4	
2	SA	0635	2.1	1239	4.3	1914	2.1			
3	SU	0116	4.5	0758	1.8	1412	4.5	2031	1.8	
4	M	0240	4.8	0907	1.4	1522	4.8	2136	1.3	
5	TU	0343	5.1	1007	1.0	1617	5.1	2233	0.9	
6	W	0437	5.4	1101	0.6	1707	5.4	2325	0.5	
7	TH	0527	5.7	1150	0.3	1755	5.6			●
8	F	0012	0.3	0615	5.8	1237	0.1	1841	5.7	
9	SA	0058	0.1	0703	5.8	1321	0.1	1925	5.7	
10	SU	0140	0.2	0748	5.7	1402	0.3	2007	5.6	
11	M	0221	0.4	0832	5.5	1442	0.6	2047	5.4	
12	TU	0301	0.7	0915	5.2	1522	1.0	2126	5.1	
13	W	0344	1.2	1001	4.8	1606	1.5	2210	4.8	
14	TH	0434	1.6	1102	4.4	1700	1.9	2319	4.5	◐
15	F	0537	2.0	1226	4.2	1810	2.2			
16	SA	0053	4.4	0709	2.1	1342	4.3	1948	2.1	
17	SU	0205	4.5	0838	1.8	1444	4.5	2103	1.8	
18	M	0302	4.7	0935	1.5	1535	4.7	2155	1.5	
19	TU	0351	4.9	1022	1.2	1618	4.9	2240	1.2	
20	W	0433	5.1	1103	1.0	1656	5.1	2319	1.0	
21	TH	0511	5.2	1140	0.9	1732	5.2	2355	0.9	
22	F	0547	5.3	1213	0.9	1806	5.3			○
23	SA	0026	0.9	0622	5.3	1242	0.9	1839	5.3	
24	SU	0054	0.9	0656	5.2	1308	1.0	1911	5.2	
25	M	0120	1.0	0728	5.1	1332	1.1	1941	5.2	
26	TU	0145	1.2	0759	5.0	1356	1.3	2010	5.1	
27	W	0212	1.3	0830	4.8	1425	1.5	2040	4.9	
28	TH	0244	1.5	0906	4.7	1500	1.7	2120	4.8	
29	F	0327	1.7	0954	4.5	1549	1.9	2214	4.6	
30	SA	0429	1.9	1056	4.4	1703	2.1	2321	4.5	◑

Chart Datum: 3·22 metres below Ordnance Datum (Newlyn)
HAT is 5·9 metres above Chart Datum

TIME ZONE (UT)
For Summer Time add ONE hour in **non-shaded areas**

PLYMOUTH (DEVONPORT)

LAT 50°22'N LONG 4°11'W

TIMES AND HEIGHTS OF HIGH AND LOW WATERS

Dates in amber are **SPRINGS**
Dates in grey are **NEAPS**

2016

MAY

Date	Day	Time	m	Time	m	Time	m	Time	m
1	SU	0601	1.9	1211	4.4	1839	2.0		
2	M	0040	4.6	0725	1.7	1336	4.6	1959	1.8
3	TU	0203	4.8	0837	1.4	1448	4.8	2108	1.4
4	W	0311	5.1	0939	1.0	1547	5.2	2207	1.0
5	TH	0409	5.4	1035	0.6	1640	5.4	2301	0.6
6	F	0503	5.6	1127	0.4	1730	5.6	● 2350	0.4
7	SA	0554	5.7	1214	0.3	1818	5.7		
8	SU	0037	0.3	0642	5.7	1300	0.3	1903	5.7
9	M	0122	0.3	0730	5.6	1343	0.4	1947	5.6
10	TU	0205	0.5	0815	5.4	1425	0.7	2028	5.4
11	W	0247	0.8	0900	5.1	1506	1.1	2108	5.2
12	TH	0330	1.1	0945	4.8	1550	1.5	2148	4.9
13	F	0417	1.5	1040	4.5	1639	1.8	◐ 2241	4.6
14	SA	0512	1.8	1152	4.3	1738	2.1		
15	SU	0007	4.4	0619	2.0	1303	4.3	1849	2.1
16	M	0122	4.4	0740	1.9	1403	4.4	2007	2.0
17	TU	0221	4.6	0848	1.7	1454	4.6	2109	1.8
18	W	0312	4.7	0939	1.5	1540	4.8	2159	1.5
19	TH	0357	4.9	1024	1.3	1621	5.0	2241	1.3
20	F	0438	5.0	1103	1.1	1700	5.1	2319	1.1
21	SA	0518	5.1	1138	1.1	1738	5.2	○ 2354	1.1
22	SU	0557	5.2	1210	1.1	1814	5.3		
23	M	0026	1.0	0634	5.1	1241	1.1	1849	5.3
24	TU	0058	1.1	0710	5.1	1312	1.2	1922	5.2
25	W	0129	1.1	0743	5.0	1342	1.2	1953	5.2
26	TH	0202	1.2	0817	4.9	1416	1.4	2027	5.1
27	F	0239	1.3	0856	4.8	1455	1.5	2108	5.0
28	SA	0323	1.5	0943	4.7	1543	1.7	2159	4.8
29	SU	0419	1.7	1039	4.6	1646	1.9	◑ 2259	4.8
30	M	0532	1.7	1147	4.5	1805	1.9		
31	TU	0011	4.7	0651	1.7	1303	4.6	1925	1.7

JUNE

Date	Day	Time	m	Time	m	Time	m	Time	m
1	W	0130	4.8	0805	1.4	1416	4.8	2038	1.5
2	TH	0242	5.0	0911	1.1	1519	5.1	2141	1.1
3	F	0344	5.2	1010	0.9	1615	5.3	2238	0.8
4	SA	0441	5.4	1105	0.6	1707	5.5	2331	0.6
5	SU	0534	5.5	1155	0.5	1757	5.6	●	
6	M	0019	0.5	0624	5.5	1242	0.5	1844	5.6
7	TU	0106	0.5	0713	5.4	1327	0.6	1928	5.6
8	W	0150	0.6	0759	5.3	1409	0.8	2010	5.4
9	TH	0232	0.8	0843	5.1	1450	1.0	2049	5.2
10	F	0314	1.1	0924	4.9	1531	1.4	2125	5.0
11	SA	0356	1.4	1006	4.6	1614	1.7	2204	4.8
12	SU	0441	1.7	1055	4.4	1702	1.9	◐ 2254	4.6
13	M	0534	1.9	1157	4.3	1758	2.1		
14	TU	0005	4.4	0633	2.0	1304	4.4	1900	2.1
15	W	0122	4.4	0738	2.0	1403	4.5	2006	2.0
16	TH	0223	4.5	0840	1.8	1456	4.7	2105	1.8
17	F	0317	4.7	0934	1.6	1544	4.9	2157	1.6
18	SA	0405	4.8	1020	1.4	1628	5.0	2242	1.4
19	SU	0450	5.0	1102	1.3	1711	5.2	2323	1.2
20	M	0533	5.1	1141	1.2	1751	5.2	○	
21	TU	0002	1.1	0614	5.1	1220	1.1	1829	5.3
22	W	0041	1.0	0654	5.1	1257	1.1	1906	5.3
23	TH	0118	1.0	0732	5.1	1334	1.1	1942	5.3
24	F	0156	1.1	0809	5.0	1411	1.2	2019	5.2
25	SA	0235	1.1	0849	5.0	1451	1.3	2100	5.2
26	SU	0318	1.2	0933	4.9	1536	1.4	2147	5.1
27	M	0407	1.4	1024	4.8	1629	1.6	◑ 2241	4.9
28	TU	0506	1.5	1123	4.7	1733	1.7	2345	4.8
29	W	0616	1.6	1233	4.7	1850	1.8		
30	TH	0101	4.8	0733	1.6	1347	4.8	2009	1.6

JULY

Date	Day	Time	m	Time	m	Time	m	Time	m
1	F	0217	4.9	0845	1.4	1454	5.0	2119	1.4
2	SA	0324	5.0	0950	1.2	1555	5.2	2220	1.1
3	SU	0424	5.2	1047	0.9	1649	5.4	2315	0.8
4	M	0518	5.3	1139	0.8	1739	5.5	●	
5	TU	0005	0.7	0609	5.3	1227	0.7	1826	5.6
6	W	0052	0.6	0656	5.3	1312	0.7	1910	5.5
7	TH	0136	0.6	0740	5.2	1353	0.8	1950	5.5
8	F	0216	0.8	0820	5.1	1431	1.0	2025	5.3
9	SA	0253	1.0	0855	5.0	1507	1.2	2057	5.1
10	SU	0329	1.3	0928	4.8	1543	1.5	2130	4.9
11	M	0405	1.6	1004	4.6	1622	1.8	2209	4.7
12	TU	0446	1.8	1048	4.5	1708	2.0	◐ 2257	4.5
13	W	0537	2.0	1145	4.4	1805	2.2	2359	4.4
14	TH	0638	2.1	1256	4.4	1910	2.2		
15	F	0119	4.4	0742	2.0	1407	4.5	2014	2.0
16	SA	0234	4.5	0844	1.9	1507	4.7	2113	1.8
17	SU	0333	4.7	0940	1.6	1559	4.9	2207	1.5
18	M	0424	4.8	1030	1.4	1645	5.1	2256	1.3
19	TU	0511	5.0	1117	1.2	1729	5.3	○ 2341	1.1
20	W	0555	5.1	1201	1.1	1811	5.4		
21	TH	0025	0.9	0637	5.2	1244	1.0	1851	5.4
22	F	0107	0.8	0719	5.2	1324	0.9	1930	5.5
23	SA	0148	0.8	0759	5.2	1404	0.9	2010	5.4
24	SU	0227	0.8	0839	5.2	1443	1.0	2051	5.4
25	M	0308	1.0	0921	5.1	1524	1.2	2134	5.2
26	TU	0351	1.2	1006	4.9	1610	1.4	◑ 2223	5.0
27	W	0441	1.4	1100	4.8	1706	1.6	2322	4.8
28	TH	0543	1.7	1206	4.6	1818	1.8		
29	F	0037	4.6	0702	1.8	1324	4.6	1944	1.8
30	SA	0159	4.6	0825	1.7	1437	4.8	2104	1.6
31	SU	0311	4.8	0936	1.5	1540	5.0	2209	1.3

AUGUST

Date	Day	Time	m	Time	m	Time	m	Time	m
1	M	0412	5.0	1035	1.2	1635	5.2	2304	1.0
2	TU	0506	5.1	1126	0.9	1724	5.4	● 2352	0.7
3	W	0554	5.2	1212	0.7	1809	5.5		
4	TH	0037	0.6	0637	5.3	1255	0.7	1849	5.5
5	F	0118	0.6	0717	5.3	1333	0.7	1925	5.5
6	SA	0155	0.7	0751	5.2	1408	0.9	1957	5.4
7	SU	0228	0.9	0821	5.1	1439	1.1	2027	5.2
8	M	0257	1.2	0852	4.9	1508	1.4	2058	5.0
9	TU	0324	1.5	0925	4.8	1537	1.7	2133	4.8
10	W	0353	1.8	1003	4.6	1610	2.0	◐ 2212	4.6
11	TH	0430	2.0	1049	4.4	1701	2.2	2303	4.4
12	F	0534	2.2	1150	4.3	1818	2.3		
13	SA	0011	4.3	0653	2.3	1310	4.3	1931	2.2
14	SU	0146	4.3	0803	2.1	1430	4.5	2038	2.0
15	M	0303	4.5	0907	1.8	1530	4.8	2138	1.6
16	TU	0400	4.8	1003	1.5	1620	5.1	2231	1.3
17	W	0448	5.0	1055	1.2	1706	5.3	2321	1.0
18	TH	0534	5.2	1143	0.9	1750	5.5	○	
19	F	0007	0.7	0618	5.3	1228	0.8	1832	5.6
20	SA	0052	0.6	0701	5.4	1310	0.6	1915	5.7
21	SU	0133	0.5	0742	5.4	1351	0.6	1956	5.6
22	M	0213	0.6	0823	5.4	1430	0.7	2038	5.5
23	TU	0252	0.8	0904	5.3	1509	1.0	2119	5.3
24	W	0332	1.1	0946	5.1	1551	1.3	2205	5.0
25	TH	0418	1.4	1036	4.8	1643	1.6	◑ 2301	4.7
26	F	0516	1.8	1142	4.6	1752	2.0		
27	SA	0020	4.5	0636	2.0	1306	4.5	1929	2.0
28	SU	0150	4.4	0813	2.0	1424	4.7	2056	1.8
29	M	0303	4.6	0927	1.7	1528	4.9	2159	1.4
30	TU	0403	4.9	1023	1.3	1621	5.2	2250	1.0
31	W	0452	5.1	1111	1.0	1707	5.4	2336	0.8

Chart Datum: 3·22 metres below Ordnance Datum (Newlyn)
HAT is 5·9 metres above Chart Datum

TIME ZONE (UT)
For Summer Time add ONE hour in **non-shaded areas**

PLYMOUTH (DEVONPORT)

LAT 50°22'N LONG 4°11'W

TIMES AND HEIGHTS OF HIGH AND LOW WATERS

Dates in amber are **SPRINGS**
Dates in grey are **NEAPS**

2016

SEPTEMBER

Date	Day	Time	m	Time	m	Time	m	Time	m	Moon
1	TH	0535	5.2	1154	0.8	1748	5.5			●
2	F	0017	0.6	0614	5.3	1234	0.7	1824	5.5	
3	SA	0055	0.6	0648	5.3	1309	0.7	1858	5.5	
4	SU	0129	0.7	0719	5.3	1341	0.9	1928	5.4	
5	M	0157	0.9	0749	5.2	1407	1.1	1958	5.3	
6	TU	0221	1.2	0819	5.1	1431	1.3	2029	5.1	
7	W	0241	1.4	0850	4.9	1452	1.6	2100	4.9	
8	TH	0301	1.7	0924	4.7	1515	1.9	2135	4.6	
9	F	0329	2.0	1005	4.5	1551	2.1	2222	4.4	◐
10	SA	0415	2.2	1059	4.4	1707	2.4	2324	4.2	
11	SU	0558	2.4	1211	4.3	1853	2.4			
12	M	0050	4.2	0728	2.3	1344	4.5	2007	2.1	
13	TU	0231	4.5	0838	2.0	1458	4.8	2110	1.7	
14	W	0333	4.8	0938	1.6	1552	5.1	2207	1.3	
15	TH	0423	5.1	1032	1.2	1640	5.4	2258	0.9	
16	F	0510	5.3	1121	0.8	1726	5.6	2346	0.6	○
17	SA	0555	5.5	1208	0.6	1811	5.8			
18	SU	0031	0.4	0638	5.6	1252	0.5	1855	5.8	
19	M	0114	0.4	0721	5.7	1333	0.5	1939	5.8	
20	TU	0155	0.5	0803	5.6	1413	0.6	2021	5.6	
21	W	0234	0.7	0844	5.5	1453	0.9	2103	5.4	
22	TH	0314	1.1	0926	5.2	1535	1.3	2148	5.0	
23	F	0358	1.5	1014	4.9	1625	1.7	2244	4.6	◑
24	SA	0454	1.9	1120	4.6	1733	2.1			
25	SU	0009	4.4	0613	2.2	1250	4.5	1915	2.2	
26	M	0140	4.4	0800	2.2	1408	4.6	2043	1.9	
27	TU	0251	4.6	0912	1.8	1511	4.9	2142	1.5	
28	W	0347	4.9	1004	1.4	1602	5.2	2230	1.1	
29	TH	0432	5.1	1050	1.1	1645	5.4	2313	0.9	
30	F	0511	5.3	1130	0.9	1723	5.5	2352	0.8	

OCTOBER

Date	Day	Time	m	Time	m	Time	m	Time	m	Moon
1	SA	0547	5.4	1208	0.8	1758	5.5			●
2	SU	0027	0.8	0618	5.4	1242	0.8	1830	5.5	
3	M	0059	0.9	0649	5.4	1311	1.0	1901	5.4	
4	TU	0124	1.0	0719	5.3	1336	1.1	1932	5.3	
5	W	0146	1.2	0750	5.2	1357	1.3	2002	5.1	
6	TH	0205	1.4	0820	5.1	1418	1.6	2032	4.9	
7	F	0225	1.7	0852	4.9	1442	1.8	2106	4.7	
8	SA	0254	1.9	0929	4.7	1517	2.0	2151	4.5	
9	SU	0337	2.2	1021	4.5	1614	2.3	2251	4.3	◐
10	M	0450	2.5	1128	4.4	1811	2.4			
11	TU	0008	4.3	0650	2.4	1251	4.5	1934	2.1	
12	W	0148	4.5	0807	2.1	1417	4.8	2041	1.7	
13	TH	0301	4.8	0911	1.6	1519	5.1	2140	1.3	
14	F	0354	5.2	1006	1.2	1611	5.4	2233	0.9	
15	SA	0443	5.4	1058	0.8	1700	5.7	2322	0.6	
16	SU	0529	5.6	1145	0.6	1748	5.8			○
17	M	0008	0.4	0614	5.8	1231	0.4	1834	5.9	
18	TU	0053	0.4	0659	5.8	1314	0.4	1920	5.8	
19	W	0135	0.5	0743	5.8	1356	0.6	2004	5.6	
20	TH	0216	0.7	0825	5.6	1438	0.9	2048	5.4	
21	F	0257	1.1	0908	5.3	1521	1.3	2135	5.0	
22	SA	0342	1.6	0955	5.0	1611	1.7	2231	4.6	◑
23	SU	0436	2.0	1059	4.7	1715	2.1	2354	4.4	
24	M	0548	2.3	1226	4.6	1847	2.2			
25	TU	0118	4.4	0727	2.3	1342	4.6	2014	2.0	
26	W	0225	4.6	0842	2.0	1443	4.8	2114	1.7	
27	TH	0319	4.8	0936	1.6	1533	5.1	2201	1.4	
28	F	0404	5.1	1021	1.3	1616	5.2	2243	1.1	
29	SA	0442	5.3	1101	1.1	1655	5.4	2322	1.0	
30	SU	0517	5.4	1138	1.0	1730	5.4	2356	1.0	●
31	M	0550	5.5	1212	1.0	1804	5.4			

NOVEMBER

Date	Day	Time	m	Time	m	Time	m	Time	m	Moon
1	TU	0027	1.0	0622	5.5	1241	1.1	1837	5.4	
2	W	0053	1.1	0655	5.4	1308	1.2	1910	5.3	
3	TH	0116	1.3	0726	5.3	1332	1.4	1941	5.1	
4	F	0139	1.5	0757	5.2	1356	1.5	2012	5.0	
5	SA	0204	1.6	0828	5.0	1424	1.7	2045	4.8	
6	SU	0236	1.8	0905	4.9	1501	1.9	2129	4.6	
7	M	0318	2.1	0954	4.7	1555	2.2	2226	4.5	◐
8	TU	0421	2.3	1056	4.6	1724	2.3	2336	4.4	
9	W	0603	2.4	1209	4.6	1857	2.1			
10	TH	0059	4.5	0730	2.1	1330	4.8	2008	1.8	
11	F	0220	4.8	0839	1.7	1442	5.1	2110	1.4	
12	SA	0322	5.2	0939	1.3	1541	5.4	2206	1.0	
13	SU	0415	5.4	1033	0.9	1635	5.6	2258	0.7	
14	M	0504	5.7	1123	0.7	1726	5.8	2346	0.5	○
15	TU	0552	5.8	1211	0.5	1815	5.8			
16	W	0033	0.5	0639	5.9	1257	0.5	1903	5.8	
17	TH	0118	0.6	0725	5.8	1342	0.6	1950	5.6	
18	F	0201	0.8	0809	5.7	1425	0.9	2036	5.3	
19	SA	0243	1.1	0853	5.4	1510	1.2	2122	5.0	
20	SU	0328	1.5	0939	5.1	1557	1.6	2215	4.7	
21	M	0417	1.9	1033	4.9	1652	1.9	2323	4.5	◑
22	TU	0516	2.2	1146	4.7	1800	2.1			
23	W	0039	4.4	0630	2.3	1301	4.6	1921	2.1	
24	TH	0145	4.5	0751	2.2	1403	4.7	2030	1.9	
25	F	0240	4.7	0855	1.9	1456	4.9	2123	1.7	
26	SA	0327	4.9	0945	1.7	1542	5.0	2208	1.5	
27	SU	0409	5.1	1028	1.4	1624	5.2	2248	1.3	
28	M	0447	5.3	1107	1.3	1703	5.3	2324	1.2	
29	TU	0524	5.4	1142	1.2	1741	5.3	2357	1.2	●
30	W	0600	5.4	1214	1.2	1817	5.3			

DECEMBER

Date	Day	Time	m	Time	m	Time	m	Time	m	Moon
1	TH	0026	1.2	0635	5.4	1245	1.3	1852	5.2	
2	F	0055	1.3	0709	5.4	1315	1.3	1926	5.1	
3	SA	0124	1.4	0741	5.3	1346	1.4	1959	5.0	
4	SU	0154	1.5	0813	5.2	1418	1.6	2033	4.9	
5	M	0229	1.7	0850	5.1	1456	1.7	2115	4.8	
6	TU	0310	1.9	0935	4.9	1545	1.9	2206	4.6	
7	W	0404	2.0	1031	4.8	1649	2.0	2308	4.6	◐
8	TH	0517	2.2	1136	4.8	1811	2.0			
9	F	0020	4.6	0645	2.1	1250	4.8	1930	1.8	
10	SA	0138	4.8	0804	1.8	1406	5.0	2039	1.5	
11	SU	0248	5.0	0911	1.5	1513	5.2	2141	1.2	
12	M	0348	5.3	1010	1.2	1613	5.4	2236	0.9	
13	TU	0443	5.6	1104	0.9	1707	5.6	2328	0.7	
14	W	0533	5.7	1155	0.7	1759	5.6			○
15	TH	0017	0.6	0622	5.8	1244	0.6	1849	5.6	
16	F	0103	0.6	0709	5.8	1329	0.6	1937	5.5	
17	SA	0147	0.8	0755	5.7	1414	0.8	2022	5.3	
18	SU	0230	1.0	0838	5.5	1456	1.1	2106	5.1	
19	M	0311	1.3	0919	5.3	1539	1.4	2149	4.9	
20	TU	0354	1.6	1000	5.0	1623	1.7	2234	4.6	
21	W	0440	2.0	1047	4.8	1713	2.0	2331	4.5	◑
22	TH	0534	2.2	1149	4.6	1812	2.1			
23	F	0041	4.4	0638	2.3	1303	4.5	1920	2.2	
24	SA	0147	4.5	0750	2.2	1407	4.6	2028	2.0	
25	SU	0243	4.7	0855	2.0	1503	4.7	2124	1.8	
26	M	0333	4.9	0948	1.8	1552	4.9	2211	1.6	
27	TU	0418	5.1	1033	1.6	1637	5.0	2252	1.4	
28	W	0500	5.2	1114	1.4	1720	5.1	2330	1.3	
29	TH	0540	5.4	1152	1.3	1800	5.2			●
30	F	0006	1.2	0618	5.4	1228	1.2	1839	5.2	
31	SA	0041	1.2	0655	5.4	1304	1.2	1916	5.2	

Chart Datum: 3·22 metres below Ordnance Datum (Newlyn)
HAT is 5·9 metres above Chart Datum

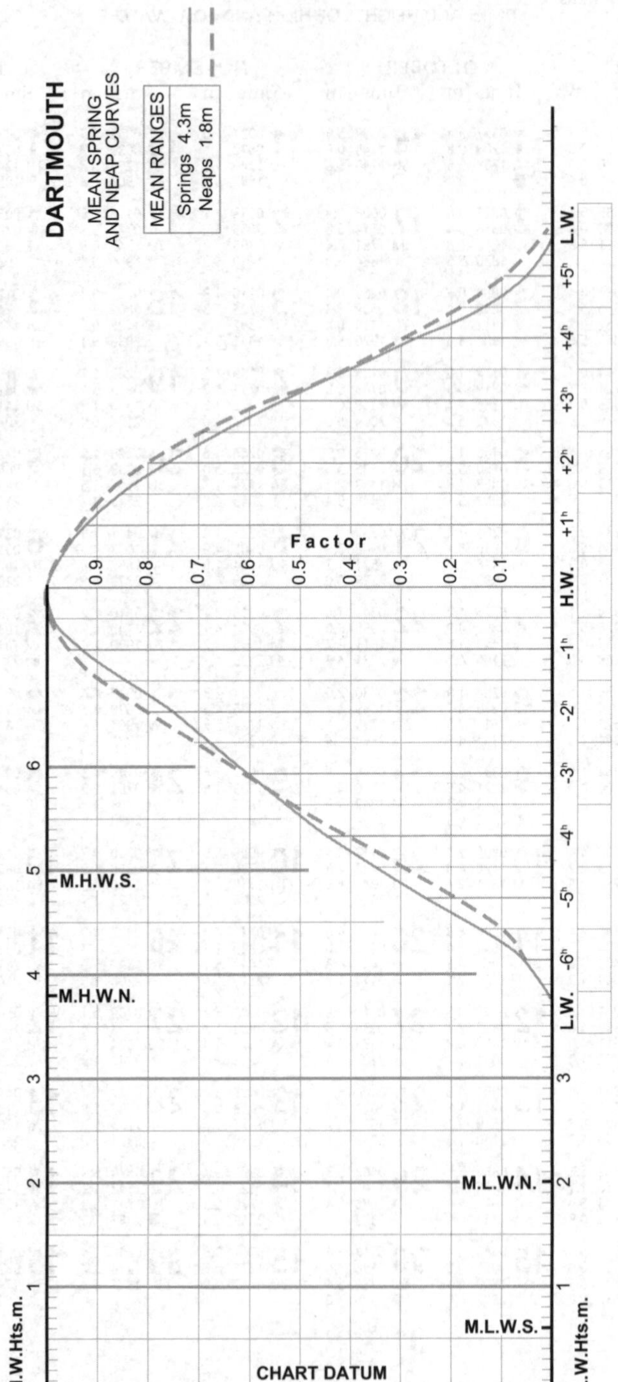
DARTMOUTH
MEAN SPRING AND NEAP CURVES
MEAN RANGES
Springs 4.3m
Neaps 1.8m
Factor
0.9 0.8 0.7 0.6 0.5 0.4 0.3 0.2 0.1
L.W. +5h +4h +3h +2h +1h H.W. -1h -2h -3h -4h -5h -6h L.W.
H.W.Hts.m.
0 1 2 3 4 5 6
M.H.W.S.
M.H.W.N.
M.L.W.N.
M.L.W.S.
L.W.Hts.m.
CHART DATUM

TIME ZONE (UT)
For Summer Time add ONE hour in **non-shaded areas**

DARTMOUTH

LAT 50°21′N LONG 3°35′W

TIMES AND HEIGHTS OF HIGH AND LOW WATERS

Dates in amber are **SPRINGS**
Dates in grey are **NEAPS**

2016

JANUARY

Date	Day	Time	m	Time	m	Time	m	Time	m	Moon
1	F	0343	1.6	1003	4.3	1609	1.7	2230	4.0	
2	SA	0424	1.9	1047	4.1	1654	1.9	2320	3.8	◑
3	SU	0516	2.1	1139	3.9	1751	2.0			
4	M	0023	3.8	0621	2.2	1247	3.9	1858	2.0	
5	TU	0140	3.8	0731	2.1	1408	3.9	2003	1.9	
6	W	0252	4.0	0836	1.9	1517	4.1	2104	1.7	
7	TH	0351	4.2	0934	1.6	1615	4.3	2158	1.4	
8	F	0443	4.5	1025	1.3	1705	4.4	2248	1.1	
9	SA	0529	4.7	1114	1.0	1753	4.6	2333	0.9	
10	SU	0614	4.8	1159	0.8	1838	4.7			●
11	M	0017	0.8	0654	4.9	1244	0.7	1918	4.7	
12	TU	0101	0.7	0736	5.0	1327	0.6	1959	4.8	
13	W	0141	0.7	0815	5.0	1407	0.6	2039	4.7	
14	TH	0222	0.8	0856	4.9	1448	0.7	2120	4.6	
15	F	0302	0.9	0938	4.8	1529	0.9	2203	4.5	
16	SA	0345	1.1	1024	4.6	1616	1.2	2251	4.3	◐
17	SU	0434	1.4	1117	4.4	1710	1.4	2350	4.1	
18	M	0536	1.6	1222	4.2	1819	1.7			
19	TU	0103	4.0	0658	1.8	1340	4.1	1944	1.7	
20	W	0223	4.1	0827	1.7	1457	4.1	2103	1.5	
21	TH	0333	4.3	0939	1.4	1604	4.3	2206	1.2	
22	F	0433	4.5	1037	1.1	1702	4.5	2300	0.9	
23	SA	0526	4.7	1127	0.8	1753	4.6	2347	0.7	
24	SU	0613	4.9	1212	0.6	1838	4.7			○
25	M	0030	0.6	0653	4.9	1255	0.5	1916	4.7	
26	TU	0109	0.6	0729	4.9	1331	0.6	1950	4.7	
27	W	0143	0.7	0801	4.9	1405	0.7	2020	4.6	
28	TH	0214	0.9	0831	4.8	1433	0.9	2050	4.5	
29	F	0241	1.1	0902	4.6	1501	1.2	2121	4.3	
30	SA	0308	1.3	0935	4.4	1527	1.4	2155	4.1	
31	SU	0334	1.6	1009	4.2	1555	1.7	2234	4.0	

FEBRUARY

Date	Day	Time	m	Time	m	Time	m	Time	m	Moon
1	M	0409	1.8	1051	4.0	1636	1.9	2322	3.8	◑
2	TU	0507	2.1	1146	3.8	1748	2.1			
3	W	0026	3.7	0634	2.1	1257	3.7	1911	2.1	
4	TH	0150	3.8	0750	2.0	1428	3.8	2022	1.8	
5	F	0311	4.0	0858	1.7	1543	4.0	2126	1.5	
6	SA	0412	4.3	0958	1.3	1641	4.3	2223	1.2	
7	SU	0503	4.6	1053	1.0	1731	4.5	2316	0.9	
8	M	0552	4.8	1143	0.6	1820	4.7			●
9	TU	0004	0.6	0637	5.0	1232	0.4	1903	4.8	
10	W	0050	0.4	0721	5.1	1316	0.3	1945	4.9	
11	TH	0132	0.3	0804	5.1	1357	0.2	2027	4.9	
12	F	0212	0.3	0845	5.1	1436	0.3	2106	4.8	
13	SA	0251	0.5	0926	4.9	1516	0.6	2146	4.7	
14	SU	0330	0.8	1008	4.7	1556	0.9	2229	4.4	
15	M	0414	1.1	1055	4.3	1643	1.3	2321	4.1	◐
16	TU	0508	1.5	1157	4.0	1743	1.7			
17	W	0034	3.9	0621	1.8	1319	3.8	1910	1.9	
18	TH	0159	3.9	0806	1.8	1442	3.9	2046	1.7	
19	F	0315	4.1	0928	1.5	1551	4.0	2154	1.4	
20	SA	0417	4.3	1024	1.1	1649	4.3	2247	1.0	
21	SU	0509	4.6	1113	0.8	1736	4.5	2331	0.7	
22	M	0553	4.8	1156	0.6	1819	4.6			○
23	TU	0012	0.6	0632	4.9	1236	0.5	1854	4.7	
24	W	0050	0.5	0706	4.9	1311	0.5	1926	4.7	
25	TH	0123	0.6	0738	4.8	1341	0.6	1955	4.6	
26	F	0149	0.7	0807	4.7	1407	0.8	2024	4.6	
27	SA	0214	0.9	0837	4.6	1428	1.0	2053	4.4	
28	SU	0234	1.1	0907	4.4	1447	1.2	2123	4.3	
29	M	0256	1.3	0937	4.2	1511	1.4	2154	4.1	

MARCH

Date	Day	Time	m	Time	m	Time	m	Time	m	Moon
1	TU	0325	1.6	1012	4.0	1544	1.7	2235	3.9	◑
2	W	0407	1.8	1102	3.8	1636	2.0	2332	3.7	
3	TH	0525	2.1	1207	3.6	1816	2.1			
4	F	0047	3.7	0709	2.0	1335	3.7	1945	1.9	
5	SA	0221	3.9	0824	1.7	1508	3.9	2057	1.6	
6	SU	0337	4.2	0932	1.3	1613	4.2	2200	1.2	
7	M	0434	4.5	1031	0.8	1706	4.5	2256	0.7	
8	TU	0526	4.8	1124	0.5	1756	4.8	2346	0.4	
9	W	0616	5.0	1212	0.2	1844	4.9			●
10	TH	0033	0.1	0702	5.2	1258	0.0	1927	5.0	
11	F	0117	0.0	0746	5.2	1340	0.0	2008	5.1	
12	SA	0157	0.1	0829	5.2	1420	0.1	2049	5.0	
13	SU	0235	0.3	0910	5.0	1458	0.4	2128	4.8	
14	M	0315	0.6	0951	4.6	1537	0.8	2206	4.5	
15	TU	0356	1.0	1036	4.3	1622	1.3	2253	4.1	◐
16	W	0446	1.5	1136	3.9	1717	1.7			
17	TH	0005	3.8	0554	1.8	1302	3.7	1838	2.0	
18	F	0137	3.8	0744	1.9	1424	3.7	2025	1.9	
19	SA	0253	3.9	0908	1.6	1532	3.9	2134	1.5	
20	SU	0354	4.2	1005	1.2	1627	4.2	2225	1.1	
21	M	0444	4.5	1051	0.8	1713	4.4	2309	0.8	
22	TU	0527	4.6	1133	0.6	1752	4.6	2349	0.6	
23	W	0606	4.7	1210	0.5	1827	4.7			○
24	TH	0024	0.5	0641	4.8	1245	0.5	1858	4.7	
25	F	0056	0.6	0712	4.8	1314	0.6	1929	4.7	
26	SA	0123	0.7	0743	4.7	1337	0.8	1958	4.6	
27	SU	0145	0.8	0813	4.6	1357	0.9	2027	4.5	
28	M	0206	1.0	0842	4.4	1418	1.1	2054	4.4	
29	TU	0228	1.2	0910	4.2	1441	1.3	2123	4.2	
30	W	0257	1.4	0944	4.0	1515	1.6	2201	4.0	
31	TH	0338	1.6	1032	3.8	1602	1.8	2256	3.8	◑

APRIL

Date	Day	Time	m	Time	m	Time	m	Time	m	Moon
1	F	0443	1.9	1136	3.6	1725	2.0			
2	SA	0006	3.8	0631	1.9	1254	3.7	1910	1.9	
3	SU	0132	3.9	0754	1.6	1429	3.9	2028	1.6	
4	M	0258	4.2	0904	1.2	1542	4.2	2134	1.1	
5	TU	0403	4.5	1005	0.8	1639	4.5	2232	0.7	
6	W	0459	4.8	1100	0.4	1730	4.8	2324	0.3	
7	TH	0551	5.1	1149	0.1	1820	5.0			●
8	F	0011	0.1	0640	5.2	1237	-0.1	1905	5.1	
9	SA	0058	-0.1	0727	5.2	1321	-0.1	1948	5.1	
10	SU	0139	0.0	0810	5.1	1401	0.1	2029	5.0	
11	M	0220	0.2	0853	4.9	1440	0.4	2108	4.8	
12	TU	0259	0.5	0935	4.6	1520	0.8	2146	4.5	
13	W	0341	1.0	1020	4.2	1603	1.3	2229	4.2	
14	TH	0430	1.4	1120	3.8	1656	1.7	2336	3.9	◐
15	F	0532	1.8	1242	3.6	1805	2.0			
16	SA	0108	3.8	0705	1.9	1358	3.7	1944	1.9	
17	SU	0222	3.9	0835	1.6	1502	3.9	2100	1.6	
18	M	0321	4.1	0933	1.3	1555	4.1	2153	1.3	
19	TU	0412	4.3	1020	1.0	1640	4.3	2239	1.0	
20	W	0455	4.5	1102	0.8	1719	4.5	2318	0.8	
21	TH	0534	4.6	1139	0.7	1756	4.6	2354	0.7	
22	F	0612	4.7	1212	0.7	1831	4.7			○
23	SA	0025	0.7	0647	4.7	1242	0.7	1903	4.7	
24	SU	0054	0.7	0720	4.6	1308	0.8	1935	4.6	
25	M	0120	0.8	0751	4.5	1331	0.9	2004	4.6	
26	TU	0144	1.0	0821	4.4	1355	1.1	2032	4.5	
27	W	0211	1.1	0851	4.2	1424	1.3	2101	4.3	
28	TH	0242	1.3	0927	4.1	1458	1.5	2140	4.2	
29	F	0325	1.5	1013	3.9	1546	1.7	2233	4.0	
30	SA	0426	1.7	1114	3.8	1659	1.9	2338	3.9	◑

Chart Datum: 2·62 metres below Ordnance Datum (Newlyn)
HAT is 5·3 metres above Chart Datum

TIME ZONE (UT)
For Summer Time add ONE hour in **non-shaded areas**

DARTMOUTH

LAT 50°21'N LONG 3°35'W

TIMES AND HEIGHTS OF HIGH AND LOW WATERS

Dates in amber are **SPRINGS**
Dates in grey are **NEAPS**

2016

MAY

Date	Day	Time	m
1	SU	0556 1227 1835	1.7 3.8 1.8
2	M	0055 0721 1352 1955	4.0 1.5 4.0 1.6
3	TU	0220 0834 1507 2105	4.2 1.2 4.2 1.2
4	W	0330 0937 1608 2205	4.5 0.8 4.6 0.8
5	TH	0430 1034 1702 2300	4.8 0.4 4.8 0.4
6	F	0526 1126 1754 ● 2349	5.0 0.2 5.0 0.2
7	SA	0619 1213 1843	5.1 0.1 5.1
8	SU	0037 0706 1300 1927	0.1 5.1 0.1 5.1
9	M	0122 0753 1342 2009	0.1 5.0 0.2 5.0
10	TU	0204 0837 1424 2050	0.3 4.8 0.5 4.8
11	W	0245 0921 1504 2129	0.6 4.5 0.9 4.6
12	TH	0327 1004 1547 2207	0.9 4.2 1.3 4.3
13	F	0414 1058 1635 ◐ 2259	1.3 3.9 1.6 4.0
14	SA	0508 1208 1733	1.6 3.7 1.9
15	SU	0023 0614 1318 1845	3.8 1.8 3.7 1.9
16	M	0138 0736 1420 2003	3.8 1.7 3.8 1.8
17	TU	0239 0845 1513 2106	4.0 1.5 4.0 1.6
18	W	0331 0937 1600 2157	4.1 1.3 4.2 1.3
19	TH	0418 1022 1643 2240	4.3 1.1 4.4 1.1
20	F	0500 1102 1723 2318	4.4 0.9 4.5 0.9
21	SA	0542 1137 1802 ○ 2353	4.5 0.9 4.6 0.9
22	SU	0622 1209 1839	4.6 0.9 4.7
23	M	0025 0658 1241 1913	0.8 4.5 0.9 4.7
24	TU	0058 0734 1312 1945	0.9 4.5 1.0 4.6
25	W	0129 0806 1341 2015	0.9 4.4 1.0 4.6
26	TH	0201 0839 1415 2049	1.0 4.3 1.2 4.5
27	F	0237 0917 1453 2129	1.1 4.2 1.3 4.4
28	SA	0321 1003 1540 2218	1.3 4.1 1.5 4.2
29	SU	0416 1057 1642 ◑ 2317	1.5 4.0 1.7 4.2
30	M	0527 1203 1800	1.5 3.9 1.7
31	TU	0027 0647 1318 1921	4.1 1.5 4.0 1.5

JUNE

Date	Day	Time	m
1	W	0146 0801 1434 2035	4.2 1.2 4.2 1.3
2	TH	0300 0908 1539 2139	4.4 0.9 4.5 0.9
3	F	0404 1008 1637 2237	4.6 0.7 4.7 0.6
4	SA	0503 1104 1730 2330	4.8 0.4 4.9 0.4
5	SU	0558 1154 1822 ●	4.9 0.3 5.0
6	M	0018 0649 1242 1908	0.3 4.9 0.3 5.0
7	TU	0106 0737 1327 1951	0.3 4.8 0.4 5.0
8	W	0149 0821 1408 2032	0.4 4.7 0.6 4.8
9	TH	0230 0904 1448 2110	0.6 4.5 0.8 4.6
10	F	0312 0944 1528 2145	0.9 4.3 1.2 4.4
11	SA	0353 1025 1611 2223	1.2 4.0 1.5 4.2
12	SU	0437 1113 1658 ◐ 2312	1.5 3.8 1.7 4.0
13	M	0529 1213 1753	1.7 3.7 1.9
14	TU	0021 0629 1319 1856	3.8 1.8 3.8 1.9
15	W	0138 0734 1420 2002	3.8 1.8 3.9 1.8
16	TH	0241 0837 1515 2102	3.9 1.6 4.1 1.6
17	F	0337 0932 1604 2155	4.1 1.4 4.3 1.4
18	SA	0426 1018 1650 2241	4.2 1.2 4.4 1.2
19	SU	0513 1101 1734 2322	4.4 1.1 4.6 1.0
20	M	0557 1140 1816 ○	4.5 1.0 4.6
21	TU	0001 0639 1219 1854	0.9 4.5 0.9 4.7
22	W	0041 0718 1257 1930	0.8 4.5 0.9 4.7
23	TH	0118 0755 1333 2005	0.8 4.5 0.9 4.7
24	F	0155 0831 1410 2041	0.9 4.4 1.0 4.6
25	SA	0233 0910 1449 2121	0.9 4.4 1.1 4.6
26	SU	0316 0953 1533 2206	1.0 4.3 1.2 4.5
27	M	0404 1043 1626 ◑ 2259	1.2 4.2 1.4 4.3
28	TU	0502 1140 1728	1.3 4.1 1.5
29	W	0001 0611 1248 1846	4.2 1.4 4.1 1.6
30	TH	0116 0729 1404 2005	4.2 1.4 4.2 1.4

JULY

Date	Day	Time	m
1	F	0235 0842 1513 2116	4.3 1.2 4.4 1.2
2	SA	0344 0948 1616 2218	4.4 1.0 4.6 0.9
3	SU	0446 1046 1712 2314	4.6 0.7 4.8 0.6
4	M	0542 1138 1803 ●	4.7 0.6 4.9
5	TU	0004 0634 1226 1851	0.5 4.7 0.5 5.0
6	W	0052 0720 1312 1934	0.4 4.7 0.5 4.9
7	TH	0135 0803 1352 2012	0.4 4.6 0.6 4.9
8	F	0215 0842 1429 2047	0.6 4.5 0.8 4.7
9	SA	0251 0916 1505 2118	0.8 4.4 1.0 4.5
10	SU	0327 0948 1540 2150	1.1 4.2 1.3 4.3
11	M	0402 1023 1619 2228	1.4 4.0 1.6 4.1
12	TU	0442 1106 1704 ◐ 2315	1.6 3.9 1.8 3.9
13	W	0532 1201 1800	1.8 3.8 2.0
14	TH	0015 0634 1311 1906	3.8 1.9 3.8 2.0
15	F	0135 0738 1424 2010	3.8 1.8 3.9 1.8
16	SA	0252 0841 1526 2110	3.9 1.7 4.1 1.6
17	SU	0353 0938 1620 2205	4.1 1.4 4.3 1.3
18	M	0446 1029 1708 2255	4.2 1.2 4.5 1.1
19	TU	0534 1116 1753 ○ 2340	4.4 1.0 4.7 0.9
20	W	0620 1200 1836	4.5 0.9 4.8
21	TH	0024 0701 1244 1915	0.7 4.6 0.8 4.8
22	F	0107 0742 1324 1953	0.6 4.6 0.7 4.9
23	SA	0147 0821 1403 2032	0.6 4.6 0.7 4.8
24	SU	0226 0900 1441 2112	0.6 4.6 0.8 4.8
25	M	0306 0941 1522 2154	0.8 4.5 1.0 4.6
26	TU	0348 1025 1607 ◑ 2242	1.0 4.3 1.2 4.4
27	W	0437 1118 1702 2339	1.2 4.2 1.4 4.2
28	TH	0538 1222 1813	1.5 4.0 1.6
29	F	0052 0658 1340 1940	4.0 1.6 4.0 1.6
30	SA	0216 0821 1455 2101	4.0 1.5 4.2 1.4
31	SU	0330 0934 1600 2207	4.2 1.3 4.4 1.1

AUGUST

Date	Day	Time	m
1	M	0433 1034 1657 2303	4.4 1.0 4.6 0.8
2	TU	0529 1125 1748 ● 2351	4.5 0.7 4.8 0.5
3	W	0619 1211 1834	4.6 0.5 4.9
4	TH	0037 0701 1255 1913	0.4 4.7 0.5 4.9
5	F	0118 0740 1332 1948	0.4 4.7 0.5 4.9
6	SA	0154 0813 1407 2019	0.5 4.6 0.7 4.8
7	SU	0227 0843 1437 2049	0.7 4.5 0.9 4.6
8	M	0255 0913 1506 2119	1.0 4.3 1.2 4.4
9	TU	0322 0945 1534 2153	1.3 4.2 1.5 4.2
10	W	0350 1022 1607 ◐ 2231	1.6 4.0 1.8 4.0
11	TH	0426 1107 1657 2321	1.8 3.8 2.0 3.8
12	F	0529 1206 1813	2.0 3.7 2.1
13	SA	0027 0649 1325 1927	3.7 2.1 3.7 2.0
14	SU	0203 0759 1448 2035	3.7 1.9 3.9 1.8
15	M	0322 0904 1550 2136	3.9 1.6 4.2 1.4
16	TU	0421 1001 1642 2230	4.2 1.3 4.5 1.1
17	W	0511 1054 1729 2320	4.4 1.0 4.7 0.8
18	TH	0558 1142 1815 ○	4.6 0.7 4.9
19	F	0006 0643 1227 1856	0.5 4.7 0.6 5.0
20	SA	0052 0725 1310 1938	0.4 4.8 0.4 5.1
21	SU	0132 0805 1350 2018	0.3 4.8 0.4 5.0
22	M	0212 0845 1428 2059	0.4 4.8 0.5 4.9
23	TU	0250 0925 1507 2139	0.6 4.7 0.8 4.7
24	W	0329 1005 1548 2224	0.9 4.5 1.1 4.4
25	TH	0415 1054 1639 ◑ 2319	1.2 4.2 1.4 4.1
26	F	0512 1159 1747	1.6 4.0 1.8
27	SA	0036 0632 1321 1925	3.9 1.8 3.9 1.8
28	SU	0207 0809 1442 2053	3.8 1.8 4.1 1.6
29	M	0322 0924 1548 2157	4.0 1.5 4.3 1.2
30	TU	0424 1021 1643 2249	4.3 1.1 4.6 0.8
31	W	0515 1110 1730 2335	4.5 0.8 4.8 0.6

Chart Datum: 2·62 metres below Ordnance Datum (Newlyn)
HAT is 5·3 metres above Chart Datum

TIME ZONE (UT)
For Summer Time add ONE hour in **non-shaded areas**

DARTMOUTH

LAT 50°21′N LONG 3°35′W

TIMES AND HEIGHTS OF HIGH AND LOW WATERS

Dates in amber are **SPRINGS**
Dates in grey are **NEAPS**

2016

SEPTEMBER

Date	Day	Time	m	Time	m	Time	m	Time	m	Moon
1	TH	0559	4.6	1153	0.6	1813	4.9			●
2	F	0016	0.4	0639	4.7	1234	0.5	1849	4.9	
3	SA	0055	0.4	0712	4.7	1309	0.5	1922	4.9	
4	SU	0129	0.5	0742	4.7	1340	0.7	1951	4.8	
5	M	0156	0.7	0811	4.6	1406	0.9	2020	4.7	
6	TU	0220	1.0	0841	4.5	1429	1.1	2051	4.5	
7	W	0239	1.2	0911	4.3	1450	1.4	2121	4.3	
8	TH	0259	1.5	0944	4.1	1513	1.7	2155	4.0	
9	F	0327	1.8	1024	3.9	1548	1.9	2241	3.8	◐
10	SA	0412	2.0	1117	3.8	1703	2.2	2341	3.6	
11	SU	0553	2.2	1227	3.7	1849	2.2			
12	M	0105	3.6	0724	2.1	1400	3.9	2003	1.9	
13	TU	0249	3.9	0835	1.8	1517	4.2	2107	1.5	
14	W	0353	4.2	0936	1.4	1613	4.5	2205	1.1	
15	TH	0445	4.5	1031	1.0	1702	4.8	2257	0.7	
16	F	0533	4.7	1120	0.6	1750	5.0	2345	0.4	○
17	SA	0620	4.9	1207	0.4	1836	5.2			
18	SU	0031	0.2	0702	5.0	1252	0.3	1919	5.2	
19	M	0114	0.2	0744	5.1	1332	0.3	2002	5.2	
20	TU	0154	0.3	0825	5.0	1412	0.4	2043	5.0	
21	W	0232	0.5	0905	4.9	1451	0.7	2124	4.8	
22	TH	0312	0.9	0946	4.6	1532	1.1	2207	4.4	
23	F	0355	1.3	1033	4.3	1622	1.5	2302	4.0	◑
24	SA	0450	1.7	1137	4.0	1728	1.9			
25	SU	0025	3.8	0608	2.0	1305	3.9	1911	2.0	
26	M	0156	3.8	0756	2.0	1425	4.0	2040	1.7	
27	TU	0310	4.0	0909	1.6	1530	4.3	2140	1.3	
28	W	0408	4.3	1002	1.2	1623	4.6	2229	0.9	
29	TH	0454	4.5	1049	0.9	1708	4.8	2312	0.7	
30	F	0534	4.7	1129	0.7	1747	4.9	2351	0.6	

OCTOBER

Date	Day	Time	m	Time	m	Time	m	Time	m	Moon
1	SA	0612	4.8	1207	0.6	1823	4.9			●
2	SU	0026	0.6	0643	4.8	1242	0.6	1854	4.9	
3	M	0059	0.7	0713	4.8	1311	0.8	1925	4.8	
4	TU	0124	0.8	0742	4.7	1335	0.9	1955	4.7	
5	W	0145	1.0	0812	4.6	1356	1.1	2024	4.5	
6	TH	0204	1.2	0842	4.5	1417	1.4	2053	4.3	
7	F	0224	1.5	0913	4.3	1440	1.6	2127	4.1	
8	SA	0252	1.7	0949	4.1	1515	1.8	2210	3.9	
9	SU	0334	2.0	1040	3.9	1611	2.1	2309	3.7	◐
10	M	0446	2.3	1145	3.8	1806	2.2			
11	TU	0024	3.7	0646	2.2	1306	3.9	1930	1.9	
12	W	0205	3.9	0803	1.9	1435	4.2	2038	1.5	
13	TH	0320	4.2	0908	1.4	1539	4.5	2138	1.1	
14	F	0415	4.6	1004	1.0	1632	4.8	2232	0.7	
15	SA	0505	4.8	1057	0.6	1723	5.1	2321	0.4	
16	SU	0553	5.0	1144	0.4	1813	5.2			○
17	M	0007	0.2	0639	5.2	1231	0.2	1858	5.3	
18	TU	0053	0.2	0723	5.2	1314	0.2	1943	5.2	
19	W	0134	0.3	0806	5.2	1355	0.4	2026	5.0	
20	TH	0215	0.5	0847	5.0	1436	0.7	2109	4.8	
21	F	0255	0.9	0929	4.7	1519	1.1	2155	4.4	
22	SA	0339	1.4	1014	4.4	1608	1.5	2249	4.0	◑
23	SU	0432	1.8	1117	4.1	1711	1.9			
24	M	0010	3.8	0543	2.1	1242	4.0	1843	2.0	
25	TU	0134	3.8	0723	2.1	1358	4.0	2010	1.8	
26	W	0243	4.0	0839	1.8	1501	4.2	2111	1.5	
27	TH	0339	4.2	0934	1.4	1553	4.5	2159	1.2	
28	F	0425	4.5	1019	1.1	1638	4.6	2242	0.9	
29	SA	0504	4.7	1100	0.9	1718	4.8	2321	0.8	
30	SU	0541	4.8	1137	0.8	1754	4.8	2355	0.8	●
31	M	0615	4.9	1211	0.8	1829	4.8			

NOVEMBER

Date	Day	Time	m	Time	m	Time	m	Time	m	Moon
1	TU	0026	0.8	0647	4.9	1241	0.9	1901	4.8	
2	W	0053	0.9	0719	4.8	1308	1.0	1934	4.7	
3	TH	0116	1.1	0749	4.7	1331	1.2	2004	4.5	
4	F	0138	1.3	0819	4.6	1355	1.3	2034	4.4	
5	SA	0203	1.4	0850	4.4	1423	1.5	2106	4.2	
6	SU	0234	1.6	0926	4.3	1459	1.7	2149	4.0	
7	M	0316	1.9	1013	4.1	1552	2.0	2245	3.9	◐
8	TU	0418	2.1	1114	4.0	1720	2.1	2353	3.8	
9	W	0558	2.2	1225	4.0	1853	1.9			
10	TH	0114	3.9	0726	1.9	1346	4.2	2004	1.6	
11	F	0238	4.2	0836	1.5	1500	4.5	2107	1.2	
12	SA	0342	4.6	0937	1.1	1601	4.8	2204	0.8	
13	SU	0437	4.8	1032	0.7	1657	5.0	2257	0.5	
14	M	0527	5.1	1122	0.5	1750	5.2	2345	0.3	○
15	TU	0617	5.2	1210	0.3	1840	5.2			
16	W	0033	0.3	0703	5.3	1257	0.3	1927	5.2	
17	TH	0118	0.4	0748	5.2	1341	0.4	2012	5.0	
18	F	0200	0.6	0831	5.1	1424	0.7	2057	4.7	
19	SA	0241	0.9	0914	4.8	1508	1.0	2142	4.4	
20	SU	0326	1.3	0959	4.5	1554	1.4	2234	4.1	
21	M	0414	1.7	1051	4.3	1648	1.7	2340	3.9	◑
22	TU	0512	2.0	1202	4.1	1755	1.9			
23	W	0054	3.8	0626	2.1	1316	4.0	1917	1.9	
24	TH	0202	3.9	0747	2.0	1420	4.1	2027	1.7	
25	F	0258	4.1	0852	1.7	1515	4.3	2120	1.5	
26	SA	0347	4.3	0943	1.5	1602	4.4	2206	1.3	
27	SU	0430	4.5	1026	1.2	1646	4.6	2247	1.1	
28	M	0510	4.7	1106	1.1	1726	4.7	2323	1.0	
29	TU	0548	4.8	1141	1.0	1805	4.7	2356	1.0	●
30	W	0625	4.8	1213	1.0	1842	4.7			

DECEMBER

Date	Day	Time	m	Time	m	Time	m	Time	m	Moon
1	TH	0025	1.0	0659	4.8	1245	1.1	1916	4.6	
2	F	0055	1.1	0733	4.8	1315	1.1	1949	4.5	
3	SA	0124	1.2	0804	4.7	1345	1.2	2021	4.4	
4	SU	0153	1.3	0835	4.6	1417	1.4	2054	4.3	
5	M	0228	1.5	0911	4.5	1454	1.5	2135	4.2	
6	TU	0308	1.7	0955	4.3	1542	1.7	2225	4.0	
7	W	0401	1.8	1049	4.2	1645	1.8	2326	4.0	◐
8	TH	0513	2.0	1153	4.2	1806	1.8			
9	F	0036	4.0	0641	1.9	1305	4.2	1926	1.6	
10	SA	0154	4.2	0800	1.6	1423	4.4	2036	1.3	
11	SU	0307	4.4	0908	1.3	1532	4.6	2139	1.0	
12	M	0409	4.7	1008	1.0	1634	4.8	2235	0.7	
13	TU	0505	5.0	1103	0.7	1730	5.0	2327	0.5	
14	W	0557	5.1	1154	0.5	1824	5.0			○
15	TH	0016	0.4	0647	5.2	1244	0.4	1913	5.0	
16	F	0103	0.4	0733	5.2	1329	0.4	2000	4.9	
17	SA	0146	0.6	0817	5.1	1413	0.6	2044	4.7	
18	SU	0228	0.8	0859	4.9	1454	0.9	2127	4.5	
19	M	0309	1.1	0939	4.7	1536	1.2	2208	4.3	
20	TU	0351	1.4	1019	4.4	1620	1.5	2252	4.0	
21	W	0436	1.8	1105	4.2	1709	1.8	2348	3.9	◑
22	TH	0529	2.0	1205	4.0	1807	1.9			
23	F	0056	3.8	0634	2.1	1318	3.9	1916	2.0	
24	SA	0204	3.9	0746	2.0	1424	4.0	2024	1.8	
25	SU	0301	4.1	0852	1.8	1522	4.1	2121	1.6	
26	M	0353	4.3	0946	1.6	1613	4.3	2209	1.4	
27	TU	0440	4.5	1032	1.4	1659	4.4	2251	1.2	
28	W	0523	4.6	1113	1.2	1744	4.5	2329	1.1	
29	TH	0604	4.8	1151	1.1	1825	4.6			●
30	F	0005	1.0	0643	4.8	1227	1.0	1903	4.6	
31	SA	0041	1.0	0719	4.8	1304	1.0	1939	4.6	

Chart Datum: 2·62 metres below Ordnance Datum (Newlyn)
HAT is 5·3 metres above Chart Datum

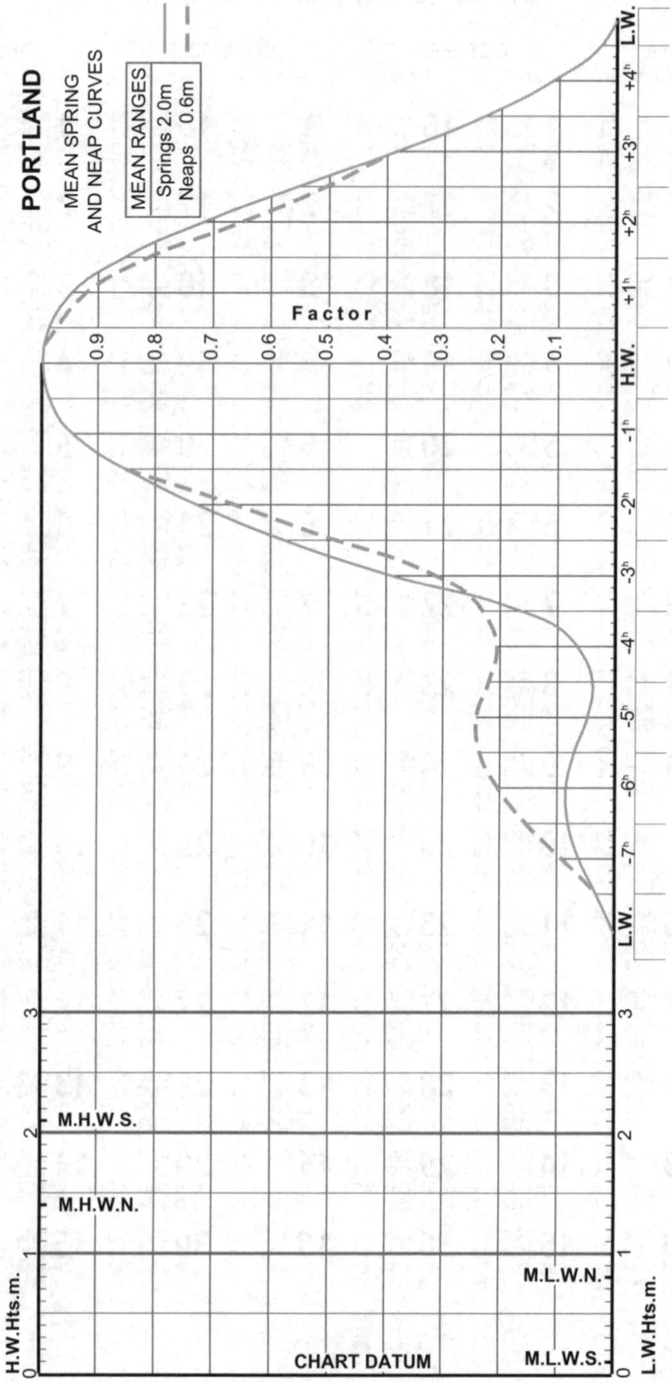
PORTLAND
MEAN SPRING
AND NEAP CURVES
MEAN RANGES
Springs 2.0m
Neaps 0.6m
Factor
0.9
0.8
0.7
0.6
0.5
0.4
0.3
0.2
0.1
L.W.
-7h
-6h
-5h
-4h
-3h
-2h
-1h
H.W.
+1h
+2h
+3h
+4h
L.W.
H.W.Hts.m.
0
1
2
3
M.H.W.S.
M.H.W.N.
CHART DATUM
M.L.W.N.
M.L.W.S.
L.W.Hts.m.

Note - Double LWs occur at Portland. The predictions are for the first LW. The second LW occurs from 3 to 4 Hrs later and may, at Springs, on occasions be lower than the first.

TIME ZONE (UT)
For Summer Time add ONE hour in **non-shaded areas**

PORTLAND

LAT 50°34'N LONG 2°26'W

TIMES AND HEIGHTS OF HIGH AND LOW WATERS

Dates in amber are **SPRINGS**
Dates in grey are **NEAPS**

2016

Day	JANUARY Time m	FEBRUARY Time m	MARCH Time m	APRIL Time m
1	F 0306 0.7 1037 1.7 1541 0.6 2305 1.5	M 0341 0.6 1111 1.5 1611 0.6 ◑ 2339 1.4	TU 0308 0.5 1033 1.5 1531 0.5 ◑ 2252 1.5	F 0435 0.6 1200 1.3 1707 0.6
2	SA 0334 0.8 1115 1.6 1613 0.7 ◑ 2349 1.4	TU 0435 0.7 1200 1.4 1709 0.6	W 0355 0.6 1120 1.4 1627 0.6 2348 1.4	SA 0031 1.4 0817 0.7 1342 1.3 1829 0.7
3	SU 0420 0.9 1202 1.4 1702 0.7	W 0042 1.4 0545 0.8 1314 1.3 1816 0.7	TH 0505 0.7 1225 1.3 1737 0.6	SU 0225 1.4 0827 0.6 1515 1.4 2022 0.6
4	M 0053 1.4 0527 0.9 1310 1.4 1916 0.7	TH 0224 1.4 0812 0.8 1456 1.4 1948 0.7	F 0109 1.3 0623 0.7 1415 1.3 1856 0.7	M 0341 1.6 0911 0.4 1619 1.6 2124 0.4
5	TU 0218 1.4 0747 0.9 1434 1.4 2010 0.7	F 0340 1.6 0904 0.7 1610 1.5 2116 0.6	SA 0301 1.5 0847 0.6 1541 1.4 2053 0.6	TU 0442 1.8 0958 0.3 1718 1.8 2215 0.3
6	W 0328 1.6 0839 0.8 1545 1.5 2057 0.6	SA 0441 1.8 0953 0.5 1712 1.7 2209 0.5	SU 0410 1.7 0934 0.5 1646 1.6 2148 0.4	W 0537 2.0 1045 0.1 1813 2.0 2303 0.2
7	TH 0425 1.8 0926 0.7 1646 1.6 2143 0.5	SU 0535 1.9 1042 0.4 1807 1.8 2258 0.3	M 0509 1.9 1022 0.3 1744 1.8 2238 0.3	TH 0630 2.2 1130 0.0 1904 2.2 ● 2348 0.0
8	F 0516 1.9 1013 0.6 1740 1.8 2228 0.5	M 0625 2.1 1128 0.3 1857 2.0 ● 2344 0.2	TU 0602 2.1 1109 0.2 1837 2.0 2326 0.1	F 0722 2.3 1213 -0.1 1952 2.3
9	SA 0602 2.0 1059 0.5 1828 1.9 2314 0.4	TU 0712 2.2 1212 0.1 1945 2.1	W 0653 2.2 1153 0.0 1929 2.1 ●	SA 0030 0.0 0813 2.4 1254 -0.1 2035 2.3
10	SU 0645 2.1 1143 0.4 1911 2.0 ● 2358 0.3	W 0027 0.1 0758 2.3 1254 0.1 2028 2.1	TH 0009 0.0 0744 2.3 1235 -0.1 2016 2.2	SU 0110 0.0 0857 2.3 1333 0.0 2110 2.2
11	M 0725 2.2 1226 0.3 1950 2.0	TH 0109 0.1 0839 2.3 1336 0.0 2103 2.1	F 0051 0.0 0831 2.4 1316 -0.1 2054 2.2	M 0149 0.1 0934 2.1 1412 0.2 2141 2.1
12	TU 0039 0.3 0803 2.2 1307 0.2 2028 2.0	F 0150 0.1 0917 2.2 1417 0.0 2136 2.0	SA 0131 0.0 0911 2.3 1356 0.0 2125 2.1	TU 0227 0.3 1009 1.9 1452 0.4 2215 1.9
13	W 0121 0.2 0841 2.2 1350 0.2 2105 2.0	SA 0230 0.2 0954 2.1 1459 0.1 2212 1.9	SU 0210 0.1 0945 2.1 1436 0.1 2155 2.0	W 0309 0.4 1051 1.6 1537 0.6 2256 1.6
14	TH 0203 0.3 0921 2.1 1434 0.2 2146 1.9	SU 0310 0.3 1035 1.9 1542 0.3 2254 1.7	M 0248 0.2 1021 1.9 1516 0.3 2231 1.8	TH 0401 0.6 1150 1.4 1636 0.8 ◐ 2352 1.5
15	F 0246 0.3 1003 2.0 1519 0.3 2230 1.8	M 0352 0.5 1123 1.7 1630 0.5 ◐ 2347 1.5	TU 0327 0.4 1105 1.6 1601 0.5 ◐ 2315 1.6	F 0526 0.8 1329 1.3 1759 0.9
16	SA 0330 0.4 1050 1.8 1608 0.4 ◐ 2320 1.7	TU 0443 0.7 1239 1.4 1731 0.7	W 0416 0.6 1215 1.4 1700 0.7	SA 0148 1.4 0650 0.8 1446 1.3 1911 0.8
17	SU 0419 0.6 1147 1.7 1701 0.5	W 0118 1.4 0603 0.8 1410 1.3 1902 0.7	TH 0030 1.4 0543 0.8 1353 1.3 1834 0.8	SU 0303 1.5 0755 0.7 1544 1.5 2012 0.7
18	M 0027 1.5 0519 0.7 1307 1.5 1806 0.6	TH 0241 1.4 0833 0.8 1523 1.4 2027 0.7	F 0220 1.4 0740 0.8 1508 1.3 1953 0.8	M 0400 1.6 0848 0.5 1635 1.6 2105 0.6
19	TU 0152 1.5 0634 0.8 1429 1.5 1928 0.7	F 0348 1.6 0918 0.7 1628 1.5 2124 0.6	SA 0329 1.5 0843 0.7 1609 1.5 2052 0.7	TU 0449 1.7 0936 0.4 1721 1.8 2155 0.4
20	W 0303 1.6 0836 0.8 1538 1.5 2049 0.6	SA 0447 1.8 1003 0.6 1724 1.7 2213 0.5	SU 0427 1.7 0931 0.5 1702 1.7 2143 0.5	W 0534 1.9 1022 0.3 1804 1.9 2241 0.3
21	TH 0406 1.7 0934 0.7 1643 1.7 2144 0.5	SU 0538 1.9 1046 0.4 1814 1.9 2258 0.3	M 0517 1.8 1015 0.4 1750 1.8 2230 0.3	TH 0616 2.0 1105 0.2 1844 2.0 2323 0.2
22	F 0503 1.9 1022 0.6 1742 1.8 2233 0.4	M 0625 2.1 1126 0.3 1900 2.0 ○ 2338 0.2	TU 0603 2.0 1057 0.2 1834 2.0 2313 0.2	F 0653 2.0 1143 0.2 1919 2.1 ○
23	SA 0554 2.1 1106 0.5 1833 1.9 2317 0.3	TU 0708 2.1 1203 0.2 1941 2.0	W 0645 2.1 1137 0.2 1915 2.0 ○ 2352 0.1	SA 0000 0.2 0727 2.0 1215 0.2 1950 2.0
24	SU 0642 2.2 1145 0.3 1920 2.0 ○ 2357 0.3	W 0015 0.1 0747 2.2 1238 0.1 2016 2.0	TH 0722 2.1 1213 0.1 1949 2.1	SU 0031 0.2 0757 2.0 1243 0.2 2017 2.0
25	M 0725 2.2 1222 0.3 2002 2.0	TH 0050 0.1 0818 2.1 1311 0.2 2041 2.0	F 0026 0.1 0754 2.1 1244 0.1 2016 2.0	M 0059 0.2 0823 1.9 1310 0.3 2039 1.9
26	TU 0034 0.2 0804 2.2 1258 0.2 2035 2.0	F 0122 0.2 0846 2.0 1340 0.2 2105 1.9	SA 0057 0.2 0822 2.0 1312 0.2 2041 1.9	TU 0127 0.3 0845 1.8 1338 0.3 2057 1.8
27	W 0110 0.2 0837 2.1 1334 0.3 2103 1.9	SA 0149 0.3 0913 1.9 1405 0.3 2128 1.7	SU 0124 0.2 0847 1.9 1336 0.3 2102 1.8	W 0157 0.3 0912 1.7 1408 0.3 2124 1.7
28	TH 0144 0.3 0908 2.0 1408 0.3 2130 1.8	SU 0213 0.3 0937 1.7 1427 0.3 2149 1.6	M 0148 0.3 0909 1.7 1400 0.3 2118 1.7	TH 0231 0.4 0951 1.5 1443 0.4 2206 1.6
29	F 0214 0.4 0938 1.9 1436 0.4 2157 1.7	M 0237 0.4 1000 1.6 1454 0.4 2214 1.5	TU 0214 0.3 0931 1.6 1426 0.3 2142 1.6	F 0315 0.4 1042 1.4 1533 0.5 2301 1.5
30	SA 0239 0.5 1007 1.7 1459 0.5 2225 1.6		W 0243 0.4 1006 1.5 1459 0.4 2222 1.5	SA 0421 0.5 1145 1.3 1648 0.6 ◑
31	SU 0304 0.6 1036 1.6 1528 0.5 2257 1.5		TH 0324 0.5 1056 1.4 1550 0.5 ◑ 2318 1.4	

Chart Datum: 0·93 metres below Ordnance Datum (Newlyn)
HAT is 2·5 metres above Chart Datum

TIME ZONE (UT)
For Summer Time add ONE hour in **non-shaded areas**

PORTLAND

LAT 50°34'N LONG 2°26'W

TIMES AND HEIGHTS OF HIGH AND LOW WATERS

Dates in amber are **SPRINGS**
Dates in grey are **NEAPS**

2016

MAY

Date	Day	Time	m
1	SU	0010 0538 1315 1807	1.4 0.6 1.3 0.7
2	M	0147 0711 1446 1937	1.5 0.5 1.5 0.6
3	TU	0308 0839 1551 2052	1.6 0.4 1.7 0.5
4	W	0411 0930 1649 2148	1.8 0.3 1.9 0.4
5	TH	0509 1019 1744 2238	2.0 0.2 2.1 0.2
6	F	0604 1106 1835 ● 2326	2.1 0.1 2.2 0.2
7	SA	0657 1150 1924	2.3 0.0 2.3
8	SU	0009 0750 1231 2010	0.1 2.3 0.0 2.3
9	M	0050 0838 1311 2051	0.1 2.2 0.1 2.2
10	TU	0130 0919 1351 2127	0.2 2.1 0.2 2.1
11	W	0211 0957 1432 2202	0.3 1.9 0.4 1.9
12	TH	0255 1036 1517 2241	0.5 1.7 0.6 1.7
13	F	0349 1122 1612 ◐ 2327	0.6 1.5 0.7 1.6
14	SA	0457 1235 1721	0.7 1.3 0.8
15	SU	0030 0608 1410 1830	1.4 0.7 1.3 0.9
16	M	0214 0711 1511 1932	1.4 0.7 1.4 0.8
17	TU	0319 0807 1601 2027	1.5 0.6 1.6 0.7
18	W	0411 0857 1647 2118	1.6 0.5 1.7 0.5
19	TH	0458 0945 1730 2207	1.7 0.4 1.9 0.4
20	F	0541 1031 1810 2253	1.8 0.3 2.0 0.4
21	SA	0622 1112 1848 ○ 2333	1.9 0.3 2.1 0.3
22	SU	0659 1147 1924	1.9 0.3 2.1
23	M	0007 0733 1218 1956	0.3 1.9 0.3 2.0
24	TU	0039 0802 1250 2022	0.3 1.9 0.3 2.0
25	W	0111 0829 1324 2046	0.3 1.8 0.3 1.9
26	TH	0147 0902 1400 2119	0.3 1.7 0.3 1.8
27	F	0228 0943 1441 2200	0.3 1.6 0.4 1.7
28	SA	0315 1032 1532 2251	0.4 1.5 0.5 1.6
29	SU	0413 1131 1635 ◑ 2353	0.5 1.4 0.6 1.5
30	M	0518 1248 1743	0.5 1.4 0.6
31	TU	0113 0630 1414 1857	1.5 0.5 1.5 0.6

JUNE

Date	Day	Time	m
1	W	0234 0751 1520 2014	1.6 0.4 1.7 0.6
2	TH	0340 0859 1619 2120	1.7 0.3 1.8 0.5
3	F	0441 0952 1715 2215	1.9 0.3 2.0 0.4
4	SA	0540 1042 1808 2305	2.0 0.2 2.2 0.3
5	SU	0635 1129 1858 ● 2352	2.1 0.1 2.3 0.2
6	M	0730 1212 1946	2.1 0.1 2.3
7	TU	0034 0821 1253 2031	0.2 2.1 0.2 2.3
8	W	0116 0904 1333 2111	0.2 2.0 0.3 2.2
9	TH	0158 0941 1414 2147	0.3 1.9 0.4 2.0
10	F	0241 1016 1457 2223	0.4 1.7 0.5 1.8
11	SA	0329 1053 1543 2301	0.5 1.6 0.7 1.7
12	SU	0423 1137 1638 ◐ 2345	0.6 1.4 0.8 1.5
13	M	0525 1237 1745	0.7 1.3 0.8
14	TU	0041 0630 1407 1853	1.4 0.7 1.4 0.8
15	W	0158 0729 1513 1952	1.4 0.6 1.5 0.8
16	TH	0312 0822 1604 2045	1.5 0.6 1.6 0.7
17	F	0411 0911 1651 2136	1.6 0.5 1.8 0.6
18	SA	0503 0958 1735 2224	1.7 0.4 1.9 0.5
19	SU	0550 1042 1818 2308	1.8 0.4 2.0 0.4
20	M	0633 1122 1859 ○ 2348	1.9 0.3 2.1 0.4
21	TU	0713 1159 1937	1.9 0.3 2.1
22	W	0024 0748 1236 2010	0.3 1.9 0.3 2.1
23	TH	0102 0819 1315 2041	0.3 1.9 0.3 2.0
24	F	0141 0855 1355 2115	0.3 1.8 0.3 1.9
25	SA	0224 0935 1438 2155	0.3 1.7 0.3 1.9
26	SU	0310 1021 1525 2240	0.3 1.6 0.4 1.8
27	M	0400 1114 1618 ◑ 2335	0.3 1.6 0.5 1.6
28	TU	0456 1220 1717	0.4 1.5 0.6
29	W	0044 0559 1341 1825	1.6 0.5 1.5 0.7
30	TH	0205 0711 1452 1941	1.6 0.5 1.6 0.7

JULY

Date	Day	Time	m
1	F	0315 0829 1553 2059	1.6 0.5 1.8 0.6
2	SA	0421 0932 1652 2202	1.7 0.4 1.9 0.5
3	SU	0523 1025 1747 2255	1.8 0.3 2.1 0.4
4	M	0621 1113 1838 ● 2342	2.0 0.2 2.2 0.3
5	TU	0715 1156 1927	2.0 0.2 2.3
6	W	0023 0806 1237 2012	0.2 2.1 0.2 2.3
7	TH	0103 0849 1316 2053	0.2 2.0 0.2 2.2
8	F	0142 0922 1355 2127	0.2 1.9 0.3 2.1
9	SA	0222 0952 1434 2200	0.3 1.8 0.4 1.9
10	SU	0302 1022 1511 2232	0.4 1.6 0.5 1.7
11	M	0340 1057 1545 2307	0.5 1.5 0.7 1.6
12	TU	0414 1137 1621 ◐ 2348	0.6 1.4 0.8 1.5
13	W	0450 1230 1715	0.7 1.4 0.8
14	TH	0040 0640 1347 1917	1.4 0.7 1.4 0.8
15	F	0156 0747 1506 2017	1.4 0.7 1.5 0.7
16	SA	0316 0839 1608 2110	1.4 0.6 1.6 0.6
17	SU	0423 0928 1700 2200	1.5 0.5 1.8 0.5
18	M	0520 1015 1749 2248	1.7 0.4 1.9 0.5
19	TU	0609 1101 1834 ○ 2332	1.8 0.4 2.1 0.4
20	W	0655 1143 1918	1.9 0.3 2.1
21	TH	0012 0737 1224 1959	0.3 1.9 0.2 2.2
22	F	0052 0814 1305 2035	0.2 1.9 0.2 2.1
23	SA	0132 0849 1346 2108	0.1 1.9 0.2 2.1
24	SU	0213 0925 1427 2145	0.1 1.9 0.2 2.0
25	M	0256 1006 1510 2226	0.2 1.8 0.3 1.9
26	TU	0341 1053 1557 ◑ 2315	0.3 1.7 0.4 1.7
27	W	0431 1150 1650	0.4 1.6 0.6
28	TH	0018 0530 1310 1756	1.5 0.5 1.5 0.7
29	F	0145 0642 1430 1922	1.5 0.6 1.5 0.8
30	SA	0302 0815 1536 2106	1.5 0.6 1.7 0.7
31	SU	0410 0920 1637 2200	1.6 0.5 1.8 0.6

AUGUST

Date	Day	Time	m
1	M	0512 1012 1732 2248	1.7 0.4 2.0 0.4
2	TU	0608 1059 1822 ● 2331	1.9 0.3 2.1 0.3
3	W	0659 1141 1909	2.0 0.2 2.2
4	TH	0010 0747 1220 1953	0.2 2.1 0.2 2.3
5	F	0047 0828 1258 2032	0.2 2.0 0.2 2.2
6	SA	0123 0859 1334 2103	0.2 2.0 0.2 2.1
7	SU	0158 0924 1408 2133	0.2 1.9 0.3 1.9
8	M	0230 0950 1438 2201	0.3 1.7 0.4 1.8
9	TU	0256 1018 1503 2231	0.4 1.6 0.6 1.6
10	W	0318 1050 1532 ◐ 2304	0.5 1.5 0.6 1.5
11	TH	0352 1131 1619 2347	0.6 1.4 0.7 1.4
12	F	0444 1227 1724	0.7 1.4 0.8
13	SA	0048 0550 1359 1959	1.3 0.7 1.4 0.8
14	SU	0225 0810 1523 2051	1.3 0.7 1.5 0.7
15	M	0347 0903 1626 2140	1.4 0.6 1.7 0.5
16	TU	0452 0952 1720 2228	1.6 0.5 1.9 0.4
17	W	0546 1040 1810 2313	1.8 0.4 2.1 0.3
18	TH	0635 1126 1857 ○ 2356	1.9 0.3 2.2 0.2
19	F	0722 1209 1942	2.0 0.2 2.3
20	SA	0036 0806 1250 2025	0.1 2.1 0.1 2.3
21	SU	0116 0841 1330 2100	0.0 2.1 0.1 2.2
22	M	0156 0913 1410 2133	0.1 2.0 0.2 2.1
23	TU	0236 0948 1451 2211	0.1 1.9 0.3 1.9
24	W	0318 1029 1533 2256	0.3 1.8 0.4 1.7
25	TH	0404 1120 1623 ◑ 2358	0.5 1.6 0.6 1.5
26	F	0501 1241 1732	0.6 1.5 0.8
27	SA	0135 0622 1414 1947	1.4 0.8 1.5 0.8
28	SU	0255 0803 1523 2055	1.4 0.7 1.6 0.7
29	M	0402 0902 1623 2143	1.5 0.6 1.8 0.6
30	TU	0500 0953 1716 2228	1.7 0.5 2.0 0.4
31	W	0551 1039 1805 2311	1.9 0.4 2.1 0.3

Chart Datum: 0·93 metres below Ordnance Datum (Newlyn)
HAT is 2·5 metres above Chart Datum

TIME ZONE (UT)
For Summer Time add ONE hour in **non-shaded areas**

PORTLAND

LAT 50°34'N LONG 2°26'W

TIMES AND HEIGHTS OF HIGH AND LOW WATERS

Dates in amber are **SPRINGS**
Dates in grey are **NEAPS**

2016

SEPTEMBER

Date	Day	Time	m	Time	m	Time	m	Time	m
1	TH	0638	2.0	1122	0.2	1850	2.2	● 2350	0.2
2	F	0722	2.1	1200	0.2	1931	2.2		
3	SA	0025	0.1	0801	2.1	1236	0.1	2007	2.2
4	SU	0058	0.1	0830	2.1	1310	0.2	2036	2.1
5	M	0129	0.2	0852	1.9	1341	0.3	2103	2.0
6	TU	0156	0.3	0916	1.8	1407	0.4	2129	1.8
7	W	0217	0.4	0941	1.7	1429	0.5	2155	1.6
8	TH	0237	0.5	1006	1.6	1456	0.6	2223	1.5
9	F	0308	0.6	1040	1.5	1537	0.7	◐ 2304	1.4
10	SA	0357	0.7	1132	1.4	1644	0.8		
11	SU	0005	1.3	0509	0.8	1250	1.4	1951	0.8
12	M	0145	1.3	0628	0.8	1443	1.5	2034	0.7
13	TU	0319	1.4	0840	0.7	1553	1.7	2119	0.5
14	W	0425	1.6	0929	0.5	1651	1.9	2204	0.4
15	TH	0521	1.8	1017	0.4	1744	2.1	2249	0.3
16	F	0612	2.0	1104	0.3	1833	2.2	○ 2333	0.1
17	SA	0700	2.1	1149	0.2	1920	2.3		
18	SU	0015	0.1	0746	2.2	1230	0.1	2006	2.4
19	M	0055	0.0	0824	2.3	1310	0.1	2046	2.3
20	TU	0134	0.1	0855	2.2	1350	0.1	2120	2.2
21	W	0213	0.2	0927	2.1	1429	0.3	2156	2.0
22	TH	0253	0.4	1006	1.9	1510	0.5	2241	1.7
23	F	0336	0.6	1054	1.7	1600	0.7	◑ 2347	1.5
24	SA	0433	0.8	1208	1.5	1721	0.8		
25	SU	0126	1.4	0607	0.9	1356	1.5	1915	0.8
26	M	0245	1.4	0733	0.9	1508	1.6	2021	0.7
27	TU	0348	1.6	0834	0.8	1606	1.8	2112	0.6
28	W	0441	1.8	0925	0.6	1657	1.9	2158	0.4
29	TH	0529	1.9	1012	0.5	1743	2.1	2241	0.3
30	F	0613	2.1	1056	0.3	1826	2.2	2322	0.2

OCTOBER

Date	Day	Time	m	Time	m	Time	m	Time	m
1	SA	0654	2.2	1135	0.2	1906	2.2	● 2358	0.2
2	SU	0730	2.2	1211	0.2	1939	2.2		
3	M	0030	0.2	0758	2.1	1243	0.2	2007	2.1
4	TU	0059	0.3	0822	2.0	1313	0.3	2034	2.0
5	W	0123	0.4	0845	1.9	1338	0.4	2059	1.8
6	TH	0144	0.4	0905	1.8	1401	0.5	2121	1.7
7	F	0205	0.5	0925	1.7	1427	0.5	2149	1.6
8	SA	0231	0.6	0959	1.6	1502	0.6	2234	1.4
9	SU	0306	0.7	1053	1.5	1610	0.7	◐ 2337	1.3
10	M	0431	0.8	1206	1.4	1943	0.8		
11	TU	0110	1.3	0558	0.9	1403	1.4	2017	0.7
12	W	0253	1.5	0808	0.8	1521	1.6	2053	0.5
13	TH	0358	1.7	0901	0.6	1621	1.8	2137	0.4
14	F	0454	1.9	0950	0.5	1715	2.0	2221	0.3
15	SA	0545	2.1	1038	0.3	1806	2.2	2306	0.2
16	SU	0632	2.3	1124	0.2	1854	2.3	○ 2350	0.1
17	M	0716	2.4	1208	0.2	1940	2.4		
18	TU	0031	0.1	0756	2.4	1248	0.1	2025	2.3
19	W	0111	0.1	0832	2.3	1328	0.2	2105	2.2
20	TH	0150	0.3	0908	2.2	1409	0.3	2146	2.0
21	F	0229	0.5	0949	2.0	1452	0.5	2233	1.8
22	SA	0313	0.7	1036	1.8	1546	0.7	◑ 2335	1.6
23	SU	0411	0.9	1138	1.6	1708	0.8		
24	M	0106	1.4	0536	1.0	1328	1.5	1830	0.9
25	TU	0225	1.5	0652	1.0	1443	1.6	1935	0.8
26	W	0327	1.6	0755	0.9	1541	1.7	2030	0.7
27	TH	0417	1.8	0848	0.8	1631	1.8	2118	0.5
28	F	0502	1.9	0937	0.6	1717	2.0	2203	0.4
29	SA	0544	2.1	1023	0.5	1759	2.1	2246	0.3
30	SU	0624	2.2	1105	0.4	1837	2.1	● 2326	0.3
31	M	0658	2.2	1143	0.3	1910	2.1		

NOVEMBER

Date	Day	Time	m	Time	m	Time	m	Time	m
1	TU	0000	0.3	0728	2.2	1218	0.3	1940	2.1
2	W	0029	0.3	0755	2.1	1247	0.4	2009	2.0
3	TH	0055	0.4	0819	2.0	1314	0.4	2034	1.8
4	F	0119	0.5	0840	1.9	1341	0.5	2058	1.7
5	SA	0145	0.5	0902	1.8	1412	0.5	2130	1.6
6	SU	0212	0.6	0937	1.7	1450	0.6	2215	1.5
7	M	0245	0.7	1029	1.6	1551	0.7	◐ 2315	1.4
8	TU	0358	0.8	1137	1.5	1708	0.7		
9	W	0036	1.4	0530	0.9	1310	1.5	2008	0.7
10	TH	0219	1.5	0656	0.8	1443	1.6	2013	0.6
11	F	0326	1.7	0821	0.7	1546	1.8	2103	0.4
12	SA	0421	1.9	0919	0.6	1643	2.0	2151	0.3
13	SU	0513	2.1	1010	0.4	1736	2.1	2238	0.2
14	M	0601	2.3	1059	0.3	1827	2.3	○ 2325	0.2
15	TU	0647	2.4	1145	0.3	1916	2.3		
16	W	0008	0.2	0730	2.4	1228	0.2	2005	2.3
17	TH	0049	0.2	0813	2.4	1310	0.3	2053	2.2
18	F	0130	0.3	0855	2.3	1353	0.4	2137	2.0
19	SA	0211	0.5	0938	2.1	1439	0.5	2221	1.8
20	SU	0255	0.7	1023	1.9	1532	0.7	2310	1.6
21	M	0348	0.9	1112	1.7	1638	0.8	◑	
22	TU	0021	1.5	0456	1.0	1220	1.6	1746	0.8
23	W	0148	1.5	0607	1.0	1359	1.5	1849	0.8
24	TH	0253	1.5	0711	1.0	1504	1.6	1946	0.7
25	F	0344	1.7	0808	0.9	1556	1.7	2037	0.6
26	SA	0431	1.8	0859	0.7	1644	1.8	2125	0.5
27	SU	0513	2.0	0947	0.6	1728	1.9	2211	0.4
28	M	0552	2.1	1034	0.5	1807	2.0	2254	0.4
29	TU	0628	2.2	1117	0.5	1844	2.0	● 2332	0.4
30	W	0702	2.2	1154	0.4	1918	2.0		

DECEMBER

Date	Day	Time	m	Time	m	Time	m	Time	m
1	TH	0004	0.4	0733	2.1	1226	0.4	1950	1.9
2	F	0033	0.4	0802	2.1	1257	0.4	2018	1.9
3	SA	0104	0.5	0827	2.0	1330	0.4	2047	1.8
4	SU	0137	0.5	0855	1.9	1407	0.5	2121	1.7
5	M	0211	0.5	0931	1.8	1449	0.5	2203	1.6
6	TU	0250	0.6	1017	1.7	1542	0.6	2256	1.5
7	W	0347	0.7	1115	1.6	1645	0.6	◐	
8	TH	0003	1.4	0503	0.8	1229	1.5	2028	0.7
9	F	0133	1.5	0617	0.8	1359	1.6	1907	0.6
10	SA	0248	1.6	0733	0.8	1510	1.7	2021	0.5
11	SU	0347	1.8	0845	0.7	1611	1.8	2121	0.4
12	M	0443	2.0	0944	0.6	1710	2.0	2214	0.3
13	TU	0535	2.2	1038	0.5	1806	2.1	2303	0.3
14	W	0624	2.3	1128	0.4	1900	2.2	○ 2350	0.2
15	TH	0712	2.4	1214	0.3	1952	2.2		
16	F	0033	0.3	0759	2.4	1257	0.3	2043	2.2
17	SA	0115	0.3	0844	2.3	1340	0.3	2125	2.0
18	SU	0156	0.4	0927	2.2	1425	0.4	2203	1.9
19	M	0238	0.6	1007	2.0	1511	0.5	2241	1.7
20	TU	0322	0.7	1046	1.8	1603	0.6	2323	1.6
21	W	0412	0.8	1130	1.6	1701	0.7	◑	
22	TH	0017	1.4	0516	0.9	1225	1.5	1804	0.8
23	F	0146	1.4	0628	1.0	1345	1.4	1905	0.7
24	SA	0258	1.5	0731	0.9	1503	1.5	2000	0.7
25	SU	0351	1.6	0827	0.8	1601	1.6	2051	0.6
26	M	0437	1.8	0917	0.7	1653	1.7	2139	0.5
27	TU	0519	1.9	1007	0.6	1738	1.8	2226	0.5
28	W	0600	2.0	1053	0.5	1821	1.9	2308	0.4
29	TH	0639	2.1	1135	0.5	1901	1.9	● 2345	0.4
30	F	0716	2.1	1212	0.4	1937	1.9		
31	SA	0020	0.4	0750	2.1	1246	0.4	2010	1.9

Chart Datum: 0·93 metres below Ordnance Datum (Newlyn)
HAT is 2·5 metres above Chart Datum

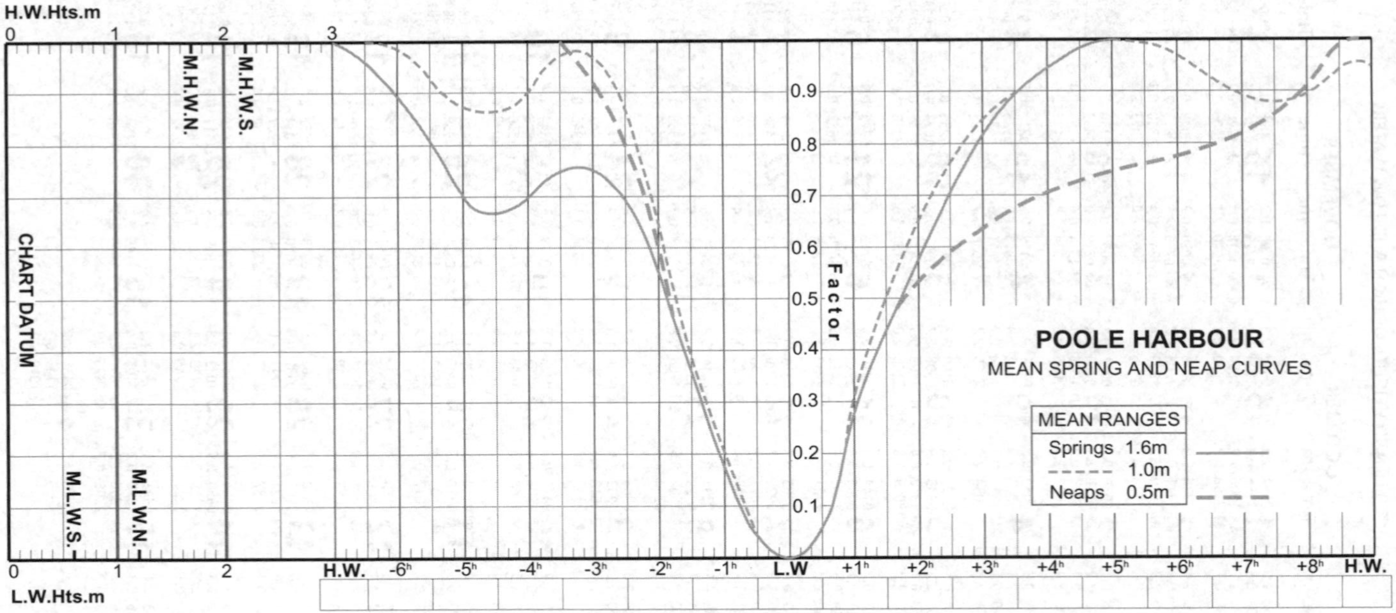

Note - Sea level is above mean tide level from 2 hrs after LW to 2 hrs before the next LW. HW occurs between 5 hrs after LW and 3 hrs before the next LW, the time shown is approximate and should be checked for suitability.

TIME ZONE (UT)
For Summer Time add ONE hour in **non-shaded areas**

POOLE HARBOUR

LAT 50°43′N LONG 1°59′W

TIMES AND HEIGHTS OF HIGH AND LOW WATERS

Dates in amber are **SPRINGS**
Dates in grey are **NEAPS**

2016

JANUARY

Date	Time	m	Date	Time	m
1 F	0832 1133 2049	1.2 1.8 1.0	16 SA	0115 0835 1322 ◐ 2059	1.9 0.9 1.9 0.8
2 SA	0001 0918 1213 ◑ 2137	1.6 1.3 1.7 1.1	17 SU	0204 0938 1410 2206	1.8 1.0 1.8 0.9
3 SU	0049 1012 1302 2235	1.6 1.3 1.6 1.2	18 M	0259 1051 1503 2320	1.7 1.1 1.7 0.9
4 M	0203 1119 1408 2345	1.5 1.3 1.5 1.2	19 TU	0803 1203 1609	2.0 1.0 1.7
5 TU	0852 1235 1556	1.8 1.2 1.5	20 W	0029 0649 1307 1901	0.9 1.9 0.9 1.8
6 W	0054 0644 1330 1714	1.2 1.8 1.1 1.6	21 TH	0131 0726 1404 1945	0.9 2.0 0.7 1.9
7 TH	0147 0548 1418 1921	1.1 1.9 0.9 1.7	22 F	0227 0805 1456 2026	0.8 2.0 0.6 1.9
8 F	0235 0627 1501 2004	0.9 2.0 0.8 1.9	23 SA	0317 0841 1543 2103	0.7 2.1 0.5 2.0
9 SA	0320 0722 1545 2050	0.8 2.1 0.6 2.0	24 SU	0403 0913 1627 ○ 2137	0.6 2.2 0.4 2.1
10 SU	0404 0854 1627 ● 2135	0.7 2.2 0.5 2.1	25 M	0446 0943 1708 2209	0.6 2.2 0.4 2.1
11 M	0447 0944 1709 2219	0.6 2.3 0.4 2.1	26 TU	0527 1013 1747 2242	0.6 2.2 0.4 2.1
12 TU	0529 1029 1750 2302	0.6 2.3 0.4 2.1	27 W	0606 1047 1824 2318	0.7 2.2 0.5 2.0
13 W	0612 1112 1832 2345	0.6 2.3 0.4 2.1	28 TH	0642 1121 1857 2358	0.8 2.0 0.6 1.9
14 TH	0656 1155 1916	0.7 2.2 0.5	29 F	0715 1044 1931 2259	0.9 1.9 0.8 1.7
15 F	0029 0743 1238 2004	2.0 0.8 2.1 0.6	30 SA	0752 1102 2009 2322	1.0 1.8 0.9 1.7
			31 SU	0833 1135 2053 2358	1.0 1.7 1.0 1.6

FEBRUARY

Date	Time	m	Date	Time	m
1 M	0921 1214 2145 ◑	1.1 1.6 1.1	16 TU	0214 1024 1433 2258	1.7 1.0 1.6 1.1
2 TU	0045 1018 1304 2246	1.6 1.2 1.6 1.2	17 W	0307 1141 1537	1.6 1.0 1.6
3 W	0159 1124 1425 2354	1.5 1.2 1.5 1.2	18 TH	0014 0836 1251 1901	1.1 1.9 0.9 1.8
4 TH	0409 1235 1629	1.6 1.1 1.5	19 F	0120 0719 1350 1940	1.0 1.8 0.8 1.8
5 F	0105 0506 1342 1917	1.1 1.7 1.0 1.7	20 SA	0216 0755 1442 2018	0.9 1.9 0.6 1.8
6 SA	0207 0559 1437 1957	1.0 1.9 0.8 1.8	21 SU	0305 0829 1528 2050	0.8 2.0 0.5 1.9
7 SU	0259 0801 1524 2041	0.8 2.0 0.5 2.0	22 M	0349 0855 1610 ○ 2116	0.6 2.1 0.4 2.0
8 M	0346 0850 1609 ● 2124	0.6 2.2 0.3 2.1	23 TU	0430 0915 1649 2140	0.6 2.1 0.4 2.1
9 TU	0430 0936 1652 2206	0.5 2.3 0.2 2.2	24 W	0507 0945 1725 2211	0.6 2.2 0.4 2.1
10 W	0513 1018 1734 2246	0.4 2.4 0.2 2.3	25 TH	0542 1022 1758 2248	0.6 2.2 0.5 2.1
11 TH	0555 1100 1815 2327	0.4 2.4 0.2 2.2	26 F	0613 1059 1827 2325	0.7 2.1 0.6 1.9
12 F	0638 1141 1858	0.5 2.3 0.3	27 SA	0643 1127 1858 2240	0.7 1.9 0.7 1.8
13 SA	0007 0723 1221 1944	2.1 0.6 2.2 0.5	28 SU	0717 1036 1934 2248	0.8 1.8 0.8 1.7
14 SU	0049 0812 1302 2035	1.9 0.8 2.0 0.7	29 M	0756 1058 2016 2312	0.9 1.8 0.9 1.7
15 M	0130 0910 1344 ◐ 2138	1.8 0.9 1.8 0.9			

MARCH

Date	Time	m	Date	Time	m
1 TU	0842 1130 2106 ◑ 2348	1.0 1.7 1.1 1.7	16 W	0116 0959 1414 2241	1.7 1.0 1.6 1.2
2 W	0937 1214 2207	1.1 1.6 1.2	17 TH	0218 1119 1959 2358	1.6 1.0 1.9 1.2
3 TH	0040 1042 1318 2316	1.6 1.1 1.5 1.2	18 F	0327 1229 2125	1.6 1.0 1.9
4 F	0250 1154 2057	1.6 1.1 1.7	19 SA	0103 0426 1328 1926	1.1 1.6 0.8 1.8
5 SA	0031 0440 1308 1909	1.2 1.7 1.0 1.7	20 SU	0157 0518 1419 2000	1.0 1.7 0.7 1.8
6 SU	0142 0543 1411 1944	1.0 1.8 0.7 1.8	21 M	0245 0614 1505 2030	0.8 1.8 0.6 1.9
7 M	0237 0750 1501 2026	0.8 2.0 0.5 2.0	22 TU	0328 0826 1547 2044	0.7 1.9 0.5 2.0
8 TU	0326 0837 1548 2107	0.6 2.2 0.3 2.2	23 W	0408 0833 1626 ○ 2101	0.6 2.1 0.5 2.1
9 W	0411 0921 1631 ● 2147	0.4 2.4 0.1 2.3	24 TH	0444 0914 1700 2138	0.6 2.1 0.5 2.2
10 TH	0453 1003 1713 2228	0.2 2.5 0.1 2.4	25 F	0516 0955 1730 2217	0.6 2.2 0.6 2.1
11 F	0535 1044 1755 2307	0.2 2.5 0.1 2.3	26 SA	0545 1034 1758 2254	0.6 2.1 0.7 2.0
12 SA	0618 1125 1838 2346	0.3 2.4 0.3 2.2	27 SU	0614 1108 1829 2241	0.7 1.9 0.7 1.9
13 SU	0702 1205 1923	0.5 2.2 0.5	28 M	0647 1015 1904 2217	0.7 1.8 0.8 1.8
14 M	0024 0750 1244 2014	2.0 0.7 2.0 0.8	29 TU	0724 1027 1945 2237	0.8 1.8 1.0 1.8
15 TU	0057 0846 1324 ◐ 2118	1.8 0.9 1.8 1.0	30 W	0808 1100 2033 2316	0.9 1.7 1.1 1.8
			31 TH	0900 1146 2133 ◑	1.0 1.7 1.2

APRIL

Date	Time	m	Date	Time	m
1 F	0007 1007 1246 2246	1.7 1.1 1.6 1.3	16 SA	0245 1158 2059	1.6 1.0 2.0
2 SA	0125 1121 2020	1.6 1.1 1.8	17 SU	0034 0353 1257 1903	1.2 1.6 0.9 1.8
3 SU	0003 0420 1236 1849	1.2 1.7 0.9 1.8	18 M	0129 0448 1350 1935	1.0 1.7 0.8 1.8
4 M	0114 0641 1341 1924	1.0 1.8 0.7 1.9	19 TU	0217 0542 1437 1827	0.9 1.8 0.7 1.9
5 TU	0212 0730 1434 2005	0.8 2.0 0.5 2.1	20 W	0301 0641 1519 1927	0.8 1.9 0.7 2.0
6 W	0301 0818 1522 2046	0.5 2.2 0.3 2.3	21 TH	0342 0749 1559 2019	0.7 2.0 0.6 2.1
7 TH	0348 0902 1607 ● 2126	0.3 2.4 0.1 2.4	22 F	0418 0843 1633 ○ 2104	0.7 2.1 0.7 2.2
8 F	0431 0945 1650 2207	0.2 2.5 0.1 2.5	23 SA	0449 0928 1702 2145	0.6 2.1 0.7 2.2
9 SA	0514 1027 1733 2247	0.2 2.5 0.2 2.4	24 SU	0518 1009 1732 2222	0.6 2.1 0.8 2.1
10 SU	0557 1108 1817 2326	0.3 2.4 0.4 2.3	25 M	0548 1045 1804 2232	0.7 2.0 0.8 2.0
11 M	0642 1149 1904	0.4 2.2 0.6	26 TU	0622 1019 1840 2204	0.7 1.9 0.9 1.9
12 TU	0002 0731 1231 1958	2.1 0.6 2.0 0.9	27 W	0659 1008 1920 2217	0.8 1.8 1.0 1.9
13 W	0025 0827 1316 2102	1.9 0.8 1.8 1.1	28 TH	0742 1041 2008 2258	0.8 1.8 1.1 1.8
14 TH	0017 0935 1838 ◐ 2219	1.7 1.0 2.0 1.2	29 F	0833 1129 2108 2351	0.9 1.7 1.2 1.8
15 F	0114 1050 1946 2331	1.6 1.0 2.0 1.2	30 SA	0937 1232 2221 ◑	1.0 1.6 1.2

Chart Datum: 1·40 metres below Ordnance Datum (Newlyn)
HAT is 2·6 metres above Chart Datum

TIDES

TIME ZONE (UT)
For Summer Time add ONE hour in **non-shaded areas**

POOLE HARBOUR

LAT 50°43'N LONG 1°59'W

TIMES AND HEIGHTS OF HIGH AND LOW WATERS

Dates in amber are **SPRINGS**
Dates in grey are **NEAPS**

2016

MAY

Date	Day	Time	m	Time	m	Time	m	Time	m
1	SU	0106	1.7	1052	1.0	1956	1.9	2336	1.2
2	M	0356	1.7	1204	0.9	1824	1.8		
3	TU	0044	1.0	0616	1.8	1308	0.7	1900	2.0
4	W	0143	0.8	0708	2.0	1405	0.5	1942	2.1
5	TH	0235	0.6	0757	2.2	1455	0.4	2024	2.3
6	F ●	0323	0.4	0843	2.3	1543	0.3	2105	2.4
7	SA	0409	0.3	0926	2.4	1628	0.2	2146	2.5
8	SU	0453	0.2	1009	2.4	1713	0.3	2227	2.4
9	M	0538	0.3	1051	2.3	1759	0.5	2306	2.3
10	TU	0624	0.4	1134	2.2	1848	0.7	2343	2.1
11	W	0714	0.6	1217	2.0	1941	0.9		
12	TH	0007	1.9	0808	0.8	1306	1.8	2042	1.1
13	F ◐	0907	0.9	1822	2.1	2148	1.2		
14	SA	0032	1.7	1014	1.0	1922	2.1	2256	1.2
15	SU	0133	1.6	1120	1.0	2025	2.0	2358	1.2
16	M	0309	1.6	1221	1.0	1841	1.8		
17	TU	0054	1.1	0415	1.6	1315	1.0	1910	1.8
18	W	0145	1.0	0511	1.7	1405	0.9	1800	1.9
19	TH	0231	0.9	0607	1.8	1449	0.9	1847	2.0
20	F	0312	0.8	0710	1.9	1529	0.8	1938	2.1
21	SA ○	0349	0.8	0812	2.0	1604	0.8	2028	2.2
22	SU	0422	0.7	0902	2.1	1636	0.8	2112	2.2
23	M	0453	0.7	0946	2.1	1709	0.8	2151	2.2
24	TU	0527	0.7	1025	2.0	1744	0.9	2219	2.1
25	W	0603	0.7	1101	1.9	1822	0.9	2227	2.0
26	TH	0642	0.7	1035	1.8	1905	1.0	2216	1.9
27	F	0725	0.8	1036	1.8	1953	1.1	2253	1.9
28	SA	0815	0.8	1122	1.7	2051	1.1	2345	1.8
29	SU ◑	0915	0.9	1225	1.7	2158	1.2		
30	M	0058	1.8	1024	0.9	1935	2.0	2308	1.1
31	TU	0327	1.8	1134	0.9	1802	1.9		

JUNE

Date	Day	Time	m	Time	m	Time	m	Time	m
1	W	0014	1.0	0435	1.8	1238	0.8	1839	2.0
2	TH	0114	0.8	0649	2.0	1336	0.6	1921	2.1
3	F	0209	0.7	0739	2.1	1430	0.5	2004	2.2
4	SA	0300	0.5	0826	2.2	1520	0.5	2047	2.3
5	SU ●	0349	0.4	0910	2.3	1609	0.4	2128	2.4
6	M	0435	0.3	0953	2.3	1656	0.5	2208	2.4
7	TU	0521	0.3	1035	2.3	1743	0.6	2247	2.3
8	W	0608	0.4	1117	2.2	1832	0.7	2324	2.2
9	TH	0655	0.5	1158	2.0	1922	0.9	2356	2.0
10	F	0744	0.7	1242	1.9	2014	1.1	2328	1.9
11	SA	0835	0.8	1336	1.7	2110	1.2		
12	SU ◐	0000	1.8	0930	1.0	1240	1.7	2211	1.2
13	M	0043	1.7	1032	1.1	1943	2.0	2315	1.3
14	TU	0138	1.6	1137	1.2	2042	2.0		
15	W	0014	1.2	0308	1.6	1236	1.2	1903	1.8
16	TH	0109	1.2	0429	1.6	1329	1.1	1850	1.9
17	F	0157	1.1	0528	1.7	1415	1.1	1816	1.9
18	SA	0240	1.0	0624	1.8	1456	1.0	1852	2.0
19	SU	0319	0.9	0741	1.9	1534	0.9	1940	2.1
20	M ○	0355	0.8	0840	2.0	1612	0.9	2038	2.2
21	TU	0432	0.7	0927	2.0	1650	0.8	2129	2.2
22	W	0510	0.6	1011	2.1	1729	0.8	2214	2.2
23	TH	0549	0.6	1054	2.1	1809	0.9	2257	2.2
24	F	0629	0.6	1136	2.0	1852	0.9	2339	2.1
25	SA	0712	0.7	1221	1.9	1939	1.0		
26	SU	0023	2.0	0759	0.7	1308	1.9	2032	1.0
27	M ◑	0111	1.9	0853	0.8	1359	1.8	2133	1.1
28	TU	0204	1.9	0956	0.9	1455	1.8	2240	1.1
29	W	0300	1.8	1105	0.9	1749	1.9	2347	1.0
30	TH	0402	1.8	1211	0.9	1825	2.0		

JULY

Date	Day	Time	m	Time	m	Time	m	Time	m
1	F	0049	0.9	0637	1.9	1312	0.8	1907	2.1
2	SA	0148	0.8	0727	2.0	1410	0.7	1950	2.2
3	SU	0242	0.6	0814	2.1	1504	0.7	2032	2.3
4	M ●	0333	0.5	0857	2.2	1555	0.6	2112	2.3
5	TU	0421	0.4	0939	2.2	1642	0.6	2151	2.4
6	W	0506	0.3	1019	2.2	1728	0.6	2228	2.3
7	TH	0551	0.4	1057	2.2	1814	0.7	2302	2.3
8	F	0635	0.5	1134	2.1	1858	0.8	2334	2.1
9	SA	0718	0.6	1211	2.0	1942	1.0	2331	2.0
10	SU	0800	0.8	1249	1.8	2026	1.1	2332	1.9
11	M	0842	1.0	1159	1.7	2112	1.2		
12	TU ◐	0006	1.8	0927	1.1	1237	1.7	2203	1.3
13	W	0049	1.7	1018	1.2	1330	1.7	2305	1.3
14	TH	0145	1.6	1122	1.3	2040	1.9		
15	F	0016	1.3	0307	1.6	1236	1.3	2147	1.9
16	SA	0115	1.2	0438	1.6	1334	1.2	1839	1.9
17	SU	0204	1.1	0539	1.7	1423	1.1	1808	2.0
18	M	0248	0.9	0738	1.8	1507	1.0	1859	2.1
19	TU ○	0331	0.8	0829	1.9	1550	0.9	2026	2.2
20	W	0412	0.6	0916	2.1	1632	0.8	2121	2.3
21	TH	0453	0.5	1000	2.2	1713	0.7	2208	2.3
22	F	0533	0.5	1042	2.2	1754	0.7	2251	2.3
23	SA	0614	0.5	1123	2.2	1836	0.7	2334	2.3
24	SU	0655	0.5	1204	2.1	1920	0.8		
25	M	0016	2.2	0740	0.6	1247	2.0	2009	0.9
26	TU ◑	0059	2.0	0829	0.7	1332	1.9	2106	1.0
27	W	0146	1.9	0928	0.9	1421	1.8	2214	1.1
28	TH	0237	1.8	1039	1.0	1521	1.8	2324	1.1
29	F	0338	1.7	1151	1.0	1821	1.9		
30	SA	0031	1.0	0633	1.8	1257	1.0	1900	2.0
31	SU	0134	0.8	0721	1.9	1358	0.9	1941	2.1

AUGUST

Date	Day	Time	m	Time	m	Time	m	Time	m
1	M	0230	0.7	0806	2.0	1453	0.8	2021	2.2
2	TU ●	0321	0.5	0847	2.1	1543	0.7	2057	2.3
3	W	0407	0.4	0925	2.2	1629	0.6	2131	2.3
4	TH	0450	0.4	0959	2.2	1711	0.6	2204	2.4
5	F	0531	0.4	1031	2.2	1752	0.7	2236	2.3
6	SA	0611	0.5	1104	2.2	1831	0.8	2309	2.2
7	SU	0648	0.6	1139	2.0	1908	0.9	2338	2.0
8	M	0723	0.8	1213	1.9	1943	1.0	2305	1.9
9	TU	0758	0.9	1125	1.8	2022	1.1	2331	1.8
10	W ◐	0839	1.1	1156	1.7	2108	1.2		
11	TH	0008	1.7	0927	1.2	1238	1.7	2202	1.3
12	F	0056	1.6	1024	1.3	1337	1.7	2304	1.3
13	SA	0203	1.6	1130	1.3	1520	1.7		
14	SU	0014	1.2	0400	1.6	1244	1.3	1833	1.8
15	M	0125	1.1	0705	1.7	1351	1.2	1744	1.9
16	TU	0219	0.9	0738	1.8	1443	1.0	1843	2.0
17	W	0307	0.7	0821	2.0	1529	0.8	2025	2.2
18	TH ○	0351	0.5	0904	2.1	1613	0.7	2112	2.4
19	F	0433	0.4	0945	2.3	1654	0.6	2156	2.5
20	SA	0514	0.3	1025	2.3	1735	0.5	2238	2.5
21	SU	0554	0.3	1105	2.3	1816	0.6	2319	2.4
22	M	0635	0.4	1145	2.3	1858	0.7		
23	TU	0001	2.3	0718	0.5	1226	2.1	1945	0.8
24	W	0043	2.1	0806	0.7	1308	2.0	2040	1.0
25	TH ◑	0128	1.9	0903	1.0	1353	1.9	2150	1.1
26	F	0221	1.8	1020	1.1	1450	1.8	2308	1.1
27	SA	0739	1.9	1139	1.2	2003	2.0		
28	SU	0019	1.0	0633	1.8	1249	1.1	1851	2.0
29	M	0122	0.9	0716	1.9	1349	1.0	1929	2.0
30	TU	0216	0.7	0757	1.9	1441	0.9	2007	2.1
31	W	0305	0.6	0834	2.0	1528	0.7	2040	2.2

Chart Datum: 1·40 metres below Ordnance Datum (Newlyn)
HAT is 2·6 metres above Chart Datum

TIME ZONE (UT)
For Summer Time add ONE hour in **non-shaded areas**

POOLE HARBOUR

LAT 50°43'N LONG 1°59'W

TIMES AND HEIGHTS OF HIGH AND LOW WATERS

Dates in amber are **SPRINGS**
Dates in grey are **NEAPS**

2016

SEPTEMBER

Date	Day	Time	m	Time	m	Time	m	Time	m
1	TH	0349	0.4	0906	2.1	1611	0.7	● 2106	2.3
2	F	0431	0.4	0932	2.2	1651	0.6	2133	2.3
3	SA	0509	0.4	1000	2.3	1728	0.7	2206	2.3
4	SU	0545	0.5	1032	2.2	1802	0.8	2242	2.2
5	M	0617	0.7	1108	2.1	1833	0.8	2317	2.1
6	TU	0647	0.8	1141	2.0	1905	0.9	2241	1.9
7	W	0720	0.9	1055	1.9	1942	1.0	2255	1.8
8	TH	0800	1.1	1116	1.8	2026	1.1	2324	1.7
9	F	0847	1.2	1147	1.8	2120	1.2	◐	
10	SA	0002	1.7	0946	1.3	1234	1.7	2223	1.3
11	SU	0106	1.6	1053	1.4	1409	1.7	2333	1.2
12	M	0836	1.8	1208	1.3	1817	1.8		
13	TU	0047	1.1	0657	1.8	1322	1.2	1846	1.9
14	W	0150	0.9	0725	1.9	1418	1.0	1925	2.1
15	TH	0240	0.7	0805	2.0	1505	0.8	2012	2.2
16	F	0327	0.4	0845	2.2	1550	0.6	○ 2056	2.4
17	SA	0410	0.3	0926	2.4	1632	0.4	2139	2.6
18	SU	0451	0.2	1006	2.5	1713	0.4	2221	2.6
19	M	0532	0.2	1046	2.5	1754	0.4	2303	2.5
20	TU	0613	0.3	1125	2.4	1837	0.6	2345	2.4
21	W	0657	0.6	1205	2.2	1923	0.7		
22	TH	0027	2.2	0745	0.8	1244	2.0	2018	0.9
23	F	0115	1.9	0845	1.1	1325	1.9	◑ 2130	1.1
24	SA	0218	1.8	1007	1.2	1420	1.8	2252	1.1
25	SU	0726	2.0	1128	1.2	1800	1.9		
26	M	0002	1.0	0623	1.9	1235	1.2	1831	1.9
27	TU	0102	0.9	0700	1.9	1332	1.1	1910	1.9
28	W	0155	0.8	0738	1.9	1422	0.9	1946	2.0
29	TH	0242	0.6	0813	2.0	1507	0.8	2015	2.1
30	F	0326	0.5	0839	2.1	1549	0.7	2029	2.2

OCTOBER

Date	Day	Time	m	Time	m	Time	m	Time	m
1	SA	0407	0.5	0854	2.2	1627	0.7	● 2057	2.3
2	SU	0444	0.5	0922	2.3	1702	0.7	2136	2.3
3	M	0517	0.6	0958	2.3	1733	0.7	2216	2.2
4	TU	0546	0.7	1036	2.2	1801	0.8	2253	2.1
5	W	0615	0.8	1107	2.0	1831	0.9	2228	1.9
6	TH	0647	1.0	1028	1.9	1907	0.9	2221	1.8
7	F	0726	1.1	1034	1.9	1949	1.0	2241	1.8
8	SA	0812	1.2	1058	1.8	2041	1.1	2320	1.7
9	SU	0910	1.3	1141	1.8	2146	1.2	◐	
10	M	0015	1.6	1022	1.4	1254	1.7	2259	1.2
11	TU	0751	1.9	1139	1.4	1756	1.8		
12	W	0012	1.1	0637	1.8	1251	1.2	1827	1.9
13	TH	0117	0.9	0704	1.9	1349	1.0	1907	2.0
14	F	0210	0.6	0742	2.1	1439	0.7	1953	2.2
15	SA	0258	0.4	0823	2.3	1524	0.5	2038	2.4
16	SU	0344	0.3	0904	2.4	1608	0.4	○ 2121	2.6
17	M	0427	0.2	0945	2.5	1650	0.3	2204	2.6
18	TU	0509	0.2	1025	2.5	1733	0.3	2246	2.5
19	W	0552	0.4	1105	2.4	1817	0.5	2329	2.4
20	TH	0638	0.6	1145	2.3	1904	0.7		
21	F	0014	2.1	0729	0.9	1223	2.1	2000	0.9
22	SA	0104	1.9	0831	1.1	1252	1.9	◑ 2109	1.0
23	SU	0609	2.1	0951	1.3	1326	1.8	2227	1.1
24	M	0716	2.1	1106	1.3	1447	1.7	2335	1.0
25	TU	0604	1.9	1209	1.2	1806	1.8		
26	W	0034	0.9	0637	1.9	1306	1.1	1639	1.8
27	TH	0127	0.8	0714	1.9	1356	1.0	1730	1.8
28	F	0215	0.8	0746	2.0	1441	0.9	1827	2.0
29	SA	0259	0.7	0802	2.1	1523	0.8	1931	2.1
30	SU	0340	0.7	0757	2.2	1602	0.7	● 2022	2.2
31	M	0417	0.7	0842	2.3	1636	0.7	2107	2.2

NOVEMBER

Date	Day	Time	m	Time	m	Time	m	Time	m
1	TU	0449	0.8	0925	2.3	1705	0.7	2150	2.2
2	W	0519	0.8	1004	2.2	1734	0.8	2230	2.1
3	TH	0548	0.9	1031	2.1	1805	0.8	2302	1.9
4	F	0622	1.0	1011	2.0	1841	0.9	2158	1.8
5	SA	0701	1.1	1005	1.9	1921	0.9	2216	1.8
6	SU	0745	1.2	1033	1.9	2010	1.0	2257	1.7
7	M	0840	1.3	1120	1.8	2111	1.1	◐ 2353	1.6
8	TU	0951	1.3	1224	1.7	2225	1.1		
9	W	0726	2.0	1107	1.3	1731	1.8	2338	1.0
10	TH	0616	1.9	1218	1.2	1804	1.9		
11	F	0042	0.9	0642	2.0	1318	1.0	1847	2.0
12	SA	0139	0.7	0720	2.1	1410	0.7	1933	2.2
13	SU	0230	0.5	0801	2.3	1458	0.5	2019	2.3
14	M	0318	0.3	0843	2.4	1545	0.3	○ 2103	2.4
15	TU	0404	0.3	0925	2.5	1629	0.3	2147	2.5
16	W	0449	0.3	1006	2.5	1714	0.3	2231	2.4
17	TH	0534	0.5	1047	2.4	1800	0.4	2315	2.3
18	F	0622	0.7	1127	2.3	1848	0.6		
19	SA	0000	2.1	0714	0.9	1205	2.1	1941	0.7
20	SU	0049	1.9	0813	1.1	1153	1.9	2043	0.9
21	M	0556	2.1	0921	1.2	1225	1.8	◑ 2151	1.0
22	TU	0655	2.1	1031	1.3	1330	1.7	2259	1.0
23	W	0759	2.1	1136	1.2	1454	1.7		
24	TH	0000	1.0	0619	1.9	1233	1.2	1558	1.7
25	F	0055	1.0	0653	1.9	1326	1.1	1655	1.7
26	SA	0145	0.9	0723	1.9	1413	1.0	1752	1.8
27	SU	0231	0.9	0627	2.0	1456	0.9	1852	1.9
28	M	0313	0.8	0714	2.1	1535	0.8	1950	2.0
29	TU	0350	0.8	0803	2.2	1610	0.8	● 2040	2.1
30	W	0424	0.8	0850	2.2	1641	0.7	2126	2.1

DECEMBER

Date	Day	Time	m	Time	m	Time	m	Time	m
1	TH	0455	0.9	0932	2.2	1712	0.7	2209	2.0
2	F	0528	0.9	1004	2.1	1746	0.7	2250	1.9
3	SA	0604	0.9	1012	2.0	1823	0.8	2327	1.8
4	SU	0644	1.0	1006	2.0	1903	0.8	2206	1.8
5	M	0728	1.1	1024	1.9	1949	0.9	2245	1.7
6	TU	0818	1.2	1109	1.9	2043	0.9	2337	1.7
7	W	0920	1.2	1206	1.8	2150	1.0	◐	
8	TH	0056	1.6	1032	1.2	1503	1.7	2301	0.9
9	F	0802	2.0	1143	1.1	1614	1.8		
10	SA	0008	0.8	0624	1.9	1246	1.0	1828	1.9
11	SU	0109	0.7	0701	2.1	1343	0.8	1916	2.0
12	M	0204	0.6	0743	2.2	1435	0.6	2003	2.2
13	TU	0255	0.5	0826	2.3	1524	0.4	2049	2.3
14	W	0344	0.4	0908	2.4	1612	0.3	○ 2133	2.3
15	TH	0432	0.4	0950	2.4	1658	0.3	2216	2.3
16	F	0519	0.5	1031	2.4	1744	0.3	2259	2.2
17	SA	0607	0.6	1110	2.3	1832	0.4	2342	2.1
18	SU	0657	0.8	1146	2.1	1921	0.6		
19	M	0025	1.9	0749	1.0	1206	2.0	2012	0.8
20	TU	0114	1.8	0844	1.1	1150	1.8	2108	0.9
21	W	0624	2.1	0945	1.2	1229	1.7	◑ 2211	1.0
22	TH	0718	2.0	1052	1.3	1323	1.6	2318	1.1
23	F	0818	2.0	1156	1.2	1456	1.6		
24	SA	0019	1.1	0648	1.8	1253	1.2	1616	1.6
25	SU	0114	1.1	0714	1.8	1344	1.1	1720	1.7
26	M	0202	1.0	0708	1.9	1429	1.0	1818	1.7
27	TU	0245	1.0	0639	2.0	1509	0.9	1920	1.8
28	W	0325	0.9	0722	2.1	1546	0.8	2018	1.9
29	TH	0401	0.9	0815	2.1	1620	0.7	● 2108	2.0
30	F	0436	0.8	0909	2.2	1656	0.6	2154	2.0
31	SA	0513	0.8	0955	2.2	1732	0.6	2237	2.0

Chart Datum: 1·40 metres below Ordnance Datum (Newlyn)
HAT is 2·6 metres above Chart Datum

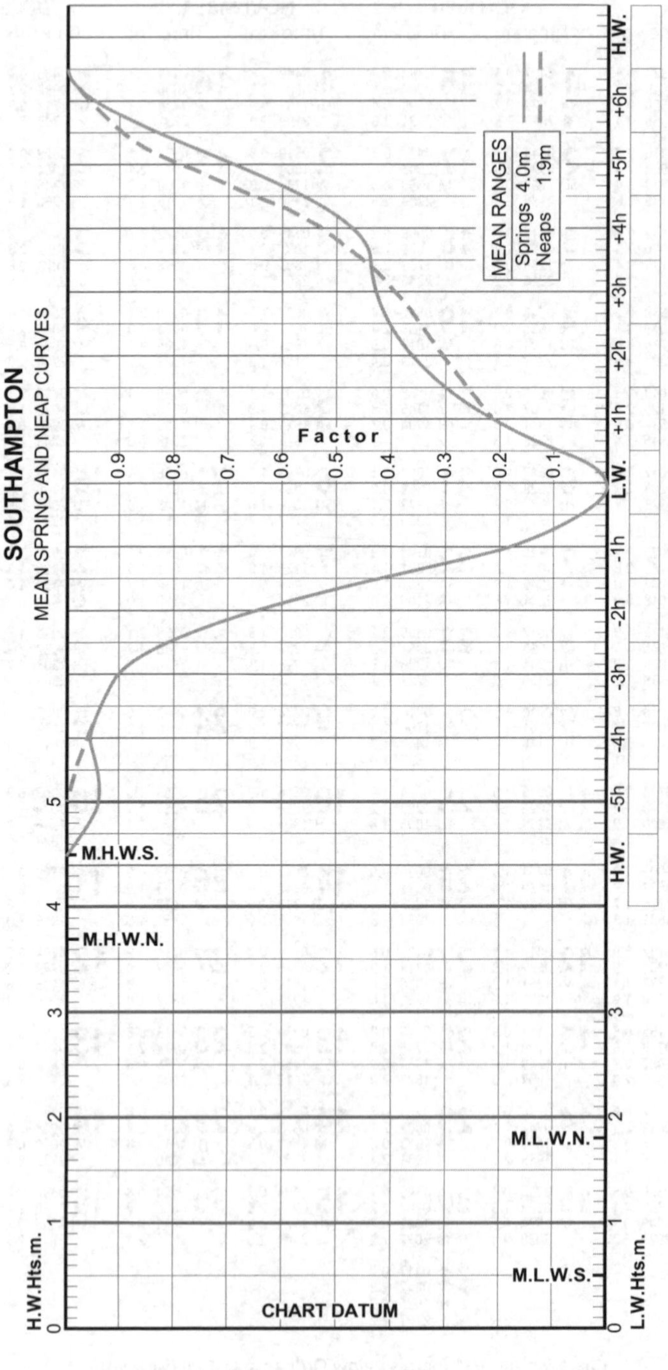

Note - Double HWs occur at Southampton. The predictions are for the first HW.

TIME ZONE (UT)
For Summer Time add ONE hour in **non-shaded areas**

SOUTHAMPTON

LAT 50°53′N LONG 1°24′W

TIMES AND HEIGHTS OF HIGH AND LOW WATERS

Dates in amber are **SPRINGS**
Dates in grey are **NEAPS**

2016

JANUARY

Date	Day	Time	m	Time	m	Time	m	Time	m
1	F	0307	4.1	0849	1.7	1516	3.9	2110	1.7
2	SA	0357	4.0	0938	1.9	1612	3.8	◑ 2204	1.9
3	SU	0527	4.0	1037	2.1	1711	3.7	2307	2.0
4	M	0548	3.9	1142	2.1	1821	3.7		
5	TU	0011	2.0	0655	3.9	1246	2.0	1928	3.7
6	W	0112	1.9	0755	4.0	1343	1.8	2029	3.9
7	TH	0205	1.7	0851	4.2	1432	1.5	2120	4.1
8	F	0253	1.5	0933	4.3	1517	1.2	2202	4.3
9	SA	0337	1.2	1012	4.5	1600	0.9	2237	4.4
10	SU	0420	1.0	1104	4.6	1643	0.7	● 2327	4.6
11	M	0503	0.8	1138	4.7	1725	0.6		
12	TU	0002	4.7	0544	0.7	1216	4.7	1805	0.5
13	W	0042	4.7	0626	0.7	1258	4.7	1847	0.5
14	TH	0126	4.7	0708	0.8	1344	4.7	1930	0.7
15	F	0214	4.6	0753	0.9	1434	4.5	2016	0.9
16	SA	0309	4.5	0843	1.2	1532	4.3	◐ 2108	1.2
17	SU	0416	4.3	0943	1.5	1618	4.1	2214	1.5
18	M	0502	4.2	1057	1.7	1732	4.0	2333	1.6
19	TU	0618	4.1	1222	1.7	1852	4.0		
20	W	0054	1.6	0805	4.2	1332	1.5	2000	4.1
21	TH	0157	1.5	0825	4.3	1428	1.2	2121	4.2
22	F	0250	1.3	0914	4.4	1517	1.0	2207	4.3
23	SA	0338	1.0	1020	4.5	1603	0.7	2250	4.4
24	SU	0423	0.8	1100	4.5	1646	0.5	○ 2333	4.4
25	M	0506	0.7	1140	4.5	1728	0.5		
26	TU	0014	4.4	0548	0.7	1218	4.4	1808	0.6
27	W	0052	4.4	0627	0.8	1255	4.4	1845	0.7
28	TH	0127	4.4	0702	1.0	1332	4.3	1918	1.0
29	F	0203	4.3	0733	1.2	1356	4.2	1947	1.2
30	SA	0241	4.2	0802	1.4	1431	4.0	2017	1.4
31	SU	0257	4.1	0837	1.6	1515	3.9	2056	1.6

FEBRUARY

Date	Day	Time	m	Time	m	Time	m	Time	m
1	M	0340	3.9	0925	1.8	1558	3.7	◑ 2151	1.9
2	TU	0429	3.8	1030	2.0	1656	3.6	2304	2.1
3	W	0531	3.6	1144	2.0	1815	3.5		
4	TH	0019	2.1	0721	3.8	1256	1.9	2009	3.8
5	F	0130	1.9	0826	4.0	1401	1.6	2059	4.0
6	SA	0229	1.6	0913	4.2	1455	1.2	2143	4.3
7	SU	0319	1.2	1011	4.4	1543	0.8	2215	4.4
8	M	0404	0.8	1043	4.6	1627	0.5	● 2307	4.6
9	TU	0448	0.6	1119	4.8	1710	0.3	2343	4.7
10	W	0530	0.4	1158	4.8	1751	0.2		
11	TH	0023	4.8	0611	0.3	1241	4.8	1831	0.2
12	F	0107	4.8	0653	0.4	1325	4.8	1913	0.4
13	SA	0154	4.7	0735	0.6	1415	4.6	1957	0.6
14	SU	0248	4.5	0821	0.9	1512	4.4	2046	1.0
15	M	0358	4.3	0915	1.3	1601	4.1	◐ 2145	1.4
16	TU	0443	4.1	1025	1.6	1717	3.9	2305	1.7
17	W	0637	4.0	1159	1.7	1832	3.9		
18	TH	0039	1.8	0703	3.9	1317	1.6	1941	3.9
19	F	0144	1.6	0804	4.0	1413	1.4	2117	4.0
20	SA	0236	1.4	0927	4.2	1501	1.1	2200	4.2
21	SU	0322	1.1	1006	4.3	1545	0.8	2238	4.3
22	M	0406	0.8	1043	4.3	1627	0.5	○ 2315	4.4
23	TU	0447	0.6	1120	4.4	1708	0.5	2353	4.4
24	W	0527	0.6	1156	4.4	1747	0.5		
25	TH	0026	4.4	0605	0.7	1231	4.3	1822	0.7
26	F	0056	4.3	0636	0.9	1304	4.3	1850	0.9
27	SA	0126	4.3	0659	1.0	1336	4.3	1910	1.0
28	SU	0156	4.3	0723	1.1	1410	4.2	1937	1.1
29	M	0232	4.2	0756	1.2	1450	4.1	2015	1.3

MARCH

Date	Day	Time	m	Time	m	Time	m	Time	m
1	TU	0313	4.1	0838	1.4	1521	3.9	◑ 2101	1.6
2	W	0343	3.8	0932	1.7	1631	3.7	2204	1.9
3	TH	0503	3.7	1049	1.9	1711	3.5	2332	2.1
4	F	0546	3.5	1216	1.9	2018	3.8		
5	SA	0058	1.9	0834	3.9	1334	1.6	2110	4.0
6	SU	0208	1.6	0915	4.1	1434	1.2	2119	4.3
7	M	0300	1.1	0946	4.4	1523	0.7	2151	4.5
8	TU	0346	0.7	1019	4.6	1608	0.4	2243	4.7
9	W	0429	0.4	1057	4.8	1651	0.1	● 2321	4.8
10	TH	0511	0.1	1137	4.9	1732	0.0		
11	F	0002	4.9	0552	0.1	1221	4.9	1812	0.0
12	SA	0046	4.8	0633	0.2	1306	4.8	1854	0.2
13	SU	0133	4.7	0715	0.4	1355	4.6	1937	0.5
14	M	0226	4.5	0800	0.7	1456	4.4	2024	1.0
15	TU	0309	4.2	0852	1.2	1545	4.1	◐ 2122	1.4
16	W	0424	4.0	0958	1.6	1703	3.9	2241	1.8
17	TH	0531	3.9	1128	1.8	1809	3.8		
18	F	0013	1.9	0634	3.7	1248	1.7	1915	3.8
19	SA	0121	1.8	0737	3.8	1348	1.5	2016	3.9
20	SU	0214	1.5	0835	3.9	1436	1.2	2106	4.1
21	M	0300	1.2	0950	4.1	1521	0.9	2225	4.2
22	TU	0343	0.9	1021	4.2	1603	0.6	2251	4.3
23	W	0424	0.7	1057	4.3	1643	0.5	○ 2325	4.4
24	TH	0503	0.6	1118	4.3	1721	0.6	2357	4.4
25	F	0539	0.7	1207	4.3	1755	0.7		
26	SA	0027	4.4	0608	0.8	1237	4.3	1820	0.9
27	SU	0054	4.4	0627	0.9	1307	4.3	1839	1.0
28	M	0123	4.3	0652	0.9	1340	4.3	1908	1.0
29	TU	0158	4.3	0726	1.0	1420	4.2	1945	1.2
30	W	0239	4.2	0807	1.2	1505	4.1	2030	1.5
31	TH	0328	4.0	0857	1.5	1559	3.9	◑ 2127	1.8

APRIL

Date	Day	Time	m	Time	m	Time	m	Time	m
1	F	0406	3.7	1006	1.8	1706	3.7	2254	2.0
2	SA	0546	3.6	1140	1.9	1803	3.6		
3	SU	0026	1.9	0658	3.7	1302	1.6	2045	4.1
4	M	0141	1.6	0849	4.1	1407	1.2	2118	4.3
5	TU	0236	1.1	0919	4.4	1458	0.7	2144	4.6
6	W	0323	0.7	0954	4.6	1544	0.4	2219	4.8
7	TH	0407	0.3	1034	4.8	1628	0.1	● 2258	4.9
8	F	0449	0.1	1116	4.9	1709	0.0	2340	4.9
9	SA	0531	0.0	1200	4.9	1751	0.0		
10	SU	0024	4.9	0613	0.1	1247	4.8	1833	0.3
11	M	0111	4.7	0656	0.3	1338	4.6	1918	0.6
12	TU	0206	4.5	0741	0.7	1446	4.4	2006	1.0
13	W	0323	4.2	0832	1.1	1530	4.1	2103	1.5
14	TH	0359	4.0	0935	1.5	1638	4.0	◐ 2215	1.8
15	F	0501	3.8	1051	1.7	1737	3.8	2333	1.9
16	SA	0558	3.7	1205	1.7	1839	3.8		
17	SU	0042	1.8	0701	3.6	1309	1.6	1939	3.8
18	M	0141	1.6	0758	3.7	1403	1.4	2034	4.0
19	TU	0230	1.3	0850	3.9	1450	1.1	2116	4.1
20	W	0315	1.0	0956	4.1	1533	0.9	2221	4.3
21	TH	0357	0.8	1031	4.2	1615	0.8	2234	4.3
22	F	0435	0.8	1049	4.2	1652	0.8	○ 2309	4.4
23	SA	0510	0.8	1145	4.3	1725	0.9		
24	SU	0000	4.4	0538	0.9	1215	4.3	1750	1.0
25	M	0027	4.4	0600	0.9	1243	4.3	1814	1.0
26	TU	0056	4.4	0628	0.9	1317	4.3	1845	1.1
27	W	0132	4.4	0704	0.9	1356	4.3	1924	1.2
28	TH	0214	4.3	0745	1.1	1443	4.2	2009	1.4
29	F	0303	4.1	0835	1.3	1538	4.0	2105	1.7
30	SA	0401	3.9	0939	1.6	1643	3.9	◑ 2225	1.9

Chart Datum: 2·74 metres below Ordnance Datum (Newlyn)
HAT is 5·0 metres above Chart Datum

TIME ZONE (UT)
For Summer Time add ONE hour in **non-shaded areas**

SOUTHAMPTON

LAT 50°53′N LONG 1°24′W

TIMES AND HEIGHTS OF HIGH AND LOW WATERS

Dates in amber are **SPRINGS**
Dates in grey are **NEAPS**

2016

MAY

Date	Day	Time	m
1	SU	0451 1107 1736 2352	3.7 1.7 3.8 1.8
2	M	0608 1226 1913	3.8 1.5 4.1
3	TU	0106 0734 1333 2012	1.6 4.0 1.2 4.3
4	W	0206 0851 1429 2119	1.1 4.3 0.8 4.6
5	TH	0257 0930 1518 2155	0.7 4.6 0.5 4.8
6	F	0343 1012 1604 ● 2236	0.4 4.7 0.3 4.9
7	SA	0427 1055 1647 2319	0.2 4.8 0.2 4.9
8	SU	0511 1141 1731	0.1 4.8 0.2
9	M	0004 0554 1230 1815	4.8 0.2 4.7 0.4
10	TU	0052 0638 1323 1901	4.6 0.4 4.5 0.7
11	W	0145 0724 1436 1949	4.4 0.7 4.4 1.0
12	TH	0250 0814 1507 2044	4.2 1.0 4.2 1.4
13	F	0327 0911 1609 ◐ 2146	4.0 1.4 4.1 1.7
14	SA	0425 1015 1702 2252	3.8 1.6 3.9 1.8
15	SU	0523 1120 1826 2358	3.7 1.7 3.9 1.9
16	M	0641 1224 1855	3.6 1.7 3.8
17	TU	0101 0747 1324 1951	1.8 3.7 1.6 3.9
18	W	0155 0812 1415 2042	1.5 3.8 1.4 4.1
19	TH	0243 0927 1501 2147	1.3 4.0 1.2 4.3
20	F	0325 1007 1543 2205	1.1 4.1 1.1 4.3
21	SA	0405 1028 1621 ○ 2243	1.0 4.2 1.0 4.4
22	SU	0440 1127 1656 2317	0.9 4.3 1.0 4.4
23	M	0510 1158 1726 2350	0.9 4.3 1.1 4.4
24	TU	0540 1226 1756	0.9 4.4 1.1
25	W	0036 0612 1259 1830	4.4 0.9 4.4 1.1
26	TH	0112 0649 1340 1910	4.4 0.9 4.4 1.2
27	F	0155 0732 1426 1957	4.3 1.0 4.3 1.3
28	SA	0244 0821 1520 2052	4.2 1.2 4.2 1.5
29	SU	0341 0921 1621 ◑ 2201	4.1 1.4 4.1 1.7
30	M	0426 1035 1736 2317	3.9 1.5 4.1 1.7
31	TU	0538 1150 1825	3.9 1.5 4.1

JUNE

Date	Day	Time	m
1	W	0030 0654 1258 1936	1.5 4.0 1.3 4.3
2	TH	0135 0802 1359 2056	1.2 4.3 1.0 4.6
3	F	0231 0910 1453 2135	0.9 4.5 0.8 4.7
4	SA	0321 0955 1542 2217	0.6 4.6 0.6 4.8
5	SU	0409 1040 1629 ● 2302	0.4 4.6 0.5 4.7
6	M	0454 1128 1715 2348	0.3 4.6 0.5 4.7
7	TU	0539 1217 1800	0.3 4.6 0.6
8	W	0034 0624 1310 1846	4.6 0.5 4.5 0.8
9	TH	0124 0709 1343 1933	4.4 0.7 4.3 1.0
10	F	0217 0755 1439 2021	4.2 0.9 4.2 1.3
11	SA	0250 0844 1534 2114	4.0 1.2 4.1 1.5
12	SU	0347 0938 1628 ◐ 2211	3.9 1.5 4.0 1.7
13	M	0441 1036 1718 2311	3.7 1.7 3.9 1.9
14	TU	0536 1137 1811	3.6 1.8 3.9
15	W	0013 0701 1237 1933	1.9 3.7 1.8 3.9
16	TH	0114 0804 1335 2028	1.8 3.8 1.7 4.0
17	F	0206 0901 1425 2057	1.6 3.9 1.5 4.1
18	SA	0252 0948 1510 2140	1.4 4.1 1.4 4.3
19	SU	0333 1007 1551 2221	1.2 4.2 1.2 4.3
20	M	0411 1047 1630 ○ 2257	1.0 4.3 1.1 4.4
21	TU	0448 1143 1707 2332	0.9 4.4 1.1 4.4
22	W	0524 1211 1743	0.9 4.4 1.0
23	TH	0019 0601 1244 1821	4.5 0.8 4.5 1.0
24	F	0056 0640 1324 1902	4.5 0.8 4.5 1.0
25	SA	0139 0722 1409 1947	4.5 0.9 4.5 1.1
26	SU	0227 0809 1501 2037	4.4 1.0 4.4 1.3
27	M	0321 0902 1600 ◑ 2136	4.2 1.2 4.3 1.4
28	TU	0422 1005 1708 2245	4.1 1.3 4.2 1.5
29	W	0513 1116 1755 2358	4.0 1.4 4.2 1.5
30	TH	0623 1228 1907	4.0 1.4 4.3

JULY

Date	Day	Time	m
1	F	0109 0739 1336 2043	1.4 4.1 1.3 4.5
2	SA	0211 0836 1435 2104	1.1 4.3 1.1 4.5
3	SU	0305 0927 1527 2152	0.9 4.4 0.9 4.6
4	M	0354 1033 1616 ● 2250	0.6 4.5 0.7 4.6
5	TU	0441 1120 1702 2334	0.5 4.5 0.7 4.6
6	W	0525 1207 1747	0.4 4.5 0.7
7	TH	0017 0609 1254 1831	4.5 0.5 4.4 0.8
8	F	0101 0652 1345 1913	4.4 0.6 4.4 0.9
9	SA	0146 0733 1407 1956	4.2 0.9 4.3 1.2
10	SU	0235 0815 1451 2039	4.1 1.1 4.2 1.4
11	M	0304 0859 1542 2126	3.9 1.4 4.1 1.7
12	TU	0357 0949 1632 ◐ 2219	3.8 1.7 4.0 1.8
13	W	0450 1045 1758 2318	3.7 1.9 3.9 2.0
14	TH	0552 1145 1826	3.6 2.0 3.8
15	F	0019 0704 1247 1932	1.9 3.7 1.9 3.9
16	SA	0121 0807 1346 2028	1.8 3.8 1.8 4.0
17	SU	0215 0901 1438 2116	1.6 4.0 1.6 4.2
18	M	0303 0947 1525 2201	1.3 4.2 1.4 4.3
19	TU	0347 1027 1608 ○ 2255	1.1 4.3 1.1 4.5
20	W	0429 1102 1649 2327	0.9 4.4 1.0 4.5
21	TH	0510 1137 1729	0.7 4.5 0.8
22	F	0000 0550 1226 1810	4.6 0.6 4.6 0.8
23	SA	0039 0628 1306 1849	4.6 0.6 4.6 0.8
24	SU	0121 0709 1350 1932	4.6 0.6 4.6 0.9
25	M	0207 0753 1440 2018	4.5 0.8 4.5 1.0
26	TU	0300 0841 1537 ◑ 2112	4.4 1.0 4.4 1.3
27	W	0400 0938 1649 2216	4.2 1.3 4.3 1.5
28	TH	0451 1048 1733 2333	4.0 1.5 4.2 1.6
29	F	0606 1207 1939	4.0 1.6 4.2
30	SA	0053 0727 1322 2031	1.6 4.0 1.6 4.3
31	SU	0200 0830 1424 2051	1.3 4.2 1.4 4.3

AUGUST

Date	Day	Time	m
1	M	0254 0945 1516 2137	1.1 4.3 1.1 4.4
2	TU	0342 1028 1603 ● 2238	0.8 4.4 0.9 4.5
3	W	0427 1111 1648 2319	0.6 4.5 0.7 4.5
4	TH	0510 1153 1731 2359	0.5 4.5 0.7 4.4
5	F	0551 1235 1812	0.5 4.4 0.7
6	SA	0037 0631 1315 1851	4.4 0.6 4.4 0.9
7	SU	0117 0709 1355 1927	4.3 0.8 4.3 1.1
8	M	0157 0743 1437 2000	4.2 1.1 4.3 1.3
9	TU	0220 0816 1522 2034	4.0 1.4 4.2 1.6
10	W	0302 0852 1533 ◐ 2118	3.9 1.6 4.0 1.8
11	TH	0345 0943 1620 2217	3.7 1.9 3.8 2.0
12	F	0440 1050 1719 2326	3.6 2.1 3.7 2.1
13	SA	0600 1200 1855	3.5 2.1 3.8
14	SU	0034 0745 1309 2002	2.0 3.7 2.0 3.9
15	M	0142 0843 1411 2055	1.8 4.0 1.8 4.1
16	TU	0238 0927 1502 2158	1.4 4.2 1.4 4.4
17	W	0326 1008 1548 2231	1.1 4.4 1.1 4.5
18	TH	0410 1042 1631 ○ 2303	0.7 4.6 0.8 4.7
19	F	0452 1129 1712 2339	0.5 4.7 0.6 4.8
20	SA	0532 1205 1752	0.4 4.8 0.5
21	SU	0018 0612 1245 1832	4.8 0.3 4.8 0.5
22	M	0101 0652 1329 1913	4.8 0.4 4.7 0.6
23	TU	0147 0733 1418 1957	4.7 0.6 4.6 0.9
24	W	0239 0819 1517 2048	4.5 1.0 4.4 1.2
25	TH	0324 0914 1602 ◑ 2151	4.2 1.4 4.2 1.6
26	F	0435 1026 1724 2317	4.0 1.7 4.1 1.8
27	SA	0559 1157 1833	3.9 1.9 4.0
28	SU	0043 0711 1313 1941	1.7 3.9 1.8 4.1
29	M	0147 0817 1412 2036	1.5 4.1 1.5 4.2
30	TU	0239 0944 1501 2145	1.2 4.3 1.3 4.3
31	W	0325 1019 1546 2223	0.9 4.4 1.0 4.4

Chart Datum: 2·74 metres below Ordnance Datum (Newlyn)
HAT is 5·0 metres above Chart Datum

TIME ZONE (UT)
For Summer Time add ONE hour in **non-shaded areas**

SOUTHAMPTON

LAT 50°53′N LONG 1°24′W

TIMES AND HEIGHTS OF HIGH AND LOW WATERS

Dates in amber are **SPRINGS**
Dates in grey are **NEAPS**

2016

SEPTEMBER

Date	Day	Time	m
1	TH	0408 1056 1629 ● 2300	0.6 4.5 0.7 4.4
2	F	0449 1135 1710 2338	0.5 4.5 0.7 4.4
3	SA	0529 1212 1749	0.5 4.5 0.7
4	SU	0013 0607 1245 1826	4.4 0.7 4.4 0.9
5	M	0048 0642 1316 1856	4.3 0.9 4.4 1.1
6	TU	0122 0708 1347 1919	4.3 1.1 4.3 1.3
7	W	0157 0730 1421 1945	4.2 1.3 4.2 1.4
8	TH	0235 0800 1441 2022	4.1 1.5 4.1 1.6
9	F	0300 0843 1528 ◐ 2113	3.9 1.8 3.9 1.9
10	SA	0415 0944 1620 2233	3.8 2.1 3.7 2.1
11	SU	0450 1117 1725 2357	3.6 2.3 3.6 2.1
12	M	0718 1237 1933	3.7 2.2 3.8
13	TU	0112 0819 1346 2058	1.9 4.0 1.9 4.1
14	W	0212 0904 1439 2133	1.5 4.3 1.4 4.4
15	TH	0302 0942 1525 2204	1.1 4.5 1.0 4.6
16	F	0347 1030 1608 ○ 2238	0.7 4.7 0.7 4.8
17	SA	0429 1103 1650 2316	0.4 4.9 0.4 4.9
18	SU	0510 1142 1731 2357	0.2 4.9 0.3 5.0
19	M	0550 1223 1811	0.2 4.9 0.4
20	TU	0040 0631 1307 1853	4.9 0.4 4.8 0.5
21	W	0127 0713 1357 1936	4.8 0.6 4.7 0.8
22	TH	0221 0759 1459 2026	4.5 1.0 4.4 1.2
23	F	0336 0854 1547 ◑ 2131	4.3 1.5 4.2 1.6
24	SA	0428 1011 1706 2302	4.0 1.9 4.0 1.8
25	SU	0542 1142 1811	3.9 2.0 3.9
26	M	0021 0646 1252 1910	1.8 3.9 1.9 3.9
27	TU	0123 0755 1349 2011	1.6 4.0 1.7 4.0
28	W	0214 0850 1438 2138	1.4 4.2 1.4 4.2
29	TH	0300 0931 1522 2205	1.1 4.3 1.1 4.3
30	F	0343 1039 1605 2239	0.8 4.5 0.8 4.4

OCTOBER

Date	Day	Time	m
1	SA	0424 1112 1645 ● 2315	0.7 4.5 0.7 4.4
2	SU	0504 1120 1724 2335	0.7 4.5 0.8 4.4
3	M	0541 1215 1758	0.8 4.5 1.0
4	TU	0022 0612 1242 1823	4.4 1.0 4.4 1.1
5	W	0052 0632 1311 1841	4.4 1.2 4.4 1.2
6	TH	0125 0654 1343 1909	4.3 1.3 4.4 1.3
7	F	0201 0727 1421 1946	4.3 1.4 4.2 1.5
8	SA	0245 0808 1508 2033	4.1 1.7 4.1 1.7
9	SU	0338 0900 1545 ◐ 2138	3.9 2.0 3.8 2.1
10	M	0443 1031 1723 2319	3.8 2.3 3.7 2.1
11	TU	0531 1204 1818	3.7 2.2 3.7
12	W	0038 0827 1315 1954	1.9 4.1 1.9 4.1
13	TH	0142 0909 1411 2106	1.5 4.4 1.5 4.4
14	F	0234 0908 1459 2136	1.1 4.6 1.0 4.6
15	SA	0320 1002 1543 2213	0.7 4.8 0.6 4.9
16	SU	0404 1038 1626 ○ 2253	0.4 5.0 0.4 5.0
17	M	0446 1117 1708 2335	0.2 5.0 0.3 5.0
18	TU	0528 1200 1750	0.2 5.0 0.3
19	W	0020 0610 1245 1833	4.9 0.4 4.9 0.5
20	TH	0109 0654 1336 1917	4.8 0.7 4.7 0.8
21	F	0205 0741 1440 2007	4.5 1.1 4.4 1.2
22	SA	0339 0837 1525 ◑ 2110	4.3 1.5 4.2 1.6
23	SU	0413 0950 1638 2231	4.1 1.9 4.0 1.8
24	M	0513 1110 1739 2345	4.0 2.0 3.9 1.9
25	TU	0613 1218 1836	3.9 2.0 3.8
26	W	0047 0716 1317 1936	1.8 4.0 1.8 3.9
27	TH	0141 0814 1408 2030	1.6 4.1 1.5 4.0
28	F	0230 0902 1454 2152	1.3 4.3 1.2 4.2
29	SA	0314 0938 1537 2218	1.1 4.4 1.0 4.3
30	SU	0356 1043 1618 ● 2233	0.9 4.5 0.9 4.4
31	M	0436 1056 1656 2329	0.9 4.5 0.9 4.4

NOVEMBER

Date	Day	Time	m
1	TU	0513 1148 1729	1.0 4.5 1.0
2	W	0001 0542 1216 1753	4.4 1.2 4.5 1.1
3	TH	0030 0603 1244 1814	4.4 1.3 4.5 1.2
4	F	0101 0629 1316 1845	4.4 1.3 4.4 1.2
5	SA	0137 0704 1354 1923	4.4 1.4 4.3 1.3
6	SU	0221 0746 1440 2009	4.3 1.6 4.2 1.6
7	M	0313 0837 1535 ◐ 2106	4.1 1.9 4.0 1.8
8	TU	0414 0950 1621 2235	4.0 2.1 3.8 2.0
9	W	0500 1123 1731 2358	3.9 2.1 3.8 1.9
10	TH	0627 1237 1902	4.0 1.9 4.0
11	F	0105 0752 1338 2006	1.6 4.3 1.5 4.3
12	SA	0202 0835 1430 2110	1.2 4.6 1.1 4.6
13	SU	0252 0935 1517 2149	0.8 4.8 0.7 4.8
14	M	0338 1014 1603 ○ 2232	0.5 5.0 0.4 4.9
15	TU	0423 1055 1647 2316	0.4 5.0 0.3 5.0
16	W	0507 1140 1731	0.4 5.0 0.3
17	TH	0003 0552 1227 1815	4.9 0.5 4.9 0.5
18	F	0053 0637 1317 1901	4.7 0.8 4.7 0.8
19	SA	0151 0726 1416 1951	4.6 1.1 4.4 1.1
20	SU	0236 0819 1528 2047	4.3 1.4 4.2 1.4
21	M	0342 0921 1601 ◑ 2154	4.2 1.7 4.0 1.7
22	TU	0444 1030 1701 2302	4.1 1.9 3.9 1.8
23	W	0612 1136 1824	4.0 2.0 3.8
24	TH	0005 0633 1239 1856	1.8 4.0 1.9 3.8
25	F	0104 0730 1334 1952	1.7 4.0 1.7 3.9
26	SA	0156 0824 1424 2041	1.5 4.2 1.4 4.0
27	SU	0243 0907 1508 2159	1.3 4.3 1.2 4.2
28	M	0327 1014 1550 2236	1.2 4.4 1.1 4.3
29	TU	0407 1032 1628 ● 2317	1.1 4.5 1.0 4.4
30	W	0445 1108 1702 2351	1.2 4.5 1.1 4.4

DECEMBER

Date	Day	Time	m
1	TH	0516 1139 1729	1.2 4.5 1.1
2	F	0017 0543 1225 1757	4.4 1.3 4.5 1.1
3	SA	0045 0613 1256 1829	4.4 1.3 4.5 1.1
4	SU	0120 0649 1335 1909	4.4 1.3 4.4 1.2
5	M	0203 0731 1420 1953	4.4 1.4 4.3 1.3
6	TU	0252 0820 1511 2046	4.3 1.6 4.2 1.5
7	W	0348 0921 1612 ◐ 2154	4.2 1.8 4.0 1.7
8	TH	0453 1039 1701 2314	4.1 1.9 3.9 1.7
9	F	0543 1156 1812	4.1 1.8 4.0
10	SA	0027 0659 1305 1928	1.6 4.3 1.5 4.2
11	SU	0131 0807 1404 2028	1.3 4.5 1.2 4.4
12	M	0226 0855 1455 2132	1.0 4.7 0.8 4.6
13	TU	0317 0956 1544 2217	0.8 4.9 0.6 4.7
14	W	0405 1039 1631 ○ 2303	0.6 4.9 0.4 4.8
15	TH	0451 1125 1716 2350	0.5 4.9 0.4 4.7
16	F	0537 1211 1802	0.6 4.8 0.4
17	SA	0040 0624 1259 1847	4.7 0.7 4.6 0.6
18	SU	0134 0710 1350 1933	4.5 0.9 4.4 0.9
19	M	0239 0757 1448 2021	4.4 1.2 4.2 1.2
20	TU	0307 0850 1525 2116	4.2 1.5 4.0 1.5
21	W	0406 0947 1619 ◑ 2215	4.1 1.8 3.9 1.7
22	TH	0459 1050 1718 2319	4.0 1.9 3.8 1.9
23	F	0553 1156 1817	3.9 2.0 3.7
24	SA	0022 0715 1258 1946	1.9 4.0 1.9 3.8
25	SU	0121 0814 1353 2011	1.8 4.0 1.7 3.9
26	M	0212 0906 1440 2107	1.6 4.2 1.5 4.0
27	TU	0258 0925 1523 2152	1.5 4.3 1.3 4.2
28	W	0341 1011 1602 2237	1.3 4.4 1.1 4.3
29	TH	0420 1050 1639 ● 2312	1.2 4.5 1.0 4.4
30	F	0455 1122 1713	1.2 4.5 1.0
31	SA	0006 0529 1154 1746	4.4 1.1 4.5 0.9

Chart Datum: 2·74 metres below Ordnance Datum (Newlyn)
HAT is 5·0 metres above Chart Datum

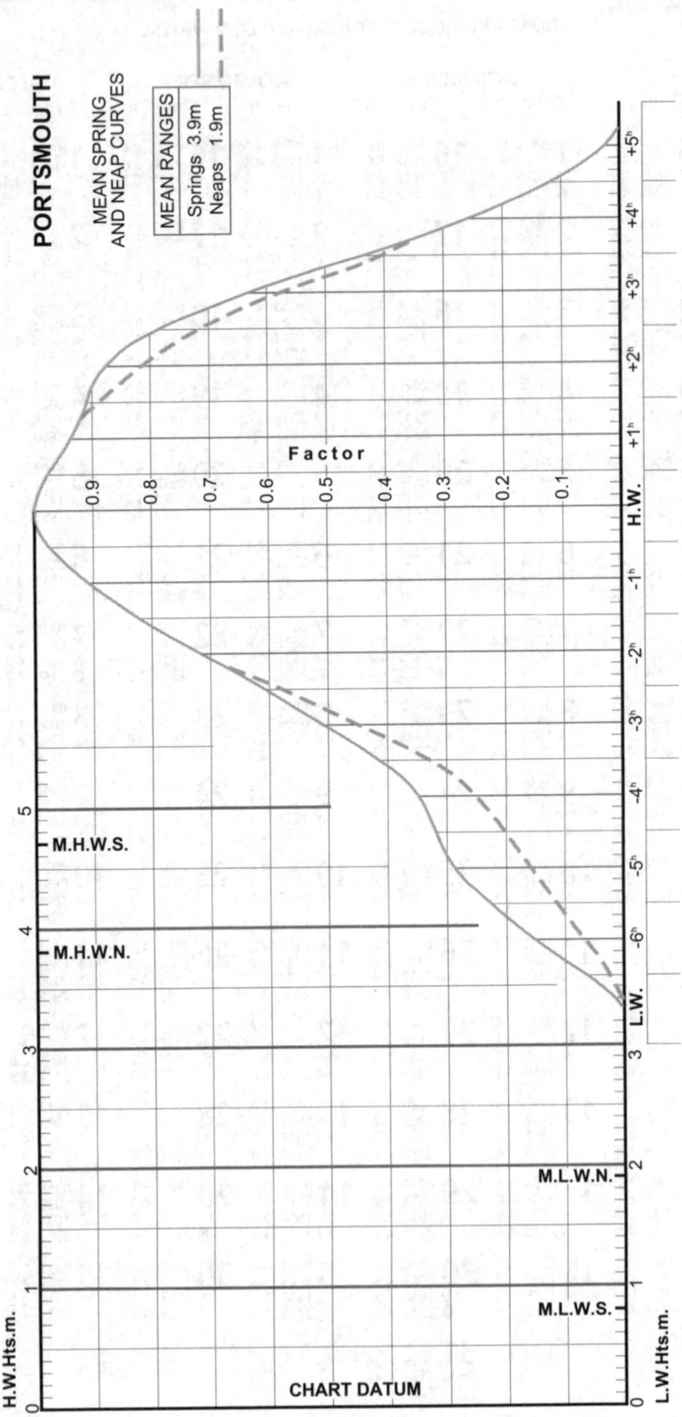
PORTSMOUTH
MEAN SPRING AND NEAP CURVES
MEAN RANGES
Springs 3.9m
Neaps 1.9m
Factor
0.9
0.8
0.7
0.6
0.5
0.4
0.3
0.2
0.1
H.W.
+1ʰ
+2ʰ
+3ʰ
+4ʰ
+5ʰ
-1ʰ
-2ʰ
-3ʰ
-4ʰ
-5ʰ
-6ʰ
L.W.
M.H.W.S.
M.H.W.N.
M.L.W.N.
M.L.W.S.
H.W.Hts.m.
L.W.Hts.m.
CHART DATUM
0
1
2
3
4
5

TIME ZONE (UT)
For Summer Time add ONE hour in **non-shaded areas**

PORTSMOUTH

LAT 50°48′N LONG 1°07′W

TIMES AND HEIGHTS OF HIGH AND LOW WATERS

Dates in amber are **SPRINGS**
Dates in grey are **NEAPS**

2016

JANUARY

Day	Time	m	Day	Time	m
1 F	0350 0853 1556 2112	4.3 1.7 4.0 1.7	16 SA	0352 0852 1607 ◐ 2118	4.6 1.2 4.3 1.2
2 SA	0433 0945 1645 ◑ 2209	4.1 1.9 3.9 1.9	17 SU	0452 0956 1712 2228	4.4 1.4 4.2 1.4
3 SU	0522 1059 1747 2326	4.0 2.0 3.7 2.0	18 M	0553 1118 1818 2352	4.3 1.6 4.1 1.6
4 M	0626 1210 1913	3.9 2.0 3.7	19 TU	0657 1235 1926	4.3 1.6 4.1
5 TU	0030 0746 1307 2025	1.9 4.0 1.9 3.8	20 W	0101 0801 1338 2030	1.5 4.3 1.4 4.2
6 W	0124 0847 1356 2121	1.8 4.1 1.7 4.0	21 TH	0202 0859 1433 2131	1.4 4.4 1.2 4.3
7 TH	0213 0936 1441 2207	1.7 4.3 1.4 4.2	22 F	0255 0951 1523 2224	1.3 4.5 1.0 4.4
8 F	0259 1016 1525 2246	1.4 4.4 1.2 4.4	23 SA	0344 1037 1609 2310	1.1 4.6 0.8 4.5
9 SA	0344 1052 1608 2321	1.2 4.6 0.9 4.6	24 SU	0430 1119 1653 ○ 2353	1.0 4.6 0.7 4.6
10 SU	0427 1127 1650 ● 2356	1.0 4.7 0.8 4.7	25 M	0513 1201 1735	0.9 4.6 0.7
11 M	0510 1203 1732	0.9 4.7 0.6	26 TU	0035 0553 1243 1813	4.6 0.9 4.6 0.7
12 TU	0033 0550 1242 1812	4.7 0.8 4.7 0.6	27 W	0117 0631 1323 1848	4.6 0.9 4.5 0.8
13 W	0115 0632 1323 1853	4.7 0.8 4.7 0.6	28 TH	0157 0705 1402 1920	4.5 1.1 4.4 1.0
14 TH	0201 0714 1410 1936	4.7 0.8 4.6 0.7	29 F	0233 0736 1437 1951	4.5 1.2 4.3 1.2
15 F	0254 0800 1504 2023	4.7 1.0 4.5 0.9	30 SA	0306 0808 1513 2025	4.4 1.4 4.2 1.4
			31 SU	0342 0846 1554 2106	4.2 1.6 4.0 1.6

FEBRUARY

Day	Time	m	Day	Time	m
1 M	0425 0933 1644 ◑ 2158	4.1 1.8 3.8 1.8	16 TU	0527 1049 1757 2329	4.2 1.5 4.0 1.6
2 TU	0516 1036 1745 2312	3.9 1.9 3.7 2.0	17 W	0634 1213 1909	4.1 1.6 3.9
3 W	0621 1204 1932	3.8 2.0 3.6	18 TH	0045 0742 1321 2020	1.7 4.1 1.5 4.0
4 TH	0040 0803 1318 2052	2.0 3.9 1.8 3.8	19 F	0149 0845 1419 2127	1.6 4.1 1.3 4.2
5 F	0143 0906 1414 2141	1.8 4.1 1.5 4.1	20 SA	0244 0938 1509 2218	1.4 4.3 1.1 4.3
6 SA	0237 0950 1503 2221	1.5 4.3 1.2 4.3	21 SU	0331 1022 1554 2255	1.2 4.4 0.9 4.4
7 SU	0325 1028 1549 2257	1.2 4.5 0.9 4.5	22 M	0415 1102 1635 ○ 2333	1.0 4.5 0.7 4.5
8 M	0410 1105 1633 ● 2334	0.9 4.7 0.6 4.7	23 TU	0456 1142 1715	0.8 4.5 0.6
9 TU	0454 1143 1716	0.7 4.8 0.4	24 W	0011 0533 1222 1751	4.6 0.8 4.5 0.7
10 W	0014 0535 1224 1757	4.8 0.5 4.8 0.3	25 TH	0050 0608 1301 1823	4.6 0.8 4.5 0.8
11 TH	0056 0617 1306 1838	4.9 0.5 4.8 0.3	26 F	0126 0638 1336 1852	4.5 0.9 4.4 0.9
12 F	0142 0659 1353 1920	4.8 0.5 4.8 0.5	27 SA	0158 0704 1406 1919	4.5 1.0 4.4 1.0
13 SA	0233 0743 1446 2004	4.8 0.7 4.6 0.7	28 SU	0227 0733 1438 1949	4.4 1.1 4.3 1.2
14 SU	0329 0831 1546 2054	4.6 1.0 4.4 1.0	29 M	0301 0807 1517 2026	4.3 1.3 4.1 1.4
15 M	0427 0929 1650 ◐ 2200	4.5 1.3 4.2 1.4			

MARCH

Day	Time	m	Day	Time	m
1 TU	0343 0849 1604 ◑ 2111	4.1 1.5 3.9 1.6	16 W	0502 1024 1739 2308	4.2 1.5 4.0 1.7
2 W	0433 0942 1700 2211	3.9 1.7 3.7 1.9	17 TH	0610 1148 1851	3.9 1.7 3.9
3 TH	0533 1055 1814 2347	3.7 1.9 3.6 2.0	18 F	0024 0721 1257 2006	1.8 3.9 1.6 3.9
4 F	0655 1241 2014	3.7 1.9 3.8	19 SA	0129 0828 1356 2144	1.7 3.9 1.5 4.1
5 SA	0118 0831 1348 2110	1.9 3.9 1.6 4.0	20 SU	0224 0924 1447 2245	1.5 4.1 1.2 4.3
6 SU	0216 0920 1441 2151	1.5 4.2 1.2 4.3	21 M	0311 1003 1531 2235	1.2 4.2 1.0 4.4
7 M	0306 1001 1528 2230	1.2 4.5 0.8 4.6	22 TU	0353 1041 1612 2309	1.0 4.4 0.8 4.5
8 TU	0351 1040 1613 2309	0.8 4.7 0.5 4.8	23 W	0433 1120 1650 ○ 2345	0.8 4.4 0.7 4.5
9 W	0435 1121 1656 ● 2350	0.5 4.8 0.3 4.9	24 TH	0509 1159 1725	0.8 4.5 0.7
10 TH	0517 1202 1738	0.3 4.9 0.2	25 F	0022 0542 1238 1756	4.5 0.8 4.5 0.8
11 F	0032 0558 1246 1819	4.9 0.3 4.9 0.2	26 SA	0057 0610 1311 1824	4.5 0.9 4.5 0.9
12 SA	0118 0640 1333 1900	4.9 0.3 4.9 0.4	27 SU	0126 0636 1340 1851	4.5 0.9 4.4 1.0
13 SU	0208 0723 1427 1944	4.8 0.5 4.7 0.6	28 M	0154 0704 1410 1920	4.4 1.0 4.4 1.1
14 M	0303 0809 1528 2034	4.7 0.8 4.5 1.0	29 TU	0227 0736 1448 1955	4.3 1.1 4.2 1.3
15 TU	0402 0905 1633 ◐ 2138	4.4 1.2 4.3 1.4	30 W	0307 0816 1534 2039	4.2 1.3 4.1 1.5
			31 TH	0357 0906 1630 ◑ 2135	4.0 1.5 3.9 1.8

APRIL

Day	Time	m	Day	Time	m
1 F	0458 1013 1741 2258	3.8 1.8 3.8 2.0	16 SA	0653 1224 1943	3.8 1.7 4.0
2 SA	0615 1202 1919	3.7 1.8 3.8	17 SU	0058 0802 1324 2123	1.8 3.8 1.6 4.1
3 SU	0051 0747 1320 2032	1.8 3.9 1.5 4.1	18 M	0156 0902 1416 2215	1.6 4.0 1.4 4.3
4 M	0152 0846 1415 2119	1.5 4.2 1.2 4.4	19 TU	0243 0940 1502 2208	1.4 4.1 1.2 4.4
5 TU	0242 0931 1503 2201	1.1 4.5 0.8 4.7	20 W	0326 1018 1543 2241	1.1 4.3 1.0 4.5
6 W	0328 1014 1549 2242	0.7 4.7 0.5 4.9	21 TH	0405 1057 1621 2318	1.0 4.4 0.9 4.5
7 TH	0412 1056 1633 ● 2324	0.4 4.9 0.3 5.0	22 F	0441 1137 1656 ○ 2355	0.9 4.4 0.9 4.5
8 F	0455 1140 1716	0.3 4.9 0.2	23 SA	0513 1215 1728	0.9 4.5 1.0
9 SA	0008 0537 1226 1758	5.0 0.2 5.0 0.2	24 SU	0028 0542 1249 1757	4.5 0.9 4.5 1.0
10 SU	0054 0620 1315 1841	5.0 0.3 4.9 0.4	25 M	0058 0611 1318 1826	4.5 0.9 4.5 1.1
11 M	0143 0704 1410 1926	4.8 0.5 4.8 0.7	26 TU	0127 0640 1350 1858	4.5 1.0 4.4 1.1
12 TU	0238 0750 1515 2016	4.7 0.8 4.6 1.1	27 W	0200 0714 1427 1934	4.4 1.0 4.3 1.3
13 W	0336 0845 1618 2119	4.4 1.2 4.3 1.5	28 TH	0240 0754 1514 2018	4.2 1.2 4.2 1.4
14 TH	0436 0959 1719 ◐ 2241	4.1 1.5 4.1 1.8	29 F	0330 0843 1611 2114	4.1 1.4 4.0 1.7
15 F	0542 1117 1827 2353	3.9 1.7 4.0 1.9	30 SA	0432 0947 1719 ◑ 2230	3.9 1.6 4.0 1.8

Chart Datum: 2·73 metres below Ordnance Datum (Newlyn)
HAT is 5·1 metres above Chart Datum

TIME ZONE (UT)
For Summer Time add ONE hour in **non-shaded areas**

PORTSMOUTH

LAT 50°48′N LONG 1°07′W

TIMES AND HEIGHTS OF HIGH AND LOW WATERS

Dates in amber are **SPRINGS**
Dates in grey are **NEAPS**

2016

MAY

Date	Day	Time	m	Time	m	Time	m	Time	m
1	SU	0546	3.8	1118	1.7	1838	4.0		
2	M	0013	1.8	0705	3.9	1246	1.5	1951	4.2
3	TU	0121	1.5	0810	4.2	1344	1.2	2045	4.5
4	W	0214	1.1	0900	4.5	1435	0.9	2131	4.7
5	TH	0302	0.8	0947	4.7	1523	0.6	2215	4.9
6	F	0348	0.5	1032	4.8	1609	0.4	● 2300	5.0
7	SA	0433	0.4	1119	4.9	1654	0.4	2345	5.0
8	SU	0517	0.3	1207	4.9	1738	0.4		
9	M	0032	4.9	0601	0.4	1300	4.8	1823	0.6
10	TU	0121	4.8	0646	0.6	1358	4.7	1909	0.8
11	W	0214	4.6	0733	0.8	1505	4.6	1959	1.1
12	TH	0311	4.4	0825	1.1	1601	4.4	2058	1.5
13	F	0407	4.2	0929	1.4	1654	4.2	◐ 2207	1.7
14	SA	0507	3.9	1039	1.6	1753	4.1	2314	1.8
15	SU	0613	3.8	1144	1.7	1900	4.0		
16	M	0018	1.8	0720	3.8	1245	1.7	2004	4.1
17	TU	0118	1.7	0820	3.9	1339	1.6	2053	4.2
18	W	0209	1.5	0908	4.0	1426	1.4	2133	4.3
19	TH	0253	1.3	0952	4.2	1508	1.3	2213	4.4
20	F	0333	1.2	1034	4.3	1548	1.2	2252	4.5
21	SA	0410	1.1	1116	4.4	1625	1.1	○ 2329	4.5
22	SU	0444	1.0	1155	4.5	1701	1.1		
23	M	0003	4.5	0517	1.0	1230	4.5	1734	1.1
24	TU	0035	4.5	0550	0.9	1301	4.5	1807	1.1
25	W	0106	4.5	0623	1.0	1335	4.5	1842	1.1
26	TH	0141	4.4	0659	1.0	1414	4.4	1921	1.2
27	F	0222	4.3	0741	1.1	1502	4.3	2006	1.3
28	SA	0311	4.2	0829	1.2	1558	4.2	2100	1.5
29	SU	0412	4.1	0928	1.4	1701	4.2	◑ 2208	1.6
30	M	0521	4.0	1043	1.5	1808	4.2	2331	1.6
31	TU	0632	4.1	1206	1.4	1914	4.3		

JUNE

Date	Day	Time	m	Time	m	Time	m	Time	m
1	W	0044	1.4	0736	4.2	1312	1.2	2012	4.5
2	TH	0144	1.2	0832	4.4	1407	1.0	2104	4.7
3	F	0236	0.9	0924	4.6	1458	0.8	2152	4.8
4	SA	0326	0.7	1014	4.7	1547	0.7	2240	4.9
5	SU	0414	0.6	1104	4.8	1635	0.6	● 2327	4.9
6	M	0500	0.5	1155	4.8	1722	0.6		
7	TU	0014	4.8	0545	0.5	1248	4.8	1807	0.7
8	W	0103	4.7	0631	0.6	1347	4.7	1853	0.9
9	TH	0153	4.6	0716	0.8	1448	4.6	1941	1.1
10	F	0245	4.4	0804	1.1	1536	4.5	2032	1.4
11	SA	0337	4.2	0856	1.3	1622	4.3	2128	1.6
12	SU	0430	4.0	0956	1.6	1711	4.2	◐ 2230	1.8
13	M	0527	3.9	1058	1.7	1807	4.0	2333	1.9
14	TU	0632	3.8	1158	1.8	1909	4.0		
15	W	0033	1.8	0736	3.8	1255	1.7	2007	4.1
16	TH	0128	1.7	0834	3.9	1346	1.6	2059	4.2
17	F	0215	1.5	0926	4.1	1432	1.5	2145	4.3
18	SA	0258	1.4	1013	4.2	1515	1.4	2227	4.4
19	SU	0338	1.2	1056	4.4	1556	1.3	2305	4.5
20	M	0417	1.1	1135	4.5	1636	1.2	○ 2340	4.5
21	TU	0456	1.0	1211	4.5	1715	1.1		
22	W	0013	4.5	0533	0.9	1245	4.5	1752	1.0
23	TH	0048	4.5	0610	0.9	1321	4.6	1830	1.0
24	F	0125	4.5	0649	0.9	1402	4.5	1910	1.1
25	SA	0206	4.5	0730	0.9	1450	4.5	1954	1.1
26	SU	0255	4.4	0816	1.0	1543	4.4	2045	1.3
27	M	0354	4.3	0910	1.2	1641	4.4	◑ 2145	1.4
28	TU	0458	4.2	1015	1.3	1742	4.3	2257	1.5
29	W	0604	4.1	1132	1.4	1845	4.4		
30	TH	0012	1.5	0709	4.2	1243	1.4	1946	4.4

JULY

Date	Day	Time	m	Time	m	Time	m	Time	m
1	F	0118	1.3	0811	4.3	1344	1.2	2043	4.6
2	SA	0216	1.1	0909	4.4	1440	1.1	2136	4.7
3	SU	0309	0.9	1003	4.6	1532	1.0	2226	4.7
4	M	0359	0.7	1055	4.6	1621	0.8	● 2313	4.8
5	TU	0447	0.6	1145	4.7	1708	0.8	2359	4.7
6	W	0532	0.6	1236	4.7	1753	0.8		
7	TH	0044	4.7	0615	0.7	1327	4.7	1837	0.9
8	F	0131	4.6	0658	0.8	1418	4.6	1920	1.1
9	SA	0218	4.4	0739	1.0	1503	4.5	2002	1.3
10	SU	0305	4.3	0821	1.2	1544	4.4	2046	1.5
11	M	0350	4.1	0906	1.5	1625	4.2	2135	1.7
12	TU	0437	3.9	0958	1.7	1709	4.1	◐ 2233	1.8
13	W	0532	3.8	1102	1.9	1803	4.0	2338	1.9
14	TH	0645	3.7	1206	1.9	1916	3.9		
15	F	0040	1.9	0759	3.8	1305	1.9	2024	4.0
16	SA	0135	1.7	0901	3.9	1357	1.7	2118	4.2
17	SU	0224	1.5	0951	4.1	1446	1.6	2203	4.3
18	M	0310	1.3	1035	4.3	1532	1.4	2242	4.4
19	TU	0354	1.1	1113	4.5	1615	1.2	○ 2317	4.5
20	W	0436	0.9	1148	4.6	1657	1.0	2352	4.6
21	TH	0517	0.7	1223	4.6	1737	0.9		
22	F	0028	4.6	0556	0.7	1302	4.7	1816	0.8
23	SA	0107	4.6	0635	0.6	1344	4.7	1856	0.8
24	SU	0148	4.6	0716	0.7	1431	4.7	1939	0.9
25	M	0237	4.5	0759	0.8	1524	4.6	2026	1.1
26	TU	0334	4.4	0849	1.0	1619	4.5	◑ 2121	1.3
27	W	0437	4.3	0948	1.3	1718	4.4	2230	1.5
28	TH	0542	4.2	1106	1.5	1821	4.3	2349	1.5
29	F	0650	4.1	1224	1.6	1927	4.3		
30	SA	0101	1.5	0758	4.2	1330	1.5	2030	4.4
31	SU	0203	1.3	0902	4.3	1429	1.3	2125	4.5

AUGUST

Date	Day	Time	m	Time	m	Time	m	Time	m
1	M	0258	1.1	0959	4.4	1522	1.2	2214	4.6
2	TU	0347	0.9	1048	4.6	1610	1.0	● 2259	4.6
3	W	0433	0.7	1133	4.6	1655	0.9	2342	4.6
4	TH	0516	0.6	1217	4.7	1737	0.8		
5	F	0024	4.6	0557	0.7	1301	4.7	1817	0.9
6	SA	0108	4.5	0636	0.8	1345	4.6	1855	1.0
7	SU	0150	4.5	0712	1.0	1425	4.5	1930	1.2
8	M	0230	4.3	0745	1.2	1502	4.4	2003	1.4
9	TU	0308	4.2	0818	1.4	1536	4.3	2038	1.6
10	W	0346	4.1	0857	1.6	1614	4.1	◐ 2122	1.8
11	TH	0431	3.9	0947	1.9	1659	4.0	2221	1.9
12	F	0527	3.7	1100	2.0	1757	3.8	2343	2.0
13	SA	0711	3.7	1225	2.1	1940	3.8		
14	SU	0057	1.9	0834	3.8	1328	1.9	2050	4.0
15	M	0155	1.7	0928	4.1	1422	1.7	2138	4.2
16	TU	0245	1.4	1010	4.3	1510	1.4	2216	4.4
17	W	0332	1.1	1046	4.5	1555	1.1	2252	4.6
18	TH	0415	0.8	1121	4.7	1637	0.9	○ 2328	4.7
19	F	0457	0.6	1158	4.8	1718	0.7		
20	SA	0005	4.8	0537	0.5	1238	4.8	1758	0.6
21	SU	0045	4.8	0617	0.4	1320	4.8	1838	0.6
22	M	0127	4.8	0657	0.5	1406	4.8	1920	0.7
23	TU	0215	4.7	0740	0.7	1459	4.7	2005	0.9
24	W	0313	4.5	0827	1.0	1556	4.6	2058	1.2
25	TH	0417	4.3	0925	1.4	1655	4.4	◑ 2208	1.5
26	F	0524	4.2	1051	1.7	1800	4.2	2335	1.7
27	SA	0636	4.0	1213	1.8	1911	4.1		
28	SU	0048	1.6	0751	4.1	1320	1.7	2018	4.2
29	M	0151	1.5	0901	4.2	1419	1.5	2115	4.3
30	TU	0244	1.2	0958	4.4	1509	1.3	2201	4.5
31	W	0332	1.0	1038	4.6	1554	1.0	2242	4.6

Chart Datum: 2·73 metres below Ordnance Datum (Newlyn)
HAT is 5·1 metres above Chart Datum

TIME ZONE (UT)
For Summer Time add ONE hour in **non-shaded areas**

PORTSMOUTH

LAT 50°48′N LONG 1°07′W

TIMES AND HEIGHTS OF HIGH AND LOW WATERS

Dates in amber are **SPRINGS**
Dates in grey are **NEAPS**

2016

SEPTEMBER

Day	Time	m	Day	Time	m
1 TH	0415 1115 1637 ● 2322	0.8 4.6 0.9 4.6	16 F	0351 1053 1614 ○ 2301	0.7 4.8 0.8 4.8
2 F	0456 1154 1717	0.7 4.7 0.8	17 SA	0434 1130 1656 2340	0.5 4.9 0.5 4.9
3 SA	0002 0535 1234 1754	4.6 0.7 4.7 0.9	18 SU	0515 1210 1737	0.4 5.0 0.5
4 SU	0043 0610 1312 1828	4.6 0.8 4.6 1.0	19 M	0020 0556 1253 1817	5.0 0.4 5.0 0.5
5 M	0122 0642 1348 1857	4.5 1.0 4.6 1.1	20 TU	0105 0636 1339 1859	4.9 0.5 4.9 0.6
6 TU	0156 0710 1419 1924	4.4 1.2 4.5 1.3	21 W	0154 0719 1432 1944	4.8 0.7 4.8 0.9
7 W	0228 0738 1451 1955	4.3 1.3 4.4 1.4	22 TH	0253 0806 1531 2036	4.6 1.1 4.6 1.2
8 TH	0303 0812 1529 2034	4.2 1.5 4.2 1.6	23 F	0401 0906 1634 ◑ 2150	4.4 1.5 4.3 1.6
9 F	0348 0855 1615 ◐ 2125	4.0 1.8 4.0 1.9	24 SA	0510 1039 1741 2319	4.2 1.8 4.1 1.7
10 SA	0442 0954 1711 2238	3.8 2.1 3.8 2.1	25 SU	0622 1157 1852	4.1 1.9 4.0
11 SU	0551 1144 1824	3.7 2.2 3.7	26 M	0028 0741 1302 2003	1.7 4.1 1.8 4.1
12 M	0023 0800 1304 2016	2.0 3.8 2.0 3.9	27 TU	0130 0921 1400 2106	1.6 4.3 1.6 4.2
13 TU	0129 0859 1359 2108	1.8 4.1 1.8 4.2	28 W	0223 1025 1449 2147	1.4 4.5 1.4 4.4
14 W	0221 0941 1447 2147	1.4 4.4 1.4 4.4	29 TH	0309 1107 1533 2223	1.1 4.6 1.1 4.5
15 TH	0307 1017 1532 2223	1.1 4.6 1.1 4.7	30 F	0352 1054 1614 2301	0.9 4.6 1.0 4.6

OCTOBER

Day	Time	m	Day	Time	m
1 SA	0432 1128 1653 ● 2340	0.8 4.7 0.9 4.6	16 SU	0408 1102 1632 ○ 2315	0.5 5.1 0.5 5.0
2 SU	0509 1205 1728	0.8 4.7 0.9	17 M	0451 1143 1714 2358	0.4 5.1 0.4 5.1
3 M	0019 0542 1241 1759	4.6 0.9 4.7 1.0	18 TU	0533 1226 1757	0.4 5.1 0.4
4 TU	0055 0612 1314 1826	4.6 1.1 4.6 1.1	19 W	0044 0616 1313 1839	5.0 0.5 5.0 0.6
5 W	0126 0638 1342 1852	4.5 1.2 4.5 1.2	20 TH	0136 0700 1406 1925	4.9 0.8 4.8 0.9
6 TH	0155 0706 1413 1921	4.4 1.3 4.4 1.3	21 F	0237 0748 1506 2017	4.7 1.2 4.6 1.2
7 F	0230 0738 1451 1958	4.3 1.5 4.3 1.5	22 SA	0348 0849 1611 ◑ 2129	4.5 1.6 4.3 1.6
8 SA	0314 0818 1538 2044	4.2 1.7 4.1 1.8	23 SU	0454 1017 1717 2253	4.3 1.9 4.1 1.8
9 SU	0409 0911 1635 ◐ 2148	4.0 2.0 3.9 2.0	24 M	0602 1131 1827	4.1 1.9 4.0
10 M	0516 1037 1745 2345	3.8 2.2 3.8 2.1	25 TU	0000 0721 1234 1940	1.8 4.1 1.9 4.0
11 TU	0652 1237 1922	3.8 2.1 3.9	26 W	0100 0908 1332 2136	1.7 4.3 1.7 4.1
12 W	0059 0820 1332 2030	1.8 4.1 1.8 4.2	27 TH	0154 1003 1422 2224	1.5 4.4 1.5 4.3
13 TH	0152 0906 1420 2113	1.4 4.4 1.4 4.5	28 F	0241 1042 1506 2202	1.3 4.5 1.3 4.4
14 F	0240 0944 1505 2153	1.1 4.7 1.0 4.7	29 SA	0323 1028 1547 2239	1.1 4.6 1.1 4.5
15 SA	0325 1022 1549 2233	0.7 4.9 0.7 4.9	30 SU	0403 1102 1625 ● 2318	1.0 4.7 1.0 4.6
			31 M	0440 1138 1700 2357	1.0 4.7 1.0 4.6

NOVEMBER

Day	Time	m	Day	Time	m
1 TU	0514 1213 1731	1.1 4.7 1.1	16 W	0513 1205 1738	0.5 5.1 0.5
2 W	0033 0544 1245 1759	4.6 1.2 4.6 1.1	17 TH	0029 0557 1253 1822	5.0 0.6 5.0 0.6
3 TH	0104 0612 1313 1826	4.6 1.3 4.6 1.2	18 F	0122 0643 1344 1909	4.9 0.9 4.8 0.8
4 F	0132 0641 1343 1857	4.5 1.4 4.5 1.3	19 SA	0226 0733 1442 2000	4.7 1.2 4.6 1.2
5 SA	0206 0714 1420 1933	4.4 1.5 4.3 1.4	20 SU	0335 0830 1544 2102	4.6 1.5 4.4 1.5
6 SU	0250 0754 1507 2018	4.3 1.7 4.2 1.6	21 M	0433 0942 1646 ◑ 2216	4.4 1.8 4.1 1.7
7 M	0344 0845 1604 ◐ 2116	4.1 1.9 4.0 1.8	22 TU	0532 1054 1750 2323	4.2 1.9 3.9 1.8
8 TU	0450 0955 1713 2240	4.0 2.1 3.9 1.9	23 W	0638 1159 1857	4.1 1.9 3.9
9 W	0605 1152 1832	4.0 2.0 3.9	24 TH	0023 0752 1258 2001	1.8 4.2 1.8 4.0
10 TH	0020 0724 1258 1943	1.8 4.2 1.8 4.2	25 F	0119 0911 1351 2054	1.7 4.3 1.7 4.1
11 F	0119 0823 1350 2037	1.5 4.5 1.4 4.4	26 SA	0208 0925 1436 2137	1.5 4.4 1.5 4.3
12 SA	0209 0909 1437 2123	1.1 4.7 1.1 4.7	27 SU	0252 0959 1518 2218	1.4 4.5 1.3 4.4
13 SU	0257 0952 1523 2208	0.8 4.9 0.8 4.9	28 M	0333 1037 1556 2300	1.3 4.6 1.2 4.5
14 M	0343 1036 1608 ○ 2253	0.6 5.1 0.5 5.0	29 TU	0411 1115 1632 ● 2340	1.2 4.6 1.1 4.6
15 TU	0428 1120 1653 2340	0.5 5.1 0.4 5.0	30 W	0447 1150 1706	1.2 4.6 1.1

DECEMBER

Day	Time	m	Day	Time	m
1 TH	0016 0520 1223 1737	4.6 1.2 4.6 1.1	16 F	0019 0543 1237 1808	4.9 0.7 4.9 0.6
2 F	0048 0552 1252 1809	4.6 1.3 4.6 1.1	17 SA	0113 0630 1326 1854	4.8 0.9 4.8 0.7
3 SA	0118 0624 1323 1842	4.5 1.3 4.5 1.1	18 SU	0213 0717 1419 1941	4.7 1.1 4.6 1.0
4 SU	0152 0659 1359 1918	4.5 1.4 4.4 1.2	19 M	0314 0807 1515 2032	4.6 1.3 4.4 1.3
5 M	0233 0740 1443 2001	4.4 1.5 4.3 1.3	20 TU	0404 0903 1610 2131	4.5 1.6 4.2 1.5
6 TU	0325 0828 1537 2054	4.3 1.6 4.1 1.5	21 W	0453 1008 1707 ◑ 2237	4.3 1.8 4.0 1.7
7 W	0426 0928 1643 ◐ 2159	4.2 1.8 4.0 1.7	22 TH	0547 1115 1808 2341	4.1 1.9 3.8 1.8
8 TH	0533 1049 1755 2326	4.2 1.9 4.0 1.7	23 F	0647 1218 1913	4.1 1.9 3.8
9 F	0641 1215 1904	4.3 1.7 4.1	24 SA	0039 0747 1316 2014	1.8 4.1 1.8 3.9
10 SA	0041 0744 1318 2004	1.5 4.4 1.4 4.3	25 SU	0132 0842 1405 2109	1.8 4.2 1.6 4.0
11 SU	0139 0838 1411 2058	1.3 4.7 1.1 4.6	26 M	0220 0930 1449 2158	1.6 4.3 1.5 4.2
12 M	0231 0928 1501 2149	1.0 4.8 0.9 4.7	27 TU	0304 1014 1529 2243	1.5 4.4 1.3 4.4
13 TU	0321 1016 1549 2238	0.8 5.0 0.7 4.8	28 W	0345 1054 1608 2323	1.4 4.5 1.2 4.5
14 W	0409 1102 1636 ○ 2328	0.7 5.0 0.5 4.9	29 TH	0424 1130 1645 ●	1.3 4.6 1.0
15 TH	0457 1149 1723	0.7 5.0 0.5	30 F	0000 0501 1203 1720	4.5 1.2 4.6 1.0
			31 SA	0033 0536 1235 1755	4.6 1.1 4.6 0.9

Chart Datum: 2·73 metres below Ordnance Datum (Newlyn)
HAT is 5·1 metres above Chart Datum

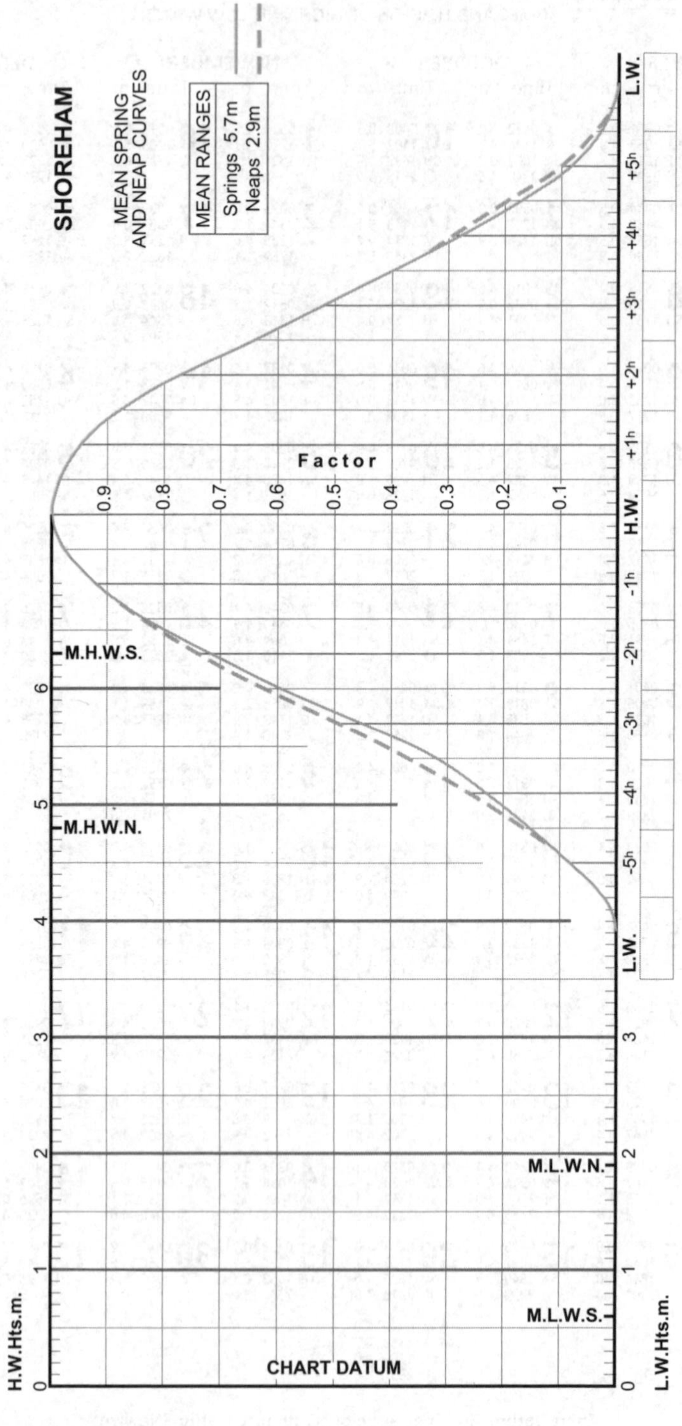
SHOREHAM
MEAN SPRING AND NEAP CURVES
MEAN RANGES
Springs 5.7m
Neaps 2.9m
M.H.W.S.
M.H.W.N.
M.L.W.N.
M.L.W.S.
CHART DATUM
H.W.Hts.m.
L.W.Hts.m.
Factor
0.9
0.8
0.7
0.6
0.5
0.4
0.3
0.2
0.1
L.W.
-5h
-4h
-3h
-2h
-1h
H.W.
+1h
+2h
+3h
+4h
+5h
L.W.
0
1
2
3
4
5
6

TIME ZONE (UT)
For Summer Time add ONE hour in **non-shaded areas**

SHOREHAM

LAT 50°50′N LONG 0°15′W

TIMES AND HEIGHTS OF HIGH AND LOW WATERS

Dates in amber are **SPRINGS**
Dates in grey are **NEAPS**

2016

JANUARY

Date	Day	Time	m	Date	Day	Time	m
1		0325	5.5	16		0312	6.0
		0929	1.6			0935	1.1
	F	1539	5.2		SA	1535	5.8
		2153	1.6		◐	2203	1.1
2		0412	5.3	17		0408	5.8
		1019	1.8			1037	1.3
	SA	1633	4.9		SU	1636	5.5
	◑	2245	1.9			2307	1.4
3		0508	5.0	18		0514	5.5
		1117	2.0			1148	1.5
	SU	1736	4.8		M	1751	5.2
		2345	2.0				
4		0610	4.9	19		0021	1.5
		1224	2.0			0632	5.4
	M	1840	4.8		TU	1303	1.5
						1915	5.2
5		0056	2.0	20		0136	1.5
		0711	5.0			0751	5.4
	TU	1340	1.9		W	1412	1.4
		1941	4.9			2031	5.4
6		0209	1.9	21		0241	1.4
		0809	5.3			0858	5.7
	W	1442	1.7		TH	1512	1.1
		2037	5.2			2133	5.7
7		0304	1.6	22		0337	1.1
		0900	5.5			0954	5.9
	TH	1530	1.4		F	1604	0.9
		2126	5.5			2225	6.0
8		0350	1.4	23		0426	0.9
		0945	5.8			1043	6.1
	F	1612	1.1		SA	1650	0.7
		2211	5.8			2312	6.2
9		0431	1.2	24		0511	0.8
		1027	6.1			1127	6.2
	SA	1653	0.9		SU	1734	0.6
		2253	6.1		○	2354	6.3
10		0510	1.0	25		0552	0.8
		1108	6.2			1208	6.3
	SU	1732	0.8		M	1814	0.6
	●	2334	6.2				
11		0549	0.9	26		0033	6.3
		1148	6.3			0631	0.8
	M	1812	0.7		TU	1245	6.2
						1851	0.7
12		0014	6.3	27		0110	6.2
		0629	0.8			0706	0.9
	TU	1230	6.4		W	1319	6.1
		1852	0.6			1926	0.8
13		0056	6.4	28		0142	6.1
		0711	0.7			0740	1.0
	W	1312	6.3		TH	1349	5.9
		1935	0.6			2000	0.9
14		0139	6.3	29		0212	5.9
		0755	0.8			0815	1.1
	TH	1355	6.2		F	1418	5.7
		2019	0.7			2035	1.1
15		0223	6.2	30		0239	5.7
		0842	0.9			0852	1.3
	F	1442	6.0		SA	1448	5.5
		2108	0.8			2113	1.4
				31		0309	5.4
						0933	1.6
					SU	1525	5.2
						2155	1.6

FEBRUARY

Date	Day	Time	m	Date	Day	Time	m
1		0350	5.2	16		0445	5.4
		1022	1.8			1119	1.5
	M	1615	4.9		TU	1722	5.1
	◑	2247	1.9			2355	1.6
2		0452	4.9	17		0601	5.1
		1123	2.0			1240	1.7
	TU	1740	4.7		W	1851	5.0
		2354	2.1				
3		0620	4.8	18		0117	1.7
		1235	2.1			0731	5.1
	W	1857	4.7		TH	1356	1.6
						2018	5.1
4		0112	2.1	19		0227	1.6
		0729	4.9			0848	5.3
	TH	1354	1.9		F	1459	1.3
		2001	5.0			2123	5.5
5		0227	1.8	20		0325	1.3
		0828	5.3			0945	5.7
	F	1458	1.5		SA	1550	1.0
		2058	5.4			2214	5.8
6		0323	1.5	21		0413	1.0
		0920	5.6			1032	5.9
	SA	1547	1.2		SU	1635	0.8
		2148	5.7			2258	6.1
7		0408	1.1	22		0455	0.8
		1006	6.0			1114	6.1
	SU	1630	0.8		M	1715	0.7
		2233	6.1		○	2337	6.2
8		0450	0.9	23		0534	0.7
		1050	6.3			1152	6.2
	M	1712	0.6		TU	1753	0.6
	●	2317	6.3				
9		0531	0.7	24		0014	6.3
		1134	6.5			0609	0.7
	TU	1754	0.4		W	1226	6.2
						1827	0.6
10		0000	6.5	25		0047	6.2
		0613	0.5			0642	0.7
	W	1217	6.6		TH	1256	6.1
		1836	0.3			1900	0.7
11		0043	6.6	26		0114	6.1
		0656	0.4			0714	0.8
	TH	1300	6.6		F	1320	6.0
		1920	0.3			1932	0.8
12		0126	6.6	27		0136	6.0
		0741	0.4			0746	0.9
	F	1343	6.5		SA	1344	5.8
		2004	0.4			2004	1.0
13		0208	6.5	28		0158	5.8
		0826	0.6			0817	1.1
	SA	1428	6.3		SU	1411	5.7
		2051	0.6			2035	1.2
14		0254	6.2	29		0227	5.6
		0915	0.8			0850	1.3
	SU	1516	6.0		M	1444	5.4
		2141	0.9			2107	1.5
15		0344	5.9				
		1011	1.1				
	M	1612	5.5				
	◐	2240	1.3				

MARCH

Date	Day	Time	m	Date	Day	Time	m
1		0303	5.3	16		0421	5.4
		0929	1.6			1052	1.5
	TU	1526	5.1		W	1701	5.1
	◑	2150	1.8			2331	1.7
2		0350	5.0	17		0534	5.0
		1022	1.9			1218	1.8
	W	1623	4.8		TH	1828	4.9
		2255	2.1				
3		0501	4.7	18		0059	1.9
		1139	2.0			0709	4.8
	TH	1811	4.6		F	1338	1.7
						2001	5.0
4		0023	2.1	19		0211	1.7
		0650	4.7			0832	5.1
	F	1307	1.9		SA	1440	1.4
		1928	4.8			2106	5.4
5		0149	1.9	20		0307	1.4
		0758	5.1			0928	5.4
	SA	1424	1.6		SU	1531	1.1
		2031	5.3			2155	5.7
6		0254	1.5	21		0354	1.1
		0855	5.5			1013	5.8
	SU	1519	1.2		M	1614	0.9
		2124	5.7			2236	6.0
7		0343	1.1	22		0434	0.9
		0945	6.0			1053	6.0
	M	1605	0.8		TU	1652	0.8
		2212	6.2			2314	6.1
8		0427	0.7	23		0510	0.8
		1031	6.3			1130	6.1
	TU	1649	0.5		W	1728	0.7
		2258	6.5		○	2349	6.2
9		0510	0.4	24		0545	0.7
		1117	6.5			1202	6.1
	W	1732	0.3		TH	1802	0.7
	●	2343	6.7				
10		0554	0.3	25		0019	6.2
		1202	6.7			0617	0.7
	TH	1817	0.1		F	1229	6.0
						1834	0.7
11		0026	6.8	26		0043	6.1
		0638	0.2			0648	0.8
	F	1246	6.7		SA	1252	6.0
		1901	0.1			1905	0.8
12		0109	6.8	27		0103	6.0
		0723	0.2			0719	0.8
	SA	1330	6.6		SU	1316	5.9
		1946	0.2			1935	0.9
13		0152	6.6	28		0127	5.9
		0808	0.4			0747	1.0
	SU	1413	6.4		M	1344	5.8
		2031	0.5			2003	1.1
14		0235	6.3	29		0157	5.7
		0855	0.7			0817	1.1
	M	1500	6.0		TU	1416	5.6
		2120	0.9			2034	1.3
15		0323	5.9	30		0232	5.5
		0948	1.1			0854	1.4
	TU	1554	5.6		W	1456	5.3
	◐	2217	1.3			2117	1.6
				31		0316	5.1
						0944	1.7
					TH	1549	5.0
					◑	2216	1.9

APRIL

Date	Day	Time	m	Date	Day	Time	m
1		0417	4.8	16		0034	1.9
		1053	1.9			0635	4.7
	F	1716	4.7		SA	1311	1.7
		2340	2.1			1930	5.0
2		0608	4.7	17		0145	1.7
		1223	1.9			0803	4.9
	SA	1856	4.9		SU	1413	1.5
						2036	5.3
3		0111	1.9	18		0241	1.5
		0727	5.0			0901	5.2
	SU	1347	1.6		M	1503	1.3
		2002	5.3			2126	5.6
4		0222	1.4	19		0327	1.2
		0828	5.5			0947	5.5
	M	1448	1.1		TU	1546	1.1
		2058	5.8			2208	5.8
5		0315	1.0	20		0407	1.0
		0921	5.9			1027	5.8
	TU	1538	0.7		W	1624	0.9
		2149	6.2			2245	6.0
6		0402	0.6	21		0444	0.9
		1010	6.3			1102	5.9
	W	1623	0.4		TH	1700	0.8
		2236	6.5			2318	6.1
7		0447	0.3	22		0518	0.8
		1057	6.6			1133	6.0
	TH	1709	0.2		F	1735	0.8
	●	2322	6.7		○	2346	6.1
8		0532	0.2	23		0552	0.8
		1144	6.7			1200	6.0
	F	1755	0.1		SA	1808	0.8
9		0007	6.8	24		0010	6.0
		0618	0.1			0624	0.8
	SA	1231	6.7		SU	1226	6.0
		1840	0.1			1840	0.9
10		0051	6.8	25		0035	6.0
		0704	0.2			0655	0.8
	SU	1316	6.6		M	1254	5.9
		1926	0.3			1910	1.0
11		0135	6.6	26		0103	5.9
		0750	0.3			0724	0.9
	M	1400	6.4		TU	1324	5.8
		2012	0.5			1939	1.1
12		0219	6.3	27		0135	5.8
		0837	0.6			0755	1.1
	TU	1447	6.0		W	1358	5.7
		2101	0.9			2013	1.3
13		0306	5.8	28		0211	5.6
		0927	1.0			0833	1.2
	W	1540	5.6		TH	1438	5.5
		2155	1.3			2057	1.5
14		0401	5.3	29		0256	5.3
		1028	1.5			0922	1.5
	TH	1642	5.2		F	1530	5.2
	◐	2306	1.7			2155	1.7
15		0508	4.9	30		0354	5.0
		1151	1.7			1026	1.7
	F	1757	4.9		SA	1643	5.0
					◑	2310	1.8

Chart Datum: 3·27 metres below Ordnance Datum (Newlyn)
HAT is 6·9 metres above Chart Datum

TIME ZONE (UT)
For Summer Time add ONE hour in **non-shaded areas**

SHOREHAM

LAT 50°50'N LONG 0°15'W

TIMES AND HEIGHTS OF HIGH AND LOW WATERS

Dates in amber are **SPRINGS**
Dates in grey are **NEAPS**

2016

MAY

Date	Day	Time	m	Time	m	Time	m	Time	m
1	SU	0523	4.8	1146	1.7	1819	5.1		
2	M	0035	1.7	0653	5.0	1309	1.5	1930	5.4
3	TU	0148	1.4	0759	5.4	1415	1.1	2030	5.8
4	W	0246	1.0	0855	5.9	1509	0.7	2123	6.2
5	TH	0336	0.6	0947	6.2	1558	0.5	2212	6.5
6	F	0424	0.3	1037	6.5	1646	0.3	● 2300	6.7
7	SA	0511	0.2	1126	6.6	1734	0.2	2347	6.7
8	SU	0559	0.2	1214	6.6	1821	0.3		
9	M	0033	6.7	0645	0.2	1302	6.6	1908	0.4
10	TU	0119	6.5	0732	0.4	1348	6.4	1955	0.6
11	W	0204	6.2	0819	0.7	1435	6.1	2042	0.9
12	TH	0250	5.8	0908	1.0	1524	5.7	2134	1.3
13	F	0342	5.4	1003	1.4	1619	5.4	◐ 2235	1.6
14	SA	0440	5.0	1111	1.6	1721	5.1	2355	1.8
15	SU	0548	4.8	1230	1.8	1835	5.0		
16	M	0108	1.8	0712	4.8	1335	1.7	1951	5.1
17	TU	0206	1.6	0821	5.0	1427	1.5	2046	5.4
18	W	0254	1.4	0911	5.3	1513	1.3	2131	5.6
19	TH	0336	1.2	0952	5.5	1553	1.2	2209	5.8
20	F	0415	1.0	1027	5.7	1631	1.0	2242	5.9
21	SA	0451	0.9	1059	5.8	1708	1.0	○ 2312	5.9
22	SU	0527	0.9	1131	5.9	1744	1.0	2342	6.0
23	M	0601	0.8	1203	5.9	1818	1.0		
24	TU	0012	6.0	0634	0.9	1235	5.9	1851	1.0
25	W	0045	5.9	0706	0.9	1309	5.9	1923	1.1
26	TH	0119	5.8	0740	1.0	1345	5.8	2000	1.2
27	F	0158	5.7	0820	1.1	1428	5.7	2044	1.3
28	SA	0244	5.5	0908	1.2	1518	5.5	2139	1.5
29	SU	0339	5.3	1007	1.4	1621	5.3	◑ 2246	1.6
30	M	0450	5.1	1117	1.5	1739	5.3		
31	TU	0002	1.5	0614	5.2	1235	1.4	1854	5.5

JUNE

Date	Day	Time	m	Time	m	Time	m	Time	m
1	W	0115	1.3	0727	5.4	1344	1.1	2000	5.8
2	TH	0218	1.0	0829	5.7	1443	0.9	2058	6.1
3	F	0313	0.7	0926	6.0	1537	0.6	2151	6.3
4	SA	0404	0.5	1020	6.3	1627	0.5	2242	6.5
5	SU	0453	0.4	1111	6.4	1717	0.4	● 2331	6.5
6	M	0542	0.3	1201	6.5	1805	0.4		
7	TU	0018	6.5	0629	0.4	1249	6.5	1851	0.5
8	W	0104	6.4	0716	0.5	1335	6.3	1937	0.7
9	TH	0149	6.1	0802	0.7	1419	6.1	2023	0.9
10	F	0233	5.8	0847	0.9	1504	5.9	2109	1.2
11	SA	0319	5.5	0933	1.2	1551	5.6	2158	1.5
12	SU	0408	5.2	1024	1.5	1642	5.3	◐ 2255	1.7
13	M	0503	4.9	1124	1.7	1738	5.1		
14	TU	0006	1.8	0603	4.8	1236	1.8	1838	5.0
15	W	0118	1.8	0708	4.8	1342	1.8	1942	5.1
16	TH	0215	1.6	0812	5.0	1436	1.6	2038	5.3
17	F	0302	1.4	0904	5.2	1522	1.4	2124	5.5
18	SA	0345	1.2	0947	5.5	1603	1.3	2203	5.7
19	SU	0424	1.1	1026	5.7	1643	1.1	2241	5.8
20	M	0502	1.0	1104	5.8	1721	1.0	○ 2317	5.9
21	TU	0540	0.9	1141	5.9	1758	1.0	2353	6.0
22	W	0616	0.8	1218	6.0	1834	1.0		
23	TH	0029	6.0	0652	0.8	1255	6.0	1910	1.0
24	F	0107	6.0	0729	0.8	1334	6.0	1949	1.0
25	SA	0148	5.9	0809	0.9	1417	5.9	2033	1.1
26	SU	0233	5.8	0855	1.0	1505	5.8	2124	1.2
27	M	0324	5.6	0949	1.1	1600	5.7	◑ 2224	1.3
28	TU	0425	5.4	1053	1.3	1704	5.5	2334	1.4
29	W	0537	5.3	1205	1.3	1818	5.5		
30	TH	0046	1.3	0655	5.3	1318	1.3	1931	5.6

JULY

Date	Day	Time	m	Time	m	Time	m	Time	m
1	F	0154	1.2	0807	5.5	1423	1.1	2037	5.8
2	SA	0254	0.9	0911	5.8	1521	0.9	2136	6.1
3	SU	0349	0.7	1008	6.0	1613	0.7	2229	6.2
4	M	0439	0.6	1100	6.2	1703	0.6	● 2319	6.3
5	TU	0528	0.5	1149	6.4	1750	0.6		
6	W	0006	6.3	0614	0.5	1236	6.4	1835	0.7
7	TH	0050	6.3	0658	0.6	1319	6.3	1918	0.8
8	F	0132	6.1	0740	0.7	1400	6.2	2000	0.9
9	SA	0211	5.9	0820	0.9	1439	6.0	2039	1.1
10	SU	0250	5.6	0859	1.1	1518	5.7	2120	1.3
11	M	0331	5.3	0941	1.4	1601	5.4	2204	1.6
12	TU	0418	5.1	1027	1.6	1649	5.2	◐ 2256	1.8
13	W	0513	4.8	1122	1.9	1745	5.0	2358	1.9
14	TH	0614	4.7	1228	2.0	1846	4.9		
15	F	0113	1.9	0717	4.8	1346	1.9	1946	5.1
16	SA	0224	1.7	0817	5.0	1448	1.7	2042	5.3
17	SU	0315	1.5	0911	5.3	1536	1.5	2131	5.6
18	M	0358	1.2	0958	5.6	1619	1.2	2214	5.8
19	TU	0439	1.0	1040	5.9	1659	1.1	○ 2255	6.0
20	W	0518	0.8	1121	6.0	1738	0.9	2334	6.1
21	TH	0557	0.7	1201	6.2	1816	0.8		
22	F	0014	6.2	0635	0.7	1241	6.3	1855	0.8
23	SA	0054	6.2	0715	0.6	1321	6.3	1936	0.8
24	SU	0135	6.2	0756	0.7	1403	6.2	2020	0.8
25	M	0219	6.1	0841	0.8	1448	6.1	2107	0.9
26	TU	0307	5.9	0931	0.9	1538	5.9	◑ 2202	1.1
27	W	0402	5.6	1030	1.2	1637	5.6	2308	1.3
28	TH	0509	5.3	1140	1.4	1748	5.4		
29	F	0022	1.5	0630	5.2	1257	1.5	1908	5.4
30	SA	0137	1.4	0753	5.3	1409	1.4	2024	5.5
31	SU	0242	1.2	0903	5.6	1510	1.2	2127	5.8

AUGUST

Date	Day	Time	m	Time	m	Time	m	Time	m
1	M	0338	0.9	1001	5.9	1603	0.9	2221	6.1
2	TU	0428	0.7	1051	6.2	1651	0.8	● 2309	6.2
3	W	0514	0.6	1137	6.3	1735	0.7	2353	6.3
4	TH	0557	0.6	1219	6.4	1817	0.7		
5	F	0033	6.2	0637	0.6	1259	6.3	1856	0.8
6	SA	0111	6.1	0714	0.7	1335	6.2	1932	0.9
7	SU	0145	6.0	0750	0.9	1409	6.0	2006	1.0
8	M	0216	5.8	0824	1.0	1440	5.8	2042	1.2
9	TU	0247	5.5	0901	1.3	1510	5.5	2121	1.5
10	W	0322	5.2	0942	1.6	1547	5.2	◐ 2207	1.7
11	TH	0409	4.9	1031	1.9	1643	5.0	2303	2.0
12	F	0523	4.7	1133	2.1	1758	4.8		
13	SA	0012	2.1	0635	4.7	1249	2.1	1907	4.9
14	SU	0134	2.0	0742	4.9	1411	1.9	2009	5.1
15	M	0244	1.6	0841	5.2	1509	1.6	2103	5.5
16	TU	0333	1.3	0932	5.6	1554	1.3	2150	5.8
17	W	0415	1.0	1017	6.0	1635	1.0	2233	6.1
18	TH	0455	0.8	1100	6.2	1715	0.8	○ 2315	6.3
19	F	0535	0.6	1141	6.4	1756	0.7	2357	6.4
20	SA	0615	0.5	1222	6.5	1837	0.6		
21	SU	0038	6.5	0656	0.4	1304	6.5	1919	0.6
22	M	0120	6.4	0739	0.5	1346	6.5	2003	0.6
23	TU	0203	6.3	0824	0.6	1429	6.3	2049	0.8
24	W	0249	6.0	0912	0.9	1517	6.0	2141	1.1
25	TH	0342	5.7	1009	1.2	1614	5.6	◑ 2244	1.4
26	F	0448	5.3	1119	1.6	1725	5.3		
27	SA	0002	1.7	0613	5.0	1242	1.7	1852	5.1
28	SU	0124	1.6	0745	5.1	1358	1.6	2017	5.3
29	M	0232	1.4	0857	5.5	1500	1.4	2120	5.6
30	TU	0327	1.1	0952	5.8	1551	1.1	2211	6.0
31	W	0414	0.9	1038	6.2	1635	0.9	2255	6.2

Chart Datum: 3·27 metres below Ordnance Datum (Newlyn)
HAT is 6·9 metres above Chart Datum

TIME ZONE (UT)
For Summer Time add ONE hour in **non-shaded areas**

SHOREHAM

LAT 50°50′N LONG 0°15′W

TIMES AND HEIGHTS OF HIGH AND LOW WATERS

Dates in amber are **SPRINGS**
Dates in grey are **NEAPS**

2016

SEPTEMBER

Date	Day	Time	m	Time	m	Time	m	Time	m
1	TH	0456	0.7	1120	6.3	1716	0.8	● 2335	6.3
2	F	0535	0.7	1158	6.4	1754	0.7		
3	SA	0013	6.2	0611	0.7	1234	6.3	1829	0.8
4	SU	0046	6.2	0646	0.8	1306	6.2	1902	0.9
5	M	0114	6.0	0718	0.9	1333	6.1	1934	1.0
6	TU	0139	5.9	0750	1.0	1355	5.9	2007	1.1
7	W	0204	5.7	0823	1.2	1420	5.7	2041	1.4
8	TH	0234	5.4	0859	1.5	1453	5.4	2120	1.7
9	F	0313	5.1	0942	1.9	1537	5.0	◐ 2211	2.0
10	SA	0408	4.8	1043	2.1	1649	4.7	2322	2.2
11	SU	0555	4.6	1204	2.3	1831	4.7		
12	M	0047	2.1	0710	4.8	1331	2.1	1939	5.0
13	TU	0209	1.8	0812	5.2	1440	1.7	2036	5.4
14	W	0304	1.4	0906	5.7	1528	1.3	2125	5.9
15	TH	0348	1.0	0952	6.1	1610	0.9	2210	6.2
16	F	0429	0.7	1036	6.4	1650	0.7	○ 2254	6.5
17	SA	0510	0.5	1119	6.6	1732	0.5	2337	6.6
18	SU	0552	0.4	1201	6.7	1815	0.4		
19	M	0020	6.7	0634	0.3	1244	6.7	1858	0.4
20	TU	0103	6.6	0719	0.4	1326	6.6	1943	0.5
21	W	0146	6.4	0805	0.6	1410	6.4	2030	0.8
22	TH	0233	6.1	0853	0.9	1458	6.0	2122	1.1
23	F	0326	5.7	0949	1.3	1555	5.6	◑ 2223	1.5
24	SA	0433	5.3	1100	1.7	1707	5.1	2344	1.8
25	SU	0558	5.0	1227	1.9	1838	5.0		
26	M	0109	1.8	0732	5.1	1344	1.8	2005	5.2
27	TU	0217	1.6	0842	5.5	1445	1.5	2106	5.5
28	W	0311	1.3	0933	5.8	1533	1.2	2153	5.9
29	TH	0355	1.0	1017	6.1	1615	0.9	2235	6.1
30	F	0434	0.8	1056	6.3	1653	0.8	2313	6.2

OCTOBER

Date	Day	Time	m	Time	m	Time	m	Time	m
1	SA	0510	0.8	1132	6.4	1729	0.8	● 2348	6.2
2	SU	0545	0.8	1205	6.3	1803	0.8		
3	M	0017	6.2	0617	0.8	1233	6.2	1834	0.9
4	TU	0042	6.1	0649	0.9	1255	6.1	1905	1.0
5	W	0106	6.0	0720	1.1	1318	5.9	1936	1.1
6	TH	0132	5.8	0751	1.3	1344	5.8	2007	1.3
7	F	0202	5.6	0823	1.5	1417	5.5	2042	1.6
8	SA	0238	5.3	0903	1.8	1458	5.2	2129	1.9
9	SU	0327	5.0	1001	2.1	1556	4.8	◐ 2235	2.1
10	M	0455	4.7	1121	2.3	1751	4.7		
11	TU	0002	2.1	0635	4.9	1250	2.1	1907	5.0
12	W	0127	1.9	0741	5.3	1404	1.7	2007	5.4
13	TH	0230	1.4	0837	5.7	1456	1.3	2059	5.9
14	F	0318	1.0	0925	6.2	1541	0.9	2146	6.3
15	SA	0401	0.7	1010	6.5	1624	0.6	2231	6.6
16	SU	0444	0.5	1055	6.8	1707	0.4	○ 2316	6.7
17	M	0528	0.3	1139	6.9	1752	0.3		
18	TU	0001	6.8	0612	0.3	1223	6.8	1837	0.3
19	W	0047	6.7	0659	0.4	1307	6.7	1924	0.5
20	TH	0132	6.5	0746	0.7	1352	6.4	2012	0.8
21	F	0220	6.2	0835	1.0	1441	6.0	2103	1.1
22	SA	0314	5.8	0931	1.4	1538	5.5	◑ 2203	1.5
23	SU	0418	5.4	1039	1.8	1646	5.1	2321	1.8
24	M	0535	5.1	1205	2.0	1811	4.9		
25	TU	0044	1.9	0704	5.1	1321	1.8	1938	5.1
26	W	0151	1.7	0814	5.4	1420	1.6	2040	5.4
27	TH	0244	1.4	0905	5.7	1508	1.3	2128	5.7
28	F	0329	1.2	0949	6.0	1550	1.1	2209	5.9
29	SA	0408	1.0	1027	6.2	1627	0.9	2246	6.1
30	SU	0444	0.9	1103	6.2	1703	0.9	● 2319	6.1
31	M	0519	0.9	1133	6.2	1737	0.9	2348	6.1

NOVEMBER

Date	Day	Time	m	Time	m	Time	m	Time	m
1	TU	0552	0.9	1159	6.2	1810	0.9		
2	W	0013	6.1	0624	1.0	1224	6.1	1841	1.0
3	TH	0040	6.0	0655	1.1	1250	6.0	1912	1.1
4	F	0109	5.9	0725	1.3	1319	5.8	1942	1.3
5	SA	0139	5.8	0758	1.5	1353	5.6	2017	1.5
6	SU	0216	5.5	0838	1.7	1434	5.3	2102	1.7
7	M	0304	5.3	0932	1.9	1527	5.0	◐ 2201	1.9
8	TU	0410	5.0	1043	2.1	1649	4.8	2317	2.0
9	W	0552	5.0	1206	2.0	1829	5.0		
10	TH	0040	1.8	0705	5.3	1322	1.7	1934	5.4
11	F	0150	1.5	0805	5.7	1421	1.3	2030	5.8
12	SA	0245	1.1	0857	6.2	1512	0.9	2121	6.2
13	SU	0334	0.8	0945	6.5	1559	0.6	2209	6.5
14	M	0420	0.5	1031	6.7	1645	0.4	○ 2257	6.7
15	TU	0507	0.4	1118	6.8	1732	0.3	2345	6.7
16	W	0554	0.4	1204	6.8	1820	0.4		
17	TH	0032	6.7	0641	0.5	1251	6.6	1907	0.5
18	F	0120	6.5	0729	0.7	1338	6.4	1956	0.7
19	SA	0209	6.3	0818	1.0	1426	6.0	2046	1.0
20	SU	0300	5.9	0911	1.3	1520	5.6	2141	1.4
21	M	0357	5.6	1012	1.7	1620	5.2	◑ 2247	1.7
22	TU	0501	5.3	1128	1.9	1729	5.0		
23	W	0004	1.9	0614	5.2	1244	1.9	1850	5.0
24	TH	0113	1.8	0730	5.3	1345	1.7	2001	5.1
25	F	0209	1.7	0828	5.5	1436	1.5	2054	5.4
26	SA	0257	1.5	0915	5.7	1521	1.3	2138	5.6
27	SU	0340	1.3	0955	5.9	1601	1.1	2216	5.8
28	M	0418	1.2	1030	6.0	1638	1.0	2249	6.0
29	TU	0454	1.1	1101	6.1	1714	1.0	● 2320	6.0
30	W	0529	1.1	1130	6.1	1748	0.9	2350	6.1

DECEMBER

Date	Day	Time	m	Time	m	Time	m	Time	m
1	TH	0604	1.1	1159	6.1	1822	1.0		
2	F	0020	6.0	0636	1.1	1230	6.0	1854	1.0
3	SA	0052	6.0	0707	1.2	1302	5.9	1926	1.1
4	SU	0125	5.9	0741	1.3	1337	5.8	2000	1.3
5	M	0203	5.7	0820	1.5	1418	5.6	2043	1.4
6	TU	0247	5.6	0909	1.6	1508	5.3	2135	1.6
7	W	0343	5.4	1010	1.8	1610	5.1	◐ 2239	1.7
8	TH	0456	5.3	1124	1.8	1734	5.1	2356	1.7
9	F	0620	5.4	1240	1.6	1855	5.3		
10	SA	0110	1.5	0729	5.6	1347	1.3	1959	5.6
11	SU	0214	1.2	0828	6.0	1445	1.0	2057	6.0
12	M	0310	0.9	0922	6.3	1538	0.7	2150	6.3
13	TU	0401	0.7	1012	6.6	1628	0.5	2242	6.5
14	W	0450	0.6	1102	6.7	1717	0.4	○ 2332	6.6
15	TH	0539	0.5	1150	6.7	1805	0.4		
16	F	0021	6.6	0626	0.6	1238	6.6	1853	0.5
17	SA	0110	6.5	0714	0.7	1325	6.4	1940	0.6
18	SU	0156	6.3	0801	0.9	1411	6.1	2027	0.9
19	M	0243	6.1	0849	1.2	1458	5.8	2115	1.2
20	TU	0331	5.8	0939	1.5	1548	5.4	2205	1.5
21	W	0422	5.5	1035	1.7	1643	5.1	◑ 2303	1.7
22	TH	0518	5.2	1144	1.9	1743	4.9		
23	F	0014	1.9	0619	5.1	1258	1.9	1850	4.9
24	SA	0124	1.9	0727	5.2	1358	1.8	2002	5.0
25	SU	0221	1.8	0828	5.3	1450	1.6	2058	5.2
26	M	0310	1.6	0916	5.6	1534	1.4	2141	5.5
27	TU	0353	1.4	0956	5.8	1615	1.2	2219	5.7
28	W	0432	1.2	1031	5.9	1653	1.0	2254	5.9
29	TH	0509	1.1	1106	6.0	1729	1.0	● 2329	6.0
30	F	0545	1.1	1139	6.1	1805	0.9		
31	SA	0003	6.1	0619	1.1	1214	6.1	1839	0.9

Chart Datum: 3·27 metres below Ordnance Datum (Newlyn)
HAT is 6·9 metres above Chart Datum

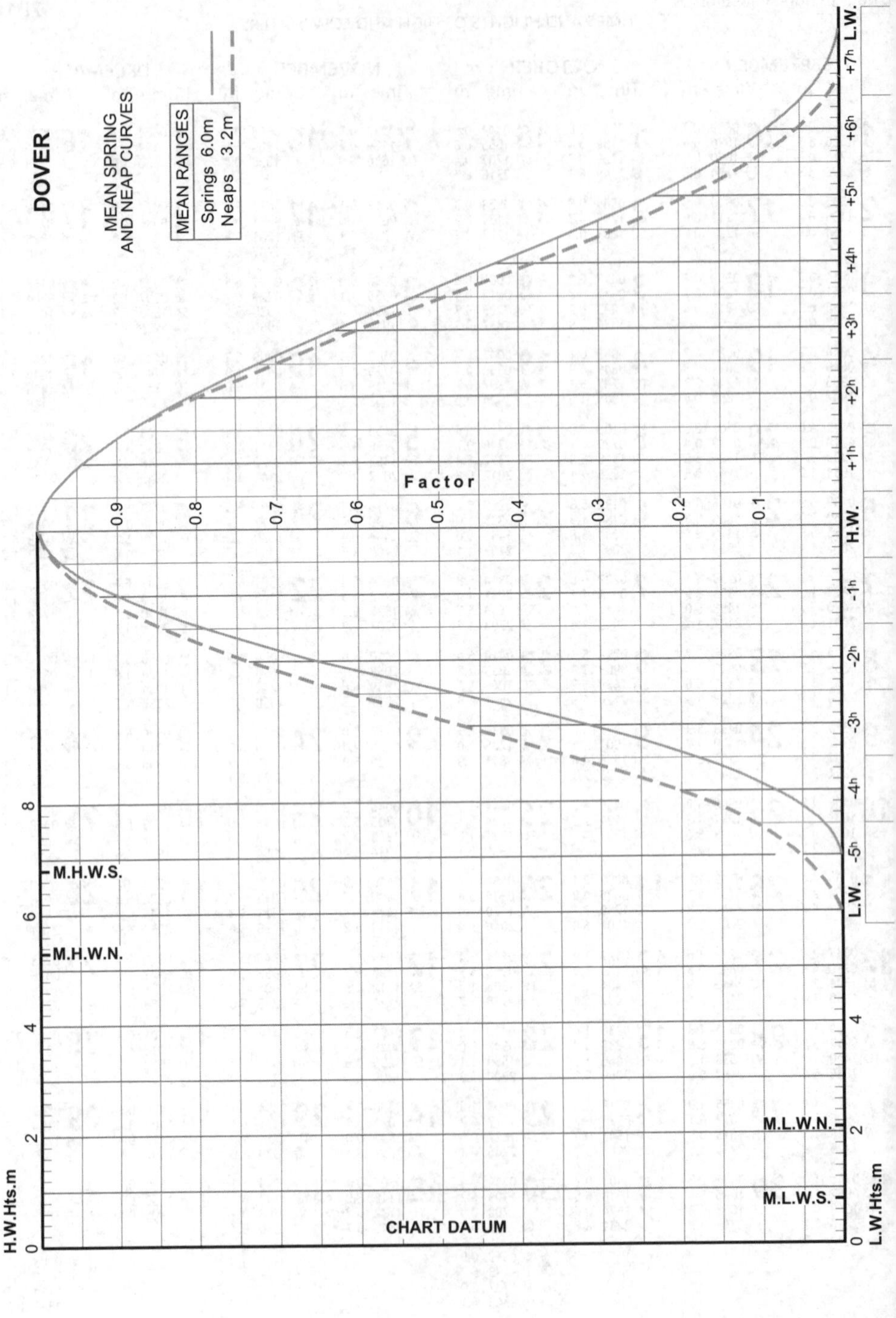
DOVER
MEAN SPRING AND NEAP CURVES
MEAN RANGES
Springs 6.0m
Neaps 3.2m
Factor
0.9
0.8
0.7
0.6
0.5
0.4
0.3
0.2
0.1
H.W.Hts.m
0
2
4
6
8
M.H.W.S.
M.H.W.N.
CHART DATUM
L.W.Hts.m
M.L.W.S.
M.L.W.N.
L.W.
-5h
-4h
-3h
-2h
-1h
H.W.
+1h
+2h
+3h
+4h
+5h
+6h
+7h
L.W.

TIME ZONE (UT)
or Summer Time add ONE hour in **non-shaded areas**

DOVER

LAT 51°07′N LONG 1°19′E

TIMES AND HEIGHTS OF HIGH AND LOW WATERS

Dates in amber are **SPRINGS**
Dates in grey are **NEAPS**

2016

JANUARY

Date	Day	Time	m	Time	m	Time	m	Time	m
1	F	0313	6.1	1019	1.7	1541	5.7	2226	2.0
2	SA	0401	5.8	1101	1.9	1637	5.4	◑ 2314	2.2
3	SU	0459	5.5	1159	2.1	1742	5.3		
4	M	0023	2.4	0604	5.4	1310	2.1	1848	5.3
5	TU	0142	2.3	0708	5.5	1417	2.0	1947	5.5
6	W	0249	2.1	0804	5.6	1516	1.8	2037	5.7
7	TH	0345	1.8	0852	5.9	1609	1.5	2120	6.0
8	F	0436	1.5	0934	6.1	1658	1.3	2200	6.3
9	SA	0522	1.3	1015	6.4	1744	1.1	2239	6.5
10	SU	0607	1.1	1055	6.5	1828	1.0	● 2318	6.7
11	M	0651	1.0	1135	6.7	1911	0.9	2357	6.8
12	TU	0734	0.9	1215	6.7	1952	0.9		
13	W	0038	6.9	0816	0.8	1257	6.7	2032	0.9
14	TH	0121	6.9	0858	0.9	1342	6.6	2112	1.0
15	F	0208	6.8	0941	1.0	1431	6.4	2155	1.2
16	SA	0258	6.6	1027	1.2	1526	6.2	◐ 2244	1.4
17	SU	0356	6.3	1120	1.4	1632	5.9	2342	1.6
18	M	0504	6.0	1224	1.6	1753	5.7		
19	TU	0052	1.8	0624	5.8	1334	1.7	1915	5.6
20	W	0205	1.8	0744	5.8	1447	1.7	2025	5.8
21	TH	0319	1.7	0852	6.0	1608	1.5	2125	6.1
22	F	0436	1.4	0950	6.2	1719	1.2	2215	6.3
23	SA	0538	1.1	1038	6.4	1811	1.1	2257	6.5
24	SU	0628	0.9	1119	6.5	1855	1.0	○ 2336	6.7
25	M	0711	0.9	1157	6.6	1933	1.0		
26	TU	0014	6.8	0749	0.9	1233	6.5	2004	1.0
27	W	0051	6.7	0821	0.9	1309	6.4	2031	1.1
28	TH	0127	6.6	0849	1.1	1343	6.3	2053	1.3
29	F	0159	6.5	0913	1.2	1415	6.1	2117	1.4
30	SA	0229	6.2	0940	1.4	1445	5.9	2148	1.6
31	SU	0300	6.0	1014	1.6	1520	5.6	2227	1.9

FEBRUARY

Date	Day	Time	m	Time	m	Time	m	Time	m
1	M	0341	5.7	1057	1.9	1614	5.3	◑ 2316	2.2
2	TU	0448	5.4	1159	2.1	1747	5.1		
3	W	0032	2.4	0614	5.3	1324	2.2	1901	5.2
4	TH	0201	2.3	0724	5.4	1437	2.0	2002	5.5
5	F	0309	2.0	0822	5.7	1538	1.7	2053	5.8
6	SA	0407	1.6	0911	6.0	1633	1.4	2138	6.2
7	SU	0459	1.3	0956	6.3	1724	1.1	2220	6.5
8	M	0549	1.0	1039	6.6	1813	0.9	● 2301	6.8
9	TU	0638	0.8	1120	6.8	1859	0.8	2342	7.0
10	W	0725	0.6	1201	6.9	1943	0.7		
11	TH	0024	7.1	0808	0.5	1244	6.9	2023	0.6
12	F	0107	7.1	0849	0.5	1327	6.8	2101	0.7
13	SA	0151	7.0	0928	0.7	1413	6.7	2141	0.8
14	SU	0239	6.8	1010	0.9	1504	6.3	2225	1.1
15	M	0332	6.4	1058	1.3	1604	5.9	◐ 2318	1.5
16	TU	0435	6.0	1157	1.7	1718	5.6		
17	W	0024	1.9	0554	5.6	1308	1.9	1846	5.4
18	TH	0141	2.0	0727	5.5	1426	1.9	2010	5.5
19	F	0301	1.8	0847	5.7	1600	1.7	2116	5.8
20	SA	0428	1.5	0947	6.0	1710	1.4	2206	6.2
21	SU	0530	1.2	1032	6.3	1800	1.1	2245	6.4
22	M	0617	0.9	1108	6.4	1841	1.0	○ 2321	6.6
23	TU	0656	0.8	1141	6.5	1915	1.0	2356	6.7
24	W	0729	0.8	1214	6.5	1942	1.0		
25	TH	0030	6.7	0756	0.9	1246	6.5	2003	1.0
26	F	0102	6.6	0819	1.0	1314	6.4	2023	1.1
27	SA	0127	6.5	0841	1.1	1337	6.2	2048	1.2
28	SU	0147	6.3	0907	1.2	1358	6.1	2118	1.4
29	M	0212	6.2	0939	1.4	1427	5.9	2153	1.6

MARCH

Date	Day	Time	m	Time	m	Time	m	Time	m
1	TU	0248	5.9	1016	1.7	1508	5.6	◑ 2234	1.9
2	W	0336	5.6	1104	2.0	1606	5.3	2331	2.2
3	TH	0502	5.2	1220	2.3	1817	5.1		
4	F	0110	2.3	0650	5.2	1359	2.2	1929	5.3
5	SA	0234	2.1	0756	5.6	1508	1.8	2026	5.7
6	SU	0337	1.6	0850	6.0	1607	1.4	2115	6.2
7	M	0434	1.2	0937	6.4	1701	1.1	2200	6.6
8	TU	0529	0.9	1021	6.7	1754	0.8	2242	6.9
9	W	0621	0.6	1103	6.9	1843	0.6	● 2324	7.1
10	TH	0710	0.4	1144	7.0	1928	0.5		
11	F	0006	7.2	0754	0.3	1227	7.1	2008	0.4
12	SA	0049	7.2	0834	0.3	1309	7.0	2046	0.5
13	SU	0133	7.1	0912	0.5	1355	6.8	2125	0.7
14	M	0220	6.8	0952	0.8	1445	6.5	2208	1.0
15	TU	0312	6.4	1037	1.3	1543	6.0	◐ 2258	1.5
16	W	0413	5.9	1134	1.7	1651	5.6		
17	TH	0003	1.9	0528	5.5	1247	2.1	1814	5.3
18	F	0121	2.0	0709	5.4	1408	2.1	1949	5.4
19	SA	0245	1.9	0838	5.6	1541	1.8	2059	5.8
20	SU	0412	1.6	0934	5.9	1649	1.5	2147	6.1
21	M	0511	1.2	1015	6.2	1737	1.2	2225	6.4
22	TU	0556	1.0	1049	6.4	1816	1.1	2300	6.6
23	W	0632	0.9	1120	6.5	1848	1.0	○ 2334	6.6
24	TH	0702	0.9	1150	6.5	1913	1.0		
25	F	0006	6.6	0725	0.9	1220	6.5	1932	1.0
26	SA	0035	6.5	0747	1.0	1246	6.4	1955	1.0
27	SU	0055	6.4	0812	1.0	1304	6.3	2022	1.1
28	M	0113	6.4	0840	1.1	1325	6.3	2053	1.3
29	TU	0140	6.3	0911	1.3	1356	6.2	2126	1.5
30	W	0215	6.1	0946	1.6	1437	5.9	2206	1.8
31	TH	0301	5.7	1030	1.9	1530	5.5	◑ 2257	2.1

APRIL

Date	Day	Time	m	Time	m	Time	m	Time	m
1	F	0407	5.3	1131	2.2	1716	5.2		
2	SA	0020	2.2	0618	5.3	1317	2.2	1855	5.4
3	SU	0158	2.0	0729	5.6	1435	1.9	1957	5.8
4	M	0306	1.6	0826	6.0	1537	1.5	2050	6.2
5	TU	0406	1.2	0916	6.4	1634	1.1	2137	6.6
6	W	0504	0.8	1001	6.7	1729	0.8	2221	6.9
7	TH	0600	0.6	1044	6.9	1821	0.6	● 2304	7.2
8	F	0651	0.4	1126	7.1	1908	0.4	2347	7.2
9	SA	0737	0.3	1208	7.1	1951	0.4		
10	SU	0030	7.2	0818	0.3	1253	7.0	2030	0.4
11	M	0116	7.1	0857	0.5	1339	6.8	2111	0.7
12	TU	0203	6.8	0937	0.9	1429	6.5	2154	1.0
13	W	0255	6.4	1021	1.3	1525	6.1	2244	1.5
14	TH	0354	5.9	1116	1.8	1627	5.7	◐ 2347	1.8
15	F	0503	5.5	1226	2.1	1739	5.4		
16	SA	0101	2.0	0634	5.3	1343	2.1	1909	5.4
17	SU	0219	1.9	0810	5.5	1501	1.9	2026	5.7
18	M	0335	1.6	0906	5.8	1609	1.6	2116	6.0
19	TU	0435	1.3	0947	6.0	1659	1.4	2157	6.3
20	W	0521	1.1	1021	6.2	1740	1.2	2234	6.4
21	TH	0557	1.0	1052	6.4	1812	1.1	2307	6.5
22	F	0626	1.0	1123	6.4	1838	1.1	○ 2338	6.5
23	SA	0652	1.0	1152	6.4	1903	1.1		
24	SU	0005	6.4	0718	1.0	1218	6.4	1930	1.1
25	M	0027	6.4	0747	1.0	1239	6.4	2001	1.1
26	TU	0049	6.3	0818	1.1	1303	6.4	2033	1.2
27	W	0117	6.3	0850	1.3	1336	6.3	2107	1.4
28	TH	0154	6.1	0925	1.5	1418	6.1	2147	1.6
29	F	0241	5.9	1008	1.8	1512	5.8	2237	1.9
30	SA	0345	5.5	1105	2.0	1634	5.5	◑ 2348	2.0

Chart Datum: 3·67 metres below Ordnance Datum (Newlyn)
HAT is 7·4 metres above Chart Datum

TIME ZONE (UT)
For Summer Time add ONE hour in **non-shaded areas**

DOVER

LAT 51°07′N LONG 1°19′E

TIMES AND HEIGHTS OF HIGH AND LOW WATERS

Dates in amber are **SPRING**
Dates in grey are **NEAPS**

201

MAY

Date	Day	Time	m	Time	m	Time	m	Time	m
1	SU	0540	5.4	1233	2.1	1816	5.5		
2	M	0121	1.9	0659	5.6	1359	1.8	1924	5.8
3	TU	0232	1.6	0759	6.0	1503	1.5	2021	6.2
4	W	0334	1.2	0851	6.3	1602	1.1	2111	6.6
5	TH	0435	0.9	0939	6.6	1701	0.9	2159	6.9
6	F	0535	0.6	1024	6.8	1756	0.6	● 2245	7.1
7	SA	0630	0.5	1109	7.0	1847	0.5	2330	7.1
8	SU	0719	0.4	1153	7.0	1934	0.4		
9	M	0015	7.1	0802	0.4	1238	7.0	2017	0.5
10	TU	0101	6.9	0844	0.6	1325	6.8	2059	0.7
11	W	0149	6.7	0925	0.9	1414	6.6	2143	1.0
12	TH	0240	6.3	1008	1.3	1506	6.3	2231	1.4
13	F	0335	5.9	1058	1.7	1602	5.9	◐ 2328	1.7
14	SA	0435	5.6	1159	2.0	1703	5.6		
15	SU	0033	1.9	0547	5.4	1307	2.1	1816	5.5
16	M	0141	1.9	0716	5.4	1414	2.0	1935	5.6
17	TU	0245	1.7	0821	5.6	1515	1.8	2035	5.8
18	W	0342	1.5	0908	5.8	1609	1.6	2122	6.1
19	TH	0431	1.4	0946	6.0	1654	1.4	2201	6.2
20	F	0512	1.2	1020	6.2	1731	1.3	2235	6.3
21	SA	0547	1.2	1052	6.3	1803	1.2	○ 2306	6.3
22	SU	0620	1.1	1123	6.4	1836	1.1	2336	6.3
23	M	0653	1.1	1152	6.4	1910	1.1		
24	TU	0003	6.3	0727	1.1	1220	6.4	1944	1.1
25	W	0032	6.3	0801	1.1	1250	6.4	2020	1.2
26	TH	0104	6.3	0836	1.3	1326	6.4	2056	1.3
27	F	0143	6.2	0912	1.4	1409	6.2	2137	1.5
28	SA	0232	6.0	0955	1.6	1503	6.0	2225	1.6
29	SU	0332	5.8	1048	1.8	1611	5.8	◑ 2329	1.7
30	M	0455	5.6	1200	1.8	1731	5.8		
31	TU	0047	1.7	0621	5.7	1321	1.8	1847	5.9

JUNE

Date	Day	Time	m	Time	m	Time	m	Time	m
1	W	0158	1.5	0729	5.9	1428	1.5	1951	6.2
2	TH	0302	1.2	0826	6.2	1531	1.3	2047	6.5
3	F	0406	1.0	0919	6.4	1633	1.0	2140	6.7
4	SA	0512	0.8	1008	6.6	1734	0.8	2230	6.8
5	SU	0611	0.7	1056	6.8	1829	0.7	● 2318	6.9
6	M	0703	0.6	1141	6.9	1919	0.6		
7	TU	0004	6.9	0749	0.6	1226	6.9	2005	0.6
8	W	0050	6.8	0832	0.8	1311	6.8	2049	0.7
9	TH	0135	6.6	0913	1.0	1357	6.6	2131	1.0
10	F	0222	6.3	0953	1.3	1444	6.4	2214	1.3
11	SA	0312	6.0	1034	1.6	1534	6.1	2301	1.5
12	SU	0405	5.7	1121	1.9	1627	5.8	◐ 2353	1.8
13	M	0504	5.5	1218	2.1	1727	5.6		
14	TU	0051	1.9	0610	5.4	1320	2.1	1834	5.5
15	W	0151	1.9	0720	5.4	1421	2.0	1941	5.6
16	TH	0248	1.8	0818	5.6	1517	1.8	2036	5.8
17	F	0340	1.6	0905	5.8	1608	1.6	2121	6.0
18	SA	0427	1.4	0945	6.0	1652	1.4	2159	6.1
19	SU	0511	1.3	1021	6.2	1733	1.3	2234	6.2
20	M	0552	1.2	1056	6.3	1812	1.1	○ 2309	6.3
21	TU	0632	1.1	1129	6.4	1852	1.1	2343	6.3
22	W	0711	1.1	1203	6.5	1931	1.1		
23	TH	0018	6.4	0749	1.1	1239	6.5	2010	1.1
24	F	0055	6.4	0827	1.1	1318	6.5	2050	1.1
25	SA	0136	6.3	0905	1.2	1401	6.5	2131	1.2
26	SU	0222	6.2	0946	1.3	1451	6.4	2216	1.3
27	M	0316	6.1	1034	1.5	1548	6.2	◑ 2310	1.5
28	TU	0422	5.9	1133	1.6	1655	6.0		
29	W	0016	1.5	0540	5.8	1245	1.7	1809	6.0
30	TH	0126	1.5	0659	5.8	1356	1.6	1923	6.0

JULY

Date	Day	Time	m	Time	m	Time	m	Time	m
1	F	0233	1.4	0805	6.0	1503	1.4	2029	6.2
2	SA	0342	1.3	0905	6.2	1611	1.2	2128	6.4
3	SU	0454	1.1	0959	6.4	1718	1.0	2222	6.6
4	M	0558	0.9	1047	6.6	1817	0.8	● 2311	6.7
5	TU	0651	0.8	1132	6.7	1908	0.7	2356	6.7
6	W	0738	0.8	1214	6.8	1954	0.7		
7	TH	0038	6.6	0819	0.9	1256	6.8	2036	0.8
8	F	0119	6.5	0856	1.0	1338	6.7	2114	0.9
9	SA	0201	6.3	0929	1.2	1420	6.5	2149	1.2
10	SU	0244	6.1	1000	1.5	1503	6.3	2223	1.4
11	M	0329	5.9	1030	1.7	1549	6.0	2300	1.7
12	TU	0420	5.6	1109	2.0	1640	5.7	◐ 2347	1.9
13	W	0518	5.4	1206	2.2	1739	5.5		
14	TH	0050	2.1	0623	5.3	1320	2.2	1844	5.4
15	F	0156	2.0	0727	5.4	1428	2.1	1947	5.5
16	SA	0257	1.8	0823	5.6	1527	1.8	2040	5.7
17	SU	0351	1.6	0910	5.9	1619	1.6	2125	6.0
18	M	0441	1.4	0952	6.1	1706	1.3	2206	6.2
19	TU	0527	1.2	1030	6.3	1751	1.2	○ 2246	6.3
20	W	0612	1.1	1108	6.5	1835	1.0	2324	6.5
21	TH	0655	1.0	1145	6.6	1918	0.9		
22	F	0002	6.5	0737	1.0	1224	6.7	2000	0.9
23	SA	0041	6.6	0816	1.0	1304	6.8	2041	0.9
24	SU	0122	6.6	0855	1.0	1347	6.8	2120	0.9
25	M	0207	6.5	0934	1.1	1433	6.6	2202	1.1
26	TU	0257	6.3	1018	1.3	1526	6.4	◑ 2250	1.3
27	W	0355	6.0	1109	1.5	1627	6.2	2348	1.5
28	TH	0508	5.8	1214	1.7	1740	5.9		
29	F	0057	1.7	0633	5.7	1328	1.8	1903	5.8
30	SA	0210	1.7	0750	5.8	1442	1.7	2019	6.0
31	SU	0326	1.5	0856	6.0	1557	1.5	2124	6.2

AUGUST

Date	Day	Time	m	Time	m	Time	m	Time	m
1	M	0447	1.3	0952	6.3	1710	1.2	2219	6.4
2	TU	0550	1.1	1039	6.5	1808	0.9	● 2305	6.6
3	W	0640	0.9	1120	6.7	1857	0.8	2345	6.6
4	TH	0724	0.9	1159	6.8	1939	0.7		
5	F	0022	6.6	0800	0.9	1238	6.8	2016	0.8
6	SA	0059	6.5	0832	1.0	1316	6.8	2048	0.9
7	SU	0135	6.4	0857	1.2	1353	6.6	2114	1.1
8	M	0211	6.2	0918	1.4	1428	6.4	2138	1.3
9	TU	0247	6.0	0942	1.6	1503	6.1	2206	1.6
10	W	0327	5.7	1015	1.8	1544	5.8	◐ 2244	1.9
11	TH	0420	5.4	1100	2.1	1643	5.5	2338	2.1
12	F	0533	5.2	1207	2.4	1756	5.3		
13	SA	0102	2.3	0644	5.2	1340	2.4	1906	5.3
14	SU	0219	2.1	0746	5.4	1451	2.1	2007	5.6
15	M	0321	1.8	0839	5.8	1549	1.7	2057	5.9
16	TU	0415	1.5	0924	6.1	1641	1.4	2142	6.2
17	W	0504	1.3	1006	6.4	1729	1.1	2224	6.5
18	TH	0552	1.1	1045	6.7	1816	0.9	○ 2304	6.7
19	F	0637	0.9	1125	6.9	1902	0.8	2343	6.8
20	SA	0721	0.9	1204	7.0	1945	0.7		
21	SU	0022	6.8	0800	0.8	1245	7.1	2026	0.7
22	M	0104	6.8	0839	0.8	1328	7.0	2104	0.7
23	TU	0147	6.7	0917	0.9	1413	6.8	2144	0.9
24	W	0236	6.5	0959	1.1	1504	6.6	2228	1.2
25	TH	0333	6.1	1047	1.5	1604	6.2	◑ 2323	1.6
26	F	0444	5.8	1150	1.8	1719	5.8		
27	SA	0033	1.9	0611	5.5	1307	2.0	1849	5.6
28	SU	0154	2.0	0737	5.6	1428	1.9	2015	5.8
29	M	0324	1.8	0848	5.9	1555	1.6	2123	6.1
30	TU	0444	1.5	0943	6.2	1705	1.2	2213	6.3
31	W	0539	1.2	1026	6.5	1757	1.0	2254	6.5

Chart Datum: 3·67 metres below Ordnance Datum (Newlyn)
HAT is 7·4 metres above Chart Datum

DOVER

TIME ZONE (UT)
For Summer Time add ONE hour in **non-shaded areas**

LAT 51°07'N LONG 1°19'E

TIMES AND HEIGHTS OF HIGH AND LOW WATERS

Dates in amber are **SPRINGS**
Dates in grey are **NEAPS**

2016

SEPTEMBER

Date	Day	Moon	Time	m	Time	m	Time	m	Time	m
1	TH	●	0624	1.0	1104	6.7	1841	0.8	2328	6.6
2	F		0703	1.0	1140	6.8	1918	0.8		
3	SA		0001	6.6	0734	1.0	1216	6.8	1949	0.9
4	SU		0034	6.6	0800	1.1	1251	6.8	2014	1.0
5	M		0106	6.5	0819	1.2	1322	6.6	2034	1.2
6	TU		0135	6.3	0838	1.3	1348	6.4	2056	1.3
7	W		0158	6.1	0905	1.5	1410	6.2	2125	1.5
8	TH		0222	5.9	0938	1.7	1440	5.9	2200	1.8
9	F	◐	0257	5.6	1018	2.0	1526	5.6	2245	2.1
10	SA		0357	5.3	1110	2.3	1707	5.2	2352	2.4
11	SU		0604	5.2	1244	2.5	1834	5.2		
12	M		0139	2.4	0713	5.4	1416	2.3	1938	5.5
13	TU		0251	2.0	0809	5.7	1519	1.8	2032	5.9
14	W		0348	1.6	0857	6.2	1614	1.4	2118	6.3
15	TH		0439	1.3	0940	6.5	1705	1.1	2200	6.6
16	F	○	0528	1.1	1021	6.9	1754	0.9	2241	6.9
17	SA		0615	0.9	1101	7.1	1841	0.7	2321	7.0
18	SU		0659	0.7	1142	7.2	1926	0.6		
19	M		0001	7.1	0740	0.7	1224	7.3	2006	0.6
20	TU		0043	7.0	0819	0.7	1307	7.2	2045	0.7
21	W		0127	6.9	0859	0.8	1353	6.9	2124	0.9
22	TH		0217	6.6	0941	1.1	1445	6.6	2208	1.3
23	F	◑	0314	6.2	1029	1.5	1546	6.1	2302	1.8
24	SA		0424	5.8	1131	1.9	1701	5.7		
25	SU		0014	2.1	0546	5.5	1251	2.1	1834	5.5
26	M		0141	2.2	0718	5.6	1419	2.0	2008	5.7
27	TU		0317	1.9	0832	5.9	1547	1.7	2112	6.0
28	W		0427	1.6	0925	6.2	1649	1.3	2157	6.3
29	TH		0517	1.3	1006	6.5	1736	1.0	2233	6.5
30	F		0559	1.1	1042	6.7	1816	0.9	2305	6.6

OCTOBER

Date	Day	Moon	Time	m	Time	m	Time	m	Time	m
1	SA	●	0634	1.1	1116	6.8	1849	1.0	2335	6.7
2	SU		0702	1.1	1150	6.8	1915	1.0		
3	M		0006	6.6	0723	1.2	1223	6.7	1936	1.1
4	TU		0036	6.6	0743	1.2	1250	6.6	1958	1.2
5	W		0100	6.4	0807	1.3	1309	6.4	2023	1.3
6	TH		0117	6.3	0836	1.4	1329	6.3	2053	1.5
7	F		0142	6.2	0909	1.6	1400	6.0	2128	1.8
8	SA		0218	5.9	0947	1.9	1442	5.7	2209	2.1
9	SU	◐	0307	5.6	1035	2.3	1544	5.3	2304	2.4
10	M		0512	5.2	1146	2.5	1801	5.2		
11	TU		0046	2.5	0636	5.4	1336	2.3	1909	5.5
12	W		0215	2.2	0737	5.7	1446	1.9	2005	5.9
13	TH		0317	1.8	0827	6.2	1543	1.5	2052	6.3
14	F		0410	1.4	0912	6.6	1636	1.1	2136	6.7
15	SA		0501	1.1	0955	7.0	1728	0.8	2217	7.0
16	SU	○	0549	0.8	1037	7.2	1817	0.6	2258	7.1
17	M		0636	0.7	1119	7.3	1904	0.5	2340	7.2
18	TU		0719	0.6	1202	7.3	1947	0.5		
19	W		0023	7.1	0801	0.7	1247	7.2	2027	0.7
20	TH		0109	7.0	0843	0.8	1334	6.9	2108	1.0
21	F		0200	6.7	0926	1.1	1428	6.5	2152	1.4
22	SA	◑	0257	6.3	1016	1.5	1529	6.1	2246	1.8
23	SU		0402	5.9	1117	1.9	1640	5.7	2356	2.2
24	M		0515	5.6	1234	2.1	1807	5.5		
25	TU		0119	2.3	0641	5.6	1358	2.0	1943	5.6
26	W		0244	2.1	0801	5.8	1517	1.7	2046	5.9
27	TH		0353	1.7	0855	6.1	1618	1.4	2130	6.2
28	F		0444	1.5	0937	6.4	1704	1.2	2205	6.4
29	SA		0525	1.3	1015	6.6	1742	1.1	2237	6.5
30	SU	●	0559	1.2	1049	6.7	1813	1.1	2308	6.6
31	M		0627	1.2	1122	6.7	1838	1.1	2339	6.6

NOVEMBER

Date	Day	Moon	Time	m	Time	m	Time	m	Time	m
1	TU		0650	1.2	1153	6.6	1903	1.2		
2	W		0007	6.6	0714	1.2	1219	6.5	1929	1.2
3	TH		0030	6.5	0743	1.3	1239	6.4	1958	1.3
4	F		0050	6.4	0815	1.4	1303	6.3	2030	1.5
5	SA		0118	6.3	0848	1.6	1335	6.1	2105	1.7
6	SU		0155	6.1	0926	1.8	1417	5.9	2145	2.0
7	M	◐	0244	5.8	1011	2.1	1513	5.6	2235	2.2
8	TU		0354	5.5	1112	2.2	1713	5.4	2347	2.4
9	W		0549	5.5	1247	2.2	1834	5.5		
10	TH		0129	2.2	0659	5.8	1406	1.9	1934	5.9
11	F		0238	1.8	0754	6.2	1508	1.5	2025	6.3
12	SA		0336	1.5	0844	6.6	1605	1.1	2111	6.6
13	SU		0431	1.1	0929	6.9	1700	0.9	2155	6.9
14	M	○	0523	0.9	1014	7.1	1754	0.7	2238	7.1
15	TU		0614	0.7	1059	7.2	1844	0.6	2323	7.1
16	W		0702	0.6	1144	7.2	1931	0.6		
17	TH		0008	7.1	0747	0.7	1231	7.1	2014	0.8
18	F		0056	7.0	0832	0.8	1320	6.8	2057	1.0
19	SA		0146	6.8	0918	1.1	1412	6.5	2141	1.4
20	SU		0239	6.5	1007	1.4	1510	6.1	2231	1.8
21	M	◑	0337	6.1	1103	1.7	1613	5.8	2332	2.1
22	TU		0440	5.8	1208	2.0	1724	5.5		
23	W		0041	2.3	0551	5.7	1318	2.0	1851	5.5
24	TH		0153	2.2	0710	5.7	1427	1.9	2001	5.6
25	F		0300	2.0	0814	5.9	1528	1.7	2052	5.9
26	SA		0357	1.8	0903	6.1	1619	1.5	2132	6.1
27	SU		0443	1.5	0944	6.3	1700	1.3	2207	6.3
28	M		0521	1.4	1020	6.4	1734	1.3	2240	6.4
29	TU	●	0552	1.3	1054	6.5	1805	1.2	2312	6.5
30	W		0622	1.2	1124	6.4	1836	1.2	2342	6.5

DECEMBER

Date	Day	Moon	Time	m	Time	m	Time	m	Time	m
1	TH		0653	1.2	1152	6.4	1908	1.2		
2	F		0008	6.5	0726	1.2	1219	6.3	1941	1.3
3	SA		0035	6.5	0800	1.3	1248	6.3	2015	1.4
4	SU		0105	6.4	0836	1.4	1321	6.2	2050	1.5
5	M		0143	6.3	0913	1.6	1403	6.1	2129	1.7
6	TU		0230	6.1	0956	1.8	1455	5.8	2215	1.9
7	W	◐	0329	5.9	1050	1.9	1605	5.6	2314	2.1
8	TH		0446	5.8	1202	1.9	1742	5.6		
9	F		0035	2.1	0611	5.8	1322	1.8	1857	5.8
10	SA		0154	1.9	0719	6.1	1429	1.5	1956	6.1
11	SU		0259	1.6	0816	6.4	1532	1.3	2048	6.4
12	M		0400	1.3	0908	6.7	1634	1.0	2138	6.6
13	TU		0500	1.0	0958	6.9	1735	0.8	2226	6.8
14	W	○	0557	0.8	1047	7.0	1830	0.7	2313	7.0
15	TH		0650	0.7	1134	7.0	1921	0.7	2359	7.0
16	F		0739	0.7	1221	6.9	2007	0.8		
17	SA		0045	7.0	0826	0.8	1308	6.7	2049	1.0
18	SU		0132	6.8	0910	0.9	1356	6.5	2130	1.2
19	M		0220	6.6	0954	1.2	1447	6.2	2212	1.5
20	TU		0310	6.3	1040	1.5	1540	5.9	2257	1.9
21	W	◑	0404	6.0	1130	1.8	1639	5.6	2351	2.1
22	TH		0503	5.7	1227	2.0	1746	5.4		
23	F		0054	2.3	0610	5.6	1329	2.0	1858	5.4
24	SA		0159	2.2	0720	5.6	1429	1.9	2002	5.5
25	SU		0301	2.1	0821	5.8	1525	1.8	2053	5.8
26	M		0355	1.8	0910	5.9	1614	1.6	2135	6.0
27	TU		0441	1.6	0950	6.1	1657	1.4	2212	6.2
28	W		0521	1.4	1025	6.2	1736	1.3	2247	6.3
29	TH	●	0558	1.3	1059	6.3	1814	1.2	2319	6.4
30	F		0635	1.2	1131	6.4	1852	1.2	2350	6.5
31	SA		0712	1.1	1204	6.4	1929	1.2		

Chart Datum: 3·67 metres below Ordnance Datum (Newlyn)
HAT is 7·4 metres above Chart Datum

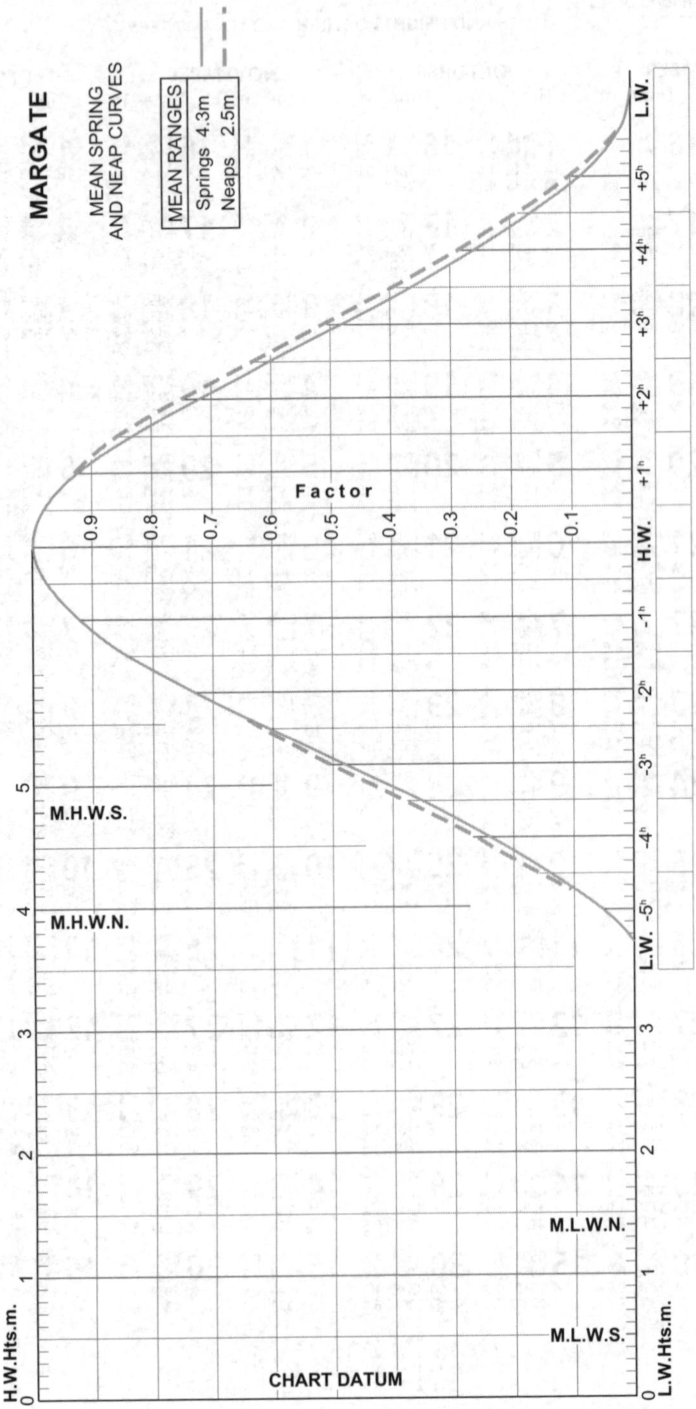
MARGATE
MEAN SPRING AND NEAP CURVES
MEAN RANGES
Springs 4.3m
Neaps 2.5m
Factor
0.9 0.8 0.7 0.6 0.5 0.4 0.3 0.2 0.1
L.W. -5h -4h -3h -2h -1h H.W. +1h +2h +3h +4h +5h L.W.
H.W.Hts.m.
0 1 2 3 4 5
M.H.W.S.
M.H.W.N.
CHART DATUM
M.L.W.N.
M.L.W.S.
L.W.Hts.m.

TIME ZONE (UT)
For Summer Time add ONE hour in **non-shaded areas**

MARGATE

LAT 51°23'N LONG 1°23'E

TIMES AND HEIGHTS OF HIGH AND LOW WATERS

Dates in amber are **SPRINGS**
Dates in grey are **NEAPS**

2016

JANUARY

Date	Day	Time	m	Time	m	Time	m	Time	m
1	F	0357	4.3	1023	0.9	1631	4.1	2225	1.4
2	SA ◑	0441	4.2	1109	1.1	1718	4.0	2317	1.5
3	SU	0534	4.0	1207	1.2	1823	3.9		
4	M	0023	1.6	0650	3.9	1321	1.3	1939	3.9
5	TU	0158	1.6	0804	3.9	1430	1.2	2041	4.0
6	W	0305	1.4	0905	4.0	1526	1.1	2136	4.2
7	TH	0359	1.2	0959	4.2	1615	1.0	2224	4.4
8	F	0447	1.0	1047	4.4	1659	0.9	2306	4.5
9	SA	0531	0.8	1129	4.5	1739	0.9	2346	4.6
10	SU ●	0612	0.7	1211	4.6	1817	0.8		
11	M	0025	4.7	0651	0.6	1253	4.7	1855	0.7
12	TU	0106	4.8	0732	0.5	1338	4.8	1935	0.7
13	W	0147	4.8	0813	0.4	1422	4.8	2018	0.7
14	TH	0230	4.8	0856	0.4	1507	4.7	2102	0.8
15	F	0312	4.7	0941	0.5	1551	4.6	2148	0.9
16	SA ◐	0357	4.6	1029	0.6	1639	4.4	2239	1.0
17	SU	0449	4.5	1125	0.7	1737	4.3	2341	1.1
18	M	0552	4.4	1232	0.8	1850	4.2		
19	TU	0057	1.2	0709	4.3	1345	0.9	2005	4.2
20	W	0216	1.2	0826	4.3	1456	1.0	2116	4.3
21	TH	0329	1.0	0939	4.4	1601	1.0	2220	4.4
22	F	0437	0.9	1043	4.5	1658	0.9	2313	4.5
23	SA	0534	0.7	1134	4.6	1745	0.9	2357	4.6
24	SU ○	0621	0.5	1219	4.7	1825	0.8		
25	M	0035	4.7	0701	0.5	1259	4.7	1901	0.8
26	TU	0110	4.7	0738	0.5	1336	4.7	1934	0.8
27	W	0145	4.7	0811	0.5	1411	4.6	2007	0.9
28	TH	0220	4.7	0841	0.6	1445	4.5	2039	1.0
29	F	0254	4.6	0912	0.7	1517	4.4	2112	1.0
30	SA	0327	4.5	0944	0.8	1551	4.3	2148	1.2
31	SU	0403	4.3	1021	0.9	1629	4.1	2230	1.3

FEBRUARY

Date	Day	Time	m	Time	m	Time	m	Time	m
1	M ◑	0444	4.1	1106	1.1	1715	3.9	2322	1.5
2	TU	0536	3.9	1205	1.3	1813	3.8		
3	W	0033	1.6	0645	3.8	1323	1.4	1939	3.8
4	TH	0208	1.5	0814	3.9	1442	1.3	2055	4.0
5	F	0321	1.3	0924	4.0	1543	1.1	2154	4.2
6	SA	0418	1.0	1022	4.3	1634	1.0	2244	4.4
7	SU	0508	0.8	1111	4.5	1719	0.9	2328	4.6
8	M ●	0554	0.6	1155	4.6	1801	0.8		
9	TU	0009	4.7	0636	0.5	1240	4.8	1842	0.7
10	W	0051	4.9	0718	0.3	1324	4.9	1923	0.6
11	TH	0134	4.9	0759	0.3	1409	4.9	2005	0.6
12	F	0216	4.9	0840	0.3	1453	4.8	2047	0.6
13	SA	0258	4.9	0921	0.4	1535	4.7	2130	0.7
14	SU	0341	4.8	1004	0.5	1618	4.5	2218	0.9
15	M ◐	0429	4.6	1055	0.7	1710	4.3	2315	1.0
16	TU	0529	4.4	1159	0.9	1821	4.1		
17	W	0031	1.2	0647	4.2	1318	1.1	1941	4.0
18	TH	0156	1.2	0811	4.2	1439	1.2	2059	4.1
19	F	0321	1.1	0932	4.3	1553	1.1	2208	4.3
20	SA	0434	0.9	1038	4.4	1652	1.0	2303	4.5
21	SU	0527	0.7	1128	4.5	1736	0.9	2346	4.6
22	M ○	0609	0.6	1209	4.6	1810	0.9		
23	TU	0021	4.6	0643	0.5	1243	4.6	1841	0.8
24	W	0052	4.7	0713	0.5	1313	4.6	1913	0.8
25	TH	0122	4.7	0742	0.5	1344	4.6	1945	0.8
26	F	0155	4.7	0811	0.5	1415	4.5	2015	0.8
27	SA	0228	4.6	0839	0.6	1447	4.5	2046	0.9
28	SU	0300	4.5	0908	0.7	1519	4.3	2117	1.0
29	M	0332	4.4	0940	0.9	1553	4.2	2153	1.1

MARCH

Date	Day	Time	m	Time	m	Time	m	Time	m
1	TU ◑	0408	4.2	1019	1.1	1633	4.0	2238	1.3
2	W	0454	4.0	1111	1.3	1724	3.9	2340	1.4
3	TH	0554	3.8	1224	1.4	1833	3.8		
4	F	0110	1.5	0718	3.8	1354	1.4	2007	3.9
5	SA	0240	1.3	0847	4.0	1509	1.2	2120	4.1
6	SU	0347	1.0	0955	4.2	1607	1.0	2217	4.4
7	M	0442	0.7	1049	4.5	1657	0.8	2305	4.6
8	TU	0531	0.5	1136	4.7	1741	0.7	2349	4.8
9	W ●	0615	0.4	1221	4.8	1824	0.6		
10	TH	0031	4.9	0657	0.2	1306	4.9	1907	0.5
11	F	0116	5.0	0739	0.2	1351	4.9	1949	0.5
12	SA	0200	5.1	0819	0.2	1434	4.9	2032	0.5
13	SU	0243	5.0	0858	0.3	1515	4.7	2114	0.6
14	M	0326	4.9	0939	0.5	1556	4.5	2200	0.8
15	TU ◐	0414	4.6	1027	0.8	1646	4.3	2256	0.9
16	W	0513	4.4	1130	1.1	1754	4.1		
17	TH	0010	1.1	0630	4.1	1253	1.3	1917	4.0
18	F	0138	1.2	0757	4.1	1421	1.3	2036	4.1
19	SA	0308	1.0	0919	4.2	1538	1.2	2147	4.2
20	SU	0418	0.8	1023	4.4	1635	1.1	2243	4.4
21	M	0508	0.7	1112	4.5	1716	1.0	2326	4.5
22	TU	0546	0.6	1150	4.5	1748	0.9	2359	4.6
23	W ○	0615	0.5	1220	4.5	1819	0.8		
24	TH	0027	4.7	0642	0.5	1246	4.6	1850	0.7
25	F	0057	4.7	0711	0.5	1314	4.6	1922	0.7
26	SA	0129	4.7	0740	0.5	1346	4.6	1953	0.7
27	SU	0203	4.6	0808	0.6	1419	4.5	2023	0.8
28	M	0236	4.5	0837	0.7	1451	4.4	2053	0.9
29	TU	0307	4.4	0908	0.8	1522	4.3	2127	1.0
30	W	0340	4.2	0944	1.0	1559	4.1	2208	1.1
31	TH ◑	0423	4.1	1032	1.2	1648	4.0	2306	1.2

APRIL

Date	Day	Time	m	Time	m	Time	m	Time	m
1	F	0522	3.9	1141	1.4	1753	3.9		
2	SA	0029	1.3	0639	3.9	1310	1.4	1920	3.9
3	SU	0201	1.2	0810	4.0	1434	1.2	2042	4.1
4	M	0314	0.9	0924	4.3	1538	1.0	2144	4.3
5	TU	0412	0.6	1022	4.5	1630	0.8	2236	4.6
6	W	0503	0.4	1112	4.7	1717	0.6	2323	4.8
7	TH ●	0549	0.3	1158	4.8	1803	0.5		
8	F	0007	4.9	0632	0.2	1244	4.9	1847	0.5
9	SA	0054	5.1	0715	0.2	1329	4.9	1933	0.4
10	SU	0141	5.1	0756	0.3	1413	4.9	2017	0.4
11	M	0227	5.0	0836	0.4	1455	4.7	2100	0.5
12	TU	0313	4.9	0917	0.6	1537	4.5	2147	0.7
13	W	0401	4.6	1003	0.9	1625	4.3	2241	0.8
14	TH ◐	0458	4.4	1102	1.2	1728	4.1	2351	1.0
15	F	0612	4.1	1223	1.4	1848	4.0		
16	SA	0114	1.1	0733	4.1	1352	1.4	2003	4.0
17	SU	0237	1.0	0850	4.1	1506	1.3	2111	4.2
18	M	0344	0.8	0953	4.3	1603	1.1	2208	4.3
19	TU	0433	0.7	1042	4.4	1645	1.0	2253	4.4
20	W	0509	0.7	1120	4.4	1720	0.9	2327	4.5
21	TH	0540	0.6	1149	4.5	1753	0.8	2358	4.6
22	F ○	0610	0.6	1214	4.5	1827	0.7		
23	SA	0029	4.6	0641	0.5	1245	4.6	1900	0.7
24	SU	0103	4.7	0711	0.6	1318	4.6	1932	0.7
25	M	0139	4.6	0740	0.6	1353	4.6	2003	0.7
26	TU	0214	4.5	0810	0.7	1427	4.5	2035	0.8
27	W	0248	4.4	0844	0.8	1500	4.3	2111	0.8
28	TH	0323	4.3	0922	0.9	1537	4.2	2153	0.9
29	F	0406	4.2	1010	1.1	1625	4.1	2248	1.0
30	SA ◑	0501	4.1	1113	1.2	1725	4.0		

Chart Datum: 2·50 metres below Ordnance Datum (Newlyn)
HAT is 5·2 metres above Chart Datum

TIME ZONE (UT)
For Summer Time add ONE hour in **non-shaded areas**

MARGATE

LAT 51°23′N LONG 1°23′E

TIMES AND HEIGHTS OF HIGH AND LOW WATERS

Dates in amber are **SPRINGS**
Dates in grey are **NEAPS**

201

MAY

Date	Day	Moon	Time	m	Time	m	Time	m	Time	m
1	SU		0002	1.1	0612	4.0	1234	1.3	1841	4.0
2	M		0127	1.0	0736	4.1	1358	1.2	2003	4.1
3	TU		0241	0.8	0851	4.3	1506	1.0	2109	4.4
4	W		0341	0.6	0952	4.5	1602	0.8	2205	4.6
5	TH		0433	0.4	1045	4.7	1652	0.6	2255	4.8
6	F	●	0521	0.3	1133	4.8	1741	0.5	2344	4.9
7	SA		0607	0.3	1220	4.8	1829	0.4		
8	SU		0034	5.0	0652	0.3	1307	4.9	1917	0.4
9	M		0124	5.0	0735	0.4	1352	4.8	2004	0.4
10	TU		0212	5.0	0817	0.5	1436	4.7	2050	0.5
11	W		0259	4.8	0858	0.7	1518	4.6	2136	0.6
12	TH		0347	4.6	0942	1.0	1604	4.4	2227	0.7
13	F	◐	0440	4.3	1035	1.2	1700	4.2	2328	0.9
14	SA		0545	4.1	1143	1.4	1811	4.1		
15	SU		0040	1.0	0659	4.0	1309	1.5	1921	4.0
16	M		0153	1.0	0806	4.1	1421	1.4	2024	4.1
17	TU		0254	0.9	0906	4.2	1519	1.2	2121	4.2
18	W		0344	0.8	0958	4.3	1607	1.1	2210	4.3
19	TH		0426	0.8	1039	4.3	1648	0.9	2252	4.4
20	F		0504	0.7	1114	4.4	1727	0.8	2328	4.5
21	SA	○	0540	0.7	1145	4.5	1804	0.7		
22	SU		0003	4.6	0613	0.6	1218	4.6	1839	0.7
23	M		0039	4.6	0645	0.6	1254	4.6	1913	0.7
24	TU		0117	4.6	0717	0.7	1331	4.6	1947	0.6
25	W		0155	4.6	0751	0.7	1409	4.5	2022	0.7
26	TH		0234	4.5	0828	0.8	1446	4.4	2101	0.7
27	F		0313	4.4	0909	0.9	1525	4.4	2145	0.8
28	SA		0356	4.3	0956	1.0	1610	4.3	2237	0.8
29	SU	◑	0447	4.2	1053	1.1	1704	4.2	2341	0.9
30	M		0550	4.1	1202	1.2	1810	4.2		
31	TU		0055	0.8	0705	4.2	1322	1.1	1925	4.3

JUNE

Date	Day	Moon	Time	m	Time	m	Time	m	Time	m
1	W		0208	0.7	0818	4.3	1433	1.0	2035	4.4
2	TH		0310	0.6	0923	4.5	1534	0.8	2136	4.6
3	F		0406	0.5	1020	4.6	1629	0.7	2232	4.7
4	SA		0457	0.4	1112	4.7	1722	0.6	2326	4.9
5	SU	●	0546	0.4	1200	4.8	1815	0.5		
6	M		0018	4.9	0633	0.5	1247	4.8	1905	0.4
7	TU		0109	5.0	0719	0.5	1333	4.8	1954	0.4
8	W		0157	4.9	0802	0.7	1417	4.7	2040	0.4
9	TH		0244	4.8	0842	0.8	1459	4.6	2124	0.5
10	F		0329	4.6	0922	1.0	1542	4.5	2208	0.7
11	SA		0416	4.4	1006	1.1	1628	4.3	2257	0.8
12	SU	◐	0509	4.2	1057	1.3	1725	4.2	2355	1.0
13	M		0613	4.0	1205	1.4	1833	4.1		
14	TU		0101	1.0	0717	4.0	1327	1.5	1936	4.0
15	W		0203	1.0	0816	4.0	1433	1.4	2034	4.1
16	TH		0258	1.0	0909	4.1	1528	1.2	2128	4.2
17	F		0347	0.9	0958	4.2	1616	1.0	2217	4.3
18	SA		0432	0.8	1041	4.4	1701	0.9	2300	4.4
19	SU		0513	0.8	1119	4.5	1742	0.8	2340	4.5
20	M	○	0550	0.8	1155	4.5	1820	0.7		
21	TU		0018	4.6	0624	0.7	1233	4.6	1856	0.6
22	W		0057	4.6	0659	0.7	1312	4.6	1933	0.6
23	TH		0138	4.6	0735	0.7	1352	4.6	2011	0.6
24	F		0220	4.6	0815	0.7	1432	4.6	2052	0.6
25	SA		0303	4.5	0857	0.8	1513	4.5	2136	0.6
26	SU		0346	4.4	0943	0.9	1556	4.5	2224	0.7
27	M	◑	0433	4.3	1035	1.0	1645	4.4	2320	0.7
28	TU		0528	4.3	1135	1.1	1743	4.4		
29	W		0026	0.7	0635	4.2	1248	1.1	1852	4.4
30	TH		0136	0.7	0749	4.3	1403	1.1	2005	4.4

JULY

Date	Day	Moon	Time	m	Time	m	Time	m	Time	m
1	F		0243	0.7	0858	4.4	1510	0.9	2113	4.5
2	SA		0344	0.7	1000	4.5	1612	0.8	2217	4.6
3	SU		0440	0.7	1056	4.6	1711	0.6	2315	4.7
4	M	●	0532	0.6	1146	4.7	1806	0.5		
5	TU		0007	4.8	0620	0.7	1233	4.7	1856	0.4
6	W		0056	4.8	0704	0.7	1316	4.8	1943	0.4
7	TH		0142	4.8	0745	0.8	1358	4.8	2025	0.4
8	F		0225	4.7	0823	0.8	1438	4.7	2104	0.5
9	SA		0306	4.6	0858	1.0	1516	4.6	2140	0.6
10	SU		0345	4.4	0935	1.1	1554	4.5	2218	0.8
11	M		0425	4.2	1016	1.2	1635	4.3	2301	0.9
12	TU	◐	0510	4.1	1104	1.4	1725	4.1	2355	1.1
13	W		0610	3.9	1206	1.5	1832	4.0		
14	TH		0103	1.2	0720	3.9	1336	1.5	1943	4.0
15	F		0211	1.2	0823	4.0	1446	1.4	2046	4.1
16	SA		0310	1.1	0919	4.1	1543	1.2	2143	4.2
17	SU		0401	1.0	1010	4.3	1634	1.0	2234	4.3
18	M		0447	0.9	1055	4.4	1720	0.8	2318	4.5
19	TU	○	0528	0.9	1135	4.5	1801	0.7	2359	4.6
20	W		0606	0.8	1214	4.6	1840	0.6		
21	TH		0039	4.7	0643	0.7	1254	4.7	1919	0.5
22	F		0122	4.7	0721	0.7	1335	4.8	1958	0.5
23	SA		0206	4.7	0802	0.7	1416	4.8	2039	0.4
24	SU		0249	4.7	0844	0.7	1457	4.7	2121	0.5
25	M		0331	4.6	0927	0.8	1538	4.7	2205	0.6
26	TU	◑	0415	4.5	1014	0.9	1624	4.6	2255	0.7
27	W		0504	4.3	1109	1.1	1718	4.5	2355	0.8
28	TH		0606	4.2	1218	1.1	1825	4.4		
29	F		0107	0.9	0723	4.2	1338	1.2	1944	4.3
30	SA		0221	1.0	0838	4.2	1454	1.1	2100	4.4
31	SU		0329	0.9	0947	4.4	1605	0.9	2212	4.5

AUGUST

Date	Day	Moon	Time	m	Time	m	Time	m	Time	m
1	M		0431	0.9	1047	4.5	1708	0.7	2311	4.7
2	TU	●	0524	0.8	1137	4.6	1800	0.6		
3	W		0000	4.7	0608	0.8	1221	4.7	1845	0.5
4	TH		0044	4.8	0648	0.8	1259	4.8	1925	0.4
5	F		0124	4.7	0724	0.8	1336	4.8	2002	0.5
6	SA		0202	4.7	0759	0.9	1412	4.8	2035	0.6
7	SU		0237	4.6	0833	0.9	1446	4.7	2106	0.7
8	M		0310	4.5	0906	1.0	1520	4.6	2137	0.8
9	TU		0343	4.3	0940	1.1	1556	4.4	2212	0.9
10	W	◐	0419	4.2	1020	1.3	1636	4.3	2255	1.1
11	TH		0503	4.0	1109	1.4	1725	4.1	2351	1.3
12	F		0559	3.9	1216	1.6	1831	3.9		
13	SA		0108	1.4	0723	3.8	1353	1.5	1956	3.9
14	SU		0228	1.4	0838	4.0	1507	1.3	2108	4.1
15	M		0330	1.2	0938	4.2	1605	1.1	2207	4.3
16	TU		0422	1.1	1029	4.4	1654	0.9	2256	4.5
17	W		0506	0.9	1113	4.6	1739	0.7	2339	4.6
18	TH	○	0547	0.8	1153	4.7	1820	0.6		
19	F		0020	4.8	0626	0.7	1233	4.8	1900	0.5
20	SA		0103	4.8	0705	0.7	1314	4.9	1940	0.4
21	SU		0146	4.9	0746	0.7	1356	5.0	2020	0.4
22	M		0230	4.8	0827	0.7	1437	4.9	2059	0.4
23	TU		0311	4.7	0909	0.8	1519	4.8	2140	0.6
24	W		0352	4.5	0954	0.9	1604	4.7	2226	0.8
25	TH	◑	0439	4.4	1046	1.0	1657	4.6	2325	1.0
26	F		0541	4.2	1155	1.2	1807	4.4		
27	SA		0042	1.2	0702	4.1	1319	1.2	1931	4.3
28	SU		0205	1.2	0822	4.2	1444	1.1	2055	4.3
29	M		0322	1.2	0936	4.3	1602	0.9	2209	4.5
30	TU		0425	1.0	1037	4.5	1702	0.7	2306	4.6
31	W		0514	1.0	1126	4.6	1749	0.6	2351	4.7

Chart Datum: 2·50 metres below Ordnance Datum (Newlyn)
HAT is 5·2 metres above Chart Datum

TIME ZONE (UT)
or Summer Time add ONE
hour in **non-shaded areas**

MARGATE

LAT 51°23'N LONG 1°23'E

TIMES AND HEIGHTS OF HIGH AND LOW WATERS

Dates in amber are **SPRINGS**
Dates in grey are **NEAPS**

2016

SEPTEMBER

Date	Day	Time	m	Time	m	Time	m	Time	m	Moon
1	TH	0553	0.9	1205	4.7	1827	0.5			●
2	F	0028	4.7	0627	0.9	1239	4.8	1900	0.5	
3	SA	0101	4.7	0701	0.8	1310	4.8	1931	0.5	
4	SU	0131	4.7	0734	0.8	1342	4.8	2001	0.6	
5	M	0202	4.6	0807	0.9	1416	4.7	2030	0.7	
6	TU	0234	4.5	0838	1.0	1449	4.6	2059	0.8	
7	W	0306	4.4	0909	1.1	1523	4.5	2129	1.0	
8	TH	0340	4.3	0943	1.2	1559	4.3	2206	1.2	
9	F	0419	4.1	1025	1.3	1643	4.1	2255	1.4	◐
10	SA	0508	3.9	1123	1.5	1739	3.9			
11	SU	0004	1.6	0614	3.8	1249	1.6	1857	3.9	
12	M	0137	1.6	0747	3.9	1423	1.4	2027	4.0	
13	TU	0255	1.4	0901	4.1	1531	1.1	2136	4.3	
14	W	0353	1.1	0958	4.4	1625	0.9	2229	4.5	
15	TH	0441	1.0	1046	4.6	1712	0.7	2314	4.7	
16	F	0523	0.8	1127	4.8	1754	0.5	2357	4.8	○
17	SA	0605	0.7	1207	4.9	1835	0.4			
18	SU	0039	4.9	0645	0.6	1249	5.0	1915	0.4	
19	M	0122	5.0	0727	0.6	1332	5.1	1955	0.4	
20	TU	0205	4.9	0809	0.6	1416	5.0	2034	0.5	
21	W	0247	4.8	0851	0.7	1500	4.9	2114	0.6	
22	TH	0329	4.6	0936	0.8	1547	4.8	2159	0.9	
23	F	0416	4.4	1028	1.0	1642	4.5	2258	1.1	◑
24	SA	0518	4.2	1138	1.1	1754	4.3			
25	SU	0019	1.4	0641	4.1	1304	1.2	1921	4.2	
26	M	0150	1.4	0804	4.1	1433	1.1	2047	4.3	
27	TU	0309	1.3	0918	4.3	1548	0.9	2157	4.5	
28	W	0411	1.2	1019	4.5	1644	0.7	2251	4.6	
29	TH	0457	1.0	1106	4.6	1727	0.6	2333	4.7	
30	F	0532	1.0	1143	4.7	1800	0.6			

OCTOBER

Date	Day	Time	m	Time	m	Time	m	Time	m	Moon
1	SA	0005	4.7	0604	0.9	1213	4.7	1828	0.6	●
2	SU	0031	4.7	0637	0.8	1241	4.8	1858	0.6	
3	M	0057	4.7	0710	0.8	1313	4.8	1928	0.6	
4	TU	0128	4.7	0742	0.8	1347	4.7	1956	0.7	
5	W	0201	4.6	0812	0.9	1421	4.6	2024	0.9	
6	TH	0234	4.5	0842	1.0	1454	4.5	2054	1.0	
7	F	0306	4.4	0914	1.1	1528	4.3	2128	1.2	
8	SA	0342	4.2	0953	1.2	1609	4.2	2213	1.4	
9	SU	0428	4.0	1046	1.4	1703	4.0	2316	1.6	◐
10	M	0528	3.9	1201	1.4	1814	3.9			
11	TU	0041	1.6	0650	3.9	1335	1.4	1942	4.0	
12	W	0212	1.5	0817	4.0	1452	1.1	2059	4.3	
13	TH	0318	1.2	0921	4.3	1550	0.8	2157	4.6	
14	F	0410	1.0	1012	4.6	1640	0.6	2245	4.8	
15	SA	0456	0.8	1057	4.8	1725	0.5	2329	4.9	
16	SU	0540	0.7	1139	5.0	1807	0.4			○
17	M	0012	5.0	0623	0.6	1223	5.1	1848	0.4	
18	TU	0056	5.0	0708	0.5	1310	5.1	1930	0.4	
19	W	0141	4.9	0752	0.5	1358	5.1	2010	0.5	
20	TH	0224	4.8	0836	0.6	1446	5.0	2052	0.7	
21	F	0308	4.7	0923	0.7	1535	4.8	2138	1.0	
22	SA	0356	4.4	1016	0.9	1630	4.5	2234	1.3	◑
23	SU	0456	4.2	1123	1.0	1740	4.3	2352	1.5	
24	M	0616	4.1	1244	1.1	1904	4.2			
25	TU	0123	1.5	0735	4.1	1408	1.0	2023	4.3	
26	W	0241	1.4	0846	4.2	1518	0.9	2130	4.4	
27	TH	0343	1.3	0947	4.4	1613	0.8	2223	4.6	
28	F	0429	1.1	1035	4.5	1653	0.7	2304	4.6	
29	SA	0506	1.0	1113	4.6	1725	0.7	2334	4.6	
30	SU	0539	0.9	1143	4.7	1756	0.7	2359	4.7	●
31	M	0613	0.8	1213	4.7	1827	0.7			

NOVEMBER

Date	Day	Time	m	Time	m	Time	m	Time	m	Moon
1	TU	0026	4.7	0647	0.8	1246	4.7	1857	0.7	
2	W	0058	4.7	0720	0.8	1321	4.7	1926	0.8	
3	TH	0133	4.7	0750	0.8	1357	4.6	1955	0.9	
4	F	0207	4.6	0821	0.9	1431	4.5	2027	1.0	
5	SA	0240	4.4	0854	0.9	1506	4.3	2103	1.1	
6	SU	0313	4.3	0933	1.0	1546	4.2	2146	1.3	
7	M	0357	4.2	1023	1.1	1637	4.1	2243	1.4	◐
8	TU	0454	4.0	1128	1.2	1740	4.0	2357	1.5	
9	W	0603	4.0	1250	1.2	1859	4.1			
10	TH	0123	1.5	0727	4.1	1409	1.0	2018	4.3	
11	F	0238	1.2	0839	4.3	1513	0.8	2122	4.5	
12	SA	0337	1.0	0936	4.6	1606	0.6	2215	4.7	
13	SU	0428	0.8	1027	4.8	1654	0.5	2303	4.9	
14	M	0516	0.7	1114	4.9	1740	0.4	2348	4.9	○
15	TU	0603	0.6	1202	5.1	1825	0.5			
16	W	0033	5.0	0651	0.5	1253	5.1	1909	0.5	
17	TH	0120	4.9	0739	0.5	1344	5.1	1952	0.6	
18	F	0206	4.8	0826	0.5	1433	5.0	2035	0.8	
19	SA	0251	4.7	0914	0.6	1523	4.8	2120	1.0	
20	SU	0338	4.5	1005	0.7	1616	4.5	2211	1.3	
21	M	0432	4.3	1104	0.9	1719	4.3	2316	1.5	◑
22	TU	0542	4.1	1214	1.0	1833	4.2			
23	W	0040	1.6	0656	4.1	1328	1.0	1943	4.2	
24	TH	0158	1.5	0802	4.1	1433	1.0	2047	4.3	
25	F	0301	1.4	0902	4.2	1527	0.9	2141	4.4	
26	SA	0352	1.2	0955	4.4	1611	0.9	2225	4.5	
27	SU	0435	1.1	1038	4.5	1650	0.8	2301	4.5	
28	M	0514	0.9	1115	4.5	1726	0.8	2331	4.6	
29	TU	0551	0.8	1149	4.6	1800	0.8			●
30	W	0001	4.6	0626	0.8	1224	4.6	1832	0.8	

DECEMBER

Date	Day	Time	m	Time	m	Time	m	Time	m	Moon
1	TH	0035	4.7	0700	0.7	1300	4.6	1902	0.8	
2	F	0110	4.7	0732	0.7	1337	4.6	1933	0.9	
3	SA	0147	4.6	0805	0.7	1414	4.5	2008	0.9	
4	SU	0222	4.5	0841	0.8	1452	4.4	2046	1.0	
5	M	0258	4.4	0921	0.8	1532	4.3	2129	1.1	
6	TU	0338	4.3	1007	0.9	1617	4.2	2220	1.3	
7	W	0428	4.2	1103	1.0	1712	4.2	2322	1.4	◐
8	TH	0528	4.2	1211	1.0	1819	4.2			
9	F	0036	1.4	0639	4.2	1327	0.9	1937	4.3	
10	SA	0156	1.2	0756	4.3	1435	0.8	2047	4.4	
11	SU	0303	1.0	0903	4.5	1535	0.7	2148	4.6	
12	M	0401	0.9	1002	4.7	1628	0.6	2241	4.7	
13	TU	0455	0.7	1057	4.8	1718	0.6	2331	4.8	
14	W	0548	0.6	1149	4.9	1807	0.6			○
15	TH	0018	4.9	0640	0.5	1242	5.0	1854	0.6	
16	F	0105	4.9	0730	0.4	1332	5.0	1940	0.7	
17	SA	0151	4.8	0818	0.4	1421	4.9	2022	0.8	
18	SU	0236	4.7	0904	0.5	1509	4.7	2103	1.0	
19	M	0320	4.6	0949	0.6	1556	4.5	2146	1.2	
20	TU	0405	4.4	1036	0.8	1647	4.3	2235	1.4	
21	W	0459	4.3	1131	0.9	1748	4.1	2335	1.5	◑
22	TH	0607	4.1	1234	1.1	1854	4.0			
23	F	0058	1.6	0713	4.0	1340	1.1	1955	4.1	
24	SA	0211	1.5	0814	4.1	1438	1.1	2052	4.1	
25	SU	0311	1.4	0912	4.1	1530	1.1	2144	4.3	
26	M	0403	1.2	1004	4.3	1617	1.0	2229	4.4	
27	TU	0449	1.0	1050	4.4	1659	0.9	2307	4.5	
28	W	0531	0.9	1129	4.5	1737	0.9	2342	4.6	
29	TH	0608	0.8	1205	4.5	1812	0.9			●
30	F	0016	4.6	0643	0.7	1242	4.6	1843	0.8	
31	SA	0053	4.7	0716	0.6	1320	4.6	1917	0.8	

Chart Datum: 2·50 metres below Ordnance Datum (Newlyn)
HAT is 5·2 metres above Chart Datum

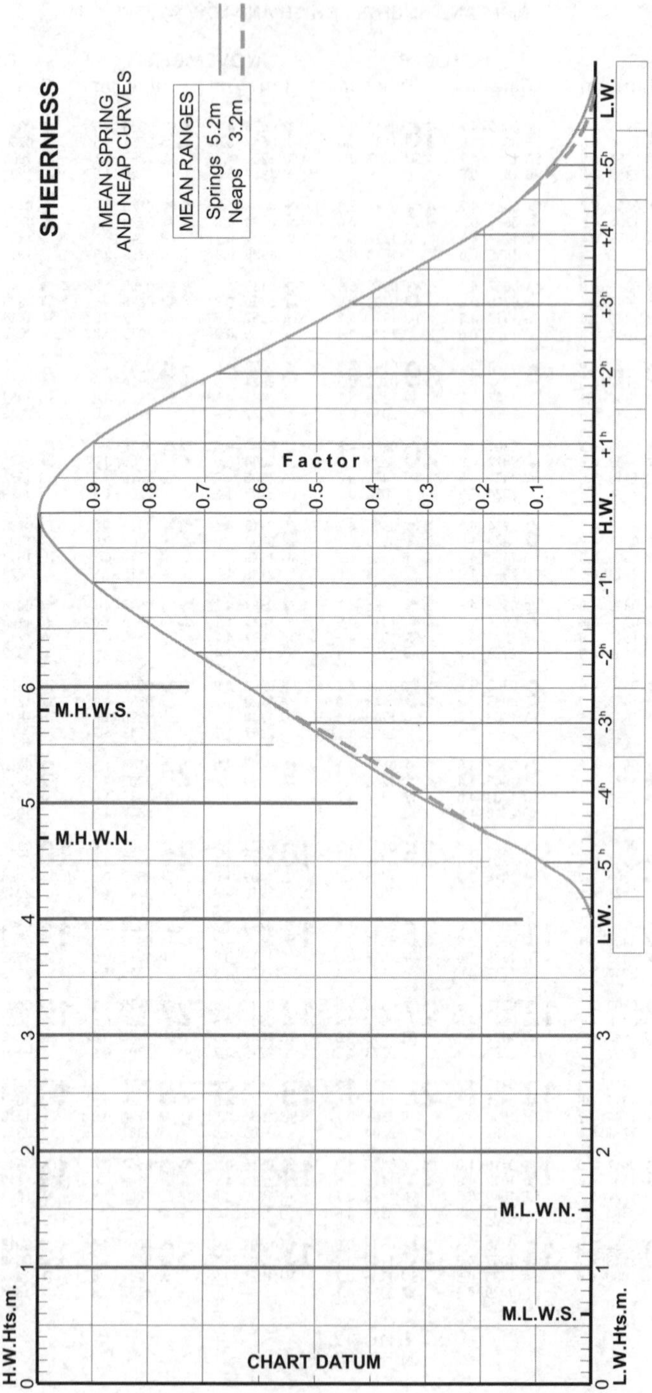
SHEERNESS
MEAN SPRING AND NEAP CURVES
MEAN RANGES
Springs 5.2m
Neaps 3.2m
Factor
0.9 0.8 0.7 0.6 0.5 0.4 0.3 0.2 0.1
L.W. -5h -4h -3h -2h -1h H.W. +1h +2h +3h +4h +5h L.W.
H.W.Hts.m.
0 1 2 3 4 5 6
M.H.W.S.
M.H.W.N.
CHART DATUM
L.W.Hts.m.
0 1 2 3
M.L.W.S.
M.L.W.N.

TIME ZONE (UT)
For Summer Time add ONE hour in **non-shaded areas**

SHEERNESS

LAT 51°27′N LONG 0°45′E

TIMES AND HEIGHTS OF HIGH AND LOW WATERS

Dates in amber are **SPRINGS**
Dates in grey are **NEAPS**

2016

JANUARY

Day	Time	m	Time	m	Time	m	Time	m
1 F	0434	5.2	1039	1.1	1707	5.1	2241	1.5
2 SA	0517	5.0	1120	1.2	1754	4.9	◑ 2329	1.6
3 SU	0609	4.8	1214	1.4	1849	4.7		
4 M	0031	1.8	0713	4.7	1329	1.5	1953	4.7
5 TU	0155	1.8	0823	4.7	1446	1.4	2059	4.8
6 W	0311	1.6	0929	4.8	1546	1.3	2159	5.1
7 TH	0410	1.3	1027	5.1	1638	1.1	2252	5.3
8 F	0501	1.1	1117	5.3	1724	1.0	2338	5.5
9 SA	0549	0.9	1202	5.5	1808	0.9		
10 SU	0021	5.7	0635	0.8	1244	5.7	● 1850	0.8
11 M	0101	5.8	0720	0.7	1326	5.8	1933	0.7
12 TU	0141	5.8	0806	0.5	1407	5.9	2016	0.7
13 W	0220	5.9	0851	0.5	1449	5.9	2058	0.7
14 TH	0301	5.8	0934	0.5	1533	5.8	2137	0.8
15 F	0343	5.8	1014	0.6	1619	5.7	2218	0.9
16 SA	0429	5.6	1055	0.7	1709	5.5	◐ 2302	1.1
17 SU	0521	5.5	1142	0.9	1807	5.3	2357	1.2
18 M	0623	5.3	1244	1.0	1914	5.1		
19 TU	0108	1.3	0736	5.1	1402	1.1	2026	5.1
20 W	0229	1.3	0853	5.1	1519	1.1	2137	5.2
21 TH	0347	1.2	1005	5.3	1630	1.1	2242	5.4
22 F	0500	1.0	1108	5.5	1731	1.0	2337	5.5
23 SA	0601	0.8	1202	5.6	1819	0.9		
24 SU	0024	5.7	0650	0.6	1249	5.8	○ 1859	0.9
25 M	0107	5.7	0732	0.5	1330	5.8	1936	0.8
26 TU	0146	5.7	0810	0.5	1409	5.8	2009	0.9
27 W	0222	5.7	0845	0.6	1445	5.7	2040	0.9
28 TH	0255	5.6	0914	0.7	1519	5.6	2107	1.0
29 F	0327	5.5	0940	0.8	1552	5.4	2135	1.1
30 SA	0400	5.4	1007	0.9	1626	5.2	2206	1.2
31 SU	0435	5.2	1039	1.1	1704	5.0	2243	1.4

FEBRUARY

Day	Time	m	Time	m	Time	m	Time	m
1 M	0516	5.0	1119	1.3	1749	4.8	◑ 2331	1.5
2 TU	0609	4.7	1214	1.5	1848	4.7		
3 W	0035	1.7	0719	4.6	1335	1.6	2000	4.7
4 TH	0210	1.7	0839	4.6	1501	1.5	2114	4.8
5 F	0330	1.4	0950	4.9	1604	1.2	2219	5.1
6 SA	0432	1.2	1050	5.2	1658	1.0	2313	5.4
7 SU	0527	0.9	1141	5.5	1748	0.9		
8 M	0000	5.6	0619	0.7	1227	5.8	● 1834	0.7
9 TU	0044	5.8	0708	0.5	1310	6.0	1920	0.6
10 W	0125	5.9	0755	0.4	1352	6.1	2004	0.5
11 TH	0205	6.0	0840	0.2	1434	6.1	2046	0.5
12 F	0245	6.0	0922	0.3	1516	6.0	2126	0.6
13 SA	0327	6.0	1001	0.4	1600	5.8	2203	0.7
14 SU	0411	5.8	1038	0.6	1647	5.6	2243	0.9
15 M	0501	5.6	1118	0.8	1741	5.3	◐ 2332	1.1
16 TU	0600	5.3	1212	1.1	1846	5.1		
17 W	0039	1.3	0713	5.1	1331	1.3	2000	4.9
18 TH	0208	1.3	0836	5.0	1456	1.3	2118	5.0
19 F	0335	1.2	0955	5.2	1614	1.2	2228	5.2
20 SA	0454	1.0	1100	5.4	1717	1.1	2324	5.4
21 SU	0552	0.8	1152	5.6	1805	1.0		
22 M	0011	5.6	0636	0.6	1235	5.7	○ 1842	0.9
23 TU	0051	5.7	0714	0.6	1313	5.8	1916	0.8
24 W	0126	5.7	0748	0.5	1348	5.8	1947	0.8
25 TH	0159	5.7	0819	0.5	1419	5.7	2017	0.8
26 F	0229	5.7	0847	0.6	1449	5.7	2045	0.8
27 SA	0259	5.6	0913	0.7	1519	5.6	2111	0.9
28 SU	0329	5.5	0938	0.8	1550	5.4	2137	1.0
29 M	0401	5.3	1006	1.0	1624	5.2	2207	1.2

MARCH

Day	Time	m	Time	m	Time	m	Time	m
1 TU	0438	5.1	1039	1.2	1703	5.0	◑ 2247	1.3
2 W	0524	4.9	1124	1.4	1754	4.8	2342	1.5
3 TH	0625	4.7	1232	1.6	1904	4.6		
4 F	0106	1.6	0748	4.6	1412	1.6	2029	4.7
5 SA	0250	1.5	0913	4.8	1530	1.3	2144	5.0
6 SU	0402	1.2	1021	5.2	1630	1.1	2245	5.3
7 M	0503	0.9	1117	5.6	1725	0.9	2336	5.6
8 TU	0600	0.6	1204	5.9	1815	0.7		
9 W	0021	5.9	0651	0.4	1249	6.1	● 1903	0.5
10 TH	0103	6.0	0738	0.2	1332	6.2	1948	0.4
11 F	0145	6.2	0822	0.1	1414	6.2	2031	0.4
12 SA	0226	6.2	0904	0.2	1456	6.1	2111	0.5
13 SU	0309	6.1	0941	0.3	1539	5.9	2149	0.6
14 M	0353	5.9	1017	0.6	1625	5.6	2227	0.8
15 TU	0443	5.7	1055	0.9	1716	5.3	◐ 2314	1.0
16 W	0541	5.3	1146	1.2	1819	5.0		
17 TH	0018	1.2	0654	5.0	1303	1.4	1935	4.8
18 F	0151	1.3	0818	5.0	1433	1.5	2056	4.9
19 SA	0321	1.2	0939	5.1	1553	1.4	2208	5.1
20 SU	0437	0.9	1043	5.4	1657	1.2	2304	5.4
21 M	0532	0.8	1133	5.6	1743	1.0	2350	5.5
22 TU	0614	0.7	1214	5.7	1819	0.9		
23 W	0028	5.6	0648	0.6	1250	5.7	○ 1851	0.8
24 TH	0102	5.7	0719	0.6	1322	5.7	1922	0.8
25 F	0133	5.7	0748	0.6	1351	5.7	1952	0.7
26 SA	0202	5.7	0817	0.6	1419	5.7	2022	0.8
27 SU	0232	5.7	0845	0.7	1448	5.7	2049	0.8
28 M	0302	5.6	0912	0.8	1518	5.5	2116	0.9
29 TU	0334	5.4	0939	1.0	1551	5.4	2143	1.1
30 W	0410	5.2	1008	1.2	1630	5.2	2218	1.2
31 TH	0454	5.0	1050	1.4	1717	5.0	◑ 2309	1.3

APRIL

Day	Time	m	Time	m	Time	m	Time	m
1 F	0551	4.8	1152	1.5	1821	4.7		
2 SA	0025	1.5	0708	4.7	1326	1.6	1945	4.7
3 SU	0210	1.4	0836	4.9	1454	1.4	2107	5.0
4 M	0329	1.1	0950	5.3	1559	1.1	2213	5.3
5 TU	0435	0.8	1049	5.7	1657	0.9	2307	5.6
6 W	0535	0.6	1139	5.9	1751	0.7	2355	5.9
7 TH ●	0629	0.4	1225	6.1	1842	0.5		
8 F	0039	6.1	0716	0.2	1310	6.2	1929	0.4
9 SA	0123	6.2	0801	0.2	1353	6.2	2013	0.3
10 SU	0207	6.3	0842	0.2	1435	6.1	2055	0.4
11 M	0251	6.2	0920	0.4	1519	5.9	2135	0.5
12 TU	0337	6.0	0957	0.7	1604	5.7	2215	0.7
13 W	0428	5.7	1035	1.0	1654	5.3	2301	0.9
14 TH ◐	0526	5.4	1123	1.3	1754	5.0		
15 F	0002	1.1	0635	5.1	1234	1.5	1907	4.8
16 SA	0131	1.2	0753	5.0	1401	1.6	2026	4.9
17 SU	0255	1.1	0911	5.1	1518	1.5	2138	5.0
18 M	0405	1.0	1015	5.3	1622	1.3	2235	5.3
19 TU	0500	0.8	1106	5.5	1710	1.1	2321	5.4
20 W	0541	0.8	1147	5.6	1748	1.0		
21 TH	0000	5.5	0614	0.7	1222	5.6	1822	0.9
22 F	0034	5.6	0646	0.7	1252	5.7	○ 1855	0.8
23 SA	0105	5.7	0717	0.6	1321	5.7	1927	0.7
24 SU	0136	5.7	0748	0.7	1351	5.7	1959	0.7
25 M	0207	5.7	0819	0.7	1421	5.7	2030	0.8
26 TU	0239	5.6	0849	0.8	1453	5.6	2100	0.9
27 W	0313	5.5	0919	1.0	1527	5.5	2130	1.0
28 TH	0351	5.3	0950	1.1	1606	5.3	2205	1.1
29 F	0436	5.2	1031	1.3	1653	5.1	2254	1.2
30 SA ◑	0531	5.0	1130	1.4	1753	4.9		

Chart Datum: 2·90 metres below Ordnance Datum (Newlyn)
HAT is 6·3 metres above Chart Datum

TIME ZONE (UT)
For Summer Time add ONE hour in **non-shaded areas**

SHEERNESS

LAT 51°27′N LONG 0°45′E

TIMES AND HEIGHTS OF HIGH AND LOW WATERS

Dates in amber are **SPRINGS**
Dates in grey are **NEAPS**

201

MAY

Date	Day	Time	m	Time	m	Time	m	Time	m	Moon
1	SU	0003	1.3	0641	5.0	1251	1.5	1909	4.9	
2	M	0134	1.2	0803	5.1	1416	1.4	2030	5.0	
3	TU	0256	1.0	0917	5.4	1524	1.1	2138	5.3	
4	W	0404	0.8	1019	5.7	1626	0.9	2236	5.6	
5	TH	0507	0.6	1113	5.9	1724	0.7	2328	5.9	
6	F	0603	0.4	1201	6.1	1819	0.5			●
7	SA	0016	6.1	0653	0.3	1248	6.1	1909	0.4	
8	SU	0103	6.2	0738	0.3	1332	6.2	1956	0.3	
9	M	0150	6.2	0821	0.4	1416	6.1	2041	0.3	
10	TU	0236	6.1	0900	0.5	1501	5.9	2123	0.5	
11	W	0324	5.9	0938	0.8	1546	5.6	2205	0.6	
12	TH	0414	5.7	1016	1.1	1634	5.4	2249	0.9	
13	F	0508	5.4	1100	1.3	1729	5.1	2344	1.1	◐
14	SA	0610	5.1	1159	1.5	1834	4.9			
15	SU	0058	1.2	0718	5.0	1317	1.6	1945	4.8	
16	M	0214	1.2	0830	5.0	1432	1.6	2055	4.9	
17	TU	0319	1.1	0935	5.1	1535	1.4	2156	5.1	
18	W	0413	1.0	1028	5.3	1628	1.2	2246	5.3	
19	TH	0458	0.9	1112	5.4	1712	1.1	2327	5.4	
20	F	0537	0.8	1149	5.5	1751	0.9			
21	SA	0004	5.5	0612	0.8	1222	5.6	1828	0.8	○
22	SU	0039	5.6	0646	0.8	1254	5.7	1903	0.8	
23	M	0112	5.6	0720	0.7	1327	5.7	1939	0.7	
24	TU	0146	5.6	0755	0.8	1400	5.7	2015	0.7	
25	W	0221	5.6	0830	0.8	1434	5.6	2051	0.8	
26	TH	0258	5.6	0905	1.0	1510	5.5	2127	0.9	
27	F	0338	5.5	0941	1.1	1550	5.4	2205	1.0	
28	SA	0423	5.4	1022	1.2	1636	5.3	2251	1.0	
29	SU	0516	5.2	1115	1.3	1732	5.1	2350	1.1	◑
30	M	0620	5.2	1221	1.4	1839	5.1			
31	TU	0105	1.0	0733	5.2	1338	1.3	1954	5.2	

JUNE

Date	Day	Time	m	Time	m	Time	m	Time	m	Moon
1	W	0223	0.9	0845	5.4	1450	1.2	2105	5.3	
2	TH	0333	0.8	0950	5.6	1555	1.0	2208	5.6	
3	F	0438	0.7	1047	5.8	1658	0.8	2305	5.8	
4	SA	0538	0.6	1140	5.9	1758	0.6	2357	5.9	
5	SU	0631	0.5	1228	6.0	1853	0.5			●
6	M	0047	6.0	0718	0.5	1315	6.0	1942	0.4	
7	TU	0136	6.1	0801	0.6	1401	6.0	2029	0.4	
8	W	0224	6.0	0842	0.7	1445	5.8	2113	0.5	
9	TH	0311	5.9	0920	0.9	1529	5.7	2154	0.6	
10	F	0358	5.7	0956	1.1	1614	5.5	2234	0.8	
11	SA	0446	5.4	1034	1.3	1701	5.2	2318	1.0	
12	SU	0537	5.2	1120	1.5	1754	5.0			◐
13	M	0011	1.1	0634	5.0	1219	1.6	1854	4.9	
14	TU	0118	1.2	0736	4.9	1333	1.7	2000	4.8	
15	W	0224	1.2	0840	4.9	1443	1.6	2105	4.9	
16	TH	0322	1.2	0940	5.0	1542	1.4	2202	5.0	
17	F	0413	1.1	1030	5.2	1634	1.2	2251	5.2	
18	SA	0458	1.0	1114	5.4	1720	1.1	2334	5.4	
19	SU	0540	0.9	1153	5.5	1802	0.9			
20	M	0014	5.5	0619	0.9	1231	5.6	1842	0.8	○
21	TU	0052	5.6	0657	0.8	1307	5.7	1922	0.8	
22	W	0130	5.7	0736	0.8	1343	5.7	2003	0.7	
23	TH	0207	5.7	0815	0.8	1420	5.7	2045	0.7	
24	F	0246	5.7	0855	0.9	1458	5.7	2126	0.7	
25	SA	0328	5.7	0934	1.0	1538	5.6	2206	0.8	
26	SU	0412	5.6	1014	1.1	1623	5.5	2248	0.8	
27	M	0502	5.4	1100	1.2	1713	5.4	2337	0.9	◑
28	TU	0559	5.3	1155	1.3	1813	5.3			
29	W	0037	1.0	0704	5.3	1303	1.3	1923	5.2	
30	TH	0151	1.0	0815	5.3	1418	1.2	2036	5.3	

JULY

Date	Day	Time	m	Time	m	Time	m	Time	m	Moon
1	F	0305	0.9	0923	5.4	1530	1.1	2145	5.4	
2	SA	0414	0.9	1026	5.6	1639	0.9	2248	5.6	
3	SU	0518	0.8	1123	5.7	1745	0.7	2345	5.8	
4	M	0613	0.7	1215	5.8	1842	0.6			●
5	TU	0037	5.9	0701	0.7	1303	5.9	1931	0.4	
6	W	0126	6.0	0744	0.7	1347	5.9	2017	0.4	
7	TH	0212	6.0	0824	0.8	1429	5.8	2059	0.5	
8	F	0255	5.9	0900	0.9	1510	5.7	2137	0.6	
9	SA	0337	5.7	0934	1.1	1549	5.6	2211	0.7	
10	SU	0418	5.5	1005	1.2	1629	5.4	2244	0.9	
11	M	0459	5.3	1040	1.4	1710	5.2	2319	1.1	
12	TU	0544	5.1	1122	1.5	1759	5.0			◐
13	W	0006	1.3	0635	4.9	1219	1.7	1857	4.8	
14	TH	0112	1.4	0735	4.8	1335	1.7	2004	4.7	
15	F	0226	1.4	0840	4.8	1453	1.6	2112	4.8	
16	SA	0329	1.3	0943	5.0	1556	1.4	2214	5.0	
17	SU	0423	1.2	1039	5.3	1649	1.2	2306	5.3	
18	M	0511	1.0	1126	5.5	1738	1.0	2351	5.5	
19	TU	0555	1.0	1209	5.6	1824	0.9			○
20	W	0033	5.6	0637	0.9	1249	5.7	1907	0.7	
21	TH	0113	5.8	0719	0.8	1328	5.8	1952	0.6	
22	F	0153	5.9	0801	0.8	1406	5.8	2036	0.5	
23	SA	0233	5.9	0844	0.8	1444	5.8	2119	0.5	
24	SU	0314	5.9	0924	0.8	1524	5.8	2159	0.6	
25	M	0357	5.8	1002	0.9	1607	5.7	2238	0.7	
26	TU	0443	5.6	1043	1.1	1654	5.6	2319	0.8	◑
27	W	0536	5.4	1130	1.2	1749	5.4			
28	TH	0011	1.0	0637	5.3	1233	1.3	1856	5.3	
29	F	0122	1.1	0748	5.2	1352	1.3	2014	5.2	
30	SA	0242	1.2	0901	5.2	1513	1.2	2130	5.3	
31	SU	0356	1.1	1011	5.4	1630	1.0	2240	5.5	

AUGUST

Date	Day	Time	m	Time	m	Time	m	Time	m	Moon
1	M	0504	1.0	1112	5.6	1738	0.8	2339	5.7	
2	TU	0600	0.9	1204	5.7	1833	0.6			●
3	W	0029	5.8	0646	0.9	1250	5.8	1919	0.5	
4	TH	0115	5.9	0727	0.9	1332	5.9	2001	0.5	
5	F	0156	5.9	0803	0.9	1410	5.9	2038	0.5	
6	SA	0234	5.9	0837	0.9	1446	5.8	2112	0.6	
7	SU	0311	5.7	0907	1.0	1521	5.7	2141	0.7	
8	M	0345	5.6	0935	1.1	1554	5.5	2207	0.9	
9	TU	0419	5.4	1003	1.3	1629	5.3	2235	1.1	
10	W	0455	5.2	1037	1.4	1708	5.1	2312	1.3	◐
11	TH	0538	5.0	1121	1.6	1757	4.8			
12	F	0002	1.5	0631	4.8	1222	1.7	1902	4.6	
13	SA	0117	1.6	0740	4.7	1353	1.8	2020	4.6	
14	SU	0243	1.6	0855	4.8	1516	1.6	2135	4.9	
15	M	0349	1.4	1003	5.1	1619	1.3	2236	5.2	
16	TU	0443	1.2	1058	5.4	1714	1.0	2327	5.5	
17	W	0532	1.0	1145	5.6	1804	0.8			
18	TH	0012	5.7	0617	0.9	1228	5.8	1850	0.7	○
19	F	0054	5.9	0701	0.8	1308	5.9	1936	0.5	
20	SA	0134	6.0	0745	0.7	1347	6.0	2021	0.4	
21	SU	0215	6.1	0828	0.7	1426	6.1	2103	0.4	
22	M	0256	6.1	0909	0.7	1506	6.0	2143	0.5	
23	TU	0338	5.9	0947	0.8	1548	5.9	2220	0.6	
24	W	0422	5.7	1024	1.0	1634	5.7	2257	0.9	
25	TH	0512	5.5	1109	1.1	1728	5.5	2345	1.1	◑
26	F	0612	5.2	1208	1.3	1837	5.2			
27	SA	0055	1.3	0724	5.1	1333	1.4	1958	5.1	
28	SU	0223	1.4	0843	5.1	1503	1.3	2121	5.2	
29	M	0343	1.3	0958	5.3	1624	1.0	2232	5.5	
30	TU	0453	1.2	1100	5.5	1730	0.8	2330	5.7	
31	W	0547	1.1	1150	5.7	1820	0.7			

Chart Datum: 2·90 metres below Ordnance Datum (Newlyn)
HAT is 6·3 metres above Chart Datum

TIME ZONE (UT)
For Summer Time add ONE hour in **non-shaded areas**

SHEERNESS

LAT 51°27′N LONG 0°45′E

TIMES AND HEIGHTS OF HIGH AND LOW WATERS

Dates in amber are **SPRINGS**
Dates in grey are **NEAPS**

2016

SEPTEMBER

Date	Day	Time	m	Time	m	Time	m	Time	m
1	TH	0017	5.8	0629	1.0	1234	5.8	● 1901	0.6
2	F	0058	5.9	0705	0.9	1312	5.9	1937	0.6
3	SA	0135	5.9	0738	0.9	1346	5.9	2010	0.6
4	SU	0208	5.8	0810	0.9	1419	5.8	2040	0.6
5	M	0240	5.8	0839	1.0	1450	5.7	2107	0.8
6	TU	0310	5.7	0906	1.1	1520	5.6	2132	0.9
7	W	0340	5.5	0931	1.2	1552	5.4	2158	1.1
8	TH	0413	5.3	0959	1.3	1628	5.2	2230	1.3
9	F	0450	5.1	1037	1.5	1711	4.9	◐ 2312	1.5
10	SA	0538	4.9	1129	1.7	1808	4.7		
11	SU	0015	1.7	0642	4.7	1247	1.8	1927	4.6
12	M	0151	1.8	0806	4.7	1433	1.7	2053	4.8
13	TU	0312	1.5	0924	5.0	1546	1.3	2203	5.2
14	W	0412	1.3	1026	5.4	1645	1.0	2258	5.6
15	TH	0505	1.0	1117	5.7	1739	0.8	2346	5.9
16	F	0553	0.9	1202	5.9	1829	0.6	○	
17	SA	0029	6.1	0640	0.7	1243	6.0	1915	0.4
18	SU	0111	6.2	0725	0.6	1324	6.2	1959	0.3
19	M	0152	6.2	0809	0.6	1404	6.2	2042	0.3
20	TU	0234	6.2	0850	0.6	1446	6.2	2121	0.5
21	W	0316	6.0	0929	0.7	1529	6.0	2158	0.7
22	TH	0400	5.8	1008	0.9	1616	5.8	2235	1.0
23	F	0449	5.5	1052	1.1	1712	5.5	◑ 2322	1.3
24	SA	0548	5.2	1152	1.3	1821	5.2		
25	SU	0031	1.5	0701	5.0	1320	1.4	1944	5.1
26	M	0202	1.6	0823	5.0	1452	1.3	2107	5.2
27	TU	0324	1.5	0939	5.2	1611	1.0	2217	5.5
28	W	0433	1.3	1041	5.5	1712	0.8	2312	5.7
29	TH	0525	1.1	1130	5.7	1758	0.7	2357	5.8
30	F	0605	1.0	1211	5.8	1835	0.7		

OCTOBER

Date	Day	Time	m	Time	m	Time	m	Time	m
1	SA	0035	5.8	0638	1.0	1247	5.8	● 1906	0.7
2	SU	0108	5.8	0709	0.9	1319	5.8	1936	0.7
3	M	0139	5.8	0741	0.9	1350	5.8	2005	0.7
4	TU	0208	5.8	0810	0.9	1420	5.8	2033	0.8
5	W	0236	5.7	0838	1.0	1450	5.7	2059	0.9
6	TH	0306	5.6	0904	1.1	1522	5.5	2126	1.1
7	F	0338	5.4	0931	1.2	1557	5.3	2155	1.3
8	SA	0414	5.2	1004	1.4	1638	5.1	2234	1.5
9	SU	0458	5.0	1052	1.5	1731	4.9	◐ 2331	1.7
10	M	0556	4.8	1201	1.7	1842	4.7		
11	TU	0055	1.8	0715	4.7	1342	1.6	2009	4.8
12	W	0229	1.6	0841	4.9	1507	1.3	2125	5.2
13	TH	0336	1.3	0949	5.3	1611	1.0	2225	5.6
14	F	0432	1.1	1044	5.6	1708	0.8	2316	5.9
15	SA	0524	0.9	1132	5.9	1801	0.6		
16	SU	0002	6.1	0614	0.7	1216	6.1	○ 1849	0.4
17	M	0046	6.2	0702	0.6	1259	6.2	1935	0.4
18	TU	0129	6.3	0748	0.5	1342	6.3	2018	0.4
19	W	0211	6.2	0832	0.6	1427	6.2	2058	0.5
20	TH	0255	6.0	0913	0.6	1512	6.1	2136	0.8
21	F	0339	5.8	0955	0.8	1602	5.8	2214	1.1
22	SA	0429	5.5	1040	1.0	1658	5.5	◑ 2300	1.4
23	SU	0527	5.2	1139	1.2	1805	5.2		
24	M	0005	1.6	0637	5.0	1303	1.3	1922	5.1
25	TU	0132	1.7	0755	5.0	1429	1.2	2041	5.2
26	W	0252	1.6	0910	5.1	1543	1.1	2150	5.4
27	TH	0359	1.4	1012	5.4	1641	0.9	2245	5.6
28	F	0452	1.2	1102	5.5	1726	0.8	2329	5.7
29	SA	0533	1.1	1143	5.6	1801	0.8		
30	SU	0007	5.7	0607	1.0	1219	5.7	● 1831	0.8
31	M	0039	5.8	0640	0.9	1252	5.7	1901	0.8

NOVEMBER

Date	Day	Time	m	Time	m	Time	m	Time	m
1	TU	0109	5.8	0712	0.9	1322	5.8	1931	0.8
2	W	0138	5.8	0744	0.9	1353	5.7	2001	0.8
3	TH	0207	5.7	0814	0.9	1425	5.7	2031	0.9
4	F	0238	5.7	0844	1.0	1459	5.5	2101	1.1
5	SA	0310	5.5	0913	1.1	1535	5.4	2132	1.3
6	SU	0347	5.3	0946	1.2	1616	5.2	2209	1.4
7	M	0430	5.2	1030	1.4	1706	5.0	◐ 2300	1.6
8	TU	0524	5.0	1131	1.5	1810	4.9		
9	W	0012	1.7	0633	4.9	1255	1.4	1928	5.0
10	TH	0139	1.6	0755	5.0	1423	1.3	2045	5.2
11	F	0254	1.4	0908	5.3	1533	1.0	2150	5.6
12	SA	0355	1.1	1008	5.6	1634	0.8	2245	5.9
13	SU	0453	0.9	1101	5.8	1731	0.6	2335	6.0
14	M	0548	0.7	1150	6.1	1823	0.5	○	
15	TU	0022	6.2	0640	0.6	1238	6.2	1911	0.4
16	W	0107	6.2	0729	0.5	1324	6.3	1955	0.5
17	TH	0152	6.1	0816	0.5	1411	6.2	2037	0.6
18	F	0237	6.0	0901	0.5	1459	6.1	2116	0.8
19	SA	0322	5.8	0945	0.7	1549	5.8	2155	1.1
20	SU	0411	5.5	1030	0.9	1643	5.5	2239	1.3
21	M	0505	5.3	1123	1.1	1744	5.3	◑ 2333	1.6
22	TU	0607	5.0	1232	1.2	1851	5.1		
23	W	0046	1.7	0717	4.9	1349	1.3	2002	5.1
24	TH	0205	1.7	0828	5.0	1457	1.2	2110	5.2
25	F	0312	1.6	0933	5.1	1555	1.1	2208	5.3
26	SA	0408	1.4	1027	5.3	1643	1.0	2256	5.4
27	SU	0455	1.2	1112	5.4	1722	0.9	2335	5.5
28	M	0535	1.1	1150	5.5	1757	0.9		
29	TU	0009	5.6	0611	1.0	1226	5.6	● 1829	0.9
30	W	0042	5.7	0647	0.9	1259	5.6	1902	0.8

DECEMBER

Date	Day	Time	m	Time	m	Time	m	Time	m
1	TH	0113	5.7	0721	0.8	1332	5.7	1935	0.9
2	F	0144	5.7	0755	0.8	1406	5.6	2009	0.9
3	SA	0217	5.7	0830	0.9	1441	5.6	2042	1.0
4	SU	0251	5.6	0904	1.0	1519	5.5	2117	1.1
5	M	0328	5.4	0940	1.1	1600	5.4	2154	1.3
6	TU	0410	5.3	1020	1.1	1648	5.2	2239	1.4
7	W	0500	5.2	1111	1.2	1744	5.1	◐ 2338	1.5
8	TH	0600	5.1	1216	1.2	1852	5.1		
9	F	0050	1.5	0712	5.1	1337	1.2	2006	5.2
10	SA	0209	1.4	0827	5.2	1453	1.0	2115	5.4
11	SU	0318	1.2	0934	5.5	1601	0.8	2216	5.7
12	M	0422	1.0	1034	5.7	1703	0.7	2311	5.8
13	TU	0524	0.8	1129	5.9	1800	0.6		
14	W	0002	6.0	0622	0.6	1221	6.0	○ 1850	0.6
15	TH	0050	6.0	0715	0.5	1311	6.1	1937	0.6
16	F	0137	6.0	0805	0.4	1400	6.1	2020	0.7
17	SA	0222	5.9	0851	0.4	1448	6.0	2100	0.8
18	SU	0307	5.8	0935	0.6	1536	5.8	2137	1.0
19	M	0353	5.6	1016	0.7	1624	5.6	2215	1.2
20	TU	0440	5.4	1059	0.9	1715	5.3	2257	1.4
21	W	0531	5.2	1148	1.1	1810	5.1	◑ 2350	1.6
22	TH	0629	5.0	1249	1.3	1911	4.9		
23	F	0059	1.7	0734	4.8	1358	1.3	2015	4.9
24	SA	0214	1.7	0842	4.8	1500	1.3	2119	4.9
25	SU	0319	1.6	0944	5.0	1554	1.2	2215	5.1
26	M	0415	1.4	1037	5.1	1642	1.1	2301	5.3
27	TU	0504	1.2	1122	5.3	1724	1.0	2341	5.4
28	W	0547	1.0	1202	5.4	1803	0.9		
29	TH	0018	5.6	0625	0.9	1240	5.5	● 1839	0.9
30	F	0053	5.6	0703	0.8	1315	5.6	1915	0.9
31	SA	0128	5.7	0742	0.8	1351	5.7	1952	0.8

Chart Datum: 2·90 metres below Ordnance Datum (Newlyn)
HAT is 6·3 metres above Chart Datum

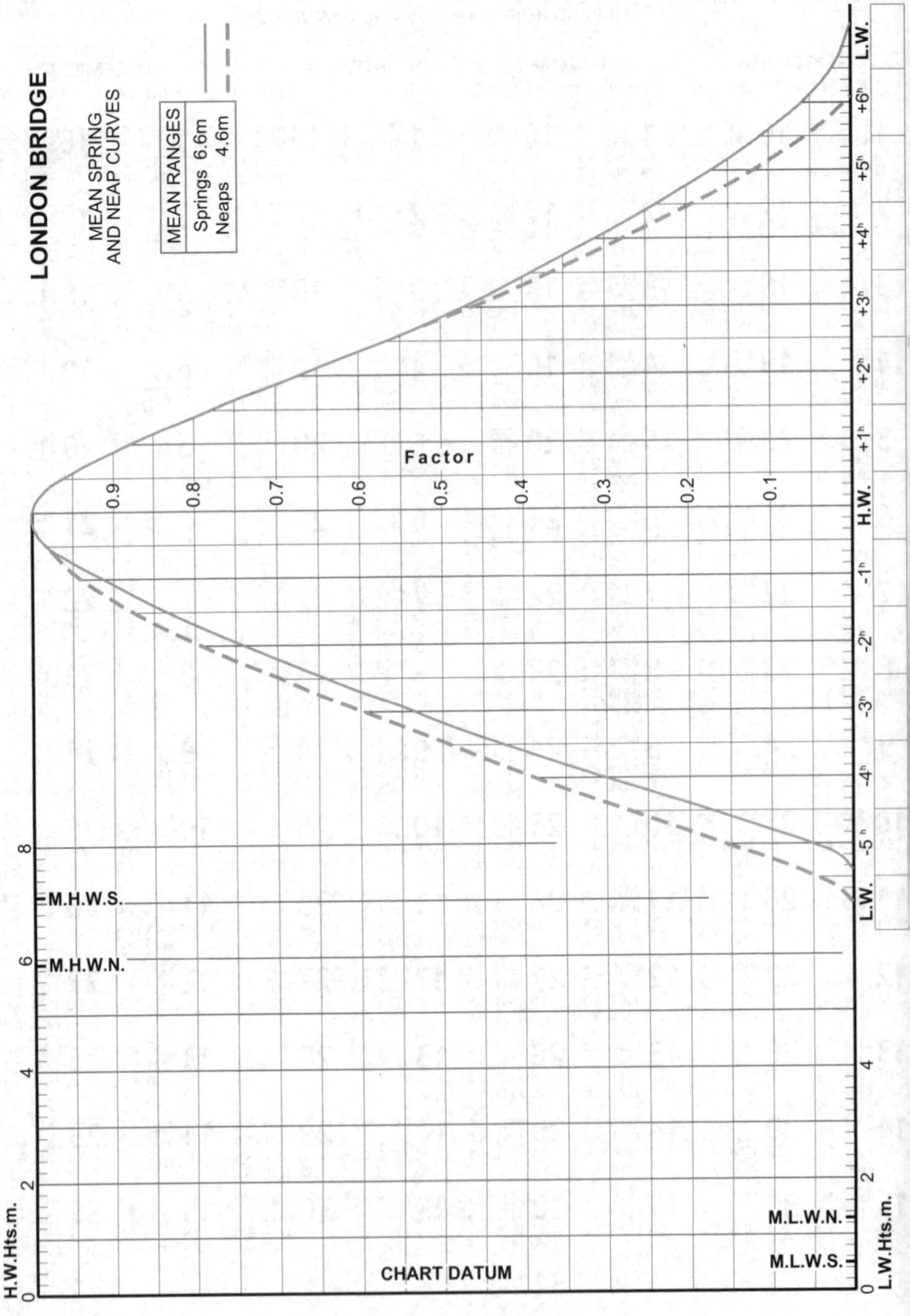
LONDON BRIDGE
MEAN SPRING AND NEAP CURVES
MEAN RANGES
Springs 6.6m
Neaps 4.6m
Factor
0.9
0.8
0.7
0.6
0.5
0.4
0.3
0.2
0.1
H.W.Hts.m.
0
2
4
6
8
M.H.W.S.
M.H.W.N.
CHART DATUM
M.L.W.N.
M.L.W.S.
L.W.Hts.m.
L.W.
-5h
-4h
-3h
-2h
-1h
H.W.
+1h
+2h
+3h
+4h
+5h
+6h
L.W.

TIME ZONE (UT)
For Summer Time add ONE hour in **non-shaded areas**

LONDON BRIDGE

LAT 51°30'N LONG 0°05'W

TIMES AND HEIGHTS OF HIGH AND LOW WATERS

Dates in amber are **SPRINGS**
Dates in grey are **NEAPS**

2016

JANUARY

Date	Day	Time	m	Time	m	Time	m	Time	m	Moon
1	F	0547	6.3	1210	1.0	1816	6.2			
2	SA	0015	1.5	0624	6.0	1248	1.1	1900	6.0	◑
3	SU	0057	1.6	0712	5.8	1333	1.3	1958	5.8	
4	M	0148	1.8	0829	5.6	1437	1.5	2108	5.8	
5	TU	0301	1.9	0946	5.7	1602	1.5	2214	5.9	
6	W	0438	1.7	1049	6.0	1706	1.3	2316	6.2	
7	TH	0543	1.4	1146	6.3	1804	1.1			
8	F	0011	6.5	0641	1.1	1236	6.6	1857	1.0	
9	SA	0100	6.7	0735	0.9	1321	6.8	1948	0.9	
10	SU	0145	6.8	0826	0.7	1404	7.0	2036	0.9	●
11	M	0227	6.9	0914	0.6	1446	7.2	2122	0.8	
12	TU	0308	7.0	0959	0.4	1528	7.3	2205	0.8	
13	W	0348	7.0	1041	0.3	1610	7.3	2245	0.7	
14	TH	0427	7.0	1119	0.4	1652	7.1	2323	0.8	
15	F	0508	6.9	1153	0.5	1737	6.9			
16	SA	0003	0.9	0551	6.8	1229	0.6	1826	6.7	◐
17	SU	0047	1.1	0641	6.6	1313	0.8	1924	6.5	
18	M	0140	1.3	0743	6.4	1413	1.0	2032	6.3	
19	TU	0248	1.4	0859	6.3	1526	1.1	2142	6.3	
20	W	0405	1.4	1013	6.3	1641	1.2	2255	6.3	
21	TH	0526	1.2	1125	6.5	1804	1.1			
22	F	0005	6.5	0641	0.9	1229	6.7	1909	1.0	
23	SA	0102	6.7	0742	0.6	1323	6.9	2002	0.9	
24	SU	0150	6.8	0833	0.5	1409	7.0	2047	0.9	○
25	M	0233	6.9	0918	0.4	1451	7.1	2127	0.9	
26	TU	0311	7.0	0957	0.5	1529	7.1	2201	1.0	
27	W	0345	6.9	1029	0.5	1604	7.0	2226	1.0	
28	TH	0417	6.9	1052	0.6	1636	6.8	2249	1.0	
29	F	0447	6.7	1114	0.7	1707	6.6	2317	1.1	
30	SA	0517	6.5	1141	0.8	1738	6.4	2347	1.2	
31	SU	0549	6.3	1209	0.9	1813	6.2			

FEBRUARY

Date	Day	Time	m	Time	m	Time	m	Time	m	Moon
1	M	0019	1.4	0626	6.1	1242	1.1	1854	6.0	◑
2	TU	0057	1.5	0713	5.8	1322	1.4	1950	5.7	
3	W	0147	1.7	0821	5.6	1423	1.6	2115	5.7	
4	TH	0303	1.8	0957	5.7	1612	1.6	2231	5.9	
5	F	0457	1.5	1107	6.1	1725	1.3	2338	6.3	
6	SA	0606	1.2	1206	6.5	1827	1.1			
7	SU	0035	6.6	0709	0.9	1258	6.8	1928	1.0	
8	M	0125	6.9	0809	0.6	1346	7.1	2025	0.8	●
9	TU	0210	7.0	0902	0.4	1430	7.3	2115	0.7	
10	W	0253	7.2	0949	0.2	1514	7.4	2200	0.6	
11	TH	0334	7.3	1032	0.1	1556	7.4	2241	0.5	
12	F	0414	7.3	1110	0.1	1638	7.3	2319	0.6	
13	SA	0454	7.2	1143	0.2	1721	7.0	2354	0.7	
14	SU	0535	7.0	1214	0.5	1806	6.7			
15	M	0032	0.9	0622	6.8	1251	0.7	1858	6.4	◐
16	TU	0117	1.1	0719	6.5	1341	1.0	2002	6.2	
17	W	0217	1.3	0831	6.3	1452	1.3	2115	6.0	
18	TH	0335	1.4	0950	6.2	1611	1.4	2235	6.1	
19	F	0459	1.3	1110	6.3	1741	1.3	2351	6.3	
20	SA	0625	0.9	1218	6.6	1851	1.0			
21	SU	0049	6.6	0726	0.6	1312	6.8	1943	0.9	
22	M	0136	6.8	0814	0.5	1356	7.0	2027	0.9	○
23	TU	0216	6.9	0856	0.4	1435	7.0	2106	0.9	
24	W	0251	7.0	0932	0.5	1509	7.0	2139	0.9	
25	TH	0323	7.0	1001	0.5	1539	7.0	2205	0.9	
26	F	0352	7.0	1024	0.5	1607	6.9	2229	0.9	
27	SA	0420	6.9	1047	0.5	1635	6.8	2256	0.9	
28	SU	0450	6.8	1112	0.6	1705	6.6	2323	1.0	
29	M	0520	6.6	1137	0.8	1738	6.4	2349	1.1	

MARCH

Date	Day	Time	m	Time	m	Time	m	Time	m	Moon
1	TU	0555	6.3	1203	1.0	1815	6.1			◑
2	W	0019	1.3	0637	6.1	1238	1.2	1902	5.9	
3	TH	0102	1.4	0731	5.8	1328	1.5	2009	5.7	
4	F	0205	1.6	0856	5.7	1454	1.7	2145	5.7	
5	SA	0404	1.6	1026	6.0	1645	1.4	2303	6.1	
6	SU	0528	1.2	1135	6.5	1755	1.1			
7	M	0006	6.6	0640	0.8	1233	6.9	1905	0.9	
8	TU	0100	6.9	0748	0.5	1323	7.2	2007	0.7	
9	W	0147	7.2	0843	0.3	1410	7.4	2100	0.6	●
10	TH	0231	7.4	0931	0.1	1454	7.5	2146	0.4	
11	F	0313	7.5	1014	0.0	1537	7.5	2228	0.3	
12	SA	0355	7.5	1052	0.0	1619	7.4	2306	0.4	
13	SU	0435	7.5	1124	0.2	1701	7.1	2340	0.5	
14	M	0518	7.2	1152	0.5	1745	6.7			
15	TU	0014	0.7	0604	6.9	1226	0.8	1834	6.4	◐
16	W	0055	0.9	0658	6.6	1311	1.1	1933	6.1	
17	TH	0150	1.2	0808	6.3	1420	1.5	2048	5.9	
18	F	0306	1.3	0927	6.1	1543	1.5	2211	5.9	
19	SA	0430	1.2	1050	6.3	1713	1.4	2329	6.2	
20	SU	0602	0.9	1159	6.6	1826	1.1			
21	M	0028	6.6	0702	0.6	1252	6.8	1918	0.9	
22	TU	0114	6.8	0748	0.5	1335	6.9	2001	0.9	
23	W	0152	6.9	0826	0.5	1411	6.9	2039	0.8	○
24	TH	0226	7.0	0859	0.5	1443	7.0	2112	0.8	
25	F	0256	7.0	0928	0.5	1511	7.0	2141	0.8	
26	SA	0324	7.1	0953	0.5	1537	7.0	2208	0.7	
27	SU	0353	7.0	1018	0.5	1606	6.9	2235	0.8	
28	M	0423	6.9	1045	0.6	1637	6.7	2302	0.9	
29	TU	0455	6.7	1109	0.8	1710	6.5	2326	1.0	
30	W	0530	6.5	1135	0.9	1746	6.2	2353	1.0	
31	TH	0611	6.3	1208	1.1	1831	6.0			◑

APRIL

Date	Day	Time	m	Time	m	Time	m	Time	m	Moon
1	F	0033	1.1	0703	6.0	1256	1.3	1931	5.8	
2	SA	0131	1.3	0816	5.9	1410	1.6	2101	5.8	
3	SU	0312	1.4	0949	6.1	1609	1.4	2226	6.1	
4	M	0451	1.1	1102	6.5	1723	1.1	2334	6.6	
5	TU	0606	0.7	1203	6.9	1836	0.8			
6	W	0031	7.0	0721	0.4	1257	7.2	1944	0.7	
7	TH	0121	7.2	0819	0.2	1346	7.4	2039	0.5	●
8	F	0207	7.5	0908	0.1	1432	7.5	2127	0.3	
9	SA	0250	7.6	0952	0.1	1516	7.5	2210	0.2	
10	SU	0334	7.7	1030	0.1	1559	7.3	2249	0.2	
11	M	0417	7.6	1102	0.3	1642	7.1	2323	0.4	
12	TU	0501	7.3	1130	0.6	1726	6.7	2356	0.6	
13	W	0548	7.0	1202	0.9	1813	6.4			
14	TH	0034	0.8	0641	6.6	1246	1.2	1908	6.1	◐
15	F	0125	1.1	0746	6.3	1349	1.5	2019	5.9	
16	SA	0237	1.2	0900	6.1	1511	1.6	2138	5.9	
17	SU	0356	1.2	1018	6.2	1633	1.4	2255	6.1	
18	M	0515	1.0	1129	6.5	1747	1.2	2356	6.4	
19	TU	0622	0.7	1223	6.7	1843	1.0			
20	W	0043	6.7	0709	0.6	1306	6.8	1928	0.9	
21	TH	0123	6.8	0747	0.6	1342	6.8	2007	0.8	
22	F	0157	6.9	0822	0.6	1414	6.9	2043	0.8	○
23	SA	0228	7.0	0853	0.6	1442	6.9	2115	0.7	
24	SU	0258	7.1	0923	0.5	1510	6.9	2146	0.7	
25	M	0328	7.1	0951	0.6	1541	6.9	2216	0.7	
26	TU	0400	7.0	1020	0.6	1614	6.7	2244	0.8	
27	W	0434	6.8	1047	0.8	1648	6.5	2309	0.8	
28	TH	0511	6.6	1116	0.9	1726	6.3	2338	0.9	
29	F	0554	6.4	1151	1.1	1811	6.1			
30	SA	0017	1.0	0645	6.2	1239	1.3	1908	5.9	◑

Chart Datum: 3·20 metres below Ordnance Datum (Newlyn)
HAT is 7·7 metres above Chart Datum

TIME ZONE (UT)
For Summer Time add ONE hour in **non-shaded areas**

LONDON BRIDGE

LAT 51°30'N LONG 0°05'W

TIMES AND HEIGHTS OF HIGH AND LOW WATERS

Dates in amber are **SPRINGS**
Dates in grey are **NEAPS**

2016

MAY

Date	Day	Time	m	Time	m	Time	m	Time	m
1	SU	0113	1.1	0753	6.1	1351	1.5	2027	5.9
2	M	0241	1.2	0918	6.2	1535	1.4	2152	6.2
3	TU	0418	0.9	1030	6.6	1651	1.1	2301	6.6
4	W	0530	0.7	1134	6.9	1805	0.8		
5	TH	0001	6.9	0648	0.5	1231	7.2	1916	0.7
6	F	0054	7.2	0751	0.3	1322	7.3	● 2014	0.5
7	SA	0142	7.4	0842	0.2	1410	7.3	2105	0.3
8	SU	0229	7.6	0928	0.3	1455	7.3	2150	0.2
9	M	0314	7.6	1008	0.4	1540	7.2	2232	0.2
10	TU	0359	7.5	1042	0.5	1624	7.0	2308	0.3
11	W	0445	7.3	1111	0.8	1708	6.7	2342	0.5
12	TH	0532	7.0	1143	1.0	1754	6.4		
13	F	0017	0.7	0623	6.6	1224	1.2	◐ 1844	6.1
14	SA	0103	0.9	0721	6.3	1317	1.5	1946	5.9
15	SU	0205	1.1	0827	6.1	1429	1.6	2057	5.9
16	M	0317	1.1	0935	6.1	1546	1.5	2207	6.0
17	TU	0422	1.0	1043	6.2	1655	1.3	2311	6.2
18	W	0522	0.9	1142	6.4	1756	1.1		
19	TH	0004	6.5	0615	0.8	1230	6.6	1847	1.0
20	F	0048	6.7	0702	0.7	1309	6.7	1932	0.8
21	SA	0126	6.8	0744	0.7	1344	6.8	○ 2013	0.7
22	SU	0201	6.9	0822	0.7	1416	6.8	2051	0.7
23	M	0234	7.0	0857	0.7	1448	6.9	2127	0.6
24	TU	0306	7.0	0929	0.7	1522	6.8	2201	0.6
25	W	0341	7.0	1001	0.7	1557	6.7	2232	0.6
26	TH	0418	6.9	1032	0.8	1634	6.6	2301	0.7
27	F	0458	6.7	1106	0.9	1713	6.4	2332	0.8
28	SA	0542	6.6	1145	1.0	1758	6.3		
29	SU	0012	0.8	0632	6.4	1234	1.2	◑ 1852	6.2
30	M	0104	0.9	0735	6.3	1340	1.4	2001	6.1
31	TU	0221	1.0	0851	6.4	1505	1.3	2120	6.3

JUNE

Date	Day	Time	m	Time	m	Time	m	Time	m
1	W	0347	0.9	1001	6.6	1622	1.1	2230	6.6
2	TH	0458	0.7	1106	6.8	1736	0.9	2333	6.9
3	F	0613	0.6	1206	7.0	1850	0.7		
4	SA	0030	7.1	0723	0.5	1301	7.1	1951	0.5
5	SU	0122	7.3	0818	0.5	1351	7.1	● 2045	0.3
6	M	0211	7.4	0906	0.5	1439	7.2	2133	0.2
7	TU	0259	7.5	0949	0.6	1525	7.1	2217	0.2
8	W	0345	7.4	1026	0.7	1609	7.0	2256	0.3
9	TH	0431	7.2	1057	0.9	1652	6.8	2330	0.5
10	F	0516	6.9	1127	1.0	1734	6.5		
11	SA	0002	0.7	0602	6.6	1202	1.2	1818	6.3
12	SU	0039	0.8	0651	6.3	1245	1.4	◐ 1909	6.0
13	M	0127	1.0	0747	6.1	1338	1.6	2010	5.9
14	TU	0227	1.1	0847	6.0	1447	1.6	2116	5.9
15	W	0332	1.1	0948	6.0	1602	1.5	2219	6.0
16	TH	0432	1.0	1049	6.1	1706	1.3	2318	6.3
17	F	0528	0.9	1145	6.4	1804	1.1		
18	SA	0010	6.5	0621	0.8	1234	6.6	1857	0.9
19	SU	0056	6.7	0711	0.8	1316	6.7	1945	0.8
20	M	0136	6.8	0756	0.8	1355	6.8	○ 2029	0.7
21	TU	0213	6.9	0837	0.8	1432	6.8	2111	0.6
22	W	0250	7.0	0915	0.8	1509	6.8	2151	0.5
23	TH	0327	7.0	0952	0.7	1546	6.8	2229	0.5
24	F	0406	7.0	1029	0.7	1624	6.7	2304	0.5
25	SA	0447	6.9	1107	0.8	1703	6.6	2336	0.6
26	SU	0530	6.8	1146	0.9	1746	6.5		
27	M	0013	0.7	0618	6.6	1232	1.1	◑ 1835	6.4
28	TU	0059	0.8	0715	6.5	1328	1.2	1935	6.3
29	W	0200	0.9	0824	6.4	1438	1.3	2050	6.3
30	TH	0316	0.9	0933	6.4	1554	1.2	2202	6.5

JULY

Date	Day	Time	m	Time	m	Time	m	Time	m
1	F	0429	0.9	1040	6.5	1709	1.0	2308	6.7
2	SA	0544	0.8	1146	6.7	1826	0.8		
3	SU	0011	6.9	0658	0.7	1246	6.8	1931	0.5
4	M	0108	7.1	0757	0.7	1339	6.9	● 2028	0.3
5	TU	0159	7.2	0848	0.7	1427	7.0	2118	0.2
6	W	0247	7.3	0933	0.7	1512	7.1	2203	0.2
7	TH	0332	7.3	1012	0.8	1554	7.0	2243	0.3
8	F	0415	7.2	1045	0.9	1633	6.9	2316	0.4
9	SA	0456	7.0	1112	1.0	1711	6.7	2343	0.6
10	SU	0535	6.7	1140	1.1	1748	6.4		
11	M	0010	0.7	0614	6.4	1213	1.3	1826	6.2
12	TU	0044	0.9	0658	6.1	1252	1.4	◐ 1914	6.0
13	W	0127	1.1	0751	5.9	1340	1.6	2018	5.8
14	TH	0225	1.3	0852	5.8	1448	1.7	2127	5.8
15	F	0340	1.3	0956	5.9	1616	1.6	2231	6.0
16	SA	0446	1.2	1059	6.1	1723	1.3	2332	6.3
17	SU	0545	1.1	1158	6.4	1822	1.0		
18	M	0025	6.6	0640	0.9	1249	6.6	1917	0.8
19	TU	0111	6.8	0733	0.9	1334	6.8	○ 2009	0.7
20	W	0154	6.9	0821	0.9	1415	6.9	2057	0.5
21	TH	0234	7.1	0907	0.8	1455	7.0	2143	0.4
22	F	0314	7.2	0950	0.7	1534	7.0	2225	0.3
23	SA	0354	7.2	1031	0.7	1612	7.0	2304	0.3
24	SU	0434	7.1	1109	0.7	1650	6.9	2338	0.4
25	M	0516	7.0	1146	0.8	1731	6.8		
26	TU	0010	0.5	0600	6.7	1225	1.0	◑ 1815	6.7
27	W	0047	0.7	0652	6.5	1312	1.1	1910	6.5
28	TH	0136	0.9	0756	6.3	1412	1.3	2020	6.4
29	F	0246	1.1	0907	6.2	1527	1.3	2136	6.4
30	SA	0402	1.1	1018	6.3	1645	1.1	2249	6.5
31	SU	0521	1.1	1131	6.4	1806	0.9	2359	6.7

AUGUST

Date	Day	Time	m	Time	m	Time	m	Time	m
1	M	0641	0.9	1236	6.7	1917	0.6		
2	TU	0059	7.0	0741	0.8	1329	6.9	● 2013	0.3
3	W	0150	7.1	0831	0.7	1415	7.0	2102	0.2
4	TH	0235	7.2	0916	0.8	1457	7.1	2146	0.2
5	F	0317	7.2	0955	0.8	1535	7.1	2223	0.3
6	SA	0355	7.2	1028	0.9	1610	7.0	2253	0.4
7	SU	0430	7.0	1052	1.0	1643	6.9	2315	0.6
8	M	0503	6.8	1115	1.0	1714	6.7	2337	0.7
9	TU	0534	6.5	1143	1.1	1746	6.4		
10	W	0004	0.9	0607	6.2	1214	1.3	◐ 1821	6.2
11	TH	0035	1.1	0646	6.0	1250	1.5	1906	5.9
12	F	0114	1.4	0740	5.7	1337	1.7	2015	5.7
13	SA	0212	1.6	0859	5.6	1454	1.8	2142	5.7
14	SU	0356	1.6	1014	5.8	1640	1.5	2252	6.0
15	M	0508	1.3	1123	6.2	1747	1.1	2353	6.4
16	TU	0610	1.1	1221	6.5	1849	0.8		
17	W	0044	6.8	0709	0.9	1310	6.8	1948	0.6
18	TH	0131	7.0	0804	0.9	1354	7.0	○ 2040	0.4
19	F	0214	7.2	0855	0.8	1435	7.1	2128	0.3
20	SA	0255	7.3	0941	0.7	1515	7.2	2212	0.2
21	SU	0336	7.4	1023	0.6	1554	7.3	2251	0.1
22	M	0416	7.3	1101	0.6	1632	7.2	2326	0.3
23	TU	0457	7.1	1137	0.7	1712	7.1	2355	0.5
24	W	0540	6.8	1212	0.9	1756	6.9		
25	TH	0027	0.7	0627	6.5	1253	1.1	◑ 1847	6.6
26	F	0110	1.0	0727	6.2	1347	1.2	1954	6.4
27	SA	0216	1.3	0841	6.0	1501	1.3	2115	6.3
28	SU	0338	1.4	0959	6.1	1623	1.2	2234	6.4
29	M	0503	1.3	1118	6.3	1751	0.9	2348	6.7
30	TU	0625	1.0	1224	6.6	1903	0.5		
31	W	0048	7.0	0723	0.8	1316	6.9	1956	0.3

Chart Datum: 3·20 metres below Ordnance Datum (Newlyn)
HAT is 7·7 metres above Chart Datum

TIME ZONE (UT)
For Summer Time add ONE hour in **non-shaded areas**

LONDON BRIDGE

LAT 51°30′N LONG 0°05′W

TIMES AND HEIGHTS OF HIGH AND LOW WATERS

Dates in amber are **SPRINGS**
Dates in grey are **NEAPS**

2016

SEPTEMBER

Date	Day	Time	m	Time	m	Time	m	Time	m
1	TH	0137	7.1	0812	0.8	1359	7.0	● 2042	0.3
2	F	0218	7.2	0854	0.8	1437	7.1	2121	0.3
3	SA	0256	7.2	0932	0.8	1511	7.1	2155	0.4
4	SU	0329	7.1	1003	0.9	1542	7.1	2221	0.5
5	M	0359	7.0	1027	0.9	1612	7.0	2241	0.6
6	TU	0427	6.8	1049	0.9	1641	6.8	2303	0.7
7	W	0456	6.6	1115	1.0	1711	6.6	2328	0.9
8	TH	0526	6.4	1142	1.2	1744	6.3	2353	1.1
9	F	0601	6.1	1209	1.3	1823	6.1	◐	
10	SA	0023	1.3	0644	5.8	1246	1.5	1913	5.8
11	SU	0108	1.6	0745	5.6	1343	1.7	2032	5.6
12	M	0224	1.8	0923	5.6	1546	1.7	2207	5.9
13	TU	0427	1.6	1043	6.0	1709	1.2	2316	6.3
14	W	0536	1.2	1147	6.5	1816	0.8		
15	TH	0013	6.8	0640	1.0	1240	6.8	1921	0.6
16	F	0103	7.1	0742	0.8	1326	7.1	○ 2017	0.4
17	SA	0148	7.3	0835	0.7	1410	7.3	2107	0.2
18	SU	0232	7.5	0923	0.6	1451	7.4	2151	0.1
19	M	0314	7.5	1007	0.5	1531	7.5	2231	0.2
20	TU	0355	7.4	1046	0.5	1611	7.5	2305	0.3
21	W	0436	7.1	1122	0.6	1652	7.3	2334	0.6
22	TH	0518	6.8	1156	0.7	1737	7.0		
23	F	0004	0.9	0605	6.4	1235	0.9	◑ 1828	6.7
24	SA	0046	1.2	0702	6.1	1325	1.2	1935	6.4
25	SU	0150	1.5	0816	5.9	1438	1.3	2055	6.2
26	M	0314	1.6	0939	6.0	1601	1.2	2216	6.3
27	TU	0442	1.4	1059	6.2	1732	0.9	2331	6.7
28	W	0602	1.1	1204	6.6	1841	0.6		
29	TH	0030	7.0	0659	0.9	1254	6.9	1931	0.4
30	F	0116	7.1	0746	0.8	1336	7.0	2013	0.4

OCTOBER

Date	Day	Time	m	Time	m	Time	m	Time	m
1	SA	0155	7.1	0827	0.8	1411	7.0	● 2049	0.5
2	SU	0229	7.1	0903	0.8	1443	7.1	2119	0.5
3	M	0259	7.1	0933	0.8	1512	7.1	2143	0.6
4	TU	0326	7.0	0959	0.8	1541	7.1	2206	0.6
5	W	0354	6.9	1024	0.8	1611	6.9	2231	0.7
6	TH	0423	6.7	1050	0.9	1642	6.7	2256	0.9
7	F	0454	6.5	1115	1.1	1715	6.5	2320	1.1
8	SA	0527	6.2	1139	1.2	1753	6.2	2348	1.3
9	SU	0608	6.0	1212	1.3	1840	6.0	◐	
10	M	0030	1.5	0702	5.7	1303	1.5	1944	5.8
11	TU	0132	1.8	0822	5.6	1424	1.6	2119	5.9
12	W	0337	1.8	0958	5.9	1627	1.3	2236	6.3
13	TH	0456	1.3	1108	6.4	1736	0.9	2338	6.8
14	F	0604	1.0	1205	6.8	1846	0.6		
15	SA	0032	7.2	0712	0.8	1256	7.2	1948	0.4
16	SU	0121	7.4	0810	0.7	1342	7.4	○ 2041	0.3
17	M	0206	7.5	0901	0.5	1426	7.6	2127	0.3
18	TU	0251	7.5	0947	0.4	1509	7.6	2208	0.3
19	W	0334	7.4	1028	0.4	1551	7.6	2243	0.5
20	TH	0417	7.1	1105	0.5	1635	7.4	2313	0.7
21	F	0500	6.8	1140	0.6	1722	7.1	2343	1.0
22	SA	0546	6.4	1217	0.8	1814	6.7	◑	
23	SU	0024	1.3	0641	6.1	1306	1.1	1918	6.4
24	M	0123	1.6	0751	5.9	1415	1.2	2032	6.2
25	TU	0245	1.7	0910	5.9	1534	1.2	2148	6.3
26	W	0408	1.6	1027	6.1	1653	1.0	2302	6.5
27	TH	0526	1.3	1133	6.4	1804	0.7		
28	F	0002	6.8	0626	1.0	1225	6.7	1855	0.6
29	SA	0049	6.9	0713	0.9	1306	6.8	1935	0.6
30	SU	0127	6.9	0754	0.9	1342	6.9	● 2010	0.6
31	M	0200	7.0	0831	0.8	1414	7.0	2040	0.7

NOVEMBER

Date	Day	Time	m	Time	m	Time	m	Time	m
1	TU	0229	7.0	0903	0.8	1444	7.1	2108	0.7
2	W	0257	7.0	0933	0.8	1514	7.1	2135	0.7
3	TH	0326	6.9	1001	0.8	1545	7.0	2203	0.8
4	F	0357	6.8	1029	0.9	1617	6.8	2230	0.9
5	SA	0429	6.6	1054	1.0	1653	6.6	2257	1.1
6	SU	0504	6.4	1120	1.0	1732	6.4	2328	1.2
7	M	0544	6.2	1153	1.1	1819	6.2	◐	
8	TU	0009	1.4	0634	5.9	1241	1.2	1917	6.1
9	W	0107	1.6	0741	5.8	1349	1.4	2037	6.1
10	TH	0245	1.7	0912	5.9	1541	1.2	2157	6.4
11	F	0416	1.4	1028	6.3	1656	0.9	2302	6.8
12	SA	0528	1.1	1130	6.8	1805	0.6		
13	SU	0001	7.1	0639	0.9	1225	7.1	1915	0.5
14	M	0054	7.3	0744	0.7	1315	7.4	○ 2013	0.4
15	TU	0143	7.4	0838	0.5	1402	7.6	2102	0.4
16	W	0230	7.4	0927	0.4	1449	7.6	2146	0.5
17	TH	0315	7.3	1011	0.3	1535	7.6	2224	0.6
18	F	0400	7.1	1051	0.4	1621	7.4	2256	0.9
19	SA	0445	6.8	1127	0.5	1709	7.1	2328	1.1
20	SU	0531	6.5	1204	0.7	1800	6.8		
21	M	0006	1.3	0621	6.2	1248	1.0	◑ 1857	6.4
22	TU	0056	1.6	0722	6.0	1347	1.1	2002	6.2
23	W	0205	1.7	0832	5.9	1457	1.2	2110	6.2
24	TH	0323	1.7	0943	6.0	1603	1.1	2218	6.3
25	F	0435	1.5	1050	6.2	1705	1.0	2322	6.4
26	SA	0539	1.3	1146	6.4	1801	0.9		
27	SU	0013	6.6	0632	1.1	1232	6.6	1848	0.8
28	M	0055	6.7	0718	1.0	1312	6.8	1930	0.8
29	TU	0131	6.8	0759	0.8	1347	6.9	● 2007	0.8
30	W	0203	6.9	0836	0.8	1420	7.0	2041	0.8

DECEMBER

Date	Day	Time	m	Time	m	Time	m	Time	m
1	TH	0233	6.9	0911	0.8	1451	7.0	2112	0.8
2	F	0305	6.9	0944	0.8	1524	7.0	2142	0.9
3	SA	0338	6.8	1015	0.8	1559	6.9	2212	0.9
4	SU	0413	6.7	1043	0.8	1636	6.8	2244	1.0
5	M	0449	6.5	1111	0.9	1717	6.6	2319	1.1
6	TU	0529	6.4	1145	0.9	1802	6.5		
7	W	0001	1.3	0616	6.2	1230	1.0	◐ 1855	6.3
8	TH	0054	1.5	0713	6.1	1328	1.1	2003	6.2
9	F	0207	1.6	0829	6.1	1454	1.1	2121	6.4
10	SA	0336	1.5	0950	6.3	1617	1.0	2229	6.6
11	SU	0454	1.3	1057	6.6	1728	0.8	2332	6.8
12	M	0610	1.0	1158	7.0	1843	0.7		
13	TU	0030	7.0	0719	0.7	1253	7.2	1947	0.6
14	W	0123	7.1	0817	0.5	1344	7.4	○ 2040	0.6
15	TH	0213	7.2	0909	0.3	1433	7.5	2127	0.6
16	F	0301	7.2	0957	0.3	1522	7.5	2209	0.8
17	SA	0347	7.1	1040	0.3	1609	7.4	2245	0.9
18	SU	0432	6.9	1118	0.4	1655	7.1	2317	1.1
19	M	0515	6.7	1152	0.6	1742	6.8	2349	1.3
20	TU	0559	6.4	1227	0.8	1831	6.5		
21	W	0027	1.4	0647	6.1	1310	1.0	◑ 1923	6.2
22	TH	0115	1.6	0745	5.9	1406	1.2	2022	6.0
23	F	0218	1.8	0850	5.8	1509	1.2	2123	6.0
24	SA	0336	1.8	0955	5.9	1611	1.2	2226	6.0
25	SU	0444	1.6	1058	6.1	1709	1.1	2327	6.2
26	M	0545	1.3	1154	6.3	1804	1.0		
27	TU	0019	6.4	0640	1.1	1241	6.6	1855	0.9
28	W	0102	6.6	0729	0.9	1322	6.7	1941	0.9
29	TH	0141	6.7	0813	0.8	1359	6.8	● 2022	0.9
30	F	0217	6.8	0854	0.8	1434	6.9	2058	0.9
31	SA	0251	6.8	0932	0.7	1509	7.0	2132	0.9

Chart Datum: 3·20 metres below Ordnance Datum (Newlyn)
HAT is 7·7 metres above Chart Datum

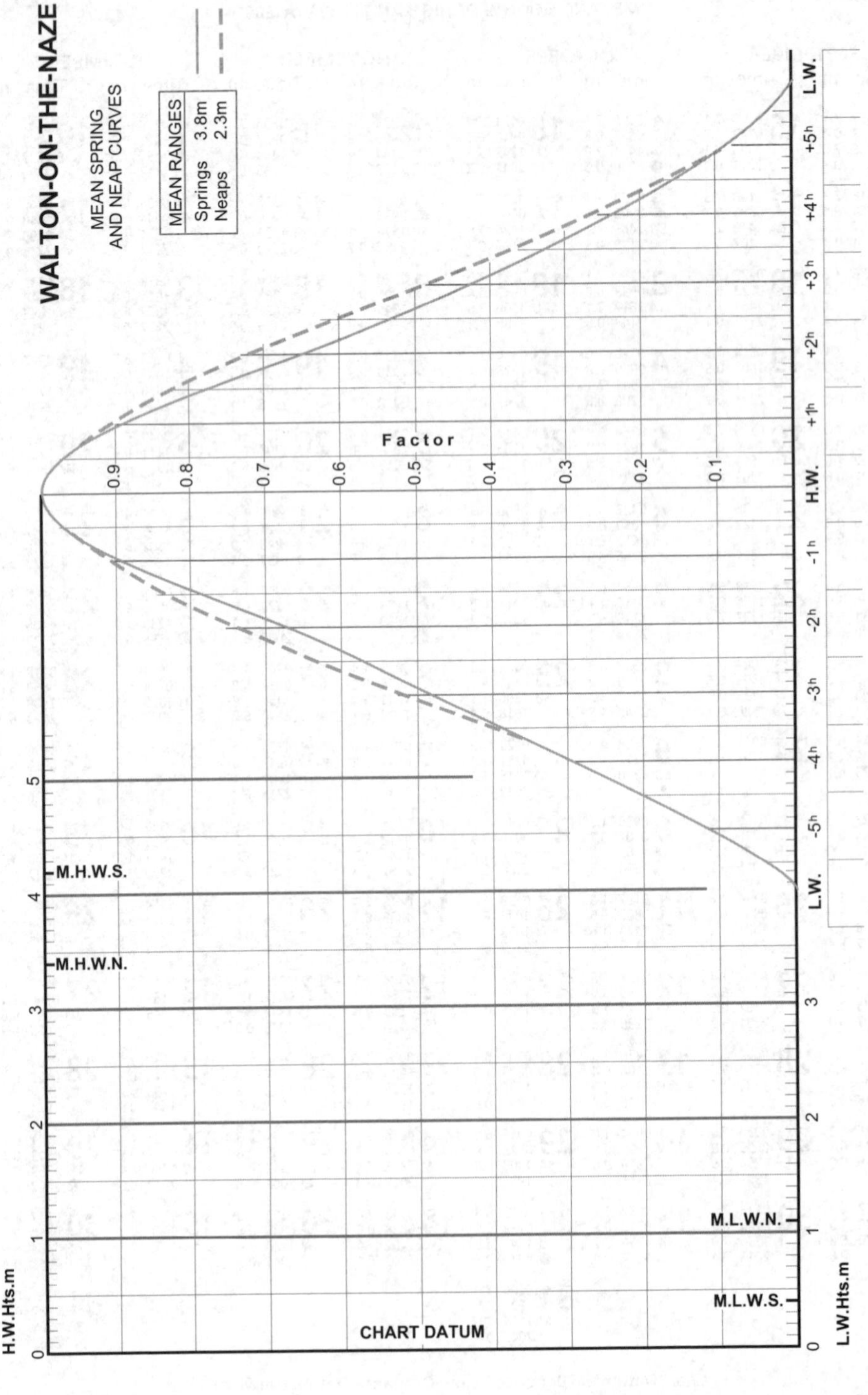
WALTON-ON-THE-NAZE
MEAN SPRING AND NEAP CURVES
MEAN RANGES
Springs 3.8m
Neaps 2.3m
Factor
0.9
0.8
0.7
0.6
0.5
0.4
0.3
0.2
0.1
L.W.
-5h
-4h
-3h
-2h
-1h
H.W.
+1h
+2h
+3h
+4h
+5h
L.W.
H.W.Hts.m
0
1
2
3
4
5
M.H.W.S.
M.H.W.N.
CHART DATUM
M.L.W.N.
M.L.W.S.
L.W.Hts.m

TIME ZONE (UT)
For Summer Time add ONE hour in **non-shaded areas**

WALTON-ON-THE-NAZE

LAT 51°51'N LONG 1°17'E

TIMES AND HEIGHTS OF HIGH AND LOW WATERS

Dates in amber are **SPRINGS**
Dates in grey are **NEAPS**

2016

JANUARY

Date	Day	Time	m	Time	m	Time	m	Time	m	Moon
1	F	0345	3.8	0956	0.7	1616	3.7	2154	1.2	
2	SA	0432	3.7	1041	0.8	1708	3.5	2246	1.3	◑
3	SU	0527	3.5	1142	0.9	1806	3.4			
4	M	0001	1.4	0628	3.4	1254	1.0	1907	3.4	
5	TU	0131	1.3	0733	3.4	1359	1.0	2010	3.5	
6	W	0237	1.2	0836	3.6	1457	0.9	2109	3.7	
7	TH	0332	1.0	0931	3.7	1548	0.8	2200	3.8	
8	F	0419	0.8	1019	3.9	1631	0.8	2245	4.0	
9	SA	0501	0.6	1103	4.0	1710	0.7	2327	4.1	
10	SU	0541	0.5	1145	4.2	1747	0.7			●
11	M	0010	4.2	0621	0.4	1228	4.3	1825	0.6	
12	TU	0052	4.3	0702	0.3	1311	4.4	1905	0.6	
13	W	0134	4.3	0744	0.2	1354	4.4	1948	0.6	
14	TH	0216	4.3	0828	0.3	1438	4.3	2033	0.7	
15	F	0258	4.2	0913	0.3	1524	4.2	2122	0.8	
16	SA	0343	4.1	1004	0.4	1615	4.0	2216	0.9	◐
17	SU	0434	4.0	1102	0.5	1714	3.8	2320	1.0	
18	M	0535	3.9	1207	0.6	1822	3.7			
19	TU	0031	1.0	0649	3.8	1317	0.7	1937	3.7	
20	W	0145	0.9	0808	3.8	1426	0.8	2051	3.8	
21	TH	0258	0.8	0917	3.9	1533	0.8	2154	3.9	
22	F	0406	0.7	1015	4.0	1631	0.8	2247	4.1	
23	SA	0503	0.5	1104	4.1	1719	0.7	2332	4.2	
24	SU	0551	0.4	1149	4.2	1801	0.7			○
25	M	0014	4.2	0632	0.3	1230	4.2	1838	0.7	
26	TU	0053	4.3	0710	0.3	1309	4.2	1913	0.7	
27	W	0130	4.2	0745	0.3	1347	4.1	1945	0.8	
28	TH	0204	4.2	0816	0.4	1423	4.0	2013	0.8	
29	F	0237	4.1	0845	0.5	1458	3.9	2042	0.9	
30	SA	0311	4.0	0915	0.6	1534	3.8	2116	1.0	
31	SU	0348	3.8	0950	0.7	1613	3.6	2157	1.1	

FEBRUARY

Date	Day	Time	m	Time	m	Time	m	Time	m	Moon
1	M	0431	3.6	1035	0.9	1702	3.5	2249	1.2	◑
2	TU	0526	3.5	1137	1.0	1804	3.4			
3	W	0008	1.3	0635	3.4	1306	1.1	1913	3.4	
4	TH	0146	1.2	0749	3.4	1417	1.1	2024	3.5	
5	F	0253	1.0	0857	3.6	1516	0.9	2128	3.7	
6	SA	0349	0.8	0954	3.8	1606	0.8	2221	3.9	
7	SU	0437	0.6	1042	4.0	1650	0.7	2308	4.1	
8	M	0522	0.4	1127	4.2	1731	0.6	2352	4.3	●
9	TU	0605	0.3	1211	4.4	1812	0.5			
10	W	0035	4.4	0647	0.2	1256	4.5	1853	0.5	
11	TH	0118	4.5	0730	0.1	1339	4.5	1935	0.5	
12	F	0200	4.5	0812	0.1	1423	4.4	2019	0.5	
13	SA	0242	4.4	0854	0.2	1508	4.2	2104	0.6	
14	SU	0325	4.3	0940	0.3	1556	4.0	2155	0.7	
15	M	0413	4.1	1033	0.5	1650	3.8	2253	0.8	◐
16	TU	0511	3.9	1137	0.7	1755	3.6			
17	W	0003	0.9	0626	3.7	1250	0.9	1914	3.5	
18	TH	0124	0.9	0751	3.6	1409	1.0	2035	3.6	
19	F	0250	0.8	0906	3.8	1525	0.9	2143	3.8	
20	SA	0404	0.7	1007	3.9	1623	0.9	2235	4.0	
21	SU	0457	0.5	1055	4.0	1707	0.8	2319	4.1	
22	M	0539	0.4	1136	4.1	1744	0.7	2358	4.2	○
23	TU	0614	0.3	1213	4.2	1818	0.7			
24	W	0033	4.2	0646	0.3	1249	4.2	1850	0.7	
25	TH	0106	4.2	0716	0.3	1323	4.1	1921	0.7	
26	F	0137	4.2	0745	0.3	1355	4.1	1948	0.7	
27	SA	0208	4.1	0811	0.4	1426	4.0	2015	0.7	
28	SU	0239	4.0	0838	0.5	1457	3.9	2046	0.8	
29	M	0312	3.9	0908	0.6	1531	3.7	2122	0.9	

MARCH

Date	Day	Time	m	Time	m	Time	m	Time	m	Moon
1	TU	0348	3.7	0945	0.8	1612	3.6	2205	1.0	◑
2	W	0433	3.6	1035	1.0	1705	3.4	2305	1.2	
3	TH	0535	3.4	1154	1.2	1818	3.3			
4	F	0049	1.2	0658	3.3	1336	1.2	1939	3.4	
5	SA	0215	1.0	0822	3.5	1444	1.0	2054	3.6	
6	SU	0317	0.8	0927	3.7	1539	0.8	2154	3.8	
7	M	0411	0.5	1019	4.0	1626	0.7	2244	4.1	
8	TU	0459	0.3	1106	4.2	1711	0.6	2330	4.3	
9	W	0544	0.2	1151	4.4	1754	0.5			●
10	TH	0013	4.5	0627	0.1	1236	4.5	1836	0.4	
11	F	0057	4.6	0709	0.0	1320	4.5	1920	0.4	
12	SA	0140	4.6	0751	0.1	1404	4.4	2003	0.4	
13	SU	0222	4.6	0831	0.2	1449	4.3	2047	0.5	
14	M	0306	4.4	0915	0.4	1535	4.0	2136	0.6	
15	TU	0353	4.2	1005	0.6	1628	3.8	2231	0.7	◐
16	W	0451	3.9	1108	0.9	1731	3.6	2340	0.8	
17	TH	0607	3.6	1223	1.0	1850	3.5			
18	F	0105	0.9	0733	3.6	1350	1.1	2014	3.5	
19	SA	0239	0.8	0851	3.7	1510	1.0	2123	3.7	
20	SU	0351	0.6	0951	3.9	1607	0.9	2215	3.9	
21	M	0440	0.5	1038	4.0	1648	0.8	2258	4.0	
22	TU	0517	0.4	1116	4.1	1722	0.7	2334	4.1	
23	W	0548	0.4	1151	4.1	1754	0.7			○
24	TH	0007	4.2	0616	0.3	1224	4.1	1826	0.6	
25	F	0039	4.2	0645	0.3	1256	4.1	1856	0.6	
26	SA	0109	4.2	0713	0.4	1326	4.1	1924	0.6	
27	SU	0140	4.2	0739	0.4	1356	4.0	1952	0.6	
28	M	0211	4.1	0805	0.5	1427	3.9	2021	0.7	
29	TU	0243	4.0	0834	0.6	1500	3.8	2055	0.7	
30	W	0318	3.8	0909	0.8	1539	3.7	2135	0.8	
31	TH	0401	3.7	0955	1.0	1628	3.5	2229	1.0	◑

APRIL

Date	Day	Time	m	Time	m	Time	m	Time	m	Moon
1	F	0457	3.5	1105	1.1	1735	3.4	2357	1.1	
2	SA	0612	3.4	1250	1.2	1856	3.4			
3	SU	0136	0.9	0743	3.5	1409	1.0	2018	3.5	
4	M	0244	0.7	0856	3.8	1508	0.8	2123	3.8	
5	TU	0341	0.4	0953	4.0	1559	0.7	2216	4.1	
6	W	0431	0.3	1042	4.3	1647	0.5	2304	4.3	
7	TH	0519	0.1	1128	4.4	1733	0.4	2349	4.5	●
8	F	0604	0.1	1213	4.5	1818	0.4			
9	SA	0033	4.6	0647	0.1	1259	4.5	1903	0.3	
10	SU	0118	4.7	0729	0.1	1344	4.4	1948	0.3	
11	M	0202	4.6	0810	0.3	1429	4.3	2033	0.4	
12	TU	0247	4.4	0853	0.5	1516	4.1	2120	0.5	
13	W	0335	4.2	0941	0.7	1607	3.8	2214	0.6	
14	TH	0433	3.9	1040	1.0	1708	3.6	2318	0.7	◐
15	F	0546	3.7	1153	1.1	1822	3.5			
16	SA	0041	0.8	0706	3.6	1319	1.2	1942	3.5	
17	SU	0211	0.8	0823	3.7	1440	1.1	2052	3.6	
18	M	0322	0.7	0924	3.8	1538	1.0	2146	3.8	
19	TU	0411	0.6	1011	3.9	1621	0.9	2229	3.9	
20	W	0447	0.5	1049	4.0	1656	0.8	2305	4.0	
21	TH	0516	0.5	1124	4.0	1729	0.7	2338	4.1	
22	F	0545	0.4	1156	4.1	1801	0.6			○
23	SA	0009	4.2	0614	0.4	1228	4.1	1832	0.5	
24	SU	0042	4.2	0643	0.4	1259	4.1	1902	0.5	
25	M	0114	4.2	0710	0.5	1331	4.1	1932	0.6	
26	TU	0147	4.1	0737	0.6	1403	4.0	2003	0.6	
27	W	0221	4.0	0808	0.7	1438	3.9	2037	0.6	
28	TH	0258	3.9	0846	0.8	1517	3.8	2117	0.7	
29	F	0341	3.8	0933	0.9	1606	3.6	2210	0.8	
30	SA	0435	3.7	1040	1.1	1707	3.5	2330	0.9	◑

Chart Datum: 2·16 metres below Ordnance Datum (Newlyn)
HAT is 4·7 metres above Chart Datum

TIME ZONE (UT)
For Summer Time add ONE hour in **non-shaded areas**

WALTON-ON-THE-NAZE

LAT 51°51'N LONG 1°17'E

TIMES AND HEIGHTS OF HIGH AND LOW WATERS

Dates in amber are **SPRINGS**
Dates in grey are **NEAPS**

2016

MAY

Date	Day	Time	m
1	SU	0544 1211 1822	3.6 1.1 3.5
2	M	0101 0707 1332 1941	0.8 3.6 1.0 3.6
3	TU	0211 0822 1435 2050	0.6 3.8 0.8 3.8
4	W	0310 0924 1531 2147	0.4 4.1 0.7 4.1
5	TH	0403 1017 1622 2238	0.3 4.2 0.5 4.3
6	F	0453 1105 1712 ● 2325	0.2 4.4 0.4 4.5
7	SA	0540 1152 1801	0.2 4.4 0.3
8	SU	0011 0626 1239 1849	4.6 0.2 4.5 0.3
9	M	0057 0710 1325 1936	4.6 0.3 4.4 0.3
10	TU	0143 0753 1411 2022	4.6 0.5 4.3 0.3
11	W	0230 0835 1458 2108	4.4 0.6 4.1 0.4
12	TH	0319 0921 1548 2158	4.2 0.8 3.9 0.5
13	F	0415 1012 1644 ◐ 2255	3.9 1.0 3.7 0.7
14	SA	0519 1115 1748	3.7 1.2 3.6
15	SU	0006 0629 1234 1857	0.8 3.6 1.2 3.5
16	M	0123 0740 1351 2007	0.8 3.6 1.2 3.6
17	TU	0233 0844 1456 2105	0.8 3.7 1.1 3.7
18	W	0327 0935 1546 2151	0.7 3.8 0.9 3.8
19	TH	0407 1017 1626 2231	0.6 3.9 0.8 3.9
20	F	0441 1053 1702 2306	0.6 4.0 0.7 4.0
21	SA	0514 1128 1737 ○ 2341	0.6 4.0 0.6 4.1
22	SU	0547 1202 1811	0.5 4.1 0.5
23	M	0016 0617 1236 1843	4.2 0.5 4.1 0.5
24	TU	0052 0647 1311 1916	4.2 0.6 4.1 0.5
25	W	0128 0718 1347 1951	4.1 0.6 4.0 0.5
26	TH	0204 0753 1424 2028	4.1 0.7 4.0 0.6
27	F	0244 0834 1504 2110	4.0 0.8 3.9 0.6
28	SA	0328 0923 1551 2203	3.9 0.9 3.8 0.7
29	SU	0420 1024 1648 ◑ 2312	3.8 1.0 3.7 0.7
30	M	0523 1139 1754	3.8 1.0 3.7
31	TU	0029 0637 1256 1907	0.6 3.8 1.0 3.8

JUNE

Date	Day	Time	m
1	W	0139 0750 1403 2018	0.5 3.9 0.9 3.9
2	TH	0240 0856 1503 2120	0.4 4.0 0.7 4.1
3	F	0336 0954 1600 2214	0.4 4.2 0.6 4.3
4	SA	0430 1046 1654 2304	0.3 4.3 0.5 4.4
5	SU	0521 1135 1747 ● 2352	0.3 4.4 0.3 4.5
6	M	0609 1222 1838	0.4 4.4 0.3
7	TU	0040 0655 1309 1926	4.6 0.5 4.4 0.3
8	W	0127 0738 1355 2012	4.5 0.6 4.3 0.3
9	TH	0214 0820 1441 2056	4.4 0.7 4.2 0.4
10	F	0302 0900 1526 2140	4.2 0.9 4.0 0.5
11	SA	0352 0943 1615 2227	3.9 1.0 3.9 0.6
12	SU	0447 1033 1708 ◐ 2322	3.8 1.1 3.7 0.7
13	M	0545 1137 1806	3.6 1.2 3.6
14	TU	0025 0646 1254 1908	0.8 3.6 1.3 3.6
15	W	0130 0749 1403 2011	0.8 3.6 1.2 3.6
16	TH	0230 0849 1503 2107	0.8 3.7 1.1 3.7
17	F	0322 0939 1553 2154	0.8 3.8 0.9 3.8
18	SA	0407 1022 1636 2236	0.7 3.9 0.8 4.0
19	SU	0448 1101 1715 2316	0.7 4.0 0.7 4.1
20	M	0524 1139 1751 ○ 2355	0.7 4.1 0.6 4.1
21	TU	0557 1217 1827	0.7 4.1 0.5
22	W	0033 0630 1256 1903	4.2 0.6 4.2 0.5
23	TH	0113 0705 1335 1942	4.2 0.6 4.2 0.4
24	F	0152 0743 1414 2022	4.2 0.7 4.1 0.4
25	SA	0233 0826 1455 2105	4.1 0.7 4.0 0.5
26	SU	0317 0913 1539 2154	4.1 0.8 4.0 0.5
27	M	0406 1008 1629 ◑ 2253	4.0 0.9 3.9 0.6
28	TU	0503 1112 1728	3.9 1.0 3.9
29	W	0000 0610 1223 1836	0.6 3.8 1.0 3.9
30	TH	0109 0722 1334 1949	0.6 3.8 0.9 3.9

JULY

Date	Day	Time	m
1	F	0213 0833 1440 2058	0.6 3.9 0.8 4.0
2	SA	0315 0937 1543 2157	0.6 4.0 0.7 4.2
3	SU	0413 1033 1643 2251	0.6 4.2 0.5 4.3
4	M	0507 1123 1738 ● 2340	0.6 4.3 0.4 4.4
5	TU	0556 1210 1829	0.6 4.3 0.3
6	W	0026 0641 1255 1915	4.4 0.6 4.3 0.3
7	TH	0113 0723 1339 1958	4.4 0.7 4.3 0.3
8	F	0157 0802 1421 2038	4.3 0.8 4.2 0.4
9	SA	0241 0837 1501 2114	4.2 0.9 4.1 0.5
10	SU	0324 0912 1542 2151	4.0 1.0 4.0 0.6
11	M	0409 0950 1626 2233	3.8 1.1 3.8 0.7
12	TU	0458 1038 1716 ◐ 2327	3.7 1.2 3.7 0.8
13	W	0552 1143 1813	3.5 1.3 3.6
14	TH	0032 0650 1306 1915	1.0 3.5 1.3 3.5
15	F	0139 0753 1416 2019	1.0 3.5 1.2 3.6
16	SA	0241 0855 1517 2118	1.0 3.6 1.0 3.7
17	SU	0336 0949 1609 2208	0.9 3.8 0.8 3.9
18	M	0424 1035 1652 2252	0.8 4.0 0.7 4.0
19	TU	0503 1117 1732 ○ 2334	0.8 4.1 0.6 4.1
20	W	0539 1158 1810	0.7 4.2 0.5
21	TH	0015 0615 1240 1849	4.2 0.7 4.3 0.4
22	F	0057 0652 1320 1929	4.3 0.6 4.3 0.3
23	SA	0138 0732 1401 2010	4.3 0.6 4.3 0.3
24	SU	0220 0814 1441 2052	4.3 0.7 4.3 0.4
25	M	0303 0859 1522 2137	4.2 0.8 4.2 0.4
26	TU	0349 0949 1609 ◑ 2229	4.1 0.9 4.1 0.5
27	W	0442 1047 1703 2332	3.9 0.9 4.0 0.6
28	TH	0545 1155 1810	3.8 1.0 3.9
29	F	0041 0657 1309 1927	0.7 3.7 1.0 3.8
30	SA	0151 0814 1422 2043	0.8 3.8 0.9 3.9
31	SU	0300 0925 1534 2147	0.8 3.9 0.7 4.1

AUGUST

Date	Day	Time	m
1	M	0404 1023 1639 2242	0.8 4.1 0.6 4.2
2	TU	0458 1113 1732 ● 2330	0.7 4.2 0.4 4.3
3	W	0544 1158 1818	0.7 4.3 0.3
4	TH	0014 0625 1240 1859	4.4 0.7 4.3 0.3
5	F	0056 0703 1319 1937	4.3 0.7 4.3 0.3
6	SA	0136 0739 1356 2010	4.3 0.8 4.3 0.4
7	SU	0214 0811 1431 2041	4.2 0.8 4.2 0.5
8	M	0251 0841 1505 2111	4.0 0.9 4.1 0.6
9	TU	0328 0912 1542 2144	3.9 1.0 3.9 0.7
10	W	0408 0950 1625 ◐ 2226	3.7 1.1 3.8 0.9
11	TH	0455 1040 1718 2326	3.6 1.2 3.6 1.1
12	F	0553 1154 1823	3.4 1.3 3.5
13	SA	0049 0659 1327 1935	1.2 3.4 1.3 3.5
14	SU	0203 0810 1438 2043	1.2 3.5 1.1 3.6
15	M	0306 0915 1537 2140	1.0 3.7 0.9 3.8
16	TU	0358 1008 1626 2229	0.9 3.9 0.7 4.0
17	W	0441 1053 1709 2313	0.8 4.1 0.6 4.2
18	TH	0519 1136 1749 ○ 2355	0.7 4.2 0.4 4.3
19	F	0557 1218 1830	0.7 4.4 0.3
20	SA	0037 0636 1259 1910	4.4 0.6 4.5 0.3
21	SU	0119 0716 1340 1950	4.5 0.6 4.5 0.3
22	M	0202 0758 1421 2031	4.4 0.6 4.5 0.3
23	TU	0244 0842 1502 2113	4.3 0.7 4.4 0.4
24	W	0329 0929 1547 2203	4.1 0.8 4.2 0.6
25	TH	0420 1025 1640 ◑ 2304	3.9 0.9 4.1 0.8
26	F	0521 1131 1748	3.7 0.9 3.9
27	SA	0017 0636 1249 1912	0.9 3.6 1.0 3.8
28	SU	0135 0800 1412 2033	1.0 3.6 0.9 3.9
29	M	0252 0914 1532 2139	1.0 3.8 0.7 4.0
30	TU	0358 1012 1633 2233	0.9 4.0 0.6 4.2
31	W	0448 1100 1721 2318	0.9 4.2 0.4 4.3

Chart Datum: 2·16 metres below Ordnance Datum (Newlyn)
HAT is 4·7 metres above Chart Datum

TIME ZONE (UT)
For Summer Time add ONE hour in **non-shaded areas**

WALTON-ON-THE-NAZE

LAT 51°51′N LONG 1°17′E

TIMES AND HEIGHTS OF HIGH AND LOW WATERS

Dates in amber are **SPRINGS**
Dates in grey are **NEAPS**

2016

SEPTEMBER

Date	Time	m	Date	Time	m
1 TH	0529 1141 1800 ● 2357	0.8 4.3 0.4 4.3	16 F	0454 1109 1723 ○ 2330	0.7 4.3 0.4 4.4
2 F	0605 1218 1835	0.7 4.3 0.4	17 SA	0535 1151 1805	0.6 4.4 0.3
3 SA	0034 0640 1253 1907	4.3 0.7 4.3 0.4	18 SU	0013 0615 1234 1846	4.5 0.6 4.6 0.2
4 SU	0110 0713 1326 1937	4.3 0.7 4.3 0.4	19 M	0057 0657 1316 1926	4.6 0.5 4.6 0.2
5 M	0144 0744 1358 2005	4.2 0.8 4.3 0.5	20 TU	0140 0740 1358 2006	4.5 0.5 4.6 0.3
6 TU	0216 0811 1430 2031	4.1 0.8 4.1 0.6	21 W	0223 0824 1441 2048	4.4 0.6 4.5 0.5
7 W	0248 0840 1503 2059	3.9 0.9 4.0 0.8	22 TH	0308 0911 1526 2137	4.2 0.7 4.3 0.7
8 TH	0320 0914 1539 2133	3.8 1.0 3.8 0.9	23 F	0358 1006 1620 ◑ 2238	3.9 0.8 4.1 1.0
9 F	0359 0955 1622 ◐ 2220	3.6 1.1 3.6 1.2	24 SA	0459 1112 1731 2353	3.7 0.9 3.8 1.1
10 SA	0449 1052 1722 2336	3.5 1.2 3.5 1.3	25 SU	0616 1233 1858	3.6 0.9 3.7
11 SU	0601 1229 1845	3.4 1.3 3.4	26 M	0117 0741 1401 2019	1.2 3.6 0.9 3.9
12 M	0121 0721 1357 2006	1.3 3.4 1.2 3.5	27 TU	0238 0856 1520 2125	1.1 3.8 0.7 4.0
13 TU	0231 0836 1501 2110	1.2 3.6 0.9 3.8	28 W	0343 0953 1617 2217	1.0 4.0 0.6 4.2
14 W	0327 0936 1554 2201	1.0 3.8 0.7 4.0	29 TH	0430 1039 1700 2258	0.9 4.1 0.5 4.2
15 TH	0412 1025 1640 2247	0.8 4.1 0.5 4.3	30 F	0507 1118 1735 2335	0.8 4.2 0.5 4.3

OCTOBER

Date	Time	m	Date	Time	m
1 SA	0541 1152 1805 ●	0.8 4.3 0.4	16 SU	0510 1123 1737 ○ 2348	0.6 4.5 0.2 4.6
2 SU	0008 0614 1224 1834	4.3 0.7 4.3 0.5	17 M	0554 1207 1820	0.5 4.7 0.2
3 M	0041 0647 1255 1903	4.3 0.7 4.3 0.5	18 TU	0033 0639 1252 1902	4.6 0.4 4.7 0.3
4 TU	0113 0717 1326 1930	4.2 0.7 4.3 0.6	19 W	0118 0724 1336 1944	4.6 0.4 4.7 0.4
5 W	0143 0745 1358 1954	4.1 0.7 4.2 0.7	20 TH	0203 0810 1421 2027	4.4 0.5 4.5 0.6
6 TH	0212 0813 1430 2020	4.0 0.8 4.0 0.8	21 F	0249 0858 1509 2116	4.2 0.5 4.3 0.9
7 F	0244 0844 1504 2053	3.9 0.9 3.9 1.0	22 SA	0339 0951 1604 ◑ 2214	3.9 0.6 4.0 1.1
8 SA	0320 0922 1544 2135	3.8 1.0 3.7 1.1	23 SU	0439 1055 1715 2326	3.7 0.8 3.8 1.3
9 SU	0405 1011 1635 ◐ 2235	3.6 1.1 3.6 1.3	24 M	0552 1213 1836	3.6 0.8 3.7
10 M	0506 1130 1747	3.4 1.2 3.5	25 TU	0049 0713 1337 1954	1.3 3.6 0.8 3.8
11 TU	0022 0628 1313 1920	1.4 3.4 1.1 3.5	26 W	0209 0826 1453 2100	1.3 3.7 0.7 4.0
12 W	0149 0751 1422 2032	1.3 3.5 0.9 3.8	27 TH	0316 0925 1549 2151	1.1 3.9 0.6 4.1
13 TH	0250 0858 1518 2129	1.0 3.8 0.6 4.1	28 F	0404 1011 1631 2232	1.0 4.0 0.6 4.1
14 F	0340 0952 1607 2218	0.8 4.1 0.4 4.3	29 SA	0442 1049 1703 2308	0.9 4.1 0.6 4.2
15 SA	0425 1039 1653 2303	0.7 4.3 0.3 4.5	30 SU	0516 1123 1732 ● 2341	0.8 4.2 0.6 4.2
			31 M	0549 1154 1802	0.7 4.2 0.5

NOVEMBER

Date	Time	m	Date	Time	m
1 TU	0012 0622 1226 1831	4.2 0.6 4.3 0.6	16 W	0012 0623 1231 1843	4.6 0.4 4.7 0.4
2 W	0043 0653 1258 1858	4.2 0.6 4.2 0.6	17 TH	0059 0712 1317 1928	4.5 0.3 4.7 0.5
3 TH	0114 0722 1331 1924	4.2 0.7 4.2 0.7	18 F	0145 0759 1405 2012	4.4 0.4 4.5 0.7
4 F	0145 0751 1404 1952	4.1 0.7 4.1 0.8	19 SA	0232 0848 1454 2059	4.2 0.4 4.3 0.9
5 SA	0218 0823 1439 2026	4.0 0.7 3.9 0.9	20 SU	0322 0938 1548 2150	4.0 0.5 4.1 1.1
6 SU	0254 0900 1519 2108	3.9 0.8 3.8 1.1	21 M	0417 1035 1652 ◑ 2251	3.8 0.6 3.8 1.3
7 M	0338 0947 1609 ◐ 2204	3.7 0.9 3.7 1.2	22 TU	0521 1143 1802	3.7 0.7 3.7
8 TU	0433 1054 1711 2327	3.6 1.0 3.6 1.3	23 W	0006 0632 1256 1914	1.4 3.6 0.8 3.7
9 W	0544 1226 1831	3.5 0.9 3.6	24 TH	0124 0744 1407 2022	1.3 3.6 0.8 3.8
10 TH	0059 0704 1341 1950	1.3 3.6 0.8 3.8	25 F	0234 0846 1508 2117	1.2 3.7 0.8 3.9
11 F	0209 0817 1441 2054	1.1 3.8 0.6 4.1	26 SA	0330 0936 1553 2201	1.1 3.9 0.7 4.0
12 SA	0305 0917 1534 2148	0.9 4.0 0.4 4.3	27 SU	0413 1017 1628 2239	0.9 4.0 0.7 4.1
13 SU	0357 1009 1624 2238	0.7 4.3 0.3 4.4	28 M	0450 1052 1701 2314	0.8 4.0 0.7 4.1
14 M	0446 1057 1712 ○ 2325	0.6 4.5 0.3 4.5	29 TU	0526 1126 1734 ● 2347	0.7 4.1 0.6 4.2
15 TU	0535 1144 1758	0.4 4.6 0.3	30 W	0600 1201 1806	0.6 4.2 0.7

DECEMBER

Date	Time	m	Date	Time	m
1 TH	0019 0632 1236 1834	4.2 0.6 4.2 0.7	16 F	0044 0702 1303 1916	4.5 0.3 4.6 0.6
2 F	0053 0703 1310 1902	4.2 0.6 4.2 0.7	17 SA	0131 0751 1351 2000	4.4 0.3 4.5 0.7
3 SA	0126 0736 1345 1934	4.1 0.6 4.1 0.8	18 SU	0217 0837 1439 2042	4.3 0.3 4.3 0.9
4 SU	0201 0810 1422 2010	4.1 0.6 4.0 0.9	19 M	0303 0922 1529 2125	4.1 0.4 4.1 1.0
5 M	0239 0849 1503 2053	4.0 0.6 3.9 1.0	20 TU	0351 1009 1622 2212	3.9 0.5 3.9 1.2
6 TU	0321 0934 1550 2146	3.9 0.7 3.9 1.1	21 W	0444 1101 1720 ◑ 2310	3.8 0.7 3.7 1.3
7 W	0411 1031 1646 ◐ 2253	3.8 0.8 3.8 1.2	22 TH	0542 1201 1822	3.6 0.8 3.6
8 TH	0511 1145 1754	3.7 0.8 3.8	23 F	0024 0645 1305 1927	1.4 3.5 0.9 3.6
9 F	0012 0622 1300 1909	1.2 3.7 0.7 3.8	24 SA	0138 0752 1407 2031	1.3 3.5 0.9 3.6
10 SA	0128 0737 1405 2020	1.1 3.8 0.6 4.0	25 SU	0244 0852 1504 2124	1.2 3.6 0.9 3.8
11 SU	0233 0845 1504 2122	0.9 4.0 0.5 4.1	26 M	0339 0941 1553 2209	1.0 3.8 0.8 3.9
12 M	0331 0944 1559 2217	0.7 4.2 0.4 4.3	27 TU	0425 1023 1635 2248	0.8 3.9 0.8 4.0
13 TU	0426 1036 1651 2308	0.6 4.4 0.4 4.4	28 W	0504 1102 1712 2324	0.7 4.0 0.7 4.1
14 W	0520 1126 1742 ○ 2356	0.4 4.5 0.4 4.4	29 TH	0540 1140 1746 ●	0.6 4.1 0.7
15 TH	0612 1214 1830	0.3 4.6 0.5	30 F	0001 0613 1218 1816	4.1 0.5 4.1 0.7
			31 SA	0037 0647 1254 1848	4.2 0.5 4.2 0.7

Chart Datum: 2·16 metres below Ordnance Datum (Newlyn)
HAT is 4·7 metres above Chart Datum

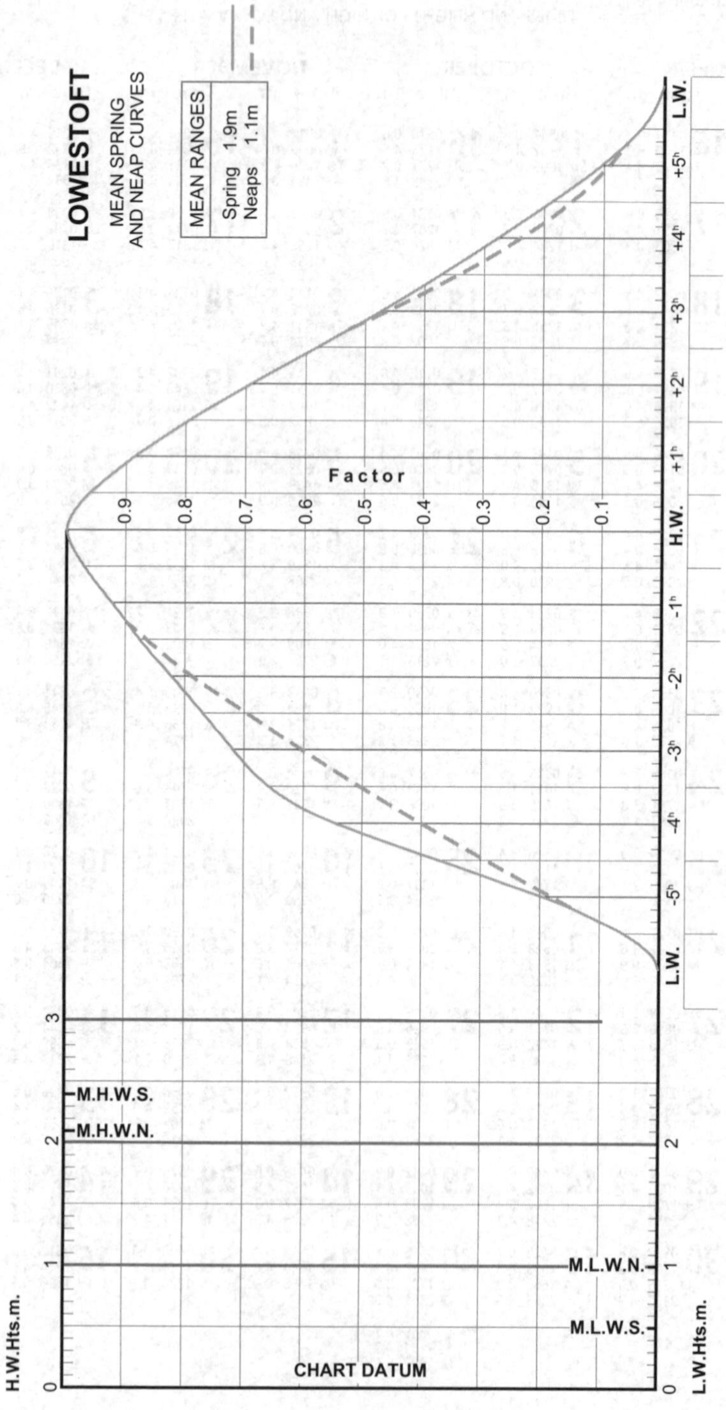
LOWESTOFT
MEAN SPRING
AND NEAP CURVES
MEAN RANGES
Spring 1.9m
Neaps 1.1m
Factor
0.9
0.8
0.7
0.6
0.5
0.4
0.3
0.2
0.1
L.W.
-5h
-4h
-3h
-2h
-1h
H.W.
+1h
+2h
+3h
+4h
+5h
L.W.
H.W.Hts.m.
M.H.W.S.
M.H.W.N.
M.L.W.N.
M.L.W.S.
CHART DATUM
L.W.Hts.m.
0
1
2
3

TIME ZONE (UT)
For Summer Time add ONE hour in **non-shaded areas**

LOWESTOFT

LAT 52°28′N LONG 1°45′E

TIMES AND HEIGHTS OF HIGH AND LOW WATERS

Dates in amber are **SPRINGS**
Dates in grey are **NEAPS**

2016

JANUARY

Date	Day	Time	m	Time	m	Time	m	Time	m
1	F	0125	2.4	0800	0.8	1428	2.1	1941	1.2
2	SA	0211	2.4	0849	0.9	1538	2.1	◑ 2028	1.3
3	SU	0304	2.3	0955	1.0	1643	2.1	2132	1.4
4	M	0414	2.2	1104	1.0	1737	2.2	2320	1.4
5	TU	0523	2.2	1158	1.0	1826	2.2		
6	W	0021	1.2	0621	2.2	1244	1.0	1910	2.3
7	TH	0109	1.1	0715	2.2	1325	0.9	1950	2.4
8	F	0154	1.0	0805	2.3	1406	0.9	2028	2.4
9	SA	0238	0.8	0850	2.4	1448	0.8	2106	2.5
10	SU	0323	0.7	0933	2.4	1531	0.7	● 2145	2.6
11	M	0409	0.6	1015	2.5	1615	0.7	2225	2.6
12	TU	0454	0.5	1057	2.5	1658	0.7	2306	2.6
13	W	0539	0.5	1140	2.5	1740	0.8	2347	2.7
14	TH	0623	0.5	1224	2.4	1822	0.8		
15	F	0031	2.6	0708	0.5	1311	2.3	1905	0.9
16	SA	0117	2.6	0756	0.6	1403	2.3	◐ 1953	1.0
17	SU	0207	2.5	0852	0.7	1512	2.2	2050	1.1
18	M	0309	2.4	1001	0.8	1639	2.2	2208	1.1
19	TU	0431	2.4	1114	0.8	1742	2.3	2334	1.1
20	W	0546	2.4	1219	0.9	1839	2.3		
21	TH	0044	0.9	0654	2.4	1320	0.9	1932	2.4
22	F	0150	0.8	0800	2.4	1416	0.9	2021	2.5
23	SA	0247	0.7	0855	2.4	1505	0.8	2105	2.5
24	SU	0335	0.5	0942	2.4	1547	0.8	○ 2146	2.6
25	M	0418	0.5	1024	2.4	1625	0.8	2226	2.6
26	TU	0458	0.5	1105	2.4	1659	0.8	2304	2.6
27	W	0535	0.5	1142	2.3	1730	0.9	2341	2.6
28	TH	0610	0.6	1217	2.3	1759	0.9		
29	F	0016	2.5	0643	0.7	1252	2.2	1829	1.0
30	SA	0053	2.5	0717	0.8	1328	2.2	1905	1.1
31	SU	0134	2.4	0753	0.9	1409	2.1	1948	1.1

FEBRUARY

Date	Day	Time	m	Time	m	Time	m	Time	m
1	M	0220	2.3	0837	1.0	1505	2.1	◑ 2039	1.2
2	TU	0318	2.2	0938	1.1	1630	2.1	2150	1.3
3	W	0441	2.1	1105	1.1	1735	2.1	2335	1.2
4	TH	0552	2.1	1206	1.1	1829	2.2		
5	F	0036	1.1	0652	2.2	1257	1.0	1917	2.3
6	SA	0127	0.9	0747	2.2	1343	0.9	2002	2.4
7	SU	0216	0.8	0834	2.3	1429	0.8	2043	2.5
8	M	0305	0.6	0917	2.4	1515	0.7	● 2124	2.6
9	TU	0353	0.5	0959	2.5	1600	0.6	2205	2.7
10	W	0439	0.4	1040	2.5	1644	0.6	2247	2.7
11	TH	0523	0.3	1121	2.5	1726	0.6	2329	2.7
12	F	0606	0.3	1204	2.5	1807	0.7		
13	SA	0012	2.7	0649	0.4	1249	2.4	1848	0.8
14	SU	0058	2.6	0733	0.5	1337	2.3	1934	0.8
15	M	0149	2.5	0824	0.7	1436	2.2	◐ 2029	0.9
16	TU	0253	2.4	0930	0.9	1601	2.2	2146	1.0
17	W	0424	2.3	1053	1.0	1714	2.2	2320	1.0
18	TH	0545	2.3	1206	1.0	1818	2.2		
19	F	0035	0.9	0702	2.3	1313	1.0	1918	2.3
20	SA	0142	0.8	0805	2.3	1409	1.0	2008	2.4
21	SU	0236	0.6	0851	2.4	1454	0.9	2050	2.5
22	M	0320	0.5	0931	2.4	1532	0.8	○ 2129	2.5
23	TU	0359	0.5	1007	2.4	1606	0.8	2205	2.6
24	W	0435	0.5	1041	2.4	1637	0.8	2241	2.6
25	TH	0509	0.5	1113	2.3	1706	0.8	2315	2.6
26	F	0540	0.6	1143	2.3	1733	0.8	2349	2.5
27	SA	0609	0.6	1213	2.3	1802	0.8		
28	SU	0024	2.4	0638	0.7	1247	2.2	1836	0.9
29	M	0102	2.4	0711	0.8	1325	2.2	1916	1.0

MARCH

Date	Day	Time	m	Time	m	Time	m	Time	m
1	TU	0146	2.3	0750	1.0	1411	2.1	◑ 2004	1.1
2	W	0237	2.2	0840	1.1	1509	2.1	2104	1.2
3	TH	0353	2.1	0951	1.2	1636	2.1	2245	1.2
4	F	0526	2.1	1128	1.2	1747	2.1		
5	SA	0004	1.0	0631	2.2	1229	1.1	1842	2.2
6	SU	0100	0.9	0727	2.2	1320	1.0	1931	2.3
7	M	0152	0.7	0815	2.3	1409	0.8	2016	2.4
8	TU	0243	0.5	0857	2.4	1456	0.7	2100	2.6
9	W	0332	0.4	0938	2.5	1543	0.6	● 2142	2.7
10	TH	0418	0.2	1019	2.5	1627	0.5	2226	2.8
11	F	0503	0.2	1100	2.5	1709	0.5	2309	2.8
12	SA	0545	0.2	1142	2.5	1751	0.5	2354	2.7
13	SU	0627	0.4	1225	2.4	1834	0.6		
14	M	0042	2.6	0710	0.6	1313	2.3	1920	0.7
15	TU	0136	2.5	0758	0.8	1407	2.2	◐ 2015	0.8
16	W	0248	2.3	0900	1.0	1521	2.2	2134	0.9
17	TH	0424	2.2	1033	1.1	1642	2.1	2307	0.9
18	F	0544	2.2	1152	1.1	1751	2.2		
19	SA	0020	0.8	0700	2.3	1300	1.1	1857	2.2
20	SU	0124	0.7	0757	2.3	1354	1.0	1949	2.3
21	M	0215	0.6	0838	2.3	1436	0.9	2030	2.4
22	TU	0257	0.6	0913	2.4	1512	0.8	2107	2.4
23	W	0334	0.5	0945	2.4	1543	0.8	○ 2141	2.5
24	TH	0407	0.5	1015	2.4	1613	0.7	2215	2.5
25	F	0438	0.5	1043	2.4	1641	0.7	2249	2.5
26	SA	0507	0.6	1111	2.4	1709	0.7	2323	2.4
27	SU	0535	0.7	1141	2.3	1739	0.8	2358	2.4
28	M	0604	0.7	1214	2.3	1813	0.8		
29	TU	0035	2.3	0636	0.8	1252	2.3	1851	0.9
30	W	0117	2.2	0715	0.9	1335	2.2	1937	0.9
31	TH	0207	2.1	0802	1.1	1427	2.1	◑ 2035	1.0

APRIL

Date	Day	Time	m	Time	m	Time	m	Time	m
1	F	0313	2.1	0904	1.2	1532	2.1	2201	1.0
2	SA	0459	2.1	1041	1.2	1658	2.1	2331	0.9
3	SU	0607	2.2	1157	1.1	1804	2.2		
4	M	0030	0.8	0703	2.3	1253	1.0	1857	2.3
5	TU	0125	0.6	0751	2.4	1344	0.8	1946	2.4
6	W	0217	0.4	0834	2.5	1434	0.7	2032	2.5
7	TH	0307	0.3	0915	2.5	1522	0.6	● 2118	2.7
8	F	0355	0.2	0956	2.6	1608	0.5	2204	2.7
9	SA	0439	0.2	1038	2.6	1652	0.4	2251	2.7
10	SU	0522	0.3	1120	2.5	1736	0.4	2339	2.7
11	M	0605	0.4	1204	2.5	1821	0.5		
12	TU	0030	2.6	0647	0.6	1252	2.4	1908	0.6
13	W	0129	2.4	0734	0.9	1344	2.3	2005	0.7
14	TH	0245	2.3	0832	1.1	1448	2.2	◐ 2120	0.8
15	F	0413	2.2	1003	1.2	1605	2.2	2245	0.8
16	SA	0529	2.2	1126	1.2	1716	2.2	2353	0.7
17	SU	0641	2.3	1232	1.2	1823	2.2		
18	M	0053	0.7	0735	2.3	1327	1.1	1920	2.2
19	TU	0144	0.7	0816	2.3	1410	1.0	2003	2.3
20	W	0226	0.6	0850	2.3	1445	0.9	2040	2.3
21	TH	0302	0.6	0919	2.4	1517	0.8	2115	2.4
22	F	0335	0.6	0946	2.4	1547	0.7	○ 2150	2.4
23	SA	0405	0.6	1013	2.4	1617	0.7	2224	2.4
24	SU	0434	0.6	1042	2.4	1648	0.7	2300	2.4
25	M	0504	0.7	1114	2.4	1720	0.7	2336	2.3
26	TU	0535	0.8	1148	2.4	1756	0.7		
27	W	0014	2.3	0609	0.8	1226	2.3	1834	0.8
28	TH	0056	2.2	0649	0.9	1308	2.3	1919	0.8
29	F	0145	2.2	0736	1.1	1358	2.2	2015	0.9
30	SA	0246	2.1	0834	1.2	1456	2.2	◑ 2131	0.9

Chart Datum: 1·50 metres below Ordnance Datum (Newlyn)
HAT is 2·9 metres above Chart Datum

TIME ZONE (UT)
For Summer Time add ONE hour in **non-shaded areas**

LOWESTOFT

LAT 52°28′N LONG 1°45′E

TIMES AND HEIGHTS OF HIGH AND LOW WATERS

Dates in amber are **SPRINGS**
Dates in grey are **NEAPS**

2016

MAY

Date	Day	Time	m	Time	m	Time	m	Time	m
1	SU	0428	2.1	0952	1.2	1606	2.2	2257	0.8
2	M	0540	2.2	1119	1.1	1723	2.2		
3	TU	0000	0.7	0635	2.3	1222	1.0	1822	2.3
4	W	0056	0.5	0724	2.4	1316	0.9	1915	2.4
5	TH	0149	0.4	0808	2.5	1409	0.7	2006	2.5
6	F	0241	0.3	0851	2.5	1500	0.6	● 2056	2.6
7	SA	0331	0.3	0934	2.6	1549	0.5	2146	2.7
8	SU	0417	0.3	1017	2.6	1636	0.4	2236	2.7
9	M	0501	0.4	1101	2.6	1723	0.4	2328	2.6
10	TU	0544	0.6	1146	2.5	1809	0.4		
11	W	0021	2.5	0626	0.7	1233	2.5	1857	0.5
12	TH	0120	2.4	0711	0.9	1323	2.4	1952	0.6
13	F	0232	2.3	0802	1.1	1418	2.3	◐ 2058	0.7
14	SA	0350	2.2	0913	1.3	1524	2.2	2213	0.7
15	SU	0500	2.2	1044	1.3	1634	2.2	2318	0.7
16	M	0606	2.2	1152	1.3	1738	2.2		
17	TU	0015	0.7	0703	2.2	1248	1.2	1836	2.2
18	W	0105	0.7	0747	2.3	1335	1.1	1927	2.2
19	TH	0148	0.7	0822	2.3	1413	1.0	2009	2.3
20	F	0226	0.7	0851	2.3	1447	0.9	2048	2.3
21	SA	0300	0.7	0918	2.4	1520	0.8	○ 2125	2.3
22	SU	0332	0.7	0945	2.4	1554	0.7	2202	2.3
23	M	0404	0.7	1016	2.5	1628	0.7	2239	2.3
24	TU	0437	0.7	1051	2.5	1705	0.7	2317	2.3
25	W	0513	0.8	1127	2.4	1744	0.7	2357	2.3
26	TH	0550	0.8	1206	2.4	1824	0.7		
27	F	0039	2.2	0630	0.9	1248	2.4	1909	0.7
28	SA	0128	2.2	0716	1.0	1335	2.3	2002	0.8
29	SU	0224	2.2	0810	1.1	1428	2.3	◑ 2107	0.8
30	M	0345	2.2	0915	1.2	1529	2.3	2223	0.7
31	TU	0508	2.2	1037	1.1	1642	2.3	2330	0.6

JUNE

Date	Day	Time	m	Time	m	Time	m	Time	m
1	W	0606	2.3	1148	1.1	1751	2.4		
2	TH	0028	0.6	0656	2.4	1249	0.9	1848	2.4
3	F	0124	0.5	0744	2.4	1346	0.8	1944	2.5
4	SA	0218	0.5	0829	2.5	1442	0.6	2038	2.6
5	SU	0309	0.5	0914	2.6	1534	0.5	● 2133	2.6
6	M	0357	0.5	0959	2.6	1624	0.4	2226	2.6
7	TU	0442	0.6	1044	2.6	1711	0.4	2318	2.5
8	W	0525	0.7	1129	2.6	1757	0.4		
9	TH	0010	2.4	0606	0.8	1214	2.5	1843	0.4
10	F	0104	2.3	0647	1.0	1300	2.5	1932	0.5
11	SA	0203	2.2	0730	1.1	1348	2.4	2026	0.6
12	SU	0313	2.2	0819	1.2	1440	2.3	◐ 2130	0.7
13	M	0420	2.2	0926	1.3	1541	2.2	2236	0.8
14	TU	0521	2.2	1058	1.3	1648	2.2	2334	0.8
15	W	0618	2.2	1202	1.3	1748	2.2		
16	TH	0024	0.9	0708	2.2	1254	1.2	1844	2.2
17	F	0109	0.9	0748	2.3	1338	1.1	1936	2.2
18	SA	0149	0.8	0820	2.3	1417	0.9	2022	2.2
19	SU	0225	0.8	0849	2.4	1454	0.8	2103	2.3
20	M	0301	0.8	0920	2.5	1532	0.7	○ 2143	2.3
21	TU	0338	0.8	0954	2.5	1612	0.7	2222	2.3
22	W	0416	0.7	1031	2.5	1653	0.6	2301	2.4
23	TH	0455	0.8	1109	2.5	1734	0.6	2342	2.3
24	F	0535	0.8	1149	2.5	1817	0.6		
25	SA	0024	2.3	0616	0.9	1231	2.5	1900	0.6
26	SU	0110	2.3	0700	1.0	1315	2.5	1948	0.6
27	M	0201	2.2	0748	1.0	1404	2.5	◑ 2044	0.7
28	TU	0305	2.2	0845	1.1	1459	2.4	2151	0.7
29	W	0433	2.2	0955	1.1	1609	2.4	2301	0.7
30	TH	0537	2.3	1117	1.1	1725	2.4		

JULY

Date	Day	Time	m	Time	m	Time	m	Time	m
1	F	0003	0.7	0630	2.4	1226	1.0	1829	2.4
2	SA	0103	0.7	0721	2.4	1329	0.8	1930	2.5
3	SU	0159	0.7	0810	2.5	1429	0.7	2030	2.5
4	M	0253	0.7	0857	2.6	1524	0.5	● 2127	2.5
5	TU	0342	0.7	0943	2.6	1613	0.4	2218	2.5
6	W	0426	0.7	1028	2.7	1659	0.4	2306	2.5
7	TH	0507	0.8	1111	2.7	1743	0.4	2353	2.4
8	F	0545	0.8	1153	2.6	1825	0.4		
9	SA	0038	2.3	0621	0.9	1234	2.6	1906	0.5
10	SU	0125	2.2	0657	1.0	1315	2.5	1949	0.7
11	M	0216	2.2	0735	1.1	1359	2.4	2036	0.8
12	TU	0320	2.1	0819	1.3	1449	2.3	◐ 2134	0.9
13	W	0424	2.1	0916	1.3	1553	2.2	2243	1.0
14	TH	0520	2.1	1102	1.3	1705	2.2	2342	1.0
15	F	0612	2.2	1211	1.3	1807	2.2		
16	SA	0031	1.0	0700	2.3	1302	1.1	1906	2.2
17	SU	0114	1.0	0742	2.3	1346	1.0	2000	2.2
18	M	0155	0.9	0819	2.4	1429	0.9	2045	2.3
19	TU	0235	0.9	0856	2.5	1512	0.8	○ 2126	2.3
20	W	0316	0.8	0933	2.5	1555	0.6	2205	2.4
21	TH	0358	0.8	1011	2.6	1639	0.6	2244	2.4
22	F	0440	0.7	1050	2.6	1722	0.5	2324	2.4
23	SA	0522	0.8	1130	2.7	1804	0.5		
24	SU	0005	2.4	0602	0.8	1212	2.7	1846	0.5
25	M	0049	2.4	0643	0.9	1255	2.6	1930	0.6
26	TU	0136	2.3	0728	1.0	1341	2.6	◑ 2019	0.6
27	W	0232	2.3	0820	1.0	1435	2.5	2119	0.7
28	TH	0351	2.2	0925	1.1	1547	2.4	2234	0.8
29	F	0507	2.3	1053	1.1	1710	2.4	2344	0.9
30	SA	0607	2.3	1211	1.0	1821	2.4		
31	SU	0048	0.9	0702	2.4	1319	0.8	1930	2.4

AUGUST

Date	Day	Time	m	Time	m	Time	m	Time	m
1	M	0149	0.9	0755	2.5	1422	0.7	2031	2.4
2	TU	0243	0.9	0843	2.6	1515	0.5	● 2122	2.5
3	W	0329	0.8	0927	2.6	1601	0.4	2207	2.5
4	TH	0410	0.8	1009	2.7	1643	0.4	2249	2.5
5	F	0448	0.8	1049	2.7	1722	0.4	2329	2.4
6	SA	0522	0.9	1128	2.7	1759	0.5		
7	SU	0007	2.4	0553	0.9	1206	2.6	1834	0.6
8	M	0044	2.3	0624	1.0	1243	2.5	1908	0.7
9	TU	0120	2.2	0658	1.1	1322	2.5	1944	0.8
10	W	0200	2.2	0737	1.2	1407	2.4	◐ 2025	1.0
11	TH	0252	2.2	0826	1.3	1503	2.2	2119	1.1
12	F	0409	2.2	0931	1.3	1623	2.2	2244	1.2
13	SA	0516	2.2	1123	1.3	1737	2.2	2352	1.2
14	SU	0611	2.3	1226	1.2	1841	2.2		
15	M	0042	1.1	0702	2.3	1317	1.0	1939	2.3
16	TU	0128	1.0	0747	2.4	1403	0.9	2025	2.3
17	W	0212	0.9	0828	2.5	1449	0.7	2105	2.4
18	TH	0256	0.8	0908	2.6	1535	0.6	○ 2144	2.5
19	F	0340	0.8	0948	2.7	1619	0.5	2223	2.5
20	SA	0424	0.7	1028	2.8	1703	0.4	2302	2.6
21	SU	0505	0.7	1109	2.8	1745	0.4	2343	2.5
22	M	0546	0.7	1150	2.8	1826	0.4		
23	TU	0025	2.5	0626	0.8	1234	2.7	1908	0.5
24	W	0111	2.4	0710	0.9	1322	2.6	1954	0.7
25	TH	0203	2.3	0801	1.0	1418	2.5	◑ 2050	0.9
26	F	0312	2.3	0906	1.0	1538	2.4	2209	1.0
27	SA	0436	2.3	1041	1.0	1709	2.4	2330	1.1
28	SU	0543	2.3	1201	0.9	1825	2.4		
29	M	0038	1.1	0643	2.4	1311	0.8	1937	2.4
30	TU	0141	1.0	0739	2.5	1411	0.7	2030	2.5
31	W	0232	1.0	0826	2.6	1500	0.6	2112	2.5

Chart Datum: 1·50 metres below Ordnance Datum (Newlyn)
HAT is 2·9 metres above Chart Datum

TIME ZONE (UT)
For Summer Time add ONE hour in **non-shaded areas**

LOWESTOFT

LAT 52°28'N LONG 1°45'E

TIMES AND HEIGHTS OF HIGH AND LOW WATERS

Dates in amber are **SPRINGS**
Dates in grey are **NEAPS**

2016

SEPTEMBER

Day	Time	m	Day	Time	m
1	0314	0.9	16	0233	0.9
	0908	2.6		0839	2.6
TH	1542	0.5	F	1509	0.5
●	2150	2.5	○	2119	2.6
2	0351	0.9	17	0319	0.8
	0947	2.7		0921	2.7
F	1620	0.5	SA	1555	0.4
	2226	2.5		2158	2.6
3	0425	0.8	18	0403	0.7
	1025	2.7		1003	2.8
SA	1656	0.5	SU	1639	0.3
	2301	2.5		2238	2.6
4	0456	0.9	19	0446	0.7
	1101	2.7		1046	2.9
SU	1729	0.6	M	1721	0.3
	2333	2.4		2319	2.6
5	0526	0.9	20	0528	0.7
	1136	2.6		1130	2.8
M	1759	0.7	TU	1803	0.4
6	0004	2.4	21	0002	2.6
	0554	0.9		0610	0.7
TU	1212	2.6	W	1216	2.8
	1828	0.8		1844	0.6
7	0037	2.3	22	0047	2.5
	0627	1.0		0656	0.8
W	1250	2.5	TH	1307	2.6
	1859	0.9		1930	0.8
8	0114	2.3	23	0138	2.4
	0705	1.1		0749	0.9
TH	1332	2.4	F	1410	2.5
	1936	1.0	◑	2025	1.0
9	0158	2.3	24	0242	2.3
	0750	1.2		0857	1.0
F	1423	2.3	SA	1542	2.4
◐	2021	1.2		2146	1.2
10	0252	2.2	25	0404	2.3
	0847	1.3		1031	1.0
SA	1536	2.2	SU	1709	2.4
	2123	1.3		2315	1.2
11	0411	2.2	26	0516	2.3
	1022	1.3		1148	0.9
SU	1710	2.2	M	1826	2.4
	2304	1.3			
12	0525	2.3	27	0025	1.2
	1150	1.2		0620	2.4
M	1817	2.2	TU	1254	0.8
				1931	2.4
13	0010	1.2	28	0126	1.1
	0622	2.3		0718	2.4
TU	1245	1.0	W	1351	0.7
	1913	2.3		2017	2.5
14	0100	1.1	29	0214	1.1
	0712	2.4		0805	2.5
W	1334	0.8	TH	1437	0.6
	2000	2.4		2054	2.5
15	0147	1.0	30	0253	1.0
	0757	2.5		0844	2.6
TH	1422	0.7	F	1516	0.6
	2041	2.5		2128	2.5

OCTOBER

Day	Time	m	Day	Time	m
1	0327	0.9	16	0255	0.8
	0922	2.6		0853	2.8
SA	1552	0.6	SU	1528	0.4
●	2200	2.5	○	2133	2.7
2	0400	0.9	17	0341	0.7
	0958	2.7		0939	2.8
SU	1625	0.6	M	1613	0.3
	2230	2.5		2214	2.7
3	0430	0.8	18	0427	0.6
	1034	2.6		1025	2.9
M	1655	0.7	TU	1657	0.4
	2259	2.5		2256	2.7
4	0459	0.9	19	0512	0.6
	1109	2.6		1112	2.8
TU	1723	0.7	W	1740	0.5
	2329	2.5		2340	2.6
5	0529	0.9	20	0557	0.6
	1144	2.5		1202	2.7
W	1751	0.8	TH	1823	0.7
6	0001	2.4	21	0026	2.6
	0601	0.9		0645	0.7
TH	1222	2.4	F	1258	2.6
	1821	0.9		1908	0.9
7	0038	2.4	22	0117	2.5
	0638	1.0		0739	0.8
F	1303	2.3	SA	1406	2.4
	1858	1.1	◑	2001	1.1
8	0120	2.4	23	0216	2.4
	0722	1.1		0847	0.8
SA	1351	2.2	SU	1538	2.4
	1942	1.2		2116	1.3
9	0210	2.3	24	0329	2.4
	0816	1.2		1012	0.9
SU	1454	2.2	M	1657	2.4
◐	2038	1.3		2248	1.3
10	0310	2.3	25	0444	2.3
	0933	1.2		1124	0.8
M	1640	2.2	TU	1809	2.4
	2158	1.4		2358	1.3
11	0430	2.3	26	0550	2.4
	1110	1.1		1226	0.8
TU	1749	2.3	W	1910	2.4
	2330	1.3			
12	0540	2.3	27	0058	1.2
	1210	0.9		0649	2.4
W	1844	2.4	TH	1321	0.7
				1955	2.4
13	0028	1.2	28	0147	1.1
	0634	2.4		0738	2.4
TH	1302	0.8	F	1406	0.7
	1931	2.4		2031	2.5
14	0118	1.0	29	0226	1.0
	0723	2.5		0818	2.5
F	1352	0.6	SA	1445	0.7
	2013	2.5		2103	2.5
15	0207	0.9	30	0301	1.0
	0808	2.6		0856	2.5
SA	1441	0.5	SU	1519	0.7
	2053	2.6	●	2132	2.5
			31	0333	0.9
				0932	2.6
			M	1551	0.7
				2200	2.5

NOVEMBER

Day	Time	m	Day	Time	m
1	0404	0.8	16	0410	0.6
	1008	2.5		1008	2.8
TU	1620	0.7	W	1635	0.5
	2228	2.5		2236	2.7
2	0435	0.8	17	0458	0.5
	1044	2.5		1100	2.7
W	1649	0.8	TH	1720	0.6
	2259	2.5		2321	2.7
3	0507	0.8	18	0546	0.5
	1120	2.4		1153	2.6
TH	1719	0.9	F	1804	0.8
	2332	2.5			
4	0541	0.9	19	0008	2.6
	1157	2.4		0635	0.6
F	1751	0.9	SA	1250	2.5
				1848	1.0
5	0009	2.5	20	0058	2.5
	0618	0.9		0728	0.6
SA	1238	2.3	SU	1355	2.4
	1829	1.0		1937	1.1
6	0050	2.4	21	0152	2.5
	0701	1.0		0830	0.7
SU	1325	2.3	M	1516	2.3
	1913	1.2	◑	2037	1.3
7	0137	2.4	22	0253	2.4
	0753	1.0		0943	0.8
M	1421	2.2	TU	1631	2.3
◐	2006	1.3		2203	1.4
8	0232	2.3	23	0404	2.3
	0900	1.0		1051	0.8
TU	1551	2.2	W	1738	2.3
	2112	1.3		2319	1.4
9	0336	2.3	24	0511	2.3
	1026	1.0		1151	0.8
W	1715	2.3	TH	1838	2.3
	2241	1.3			
10	0452	2.3	25	0020	1.3
	1134	0.8		0611	2.3
TH	1812	2.4	F	1244	0.8
	2351	1.2		1927	2.4
11	0556	2.4	26	0112	1.2
	1229	0.7		0704	2.4
F	1900	2.5	SA	1330	0.8
				2005	2.4
12	0047	1.1	27	0155	1.1
	0649	2.5		0750	2.4
SA	1321	0.6	SU	1410	0.8
	1944	2.5		2037	2.4
13	0139	0.9	28	0232	1.0
	0739	2.6		0831	2.4
SU	1412	0.5	M	1445	0.8
	2027	2.6		2105	2.5
14	0230	0.8	29	0307	0.9
	0828	2.7		0909	2.4
M	1502	0.4	TU	1518	0.8
○	2109	2.7	●	2132	2.5
15	0321	0.6	30	0340	0.8
	0918	2.8		0946	2.4
TU	1550	0.4	W	1548	0.8
	2152	2.7		2201	2.5

DECEMBER

Day	Time	m	Day	Time	m
1	0414	0.8	16	0447	0.4
	1023	2.4		1051	2.6
TH	1620	0.8	F	1703	0.7
	2234	2.6		2305	2.7
2	0449	0.8	17	0535	0.4
	1100	2.4		1143	2.6
F	1653	0.9	SA	1746	0.8
	2309	2.5		2351	2.7
3	0526	0.8	18	0623	0.5
	1139	2.4		1235	2.5
SA	1729	0.9	SU	1828	0.9
	2347	2.5			
4	0605	0.8	19	0037	2.6
	1219	2.3		0711	0.5
SU	1808	1.0	M	1332	2.3
				1910	1.1
5	0027	2.5	20	0125	2.5
	0647	0.9		0803	0.6
M	1304	2.3	TU	1438	2.2
	1851	1.1		1956	1.2
6	0112	2.4	21	0216	2.4
	0736	0.9		0902	0.8
TU	1354	2.2	W	1552	2.2
	1940	1.2	◑	2052	1.3
7	0202	2.4	22	0315	2.3
	0833	0.9		1009	0.9
W	1457	2.2	TH	1656	2.2
◐	2038	1.2		2219	1.4
8	0257	2.4	23	0424	2.3
	0945	0.9		1111	0.9
TH	1633	2.2	F	1755	2.2
	2150	1.3		2335	1.3
9	0404	2.4	24	0529	2.3
	1057	0.8		1205	0.9
F	1737	2.3	SA	1849	2.3
	2310	1.2			
10	0518	2.4	25	0033	1.3
	1158	0.7		0627	2.2
SA	1829	2.4	SU	1254	0.9
				1933	2.3
11	0015	1.1	26	0123	1.1
	0619	2.5		0722	2.3
SU	1254	0.6	M	1336	0.9
	1917	2.5		2009	2.4
12	0114	0.9	27	0205	1.0
	0714	2.6		0811	2.3
M	1347	0.6	TU	1413	0.9
	2003	2.5		2038	2.4
13	0210	0.8	28	0243	0.9
	0809	2.6		0853	2.3
TU	1440	0.6	W	1448	0.9
	2048	2.6		2107	2.5
14	0305	0.6	29	0319	0.8
	0903	2.7		0930	2.4
W	1530	0.6	TH	1522	0.8
○	2133	2.7	●	2139	2.5
15	0358	0.5	30	0357	0.8
	0958	2.7		1007	2.4
TH	1618	0.6	F	1558	0.8
	2219	2.7		2214	2.6
			31	0435	0.7
				1044	2.4
			SA	1635	0.8
				2251	2.6

Chart Datum: 1·50 metres below Ordnance Datum (Newlyn)
HAT is 2·9 metres above Chart Datum

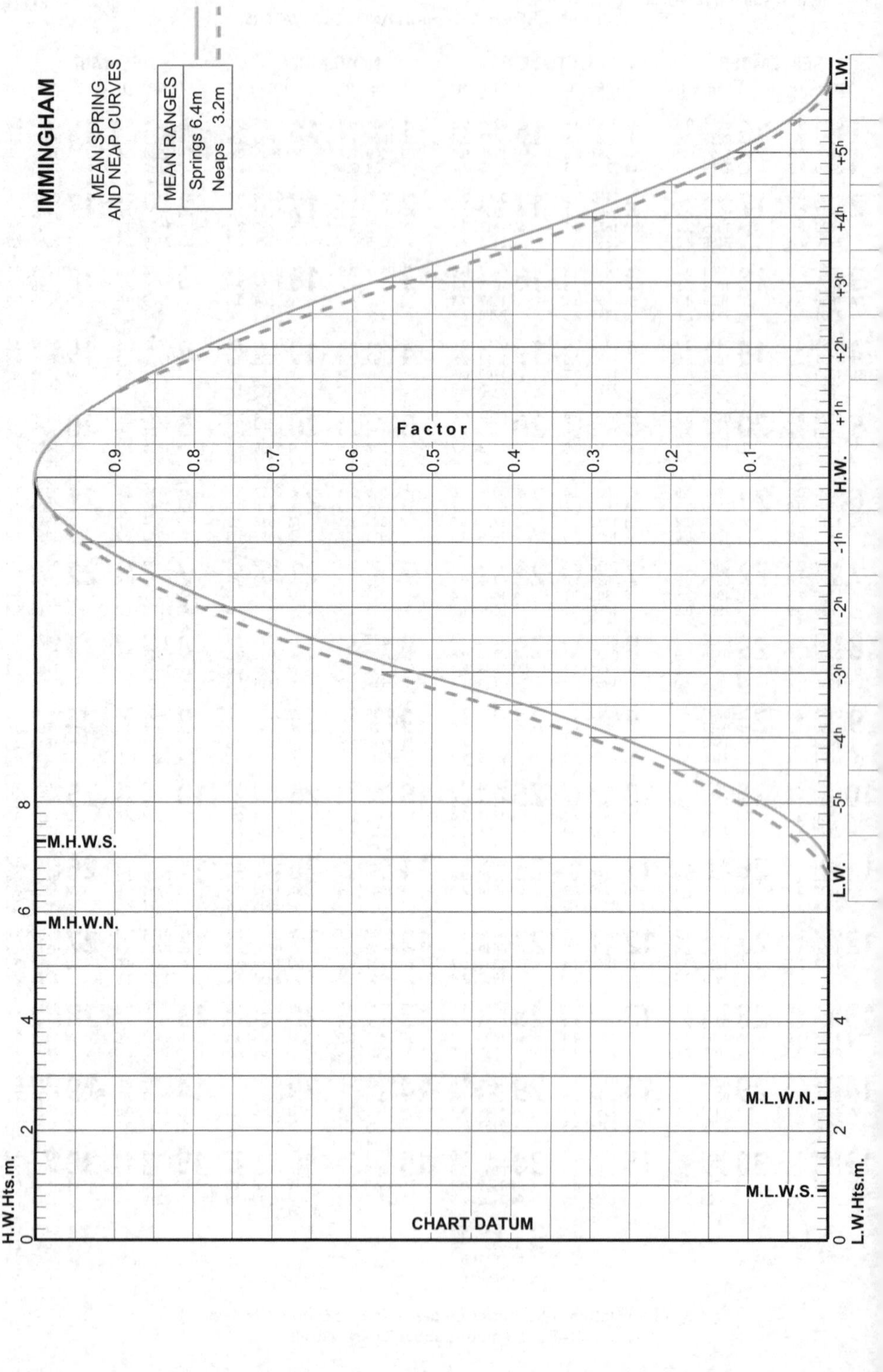
IMMINGHAM
MEAN SPRING
AND NEAP CURVES
MEAN RANGES
Springs 6.4m
Neaps 3.2m
Factor
0.9
0.8
0.7
0.6
0.5
0.4
0.3
0.2
0.1
L.W.
-5h
-4h
-3h
-2h
-1h
H.W.
+1h
+2h
+3h
+4h
+5h
L.W.
H.W.Hts.m.
0
2
4
6
8
M.H.W.S.
M.H.W.N.
CHART DATUM
L.W.Hts.m.
0
2
4
M.L.W.S.
M.L.W.N.

TIME ZONE (UT)
For Summer Time add ONE hour in **non-shaded areas**

IMMINGHAM

LAT 53°38′N LONG 0°11′W

TIMES AND HEIGHTS OF HIGH AND LOW WATERS

Dates in amber are **SPRINGS**
Dates in grey are **NEAPS**

2016

JANUARY

Date	Day	Moon	Time	m	Time	m	Time	m	Time	m
1	F		0411	1.9	1019	6.1	1610	2.4	2221	6.2
2	SA	◑	0456	2.2	1111	5.8	1659	2.7	2320	5.9
3	SU		0550	2.4	1215	5.7	1800	2.8		
4	M		0031	5.8	0652	2.5	1322	5.7	1908	2.9
5	TU		0141	5.8	0758	2.4	1424	5.9	2020	2.7
6	W		0244	5.9	0900	2.2	1519	6.2	2126	2.4
7	TH		0338	6.2	0955	2.0	1606	6.5	2221	2.0
8	F		0426	6.4	1043	1.7	1649	6.7	2310	1.7
9	SA		0511	6.7	1128	1.5	1730	7.0	2356	1.4
10	SU	●	0555	6.9	1211	1.4	1810	7.2		
11	M		0040	1.2	0637	7.0	1253	1.2	1849	7.3
12	TU		0123	1.0	0719	7.1	1334	1.2	1927	7.4
13	W		0204	0.9	0800	7.1	1414	1.2	2006	7.4
14	TH		0246	1.0	0842	7.0	1455	1.3	2048	7.3
15	F		0328	1.1	0927	6.8	1538	1.5	2134	7.1
16	SA	◐	0415	1.3	1018	6.5	1628	1.8	2228	6.8
17	SU		0509	1.6	1120	6.3	1727	2.1	2333	6.5
18	M		0613	1.9	1232	6.1	1839	2.3		
19	TU		0050	6.3	0726	2.1	1346	6.1	1959	2.3
20	W		0209	6.3	0840	2.0	1455	6.2	2114	2.1
21	TH		0321	6.4	0944	1.9	1556	6.5	2217	1.7
22	F		0424	6.6	1040	1.6	1647	6.8	2312	1.3
23	SA		0518	6.8	1130	1.5	1733	7.0		
24	SU	○	0002	1.1	0605	7.0	1215	1.3	1814	7.2
25	M		0048	1.0	0646	7.0	1256	1.3	1853	7.3
26	TU		0129	0.9	0724	7.0	1333	1.3	1930	7.3
27	W		0205	1.0	0759	6.9	1405	1.4	2003	7.2
28	TH		0237	1.2	0830	6.7	1434	1.6	2033	7.0
29	F		0306	1.5	0859	6.5	1503	1.8	2104	6.7
30	SA		0337	1.7	0931	6.3	1535	2.0	2139	6.4
31	SU		0411	2.0	1010	6.1	1613	2.3	2221	6.1

FEBRUARY

Date	Day	Moon	Time	m	Time	m	Time	m	Time	m
1	M	◑	0455	2.3	1100	5.8	1703	2.6	2316	5.8
2	TU		0553	2.5	1209	5.6	1809	2.8		
3	W		0035	5.6	0700	2.6	1329	5.6	1922	2.8
4	TH		0200	5.7	0812	2.5	1438	5.9	2037	2.6
5	F		0308	5.9	0918	2.2	1535	6.2	2147	2.2
6	SA		0404	6.3	1015	1.9	1624	6.6	2246	1.7
7	SU		0453	6.6	1106	1.6	1709	6.9	2337	1.3
8	M	●	0539	6.9	1153	1.3	1751	7.2		
9	TU		0025	1.0	0623	7.1	1238	1.1	1832	7.5
10	W		0110	0.7	0705	7.3	1321	0.9	1912	7.7
11	TH		0153	0.6	0745	7.3	1402	0.9	1953	7.7
12	F		0233	0.6	0825	7.3	1443	0.9	2034	7.6
13	SA		0314	0.8	0907	7.1	1524	1.2	2118	7.4
14	SU		0355	1.1	0953	6.7	1608	1.5	2209	7.0
15	M	◐	0442	1.6	1047	6.3	1701	1.9	2310	6.5
16	TU		0541	2.0	1156	6.0	1810	2.3		
17	W		0028	6.1	0658	2.4	1315	5.9	1937	2.4
18	TH		0156	6.0	0821	2.4	1431	6.0	2101	2.2
19	F		0315	6.1	0930	2.2	1538	6.3	2206	1.8
20	SA		0421	6.4	1026	1.9	1632	6.6	2259	1.4
21	SU		0512	6.7	1114	1.6	1716	6.9	2346	1.1
22	M	○	0553	6.8	1157	1.4	1756	7.1		
23	TU		0028	1.0	0629	6.9	1237	1.3	1833	7.2
24	W		0107	0.9	0702	6.9	1312	1.3	1908	7.2
25	TH		0141	1.0	0732	6.9	1344	1.3	1939	7.1
26	F		0211	1.1	0759	6.8	1411	1.4	2007	7.0
27	SA		0238	1.3	0825	6.7	1437	1.5	2036	6.8
28	SU		0304	1.6	0854	6.5	1504	1.7	2106	6.6
29	M		0332	1.8	0927	6.3	1536	2.0	2140	6.2

MARCH

Date	Day	Moon	Time	m	Time	m	Time	m	Time	m
1	TU	◑	0407	2.1	1007	6.0	1619	2.3	2224	5.9
2	W		0458	2.5	1100	5.7	1720	2.6	2328	5.6
3	TH		0609	2.7	1224	5.5	1837	2.7		
4	F		0114	5.5	0728	2.7	1357	5.7	1957	2.5
5	SA		0241	5.8	0843	2.4	1504	6.0	2114	2.1
6	SU		0344	6.2	0948	2.0	1557	6.5	2221	1.6
7	M		0435	6.6	1043	1.6	1644	6.9	2316	1.1
8	TU		0521	7.0	1132	1.2	1728	7.3		
9	W	●	0005	0.7	0604	7.3	1220	0.9	1811	7.6
10	TH		0051	0.5	0646	7.5	1304	0.7	1853	7.8
11	F		0134	0.3	0726	7.5	1347	0.6	1936	7.9
12	SA		0215	0.4	0805	7.5	1428	0.6	2018	7.8
13	SU		0255	0.6	0845	7.2	1508	0.9	2103	7.4
14	M		0334	1.1	0928	6.9	1551	1.3	2152	6.9
15	TU	◐	0418	1.6	1019	6.4	1641	1.8	2253	6.4
16	W		0512	2.2	1124	6.0	1747	2.2		
17	TH		0014	5.9	0629	2.6	1248	5.7	1919	2.4
18	F		0144	5.8	0800	2.7	1407	5.8	2045	2.2
19	SA		0305	6.0	0911	2.4	1516	6.1	2147	1.8
20	SU		0409	6.3	1006	2.0	1610	6.5	2238	1.4
21	M		0455	6.6	1052	1.7	1654	6.8	2322	1.2
22	TU		0532	6.7	1134	1.5	1733	7.0		
23	W	○	0002	1.0	0604	6.9	1213	1.3	1808	7.1
24	TH		0040	1.0	0635	6.9	1249	1.2	1842	7.1
25	F		0113	1.0	0702	6.9	1320	1.3	1913	7.0
26	SA		0143	1.1	0729	6.9	1348	1.3	1942	6.9
27	SU		0210	1.3	0755	6.8	1413	1.4	2011	6.8
28	M		0235	1.5	0824	6.7	1440	1.6	2040	6.6
29	TU		0300	1.7	0854	6.5	1510	1.8	2112	6.3
30	W		0332	2.0	0930	6.2	1550	2.1	2154	6.0
31	TH	◑	0419	2.4	1018	5.9	1647	2.3	2252	5.7

APRIL

Date	Day	Moon	Time	m	Time	m	Time	m	Time	m
1	F		0527	2.6	1127	5.6	1804	2.5		
2	SA		0028	5.5	0649	2.7	1309	5.7	1924	2.4
3	SU		0213	5.7	0809	2.5	1428	6.0	2043	2.0
4	M		0319	6.2	0918	2.0	1526	6.5	2152	1.5
5	TU		0412	6.7	1016	1.6	1616	7.0	2249	1.0
6	W		0459	7.0	1108	1.1	1703	7.4	2340	0.6
7	TH	●	0543	7.3	1157	0.8	1749	7.7		
8	F		0027	0.4	0624	7.5	1244	0.5	1834	7.8
9	SA		0112	0.3	0704	7.6	1329	0.4	1918	7.9
10	SU		0154	0.4	0744	7.5	1412	0.5	2003	7.7
11	M		0235	0.7	0824	7.3	1454	0.8	2049	7.4
12	TU		0314	1.1	0907	6.9	1538	1.2	2139	6.9
13	W		0356	1.7	0955	6.5	1627	1.7	2240	6.3
14	TH	◐	0447	2.3	1058	6.0	1731	2.1		
15	F		0000	5.9	0557	2.7	1219	5.8	1856	2.3
16	SA		0124	5.7	0728	2.8	1338	5.8	2017	2.1
17	SU		0238	5.9	0842	2.6	1445	6.0	2118	1.9
18	M		0339	6.2	0937	2.2	1540	6.3	2207	1.6
19	TU		0425	6.4	1024	1.9	1625	6.6	2250	1.3
20	W		0502	6.6	1106	1.6	1705	6.8	2330	1.2
21	TH		0535	6.8	1145	1.4	1741	6.8		
22	F	○	0007	1.1	0604	6.9	1222	1.3	1814	6.9
23	SA		0043	1.2	0632	6.9	1255	1.3	1846	6.9
24	SU		0115	1.2	0701	6.9	1325	1.3	1919	6.8
25	M		0144	1.3	0731	6.9	1353	1.4	1950	6.7
26	TU		0210	1.5	0800	6.8	1422	1.5	2022	6.6
27	W		0238	1.7	0831	6.6	1454	1.7	2056	6.4
28	TH		0312	1.9	0907	6.4	1535	1.9	2139	6.1
29	F		0357	2.2	0954	6.1	1630	2.1	2236	5.8
30	SA	◑	0500	2.5	1057	5.9	1741	2.2		

Chart Datum: 3·90 metres below Ordnance Datum (Newlyn)
HAT is 8·0 metres above Chart Datum

TIME ZONE (UT)
For Summer Time add ONE hour in **non-shaded areas**

IMMINGHAM

LAT 53°38′N LONG 0°11′W

TIMES AND HEIGHTS OF HIGH AND LOW WATERS

Dates in amber are **SPRINGS**
Dates in grey are **NEAPS**

2016

MAY

Day	Time	m	Day	Time	m
1 SU	0000 0617 1222 1857	5.7 2.6 5.9 2.1	16 M	0156 0756 1406 2036	5.8 2.7 5.9 2.0
2 M	0141 0735 1348 2012	5.9 2.4 6.1 1.8	17 TU	0256 0859 1503 2128	6.0 2.4 6.1 1.8
3 TU	0249 0846 1452 2120	6.2 2.0 6.5 1.4	18 W	0345 0949 1551 2213	6.2 2.1 6.3 1.6
4 W	0344 0948 1547 2220	6.7 1.6 6.9 1.0	19 TH	0426 1033 1633 2254	6.5 1.8 6.5 1.5
5 TH	0433 1043 1638 2313	7.0 1.2 7.3 0.7	20 F	0501 1114 1711 2334	6.6 1.6 6.6 1.4
6 F ●	0519 1135 1728	7.3 0.8 7.6	21 SA ○	0533 1153 1746	6.8 1.5 6.7
7 SA	0003 0602 1225 1816	0.5 7.5 0.6 7.7	22 SU	0012 0604 1230 1822	1.3 6.9 1.4 6.7
8 SU	0050 0644 1312 1904	0.5 7.5 0.5 7.7	23 M	0048 0637 1305 1858	1.3 6.9 1.4 6.7
9 M	0134 0726 1357 1951	0.6 7.5 0.5 7.5	24 TU	0120 0711 1337 1935	1.4 6.9 1.4 6.7
10 TU	0216 0807 1442 2038	0.8 7.3 0.7 7.2	25 W	0151 0743 1410 2011	1.5 6.9 1.4 6.6
11 W	0256 0850 1526 2128	1.2 7.0 1.1 6.8	26 TH	0223 0816 1446 2048	1.6 6.8 1.5 6.5
12 TH	0338 0936 1615 2227	1.7 6.6 1.5 6.3	27 F	0300 0854 1528 2132	1.8 6.6 1.6 6.3
13 F	0424 1033 1711 ◐ 2337	2.2 6.2 1.9 5.9	28 SA	0345 0940 1621 2227	2.0 6.4 1.8 6.1
14 SA	0522 1145 1820	2.6 5.9 2.1	29 SU	0441 1038 1723 ◑ 2339	2.2 6.2 1.8 5.9
15 SU	0050 0637 1300 1934	5.8 2.8 5.8 2.2	30 M	0550 1150 1832	2.3 6.2 1.8
			31 TU	0104 0703 1310 1943	6.0 2.3 6.3 1.7

JUNE

Day	Time	m	Day	Time	m
1 W	0215 0814 1420 2051	6.3 2.0 6.5 1.4	16 TH	0258 0904 1511 2130	6.0 2.4 6.1 1.9
2 TH	0315 0920 1521 2153	6.6 1.7 6.8 1.2	17 F	0345 0956 1558 2217	6.2 2.1 6.2 1.8
3 F	0408 1020 1617 2249	6.9 1.3 7.1 1.0	18 SA	0425 1042 1641 2301	6.5 1.8 6.4 1.6
4 SA	0457 1115 1711 2341	7.1 1.0 7.3 0.8	19 SU	0503 1126 1721 2343	6.7 1.6 6.6 1.5
5 SU ●	0543 1207 1803	7.3 0.7 7.4	20 M ○	0539 1207 1802	6.8 1.5 6.7
6 M	0030 0627 1258 1853	0.8 7.4 0.6 7.4	21 TU	0023 0616 1247 1842	1.4 6.9 1.4 6.7
7 TU	0116 0710 1345 1942	0.8 7.4 0.6 7.3	22 W	0101 0654 1325 1922	1.4 7.0 1.3 6.8
8 W	0159 0752 1430 2028	1.0 7.3 0.8 7.1	23 TH	0136 0730 1403 2001	1.4 7.0 1.2 6.8
9 TH	0239 0834 1514 2116	1.3 7.1 1.0 6.8	24 F	0213 0806 1442 2041	1.5 7.0 1.3 6.7
10 F	0319 0918 1558 2206	1.7 6.8 1.4 6.4	25 SA	0251 0845 1523 2124	1.6 6.9 1.3 6.5
11 SA	0359 1006 1645 2302	2.0 6.4 1.7 6.1	26 SU	0334 0929 1611 2215	1.7 6.8 1.4 6.4
12 SU ◐	0445 1104 1736	2.4 6.1 2.0	27 M	0425 1021 1705 ◑ 2316	1.9 6.6 1.6 6.2
13 M	0003 0540 1210 1834	5.8 2.6 5.9 2.2	28 TU	0524 1125 1808	2.1 6.5 1.7
14 TU	0105 0646 1316 1937	5.7 2.7 5.8 2.2	29 W	0028 0633 1239 1915	6.1 2.2 6.4 1.7
15 W	0204 0759 1417 2037	5.8 2.7 5.9 2.1	30 TH	0141 0746 1353 2025	6.2 2.1 6.5 1.6

JULY

Day	Time	m	Day	Time	m
1 F	0247 0857 1501 2131	6.4 1.9 6.6 1.5	16 SA	0302 0911 1524 2140	6.0 2.4 6.0 2.1
2 SA	0346 1002 1604 2230	6.7 1.5 6.8 1.3	17 SU	0351 1010 1614 2231	6.3 2.1 6.3 1.8
3 SU	0439 1100 1702 2324	6.9 1.2 7.0 1.2	18 M	0435 1100 1700 2318	6.6 1.8 6.5 1.6
4 M ●	0528 1155 1756	7.1 0.9 7.1	19 TU ○	0517 1147 1744	6.8 1.5 6.7
5 TU	0014 0613 1246 1846	1.1 7.3 0.7 7.2	20 W	0002 0557 1231 1826	1.5 7.0 1.3 6.9
6 W	0100 0656 1333 1932	1.1 7.3 0.7 7.2	21 TH	0043 0636 1314 1908	1.3 7.2 1.1 7.0
7 TH	0143 0737 1416 2015	1.2 7.3 0.8 7.0	22 F	0123 0715 1354 1948	1.3 7.3 1.0 7.0
8 F	0221 0817 1457 2055	1.3 7.2 1.0 6.8	23 SA	0201 0753 1433 2028	1.2 7.3 0.9 7.0
9 SA	0257 0856 1535 2135	1.6 7.0 1.3 6.5	24 SU	0240 0832 1513 2110	1.3 7.3 1.0 6.9
10 SU	0331 0935 1611 2217	1.9 6.7 1.6 6.2	25 M	0321 0915 1556 2155	1.4 7.2 1.2 6.7
11 M	0408 1018 1651 2303	2.2 6.3 1.9 6.0	26 TU	0407 1004 1644 ◑ 2249	1.6 6.9 1.4 6.4
12 TU	0451 1111 1738 ◐ 2359	2.4 6.0 2.2 5.8	27 W	0500 1102 1741 2355	1.9 6.6 1.7 6.2
13 W	0544 1214 1834	2.7 5.8 2.4	28 TH	0605 1214 1850	2.2 6.4 1.9
14 TH	0101 0647 1322 1936	5.7 2.8 5.7 2.4	29 F	0109 0722 1333 2005	6.1 2.2 6.3 2.0
15 F	0204 0759 1427 2042	5.8 2.7 5.8 2.3	30 SA	0222 0841 1450 2115	6.2 2.1 6.4 1.9
			31 SU	0328 0950 1559 2216	6.4 1.7 6.6 1.7

AUGUST

Day	Time	m	Day	Time	m
1 M	0425 1050 1659 2310	6.7 1.4 6.8 1.5	16 TU	0409 1036 1641 2254	6.5 1.8 6.5 1.7
2 TU	0514 1143 1751 ● 2359	7.0 1.0 7.0 1.3	17 W	0453 1126 1726 2341	6.9 1.4 6.8 1.5
3 W	0558 1232 1836	7.2 0.8 7.1	18 TH ○	0535 1212 1809	7.1 1.1 7.0
4 TH	0043 0639 1317 1916	1.2 7.3 0.7 7.1	19 F	0024 0616 1256 1850	1.3 7.4 0.9 7.2
5 F	0124 0718 1357 1953	1.2 7.3 0.8 7.0	20 SA	0106 0656 1338 1930	1.1 7.6 0.7 7.3
6 SA	0200 0755 1433 2027	1.3 7.3 1.0 6.9	21 SU	0146 0735 1417 2009	1.0 7.6 0.7 7.3
7 SU	0232 0829 1505 2059	1.5 7.1 1.2 6.7	22 M	0225 0815 1456 2049	1.0 7.6 0.8 7.1
8 M	0302 0902 1535 2129	1.7 6.8 1.6 6.4	23 TU	0305 0858 1536 2131	1.2 7.4 1.1 6.9
9 TU	0332 0936 1608 2205	1.9 6.5 1.9 6.2	24 W	0348 0945 1620 2221	1.5 7.1 1.5 6.5
10 W	0407 1017 1647 ◐ 2250	2.2 6.2 2.2 5.9	25 TH	0438 1042 1714 ◑ 2324	1.8 6.7 1.9 6.2
11 TH	0453 1111 1738 2354	2.5 5.8 2.5 5.7	26 F	0542 1155 1825	2.2 6.2 2.3
12 F	0553 1225 1842	2.8 5.6 2.6	27 SA	0042 0704 1322 1948	6.0 2.4 6.0 2.4
13 SA	0111 0704 1345 1953	5.7 2.8 5.6 2.6	28 SU	0201 0831 1445 2104	6.0 2.2 6.1 2.3
14 SU	0221 0822 1455 2104	5.8 2.6 5.8 2.4	29 M	0312 0941 1557 2204	6.3 1.8 6.4 2.0
15 M	0320 0937 1552 2204	6.2 2.3 6.2 2.0	30 TU	0410 1038 1654 2255	6.7 1.4 6.7 1.7
			31 W	0457 1127 1739 2341	7.0 1.1 6.9 1.4

Chart Datum: 3·90 metres below Ordnance Datum (Newlyn)
HAT is 8·0 metres above Chart Datum

TIME ZONE (UT)
For Summer Time add ONE hour in **non-shaded areas**

IMMINGHAM

LAT 53°38′N LONG 0°11′W

TIMES AND HEIGHTS OF HIGH AND LOW WATERS

Dates in amber are **SPRINGS**
Dates in grey are **NEAPS**

2016

SEPTEMBER

Date	Day	Time	m	Time	m	Time	m	Time	m	Moon
1	TH	0538	7.2	1212	0.9	1817	7.1			●
2	F	0023	1.3	0617	7.3	1254	0.8	1852	7.1	
3	SA	0102	1.3	0654	7.3	1331	0.9	1925	7.0	
4	SU	0135	1.3	0728	7.3	1404	1.1	1954	7.0	
5	M	0205	1.4	0800	7.1	1432	1.3	2021	6.8	
6	TU	0232	1.6	0829	6.9	1459	1.6	2048	6.7	
7	W	0258	1.8	0900	6.6	1526	1.8	2119	6.4	
8	TH	0329	2.1	0934	6.3	1558	2.2	2157	6.1	
9	F	0409	2.4	1018	5.9	1645	2.5	2249	5.8	◐
10	SA	0506	2.7	1126	5.6	1750	2.8			
11	SU	0013	5.6	0619	2.8	1306	5.5	1908	2.8	
12	M	0142	5.7	0740	2.7	1426	5.7	2027	2.6	
13	TU	0248	6.1	0902	2.3	1528	6.1	2134	2.2	
14	W	0340	6.5	1007	1.8	1619	6.6	2228	1.8	
15	TH	0426	6.9	1100	1.3	1704	6.9	2315	1.5	
16	F	0509	7.3	1147	1.0	1747	7.2			○
17	SA	0001	1.2	0551	7.6	1232	0.7	1827	7.4	
18	SU	0044	0.9	0632	7.8	1315	0.5	1907	7.5	
19	M	0126	0.8	0714	7.9	1355	0.5	1945	7.5	
20	TU	0207	0.8	0756	7.8	1435	0.7	2025	7.4	
21	W	0248	1.0	0840	7.6	1514	1.1	2106	7.1	
22	TH	0330	1.3	0928	7.1	1556	1.6	2154	6.6	
23	F	0419	1.8	1026	6.6	1647	2.1	2255	6.2	◑
24	SA	0523	2.2	1142	6.1	1800	2.6			
25	SU	0016	5.9	0649	2.4	1313	5.9	1930	2.7	
26	M	0139	6.0	0818	2.2	1436	6.1	2047	2.5	
27	TU	0251	6.2	0925	1.8	1546	6.4	2145	2.2	
28	W	0348	6.6	1018	1.5	1637	6.7	2234	1.8	
29	TH	0434	6.9	1104	1.2	1716	6.9	2317	1.5	
30	F	0514	7.1	1146	1.0	1751	7.0	2357	1.4	

OCTOBER

Date	Day	Time	m	Time	m	Time	m	Time	m	Moon
1	SA	0552	7.2	1224	1.0	1823	7.1			●
2	SU	0035	1.3	0627	7.3	1300	1.0	1853	7.1	
3	M	0108	1.3	0700	7.2	1331	1.2	1921	7.0	
4	TU	0137	1.4	0731	7.1	1359	1.4	1947	7.0	
5	W	0203	1.5	0800	6.9	1425	1.6	2014	6.8	
6	TH	0229	1.7	0830	6.7	1450	1.8	2043	6.6	
7	F	0258	1.9	0902	6.4	1519	2.1	2117	6.3	
8	SA	0335	2.2	0942	6.0	1601	2.5	2201	6.0	
9	SU	0428	2.5	1039	5.7	1703	2.8	2307	5.7	◐
10	M	0542	2.7	1221	5.5	1824	2.9			
11	TU	0053	5.7	0702	2.6	1354	5.7	1946	2.8	
12	W	0210	6.0	0822	2.3	1459	6.2	2057	2.4	
13	TH	0307	6.5	0931	1.8	1552	6.6	2155	1.9	
14	F	0355	6.9	1027	1.3	1638	7.0	2246	1.5	
15	SA	0440	7.3	1117	0.9	1721	7.3	2334	1.1	
16	SU	0525	7.7	1204	0.6	1802	7.5			○
17	M	0020	0.8	0609	7.9	1249	0.5	1842	7.6	
18	TU	0105	0.7	0653	7.9	1331	0.5	1922	7.6	
19	W	0149	0.7	0738	7.8	1412	0.8	2002	7.5	
20	TH	0231	0.9	0824	7.6	1452	1.2	2044	7.2	
21	F	0315	1.2	0914	7.1	1534	1.7	2131	6.8	
22	SA	0404	1.7	1012	6.6	1623	2.2	2230	6.3	◑
23	SU	0507	2.1	1129	6.1	1731	2.7	2348	6.0	
24	M	0630	2.3	1254	5.9	1859	2.9			
25	TU	0110	6.0	0752	2.2	1410	6.0	2017	2.7	
26	W	0220	6.2	0857	1.9	1516	6.3	2117	2.4	
27	TH	0318	6.5	0949	1.6	1606	6.6	2206	2.0	
28	F	0406	6.8	1033	1.4	1645	6.8	2249	1.7	
29	SA	0447	6.9	1114	1.3	1720	7.0	2329	1.5	
30	SU	0524	7.1	1151	1.2	1752	7.0			●
31	M	0006	1.4	0559	7.1	1227	1.2	1821	7.1	

NOVEMBER

Date	Day	Time	m	Time	m	Time	m	Time	m	Moon
1	TU	0041	1.4	0632	7.1	1300	1.3	1850	7.1	
2	W	0111	1.4	0705	7.0	1329	1.4	1919	7.0	
3	TH	0139	1.5	0737	6.9	1356	1.6	1947	6.9	
4	F	0206	1.7	0809	6.7	1422	1.8	2017	6.8	
5	SA	0237	1.8	0841	6.4	1453	2.0	2049	6.5	
6	SU	0314	2.0	0920	6.2	1533	2.4	2130	6.2	
7	M	0403	2.3	1013	5.9	1628	2.7	2227	6.0	◐
8	TU	0510	2.5	1134	5.7	1742	2.8	2349	5.9	
9	W	0627	2.4	1312	5.8	1903	2.7			
10	TH	0120	6.0	0742	2.1	1422	6.1	2016	2.4	
11	F	0227	6.4	0852	1.7	1519	6.6	2120	2.0	
12	SA	0322	6.9	0952	1.3	1608	7.0	2216	1.5	
13	SU	0412	7.3	1045	1.0	1654	7.3	2308	1.2	
14	M	0500	7.6	1135	0.8	1738	7.5	2357	0.9	○
15	TU	0549	7.8	1223	0.7	1820	7.6			
16	W	0045	0.7	0636	7.8	1309	0.7	1902	7.6	
17	TH	0132	0.7	0724	7.7	1352	0.9	1944	7.5	
18	F	0218	0.8	0812	7.5	1433	1.2	2026	7.3	
19	SA	0303	1.1	0902	7.1	1515	1.7	2112	6.9	
20	SU	0352	1.5	0959	6.6	1601	2.2	2206	6.5	
21	M	0448	1.9	1107	6.2	1656	2.6	2315	6.2	◑
22	TU	0556	2.2	1221	5.9	1809	2.9			
23	W	0031	6.0	0711	2.2	1329	5.9	1929	2.9	
24	TH	0140	6.1	0816	2.1	1431	6.1	2038	2.6	
25	F	0241	6.2	0911	1.9	1524	6.3	2131	2.3	
26	SA	0333	6.5	0957	1.7	1609	6.6	2217	2.0	
27	SU	0417	6.6	1038	1.6	1647	6.8	2259	1.7	
28	M	0457	6.8	1118	1.5	1721	6.9	2338	1.6	
29	TU	0533	6.8	1155	1.4	1753	7.0			●
30	W	0014	1.5	0608	6.9	1231	1.4	1824	7.1	

DECEMBER

Date	Day	Time	m	Time	m	Time	m	Time	m	Moon
1	TH	0049	1.5	0643	6.9	1303	1.5	1857	7.1	
2	F	0120	1.5	0718	6.8	1333	1.6	1929	7.0	
3	SA	0151	1.6	0753	6.7	1403	1.7	2000	6.9	
4	SU	0224	1.7	0829	6.5	1436	1.9	2032	6.7	
5	M	0301	1.8	0908	6.3	1515	2.1	2112	6.5	
6	TU	0347	1.9	0956	6.1	1604	2.3	2202	6.3	
7	W	0444	2.1	1059	5.9	1707	2.5	2307	6.2	◐
8	TH	0552	2.1	1221	5.9	1821	2.6			
9	F	0025	6.2	0704	2.0	1339	6.1	1935	2.4	
10	SA	0143	6.4	0814	1.8	1443	6.4	2045	2.1	
11	SU	0249	6.7	0919	1.5	1539	6.8	2148	1.7	
12	M	0347	7.1	1018	1.2	1629	7.1	2245	1.3	
13	TU	0442	7.3	1111	1.0	1717	7.3	2339	1.0	
14	W	0534	7.5	1202	0.9	1803	7.5			○
15	TH	0030	0.8	0625	7.6	1250	0.9	1846	7.6	
16	F	0119	0.7	0715	7.5	1335	1.0	1929	7.5	
17	SA	0206	0.7	0803	7.3	1417	1.2	2012	7.4	
18	SU	0251	1.0	0850	7.0	1457	1.6	2055	7.1	
19	M	0336	1.3	0940	6.7	1537	1.9	2142	6.7	
20	TU	0422	1.6	1035	6.3	1621	2.3	2236	6.4	
21	W	0513	2.0	1135	6.0	1712	2.7	2341	6.1	◑
22	TH	0611	2.3	1237	5.8	1815	2.9			
23	F	0049	5.9	0715	2.4	1339	5.8	1930	2.9	
24	SA	0155	6.0	0819	2.3	1436	6.0	2044	2.7	
25	SU	0254	6.1	0914	2.1	1528	6.2	2141	2.3	
26	M	0345	6.3	1001	1.9	1612	6.5	2228	2.0	
27	TU	0430	6.4	1045	1.7	1651	6.7	2311	1.8	
28	W	0509	6.6	1126	1.6	1727	6.9	2351	1.6	
29	TH	0547	6.7	1205	1.5	1803	7.0			●
30	F	0030	1.5	0625	6.8	1242	1.5	1839	7.1	
31	SA	0107	1.4	0703	6.8	1316	1.5	1913	7.1	

Chart Datum: 3·90 metres below Ordnance Datum (Newlyn)
HAT is 8·0 metres above Chart Datum

TIDES

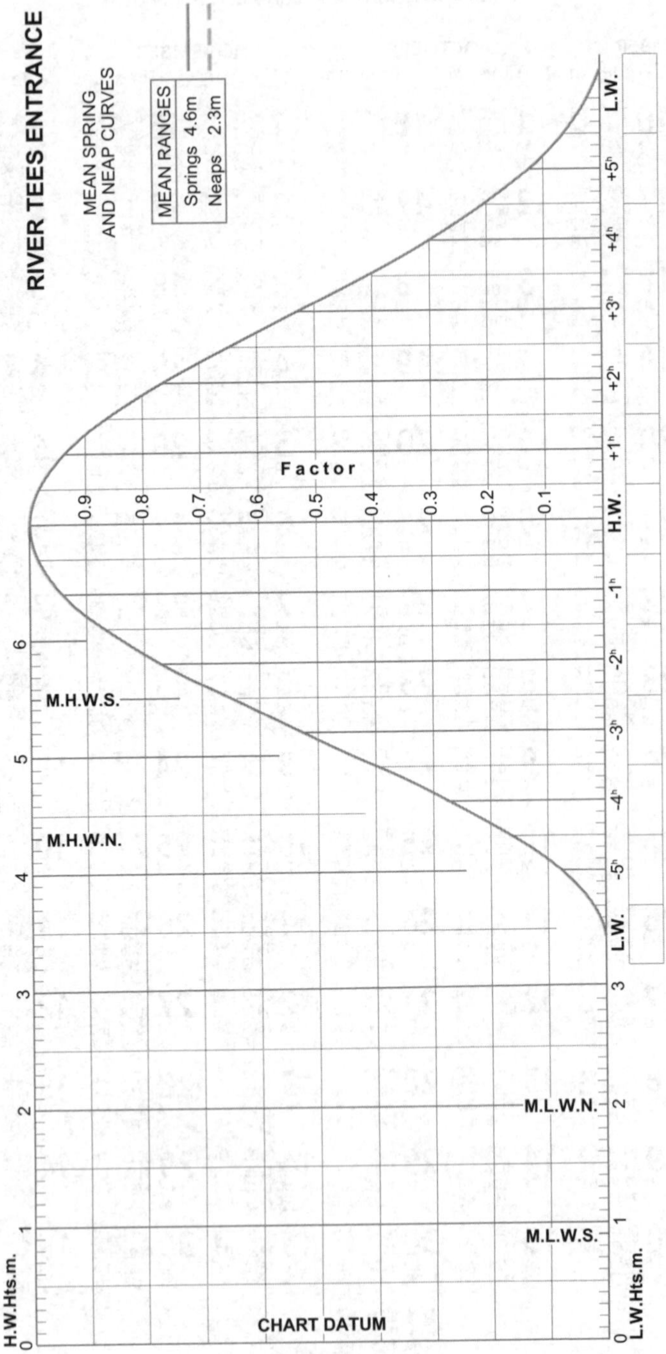
RIVER TEES ENTRANCE
MEAN SPRING AND NEAP CURVES
MEAN RANGES
Springs 4.6m
Neaps 2.3m
Factor
0.9
0.8
0.7
0.6
0.5
0.4
0.3
0.2
0.1
L.W.
-5h
-4h
-3h
-2h
-1h
H.W.
+1h
+2h
+3h
+4h
+5h
L.W.
H.W.Hts.m.
M.H.W.S.
M.H.W.N.
CHART DATUM
M.L.W.N.
M.L.W.S.
L.W.Hts.m.

TIME ZONE (UT)
For Summer Time add ONE hour in **non-shaded areas**

RIVER TEES

LAT 54°38′N LONG 1°09′W

TIMES AND HEIGHTS OF HIGH AND LOW WATERS

Dates in amber are **SPRINGS**
Dates in grey are **NEAPS**

2016

JANUARY

Date	Time	m	Date	Time	m
1 F	0201	1.5	16 SA	0156	1.0
	0812	4.5		0811	4.9
	1403	2.0		1413	1.5
	2022	4.7		◐ 2018	5.1
2 SA	0249	1.7	17 SU	0252	1.2
	0904	4.4		0910	4.7
	1458	2.2		1515	1.7
	◑ 2118	4.5		2122	4.9
3 SU	0347	1.9	18 M	0357	1.5
	1002	4.3		1016	4.6
	1610	2.3		1628	1.8
	2222	4.3		2233	4.7
4 M	0454	2.0	19 TU	0511	1.6
	1105	4.3		1126	4.6
	1725	2.3		1746	1.8
	2329	4.3		2349	4.7
5 TU	0600	2.0	20 W	0629	1.6
	1207	4.4		1238	4.7
	1831	2.1		1902	1.6
6 W	0032	4.4	21 TH	0103	4.8
	0657	1.8		0735	1.5
	1302	4.6		1341	4.9
	1925	1.9		2004	1.3
7 TH	0127	4.6	22 F	0206	5.0
	0746	1.6		0830	1.3
	1348	4.8		1433	5.1
	2011	1.6		2057	1.1
8 F	0214	4.8	23 SA	0258	5.1
	0829	1.4		0916	1.2
	1430	5.0		1518	5.3
	2054	1.3		2143	0.9
9 SA	0257	5.0	24 SU	0342	5.2
	0910	1.2		0958	1.1
	1510	5.2		1559	5.4
	2135	1.1		○ 2224	0.8
10 SU	0338	5.1	25 M	0423	5.3
	0950	1.1		1036	1.1
	1548	5.4		1636	5.4
	● 2216	0.9		2302	0.7
11 M	0418	5.3	26 TU	0501	5.2
	1030	1.0		1111	1.2
	1627	5.5		1710	5.4
	2256	0.7		2337	0.8
12 TU	0500	5.3	27 W	0537	5.2
	1110	1.0		1143	1.2
	1707	5.6		1745	5.4
	2338	0.6			
13 W	0543	5.3	28 TH	0011	0.9
	1151	1.0		0612	5.0
	1749	5.6		1215	1.4
				1820	5.2
14 TH	0021	0.7	29 F	0045	1.1
	0628	5.2		0648	4.9
	1235	1.1		1246	1.5
	1833	5.5		1858	5.0
15 F	0106	0.8	30 SA	0119	1.3
	0717	5.1		0727	4.7
	1321	1.3		1320	1.7
	1922	5.3		1939	4.8
			31 SU	0156	1.6
				0811	4.5
				1401	1.9
				2027	4.5

FEBRUARY

Date	Time	m	Date	Time	m
1 M	0241	1.8	16 TU	0328	1.6
	0902	4.3		0946	4.5
	1454	2.2		1601	1.8
	◑ 2124	4.3		2212	4.5
2 TU	0341	2.0	17 W	0446	1.8
	1002	4.2		1101	4.4
	1609	2.3		1728	1.8
	2231	4.2		2335	4.4
3 W	0457	2.1	18 TH	0615	1.9
	1109	4.2		1222	4.5
	1734	2.2		1854	1.7
	2344	4.2			
4 TH	0613	2.0	19 F	0059	4.6
	1215	4.3		0726	1.7
	1847	2.0		1330	4.7
				1958	1.4
5 F	0051	4.4	20 SA	0201	4.8
	0714	1.8		0820	1.5
	1314	4.6		1422	5.0
	1944	1.7		2048	1.1
6 SA	0148	4.6	21 SU	0249	5.0
	0805	1.5		0903	1.3
	1403	4.9		1505	5.2
	2033	1.3		2130	0.9
7 SU	0235	4.9	22 M	0329	5.1
	0851	1.3		0942	1.2
	1447	5.2		1543	5.3
	2117	1.0		○ 2206	0.8
8 M	0319	5.2	23 TU	0405	5.2
	0934	1.0		1016	1.1
	1529	5.4		1617	5.4
	● 2200	0.7		2239	0.7
9 TU	0401	5.4	24 W	0439	5.2
	1016	0.8		1047	1.1
	1609	5.6		1648	5.4
	2242	0.4		2311	0.8
10 W	0443	5.5	25 TH	0510	5.2
	1057	0.7		1117	1.1
	1650	5.8		1719	5.3
	2324	0.3		2341	0.9
11 TH	0526	5.5	26 F	0541	5.1
	1137	0.7		1145	1.2
	1732	5.8		1751	5.2
12 F	0005	0.3	27 SA	0010	1.0
	0609	5.5		0613	5.0
	1219	0.8		1215	1.3
	1815	5.7		1825	5.1
13 SA	0048	0.5	28 SU	0041	1.2
	0656	5.3		0648	4.8
	1302	1.0		1247	1.4
	1903	5.5		1903	4.9
14 SU	0134	0.8	29 M	0115	1.4
	0745	5.0		0728	4.6
	1350	1.2		1325	1.7
	1957	5.2		1946	4.6
15 M	0225	1.2			
	0841	4.7			
	1448	1.5			
	◐ 2059	4.8			

MARCH

Date	Time	m	Date	Time	m
1 TU	0156	1.7	16 W	0302	1.7
	0815	4.4		0919	4.5
	1410	1.9		1540	1.7
	◑ 2038	4.4		2155	4.4
2 W	0247	2.0	17 TH	0424	2.0
	0912	4.2		1036	4.3
	1510	2.1		1712	1.8
	2143	4.2		2323	4.3
3 TH	0400	2.2	18 F	0558	2.0
	1018	4.1		1201	4.4
	1638	2.2		1840	1.6
	2258	4.1			
4 F	0528	2.1	19 SA	0047	4.4
	1129	4.2		0709	1.9
	1806	2.0		1311	4.6
				1942	1.4
5 SA	0014	4.3	20 SU	0146	4.6
	0642	1.9		0801	1.6
	1236	4.4		1402	4.8
	1913	1.6		2029	1.1
6 SU	0118	4.6	21 M	0231	4.8
	0739	1.6		0843	1.4
	1333	4.8		1444	5.0
	2007	1.2		2107	0.9
7 M	0210	4.9	22 TU	0308	5.0
	0828	1.2		0919	1.2
	1421	5.2		1521	5.2
	2055	0.8		2141	0.8
8 TU	0256	5.2	23 W	0342	5.1
	0913	0.9		0951	1.1
	1505	5.5		1553	5.3
	2140	0.5		○ 2212	0.8
9 W	0339	5.5	24 TH	0412	5.1
	0956	0.7		1021	1.0
	1547	5.7		1624	5.3
	● 2222	0.2		2241	0.8
10 TH	0422	5.6	25 F	0441	5.2
	1038	0.5		1050	1.0
	1630	5.9		1653	5.2
	2304	0.1		2310	0.9
11 F	0505	5.7	26 SA	0509	5.1
	1119	0.5		1118	1.0
	1713	5.9		1723	5.2
	2346	0.2		2338	1.0
12 SA	0548	5.6	27 SU	0540	5.1
	1200	0.5		1148	1.1
	1758	5.8		1756	5.0
13 SU	0028	0.4	28 M	0009	1.1
	0633	5.4		0614	4.9
	1244	0.7		1221	1.3
	1846	5.5		1832	4.9
14 M	0112	0.8	29 TU	0044	1.3
	0721	5.1		0653	4.7
	1331	1.0		1257	1.5
	1939	5.2		1915	4.6
15 TU	0201	1.2	30 W	0123	1.6
	0815	4.8		0738	4.5
	1427	1.4		1340	1.7
	◐ 2041	4.7		2005	4.4
			31 TH	0211	1.9
				0832	4.3
				1436	1.9
				◑ 2108	4.2

APRIL

Date	Time	m	Date	Time	m
1 F	0317	2.1	16 SA	0526	2.1
	0937	4.2		1128	4.3
	1556	2.0		1809	1.6
	2222	4.1			
2 SA	0447	2.1	17 SU	0019	4.3
	1049	4.2		0638	2.0
	1726	1.9		1239	4.5
	2338	4.3		1910	1.4
3 SU	0606	1.9	18 M	0118	4.5
	1158	4.4		0731	1.8
	1839	1.5		1332	4.7
				1957	1.2
4 M	0046	4.6	19 TU	0203	4.7
	0708	1.6		0813	1.5
	1259	4.8		1415	4.9
	1937	1.1		2036	1.1
5 TU	0141	4.9	20 W	0240	4.9
	0800	1.2		0850	1.3
	1351	5.2		1452	5.0
	2028	0.7		2110	1.0
6 W	0229	5.3	21 TH	0313	5.0
	0847	0.9		0923	1.2
	1438	5.5		1526	5.1
	2114	0.4		2141	0.9
7 TH	0314	5.5	22 F	0343	5.1
	0933	0.6		0954	1.1
	1523	5.8		1557	5.1
	● 2159	0.2		○ 2212	0.9
8 F	0358	5.7	23 SA	0412	5.1
	1016	0.4		1024	1.0
	1609	5.9		1628	5.1
	2243	0.1		2241	0.9
9 SA	0442	5.7	24 SU	0440	5.1
	1100	0.3		1054	1.0
	1654	5.9		1659	5.1
	2325	0.2		2311	1.0
10 SU	0526	5.6	25 M	0512	5.1
	1143	0.4		1126	1.1
	1742	5.7		1732	5.0
				2343	1.1
11 M	0008	0.5	26 TU	0547	5.0
	0610	5.4		1200	1.2
	1228	0.6		1810	4.9
	1831	5.5			
12 TU	0053	0.8	27 W	0019	1.3
	0658	5.1		0625	4.8
	1316	0.9		1238	1.3
	1925	5.1		1852	4.7
13 W	0141	1.3	28 TH	0059	1.6
	0751	4.8		0709	4.7
	1412	1.3		1322	1.5
	2026	4.7		1943	4.5
14 TH	0241	1.8	29 F	0146	1.8
	0853	4.5		0801	4.5
	1522	1.6		1417	1.7
	◐ 2138	4.4		2043	4.3
15 F	0358	2.1	30 SA	0249	2.0
	1007	4.3		0903	4.4
	1646	1.7		1529	1.7
	2259	4.2		◑ 2153	4.3

Chart Datum: 2·85 metres below Ordnance Datum (Newlyn)
HAT is 6·1 metres above Chart Datum

TIME ZONE (UT)
For Summer Time add ONE hour in **non-shaded areas**

RIVER TEES

LAT 54°38′N LONG 1°09′W

TIMES AND HEIGHTS OF HIGH AND LOW WATERS

Dates in amber are **SPRINGS**
Dates in grey are **NEAPS**

2016

MAY

Date	Day	Time	m
1		0411	2.1
		1013	4.4
	SU	1650	1.6
		2306	4.4
2		0529	1.9
		1122	4.6
	M	1802	1.4
3		0013	4.6
		0633	1.6
	TU	1225	4.9
		1903	1.0
4		0111	4.9
		0729	1.2
	W	1321	5.2
		1958	0.7
5		0202	5.2
		0820	0.9
	TH	1412	5.5
		2048	0.4
6		0250	5.5
		0909	0.6
	F	1501	5.7
		● 2136	0.3
7		0335	5.6
		0956	0.4
	SA	1550	5.8
		2222	0.3
8		0421	5.6
		1042	0.4
	SU	1639	5.8
		2307	0.4
9		0506	5.6
		1128	0.4
	M	1728	5.6
		2351	0.6
10		0551	5.4
		1214	0.6
	TU	1819	5.4
11		0035	1.0
		0638	5.2
	W	1304	0.8
		1912	5.0
12		0124	1.4
		0729	4.9
	TH	1358	1.1
		2009	4.7
13		0218	1.8
		0827	4.6
	F	1459	1.4
		◐ 2113	4.4
14		0325	2.0
		0933	4.4
	SA	1610	1.6
		2223	4.3
15		0441	2.2
		1045	4.4
	SU	1723	1.6
		2334	4.3
16		0552	2.1
		1154	4.4
	M	1826	1.5
17		0035	4.4
		0650	1.9
	TU	1252	4.6
		1916	1.4
18		0125	4.6
		0737	1.7
	W	1339	4.7
		1958	1.3
19		0206	4.8
		0817	1.5
	TH	1420	4.9
		2036	1.2
20		0241	4.9
		0853	1.3
	F	1457	5.0
		2111	1.1
21		0314	5.0
		0927	1.2
	SA	1532	5.0
		○ 2143	1.0
22		0344	5.1
		1000	1.1
	SU	1605	5.0
		2215	1.0
23		0415	5.1
		1034	1.0
	M	1639	5.0
		2248	1.1
24		0449	5.1
		1108	1.0
	TU	1714	5.0
		2323	1.1
25		0525	5.1
		1145	1.1
	W	1754	4.9
26		0001	1.3
		0604	5.0
	TH	1225	1.2
		1837	4.8
27		0042	1.5
		0647	4.9
	F	1310	1.3
		1927	4.7
28		0130	1.7
		0738	4.7
	SA	1404	1.4
		2024	4.5
29		0228	1.8
		0836	4.6
	SU	1508	1.5
		◑ 2128	4.5
30		0339	1.9
		0942	4.6
	M	1619	1.4
		2236	4.5
31		0453	1.8
		1050	4.7
	TU	1728	1.3
		2341	4.7

JUNE

Date	Day	Time	m
1		0559	1.6
		1155	4.9
	W	1832	1.1
2		0042	4.9
		0659	1.3
	TH	1255	5.1
		1931	0.8
3		0137	5.1
		0756	1.0
	F	1352	5.4
		2025	0.7
4		0228	5.3
		0849	0.8
	SA	1445	5.5
		2117	0.6
5		0317	5.5
		0940	0.6
	SU	1537	5.6
		● 2205	0.6
6		0403	5.5
		1028	0.5
	M	1627	5.6
		2251	0.6
7		0449	5.5
		1116	0.5
	TU	1716	5.5
		2336	0.8
8		0534	5.4
		1202	0.6
	W	1805	5.3
9		0020	1.1
		0619	5.3
	TH	1249	0.8
		1854	5.1
10		0104	1.4
		0706	5.1
	F	1338	1.0
		1945	4.8
11		0151	1.7
		0756	4.8
	SA	1429	1.3
		2039	4.5
12		0245	1.9
		0853	4.6
	SU	1526	1.5
		◐ 2137	4.3
13		0348	2.1
		0956	4.4
	M	1628	1.7
		2239	4.3
14		0456	2.2
		1101	4.4
	TU	1732	1.7
		2341	4.3
15		0600	2.1
		1203	4.4
	W	1829	1.7
16		0038	4.4
		0655	1.9
	TH	1259	4.5
		1918	1.6
17		0126	4.6
		0742	1.7
	F	1347	4.7
		2002	1.4
18		0208	4.8
		0824	1.5
	SA	1430	4.8
		2041	1.3
19		0245	4.9
		0903	1.3
	SU	1509	4.9
		2118	1.2
20		0320	5.1
		0940	1.1
	M	1546	5.0
		○ 2154	1.1
21		0355	5.2
		1016	1.0
	TU	1622	5.1
		2231	1.1
22		0430	5.2
		1054	1.0
	W	1700	5.1
		2309	1.1
23		0507	5.2
		1133	0.9
	TH	1740	5.1
		2348	1.2
24		0547	5.2
		1214	1.0
	F	1824	5.0
25		0030	1.3
		0629	5.1
	SA	1300	1.0
		1912	4.9
26		0116	1.4
		0717	5.0
	SU	1349	1.1
		2005	4.8
27		0208	1.6
		0812	4.9
	M	1446	1.2
		◑ 2103	4.7
28		0310	1.7
		0914	4.8
	TU	1550	1.3
		2207	4.6
29		0419	1.7
		1021	4.8
	W	1657	1.3
		2312	4.7
30		0529	1.6
		1130	4.9
	TH	1805	1.3

JULY

Date	Day	Time	m
1		0017	4.8
		0635	1.4
	F	1237	5.0
		1910	1.1
2		0119	5.0
		0738	1.2
	SA	1339	5.2
		2010	1.0
3		0214	5.2
		0836	0.9
	SU	1436	5.3
		2103	0.9
4		0304	5.4
		0929	0.7
	M	1528	5.4
		● 2152	0.9
5		0351	5.5
		1018	0.6
	TU	1617	5.4
		2238	0.9
6		0435	5.5
		1103	0.6
	W	1703	5.4
		2320	1.0
7		0517	5.5
		1147	0.6
	TH	1748	5.3
8		0000	1.1
		0557	5.4
	F	1229	0.8
		1831	5.1
9		0040	1.3
		0639	5.2
	SA	1310	1.0
		1914	4.9
10		0118	1.5
		0722	5.0
	SU	1353	1.2
		1959	4.7
11		0200	1.8
		0810	4.8
	M	1439	1.5
		2048	4.5
12		0249	2.0
		0904	4.5
	TU	1531	1.8
		◐ 2142	4.3
13		0351	2.2
		1006	4.4
	W	1632	1.9
		2242	4.2
14		0502	2.2
		1112	4.3
	TH	1737	1.9
		2345	4.3
15		0610	2.1
		1216	4.4
	F	1838	1.8
16		0043	4.4
		0707	1.9
	SA	1314	4.5
		1929	1.7
17		0134	4.6
		0756	1.6
	SU	1403	4.7
		2015	1.5
18		0218	4.9
		0840	1.4
	M	1446	4.9
		2057	1.3
19		0257	5.1
		0921	1.2
	TU	1526	5.1
		○ 2136	1.2
20		0335	5.2
		1000	1.0
	W	1605	5.2
		2216	1.1
21		0412	5.4
		1040	0.8
	TH	1644	5.3
		2255	1.0
22		0450	5.4
		1120	0.7
	F	1725	5.3
		2335	1.0
23		0529	5.5
		1201	0.7
	SA	1808	5.3
24		0015	1.1
		0611	5.4
	SU	1245	0.7
		1853	5.2
25		0059	1.2
		0656	5.3
	M	1331	0.9
		1942	5.0
26		0147	1.4
		0748	5.2
	TU	1423	1.1
		◑ 2037	4.8
27		0243	1.6
		0849	5.0
	W	1523	1.3
		2139	4.7
28		0350	1.7
		0958	4.8
	TH	1631	1.5
		2247	4.6
29		0505	1.7
		1112	4.7
	F	1746	1.6
		2358	4.6
30		0622	1.6
		1227	4.8
	SA	1859	1.5
31		0106	4.8
		0731	1.3
	SU	1336	5.0
		2001	1.3

AUGUST

Date	Day	Time	m
1		0205	5.1
		0830	1.1
	M	1433	5.2
		2054	1.2
2		0255	5.3
		0921	0.8
	TU	1522	5.3
		● 2140	1.1
3		0339	5.4
		1006	0.7
	W	1606	5.4
		2222	1.0
4		0419	5.5
		1047	0.6
	TH	1646	5.4
		2300	1.0
5		0457	5.5
		1125	0.7
	F	1725	5.3
		2336	1.1
6		0533	5.4
		1201	0.8
	SA	1802	5.2
7		0009	1.2
		0609	5.3
	SU	1237	1.0
		1838	5.0
8		0042	1.4
		0647	5.1
	M	1312	1.2
		1917	4.8
9		0115	1.6
		0728	4.9
	TU	1349	1.5
		1959	4.6
10		0154	1.9
		0815	4.6
	W	1432	1.8
		◐ 2047	4.4
11		0244	2.1
		0912	4.4
	TH	1529	2.0
		2144	4.3
12		0356	2.3
		1019	4.2
	F	1641	2.1
		2250	4.2
13		0520	2.2
		1132	4.2
	SA	1756	2.1
		2358	4.3
14		0633	2.0
		1240	4.4
	SU	1859	1.9
15		0059	4.5
		0729	1.7
	M	1336	4.6
		1950	1.6
16		0149	4.8
		0817	1.4
	TU	1423	4.9
		2035	1.4
17		0232	5.1
		0900	1.1
	W	1504	5.1
		2117	1.2
18		0312	5.3
		0941	0.8
	TH	1544	5.3
		○ 2158	1.0
19		0351	5.5
		1022	0.6
	F	1624	5.5
		2238	0.8
20		0430	5.7
		1102	0.5
	SA	1705	5.5
		2317	0.8
21		0509	5.7
		1143	0.4
	SU	1747	5.5
		2357	0.8
22		0551	5.7
		1224	0.5
	M	1831	5.4
23		0039	0.9
		0636	5.6
	TU	1309	0.8
		1918	5.2
24		0125	1.2
		0728	5.3
	W	1358	1.1
		2012	4.9
25		0219	1.4
		0828	5.0
	TH	1457	1.5
		◑ 2113	4.7
26		0327	1.7
		0939	4.7
	F	1610	1.8
		2224	4.5
27		0450	1.8
		1101	4.6
	SA	1735	1.9
		2343	4.5
28		0617	1.7
		1226	4.7
	SU	1854	1.8
29		0058	4.7
		0727	1.4
	M	1334	4.9
		1953	1.5
30		0156	5.0
		0822	1.1
	TU	1426	5.1
		2042	1.4
31		0243	5.2
		0908	0.9
	W	1510	5.2
		2124	1.2

Chart Datum: 2·85 metres below Ordnance Datum (Newlyn)
HAT is 6·1 metres above Chart Datum

TIME ZONE (UT)
For Summer Time add ONE hour in **non-shaded areas**

RIVER TEES

LAT 54°38'N LONG 1°09'W

TIMES AND HEIGHTS OF HIGH AND LOW WATERS

Dates in amber are **SPRINGS**
Dates in grey are **NEAPS**

2016

SEPTEMBER

Date	Day	Time	m	Time	m	Time	m	Time	m
1	TH	0324	5.4	0948	0.7	1548	5.3	● 2201	1.1
2	F	0400	5.5	1024	0.7	1624	5.3	2235	1.1
3	SA	0433	5.5	1058	0.8	1657	5.3	2307	1.1
4	SU	0506	5.4	1129	0.9	1729	5.2	2337	1.2
5	M	0538	5.3	1200	1.0	1802	5.1		
6	TU	0007	1.3	0612	5.2	1231	1.2	1836	5.0
7	W	0038	1.5	0650	4.9	1305	1.5	1915	4.8
8	TH	0114	1.7	0734	4.7	1344	1.8	2001	4.5
9	F	0157	2.0	0825	4.4	1434	2.1	◐ 2055	4.3
10	SA	0257	2.2	0930	4.2	1545	2.3	2200	4.2
11	SU	0428	2.3	1047	4.2	1713	2.3	2312	4.2
12	M	0555	2.1	1204	4.3	1826	2.1		
13	TU	0020	4.5	0659	1.8	1306	4.6	1922	1.8
14	W	0117	4.8	0750	1.4	1355	4.9	2009	1.4
15	TH	0203	5.1	0835	1.0	1438	5.2	2053	1.1
16	F	0245	5.4	0917	0.7	1519	5.5	○ 2135	0.9
17	SA	0326	5.7	0959	0.4	1600	5.7	2216	0.7
18	SU	0406	5.9	1040	0.3	1641	5.7	2257	0.6
19	M	0448	5.9	1121	0.3	1723	5.7	2337	0.6
20	TU	0531	5.9	1203	0.5	1808	5.5		
21	W	0020	0.8	0618	5.7	1247	0.8	1854	5.3
22	TH	0107	1.0	0711	5.3	1336	1.2	1947	5.0
23	F	0201	1.4	0812	4.9	1434	1.6	◑ 2049	4.7
24	SA	0311	1.7	0926	4.6	1551	2.0	2202	4.5
25	SU	0438	1.8	1052	4.5	1723	2.1	2326	4.5
26	M	0608	1.7	1220	4.6	1841	1.9		
27	TU	0042	4.7	0715	1.4	1323	4.8	1938	1.7
28	W	0139	5.0	0806	1.1	1411	5.0	2023	1.5
29	TH	0223	5.2	0848	1.0	1451	5.2	2102	1.3
30	F	0302	5.3	0924	0.9	1526	5.3	2136	1.2

OCTOBER

Date	Day	Time	m	Time	m	Time	m	Time	m
1	SA	0336	5.4	0956	0.8	1558	5.3	● 2208	1.1
2	SU	0408	5.4	1027	0.9	1628	5.3	2238	1.1
3	M	0438	5.4	1057	1.0	1656	5.3	2307	1.1
4	TU	0509	5.3	1125	1.1	1727	5.2	2337	1.2
5	W	0542	5.1	1155	1.3	1801	5.1		
6	TH	0009	1.4	0618	5.0	1229	1.5	1839	4.9
7	F	0044	1.6	0700	4.7	1307	1.8	1923	4.7
8	SA	0126	1.8	0750	4.5	1354	2.1	2015	4.4
9	SU	0219	2.1	0851	4.3	1458	2.3	◐ 2117	4.3
10	M	0338	2.2	1005	4.2	1628	2.4	2228	4.3
11	TU	0511	2.1	1123	4.3	1748	2.2	2338	4.5
12	W	0622	1.7	1230	4.6	1849	1.8		
13	TH	0039	4.8	0717	1.3	1323	5.0	1939	1.5
14	F	0130	5.2	0805	0.9	1409	5.3	2025	1.1
15	SA	0216	5.5	0850	0.6	1452	5.6	2109	0.8
16	SU	0300	5.8	0933	0.4	1534	5.7	○ 2153	0.6
17	M	0343	5.9	1016	0.3	1617	5.8	2236	0.5
18	TU	0428	6.0	1059	0.3	1701	5.8	2319	0.5
19	W	0515	5.9	1142	0.5	1746	5.6		
20	TH	0004	0.7	0604	5.6	1227	0.9	1833	5.4
21	F	0052	0.9	0658	5.3	1316	1.3	1925	5.1
22	SA	0147	1.2	0759	4.9	1415	1.8	◑ 2026	4.8
23	SU	0256	1.6	0911	4.6	1530	2.1	2137	4.5
24	M	0418	1.7	1034	4.4	1657	2.2	2258	4.5
25	TU	0543	1.6	1156	4.5	1814	2.1		
26	W	0013	4.6	0648	1.4	1259	4.7	1911	1.9
27	TH	0111	4.8	0738	1.3	1346	4.9	1956	1.7
28	F	0156	5.0	0819	1.1	1424	5.1	2035	1.5
29	SA	0235	5.2	0854	1.0	1459	5.2	2109	1.3
30	SU	0310	5.3	0926	1.0	1530	5.3	● 2141	1.2
31	M	0343	5.3	0957	1.0	1559	5.3	2212	1.1

NOVEMBER

Date	Day	Time	m	Time	m	Time	m	Time	m
1	TU	0414	5.3	1026	1.1	1627	5.3	2242	1.1
2	W	0445	5.2	1055	1.2	1658	5.3	2313	1.2
3	TH	0518	5.1	1127	1.3	1732	5.2	2346	1.3
4	F	0555	4.9	1201	1.5	1810	5.0		
5	SA	0022	1.5	0636	4.8	1240	1.7	1852	4.8
6	SU	0104	1.7	0724	4.6	1325	2.0	1942	4.6
7	M	0155	1.8	0822	4.4	1423	2.2	◐ 2040	4.5
8	TU	0302	2.0	0929	4.3	1542	2.3	2146	4.4
9	W	0424	1.9	1042	4.4	1703	2.2	2255	4.6
10	TH	0538	1.6	1150	4.6	1809	1.9	2359	4.8
11	F	0640	1.3	1248	4.9	1905	1.5		
12	SA	0055	5.1	0733	1.0	1338	5.3	1956	1.2
13	SU	0147	5.5	0822	0.7	1425	5.5	2044	0.9
14	M	0236	5.7	0909	0.5	1511	5.7	○ 2131	0.6
15	TU	0324	5.8	0955	0.4	1556	5.8	2218	0.5
16	W	0412	5.9	1041	0.5	1641	5.8	2304	0.5
17	TH	0502	5.8	1126	0.7	1727	5.7	2351	0.6
18	F	0553	5.6	1211	1.0	1815	5.5		
19	SA	0041	0.8	0647	5.3	1300	1.4	1905	5.2
20	SU	0134	1.1	0745	4.9	1355	1.8	2001	4.9
21	M	0235	1.4	0848	4.6	1459	2.1	◑ 2105	4.7
22	TU	0344	1.6	0959	4.4	1614	2.3	2216	4.5
23	W	0500	1.7	1113	4.4	1730	2.2	2328	4.5
24	TH	0608	1.6	1218	4.5	1833	2.1		
25	F	0031	4.7	0701	1.5	1310	4.7	1923	1.9
26	SA	0122	4.8	0745	1.4	1353	4.9	2005	1.7
27	SU	0205	4.9	0823	1.3	1429	5.0	2042	1.5
28	M	0244	5.0	0858	1.2	1503	5.2	2117	1.3
29	TU	0320	5.1	0930	1.2	1533	5.2	● 2150	1.2
30	W	0354	5.1	1001	1.2	1603	5.3	2222	1.2

DECEMBER

Date	Day	Time	m	Time	m	Time	m	Time	m
1	TH	0427	5.1	1033	1.2	1635	5.3	2255	1.2
2	F	0501	5.1	1106	1.3	1710	5.2	2330	1.2
3	SA	0537	5.0	1142	1.4	1747	5.1		
4	SU	0007	1.3	0618	4.9	1221	1.6	1828	5.0
5	M	0049	1.4	0704	4.7	1304	1.8	1914	4.8
6	TU	0136	1.5	0757	4.6	1356	2.0	2007	4.7
7	W	0234	1.6	0858	4.5	1501	2.1	◐ 2108	4.7
8	TH	0343	1.7	1004	4.5	1617	2.1	2215	4.7
9	F	0455	1.6	1111	4.6	1727	1.9	2321	4.8
10	SA	0601	1.4	1213	4.9	1831	1.6		
11	SU	0024	5.0	0702	1.1	1310	5.1	1929	1.3
12	M	0123	5.3	0758	0.9	1402	5.4	2023	1.0
13	TU	0218	5.5	0850	0.7	1452	5.6	2115	0.8
14	W	0311	5.6	0939	0.7	1539	5.7	○ 2205	0.6
15	TH	0402	5.7	1027	0.7	1626	5.7	2254	0.5
16	F	0452	5.6	1113	0.8	1712	5.7	2341	0.5
17	SA	0542	5.5	1158	1.0	1758	5.5		
18	SU	0028	0.7	0632	5.3	1243	1.3	1844	5.3
19	M	0116	0.9	0723	5.0	1330	1.6	1934	5.1
20	TU	0207	1.2	0817	4.7	1421	1.9	2028	4.8
21	W	0302	1.5	0915	4.5	1521	2.2	◑ 2128	4.6
22	TH	0404	1.7	1017	4.4	1630	2.3	2233	4.5
23	F	0511	1.8	1122	4.3	1741	2.2	2340	4.4
24	SA	0614	1.8	1222	4.5	1842	2.1		
25	SU	0041	4.5	0706	1.7	1315	4.6	1932	1.9
26	M	0134	4.7	0751	1.6	1358	4.8	2015	1.6
27	TU	0219	4.8	0831	1.5	1437	5.0	2054	1.4
28	W	0259	4.9	0907	1.4	1511	5.1	2131	1.3
29	TH	0336	5.0	0942	1.3	1544	5.2	● 2206	1.2
30	F	0412	5.1	1016	1.2	1617	5.3	2241	1.1
31	SA	0447	5.1	1051	1.2	1652	5.3	2317	1.0

Chart Datum: 2·85 metres below Ordnance Datum (Newlyn)
HAT is 6·1 metres above Chart Datum

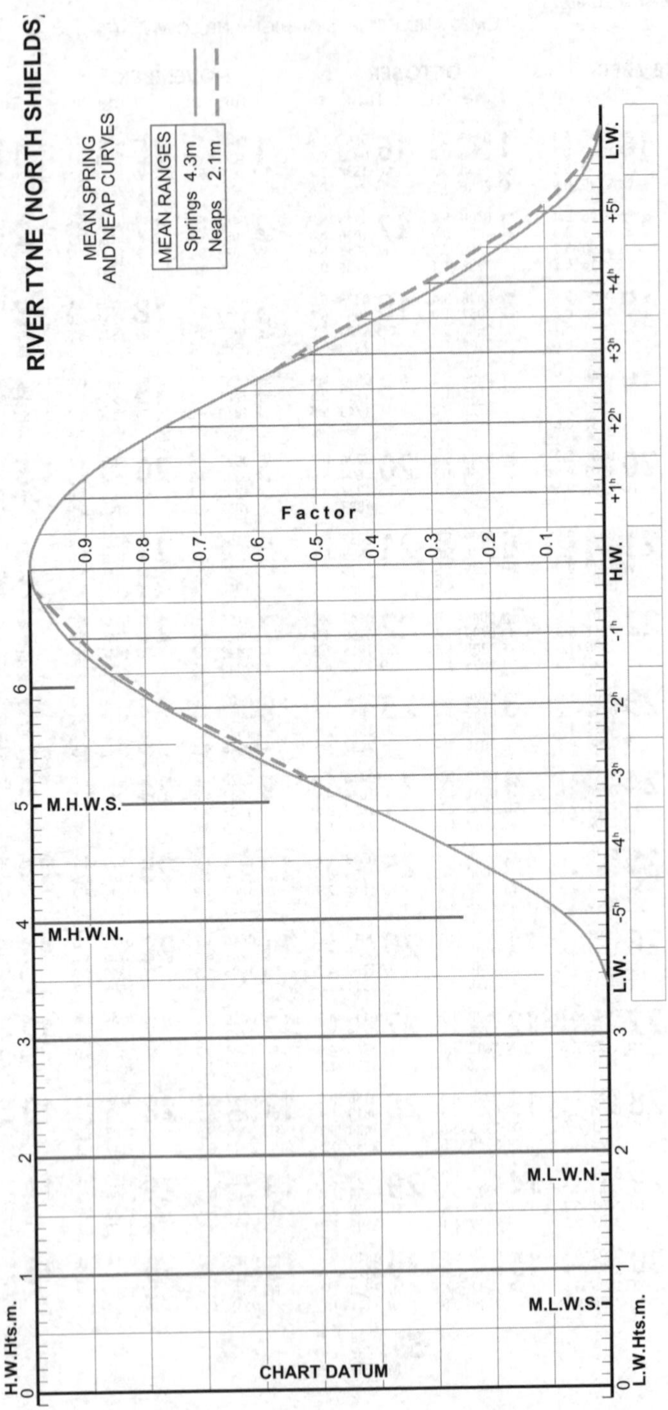
RIVER TYNE (NORTH SHIELDS)
MEAN SPRING AND NEAP CURVES
MEAN RANGES
Springs 4.3m
Neaps 2.1m
Factor
0.9
0.8
0.7
0.6
0.5
0.4
0.3
0.2
0.1
L.W.
-5h
-4h
-3h
-2h
-1h
H.W.
+1h
+2h
+3h
+4h
+5h
L.W.
H.W.Hts.m.
M.H.W.S.
M.H.W.N.
CHART DATUM
M.L.W.N.
M.L.W.S.
L.W.Hts.m.

TIME ZONE (UT)
For Summer Time add ONE hour in **non-shaded areas**

NORTH SHIELDS

LAT 55°00′N LONG 1°26′W

TIMES AND HEIGHTS OF HIGH AND LOW WATERS

Dates in amber are **SPRINGS**
Dates in grey are **NEAPS**

2016

JANUARY

Date	Day	Time	m	Time	m	Time	m	Time	m
1	F	0146	1.4	0759	4.3	1348	1.9	2008	4.4
2	SA	0235	1.7	0852	4.1	1443	2.1	◑ 2105	4.2
3	SU	0334	1.8	0950	4.0	1554	2.2	2209	4.1
4	M	0440	1.9	1055	4.0	1711	2.2	2318	4.1
5	TU	0546	1.9	1200	4.1	1820	2.1		
6	W	0024	4.2	0645	1.7	1256	4.3	1916	1.8
7	TH	0120	4.3	0735	1.6	1342	4.5	2003	1.6
8	F	0205	4.5	0818	1.4	1422	4.7	2044	1.3
9	SA	0246	4.7	0859	1.2	1500	4.9	2124	1.1
10	SU	0325	4.9	0938	1.1	1536	5.1	● 2204	0.9
11	M	0404	5.0	1018	1.0	1613	5.2	2245	0.7
12	TU	0444	5.1	1057	0.9	1652	5.3	2327	0.6
13	W	0526	5.1	1138	1.0	1733	5.3		
14	TH	0010	0.7	0610	5.0	1220	1.1	1817	5.2
15	F	0055	0.8	0659	4.8	1305	1.3	1906	5.0
16	SA	0144	1.0	0753	4.6	1357	1.5	◐ 2002	4.9
17	SU	0241	1.2	0855	4.5	1500	1.6	2108	4.6
18	M	0348	1.4	1003	4.3	1616	1.7	2222	4.5
19	TU	0502	1.5	1116	4.3	1736	1.7	2340	4.5
20	W	0616	1.5	1226	4.5	1850	1.5		
21	TH	0052	4.6	0722	1.4	1327	4.7	1953	1.3
22	F	0153	4.7	0817	1.3	1417	4.9	2046	1.0
23	SA	0243	4.9	0904	1.2	1501	5.0	2131	0.8
24	SU	0327	4.9	0945	1.1	1541	5.1	○ 2213	0.7
25	M	0408	5.0	1022	1.1	1618	5.2	2250	0.7
26	TU	0446	4.9	1056	1.1	1654	5.1	2325	0.8
27	W	0522	4.9	1127	1.2	1729	5.0	2358	0.9
28	TH	0558	4.7	1158	1.3	1805	4.9		
29	F	0031	1.0	0634	4.6	1231	1.4	1842	4.7
30	SA	0106	1.2	0712	4.4	1306	1.6	1923	4.5
31	SU	0146	1.5	0756	4.2	1348	1.8	2010	4.3

FEBRUARY

Date	Day	Time	m	Time	m	Time	m	Time	m
1	M	0233	1.7	0848	4.0	1443	2.1	◑ 2108	4.1
2	TU	0334	1.9	0949	3.9	1559	2.2	2217	3.9
3	W	0448	2.0	1100	3.9	1724	2.1	2335	4.0
4	TH	0601	1.9	1211	4.1	1838	1.9		
5	F	0045	4.1	0704	1.7	1310	4.3	1935	1.6
6	SA	0140	4.4	0755	1.5	1357	4.6	2022	1.3
7	SU	0225	4.7	0839	1.2	1437	4.9	2106	0.9
8	M	0306	4.9	0921	1.0	1516	5.1	● 2148	0.6
9	TU	0346	5.1	1002	0.8	1554	5.3	2230	0.4
10	W	0427	5.2	1042	0.7	1634	5.4	2312	0.3
11	TH	0509	5.2	1123	0.7	1716	5.5	2354	0.4
12	F	0552	5.1	1204	0.8	1800	5.4		
13	SA	0037	0.5	0637	5.0	1247	1.0	1848	5.2
14	SU	0123	0.8	0728	4.7	1336	1.2	1942	4.9
15	M	0215	1.1	0826	4.5	1434	1.5	◐ 2047	4.6
16	TU	0319	1.5	0934	4.3	1550	1.7	2203	4.3
17	W	0438	1.7	1051	4.2	1718	1.7	2328	4.3
18	TH	0602	1.7	1209	4.3	1841	1.5		
19	F	0046	4.4	0714	1.6	1315	4.5	1946	1.3
20	SA	0148	4.5	0808	1.4	1407	4.7	2036	1.0
21	SU	0235	4.7	0852	1.3	1449	4.9	2118	0.8
22	M	0315	4.8	0929	1.1	1526	5.0	○ 2155	0.7
23	TU	0351	4.9	1003	1.0	1600	5.1	2228	0.7
24	W	0424	4.9	1034	1.0	1632	5.1	2300	0.7
25	TH	0455	4.9	1103	1.0	1704	5.0	2329	0.8
26	F	0527	4.8	1132	1.1	1736	4.9	2359	0.9
27	SA	0559	4.7	1201	1.2	1810	4.8		
28	SU	0030	1.1	0633	4.5	1234	1.4	1846	4.6
29	M	0105	1.3	0711	4.3	1310	1.6	1928	4.3

MARCH

Date	Day	Time	m	Time	m	Time	m	Time	m
1	TU	0145	1.6	0755	4.2	1356	1.8	◑ 2019	4.1
2	W	0237	1.9	0851	4.0	1459	2.0	2126	3.9
3	TH	0350	2.0	1002	3.9	1628	2.1	2247	3.9
4	F	0517	2.0	1121	3.9	1755	1.9		
5	SA	0009	4.0	0631	1.8	1232	4.2	1903	1.6
6	SU	0112	4.3	0729	1.5	1326	4.5	1956	1.2
7	M	0201	4.6	0816	1.2	1411	4.8	2043	0.8
8	TU	0244	4.9	0900	0.9	1452	5.1	2127	0.4
9	W	0325	5.2	0942	0.6	1532	5.4	● 2210	0.2
10	TH	0406	5.3	1023	0.5	1614	5.5	2252	0.1
11	F	0447	5.3	1105	0.4	1657	5.6	2334	0.2
12	SA	0530	5.2	1147	0.5	1742	5.4		
13	SU	0017	0.4	0615	5.0	1230	0.7	1831	5.2
14	M	0102	0.8	0704	4.8	1318	1.0	1926	4.9
15	TU	0152	1.2	0800	4.5	1416	1.3	◐ 2032	4.5
16	W	0255	1.6	0908	4.2	1532	1.6	2149	4.2
17	TH	0417	1.9	1026	4.1	1703	1.6	2315	4.1
18	F	0547	1.9	1148	4.2	1827	1.5		
19	SA	0034	4.2	0659	1.7	1257	4.3	1930	1.3
20	SU	0134	4.4	0752	1.5	1349	4.6	2018	1.1
21	M	0218	4.6	0833	1.3	1430	4.7	2057	0.9
22	TU	0255	4.7	0908	1.2	1506	4.9	2130	0.8
23	W	0328	4.8	0940	1.0	1538	5.0	○ 2201	0.7
24	TH	0358	4.9	1009	0.9	1608	5.0	2231	0.7
25	F	0427	4.9	1038	0.9	1639	5.0	2300	0.8
26	SA	0457	4.8	1107	1.0	1710	4.9	2329	0.9
27	SU	0528	4.7	1137	1.1	1743	4.7	2359	1.1
28	M	0600	4.6	1208	1.2	1819	4.6		
29	TU	0032	1.3	0635	4.5	1244	1.4	1858	4.4
30	W	0110	1.5	0717	4.3	1327	1.6	1947	4.1
31	TH	0157	1.8	0808	4.1	1425	1.8	◑ 2051	4.0

APRIL

Date	Day	Time	m	Time	m	Time	m	Time	m
1	F	0305	2.0	0916	3.9	1545	1.9	2210	3.9
2	SA	0434	2.0	1035	4.0	1714	1.7	2331	4.0
3	SU	0555	1.8	1150	4.2	1828	1.4		
4	M	0039	4.3	0657	1.5	1252	4.5	1925	1.0
5	TU	0132	4.7	0749	1.2	1341	4.8	2015	0.7
6	W	0218	5.0	0835	0.8	1426	5.2	2102	0.4
7	TH	0300	5.2	0919	0.6	1509	5.4	● 2146	0.2
8	F	0342	5.4	1003	0.4	1553	5.5	2230	0.1
9	SA	0425	5.4	1046	0.3	1639	5.5	2314	0.2
10	SU	0508	5.3	1130	0.4	1726	5.4	2357	0.5
11	M	0554	5.1	1215	0.6	1818	5.1		
12	TU	0041	0.9	0642	4.8	1305	0.9	1914	4.8
13	W	0131	1.3	0738	4.5	1402	1.2	2019	4.4
14	TH	0232	1.7	0843	4.3	1515	1.4	◐ 2131	4.2
15	F	0351	1.9	0957	4.1	1639	1.5	2251	4.1
16	SA	0518	2.0	1117	4.1	1800	1.5		
17	SU	0007	4.1	0631	1.8	1227	4.2	1901	1.3
18	M	0106	4.3	0724	1.6	1321	4.4	1948	1.2
19	TU	0151	4.5	0806	1.4	1403	4.6	2026	1.0
20	W	0227	4.6	0841	1.2	1439	4.7	2059	0.9
21	TH	0300	4.7	0913	1.1	1512	4.8	2131	0.8
22	F	0330	4.8	0944	1.0	1544	4.9	○ 2201	0.8
23	SA	0400	4.8	1015	0.9	1615	4.8	2232	0.8
24	SU	0430	4.8	1045	0.9	1648	4.8	2302	0.9
25	M	0501	4.8	1116	1.0	1722	4.7	2334	1.1
26	TU	0534	4.7	1149	1.1	1758	4.6		
27	W	0007	1.3	0609	4.6	1227	1.2	1838	4.4
28	TH	0046	1.5	0650	4.4	1310	1.4	1927	4.2
29	F	0132	1.7	0740	4.3	1405	1.5	2027	4.1
30	SA	0235	1.9	0843	4.1	1516	1.6	◑ 2140	4.0

Chart Datum: 2·60 metres below Ordnance Datum (Newlyn)
HAT is 5·7 metres above Chart Datum

TIME ZONE (UT)
For Summer Time add ONE hour in **non-shaded areas**

NORTH SHIELDS

LAT 55°00'N LONG 1°26'W

TIMES AND HEIGHTS OF HIGH AND LOW WATERS

Dates in amber are **SPRINGS**
Dates in grey are **NEAPS**

2016

MAY

Date	Time	m	Time	m	Time	m	Time	m
1 SU	0356	1.9	0956	4.1	1638	1.5	2256	4.1
2 M	0517	1.8	1110	4.3	1751	1.3		
3 TU	0005	4.4	0622	1.5	1216	4.5	1852	1.0
4 W	0102	4.7	0718	1.2	1311	4.8	1946	0.7
5 TH	0151	5.0	0809	0.9	1400	5.1	2036	0.4
6 F	0236	5.2	0857	0.6	1448	5.3	● 2123	0.3
7 SA	0320	5.3	0943	0.4	1535	5.4	2209	0.3
8 SU	0404	5.3	1030	0.3	1623	5.4	2254	0.4
9 M	0448	5.3	1116	0.4	1713	5.3	2338	0.7
10 TU	0534	5.1	1203	0.5	1805	5.0		
11 W	0023	1.0	0623	4.9	1253	0.8	1901	4.7
12 TH	0111	1.3	0716	4.6	1347	1.0	2001	4.4
13 F	0206	1.7	0816	4.4	1450	1.3	◐ 2105	4.2
14 SA	0315	1.9	0923	4.2	1602	1.5	2214	4.1
15 SU	0433	2.0	1034	4.1	1715	1.5	2324	4.1
16 M	0546	1.9	1143	4.2	1818	1.4		
17 TU	0025	4.2	0644	1.8	1242	4.3	1908	1.3
18 W	0114	4.3	0730	1.6	1329	4.4	1949	1.2
19 TH	0154	4.5	0809	1.4	1409	4.5	2025	1.1
20 F	0230	4.6	0845	1.2	1445	4.6	2100	1.0
21 SA	0303	4.7	0919	1.1	1520	4.7	○ 2133	1.0
22 SU	0334	4.8	0952	1.0	1554	4.7	2206	1.0
23 M	0406	4.8	1025	0.9	1628	4.7	2239	1.0
24 TU	0439	4.8	1100	0.9	1704	4.7	2313	1.1
25 W	0513	4.8	1136	1.0	1742	4.6	2349	1.2
26 TH	0550	4.7	1215	1.1	1824	4.5		
27 F	0029	1.4	0631	4.6	1300	1.2	1911	4.4
28 SA	0116	1.5	0720	4.5	1351	1.3	2008	4.3
29 SU	0212	1.7	0818	4.4	1454	1.3	◑ 2114	4.2
30 M	0322	1.8	0924	4.4	1605	1.3	2224	4.3
31 TU	0438	1.7	1035	4.4	1717	1.2	2332	4.4

JUNE

Date	Time	m	Time	m	Time	m	Time	m
1 W	0548	1.5	1142	4.6	1821	1.0		
2 TH	0033	4.6	0649	1.2	1244	4.8	1919	0.8
3 F	0127	4.9	0745	1.0	1340	5.0	2013	0.6
4 SA	0215	5.1	0838	0.7	1432	5.2	2104	0.5
5 SU	0301	5.2	0928	0.5	1522	5.3	● 2151	0.5
6 M	0346	5.2	1017	0.4	1611	5.3	2237	0.6
7 TU	0431	5.2	1104	0.4	1701	5.1	2321	0.8
8 W	0517	5.1	1151	0.5	1752	5.0		
9 TH	0005	1.1	0604	5.0	1238	0.7	1842	4.7
10 F	0049	1.3	0653	4.8	1325	1.0	1935	4.5
11 SA	0135	1.6	0745	4.6	1417	1.2	2030	4.3
12 SU	0228	1.8	0842	4.3	1514	1.4	◐ 2128	4.1
13 M	0332	2.0	0943	4.2	1617	1.6	2229	4.0
14 TU	0443	2.0	1048	4.1	1719	1.6	2332	4.1
15 W	0550	2.0	1152	4.1	1817	1.6		
16 TH	0029	4.2	0647	1.8	1249	4.2	1907	1.5
17 F	0117	4.3	0735	1.6	1337	4.4	1951	1.3
18 SA	0159	4.5	0817	1.4	1419	4.5	2031	1.2
19 SU	0236	4.7	0855	1.2	1457	4.6	2108	1.1
20 M	0311	4.8	0932	1.1	1534	4.7	○ 2144	1.1
21 TU	0345	4.9	1008	0.9	1610	4.8	2220	1.0
22 W	0419	4.9	1045	0.9	1648	4.8	2257	1.0
23 TH	0455	4.9	1124	0.8	1727	4.8	2335	1.1
24 F	0533	4.9	1204	0.8	1809	4.7		
25 SA	0016	1.2	0614	4.9	1248	0.9	1855	4.6
26 SU	0100	1.3	0701	4.8	1336	1.0	1947	4.5
27 M	0151	1.5	0755	4.7	1432	1.1	◑ 2047	4.4
28 TU	0252	1.6	0856	4.6	1536	1.2	2153	4.4
29 W	0403	1.6	1005	4.5	1646	1.2	2301	4.4
30 TH	0516	1.5	1116	4.6	1755	1.1		

JULY

Date	Time	m	Time	m	Time	m	Time	m
1 F	0007	4.5	0625	1.4	1225	4.7	1858	1.0
2 SA	0107	4.7	0728	1.1	1327	4.8	1957	0.9
3 SU	0200	4.9	0825	0.9	1422	5.0	2050	0.8
4 M	0248	5.1	0918	0.6	1513	5.1	● 2138	0.8
5 TU	0333	5.2	1006	0.5	1602	5.1	2222	0.8
6 W	0417	5.2	1052	0.5	1648	5.1	2304	0.9
7 TH	0500	5.2	1135	0.5	1733	4.9	2343	1.1
8 F	0542	5.1	1216	0.7	1817	4.8		
9 SA	0021	1.3	0625	4.9	1256	0.9	1901	4.6
10 SU	0059	1.5	0709	4.7	1338	1.1	1947	4.4
11 M	0141	1.7	0757	4.5	1423	1.4	2037	4.2
12 TU	0230	1.9	0850	4.3	1515	1.6	◐ 2131	4.0
13 W	0333	2.0	0950	4.1	1617	1.7	2232	4.0
14 TH	0446	2.1	1056	4.0	1722	1.8	2337	4.0
15 F	0558	2.0	1205	4.1	1824	1.7		
16 SA	0037	4.2	0659	1.8	1305	4.2	1918	1.6
17 SU	0127	4.4	0749	1.5	1353	4.4	2004	1.4
18 M	0210	4.6	0832	1.3	1435	4.6	2045	1.2
19 TU	0247	4.8	0911	1.1	1514	4.7	○ 2124	1.1
20 W	0323	4.9	0950	0.9	1552	4.9	2202	1.0
21 TH	0359	5.1	1029	0.7	1630	5.0	2241	0.9
22 F	0436	5.1	1109	0.6	1709	5.0	2320	0.9
23 SA	0515	5.2	1150	0.6	1751	4.9		
24 SU	0000	1.0	0556	5.1	1233	0.6	1835	4.8
25 M	0043	1.1	0641	5.1	1318	0.8	1924	4.7
26 TU	0130	1.3	0733	4.9	1409	1.0	◑ 2020	4.5
27 W	0225	1.4	0832	4.7	1509	1.2	2124	4.4
28 TH	0334	1.6	0942	4.6	1620	1.4	2235	4.4
29 F	0453	1.6	1058	4.5	1735	1.4	2347	4.4
30 SA	0610	1.5	1215	4.5	1846	1.4		
31 SU	0053	4.6	0720	1.2	1322	4.7	1948	1.2

AUGUST

Date	Time	m	Time	m	Time	m	Time	m
1 M	0150	4.8	0819	1.0	1418	4.8	2040	1.1
2 TU	0238	5.0	0909	0.7	1506	5.0	● 2125	1.0
3 W	0321	5.1	0954	0.6	1550	5.0	2206	0.9
4 TH	0401	5.2	1035	0.5	1630	5.0	2243	1.0
5 F	0439	5.2	1113	0.6	1709	4.9	2318	1.0
6 SA	0517	5.1	1148	0.7	1746	4.8	2351	1.2
7 SU	0554	5.0	1222	0.9	1824	4.7		
8 M	0023	1.3	0631	4.8	1257	1.1	1902	4.5
9 TU	0059	1.5	0712	4.6	1335	1.3	1945	4.3
10 W	0139	1.7	0759	4.4	1419	1.6	◐ 2034	4.1
11 TH	0231	2.0	0855	4.1	1515	1.8	2133	4.0
12 F	0341	2.1	1002	4.0	1626	2.0	2240	4.0
13 SA	0505	2.1	1118	3.9	1741	1.9	2352	4.1
14 SU	0621	1.9	1230	4.1	1846	1.8		
15 M	0053	4.3	0720	1.6	1327	4.3	1938	1.6
16 TU	0141	4.5	0807	1.3	1412	4.6	2023	1.3
17 W	0222	4.8	0849	1.0	1451	4.8	2103	1.1
18 TH	0259	5.0	0929	0.7	1530	5.0	○ 2143	0.9
19 F	0336	5.2	1009	0.5	1608	5.2	2222	0.8
20 SA	0414	5.4	1050	0.4	1648	5.2	2301	0.7
21 SU	0454	5.4	1131	0.4	1729	5.2	2341	0.8
22 M	0536	5.4	1212	0.5	1813	5.1		
23 TU	0023	0.9	0621	5.3	1257	0.7	1900	4.9
24 W	0110	1.1	0713	5.0	1345	1.0	1954	4.6
25 TH	0204	1.3	0813	4.7	1444	1.3	◑ 2058	4.4
26 F	0313	1.6	0926	4.5	1559	1.6	2213	4.3
27 SA	0438	1.6	1049	4.3	1722	1.7	2332	4.3
28 SU	0604	1.5	1212	4.4	1840	1.6		
29 M	0043	4.5	0715	1.3	1319	4.6	1941	1.5
30 TU	0140	4.8	0811	1.0	1412	4.8	2029	1.3
31 W	0226	5.0	0857	0.8	1455	4.9	2110	1.1

Chart Datum: 2·60 metres below Ordnance Datum (Newlyn)
HAT is 5·7 metres above Chart Datum

TIME ZONE (UT)
For Summer Time add ONE hour in **non-shaded areas**

NORTH SHIELDS

LAT 55°00′N LONG 1°26′W

TIMES AND HEIGHTS OF HIGH AND LOW WATERS

Dates in amber are **SPRINGS**
Dates in grey are **NEAPS**

2016

SEPTEMBER

Date	Day	Time	m	Time	m	Time	m	Time	m
1	TH	0306	5.1	0937	0.6	1533	5.0	● 2146	1.0
2	F	0341	5.2	1013	0.6	1608	5.0	2220	1.0
3	SA	0416	5.2	1046	0.6	1641	5.0	2251	1.0
4	SU	0449	5.1	1117	0.7	1713	4.9	2321	1.1
5	M	0522	5.0	1147	0.9	1746	4.8	2351	1.2
6	TU	0557	4.9	1218	1.1	1821	4.6		
7	W	0023	1.4	0634	4.7	1252	1.3	1858	4.5
8	TH	0100	1.6	0717	4.4	1331	1.6	1943	4.3
9	F	0145	1.8	0808	4.2	1421	1.9	◐ 2038	4.1
10	SA	0247	2.1	0914	4.0	1531	2.1	2146	4.0
11	SU	0412	2.1	1033	3.9	1656	2.1	2303	4.0
12	M	0540	2.0	1153	4.0	1812	2.0		
13	TU	0014	4.2	0647	1.7	1256	4.3	1910	1.7
14	W	0109	4.5	0738	1.3	1344	4.6	1957	1.4
15	TH	0153	4.8	0823	0.9	1426	4.9	2039	1.1
16	F	0232	5.1	0905	0.6	1505	5.2	○ 2120	0.8
17	SA	0311	5.4	0946	0.4	1544	5.3	2200	0.6
18	SU	0350	5.6	1027	0.2	1624	5.4	2241	0.6
19	M	0432	5.6	1109	0.3	1705	5.4	2322	0.6
20	TU	0516	5.5	1151	0.4	1749	5.2		
21	W	0005	0.8	0603	5.3	1235	0.7	1836	5.0
22	TH	0053	1.0	0656	5.0	1324	1.1	1930	4.7
23	F	0148	1.3	0800	4.7	1423	1.5	◑ 2035	4.5
24	SA	0259	1.5	0916	4.4	1541	1.9	2152	4.3
25	SU	0428	1.6	1041	4.3	1711	1.9	2314	4.3
26	M	0554	1.5	1204	4.4	1829	1.8		
27	TU	0027	4.5	0703	1.3	1309	4.5	1927	1.6
28	W	0124	4.7	0755	1.1	1357	4.7	2012	1.4
29	TH	0208	4.9	0837	0.9	1436	4.9	2050	1.2
30	F	0246	5.0	0913	0.8	1510	5.0	2123	1.1

OCTOBER

Date	Day	Time	m	Time	m	Time	m	Time	m
1	SA	0319	5.1	0945	0.7	1542	5.0	● 2154	1.0
2	SU	0351	5.1	1015	0.8	1612	5.0	2224	1.0
3	M	0422	5.1	1045	0.8	1642	5.0	2253	1.1
4	TU	0455	5.0	1114	1.0	1713	4.9	2323	1.2
5	W	0528	4.9	1144	1.2	1745	4.8	2355	1.3
6	TH	0604	4.7	1216	1.4	1821	4.6		
7	F	0030	1.5	0644	4.5	1253	1.6	1902	4.4
8	SA	0113	1.7	0733	4.2	1339	1.9	1952	4.2
9	SU	0209	1.9	0835	4.0	1443	2.1	◐ 2057	4.1
10	M	0326	2.0	0952	3.9	1610	2.2	2214	4.1
11	TU	0455	1.9	1112	4.1	1733	2.1	2329	4.2
12	W	0608	1.6	1220	4.3	1837	1.8		
13	TH	0030	4.5	0704	1.3	1313	4.7	1927	1.4
14	F	0120	4.9	0752	0.9	1357	5.0	2012	1.1
15	SA	0203	5.2	0837	0.6	1438	5.3	2055	0.8
16	SU	0245	5.5	0921	0.4	1519	5.4	○ 2137	0.6
17	M	0327	5.6	1004	0.3	1600	5.5	2220	0.5
18	TU	0412	5.7	1047	0.3	1642	5.5	2304	0.5
19	W	0458	5.6	1130	0.5	1727	5.3	2350	0.7
20	TH	0549	5.3	1215	0.9	1815	5.1		
21	F	0039	0.9	0644	5.0	1305	1.3	1909	4.8
22	SA	0136	1.2	0748	4.7	1403	1.7	◑ 2013	4.5
23	SU	0246	1.5	0902	4.4	1520	2.0	2128	4.3
24	M	0410	1.6	1022	4.3	1648	2.1	2248	4.3
25	TU	0532	1.5	1141	4.3	1804	2.0		
26	W	0001	4.4	0638	1.4	1245	4.5	1902	1.8
27	TH	0059	4.6	0729	1.2	1333	4.6	1947	1.6
28	F	0144	4.8	0810	1.1	1411	4.8	2024	1.4
29	SA	0221	4.9	0844	1.0	1444	4.9	2057	1.2
30	SU	0255	5.0	0915	1.0	1515	5.0	● 2129	1.1
31	M	0327	5.0	0946	0.9	1545	5.0	2200	1.1

NOVEMBER

Date	Day	Time	m	Time	m	Time	m	Time	m
1	TU	0359	5.0	1016	1.0	1615	5.0	2230	1.1
2	W	0432	5.0	1046	1.1	1646	5.0	2301	1.2
3	TH	0506	4.8	1117	1.2	1718	4.9	2334	1.3
4	F	0542	4.7	1149	1.4	1753	4.7		
5	SA	0010	1.4	0621	4.5	1226	1.6	1832	4.6
6	SU	0052	1.6	0707	4.3	1310	1.9	1919	4.4
7	M	0144	1.7	0804	4.2	1407	2.1	◐ 2018	4.3
8	TU	0251	1.8	0915	4.1	1524	2.2	2129	4.2
9	W	0410	1.8	1030	4.2	1647	2.1	2242	4.3
10	TH	0525	1.6	1140	4.4	1757	1.8	2349	4.6
11	F	0627	1.3	1238	4.7	1853	1.5		
12	SA	0045	4.9	0720	0.9	1328	5.0	1943	1.2
13	SU	0136	5.2	0810	0.7	1413	5.2	2031	0.9
14	M	0222	5.4	0857	0.5	1456	5.4	○ 2117	0.6
15	TU	0309	5.6	0942	0.4	1539	5.5	2204	0.5
16	W	0356	5.6	1028	0.5	1622	5.5	2250	0.5
17	TH	0445	5.5	1113	0.7	1708	5.3	2338	0.6
18	F	0537	5.3	1158	1.0	1756	5.2		
19	SA	0028	0.8	0632	5.0	1247	1.4	1849	4.9
20	SU	0123	1.1	0733	4.7	1341	1.7	1949	4.7
21	M	0226	1.3	0839	4.4	1447	2.0	◑ 2056	4.5
22	TU	0338	1.5	0948	4.2	1606	2.1	2208	4.3
23	W	0451	1.6	1100	4.2	1721	2.1	2320	4.3
24	TH	0558	1.6	1206	4.3	1825	2.0		
25	F	0022	4.4	0652	1.5	1258	4.5	1915	1.8
26	SA	0113	4.6	0735	1.4	1341	4.6	1955	1.6
27	SU	0155	4.7	0812	1.3	1417	4.8	2032	1.4
28	M	0232	4.8	0846	1.2	1450	4.9	2106	1.3
29	TU	0307	4.9	0919	1.1	1522	5.0	● 2139	1.2
30	W	0341	4.9	0951	1.1	1553	5.0	2212	1.1

DECEMBER

Date	Day	Time	m	Time	m	Time	m	Time	m
1	TH	0414	4.9	1023	1.2	1624	5.0	2245	1.1
2	F	0449	4.8	1056	1.2	1657	4.9	2319	1.2
3	SA	0525	4.7	1130	1.4	1732	4.9	2357	1.2
4	SU	0604	4.6	1207	1.5	1811	4.8		
5	M	0037	1.4	0647	4.5	1249	1.7	1854	4.6
6	TU	0125	1.5	0739	4.4	1340	1.9	1947	4.5
7	W	0222	1.6	0840	4.3	1443	2.0	◐ 2049	4.4
8	TH	0330	1.6	0949	4.3	1559	2.0	2159	4.4
9	F	0443	1.5	1059	4.4	1714	1.8	2308	4.6
10	SA	0550	1.3	1203	4.6	1819	1.6		
11	SU	0013	4.8	0650	1.1	1300	4.8	1917	1.3
12	M	0112	5.0	0746	0.9	1351	5.1	2011	1.0
13	TU	0205	5.2	0837	0.7	1437	5.3	2102	0.7
14	W	0256	5.4	0926	0.7	1522	5.4	○ 2152	0.6
15	TH	0346	5.4	1013	0.7	1607	5.4	2240	0.5
16	F	0436	5.4	1059	0.8	1653	5.4	2328	0.6
17	SA	0526	5.2	1143	1.1	1740	5.2		
18	SU	0016	0.7	0617	5.0	1228	1.3	1828	5.0
19	M	0105	0.9	0710	4.7	1313	1.6	1920	4.8
20	TU	0156	1.2	0806	4.5	1404	1.9	2017	4.6
21	W	0252	1.5	0904	4.2	1506	2.1	◑ 2119	4.4
22	TH	0355	1.7	1006	4.1	1618	2.2	2225	4.2
23	F	0500	1.8	1112	4.1	1730	2.1	2333	4.2
24	SA	0602	1.7	1213	4.2	1833	2.0		
25	SU	0034	4.3	0655	1.7	1306	4.4	1924	1.8
26	M	0126	4.4	0740	1.5	1349	4.5	2007	1.6
27	TU	0209	4.6	0820	1.4	1427	4.7	2046	1.4
28	W	0248	4.7	0857	1.3	1501	4.8	2122	1.2
29	TH	0324	4.8	0932	1.2	1534	4.9	● 2156	1.1
30	F	0359	4.8	1006	1.2	1607	5.0	2231	1.0
31	SA	0434	4.8	1041	1.2	1640	5.0	2307	1.0

Chart Datum: 2·60 metres below Ordnance Datum (Newlyn)
HAT is 5·7 metres above Chart Datum

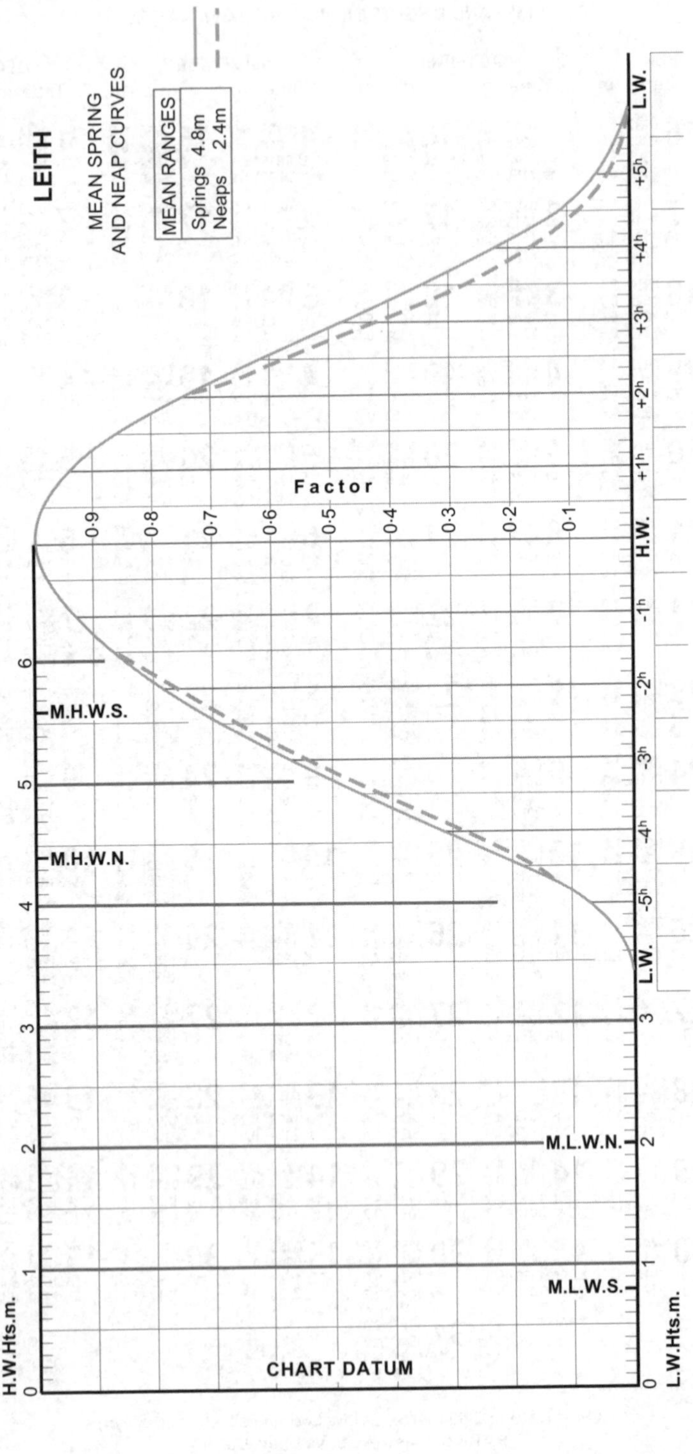
LEITH
MEAN SPRING
AND NEAP CURVES
MEAN RANGES
Springs 4.8m
Neaps 2.4m
Factor
0·9
0·8
0·7
0·6
0·5
0·4
0·3
0·2
0·1
L.W.
-5h
-4h
-3h
-2h
-1h
H.W.
+1h
+2h
+3h
+4h
+5h
L.W.
H.W.Hts.m.
0
1
2
3
4
5
6
M.H.W.S.
M.H.W.N.
CHART DATUM
M.L.W.N.
M.L.W.S.
L.W.Hts.m.

TIME ZONE (UT)
For Summer Time add ONE hour in **non-shaded areas**

SCOTLAND – LEITH

LAT 55°59′N LONG 3°11′W

TIMES AND HEIGHTS OF HIGH AND LOW WATERS

Dates in amber are **SPRINGS**
Dates in grey are **NEAPS**

2016

JANUARY

Date	Day	Time	m	Date	Day	Time	m
1	F	0009 0708 1211 1930	1.6 4.7 2.0 4.8	16	SA	0032 0658 1245 ◐ 1912	1.1 5.2 1.5 5.3
2	SA	0055 0757 1308 ◑ 2023	1.8 4.6 2.3 4.6	17	SU	0122 0758 1346 2017	1.3 5.0 1.8 5.0
3	SU	0156 0850 1427 2121	2.0 4.4 2.4 4.5	18	M	0229 0907 1504 2133	1.6 4.8 1.9 4.9
4	M	0317 0948 1557 2222	2.1 4.4 2.4 4.4	19	TU	0353 1018 1625 2247	1.7 4.8 1.8 4.9
5	TU	0435 1049 1705 2325	2.1 4.5 2.2 4.6	20	W	0511 1127 1737 2356	1.7 4.9 1.6 5.0
6	W	0532 1150 1758	1.9 4.7 1.9	21	TH	0617 1229 1843	1.6 5.1 1.4
7	TH	0024 0619 1245 1844	4.7 1.7 4.9 1.7	22	F	0057 0711 1324 1939	5.2 1.4 5.3 1.1
8	F	0115 0701 1331 1926	5.0 1.5 5.2 1.4	23	SA	0149 0757 1411 2027	5.3 1.2 5.5 0.9
9	SA	0158 0742 1412 2009	5.2 1.3 5.4 1.1	24	SU	0235 0838 1454 ○ 2110	5.5 1.1 5.6 0.7
10	SU	0238 0824 1450 ● 2052	5.4 1.1 5.5 0.9	25	M	0316 0914 1535 2147	5.5 1.1 5.6 0.7
11	M	0317 0907 1528 2136	5.5 1.0 5.6 0.7	26	TU	0356 0945 1614 2219	5.5 1.1 5.5 0.8
12	TU	0356 0950 1606 2221	5.6 0.9 5.7 0.7	27	W	0434 1009 1651 2243	5.4 1.2 5.4 0.9
13	W	0437 1034 1647 2305	5.6 1.0 5.7 0.7	28	TH	0510 1031 1727 2304	5.2 1.3 5.3 1.1
14	TH	0520 1116 1731 2348	5.6 1.1 5.6 0.8	29	F	0547 1057 1804 2332	5.0 1.5 5.1 1.3
15	F	0607 1158 1818	5.4 1.3 5.5	30	SA	0625 1129 1844	4.9 1.7 4.9
				31	SU	0007 0708 1209 1929	1.6 4.7 1.9 4.6

FEBRUARY

Date	Day	Time	m	Date	Day	Time	m
1	M	0054 0756 1305 ◑ 2024	1.9 4.5 2.2 4.4	16	TU	0153 0840 1433 2113	1.7 4.7 1.8 4.8
2	TU	0156 0853 1431 2127	2.1 4.4 2.4 4.3	17	W	0326 0955 1609 2231	1.9 4.6 1.9 4.7
3	W	0324 0957 1615 2236	2.2 4.4 2.3 4.4	18	TH	0458 1110 1734 2348	1.9 4.7 1.7 4.8
4	TH	0453 1104 1727 2345	2.1 4.5 2.1 4.5	19	F	0610 1220 1843	1.8 4.9 1.4
5	F	0552 1210 1822	1.9 4.7 1.8	20	SA	0053 0703 1316 1934	5.0 1.6 5.1 1.1
6	SA	0046 0641 1305 1909	4.8 1.6 5.0 1.4	21	SU	0143 0744 1401 2016	5.2 1.4 5.3 0.9
7	SU	0135 0725 1350 1954	5.1 1.3 5.3 1.0	22	M	0224 0820 1441 ○ 2052	5.3 1.2 5.5 0.8
8	M	0218 0809 1430 ● 2039	5.4 1.0 5.6 0.7	23	TU	0300 0852 1517 2124	5.4 1.0 5.5 0.7
9	TU	0257 0853 1509 2125	5.6 0.8 5.8 0.4	24	W	0334 0921 1552 2152	5.4 1.0 5.5 0.7
10	W	0337 0938 1548 2209	5.8 0.6 5.9 0.3	25	TH	0407 0947 1625 2215	5.3 1.0 5.4 0.8
11	TH	0418 1021 1629 2252	5.8 0.6 5.9 0.3	26	F	0440 1010 1658 2237	5.2 1.1 5.3 1.0
12	F	0501 1103 1713 2334	5.7 0.7 5.9 0.6	27	SA	0513 1031 1731 2300	5.1 1.2 5.2 1.2
13	SA	0546 1142 1800	5.6 1.0 5.7	28	SU	0549 1054 1807 2326	5.0 1.4 5.0 1.4
14	SU	0013 0635 1222 1852	0.9 5.3 1.3 5.4	29	M	0627 1123 1848	4.8 1.7 4.7
15	M	0055 0732 1313 ◐ 1956	1.3 5.0 1.6 5.0				

MARCH

Date	Day	Time	m	Date	Day	Time	m
1	TU	0000 0710 1203 ◑ 1936	1.7 4.6 1.9 4.5	16	W	0127 0817 1414 2056	1.8 4.7 1.8 4.7
2	W	0052 0803 1311 2037	2.0 4.4 2.2 4.3	17	TH	0304 0933 1600 2214	2.1 4.5 1.8 4.6
3	TH	0218 0908 1504 2151	2.3 4.3 2.3 4.3	18	F	0442 1050 1727 2334	2.1 4.6 1.7 4.7
4	F	0409 1021 1652 2306	2.3 4.3 2.1 4.4	19	SA	0554 1202 1832	1.9 4.8 1.4
5	SA	0525 1134 1757	2.0 4.6 1.7	20	SU	0040 0645 1300 1918	4.9 1.7 5.0 1.2
6	SU	0015 0618 1236 1848	4.7 1.7 4.9 1.3	21	M	0128 0723 1344 1955	5.1 1.4 5.2 1.0
7	M	0109 0704 1324 1935	5.1 1.3 5.3 0.9	22	TU	0206 0755 1421 2026	5.2 1.2 5.3 0.8
8	TU	0153 0750 1406 2022	5.5 0.9 5.6 0.5	23	W	0239 0825 1456 ○ 2054	5.3 1.0 5.4 0.8
9	W	0234 0835 1446 ● 2107	5.7 0.6 5.9 0.2	24	TH	0310 0855 1528 2121	5.3 0.9 5.4 0.7
10	TH	0315 0920 1527 2152	5.9 0.4 6.1 0.1	25	F	0340 0924 1559 2147	5.3 0.9 5.4 0.8
11	F	0356 1004 1610 2235	5.9 0.4 6.1 0.2	26	SA	0411 0950 1631 2211	5.3 1.0 5.3 0.9
12	SA	0440 1046 1655 2316	5.8 0.5 6.0 0.4	27	SU	0443 1010 1704 2231	5.2 1.1 5.2 1.1
13	SU	0525 1126 1744 2354	5.6 0.7 5.7 0.8	28	M	0517 1028 1739 2252	5.0 1.3 5.0 1.4
14	M	0614 1206 1837	5.3 1.1 5.4	29	TU	0554 1053 1818 2319	4.9 1.5 4.8 1.6
15	TU	0033 0709 1255 ◐ 1941	1.3 5.0 1.4 5.0	30	W	0635 1130 1903	4.7 1.7 4.6
				31	TH	0003 0722 1228 ◑ 2000	1.9 4.5 2.0 4.4

APRIL

Date	Day	Time	m	Date	Day	Time	m
1	F	0129 0824 1411 2111	2.2 4.4 2.1 4.3	16	SA	0410 1021 1702 2305	2.2 4.5 1.7 4.6
2	SA	0324 0940 1609 2229	2.3 4.4 2.0 4.5	17	SU	0519 1132 1803	2.0 4.7 1.5
3	SU	0451 1056 1725 2340	2.0 4.5 1.6 4.8	18	M	0011 0610 1231 1848	4.7 1.8 4.9 1.3
4	M	0549 1201 1820	1.6 4.9 1.2	19	TU	0101 0648 1317 1922	4.9 1.6 5.0 1.1
5	TU	0038 0637 1253 1910	5.1 1.2 5.3 0.8	20	W	0139 0721 1355 1952	5.1 1.3 5.2 1.0
6	W	0126 0724 1339 1958	5.5 0.9 5.6 0.4	21	TH	0212 0754 1430 2020	5.2 1.1 5.3 0.9
7	TH	0209 0812 1422 ● 2045	5.8 0.5 5.9 0.2	22	F	0243 0828 1502 ○ 2049	5.2 1.0 5.3 0.9
8	F	0251 0859 1506 2131	5.9 0.3 6.1 0.1	23	SA	0313 0900 1534 2118	5.3 0.9 5.3 0.9
9	SA	0334 0945 1551 2215	6.0 0.2 6.1 0.2	24	SU	0344 0930 1606 2146	5.3 1.0 5.2 1.0
10	SU	0418 1030 1639 2257	5.9 0.3 6.0 0.5	25	M	0417 0956 1640 2211	5.2 1.1 5.2 1.2
11	M	0505 1113 1729 2337	5.6 0.6 5.7 0.9	26	TU	0451 1017 1716 2232	5.1 1.2 5.0 1.4
12	TU	0555 1156 1824	5.3 1.0 5.3	27	W	0527 1041 1756 2300	5.0 1.3 4.9 1.6
13	W	0016 0651 1247 1927	1.4 5.0 1.3 5.0	28	TH	0607 1118 1841 2343	4.8 1.5 4.7 1.9
14	TH	0108 0757 1402 ◐ 2037	1.9 4.7 1.7 4.7	29	F	0654 1217 1935	4.7 1.7 4.6
15	F	0236 0909 1542 2149	2.2 4.6 1.8 4.5	30	SA	0106 0751 1346 ◑ 2040	2.1 4.5 1.9 4.5

Chart Datum: 2·90 metres below Ordnance Datum (Newlyn)
HAT is 6·3 metres above Chart Datum

TIME ZONE (UT)
For Summer Time add ONE hour in **non-shaded areas**

SCOTLAND – LEITH

LAT 55°59′N LONG 3°11′W

TIMES AND HEIGHTS OF HIGH AND LOW WATERS

Dates in amber are **SPRINGS**
Dates in grey are **NEAPS**

2016

MAY

Date	Day	Time	m	Time	m	Time	m	Time	m
1	SU	0247	2.1	0902	4.5	1527	1.8	2155	4.6
2	M	0413	1.9	1019	4.6	1647	1.5	2306	4.8
3	TU	0514	1.6	1125	4.9	1747	1.1		
4	W	0006	5.2	0606	1.2	1222	5.3	1840	0.8
5	TH	0057	5.5	0656	0.9	1312	5.6	1932	0.5
6	F	0143	5.7	0747	0.6	1359	5.9	● 2022	0.3
7	SA	0228	5.9	0839	0.3	1446	6.0	2110	0.3
8	SU	0313	5.9	0929	0.3	1534	6.0	2156	0.4
9	M	0359	5.8	1016	0.3	1624	5.9	2239	0.7
10	TU	0448	5.6	1102	0.6	1716	5.6	2320	1.1
11	W	0538	5.4	1147	0.9	1810	5.3	2359	1.5
12	TH	0634	5.1	1235	1.2	1909	5.0		
13	F	0043	1.8	0735	4.8	1338	1.5	◐ 2010	4.7
14	SA	0152	2.1	0839	4.7	1502	1.7	2114	4.5
15	SU	0319	2.2	0944	4.6	1615	1.7	2221	4.5
16	M	0426	2.1	1050	4.6	1714	1.6	2326	4.6
17	TU	0520	1.9	1150	4.7	1801	1.5		
18	W	0021	4.7	0604	1.7	1242	4.8	1837	1.4
19	TH	0104	4.9	0645	1.5	1324	5.0	1910	1.2
20	F	0141	5.0	0723	1.3	1401	5.1	1944	1.1
21	SA	0214	5.2	0800	1.1	1436	5.2	○ 2017	1.0
22	SU	0246	5.2	0836	1.0	1510	5.2	2051	1.0
23	M	0320	5.3	0910	1.0	1545	5.2	2124	1.1
24	TU	0354	5.3	0944	1.0	1620	5.2	2158	1.2
25	W	0429	5.2	1017	1.1	1657	5.1	2230	1.3
26	TH	0506	5.1	1050	1.2	1737	5.0	2305	1.5
27	F	0547	5.0	1130	1.3	1823	4.9	2350	1.7
28	SA	0633	4.9	1223	1.5	1914	4.8		
29	SU	0057	1.9	0726	4.8	1330	1.5	◑ 2015	4.7
30	M	0215	1.9	0831	4.7	1451	1.5	2124	4.8
31	TU	0334	1.8	0944	4.8	1610	1.4	2233	4.9

JUNE

Date	Day	Time	m	Time	m	Time	m	Time	m
1	W	0440	1.6	1053	5.0	1715	1.2	2335	5.1
2	TH	0537	1.3	1154	5.3	1812	0.9		
3	F	0030	5.4	0631	1.0	1249	5.5	1907	0.7
4	SA	0121	5.6	0727	0.7	1341	5.7	2001	0.6
5	SU	0208	5.7	0822	0.5	1431	5.8	● 2051	0.5
6	M	0256	5.8	0915	0.4	1521	5.8	2138	0.6
7	TU	0343	5.7	1003	0.4	1611	5.7	2221	0.8
8	W	0432	5.6	1050	0.5	1701	5.5	2301	1.1
9	TH	0522	5.4	1133	0.8	1752	5.3	2336	1.4
10	F	0613	5.2	1214	1.1	1844	5.0		
11	SA	0009	1.7	0706	5.0	1257	1.4	1936	4.8
12	SU	0056	2.0	0803	4.8	1352	1.7	◐ 2031	4.6
13	M	0203	2.2	0900	4.6	1504	1.8	2127	4.5
14	TU	0323	2.2	0958	4.5	1610	1.8	2226	4.5
15	W	0428	2.1	1058	4.5	1704	1.7	2325	4.6
16	TH	0523	1.9	1156	4.6	1750	1.6		
17	F	0019	4.7	0610	1.7	1248	4.8	1832	1.5
18	SA	0105	4.9	0654	1.5	1331	4.9	1911	1.3
19	SU	0145	5.1	0734	1.3	1411	5.1	1949	1.2
20	M	0222	5.2	0813	1.1	1448	5.2	○ 2027	1.1
21	TU	0258	5.3	0852	1.0	1524	5.3	2106	1.1
22	W	0334	5.4	0932	0.9	1601	5.3	2146	1.1
23	TH	0410	5.4	1012	0.9	1639	5.3	2226	1.2
24	F	0448	5.3	1053	0.9	1720	5.3	2308	1.3
25	SA	0529	5.3	1136	1.0	1805	5.2	2351	1.4
26	SU	0614	5.2	1221	1.1	1854	5.1		
27	M	0042	1.6	0705	5.1	1314	1.3	◑ 1950	4.9
28	TU	0144	1.7	0804	5.0	1419	1.4	2055	4.9
29	W	0256	1.8	0915	4.9	1535	1.4	2204	4.9
30	TH	0408	1.7	1026	5.0	1648	1.3	2309	5.0

JULY

Date	Day	Time	m	Time	m	Time	m	Time	m
1	F	0514	1.4	1133	5.1	1751	1.2		
2	SA	0009	5.2	0615	1.2	1234	5.3	1850	1.1
3	SU	0104	5.4	0715	0.9	1329	5.5	1945	0.9
4	M	0155	5.6	0812	0.6	1420	5.6	● 2035	0.8
5	TU	0243	5.7	0903	0.5	1509	5.7	2120	0.8
6	W	0330	5.7	0950	0.4	1556	5.6	2202	0.9
7	TH	0416	5.6	1033	0.5	1642	5.5	2238	1.1
8	F	0501	5.5	1111	0.7	1727	5.3	2306	1.3
9	SA	0547	5.3	1143	1.0	1812	5.1	2331	1.5
10	SU	0632	5.1	1210	1.3	1857	4.9		
11	M	0006	1.8	0719	4.9	1247	1.5	1943	4.7
12	TU	0056	2.0	0810	4.7	1338	1.8	◐ 2034	4.5
13	W	0204	2.2	0904	4.5	1448	2.0	2128	4.4
14	TH	0329	2.2	1002	4.4	1607	2.0	2226	4.5
15	F	0443	2.1	1104	4.5	1710	1.9	2327	4.6
16	SA	0540	1.9	1206	4.6	1801	1.7		
17	SU	0026	4.8	0628	1.7	1301	4.8	1845	1.5
18	M	0116	5.0	0712	1.4	1346	5.0	1926	1.3
19	TU	0159	5.2	0754	1.1	1426	5.2	○ 2007	1.2
20	W	0238	5.4	0835	0.9	1504	5.4	2049	1.0
21	TH	0315	5.5	0918	0.7	1542	5.5	2132	0.9
22	F	0352	5.6	1002	0.6	1620	5.5	2215	0.9
23	SA	0430	5.6	1045	0.6	1701	5.5	2258	1.0
24	SU	0511	5.6	1127	0.7	1745	5.4	2339	1.2
25	M	0555	5.5	1209	0.9	1833	5.3		
26	TU	0022	1.4	0644	5.3	1253	1.1	◑ 1925	5.1
27	W	0114	1.6	0741	5.1	1349	1.4	2028	4.9
28	TH	0223	1.7	0851	5.0	1505	1.6	2139	4.8
29	F	0345	1.7	1007	4.9	1629	1.6	2249	4.9
30	SA	0501	1.6	1119	5.0	1740	1.5	2355	5.1
31	SU	0610	1.3	1226	5.1	1841	1.4		

AUGUST

Date	Day	Time	m	Time	m	Time	m	Time	m
1	M	0054	5.3	0711	1.0	1323	5.3	1933	1.2
2	TU	0146	5.5	0805	0.8	1412	5.5	● 2019	1.0
3	W	0231	5.6	0852	0.6	1456	5.6	2101	0.9
4	TH	0315	5.7	0933	0.5	1539	5.5	2138	0.9
5	F	0356	5.6	1011	0.6	1619	5.5	2210	1.0
6	SA	0437	5.5	1042	0.7	1658	5.3	2233	1.2
7	SU	0516	5.4	1106	0.9	1736	5.1	2255	1.4
8	M	0555	5.2	1128	1.2	1815	5.0	2324	1.6
9	TU	0635	5.0	1159	1.4	1857	4.8		
10	W	0002	1.8	0720	4.7	1242	1.7	◐ 1944	4.6
11	TH	0056	2.1	0812	4.5	1339	2.0	2037	4.4
12	F	0214	2.3	0912	4.4	1501	2.2	2137	4.4
13	SA	0356	2.3	1016	4.3	1632	2.1	2242	4.5
14	SU	0512	2.1	1124	4.5	1734	1.9	2348	4.7
15	M	0607	1.8	1228	4.7	1823	1.7		
16	TU	0046	4.9	0652	1.4	1320	5.0	1906	1.4
17	W	0134	5.2	0735	1.1	1402	5.3	1948	1.1
18	TH	0214	5.5	0818	0.8	1441	5.5	○ 2031	0.9
19	F	0252	5.7	0902	0.5	1520	5.7	2115	0.7
20	SA	0329	5.8	0946	0.4	1559	5.8	2158	0.7
21	SU	0409	5.9	1029	0.3	1640	5.8	2241	0.7
22	M	0451	5.9	1110	0.5	1723	5.6	2321	0.9
23	TU	0536	5.7	1150	0.8	1810	5.4		
24	W	0002	1.2	0624	5.5	1232	1.1	1901	5.2
25	TH	0050	1.5	0722	5.2	1323	1.5	◑ 2004	4.9
26	F	0200	1.7	0834	4.9	1444	1.8	2118	4.8
27	SA	0332	1.8	0954	4.8	1618	1.9	2233	4.8
28	SU	0459	1.7	1112	4.8	1735	1.8	2345	5.0
29	M	0611	1.4	1222	5.0	1835	1.6		
30	TU	0046	5.2	0709	1.1	1317	5.2	1921	1.4
31	W	0136	5.4	0755	0.8	1402	5.4	2001	1.2

Chart Datum: 2·90 metres below Ordnance Datum (Newlyn)
HAT is 6·3 metres above Chart Datum

TIME ZONE (UT)
For Summer Time add ONE hour in **non-shaded areas**

SCOTLAND – LEITH

LAT 55°59′N LONG 3°11′W

TIMES AND HEIGHTS OF HIGH AND LOW WATERS

Dates in amber are **SPRINGS**
Dates in grey are **NEAPS**

2016

SEPTEMBER

Date	Day	Time	m	Time	m	Time	m	Time	m	Moon
1	TH	0218	5.6	0834	0.7	1441	5.5	2037	1.0	●
2	F	0257	5.6	0910	0.6	1517	5.5	2110	1.0	
3	SA	0334	5.6	0941	0.6	1552	5.4	2139	1.0	
4	SU	0409	5.5	1007	0.7	1626	5.4	2202	1.1	
5	M	0444	5.4	1028	0.9	1701	5.2	2223	1.2	
6	TU	0519	5.2	1049	1.1	1737	5.1	2246	1.4	
7	W	0556	5.0	1115	1.4	1815	4.9	2315	1.7	
8	TH	0638	4.8	1149	1.7	1859	4.7	2356	2.0	
9	F	0726	4.6	1240	2.1	1950	4.5			◐
10	SA	0105	2.2	0825	4.4	1400	2.3	2052	4.4	
11	SU	0251	2.4	0933	4.3	1547	2.4	2200	4.4	
12	M	0441	2.2	1045	4.4	1707	2.1	2310	4.6	
13	TU	0543	1.8	1154	4.7	1800	1.8			
14	W	0013	4.9	0630	1.4	1250	5.1	1844	1.4	
15	TH	0104	5.3	0714	1.0	1335	5.4	1926	1.1	
16	F	0147	5.6	0757	0.7	1415	5.7	2009	0.8	○
17	SA	0226	5.8	0841	0.4	1454	5.9	2053	0.6	
18	SU	0305	6.0	0925	0.2	1534	6.0	2138	0.5	
19	M	0346	6.1	1008	0.2	1616	5.9	2221	0.6	
20	TU	0430	6.0	1050	0.4	1700	5.8	2304	0.8	
21	W	0517	5.8	1131	0.8	1747	5.5	2346	1.1	
22	TH	0608	5.5	1211	1.2	1840	5.2			
23	F	0035	1.4	0708	5.2	1304	1.7	1944	4.9	◑
24	SA	0147	1.7	0822	4.9	1428	2.1	2101	4.7	
25	SU	0327	1.8	0942	4.7	1607	2.1	2217	4.7	
26	M	0456	1.7	1101	4.8	1723	2.0	2330	4.9	
27	TU	0604	1.4	1211	5.0	1820	1.8			
28	W	0031	5.2	0655	1.2	1304	5.2	1902	1.5	
29	TH	0119	5.4	0736	1.0	1345	5.3	1937	1.3	
30	F	0159	5.5	0810	0.8	1420	5.4	2008	1.1	

OCTOBER

Date	Day	Time	m	Time	m	Time	m	Time	m	Moon
1	SA	0235	5.5	0840	0.8	1453	5.5	2040	1.0	●
2	SU	0309	5.5	0907	0.8	1524	5.4	2109	1.0	
3	M	0342	5.5	0932	0.8	1556	5.4	2135	1.1	
4	TU	0415	5.4	0954	1.0	1628	5.3	2157	1.2	
5	W	0449	5.2	1015	1.2	1702	5.2	2218	1.4	
6	TH	0525	5.1	1038	1.4	1739	5.0	2243	1.6	
7	F	0605	4.9	1106	1.7	1820	4.8	2318	1.8	
8	SA	0650	4.6	1147	2.0	1908	4.6			
9	SU	0015	2.1	0745	4.5	1307	2.3	2007	4.5	◐
10	M	0155	2.3	0852	4.4	1457	2.4	2118	4.5	
11	TU	0352	2.2	1006	4.5	1631	2.2	2231	4.6	
12	W	0509	1.8	1117	4.8	1729	1.9	2337	4.9	
13	TH	0600	1.4	1216	5.1	1816	1.5			
14	F	0031	5.3	0645	1.0	1305	5.5	1859	1.1	
15	SA	0117	5.6	0730	0.6	1348	5.8	1944	0.8	
16	SU	0159	5.9	0816	0.4	1428	6.0	2030	0.5	○
17	M	0241	6.1	0902	0.2	1510	6.1	2117	0.4	
18	TU	0325	6.2	0947	0.3	1553	6.0	2204	0.5	
19	W	0412	6.1	1031	0.5	1639	5.8	2249	0.7	
20	TH	0501	5.9	1113	0.9	1728	5.6	2335	1.0	
21	F	0555	5.5	1155	1.4	1822	5.3			
22	SA	0027	1.3	0656	5.2	1247	1.9	1927	5.0	◑
23	SU	0137	1.7	0808	4.9	1406	2.2	2041	4.8	
24	M	0312	1.8	0923	4.7	1541	2.3	2154	4.8	
25	TU	0435	1.7	1037	4.7	1654	2.1	2304	4.9	
26	W	0540	1.5	1146	4.9	1751	1.9			
27	TH	0005	5.1	0629	1.3	1240	5.1	1832	1.7	
28	F	0055	5.2	0707	1.2	1321	5.2	1906	1.5	
29	SA	0135	5.3	0737	1.1	1355	5.3	1938	1.3	
30	SU	0211	5.4	0804	1.0	1427	5.4	2011	1.1	●
31	M	0245	5.4	0831	1.0	1457	5.4	2043	1.1	

NOVEMBER

Date	Day	Time	m	Time	m	Time	m	Time	m	Moon
1	TU	0317	5.4	0859	1.0	1528	5.4	2113	1.1	
2	W	0350	5.3	0926	1.1	1600	5.4	2139	1.2	
3	TH	0424	5.2	0951	1.3	1634	5.3	2203	1.3	
4	F	0500	5.1	1015	1.5	1710	5.1	2229	1.5	
5	SA	0539	5.0	1042	1.7	1749	5.0	2303	1.7	
6	SU	0623	4.8	1120	2.0	1835	4.8	2355	1.9	
7	M	0715	4.6	1226	2.3	1929	4.6			◐
8	TU	0116	2.1	0816	4.6	1410	2.4	2035	4.6	
9	W	0254	2.0	0928	4.6	1544	2.2	2150	4.7	
10	TH	0423	1.8	1039	4.8	1651	1.9	2258	4.9	
11	F	0523	1.4	1141	5.1	1743	1.6	2356	5.3	
12	SA	0614	1.1	1233	5.5	1831	1.2			
13	SU	0047	5.6	0702	0.8	1320	5.8	1919	0.9	
14	M	0134	5.9	0751	0.5	1404	6.0	2009	0.6	○
15	TU	0221	6.1	0840	0.4	1448	6.0	2100	0.5	
16	W	0308	6.1	0928	0.5	1534	6.0	2150	0.5	
17	TH	0357	6.0	1013	0.7	1621	5.9	2238	0.6	
18	F	0448	5.8	1057	1.1	1711	5.6	2326	0.9	
19	SA	0542	5.5	1140	1.5	1805	5.3			
20	SU	0016	1.2	0641	5.2	1226	1.9	1907	5.1	
21	M	0117	1.5	0745	4.9	1328	2.2	2015	4.9	◑
22	TU	0235	1.7	0852	4.7	1452	2.3	2122	4.8	
23	W	0354	1.8	0959	4.7	1606	2.3	2227	4.8	
24	TH	0458	1.7	1105	4.7	1705	2.1	2329	4.9	
25	F	0550	1.6	1203	4.9	1752	1.9			
26	SA	0022	5.0	0628	1.5	1249	5.0	1832	1.7	
27	SU	0108	5.1	0659	1.4	1327	5.2	1909	1.5	
28	M	0147	5.2	0729	1.3	1401	5.3	1945	1.3	
29	TU	0222	5.3	0800	1.2	1433	5.4	2020	1.2	●
30	W	0256	5.3	0832	1.2	1505	5.4	2053	1.2	

DECEMBER

Date	Day	Time	m	Time	m	Time	m	Time	m	Moon
1	TH	0330	5.3	0904	1.2	1538	5.4	2126	1.2	
2	F	0404	5.3	0936	1.3	1612	5.3	2157	1.2	
3	SA	0440	5.2	1007	1.4	1648	5.2	2229	1.3	
4	SU	0519	5.1	1038	1.6	1726	5.1	2304	1.5	
5	M	0602	5.0	1113	1.8	1809	5.0	2349	1.6	
6	TU	0650	4.9	1205	2.0	1858	4.9			
7	W	0049	1.7	0745	4.8	1326	2.2	1957	4.8	◐
8	TH	0205	1.8	0851	4.7	1453	2.2	2107	4.8	
9	F	0331	1.7	1001	4.9	1608	2.0	2220	4.9	
10	SA	0444	1.5	1106	5.1	1710	1.7	2325	5.2	
11	SU	0544	1.2	1204	5.3	1805	1.3			
12	M	0022	5.5	0638	1.0	1257	5.6	1859	1.0	
13	TU	0115	5.7	0731	0.8	1345	5.8	1954	0.7	
14	W	0205	5.9	0823	0.7	1431	5.9	2048	0.5	○
15	TH	0255	6.0	0912	0.7	1518	5.9	2139	0.5	
16	F	0345	5.9	0959	0.8	1606	5.8	2228	0.5	
17	SA	0435	5.8	1042	1.1	1656	5.7	2314	0.7	
18	SU	0526	5.5	1121	1.4	1747	5.5	2358	1.0	
19	M	0619	5.2	1155	1.7	1842	5.2			
20	TU	0042	1.4	0714	5.0	1233	2.0	1940	5.0	
21	W	0133	1.7	0811	4.7	1332	2.2	2040	4.8	◑
22	TH	0240	1.9	0909	4.6	1453	2.4	2140	4.7	
23	F	0352	2.0	1009	4.5	1608	2.3	2241	4.6	
24	SA	0452	1.9	1110	4.6	1709	2.2	2341	4.7	
25	SU	0541	1.8	1208	4.7	1800	1.9			
26	M	0035	4.8	0622	1.7	1256	4.9	1844	1.7	
27	TU	0121	5.0	0700	1.5	1336	5.1	1924	1.5	
28	W	0201	5.1	0736	1.4	1412	5.3	2001	1.3	
29	TH	0237	5.2	0812	1.3	1447	5.4	2037	1.2	●
30	F	0312	5.3	0848	1.2	1521	5.4	2114	1.1	
31	SA	0346	5.3	0925	1.2	1555	5.4	2151	1.0	

Chart Datum: 2·90 metres below Ordnance Datum (Newlyn)
HAT is 6·3 metres above Chart Datum

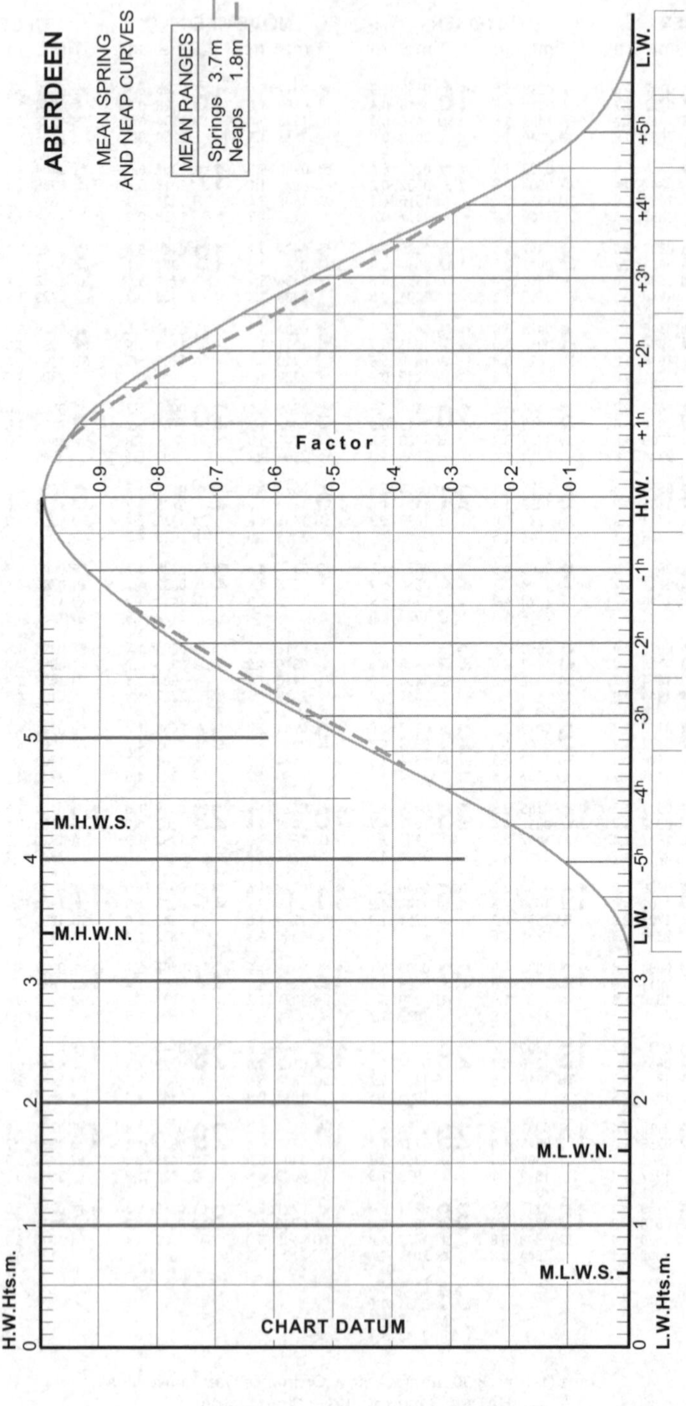
ABERDEEN
MEAN SPRING AND NEAP CURVES
MEAN RANGES
Springs 3.7m
Neaps 1.8m
Factor
0·9
0·8
0·7
0·6
0·5
0·4
0·3
0·2
0·1
L.W.
-5h
-4h
-3h
-2h
-1h
H.W.
+1h
+2h
+3h
+4h
+5h
L.W.
H.W.Hts.m.
0
1
2
3
4
5
M.H.W.N.
M.H.W.S.
CHART DATUM
L.W.Hts.m.
M.L.W.S.
M.L.W.N.

TIME ZONE (UT)
For Summer Time add ONE hour in **non-shaded areas**

SCOTLAND – ABERDEEN

LAT 57°09′N LONG 2°04′W

TIMES AND HEIGHTS OF HIGH AND LOW WATERS

Dates in amber are **SPRINGS**
Dates in grey are **NEAPS**

2016

JANUARY

Day	Time	m	Day	Time	m
1 F	0557 1130 1805	3.6 1.8 3.7	16 SA ◐	0549 1136 1757	3.9 1.3 4.1
2 SA ◑	0016 0648 1227 1900	1.5 3.5 1.9 3.6	17 SU	0019 0650 1241 1903	1.1 3.8 1.5 3.9
3 SU	0114 0745 1336 2002	1.6 3.4 2.0 3.5	18 M	0125 0757 1355 2015	1.3 3.7 1.6 3.8
4 M	0219 0850 1451 2112	1.7 3.4 2.0 3.5	19 TU	0239 0909 1515 2133	1.4 3.7 1.5 3.8
5 TU	0327 0955 1604 2219	1.7 3.5 1.9 3.6	20 W	0357 1020 1631 2246	1.4 3.8 1.4 3.9
6 W	0427 1050 1658 2313	1.6 3.7 1.7 3.7	21 TH	0502 1120 1731 2346	1.3 4.0 1.2 4.0
7 TH	0515 1135 1741 2359	1.5 3.9 1.4 3.9	22 F	0554 1210 1821	1.2 4.1 1.0
8 F	0556 1215 1821	1.3 4.0 1.2	23 SA	0037 0639 1254 1905	4.1 1.1 4.3 0.8
9 SA	0039 0634 1253 1859	4.0 1.1 4.2 1.0	24 SU ○	0122 0719 1334 1946	4.2 1.0 4.4 0.7
10 SU ●	0119 0713 1329 1938	4.1 1.0 4.3 0.8	25 M	0202 0755 1412 2024	4.2 1.0 4.4 0.7
11 M	0158 0752 1406 2019	4.2 0.9 4.4 0.7	26 TU	0240 0830 1448 2100	4.2 1.0 4.4 0.7
12 TU	0239 0832 1445 2100	4.3 0.9 4.5 0.6	27 W	0317 0903 1524 2134	4.1 1.1 4.3 0.8
13 W	0321 0913 1526 2143	4.3 0.9 4.5 0.7	28 TH	0353 0935 1559 2208	4.0 1.2 4.2 1.0
14 TH	0406 0955 1610 2229	4.2 1.0 4.4 0.7	29 F	0429 1008 1636 2243	3.9 1.3 4.0 1.2
15 F	0454 1042 1700 2320	4.1 1.2 4.3 0.9	30 SA	0508 1045 1717 2323	3.7 1.5 3.8 1.4
			31 SU	0553 1128 1806	3.6 1.7 3.6

FEBRUARY

Day	Time	m	Day	Time	m
1 M ◑	0012 0645 1225 1904	1.6 3.4 1.8 3.5	16 TU	0057 0728 1329 1957	1.3 3.6 1.5 3.7
2 TU	0113 0745 1340 2012	1.7 3.4 2.0 3.4	17 W	0214 0844 1458 2122	1.5 3.6 1.5 3.6
3 W	0225 0854 1503 2129	1.8 3.4 1.9 3.4	18 TH	0344 1004 1622 2242	1.6 3.6 1.4 3.7
4 TH	0341 1005 1620 2240	1.7 3.5 1.7 3.5	19 F	0453 1109 1723 2342	1.5 3.8 1.2 3.8
5 F	0444 1103 1715 2334	1.6 3.7 1.5 3.7	20 SA	0544 1200 1811	1.3 4.0 1.0
6 SA	0532 1150 1759	1.4 3.9 1.2	21 SU	0029 0626 1242 1852	4.0 1.2 4.1 0.8
7 SU	0019 0614 1231 1840	3.9 1.1 4.1 0.9	22 M ○	0110 0703 1319 1928	4.0 1.0 4.2 0.7
8 M ●	0101 0655 1310 1921	4.1 0.9 4.3 0.6	23 TU	0145 0737 1354 2002	4.1 1.0 4.3 0.7
9 TU	0141 0736 1348 2003	4.3 0.8 4.5 0.4	24 W	0218 0808 1426 2034	4.1 0.9 4.3 0.7
10 W	0221 0816 1428 2044	4.4 0.7 4.6 0.3	25 TH	0249 0838 1458 2104	4.1 0.9 4.2 0.7
11 TH	0303 0857 1509 2127	4.4 0.7 4.6 0.4	26 F	0320 0908 1530 2135	4.0 1.0 4.2 0.9
12 F	0346 0938 1553 2211	4.3 0.7 4.5 0.5	27 SA	0352 0938 1603 2206	3.9 1.1 4.0 1.0
13 SA	0432 1023 1642 2258	4.2 0.9 4.4 0.7	28 SU	0427 1010 1640 2241	3.8 1.2 3.9 1.2
14 SU	0523 1113 1737 2353	4.0 1.1 4.2 1.0	29 M	0505 1048 1724 2322	3.6 1.4 3.7 1.4
15 M ◐	0622 1215 1842	3.8 1.3 3.9			

MARCH

Day	Time	m	Day	Time	m
1 TU ◑	0552 1134 1818	3.5 1.6 3.5	16 W	0033 0703 1311 1943	1.4 3.6 1.4 3.6
2 W	0015 0650 1240 1925	1.7 3.4 1.8 3.3	17 TH	0153 0819 1442 2111	1.7 3.5 1.5 3.5
3 TH	0128 0759 1407 2042	1.8 3.3 1.8 3.3	18 F	0328 0943 1608 2231	1.7 3.5 1.3 3.6
4 F	0253 0914 1536 2203	1.8 3.3 1.7 3.4	19 SA	0438 1051 1707 2329	1.6 3.7 1.1 3.7
5 SA	0411 1025 1644 2306	1.6 3.5 1.4 3.6	20 SU	0527 1142 1753	1.4 3.8 1.0
6 SU	0507 1120 1733 2355	1.4 3.8 1.1 3.9	21 M	0013 0607 1223 1830	3.8 1.2 4.0 0.8
7 M	0553 1205 1817	1.1 4.1 0.7	22 TU	0049 0642 1258 1904	3.9 1.1 4.1 0.7
8 TU	0038 0634 1246 1900	4.2 0.8 4.3 0.4	23 W ○	0121 0714 1331 1936	4.0 0.9 4.2 0.7
9 W ●	0119 0716 1327 1942	4.4 0.6 4.5 0.2	24 TH	0151 0745 1402 2006	4.1 0.9 4.2 0.7
10 TH	0200 0757 1408 2024	4.5 0.5 4.7 0.2	25 F	0221 0814 1433 2035	4.1 0.8 4.2 0.7
11 F	0241 0838 1451 2107	4.5 0.4 4.7 0.2	26 SA	0250 0843 1504 2104	4.0 0.9 4.1 0.8
12 SA	0324 0920 1536 2150	4.4 0.5 4.6 0.4	27 SU	0320 0912 1537 2134	4.0 1.0 4.0 1.0
13 SU	0409 1005 1625 2237	4.2 0.7 4.4 0.7	28 M	0353 0944 1613 2207	3.9 1.1 3.8 1.2
14 M	0459 1056 1722 2330	4.0 0.9 4.1 1.1	29 TU	0429 1020 1654 2245	3.7 1.2 3.7 1.4
15 TU ◐	0556 1156 1828	3.8 1.2 3.8	30 W	0511 1104 1746 2334	3.6 1.4 3.5 1.6
			31 TH ◑	0605 1203 1852	3.4 1.6 3.3

APRIL

Day	Time	m	Day	Time	m
1 F	0044 0715 1325 2006	1.8 3.3 1.7 3.3	16 SA	0258 0911 1541 2206	1.8 3.5 1.3 3.5
2 SA	0212 0829 1453 2125	1.8 3.3 1.6 3.4	17 SU	0411 1022 1640 2303	1.6 3.6 1.2 3.6
3 SU	0334 0942 1607 2234	1.6 3.5 1.3 3.6	18 M	0501 1114 1725 2346	1.5 3.7 1.0 3.7
4 M	0437 1045 1703 2327	1.4 3.7 1.0 3.9	19 TU	0541 1156 1802	1.3 3.8 0.9
5 TU	0527 1135 1751	1.1 4.0 0.6	20 W	0022 0616 1232 1835	3.8 1.1 3.9 0.8
6 W	0012 0611 1221 1835	4.2 0.8 4.3 0.3	21 TH	0054 0649 1305 1907	3.9 1.0 4.0 0.8
7 TH ●	0055 0654 1304 1919	4.4 0.5 4.5 0.2	22 F ○	0124 0720 1337 1937	4.0 0.9 4.1 0.8
8 F	0137 0736 1348 2002	4.5 0.4 4.7 0.1	23 SA	0153 0751 1409 2007	4.1 0.8 4.1 0.8
9 SA	0218 0819 1433 2046	4.5 0.3 4.7 0.2	24 SU	0223 0821 1442 2037	4.0 0.9 4.0 0.9
10 SU	0301 0904 1520 2130	4.4 0.4 4.5 0.5	25 M	0254 0851 1516 2109	4.0 0.9 3.9 1.0
11 M	0347 0950 1612 2217	4.3 0.5 4.3 0.8	26 TU	0326 0925 1552 2142	3.9 1.0 3.8 1.1
12 TU	0437 1042 1710 2309	4.1 0.8 4.0 1.2	27 W	0402 1002 1634 2221	3.8 1.1 3.7 1.3
13 W	0534 1142 1816	3.8 1.0 3.7	28 TH	0443 1046 1725 2310	3.7 1.2 3.5 1.5
14 TH ◐	0011 0639 1253 1927	1.5 3.6 1.3 3.5	29 F	0535 1143 1828	3.5 1.4 3.4
15 F	0127 0751 1417 2048	1.7 3.5 1.4 3.4	30 SA ◑	0015 0640 1256 1937	1.7 3.4 1.4 3.4

Chart Datum: 2·25 metres below Ordnance Datum (Newlyn)
HAT is 4·8 metres above Chart Datum

TIME ZONE (UT)
For Summer Time add ONE hour in **non-shaded areas**

SCOTLAND – ABERDEEN

LAT 57°09′N LONG 2°04′W

TIMES AND HEIGHTS OF HIGH AND LOW WATERS

Dates in amber are **SPRINGS**
Dates in grey are **NEAPS**

2016

MAY

Day		Time	m	Time	m	Time	m	Time	m
1	SU	0137	1.7	0752	3.4	1416	1.3	2049	3.5
2	M	0256	1.6	0902	3.5	1529	1.1	2159	3.7
3	TU	0403	1.3	1009	3.8	1631	0.9	2257	3.9
4	W	0458	1.1	1105	4.0	1723	0.6	2346	4.2
5	TH	0547	0.8	1155	4.3	1812	0.4		
6	F	0030	4.3	0632	0.5	1243	4.5	● 1857	0.3
7	SA	0114	4.5	0718	0.4	1330	4.6	1942	0.3
8	SU	0157	4.5	0803	0.3	1418	4.6	2027	0.4
9	M	0241	4.4	0850	0.4	1507	4.4	2112	0.6
10	TU	0328	4.3	0938	0.5	1600	4.2	2159	0.9
11	W	0418	4.1	1029	0.7	1658	4.0	2249	1.2
12	TH	0513	3.9	1126	0.9	1758	3.7	2346	1.5
13	F	0614	3.7	1228	1.1	1902	3.5	◐	
14	SA	0052	1.7	0718	3.5	1339	1.3	2010	3.4
15	SU	0208	1.8	0828	3.5	1455	1.3	2123	3.4
16	M	0326	1.7	0939	3.5	1600	1.3	2223	3.5
17	TU	0425	1.6	1036	3.6	1649	1.2	2310	3.6
18	W	0510	1.4	1123	3.7	1729	1.1	2349	3.8
19	TH	0548	1.2	1202	3.8	1805	1.0		
20	F	0023	3.9	0623	1.1	1239	3.9	1838	0.9
21	SA	0056	4.0	0656	1.0	1314	3.9	○ 1910	0.9
22	SU	0128	4.0	0729	0.9	1348	4.0	1942	0.9
23	M	0159	4.1	0801	0.9	1423	4.0	2015	0.9
24	TU	0231	4.0	0835	0.9	1458	3.9	2049	1.0
25	W	0305	4.0	0911	0.9	1537	3.9	2125	1.1
26	TH	0342	3.9	0950	1.0	1619	3.8	2206	1.2
27	F	0424	3.8	1035	1.0	1709	3.7	2253	1.4
28	SA	0513	3.7	1128	1.1	1807	3.6	2353	1.5
29	SU	0614	3.7	1232	1.2	1911	3.5	◑	
30	M	0104	1.6	0720	3.6	1344	1.2	2017	3.6
31	TU	0218	1.5	0828	3.7	1454	1.1	2125	3.7

JUNE

Day		Time	m	Time	m	Time	m	Time	m
1	W	0327	1.4	0936	3.8	1559	0.9	2227	3.9
2	TH	0429	1.1	1039	4.0	1658	0.7	2321	4.1
3	F	0525	0.9	1135	4.2	1751	0.6		
4	SA	0009	4.2	0615	0.7	1227	4.3	1839	0.5
5	SU	0055	4.4	0703	0.5	1317	4.4	● 1926	0.5
6	M	0140	4.4	0751	0.4	1406	4.4	2011	0.6
7	TU	0225	4.4	0838	0.4	1456	4.3	2055	0.8
8	W	0311	4.3	0925	0.5	1547	4.2	2140	1.0
9	TH	0359	4.2	1013	0.6	1639	4.0	2225	1.2
10	F	0449	4.0	1103	0.8	1733	3.8	2314	1.4
11	SA	0543	3.8	1156	1.1	1827	3.6		
12	SU	0009	1.6	0638	3.6	1253	1.3	◐ 1923	3.4
13	M	0112	1.7	0738	3.5	1354	1.4	2025	3.4
14	TU	0221	1.8	0843	3.4	1501	1.4	2129	3.4
15	W	0333	1.7	0948	3.5	1602	1.4	2225	3.5
16	TH	0431	1.6	1044	3.5	1651	1.3	2312	3.6
17	F	0517	1.4	1131	3.7	1733	1.2	2352	3.8
18	SA	0557	1.2	1213	3.8	1810	1.1		
19	SU	0029	3.9	0633	1.1	1252	3.9	1845	1.0
20	M	0104	4.0	0708	1.0	1329	3.9	○ 1921	1.0
21	TU	0138	4.1	0744	0.9	1405	4.0	1957	1.0
22	W	0212	4.1	0821	0.8	1443	4.0	2033	1.0
23	TH	0248	4.1	0859	0.8	1522	4.0	2112	1.0
24	F	0326	4.1	0939	0.8	1605	3.9	2152	1.1
25	SA	0408	4.1	1023	0.8	1652	3.9	2238	1.2
26	SU	0455	4.0	1113	0.9	1745	3.8	2331	1.3
27	M	0550	3.9	1210	1.0	1844	3.7	◑	
28	TU	0034	1.4	0652	3.8	1315	1.1	1947	3.7
29	W	0144	1.4	0759	3.8	1423	1.1	2054	3.7
30	TH	0256	1.4	0909	3.8	1533	1.0	2201	3.8

JULY

Day		Time	m	Time	m	Time	m	Time	m
1	F	0406	1.2	1019	3.9	1639	1.0	2301	4.0
2	SA	0509	1.0	1122	4.1	1737	0.9	2353	4.1
3	SU	0604	0.8	1217	4.2	1827	0.8		
4	M	0041	4.3	0654	0.6	1308	4.3	● 1913	0.8
5	TU	0127	4.4	0741	0.5	1357	4.3	1956	0.8
6	W	0211	4.4	0826	0.4	1443	4.2	2038	0.9
7	TH	0254	4.3	0909	0.5	1529	4.1	2118	1.0
8	F	0337	4.2	0951	0.6	1614	4.0	2158	1.1
9	SA	0421	4.1	1033	0.8	1659	3.8	2238	1.3
10	SU	0506	3.9	1116	1.0	1745	3.6	2322	1.5
11	M	0554	3.7	1203	1.2	1834	3.5		
12	TU	0014	1.7	0646	3.6	1256	1.4	◐ 1927	3.4
13	W	0116	1.8	0744	3.4	1356	1.5	2027	3.4
14	TH	0227	1.8	0851	3.4	1503	1.6	2132	3.4
15	F	0343	1.8	1000	3.4	1609	1.5	2232	3.5
16	SA	0445	1.6	1059	3.5	1701	1.4	2321	3.7
17	SU	0531	1.4	1147	3.7	1744	1.3		
18	M	0003	3.9	0610	1.2	1230	3.8	1823	1.1
19	TU	0041	4.0	0648	1.0	1309	4.0	○ 1900	1.0
20	W	0117	4.1	0726	0.8	1347	4.1	1938	0.9
21	TH	0153	4.3	0804	0.7	1425	4.1	2017	0.9
22	F	0230	4.3	0844	0.6	1505	4.2	2056	0.9
23	SA	0309	4.3	0925	0.6	1547	4.1	2136	0.9
24	SU	0350	4.3	1007	0.6	1631	4.1	2219	1.0
25	M	0436	4.2	1053	0.7	1721	3.9	2308	1.2
26	TU	0528	4.1	1146	0.9	1817	3.8	◑	
27	W	0007	1.3	0628	4.0	1248	1.1	1920	3.7
28	TH	0116	1.4	0737	3.8	1357	1.2	2028	3.7
29	F	0232	1.4	0851	3.8	1514	1.3	2141	3.7
30	SA	0353	1.3	1009	3.8	1628	1.2	2247	3.9
31	SU	0502	1.1	1117	3.9	1728	1.1	2343	4.1

AUGUST

Day		Time	m	Time	m	Time	m	Time	m
1	M	0557	0.9	1213	4.1	1817	1.0		
2	TU	0031	4.2	0645	0.7	1302	4.2	● 1901	0.9
3	W	0115	4.3	0729	0.6	1345	4.2	1940	0.9
4	TH	0155	4.4	0809	0.5	1426	4.2	2018	0.9
5	F	0234	4.4	0847	0.5	1505	4.1	2053	1.0
6	SA	0312	4.3	0923	0.6	1542	4.0	2127	1.1
7	SU	0349	4.2	0959	0.8	1620	3.9	2201	1.2
8	M	0427	4.0	1034	1.0	1659	3.7	2238	1.4
9	TU	0508	3.8	1113	1.2	1742	3.6	2320	1.6
10	W	0556	3.6	1159	1.4	1832	3.5	◐	
11	TH	0014	1.7	0652	3.5	1256	1.6	1929	3.4
12	F	0125	1.9	0757	3.4	1405	1.8	2034	3.4
13	SA	0247	1.9	0912	3.3	1522	1.7	2146	3.5
14	SU	0408	1.7	1025	3.4	1629	1.6	2247	3.6
15	M	0503	1.5	1121	3.6	1719	1.4	2335	3.8
16	TU	0546	1.2	1206	3.8	1800	1.2		
17	W	0016	4.0	0625	0.9	1247	4.0	1839	1.0
18	TH	0054	4.2	0704	0.7	1325	4.2	○ 1918	0.8
19	F	0131	4.4	0744	0.5	1404	4.3	1957	0.7
20	SA	0209	4.5	0824	0.4	1443	4.4	2036	0.7
21	SU	0249	4.6	0905	0.4	1524	4.3	2117	0.7
22	M	0331	4.5	0947	0.5	1608	4.2	2159	0.8
23	TU	0416	4.4	1032	0.7	1656	4.1	2247	1.0
24	W	0508	4.2	1123	0.9	1751	3.9	2344	1.2
25	TH	0610	4.0	1223	1.2	1855	3.7	◑	
26	F	0055	1.4	0721	3.8	1336	1.4	2007	3.6
27	SA	0218	1.5	0842	3.7	1502	1.6	2125	3.7
28	SU	0347	1.4	1007	3.7	1622	1.5	2237	3.8
29	M	0455	1.2	1115	3.9	1719	1.3	2333	4.0
30	TU	0548	0.9	1207	4.0	1805	1.2		
31	W	0019	4.2	0632	0.7	1250	4.1	1845	1.1

Chart Datum: 2·25 metres below Ordnance Datum (Newlyn)
HAT is 4·8 metres above Chart Datum

TIME ZONE (UT)
For Summer Time add ONE hour in **non-shaded areas**

SCOTLAND – ABERDEEN

LAT 57°09'N LONG 2°04'W

TIMES AND HEIGHTS OF HIGH AND LOW WATERS

Dates in amber are **SPRINGS**
Dates in grey are **NEAPS**

2016

SEPTEMBER

Date	Day	Time	m	Time	m	Time	m	Time	m
1	TH ●	0059	4.3	0711	0.6	1328	4.2	1921	1.0
2	F	0136	4.4	0747	0.6	1403	4.2	1954	0.9
3	SA	0210	4.4	0820	0.6	1436	4.2	2026	0.9
4	SU	0244	4.3	0852	0.7	1508	4.1	2057	1.0
5	M	0317	4.2	0923	0.8	1541	4.0	2128	1.1
6	TU	0351	4.1	0954	1.0	1615	3.9	2200	1.3
7	W	0429	3.9	1028	1.2	1654	3.7	2238	1.5
8	TH	0513	3.7	1109	1.5	1740	3.6	2324	1.7
9	F ◐	0607	3.5	1200	1.7	1837	3.5		
10	SA	0028	1.8	0713	3.4	1311	1.9	1943	3.4
11	SU	0154	1.9	0827	3.3	1435	1.9	2056	3.4
12	M	0323	1.8	0947	3.4	1554	1.8	2207	3.6
13	TU	0431	1.5	1051	3.6	1651	1.5	2303	3.8
14	W	0518	1.2	1139	3.9	1735	1.3	2347	4.1
15	TH	0600	0.9	1221	4.1	1816	1.0		
16	F ○	0027	4.3	0639	0.6	1300	4.4	1855	0.8
17	SA	0106	4.5	0720	0.4	1339	4.5	1935	0.6
18	SU	0146	4.7	0801	0.3	1419	4.6	2015	0.6
19	M	0227	4.7	0842	0.3	1500	4.5	2056	0.6
20	TU	0311	4.7	0924	0.4	1544	4.4	2140	0.7
21	W	0358	4.5	1010	0.7	1631	4.2	2229	0.9
22	TH	0452	4.3	1101	1.0	1727	4.0	2328	1.2
23	F ◑	0557	4.0	1202	1.4	1833	3.8		
24	SA	0040	1.4	0711	3.7	1319	1.7	1946	3.7
25	SU	0207	1.5	0835	3.6	1450	1.8	2108	3.7
26	M	0337	1.4	1001	3.7	1609	1.7	2222	3.8
27	TU	0442	1.2	1105	3.8	1704	1.5	2317	4.0
28	W	0532	1.0	1152	4.0	1748	1.3		
29	TH	0001	4.1	0612	0.9	1232	4.1	1824	1.2
30	F	0039	4.3	0648	0.8	1305	4.2	1858	1.0

OCTOBER

Date	Day	Time	m	Time	m	Time	m	Time	m
1	SA ●	0113	4.3	0720	0.7	1336	4.2	1930	1.0
2	SU	0145	4.3	0751	0.7	1406	4.2	2000	1.0
3	M	0217	4.3	0821	0.8	1436	4.2	2030	1.0
4	TU	0249	4.2	0850	0.9	1506	4.1	2059	1.1
5	W	0322	4.1	0920	1.1	1539	4.0	2131	1.2
6	TH	0358	3.9	0952	1.3	1615	3.9	2207	1.4
7	F	0440	3.8	1030	1.5	1656	3.7	2250	1.6
8	SA	0531	3.6	1117	1.7	1749	3.6	2348	1.7
9	SU ◐	0636	3.4	1222	1.9	1857	3.5		
10	M	0106	1.8	0749	3.4	1349	2.0	2009	3.5
11	TU	0235	1.7	0905	3.5	1512	1.9	2121	3.6
12	W	0349	1.5	1015	3.7	1616	1.6	2224	3.8
13	TH	0444	1.2	1108	4.0	1705	1.3	2314	4.1
14	F	0530	0.9	1152	4.2	1749	1.0	2358	4.4
15	SA	0613	0.6	1233	4.5	1831	0.8		
16	SU ○	0040	4.6	0654	0.4	1314	4.6	1912	0.6
17	M	0123	4.8	0737	0.3	1355	4.7	1955	0.5
18	TU	0207	4.8	0820	0.4	1437	4.6	2038	0.5
19	W	0253	4.7	0903	0.6	1521	4.5	2125	0.7
20	TH	0344	4.5	0950	0.9	1609	4.3	2216	0.9
21	F	0440	4.3	1041	1.2	1705	4.1	2315	1.1
22	SA ◑	0546	4.0	1143	1.6	1811	3.9		
23	SU	0026	1.3	0658	3.7	1257	1.8	1923	3.7
24	M	0148	1.4	0818	3.6	1424	1.9	2041	3.7
25	TU	0313	1.4	0940	3.7	1544	1.8	2155	3.8
26	W	0418	1.3	1042	3.8	1640	1.6	2252	3.9
27	TH	0507	1.1	1128	3.9	1724	1.5	2337	4.0
28	F	0546	1.0	1206	4.0	1801	1.3		
29	SA	0014	4.1	0620	1.0	1238	4.1	1834	1.2
30	SU ●	0049	4.2	0652	0.9	1309	4.2	1906	1.1
31	M	0121	4.2	0722	0.9	1338	4.2	1937	1.0

NOVEMBER

Date	Day	Time	m	Time	m	Time	m	Time	m
1	TU	0153	4.2	0752	0.9	1408	4.2	2007	1.0
2	W	0226	4.2	0822	1.0	1438	4.2	2037	1.1
3	TH	0300	4.1	0853	1.2	1510	4.1	2110	1.2
4	F	0336	4.0	0926	1.3	1545	4.0	2146	1.3
5	SA	0417	3.8	1002	1.5	1625	3.9	2228	1.4
6	SU	0505	3.7	1047	1.7	1713	3.7	2321	1.6
7	M ◐	0605	3.5	1146	1.9	1815	3.6		
8	TU	0029	1.7	0713	3.5	1305	1.9	1926	3.6
9	W	0149	1.6	0824	3.6	1426	1.9	2035	3.7
10	TH	0303	1.4	0934	3.7	1535	1.7	2141	3.9
11	F	0405	1.2	1033	4.0	1632	1.4	2239	4.1
12	SA	0458	0.9	1122	4.2	1721	1.1	2330	4.4
13	SU	0546	0.7	1207	4.4	1808	0.8		
14	M ○	0017	4.6	0631	0.5	1250	4.6	1852	0.6
15	TU	0104	4.7	0716	0.5	1333	4.7	1938	0.5
16	W	0151	4.8	0801	0.5	1416	4.7	2024	0.5
17	TH	0240	4.7	0846	0.7	1502	4.6	2113	0.6
18	F	0332	4.5	0933	1.0	1551	4.4	2204	0.8
19	SA	0429	4.2	1023	1.3	1645	4.2	2301	1.0
20	SU	0531	4.0	1119	1.6	1747	4.0		
21	M ◑	0004	1.2	0635	3.8	1225	1.8	1852	3.8
22	TU	0114	1.4	0745	3.6	1339	1.9	2002	3.7
23	W	0229	1.5	0859	3.6	1459	1.9	2115	3.7
24	TH	0340	1.4	1004	3.7	1605	1.8	2217	3.8
25	F	0433	1.4	1055	3.8	1654	1.6	2306	3.9
26	SA	0515	1.3	1135	3.9	1734	1.5	2347	4.0
27	SU	0551	1.2	1210	4.0	1810	1.3		
28	M	0024	4.1	0624	1.1	1243	4.1	1844	1.2
29	TU ●	0100	4.1	0657	1.1	1314	4.2	1916	1.1
30	W	0134	4.1	0728	1.1	1345	4.2	1948	1.1

DECEMBER

Date	Day	Time	m	Time	m	Time	m	Time	m
1	TH	0208	4.1	0800	1.1	1417	4.2	2021	1.1
2	F	0242	4.1	0833	1.2	1449	4.2	2055	1.1
3	SA	0319	4.0	0907	1.3	1524	4.1	2132	1.2
4	SU	0359	3.9	0944	1.4	1603	4.0	2213	1.3
5	M	0444	3.8	1026	1.6	1647	3.9	2301	1.3
6	TU	0537	3.7	1118	1.7	1741	3.8	2359	1.4
7	W ◐	0639	3.6	1224	1.8	1846	3.8		
8	TH	0108	1.4	0745	3.6	1340	1.8	1954	3.8
9	F	0219	1.4	0852	3.7	1452	1.7	2101	3.9
10	SA	0326	1.2	0957	3.9	1558	1.5	2207	4.1
11	SU	0428	1.0	1054	4.1	1656	1.2	2306	4.3
12	M	0523	0.9	1144	4.3	1749	1.0		
13	TU	0000	4.4	0613	0.7	1231	4.5	1838	0.7
14	W ○	0051	4.6	0701	0.7	1316	4.6	1926	0.6
15	TH	0140	4.6	0747	0.7	1401	4.6	2014	0.5
16	F	0230	4.6	0832	0.8	1447	4.6	2102	0.6
17	SA	0321	4.4	0917	1.0	1534	4.5	2151	0.7
18	SU	0414	4.2	1003	1.2	1624	4.3	2241	0.9
19	M	0508	4.0	1051	1.5	1718	4.1	2333	1.1
20	TU	0603	3.8	1144	1.7	1814	3.9		
21	W ◑	0030	1.3	0700	3.6	1245	1.9	1914	3.7
22	TH	0131	1.5	0803	3.5	1353	2.0	2020	3.6
23	F	0238	1.6	0910	3.5	1509	1.9	2129	3.6
24	SA	0346	1.6	1010	3.6	1616	1.8	2229	3.7
25	SU	0439	1.5	1100	3.7	1706	1.6	2319	3.8
26	M	0522	1.4	1142	3.9	1747	1.5		
27	TU	0002	3.9	0559	1.3	1219	4.0	1823	1.3
28	W	0041	4.0	0635	1.2	1254	4.1	1858	1.2
29	TH ●	0117	4.0	0709	1.2	1327	4.2	1932	1.1
30	F	0152	4.1	0742	1.1	1359	4.2	2007	1.0
31	SA	0228	4.1	0817	1.1	1432	4.3	2042	1.0

Chart Datum: 2·25 metres below Ordnance Datum (Newlyn)
HAT is 4·8 metres above Chart Datum

TIDES

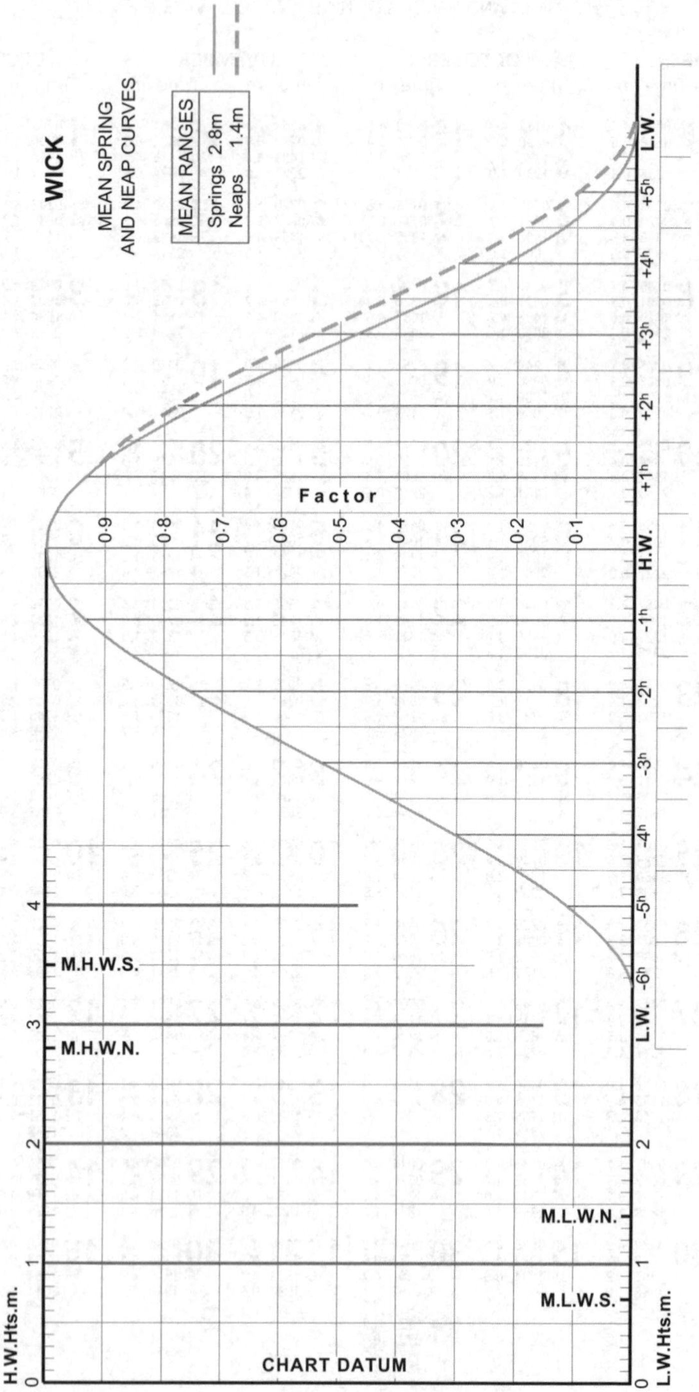
WICK
MEAN SPRING AND NEAP CURVES
MEAN RANGES
Springs 2.8m
Neaps 1.4m
Factor
0·9
0·8
0·7
0·6
0·5
0·4
0·3
0·2
0·1
L.W.
-6h
-5h
-4h
-3h
-2h
-1h
H.W.
+1h
+2h
+3h
+4h
+5h
L.W.
H.W.Hts.m.
0
1
2
3
4
M.H.W.N.
M.H.W.S.
CHART DATUM
L.W.Hts.m.
M.L.W.S.
M.L.W.N.

TIME ZONE (UT)
For Summer Time add ONE hour in **non-shaded areas**

SCOTLAND – WICK

LAT 58°26′N LONG 3°05′W

TIMES AND HEIGHTS OF HIGH AND LOW WATERS

Dates in amber are **SPRINGS**
Dates in grey are **NEAPS**

2016

JANUARY

Date	Day	Time	m	Time	m	Time	m	Time	m
1	F	0341	2.9	0904	1.5	1552	3.1	2204	1.3
2	SA	0434	2.8	1001	1.6	1647	2.9	◑ 2306	1.4
3	SU	0533	2.8	1117	1.7	1750	2.9		
4	M	0013	1.4	0635	2.8	1239	1.7	1855	2.8
5	TU	0121	1.4	0737	2.9	1354	1.6	1959	2.9
6	W	0218	1.3	0833	3.0	1448	1.4	2056	3.0
7	TH	0304	1.2	0921	3.2	1531	1.3	2145	3.1
8	F	0343	1.1	1003	3.3	1610	1.1	2229	3.3
9	SA	0420	1.0	1043	3.5	1647	0.9	2310	3.4
10	SU	0457	0.9	1122	3.6	1724	0.8	● 2351	3.5
11	M	0535	0.9	1202	3.7	1804	0.7		
12	TU	0033	3.5	0615	0.8	1243	3.7	1845	0.6
13	W	0116	3.5	0656	0.9	1325	3.7	1928	0.6
14	TH	0200	3.4	0738	0.9	1408	3.6	2014	0.7
15	F	0247	3.3	0824	1.1	1455	3.5	2106	0.8
16	SA	0338	3.2	0916	1.2	1548	3.4	◐ 2207	1.0
17	SU	0437	3.1	1024	1.3	1651	3.2	2319	1.1
18	M	0544	3.0	1144	1.4	1802	3.1		
19	TU	0035	1.2	0653	3.0	1309	1.4	1917	3.1
20	W	0151	1.2	0806	3.1	1423	1.2	2033	3.2
21	TH	0252	1.1	0909	3.2	1521	1.0	2137	3.3
22	F	0341	1.1	1001	3.4	1609	0.9	2229	3.4
23	SA	0423	1.0	1047	3.5	1652	0.7	2314	3.4
24	SU	0501	1.0	1129	3.6	1731	0.7	○ 2355	3.4
25	M	0537	0.9	1208	3.6	1809	0.6		
26	TU	0033	3.4	0611	0.9	1245	3.6	1844	0.7
27	W	0110	3.3	0644	1.0	1320	3.5	1919	0.7
28	TH	0145	3.2	0716	1.0	1355	3.4	1953	0.9
29	F	0219	3.1	0748	1.1	1430	3.3	2028	1.0
30	SA	0256	3.0	0823	1.3	1508	3.1	2107	1.2
31	SU	0337	2.9	0903	1.4	1551	3.0	2157	1.3

FEBRUARY

Date	Day	Time	m	Time	m	Time	m	Time	m
1	M	0427	2.8	0959	1.6	1646	2.8	◑ 2304	1.5
2	TU	0528	2.7	1127	1.7	1756	2.7		
3	W	0019	1.5	0637	2.7	1258	1.6	1909	2.7
4	TH	0134	1.4	0744	2.8	1415	1.5	2020	2.8
5	F	0235	1.3	0844	3.0	1507	1.3	2119	3.0
6	SA	0321	1.2	0935	3.2	1550	1.0	2207	3.2
7	SU	0401	1.0	1020	3.4	1629	0.8	2252	3.4
8	M	0440	0.9	1102	3.6	1708	0.6	● 2334	3.5
9	TU	0519	0.7	1144	3.7	1748	0.4		
10	W	0017	3.6	0559	0.6	1227	3.8	1829	0.3
11	TH	0100	3.6	0640	0.6	1309	3.8	1912	0.4
12	F	0143	3.5	0721	0.7	1352	3.7	1955	0.5
13	SA	0227	3.4	0805	0.8	1438	3.6	2042	0.7
14	SU	0314	3.2	0853	1.0	1529	3.4	2137	0.9
15	M	0408	3.0	0955	1.2	1629	3.2	◐ 2247	1.2
16	TU	0513	2.9	1119	1.3	1743	3.0		
17	W	0010	1.3	0626	2.9	1255	1.3	1904	2.9
18	TH	0139	1.3	0746	2.9	1417	1.2	2028	3.0
19	F	0245	1.3	0855	3.1	1515	1.0	2130	3.1
20	SA	0332	1.2	0948	3.3	1600	0.8	2219	3.2
21	SU	0411	1.1	1033	3.4	1638	0.7	2300	3.3
22	M	0445	0.9	1112	3.5	1713	0.6	○ 2337	3.3
23	TU	0517	0.9	1149	3.5	1746	0.6		
24	W	0011	3.3	0549	0.8	1223	3.5	1818	0.6
25	TH	0044	3.3	0620	0.8	1255	3.5	1849	0.7
26	F	0115	3.2	0650	0.9	1327	3.4	1919	0.8
27	SA	0145	3.2	0720	0.9	1358	3.3	1950	0.9
28	SU	0218	3.1	0751	1.1	1432	3.1	2023	1.0
29	M	0253	2.9	0825	1.2	1511	3.0	2101	1.2

MARCH

Date	Day	Time	m	Time	m	Time	m	Time	m
1	TU	0335	2.8	0908	1.4	1559	2.8	◑ 2154	1.4
2	W	0428	2.7	1016	1.5	1702	2.7	2320	1.5
3	TH	0538	2.7	1202	1.5	1824	2.6		
4	F	0047	1.5	0654	2.7	1334	1.4	1943	2.7
5	SA	0202	1.4	0804	2.8	1438	1.2	2050	2.9
6	SU	0256	1.2	0903	3.1	1524	0.9	2144	3.1
7	M	0340	1.0	0953	3.3	1606	0.6	2230	3.3
8	TU	0420	0.8	1039	3.5	1647	0.4	2314	3.5
9	W	0500	0.6	1123	3.7	1728	0.2	● 2356	3.6
10	TH	0541	0.4	1207	3.8	1809	0.2		
11	F	0039	3.6	0621	0.4	1251	3.8	1851	0.2
12	SA	0122	3.6	0703	0.5	1335	3.8	1934	0.4
13	SU	0205	3.4	0747	0.6	1422	3.6	2019	0.7
14	M	0250	3.2	0835	0.8	1513	3.3	2110	1.0
15	TU	0342	3.0	0937	1.0	1613	3.0	◐ 2218	1.2
16	W	0445	2.9	1103	1.2	1728	2.8	2346	1.4
17	TH	0601	2.8	1242	1.2	1853	2.8		
18	F	0124	1.4	0722	2.8	1404	1.1	2016	2.8
19	SA	0231	1.3	0834	3.0	1459	0.9	2115	3.0
20	SU	0317	1.2	0928	3.1	1542	0.8	2200	3.1
21	M	0353	1.1	1012	3.2	1616	0.7	2239	3.2
22	TU	0424	0.9	1050	3.3	1648	0.6	2313	3.2
23	W	0455	0.8	1125	3.4	1719	0.6	○ 2345	3.3
24	TH	0526	0.8	1158	3.4	1749	0.6		
25	F	0015	3.3	0556	0.7	1230	3.4	1819	0.6
26	SA	0045	3.2	0625	0.8	1300	3.3	1848	0.7
27	SU	0115	3.2	0655	0.8	1331	3.2	1918	0.8
28	M	0145	3.1	0726	0.9	1405	3.1	1949	1.0
29	TU	0219	3.0	0759	1.0	1443	2.9	2024	1.1
30	W	0259	2.9	0840	1.2	1528	2.8	2110	1.3
31	TH	0348	2.8	0936	1.3	1628	2.6	◑ 2226	1.5

APRIL

Date	Day	Time	m	Time	m	Time	m	Time	m
1	F	0451	2.7	1119	1.4	1747	2.6		
2	SA	0005	1.5	0609	2.7	1250	1.3	1908	2.7
3	SU	0125	1.4	0723	2.8	1402	1.0	2018	2.9
4	M	0226	1.1	0827	3.0	1454	0.8	2116	3.1
5	TU	0313	0.9	0923	3.2	1539	0.5	2205	3.3
6	W	0356	0.7	1013	3.5	1622	0.3	2250	3.5
7	TH	0438	0.5	1100	3.7	1704	0.2	● 2334	3.6
8	F	0520	0.3	1146	3.8	1747	0.1		
9	SA	0017	3.6	0603	0.3	1233	3.8	1829	0.2
10	SU	0100	3.6	0647	0.4	1319	3.7	1913	0.4
11	M	0143	3.4	0732	0.5	1407	3.5	1957	0.7
12	TU	0228	3.3	0823	0.7	1459	3.2	2047	1.0
13	W	0319	3.1	0926	0.9	1559	3.0	2152	1.3
14	TH	0420	2.9	1047	1.1	1711	2.8	◐ 2316	1.5
15	F	0533	2.8	1217	1.1	1830	2.7		
16	SA	0053	1.5	0649	2.8	1337	1.0	1949	2.7
17	SU	0204	1.4	0802	2.9	1432	0.9	2048	2.9
18	M	0251	1.2	0859	3.0	1513	0.8	2133	3.0
19	TU	0327	1.1	0944	3.1	1547	0.8	2211	3.1
20	W	0359	1.0	1023	3.2	1619	0.7	2245	3.2
21	TH	0431	0.8	1058	3.2	1650	0.6	2317	3.2
22	F	0502	0.8	1132	3.3	1721	0.6	○ 2347	3.3
23	SA	0533	0.7	1204	3.3	1751	0.7		
24	SU	0017	3.3	0603	0.7	1236	3.2	1821	0.7
25	M	0048	3.2	0634	0.8	1309	3.1	1851	0.8
26	TU	0120	3.2	0707	0.8	1344	3.0	1924	1.0
27	W	0154	3.1	0742	0.9	1423	2.9	2000	1.1
28	TH	0234	3.0	0824	1.0	1509	2.8	2046	1.3
29	F	0321	2.9	0920	1.1	1606	2.7	2153	1.4
30	SA	0420	2.8	1048	1.2	1719	2.7	◑ 2328	1.4

Chart Datum: 1·71 metres below Ordnance Datum (Newlyn)
HAT is 4·0 metres above Chart Datum

TIME ZONE (UT)
For Summer Time add ONE hour in **non-shaded areas**

SCOTLAND – WICK

LAT 58°26′N LONG 3°05′W

TIMES AND HEIGHTS OF HIGH AND LOW WATERS

Dates in amber are **SPRINGS**
Dates in grey are **NEAPS**

2016

MAY

Date	Day	Time	m	Time	m	Time	m	Time	m
1	SU	0533	2.8	1212	1.1	1836	2.7		
2	M	0046	1.3	0646	2.8	1324	0.9	1944	2.9
3	TU	0152	1.1	0752	3.0	1422	0.7	2045	3.1
4	W	0245	0.9	0852	3.2	1512	0.5	2137	3.3
5	TH	0332	0.7	0947	3.4	1558	0.3	2225	3.5
6	F	0417	0.5	1038	3.6	1642	0.3	● 2311	3.6
7	SA	0502	0.4	1128	3.7	1726	0.3	2355	3.6
8	SU	0547	0.3	1216	3.7	1810	0.4		
9	M	0039	3.6	0633	0.3	1304	3.6	1854	0.6
10	TU	0124	3.5	0721	0.4	1353	3.4	1939	0.8
11	W	0209	3.3	0813	0.6	1445	3.1	2027	1.1
12	TH	0259	3.1	0913	0.8	1542	2.9	2123	1.3
13	F	0355	3.0	1021	1.0	1646	2.8	◐ 2234	1.4
14	SA	0501	2.8	1135	1.1	1754	2.7	2356	1.5
15	SU	0609	2.8	1251	1.1	1904	2.7		
16	M	0117	1.4	0716	2.8	1351	1.0	2007	2.8
17	TU	0213	1.3	0818	2.9	1436	0.9	2057	2.9
18	W	0255	1.2	0909	2.9	1514	0.9	2138	3.0
19	TH	0332	1.1	0952	3.0	1548	0.8	2214	3.1
20	F	0406	0.9	1030	3.1	1622	0.8	2248	3.2
21	SA	0440	0.8	1106	3.1	1654	0.7	○ 2320	3.2
22	SU	0513	0.8	1141	3.2	1726	0.8	2353	3.3
23	M	0545	0.7	1215	3.2	1758	0.8		
24	TU	0025	3.3	0618	0.7	1251	3.1	1831	0.9
25	W	0100	3.2	0653	0.8	1328	3.1	1906	0.9
26	TH	0136	3.2	0732	0.8	1409	3.0	1946	1.0
27	F	0217	3.1	0816	0.9	1455	2.9	2033	1.2
28	SA	0303	3.0	0911	0.9	1549	2.8	2132	1.3
29	SU	0358	2.9	1023	1.0	1654	2.8	◑ 2253	1.3
30	M	0503	2.9	1139	0.9	1805	2.8		
31	TU	0008	1.3	0613	2.9	1249	0.9	1911	2.9

JUNE

Date	Day	Time	m	Time	m	Time	m	Time	m
1	W	0117	1.1	0721	3.0	1352	0.7	2014	3.1
2	TH	0217	1.0	0825	3.2	1447	0.6	2111	3.2
3	F	0311	0.8	0925	3.3	1537	0.5	2203	3.4
4	SA	0400	0.6	1021	3.5	1624	0.5	2251	3.5
5	SU	0448	0.4	1113	3.5	1709	0.5	● 2337	3.6
6	M	0536	0.4	1203	3.5	1754	0.6		
7	TU	0022	3.6	0623	0.4	1251	3.5	1837	0.7
8	W	0107	3.5	0710	0.4	1339	3.3	1920	0.9
9	TH	0151	3.4	0759	0.6	1427	3.1	2004	1.1
10	F	0237	3.2	0850	0.7	1517	3.0	2050	1.2
11	SA	0327	3.1	0944	0.9	1611	2.8	2145	1.4
12	SU	0423	2.9	1043	1.0	1709	2.7	◐ 2250	1.5
13	M	0523	2.8	1147	1.1	1809	2.7		
14	TU	0004	1.5	0625	2.8	1254	1.1	1911	2.7
15	W	0120	1.4	0728	2.8	1351	1.1	2009	2.8
16	TH	0218	1.3	0827	2.8	1438	1.0	2059	2.9
17	F	0303	1.2	0918	2.9	1518	1.0	2141	3.0
18	SA	0343	1.1	1001	3.0	1555	0.9	2219	3.1
19	SU	0419	0.9	1041	3.1	1630	0.9	2255	3.2
20	M	0455	0.8	1119	3.1	1704	0.9	○ 2330	3.3
21	TU	0529	0.8	1157	3.2	1739	0.8		
22	W	0006	3.3	0605	0.7	1235	3.2	1815	0.8
23	TH	0043	3.4	0643	0.7	1315	3.2	1853	0.9
24	F	0122	3.3	0723	0.7	1356	3.1	1934	0.9
25	SA	0203	3.3	0807	0.7	1441	3.0	2019	1.0
26	SU	0248	3.2	0857	0.8	1532	3.0	2112	1.1
27	M	0339	3.1	0958	0.8	1630	2.9	◑ 2218	1.2
28	TU	0438	3.1	1108	0.9	1735	2.9	2333	1.2
29	W	0546	3.0	1217	0.9	1841	2.9		
30	TH	0046	1.2	0655	3.0	1326	0.9	1947	3.0

JULY

Date	Day	Time	m	Time	m	Time	m	Time	m
1	F	0157	1.1	0804	3.1	1429	0.8	2050	3.2
2	SA	0257	0.9	0911	3.2	1523	0.8	2146	3.3
3	SU	0351	0.7	1011	3.3	1611	0.7	2236	3.4
4	M	0440	0.5	1103	3.4	1656	0.7	● 2323	3.5
5	TU	0526	0.4	1151	3.4	1739	0.7		
6	W	0007	3.6	0611	0.4	1238	3.4	1819	0.8
7	TH	0050	3.6	0654	0.5	1321	3.3	1858	0.9
8	F	0132	3.5	0736	0.6	1403	3.2	1936	1.0
9	SA	0213	3.3	0818	0.7	1446	3.0	2015	1.1
10	SU	0255	3.2	0901	0.9	1530	2.9	2056	1.3
11	M	0341	3.0	0949	1.0	1618	2.8	2147	1.4
12	TU	0432	2.9	1044	1.2	1713	2.7	◐ 2255	1.5
13	W	0531	2.8	1147	1.3	1812	2.7		
14	TH	0012	1.5	0634	2.7	1255	1.3	1914	2.7
15	F	0133	1.4	0740	2.7	1358	1.2	2014	2.8
16	SA	0234	1.3	0842	2.8	1449	1.2	2106	3.0
17	SU	0320	1.2	0934	2.9	1531	1.1	2150	3.1
18	M	0400	1.0	1018	3.0	1609	1.0	2230	3.2
19	TU	0437	0.9	1059	3.1	1645	0.9	○ 2309	3.4
20	W	0513	0.7	1139	3.2	1722	0.8	2347	3.5
21	TH	0550	0.6	1218	3.3	1759	0.8		
22	F	0026	3.5	0628	0.5	1259	3.3	1838	0.8
23	SA	0107	3.5	0709	0.5	1341	3.3	1919	0.8
24	SU	0148	3.5	0752	0.5	1424	3.2	2002	0.9
25	M	0231	3.4	0838	0.6	1511	3.1	2049	1.0
26	TU	0320	3.3	0932	0.8	1604	3.0	◑ 2148	1.1
27	W	0416	3.2	1038	0.9	1706	2.9	2304	1.2
28	TH	0523	3.1	1151	1.0	1814	2.9		
29	F	0025	1.2	0637	3.0	1309	1.1	1925	3.0
30	SA	0147	1.1	0754	3.0	1419	1.1	2034	3.1
31	SU	0253	1.0	0906	3.1	1516	1.0	2134	3.3

AUGUST

Date	Day	Time	m	Time	m	Time	m	Time	m
1	M	0346	0.8	1005	3.2	1602	0.9	2224	3.4
2	TU	0432	0.6	1054	3.3	1644	0.9	● 2309	3.5
3	W	0514	0.5	1139	3.4	1722	0.8	2351	3.6
4	TH	0554	0.5	1219	3.4	1759	0.8		
5	F	0030	3.6	0631	0.5	1258	3.3	1833	0.8
6	SA	0108	3.5	0707	0.6	1335	3.2	1907	0.9
7	SU	0144	3.4	0742	0.7	1410	3.1	1940	1.0
8	M	0221	3.3	0817	0.9	1447	3.0	2015	1.2
9	TU	0259	3.1	0855	1.0	1527	2.9	2054	1.3
10	W	0341	2.9	0941	1.2	1614	2.8	◐ 2147	1.5
11	TH	0434	2.8	1043	1.4	1711	2.7	2310	1.6
12	F	0541	2.7	1157	1.4	1818	2.7		
13	SA	0041	1.5	0654	2.6	1314	1.4	1925	2.8
14	SU	0202	1.4	0806	2.7	1419	1.3	2027	2.9
15	M	0256	1.2	0906	2.9	1507	1.2	2119	3.1
16	TU	0338	1.0	0954	3.0	1547	1.1	2203	3.3
17	W	0415	0.8	1037	3.2	1625	0.9	2245	3.4
18	TH	0452	0.6	1118	3.4	1702	0.8	○ 2326	3.6
19	F	0530	0.5	1158	3.5	1740	0.7		
20	SA	0006	3.7	0609	0.4	1240	3.5	1819	0.6
21	SU	0048	3.7	0649	0.3	1321	3.5	1900	0.6
22	M	0130	3.7	0731	0.4	1403	3.4	1942	0.7
23	TU	0214	3.6	0815	0.6	1448	3.3	2028	0.9
24	W	0302	3.4	0905	0.8	1539	3.1	2124	1.1
25	TH	0358	3.2	1010	1.1	1639	3.0	◑ 2243	1.2
26	F	0507	3.0	1130	1.2	1750	2.9		
27	SA	0015	1.3	0627	2.9	1259	1.3	1907	2.9
28	SU	0144	1.2	0752	3.0	1415	1.3	2022	3.1
29	M	0249	1.0	0903	3.1	1509	1.2	2121	3.3
30	TU	0338	0.8	0957	3.2	1552	1.1	2210	3.4
31	W	0420	0.7	1041	3.3	1628	1.0	2252	3.5

Chart Datum: 1·71 metres below Ordnance Datum (Newlyn)
HAT is 4·0 metres above Chart Datum

TIME ZONE (UT)
For Summer Time add ONE hour in **non-shaded areas**

SCOTLAND – WICK

LAT 58°26′N LONG 3°05′W

TIMES AND HEIGHTS OF HIGH AND LOW WATERS

Dates in amber are **SPRINGS**
Dates in grey are **NEAPS**

2016

SEPTEMBER

Date	Day	Time	m	Time	m	Time	m	Time	m
1	TH	0456	0.6	1120	3.4	1702	0.9	● 2331	3.6
2	F	0530	0.5	1157	3.4	1735	0.8		
3	SA	0007	3.6	0603	0.5	1231	3.4	1807	0.8
4	SU	0042	3.5	0635	0.6	1303	3.3	1838	0.9
5	M	0115	3.4	0707	0.7	1335	3.2	1909	1.0
6	TU	0147	3.3	0738	0.9	1407	3.1	1941	1.1
7	W	0221	3.2	0810	1.0	1442	3.0	2015	1.2
8	TH	0300	3.0	0847	1.2	1523	2.9	2058	1.4
9	F	0347	2.8	0938	1.4	1614	2.8	◐ 2206	1.5
10	SA	0449	2.7	1101	1.6	1721	2.7	2351	1.6
11	SU	0610	2.6	1228	1.6	1836	2.8		
12	M	0122	1.5	0728	2.7	1345	1.5	1945	2.9
13	TU	0225	1.2	0835	2.9	1440	1.3	2044	3.1
14	W	0310	1.0	0927	3.1	1522	1.1	2133	3.3
15	TH	0349	0.8	1011	3.3	1601	0.9	2218	3.5
16	F	0427	0.5	1053	3.5	1640	0.7	○ 2301	3.7
17	SA	0506	0.4	1135	3.6	1719	0.6	2344	3.8
18	SU	0546	0.3	1216	3.7	1759	0.5		
19	M	0026	3.9	0626	0.3	1258	3.7	1840	0.6
20	TU	0111	3.8	0708	0.4	1341	3.6	1923	0.7
21	W	0156	3.7	0752	0.7	1425	3.4	2010	0.8
22	TH	0246	3.5	0841	0.9	1515	3.2	2108	1.0
23	F	0344	3.2	0945	1.2	1615	3.0	◑ 2232	1.2
24	SA	0456	3.0	1111	1.5	1729	2.9		
25	SU	0008	1.3	0619	2.9	1248	1.5	1847	3.0
26	M	0135	1.1	0745	2.9	1404	1.4	2004	3.1
27	TU	0237	1.0	0851	3.1	1455	1.3	2103	3.2
28	W	0322	0.9	0940	3.2	1534	1.2	2150	3.4
29	TH	0359	0.8	1021	3.3	1607	1.0	2231	3.5
30	F	0432	0.7	1057	3.4	1639	0.9	2307	3.5

OCTOBER

Date	Day	Time	m	Time	m	Time	m	Time	m
1	SA	0503	0.6	1130	3.4	1710	0.9	● 2341	3.5
2	SU	0534	0.6	1201	3.4	1741	0.8		
3	M	0014	3.5	0604	0.7	1232	3.4	1812	0.9
4	TU	0046	3.4	0634	0.8	1302	3.3	1842	0.9
5	W	0118	3.3	0704	0.9	1332	3.3	1913	1.0
6	TH	0151	3.2	0734	1.1	1406	3.2	1947	1.2
7	F	0229	3.0	0809	1.3	1445	3.0	2027	1.3
8	SA	0314	2.9	0852	1.5	1532	2.9	2122	1.5
9	SU	0411	2.7	1002	1.6	1633	2.8	◐ 2305	1.5
10	M	0529	2.7	1143	1.7	1749	2.8		
11	TU	0035	1.4	0649	2.8	1304	1.6	1902	2.9
12	W	0145	1.2	0758	2.9	1406	1.4	2005	3.1
13	TH	0236	1.0	0855	3.2	1453	1.2	2059	3.3
14	F	0319	0.7	0942	3.4	1535	0.9	2148	3.6
15	SA	0400	0.5	1027	3.6	1616	0.7	2235	3.8
16	SU	0441	0.4	1110	3.7	1657	0.6	○ 2321	3.9
17	M	0522	0.3	1152	3.8	1739	0.5		
18	TU	0006	3.9	0604	0.4	1236	3.8	1822	0.5
19	W	0053	3.9	0647	0.5	1319	3.7	1908	0.6
20	TH	0141	3.7	0732	0.8	1404	3.5	1957	0.8
21	F	0232	3.4	0821	1.1	1454	3.3	2058	1.0
22	SA	0332	3.2	0922	1.4	1553	3.1	◑ 2219	1.2
23	SU	0443	3.0	1045	1.6	1705	3.0	2348	1.2
24	M	0602	2.9	1220	1.6	1820	3.0		
25	TU	0111	1.2	0721	2.9	1339	1.6	1934	3.1
26	W	0212	1.1	0826	3.0	1432	1.4	2035	3.2
27	TH	0257	1.0	0914	3.2	1511	1.3	2124	3.3
28	F	0333	0.9	0954	3.3	1544	1.2	2205	3.4
29	SA	0404	0.8	1030	3.4	1615	1.0	2241	3.4
30	SU	0435	0.8	1102	3.4	1647	1.0	● 2316	3.5
31	M	0505	0.8	1133	3.5	1718	0.9	2348	3.5

NOVEMBER

Date	Day	Time	m	Time	m	Time	m	Time	m
1	TU	0536	0.8	1203	3.5	1750	0.9		
2	W	0021	3.4	0606	0.9	1234	3.4	1821	1.0
3	TH	0054	3.3	0636	1.0	1305	3.4	1853	1.0
4	F	0128	3.2	0707	1.2	1339	3.3	1927	1.1
5	SA	0206	3.1	0742	1.3	1417	3.2	2008	1.2
6	SU	0250	3.0	0824	1.5	1502	3.1	2059	1.4
7	M	0344	2.9	0922	1.6	1557	3.0	◐ 2220	1.4
8	TU	0453	2.8	1056	1.7	1706	2.9	2348	1.4
9	W	0610	2.8	1218	1.6	1819	3.0		
10	TH	0100	1.2	0718	3.0	1326	1.4	1925	3.1
11	F	0159	1.0	0819	3.2	1421	1.2	2024	3.4
12	SA	0249	0.8	0912	3.4	1508	1.0	2119	3.6
13	SU	0334	0.6	1000	3.6	1553	0.8	2211	3.7
14	M	0418	0.5	1046	3.7	1637	0.6	○ 2300	3.9
15	TU	0501	0.5	1130	3.8	1723	0.5	2349	3.9
16	W	0545	0.5	1215	3.8	1809	0.5		
17	TH	0038	3.8	0629	0.7	1300	3.7	1857	0.6
18	F	0128	3.7	0714	0.9	1346	3.6	1948	0.8
19	SA	0220	3.4	0802	1.2	1435	3.4	2047	0.9
20	SU	0317	3.2	0857	1.4	1531	3.3	2156	1.1
21	M	0421	3.0	1006	1.6	1635	3.1	◑ 2310	1.2
22	TU	0529	2.9	1126	1.7	1744	3.1		
23	W	0028	1.2	0638	2.9	1252	1.7	1852	3.0
24	TH	0134	1.2	0745	3.0	1355	1.6	1957	3.1
25	F	0223	1.1	0839	3.1	1441	1.4	2051	3.2
26	SA	0301	1.1	0923	3.2	1519	1.3	2136	3.3
27	SU	0336	1.0	1000	3.3	1553	1.2	2215	3.3
28	M	0408	1.0	1035	3.4	1627	1.1	2252	3.4
29	TU	0440	1.0	1107	3.5	1700	1.0	● 2326	3.4
30	W	0512	1.0	1139	3.5	1733	1.0		

DECEMBER

Date	Day	Time	m	Time	m	Time	m	Time	m
1	TH	0001	3.4	0543	1.0	1211	3.5	1805	1.0
2	F	0036	3.3	0615	1.1	1244	3.5	1839	1.0
3	SA	0111	3.3	0649	1.1	1319	3.4	1915	1.0
4	SU	0150	3.2	0725	1.2	1357	3.3	1955	1.1
5	M	0232	3.1	0807	1.4	1440	3.2	2043	1.2
6	TU	0322	3.0	0857	1.5	1530	3.2	2145	1.2
7	W	0421	2.9	1007	1.6	1630	3.1	◐ 2304	1.2
8	TH	0531	2.9	1131	1.6	1739	3.1		
9	F	0016	1.2	0639	3.0	1243	1.5	1847	3.2
10	SA	0122	1.0	0743	3.2	1348	1.3	1952	3.3
11	SU	0220	0.9	0842	3.3	1444	1.1	2054	3.5
12	M	0312	0.8	0936	3.5	1535	0.9	2152	3.6
13	TU	0359	0.7	1026	3.7	1624	0.7	2246	3.7
14	W	0445	0.7	1113	3.8	1712	0.6	○ 2337	3.8
15	TH	0530	0.7	1159	3.8	1800	0.5		
16	F	0026	3.7	0614	0.8	1244	3.8	1847	0.6
17	SA	0116	3.6	0658	1.0	1330	3.7	1936	0.7
18	SU	0204	3.4	0742	1.1	1416	3.6	2027	0.8
19	M	0255	3.2	0827	1.3	1505	3.4	2121	1.0
20	TU	0348	3.1	0918	1.5	1600	3.2	2220	1.2
21	W	0445	2.9	1021	1.6	1659	3.1	◑ 2325	1.3
22	TH	0546	2.8	1135	1.7	1802	3.0		
23	F	0034	1.3	0649	2.8	1258	1.7	1907	3.0
24	SA	0137	1.3	0752	2.9	1404	1.6	2011	3.0
25	SU	0227	1.3	0846	3.0	1453	1.4	2105	3.1
26	M	0308	1.2	0930	3.2	1533	1.3	2150	3.1
27	TU	0345	1.1	1009	3.3	1610	1.2	2230	3.2
28	W	0420	1.1	1044	3.4	1645	1.1	2307	3.3
29	TH	0453	1.1	1119	3.5	1719	1.0	● 2344	3.3
30	F	0526	1.0	1153	3.5	1752	0.9		
31	SA	0019	3.3	0559	1.0	1228	3.5	1827	0.9

Chart Datum: 1·71 metres below Ordnance Datum (Newlyn)
HAT is 4·0 metres above Chart Datum

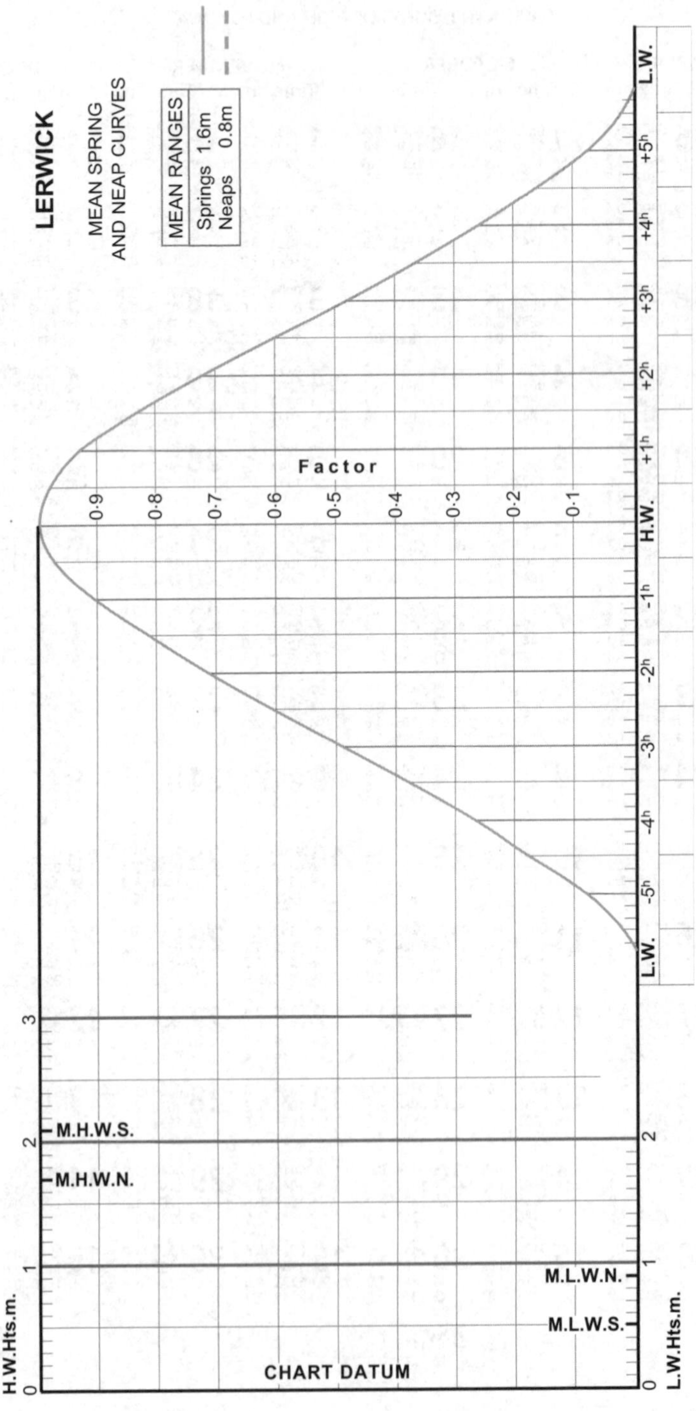
LERWICK
MEAN SPRING AND NEAP CURVES
MEAN RANGES
Springs 1.6m
Neaps 0.8m
Factor
0·9
0·8
0·7
0·6
0·5
0·4
0·3
0·2
0·1
L.W.
-5h
-4h
-3h
-2h
-1h
H.W.
+1h
+2h
+3h
+4h
+5h
L.W.
H.W.Hts.m.
0
1
2
3
M.H.W.S.
M.H.W.N.
CHART DATUM
M.L.W.N.
M.L.W.S.
L.W.Hts.m.

TIME ZONE (UT)
For Summer Time add ONE hour in **non-shaded areas**

SCOTLAND – LERWICK

LAT 60°09′N LONG 1°08′W

TIMES AND HEIGHTS OF HIGH AND LOW WATERS

Dates in amber are **SPRINGS**
Dates in grey are **NEAPS**

2016

JANUARY

Date	Day	Time	m	Time	m	Time	m	Time	m
1	F	0317	1.8	0904	1.1	1526	1.9	2152	0.9
2	SA	0405	1.8	1001	1.1	1616	1.8	◑ 2252	1.0
3	SU	0501	1.7	1119	1.2	1719	1.8	2358	1.0
4	M	0615	1.7	1236	1.1	1842	1.8		
5	TU	0100	1.0	0722	1.8	1340	1.1	1946	1.8
6	W	0154	0.9	0813	1.9	1429	1.0	2037	1.9
7	TH	0240	0.9	0856	2.0	1512	0.9	2122	2.0
8	F	0322	0.8	0937	2.1	1551	0.8	2204	2.0
9	SA	0402	0.8	1016	2.2	1631	0.6	2247	2.1
10	SU	0442	0.7	1056	2.3	1710	0.5	● 2329	2.2
11	M	0522	0.7	1136	2.3	1751	0.5		
12	TU	0012	2.2	0602	0.6	1217	2.3	1832	0.4
13	W	0056	2.2	0643	0.6	1259	2.3	1915	0.4
14	TH	0142	2.1	0727	0.7	1344	2.3	2001	0.5
15	F	0230	2.0	0814	0.8	1432	2.2	2051	0.6
16	SA	0321	2.0	0905	0.8	1527	2.1	◐ 2147	0.7
17	SU	0418	1.9	1007	0.9	1630	2.0	2257	0.8
18	M	0524	1.8	1129	1.0	1743	1.9		
19	TU	0021	0.8	0637	1.9	1257	0.9	1903	1.9
20	W	0134	0.8	0747	1.9	1406	0.8	2015	1.9
21	TH	0233	0.8	0847	2.0	1503	0.7	2117	2.0
22	F	0323	0.8	0939	2.1	1551	0.6	2211	2.1
23	SA	0407	0.7	1026	2.2	1635	0.5	2257	2.1
24	SU	0447	0.7	1108	2.3	1715	0.5	○ 2338	2.1
25	M	0526	0.7	1147	2.3	1754	0.4		
26	TU	0016	2.1	0602	0.7	1224	2.3	1830	0.5
27	W	0051	2.1	0637	0.7	1259	2.2	1906	0.5
28	TH	0125	2.0	0710	0.8	1333	2.2	1942	0.6
29	F	0159	1.9	0743	0.8	1408	2.1	2017	0.7
30	SA	0235	1.9	0818	0.9	1445	1.9	2057	0.8
31	SU	0314	1.8	0859	1.0	1528	1.8	2144	0.9

FEBRUARY

Date	Day	Time	m	Time	m	Time	m	Time	m
1	M	0400	1.7	0956	1.1	1619	1.7	◑ 2249	1.0
2	TU	0455	1.7	1129	1.1	1723	1.7		
3	W	0007	1.0	0607	1.7	1252	1.1	1854	1.7
4	TH	0114	1.0	0728	1.8	1355	1.0	2005	1.7
5	F	0211	0.9	0824	1.9	1446	0.9	2057	1.9
6	SA	0259	0.8	0911	2.0	1531	0.7	2143	2.0
7	SU	0343	0.7	0955	2.1	1612	0.5	2228	2.1
8	M	0425	0.6	1037	2.2	1653	0.4	● 2312	2.2
9	TU	0505	0.5	1120	2.3	1734	0.3	2356	2.2
10	W	0546	0.5	1202	2.4	1815	0.2		
11	TH	0039	2.2	0627	0.5	1245	2.4	1857	0.3
12	F	0123	2.2	0709	0.5	1329	2.3	1941	0.3
13	SA	0208	2.1	0754	0.6	1416	2.2	2028	0.5
14	SU	0256	2.0	0843	0.7	1509	2.1	2120	0.7
15	M	0349	1.9	0942	0.8	1609	1.9	◐ 2226	0.8
16	TU	0452	1.8	1104	0.9	1723	1.8	2359	0.9
17	W	0610	1.8	1243	0.9	1852	1.8		
18	TH	0121	0.9	0729	1.8	1358	0.8	2010	1.8
19	F	0225	0.9	0834	1.9	1455	0.7	2111	1.9
20	SA	0314	0.8	0927	2.0	1541	0.6	2200	2.0
21	SU	0355	0.7	1012	2.1	1621	0.5	2241	2.0
22	M	0432	0.7	1052	2.2	1657	0.4	○ 2318	2.1
23	TU	0507	0.6	1128	2.2	1731	0.4	2351	2.1
24	W	0540	0.6	1201	2.2	1804	0.4		
25	TH	0023	2.0	0611	0.6	1233	2.2	1835	0.5
26	F	0053	2.0	0641	0.6	1304	2.1	1907	0.5
27	SA	0123	1.9	0712	0.7	1335	2.0	1939	0.6
28	SU	0154	1.9	0744	0.8	1409	1.9	2013	0.7
29	M	0229	1.8	0822	0.8	1449	1.8	2054	0.8

MARCH

Date	Day	Time	m	Time	m	Time	m	Time	m
1	TU	0312	1.7	0908	0.9	1538	1.7	◑ 2145	1.0
2	W	0404	1.7	1015	1.0	1638	1.6	2304	1.0
3	TH	0507	1.6	1203	1.0	1756	1.6		
4	F	0036	1.0	0627	1.6	1319	0.9	1929	1.6
5	SA	0142	0.9	0747	1.7	1417	0.8	2030	1.8
6	SU	0236	0.8	0842	1.9	1505	0.6	2120	1.9
7	M	0322	0.7	0930	2.0	1549	0.4	2206	2.0
8	TU	0404	0.5	1015	2.2	1631	0.3	2250	2.2
9	W	0445	0.4	1059	2.3	1712	0.1	● 2334	2.2
10	TH	0526	0.3	1143	2.4	1754	0.1		
11	F	0017	2.2	0608	0.3	1227	2.4	1836	0.1
12	SA	0101	2.2	0651	0.3	1313	2.3	1919	0.3
13	SU	0144	2.1	0736	0.4	1401	2.2	2005	0.5
14	M	0230	2.0	0825	0.5	1453	2.0	2056	0.7
15	TU	0322	1.8	0924	0.7	1553	1.8	◐ 2159	0.8
16	W	0422	1.7	1049	0.8	1707	1.7	2338	1.0
17	TH	0541	1.7	1228	0.8	1841	1.6		
18	F	0105	1.0	0707	1.7	1342	0.7	1958	1.7
19	SA	0209	0.9	0814	1.8	1439	0.6	2055	1.8
20	SU	0257	0.8	0906	1.9	1522	0.5	2139	1.8
21	M	0337	0.7	0950	2.0	1600	0.5	2217	1.9
22	TU	0412	0.6	1028	2.0	1633	0.4	2251	2.0
23	W	0445	0.5	1103	2.1	1704	0.4	○ 2323	2.0
24	TH	0515	0.5	1135	2.1	1735	0.4	2352	2.0
25	F	0545	0.5	1206	2.1	1804	0.4		
26	SA	0021	2.0	0614	0.5	1236	2.0	1834	0.5
27	SU	0049	1.9	0645	0.6	1306	2.0	1905	0.6
28	M	0119	1.9	0718	0.6	1340	1.9	1939	0.7
29	TU	0152	1.8	0756	0.7	1419	1.8	2017	0.8
30	W	0233	1.8	0840	0.8	1508	1.7	2105	0.9
31	TH	0323	1.7	0939	0.9	1608	1.6	◑ 2210	1.0

APRIL

Date	Day	Time	m	Time	m	Time	m	Time	m
1	F	0425	1.6	1107	0.9	1721	1.5	2354	1.0
2	SA	0539	1.6	1239	0.8	1851	1.6		
3	SU	0110	0.9	0705	1.7	1343	0.7	2000	1.7
4	M	0208	0.8	0810	1.8	1435	0.5	2052	1.9
5	TU	0256	0.6	0902	2.0	1522	0.3	2140	2.0
6	W	0340	0.4	0949	2.1	1606	0.2	2225	2.1
7	TH	0423	0.3	1036	2.2	1649	0.1	● 2309	2.2
8	F	0506	0.2	1122	2.3	1731	0.1	2353	2.2
9	SA	0549	0.2	1209	2.3	1814	0.2		
10	SU	0036	2.2	0633	0.2	1257	2.2	1858	0.3
11	M	0121	2.1	0720	0.3	1347	2.1	1944	0.5
12	TU	0207	2.0	0811	0.4	1441	1.9	2035	0.7
13	W	0258	1.9	0911	0.6	1539	1.7	2137	0.9
14	TH	0356	1.7	1031	0.7	1649	1.6	◐ 2308	1.0
15	F	0508	1.7	1201	0.7	1816	1.6		
16	SA	0036	1.0	0634	1.6	1314	0.7	1929	1.6
17	SU	0142	0.9	0742	1.7	1410	0.6	2024	1.7
18	M	0232	0.8	0835	1.8	1454	0.5	2107	1.8
19	TU	0313	0.7	0920	1.8	1531	0.5	2145	1.8
20	W	0348	0.6	0959	1.9	1604	0.4	2219	1.9
21	TH	0420	0.5	1034	1.9	1634	0.4	2251	1.9
22	F	0450	0.5	1108	2.0	1704	0.4	○ 2321	2.0
23	SA	0520	0.5	1140	2.0	1734	0.4	2350	2.0
24	SU	0551	0.5	1211	1.9	1806	0.5		
25	M	0019	2.0	0623	0.5	1243	1.9	1838	0.6
26	TU	0050	1.9	0658	0.5	1318	1.8	1913	0.6
27	W	0125	1.9	0737	0.6	1359	1.7	1952	0.7
28	TH	0205	1.8	0823	0.7	1448	1.7	2040	0.8
29	F	0254	1.7	0918	0.7	1548	1.6	2142	0.9
30	SA	0355	1.6	1030	0.7	1656	1.6	◑ 2306	0.9

Chart Datum: 1·22 metres below Ordnance Datum (Local)
HAT is 2·5 metres above Chart Datum

TIME ZONE (UT)
For Summer Time add ONE hour in **non-shaded areas**

SCOTLAND – LERWICK

LAT 60°09'N LONG 1°08'W

TIMES AND HEIGHTS OF HIGH AND LOW WATERS

Dates in amber are **SPRINGS**
Dates in grey are **NEAPS**

2016

MAY

Day	Time	m	Time	m	Time	m	Time	m
1 SU	0505	1.6	1157	0.7	1815	1.6		
2 M	0033	0.8	0624	1.7	1307	0.6	1927	1.7
3 TU	0136	0.7	0736	1.8	1404	0.4	2023	1.8
4 W	0228	0.6	0833	1.9	1454	0.3	2112	2.0
5 TH	0316	0.4	0924	2.1	1541	0.2	2159	2.1
6 F	0401	0.3	1014	2.2	1626	0.2	● 2245	2.2
7 SA	0446	0.2	1103	2.2	1710	0.2	2330	2.2
8 SU	0532	0.2	1153	2.2	1754	0.2		
9 M	0015	2.2	0618	0.2	1244	2.1	1839	0.4
10 TU	0101	2.1	0706	0.2	1335	2.0	1926	0.5
11 W	0148	2.0	0757	0.4	1427	1.9	2016	0.7
12 TH	0237	1.9	0855	0.5	1521	1.7	2113	0.8
13 F	0330	1.8	1003	0.6	1621	1.6	◐ 2226	0.9
14 SA	0433	1.7	1119	0.7	1733	1.5	2349	0.9
15 SU	0549	1.6	1230	0.7	1844	1.6		
16 M	0101	0.9	0700	1.6	1330	0.7	1941	1.6
17 TU	0158	0.8	0756	1.7	1418	0.6	2028	1.7
18 W	0242	0.7	0844	1.7	1457	0.6	2108	1.8
19 TH	0320	0.7	0926	1.8	1531	0.5	2145	1.9
20 F	0353	0.6	1005	1.8	1603	0.5	2220	1.9
21 SA	0425	0.5	1041	1.9	1635	0.5	○ 2252	2.0
22 SU	0457	0.5	1116	1.9	1708	0.5	2324	2.0
23 M	0530	0.5	1150	1.9	1742	0.5	2356	2.0
24 TU	0605	0.5	1225	1.9	1817	0.6		
25 W	0029	2.0	0642	0.5	1304	1.8	1854	0.6
26 TH	0106	1.9	0723	0.5	1346	1.8	1936	0.7
27 F	0147	1.9	0809	0.5	1435	1.7	2024	0.8
28 SA	0236	1.8	0902	0.6	1531	1.7	2120	0.8
29 SU	0333	1.7	1004	0.6	1633	1.6	◑ 2229	0.8
30 M	0439	1.7	1117	0.6	1743	1.6	2350	0.8
31 TU	0551	1.7	1231	0.5	1853	1.7		

JUNE

Day	Time	m	Time	m	Time	m	Time	m
1 W	0101	0.7	0704	1.8	1334	0.5	1953	1.8
2 TH	0201	0.6	0807	1.9	1429	0.4	2046	1.9
3 F	0254	0.5	0903	2.0	1519	0.3	2136	2.0
4 SA	0343	0.4	0957	2.1	1607	0.3	2224	2.1
5 SU	0431	0.3	1050	2.1	1653	0.3	● 2311	2.2
6 M	0518	0.2	1142	2.1	1738	0.4	2358	2.2
7 TU	0605	0.2	1233	2.1	1823	0.5		
8 W	0044	2.1	0652	0.2	1322	2.0	1908	0.6
9 TH	0130	2.1	0741	0.3	1409	1.9	1954	0.7
10 F	0216	2.0	0832	0.5	1456	1.8	2044	0.8
11 SA	0303	1.9	0927	0.6	1545	1.6	2140	0.9
12 SU	0354	1.7	1027	0.7	1641	1.6	◐ 2247	0.9
13 M	0454	1.7	1131	0.7	1746	1.6		
14 TU	0002	0.9	0606	1.6	1235	0.7	1851	1.6
15 W	0111	0.9	0712	1.6	1331	0.7	1945	1.7
16 TH	0205	0.8	0806	1.7	1417	0.7	2031	1.7
17 F	0248	0.8	0853	1.7	1457	0.7	2112	1.8
18 SA	0326	0.7	0936	1.8	1534	0.6	2150	1.9
19 SU	0401	0.6	1015	1.9	1610	0.6	2226	2.0
20 M	0437	0.5	1054	1.9	1646	0.6	○ 2302	2.0
21 TU	0513	0.5	1132	1.9	1723	0.6	2337	2.0
22 W	0550	0.4	1211	1.9	1801	0.6		
23 TH	0014	2.0	0629	0.4	1252	1.9	1840	0.6
24 F	0053	2.0	0710	0.4	1335	1.9	1922	0.6
25 SA	0135	2.0	0755	0.4	1421	1.8	2008	0.7
26 SU	0221	1.9	0844	0.5	1513	1.8	2059	0.7
27 M	0315	1.9	0939	0.5	1610	1.7	◑ 2159	0.8
28 TU	0416	1.8	1044	0.6	1713	1.7	2311	0.8
29 W	0524	1.8	1158	0.6	1822	1.7		
30 TH	0031	0.8	0637	1.8	1309	0.6	1927	1.8

JULY

Day	Time	m	Time	m	Time	m	Time	m
1 F	0140	0.7	0747	1.9	1410	0.6	2025	1.9
2 SA	0238	0.6	0849	1.9	1504	0.5	2119	2.0
3 SU	0331	0.4	0947	2.0	1553	0.5	2210	2.1
4 M	0420	0.3	1042	2.1	1639	0.5	● 2258	2.2
5 TU	0507	0.3	1133	2.1	1723	0.5	2344	2.2
6 W	0552	0.3	1219	2.1	1806	0.5		
7 TH	0028	2.2	0636	0.3	1303	2.0	1847	0.6
8 F	0110	2.1	0719	0.4	1344	1.9	1929	0.7
9 SA	0151	2.0	0802	0.5	1425	1.8	2010	0.8
10 SU	0232	1.9	0847	0.6	1506	1.7	2053	0.8
11 M	0315	1.8	0934	0.7	1550	1.7	2144	0.9
12 TU	0402	1.7	1028	0.8	1640	1.6	◐ 2252	1.0
13 W	0459	1.6	1131	0.8	1744	1.6		
14 TH	0010	1.0	0615	1.6	1235	0.9	1856	1.6
15 F	0120	0.9	0727	1.6	1333	0.8	1953	1.7
16 SA	0215	0.9	0822	1.7	1423	0.8	2040	1.8
17 SU	0259	0.8	0909	1.8	1507	0.8	2122	1.9
18 M	0339	0.7	0952	1.9	1548	0.7	2202	2.0
19 TU	0417	0.6	1033	1.9	1627	0.6	○ 2241	2.1
20 W	0455	0.5	1114	2.0	1706	0.6	2320	2.1
21 TH	0534	0.4	1155	2.0	1745	0.5	2359	2.2
22 F	0614	0.3	1236	2.0	1825	0.5		
23 SA	0039	2.2	0654	0.3	1319	2.0	1906	0.6
24 SU	0121	2.1	0737	0.4	1404	2.0	1950	0.6
25 M	0206	2.1	0823	0.4	1452	1.9	2038	0.7
26 TU	0257	2.0	0915	0.5	1545	1.8	◑ 2133	0.7
27 W	0355	1.9	1014	0.6	1644	1.8	2242	0.8
28 TH	0501	1.8	1131	0.7	1753	1.8		
29 F	0010	0.8	0619	1.8	1252	0.8	1906	1.8
30 SA	0128	0.7	0737	1.8	1359	0.7	2012	1.9
31 SU	0232	0.6	0845	1.9	1456	0.7	2109	2.0

AUGUST

Day	Time	m	Time	m	Time	m	Time	m
1 M	0325	0.5	0944	2.0	1544	0.6	2200	2.1
2 TU	0412	0.4	1035	2.0	1627	0.6	● 2247	2.2
3 W	0455	0.3	1120	2.1	1708	0.6	2329	2.2
4 TH	0535	0.3	1200	2.1	1746	0.6		
5 F	0009	2.2	0614	0.3	1238	2.0	1823	0.6
6 SA	0046	2.2	0652	0.4	1314	2.0	1859	0.6
7 SU	0122	2.1	0729	0.5	1349	1.9	1934	0.7
8 M	0158	2.0	0805	0.6	1424	1.8	2010	0.8
9 TU	0236	1.9	0844	0.7	1502	1.8	2051	0.9
10 W	0317	1.8	0928	0.8	1546	1.7	◐ 2145	1.0
11 TH	0406	1.7	1028	0.9	1637	1.6	2310	1.0
12 F	0507	1.6	1144	1.0	1743	1.6		
13 SA	0034	1.0	0636	1.6	1254	1.0	1908	1.7
14 SU	0140	0.9	0751	1.7	1353	0.9	2007	1.8
15 M	0232	0.8	0843	1.8	1443	0.8	2054	1.9
16 TU	0315	0.7	0928	1.9	1527	0.7	2137	2.0
17 W	0356	0.6	1011	2.0	1607	0.6	2219	2.1
18 TH	0435	0.4	1053	2.1	1647	0.5	○ 2259	2.2
19 F	0514	0.3	1134	2.1	1726	0.5	2340	2.3
20 SA	0553	0.3	1216	2.2	1806	0.5		
21 SU	0021	2.3	0634	0.2	1259	2.1	1846	0.5
22 M	0104	2.3	0716	0.3	1342	2.1	1930	0.5
23 TU	0149	2.2	0801	0.4	1428	2.0	2017	0.6
24 W	0239	2.1	0850	0.6	1519	1.9	2112	0.7
25 TH	0338	2.0	0949	0.7	1618	1.8	◑ 2222	0.8
26 F	0446	1.8	1110	0.9	1729	1.8		
27 SA	0002	0.8	0610	1.8	1244	0.9	1850	1.8
28 SU	0124	0.8	0736	1.8	1353	0.9	2001	1.9
29 M	0226	0.7	0842	1.9	1448	0.8	2059	2.0
30 TU	0317	0.6	0935	2.0	1533	0.7	2147	2.1
31 W	0359	0.5	1020	2.0	1612	0.7	2230	2.2

Chart Datum: 1·22 metres below Ordnance Datum (Local)
HAT is 2·5 metres above Chart Datum

TIME ZONE (UT)
For Summer Time add ONE hour in **non-shaded areas**

SCOTLAND – LERWICK

LAT 60°09'N LONG 1°08'W

TIMES AND HEIGHTS OF HIGH AND LOW WATERS

Dates in amber are **SPRINGS**
Dates in grey are **NEAPS**

2016

SEPTEMBER

Date	Day	Time	m
1	TH	0438 1100 1649 ● 2309	0.4 2.1 0.6 2.2
2	F	0514 1136 1724 2345	0.4 2.1 0.6 2.2
3	SA	0548 1209 1757	0.4 2.1 0.6
4	SU	0018 0621 1241 1829	2.2 0.4 2.0 0.6
5	M	0051 0653 1311 1901	2.1 0.5 2.0 0.7
6	TU	0124 0726 1343 1934	2.1 0.6 1.9 0.8
7	W	0158 0800 1418 2011	2.0 0.8 1.9 0.9
8	TH	0237 0839 1459 2057	1.8 0.9 1.8 1.0
9	F	0325 0929 1548 ◐ 2205	1.7 1.0 1.7 1.0
10	SA	0423 1046 1648 2351	1.6 1.1 1.7 1.0
11	SU	0538 1218 1804	1.6 1.1 1.7
12	M	0104 0716 1324 1929	1.0 1.7 1.0 1.8
13	TU	0201 0815 1417 2024	0.8 1.8 0.9 1.9
14	W	0248 0902 1502 2110	0.7 1.9 0.8 2.1
15	TH	0330 0945 1544 2153	0.5 2.1 0.6 2.2
16	F	0410 1028 1624 ○ 2235	0.4 2.2 0.5 2.3
17	SA	0450 1110 1704 2318	0.3 2.2 0.4 2.4
18	SU	0531 1152 1745	0.2 2.3 0.4
19	M	0001 0611 1235 1827	2.4 0.2 2.3 0.4
20	TU	0045 0654 1318 1911	2.4 0.3 2.2 0.5
21	W	0133 0739 1404 1959	2.3 0.5 2.1 0.6
22	TH	0225 0828 1455 2056	2.1 0.7 2.0 0.7
23	F	0325 0927 1554 ◑ 2211	2.0 0.9 1.9 0.8
24	SA	0435 1055 1706 2354	1.8 1.0 1.8 0.8
25	SU	0604 1232 1833	1.8 1.0 1.8
26	M	0112 0728 1341 1945	0.8 1.8 1.0 1.9
27	TU	0213 0830 1433 2041	0.7 1.9 0.9 2.0
28	W	0300 0917 1516 2127	0.6 2.0 0.8 2.1
29	TH	0340 0958 1553 2208	0.5 2.0 0.7 2.2
30	F	0415 1034 1627 2245	0.5 2.1 0.6 2.2

OCTOBER

Date	Day	Time	m
1	SA	0448 1107 1659 ● 2318	0.5 2.1 0.6 2.2
2	SU	0519 1137 1731 2350	0.5 2.1 0.6 2.2
3	M	0550 1207 1801	0.5 2.1 0.6
4	TU	0021 0620 1236 1832	2.1 0.6 2.1 0.7
5	W	0053 0651 1306 1905	2.1 0.7 2.0 0.8
6	TH	0127 0724 1339 1942	2.0 0.8 2.0 0.8
7	F	0205 0801 1418 2026	1.9 0.9 1.9 0.9
8	SA	0253 0847 1507 2124	1.8 1.0 1.8 1.0
9	SU	0351 0951 1607 ◐ 2257	1.7 1.1 1.8 1.0
10	M	0500 1136 1717	1.7 1.1 1.7
11	TU	0025 0629 1251 1841	1.0 1.7 1.1 1.8
12	W	0126 0742 1347 1948	0.8 1.8 0.9 1.9
13	TH	0216 0832 1435 2039	0.7 2.0 0.8 2.1
14	F	0301 0917 1518 2126	0.5 2.1 0.7 2.2
15	SA	0343 1001 1600 2210	0.4 2.2 0.5 2.4
16	SU	0425 1044 1642 ○ 2255	0.3 2.3 0.4 2.4
17	M	0507 1127 1725 2341	0.2 2.4 0.4 2.5
18	TU	0550 1210 1809	0.3 2.3 0.4
19	W	0029 0633 1255 1855	2.4 0.4 2.3 0.4
20	TH	0120 0719 1342 1945	2.3 0.6 2.2 0.6
21	F	0215 0809 1434 2043	2.1 0.8 2.1 0.7
22	SA	0314 0908 1532 ◑ 2158	2.0 1.0 2.0 0.8
23	SU	0421 1032 1641 2333	1.8 1.1 1.9 0.8
24	M	0545 1207 1805	1.8 1.1 1.9
25	TU	0049 0704 1317 1917	0.8 1.8 1.1 1.9
26	W	0149 0803 1410 2014	0.8 1.9 1.0 2.0
27	TH	0236 0849 1453 2100	0.7 1.9 0.9 2.1
28	F	0315 0928 1530 2141	0.6 2.0 0.8 2.1
29	SA	0349 1004 1604 2218	0.6 2.1 0.7 2.2
30	SU	0420 1036 1636 ● 2252	0.6 2.1 0.7 2.2
31	M	0450 1107 1706 2325	0.6 2.2 0.7 2.2

NOVEMBER

Date	Day	Time	m
1	TU	0520 1137 1737 2357	0.6 2.2 0.7 2.1
2	W	0551 1206 1809	0.7 2.2 0.7
3	TH	0029 0622 1237 1843	2.1 0.8 2.1 0.7
4	F	0104 0656 1310 1921	2.0 0.8 2.1 0.8
5	SA	0143 0734 1348 2005	1.9 0.9 2.0 0.9
6	SU	0229 0818 1435 2058	1.8 1.0 1.9 0.9
7	M	0326 0916 1533 ◐ 2208	1.8 1.1 1.8 1.0
8	TU	0431 1036 1640 2336	1.7 1.1 1.8 0.9
9	W	0546 1208 1755	1.7 1.1 1.8
10	TH	0045 0701 1312 1909	0.8 1.8 1.0 1.9
11	F	0142 0759 1405 2008	0.7 2.0 0.8 2.1
12	SA	0231 0848 1452 2059	0.6 2.1 0.7 2.2
13	SU	0317 0934 1538 2147	0.5 2.3 0.6 2.4
14	M	0402 1019 1622 ○ 2236	0.4 2.3 0.5 2.4
15	TU	0446 1104 1708 2326	0.4 2.4 0.4 2.4
16	W	0531 1150 1754	0.4 2.4 0.4
17	TH	0017 0615 1236 1842	2.4 0.5 2.4 0.4
18	F	0110 0702 1324 1933	2.3 0.7 2.3 0.5
19	SA	0204 0752 1415 2029	2.1 0.9 2.2 0.6
20	SU	0259 0847 1510 2136	2.0 1.0 2.1 0.8
21	M	0358 0955 1611 ◑ 2254	1.9 1.1 2.0 0.8
22	TU	0507 1121 1723	1.8 1.2 1.9
23	W	0009 0621 1238 1837	0.9 1.8 1.1 1.9
24	TH	0113 0723 1339 1937	0.8 1.8 1.0 1.9
25	F	0204 0812 1427 2028	0.8 1.9 1.0 2.0
26	SA	0245 0855 1507 2112	0.8 2.0 0.9 2.0
27	SU	0321 0932 1542 2151	0.8 2.1 0.8 2.1
28	M	0353 1007 1614 2228	0.7 2.1 0.8 2.1
29	TU	0424 1040 1646 ● 2303	0.7 2.2 0.7 2.1
30	W	0456 1112 1718 2337	0.7 2.2 0.7 2.1

DECEMBER

Date	Day	Time	m
1	TH	0528 1144 1752	0.8 2.2 0.7
2	F	0012 0601 1216 1827	2.1 0.8 2.2 0.7
3	SA	0048 0636 1250 1906	2.0 0.9 2.2 0.7
4	SU	0127 0715 1328 1949	2.0 0.9 2.1 0.8
5	M	0212 0759 1413 2038	1.9 1.0 2.0 0.8
6	TU	0304 0851 1506 2135	1.9 1.0 2.0 0.9
7	W	0403 0953 1608 ◐ 2244	1.8 1.1 1.9 0.9
8	TH	0509 1112 1717	1.8 1.1 1.9
9	F	0001 0620 1232 1830	0.8 1.9 1.0 2.0
10	SA	0107 0726 1334 1937	0.7 2.0 0.9 2.1
11	SU	0204 0821 1429 2035	0.7 2.1 0.8 2.2
12	M	0255 0911 1519 2130	0.6 2.2 0.6 2.3
13	TU	0343 1000 1608 2223	0.5 2.3 0.5 2.3
14	W	0430 1047 1655 ○ 2316	0.5 2.4 0.4 2.4
15	TH	0516 1135 1743	0.5 2.4 0.4
16	F	0008 0601 1222 1830	2.3 0.6 2.4 0.4
17	SA	0059 0646 1309 1919	2.3 0.7 2.3 0.5
18	SU	0148 0733 1357 2010	2.1 0.8 2.3 0.6
19	M	0236 0821 1445 2104	2.0 0.9 2.1 0.7
20	TU	0326 0914 1535 2203	1.9 1.0 2.0 0.8
21	W	0420 1017 1633 ◑ 2311	1.8 1.1 1.9 0.9
22	TH	0523 1137 1742	1.7 1.1 1.8
23	F	0020 0631 1255 1853	0.9 1.8 1.1 1.8
24	SA	0121 0730 1355 1952	0.9 1.8 1.1 1.9
25	SU	0210 0820 1442 2042	0.9 1.9 1.0 1.9
26	M	0251 0902 1521 2126	0.9 2.0 0.9 2.0
27	TU	0327 0941 1556 2206	0.8 2.1 0.8 2.0
28	W	0402 1017 1630 2244	0.8 2.1 0.8 2.1
29	TH	0436 1052 1703 ● 2321	0.8 2.2 0.7 2.1
30	F	0511 1126 1738 2358	0.8 2.2 0.6 2.1
31	SA	0546 1200 1815	0.8 2.2 0.6

Chart Datum: 1·22 metres below Ordnance Datum (Local)
HAT is 2·5 metres above Chart Datum

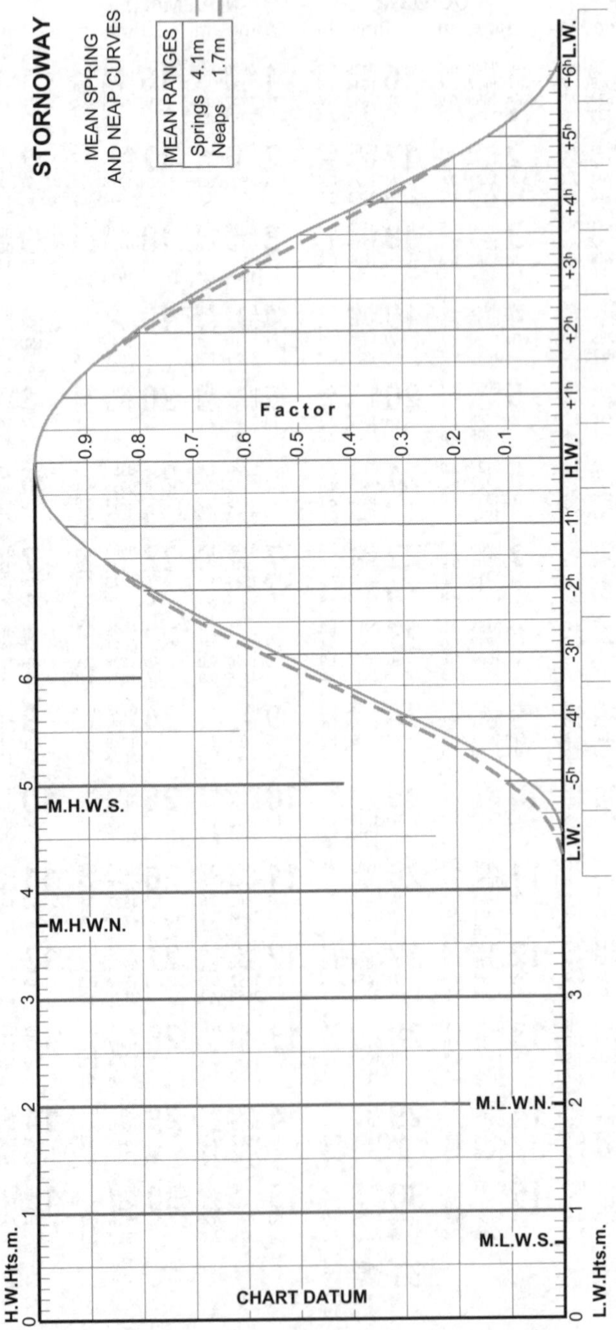
STORNOWAY
MEAN SPRING
AND NEAP CURVES
MEAN RANGES
Springs 4.1m
Neaps 1.7m
Factor
0.9
0.8
0.7
0.6
0.5
0.4
0.3
0.2
0.1
L.W.
-5h
-4h
-3h
-2h
-1h
H.W.
+1h
+2h
+3h
+4h
+5h
+6h
L.W.
H.W.Hts.m.
0
1
2
3
4
5
6
M.H.W.S.
M.H.W.N.
M.L.W.N.
M.L.W.S.
CHART DATUM
L.W.Hts.m.

TIME ZONE (UT)
For Summer Time add ONE hour in **non-shaded areas**

SCOTLAND – STORNOWAY

LAT 58°12'N LONG 6°23'W

TIMES AND HEIGHTS OF HIGH AND LOW WATERS

Dates in amber are **SPRINGS**
Dates in grey are **NEAPS**

2016

JANUARY

Date	Day	Time	m	Time	m	Time	m	Time	m	Moon
1	F	0506	1.9	1113	4.1	1754	1.8			
2	SA	0010	3.7	0556	2.1	1223	3.9	1850	2.0	◑
3	SU	0123	3.7	0658	2.3	1342	3.8	2000	2.1	
4	M	0233	3.7	0816	2.3	1453	3.8	2113	2.1	
5	TU	0334	3.8	0931	2.2	1553	3.9	2213	1.9	
6	W	0425	4.0	1031	2.0	1642	4.0	2300	1.7	
7	TH	0506	4.3	1118	1.8	1723	4.2	2341	1.5	
8	F	0543	4.5	1200	1.5	1800	4.4			
9	SA	0020	1.3	0617	4.7	1240	1.3	1835	4.5	
10	SU	0058	1.1	0652	4.9	1319	1.0	1912	4.7	●
11	M	0135	1.0	0728	5.1	1358	0.9	1951	4.8	
12	TU	0213	0.9	0807	5.1	1439	0.8	2033	4.7	
13	W	0253	0.9	0849	5.1	1520	0.8	2117	4.6	
14	TH	0334	1.0	0935	5.0	1604	0.9	2206	4.4	
15	F	0419	1.2	1027	4.8	1652	1.1	2304	4.2	
16	SA	0510	1.4	1128	4.5	1746	1.3			◐
17	SU	0013	4.0	0610	1.7	1239	4.3	1849	1.6	
18	M	0131	3.9	0725	1.9	1355	4.2	2005	1.7	
19	TU	0248	4.0	0849	1.9	1510	4.2	2125	1.7	
20	W	0358	4.1	1008	1.7	1617	4.3	2234	1.6	
21	TH	0455	4.4	1111	1.5	1714	4.4	2329	1.4	
22	F	0541	4.6	1203	1.2	1801	4.6			
23	SA	0015	1.2	0621	4.8	1249	1.0	1841	4.7	
24	SU	0057	1.0	0658	4.9	1330	0.9	1919	4.7	○
25	M	0135	1.0	0732	5.0	1408	0.8	1954	4.7	
26	TU	0211	1.0	0805	4.9	1443	0.9	2027	4.6	
27	W	0245	1.0	0836	4.8	1518	1.0	2101	4.5	
28	TH	0319	1.1	0908	4.7	1552	1.1	2135	4.3	
29	F	0354	1.3	0941	4.4	1628	1.4	2213	4.1	
30	SA	0430	1.6	1018	4.2	1706	1.6	2300	3.9	
31	SU	0509	1.8	1105	4.0	1749	1.9			

FEBRUARY

Date	Day	Time	m	Time	m	Time	m	Time	m	Moon
1	M	0004	3.7	0556	2.1	1214	3.7	1844	2.1	◑
2	TU	0126	3.6	0700	2.3	1347	3.6	2000	2.2	
3	W	0241	3.7	0828	2.3	1507	3.6	2126	2.1	
4	TH	0346	3.8	0952	2.2	1612	3.8	2229	1.9	
5	F	0437	4.1	1052	1.9	1701	4.0	2317	1.6	
6	SA	0519	4.4	1139	1.5	1742	4.3	2359	1.3	
7	SU	0557	4.7	1221	1.1	1820	4.5			
8	M	0039	1.0	0633	5.0	1302	0.8	1856	4.8	●
9	TU	0119	0.8	0710	5.2	1342	0.5	1935	4.9	
10	W	0158	0.6	0750	5.3	1423	0.4	2015	4.9	
11	TH	0238	0.5	0831	5.3	1503	0.4	2057	4.8	
12	F	0318	0.6	0915	5.2	1545	0.5	2142	4.6	
13	SA	0402	0.8	1005	4.9	1630	0.8	2235	4.4	
14	SU	0449	1.2	1103	4.6	1719	1.2	2340	4.1	
15	M	0545	1.5	1215	4.2	1817	1.6			◐
16	TU	0102	3.9	0656	1.8	1337	4.0	1932	1.9	
17	W	0227	3.8	0829	1.9	1459	3.9	2105	1.9	
18	TH	0345	4.0	1001	1.8	1612	4.0	2224	1.8	
19	F	0445	4.2	1105	1.5	1708	4.2	2319	1.5	
20	SA	0532	4.4	1154	1.2	1751	4.4			
21	SU	0003	1.3	0609	4.6	1237	1.0	1827	4.5	
22	M	0042	1.1	0642	4.8	1313	0.8	1900	4.6	○
23	TU	0118	0.9	0712	4.9	1347	0.8	1930	4.7	
24	W	0151	0.9	0741	4.9	1419	0.8	2000	4.6	
25	TH	0222	0.9	0809	4.8	1450	0.8	2029	4.5	
26	F	0253	1.0	0837	4.6	1521	1.0	2100	4.4	
27	SA	0325	1.1	0907	4.5	1552	1.2	2133	4.2	
28	SU	0357	1.3	0940	4.2	1625	1.4	2211	4.0	
29	M	0433	1.6	1019	4.0	1702	1.7	2302	3.8	

MARCH

Date	Day	Time	m	Time	m	Time	m	Time	m	Moon
1	TU	0514	1.8	1113	3.7	1746	1.9			◑
2	W	0016	3.6	0606	2.1	1241	3.5	1849	2.2	
3	TH	0145	3.6	0725	2.2	1420	3.5	2028	2.2	
4	F	0300	3.7	0908	2.1	1537	3.6	2155	2.0	
5	SA	0401	3.9	1022	1.8	1635	3.9	2251	1.7	
6	SU	0450	4.2	1114	1.4	1720	4.2	2336	1.3	
7	M	0531	4.6	1158	1.0	1759	4.5			
8	TU	0018	0.9	0609	5.0	1241	0.6	1836	4.8	
9	W	0058	0.6	0648	5.2	1321	0.3	1914	5.0	●
10	TH	0138	0.4	0728	5.4	1402	0.1	1953	5.1	
11	F	0219	0.3	0810	5.4	1442	0.1	2035	5.0	
12	SA	0300	0.4	0855	5.2	1524	0.3	2119	4.7	
13	SU	0344	0.6	0945	4.8	1607	0.7	2210	4.4	
14	M	0431	1.0	1045	4.4	1653	1.1	2314	4.1	
15	TU	0525	1.4	1200	4.1	1749	1.6			◐
16	W	0038	3.8	0636	1.7	1324	3.8	1902	1.9	
17	TH	0206	3.8	0814	1.9	1447	3.7	2043	2.0	
18	F	0326	3.9	0948	1.7	1600	3.8	2207	1.9	
19	SA	0428	4.0	1050	1.5	1654	4.0	2301	1.6	
20	SU	0513	4.3	1136	1.2	1734	4.2	2344	1.4	
21	M	0549	4.4	1215	1.0	1808	4.4			
22	TU	0021	1.1	0620	4.6	1250	0.8	1837	4.5	
23	W	0056	1.0	0648	4.7	1322	0.7	1905	4.6	○
24	TH	0127	0.9	0715	4.7	1352	0.7	1933	4.6	
25	F	0158	0.8	0742	4.6	1421	0.8	2001	4.6	
26	SA	0228	0.9	0809	4.5	1450	0.9	2030	4.5	
27	SU	0258	1.0	0838	4.4	1520	1.0	2101	4.3	
28	M	0330	1.2	0911	4.2	1551	1.3	2137	4.1	
29	TU	0405	1.4	0951	3.9	1625	1.5	2223	3.9	
30	W	0444	1.6	1042	3.7	1706	1.8	2327	3.7	
31	TH	0533	1.9	1202	3.5	1802	2.0			◑

APRIL

Date	Day	Time	m	Time	m	Time	m	Time	m	Moon
1	F	0054	3.6	0644	2.0	1341	3.4	1933	2.2	
2	SA	0215	3.7	0824	2.0	1501	3.6	2114	2.0	
3	SU	0321	3.9	0946	1.7	1604	3.8	2219	1.7	
4	M	0415	4.2	1044	1.3	1652	4.2	2308	1.3	
5	TU	0501	4.6	1131	0.8	1734	4.5	2352	0.8	
6	W	0544	4.9	1215	0.4	1813	4.8			
7	TH	0035	0.5	0624	5.2	1257	0.2	1852	5.1	●
8	F	0117	0.3	0707	5.3	1339	0.0	1932	5.1	
9	SA	0159	0.2	0751	5.3	1420	0.1	2014	5.0	
10	SU	0243	0.3	0838	5.1	1502	0.3	2059	4.8	
11	M	0327	0.5	0930	4.7	1545	0.7	2150	4.5	
12	TU	0416	0.9	1033	4.3	1632	1.2	2254	4.2	
13	W	0511	1.3	1147	3.9	1725	1.6			
14	TH	0015	3.9	0620	1.6	1306	3.7	1835	2.0	◐
15	F	0138	3.8	0750	1.8	1424	3.6	2008	2.1	
16	SA	0255	3.8	0919	1.7	1535	3.7	2134	2.0	
17	SU	0358	3.9	1021	1.5	1629	3.8	2232	1.7	
18	M	0446	4.1	1107	1.3	1709	4.0	2316	1.5	
19	TU	0522	4.2	1146	1.1	1742	4.2	2355	1.3	
20	W	0554	4.4	1220	0.9	1812	4.4			
21	TH	0029	1.1	0622	4.4	1253	0.8	1840	4.5	
22	F	0102	1.0	0650	4.5	1323	0.8	1908	4.6	○
23	SA	0133	0.9	0717	4.5	1353	0.8	1936	4.6	
24	SU	0204	0.9	0746	4.4	1422	0.9	2005	4.5	
25	M	0235	1.0	0817	4.3	1452	1.0	2037	4.4	
26	TU	0308	1.1	0853	4.1	1524	1.2	2115	4.2	
27	W	0344	1.2	0935	3.9	1559	1.4	2200	4.0	
28	TH	0424	1.4	1029	3.7	1641	1.7	2300	3.9	
29	F	0514	1.6	1143	3.6	1735	1.9			
30	SA	0016	3.8	0619	1.8	1309	3.5	1856	2.0	◑

Chart Datum: 2·71 metres below Ordnance Datum (Local)
HAT is 5·5 metres above Chart Datum

TIME ZONE (UT)
For Summer Time add ONE hour in **non-shaded areas**

SCOTLAND – STORNOWAY

LAT 58°12′N LONG 6°23′W

TIMES AND HEIGHTS OF HIGH AND LOW WATERS

Dates in amber are **SPRINGS**
Dates in grey are **NEAPS**

2016

MAY

Date	Time	m	Date	Time	m
1 SU	0134 0746 1425 2030	3.8 1.8 3.6 1.9	16 M	0317 0938 1552 2150	3.8 1.6 3.7 1.9
2 M	0242 0907 1530 2142	3.9 1.5 3.9 1.6	17 TU	0409 1029 1636 2241	3.9 1.5 3.9 1.7
3 TU	0341 1009 1623 2237	4.2 1.2 4.2 1.3	18 W	0450 1111 1713 2323	4.0 1.3 4.1 1.5
4 W	0432 1101 1708 2326	4.5 0.8 4.5 0.9	19 TH	0526 1149 1746	4.1 1.1 4.3
5 TH	0519 1148 1750	4.8 0.5 4.8	20 F	0001 0557 1223 1816	1.3 4.2 1.0 4.4
6 F	0012 0603 1234 ● 1831	0.6 5.1 0.3 5.0	21 SA	0036 0628 1256 ○ 1845	1.1 4.3 1.0 4.5
7 SA	0057 0648 1317 1913	0.4 5.1 0.2 5.1	22 SU	0110 0658 1327 1915	1.0 4.3 0.9 4.5
8 SU	0142 0735 1400 1956	0.3 5.1 0.3 5.0	23 M	0143 0729 1358 1946	1.0 4.3 1.0 4.5
9 M	0228 0824 1443 2043	0.3 4.9 0.5 4.8	24 TU	0216 0803 1431 2021	1.0 4.2 1.0 4.5
10 TU	0314 0918 1527 2134	0.5 4.6 0.8 4.5	25 W	0251 0841 1505 2100	1.0 4.1 1.2 4.4
11 W	0403 1019 1613 2234	0.8 4.2 1.2 4.3	26 TH	0329 0926 1542 2146	1.1 4.0 1.3 4.2
12 TH	0457 1126 1704 2345	1.2 3.9 1.6 4.0	27 F	0411 1019 1626 2242	1.3 3.9 1.5 4.1
13 F	0559 1236 1806 ◐	1.5 3.7 1.9	28 SA	0500 1124 1719 2348	1.4 3.7 1.7 4.0
14 SA	0100 0712 1347 1921	3.8 1.7 3.6 2.0	29 SU	0601 1238 1828 ◑	1.5 3.7 1.8
15 SU	0212 0831 1455 2043	3.8 1.7 3.6 2.0	30 M	0058 0713 1350 1950	4.0 1.5 3.7 1.8
			31 TU	0207 0828 1457 2104	4.0 1.4 3.9 1.6

JUNE

Date	Time	m	Date	Time	m
1 W	0309 0935 1555 2207	4.2 1.2 4.1 1.4	16 TH	0414 1033 1641 2249	3.8 1.6 4.0 1.7
2 TH	0406 1033 1646 2302	4.4 0.9 4.4 1.1	17 F	0457 1116 1719 2332	3.9 1.4 4.1 1.5
3 F	0459 1125 1732 2353	4.7 0.7 4.7 0.8	18 SA	0535 1154 1753	4.0 1.3 4.3
4 SA	0548 1213 1816	4.8 0.6 4.9	19 SU	0011 0609 1230 1825	1.3 4.2 1.2 4.5
5 SU	0042 0636 1259 ● 1859	0.6 4.9 0.5 5.0	20 M	0048 0642 1305 ○ 1857	1.2 4.2 1.1 4.6
6 M	0130 0724 1344 1943	0.5 4.9 0.5 4.9	21 TU	0124 0716 1339 1930	1.1 4.3 1.0 4.6
7 TU	0216 0813 1427 2028	0.5 4.7 0.7 4.8	22 W	0200 0752 1414 2007	1.0 4.3 1.0 4.6
8 W	0303 0904 1511 2116	0.6 4.5 0.9 4.6	23 TH	0238 0831 1451 2046	0.9 4.3 1.1 4.6
9 TH	0350 0956 1555 2207	0.8 4.2 1.2 4.4	24 F	0317 0914 1530 2131	0.9 4.2 1.1 4.5
10 F	0438 1052 1641 2304	1.1 4.0 1.5 4.1	25 SA	0359 1004 1613 2222	1.0 4.1 1.3 4.4
11 SA	0529 1153 1732	1.3 3.7 1.7	26 SU	0446 1101 1703 2321	1.1 4.0 1.5 4.3
12 SU	0009 0626 1257 ◐ 1831	3.9 1.6 3.6 1.9	27 M	0540 1207 1803 ◑	1.3 3.9 1.6
13 M	0118 0730 1402 1941	3.8 1.7 3.6 2.1	28 TU	0027 0642 1319 1914	4.2 1.4 3.8 1.7
14 TU	0224 0839 1504 2055	3.7 1.8 3.6 2.0	29 W	0137 0753 1428 2031	4.1 1.4 3.9 1.7
15 W	0324 0942 1557 2158	3.7 1.7 3.8 1.9	30 TH	0245 0904 1533 2142	4.2 1.3 4.1 1.5

JULY

Date	Time	m	Date	Time	m
1 F	0349 1011 1630 2246	4.3 1.2 4.3 1.3	16 SA	0429 1044 1652 2305	3.8 1.7 4.0 1.7
2 SA	0448 1108 1720 2342	4.4 1.0 4.5 1.0	17 SU	0513 1128 1730 2349	3.9 1.5 4.2 1.5
3 SU	0541 1200 1806	4.6 0.9 4.7	18 M	0551 1207 1805	4.1 1.3 4.5
4 M	0033 0629 1247 ● 1849	0.8 4.7 0.8 4.9	19 TU	0028 0626 1245 ○ 1838	1.3 4.2 1.1 4.6
5 TU	0121 0715 1331 1931	0.6 4.7 0.8 4.9	20 W	0107 0700 1322 1913	1.0 4.4 1.0 4.8
6 W	0206 0759 1413 2012	0.6 4.7 0.8 4.9	21 TH	0145 0736 1358 1950	0.8 4.5 0.9 4.9
7 TH	0249 0842 1453 2052	0.6 4.5 0.9 4.7	22 F	0223 0815 1436 2029	0.7 4.5 0.9 4.9
8 F	0330 0925 1533 2133	0.8 4.3 1.1 4.5	23 SA	0302 0856 1515 2112	0.7 4.5 0.9 4.8
9 SA	0412 1009 1614 2216	1.0 4.1 1.3 4.3	24 SU	0343 0942 1557 2159	0.7 4.4 1.0 4.7
10 SU	0454 1058 1656 2305	1.2 3.9 1.6 4.0	25 M	0427 1034 1644 2255	0.9 4.2 1.2 4.5
11 M	0539 1155 1743	1.5 3.7 1.8	26 TU	0516 1136 1738 ◑	1.1 4.0 1.5
12 TU	0006 0630 1301 ◐ 1839	3.8 1.7 3.6 2.0	27 W	0001 0612 1250 1844	4.3 1.3 3.9 1.7
13 W	0121 0731 1409 1949	3.7 1.9 3.6 2.1	28 TH	0115 0720 1406 2005	4.1 1.5 3.9 1.8
14 TH	0232 0843 1512 2107	3.6 1.9 3.7 2.1	29 F	0230 0839 1518 2128	4.0 1.6 4.0 1.7
15 F	0335 0951 1606 2214	3.7 1.8 3.8 2.0	30 SA	0342 0956 1622 2240	4.1 1.5 4.2 1.4
			31 SU	0445 1059 1714 2337	4.2 1.3 4.5 1.2

AUGUST

Date	Time	m	Date	Time	m
1 M	0537 1151 1758	4.4 1.2 4.7	16 TU	0531 1144 1742	4.1 1.4 4.5
2 TU	0026 0622 1236 ● 1838	0.9 4.6 1.0 4.9	17 W	0007 0606 1224 1816	1.2 4.3 1.1 4.8
3 W	0111 0702 1317 1915	0.7 4.6 0.9 4.9	18 TH	0046 0641 1302 ○ 1851	0.9 4.6 0.9 5.0
4 TH	0151 0739 1356 1950	0.6 4.7 0.8 4.9	19 F	0125 0716 1339 1928	0.6 4.7 0.7 5.1
5 F	0229 0815 1432 2024	0.6 4.6 0.9 4.8	20 SA	0203 0754 1418 2007	0.5 4.8 0.6 5.2
6 SA	0305 0850 1508 2057	0.7 4.4 1.0 4.6	21 SU	0242 0834 1457 2050	0.4 4.8 0.6 5.1
7 SU	0340 0926 1544 2131	0.9 4.3 1.2 4.4	22 M	0322 0917 1539 2136	0.5 4.6 0.8 4.9
8 M	0416 1004 1620 2208	1.2 4.1 1.4 4.1	23 TU	0405 1006 1624 2231	0.7 4.4 1.1 4.6
9 TU	0454 1050 1700 2254	1.4 3.8 1.7 3.9	24 W	0451 1107 1716 2340	1.0 4.2 1.4 4.3
10 W	0535 1152 1746 ◐	1.7 3.7 2.0	25 TH	0545 1226 1822 ◑	1.4 4.0 1.7
11 TH	0002 0626 1311 1845	3.7 1.9 3.6 2.2	26 F	0102 0653 1350 1948	4.0 1.7 3.9 1.9
12 F	0136 0736 1424 2009	3.5 2.1 3.6 2.3	27 SA	0224 0821 1508 2124	3.9 1.9 4.0 1.8
13 SA	0255 0903 1529 2137	3.5 2.1 3.8 2.1	28 SU	0340 0949 1615 2237	4.0 1.8 4.2 1.5
14 SU	0400 1012 1622 2239	3.6 1.9 4.0 1.9	29 M	0442 1052 1706 2331	4.1 1.6 4.4 1.2
15 M	0451 1102 1704 2326	3.8 1.7 4.2 1.6	30 TU	0530 1140 1747	4.3 1.3 4.6
			31 W	0015 0609 1222 1822	1.0 4.5 1.1 4.8

Chart Datum: 2·71 metres below Ordnance Datum (Local)
HAT is 5·5 metres above Chart Datum

TIME ZONE (UT)
For Summer Time add ONE hour in **non-shaded areas**

SCOTLAND – STORNOWAY

LAT 58°12'N LONG 6°23'W

TIMES AND HEIGHTS OF HIGH AND LOW WATERS

Dates in amber are **SPRINGS**
Dates in grey are **NEAPS**

2016

SEPTEMBER

Date	Day	Time	m	Time	m	Time	m	Time	m
1	TH ●	0055	0.8	0643	4.6	1300	1.0	1854	4.9
2	F	0131	0.7	0715	4.7	1335	0.9	1925	4.9
3	SA	0204	0.7	0746	4.7	1408	0.9	1954	4.8
4	SU	0236	0.8	0816	4.6	1441	1.0	2023	4.7
5	M	0308	0.9	0847	4.4	1513	1.1	2053	4.5
6	TU	0339	1.1	0920	4.3	1547	1.3	2126	4.2
7	W	0413	1.4	0958	4.0	1622	1.6	2205	4.0
8	TH	0449	1.7	1049	3.8	1703	1.9	2300	3.7
9	F ◐	0532	1.9	1206	3.7	1755	2.1		
10	SA	0037	3.5	0631	2.2	1334	3.6	1912	2.3
11	SU	0214	3.5	0807	2.3	1447	3.7	2055	2.2
12	M	0328	3.6	0938	2.1	1547	3.9	2209	1.9
13	TU	0423	3.8	1035	1.8	1634	4.2	2259	1.6
14	W	0506	4.1	1119	1.5	1714	4.5	2341	1.2
15	TH	0542	4.4	1159	1.1	1750	4.9		
16	F ○	0021	0.8	0617	4.7	1238	0.8	1827	5.2
17	SA	0100	0.5	0653	5.0	1317	0.6	1905	5.4
18	SU	0139	0.3	0730	5.1	1357	0.5	1945	5.4
19	M	0219	0.2	0810	5.0	1437	0.5	2028	5.3
20	TU	0259	0.4	0853	4.9	1520	0.7	2116	5.0
21	W	0342	0.7	0941	4.6	1606	1.0	2213	4.6
22	TH	0428	1.1	1043	4.3	1659	1.4	2328	4.2
23	F ◑	0520	1.5	1207	4.0	1806	1.7		
24	SA	0054	3.9	0629	1.9	1335	3.9	1938	1.9
25	SU	0217	3.8	0805	2.1	1455	4.0	2118	1.8
26	M	0333	3.9	0937	2.0	1601	4.2	2226	1.5
27	TU	0432	4.1	1037	1.7	1651	4.4	2315	1.3
28	W	0516	4.3	1123	1.5	1729	4.6	2355	1.1
29	TH	0551	4.5	1202	1.2	1802	4.7		
30	F	0031	0.9	0621	4.6	1238	1.1	1831	4.8

OCTOBER

Date	Day	Time	m	Time	m	Time	m	Time	m
1	SA ●	0105	0.8	0650	4.7	1311	1.0	1859	4.8
2	SU	0136	0.8	0718	4.7	1343	1.0	1926	4.8
3	M	0206	0.8	0746	4.7	1414	1.0	1954	4.7
4	TU	0236	1.0	0815	4.6	1445	1.1	2023	4.5
5	W	0306	1.2	0846	4.4	1517	1.3	2055	4.3
6	TH	0337	1.4	0921	4.3	1552	1.5	2133	4.0
7	F	0412	1.7	1006	4.0	1631	1.8	2224	3.8
8	SA	0451	1.9	1110	3.8	1720	2.0	2349	3.6
9	SU ◐	0544	2.2	1241	3.7	1828	2.2		
10	M	0130	3.5	0710	2.4	1401	3.8	2006	2.2
11	TU	0249	3.6	0854	2.2	1506	4.0	2130	1.9
12	W	0349	3.9	1000	1.9	1558	4.3	2225	1.5
13	TH	0436	4.2	1048	1.5	1642	4.6	2311	1.1
14	F	0515	4.6	1131	1.2	1723	4.9	2353	0.7
15	SA	0552	4.9	1212	0.8	1802	5.2		
16	SU ○	0034	0.4	0629	5.1	1254	0.6	1842	5.4
17	M	0115	0.3	0708	5.2	1336	0.4	1925	5.4
18	TU	0156	0.3	0749	5.2	1418	0.5	2010	5.3
19	W	0238	0.4	0832	5.0	1503	0.6	2101	5.0
20	TH	0321	0.8	0922	4.7	1551	0.9	2201	4.6
21	F	0407	1.2	1023	4.4	1645	1.3	2316	4.2
22	SA ◑	0500	1.6	1146	4.2	1753	1.7		
23	SU	0039	3.9	0607	2.0	1312	4.0	1920	1.9
24	M	0158	3.8	0737	2.2	1430	4.0	2052	1.8
25	TU	0312	3.9	0907	2.1	1537	4.2	2200	1.6
26	W	0411	4.0	1010	1.9	1628	4.3	2248	1.4
27	TH	0454	4.2	1057	1.7	1707	4.5	2328	1.2
28	F	0528	4.4	1137	1.4	1739	4.6		
29	SA	0004	1.1	0558	4.6	1213	1.3	1808	4.7
30	SU ●	0037	1.0	0626	4.7	1247	1.2	1836	4.7
31	M	0108	1.0	0654	4.8	1319	1.1	1904	4.7

NOVEMBER

Date	Day	Time	m	Time	m	Time	m	Time	m
1	TU	0138	1.0	0722	4.8	1350	1.1	1932	4.6
2	W	0208	1.1	0751	4.7	1421	1.2	2002	4.5
3	TH	0238	1.2	0822	4.6	1454	1.3	2036	4.3
4	F	0310	1.4	0857	4.4	1529	1.5	2115	4.1
5	SA	0344	1.6	0940	4.3	1609	1.7	2206	3.9
6	SU	0423	1.9	1036	4.1	1656	1.9	2316	3.7
7	M ◐	0513	2.1	1152	3.9	1757	2.0		
8	TU	0045	3.6	0626	2.3	1313	3.9	1919	2.1
9	W	0204	3.7	0801	2.2	1421	4.0	2042	1.9
10	TH	0310	3.9	0917	2.0	1520	4.3	2146	1.5
11	F	0403	4.2	1014	1.6	1610	4.6	2238	1.2
12	SA	0448	4.6	1102	1.3	1656	4.9	2325	0.8
13	SU	0529	4.9	1148	0.9	1740	5.2		
14	M ○	0009	0.6	0609	5.1	1233	0.7	1824	5.3
15	TU	0053	0.4	0650	5.3	1318	0.5	1910	5.3
16	W	0136	0.4	0732	5.3	1403	0.5	1958	5.2
17	TH	0220	0.6	0818	5.1	1450	0.7	2050	4.9
18	F	0304	0.9	0907	4.9	1540	0.9	2149	4.6
19	SA	0351	1.2	1005	4.6	1633	1.2	2256	4.2
20	SU	0442	1.6	1116	4.3	1734	1.6		
21	M ◑	0009	4.0	0541	2.0	1235	4.1	1845	1.8
22	TU	0123	3.8	0654	2.2	1351	4.1	2005	1.9
23	W	0234	3.8	0816	2.2	1459	4.1	2117	1.8
24	TH	0336	3.9	0929	2.1	1555	4.1	2212	1.7
25	F	0424	4.1	1024	1.9	1639	4.2	2257	1.5
26	SA	0502	4.3	1108	1.7	1715	4.4	2335	1.4
27	SU	0535	4.5	1147	1.5	1748	4.5		
28	M	0010	1.3	0605	4.6	1224	1.4	1818	4.5
29	TU ●	0043	1.2	0635	4.7	1257	1.3	1847	4.6
30	W	0115	1.2	0704	4.8	1330	1.2	1917	4.5

DECEMBER

Date	Day	Time	m	Time	m	Time	m	Time	m
1	TH	0146	1.2	0734	4.8	1403	1.2	1949	4.5
2	F	0217	1.3	0806	4.7	1437	1.3	2024	4.4
3	SA	0250	1.4	0842	4.6	1513	1.4	2104	4.2
4	SU	0325	1.5	0923	4.5	1553	1.5	2151	4.1
5	M	0405	1.7	1013	4.3	1638	1.6	2249	3.9
6	TU	0452	1.9	1114	4.2	1732	1.8		
7	W ◐	0001	3.8	0552	2.1	1226	4.1	1839	1.8
8	TH	0118	3.8	0711	2.1	1337	4.2	1954	1.8
9	F	0228	4.0	0830	2.0	1442	4.3	2105	1.6
10	SA	0330	4.2	0938	1.8	1541	4.5	2207	1.3
11	SU	0423	4.5	1036	1.4	1634	4.8	2300	1.0
12	M	0510	4.8	1128	1.1	1725	5.0	2349	0.8
13	TU	0554	5.0	1217	0.9	1813	5.1		
14	W ○	0036	0.7	0637	5.2	1306	0.7	1901	5.2
15	TH	0122	0.7	0721	5.3	1353	0.6	1949	5.1
16	F	0206	0.7	0806	5.2	1440	0.7	2039	4.9
17	SA	0250	0.9	0853	5.0	1528	0.8	2130	4.6
18	SU	0334	1.2	0942	4.8	1616	1.1	2224	4.3
19	M	0420	1.5	1037	4.5	1707	1.4	2323	4.0
20	TU	0510	1.8	1141	4.2	1802	1.7		
21	W ◑	0029	3.8	0606	2.0	1253	4.0	1905	1.9
22	TH	0139	3.7	0713	2.2	1405	3.9	2015	2.0
23	F	0247	3.8	0829	2.3	1510	3.9	2124	1.9
24	SA	0345	3.9	0941	2.2	1605	4.0	2220	1.8
25	SU	0433	4.1	1037	2.0	1651	4.1	2306	1.7
26	M	0512	4.3	1123	1.8	1729	4.2	2345	1.5
27	TU	0547	4.5	1202	1.6	1803	4.3		
28	W	0021	1.4	0618	4.6	1239	1.4	1835	4.4
29	TH ●	0055	1.3	0649	4.7	1314	1.3	1906	4.5
30	F	0128	1.2	0720	4.8	1349	1.2	1939	4.5
31	SA	0201	1.2	0753	4.8	1424	1.1	2013	4.5

Chart Datum: 2·71 metres below Ordnance Datum (Local)
HAT is 5·5 metres above Chart Datum

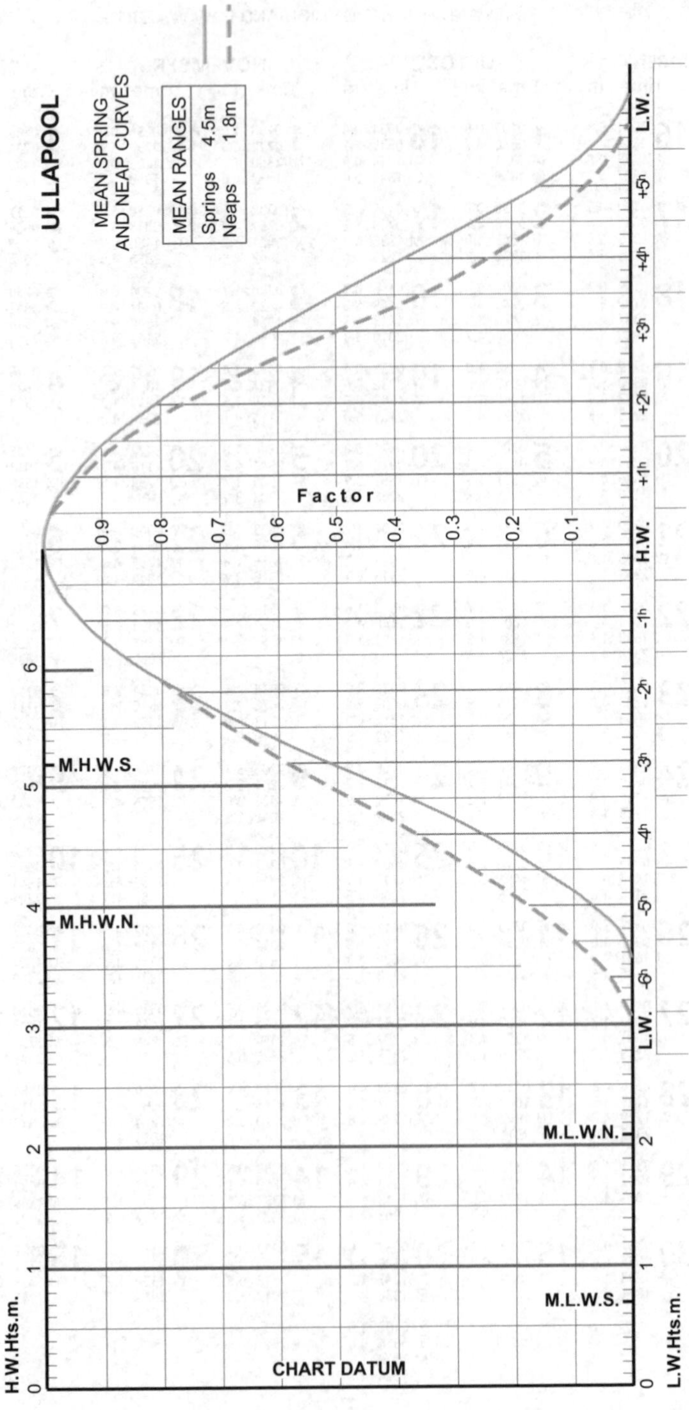
ULLAPOOL
MEAN SPRING AND NEAP CURVES
MEAN RANGES
Springs 4.5m
Neaps 1.8m
Factor
0.9
0.8
0.7
0.6
0.5
0.4
0.3
0.2
0.1
L.W.
-6h
-5h
-4h
-3h
-2h
-1h
H.W.
+1h
+2h
+3h
+4h
+5h
L.W.
H.W.Hts.m.
0
1
2
3
4
5
6
M.H.W.S.
M.H.W.N.
CHART DATUM
L.W.Hts.m.
M.L.W.S.
M.L.W.N.

TIME ZONE (UT)
For Summer Time add ONE hour in **non-shaded areas**

SCOTLAND – ULLAPOOL

LAT 57°54′N LONG 5°09′W

TIMES AND HEIGHTS OF HIGH AND LOW WATERS

Dates in amber are **SPRINGS**
Dates in grey are **NEAPS**

2016

JANUARY

Date	Day	Time	m	Time	m	Time	m	Time	m
1	F	0516	2.0	1119	4.3	1759	2.0		
2	SA	0014	4.1	0606	2.2	1227	4.1	◑ 1855	2.2
3	SU	0125	4.0	0709	2.4	1346	4.0	2005	2.3
4	M	0236	4.0	0826	2.5	1459	4.0	2118	2.2
5	TU	0339	4.1	0940	2.4	1600	4.2	2218	2.1
6	W	0430	4.4	1037	2.1	1649	4.3	2306	1.8
7	TH	0511	4.6	1124	1.9	1730	4.5	2347	1.6
8	F	0548	4.8	1206	1.6	1807	4.7		
9	SA	0026	1.4	0623	5.1	1246	1.3	1842	4.9
10	SU	0105	1.2	0658	5.3	1325	1.1	● 1919	5.1
11	M	0143	1.0	0734	5.4	1405	0.9	1958	5.1
12	TU	0221	1.0	0813	5.5	1445	0.8	2039	5.1
13	W	0301	1.0	0855	5.4	1526	0.8	2123	5.0
14	TH	0342	1.1	0941	5.3	1610	1.0	2213	4.8
15	F	0428	1.3	1033	5.1	1658	1.2	2310	4.6
16	SA	0519	1.5	1134	4.8	1752	1.4	◐	
17	SU	0018	4.4	0619	1.8	1246	4.6	1855	1.7
18	M	0133	4.3	0733	2.0	1400	4.5	2010	1.8
19	TU	0250	4.3	0856	2.0	1516	4.5	2130	1.8
20	W	0402	4.5	1014	1.8	1625	4.6	2240	1.7
21	TH	0500	4.7	1117	1.6	1721	4.8	2335	1.5
22	F	0547	5.0	1209	1.3	1808	4.9		
23	SA	0022	1.3	0627	5.2	1255	1.1	1849	5.1
24	SU	0105	1.1	0704	5.3	1336	0.9	○ 1926	5.1
25	M	0143	1.0	0738	5.3	1413	0.9	2001	5.1
26	TU	0219	1.0	0811	5.3	1449	0.9	2035	5.0
27	W	0254	1.1	0842	5.1	1523	1.0	2108	4.8
28	TH	0328	1.2	0914	5.0	1558	1.2	2143	4.7
29	F	0402	1.4	0947	4.7	1633	1.5	2220	4.4
30	SA	0438	1.7	1024	4.5	1711	1.7	2306	4.2
31	SU	0518	2.0	1110	4.2	1754	2.0		

FEBRUARY

Date	Day	Time	m	Time	m	Time	m	Time	m
1	M	0009	4.0	0605	2.2	1220	4.0	◑ 1848	2.2
2	TU	0128	3.9	0710	2.4	1350	3.9	2005	2.3
3	W	0243	3.9	0837	2.5	1511	3.9	2131	2.3
4	TH	0350	4.1	0958	2.3	1618	4.1	2235	2.0
5	F	0442	4.4	1057	2.0	1707	4.3	2324	1.7
6	SA	0525	4.7	1144	1.6	1748	4.6		
7	SU	0006	1.4	0602	5.0	1227	1.2	1826	4.9
8	M	0047	1.1	0639	5.3	1308	0.9	● 1903	5.2
9	TU	0126	0.8	0717	5.5	1349	0.6	1941	5.3
10	W	0206	0.6	0756	5.7	1429	0.4	2021	5.4
11	TH	0245	0.6	0837	5.7	1509	0.4	2103	5.3
12	F	0326	0.7	0922	5.5	1551	0.6	2149	5.0
13	SA	0410	0.9	1011	5.2	1636	0.9	2241	4.7
14	SU	0457	1.2	1110	4.9	1725	1.3	2346	4.4
15	M	0553	1.6	1221	4.5	1824	1.7	◐	
16	TU	0104	4.2	0704	1.9	1341	4.3	1939	2.0
17	W	0229	4.2	0836	2.1	1505	4.2	2111	2.0
18	TH	0350	4.3	1005	1.9	1619	4.3	2230	1.9
19	F	0451	4.5	1110	1.6	1715	4.5	2326	1.6
20	SA	0538	4.7	1200	1.3	1759	4.7		
21	SU	0011	1.4	0615	5.0	1242	1.1	1835	4.9
22	M	0050	1.1	0648	5.1	1319	0.9	○ 1907	5.0
23	TU	0126	1.0	0718	5.2	1353	0.8	1938	5.1
24	W	0159	0.9	0747	5.2	1425	0.8	2007	5.0
25	TH	0230	0.9	0815	5.1	1456	0.9	2037	4.9
26	F	0301	1.0	0843	5.0	1526	1.0	2107	4.8
27	SA	0332	1.2	0913	4.8	1557	1.2	2140	4.6
28	SU	0405	1.4	0947	4.6	1631	1.5	2218	4.3
29	M	0441	1.7	1026	4.3	1708	1.8	2307	4.1

MARCH

Date	Day	Time	m	Time	m	Time	m	Time	m
1	TU	0522	2.0	1118	4.0	1753	2.1	◑	
2	W	0019	3.9	0615	2.2	1246	3.8	1857	2.3
3	TH	0147	3.8	0734	2.4	1423	3.8	2035	2.4
4	F	0304	3.9	0914	2.3	1542	3.9	2201	2.1
5	SA	0407	4.2	1027	1.9	1641	4.2	2258	1.8
6	SU	0456	4.5	1119	1.5	1725	4.6	2343	1.4
7	M	0537	4.9	1204	1.0	1804	4.9		
8	TU	0025	1.0	0616	5.3	1247	0.6	1842	5.2
9	W	0106	0.6	0655	5.6	1327	0.3	● 1920	5.4
10	TH	0146	0.4	0735	5.8	1408	0.1	2000	5.5
11	F	0226	0.3	0817	5.7	1449	0.2	2041	5.4
12	SA	0308	0.4	0902	5.5	1530	0.4	2126	5.1
13	SU	0351	0.7	0952	5.2	1614	0.8	2217	4.8
14	M	0438	1.0	1052	4.8	1701	1.2	2321	4.4
15	TU	0533	1.5	1206	4.4	1757	1.7	◐	
16	W	0041	4.2	0643	1.8	1327	4.1	1912	2.1
17	TH	0209	4.0	0819	2.0	1453	4.0	2051	2.2
18	F	0333	4.1	0952	1.9	1607	4.1	2214	2.0
19	SA	0435	4.3	1055	1.6	1700	4.3	2309	1.7
20	SU	0520	4.5	1141	1.3	1741	4.6	2352	1.4
21	M	0556	4.7	1221	1.1	1815	4.7		
22	TU	0029	1.2	0627	4.9	1256	0.9	1844	4.9
23	W	0104	1.0	0655	5.0	1328	0.8	○ 1913	5.0
24	TH	0135	0.9	0722	5.0	1358	0.8	1940	5.0
25	F	0205	0.9	0749	5.0	1427	0.8	2008	4.9
26	SA	0235	0.9	0816	4.9	1456	0.9	2037	4.8
27	SU	0305	1.1	0846	4.7	1526	1.1	2108	4.7
28	M	0337	1.2	0919	4.5	1558	1.3	2144	4.4
29	TU	0412	1.5	0958	4.3	1633	1.6	2228	4.2
30	W	0452	1.7	1048	4.0	1715	1.9	2330	4.0
31	TH	0542	2.0	1206	3.8	1812	2.2	◑	

APRIL

Date	Day	Time	m	Time	m	Time	m	Time	m
1	F	0058	3.9	0652	2.2	1344	3.7	1943	2.3
2	SA	0219	3.9	0830	2.1	1504	3.9	2122	2.1
3	SU	0327	4.1	0952	1.8	1608	4.2	2227	1.7
4	M	0422	4.5	1049	1.4	1657	4.5	2316	1.3
5	TU	0508	4.9	1137	0.9	1739	4.9		
6	W	0000	0.9	0550	5.3	1221	0.5	1818	5.2
7	TH	0043	0.5	0631	5.6	1304	0.2	● 1858	5.5
8	F	0125	0.3	0714	5.7	1345	0.1	1938	5.5
9	SA	0207	0.2	0758	5.6	1427	0.1	2020	5.4
10	SU	0250	0.3	0845	5.4	1509	0.4	2106	5.2
11	M	0335	0.6	0938	5.1	1553	0.8	2157	4.8
12	TU	0423	0.9	1040	4.6	1641	1.2	2301	4.5
13	W	0518	1.4	1152	4.3	1735	1.7		
14	TH	0018	4.2	0626	1.7	1309	4.0	◐ 1846	2.1
15	F	0142	4.0	0754	1.9	1430	3.9	2019	2.2
16	SA	0304	4.0	0922	1.8	1542	4.0	2143	2.0
17	SU	0407	4.2	1025	1.6	1635	4.2	2240	1.8
18	M	0453	4.3	1112	1.4	1715	4.4	2325	1.5
19	TU	0530	4.5	1152	1.2	1749	4.6		
20	W	0003	1.3	0601	4.7	1227	1.0	1819	4.7
21	TH	0037	1.1	0630	4.8	1259	0.9	1847	4.9
22	F	0109	1.0	0658	4.8	1330	0.9	○ 1915	4.9
23	SA	0140	0.9	0725	4.8	1359	0.9	1943	4.9
24	SU	0211	1.0	0754	4.7	1429	1.0	2012	4.8
25	M	0242	1.0	0825	4.6	1459	1.1	2044	4.7
26	TU	0315	1.1	0900	4.5	1532	1.3	2121	4.5
27	W	0350	1.3	0942	4.3	1608	1.5	2206	4.3
28	TH	0431	1.5	1035	4.0	1650	1.8	2305	4.1
29	F	0521	1.7	1147	3.9	1746	2.0		
30	SA	0022	4.0	0626	1.9	1312	3.8	◑ 1906	2.1

Chart Datum: 2·75 metres below Ordnance Datum (Newlyn)
HAT is 5·9 metres above Chart Datum

TIME ZONE (UT)
For Summer Time add ONE hour in **non-shaded areas**

SCOTLAND – ULLAPOOL

LAT 57°54′N LONG 5°09′W

TIMES AND HEIGHTS OF HIGH AND LOW WATERS

Dates in amber are **SPRINGS**
Dates in grey are **NEAPS**

2016

MAY

Day	Time	m	Time	m	Time	m	Time	m
1 SU	0140	4.0	0751	1.9	1428	3.9	2040	2.0
2 M	0248	4.2	0913	1.6	1534	4.2	2150	1.7
3 TU	0348	4.5	1015	1.3	1627	4.5	2245	1.3
4 W	0439	4.8	1107	0.9	1713	4.9	2334	0.9
5 TH	0526	5.1	1155	0.5	1756	5.2		
6 F	0019	0.6	0610	5.4	1240	0.3	● 1837	5.4
7 SA	0105	0.4	0656	5.5	1324	0.2	1919	5.4
8 SU	0150	0.3	0742	5.4	1407	0.3	2003	5.3
9 M	0235	0.4	0832	5.2	1451	0.5	2050	5.1
10 TU	0321	0.6	0926	4.9	1536	0.9	2141	4.8
11 W	0410	0.9	1026	4.6	1623	1.2	2241	4.5
12 TH	0504	1.2	1131	4.2	1715	1.6	2350	4.2
13 F ◐	0605	1.6	1239	4.0	1818	2.0		
14 SA	0104	4.0	0717	1.8	1352	3.9	1934	2.1
15 SU	0220	4.0	0835	1.8	1501	3.9	2055	2.1
16 M	0326	4.0	0942	1.7	1558	4.0	2159	1.9
17 TU	0417	4.1	1034	1.6	1642	4.2	2249	1.7
18 W	0458	4.3	1117	1.4	1719	4.4	2331	1.5
19 TH	0534	4.4	1155	1.2	1752	4.6		
20 F	0008	1.3	0605	4.5	1230	1.1	1822	4.7
21 SA	0043	1.2	0635	4.6	1302	1.0	○ 1852	4.8
22 SU	0116	1.1	0706	4.6	1334	1.0	1922	4.9
23 M	0149	1.0	0737	4.6	1406	1.0	1953	4.8
24 TU	0223	1.0	0811	4.6	1438	1.1	2027	4.8
25 W	0258	1.1	0849	4.5	1513	1.2	2106	4.7
26 TH	0335	1.2	0933	4.3	1551	1.4	2152	4.5
27 F	0418	1.3	1025	4.2	1635	1.6	2247	4.4
28 SA	0507	1.5	1129	4.1	1729	1.8	2354	4.2
29 SU ◑	0606	1.6	1242	4.0	1839	1.9		
30 M	0106	4.2	0718	1.6	1354	4.0	1959	1.9
31 TU	0214	4.3	0834	1.5	1500	4.2	2113	1.7

JUNE

Day	Time	m	Time	m	Time	m	Time	m
1 W	0316	4.5	0941	1.3	1559	4.5	2215	1.4
2 TH	0413	4.7	1039	1.0	1650	4.7	2310	1.1
3 F	0506	5.0	1132	0.8	1737	5.0		
4 SA	0000	0.8	0555	5.2	1221	0.6	1821	5.2
5 SU	0049	0.6	0644	5.2	1307	0.5	● 1905	5.3
6 M	0136	0.5	0732	5.2	1352	0.6	1950	5.3
7 TU	0223	0.5	0821	5.1	1436	0.7	2035	5.1
8 W	0309	0.6	0911	4.9	1520	0.9	2123	4.9
9 TH	0356	0.9	1003	4.6	1605	1.2	2214	4.6
10 F	0444	1.1	1058	4.3	1652	1.5	2310	4.4
11 SA	0535	1.4	1157	4.1	1743	1.8		
12 SU	0013	4.1	0631	1.7	1300	3.9	◐ 1843	2.0
13 M	0122	4.0	0736	1.8	1406	3.9	1953	2.1
14 TU	0231	3.9	0844	1.9	1509	3.9	2105	2.1
15 W	0333	4.0	0947	1.8	1602	4.1	2206	2.0
16 TH	0423	4.1	1038	1.7	1646	4.3	2256	1.8
17 F	0505	4.2	1122	1.5	1724	4.4	2339	1.6
18 SA	0542	4.3	1201	1.4	1759	4.6		
19 SU	0017	1.4	0616	4.5	1237	1.2	1831	4.8
20 M	0055	1.2	0649	4.6	1312	1.1	○ 1903	4.9
21 TU	0131	1.1	0723	4.6	1347	1.1	1937	4.9
22 W	0207	1.0	0759	4.7	1422	1.1	2013	4.9
23 TH	0244	1.0	0838	4.6	1459	1.1	2053	4.9
24 F	0323	1.0	0921	4.6	1538	1.2	2137	4.8
25 SA	0405	1.1	1010	4.4	1622	1.4	2228	4.7
26 SU	0452	1.2	1107	4.3	1712	1.5	2328	4.5
27 M ◑	0545	1.3	1212	4.2	1812	1.7		
28 TU	0035	4.4	0647	1.5	1322	4.2	1923	1.8
29 W	0144	4.4	0758	1.5	1430	4.2	2039	1.7
30 TH	0251	4.4	0910	1.5	1535	4.4	2150	1.6

JULY

Day	Time	m	Time	m	Time	m	Time	m
1 F	0356	4.6	1017	1.3	1634	4.6	2253	1.3
2 SA	0455	4.7	1115	1.1	1725	4.9	2348	1.0
3 SU	0548	4.9	1207	1.0	1812	5.1		
4 M	0039	0.8	0637	5.0	1255	0.8	● 1855	5.2
5 TU	0127	0.6	0723	5.1	1339	0.8	1937	5.2
6 W	0212	0.6	0807	5.0	1422	0.8	2018	5.2
7 TH	0255	0.7	0850	4.9	1502	0.9	2059	5.0
8 F	0336	0.8	0933	4.7	1543	1.1	2140	4.8
9 SA	0417	1.0	1016	4.4	1623	1.4	2223	4.5
10 SU	0459	1.3	1104	4.2	1706	1.6	2311	4.3
11 M	0544	1.6	1200	4.0	1753	1.9		
12 TU	0012	4.0	0635	1.8	1304	3.9	◐ 1849	2.1
13 W	0124	3.9	0737	2.0	1411	3.9	2000	2.2
14 TH	0237	3.8	0849	2.1	1516	3.9	2116	2.2
15 F	0343	3.9	0956	2.0	1611	4.1	2220	2.0
16 SA	0436	4.0	1049	1.8	1656	4.3	2310	1.8
17 SU	0520	4.2	1134	1.6	1735	4.5	2354	1.5
18 M	0558	4.4	1214	1.4	1811	4.7		
19 TU	0034	1.3	0633	4.6	1252	1.2	○ 1845	4.9
20 W	0113	1.1	0708	4.7	1329	1.0	1920	5.1
21 TH	0151	0.9	0744	4.9	1407	0.9	1956	5.2
22 F	0229	0.7	0822	4.9	1444	0.9	2035	5.2
23 SA	0308	0.7	0903	4.9	1524	0.9	2118	5.1
24 SU	0349	0.8	0948	4.7	1606	1.1	2206	5.0
25 M	0433	0.9	1040	4.6	1653	1.3	2302	4.7
26 TU ◑	0522	1.1	1142	4.4	1747	1.5		
27 W	0008	4.5	0618	1.4	1254	4.2	1853	1.7
28 TH	0121	4.4	0726	1.6	1407	4.2	2012	1.8
29 F	0236	4.3	0845	1.7	1521	4.3	2134	1.7
30 SA	0349	4.4	1002	1.6	1626	4.5	2245	1.5
31 SU	0452	4.6	1106	1.4	1720	4.7	2343	1.2

AUGUST

Day	Time	m	Time	m	Time	m	Time	m
1 M	0545	4.8	1158	1.2	1805	5.0		
2 TU	0032	1.0	0629	4.9	1244	1.0	● 1844	5.1
3 W	0117	0.8	0709	5.0	1326	0.9	1921	5.2
4 TH	0157	0.7	0747	5.0	1404	0.9	1956	5.2
5 F	0235	0.7	0823	5.0	1441	0.9	2030	5.1
6 SA	0311	0.8	0858	4.8	1517	1.0	2103	4.9
7 SU	0346	1.0	0933	4.6	1552	1.2	2137	4.7
8 M	0422	1.2	1011	4.4	1629	1.5	2215	4.4
9 TU	0459	1.5	1056	4.2	1708	1.8	2301	4.1
10 W ◐	0541	1.8	1156	4.0	1755	2.1		
11 TH	0009	3.9	0631	2.1	1311	3.9	1854	2.3
12 F	0138	3.8	0742	2.2	1425	3.9	2017	2.4
13 SA	0259	3.8	0908	2.2	1532	4.0	2141	2.2
14 SU	0406	3.9	1018	2.1	1627	4.2	2243	2.0
15 M	0457	4.1	1109	1.8	1710	4.5	2330	1.6
16 TU	0537	4.4	1151	1.5	1747	4.8		
17 W	0012	1.3	0612	4.7	1231	1.2	1822	5.1
18 TH	0052	0.9	0647	4.9	1309	0.9	○ 1858	5.3
19 F	0130	0.7	0723	5.1	1347	0.7	1935	5.5
20 SA	0209	0.5	0800	5.2	1425	0.6	2014	5.5
21 SU	0248	0.4	0840	5.2	1505	0.7	2056	5.4
22 M	0328	0.5	0923	5.0	1546	0.8	2143	5.2
23 TU	0411	0.7	1012	4.8	1632	1.1	2238	4.9
24 W	0457	1.1	1113	4.5	1724	1.4	2348	4.6
25 TH ◑	0552	1.5	1229	4.3	1830	1.8		
26 F	0107	4.3	0700	1.8	1351	4.2	1955	2.0
27 SA	0229	4.2	0828	2.0	1513	4.2	2128	1.9
28 SU	0347	4.3	0955	1.9	1621	4.4	2241	1.6
29 M	0449	4.5	1059	1.6	1712	4.7	2336	1.3
30 TU	0537	4.7	1148	1.4	1753	4.9		
31 W	0020	1.0	0616	4.9	1230	1.1	1829	5.1

Chart Datum: 2·75 metres below Ordnance Datum (Newlyn)
HAT is 5·9 metres above Chart Datum

TIME ZONE (UT)
For Summer Time add ONE hour in **non-shaded areas**

SCOTLAND – ULLAPOOL

LAT 57°54'N LONG 5°09'W

TIMES AND HEIGHTS OF HIGH AND LOW WATERS

Dates in amber are **SPRINGS**
Dates in grey are **NEAPS**

2016

SEPTEMBER

Date	Day	Time	m	Time	m	Time	m	Time	m	Moon
1	TH	0100	0.8	0650	5.0	1308	1.0	1901	5.2	●
2	F	0136	0.7	0723	5.1	1343	0.9	1931	5.2	
3	SA	0210	0.7	0753	5.0	1416	0.9	2000	5.1	
4	SU	0242	0.8	0823	4.9	1448	1.0	2030	5.0	
5	M	0313	1.0	0854	4.8	1521	1.2	2100	4.8	
6	TU	0345	1.2	0927	4.6	1554	1.4	2133	4.5	
7	W	0418	1.5	1004	4.4	1630	1.7	2212	4.3	
8	TH	0455	1.8	1053	4.1	1711	2.0	2306	4.0	
9	F	0539	2.1	1208	3.9	1803	2.2			◐
10	SA	0039	3.8	0639	2.3	1335	3.9	1918	2.4	
11	SU	0214	3.7	0815	2.4	1450	4.0	2059	2.3	
12	M	0332	3.9	0944	2.2	1552	4.2	2212	2.0	
13	TU	0428	4.1	1041	1.9	1640	4.5	2303	1.6	
14	W	0511	4.5	1126	1.5	1720	4.8	2346	1.2	
15	TH	0548	4.8	1206	1.2	1757	5.2			
16	F	0026	0.8	0623	5.1	1246	0.8	1833	5.5	○
17	SA	0106	0.5	0659	5.4	1324	0.6	1911	5.7	
18	SU	0145	0.3	0736	5.5	1404	0.5	1951	5.7	
19	M	0225	0.3	0816	5.4	1444	0.5	2035	5.6	
20	TU	0306	0.4	0859	5.2	1527	0.7	2123	5.3	
21	W	0348	0.7	0948	4.9	1613	1.0	2220	4.9	
22	TH	0435	1.1	1049	4.6	1706	1.4	2334	4.5	
23	F	0529	1.6	1210	4.3	1813	1.8			◑
24	SA	0057	4.2	0638	2.0	1337	4.2	1943	2.0	
25	SU	0222	4.1	0813	2.2	1501	4.2	2120	1.9	
26	M	0340	4.2	0944	2.1	1608	4.4	2229	1.7	
27	TU	0438	4.4	1045	1.8	1658	4.7	2319	1.4	
28	W	0522	4.7	1131	1.5	1736	4.9			
29	TH	0001	1.1	0557	4.9	1210	1.3	1809	5.0	
30	F	0038	1.0	0628	5.0	1246	1.1	1838	5.1	

OCTOBER

Date	Day	Time	m	Time	m	Time	m	Time	m	Moon
1	SA	0111	0.9	0657	5.1	1319	1.0	1906	5.2	●
2	SU	0142	0.8	0725	5.1	1350	1.0	1933	5.1	
3	M	0212	0.9	0753	5.1	1421	1.1	2001	5.0	
4	TU	0242	1.0	0822	4.9	1452	1.2	2030	4.8	
5	W	0312	1.2	0852	4.8	1524	1.4	2103	4.6	
6	TH	0344	1.5	0928	4.6	1559	1.6	2141	4.3	
7	F	0419	1.7	1011	4.3	1638	1.9	2230	4.1	
8	SA	0500	2.0	1112	4.1	1727	2.1	2350	3.9	
9	SU	0554	2.3	1243	4.0	1834	2.3			◐
10	M	0130	3.8	0720	2.5	1404	4.0	2011	2.3	
11	TU	0251	3.9	0902	2.3	1511	4.2	2134	2.0	
12	W	0353	4.2	1007	2.0	1605	4.5	2230	1.6	
13	TH	0440	4.5	1056	1.6	1649	4.9	2316	1.2	
14	F	0520	4.9	1138	1.2	1729	5.3	2358	0.8	
15	SA	0557	5.3	1220	0.8	1809	5.6			
16	SU	0040	0.5	0635	5.5	1301	0.6	1849	5.8	○
17	M	0121	0.3	0713	5.6	1343	0.4	1931	5.8	
18	TU	0203	0.3	0754	5.6	1425	0.5	2017	5.6	
19	W	0245	0.5	0839	5.4	1510	0.7	2108	5.3	
20	TH	0328	0.8	0928	5.1	1558	1.0	2208	4.9	
21	F	0416	1.3	1030	4.7	1652	1.4	2321	4.5	
22	SA	0510	1.7	1149	4.4	1759	1.8			◑
23	SU	0041	4.2	0618	2.1	1315	4.3	1924	2.0	
24	M	0203	4.1	0747	2.3	1438	4.3	2055	2.0	
25	TU	0319	4.2	0916	2.2	1545	4.4	2203	1.8	
26	W	0416	4.4	1018	2.0	1635	4.6	2253	1.5	
27	TH	0459	4.6	1105	1.7	1714	4.7	2334	1.3	
28	F	0534	4.8	1145	1.5	1746	4.9			
29	SA	0010	1.2	0604	4.9	1221	1.3	1815	5.0	
30	SU	0044	1.1	0633	5.1	1254	1.2	1843	5.0	●
31	M	0115	1.0	0701	5.1	1326	1.2	1911	5.0	

NOVEMBER

Date	Day	Time	m	Time	m	Time	m	Time	m	Moon
1	TU	0145	1.1	0729	5.1	1356	1.2	1939	4.9	
2	W	0215	1.2	0757	5.0	1428	1.2	2009	4.8	
3	TH	0245	1.3	0828	4.9	1500	1.4	2043	4.7	
4	F	0317	1.5	0903	4.7	1535	1.6	2122	4.4	
5	SA	0352	1.7	0945	4.5	1615	1.8	2210	4.2	
6	SU	0432	2.0	1039	4.3	1702	2.0	2318	4.0	
7	M	0523	2.2	1155	4.2	1802	2.2			◐
8	TU	0047	3.9	0636	2.4	1317	4.2	1923	2.2	
9	W	0206	4.0	0810	2.4	1427	4.3	2047	2.0	
10	TH	0312	4.2	0926	2.1	1526	4.6	2152	1.6	
11	F	0407	4.6	1021	1.7	1617	4.9	2244	1.3	
12	SA	0452	4.9	1110	1.3	1703	5.2	2331	0.9	
13	SU	0533	5.3	1155	1.0	1747	5.5			
14	M	0015	0.6	0614	5.5	1240	0.7	1831	5.7	○
15	TU	0100	0.5	0655	5.7	1325	0.5	1917	5.7	
16	W	0143	0.5	0738	5.6	1410	0.5	2005	5.6	
17	TH	0227	0.6	0824	5.5	1457	0.7	2057	5.3	
18	F	0312	0.9	0914	5.2	1546	1.0	2155	4.9	
19	SA	0359	1.3	1011	4.9	1639	1.3	2301	4.6	
20	SU	0451	1.7	1120	4.6	1740	1.7			
21	M	0011	4.3	0551	2.1	1238	4.4	1850	1.9	◑
22	TU	0126	4.2	0706	2.3	1357	4.3	2008	2.0	
23	W	0241	4.2	0827	2.3	1508	4.3	2121	1.9	
24	TH	0342	4.3	0938	2.2	1603	4.4	2217	1.8	
25	F	0429	4.4	1032	2.0	1646	4.5	2302	1.6	
26	SA	0508	4.6	1116	1.8	1723	4.7	2341	1.5	
27	SU	0541	4.8	1155	1.6	1755	4.8			
28	M	0016	1.4	0611	5.0	1230	1.5	1825	4.9	
29	TU	0050	1.3	0641	5.1	1304	1.3	1855	4.9	●
30	W	0121	1.2	0710	5.1	1337	1.3	1925	4.9	

DECEMBER

Date	Day	Time	m	Time	m	Time	m	Time	m	Moon
1	TH	0153	1.3	0740	5.1	1409	1.3	1957	4.8	
2	F	0225	1.3	0812	5.0	1443	1.3	2031	4.7	
3	SA	0258	1.5	0848	4.9	1519	1.4	2110	4.6	
4	SU	0333	1.6	0928	4.8	1558	1.6	2156	4.4	
5	M	0413	1.8	1017	4.6	1643	1.7	2252	4.3	
6	TU	0501	2.0	1117	4.5	1737	1.9			
7	W	0004	4.2	0601	2.2	1231	4.4	1843	1.9	◐
8	TH	0121	4.2	0719	2.2	1343	4.4	1959	1.9	
9	F	0230	4.3	0839	2.1	1448	4.6	2110	1.7	
10	SA	0332	4.5	0946	1.8	1547	4.8	2212	1.4	
11	SU	0426	4.8	1043	1.5	1641	5.1	2306	1.1	
12	M	0514	5.1	1135	1.2	1731	5.3	2355	0.9	
13	TU	0559	5.4	1224	0.9	1820	5.5			
14	W	0043	0.7	0643	5.6	1312	0.7	1908	5.5	○
15	TH	0129	0.7	0727	5.6	1400	0.6	1956	5.5	
16	F	0214	0.8	0813	5.5	1447	0.7	2045	5.3	
17	SA	0258	1.0	0859	5.4	1534	0.9	2136	5.0	
18	SU	0343	1.2	0949	5.1	1622	1.2	2230	4.7	
19	M	0430	1.5	1043	4.8	1712	1.5	2328	4.4	
20	TU	0520	1.9	1145	4.5	1808	1.8			
21	W	0032	4.2	0617	2.2	1256	4.3	1910	2.0	◑
22	TH	0143	4.1	0725	2.3	1411	4.2	2020	2.1	
23	F	0253	4.1	0840	2.4	1519	4.2	2129	2.1	
24	SA	0351	4.2	0949	2.3	1613	4.3	2225	2.0	
25	SU	0438	4.4	1044	2.1	1658	4.4	2311	1.8	
26	M	0518	4.6	1129	1.9	1736	4.5	2351	1.6	
27	TU	0553	4.8	1208	1.7	1811	4.7			
28	W	0027	1.5	0624	5.0	1245	1.5	1842	4.8	
29	TH	0102	1.4	0656	5.1	1320	1.4	1914	4.8	●
30	F	0136	1.3	0727	5.1	1355	1.3	1946	4.9	
31	SA	0209	1.3	0759	5.2	1430	1.2	2020	4.9	

Chart Datum: 2·75 metres below Ordnance Datum (Newlyn)
HAT is 5·9 metres above Chart Datum

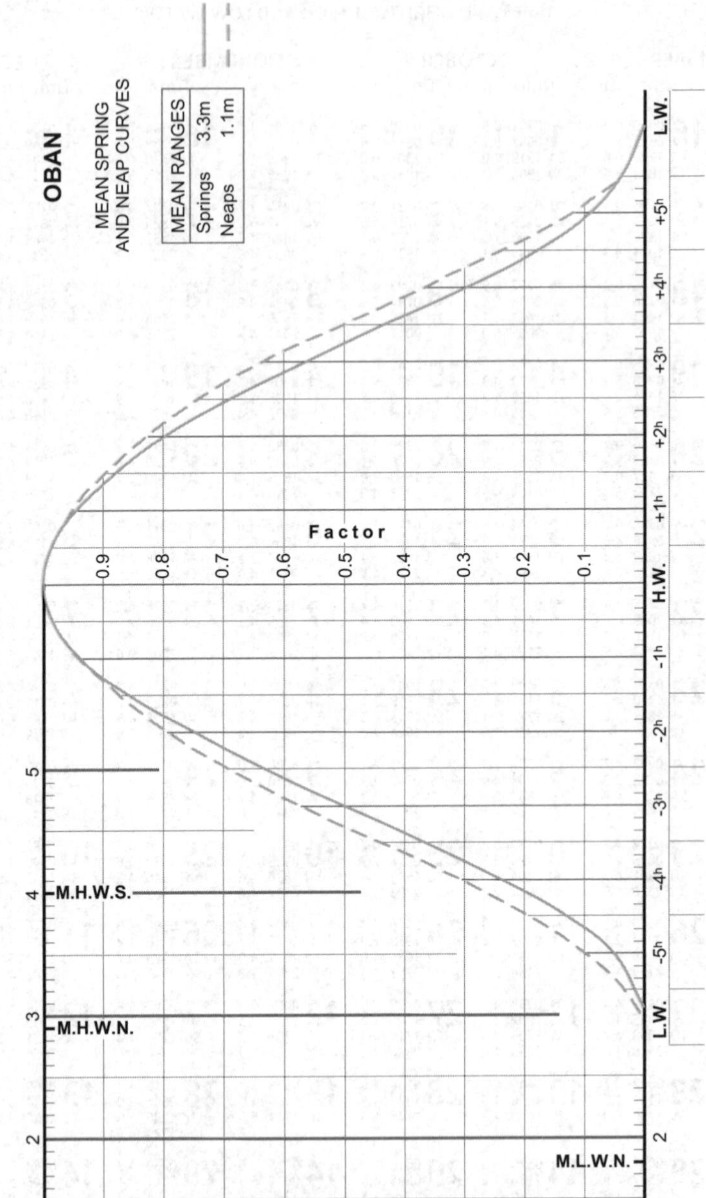
OBAN
MEAN SPRING AND NEAP CURVES
MEAN RANGES
Springs 3.3m
Neaps 1.1m
Factor
0.9
0.8
0.7
0.6
0.5
0.4
0.3
0.2
0.1
L.W.
-5h
-4h
-3h
-2h
-1h
H.W.
+1h
+2h
+3h
+4h
+5h
L.W.
H.W.Hts.m.
0
1
2
3
4
5
M.H.W.S.
M.H.W.N.
CHART DATUM
M.L.W.S.
M.L.W.N.
L.W.Hts.m.

TIME ZONE (UT)
For Summer Time add ONE hour in **non-shaded areas**

SCOTLAND – OBAN

LAT 56°25′N LONG 5°29′W

TIMES AND HEIGHTS OF HIGH AND LOW WATERS

Dates in amber are **SPRINGS**
Dates in grey are **NEAPS**

2016

JANUARY

Date	Time	m	Date	Time	m
1 F	0401 0943 1647 2215	1.5 3.4 1.9 3.2	16 SA	0358 1000 1636 ◐ 2214	1.1 3.6 1.3 3.2
2 SA	0449 1032 1743 ◑ 2317	1.7 3.2 2.0 3.0	17 SU	0459 1107 1741 2324	1.3 3.3 1.5 3.1
3 SU	0543 1139 1848	1.8 3.1 2.1	18 M	0610 1246 1852	1.4 3.2 1.5
4 M	0051 0641 1313 1959	3.0 1.9 3.1 2.0	19 TU	0100 0729 1419 2004	3.0 1.5 3.3 1.5
5 TU	0214 0744 1431 2104	3.1 1.9 3.2 1.9	20 W	0232 0851 1527 2112	3.2 1.4 3.4 1.4
6 W	0309 0849 1525 2152	3.2 1.8 3.4 1.7	21 TH	0336 1001 1619 2209	3.4 1.3 3.6 1.2
7 TH	0355 0947 1610 2231	3.4 1.6 3.5 1.4	22 F	0422 1056 1700 2257	3.6 1.1 3.7 1.0
8 F	0436 1036 1651 2307	3.6 1.4 3.7 1.2	23 SA	0503 1141 1737 2340	3.8 1.0 3.8 0.9
9 SA	0515 1120 1729 2343	3.8 1.2 3.8 1.0	24 SU ○	0541 1223 1811	4.0 1.0 3.9
10 SU ●	0552 1202 1804	4.0 1.0 3.9	25 M	0020 0617 1302 1844	0.8 4.1 1.0 3.9
11 M	0019 0628 1243 1837	0.9 4.0 0.9 3.9	26 TU	0059 0653 1339 1917	0.8 4.1 1.1 3.9
12 TU	0058 0703 1324 1912	0.8 4.1 0.8 3.9	27 W	0136 0727 1414 1949	0.8 4.0 1.2 3.8
13 W	0137 0741 1406 1951	0.7 4.0 0.9 3.8	28 TH	0212 0800 1448 2021	1.0 3.9 1.4 3.7
14 TH	0220 0822 1451 2033	0.8 3.9 1.0 3.6	29 F	0248 0832 1522 2054	1.1 3.7 1.6 3.5
15 F	0306 0908 1540 2120	0.9 3.8 1.1 3.4	30 SA	0325 0905 1600 2131	1.4 3.6 1.7 3.4
			31 SU	0405 0941 1645 2213	1.6 3.4 1.9 3.2

FEBRUARY

Date	Time	m	Date	Time	m
1 M	0452 1024 1742 ◑ 2311	1.8 3.2 2.0 3.0	16 TU	0546 1211 1819	1.4 3.0 1.5
2 TU	0549 1126 1849	1.9 3.0 2.1	17 W	0025 0706 1405 1935	2.9 1.5 3.0 1.6
3 W	0101 0654 1342 2003	2.9 2.0 3.0 2.0	18 TH	0215 0846 1527 2053	3.0 1.5 3.1 1.5
4 TH	0238 0805 1505 2113	3.0 1.9 3.1 1.8	19 F	0332 1002 1620 2156	3.2 1.4 3.3 1.3
5 F	0334 0917 1555 2204	3.2 1.7 3.3 1.5	20 SA	0415 1052 1654 2244	3.4 1.2 3.5 1.1
6 SA	0419 1017 1637 2246	3.5 1.4 3.5 1.2	21 SU	0451 1133 1724 2325	3.7 1.1 3.7 0.9
7 SU	0459 1105 1715 2324	3.7 1.1 3.7 0.9	22 M ○	0526 1209 1755	3.8 1.0 3.8
8 M ●	0538 1148 1750	4.0 0.8 3.9	23 TU	0003 0600 1243 1826	0.8 4.0 0.9 3.9
9 TU	0002 0614 1229 1823	0.6 4.1 0.6 4.0	24 W	0040 0633 1316 1856	0.7 4.0 1.0 4.0
10 W	0042 0650 1309 1858	0.4 4.2 0.5 4.0	25 TH	0114 0704 1347 1925	0.7 4.0 1.0 3.9
11 TH	0123 0727 1350 1935	0.4 4.2 0.5 3.9	26 F	0147 0734 1417 1954	0.9 3.9 1.2 3.8
12 F	0205 0806 1432 2015	0.4 4.0 0.6 3.8	27 SA	0218 0803 1446 2024	1.0 3.8 1.4 3.7
13 SA	0251 0849 1518 2058	0.6 3.8 0.8 3.5	28 SU	0249 0831 1515 2055	1.2 3.6 1.5 3.5
14 SU	0340 0936 1610 2147	0.8 3.5 1.1 3.3	29 M	0323 0901 1549 2132	1.5 3.4 1.7 3.3
15 M	0438 1035 1710 ◐ 2249	1.1 3.2 1.3 3.0			

MARCH

Date	Time	m	Date	Time	m
1 TU	0403 0937 1640 ◑ 2217	1.7 3.2 1.9 3.0	16 W	0527 1145 1750 2356	1.3 2.8 1.4 2.8
2 W	0459 1026 1752 2326	1.9 3.0 2.0 2.9	17 TH	0650 1352 1907	1.6 2.8 1.5
3 TH	0613 1151 1910	2.0 2.8 2.0	18 F	0156 0843 1522 2031	2.9 1.5 2.9 1.5
4 F	0200 0732 1444 2028	2.9 1.9 2.9 1.8	19 SA	0327 0953 1609 2137	3.1 1.4 3.1 1.3
5 SA	0311 0853 1538 2132	3.1 1.6 3.1 1.5	20 SU	0358 1038 1634 2225	3.3 1.2 3.3 1.1
6 SU	0358 0957 1619 2220	3.4 1.3 3.4 1.1	21 M	0430 1115 1701 2305	3.5 1.1 3.5 0.9
7 M	0439 1046 1656 2303	3.7 0.9 3.7 0.7	22 TU	0503 1147 1731 2341	3.7 1.0 3.7 0.8
8 TU	0517 1129 1730 2343	4.0 0.6 3.9 0.4	23 W ○	0537 1218 1802	3.9 0.9 3.9
9 W ●	0555 1210 1804	4.2 0.4 4.0	24 TH	0015 0608 1248 1831	0.7 4.0 0.9 3.9
10 TH	0024 0632 1250 1839	0.2 4.3 0.3 4.1	25 F	0048 0639 1317 1859	0.8 4.0 1.0 3.9
11 F	0107 0709 1330 1917	0.1 4.2 0.3 4.0	26 SA	0120 0708 1346 1927	0.9 3.9 1.1 3.8
12 SA	0150 0748 1412 1956	0.2 4.1 0.4 3.8	27 SU	0150 0736 1413 1956	1.0 3.8 1.2 3.7
13 SU	0236 0829 1457 2038	0.4 3.8 0.6 3.6	28 M	0218 0802 1435 2027	1.2 3.6 1.4 3.5
14 M	0325 0915 1547 2125	0.7 3.5 0.9 3.3	29 TU	0246 0831 1502 2101	1.4 3.4 1.6 3.3
15 TU	0421 1010 1644 ◐ 2223	1.0 3.1 1.2 3.0	30 W	0322 0906 1544 2144	1.6 3.2 1.7 3.1
			31 TH	0415 0953 1656 ◑ 2246	1.8 3.0 1.9 2.9

APRIL

Date	Time	m	Date	Time	m
1 F	0538 1108 1823	1.9 2.8 1.9	16 SA	0123 0821 1449 1956	2.8 1.6 2.8 1.5
2 SA	0058 0705 1408 1943	2.9 1.8 2.8 1.7	17 SU	0245 0928 1535 2105	3.0 1.5 3.0 1.4
3 SU	0237 0827 1511 2054	3.1 1.6 3.1 1.4	18 M	0326 1012 1601 2156	3.2 1.3 3.2 1.2
4 M	0329 0931 1553 2150	3.4 1.2 3.3 1.0	19 TU	0400 1048 1630 2237	3.4 1.2 3.4 1.0
5 TU	0412 1022 1630 2237	3.8 0.8 3.6 0.7	20 W	0435 1119 1702 2313	3.6 1.1 3.6 0.9
6 W	0453 1106 1706 2322	4.0 0.5 3.9 0.4	21 TH	0509 1148 1734 2347	3.7 1.0 3.8 0.9
7 TH ●	0532 1147 1742	4.2 0.3 4.0	22 F ○	0542 1217 1805	3.8 0.9 3.9
8 F	0005 0610 1228 1819	0.2 4.3 0.2 4.1	23 SA	0020 0614 1247 1834	0.9 3.9 1.0 3.9
9 SA	0050 0650 1310 1858	0.1 4.2 0.2 4.0	24 SU	0052 0644 1317 1904	0.9 3.8 1.0 3.8
10 SU	0135 0730 1352 1939	0.2 4.0 0.3 3.9	25 M	0124 0713 1344 1934	1.0 3.7 1.1 3.7
11 M	0221 0812 1437 2021	0.4 3.8 0.6 3.7	26 TU	0153 0741 1408 2005	1.2 3.6 1.3 3.6
12 TU	0311 0857 1526 2107	0.7 3.4 0.8 3.4	27 W	0223 0811 1438 2041	1.3 3.4 1.4 3.4
13 W	0406 0951 1620 2203	1.1 3.0 1.1 3.1	28 TH	0301 0849 1520 2125	1.5 3.2 1.6 3.2
14 TH	0510 1119 1722 ◐ 2325	1.4 2.8 1.4 2.9	29 F	0355 0939 1621 2225	1.6 3.0 1.7 3.1
15 F	0633 1325 1834	1.6 2.7 1.5	30 SA	0512 1051 1740 ◑ 2356	1.7 2.8 1.7 3.0

Chart Datum: 2·10 metres below Ordnance Datum (Newlyn)
HAT is 4·5 metres above Chart Datum

TIME ZONE (UT)
For Summer Time add ONE hour in **non-shaded areas**

SCOTLAND – OBAN

LAT 56°25'N LONG 5°29'W

TIMES AND HEIGHTS OF HIGH AND LOW WATERS

Dates in amber are **SPRINGS**
Dates in grey are **NEAPS**

2016

MAY

Date	Day	Time	m	Time	m	Time	m	Time	m
1	SU	0637	1.7	1247	2.8	1900	1.6		
2	M	0150	3.2	0755	1.5	1429	3.0	2014	1.4
3	TU	0254	3.5	0900	1.2	1520	3.3	2117	1.0
4	W	0343	3.7	0953	0.9	1601	3.6	2211	0.7
5	TH	0427	4.0	1040	0.6	1640	3.8	2301	0.5
6	F	0509	4.1	1124	0.4	1720	4.0	● 2348	0.3
7	SA	0551	4.2	1207	0.3	1801	4.1		
8	SU	0034	0.3	0632	4.1	1250	0.3	1842	4.0
9	M	0121	0.3	0714	4.0	1334	0.4	1924	3.9
10	TU	0209	0.5	0757	3.7	1418	0.6	2007	3.7
11	W	0258	0.8	0843	3.4	1506	0.8	2052	3.5
12	TH	0351	1.1	0934	3.1	1557	1.1	2143	3.2
13	F	0451	1.4	1043	2.8	1653	1.3	◐ 2247	3.0
14	SA	0604	1.6	1237	2.7	1755	1.5		
15	SU	0021	2.9	0735	1.7	1353	2.8	1905	1.5
16	M	0150	2.9	0848	1.6	1444	2.9	2016	1.5
17	TU	0244	3.1	0937	1.5	1522	3.1	2115	1.4
18	W	0325	3.2	1015	1.4	1556	3.3	2201	1.3
19	TH	0403	3.4	1048	1.2	1631	3.5	2239	1.2
20	F	0440	3.6	1117	1.1	1706	3.7	2315	1.1
21	SA	0516	3.7	1147	1.1	1740	3.8	○ 2351	1.0
22	SU	0551	3.7	1218	1.0	1813	3.8		
23	M	0026	1.0	0624	3.7	1251	1.0	1844	3.8
24	TU	0102	1.1	0655	3.7	1321	1.1	1917	3.7
25	W	0137	1.1	0727	3.6	1351	1.2	1951	3.6
26	TH	0212	1.2	0801	3.4	1425	1.3	2029	3.5
27	F	0253	1.4	0842	3.3	1508	1.4	2114	3.4
28	SA	0345	1.5	0932	3.1	1601	1.4	2210	3.3
29	SU	0451	1.5	1035	3.0	1708	1.5	◑ 2322	3.2
30	M	0607	1.5	1156	2.9	1823	1.5		
31	TU	0056	3.3	0721	1.4	1332	3.0	1937	1.3

JUNE

Date	Day	Time	m	Time	m	Time	m	Time	m
1	W	0217	3.4	0827	1.2	1442	3.2	2047	1.1
2	TH	0316	3.6	0925	1.0	1534	3.5	2148	0.9
3	F	0406	3.8	1016	0.8	1620	3.7	2243	0.7
4	SA	0452	4.0	1104	0.6	1703	3.9	2333	0.5
5	SU	0536	4.0	1149	0.5	1747	4.0	●	
6	M	0022	0.5	0619	4.0	1234	0.5	1829	4.0
7	TU	0110	0.6	0702	3.9	1317	0.5	1911	4.0
8	W	0157	0.7	0745	3.7	1401	0.7	1953	3.8
9	TH	0244	0.9	0828	3.5	1446	0.8	2036	3.6
10	F	0333	1.2	0912	3.2	1532	1.1	2120	3.4
11	SA	0424	1.4	1003	3.0	1620	1.3	2209	3.2
12	SU	0521	1.6	1108	2.9	1713	1.5	◐ 2308	3.0
13	M	0627	1.7	1239	2.8	1809	1.6		
14	TU	0024	2.9	0743	1.8	1348	2.9	1910	1.6
15	W	0144	3.0	0848	1.7	1439	3.0	2013	1.6
16	TH	0243	3.1	0936	1.6	1522	3.2	2111	1.5
17	F	0330	3.3	1014	1.4	1602	3.4	2200	1.4
18	SA	0413	3.4	1048	1.3	1641	3.5	2243	1.3
19	SU	0454	3.6	1121	1.2	1719	3.7	2325	1.2
20	M	0533	3.7	1154	1.1	1756	3.8	○	
21	TU	0005	1.1	0609	3.7	1229	1.0	1830	3.8
22	W	0045	1.0	0643	3.7	1303	1.0	1905	3.8
23	TH	0124	1.0	0716	3.6	1337	1.0	1940	3.8
24	F	0203	1.0	0751	3.5	1414	1.0	2019	3.7
25	SA	0245	1.1	0832	3.4	1456	1.1	2102	3.6
26	SU	0333	1.2	0919	3.3	1545	1.2	2153	3.5
27	M	0429	1.3	1013	3.1	1643	1.3	◑ 2255	3.3
28	TU	0536	1.4	1121	3.0	1752	1.4		
29	W	0015	3.3	0647	1.4	1247	3.0	1907	1.4
30	TH	0147	3.3	0757	1.3	1413	3.2	2022	1.3

JULY

Date	Day	Time	m	Time	m	Time	m	Time	m
1	F	0258	3.5	0901	1.1	1517	3.4	2131	1.1
2	SA	0355	3.6	0957	1.0	1608	3.6	2231	0.9
3	SU	0445	3.8	1048	0.8	1654	3.8	2324	0.8
4	M	0530	3.8	1135	0.7	1737	3.9	●	
5	TU	0013	0.7	0612	3.9	1220	0.6	1818	4.0
6	W	0059	0.7	0652	3.8	1302	0.6	1858	4.0
7	TH	0144	0.8	0730	3.7	1344	0.7	1937	3.9
8	F	0226	1.0	0808	3.6	1424	0.8	2015	3.8
9	SA	0308	1.2	0845	3.4	1505	1.0	2052	3.6
10	SU	0350	1.4	0923	3.3	1546	1.2	2131	3.4
11	M	0434	1.6	1007	3.1	1631	1.4	2215	3.2
12	TU	0524	1.8	1102	3.0	1720	1.6	◐ 2308	3.0
13	W	0623	1.9	1222	2.9	1815	1.7		
14	TH	0024	2.9	0733	1.9	1349	2.9	1915	1.8
15	F	0153	3.0	0845	1.8	1450	3.1	2019	1.7
16	SA	0301	3.1	0941	1.6	1538	3.2	2122	1.6
17	SU	0352	3.3	1023	1.4	1622	3.4	2217	1.4
18	M	0437	3.5	1100	1.2	1703	3.6	2304	1.2
19	TU	0519	3.6	1135	1.0	1741	3.8	○ 2348	1.0
20	W	0557	3.7	1209	0.9	1818	3.9		
21	TH	0029	0.9	0630	3.8	1245	0.8	1852	4.0
22	F	0109	0.8	0702	3.8	1321	0.7	1927	4.0
23	SA	0149	0.8	0737	3.7	1400	0.7	2004	3.9
24	SU	0230	0.8	0815	3.6	1442	0.8	2046	3.8
25	M	0315	0.9	0859	3.4	1529	0.9	2133	3.6
26	TU	0407	1.1	0949	3.3	1623	1.1	◑ 2229	3.4
27	W	0508	1.3	1050	3.1	1730	1.3	2344	3.2
28	TH	0617	1.4	1215	3.0	1845	1.4		
29	F	0129	3.1	0730	1.4	1359	3.1	2005	1.4
30	SA	0252	3.2	0842	1.3	1515	3.3	2125	1.3
31	SU	0356	3.4	0944	1.1	1608	3.5	2229	1.1

AUGUST

Date	Day	Time	m	Time	m	Time	m	Time	m
1	M	0445	3.6	1037	0.9	1650	3.7	2320	1.0
2	TU	0526	3.7	1123	0.8	1728	3.9	●	
3	W	0004	0.9	0602	3.8	1206	0.7	1805	4.0
4	TH	0045	0.8	0637	3.9	1246	0.6	1841	4.0
5	F	0124	0.9	0710	3.8	1324	0.7	1916	4.0
6	SA	0202	1.0	0743	3.8	1400	0.8	1949	3.9
7	SU	0237	1.1	0814	3.6	1435	1.0	2021	3.7
8	M	0313	1.3	0846	3.5	1512	1.2	2054	3.5
9	TU	0350	1.5	0922	3.3	1552	1.4	2129	3.3
10	W	0434	1.7	1004	3.1	1637	1.7	◐ 2209	3.1
11	TH	0528	1.9	1102	3.0	1731	1.8	2303	3.0
12	F	0634	2.0	1249	2.9	1833	1.9		
13	SA	0102	2.9	0750	1.9	1426	3.0	1942	1.9
14	SU	0242	3.0	0906	1.7	1522	3.2	2055	1.7
15	M	0339	3.2	0959	1.5	1606	3.4	2159	1.5
16	TU	0423	3.4	1039	1.2	1646	3.7	2248	1.2
17	W	0503	3.6	1115	1.0	1724	3.9	2331	0.9
18	TH	0539	3.8	1149	0.7	1801	4.0	○	
19	F	0011	0.7	0612	3.9	1225	0.5	1835	4.1
20	SA	0051	0.6	0643	3.9	1303	0.4	1909	4.1
21	SU	0130	0.5	0717	3.9	1343	0.4	1946	4.1
22	M	0211	0.6	0755	3.8	1426	0.6	2026	3.9
23	TU	0255	0.7	0836	3.6	1513	0.8	2110	3.6
24	W	0344	0.9	0924	3.3	1607	1.0	2204	3.3
25	TH	0442	1.2	1023	3.1	1713	1.3	◑ 2320	3.1
26	F	0551	1.4	1152	2.9	1829	1.5		
27	SA	0123	3.0	0707	1.5	1358	3.0	2000	1.5
28	SU	0253	3.1	0826	1.4	1519	3.2	2132	1.4
29	M	0356	3.3	0933	1.2	1606	3.4	2229	1.2
30	TU	0439	3.5	1024	1.0	1639	3.7	2312	1.1
31	W	0511	3.6	1108	0.8	1712	3.9	2349	0.9

Chart Datum: 2·10 metres below Ordnance Datum (Newlyn)
HAT is 4·5 metres above Chart Datum

TIME ZONE (UT)
For Summer Time add ONE hour in **non-shaded areas**

SCOTLAND – OBAN

LAT 56°25′N LONG 5°29′W

TIMES AND HEIGHTS OF HIGH AND LOW WATERS

Dates in amber are **SPRINGS**
Dates in grey are **NEAPS**

2016

SEPTEMBER

Date	Time	m	Date	Time	m
1 TH ●	0543 1148 1746	3.8 0.7 4.0	16 F ○	0516 1126 1737 2349	3.8 0.6 4.2 0.6
2 F	0025 0614 1225 1818	0.9 3.9 0.7 4.1	17 SA	0548 1204 1812	4.0 0.4 4.3
3 SA	0059 0645 1300 1849	0.9 3.9 0.7 4.1	18 SU	0028 0620 1244 1847	0.4 4.0 0.3 4.3
4 SU	0132 0714 1333 1920	1.0 3.9 0.8 4.0	19 M	0107 0655 1325 1924	0.4 4.0 0.3 4.2
5 M	0204 0743 1406 1950	1.1 3.8 1.0 3.9	20 TU	0149 0733 1410 2004	0.4 3.9 0.5 4.0
6 TU	0236 0812 1439 2019	1.3 3.7 1.2 3.7	21 W	0233 0815 1458 2049	0.6 3.7 0.7 3.6
7 W	0310 0845 1514 2049	1.5 3.5 1.5 3.5	22 TH	0322 0902 1553 2141	0.9 3.5 1.1 3.3
8 TH	0348 0922 1557 2123	1.7 3.3 1.7 3.2	23 F ◑	0419 1000 1659 2259	1.2 3.2 1.4 3.0
9 F ◐	0439 1010 1651 2207	1.9 3.1 1.9 3.0	24 SA	0526 1134 1818	1.4 3.0 1.6
10 SA	0546 1131 1759 2324	2.0 2.9 2.1 2.8	25 SU	0117 0642 1354 2005	2.9 1.5 3.0 1.6
11 SU	0704 1405 1916	2.0 3.0 2.0	26 M	0250 0806 1518 2128	3.0 1.5 3.2 1.5
12 M	0228 0825 1504 2035	2.9 1.8 3.2 1.8	27 TU	0348 0915 1553 2217	3.2 1.3 3.4 1.3
13 TU	0324 0927 1547 2140	3.1 1.6 3.5 1.5	28 W	0421 1005 1618 2255	3.4 1.1 3.7 1.1
14 W	0405 1011 1625 2228	3.4 1.2 3.7 1.1	29 TH	0447 1047 1648 2328	3.6 0.9 3.8 1.0
15 TH	0442 1049 1701 2310	3.6 0.9 4.0 0.8	30 F	0516 1125 1720 2359	3.8 0.8 4.0 1.0

OCTOBER

Date	Time	m	Date	Time	m
1 SA ●	0547 1200 1751	3.9 0.8 4.1	16 SU ○	0521 1142 1747	4.1 0.4 4.4
2 SU	0029 0616 1234 1821	0.9 4.0 0.8 4.1	17 M	0003 0557 1225 1825	0.4 4.2 0.3 4.4
3 M	0100 0645 1306 1851	1.0 4.0 0.9 4.0	18 TU	0045 0634 1309 1904	0.3 4.2 0.4 4.2
4 TU	0132 0714 1337 1921	1.1 4.0 1.1 3.9	19 W	0127 0715 1355 1945	0.4 4.0 0.5 4.0
5 W	0203 0743 1408 1949	1.3 3.8 1.3 3.7	20 TH	0212 0757 1445 2030	0.6 3.8 0.8 3.6
6 TH	0233 0815 1441 2017	1.5 3.6 1.6 3.5	21 F	0301 0845 1540 2122	0.9 3.6 1.1 3.3
7 F	0304 0851 1519 2049	1.7 3.4 1.8 3.3	22 SA ◑	0356 0941 1644 2236	1.1 3.3 1.5 3.0
8 SA	0346 0934 1613 2131	1.9 3.2 2.0 3.1	23 SU	0459 1106 1803	1.4 3.1 1.7
9 SU ◐	0454 1038 1728 2239	2.0 3.0 2.1 2.9	24 M	0055 0611 1328 1950	2.8 1.6 3.1 1.7
10 M	0615 1327 1850	2.0 3.0 2.1	25 TU	0226 0733 1454 2106	2.9 1.6 3.2 1.6
11 TU	0159 0735 1434 2010	2.9 1.9 3.2 1.8	26 W	0322 0845 1526 2153	3.1 1.4 3.4 1.4
12 W	0258 0844 1519 2113	3.1 1.6 3.5 1.5	27 TH	0351 0938 1550 2229	3.3 1.3 3.6 1.3
13 TH	0339 0936 1557 2201	3.4 1.3 3.8 1.1	28 F	0416 1021 1620 2301	3.5 1.1 3.8 1.2
14 F	0414 1020 1634 2244	3.6 0.9 4.1 0.8	29 SA	0446 1058 1652 2330	3.7 1.0 3.9 1.1
15 SA	0448 1101 1710 2324	3.9 0.6 4.3 0.5	30 SU ●	0518 1133 1724 2359	3.9 1.0 4.0 1.1
			31 M	0549 1206 1755	4.0 1.0 4.1

NOVEMBER

Date	Time	m	Date	Time	m
1 TU	0030 0619 1239 1826	1.1 4.1 1.1 4.0	16 W	0024 0618 1256 1847	0.4 4.2 0.5 4.2
2 W	0102 0650 1312 1857	1.1 4.0 1.2 3.9	17 TH	0108 0700 1343 1930	0.5 4.1 0.7 4.0
3 TH	0134 0721 1344 1926	1.3 3.9 1.4 3.8	18 F	0154 0744 1433 2015	0.6 4.0 0.9 3.7
4 F	0203 0753 1416 1955	1.4 3.8 1.6 3.6	19 SA	0242 0831 1526 2104	0.9 3.7 1.2 3.4
5 SA	0232 0828 1452 2029	1.6 3.6 1.8 3.4	20 SU	0334 0923 1625 2205	1.1 3.5 1.5 3.1
6 SU	0308 0910 1542 2113	1.8 3.4 1.9 3.2	21 M ◑	0430 1028 1736 2355	1.4 3.2 1.7 2.9
7 M ◐	0402 1007 1654 2216	1.9 3.2 2.0 3.0	22 TU	0534 1215 1904	1.5 3.1 1.8
8 TU	0519 1137 1816 2359	2.0 3.2 2.0 2.9	23 W	0130 0645 1353 2025	2.9 1.6 3.2 1.8
9 W	0638 1346 1933	1.9 3.3 1.8	24 TH	0231 0758 1444 2118	3.0 1.6 3.3 1.7
10 TH	0214 0752 1442 2037	3.1 1.7 3.6 1.5	25 F	0310 0900 1518 2158	3.2 1.5 3.4 1.5
11 F	0303 0856 1526 2129	3.3 1.4 3.8 1.2	26 SA	0343 0949 1551 2232	3.4 1.4 3.6 1.4
12 SA	0342 0948 1606 2215	3.6 1.1 4.1 0.9	27 SU	0416 1029 1624 2302	3.6 1.3 3.8 1.3
13 SU	0419 1036 1646 2259	3.9 0.8 4.3 0.6	28 M	0451 1105 1659 2332	3.8 1.3 3.9 1.2
14 M ○	0457 1123 1726 2341	4.1 0.6 4.4 0.5	29 TU ●	0525 1140 1734	3.9 1.2 4.0
15 TU	0537 1209 1806	4.2 0.5 4.4	30 W	0004 0558 1215 1808	1.2 4.0 1.2 4.0

DECEMBER

Date	Time	m	Date	Time	m
1 TH	0038 0632 1251 1840	1.2 4.0 1.3 3.9	16 F	0054 0649 1334 1919	0.6 4.2 0.8 4.0
2 F	0111 0704 1326 1912	1.2 3.9 1.4 3.8	17 SA	0139 0733 1421 2002	0.6 4.1 1.0 3.8
3 SA	0142 0738 1400 1943	1.3 3.8 1.5 3.7	18 SU	0224 0816 1509 2045	0.8 3.9 1.2 3.5
4 SU	0212 0813 1436 2019	1.4 3.7 1.6 3.5	19 M	0311 0901 1600 2132	1.0 3.6 1.5 3.3
5 M	0247 0853 1521 2101	1.6 3.6 1.7 3.3	20 TU	0400 0949 1655 2228	1.3 3.4 1.7 3.1
6 TU	0333 0943 1619 2155	1.7 3.4 1.8 3.2	21 W ◑	0452 1047 1758 2351	1.5 3.2 1.9 3.0
7 W ◐	0433 1048 1732 2305	1.7 3.3 1.9 3.1	22 TH	0549 1206 1912	1.6 3.1 1.9
8 TH	0546 1218 1847	1.8 3.3 1.8	23 F	0121 0652 1340 2026	3.0 1.7 3.1 1.9
9 F	0037 0702 1354 1955	3.1 1.7 3.5 1.6	24 SA	0221 0801 1439 2121	3.1 1.8 3.2 1.8
10 SA	0210 0815 1454 2056	3.2 1.5 3.7 1.3	25 SU	0308 0906 1522 2202	3.2 1.7 3.4 1.6
11 SU	0308 0920 1543 2148	3.5 1.2 3.9 1.1	26 M	0349 0957 1601 2237	3.4 1.6 3.5 1.5
12 M	0355 1017 1628 2237	3.8 1.0 4.1 0.8	27 TU	0428 1039 1640 2310	3.6 1.5 3.7 1.3
13 TU	0440 1109 1711 2323	4.0 0.8 4.2 0.7	28 W	0506 1118 1719 2344	3.8 1.4 3.8 1.2
14 W ○	0523 1158 1754	4.1 0.7 4.2	29 TH ●	0543 1156 1756	3.9 1.3 3.9
15 TH	0008 0606 1246 1836	0.6 4.2 0.7 4.1	30 F	0018 0619 1234 1829	1.2 4.0 1.2 3.9
			31 SA	0052 0652 1311 1900	1.1 4.0 1.2 3.8

Chart Datum: 2·10 metres below Ordnance Datum (Newlyn)
HAT is 4·5 metres above Chart Datum

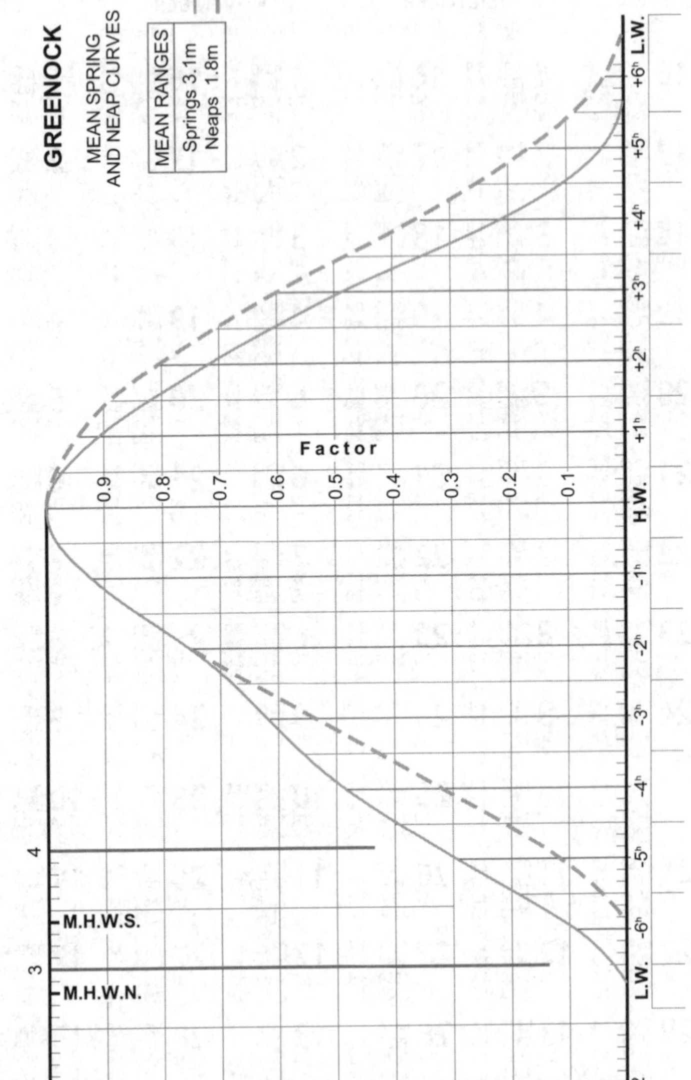
GREENOCK
MEAN SPRING AND NEAP CURVES
MEAN RANGES
Springs 3.1m
Neaps 1.8m
Factor
0.9
0.8
0.7
0.6
0.5
0.4
0.3
0.2
0.1
L.W.
-6h
-5h
-4h
-3h
-2h
-1h
H.W.
+1h
+2h
+3h
+4h
+5h
+6h
L.W.
H.W.Hts.m.
0
1
2
3
4
M.H.W.S.
M.H.W.N.
CHART DATUM
M.L.W.S.
M.L.W.N.
L.W.Hts.m.

TIME ZONE (UT)
For Summer Time add ONE hour in **non-shaded areas**

SCOTLAND – GREENOCK

LAT 55°57′N LONG 4°46′W

TIMES AND HEIGHTS OF HIGH AND LOW WATERS

Dates in amber are **SPRINGS**
Dates in grey are **NEAPS**

2016

JANUARY

Date	Time	m	Date	Time	m
1 F	0451 1016 1645 2238	3.1 0.9 3.4 0.8	16 SA	0429 1008 1648 ◐ 2248	3.4 0.6 3.6 0.4
2 SA	0538 1110 1730 ◑ 2336	3.0 1.1 3.3 1.0	17 SU	0516 1106 1742 2352	3.3 0.7 3.4 0.6
3 SU	0630 1213 1822	2.9 1.2 3.1	18 M	0611 1213 1850	3.2 0.9 3.2
4 M	0042 0732 1324 1922	1.0 2.9 1.2 3.0	19 TU	0104 0724 1331 2019	0.7 3.0 0.9 3.1
5 TU	0150 0842 1432 2031	1.0 3.0 1.1 3.0	20 W	0216 0857 1446 2144	0.7 3.1 0.8 3.1
6 W	0249 0948 1526 2139	1.0 3.1 1.0 3.1	21 TH	0319 1009 1548 2249	0.6 3.2 0.6 3.3
7 TH	0339 1041 1612 2236	0.9 3.3 0.8 3.2	22 F	0414 1105 1640 2343	0.5 3.4 0.5 3.4
8 F	0421 1125 1652 2324	0.8 3.4 0.6 3.3	23 SA	0502 1152 1725	0.4 3.5 0.3
9 SA	0500 1204 1729	0.7 3.5 0.5	24 SU	0032 0546 1235 ○ 1804	3.4 0.4 3.6 0.3
10 SU	0008 0536 1240 ● 1805	3.4 0.6 3.6 0.4	25 M	0116 0626 1314 1841	3.4 0.4 3.7 0.3
11 M	0052 0614 1316 1843	3.4 0.5 3.7 0.3	26 TU	0155 0704 1351 1916	3.3 0.4 3.7 0.3
12 TU	0135 0656 1354 1925	3.5 0.5 3.8 0.3	27 W	0231 0740 1426 1951	3.3 0.4 3.7 0.4
13 W	0218 0740 1434 2010	3.5 0.4 3.8 0.2	28 TH	0304 0816 1501 2028	3.3 0.5 3.7 0.4
14 TH	0301 0827 1517 2058	3.5 0.4 3.8 0.2	29 F	0340 0854 1537 2108	3.3 0.6 3.6 0.5
15 F	0344 0916 1601 2150	3.5 0.5 3.7 0.3	30 SA	0417 0935 1614 2151	3.2 0.7 3.5 0.7
			31 SU	0457 1019 1654 2237	3.1 0.8 3.3 0.8

FEBRUARY

Date	Time	m	Date	Time	m
1 M	0540 1111 1739 ◑ 2332	3.0 1.0 3.1 1.0	16 TU	0539 1147 1819	3.2 0.7 3.1
2 TU	0631 1214 1833	2.9 1.1 3.0	17 W	0041 0638 1311 1955	0.7 3.0 0.8 2.9
3 W	0040 0736 1331 1937	1.1 2.8 1.2 2.9	18 TH	0159 0825 1433 2140	0.8 2.9 0.8 2.9
4 TH	0156 0858 1446 2053	1.1 2.9 1.0 2.9	19 F	0306 0954 1537 2244	0.7 3.0 0.6 3.1
5 F	0303 1008 1543 2207	1.0 3.0 0.8 3.0	20 SA	0402 1051 1628 2335	0.5 3.2 0.4 3.2
6 SA	0354 1059 1628 2305	0.8 3.2 0.6 3.1	21 SU	0450 1138 1711	0.4 3.4 0.3
7 SU	0437 1141 1707 2353	0.6 3.4 0.4 3.3	22 M	0020 0531 1221 ○ 1749	3.3 0.3 3.5 0.3
8 M	0517 1220 1746 ●	0.5 3.5 0.2	23 TU	0100 0609 1258 1822	3.3 0.3 3.6 0.3
9 TU	0037 0557 1300 1825	3.3 0.3 3.6 0.1	24 W	0136 0643 1332 1852	3.3 0.3 3.6 0.3
10 W	0121 0638 1340 1906	3.4 0.2 3.7 0.0	25 TH	0207 0714 1404 1923	3.3 0.3 3.6 0.3
11 TH	0204 0722 1422 1951	3.5 0.2 3.8 0.0	26 F	0237 0746 1436 1957	3.3 0.4 3.6 0.4
12 F	0245 0808 1504 2038	3.5 0.2 3.8 0.0	27 SA	0309 0820 1510 2032	3.3 0.4 3.5 0.4
13 SA	0327 0855 1547 2128	3.5 0.2 3.7 0.1	28 SU	0343 0857 1545 2109	3.3 0.5 3.5 0.5
14 SU	0408 0946 1632 2223	3.5 0.3 3.6 0.3	29 M	0418 0938 1623 2151	3.2 0.6 3.3 0.7
15 M	0451 1041 1721 ◐ 2326	3.3 0.5 3.4 0.5			

MARCH

Date	Time	m	Date	Time	m
1 TU	0456 1024 1705 ◑ 2239	3.1 0.8 3.1 0.9	16 W	0513 1127 1800	3.2 0.6 2.9
2 W	0539 1121 1755 2338	2.9 0.9 2.9 1.0	17 TH	0021 0607 1256 1941	0.8 2.9 0.7 2.7
3 TH	0637 1231 1856	2.7 1.0 2.8	18 F	0140 0747 1415 2130	0.8 2.8 0.7 2.8
4 F	0053 0756 1357 2012	1.1 2.7 1.0 2.8	19 SA	0247 0932 1518 2229	0.8 2.9 0.5 3.0
5 SA	0218 0927 1508 2140	1.0 2.8 0.7 2.9	20 SU	0343 1030 1608 2316	0.6 3.1 0.4 3.1
6 SU	0323 1028 1559 2245	0.8 3.1 0.4 3.1	21 M	0430 1117 1650 2358	0.4 3.3 0.3 3.2
7 M	0412 1115 1642 2334	0.6 3.3 0.2 3.2	22 TU	0512 1158 1727	0.3 3.4 0.2
8 TU	0455 1157 1722	0.3 3.5 0.0	23 W	0036 0548 1236 ○ 1758	3.3 0.3 3.4 0.3
9 W	0019 0536 1241 ● 1802	3.3 0.2 3.6 -0.2	24 TH	0109 0620 1308 1826	3.3 0.3 3.4 0.3
10 TH	0103 0618 1324 1845	3.4 0.0 3.7 -0.2	25 F	0139 0648 1339 1855	3.3 0.3 3.4 0.3
11 F	0145 0702 1407 1929	3.5 0.0 3.8 -0.2	26 SA	0208 0717 1410 1926	3.3 0.3 3.4 0.4
12 SA	0226 0747 1450 2016	3.5 0.0 3.8 -0.1	27 SU	0239 0749 1443 1959	3.4 0.3 3.4 0.4
13 SU	0306 0834 1533 2106	3.6 0.0 3.7 0.1	28 M	0310 0824 1518 2037	3.3 0.4 3.4 0.4
14 M	0346 0924 1617 2200	3.5 0.2 3.5 0.3	29 TU	0342 0905 1555 2119	3.3 0.5 3.3 0.6
15 TU	0427 1019 1704 ◐ 2303	3.4 0.4 3.3 0.6	30 W	0417 0951 1637 2207	3.1 0.6 3.1 0.7
			31 TH	0456 1047 1725 ◑ 2304	3.0 0.8 2.9 0.9

APRIL

Date	Time	m	Date	Time	m
1 F	0547 1153 1824	2.8 0.8 2.8	16 SA	0111 0708 1348 2102	0.9 2.8 0.6 2.7
2 SA	0012 0701 1312 1938	1.1 2.7 0.8 2.7	17 SU	0218 0856 1448 2201	0.8 2.9 0.5 2.9
3 SU	0133 0838 1427 2108	1.0 2.8 0.6 2.8	18 M	0315 0958 1539 2247	0.7 3.1 0.4 3.1
4 M	0247 0952 1525 2218	0.8 3.0 0.3 3.0	19 TU	0404 1047 1622 2328	0.5 3.2 0.3 3.2
5 TU	0343 1044 1612 2310	0.5 3.2 0.0 3.2	20 W	0446 1128 1658	0.4 3.3 0.3
6 W	0431 1131 1656 2356	0.3 3.4 -0.2 3.3	21 TH	0005 0522 1206 1730	3.2 0.3 3.3 0.3
7 TH	0515 1217 1739 ●	0.1 3.6 -0.3	22 F	0039 0554 1239 ○ 1759	3.3 0.3 3.3 0.4
8 F	0040 0558 1304 1823	3.4 -0.1 3.6 -0.3	23 SA	0110 0622 1310 1827	3.3 0.3 3.3 0.4
9 SA	0123 0642 1350 1908	3.5 -0.1 3.7 -0.2	24 SU	0140 0651 1342 1858	3.4 0.3 3.3 0.4
10 SU	0205 0727 1435 1956	3.6 -0.1 3.7 -0.1	25 M	0209 0722 1416 1933	3.4 0.3 3.4 0.4
11 M	0245 0814 1520 2046	3.6 -0.1 3.6 0.1	26 TU	0240 0759 1453 2012	3.4 0.3 3.3 0.5
12 TU	0325 0904 1604 2140	3.6 0.1 3.4 0.3	27 W	0312 0840 1532 2057	3.4 0.4 3.3 0.5
13 W	0406 1000 1653 2242	3.4 0.3 3.2 0.6	28 TH	0346 0928 1614 2146	3.3 0.5 3.2 0.7
14 TH	0451 1109 1750 ◐ 2356	3.2 0.5 2.9 0.8	29 F	0425 1023 1702 2243	3.1 0.6 3.0 0.8
15 F	0545 1233 1922	3.0 0.6 2.7	30 SA	0512 1127 1758 ◑ 2347	3.0 0.6 2.9 0.9

Chart Datum: 1·62 metres below Ordnance Datum (Newlyn)
HAT is 3·9 metres above Chart Datum

TIME ZONE (UT)
For Summer Time add ONE hour in **non-shaded areas**

SCOTLAND – GREENOCK

LAT 55°57′N LONG 4°46′W

TIMES AND HEIGHTS OF HIGH AND LOW WATERS

Dates in amber are **SPRINGS**
Dates in grey are **NEAPS**

2016

MAY

Date	Day	Time	m	Date	Day	Time	m
1	SU	0620 1239 1908	2.8 0.6 2.8	16	M	0139 0758 1410 2116	0.9 2.9 0.6 2.8
2	M	0058 0752 1350 2031	0.9 2.8 0.4 2.9	17	TU	0239 0913 1502 2207	0.8 3.0 0.5 3.0
3	TU	0211 0913 1451 2145	0.8 3.0 0.2 3.1	18	W	0331 1007 1546 2251	0.6 3.1 0.4 3.1
4	W	0314 1013 1543 2241	0.5 3.2 0.0 3.2	19	TH	0416 1052 1625 2330	0.5 3.2 0.4 3.2
5	TH	0406 1105 1631 2330	0.3 3.4 -0.2 3.4	20	F	0454 1131 1700	0.4 3.2 0.4
6	F ●	0453 1154 1717	0.1 3.5 -0.2	21	SA ○	0007 0528 1207 1732	3.3 0.4 3.2 0.5
7	SA	0016 0538 1244 1802	3.5 -0.1 3.6 -0.2	22	SU	0041 0559 1240 1803	3.4 0.4 3.2 0.5
8	SU	0101 0623 1333 1849	3.6 -0.1 3.6 -0.1	23	M	0113 0629 1314 1836	3.4 0.4 3.3 0.5
9	M	0144 0709 1420 1938	3.6 -0.1 3.6 0.0	24	TU	0143 0702 1351 1913	3.5 0.3 3.3 0.5
10	TU	0225 0756 1507 2028	3.6 -0.1 3.5 0.2	25	W	0214 0739 1430 1954	3.5 0.3 3.3 0.5
11	W	0306 0846 1553 2121	3.6 0.1 3.3 0.4	26	TH	0248 0822 1512 2040	3.5 0.3 3.3 0.5
12	TH	0348 0941 1642 2219	3.5 0.3 3.1 0.6	27	F	0325 0910 1555 2130	3.4 0.4 3.2 0.6
13	F ◐	0433 1044 1738 2323	3.3 0.4 2.9 0.8	28	SA	0404 1004 1643 2225	3.3 0.4 3.1 0.7
14	SA	0524 1157 1847	3.1 0.6 2.7	29	SU ◑	0451 1105 1736 2324	3.2 0.5 3.0 0.8
15	SU	0032 0630 1309 2009	0.9 2.9 0.6 2.7	30	M	0551 1211 1839	3.0 0.4 3.0
				31	TU	0029 0713 1318 1953	0.8 3.0 0.4 3.0

JUNE

Date	Day	Time	m	Date	Day	Time	m
1	W	0139 0836 1420 2109	0.7 3.1 0.2 3.1	16	TH	0252 0912 1507 2206	0.8 2.9 0.6 3.0
2	TH	0245 0944 1517 2212	0.6 3.2 0.1 3.2	17	F	0342 1008 1552 2254	0.7 3.0 0.6 3.2
3	F	0343 1041 1609 2306	0.4 3.4 0.0 3.3	18	SA	0425 1053 1631 2336	0.5 3.1 0.5 3.3
4	SA	0435 1135 1658 2355	0.2 3.4 -0.1 3.5	19	SU	0504 1133 1708	0.5 3.1 0.5
5	SU ●	0523 1226 1746	0.0 3.5 0.0	20	M ○	0014 0539 1211 1742	3.4 0.4 3.2 0.5
6	M	0041 0608 1318 1833	3.5 0.0 3.5 0.0	21	TU	0048 0612 1249 1817	3.4 0.4 3.2 0.5
7	TU	0125 0654 1407 1921	3.6 -0.1 3.4 0.1	22	W	0120 0646 1329 1855	3.5 0.3 3.2 0.5
8	W	0208 0740 1454 2010	3.6 0.0 3.3 0.3	23	TH	0153 0724 1411 1938	3.5 0.3 3.3 0.5
9	TH	0249 0826 1540 2059	3.6 0.1 3.2 0.4	24	F	0229 0806 1454 2024	3.5 0.3 3.3 0.4
10	F	0330 0916 1627 2150	3.5 0.2 3.1 0.5	25	SA	0308 0853 1538 2113	3.5 0.3 3.3 0.5
11	SA	0413 1010 1715 2244	3.4 0.4 3.0 0.7	26	SU	0349 0945 1624 2205	3.5 0.3 3.2 0.5
12	SU ◐	0459 1110 1806 2343	3.2 0.5 2.9 0.8	27	M ◑	0434 1042 1714 2301	3.4 0.3 3.2 0.6
13	M	0551 1216 1904	3.0 0.6 2.8	28	TU	0528 1144 1810	3.2 0.3 3.1
14	TU	0047 0653 1320 2007	0.9 2.9 0.7 2.8	29	W	0002 0637 1249 1915	0.7 3.1 0.4 3.0
15	W	0153 0804 1418 2111	0.9 2.9 0.7 2.9	30	TH	0109 0801 1354 2033	0.7 3.1 0.3 3.0

JULY

Date	Day	Time	m	Date	Day	Time	m
1	F	0220 0919 1456 2146	0.7 3.1 0.3 3.1	16	SA	0306 0915 1519 2217	0.8 2.9 0.7 3.1
2	SA	0325 1025 1553 2246	0.5 3.2 0.2 3.3	17	SU	0357 1016 1605 2307	0.7 3.0 0.7 3.2
3	SU	0421 1122 1645 2339	0.3 3.3 0.1 3.4	18	M	0441 1105 1645 2348	0.5 3.1 0.6 3.3
4	M ●	0511 1216 1733	0.1 3.4 0.1	19	TU ○	0519 1147 1722	0.4 3.1 0.5
5	TU	0026 0557 1307 1820	3.5 0.1 3.3 0.2	20	W	0025 0554 1229 1758	3.4 0.3 3.2 0.5
6	W	0111 0640 1355 1905	3.6 0.0 3.3 0.2	21	TH	0059 0629 1310 1837	3.5 0.2 3.2 0.4
7	TH	0152 0722 1440 1949	3.6 0.1 3.2 0.3	22	F	0135 0706 1353 1920	3.6 0.2 3.3 0.4
8	F	0231 0804 1522 2033	3.6 0.1 3.2 0.4	23	SA	0213 0748 1436 2005	3.6 0.1 3.3 0.3
9	SA	0310 0846 1601 2117	3.6 0.2 3.1 0.5	24	SU	0253 0833 1520 2052	3.6 0.1 3.3 0.3
10	SU	0349 0932 1642 2203	3.5 0.4 3.0 0.6	25	M	0334 0922 1604 2142	3.6 0.1 3.3 0.4
11	M	0429 1022 1725 2253	3.3 0.5 3.0 0.7	26	TU ◑	0418 1017 1650 2236	3.5 0.2 3.3 0.5
12	TU ◐	0512 1118 1811 2348	3.2 0.7 2.9 0.9	27	W	0507 1117 1739 2335	3.3 0.4 3.2 0.6
13	W	0601 1220 1904	3.0 0.8 2.8	28	TH	0606 1224 1838	3.1 0.5 3.1
14	TH	0053 0657 1325 2006	1.0 2.9 0.8 2.8	29	F	0044 0728 1335 1957	0.7 3.0 0.5 3.0
15	F	0204 0804 1426 2115	1.0 2.8 0.8 2.9	30	SA	0202 0904 1443 2126	0.8 3.0 0.5 3.0
				31	SU	0314 1019 1543 2234	0.6 3.1 0.4 3.2

AUGUST

Date	Day	Time	m	Date	Day	Time	m
1	M	0413 1117 1635 2327	0.4 3.2 0.3 3.4	16	TU	0416 1043 1622 2322	0.6 3.0 0.6 3.3
2	TU ●	0503 1209 1723	0.2 3.3 0.3	17	W	0456 1129 1700	0.4 3.1 0.5
3	W	0014 0546 1257 1806	3.5 0.1 3.3 0.3	18	TH ○	0001 0532 1211 1737	3.4 0.2 3.2 0.4
4	TH	0057 0625 1341 1847	3.6 0.1 3.2 0.3	19	F	0038 0608 1253 1816	3.5 0.1 3.3 0.3
5	F	0135 0702 1420 1925	3.6 0.1 3.2 0.3	20	SA	0117 0645 1335 1858	3.6 0.0 3.3 0.3
6	SA	0211 0737 1454 2003	3.6 0.2 3.2 0.4	21	SU	0157 0726 1417 1943	3.7 0.0 3.4 0.2
7	SU	0246 0814 1528 2041	3.6 0.3 3.1 0.4	22	M	0238 0811 1459 2030	3.7 0.0 3.4 0.2
8	M	0321 0853 1604 2122	3.5 0.4 3.1 0.5	23	TU	0319 0859 1541 2119	3.7 0.1 3.4 0.3
9	TU	0358 0936 1643 2206	3.4 0.5 3.1 0.7	24	W	0402 0951 1624 2212	3.6 0.3 3.4 0.4
10	W ◐	0436 1023 1725 2255	3.3 0.7 3.0 0.8	25	TH ◑	0448 1052 1711 2312	3.4 0.5 3.3 0.6
11	TH	0519 1118 1813 2355	3.1 0.9 2.9 1.0	26	F	0542 1204 1806	3.1 0.6 3.1
12	F	0611 1225 1910	2.9 1.0 2.8	27	SA	0026 0702 1323 1923	0.8 2.9 0.7 3.0
13	SA	0108 0713 1340 2021	1.1 2.8 1.0 2.8	28	SU	0153 0904 1434 2113	0.8 2.9 0.7 3.0
14	SU	0228 0826 1446 2138	1.0 2.8 0.9 3.0	29	M	0306 1017 1533 2222	0.7 3.0 0.6 3.2
15	M	0329 0944 1539 2237	0.8 2.9 0.8 3.1	30	TU	0404 1111 1624 2314	0.5 3.2 0.4 3.4
				31	W	0451 1158 1709 2358	0.3 3.3 0.3 3.5

Chart Datum: 1·62 metres below Ordnance Datum (Newlyn)
HAT is 3·9 metres above Chart Datum

TIME ZONE (UT)
For Summer Time add ONE hour in **non-shaded areas**

SCOTLAND – GREENOCK

LAT 55°57′N LONG 4°46′W

TIMES AND HEIGHTS OF HIGH AND LOW WATERS

Dates in amber are **SPRINGS**
Dates in grey are **NEAPS**

2016

SEPTEMBER

Day	Time	m	Time	m	Time	m	Time	m
1 TH ●	0531	0.2	1240	3.3	1750	0.3		
2 F	0038	3.6	0607	0.2	1319	3.3	1826	0.3
3 SA	0115	3.6	0638	0.2	1352	3.2	1859	0.4
4 SU	0148	3.6	0709	0.3	1422	3.2	1931	0.4
5 M	0220	3.6	0741	0.4	1453	3.3	2006	0.5
6 TU	0253	3.6	0816	0.4	1527	3.3	2043	0.5
7 W	0327	3.5	0853	0.5	1603	3.2	2123	0.6
8 TH	0404	3.4	0934	0.7	1642	3.1	2209	0.8
9 F	0445	3.2	1021	0.9	1727	3.0	◐ 2303	1.0
10 SA	0535	3.0	1122	1.1	1821	2.9		
11 SU	0014	1.1	0635	2.8	1243	1.2	1929	2.8
12 M	0144	1.1	0749	2.8	1407	1.1	2054	2.9
13 TU	0256	0.9	0916	2.9	1509	0.9	2203	3.1
14 W	0347	0.6	1022	3.1	1555	0.7	2251	3.3
15 TH	0428	0.3	1110	3.2	1635	0.5	2333	3.5
16 F ○	0506	0.1	1152	3.3	1714	0.3		
17 SA	0014	3.6	0543	0.0	1233	3.4	1754	0.2
18 SU	0056	3.7	0622	-0.1	1314	3.5	1836	0.2
19 M	0139	3.8	0704	-0.1	1356	3.5	1921	0.1
20 TU	0222	3.8	0748	0.0	1437	3.6	2007	0.2
21 W	0305	3.8	0836	0.1	1519	3.6	2057	0.3
22 TH	0348	3.6	0929	0.4	1601	3.5	2150	0.5
23 F	0434	3.4	1031	0.6	1647	3.4	◑ 2254	0.7
24 SA	0527	3.1	1148	0.8	1741	3.2		
25 SU	0017	0.8	0653	2.8	1310	0.9	1857	3.0
26 M	0143	0.8	0901	2.9	1419	0.9	2055	3.0
27 TU	0251	0.7	1006	3.1	1517	0.7	2202	3.2
28 W	0346	0.5	1055	3.3	1607	0.5	2253	3.4
29 TH	0431	0.4	1138	3.4	1650	0.4	2336	3.5
30 F	0510	0.3	1216	3.4	1729	0.4		

OCTOBER

Day	Time	m	Time	m	Time	m	Time	m
1 SA	0015	3.6	0543	0.3	1251	3.4	● 1803	0.4
2 SU	0050	3.6	0613	0.4	1321	3.4	1833	0.4
3 M	0121	3.6	0641	0.4	1349	3.4	1902	0.5
4 TU	0153	3.6	0711	0.5	1420	3.4	1934	0.5
5 W	0225	3.6	0744	0.5	1453	3.5	2009	0.6
6 TH	0300	3.5	0819	0.6	1527	3.4	2048	0.7
7 F	0337	3.4	0859	0.8	1604	3.3	2133	0.8
8 SA	0418	3.3	0944	1.0	1645	3.2	2225	1.0
9 SU	0505	3.1	1040	1.2	1736	3.0	◐ 2331	1.1
10 M	0603	2.9	1151	1.3	1843	2.9		
11 TU	0054	1.1	0716	2.8	1318	1.3	2005	2.9
12 W	0214	0.9	0844	2.9	1431	1.1	2122	3.1
13 TH	0311	0.6	0955	3.1	1524	0.8	2217	3.4
14 F	0356	0.3	1045	3.3	1609	0.5	2304	3.5
15 SA	0437	0.1	1128	3.5	1651	0.3	2349	3.7
16 SU ○	0518	0.0	1210	3.6	1733	0.2		
17 M	0035	3.8	0559	-0.1	1253	3.6	1816	0.1
18 TU	0121	3.8	0643	0.0	1335	3.7	1901	0.1
19 W	0206	3.8	0729	0.1	1417	3.7	1948	0.2
20 TH	0251	3.8	0817	0.3	1459	3.7	2038	0.3
21 F	0336	3.6	0911	0.5	1542	3.6	2132	0.5
22 SA	0424	3.4	1012	0.8	1628	3.5	◑ 2238	0.7
23 SU	0521	3.1	1127	1.0	1721	3.3		
24 M	0002	0.8	0648	2.9	1246	1.1	1834	3.1
25 TU	0121	0.8	0837	2.9	1354	1.0	2019	3.1
26 W	0226	0.7	0940	3.1	1452	0.8	2131	3.2
27 TH	0320	0.6	1028	3.3	1543	0.7	2223	3.4
28 F	0405	0.5	1110	3.4	1627	0.5	2307	3.5
29 SA	0444	0.4	1147	3.5	1705	0.5	2346	3.5
30 SU ●	0518	0.5	1220	3.5	1739	0.5		
31 M	0021	3.5	0547	0.5	1251	3.5	1809	0.5

NOVEMBER

Day	Time	m	Time	m	Time	m	Time	m
1 TU	0054	3.5	0616	0.6	1321	3.6	1837	0.6
2 W	0126	3.5	0645	0.6	1352	3.6	1908	0.6
3 TH	0200	3.5	0718	0.6	1424	3.6	1943	0.6
4 F	0236	3.5	0754	0.7	1458	3.6	2022	0.7
5 SA	0314	3.5	0835	0.8	1533	3.5	2107	0.8
6 SU	0355	3.3	0921	1.0	1612	3.3	2159	0.9
7 M	0441	3.2	1015	1.1	1659	3.2	◐ 2300	1.0
8 TU	0535	3.0	1118	1.3	1800	3.1		
9 W	0011	1.0	0643	3.0	1232	1.3	1917	3.1
10 TH	0127	0.8	0804	3.0	1347	1.1	2037	3.2
11 F	0230	0.6	0919	3.2	1449	0.9	2142	3.4
12 SA	0323	0.4	1015	3.4	1541	0.6	2236	3.6
13 SU	0410	0.2	1103	3.5	1628	0.4	2326	3.7
14 M ○	0455	0.0	1148	3.7	1714	0.2		
15 TU	0015	3.8	0539	0.0	1233	3.7	1758	0.2
16 W	0104	3.8	0625	0.1	1317	3.8	1844	0.1
17 TH	0153	3.8	0712	0.2	1400	3.9	1932	0.2
18 F	0240	3.7	0801	0.4	1443	3.8	2021	0.3
19 SA	0327	3.5	0854	0.6	1526	3.7	2115	0.5
20 SU	0417	3.4	0951	0.8	1612	3.6	2217	0.6
21 M	0512	3.1	1057	1.0	1704	3.4	◑ 2330	0.8
22 TU	0622	3.0	1209	1.1	1806	3.2		
23 W	0046	0.9	0746	2.9	1318	1.1	1926	3.1
24 TH	0151	0.8	0857	3.0	1420	1.0	2044	3.2
25 F	0246	0.7	0951	3.2	1513	0.8	2145	3.3
26 SA	0334	0.7	1035	3.3	1559	0.7	2233	3.4
27 SU	0415	0.6	1115	3.5	1640	0.6	2315	3.4
28 M	0451	0.6	1151	3.5	1716	0.6	2353	3.4
29 TU ●	0524	0.6	1225	3.6	1749	0.6		
30 W	0027	3.5	0555	0.7	1258	3.6	1819	0.6

DECEMBER

Day	Time	m	Time	m	Time	m	Time	m
1 TH	0102	3.5	0625	0.7	1329	3.7	1850	0.6
2 F	0138	3.5	0658	0.7	1401	3.7	1924	0.6
3 SA	0215	3.5	0735	0.7	1435	3.7	2003	0.7
4 SU	0255	3.5	0817	0.8	1511	3.6	2047	0.7
5 M	0336	3.4	0903	0.9	1550	3.5	2137	0.8
6 TU	0421	3.3	0954	1.0	1634	3.4	2233	0.8
7 W	0510	3.2	1051	1.1	1726	3.3	◐ 2336	0.8
8 TH	0608	3.1	1156	1.1	1833	3.2		
9 F	0044	0.8	0719	3.1	1306	1.1	1953	3.2
10 SA	0151	0.6	0837	3.2	1415	0.9	2108	3.3
11 SU	0252	0.5	0944	3.3	1515	0.7	2211	3.5
12 M	0346	0.3	1039	3.5	1609	0.5	2307	3.6
13 TU	0435	0.2	1129	3.6	1658	0.3		
14 W	0000	3.7	0523	0.2	1217	3.7	○ 1744	0.2
15 TH	0052	3.7	0610	0.2	1302	3.8	1831	0.2
16 F	0142	3.7	0658	0.3	1346	3.9	1918	0.2
17 SA	0230	3.6	0746	0.4	1429	3.9	2005	0.3
18 SU	0317	3.5	0835	0.5	1512	3.8	2054	0.4
19 M	0404	3.3	0926	0.7	1556	3.7	2147	0.5
20 TU	0452	3.2	1020	0.8	1643	3.5	2245	0.7
21 W	0543	3.1	1121	1.0	1733	3.3	◑ 2352	0.8
22 TH	0641	3.0	1229	1.1	1830	3.2		
23 F	0102	0.9	0747	2.9	1337	1.1	1936	3.1
24 SA	0205	0.9	0855	3.0	1438	1.0	2048	3.1
25 SU	0258	0.9	0954	3.2	1529	0.9	2152	3.2
26 M	0345	0.8	1042	3.3	1614	0.7	2243	3.2
27 TU	0426	0.7	1124	3.5	1654	0.7	2326	3.3
28 W	0503	0.7	1203	3.6	1731	0.6		
29 TH	0005	3.3	0537	0.7	1238	3.6	● 1804	0.6
30 F	0043	3.4	0609	0.7	1310	3.7	1836	0.6
31 SA	0120	3.4	0642	0.7	1342	3.7	1909	0.6

Chart Datum: 1·62 metres below Ordnance Datum (Newlyn)
HAT is 3·9 metres above Chart Datum

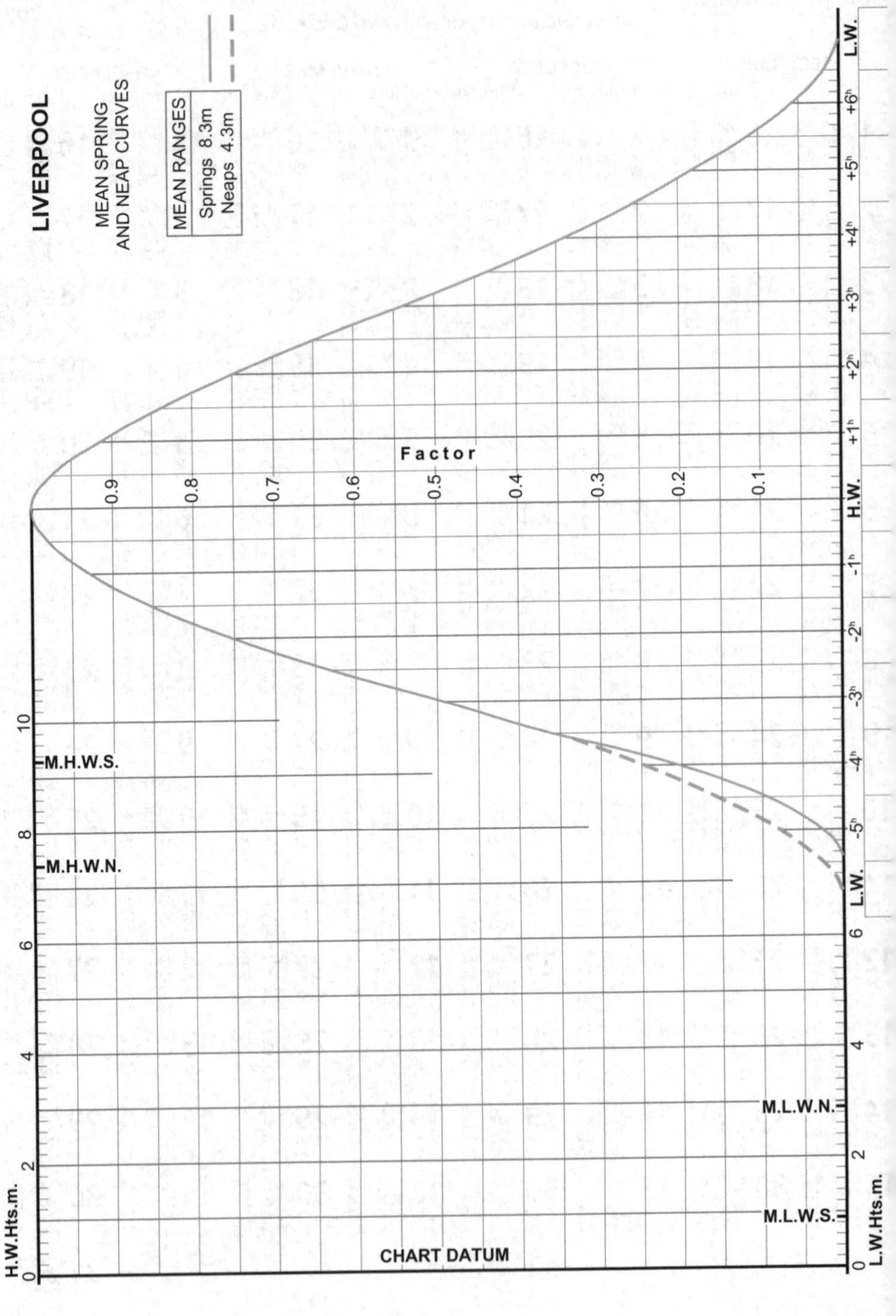
LIVERPOOL
MEAN SPRING
AND NEAP CURVES
MEAN RANGES
Springs 8.3m
Neaps 4.3m
Factor
0.9
0.8
0.7
0.6
0.5
0.4
0.3
0.2
0.1
L.W.
-5h
-4h
-3h
-2h
-1h
H.W.
+1h
+2h
+3h
+4h
+5h
+6h
L.W.
H.W.Hts.m.
0
2
4
6
8
10
M.H.W.S.
M.H.W.N.
CHART DATUM
L.W.Hts.m.
M.L.W.S.
M.L.W.N.

TIME ZONE (UT)
For Summer Time add ONE hour in **non-shaded areas**

LIVERPOOL (GLADSTONE DOCK)

LAT 53°27′N LONG 3°01′W

TIMES AND HEIGHTS OF HIGH AND LOW WATERS

Dates in amber are **SPRINGS**
Dates in yellow are **NEAPS**

2016

JANUARY

Date	Day	Time m	Time m	Time m	Time m
1	F	0314 8.0	0943 2.9	1534 8.1	2226 2.9
2	SA	0404 7.6	1030 3.3	1629 7.7	◑ 2319 3.2
3	SU	0504 7.3	1131 3.5	1734 7.4	
4	M	0026 3.3	0612 7.3	1245 3.6	1843 7.4
5	TU	0135 3.2	0720 7.4	1357 3.3	1948 7.6
6	W	0235 2.9	0819 7.8	1457 2.9	2044 7.9
7	TH	0327 2.5	0908 8.2	1548 2.5	2131 8.3
8	F	0413 2.1	0951 8.6	1636 2.0	2212 8.6
9	SA	0457 1.8	1031 9.0	1721 1.7	2252 8.9
10	SU	0540 1.5	1110 9.3	1805 1.4	● 2332 9.1
11	M	0622 1.3	1149 9.5	1848 1.2	
12	TU	0012 9.3	0704 1.2	1231 9.6	1931 1.1
13	W	0055 9.3	0745 1.3	1314 9.6	2012 1.1
14	TH	0138 9.2	0826 1.4	1358 9.5	2054 1.3
15	F	0224 9.0	0909 1.7	1446 9.2	2139 1.6
16	SA	0314 8.7	0956 2.1	1539 8.9	◐ 2229 2.0
17	SU	0411 8.3	1052 2.4	1640 8.5	2329 2.3
18	M	0518 8.0	1200 2.6	1751 8.3	
19	TU	0042 2.5	0634 7.9	1320 2.7	1906 8.2
20	W	0200 2.5	0748 8.1	1438 2.4	2018 8.4
21	TH	0310 2.2	0853 8.5	1546 2.0	2120 8.6
22	F	0410 1.9	0948 8.8	1644 1.6	2213 8.9
23	SA	0502 1.7	1036 9.1	1734 1.3	2259 9.1
24	SU	0547 1.5	1118 9.3	1818 1.2	○ 2340 9.2
25	M	0627 1.4	1156 9.4	1858 1.1	
26	TU	0017 9.2	0702 1.4	1233 9.4	1933 1.3
27	W	0052 9.1	0734 1.6	1306 9.2	2005 1.5
28	TH	0125 8.9	0804 1.8	1339 9.0	2035 1.8
29	F	0159 8.6	0833 2.1	1413 8.7	2103 2.1
30	SA	0235 8.3	0905 2.5	1450 8.3	2135 2.5
31	SU	0314 7.9	0942 2.8	1532 7.9	2215 2.9

FEBRUARY

Date	Day	Time m	Time m	Time m	Time m
1	M	0402 7.5	1030 3.2	1624 7.5	◑ 2310 3.3
2	TU	0503 7.2	1135 3.5	1734 7.2	
3	W	0026 3.4	0618 7.2	1259 3.5	1854 7.2
4	TH	0147 3.2	0732 7.4	1416 3.2	2006 7.5
5	F	0252 2.8	0834 7.9	1519 2.6	2103 8.0
6	SA	0347 2.3	0924 8.4	1613 2.1	2151 8.5
7	SU	0436 1.8	1009 8.9	1703 1.5	2234 8.9
8	M	0523 1.4	1051 9.4	1750 1.1	● 2315 9.3
9	TU	0608 1.0	1132 9.7	1835 0.7	2357 9.6
10	W	0651 0.8	1214 9.9	1918 0.6	
11	TH	0039 9.7	0733 0.8	1258 10.0	1959 0.6
12	F	0122 9.6	0813 0.9	1341 9.9	2039 0.8
13	SA	0206 9.3	0854 1.2	1427 9.5	2120 1.2
14	SU	0252 8.9	0937 1.6	1516 9.1	2205 1.8
15	M	0345 8.5	1029 2.1	1614 8.5	◐ 2301 2.3
16	TU	0449 8.0	1135 2.6	1726 8.0	
17	W	0013 2.7	0608 7.7	1300 2.8	1847 7.8
18	TH	0139 2.8	0730 7.8	1425 2.6	2007 7.9
19	F	0257 2.6	0841 8.2	1537 2.1	2112 8.3
20	SA	0400 2.2	0937 8.6	1635 1.7	2204 8.6
21	SU	0451 1.8	1023 8.9	1722 1.4	2246 8.9
22	M	0533 1.6	1102 9.2	1801 1.2	○ 2323 9.1
23	TU	0608 1.4	1137 9.3	1836 1.1	2356 9.1
24	W	0640 1.4	1210 9.3	1907 1.2	
25	TH	0027 9.1	0709 1.4	1241 9.2	1935 1.3
26	F	0058 9.0	0737 1.5	1312 9.1	2001 1.5
27	SA	0128 8.8	0805 1.7	1342 8.8	2028 1.8
28	SU	0200 8.6	0835 2.0	1413 8.5	2058 2.2
29	M	0234 8.2	0909 2.4	1448 8.1	2133 2.6

MARCH

Date	Day	Time m	Time m	Time m	Time m
1	TU	0313 7.8	0950 2.9	1530 7.6	◑ 2218 3.1
2	W	0404 7.4	1044 3.2	1630 7.2	2324 3.4
3	TH	0517 7.1	1203 3.4	1756 7.0	
4	F	0054 3.4	0642 7.2	1334 3.2	1924 7.3
5	SA	0215 3.0	0756 7.7	1447 2.6	2032 7.8
6	SU	0318 2.4	0854 8.3	1548 2.0	2125 8.4
7	M	0413 1.8	0943 8.9	1641 1.4	2211 9.0
8	TU	0503 1.2	1028 9.5	1730 0.8	2254 9.5
9	W	0550 0.8	1111 9.9	1816 0.4	● 2337 9.8
10	TH	0634 0.5	1154 10.1	1859 0.2	
11	F	0019 9.9	0716 0.4	1238 10.2	1940 0.2
12	SA	0102 9.8	0757 0.5	1322 10.0	2020 0.5
13	SU	0145 9.5	0838 0.8	1407 9.6	2100 1.1
14	M	0231 9.1	0921 1.4	1456 9.1	2143 1.7
15	TU	0321 8.5	1011 2.0	1553 8.4	◐ 2236 2.4
16	W	0424 8.0	1117 2.5	1705 7.8	2348 2.9
17	TH	0544 7.6	1243 2.8	1830 7.5	
18	F	0118 3.0	0709 7.6	1409 2.6	1952 7.7
19	SA	0240 2.8	0822 8.0	1520 2.2	2057 8.1
20	SU	0343 2.3	0918 8.4	1615 1.8	2146 8.5
21	M	0432 2.0	1002 8.7	1700 1.5	2225 8.8
22	TU	0511 1.7	1040 9.0	1736 1.3	2259 9.0
23	W	0544 1.5	1113 9.1	1808 1.2	○ 2330 9.1
24	TH	0614 1.4	1144 9.2	1837 1.2	
25	F	0000 9.1	0641 1.3	1215 9.1	1903 1.3
26	SA	0030 9.1	0710 1.4	1245 9.0	1931 1.4
27	SU	0100 8.9	0739 1.5	1314 8.8	1959 1.7
28	M	0130 8.7	0811 1.8	1344 8.5	2029 2.0
29	TU	0202 8.4	0844 2.1	1417 8.2	2103 2.4
30	W	0239 8.1	0922 2.5	1458 7.8	2144 2.9
31	TH	0326 7.7	1011 2.9	1553 7.4	◑ 2242 3.3

APRIL

Date	Day	Time m	Time m	Time m	Time m
1	F	0433 7.4	1122 3.2	1712 7.1	
2	SA	0006 3.4	0557 7.3	1252 3.0	1842 7.3
3	SU	0135 3.0	0716 7.7	1412 2.5	1957 7.8
4	M	0245 2.4	0821 8.3	1517 1.9	2056 8.5
5	TU	0345 1.8	0914 9.0	1614 1.2	2145 9.1
6	W	0438 1.2	1002 9.5	1706 0.7	2230 9.5
7	TH	0527 0.7	1047 9.9	1753 0.3	● 2314 9.9
8	F	0613 0.4	1132 10.2	1837 0.1	2357 10.0
9	SA	0657 0.2	1217 10.2	1919 0.2	
10	SU	0041 9.9	0739 0.3	1303 9.9	2000 0.6
11	M	0125 9.6	0822 0.7	1350 9.5	2040 1.1
12	TU	0211 9.1	0907 1.2	1439 8.9	2124 1.8
13	W	0302 8.6	0958 1.8	1535 8.3	2216 2.4
14	TH	0403 8.0	1102 2.4	1644 7.7	◐ 2325 3.0
15	F	0518 7.7	1221 2.7	1803 7.5	
16	SA	0050 3.1	0637 7.6	1341 2.6	1923 7.6
17	SU	0209 2.9	0750 7.8	1449 2.3	2029 7.9
18	M	0312 2.6	0848 8.2	1543 2.0	2117 8.3
19	TU	0401 2.2	0933 8.5	1627 1.7	2156 8.6
20	W	0440 1.9	1011 8.7	1703 1.5	2230 8.8
21	TH	0513 1.7	1044 8.9	1735 1.4	2301 8.9
22	F	0544 1.5	1117 8.9	1805 1.3	○ 2332 9.0
23	SA	0614 1.4	1148 9.0	1834 1.3	
24	SU	0003 9.0	0644 1.4	1219 8.9	1903 1.4
25	M	0034 8.9	0717 1.5	1250 8.7	1934 1.6
26	TU	0105 8.8	0750 1.7	1322 8.5	2007 1.9
27	W	0139 8.6	0826 1.9	1357 8.3	2042 2.3
28	TH	0217 8.3	0904 2.3	1439 8.0	2123 2.6
29	F	0304 8.0	0952 2.6	1533 7.6	2217 3.0
30	SA	0406 7.7	1055 2.8	1644 7.4	◑ 2331 3.1

Chart Datum: 4·93 metres below Ordnance Datum (Newlyn)
HAT is 10·3m above Chart Datum

TIME ZONE (UT)
For Summer Time add ONE hour in **non-shaded areas**

LIVERPOOL (GLADSTONE DOCK)

LAT 53°27′N LONG 3°01′W

TIMES AND HEIGHTS OF HIGH AND LOW WATERS

Dates in amber are **SPRINGS**
Dates in yellow are **NEAPS**

2016

MAY

Date	Day	Time	m	Time	m	Time	m	Time	m
1	SU	0523	7.7	1215	2.7	1806	7.5		
2	M	0054	2.9	0639	7.9	1334	2.3	1921	8.0
3	TU	0209	2.4	0746	8.4	1443	1.8	2024	8.5
4	W	0313	1.8	0843	9.0	1544	1.3	2117	9.0
5	TH	0410	1.3	0935	9.4	1638	0.8	2205	9.5
6	F	0502	0.8	1024	9.8	1728	0.5	● 2251	9.7
7	SA	0551	0.5	1112	10.0	1814	0.4	2337	9.9
8	SU	0638	0.3	1159	9.9	1858	0.4		
9	M	0022	9.8	0723	0.4	1247	9.7	1940	0.7
10	TU	0108	9.5	0808	0.7	1334	9.3	2023	1.2
11	W	0154	9.1	0854	1.2	1423	8.8	2107	1.8
12	TH	0243	8.7	0945	1.7	1516	8.3	2156	2.4
13	F	0340	8.2	1042	2.2	1617	7.8	◐ 2256	2.9
14	SA	0445	7.8	1150	2.6	1726	7.5		
15	SU	0008	3.1	0555	7.6	1300	2.6	1838	7.5
16	M	0122	3.1	0705	7.7	1405	2.5	1945	7.7
17	TU	0226	2.9	0806	7.9	1500	2.3	2038	8.0
18	W	0318	2.6	0855	8.1	1546	2.1	2121	8.3
19	TH	0401	2.3	0937	8.4	1625	1.9	2158	8.6
20	F	0438	2.0	1014	8.6	1700	1.7	2232	8.8
21	SA	0513	1.7	1049	8.7	1733	1.6	○ 2305	8.9
22	SU	0548	1.6	1123	8.8	1806	1.5	2338	9.0
23	M	0622	1.5	1156	8.8	1840	1.5		
24	TU	0011	9.0	0658	1.5	1230	8.7	1914	1.6
25	W	0046	8.9	0735	1.6	1305	8.6	1950	1.8
26	TH	0122	8.8	0813	1.7	1344	8.4	2028	2.1
27	F	0203	8.6	0853	2.0	1427	8.2	2110	2.3
28	SA	0250	8.3	0940	2.2	1519	8.0	2201	2.6
29	SU	0348	8.1	1036	2.3	1623	7.8	◑ 2304	2.7
30	M	0455	8.1	1144	2.3	1735	7.8		
31	TU	0017	2.7	0606	8.2	1258	2.2	1847	8.1

JUNE

Date	Day	Time	m	Time	m	Time	m	Time	m
1	W	0131	2.4	0714	8.5	1409	1.8	1953	8.5
2	TH	0240	2.0	0815	8.9	1513	1.5	2051	8.9
3	F	0342	1.5	0912	9.2	1611	1.1	2143	9.2
4	SA	0439	1.1	1005	9.5	1704	0.9	2232	9.5
5	SU	0532	0.8	1055	9.6	1753	0.7	● 2320	9.6
6	M	0622	0.6	1144	9.6	1840	0.8		
7	TU	0006	9.6	0709	0.6	1232	9.5	1923	1.0
8	W	0052	9.5	0755	0.8	1319	9.2	2006	1.4
9	TH	0137	9.2	0841	1.2	1405	8.8	2048	1.8
10	F	0223	8.8	0926	1.6	1452	8.4	2132	2.3
11	SA	0311	8.4	1014	2.1	1542	8.0	2220	2.7
12	SU	0405	8.0	1107	2.5	1639	7.6	◐ 2316	3.1
13	M	0506	7.7	1207	2.7	1742	7.4		
14	TU	0021	3.2	0610	7.6	1309	2.8	1848	7.4
15	W	0127	3.2	0714	7.6	1408	2.7	1949	7.7
16	TH	0227	2.9	0812	7.8	1459	2.5	2041	8.0
17	F	0318	2.6	0901	8.0	1545	2.2	2124	8.3
18	SA	0402	2.3	0944	8.3	1625	2.0	2203	8.6
19	SU	0444	2.0	1023	8.5	1704	1.8	2240	8.8
20	M	0524	1.7	1100	8.6	1742	1.6	○ 2315	8.9
21	TU	0604	1.5	1136	8.7	1820	1.5	2352	9.1
22	W	0643	1.4	1212	8.8	1859	1.5		
23	TH	0029	9.1	0723	1.4	1251	8.8	1937	1.6
24	F	0109	9.0	0803	1.5	1332	8.7	2017	1.7
25	SA	0151	8.9	0844	1.6	1416	8.6	2059	2.0
26	SU	0237	8.8	0928	1.8	1505	8.4	2146	2.2
27	M	0329	8.6	1018	1.9	1601	8.2	◑ 2241	2.4
28	TU	0429	8.4	1117	2.1	1706	8.1	2346	2.5
29	W	0536	8.3	1225	2.1	1817	8.1		
30	TH	0058	2.4	0646	8.4	1338	2.0	1926	8.3

JULY

Date	Day	Time	m	Time	m	Time	m	Time	m
1	F	0212	2.2	0753	8.6	1447	1.8	2030	8.6
2	SA	0321	1.8	0855	8.9	1550	1.6	2127	8.9
3	SU	0423	1.4	0952	9.1	1646	1.3	2219	9.2
4	M	0519	1.1	1044	9.3	1737	1.2	● 2307	9.4
5	TU	0610	0.9	1133	9.3	1824	1.1	2353	9.5
6	W	0657	0.8	1218	9.3	1908	1.2		
7	TH	0036	9.4	0740	0.9	1301	9.1	1948	1.4
8	F	0118	9.2	0822	1.2	1342	8.8	2026	1.7
9	SA	0157	8.9	0901	1.6	1421	8.5	2102	2.1
10	SU	0238	8.6	0938	2.0	1503	8.2	2139	2.5
11	M	0322	8.2	1017	2.4	1549	7.8	2220	2.9
12	TU	0412	7.8	1103	2.8	1644	7.5	◐ 2312	3.2
13	W	0511	7.5	1201	3.0	1747	7.3		
14	TH	0019	3.4	0618	7.3	1308	3.1	1855	7.4
15	F	0131	3.3	0726	7.4	1411	2.9	1958	7.6
16	SA	0235	3.0	0826	7.7	1506	2.6	2051	8.0
17	SU	0329	2.6	0916	8.0	1554	2.3	2136	8.4
18	M	0418	2.2	0959	8.3	1639	1.9	2216	8.7
19	TU	0503	1.8	1039	8.6	1722	1.7	○ 2255	9.0
20	W	0547	1.5	1117	8.8	1804	1.5	2333	9.2
21	TH	0630	1.2	1156	9.0	1845	1.3		
22	F	0012	9.4	0711	1.1	1236	9.1	1926	1.3
23	SA	0053	9.4	0752	1.1	1317	9.1	2006	1.3
24	SU	0135	9.4	0832	1.2	1400	9.0	2046	1.5
25	M	0220	9.2	0913	1.4	1446	8.7	2130	1.8
26	TU	0308	9.0	0958	1.7	1538	8.5	◑ 2219	2.1
27	W	0404	8.6	1051	2.0	1638	8.2	2320	2.4
28	TH	0510	8.3	1157	2.3	1751	8.0		
29	F	0034	2.5	0624	8.2	1314	2.4	1906	8.0
30	SA	0155	2.4	0739	8.2	1429	2.2	2017	8.3
31	SU	0309	2.1	0847	8.5	1536	2.0	2118	8.7

AUGUST

Date	Day	Time	m	Time	m	Time	m	Time	m
1	M	0414	1.7	0946	8.8	1635	1.7	2210	9.1
2	TU	0510	1.3	1036	9.0	1725	1.4	● 2256	9.3
3	W	0559	1.0	1121	9.2	1810	1.3	2338	9.4
4	TH	0642	0.9	1201	9.2	1850	1.3		
5	F	0017	9.4	0720	1.0	1239	9.1	1925	1.4
6	SA	0053	9.3	0756	1.2	1314	8.9	1958	1.6
7	SU	0128	9.1	0828	1.5	1348	8.7	2029	1.9
8	M	0202	8.8	0858	1.9	1423	8.4	2059	2.3
9	TU	0239	8.4	0928	2.3	1503	8.1	2133	2.7
10	W	0320	8.0	1003	2.7	1549	7.7	◐ 2217	3.1
11	TH	0411	7.5	1052	3.1	1646	7.3	2316	3.4
12	F	0517	7.2	1201	3.4	1758	7.2		
13	SA	0034	3.5	0635	7.1	1321	3.3	1913	7.4
14	SU	0153	3.2	0749	7.3	1429	3.0	2017	7.8
15	M	0258	2.8	0848	7.8	1525	2.5	2108	8.3
16	TU	0353	2.2	0936	8.2	1615	2.0	2152	8.8
17	W	0442	1.7	1017	8.7	1702	1.6	2232	9.2
18	TH	0529	1.3	1057	9.1	1746	1.3	○ 2312	9.5
19	F	0613	1.0	1136	9.3	1829	1.0	2352	9.7
20	SA	0656	0.7	1216	9.5	1911	0.9		
21	SU	0033	9.8	0736	0.7	1258	9.5	1951	1.0
22	M	0116	9.8	0816	0.8	1340	9.3	2031	1.2
23	TU	0200	9.5	0855	1.1	1425	9.0	2113	1.6
24	W	0247	9.2	0938	1.6	1515	8.6	2200	2.0
25	TH	0342	8.7	1028	2.1	1614	8.2	◑ 2300	2.4
26	F	0449	8.2	1133	2.6	1730	7.8		
27	SA	0019	2.7	0609	7.9	1257	2.8	1852	7.8
28	SU	0146	2.6	0731	7.9	1419	2.6	2008	8.2
29	M	0302	2.2	0842	8.3	1528	2.3	2109	8.6
30	TU	0406	1.7	0939	8.6	1625	1.[illegible]	2159	9.[illegible]
31	W	0459	1.4	1025	8.[illegible]	1712	1.6	2241	9.2

Chart Datum: 4·93 metres below Ordnance Datum (Newlyn)
HAT is 10·3m above Chart Datum

TIME ZONE (UT)
For Summer Time add ONE hour in **non-shaded areas**

LIVERPOOL (GLADSTONE DOCK)

LAT 53°27'N LONG 3°01'W

TIMES AND HEIGHTS OF HIGH AND LOW WATERS

Dates in amber are **SPRINGS**
Dates in yellow are **NEAPS**

2016

SEPTEMBER

Date	Day	Time	m	Time	m	Time	m	Time	m	Moon
1	TH	0543	1.1	1104	9.1	1752	1.4	2319	9.4	●
2	F	0621	1.1	1140	9.2	1827	1.4	2353	9.4	
3	SA	0655	1.1	1212	9.2	1859	1.4			
4	SU	0026	9.3	0724	1.3	1244	9.1	1927	1.6	
5	M	0057	9.1	0752	1.5	1315	8.9	1955	1.8	
6	TU	0128	8.9	0819	1.8	1347	8.6	2024	2.1	
7	W	0201	8.5	0846	2.2	1422	8.3	2057	2.5	
8	TH	0236	8.1	0919	2.6	1501	7.9	2136	2.9	
9	F	0318	7.6	1002	3.1	1550	7.5	2228	3.3	◐
10	SA	0416	7.2	1103	3.5	1701	7.2	2343	3.5	
11	SU	0540	6.9	1229	3.6	1825	7.2			
12	M	0111	3.4	0708	7.1	1351	3.2	1939	7.6	
13	TU	0225	2.8	0817	7.7	1455	2.7	2037	8.2	
14	W	0325	2.2	0909	8.3	1550	2.1	2124	8.8	
15	TH	0418	1.6	0952	8.8	1639	1.6	2207	9.4	
16	F	0506	1.1	1033	9.3	1725	1.1	2248	9.8	○
17	SA	0552	0.7	1113	9.6	1810	0.8	2329	10.0	
18	SU	0635	0.5	1154	9.8	1852	0.7			
19	M	0011	10.1	0716	0.5	1236	9.8	1933	0.7	
20	TU	0055	10.0	0756	0.7	1319	9.6	2014	1.0	
21	W	0140	9.7	0836	1.1	1404	9.2	2057	1.4	
22	TH	0228	9.2	0918	1.7	1454	8.7	2146	2.0	
23	F	0323	8.6	1008	2.3	1554	8.2	2248	2.5	◑
24	SA	0433	8.0	1116	2.9	1712	7.8			
25	SU	0010	2.8	0556	7.7	1243	3.1	1836	7.8	
26	M	0136	2.6	0721	7.8	1407	2.9	1953	8.1	
27	TU	0250	2.2	0831	8.2	1515	2.4	2054	8.5	
28	W	0350	1.8	0924	8.6	1609	2.1	2141	8.9	
29	TH	0439	1.5	1006	8.9	1652	1.8	2221	9.1	
30	F	0519	1.3	1042	9.1	1728	1.6	2255	9.3	

OCTOBER

Date	Day	Time	m	Time	m	Time	m	Time	m	Moon
1	SA	0553	1.3	1114	9.2	1800	1.5	2327	9.3	●
2	SU	0623	1.3	1145	9.2	1829	1.5	2358	9.2	
3	M	0651	1.4	1214	9.2	1857	1.6			
4	TU	0028	9.1	0718	1.6	1245	9.0	1926	1.8	
5	W	0059	8.9	0745	1.8	1316	8.8	1956	2.0	
6	TH	0130	8.6	0814	2.2	1348	8.5	2029	2.4	
7	F	0203	8.2	0847	2.6	1424	8.1	2107	2.8	
8	SA	0242	7.8	0927	3.0	1509	7.7	2155	3.1	
9	SU	0334	7.4	1021	3.5	1612	7.4	2302	3.4	◐
10	M	0450	7.1	1141	3.6	1736	7.3			
11	TU	0029	3.3	0621	7.2	1310	3.4	1856	7.7	
12	W	0149	2.8	0738	7.7	1421	2.8	2000	8.2	
13	TH	0253	2.2	0836	8.3	1519	2.2	2052	8.9	
14	F	0349	1.6	0923	9.0	1612	1.6	2138	9.5	
15	SA	0439	1.0	1007	9.5	1701	1.1	2222	9.9	
16	SU	0527	0.6	1049	9.8	1747	0.8	2306	10.2	○
17	M	0612	0.4	1132	10.0	1832	0.6	2350	10.2	
18	TU	0654	0.4	1215	10.0	1915	0.6			
19	W	0035	10.1	0736	0.7	1259	9.7	1959	0.9	
20	TH	0123	9.7	0817	1.2	1345	9.4	2044	1.3	
21	F	0212	9.2	0901	1.8	1436	8.8	2135	1.9	
22	SA	0308	8.5	0952	2.4	1537	8.3	2238	2.4	◑
23	SU	0416	8.0	1058	3.0	1651	7.9	2355	2.7	
24	M	0536	7.6	1221	3.2	1811	7.8			
25	TU	0114	2.6	0657	7.7	1342	3.0	1926	8.0	
26	W	0225	2.3	0807	8.0	1448	2.7	2027	8.4	
27	TH	0322	2.0	0859	8.4	1541	2.3	2115	8.7	
28	F	0409	1.8	0941	8.7	1623	2.1	2154	8.9	
29	SA	0448	1.6	1016	8.9	1659	1.9	2229	9.1	
30	SU	0521	1.6	1047	9.1	1730	1.8	2301	9.1	●
31	M	0551	1.5	1118	9.2	1800	1.7	2332	9.1	

NOVEMBER

Date	Day	Time	m	Time	m	Time	m	Time	m	Moon
1	TU	0619	1.6	1148	9.2	1830	1.7			
2	W	0003	9.0	0648	1.7	1219	9.1	1901	1.8	
3	TH	0035	8.9	0718	1.8	1250	8.9	1934	1.9	
4	F	0107	8.6	0750	2.1	1323	8.7	2009	2.2	
5	SA	0140	8.3	0824	2.5	1359	8.4	2047	2.6	
6	SU	0220	8.0	0904	2.9	1443	8.1	2133	2.9	
7	M	0309	7.7	0954	3.3	1540	7.8	2232	3.1	◐
8	TU	0414	7.4	1102	3.5	1654	7.6	2348	3.1	
9	W	0536	7.4	1225	3.3	1812	7.8			
10	TH	0107	2.8	0654	7.8	1341	2.9	1920	8.3	
11	F	0216	2.2	0759	8.3	1445	2.3	2018	8.9	
12	SA	0316	1.7	0853	8.9	1542	1.7	2110	9.4	
13	SU	0411	1.2	0941	9.4	1635	1.2	2158	9.8	
14	M	0501	0.8	1026	9.8	1725	0.9	2245	10.1	○
15	TU	0548	0.6	1112	10.0	1813	0.7	2333	10.1	
16	W	0634	0.6	1157	10.0	1900	0.7			
17	TH	0020	10.0	0717	0.8	1243	9.8	1946	0.9	
18	F	0109	9.6	0801	1.3	1330	9.5	2033	1.2	
19	SA	0159	9.1	0846	1.8	1421	9.0	2125	1.7	
20	SU	0253	8.6	0936	2.4	1517	8.5	2222	2.2	
21	M	0353	8.1	1035	2.9	1621	8.1	2328	2.6	◑
22	TU	0501	7.7	1146	3.2	1732	7.9			
23	W	0038	2.7	0615	7.6	1300	3.2	1843	7.9	
24	TH	0145	2.6	0726	7.8	1407	3.0	1948	8.0	
25	F	0243	2.4	0823	8.1	1502	2.8	2040	8.3	
26	SA	0332	2.2	0909	8.4	1548	2.5	2124	8.5	
27	SU	0412	2.0	0946	8.7	1626	2.2	2202	8.7	
28	M	0448	1.9	1021	8.9	1701	2.0	2237	8.9	
29	TU	0520	1.8	1053	9.0	1735	1.9	2310	8.9	●
30	W	0552	1.7	1125	9.1	1808	1.8	2343	8.9	

DECEMBER

Date	Day	Time	m	Time	m	Time	m	Time	m	Moon
1	TH	0624	1.7	1158	9.1	1842	1.8			
2	F	0016	8.8	0657	1.8	1231	9.0	1918	1.8	
3	SA	0050	8.7	0732	2.0	1306	8.9	1955	2.0	
4	SU	0125	8.5	0808	2.3	1343	8.7	2034	2.2	
5	M	0205	8.3	0848	2.6	1425	8.5	2117	2.5	
6	TU	0251	8.0	0934	2.9	1516	8.2	2209	2.7	
7	W	0348	7.8	1032	3.1	1619	8.1	2312	2.7	◐
8	TH	0457	7.7	1142	3.1	1730	8.1			
9	F	0024	2.6	0611	7.9	1258	2.9	1841	8.3	
10	SA	0137	2.3	0722	8.3	1409	2.5	1946	8.7	
11	SU	0244	1.9	0823	8.7	1513	2.0	2045	9.1	
12	M	0343	1.5	0918	9.2	1612	1.5	2139	9.5	
13	TU	0438	1.1	1008	9.5	1706	1.1	2230	9.7	
14	W	0529	0.9	1056	9.8	1758	0.8	2320	9.8	○
15	TH	0617	0.9	1144	9.9	1847	0.7			
16	F	0009	9.8	0702	1.0	1231	9.8	1935	0.8	
17	SA	0057	9.5	0747	1.3	1317	9.5	2022	1.1	
18	SU	0144	9.2	0831	1.7	1404	9.2	2109	1.5	
19	M	0232	8.7	0916	2.2	1452	8.8	2157	2.0	
20	TU	0321	8.3	1003	2.7	1544	8.4	2250	2.5	
21	W	0416	7.8	1057	3.1	1643	8.0	2348	2.8	◑
22	TH	0519	7.6	1201	3.3	1748	7.7			
23	F	0051	2.9	0627	7.5	1310	3.4	1855	7.7	
24	SA	0153	2.9	0734	7.6	1413	3.2	1958	7.8	
25	SU	0248	2.7	0830	7.9	1508	2.9	2051	8.1	
26	M	0335	2.5	0916	8.3	1554	2.6	2136	8.3	
27	TU	0416	2.2	0955	8.6	1635	2.3	2215	8.5	
28	W	0454	2.0	1032	8.8	1713	2.0	2251	8.7	
29	TH	0530	1.8	1106	9.0	1751	1.8	2326	8.8	●
30	F	0606	1.7	1141	9.1	1828	1.7			
31	SA	0000	8.9	0642	1.7	1216	9.2	1906	1.6	

Chart Datum: 4·93 metres below Ordnance Datum (Newlyn)
HAT is 10·3m above Chart Datum

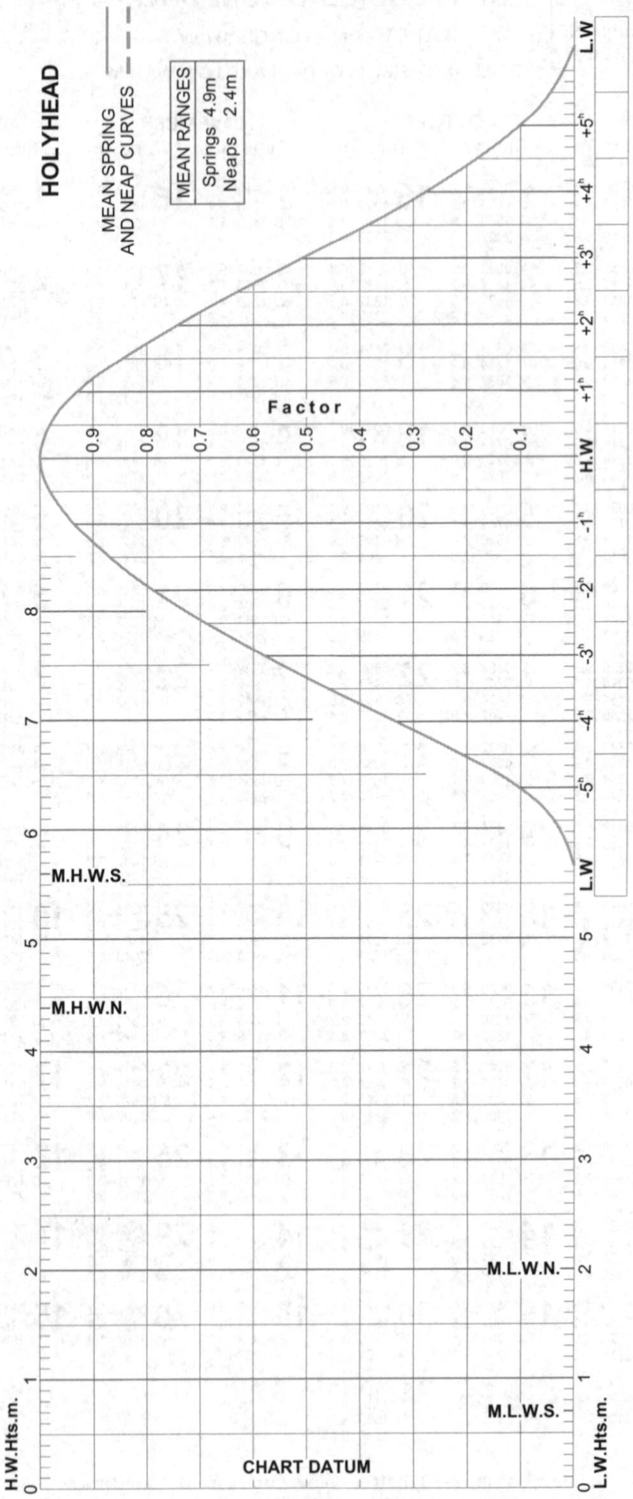
HOLYHEAD
MEAN SPRING AND NEAP CURVES
MEAN RANGES
Springs 4.9m
Neaps 2.4m
Factor
0.9
0.8
0.7
0.6
0.5
0.4
0.3
0.2
0.1
L.W
-5h
-4h
-3h
-2h
-1h
H.W
+1h
+2h
+3h
+4h
+5h
L.W
H.W.Hts.m.
L.W.Hts.m.
M.H.W.S.
M.H.W.N.
M.L.W.N.
M.L.W.S.
CHART DATUM

TIME ZONE (UT)
For Summer Time add ONE hour in **non-shaded areas**

WALES – HOLYHEAD

LAT 53°19′N LONG 4°37′W

TIMES AND HEIGHTS OF HIGH AND LOW WATERS

Dates in amber are **SPRINGS**
Dates in yellow are **NEAPS**

2016

JANUARY

Date	Day	Time	m	Time	m	Time	m	Time	m
1	F	0235	4.8	0835	1.9	1450	4.9	2117	1.8
2	SA	0327	4.6	0927	2.2	1544	4.7	◑ 2215	2.0
3	SU	0430	4.4	1031	2.4	1650	4.6	2321	2.1
4	M	0540	4.4	1143	2.4	1802	4.6		
5	TU	0026	2.1	0647	4.6	1250	2.2	1908	4.7
6	W	0123	1.9	0743	4.8	1346	2.0	2003	4.8
7	TH	0211	1.7	0828	5.0	1433	1.7	2048	5.0
8	F	0253	1.5	0908	5.3	1514	1.4	2128	5.2
9	SA	0332	1.2	0946	5.5	1554	1.1	2207	5.4
10	SU	0410	1.0	1023	5.7	1633	0.9	● 2245	5.5
11	M	0449	0.9	1102	5.8	1713	0.8	2325	5.6
12	TU	0529	0.8	1142	5.9	1754	0.7		
13	W	0007	5.6	0610	0.8	1225	5.9	1837	0.7
14	TH	0052	5.5	0654	0.9	1310	5.8	1924	0.8
15	F	0139	5.4	0742	1.1	1358	5.6	2014	1.0
16	SA	0230	5.2	0836	1.3	1452	5.4	◐ 2112	1.2
17	SU	0330	4.9	0938	1.6	1555	5.2	2218	1.4
18	M	0442	4.8	1051	1.7	1709	5.0	2331	1.6
19	TU	0600	4.8	1208	1.7	1827	5.0		
20	W	0043	1.5	0712	4.9	1319	1.6	1937	5.1
21	TH	0149	1.4	0813	5.2	1422	1.3	2037	5.2
22	F	0245	1.2	0903	5.4	1515	1.1	2127	5.4
23	SA	0332	1.1	0948	5.6	1601	0.9	2211	5.5
24	SU	0414	1.0	1029	5.7	1643	0.8	○ 2252	5.5
25	M	0452	0.9	1107	5.8	1721	0.8	2329	5.5
26	TU	0529	0.9	1144	5.7	1758	0.8		
27	W	0005	5.4	0603	1.0	1220	5.6	1833	1.0
28	TH	0040	5.3	0638	1.2	1254	5.5	1908	1.1
29	F	0115	5.1	0714	1.4	1328	5.3	1945	1.4
30	SA	0151	4.9	0752	1.6	1406	5.1	2025	1.6
31	SU	0232	4.7	0836	1.9	1449	4.8	2112	1.9

FEBRUARY

Date	Day	Time	m	Time	m	Time	m	Time	m
1	M	0322	4.5	0928	2.1	1543	4.6	◑ 2210	2.1
2	TU	0427	4.4	1035	2.3	1657	4.4	2322	2.2
3	W	0546	4.4	1154	2.3	1819	4.4		
4	TH	0036	2.1	0659	4.5	1306	2.1	1930	4.6
5	F	0138	1.9	0757	4.8	1404	1.8	2024	4.8
6	SA	0228	1.6	0844	5.1	1452	1.4	2109	5.1
7	SU	0311	1.2	0924	5.4	1534	1.0	2149	5.4
8	M	0351	0.9	1004	5.7	1614	0.7	● 2228	5.6
9	TU	0431	0.7	1043	5.9	1655	0.5	2308	5.7
10	W	0511	0.5	1124	6.1	1736	0.3	2350	5.8
11	TH	0553	0.5	1207	6.1	1819	0.3		
12	F	0032	5.7	0636	0.5	1252	6.0	1903	0.5
13	SA	0118	5.5	0722	0.7	1338	5.8	1952	0.8
14	SU	0206	5.3	0813	1.0	1430	5.5	2046	1.1
15	M	0302	5.0	0914	1.4	1530	5.1	◐ 2150	1.5
16	TU	0411	4.8	1027	1.6	1647	4.8	2307	1.7
17	W	0535	4.6	1150	1.7	1814	4.7		
18	TH	0027	1.8	0657	4.7	1309	1.6	1933	4.8
19	F	0140	1.6	0803	5.0	1416	1.4	2034	5.0
20	SA	0237	1.4	0855	5.2	1508	1.1	2120	5.2
21	SU	0322	1.2	0937	5.4	1550	0.9	2159	5.3
22	M	0401	1.0	1014	5.6	1627	0.8	○ 2234	5.4
23	TU	0435	0.9	1048	5.6	1701	0.7	2307	5.4
24	W	0507	0.9	1121	5.6	1732	0.8	2339	5.4
25	TH	0539	0.9	1153	5.6	1804	0.9		
26	F	0010	5.4	0610	1.0	1225	5.5	1835	1.0
27	SA	0042	5.3	0643	1.1	1256	5.3	1908	1.2
28	SU	0115	5.1	0717	1.3	1330	5.1	1943	1.4
29	M	0151	4.9	0756	1.6	1408	4.9	2024	1.7

MARCH

Date	Day	Time	m	Time	m	Time	m	Time	m
1	TU	0233	4.7	0842	1.9	1454	4.6	◑ 2114	2.0
2	W	0327	4.5	0942	2.1	1558	4.3	2222	2.2
3	TH	0444	4.3	1100	2.2	1730	4.3	2346	2.2
4	F	0611	4.4	1224	2.1	1855	4.4		
5	SA	0102	2.0	0721	4.7	1332	1.7	1957	4.7
6	SU	0200	1.6	0815	5.0	1425	1.3	2045	5.1
7	M	0247	1.2	0859	5.4	1509	0.8	2127	5.4
8	TU	0329	0.8	0940	5.7	1551	0.5	2207	5.7
9	W	0409	0.5	1021	6.0	1632	0.2	● 2247	5.8
10	TH	0450	0.3	1103	6.2	1714	0.1	2329	5.9
11	F	0533	0.2	1147	6.2	1757	0.1		
12	SA	0012	5.9	0616	0.3	1232	6.1	1842	0.3
13	SU	0057	5.7	0703	0.5	1320	5.8	1930	0.7
14	M	0144	5.4	0755	0.8	1411	5.4	2023	1.1
15	TU	0238	5.1	0855	1.2	1512	5.0	◐ 2126	1.5
16	W	0345	4.8	1009	1.6	1631	4.7	2245	1.9
17	TH	0510	4.6	1133	1.7	1803	4.5		
18	F	0009	1.9	0638	4.6	1255	1.6	1923	4.6
19	SA	0124	1.8	0747	4.8	1400	1.4	2021	4.8
20	SU	0221	1.5	0838	5.1	1450	1.2	2105	5.0
21	M	0305	1.3	0918	5.3	1530	1.0	2140	5.2
22	TU	0341	1.1	0952	5.4	1604	0.8	2212	5.3
23	W	0413	0.9	1024	5.5	1635	0.8	○ 2242	5.4
24	TH	0443	0.9	1055	5.5	1705	0.8	2311	5.4
25	F	0513	0.8	1126	5.5	1734	0.8	2341	5.4
26	SA	0544	0.9	1157	5.4	1804	1.0		
27	SU	0012	5.3	0615	1.0	1229	5.3	1836	1.1
28	M	0045	5.2	0649	1.2	1302	5.1	1909	1.3
29	TU	0120	5.0	0726	1.4	1339	4.9	1948	1.6
30	W	0159	4.8	0810	1.6	1422	4.6	2035	1.9
31	TH	0249	4.6	0906	1.9	1521	4.4	◑ 2139	2.1

APRIL

Date	Day	Time	m	Time	m	Time	m	Time	m
1	F	0356	4.4	1019	2.0	1647	4.3	2302	2.2
2	SA	0524	4.4	1144	1.9	1818	4.4		
3	SU	0023	2.0	0641	4.6	1256	1.6	1926	4.7
4	M	0127	1.6	0740	5.0	1353	1.1	2017	5.1
5	TU	0218	1.2	0829	5.4	1441	0.7	2101	5.4
6	W	0303	0.7	0914	5.7	1525	0.4	2143	5.7
7	TH	0346	0.4	0957	6.0	1608	0.1	● 2224	5.9
8	F	0429	0.2	1041	6.2	1652	0.0	2307	6.0
9	SA	0513	0.1	1127	6.2	1736	0.1	2351	5.9
10	SU	0559	0.2	1214	6.0	1822	0.4		
11	M	0037	5.7	0647	0.4	1304	5.7	1910	0.7
12	TU	0126	5.5	0740	0.7	1357	5.3	2003	1.2
13	W	0219	5.1	0840	1.1	1458	4.9	2105	1.6
14	TH	0323	4.8	0951	1.5	1614	4.6	◐ 2219	1.9
15	F	0442	4.6	1110	1.6	1740	4.5	2341	2.0
16	SA	0607	4.6	1227	1.6	1858	4.5		
17	SU	0055	1.9	0717	4.7	1332	1.5	1956	4.7
18	M	0154	1.7	0809	4.9	1422	1.3	2039	4.9
19	TU	0238	1.5	0850	5.1	1502	1.1	2114	5.1
20	W	0315	1.3	0925	5.2	1536	1.0	2145	5.2
21	TH	0347	1.1	0957	5.3	1606	0.9	2215	5.3
22	F	0417	1.0	1029	5.4	1636	0.9	○ 2244	5.4
23	SA	0448	0.9	1100	5.4	1706	0.9	2315	5.4
24	SU	0519	0.9	1132	5.3	1737	1.0	2347	5.4
25	M	0552	1.0	1205	5.2	1809	1.1		
26	TU	0020	5.3	0627	1.1	1240	5.1	1844	1.3
27	W	0057	5.2	0705	1.3	1318	4.9	1923	1.5
28	TH	0137	5.0	0749	1.5	1403	4.7	2010	1.7
29	F	0225	4.8	0843	1.6	1459	4.5	2110	1.9
30	SA	0327	4.6	0950	1.7	1615	4.4	◑ 2226	2.0

Chart Datum: 3·05 metres below Ordnance Datum (Newlyn)
HAT is 6·3m above Chart Datum

TIME ZONE (UT)
For Summer Time add ONE hour in **non-shaded areas**

WALES – HOLYHEAD

LAT 53°19'N LONG 4°37'W

TIMES AND HEIGHTS OF HIGH AND LOW WATERS

Dates in amber are **SPRINGS**
Dates in yellow are **NEAPS**

2016

MAY

Date	Day	Time	m	Time	m	Time	m	Time	m
1	SU	0444	4.6	1108	1.7	1741	4.5	2345	1.9
2	M	0601	4.8	1219	1.4	1851	4.8		
3	TU	0052	1.6	0704	5.0	1320	1.1	1946	5.1
4	W	0147	1.2	0758	5.4	1412	0.7	2034	5.4
5	TH	0236	0.8	0847	5.7	1459	0.4	2118	5.7
6	F	0323	0.5	0934	5.9	1545	0.2	● 2202	5.8
7	SA	0409	0.3	1022	6.0	1631	0.2	2247	5.9
8	SU	0456	0.2	1110	6.0	1717	0.3	2333	5.9
9	M	0544	0.3	1159	5.8	1804	0.5		
10	TU	0020	5.8	0634	0.5	1250	5.6	1853	0.8
11	W	0109	5.5	0726	0.7	1342	5.2	1944	1.2
12	TH	0201	5.2	0823	1.1	1440	4.9	2041	1.6
13	F	0300	5.0	0927	1.4	1547	4.6	◐ 2147	1.9
14	SA	0407	4.7	1037	1.6	1701	4.5	2301	2.0
15	SU	0521	4.6	1147	1.7	1815	4.5		
16	M	0012	2.0	0632	4.6	1251	1.6	1916	4.6
17	TU	0113	1.9	0729	4.7	1344	1.5	2003	4.8
18	W	0203	1.7	0815	4.9	1427	1.3	2041	5.0
19	TH	0243	1.5	0854	5.0	1504	1.2	2115	5.1
20	F	0319	1.3	0929	5.1	1537	1.1	2147	5.2
21	SA	0351	1.2	1003	5.2	1609	1.0	○ 2219	5.3
22	SU	0424	1.1	1036	5.2	1640	1.0	2251	5.4
23	M	0458	1.0	1110	5.2	1713	1.1	2325	5.4
24	TU	0533	1.0	1145	5.2	1748	1.1		
25	W	0001	5.4	0609	1.1	1223	5.1	1825	1.2
26	TH	0039	5.3	0649	1.2	1303	5.0	1906	1.4
27	F	0121	5.2	0734	1.3	1349	4.8	1953	1.6
28	SA	0209	5.0	0826	1.4	1443	4.7	2049	1.7
29	SU	0305	4.9	0927	1.5	1549	4.6	◑ 2157	1.8
30	M	0412	4.9	1036	1.4	1704	4.6	2310	1.7
31	TU	0524	4.9	1145	1.3	1815	4.8		

JUNE

Date	Day	Time	m	Time	m	Time	m	Time	m
1	W	0018	1.5	0631	5.1	1249	1.1	1916	5.0
2	TH	0118	1.2	0731	5.3	1346	0.8	2009	5.3
3	F	0213	0.9	0825	5.5	1437	0.6	2058	5.5
4	SA	0304	0.7	0917	5.7	1527	0.5	2145	5.7
5	SU	0353	0.5	1007	5.8	1614	0.5	● 2231	5.8
6	M	0443	0.4	1056	5.8	1702	0.5	2318	5.8
7	TU	0532	0.4	1146	5.7	1749	0.7		
8	W	0005	5.7	0620	0.5	1235	5.5	1835	0.9
9	TH	0052	5.6	0710	0.8	1324	5.2	1923	1.2
10	F	0140	5.3	0801	1.0	1415	4.9	2013	1.5
11	SA	0230	5.1	0855	1.3	1509	4.7	2107	1.8
12	SU	0325	4.8	0953	1.6	1610	4.5	◐ 2209	2.0
13	M	0426	4.6	1056	1.7	1715	4.4	2317	2.1
14	TU	0532	4.5	1159	1.8	1821	4.5		
15	W	0021	2.1	0637	4.6	1257	1.7	1917	4.6
16	TH	0119	1.9	0733	4.7	1347	1.6	2004	4.8
17	F	0207	1.7	0821	4.8	1430	1.5	2045	5.0
18	SA	0249	1.5	0902	4.9	1508	1.3	2121	5.1
19	SU	0327	1.3	0939	5.1	1543	1.2	2155	5.3
20	M	0403	1.2	1014	5.1	1618	1.1	○ 2230	5.4
21	TU	0439	1.0	1050	5.2	1653	1.1	2306	5.5
22	W	0516	1.0	1128	5.2	1730	1.0	2344	5.5
23	TH	0555	0.9	1207	5.2	1809	1.1		
24	F	0024	5.5	0635	0.9	1249	5.1	1851	1.2
25	SA	0106	5.4	0719	1.0	1334	5.0	1937	1.3
26	SU	0153	5.3	0808	1.1	1424	4.9	2029	1.4
27	M	0244	5.2	0903	1.2	1522	4.8	◑ 2129	1.6
28	TU	0344	5.1	1006	1.3	1631	4.8	2238	1.6
29	W	0452	5.0	1115	1.3	1743	4.8	2348	1.5
30	TH	0603	5.1	1222	1.2	1850	5.0		

JULY

Date	Day	Time	m	Time	m	Time	m	Time	m
1	F	0055	1.4	0710	5.2	1325	1.1	1950	5.2
2	SA	0156	1.1	0811	5.3	1422	0.9	2043	5.4
3	SU	0252	0.9	0906	5.5	1514	0.8	2132	5.6
4	M	0344	0.7	0957	5.6	1602	0.7	● 2219	5.7
5	TU	0433	0.5	1045	5.6	1648	0.7	2304	5.8
6	W	0520	0.5	1131	5.5	1732	0.8	2348	5.7
7	TH	0605	0.6	1216	5.4	1815	0.9		
8	F	0031	5.6	0648	0.8	1300	5.2	1856	1.1
9	SA	0114	5.4	0731	1.0	1342	5.0	1939	1.4
10	SU	0156	5.2	0815	1.3	1425	4.8	2024	1.6
11	M	0240	5.0	0903	1.5	1513	4.6	2113	1.9
12	TU	0329	4.7	0956	1.8	1609	4.4	◐ 2212	2.1
13	W	0429	4.5	1058	1.9	1714	4.4	2320	2.2
14	TH	0537	4.4	1202	2.0	1822	4.4		
15	F	0029	2.1	0646	4.5	1303	1.9	1923	4.6
16	SA	0129	2.0	0747	4.6	1356	1.7	2013	4.8
17	SU	0220	1.7	0836	4.8	1440	1.5	2055	5.1
18	M	0303	1.4	0917	5.0	1520	1.3	2133	5.3
19	TU	0342	1.2	0955	5.1	1557	1.1	○ 2209	5.4
20	W	0420	1.0	1032	5.3	1634	1.0	2246	5.6
21	TH	0458	0.8	1110	5.4	1712	0.9	2325	5.7
22	F	0537	0.7	1150	5.4	1752	0.8		
23	SA	0006	5.7	0617	0.7	1232	5.4	1833	0.9
24	SU	0048	5.7	0700	0.7	1315	5.3	1918	1.0
25	M	0133	5.6	0747	0.9	1403	5.2	2007	1.2
26	TU	0222	5.4	0839	1.0	1456	5.0	◑ 2104	1.4
27	W	0319	5.2	0939	1.3	1600	4.8	2211	1.6
28	TH	0427	5.0	1049	1.4	1715	4.8	2326	1.6
29	F	0544	4.9	1202	1.5	1831	4.8		
30	SA	0040	1.5	0659	5.0	1312	1.4	1938	5.0
31	SU	0149	1.3	0806	5.1	1414	1.2	2035	5.3

AUGUST

Date	Day	Time	m	Time	m	Time	m	Time	m
1	M	0248	1.0	0902	5.3	1507	1.1	2123	5.5
2	TU	0338	0.8	0950	5.4	1552	0.9	● 2207	5.7
3	W	0423	0.7	1033	5.5	1634	0.8	2249	5.7
4	TH	0504	0.6	1113	5.5	1713	0.8	2328	5.7
5	F	0543	0.7	1152	5.4	1751	0.9		
6	SA	0006	5.6	0620	0.8	1229	5.3	1827	1.0
7	SU	0043	5.5	0657	1.0	1305	5.1	1903	1.3
8	M	0119	5.3	0734	1.2	1342	5.0	1942	1.5
9	TU	0156	5.1	0814	1.5	1422	4.8	2025	1.8
10	W	0238	4.8	0859	1.8	1509	4.6	◐ 2115	2.0
11	TH	0329	4.6	0954	2.0	1609	4.4	2218	2.2
12	F	0438	4.4	1102	2.2	1724	4.4	2335	2.3
13	SA	0558	4.3	1216	2.1	1838	4.5		
14	SU	0050	2.1	0713	4.5	1321	2.0	1940	4.7
15	M	0150	1.8	0810	4.7	1412	1.7	2028	5.0
16	TU	0238	1.5	0855	4.9	1456	1.4	2109	5.3
17	W	0319	1.1	0934	5.2	1535	1.1	2146	5.5
18	TH	0358	0.8	1011	5.4	1613	0.8	○ 2224	5.8
19	F	0436	0.6	1049	5.6	1651	0.7	2303	5.9
20	SA	0515	0.4	1128	5.7	1731	0.6	2344	6.0
21	SU	0556	0.4	1210	5.6	1812	0.6		
22	M	0027	5.9	0638	0.5	1253	5.5	1856	0.8
23	TU	0112	5.8	0724	0.7	1340	5.4	1945	1.0
24	W	0201	5.5	0815	1.0	1431	5.1	2042	1.3
25	TH	0258	5.2	0914	1.3	1535	4.9	◑ 2150	1.6
26	F	0408	4.9	1027	1.6	1654	4.7	2312	1.7
27	SA	0534	4.8	1148	1.8	1819	4.8		
28	SU	0033	1.6	0657	4.8	1304	1.7	1930	5.0
29	M	0145	1.4	0805	5.0	1408	1.5	2027	5.2
30	TU	0242	1.1	0857	5.2	1458	1.2	2113	5.5
31	W	0328	0.9	0939	5.3	1539	1.1	2153	5.6

Chart Datum: 3·05 metres below Ordnance Datum (Newlyn)
HAT is 6·3m above Chart Datum

TIME ZONE (UT)
For Summer Time add ONE hour in **non-shaded areas**

WALES – HOLYHEAD

LAT 53°19′N LONG 4°37′W

TIMES AND HEIGHTS OF HIGH AND LOW WATERS

Dates in amber are **SPRINGS**
Dates in yellow are **NEAPS**

2016

SEPTEMBER

Date	Day	Time	m	Time	m	Time	m	Time	m
1	TH ●	0407	0.8	1016	5.4	1616	0.9	2229	5.7
2	F	0443	0.7	1051	5.5	1651	0.9	2304	5.7
3	SA	0517	0.7	1124	5.5	1724	0.9	2338	5.6
4	SU	0550	0.8	1157	5.4	1757	1.0		
5	M	0011	5.5	0622	1.0	1230	5.3	1830	1.2
6	TU	0044	5.3	0655	1.2	1303	5.1	1905	1.4
7	W	0118	5.1	0731	1.5	1339	5.0	1944	1.7
8	TH	0156	4.9	0811	1.8	1421	4.7	2030	2.0
9	F ◐	0241	4.6	0900	2.0	1514	4.5	2128	2.2
10	SA	0343	4.4	1005	2.3	1627	4.4	2244	2.3
11	SU	0512	4.3	1126	2.3	1752	4.5		
12	M	0008	2.2	0638	4.4	1244	2.1	1903	4.7
13	TU	0116	1.9	0742	4.7	1342	1.8	1957	5.0
14	W	0208	1.5	0829	5.0	1428	1.4	2040	5.4
15	TH	0252	1.1	0909	5.3	1509	1.1	2120	5.7
16	F ○	0331	0.7	0947	5.6	1548	0.7	2159	5.9
17	SA	0410	0.4	1025	5.8	1627	0.5	2239	6.1
18	SU	0450	0.3	1105	5.9	1708	0.4	2321	6.2
19	M	0532	0.3	1147	5.9	1751	0.4		
20	TU	0005	6.1	0615	0.4	1231	5.8	1836	0.6
21	W	0052	5.9	0702	0.7	1318	5.5	1926	0.9
22	TH	0143	5.6	0753	1.1	1410	5.3	2025	1.3
23	F ◑	0242	5.2	0854	1.5	1514	5.0	2136	1.6
24	SA	0357	4.8	1010	1.9	1636	4.8	2300	1.7
25	SU	0528	4.7	1134	2.0	1804	4.8		
26	M	0023	1.7	0652	4.8	1252	1.9	1917	5.0
27	TU	0133	1.5	0756	5.0	1355	1.6	2013	5.2
28	W	0227	1.2	0844	5.2	1442	1.4	2056	5.4
29	TH	0310	1.0	0922	5.3	1521	1.2	2133	5.6
30	F	0346	0.9	0955	5.4	1555	1.1	2206	5.6

OCTOBER

Date	Day	Time	m	Time	m	Time	m	Time	m
1	SA ●	0419	0.9	1026	5.5	1626	1.0	2238	5.6
2	SU	0449	0.9	1056	5.5	1657	1.0	2310	5.6
3	M	0519	0.9	1127	5.5	1728	1.1	2341	5.5
4	TU	0550	1.1	1158	5.4	1801	1.2		
5	W	0013	5.4	0621	1.3	1231	5.3	1835	1.4
6	TH	0047	5.2	0655	1.5	1306	5.1	1912	1.6
7	F	0123	5.0	0733	1.8	1345	4.9	1955	1.9
8	SA	0206	4.7	0818	2.0	1434	4.7	2050	2.1
9	SU ◐	0303	4.4	0919	2.3	1538	4.5	2201	2.2
10	M	0426	4.3	1039	2.4	1704	4.5	2325	2.1
11	TU	0559	4.4	1201	2.2	1821	4.7		
12	W	0037	1.8	0707	4.7	1306	1.9	1920	5.1
13	TH	0134	1.4	0758	5.1	1357	1.5	2008	5.4
14	F	0221	1.0	0841	5.4	1441	1.1	2051	5.8
15	SA	0303	0.7	0921	5.7	1522	0.7	2133	6.0
16	SU ○	0344	0.4	1000	5.9	1604	0.5	2215	6.2
17	M	0426	0.2	1042	6.0	1647	0.4	2300	6.3
18	TU	0509	0.3	1125	6.0	1732	0.4	2346	6.2
19	W	0555	0.5	1211	5.9	1820	0.6		
20	TH	0035	5.9	0642	0.8	1259	5.7	1912	0.9
21	F	0129	5.5	0735	1.2	1353	5.4	2012	1.2
22	SA ◑	0229	5.1	0836	1.6	1456	5.1	2122	1.5
23	SU	0344	4.8	0949	2.0	1614	4.9	2242	1.7
24	M	0511	4.7	1111	2.1	1739	4.9		
25	TU	0000	1.7	0631	4.7	1228	2.0	1851	5.0
26	W	0109	1.6	0734	4.9	1330	1.8	1948	5.1
27	TH	0202	1.4	0821	5.1	1419	1.6	2032	5.3
28	F	0245	1.2	0858	5.3	1458	1.4	2108	5.4
29	SA	0320	1.1	0930	5.4	1531	1.3	2141	5.5
30	SU ●	0352	1.0	1000	5.5	1602	1.2	2213	5.5
31	M	0422	1.0	1030	5.5	1633	1.1	2244	5.5

NOVEMBER

Date	Day	Time	m	Time	m	Time	m	Time	m
1	TU	0451	1.1	1100	5.6	1704	1.2	2316	5.5
2	W	0522	1.2	1131	5.5	1737	1.2	2348	5.4
3	TH	0554	1.3	1205	5.4	1812	1.4		
4	F	0023	5.2	0627	1.5	1240	5.3	1849	1.5
5	SA	0100	5.0	0705	1.7	1320	5.1	1931	1.7
6	SU	0143	4.8	0749	2.0	1406	4.9	2022	1.9
7	M ◐	0236	4.6	0845	2.2	1504	4.8	2126	2.0
8	TU	0347	4.5	0957	2.3	1617	4.7	2242	2.0
9	W	0514	4.5	1117	2.2	1735	4.8	2355	1.8
10	TH	0627	4.8	1226	1.9	1841	5.1		
11	F	0056	1.4	0724	5.1	1323	1.5	1935	5.4
12	SA	0149	1.0	0812	5.4	1412	1.2	2023	5.7
13	SU	0235	0.7	0855	5.7	1458	0.8	2109	6.0
14	M ○	0320	0.5	0938	5.9	1543	0.5	2155	6.2
15	TU	0405	0.4	1022	6.1	1629	0.4	2243	6.2
16	W	0451	0.4	1108	6.1	1717	0.4	2332	6.1
17	TH	0538	0.6	1155	6.0	1808	0.6		
18	F	0022	5.8	0627	0.9	1244	5.8	1900	0.8
19	SA	0116	5.5	0718	1.2	1337	5.5	1958	1.1
20	SU	0214	5.2	0815	1.6	1435	5.3	2101	1.4
21	M ◑	0321	4.9	0920	1.9	1543	5.0	2212	1.7
22	TU	0436	4.7	1034	2.1	1658	4.9	2324	1.8
23	W	0552	4.7	1147	2.2	1810	4.9		
24	TH	0030	1.7	0657	4.8	1253	2.1	1911	5.0
25	F	0127	1.6	0748	4.9	1346	1.9	2000	5.1
26	SA	0213	1.5	0829	5.1	1430	1.7	2041	5.2
27	SU	0251	1.4	0904	5.3	1506	1.5	2117	5.3
28	M	0325	1.3	0936	5.4	1540	1.4	2150	5.4
29	TU ●	0357	1.2	1007	5.5	1612	1.3	2223	5.4
30	W	0428	1.2	1038	5.6	1645	1.2	2255	5.4

DECEMBER

Date	Day	Time	m	Time	m	Time	m	Time	m
1	TH	0500	1.2	1111	5.6	1719	1.2	2329	5.3
2	F	0533	1.3	1145	5.5	1754	1.3		
3	SA	0005	5.2	0608	1.4	1222	5.5	1832	1.4
4	SU	0044	5.1	0646	1.6	1301	5.3	1913	1.5
5	M	0126	5.0	0729	1.7	1345	5.2	2001	1.6
6	TU	0215	4.8	0820	1.9	1437	5.1	2057	1.7
7	W ◐	0315	4.7	0922	2.0	1539	5.0	2202	1.7
8	TH	0428	4.7	1034	2.0	1650	5.0	2313	1.6
9	F	0544	4.8	1145	1.9	1800	5.1		
10	SA	0019	1.4	0648	5.0	1250	1.6	1903	5.3
11	SU	0119	1.2	0744	5.3	1346	1.3	1959	5.6
12	M	0212	0.9	0834	5.6	1438	1.0	2051	5.8
13	TU	0302	0.7	0921	5.8	1528	0.7	2141	6.0
14	W ○	0350	0.6	1007	6.0	1618	0.5	2231	6.0
15	TH	0437	0.6	1054	6.1	1707	0.5	2321	5.9
16	F	0525	0.7	1141	6.0	1757	0.6		
17	SA	0010	5.8	0612	0.9	1230	5.9	1846	0.7
18	SU	0101	5.5	0700	1.1	1318	5.7	1938	1.0
19	M	0152	5.2	0750	1.5	1409	5.4	2032	1.3
20	TU	0246	4.9	0844	1.8	1503	5.1	2130	1.6
21	W ◑	0346	4.7	0944	2.0	1604	4.9	2234	1.8
22	TH	0453	4.6	1052	2.2	1712	4.7	2339	1.9
23	F	0602	4.5	1201	2.2	1820	4.7		
24	SA	0040	1.9	0704	4.7	1304	2.1	1921	4.8
25	SU	0135	1.8	0754	4.9	1357	2.0	2011	4.9
26	M	0221	1.7	0836	5.1	1441	1.7	2053	5.0
27	TU	0300	1.5	0913	5.2	1519	1.5	2131	5.2
28	W	0335	1.4	0947	5.4	1554	1.4	2205	5.3
29	TH ●	0408	1.3	1020	5.5	1628	1.2	2239	5.3
30	F	0442	1.2	1053	5.6	1703	1.1	2314	5.3
31	SA	0516	1.2	1129	5.6	1739	1.1	2350	5.3

Chart Datum: 3·05 metres below Ordnance Datum (Newlyn)
HAT is 6·3m above Chart Datum

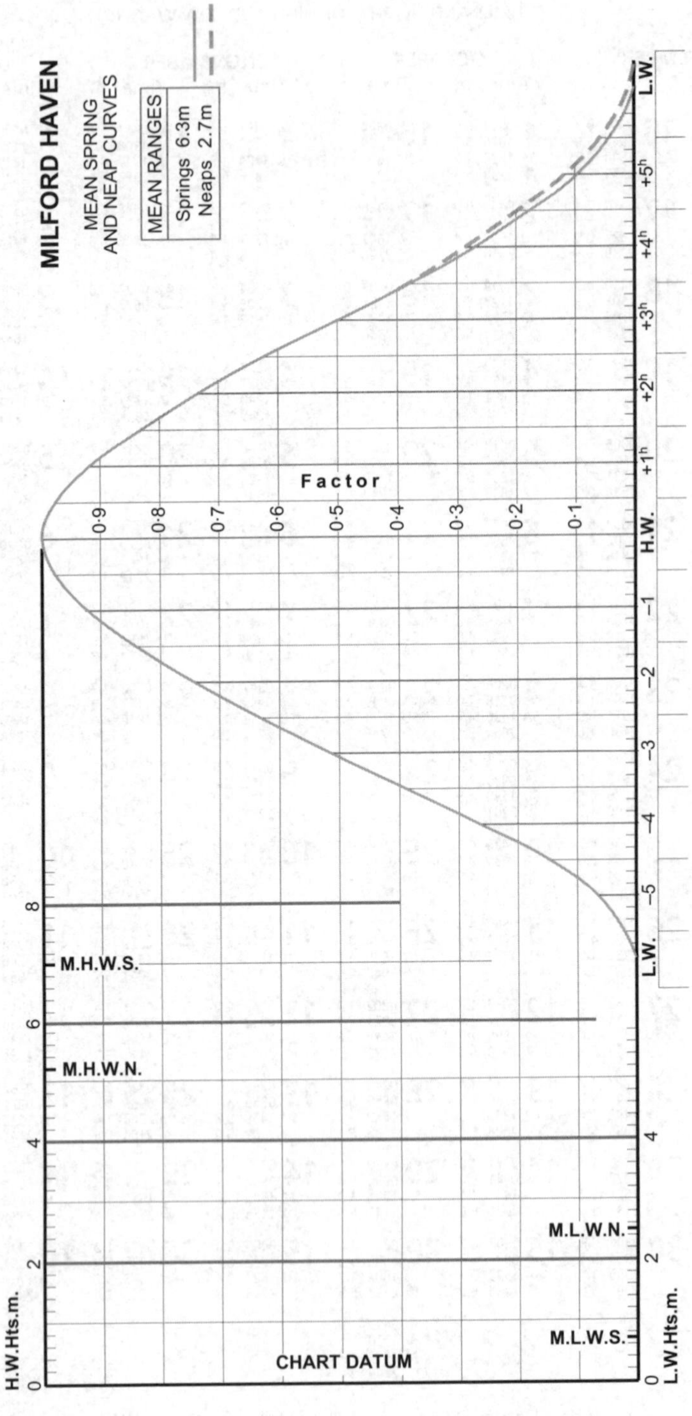
MILFORD HAVEN
MEAN SPRING AND NEAP CURVES
MEAN RANGES
Springs 6.3m
Neaps 2.7m
Factor
0·9
0·8
0·7
0·6
0·5
0·4
0·3
0·2
0·1
L.W.
−5
−4
−3
−2
−1
H.W.
+1h
+2h
+3h
+4h
+5h
L.W.
H.W.Hts.m.
0
2
4
6
8
M.H.W.S.
M.H.W.N.
CHART DATUM
M.L.W.N.
M.L.W.S.
L.W.Hts.m.
0
2
4

TIME ZONE (UT)
For Summer Time add ONE hour in **non-shaded areas**

WALES – MILFORD HAVEN

LAT 51°42'N LONG 5°03'W

TIMES AND HEIGHTS OF HIGH AND LOW WATERS

Dates in amber are **SPRINGS**
Dates in yellow are **NEAPS**

2016

JANUARY

Day	Time	m	Time	m	Time	m	Time	m
1 F	0419	2.1	1030	5.9	1650	2.2	2256	5.5
2 SA	0506	2.4	1117	5.6	1742	2.5	◑ 2350	5.3
3 SU	0606	2.6	1217	5.4	1850	2.6		
4 M	0100	5.2	0719	2.7	1332	5.3	2003	2.6
5 TU	0215	5.3	0833	2.6	1442	5.4	2110	2.4
6 W	0317	5.6	0935	2.3	1540	5.7	2204	2.1
7 TH	0408	5.9	1026	1.9	1628	6.0	2249	1.7
8 F	0452	6.3	1111	1.6	1712	6.4	2331	1.4
9 SA	0534	6.7	1152	1.3	1753	6.6		
10 SU	0011	1.2	0614	6.9	1234	1.0	● 1834	6.9
11 M	0052	1.0	0654	7.1	1315	0.8	1915	7.0
12 TU	0132	0.8	0736	7.2	1357	0.7	1957	7.0
13 W	0214	0.8	0818	7.2	1439	0.8	2039	6.9
14 TH	0255	0.9	0902	7.1	1522	0.9	2124	6.7
15 F	0339	1.1	0948	6.8	1607	1.2	2211	6.4
16 SA	0426	1.4	1039	6.5	1658	1.5	◐ 2305	6.1
17 SU	0522	1.8	1136	6.2	1759	1.8		
18 M	0008	5.8	0630	2.0	1245	5.9	1912	2.0
19 TU	0122	5.7	0753	2.1	1400	5.8	2031	2.0
20 W	0239	5.8	0911	1.9	1514	6.0	2142	1.8
21 TH	0349	6.1	1018	1.6	1620	6.2	2241	1.5
22 F	0449	6.4	1113	1.3	1715	6.5	2331	1.2
23 SA	0538	6.8	1201	1.1	1802	6.8		
24 SU	0016	1.0	0621	7.0	1244	0.9	○ 1843	6.9
25 M	0056	0.9	0700	7.0	1322	0.9	1921	6.9
26 TU	0133	0.9	0737	7.0	1357	0.9	1956	6.8
27 W	0207	1.0	0811	6.9	1430	1.1	2029	6.6
28 TH	0240	1.2	0844	6.7	1502	1.3	2102	6.4
29 F	0311	1.4	0916	6.5	1532	1.6	2135	6.1
30 SA	0343	1.7	0950	6.1	1605	1.9	2210	5.8
31 SU	0418	2.0	1028	5.8	1643	2.2	2252	5.5

FEBRUARY

Day	Time	m	Time	m	Time	m	Time	m
1 M	0502	2.3	1113	5.5	1733	2.5	◑ 2346	5.2
2 TU	0604	2.6	1214	5.2	1847	2.7		
3 W	0100	5.1	0729	2.7	1337	5.1	2014	2.6
4 TH	0226	5.2	0850	2.5	1457	5.3	2126	2.3
5 F	0333	5.6	0954	2.1	1558	5.7	2221	1.9
6 SA	0425	6.1	1046	1.6	1649	6.2	2309	1.4
7 SU	0512	6.6	1132	1.2	1734	6.6	2353	1.0
8 M ●	0556	7.0	1216	0.8	1818	7.0		
9 TU	0035	0.7	0638	7.3	1300	0.5	1900	7.2
10 W	0118	0.5	0721	7.5	1342	0.3	1942	7.3
11 TH	0200	0.4	0803	7.5	1424	0.3	2024	7.3
12 F	0241	0.5	0846	7.4	1506	0.5	2107	7.0
13 SA	0323	0.7	0930	7.1	1548	0.8	2151	6.7
14 SU	0407	1.1	1017	6.7	1634	1.3	2240	6.3
15 M	0457	1.5	1110	6.2	1728	1.8	◐ 2338	5.8
16 TU	0601	2.0	1216	5.7	1840	2.1		
17 W	0052	5.5	0728	2.2	1336	5.5	2008	2.2
18 TH	0219	5.5	0857	2.1	1500	5.6	2128	2.0
19 F	0338	5.8	1008	1.8	1610	5.9	2230	1.7
20 SA	0438	6.2	1103	1.4	1704	6.3	2319	1.3
21 SU	0525	6.6	1148	1.1	1747	6.6		
22 M	0001	1.1	0605	6.8	1227	0.9	○ 1825	6.8
23 TU	0038	0.9	0641	6.9	1301	0.8	1859	6.8
24 W	0111	0.8	0715	7.0	1333	0.8	1931	6.8
25 TH	0143	0.9	0746	6.9	1403	0.9	2002	6.7
26 F	0213	1.0	0815	6.8	1431	1.1	2031	6.6
27 SA	0242	1.1	0845	6.6	1459	1.3	2101	6.4
28 SU	0311	1.4	0915	6.3	1528	1.6	2132	6.1
29 M	0342	1.7	0947	6.0	1600	1.9	2207	5.7

MARCH

Day	Time	m	Time	m	Time	m	Time	m
1 TU	0419	2.1	1026	5.6	1640	2.3	◑ 2252	5.4
2 W	0508	2.4	1118	5.2	1737	2.6	2357	5.1
3 TH	0624	2.7	1234	5.0	1913	2.7		
4 F	0127	5.1	0804	2.6	1410	5.1	2045	2.5
5 SA	0253	5.4	0920	2.2	1526	5.6	2151	2.0
6 SU	0355	6.0	1019	1.6	1623	6.1	2243	1.4
7 M	0446	6.5	1108	1.1	1711	6.6	2330	0.9
8 TU	0533	7.0	1155	0.6	1756	7.1		
9 W	0015	0.5	0617	7.4	1239	0.2	● 1839	7.4
10 TH	0059	0.2	0701	7.7	1323	0.1	1922	7.5
11 F	0142	0.1	0744	7.7	1405	0.1	2004	7.5
12 SA	0224	0.2	0827	7.6	1446	0.3	2047	7.2
13 SU	0306	0.5	0911	7.2	1528	0.7	2130	6.9
14 M	0349	0.9	0956	6.7	1612	1.2	2217	6.4
15 TU	0437	1.5	1048	6.1	1703	1.8	◐ 2313	5.8
16 W	0538	2.0	1151	5.6	1812	2.2		
17 TH	0027	5.4	0706	2.3	1314	5.3	1945	2.4
18 F	0157	5.4	0839	2.2	1442	5.4	2109	2.2
19 SA	0319	5.7	0951	1.9	1553	5.8	2211	1.8
20 SU	0418	6.1	1044	1.5	1644	6.1	2259	1.4
21 M	0504	6.4	1126	1.2	1725	6.5	2338	1.2
22 TU	0543	6.7	1202	1.0	1801	6.7		
23 W	0013	1.0	0616	6.8	1235	0.9	○ 1833	6.8
24 TH	0046	0.9	0648	6.9	1305	0.9	1904	6.8
25 F	0116	0.9	0718	6.8	1334	0.9	1933	6.8
26 SA	0146	0.9	0747	6.8	1402	1.0	2002	6.7
27 SU	0214	1.1	0815	6.6	1430	1.2	2031	6.5
28 M	0244	1.3	0845	6.4	1458	1.5	2101	6.2
29 TU	0315	1.6	0916	6.1	1530	1.8	2135	5.9
30 W	0351	1.9	0953	5.7	1607	2.1	2217	5.6
31 TH	0436	2.2	1042	5.4	1658	2.4	◑ 2316	5.3

APRIL

Day	Time	m	Time	m	Time	m	Time	m
1 F	0541	2.5	1153	5.1	1819	2.6		
2 SA	0041	5.2	0719	2.5	1326	5.1	2002	2.5
3 SU	0211	5.4	0843	2.1	1450	5.5	2116	2.0
4 M	0321	6.0	0947	1.5	1552	6.1	2214	1.4
5 TU	0417	6.5	1040	1.0	1644	6.7	2304	0.9
6 W	0506	7.1	1129	0.5	1731	7.1	2351	0.4
7 TH ●	0553	7.5	1215	0.2	1816	7.5		
8 F	0037	0.2	0638	7.7	1301	0.0	1900	7.6
9 SA	0122	0.1	0723	7.7	1344	0.1	1944	7.6
10 SU	0205	0.2	0807	7.5	1426	0.3	2027	7.3
11 M	0248	0.5	0852	7.1	1508	0.7	2111	6.9
12 TU	0333	0.9	0938	6.6	1552	1.3	2158	6.4
13 W	0421	1.5	1028	6.1	1642	1.8	2252	5.9
14 TH ◐	0520	2.0	1129	5.5	1747	2.3		
15 F	0001	5.5	0641	2.3	1247	5.2	1914	2.4
16 SA	0126	5.4	0810	2.3	1411	5.3	2038	2.3
17 SU	0245	5.6	0920	2.0	1521	5.6	2140	2.0
18 M	0346	5.9	1013	1.7	1613	6.0	2228	1.6
19 TU	0433	6.2	1055	1.4	1655	6.3	2308	1.4
20 W	0512	6.5	1131	1.2	1732	6.5	2344	1.2
21 TH	0547	6.6	1204	1.1	1805	6.7		
22 F	0017	1.1	0619	6.7	1236	1.0	○ 1835	6.7
23 SA	0049	1.0	0650	6.7	1306	1.0	1905	6.8
24 SU	0119	1.0	0720	6.7	1335	1.1	1935	6.7
25 M	0150	1.1	0749	6.6	1405	1.2	2006	6.6
26 TU	0222	1.2	0821	6.4	1436	1.4	2038	6.4
27 W	0255	1.5	0854	6.2	1509	1.7	2113	6.1
28 TH	0333	1.7	0933	5.9	1548	2.0	2157	5.8
29 F	0419	2.0	1022	5.6	1639	2.2	2254	5.6
30 SA ◑	0520	2.2	1129	5.3	1749	2.4		

Chart Datum: 3·71 metres below Ordnance Datum (Newlyn)
HAT is 7·9m above Chart Datum

TIME ZONE (UT)
For Summer Time add ONE hour in **non-shaded areas**

WALES – MILFORD HAVEN

LAT 51°42'N LONG 5°03'W

TIMES AND HEIGHTS OF HIGH AND LOW WATERS

Dates in amber are **SPRINGS**
Dates in yellow are **NEAPS**

2016

MAY

Date	Day	Time	m	Time	m	Time	m	Time	m
1	SU	0010	5.5	0642	2.2	1252	5.3	1921	2.3
2	M	0133	5.6	0805	2.0	1413	5.6	2039	1.9
3	TU	0245	6.0	0913	1.5	1519	6.1	2142	1.5
4	W	0345	6.5	1010	1.0	1614	6.6	2236	1.0
5	TH	0439	7.0	1102	0.6	1705	7.1	2327	0.6
6	F ●	0529	7.3	1151	0.3	1753	7.4		
7	SA	0015	0.3	0616	7.5	1238	0.2	1839	7.5
8	SU	0102	0.2	0703	7.5	1323	0.3	1924	7.5
9	M	0148	0.3	0749	7.3	1407	0.5	2009	7.3
10	TU	0233	0.6	0835	7.0	1451	0.9	2054	6.9
11	W	0318	1.0	0921	6.6	1535	1.3	2141	6.5
12	TH	0406	1.4	1010	6.1	1623	1.8	2232	6.0
13	F ◐	0500	1.9	1105	5.6	1720	2.2	2332	5.7
14	SA	0607	2.2	1211	5.3	1832	2.4		
15	SU	0044	5.5	0723	2.3	1327	5.3	1949	2.4
16	M	0158	5.5	0833	2.2	1436	5.5	2056	2.2
17	TU	0302	5.7	0930	1.9	1532	5.7	2149	1.9
18	W	0353	6.0	1016	1.7	1618	6.0	2233	1.7
19	TH	0437	6.2	1056	1.5	1658	6.3	2312	1.4
20	F	0515	6.4	1132	1.3	1734	6.5	2348	1.3
21	SA ○	0550	6.5	1206	1.2	1808	6.6		
22	SU	0022	1.2	0623	6.6	1239	1.2	1840	6.7
23	M	0056	1.1	0656	6.6	1312	1.2	1913	6.7
24	TU	0130	1.1	0729	6.5	1345	1.2	1946	6.6
25	W	0205	1.2	0803	6.4	1419	1.4	2022	6.5
26	TH	0242	1.4	0840	6.3	1456	1.5	2101	6.3
27	F	0322	1.5	0922	6.1	1538	1.7	2146	6.1
28	SA	0408	1.7	1011	5.8	1627	2.0	2241	5.9
29	SU ◑	0504	1.9	1111	5.6	1729	2.1	2347	5.8
30	M	0613	1.9	1223	5.6	1846	2.1		
31	TU	0059	5.9	0729	1.8	1338	5.8	2003	1.9

JUNE

Date	Day	Time	m	Time	m	Time	m	Time	m
1	W	0211	6.1	0839	1.5	1446	6.1	2110	1.5
2	TH	0315	6.4	0941	1.2	1546	6.5	2210	1.2
3	F	0413	6.8	1037	0.9	1641	6.8	2305	0.8
4	SA	0507	7.0	1129	0.7	1733	7.1	2356	0.6
5	SU ●	0559	7.2	1218	0.5	1822	7.3		
6	M	0045	0.5	0647	7.2	1306	0.5	1908	7.3
7	TU	0133	0.5	0734	7.1	1351	0.7	1954	7.2
8	W	0218	0.7	0819	6.9	1434	0.9	2038	6.9
9	TH	0303	1.0	0904	6.5	1517	1.3	2123	6.6
10	F	0347	1.4	0948	6.2	1601	1.6	2208	6.2
11	SA	0433	1.7	1035	5.8	1648	2.0	2257	5.9
12	SU ◐	0525	2.1	1128	5.5	1743	2.3	2354	5.6
13	M	0625	2.3	1231	5.3	1848	2.4		
14	TU	0100	5.4	0731	2.3	1340	5.3	1957	2.4
15	W	0208	5.5	0836	2.2	1443	5.5	2100	2.2
16	TH	0307	5.6	0932	2.0	1537	5.7	2153	2.0
17	F	0358	5.8	1019	1.8	1623	6.0	2238	1.7
18	SA	0442	6.1	1100	1.6	1704	6.3	2319	1.5
19	SU	0522	6.3	1139	1.4	1742	6.5	2357	1.3
20	M ○	0559	6.4	1215	1.3	1818	6.6		
21	TU	0035	1.2	0635	6.5	1252	1.2	1854	6.7
22	W	0113	1.1	0712	6.6	1328	1.1	1931	6.8
23	TH	0151	1.1	0750	6.6	1406	1.2	2010	6.7
24	F	0230	1.1	0830	6.5	1446	1.3	2051	6.6
25	SA	0312	1.2	0912	6.4	1528	1.4	2136	6.5
26	SU	0357	1.4	0959	6.2	1615	1.6	2226	6.3
27	M ◑	0447	1.5	1053	6.0	1709	1.8	2324	6.1
28	TU	0546	1.7	1155	5.8	1815	1.9		
29	W	0030	6.0	0655	1.8	1306	5.8	1930	1.9
30	TH	0141	6.0	0808	1.7	1417	5.9	2044	1.7

JULY

Date	Day	Time	m	Time	m	Time	m	Time	m
1	F	0250	6.2	0917	1.5	1523	6.2	2150	1.4
2	SA	0354	6.4	1018	1.2	1624	6.5	2250	1.1
3	SU	0453	6.7	1113	1.0	1719	6.8	2343	0.9
4	M ●	0546	6.9	1203	0.8	1809	7.0		
5	TU	0033	0.7	0635	7.0	1251	0.7	1855	7.1
6	W	0119	0.7	0720	7.0	1334	0.8	1939	7.1
7	TH	0202	0.8	0802	6.8	1416	0.9	2020	6.9
8	F	0243	1.0	0842	6.6	1455	1.2	2100	6.7
9	SA	0322	1.3	0921	6.3	1533	1.5	2138	6.4
10	SU	0400	1.6	1001	6.0	1611	1.8	2218	6.1
11	M	0439	1.9	1043	5.7	1653	2.1	2303	5.7
12	TU ◐	0525	2.2	1132	5.4	1745	2.4	2356	5.4
13	W	0622	2.4	1233	5.2	1851	2.5		
14	TH	0102	5.3	0731	2.5	1346	5.2	2003	2.5
15	F	0215	5.3	0841	2.4	1453	5.4	2110	2.3
16	SA	0318	5.5	0941	2.1	1548	5.7	2206	2.0
17	SU	0411	5.8	1030	1.8	1636	6.1	2253	1.7
18	M	0456	6.1	1113	1.5	1718	6.4	2335	1.4
19	TU ○	0537	6.4	1153	1.3	1758	6.7		
20	W	0016	1.2	0617	6.6	1233	1.1	1836	6.9
21	TH	0056	1.0	0656	6.8	1313	0.9	1916	7.0
22	F	0136	0.8	0736	6.8	1353	0.9	1957	7.1
23	SA	0217	0.8	0817	6.8	1433	0.9	2038	7.0
24	SU	0258	0.9	0859	6.7	1515	1.0	2122	6.8
25	M	0341	1.0	0943	6.5	1559	1.3	2209	6.6
26	TU ◑	0427	1.3	1032	6.2	1648	1.6	2301	6.3
27	W	0521	1.6	1129	5.9	1748	1.8		
28	TH	0003	6.0	0626	1.9	1238	5.7	1903	2.0
29	F	0116	5.8	0744	1.9	1354	5.7	2026	2.0
30	SA	0232	5.9	0901	1.8	1509	5.9	2140	1.7
31	SU	0343	6.1	1007	1.6	1615	6.3	2242	1.4

AUGUST

Date	Day	Time	m	Time	m	Time	m	Time	m
1	M	0445	6.4	1103	1.3	1711	6.6	2335	1.1
2	TU ●	0537	6.7	1152	1.0	1758	6.9		
3	W	0021	0.9	0622	6.8	1236	0.9	1841	7.1
4	TH	0104	0.8	0703	6.9	1316	0.8	1920	7.1
5	F	0142	0.8	0741	6.8	1353	0.9	1957	7.0
6	SA	0218	0.9	0816	6.7	1428	1.1	2032	6.8
7	SU	0251	1.2	0850	6.5	1501	1.3	2105	6.5
8	M	0323	1.4	0924	6.2	1533	1.6	2139	6.2
9	TU	0355	1.7	0959	5.9	1607	1.9	2215	5.9
10	W ◐	0430	2.1	1039	5.6	1648	2.3	2259	5.5
11	TH	0516	2.4	1129	5.3	1745	2.6	2355	5.2
12	F	0623	2.6	1237	5.1	1905	2.7		
13	SA	0112	5.1	0748	2.7	1404	5.2	2027	2.6
14	SU	0237	5.2	0903	2.4	1514	5.5	2134	2.2
15	M	0341	5.6	1001	2.0	1608	5.9	2227	1.8
16	TU	0431	6.0	1049	1.6	1654	6.4	2313	1.4
17	W	0515	6.4	1132	1.2	1736	6.8	2355	1.0
18	TH ○	0557	6.8	1213	0.9	1817	7.1		
19	F	0036	0.7	0637	7.0	1254	0.7	1857	7.3
20	SA	0118	0.5	0718	7.2	1335	0.6	1939	7.4
21	SU	0159	0.5	0759	7.2	1416	0.6	2020	7.4
22	M	0241	0.6	0841	7.0	1458	0.8	2103	7.1
23	TU	0322	0.8	0924	6.8	1540	1.1	2149	6.8
24	W	0406	1.2	1010	6.4	1628	1.5	2239	6.3
25	TH ◑	0457	1.6	1105	6.0	1726	1.9	2340	5.9
26	F	0601	2.0	1214	5.7	1846	2.2		
27	SA	0056	5.6	0726	2.2	1338	5.6	2017	2.2
28	SU	0221	5.6	0851	2.1	1501	5.8	2135	1.9
29	M	0338	5.9	0959	1.8	1608	6.2	2235	1.5
30	TU	0437	6.3	1053	1.4	1700	6.6	2324	1.2
31	W	0524	6.6	1138	1.1	1744	6.9		

Chart Datum: 3·71 metres below Ordnance Datum (Newlyn)
HAT is 7·9m above Chart Datum

TIME ZONE (UT)
For Summer Time add ONE hour in **non-shaded areas**

WALES – MILFORD HAVEN

LAT 51°42'N LONG 5°03'W

TIMES AND HEIGHTS OF HIGH AND LOW WATERS

Dates in amber are **SPRINGS**
Dates in yellow are **NEAPS**

2016

SEPTEMBER

Date	Time	m	Date	Time	m
1 TH ●	0006 0605 1218 1822	1.0 6.8 0.9 7.0	16 F ○	0533 1150 1753	7.0 0.8 7.3
2 F	0043 0642 1254 1858	0.9 6.9 0.9 7.1	17 SA	0014 0615 1233 1835	0.5 7.3 0.5 7.6
3 SA	0117 0716 1327 1930	0.9 6.9 0.9 7.0	18 SU	0057 0657 1315 1918	0.3 7.5 0.4 7.7
4 SU	0149 0747 1359 2001	0.9 6.8 1.0 6.9	19 M	0139 0738 1357 2000	0.3 7.5 0.4 7.6
5 M	0218 0818 1429 2031	1.1 6.6 1.2 6.6	20 TU	0221 0820 1439 2044	0.4 7.3 0.6 7.3
6 TU	0247 0848 1458 2102	1.4 6.4 1.5 6.4	21 W	0302 0904 1523 2129	0.8 7.0 1.0 6.9
7 W	0315 0919 1529 2134	1.7 6.1 1.8 6.0	22 TH	0346 0950 1611 2220	1.2 6.5 1.5 6.3
8 TH	0347 0954 1605 2212	2.0 5.8 2.2 5.6	23 F ◑	0436 1045 1710 2321	1.8 6.0 2.0 5.8
9 F ◐	0425 1037 1652 2301	2.4 5.4 2.5 5.3	24 SA	0541 1155 1834	2.2 5.6 2.3
10 SA	0519 1139 1805	2.7 5.1 2.8	25 SU	0040 0712 1324 2009	5.4 2.4 5.5 2.3
11 SU	0013 0650 1307 1945	5.0 2.9 5.1 2.8	26 M	0210 0840 1449 2125	5.5 2.3 5.8 2.0
12 M	0150 0825 1436 2102	5.0 2.6 5.4 2.4	27 TU	0326 0946 1554 2222	5.8 1.9 6.2 1.6
13 TU	0309 0931 1538 2159	5.5 2.2 5.9 1.9	28 W	0421 1037 1642 2306	6.2 1.5 6.6 1.3
14 W	0404 1022 1627 2247	6.0 1.7 6.4 1.3	29 TH	0505 1119 1723 2344	6.6 1.3 6.8 1.1
15 TH	0450 1107 1711 2331	6.5 1.2 6.9 0.9	30 F	0543 1155 1759	6.8 1.1 7.0

OCTOBER

Date	Time	m	Date	Time	m
1 SA ●	0017 0617 1229 1832	1.0 6.9 1.0 7.0	16 SU ○	0551 1210 1813	7.4 0.5 7.7
2 SU	0049 0648 1300 1902	1.0 6.9 1.0 7.0	17 M	0034 0634 1255 1856	0.3 7.6 0.3 7.8
3 M	0119 0718 1330 1932	1.0 6.9 1.1 6.9	18 TU	0118 0717 1339 1941	0.3 7.6 0.4 7.7
4 TU	0147 0747 1359 2001	1.2 6.8 1.2 6.7	19 W	0201 0801 1423 2026	0.4 7.5 0.6 7.3
5 W	0215 0816 1428 2030	1.4 6.6 1.5 6.5	20 TH	0244 0846 1508 2113	0.8 7.1 1.0 6.9
6 TH	0243 0847 1459 2101	1.6 6.3 1.8 6.1	21 F	0329 0934 1557 2204	1.3 6.6 1.5 6.3
7 F	0314 0920 1535 2136	1.9 6.0 2.1 5.8	22 SA ◑	0419 1029 1657 2304	1.8 6.2 2.0 5.8
8 SA	0350 1000 1619 2222	2.3 5.7 2.5 5.4	23 SU	0523 1136 1817	2.3 5.7 2.4
9 SU ◐	0438 1056 1721 2329	2.6 5.3 2.7 5.1	24 M	0020 0649 1300 1947	5.4 2.5 5.6 2.4
10 M	0555 1217 1900	2.9 5.2 2.8	25 TU	0145 0815 1421 2100	5.4 2.4 5.7 2.1
11 TU	0102 0742 1351 2024	5.1 2.7 5.4 2.4	26 W	0259 0921 1526 2155	5.7 2.1 6.1 1.8
12 W	0230 0856 1501 2127	5.4 2.3 5.9 1.9	27 TH	0355 1011 1615 2239	6.1 1.8 6.4 1.5
13 TH	0331 0952 1555 2218	6.0 1.7 6.5 1.3	28 F	0439 1052 1656 2316	6.4 1.5 6.6 1.3
14 F	0421 1040 1643 2305	6.6 1.2 7.0 0.8	29 SA	0516 1128 1732 2349	6.7 1.3 6.8 1.2
15 SA	0507 1126 1728 2350	7.1 0.8 7.4 0.5	30 SU ●	0550 1202 1805	6.8 1.2 6.9
			31 M	0021 0621 1234 1835	1.2 6.9 1.2 6.9

NOVEMBER

Date	Time	m	Date	Time	m
1 TU	0051 0651 1304 1905	1.2 6.9 1.2 6.8	16 W	0059 0700 1323 1925	0.4 7.6 0.5 7.6
2 W	0120 0721 1335 1935	1.2 6.8 1.3 6.7	17 TH	0144 0746 1410 2012	0.6 7.5 0.6 7.3
3 TH	0149 0751 1406 2006	1.4 6.7 1.5 6.5	18 F	0229 0832 1456 2059	0.9 7.2 1.0 6.8
4 F	0220 0823 1439 2038	1.6 6.5 1.7 6.3	19 SA	0315 0920 1546 2149	1.3 6.8 1.4 6.4
5 SA	0252 0857 1515 2114	1.9 6.2 2.0 6.0	20 SU	0404 1012 1641 2244	1.8 6.3 1.9 5.9
6 SU	0329 0937 1559 2159	2.2 5.9 2.3 5.6	21 M ◑	0501 1111 1747 2348	2.2 5.9 2.2 5.5
7 M ◐	0415 1030 1655 2301	2.5 5.6 2.5 5.4	22 TU	0612 1221 1905	2.5 5.7 2.4
8 TU	0520 1141 1815	2.7 5.5 2.6	23 W	0103 0730 1337 2017	5.4 2.5 5.7 2.3
9 W	0021 0653 1305 1941	5.3 2.7 5.6 2.3	24 TH	0216 0840 1444 2117	5.5 2.3 5.8 2.1
10 TH	0146 0815 1420 2049	5.5 2.3 5.9 1.9	25 F	0317 0935 1539 2204	5.8 2.1 6.1 1.8
11 F	0254 0917 1521 2146	6.0 1.8 6.5 1.4	26 SA	0405 1021 1624 2245	6.1 1.8 6.3 1.6
12 SA	0350 1012 1614 2238	6.5 1.3 6.9 1.0	27 SU	0446 1100 1703 2321	6.4 1.6 6.5 1.5
13 SU	0440 1101 1703 2326	7.0 0.9 7.3 0.6	28 M	0523 1136 1739 2355	6.6 1.5 6.6 1.4
14 M ○	0528 1149 1751	7.4 0.6 7.6	29 TU ●	0557 1210 1812	6.7 1.4 6.7
15 TU	0013 0614 1237 1838	0.4 7.6 0.4 7.7	30 W	0027 0629 1244 1844	1.3 6.8 1.3 6.7

DECEMBER

Date	Time	m	Date	Time	m
1 TH	0059 0701 1316 1916	1.3 6.8 1.3 6.6	16 F	0130 0734 1359 2000	0.6 7.4 0.7 7.2
2 F	0131 0733 1350 1949	1.4 6.8 1.4 6.5	17 SA	0215 0820 1445 2045	0.8 7.2 0.9 6.9
3 SA	0203 0807 1425 2024	1.5 6.6 1.5 6.4	18 SU	0300 0905 1530 2131	1.1 6.9 1.2 6.5
4 SU	0238 0843 1503 2102	1.7 6.5 1.7 6.2	19 M	0344 0951 1617 2217	1.5 6.5 1.6 6.1
5 M	0317 0924 1546 2146	1.9 6.2 1.9 5.9	20 TU	0431 1039 1707 2309	1.9 6.2 2.0 5.7
6 TU	0401 1013 1636 2240	2.1 6.0 2.1 5.7	21 W ◑	0524 1134 1806	2.3 5.8 2.3
7 W ◐	0457 1114 1739 2347	2.3 5.8 2.2 5.6	22 TH	0009 0627 1239 1913	5.4 2.5 5.6 2.5
8 TH	0608 1224 1856	2.4 5.8 2.2	23 F	0119 0739 1349 2023	5.3 2.5 5.5 2.4
9 F	0102 0729 1339 2009	5.6 2.3 6.0 1.9	24 SA	0227 0847 1453 2122	5.5 2.4 5.6 2.2
10 SA	0215 0841 1446 2114	5.9 1.9 6.3 1.6	25 SU	0326 0944 1548 2211	5.7 2.2 5.8 2.0
11 SU	0319 0944 1546 2213	6.3 1.5 6.7 1.2	26 M	0415 1031 1634 2254	6.0 1.9 6.1 1.8
12 M	0416 1040 1642 2306	6.8 1.1 7.0 0.9	27 TU	0457 1112 1715 2332	6.3 1.7 6.3 1.5
13 TU	0508 1133 1735 2356	7.1 0.8 7.3 0.7	28 W	0535 1150 1752	6.5 1.5 6.5
14 W ○	0559 1223 1825	7.4 0.6 7.4	29 TH ●	0007 0610 1226 1827	1.4 6.7 1.3 6.6
15 TH	0044 0647 1312 1913	0.6 7.5 0.5 7.4	30 F	0042 0645 1302 1901	1.3 6.8 1.2 6.6
			31 SA	0116 0719 1337 1936	1.2 6.8 1.2 6.6

Chart Datum: 3·71 metres below Ordnance Datum (Newlyn)
HAT is 7·9m above Chart Datum

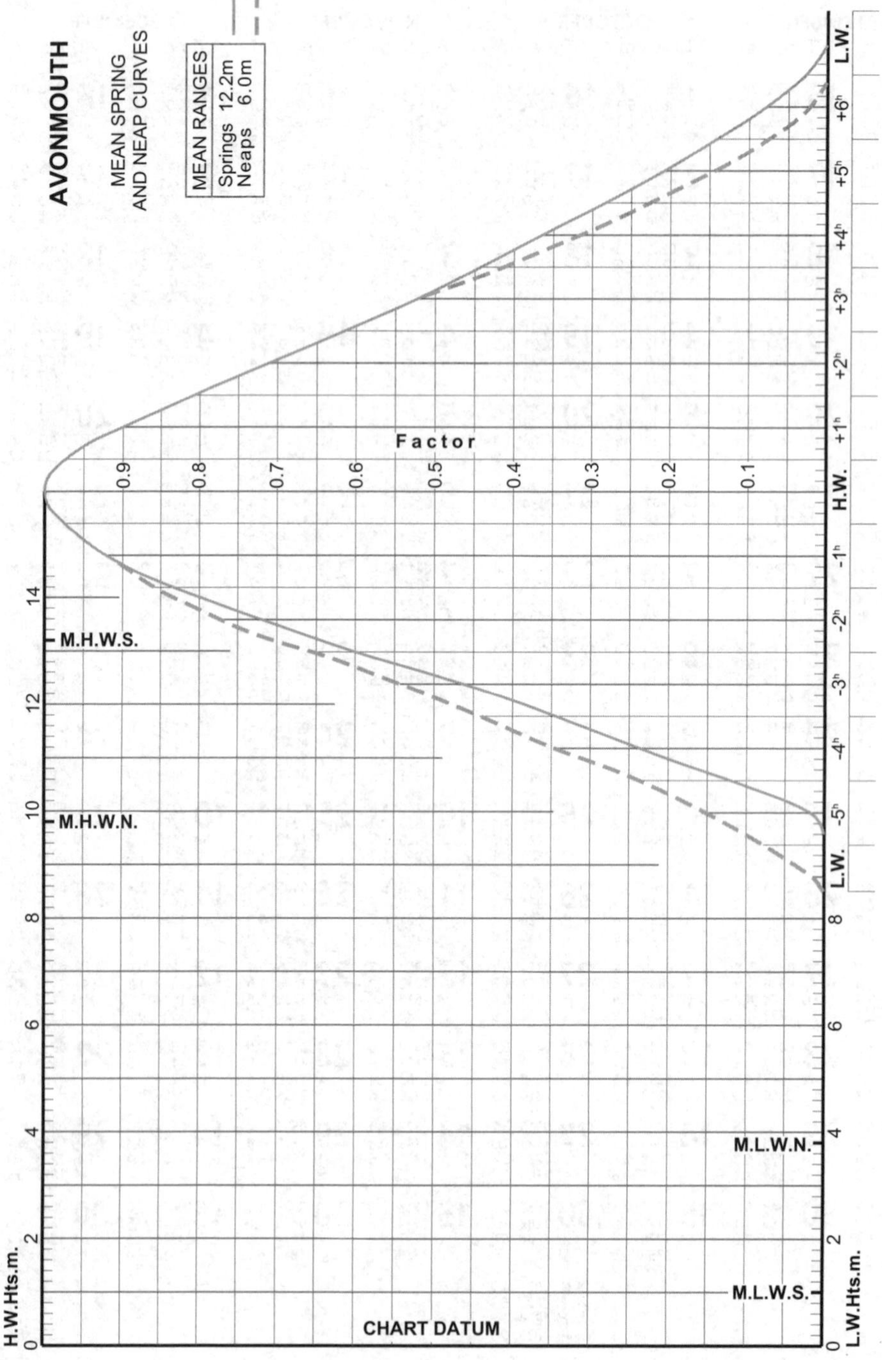
AVONMOUTH
MEAN SPRING
AND NEAP CURVES
MEAN RANGES
Springs 12.2m
Neaps 6.0m
Factor
0.9
0.8
0.7
0.6
0.5
0.4
0.3
0.2
0.1
L.W.
-5h
-4h
-3h
-2h
-1h
H.W.
+1h
+2h
+3h
+4h
+5h
+6h
L.W.
H.W.Hts.m.
0
2
4
6
8
10
12
14
M.H.W.S.
M.H.W.N.
CHART DATUM
L.W.Hts.m.
M.L.W.S.
M.L.W.N.

TIME ZONE (UT)
For Summer Time add ONE hour in **non-shaded areas**

AVONMOUTH

LAT 51°30′N LONG 2°44′W

TIMES AND HEIGHTS OF HIGH AND LOW WATERS

Dates in amber are **SPRINGS**
Dates in yellow are **NEAPS**

2016

JANUARY

Date	Day	Time	m	Time	m	Time	m	Time	m	Moon
1	F	0513	2.6	1113	11.1	1735	2.9	2335	10.6	
2	SA	0553	3.0	1156	10.5	1819	3.2			◑
3	SU	0022	10.1	0643	3.5	1253	10.1	1915	3.6	
4	M	0129	9.8	0749	3.8	1408	9.9	2025	3.7	
5	TU	0248	9.9	0904	3.7	1522	10.2	2141	3.5	
6	W	0357	10.4	1017	3.2	1624	10.8	2252	2.9	
7	TH	0454	11.2	1121	2.5	1718	11.5	2352	2.3	
8	F	0544	12.0	1217	2.0	1806	12.1			
9	SA	0045	1.8	0629	12.6	1310	1.6	1851	12.6	
10	SU	0136	1.6	0712	13.0	1400	1.5	1935	12.9	●
11	M	0223	1.5	0755	13.2	1447	1.4	2019	13.1	
12	TU	0306	1.4	0837	13.4	1529	1.3	2101	13.2	
13	W	0344	1.5	0919	13.4	1607	1.3	2142	13.1	
14	TH	0418	1.5	1001	13.2	1642	1.4	2223	12.9	
15	F	0452	1.7	1043	12.9	1717	1.6	2305	12.5	
16	SA	0528	2.0	1129	12.3	1757	2.0	2352	11.8	◐
17	SU	0611	2.4	1222	11.6	1845	2.5			
18	M	0049	11.1	0705	3.0	1332	11.0	1949	3.1	
19	TU	0207	10.7	0833	3.5	1456	10.8	2127	3.3	
20	W	0330	10.8	1013	3.3	1609	11.1	2246	2.8	
21	TH	0439	11.3	1122	2.6	1712	11.7	2349	2.1	
22	F	0537	12.1	1220	1.9	1807	12.4			
23	SA	0044	1.5	0628	12.8	1314	1.4	1856	12.9	
24	SU	0136	1.1	0714	13.2	1404	1.1	1941	13.2	○
25	M	0223	0.9	0757	13.4	1450	1.1	2022	13.2	
26	TU	0306	1.0	0836	13.3	1529	1.3	2100	13.0	
27	W	0341	1.3	0911	13.0	1600	1.6	2132	12.6	
28	TH	0406	1.7	0942	12.6	1620	2.0	2200	12.2	
29	F	0424	1.9	1011	12.2	1637	2.2	2227	11.7	
30	SA	0446	2.1	1040	11.7	1701	2.3	2257	11.2	
31	SU	0516	2.4	1112	11.1	1734	2.6	2332	10.7	

FEBRUARY

Date	Day	Time	m	Time	m	Time	m	Time	m	Moon
1	M	0554	2.9	1152	10.5	1817	3.1			◑
2	TU	0019	10.1	0645	3.4	1250	9.9	1917	3.7	
3	W	0128	9.7	0803	3.8	1411	9.7	2043	3.9	
4	TH	0259	9.8	0929	3.6	1538	10.1	2207	3.4	
5	F	0417	10.6	1044	3.0	1647	11.0	2319	2.7	
6	SA	0516	11.5	1149	2.2	1743	11.9			
7	SU	0020	2.0	0607	12.4	1248	1.7	1832	12.6	
8	M	0117	1.5	0654	13.1	1343	1.3	1919	13.2	●
9	TU	0209	1.2	0739	13.6	1434	1.0	2004	13.6	
10	W	0257	1.0	0823	13.9	1520	0.8	2047	13.8	
11	TH	0338	0.8	0906	14.0	1600	0.7	2128	13.8	
12	F	0414	0.9	0947	13.9	1634	0.8	2208	13.5	
13	SA	0445	1.1	1028	13.5	1704	1.2	2247	13.0	
14	SU	0515	1.5	1110	12.7	1736	1.7	2329	12.2	
15	M	0549	2.1	1157	11.8	1815	2.4			◐
16	TU	0019	11.2	0633	2.9	1259	10.8	1908	3.2	
17	W	0132	10.4	0740	3.7	1430	10.2	2043	3.7	
18	TH	0306	10.2	0948	3.7	1550	10.4	2223	3.3	
19	F	0420	10.7	1103	3.0	1656	11.1	2328	2.5	
20	SA	0521	11.6	1201	2.1	1752	12.0			
21	SU	0023	1.7	0611	12.4	1254	1.4	1839	12.7	
22	M	0114	1.1	0657	13.0	1343	1.0	1922	13.1	○
23	TU	0202	0.8	0738	13.3	1428	0.9	2002	13.2	
24	W	0245	0.8	0815	13.3	1508	1.0	2036	13.0	
25	TH	0321	1.0	0848	13.1	1540	1.4	2106	12.7	
26	F	0348	1.4	0917	12.7	1600	1.8	2133	12.4	
27	SA	0404	1.7	0943	12.4	1611	1.9	2158	12.0	
28	SU	0419	1.8	1009	12.0	1629	2.0	2223	11.6	
29	M	0444	2.0	1037	11.5	1658	2.2	2254	11.1	

MARCH

Date	Day	Time	m	Time	m	Time	m	Time	m	Moon
1	TU	0517	2.4	1112	10.9	1734	2.7	2335	10.5	◑
2	W	0559	3.0	1201	10.2	1822	3.4			
3	TH	0032	9.9	0701	3.7	1310	9.7	1936	4.0	
4	F	0155	9.6	0839	3.9	1446	9.8	2124	3.8	
5	SA	0336	10.1	1009	3.3	1616	10.6	2249	3.0	
6	SU	0448	11.2	1124	2.4	1719	11.7	2357	2.2	
7	M	0544	12.3	1227	1.6	1812	12.7			
8	TU	0056	1.5	0633	13.2	1324	1.0	1859	13.5	
9	W	0151	0.9	0720	13.9	1416	0.6	1944	14.0	●
10	TH	0240	0.6	0805	14.3	1503	0.3	2028	14.2	
11	F	0323	0.4	0848	14.4	1543	0.3	2109	14.2	
12	SA	0400	0.4	0930	14.3	1617	0.5	2149	13.9	
13	SU	0431	0.7	1010	13.7	1646	1.0	2227	13.3	
14	M	0458	1.3	1050	12.8	1714	1.6	2307	12.3	
15	TU	0528	2.0	1134	11.7	1749	2.4	2353	11.2	◐
16	W	0608	2.8	1232	10.5	1838	3.3			
17	TH	0102	10.1	0708	3.7	1407	9.8	1959	4.0	
18	F	0243	9.9	0920	4.0	1529	10.0	2158	3.7	
19	SA	0357	10.4	1040	3.2	1634	10.8	2304	2.7	
20	SU	0458	11.3	1137	2.2	1729	11.7	2358	1.8	
21	M	0549	12.1	1227	1.5	1816	12.4			
22	TU	0047	1.1	0633	12.8	1315	1.0	1857	12.9	
23	W	0134	0.8	0712	13.1	1400	0.8	1934	13.1	○
24	TH	0218	0.7	0748	13.1	1440	1.0	2008	13.0	
25	F	0255	0.9	0821	12.9	1514	1.3	2038	12.7	
26	SA	0325	1.3	0850	12.6	1536	1.7	2105	12.4	
27	SU	0342	1.6	0917	12.3	1546	1.9	2130	12.1	
28	M	0355	1.7	0941	12.0	1602	1.9	2154	11.8	
29	TU	0419	1.8	1009	11.7	1630	2.0	2225	11.4	
30	W	0450	2.1	1045	11.2	1704	2.4	2306	10.9	
31	TH	0530	2.6	1132	10.6	1748	3.1	2359	10.2	◑

APRIL

Date	Day	Time	m	Time	m	Time	m	Time	m	Moon
1	F	0624	3.3	1235	10.0	1851	3.7			
2	SA	0113	9.8	0749	3.7	1401	9.8	2035	3.9	
3	SU	0252	10.1	0933	3.3	1541	10.5	2217	3.2	
4	M	0417	11.1	1056	2.4	1652	11.6	2331	2.2	
5	TU	0518	12.3	1202	1.6	1747	12.7			
6	W	0031	1.4	0609	13.3	1300	0.9	1836	13.6	
7	TH	0126	0.8	0657	14.0	1352	0.4	1922	14.2	●
8	F	0216	0.4	0743	14.4	1440	0.1	2006	14.4	
9	SA	0301	0.2	0828	14.5	1521	0.1	2048	14.4	
10	SU	0340	0.3	0910	14.3	1557	0.4	2129	14.0	
11	M	0414	0.7	0952	13.7	1627	1.0	2208	13.3	
12	TU	0443	1.3	1033	12.7	1656	1.7	2248	12.3	
13	W	0512	2.0	1116	11.6	1729	2.5	2333	11.2	
14	TH	0551	2.8	1211	10.5	1815	3.3			◐
15	F	0039	10.2	0647	3.6	1340	9.8	1926	4.0	
16	SA	0216	9.8	0823	3.9	1500	9.9	2117	3.8	
17	SU	0327	10.3	1005	3.3	1603	10.5	2230	3.0	
18	M	0426	11.0	1104	2.5	1657	11.3	2325	2.1	
19	TU	0517	11.8	1154	1.8	1744	12.1			
20	W	0014	1.4	0601	12.3	1242	1.3	1825	12.6	
21	TH	0101	1.0	0641	12.7	1326	1.1	1902	12.8	
22	F	0145	1.0	0717	12.7	1408	1.1	1937	12.8	○
23	SA	0224	1.1	0752	12.6	1443	1.4	2009	12.6	
24	SU	0257	1.4	0823	12.5	1510	1.7	2038	12.4	
25	M	0320	1.7	0852	12.2	1525	1.9	2106	12.2	
26	TU	0337	1.8	0920	12.0	1543	1.9	2133	11.9	
27	W	0401	1.8	0951	11.8	1611	2.0	2207	11.6	
28	TH	0434	2.0	1029	11.4	1646	2.3	2248	11.2	
29	F	0514	2.4	1115	10.9	1730	2.8	2341	10.7	
30	SA	0606	2.9	1215	10.4	1828	3.4			◑

Chart Datum: 6·50 metres below Ordnance Datum (Newlyn)
HAT is 14·7m above Chart Datum

TIME ZONE (UT)
For Summer Time add ONE hour in **non-shaded areas**

AVONMOUTH

LAT 51°30'N LONG 2°44'W

TIMES AND HEIGHTS OF HIGH AND LOW WATERS

Dates in amber are **SPRINGS**
Dates in yellow are **NEAPS**

2016

MAY

Date	Day	Time	m	Time	m	Time	m	Time	m
1	SU	0049	10.3	0718	3.3	1331	10.2	1954	3.6
2	M	0215	10.4	0855	3.1	1501	10.6	2141	3.2
3	TU	0341	11.2	1022	2.4	1619	11.5	2259	2.3
4	W	0448	12.2	1131	1.7	1719	12.6		
5	TH	0002	1.5	0543	13.1	1231	1.0	1810	13.4
6	F	0059	0.9	0633	13.8	1325	0.5	● 1858	14.0
7	SA	0150	0.5	0721	14.2	1414	0.3	1943	14.3
8	SU	0238	0.3	0808	14.2	1458	0.3	2027	14.2
9	M	0321	0.4	0852	14.0	1537	0.6	2110	13.8
10	TU	0358	0.8	0936	13.4	1611	1.1	2152	13.1
11	W	0430	1.4	1018	12.6	1641	1.7	2232	12.3
12	TH	0501	2.0	1101	11.6	1714	2.4	2317	11.3
13	F	0538	2.7	1150	10.7	1756	3.1	◐	
14	SA	0013	10.4	0626	3.3	1300	10.0	1854	3.6
15	SU	0136	10.0	0732	3.6	1419	9.9	2009	3.7
16	M	0247	10.2	0853	3.5	1522	10.2	2133	3.3
17	TU	0346	10.7	1013	3.0	1617	10.9	2240	2.6
18	W	0437	11.2	1111	2.3	1705	11.5	2334	2.0
19	TH	0524	11.8	1201	1.8	1749	12.1		
20	F	0022	1.5	0605	12.2	1248	1.5	1828	12.4
21	SA	0108	1.3	0645	12.4	1332	1.4	○ 1905	12.5
22	SU	0150	1.3	0722	12.4	1411	1.5	1941	12.5
23	M	0229	1.5	0758	12.3	1445	1.7	2015	12.4
24	TU	0301	1.7	0833	12.2	1510	1.9	2048	12.3
25	W	0326	1.8	0906	12.1	1533	2.0	2120	12.1
26	TH	0353	1.9	0941	12.0	1602	2.0	2157	11.9
27	F	0427	1.9	1020	11.7	1639	2.2	2239	11.6
28	SA	0508	2.2	1106	11.4	1722	2.5	2330	11.2
29	SU	0557	2.5	1200	11.0	1816	2.9	◑	
30	M	0031	10.9	0659	2.8	1306	10.8	1927	3.2
31	TU	0146	10.9	0818	2.8	1425	10.9	2102	3.0

JUNE

Date	Day	Time	m	Time	m	Time	m	Time	m
1	W	0307	11.3	0946	2.5	1544	11.4	2227	2.5
2	TH	0417	11.9	1100	1.9	1650	12.2	2333	1.8
3	F	0518	12.7	1202	1.3	1746	13.0		
4	SA	0032	1.2	0611	13.3	1259	0.9	1836	13.5
5	SU	0126	0.8	0701	13.6	1351	0.6	● 1923	13.8
6	M	0217	0.6	0750	13.7	1439	0.6	2009	13.8
7	TU	0304	0.7	0836	13.6	1522	0.8	2054	13.6
8	W	0345	1.0	0921	13.2	1559	1.2	2136	13.1
9	TH	0421	1.5	1003	12.6	1630	1.7	2217	12.4
10	F	0451	2.0	1044	11.8	1700	2.2	2257	11.6
11	SA	0522	2.4	1124	11.1	1736	2.7	2341	10.9
12	SU	0601	2.9	1212	10.4	1821	3.1	◐	
13	M	0037	10.3	0650	3.2	1314	10.0	1917	3.4
14	TU	0148	10.1	0749	3.4	1424	10.0	2023	3.5
15	W	0253	10.2	0855	3.3	1526	10.3	2133	3.2
16	TH	0350	10.6	1006	2.9	1621	10.9	2241	2.6
17	F	0442	11.1	1112	2.4	1710	11.5	2339	2.1
18	SA	0530	11.6	1206	2.0	1755	12.0		
19	SU	0030	1.7	0613	12.0	1256	1.7	1836	12.3
20	M	0118	1.5	0656	12.2	1341	1.6	○ 1917	12.5
21	TU	0202	1.5	0737	12.3	1423	1.7	1956	12.6
22	W	0244	1.6	0816	12.4	1500	1.8	2034	12.5
23	TH	0321	1.7	0855	12.3	1532	1.9	2112	12.5
24	F	0354	1.8	0934	12.3	1602	1.9	2150	12.4
25	SA	0427	1.8	1014	12.2	1637	2.0	2232	12.2
26	SU	0505	1.9	1057	12.0	1717	2.1	2319	11.9
27	M	0549	2.1	1145	11.6	1804	2.5	◑	
28	TU	0013	11.5	0640	2.4	1243	11.2	1902	2.8
29	W	0119	11.2	0745	2.6	1353	11.0	2021	3.1
30	TH	0236	11.2	0910	2.7	1513	11.1	2157	2.8

JULY

Date	Day	Time	m	Time	m	Time	m	Time	m
1	F	0351	11.5	1031	2.4	1624	11.7	2309	2.3
2	SA	0456	12.0	1138	1.9	1724	12.3		
3	SU	0010	1.7	0553	12.6	1237	1.4	1818	13.0
4	M	0107	1.2	0645	13.1	1332	1.0	● 1907	13.4
5	TU	0200	0.9	0735	13.3	1422	0.8	1954	13.5
6	W	0249	0.9	0822	13.3	1508	0.9	2038	13.4
7	TH	0334	1.0	0906	13.1	1548	1.2	2120	13.1
8	F	0411	1.4	0946	12.7	1619	1.6	2158	12.6
9	SA	0439	1.9	1021	12.1	1644	2.0	2232	12.0
10	SU	0502	2.2	1054	11.5	1711	2.3	2306	11.4
11	M	0531	2.5	1129	10.9	1745	2.7	2345	10.8
12	TU	0609	2.8	1211	10.4	1830	3.1	◐	
13	W	0036	10.2	0657	3.2	1308	10.0	1927	3.5
14	TH	0143	9.9	0759	3.4	1421	9.9	2036	3.5
15	F	0255	10.0	0909	3.4	1531	10.2	2149	3.2
16	SA	0359	10.5	1021	3.0	1632	10.9	2257	2.6
17	SU	0456	11.1	1127	2.4	1724	11.6	2356	2.0
18	M	0546	11.7	1224	2.0	1811	12.2		
19	TU	0049	1.7	0632	12.2	1316	1.7	○ 1855	12.6
20	W	0141	1.5	0717	12.5	1405	1.6	1938	12.9
21	TH	0230	1.4	0801	12.7	1451	1.6	2020	13.0
22	F	0314	1.4	0843	12.8	1531	1.6	2101	13.0
23	SA	0353	1.4	0923	12.8	1605	1.6	2141	13.0
24	SU	0427	1.5	1003	12.8	1636	1.7	2221	12.8
25	M	0459	1.5	1043	12.5	1709	1.8	2304	12.4
26	TU	0535	1.8	1127	12.1	1748	2.2	◑ 2352	11.9
27	W	0618	2.2	1218	11.5	1836	2.7		
28	TH	0052	11.2	0712	2.7	1324	10.9	1942	3.3
29	F	0211	10.8	0834	3.1	1447	10.7	2132	3.4
30	SA	0331	10.9	1009	3.0	1604	11.1	2251	2.8
31	SU	0440	11.4	1119	2.4	1708	11.8	2354	2.1

AUGUST

Date	Day	Time	m	Time	m	Time	m	Time	m
1	M	0540	12.1	1219	1.7	1804	12.5		
2	TU	0051	1.4	0632	12.7	1314	1.2	● 1853	13.1
3	W	0144	1.0	0720	13.1	1405	0.9	1939	13.4
4	TH	0233	0.8	0805	13.2	1452	0.8	2021	13.4
5	F	0317	0.9	0847	13.1	1532	1.0	2100	13.2
6	SA	0354	1.3	0923	12.8	1604	1.4	2134	12.8
7	SU	0421	1.7	0954	12.3	1625	1.8	2203	12.3
8	M	0438	2.1	1022	11.8	1644	2.1	2232	11.8
9	TU	0458	2.3	1050	11.3	1709	2.4	2302	11.1
10	W	0526	2.6	1123	10.7	1743	2.8	◐ 2339	10.5
11	TH	0604	3.0	1206	10.1	1830	3.4		
12	F	0032	9.9	0658	3.6	1310	9.7	1941	3.9
13	SA	0151	9.6	0817	3.9	1440	9.7	2105	3.8
14	SU	0318	9.9	0940	3.6	1557	10.3	2222	3.2
15	M	0426	10.7	1054	2.9	1657	11.2	2329	2.4
16	TU	0522	11.5	1158	2.2	1748	12.1		
17	W	0027	1.8	0611	12.3	1255	1.8	1834	12.8
18	TH	0122	1.4	0658	12.8	1348	1.5	○ 1919	13.3
19	F	0214	1.2	0742	13.2	1438	1.3	2003	13.6
20	SA	0302	1.0	0826	13.4	1521	1.2	2044	13.7
21	SU	0343	1.0	0907	13.4	1558	1.2	2125	13.6
22	M	0418	1.1	0946	13.3	1629	1.3	2205	13.4
23	TU	0448	1.3	1026	13.0	1657	1.6	2246	12.8
24	W	0517	1.7	1107	12.3	1729	2.1	2331	12.0
25	TH	0554	2.3	1154	11.5	1810	2.8	◑	
26	F	0027	11.0	0641	3.0	1258	10.6	1909	3.6
27	SA	0151	10.3	0801	3.7	1430	10.3	2116	3.9
28	SU	0318	10.4	0953	3.5	1550	10.7	2238	3.2
29	M	0428	11.0	1104	2.7	1655	11.5	2339	2.2
30	TU	0526	11.8	1201	1.9	1749	12.4		
31	W	0033	1.4	0617	12.6	1254	1.2	1836	13.1

Chart Datum: 6·50 metres below Ordnance Datum (Newlyn)
HAT is 14·7m above Chart Datum

TIME ZONE (UT)
For Summer Time add ONE hour in **non-shaded areas**

AVONMOUTH

LAT 51°30′N LONG 2°44′W

TIMES AND HEIGHTS OF HIGH AND LOW WATERS

Dates in amber are **SPRINGS**
Dates in yellow are **NEAPS**

2016

SEPTEMBER

Date	Day	Phase	Time	m	Time	m	Time	m	Time	m
1	TH	●	0123	0.9	0702	13.1	1344	0.8	1920	13.4
2	F		0211	0.7	0744	13.3	1429	0.7	1959	13.5
3	SA		0254	0.8	0822	13.2	1510	0.9	2035	13.3
4	SU		0331	1.2	0855	12.9	1542	1.3	2106	12.9
5	M		0358	1.7	0924	12.5	1602	1.8	2133	12.4
6	TU		0411	2.1	0949	12.0	1615	2.1	2158	11.9
7	W		0423	2.3	1014	11.6	1635	2.3	2224	11.4
8	TH		0446	2.5	1042	11.0	1704	2.6	2256	10.8
9	F	◐	0518	2.9	1118	10.4	1742	3.2	2339	10.1
10	SA		0602	3.5	1211	9.8	1838	3.9		
11	SU		0045	9.5	0711	4.1	1336	9.4	2018	4.2
12	M		0230	9.5	0858	4.1	1522	9.9	2150	3.6
13	TU		0357	10.3	1025	3.3	1630	11.0	2304	2.7
14	W		0458	11.4	1134	2.5	1724	12.1		
15	TH		0005	1.8	0549	12.4	1233	1.8	1812	13.0
16	F	○	0101	1.3	0636	13.1	1327	1.3	1857	13.7
17	SA		0154	0.9	0721	13.6	1417	1.0	1942	14.1
18	SU		0241	0.7	0804	13.9	1502	0.8	2024	14.2
19	M		0324	0.6	0846	14.0	1541	0.9	2106	14.1
20	TU		0400	0.8	0926	13.7	1614	1.1	2147	13.7
21	W		0430	1.2	1006	13.3	1642	1.5	2227	13.0
22	TH		0458	1.7	1047	12.5	1711	2.2	2311	11.9
23	F	◑	0531	2.5	1132	11.4	1749	3.0		
24	SA		0006	10.8	0615	3.3	1237	10.4	1845	3.9
25	SU		0136	10.0	0733	4.1	1417	10.0	2101	4.1
26	M		0303	10.1	0936	3.8	1533	10.5	2220	3.3
27	TU		0410	10.8	1043	2.9	1635	11.4	2318	2.3
28	W		0506	11.7	1138	2.0	1728	12.3		
29	TH		0008	1.5	0554	12.5	1229	1.2	1813	13.0
30	F		0057	1.0	0638	13.0	1316	0.8	1855	13.3

OCTOBER

Date	Day	Phase	Time	m	Time	m	Time	m	Time	m
1	SA	●	0142	0.7	0717	13.2	1401	0.8	1933	13.4
2	SU		0225	0.8	0753	13.2	1441	1.0	2007	13.2
3	M		0302	1.2	0825	12.9	1515	1.4	2037	12.8
4	TU		0329	1.7	0853	12.5	1537	1.9	2104	12.4
5	W		0343	2.1	0918	12.1	1548	2.1	2129	12.0
6	TH		0352	2.3	0942	11.7	1607	2.3	2154	11.6
7	F		0415	2.4	1010	11.3	1635	2.5	2226	11.1
8	SA		0446	2.7	1046	10.7	1710	3.0	2308	10.4
9	SU	◐	0526	3.3	1135	10.1	1758	3.7		
10	M		0007	9.8	0622	4.0	1247	9.6	1919	4.2
11	TU		0134	9.5	0802	4.3	1434	9.8	2111	3.9
12	W		0320	10.2	0950	3.7	1557	10.9	2233	2.9
13	TH		0429	11.3	1105	2.7	1656	12.0	2338	2.0
14	F		0523	12.4	1206	1.9	1747	13.1		
15	SA		0035	1.3	0611	13.3	1301	1.3	1833	13.8
16	SU	○	0127	0.8	0657	13.9	1351	0.9	1919	14.3
17	M		0216	0.5	0741	14.2	1438	0.7	2003	14.5
18	TU		0259	0.5	0824	14.3	1519	0.7	2046	14.3
19	W		0338	0.7	0906	14.0	1556	1.0	2129	13.8
20	TH		0411	1.2	0947	13.4	1627	1.5	2211	13.0
21	F		0441	1.8	1029	12.6	1658	2.2	2255	11.9
22	SA	◑	0514	2.6	1115	11.5	1735	3.0	2349	10.8
23	SU		0557	3.4	1218	10.5	1830	3.8		
24	M		0114	10.0	0705	4.1	1354	10.1	2019	4.2
25	TU		0238	10.0	0903	4.0	1507	10.5	2150	3.6
26	W		0342	10.6	1013	3.2	1606	11.2	2247	2.7
27	TH		0437	11.4	1107	2.3	1658	12.0	2337	1.9
28	F		0525	12.2	1157	1.6	1744	12.6		
29	SA		0024	1.3	0608	12.8	1244	1.2	1825	13.0
30	SU	●	0109	1.0	0646	13.0	1328	1.0	1903	13.1
31	M		0152	1.1	0722	13.0	1409	1.2	1938	13.0

NOVEMBER

Date	Day	Phase	Time	m	Time	m	Time	m	Time	m
1	TU		0229	1.3	0755	12.8	1444	1.5	2010	12.7
2	W		0300	1.7	0825	12.6	1511	1.9	2040	12.4
3	TH		0319	2.1	0853	12.2	1528	2.2	2107	12.1
4	F		0331	2.3	0920	11.9	1548	2.3	2134	11.7
5	SA		0355	2.4	0949	11.6	1617	2.4	2208	11.4
6	SU		0427	2.6	1027	11.1	1653	2.8	2250	10.9
7	M	◐	0507	3.0	1115	10.6	1739	3.3	2344	10.3
8	TU		0558	3.6	1218	10.2	1844	3.8		
9	W		0056	10.0	0713	4.0	1342	10.2	2020	3.8
10	TH		0228	10.2	0902	3.8	1514	10.8	2153	3.1
11	F		0351	11.1	1028	3.0	1622	11.8	2305	2.2
12	SA		0452	12.2	1134	2.1	1718	12.8		
13	SU		0004	1.5	0544	13.1	1231	1.4	1809	13.6
14	M	○	0059	0.9	0632	13.9	1324	1.0	1856	14.2
15	TU		0149	0.6	0719	14.2	1413	0.7	1943	14.3
16	W		0235	0.5	0804	14.3	1459	0.7	2029	14.2
17	TH		0318	0.7	0848	14.1	1539	1.0	2114	13.8
18	F		0355	1.1	0931	13.5	1616	1.5	2158	13.0
19	SA		0429	1.7	1015	12.7	1650	2.1	2242	12.1
20	SU		0502	2.4	1100	11.8	1725	2.8	2331	11.1
21	M	◑	0542	3.1	1155	10.9	1811	3.4		
22	TU		0037	10.3	0634	3.7	1314	10.3	1914	3.9
23	W		0158	10.0	0748	4.0	1429	10.4	2044	3.8
24	TH		0304	10.3	0919	3.7	1529	10.8	2201	3.3
25	F		0400	10.9	1025	3.0	1622	11.4	2257	2.6
26	SA		0450	11.6	1119	2.3	1710	11.9	2347	2.0
27	SU		0535	12.1	1207	1.8	1753	12.4		
28	M		0033	1.6	0615	12.6	1252	1.5	1833	12.6
29	TU	●	0117	1.4	0652	12.8	1335	1.4	1910	12.7
30	W		0157	1.5	0728	12.7	1414	1.6	1946	12.6

DECEMBER

Date	Day	Phase	Time	m	Time	m	Time	m	Time	m
1	TH		0232	1.7	0802	12.6	1448	1.8	2020	12.4
2	F		0300	2.0	0835	12.4	1515	2.1	2052	12.2
3	SA		0321	2.2	0906	12.1	1539	2.2	2123	12.0
4	SU		0345	2.3	0939	11.9	1608	2.3	2159	11.7
5	M		0418	2.4	1017	11.6	1645	2.5	2240	11.4
6	TU		0457	2.7	1102	11.3	1729	2.8	2329	11.0
7	W	◐	0545	3.1	1157	10.9	1823	3.1		
8	TH		0028	10.7	0645	3.4	1305	10.7	1933	3.3
9	F		0142	10.6	0805	3.6	1427	10.9	2104	3.2
10	SA		0307	11.0	0945	3.2	1545	11.5	2228	2.6
11	SU		0419	11.8	1102	2.5	1650	12.3	2334	1.9
12	M		0519	12.6	1204	1.8	1746	13.1		
13	TU		0032	1.3	0611	13.4	1300	1.2	1837	13.7
14	W	○	0126	0.8	0700	13.9	1353	0.9	1927	14.0
15	TH		0216	0.7	0747	14.1	1442	0.8	2014	14.0
16	F		0302	0.7	0833	14.0	1527	0.9	2101	13.7
17	SA		0343	1.0	0918	13.6	1607	1.3	2145	13.2
18	SU		0419	1.5	1001	13.0	1641	1.8	2227	12.4
19	M		0451	2.1	1042	12.3	1712	2.4	2308	11.6
20	TU		0523	2.6	1126	11.5	1747	2.9	2353	10.8
21	W	◑	0603	3.1	1217	10.8	1830	3.3		
22	TH		0051	10.2	0653	3.5	1326	10.3	1925	3.6
23	F		0205	10.0	0755	3.7	1436	10.2	2031	3.7
24	SA		0310	10.2	0907	3.6	1537	10.5	2148	3.4
25	SU		0407	10.7	1023	3.1	1631	11.0	2258	2.8
26	M		0458	11.3	1124	2.5	1719	11.6	2353	2.2
27	TU		0543	11.9	1215	2.0	1804	12.0		
28	W		0041	1.8	0625	12.4	1302	1.7	1845	12.3
29	TH	●	0127	1.6	0705	12.6	1347	1.6	1925	12.5
30	F		0209	1.7	0743	12.7	1429	1.7	2003	12.5
31	SA		0247	1.8	0820	12.6	1506	1.9	2040	12.4

Chart Datum: 6·50 metres below Ordnance Datum (Newlyn)
HAT is 14·7m above Chart Datum

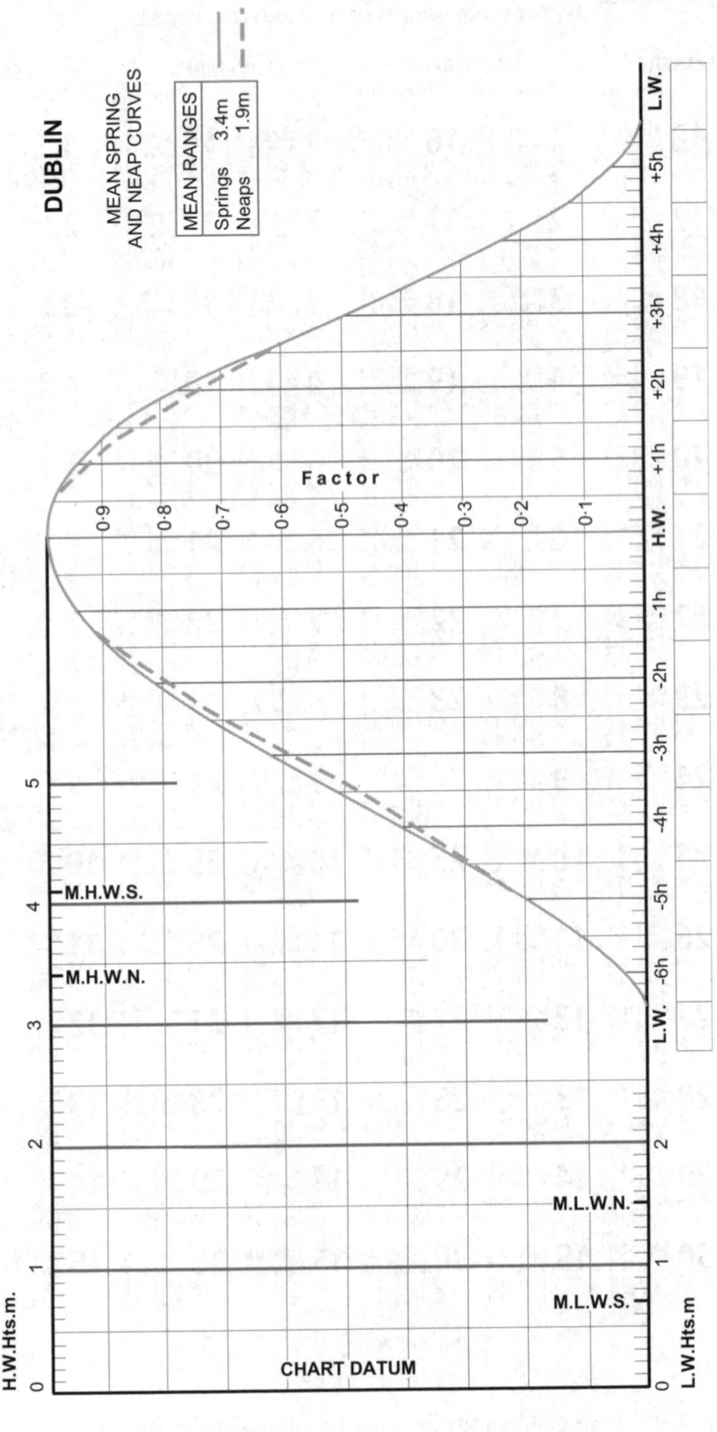
DUBLIN
MEAN SPRING AND NEAP CURVES
MEAN RANGES
Springs 3.4m
Neaps 1.9m
Factor
0·9
0·8
0·7
0·6
0·5
0·4
0·3
0·2
0·1
L.W.
-6h
-5h
-4h
-3h
-2h
-1h
H.W.
+1h
+2h
+3h
+4h
+5h
L.W.
H.W.Hts.m.
M.H.W.S.
M.H.W.N.
CHART DATUM
M.L.W.N.
M.L.W.S.
L.W.Hts.m

TIME ZONE (UT)
For Summer Time add ONE hour in **non-shaded areas**

IRELAND – DUBLIN (NORTH WALL)

LAT 53°21'N LONG 6°13'W

TIMES AND HEIGHTS OF HIGH AND LOW WATERS

Dates in amber are **SPRINGS**
Dates in yellow are **NEAPS**

2016

JANUARY

Date	Day	Time	m	Time	m	Time	m	Time	m
1	F	0408	3.5	0945	1.4	1627	3.7	2223	1.2
2	SA	0508	3.4	1044	1.6	1727	3.5	◑ 2319	1.3
3	SU	0612	3.3	1146	1.6	1832	3.4		
4	M	0018	1.4	0713	3.4	1251	1.7	1935	3.4
5	TU	0121	1.4	0810	3.5	1353	1.6	2032	3.5
6	W	0218	1.4	0900	3.6	1447	1.4	2122	3.6
7	TH	0305	1.2	0944	3.8	1530	1.3	2206	3.7
8	F	0344	1.1	1022	3.9	1606	1.1	2245	3.8
9	SA	0419	0.9	1057	4.0	1641	0.9	2322	3.9
10	SU	0454	0.8	1132	4.1	1717	0.7	● 2359	4.0
11	M	0531	0.7	1210	4.2	1756	0.6		
12	TU	0039	4.0	0610	0.7	1253	4.3	1838	0.5
13	W	0123	4.0	0654	0.7	1338	4.3	1925	0.5
14	TH	0211	4.0	0742	0.8	1426	4.2	2015	0.6
15	F	0302	3.9	0835	0.9	1518	4.2	2110	0.7
16	SA	0357	3.8	0933	1.0	1613	4.0	◐ 2209	0.8
17	SU	0458	3.7	1037	1.2	1715	3.9	2315	1.0
18	M	0608	3.7	1148	1.3	1826	3.8		
19	TU	0028	1.1	0721	3.7	1303	1.3	1941	3.7
20	W	0142	1.2	0829	3.8	1414	1.2	2053	3.7
21	TH	0249	1.1	0932	3.9	1517	1.0	2157	3.8
22	F	0345	1.0	1026	4.0	1609	0.8	2251	3.9
23	SA	0431	0.9	1113	4.1	1655	0.7	2335	3.9
24	SU	0511	0.8	1153	4.1	1736	0.6	○	
25	M	0012	3.9	0547	0.8	1227	4.1	1814	0.6
26	TU	0044	3.8	0621	0.8	1259	4.1	1851	0.6
27	W	0117	3.8	0656	0.8	1335	4.0	1929	0.7
28	TH	0154	3.7	0733	0.9	1413	4.0	2008	0.8
29	F	0233	3.7	0813	1.0	1454	3.8	2049	0.9
30	SA	0315	3.6	0856	1.2	1537	3.7	2133	1.1
31	SU	0402	3.4	0946	1.3	1625	3.5	2222	1.3

FEBRUARY

Date	Day	Time	m	Time	m	Time	m	Time	m
1	M	0457	3.3	1046	1.5	1723	3.3	◑ 2320	1.4
2	TU	0607	3.2	1153	1.6	1839	3.2		
3	W	0025	1.5	0719	3.3	1301	1.6	1950	3.3
4	TH	0131	1.5	0820	3.4	1405	1.5	2050	3.4
5	F	0230	1.3	0911	3.6	1458	1.2	2140	3.5
6	SA	0317	1.1	0955	3.8	1541	1.0	2222	3.7
7	SU	0357	0.9	1034	4.0	1619	0.7	2301	3.9
8	M	0435	0.7	1112	4.2	1657	0.5	● 2339	4.0
9	TU	0513	0.5	1150	4.3	1737	0.3		
10	W	0018	4.1	0552	0.4	1232	4.4	1819	0.2
11	TH	0101	4.1	0634	0.4	1317	4.4	1904	0.2
12	F	0146	4.1	0721	0.5	1404	4.3	1953	0.4
13	SA	0235	4.0	0812	0.6	1455	4.2	2046	0.5
14	SU	0328	3.9	0909	0.8	1550	4.0	2143	0.8
15	M	0428	3.7	1012	1.0	1653	3.8	◐ 2246	1.0
16	TU	0540	3.6	1123	1.2	1809	3.6		
17	W	0000	1.3	0657	3.5	1242	1.3	1929	3.5
18	TH	0123	1.3	0811	3.6	1401	1.2	2044	3.6
19	F	0238	1.2	0918	3.7	1507	1.0	2150	3.6
20	SA	0334	1.1	1015	3.9	1558	0.8	2244	3.7
21	SU	0418	0.9	1102	4.0	1641	0.7	2326	3.8
22	M	0457	0.8	1141	4.0	1719	0.6	○ 2358	3.8
23	TU	0531	0.7	1210	4.0	1754	0.6		
24	W	0021	3.8	0602	0.7	1237	4.0	1827	0.6
25	TH	0049	3.8	0633	0.7	1308	4.0	1859	0.6
26	F	0121	3.7	0704	0.7	1342	3.9	1932	0.7
27	SA	0155	3.7	0736	0.8	1419	3.8	2005	0.8
28	SU	0233	3.6	0812	0.9	1459	3.7	2042	1.0
29	M	0315	3.5	0853	1.1	1544	3.5	2124	1.2

MARCH

Date	Day	Time	m	Time	m	Time	m	Time	m
1	TU	0403	3.4	0941	1.3	1635	3.3	◑ 2217	1.4
2	W	0500	3.2	1047	1.5	1739	3.2	2329	1.5
3	TH	0614	3.2	1210	1.5	1904	3.1		
4	F	0046	1.5	0734	3.2	1323	1.4	2016	3.3
5	SA	0154	1.4	0835	3.4	1425	1.1	2112	3.5
6	SU	0249	1.1	0925	3.7	1514	0.8	2158	3.7
7	M	0334	0.8	1008	3.9	1556	0.5	2238	3.9
8	TU	0414	0.5	1049	4.2	1636	0.2	2317	4.1
9	W	0453	0.3	1129	4.3	1717	0.1	● 2356	4.2
10	TH	0533	0.2	1211	4.4	1759	0.0		
11	F	0037	4.2	0615	0.2	1256	4.4	1843	0.1
12	SA	0122	4.1	0701	0.2	1344	4.3	1930	0.3
13	SU	0210	4.0	0752	0.4	1436	4.1	2022	0.5
14	M	0302	3.9	0850	0.6	1532	3.9	2119	0.8
15	TU	0401	3.7	0953	0.8	1638	3.7	◐ 2221	1.1
16	W	0514	3.6	1102	1.1	1756	3.5	2333	1.3
17	TH	0634	3.5	1220	1.2	1916	3.4		
18	F	0059	1.4	0749	3.5	1343	1.1	2031	3.5
19	SA	0219	1.3	0858	3.6	1449	1.0	2136	3.6
20	SU	0315	1.2	0956	3.8	1539	0.8	2227	3.6
21	M	0359	1.0	1043	3.9	1620	0.7	2307	3.7
22	TU	0436	0.8	1120	3.9	1656	0.6	2336	3.7
23	W	0510	0.7	1149	3.9	1729	0.6	○ 2357	3.7
24	TH	0541	0.7	1214	3.9	1800	0.6		
25	F	0021	3.7	0609	0.7	1243	3.9	1829	0.6
26	SA	0050	3.8	0636	0.7	1315	3.8	1857	0.7
27	SU	0123	3.8	0706	0.7	1351	3.7	1928	0.8
28	M	0201	3.7	0740	0.8	1431	3.6	2005	0.9
29	TU	0243	3.6	0821	0.9	1515	3.5	2048	1.1
30	W	0329	3.5	0908	1.1	1604	3.3	2138	1.3
31	TH	0422	3.3	1007	1.2	1704	3.2	◑ 2243	1.4

APRIL

Date	Day	Time	m	Time	m	Time	m	Time	m
1	F	0526	3.2	1125	1.3	1820	3.1		
2	SA	0004	1.5	0643	3.2	1245	1.2	1938	3.3
3	SU	0118	1.3	0755	3.4	1351	1.0	2039	3.5
4	M	0218	1.1	0852	3.7	1445	0.7	2129	3.7
5	TU	0307	0.8	0940	3.9	1532	0.4	2213	3.9
6	W	0350	0.5	1025	4.1	1614	0.1	2254	4.1
7	TH	0432	0.2	1108	4.3	1656	0.0	● 2334	4.2
8	F	0514	0.1	1152	4.4	1739	0.0		
9	SA	0016	4.2	0558	0.1	1239	4.3	1823	0.1
10	SU	0101	4.2	0645	0.2	1328	4.2	1910	0.3
11	M	0149	4.1	0737	0.3	1421	4.1	2002	0.6
12	TU	0241	3.9	0834	0.5	1519	3.9	2058	0.9
13	W	0341	3.8	0936	0.7	1625	3.6	2158	1.1
14	TH	0451	3.6	1042	0.9	1739	3.5	◐ 2306	1.4
15	F	0607	3.5	1155	1.1	1854	3.4		
16	SA	0025	1.5	0720	3.5	1314	1.1	2006	3.4
17	SU	0146	1.4	0829	3.6	1420	1.0	2110	3.5
18	M	0246	1.3	0927	3.7	1511	0.9	2159	3.6
19	TU	0332	1.1	1014	3.8	1553	0.8	2237	3.6
20	W	0411	0.9	1052	3.8	1629	0.7	2306	3.7
21	TH	0445	0.8	1122	3.8	1702	0.7	2331	3.7
22	F	0517	0.8	1151	3.8	1732	0.7	○ 2355	3.8
23	SA	0545	0.7	1219	3.8	1759	0.7		
24	SU	0023	3.8	0611	0.7	1251	3.8	1826	0.8
25	M	0057	3.8	0640	0.8	1327	3.7	1859	0.8
26	TU	0135	3.8	0716	0.8	1408	3.6	1937	0.9
27	W	0218	3.7	0759	0.9	1453	3.6	2022	1.0
28	TH	0305	3.6	0848	1.0	1542	3.4	2114	1.2
29	F	0356	3.5	0946	1.1	1639	3.3	2216	1.3
30	SA	0456	3.4	1056	1.1	1747	3.3	◑ 2328	1.4

Chart Datum: 0·20 metres above Ordnance Datum (Dublin)
HAT is 4·5m above Chart Datum

TIME ZONE (UT)
For Summer Time add ONE hour in **non-shaded areas**

IRELAND – DUBLIN (NORTH WALL)

LAT 53°21'N LONG 6°13'W

TIMES AND HEIGHTS OF HIGH AND LOW WATERS

Dates in amber are **SPRINGS**
Dates in yellow are **NEAPS**

2016

MAY

Date	Day	Time	m
1	SU	0605 1210 1900	3.4 1.1 3.4
2	M	0040 0715 1318 2004	1.3 3.5 0.9 3.5
3	TU	0144 0817 1416 2059	1.1 3.7 0.6 3.7
4	W	0238 0912 1507 2147	0.8 3.9 0.4 3.9
5	TH	0327 1002 1553 2232	0.5 4.1 0.2 4.1
6	F	0412 1050 1638 ● 2315	0.3 4.3 0.1 4.2
7	SA	0457 1137 1722 2359	0.2 4.3 0.1 4.2
8	SU	0544 1225 1806	0.2 4.3 0.2
9	M	0044 0632 1315 1853	4.2 0.2 4.2 0.4
10	TU	0132 0724 1408 1943	4.1 0.3 4.0 0.7
11	W	0224 0819 1505 2037	4.0 0.5 3.8 0.9
12	TH	0322 0918 1607 2134	3.8 0.7 3.6 1.2
13	F	0427 1019 1713 ◐ 2236	3.7 0.9 3.5 1.4
14	SA	0536 1124 1821 2343	3.6 1.0 3.4 1.5
15	SU	0645 1233 1928	3.5 1.1 3.4
16	M	0058 0749 1340 2028	1.5 3.6 1.1 3.4
17	TU	0205 0847 1435 2118	1.4 3.6 1.0 3.5
18	W	0258 0936 1520 2158	1.2 3.7 0.9 3.6
19	TH	0340 1017 1558 2232	1.1 3.7 0.9 3.7
20	F	0417 1053 1632 2303	1.0 3.7 0.8 3.8
21	SA	0450 1125 1703 ○ 2330	0.9 3.7 0.8 3.8
22	SU	0520 1156 1731 2359	0.9 3.7 0.8 3.8
23	M	0547 1229 1800	0.8 3.7 0.8
24	TU	0033 0618 1306 1835	3.9 0.8 3.7 0.9
25	W	0114 0656 1348 1915	3.9 0.8 3.7 0.9
26	TH	0157 0741 1433 2001	3.9 0.8 3.7 1.0
27	F	0245 0832 1523 2054	3.8 0.9 3.6 1.1
28	SA	0336 0929 1618 2152	3.7 0.9 3.5 1.2
29	SU	0432 1032 1719 ◑ 2257	3.7 1.0 3.5 1.2
30	M	0534 1139 1825	3.6 0.9 3.5
31	TU	0005 0640 1246 1930	1.2 3.7 0.8 3.6

JUNE

Date	Day	Time	m
1	W	0110 0745 1348 2030	1.1 3.8 0.7 3.8
2	TH	0210 0846 1444 2124	0.9 3.9 0.6 3.9
3	F	0305 0942 1535 2214	0.7 4.1 0.4 4.0
4	SA	0356 1035 1623 2301	0.5 4.2 0.4 4.1
5	SU	0445 1125 1708 ● 2345	0.4 4.2 0.4 4.2
6	M	0533 1214 1753	0.3 4.2 0.5
7	TU	0030 0620 1303 1837	4.2 0.4 4.1 0.6
8	W	0117 0710 1352 1924	4.1 0.4 3.9 0.8
9	TH	0206 0802 1444 2013	4.0 0.5 3.8 0.9
10	F	0258 0856 1538 2106	3.9 0.7 3.6 1.1
11	SA	0355 0951 1636 2202	3.8 0.9 3.5 1.3
12	SU	0457 1048 1738 ◐ 2302	3.7 1.0 3.4 1.4
13	M	0601 1147 1839	3.6 1.1 3.3
14	TU	0005 0703 1250 1937	1.5 3.5 1.2 3.4
15	W	0112 0801 1349 2030	1.5 3.5 1.2 3.5
16	TH	0214 0854 1441 2117	1.4 3.6 1.1 3.6
17	F	0305 0941 1524 2158	1.3 3.6 1.1 3.7
18	SA	0346 1022 1601 2234	1.2 3.7 1.0 3.8
19	SU	0422 1100 1634 2306	1.1 3.7 0.9 3.9
20	M	0453 1134 1705 ○ 2337	1.0 3.7 0.9 3.9
21	TU	0524 1208 1738	0.9 3.8 0.8
22	W	0012 0558 1246 1814	4.0 0.8 3.8 0.8
23	TH	0053 0638 1328 1855	4.0 0.8 3.8 0.8
24	F	0137 0723 1413 1941	4.0 0.7 3.8 0.9
25	SA	0224 0813 1502 2032	4.0 0.7 3.8 1.0
26	SU	0314 0908 1554 2127	4.0 0.8 3.7 1.0
27	M	0408 1007 1651 ◑ 2228	3.9 0.8 3.6 1.1
28	TU	0507 1111 1754 2333	3.8 0.9 3.6 1.2
29	W	0612 1217 1901	3.8 0.9 3.6
30	TH	0041 0720 1323 2006	1.1 3.8 0.9 3.7

JULY

Date	Day	Time	m
1	F	0147 0827 1425 2106	1.1 3.9 0.8 3.9
2	SA	0250 0930 1522 2201	0.9 3.9 0.7 4.0
3	SU	0346 1027 1613 2250	0.7 4.0 0.7 4.1
4	M	0437 1118 1658 ● 2335	0.6 4.1 0.6 4.2
5	TU	0524 1204 1740	0.5 4.0 0.6
6	W	0017 0609 1248 1821	4.2 0.5 4.0 0.7
7	TH	0059 0654 1331 1902	4.1 0.5 3.9 0.8
8	F	0142 0740 1415 1946	4.1 0.6 3.8 0.9
9	SA	0227 0828 1501 2033	4.0 0.7 3.6 1.0
10	SU	0315 0917 1550 2124	3.8 0.9 3.5 1.2
11	M	0408 1008 1644 2219	3.7 1.0 3.4 1.4
12	TU	0507 1101 1745 ◐ 2317	3.5 1.2 3.3 1.5
13	W	0612 1158 1847	3.4 1.3 3.3
14	TH	0020 0716 1257 1945	1.6 3.4 1.4 3.4
15	F	0124 0814 1356 2038	1.5 3.4 1.3 3.5
16	SA	0225 0907 1448 2125	1.4 3.5 1.3 3.6
17	SU	0315 0954 1531 2206	1.3 3.6 1.1 3.8
18	M	0354 1035 1608 2242	1.1 3.7 1.0 3.9
19	TU	0429 1112 1642 ○ 2316	1.0 3.8 0.9 4.0
20	W	0502 1147 1716 2351	0.8 3.8 0.8 4.1
21	TH	0538 1224 1753	0.7 3.9 0.7
22	F	0030 0618 1306 1833	4.2 0.6 3.9 0.7
23	SA	0114 0702 1350 1918	4.2 0.5 3.9 0.7
24	SU	0200 0750 1437 2007	4.2 0.6 3.9 0.8
25	M	0250 0844 1528 2101	4.1 0.6 3.8 0.9
26	TU	0343 0941 1623 ◑ 2201	4.0 0.8 3.8 1.0
27	W	0441 1043 1726 2306	3.9 0.9 3.7 1.1
28	TH	0548 1151 1837	3.8 1.0 3.6
29	F	0018 0703 1302 1948	1.2 3.7 1.1 3.7
30	SA	0132 0818 1412 2054	1.2 3.7 1.1 3.8
31	SU	0241 0925 1513 2153	1.0 3.8 1.0 3.9

AUGUST

Date	Day	Time	m
1	M	0340 1023 1604 2243	0.9 3.9 0.9 4.1
2	TU	0430 1113 1648 ● 2326	0.7 3.9 0.8 4.1
3	W	0515 1155 1727	0.6 3.9 0.7
4	TH	0003 0555 1231 1803	4.1 0.5 3.9 0.7
5	F	0037 0634 1305 1839	4.1 0.5 3.8 0.8
6	SA	0113 0714 1341 1917	4.1 0.6 3.8 0.8
7	SU	0153 0754 1421 1957	4.0 0.7 3.7 1.0
8	M	0234 0838 1503 2042	3.9 0.9 3.6 1.1
9	TU	0319 0924 1548 2132	3.7 1.0 3.5 1.3
10	W	0409 1014 1641 ◐ 2228	3.5 1.2 3.4 1.4
11	TH	0511 1109 1746 2332	3.4 1.4 3.3 1.6
12	F	0627 1210 1858	3.3 1.5 3.3
13	SA	0039 0737 1313 2001	1.6 3.3 1.5 3.4
14	SU	0146 0837 1413 2054	1.5 3.4 1.4 3.6
15	M	0244 0928 1503 2139	1.3 3.5 1.2 3.7
16	TU	0328 1012 1543 2217	1.1 3.7 1.0 3.9
17	W	0404 1049 1619 2253	0.8 3.8 0.8 4.1
18	TH	0440 1125 1654 ○ 2329	0.6 3.9 0.6 4.2
19	F	0516 1202 1732	0.4 4.0 0.5
20	SA	0007 0555 1242 1811	4.3 0.3 4.1 0.5
21	SU	0049 0638 1324 1855	4.4 0.3 4.1 0.5
22	M	0135 0726 1411 1943	4.3 0.4 4.0 0.6
23	TU	0224 0817 1501 2037	4.2 0.6 3.9 0.8
24	W	0318 0915 1556 2138	4.1 0.8 3.8 1.0
25	TH	0418 1018 1700 ◑ 2245	3.9 1.0 3.7 1.1
26	F	0531 1128 1817	3.7 1.2 3.6
27	SA	0001 0655 1245 1933	1.3 3.6 1.3 3.6
28	SU	0122 0813 1400 2043	1.2 3.6 1.3 3.8
29	M	0235 0921 1503 2144	1.1 3.7 1.1 3.9
30	TU	0332 1019 1552 2234	0.9 3.8 1.0 4.0
31	W	0419 1105 1634 2315	0.7 3.9 0.9 4.1

Chart Datum: 0·20 metres above Ordnance Datum (Dublin)
HAT is 4·5m above Chart Datum

TIME ZONE (UT)
For Summer Time add ONE hour in **non-shaded areas**

IRELAND – DUBLIN (NORTH WALL)

LAT 53°21′N LONG 6°13′W

TIMES AND HEIGHTS OF HIGH AND LOW WATERS

Dates in amber are **SPRINGS**
Dates in yellow are **NEAPS**

2016

SEPTEMBER

Date	Day	Moon	Time	m	Time	m	Time	m	Time	m
1	TH	●	0459	0.6	1143	3.9	1710	0.8	2347	4.1
2	F		0536	0.5	1211	3.8	1744	0.7		
3	SA		0014	4.1	0610	0.6	1238	3.8	1815	0.7
4	SU		0046	4.0	0644	0.6	1309	3.8	1848	0.8
5	M		0121	4.0	0719	0.7	1344	3.8	1923	0.9
6	TU		0159	3.9	0755	0.9	1423	3.7	2001	1.0
7	W		0240	3.7	0835	1.0	1504	3.6	2043	1.2
8	TH		0326	3.6	0921	1.2	1550	3.5	2133	1.4
9	F	◐	0419	3.4	1017	1.4	1645	3.3	2240	1.5
10	SA		0530	3.2	1124	1.6	1759	3.3	2357	1.6
11	SU		0658	3.2	1234	1.6	1919	3.3		
12	M		0108	1.5	0807	3.3	1340	1.5	2020	3.5
13	TU		0212	1.3	0902	3.5	1434	1.3	2109	3.7
14	W		0300	1.0	0947	3.7	1517	1.0	2150	3.9
15	TH		0339	0.7	1025	3.9	1555	0.7	2228	4.2
16	F	○	0416	0.4	1101	4.1	1632	0.5	2305	4.3
17	SA		0454	0.2	1138	4.2	1710	0.4	2344	4.4
18	SU		0534	0.1	1217	4.2	1751	0.3		
19	M		0026	4.5	0615	0.2	1259	4.2	1834	0.3
20	TU		0112	4.4	0701	0.3	1346	4.1	1922	0.5
21	W		0202	4.2	0753	0.6	1436	4.0	2017	0.7
22	TH		0258	4.0	0850	0.8	1533	3.9	2119	0.9
23	F	◑	0402	3.8	0955	1.1	1639	3.7	2229	1.1
24	SA		0522	3.6	1106	1.3	1758	3.6	2346	1.2
25	SU		0646	3.5	1226	1.5	1916	3.7		
26	M		0109	1.2	0803	3.6	1345	1.4	2026	3.8
27	TU		0221	1.1	0911	3.7	1446	1.3	2127	3.9
28	W		0316	0.9	1005	3.8	1534	1.1	2217	4.0
29	TH		0400	0.7	1049	3.9	1614	0.9	2258	4.1
30	F		0439	0.6	1124	3.9	1650	0.8	2328	4.1

OCTOBER

Date	Day	Moon	Time	m	Time	m	Time	m	Time	m
1	SA	●	0513	0.6	1149	3.9	1723	0.8	2354	4.0
2	SU		0545	0.6	1212	3.8	1754	0.8		
3	M		0022	4.0	0615	0.7	1241	3.9	1823	0.8
4	TU		0055	3.9	0645	0.8	1314	3.8	1854	0.9
5	W		0131	3.9	0716	0.9	1350	3.8	1928	1.0
6	TH		0211	3.7	0753	1.1	1431	3.7	2008	1.1
7	F		0255	3.6	0835	1.2	1516	3.6	2054	1.3
8	SA		0346	3.4	0928	1.4	1607	3.5	2153	1.4
9	SU	◐	0448	3.2	1037	1.6	1709	3.3	2311	1.5
10	M		0611	3.2	1154	1.7	1826	3.3		
11	TU		0029	1.5	0729	3.3	1303	1.5	1936	3.5
12	W		0135	1.2	0829	3.5	1401	1.3	2032	3.7
13	TH		0228	0.9	0917	3.7	1448	1.0	2119	4.0
14	F		0312	0.6	0958	4.0	1530	0.7	2201	4.2
15	SA		0353	0.3	1036	4.1	1610	0.5	2242	4.4
16	SU	○	0432	0.2	1115	4.3	1650	0.3	2324	4.5
17	M		0513	0.1	1155	4.3	1732	0.2		
18	TU		0007	4.5	0555	0.2	1238	4.3	1817	0.3
19	W		0055	4.4	0641	0.4	1325	4.2	1907	0.4
20	TH		0147	4.2	0732	0.6	1417	4.1	2002	0.6
21	F		0245	4.0	0829	0.9	1515	4.0	2104	0.9
22	SA	◑	0352	3.8	0932	1.2	1621	3.8	2211	1.1
23	SU		0509	3.6	1042	1.4	1736	3.7	2325	1.2
24	M		0627	3.5	1159	1.5	1850	3.7		
25	TU		0045	1.2	0742	3.6	1318	1.5	2000	3.8
26	W		0156	1.1	0848	3.7	1421	1.4	2101	3.9
27	TH		0251	1.0	0941	3.8	1510	1.2	2152	4.0
28	F		0336	0.8	1024	3.9	1552	1.1	2233	4.0
29	SA		0414	0.8	1058	3.9	1629	1.0	2305	4.0
30	SU	●	0448	0.7	1124	3.9	1702	0.9	2334	4.0
31	M		0520	0.8	1149	3.9	1734	0.9		

NOVEMBER

Date	Day	Moon	Time	m	Time	m	Time	m	Time	m
1	TU		0002	3.9	0548	0.8	1217	3.9	1803	0.9
2	W		0034	3.9	0616	0.9	1249	3.9	1832	0.9
3	TH		0109	3.8	0646	1.0	1325	3.9	1904	1.0
4	F		0148	3.7	0722	1.1	1405	3.8	1943	1.1
5	SA		0232	3.6	0804	1.2	1450	3.7	2029	1.2
6	SU		0322	3.5	0855	1.4	1539	3.6	2123	1.3
7	M	◐	0419	3.4	0956	1.5	1635	3.5	2230	1.4
8	TU		0528	3.3	1110	1.6	1739	3.5	2345	1.3
9	W		0643	3.4	1222	1.5	1848	3.6		
10	TH		0054	1.2	0748	3.6	1324	1.4	1950	3.7
11	F		0154	0.9	0841	3.8	1417	1.1	2045	4.0
12	SA		0244	0.7	0928	4.0	1504	0.8	2135	4.2
13	SU		0330	0.4	1012	4.2	1549	0.6	2222	4.3
14	M	○	0413	0.3	1055	4.3	1633	0.4	2308	4.4
15	TU		0456	0.2	1138	4.4	1718	0.3	2354	4.4
16	W		0540	0.3	1222	4.4	1805	0.3		
17	TH		0043	4.3	0625	0.5	1310	4.3	1855	0.4
18	F		0136	4.2	0715	0.7	1402	4.2	1949	0.6
19	SA		0234	4.0	0809	1.0	1458	4.1	2048	0.8
20	SU		0337	3.8	0909	1.2	1600	3.9	2150	1.0
21	M	◑	0446	3.6	1012	1.4	1708	3.8	2255	1.1
22	TU		0557	3.5	1122	1.6	1816	3.7		
23	W		0007	1.2	0706	3.5	1237	1.6	1922	3.7
24	TH		0118	1.2	0810	3.6	1345	1.5	2024	3.8
25	F		0218	1.1	0905	3.7	1441	1.4	2117	3.8
26	SA		0307	1.0	0949	3.8	1527	1.2	2202	3.9
27	SU		0348	1.0	1025	3.9	1606	1.1	2239	3.9
28	M		0423	0.9	1057	3.9	1642	1.0	2313	3.9
29	TU	●	0455	0.9	1127	4.0	1714	1.0	2344	3.9
30	W		0525	0.9	1156	4.0	1744	1.0		

DECEMBER

Date	Day	Moon	Time	m	Time	m	Time	m	Time	m
1	TH		0015	3.8	0552	1.0	1227	4.0	1812	1.0
2	F		0050	3.8	0622	1.0	1302	4.0	1845	1.0
3	SA		0128	3.8	0658	1.1	1343	4.0	1924	1.0
4	SU		0212	3.7	0740	1.2	1427	3.9	2008	1.0
5	M		0259	3.6	0828	1.3	1515	3.8	2059	1.1
6	TU		0352	3.6	0924	1.4	1607	3.8	2157	1.1
7	W	◐	0451	3.5	1027	1.5	1704	3.7	2302	1.2
8	TH		0557	3.5	1136	1.5	1806	3.7		
9	F		0012	1.1	0704	3.6	1244	1.4	1911	3.8
10	SA		0118	1.0	0805	3.8	1345	1.2	2013	3.9
11	SU		0217	0.8	0900	3.9	1441	1.0	2112	4.1
12	M		0310	0.6	0951	4.1	1532	0.7	2206	4.2
13	TU		0358	0.5	1039	4.3	1621	0.5	2257	4.3
14	W	○	0444	0.5	1125	4.4	1709	0.4	2346	4.3
15	TH		0528	0.5	1210	4.4	1756	0.4		
16	F		0035	4.2	0612	0.6	1257	4.4	1844	0.4
17	SA		0125	4.1	0659	0.7	1346	4.3	1935	0.5
18	SU		0218	4.0	0748	0.9	1438	4.2	2027	0.7
19	M		0313	3.8	0842	1.1	1532	4.0	2122	0.8
20	TU		0412	3.6	0939	1.3	1631	3.9	2219	1.0
21	W	◑	0515	3.5	1040	1.5	1734	3.7	2320	1.2
22	TH		0619	3.5	1145	1.6	1837	3.6		
23	F		0026	1.3	0720	3.5	1257	1.6	1938	3.6
24	SA		0134	1.3	0817	3.6	1404	1.5	2036	3.6
25	SU		0232	1.3	0907	3.7	1459	1.4	2127	3.7
26	M		0319	1.2	0951	3.8	1543	1.3	2211	3.7
27	TU		0358	1.1	1029	3.9	1621	1.2	2250	3.7
28	W		0431	1.1	1104	3.9	1654	1.1	2325	3.8
29	TH	●	0502	1.0	1136	4.0	1724	1.0	2357	3.8
30	F		0531	1.0	1206	4.0	1753	0.9		
31	SA		0030	3.8	0601	0.9	1241	4.1	1825	0.9

Chart Datum: 0·20 metres above Ordnance Datum (Dublin)
HAT is 4·5m above Chart Datum

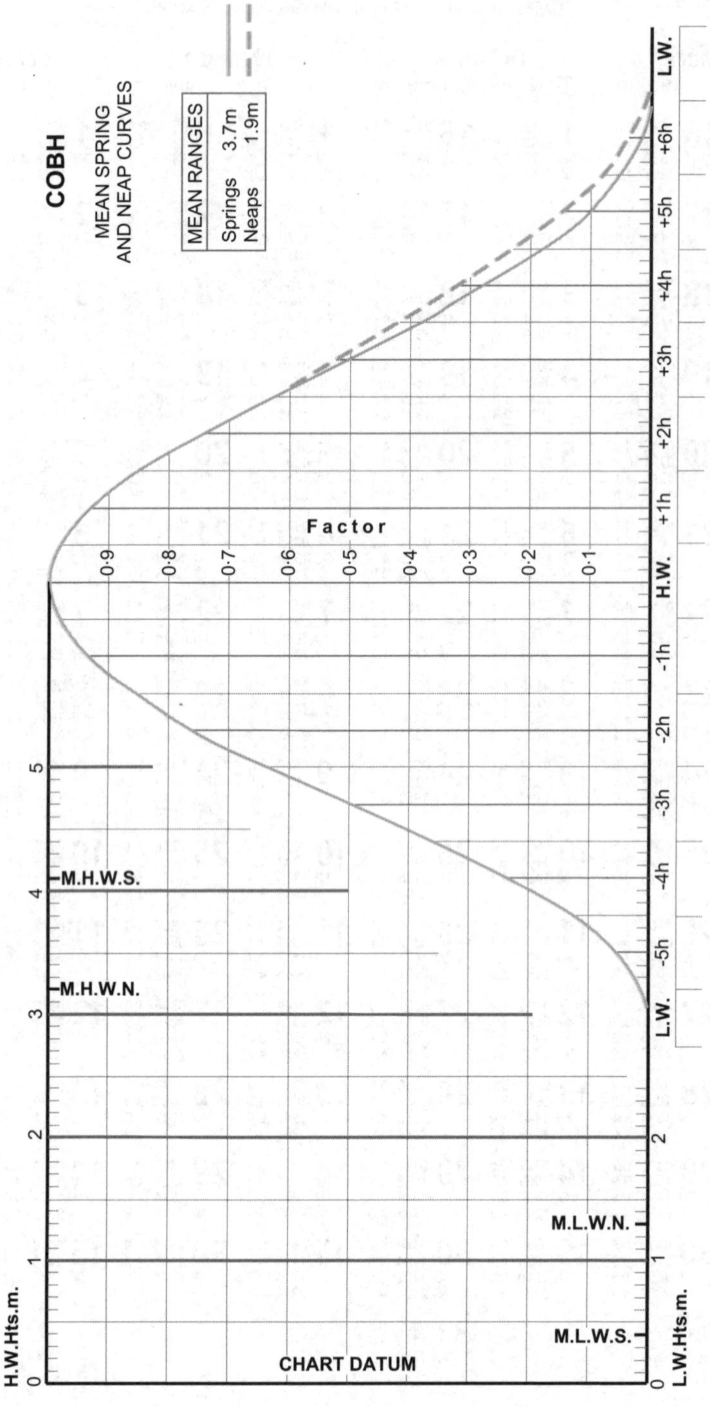
COBH
MEAN SPRING AND NEAP CURVES
MEAN RANGES
Springs 3.7m
Neaps 1.9m
Factor
0·9
0·8
0·7
0·6
0·5
0·4
0·3
0·2
0·1
H.W.Hts.m.
0
1
2
3
4
5
M.H.W.S.
M.H.W.N.
CHART DATUM
M.L.W.S.
M.L.W.N.
L.W.Hts.m.
L.W.
-5h
-4h
-3h
-2h
-1h
H.W.
+1h
+2h
+3h
+4h
+5h
+6h
L.W.

TIME ZONE (UT)
For Summer Time add ONE hour in **non-shaded areas**

IRELAND – COBH

LAT 51°51′N LONG 8°18′W

TIMES AND HEIGHTS OF HIGH AND LOW WATERS

Dates in amber are **SPRINGS**
Dates in yellow are **NEAPS**

2016

JANUARY

Date	Day	Time	m	Time	m	Time	m	Time	m
1	F	0357	1.1	0948	3.6	1625	1.2	2203	3.5
2	SA	0447	1.2	1036	3.5	1717	1.4	◑ 2255	3.4
3	SU	0543	1.3	1132	3.4	1817	1.4	2358	3.4
4	M	0646	1.4	1238	3.4	1920	1.4		
5	TU	0108	3.4	0747	1.3	1346	3.5	2019	1.3
6	W	0215	3.5	0846	1.2	1446	3.6	2115	1.1
7	TH	0312	3.7	0940	1.1	1539	3.7	2206	1.0
8	F	0403	3.9	1029	0.9	1625	3.9	2251	0.8
9	SA	0448	4.0	1113	0.7	1707	4.0	2332	0.6
10	SU	0530	4.2	1154	0.6	1746	4.1	●	
11	M	0012	0.5	0610	4.2	1234	0.6	1825	4.1
12	TU	0052	0.5	0650	4.2	1314	0.5	1905	4.1
13	W	0134	0.5	0732	4.2	1357	0.6	1948	4.1
14	TH	0218	0.5	0817	4.2	1441	0.6	2033	4.0
15	F	0305	0.6	0904	4.1	1528	0.7	2121	3.9
16	SA	0355	0.8	0954	3.9	1619	0.9	◐ 2213	3.8
17	SU	0450	0.9	1049	3.8	1717	1.0	2312	3.6
18	M	0554	1.0	1152	3.6	1825	1.1		
19	TU	0020	3.5	0707	1.1	1304	3.6	1941	1.1
20	W	0137	3.5	0824	1.0	1417	3.6	2056	1.0
21	TH	0252	3.7	0936	0.9	1524	3.7	2201	0.8
22	F	0356	3.9	1035	0.7	1621	3.9	2255	0.6
23	SA	0448	4.0	1124	0.5	1709	4.0	2340	0.5
24	SU	0533	4.2	1207	0.5	1751	4.1	○	
25	M	0020	0.4	0613	4.2	1245	0.5	1828	4.1
26	TU	0056	0.5	0649	4.2	1320	0.6	1903	4.1
27	W	0130	0.5	0724	4.1	1353	0.7	1935	4.0
28	TH	0204	0.7	0758	4.0	1426	0.8	2009	3.9
29	F	0238	0.8	0832	3.9	1501	0.9	2044	3.8
30	SA	0314	0.9	0909	3.8	1538	1.1	2123	3.7
31	SU	0355	1.1	0949	3.6	1621	1.2	2207	3.5

FEBRUARY

Date	Day	Time	m	Time	m	Time	m	Time	m
1	M	0444	1.3	1035	3.5	1715	1.4	◑ 2300	3.4
2	TU	0545	1.4	1131	3.4	1821	1.4		
3	W	0005	3.3	0654	1.4	1242	3.3	1932	1.4
4	TH	0121	3.3	0803	1.3	1359	3.4	2038	1.3
5	F	0234	3.5	0907	1.1	1506	3.5	2137	1.0
6	SA	0334	3.7	1004	0.9	1601	3.8	2228	0.8
7	SU	0425	3.9	1053	0.7	1647	3.9	2313	0.5
8	M	0510	4.1	1137	0.5	1730	4.1	● 2355	0.4
9	TU	0552	4.3	1218	0.3	1810	4.2		
10	W	0035	0.3	0634	4.3	1259	0.3	1850	4.2
11	TH	0117	0.2	0716	4.3	1340	0.3	1932	4.2
12	F	0200	0.3	0759	4.2	1423	0.4	2015	4.1
13	SA	0246	0.4	0844	4.1	1508	0.5	2100	4.0
14	SU	0333	0.5	0931	3.9	1555	0.7	2149	3.8
15	M	0425	0.7	1022	3.7	1649	0.9	◐ 2243	3.6
16	TU	0525	0.9	1123	3.5	1754	1.1	2351	3.4
17	W	0638	1.1	1237	3.3	1913	1.2		
18	TH	0114	3.3	0804	1.1	1359	3.4	2039	1.1
19	F	0237	3.5	0924	0.9	1510	3.5	2151	0.9
20	SA	0342	3.7	1024	0.7	1607	3.7	2245	0.6
21	SU	0434	3.9	1112	0.5	1654	3.9	2328	0.5
22	M	0516	4.1	1152	0.4	1735	4.0	○	
23	TU	0004	0.4	0554	4.1	1226	0.4	1809	4.1
24	W	0036	0.4	0627	4.1	1257	0.5	1841	4.0
25	TH	0105	0.5	0659	4.1	1325	0.6	1910	4.0
26	F	0133	0.6	0729	4.0	1354	0.7	1940	3.9
27	SA	0203	0.7	0759	3.9	1424	0.8	2013	3.9
28	SU	0236	0.8	0832	3.8	1458	0.9	2048	3.8
29	M	0313	1.0	0908	3.7	1536	1.1	2128	3.6

MARCH

Date	Day	Time	m	Time	m	Time	m	Time	m
1	TU	0357	1.1	0951	3.5	1623	1.3	◑ 2216	3.5
2	W	0453	1.3	1043	3.4	1726	1.4	2316	3.3
3	TH	0605	1.4	1149	3.2	1844	1.4		
4	F	0031	3.3	0721	1.3	1310	3.2	1959	1.3
5	SA	0153	3.4	0832	1.1	1429	3.4	2104	1.0
6	SU	0302	3.6	0934	0.9	1532	3.6	2201	0.7
7	M	0357	3.9	1028	0.6	1623	3.9	2249	0.4
8	TU	0445	4.1	1114	0.3	1708	4.1	2334	0.2
9	W	0530	4.3	1158	0.1	1750	4.2	●	
10	TH	0016	0.1	0612	4.3	1240	0.1	1831	4.3
11	F	0059	0.0	0655	4.3	1322	0.1	1913	4.3
12	SA	0142	0.1	0738	4.3	1404	0.1	1956	4.2
13	SU	0227	0.2	0823	4.1	1449	0.3	2040	4.0
14	M	0314	0.4	0909	3.9	1536	0.5	2127	3.8
15	TU	0405	0.6	0959	3.6	1628	0.8	◐ 2220	3.6
16	W	0503	0.9	1058	3.4	1730	1.0	2327	3.3
17	TH	0615	1.1	1214	3.2	1850	1.1		
18	F	0055	3.2	0743	1.1	1339	3.2	2021	1.1
19	SA	0219	3.3	0905	0.9	1451	3.4	2134	0.8
20	SU	0322	3.6	1005	0.7	1547	3.6	2227	0.6
21	M	0412	3.8	1051	0.5	1633	3.8	2309	0.5
22	TU	0453	4.0	1130	0.4	1713	4.0	2343	0.4
23	W	0530	4.0	1202	0.4	1747	4.0	○	
24	TH	0012	0.4	0603	4.0	1231	0.5	1817	4.0
25	F	0038	0.5	0632	4.0	1256	0.5	1845	4.0
26	SA	0103	0.6	0700	3.9	1323	0.6	1913	3.9
27	SU	0132	0.6	0728	3.9	1353	0.7	1944	3.9
28	M	0205	0.8	0800	3.8	1426	0.8	2018	3.8
29	TU	0242	0.9	0835	3.7	1503	1.0	2057	3.7
30	W	0325	1.0	0917	3.6	1548	1.2	2143	3.5
31	TH	0417	1.2	1008	3.4	1647	1.3	◑ 2240	3.4

APRIL

Date	Day	Time	m	Time	m	Time	m	Time	m
1	F	0525	1.3	1113	3.2	1803	1.4	2352	3.3
2	SA	0643	1.3	1230	3.2	1921	1.2		
3	SU	0113	3.4	0756	1.1	1350	3.3	2029	1.0
4	M	0226	3.6	0901	0.8	1457	3.6	2129	0.7
5	TU	0325	3.8	0958	0.5	1553	3.9	2222	0.4
6	W	0417	4.1	1048	0.2	1642	4.1	2310	0.1
7	TH	0504	4.2	1135	0.1	1727	4.2	● 2355	0.0
8	F	0550	4.3	1219	0.0	1811	4.3		
9	SA	0040	-0.1	0634	4.3	1303	0.0	1854	4.3
10	SU	0125	0.0	0719	4.2	1348	0.1	1938	4.2
11	M	0211	0.1	0804	4.1	1433	0.2	2023	4.0
12	TU	0259	0.3	0850	3.9	1521	0.4	2110	3.8
13	W	0349	0.5	0940	3.6	1613	0.7	2203	3.5
14	TH	0446	0.8	1038	3.3	1713	0.9	◐ 2308	3.3
15	F	0555	1.0	1150	3.1	1828	1.1		
16	SA	0031	3.2	0716	1.0	1312	3.1	1951	1.0
17	SU	0150	3.3	0833	0.9	1422	3.3	2102	0.9
18	M	0251	3.5	0932	0.8	1517	3.5	2156	0.7
19	TU	0341	3.7	1020	0.6	1604	3.7	2239	0.6
20	W	0424	3.8	1100	0.5	1644	3.8	2314	0.5
21	TH	0502	3.9	1133	0.5	1719	3.9	2343	0.5
22	F	0535	3.9	1201	0.5	1751	3.9	○	
23	SA	0009	0.5	0605	3.9	1228	0.6	1819	3.9
24	SU	0036	0.6	0633	3.9	1256	0.6	1849	3.9
25	M	0106	0.7	0702	3.9	1328	0.7	1920	3.9
26	TU	0141	0.7	0734	3.8	1403	0.8	1955	3.8
27	W	0220	0.8	0812	3.7	1442	0.9	2035	3.7
28	TH	0304	1.0	0855	3.6	1528	1.0	2121	3.6
29	F	0355	1.1	0946	3.5	1624	1.2	2217	3.5
30	SA	0457	1.2	1047	3.4	1732	1.2	◑ 2324	3.4

Chart Datum: 0·13 metres above Ordnance Datum (Dublin)
HAT is 4·5m above Chart Datum

TIME ZONE (UT)
For Summer Time add ONE hour in **non-shaded areas**

IRELAND – COBH

LAT 51°51′N LONG 8°18′W

TIMES AND HEIGHTS OF HIGH AND LOW WATERS

Dates in amber are **SPRINGS**
Dates in yellow are **NEAPS**

2016

MAY

Date	Day	Time	m	Time	m	Time	m	Time	m
1	SU	0609	1.2	1159	3.3	1846	1.1		
2	M	0039	3.5	0721	1.0	1314	3.4	1955	0.9
3	TU	0151	3.6	0827	0.8	1422	3.6	2057	0.7
4	W	0253	3.8	0927	0.5	1521	3.9	2154	0.4
5	TH	0348	4.0	1022	0.3	1615	4.1	2247	0.2
6	F	0440	4.2	1112	0.1	1704	4.2	● 2336	0.0
7	SA	0529	4.3	1200	0.0	1752	4.3		
8	SU	0023	0.0	0615	4.3	1247	0.0	1837	4.3
9	M	0110	0.0	0701	4.2	1333	0.1	1922	4.2
10	TU	0157	0.1	0747	4.0	1419	0.2	2007	4.0
11	W	0245	0.3	0834	3.8	1507	0.4	2055	3.8
12	TH	0335	0.5	0922	3.6	1558	0.7	2146	3.6
13	F	0429	0.8	1016	3.4	1655	0.9	◐ 2245	3.4
14	SA	0530	1.0	1119	3.2	1759	1.0	2355	3.3
15	SU	0639	1.0	1231	3.2	1910	1.0		
16	M	0108	3.3	0747	1.0	1340	3.3	2015	1.0
17	TU	0210	3.4	0846	0.9	1437	3.4	2111	0.9
18	W	0302	3.5	0937	0.8	1526	3.6	2158	0.8
19	TH	0347	3.7	1021	0.7	1609	3.7	2237	0.7
20	F	0429	3.8	1058	0.7	1648	3.8	2310	0.6
21	SA	0506	3.8	1131	0.6	1723	3.9	○ 2341	0.6
22	SU	0539	3.9	1202	0.6	1756	3.9		
23	M	0012	0.6	0609	3.9	1234	0.6	1828	3.9
24	TU	0046	0.7	0641	3.9	1309	0.7	1902	3.9
25	W	0123	0.7	0716	3.8	1347	0.7	1939	3.9
26	TH	0204	0.8	0756	3.8	1428	0.8	2020	3.8
27	F	0249	0.9	0840	3.7	1515	0.9	2107	3.8
28	SA	0339	0.9	0931	3.6	1607	1.0	2200	3.7
29	SU	0435	1.0	1028	3.5	1708	1.0	◑ 2302	3.6
30	M	0540	1.0	1132	3.5	1815	1.0		
31	TU	0009	3.6	0648	1.0	1241	3.5	1923	0.9

JUNE

Date	Day	Time	m	Time	m	Time	m	Time	m
1	W	0119	3.7	0755	0.8	1349	3.7	2028	0.7
2	TH	0223	3.8	0858	0.6	1451	3.8	2129	0.5
3	F	0322	4.0	0958	0.4	1550	4.0	2226	0.3
4	SA	0419	4.1	1053	0.3	1645	4.1	2319	0.2
5	SU	0511	4.2	1144	0.2	1735	4.2	●	
6	M	0009	0.1	0559	4.2	1232	0.1	1822	4.2
7	TU	0056	0.1	0646	4.1	1319	0.2	1907	4.1
8	W	0143	0.2	0731	4.0	1404	0.3	1952	4.0
9	TH	0229	0.4	0816	3.9	1451	0.5	2037	3.9
10	F	0316	0.6	0901	3.7	1538	0.6	2123	3.7
11	SA	0405	0.8	0948	3.5	1628	0.8	2213	3.5
12	SU	0457	0.9	1039	3.4	1722	1.0	◐ 2310	3.4
13	M	0554	1.1	1138	3.3	1821	1.1		
14	TU	0014	3.3	0654	1.1	1244	3.3	1921	1.1
15	W	0118	3.3	0752	1.1	1346	3.3	2017	1.0
16	TH	0216	3.4	0846	1.0	1441	3.5	2109	0.9
17	F	0307	3.5	0936	0.9	1530	3.6	2155	0.9
18	SA	0354	3.7	1021	0.8	1615	3.7	2237	0.8
19	SU	0436	3.8	1102	0.7	1656	3.9	2315	0.7
20	M	0515	3.8	1139	0.7	1734	3.9	○ 2352	0.6
21	TU	0550	3.9	1215	0.6	1811	4.0		
22	W	0029	0.6	0625	3.9	1253	0.6	1847	4.0
23	TH	0108	0.6	0703	3.9	1332	0.6	1926	4.0
24	F	0150	0.7	0743	3.9	1415	0.7	2008	3.9
25	SA	0234	0.7	0828	3.8	1500	0.7	2054	3.9
26	SU	0322	0.8	0916	3.8	1549	0.8	2144	3.8
27	M	0413	0.8	1009	3.7	1643	0.8	◑ 2239	3.7
28	TU	0511	0.9	1107	3.6	1745	0.9	2341	3.7
29	W	0616	0.9	1211	3.6	1852	0.9		
30	TH	0048	3.7	0725	0.9	1319	3.6	2001	0.8

JULY

Date	Day	Time	m	Time	m	Time	m	Time	m
1	F	0156	3.7	0833	0.8	1427	3.7	2108	0.7
2	SA	0301	3.8	0938	0.6	1531	3.9	2210	0.5
3	SU	0402	3.9	1037	0.5	1630	4.0	2306	0.4
4	M	0456	4.0	1130	0.3	1722	4.1	● 2356	0.3
5	TU	0546	4.1	1218	0.3	1809	4.2		
6	W	0042	0.3	0630	4.1	1303	0.3	1851	4.1
7	TH	0125	0.3	0713	4.0	1345	0.3	1933	4.0
8	F	0208	0.5	0753	3.9	1427	0.5	2013	3.9
9	SA	0250	0.6	0833	3.8	1509	0.6	2054	3.8
10	SU	0332	0.8	0914	3.6	1551	0.8	2136	3.6
11	M	0416	0.9	0956	3.5	1636	1.0	2221	3.5
12	TU	0504	1.1	1044	3.4	1726	1.1	◐ 2312	3.4
13	W	0558	1.2	1140	3.3	1823	1.2		
14	TH	0013	3.3	0657	1.2	1246	3.3	1922	1.2
15	F	0121	3.3	0757	1.2	1352	3.4	2021	1.1
16	SA	0224	3.4	0854	1.1	1452	3.5	2116	1.0
17	SU	0319	3.5	0947	0.9	1544	3.7	2207	0.9
18	M	0408	3.7	1035	0.8	1631	3.8	2252	0.7
19	TU	0452	3.8	1117	0.7	1713	3.9	○ 2333	0.6
20	W	0532	3.9	1156	0.5	1752	4.0		
21	TH	0012	0.5	0609	4.0	1235	0.5	1831	4.1
22	F	0052	0.5	0648	4.0	1315	0.5	1910	4.1
23	SA	0133	0.5	0728	4.0	1357	0.5	1952	4.1
24	SU	0216	0.5	0812	3.9	1441	0.5	2036	4.0
25	M	0302	0.6	0858	3.9	1528	0.6	2124	3.9
26	TU	0350	0.7	0947	3.8	1618	0.7	◑ 2216	3.8
27	W	0444	0.8	1041	3.7	1716	0.8	2314	3.7
28	TH	0545	0.9	1143	3.6	1823	0.9		
29	F	0021	3.5	0657	1.0	1255	3.5	1937	0.9
30	SA	0135	3.5	0813	0.9	1410	3.6	2052	0.8
31	SU	0246	3.6	0925	0.8	1520	3.7	2200	0.7

AUGUST

Date	Day	Time	m	Time	m	Time	m	Time	m
1	M	0349	3.8	1027	0.6	1620	3.9	2256	0.5
2	TU	0444	3.9	1119	0.4	1710	4.1	● 2343	0.4
3	W	0531	4.0	1203	0.3	1753	4.1		
4	TH	0025	0.3	0612	4.1	1244	0.3	1832	4.1
5	F	0104	0.4	0651	4.0	1321	0.4	1909	4.1
6	SA	0141	0.5	0727	3.9	1357	0.5	1944	4.0
7	SU	0216	0.6	0802	3.8	1432	0.6	2020	3.8
8	M	0252	0.8	0837	3.7	1508	0.8	2056	3.7
9	TU	0329	0.9	0915	3.6	1546	1.0	2135	3.6
10	W	0410	1.1	0957	3.5	1629	1.1	◐ 2218	3.5
11	TH	0459	1.2	1046	3.4	1723	1.3	2310	3.3
12	F	0601	1.3	1146	3.3	1829	1.3		
13	SA	0017	3.2	0709	1.3	1300	3.2	1937	1.3
14	SU	0135	3.3	0815	1.2	1414	3.4	2041	1.1
15	M	0245	3.4	0915	1.0	1515	3.6	2138	0.9
16	TU	0341	3.6	1007	0.8	1605	3.8	2228	0.7
17	W	0428	3.8	1053	0.6	1650	4.0	2311	0.5
18	TH	0510	4.0	1134	0.4	1731	4.1	○ 2352	0.4
19	F	0549	4.0	1213	0.3	1811	4.2		
20	SA	0032	0.3	0628	4.1	1254	0.3	1850	4.2
21	SU	0113	0.3	0709	4.1	1336	0.3	1932	4.2
22	M	0155	0.4	0752	4.0	1419	0.3	2015	4.1
23	TU	0240	0.4	0836	4.0	1505	0.5	2102	4.0
24	W	0327	0.6	0924	3.8	1555	0.6	2152	3.8
25	TH	0419	0.8	1017	3.7	1651	0.8	◑ 2249	3.6
26	F	0520	1.0	1119	3.5	1758	1.0	2358	3.4
27	SA	0635	1.1	1237	3.4	1919	1.1		
28	SU	0119	3.4	0759	1.0	1401	3.4	2044	1.0
29	M	0236	3.5	0917	0.8	1512	3.6	2152	0.7
30	TU	0338	3.7	1018	0.6	1608	3.9	2245	0.5
31	W	0430	3.9	1106	0.4	1655	4.0	2329	0.4

Chart Datum: 0·13 metres above Ordnance Datum (Dublin)
HAT is 4·5m above Chart Datum

TIME ZONE (UT)
For Summer Time add ONE hour in **non-shaded areas**

IRELAND – COBH

LAT 51°51′N LONG 8°18′W

TIMES AND HEIGHTS OF HIGH AND LOW WATERS

Dates in amber are **SPRINGS**
Dates in yellow are **NEAPS**

2016

SEPTEMBER

Date	Day	Time	m	Time	m	Time	m	Time	m
1	TH ●	0514	4.0	1147	0.4	1735	4.1		
2	F	0006	0.4	0552	4.1	1222	0.4	1810	4.1
3	SA	0040	0.4	0627	4.0	1254	0.4	1843	4.1
4	SU	0110	0.5	0658	4.0	1323	0.5	1914	4.0
5	M	0140	0.7	0729	3.9	1353	0.7	1945	3.9
6	TU	0210	0.8	0801	3.8	1424	0.8	2017	3.8
7	W	0244	0.9	0837	3.7	1459	1.0	2052	3.7
8	TH	0321	1.1	0916	3.6	1540	1.1	2133	3.5
9	F ◐	0407	1.2	1002	3.4	1631	1.3	2222	3.4
10	SA	0507	1.4	1059	3.3	1739	1.4	2324	3.2
11	SU	0623	1.4	1211	3.2	1855	1.4		
12	M	0043	3.2	0737	1.3	1334	3.3	2006	1.2
13	TU	0206	3.4	0842	1.1	1443	3.5	2107	1.0
14	W	0309	3.6	0937	0.8	1536	3.8	2200	0.7
15	TH	0359	3.8	1026	0.6	1623	4.0	2246	0.5
16	F ○	0443	4.0	1109	0.3	1705	4.2	2329	0.3
17	SA	0525	4.2	1151	0.2	1747	4.3		
18	SU	0010	0.2	0606	4.2	1232	0.1	1828	4.3
19	M	0052	0.2	0648	4.2	1315	0.2	1910	4.3
20	TU	0135	0.2	0731	4.2	1359	0.2	1954	4.2
21	W	0220	0.4	0816	4.0	1446	0.4	2040	4.0
22	TH	0308	0.5	0904	3.9	1536	0.6	2130	3.8
23	F ◑	0401	0.8	0957	3.6	1632	0.9	2228	3.5
24	SA	0502	1.0	1102	3.4	1740	1.1	2340	3.3
25	SU	0619	1.1	1225	3.3	1906	1.1		
26	M	0105	3.3	0749	1.1	1351	3.4	2033	1.0
27	TU	0222	3.4	0906	0.9	1458	3.6	2138	0.8
28	W	0322	3.7	1003	0.7	1550	3.8	2227	0.6
29	TH	0410	3.9	1048	0.5	1634	4.0	2308	0.5
30	F	0452	4.0	1126	0.4	1712	4.1	2343	0.5

OCTOBER

Date	Day	Time	m	Time	m	Time	m	Time	m
1	SA ●	0529	4.1	1158	0.5	1746	4.1		
2	SU	0012	0.5	0601	4.1	1225	0.5	1816	4.1
3	M	0039	0.6	0630	4.0	1251	0.6	1844	4.0
4	TU	0105	0.7	0659	3.9	1318	0.7	1912	3.9
5	W	0134	0.8	0730	3.9	1348	0.9	1942	3.9
6	TH	0206	0.9	0804	3.8	1423	1.0	2017	3.8
7	F	0244	1.1	0842	3.7	1504	1.2	2057	3.6
8	SA	0329	1.2	0927	3.5	1554	1.3	2145	3.5
9	SU ◐	0426	1.4	1022	3.4	1658	1.4	2246	3.3
10	M	0540	1.5	1131	3.3	1815	1.5		
11	TU	0001	3.3	0657	1.4	1251	3.4	1930	1.3
12	W	0123	3.4	0806	1.2	1405	3.6	2034	1.0
13	TH	0232	3.6	0905	0.9	1503	3.9	2130	0.7
14	F	0327	3.9	0957	0.6	1553	4.1	2220	0.5
15	SA	0415	4.1	1044	0.3	1639	4.3	2305	0.3
16	SU ○	0500	4.3	1129	0.2	1723	4.4	2349	0.2
17	M	0544	4.3	1213	0.1	1807	4.4		
18	TU	0033	0.1	0628	4.3	1258	0.1	1851	4.3
19	W	0118	0.2	0713	4.3	1344	0.2	1936	4.2
20	TH	0204	0.3	0759	4.1	1432	0.4	2023	4.0
21	F	0253	0.5	0848	3.9	1522	0.7	2113	3.8
22	SA ◑	0347	0.8	0942	3.7	1619	0.9	2210	3.5
23	SU	0448	1.0	1046	3.5	1726	1.1	2320	3.3
24	M	0602	1.1	1206	3.3	1848	1.2		
25	TU	0042	3.3	0728	1.1	1327	3.4	2009	1.1
26	W	0158	3.4	0841	1.0	1432	3.6	2111	0.9
27	TH	0256	3.6	0936	0.8	1523	3.8	2200	0.8
28	F	0344	3.8	1021	0.7	1606	3.9	2241	0.7
29	SA	0426	4.0	1059	0.6	1645	4.0	2315	0.6
30	SU ●	0503	4.0	1131	0.6	1719	4.1	2344	0.6
31	M	0536	4.1	1157	0.7	1750	4.1		

NOVEMBER

Date	Day	Time	m	Time	m	Time	m	Time	m
1	TU	0010	0.7	0605	4.0	1223	0.7	1817	4.0
2	W	0037	0.8	0634	4.0	1251	0.8	1845	4.0
3	TH	0107	0.8	0705	4.0	1323	0.9	1915	3.9
4	F	0141	0.9	0739	3.9	1400	1.0	1950	3.9
5	SA	0219	1.1	0818	3.8	1441	1.2	2031	3.7
6	SU	0305	1.2	0903	3.7	1530	1.3	2119	3.6
7	M ◐	0359	1.3	0956	3.6	1629	1.4	2218	3.5
8	TU	0506	1.4	1100	3.5	1739	1.4	2327	3.4
9	W	0619	1.4	1212	3.5	1853	1.3		
10	TH	0042	3.5	0729	1.2	1325	3.7	2000	1.1
11	F	0153	3.7	0832	0.9	1427	3.9	2059	0.8
12	SA	0253	3.9	0928	0.7	1522	4.1	2154	0.6
13	SU	0347	4.1	1021	0.4	1613	4.3	2244	0.4
14	M ○	0437	4.3	1111	0.3	1702	4.4	2332	0.2
15	TU	0526	4.4	1158	0.2	1749	4.4		
16	W	0018	0.2	0612	4.4	1245	0.2	1835	4.3
17	TH	0104	0.2	0659	4.3	1332	0.3	1921	4.2
18	F	0152	0.4	0746	4.2	1420	0.5	2008	4.0
19	SA	0241	0.5	0835	4.0	1511	0.7	2057	3.8
20	SU	0333	0.8	0927	3.8	1604	0.9	2150	3.6
21	M ◑	0430	1.0	1026	3.6	1705	1.1	2252	3.4
22	TU	0536	1.1	1133	3.4	1815	1.2		
23	W	0004	3.3	0649	1.2	1247	3.4	1927	1.2
24	TH	0117	3.4	0759	1.1	1352	3.5	2030	1.1
25	F	0218	3.5	0857	1.0	1446	3.7	2122	1.0
26	SA	0309	3.7	0945	0.9	1532	3.8	2206	0.9
27	SU	0354	3.9	1026	0.8	1614	3.9	2244	0.8
28	M	0434	4.0	1101	0.8	1652	4.0	2317	0.8
29	TU ●	0510	4.0	1132	0.8	1726	4.0	2346	0.8
30	W	0544	4.1	1201	0.8	1756	4.0		

DECEMBER

Date	Day	Time	m	Time	m	Time	m	Time	m
1	TH	0016	0.8	0615	4.1	1232	0.8	1825	4.0
2	F	0048	0.8	0648	4.0	1307	0.9	1857	4.0
3	SA	0124	0.9	0723	4.0	1345	1.0	1933	3.9
4	SU	0204	1.0	0802	3.9	1426	1.1	2014	3.8
5	M	0248	1.1	0846	3.9	1513	1.2	2101	3.7
6	TU	0339	1.2	0936	3.8	1606	1.3	2155	3.6
7	W ◐	0437	1.3	1034	3.7	1707	1.3	2257	3.6
8	TH	0543	1.3	1138	3.7	1815	1.3		
9	F	0005	3.6	0652	1.2	1247	3.7	1924	1.1
10	SA	0115	3.7	0759	1.0	1353	3.9	2029	0.9
11	SU	0220	3.9	0902	0.8	1454	4.0	2130	0.7
12	M	0321	4.1	1001	0.6	1551	4.2	2225	0.5
13	TU	0418	4.2	1056	0.4	1645	4.3	2317	0.4
14	W ○	0511	4.3	1146	0.3	1735	4.3		
15	TH	0006	0.3	0600	4.4	1235	0.3	1822	4.3
16	F	0053	0.3	0647	4.4	1321	0.3	1908	4.2
17	SA	0139	0.4	0733	4.2	1408	0.5	1953	4.1
18	SU	0226	0.5	0819	4.1	1455	0.6	2038	3.9
19	M	0314	0.7	0906	3.9	1543	0.8	2124	3.7
20	TU	0404	0.9	0956	3.7	1634	1.0	2214	3.5
21	W ◑	0458	1.1	1050	3.5	1731	1.2	2311	3.4
22	TH	0558	1.2	1151	3.4	1833	1.3		
23	F	0017	3.3	0702	1.2	1258	3.4	1935	1.3
24	SA	0126	3.4	0803	1.2	1359	3.5	2033	1.2
25	SU	0226	3.5	0859	1.1	1453	3.6	2125	1.1
26	M	0318	3.7	0949	1.0	1542	3.8	2211	1.0
27	TU	0405	3.8	1032	0.9	1626	3.9	2251	0.9
28	W	0447	4.0	1110	0.9	1705	4.0	2327	0.8
29	TH ●	0525	4.1	1144	0.8	1740	4.0		
30	F	0000	0.7	0600	4.1	1219	0.8	1812	4.0
31	SA	0034	0.7	0634	4.1	1254	0.8	1845	4.0

Chart Datum: 0·13 metres above Ordnance Datum (Dublin)
HAT is 4·5m above Chart Datum

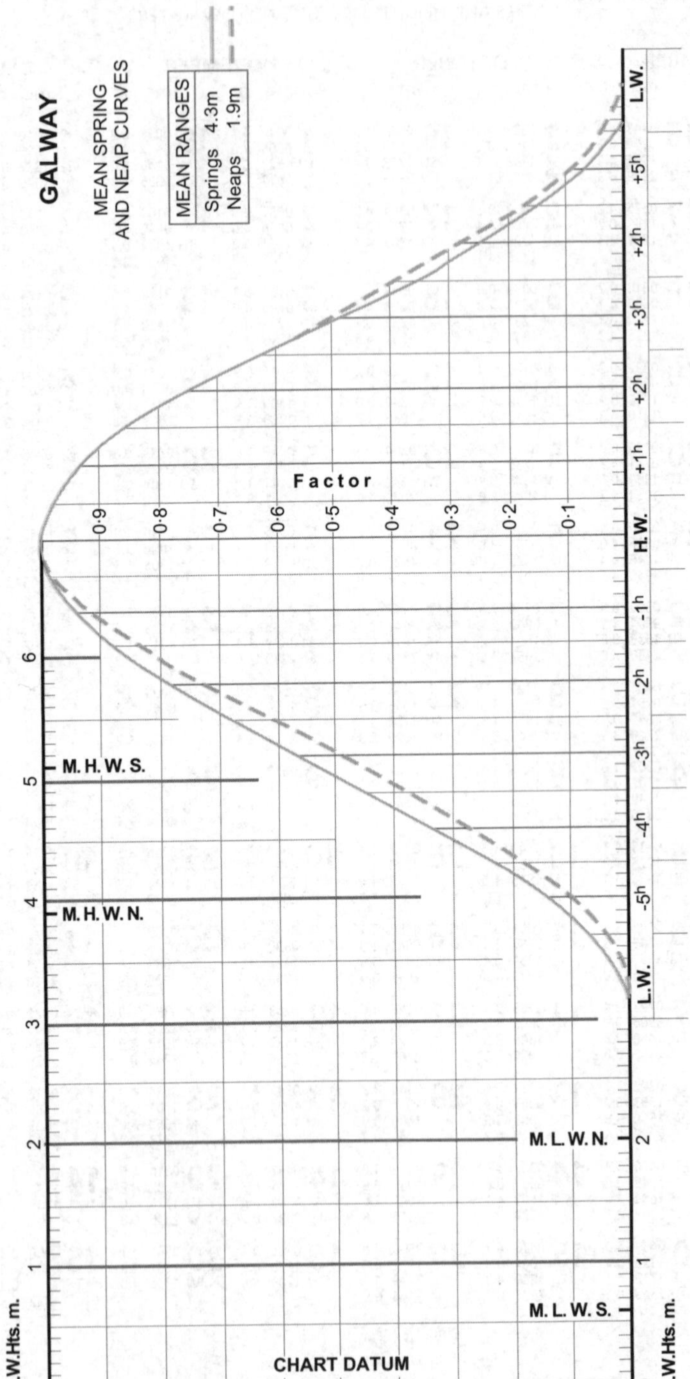
GALWAY
MEAN SPRING AND NEAP CURVES
MEAN RANGES
Springs 4.3m
Neaps 1.9m
Factor
0·9
0·8
0·7
0·6
0·5
0·4
0·3
0·2
0·1
H.W.Hts. m.
0
1
2
3
4
5
6
M. H. W. S.
M. H. W. N.
M. L. W. N.
M. L. W. S.
CHART DATUM
L.W.Hts. m.
L.W.
-5h
-4h
-3h
-2h
-1h
H.W.
+1h
+2h
+3h
+4h
+5h
L.W.

TIME ZONE (UT)
For Summer Time add ONE hour in **non-shaded areas**

IRELAND – GALWAY

LAT 53°16′N LONG 9°03′W

TIMES AND HEIGHTS OF HIGH AND LOW WATERS

Dates in amber are **SPRINGS**
Dates in yellow are **NEAPS**

2016

JANUARY

Date	Day	Time	m	Time	m	Time	m	Time	m
1	F	0307	1.9	0936	4.4	1544	1.8	2209	4.2
2	SA	0412	2.1	1026	4.2	1653	2.0	◑ 2301	4.1
3	SU	0531	2.2	1121	4.0	1804	2.1		
4	M	0000	4.0	0636	2.2	1226	4.0	1904	2.0
5	TU	0113	4.1	0733	2.1	1348	4.1	1958	1.9
6	W	0219	4.3	0824	1.9	1447	4.3	2046	1.7
7	TH	0306	4.5	0910	1.6	1532	4.5	2129	1.5
8	F	0348	4.8	0951	1.3	1613	4.7	2208	1.3
9	SA	0427	5.0	1029	1.1	1653	4.9	2244	1.1
10	SU	0507	5.2	1106	0.9	1733	5.1	● 2320	1.0
11	M	0547	5.3	1143	0.7	1814	5.1	2358	0.9
12	TU	0627	5.4	1223	0.6	1855	5.2		
13	W	0040	0.9	0709	5.4	1305	0.7	1938	5.1
14	TH	0124	0.9	0754	5.2	1350	0.8	2024	4.9
15	F	0212	1.1	0842	5.1	1438	1.0	2114	4.7
16	SA	0303	1.3	0935	4.8	1532	1.3	◐ 2210	4.5
17	SU	0402	1.6	1035	4.6	1633	1.5	2315	4.4
18	M	0511	1.8	1147	4.4	1745	1.7		
19	TU	0034	4.3	0636	1.8	1310	4.3	1915	1.7
20	W	0150	4.4	0806	1.6	1421	4.5	2030	1.6
21	TH	0251	4.7	0907	1.4	1518	4.7	2123	1.4
22	F	0342	4.9	0955	1.1	1608	4.9	2207	1.2
23	SA	0428	5.2	1036	0.9	1653	5.1	2245	1.1
24	SU	0511	5.3	1111	0.8	1735	5.2	○ 2319	1.0
25	M	0551	5.3	1143	0.8	1815	5.2	2353	1.0
26	TU	0629	5.3	1216	0.8	1854	5.1		
27	W	0028	1.1	0706	5.2	1252	0.9	1930	5.0
28	TH	0105	1.2	0742	5.0	1328	1.1	2007	4.8
29	F	0141	1.4	0821	4.8	1405	1.4	2047	4.6
30	SA	0219	1.6	0902	4.6	1443	1.6	2130	4.4
31	SU	0258	1.9	0948	4.3	1524	1.9	2217	4.2

FEBRUARY

Date	Day	Time	m	Time	m	Time	m	Time	m
1	M	0344	2.1	1038	4.1	1615	2.1	◑ 2308	4.1
2	TU	0453	2.3	1133	3.9	1823	2.2		
3	W	0006	4.0	0700	2.2	1238	3.9	1929	2.1
4	TH	0114	4.1	0758	2.0	1356	4.0	2023	1.9
5	F	0225	4.3	0849	1.7	1501	4.3	2110	1.6
6	SA	0319	4.6	0933	1.4	1548	4.6	2152	1.3
7	SU	0403	4.9	1014	1.0	1631	4.9	2230	1.0
8	M	0445	5.2	1051	0.7	1712	5.2	● 2306	0.8
9	TU	0526	5.5	1128	0.5	1753	5.3	2344	0.6
10	W	0609	5.6	1206	0.3	1836	5.4		
11	TH	0024	0.5	0652	5.6	1247	0.3	1918	5.3
12	F	0106	0.6	0736	5.5	1330	0.5	2003	5.2
13	SA	0152	0.8	0823	5.2	1416	0.8	2051	4.9
14	SU	0241	1.1	0914	4.9	1507	1.1	2143	4.6
15	M	0337	1.4	1012	4.5	1606	1.5	◐ 2245	4.3
16	TU	0446	1.7	1124	4.2	1720	1.8		
17	W	0008	4.2	0615	1.8	1255	4.1	1856	1.9
18	TH	0135	4.2	0756	1.7	1411	4.2	2020	1.8
19	F	0240	4.4	0902	1.4	1509	4.5	2116	1.5
20	SA	0332	4.7	0949	1.2	1557	4.8	2158	1.3
21	SU	0416	5.0	1027	1.0	1639	5.0	2232	1.1
22	M	0457	5.1	1057	0.8	1718	5.1	○ 2301	1.0
23	TU	0534	5.2	1121	0.8	1755	5.1	2330	0.9
24	W	0610	5.2	1150	0.7	1830	5.1		
25	TH	0003	0.9	0644	5.2	1223	0.8	1904	5.0
26	F	0037	1.0	0718	5.0	1256	0.9	1938	4.9
27	SA	0110	1.1	0753	4.8	1330	1.1	2015	4.7
28	SU	0145	1.3	0831	4.6	1404	1.4	2054	4.5
29	M	0222	1.6	0913	4.3	1443	1.7	2138	4.3

MARCH

Date	Day	Time	m	Time	m	Time	m	Time	m
1	TU	0304	1.8	1000	4.1	1527	1.9	◑ 2227	4.1
2	W	0353	2.1	1054	3.9	1621	2.2	2324	3.9
3	TH	0457	2.2	1156	3.8	1900	2.3		
4	F	0026	3.9	0732	2.1	1306	3.9	2000	2.0
5	SA	0138	4.1	0826	1.7	1426	4.2	2049	1.6
6	SU	0247	4.5	0912	1.3	1522	4.6	2132	1.2
7	M	0337	4.9	0954	0.8	1606	4.9	2210	0.8
8	TU	0421	5.3	1031	0.5	1648	5.3	2247	0.5
9	W	0504	5.6	1108	0.2	1730	5.5	● 2324	0.3
10	TH	0548	5.7	1145	0.1	1813	5.6		
11	F	0004	0.2	0632	5.7	1226	0.1	1856	5.5
12	SA	0046	0.3	0717	5.6	1308	0.3	1941	5.3
13	SU	0131	0.5	0805	5.3	1353	0.7	2028	5.0
14	M	0220	0.9	0855	4.9	1443	1.1	2119	4.7
15	TU	0316	1.3	0953	4.5	1544	1.6	◐ 2218	4.3
16	W	0427	1.6	1104	4.1	1702	1.9	2343	4.0
17	TH	0557	1.8	1241	4.0	1834	2.0		
18	F	0119	4.1	0734	1.7	1358	4.1	1958	1.9
19	SA	0225	4.3	0845	1.5	1454	4.3	2057	1.6
20	SU	0316	4.5	0931	1.2	1540	4.6	2139	1.3
21	M	0359	4.7	1007	1.0	1620	4.8	2211	1.1
22	TU	0437	4.9	1033	0.9	1657	5.0	2238	0.9
23	W	0513	5.0	1055	0.8	1731	5.0	○ 2306	0.8
24	TH	0547	5.0	1123	0.7	1804	5.1	2337	0.8
25	F	0621	5.0	1154	0.8	1838	5.0		
26	SA	0010	0.8	0654	4.9	1227	0.9	1910	4.9
27	SU	0044	0.9	0728	4.8	1300	1.0	1944	4.7
28	M	0118	1.1	0803	4.6	1335	1.2	2020	4.5
29	TU	0155	1.3	0841	4.3	1413	1.5	2101	4.3
30	W	0236	1.6	0927	4.1	1457	1.8	2150	4.1
31	TH	0324	1.8	1021	3.9	1549	2.1	◑ 2247	3.9

APRIL

Date	Day	Time	m	Time	m	Time	m	Time	m
1	F	0422	2.0	1122	3.8	1656	2.2	2349	3.9
2	SA	0657	2.0	1230	3.9	1932	2.0		
3	SU	0058	4.1	0758	1.6	1348	4.1	2024	1.6
4	M	0211	4.4	0846	1.2	1452	4.5	2107	1.2
5	TU	0308	4.8	0928	0.7	1540	5.0	2146	0.7
6	W	0356	5.2	1007	0.4	1623	5.3	2224	0.4
7	TH	0441	5.5	1044	0.1	1706	5.6	● 2303	0.2
8	F	0527	5.7	1123	0.1	1750	5.6	2344	0.1
9	SA	0613	5.7	1203	0.1	1835	5.6		
10	SU	0026	0.2	0659	5.5	1246	0.4	1920	5.4
11	M	0112	0.4	0747	5.2	1332	0.8	2007	5.1
12	TU	0202	0.8	0838	4.8	1424	1.2	2058	4.7
13	W	0259	1.2	0935	4.4	1526	1.6	2155	4.3
14	TH	0411	1.5	1044	4.1	1645	1.9	◐ 2311	4.0
15	F	0532	1.7	1220	3.9	1806	2.0		
16	SA	0054	4.0	0651	1.7	1335	4.0	1919	1.9
17	SU	0201	4.1	0805	1.5	1430	4.2	2021	1.7
18	M	0252	4.3	0856	1.3	1516	4.5	2106	1.4
19	TU	0335	4.5	0932	1.2	1555	4.6	2141	1.2
20	W	0413	4.7	0959	1.0	1630	4.8	2211	1.0
21	TH	0447	4.8	1026	0.9	1703	4.9	2241	0.9
22	F	0521	4.8	1056	0.8	1737	5.0	○ 2313	0.8
23	SA	0556	4.8	1127	0.8	1811	4.9	2346	0.8
24	SU	0631	4.8	1200	0.9	1844	4.9		
25	M	0019	0.9	0704	4.7	1234	1.0	1917	4.7
26	TU	0055	1.0	0738	4.5	1310	1.2	1950	4.6
27	W	0134	1.2	0815	4.4	1350	1.4	2029	4.4
28	TH	0215	1.4	0859	4.2	1434	1.7	2118	4.2
29	F	0303	1.6	0953	4.0	1527	1.9	2215	4.1
30	SA	0401	1.7	1053	3.9	1633	2.0	◑ 2317	4.0

Chart Datum: 0·20 metres above Ordnance Datum (Dublin)
HAT is 5·9m above Chart Datum

TIME ZONE (UT)
For Summer Time add ONE hour in **non-shaded areas**

IRELAND – GALWAY

LAT 53°16′N LONG 9°03′W

TIMES AND HEIGHTS OF HIGH AND LOW WATERS

Dates in amber are **SPRING**
Dates in yellow are **NEAPS**

201

MAY

Date	Day	Time	m	Date	Day	Time	m
1	SU	0515 1159 1820	1.8 4.0 2.0	16	M	0125 0709 1357 1935	4.0 1.7 4.1 1.8
2	M	0024 0715 1313 1949	4.1 1.5 4.2 1.6	17	TU	0220 0803 1444 2025	4.1 1.5 4.3 1.6
3	TU	0136 0813 1420 2037	4.4 1.2 4.6 1.2	18	W	0305 0847 1524 2106	4.3 1.4 4.5 1.4
4	W	0240 0858 1512 2120	4.8 0.8 5.0 0.7	19	TH	0343 0924 1600 2142	4.4 1.2 4.6 1.2
5	TH	0332 0940 1559 2201	5.2 0.5 5.3 0.4	20	F	0419 0958 1634 2217	4.5 1.1 4.8 1.1
6	F	0420 1020 1644 ● 2243	5.4 0.3 5.5 0.2	21	SA	0455 1031 1709 ○ 2251	4.7 1.0 4.9 1.0
7	SA	0507 1101 1729 2325	5.6 0.2 5.6 0.2	22	SU	0531 1104 1744 2324	4.7 1.0 4.9 0.9
8	SU	0555 1143 1815	5.6 0.3 5.5	23	M	0607 1137 1819 2359	4.7 1.0 4.9 0.9
9	M	0010 0642 1228 1901	0.3 5.4 0.6 5.4	24	TU	0643 1213 1852	4.7 1.1 4.8
10	TU	0057 0731 1315 1948	0.5 5.1 0.9 5.1	25	W	0037 0717 1251 1926	1.0 4.6 1.2 4.7
11	W	0147 0822 1407 2038	0.8 4.8 1.3 4.8	26	TH	0117 0754 1333 2005	1.0 4.5 1.3 4.6
12	TH	0243 0916 1508 2132	1.1 4.5 1.6 4.4	27	F	0200 0838 1419 2053	1.2 4.3 1.5 4.4
13	F	0350 1018 1620 ◐ 2234	1.4 4.2 1.9 4.1	28	SA	0248 0929 1511 2148	1.3 4.2 1.7 4.3
14	SA	0500 1139 1732	1.6 4.0 2.0	29	SU	0344 1027 1614 ◑ 2249	1.4 4.1 1.8 4.2
15	SU	0009 0607 1258 1836	4.0 1.7 4.0 1.9	30	M	0448 1131 1727 2354	1.5 4.1 1.8 4.3
				31	TU	0604 1241 1853	1.5 4.3 1.6

JUNE

Date	Day	Time	m	Date	Day	Time	m
1	W	0106 0726 1350 2002	4.4 1.2 4.6 1.3	16	TH	0227 0808 1447 2032	4.1 1.7 4.3 1.6
2	TH	0214 0827 1448 2054	4.7 1.0 4.9 0.9	17	F	0310 0853 1527 2115	4.2 1.5 4.5 1.5
3	F	0311 0916 1538 2141	5.0 0.7 5.2 0.6	18	SA	0349 0933 1604 2155	4.4 1.4 4.7 1.3
4	SA	0403 1001 1626 2227	5.2 0.6 5.4 0.5	19	SU	0427 1011 1641 2232	4.5 1.3 4.8 1.1
5	SU	0452 1045 1712 ● 2311	5.4 0.5 5.5 0.4	20	M	0506 1046 1718 ○ 2307	4.6 1.2 4.9 1.0
6	M	0541 1129 1759 2357	5.4 0.6 5.5 0.4	21	TU	0544 1120 1755 2343	4.7 1.1 5.0 0.9
7	TU	0628 1213 1845	5.3 0.8 5.4	22	W	0621 1156 1831	4.8 1.1 5.0
8	W	0042 0716 1259 1931	0.6 5.1 1.0 5.1	23	TH	0021 0658 1236 1907	0.8 4.7 1.1 4.9
9	TH	0130 0804 1347 2018	0.8 4.9 1.3 4.9	24	F	0102 0736 1318 1947	0.9 4.7 1.2 4.9
10	F	0221 0853 1440 2106	1.1 4.6 1.6 4.6	25	SA	0146 0819 1404 2033	0.9 4.6 1.3 4.7
11	SA	0317 0944 1542 2157	1.4 4.3 1.8 4.3	26	SU	0233 0907 1455 2126	1.0 4.5 1.4 4.6
12	SU	0419 1041 1650 ◐ 2254	1.6 4.1 2.0 4.1	27	M	0325 1002 1553 ◑ 2224	1.2 4.4 1.6 4.5
13	M	0522 1150 1754	1.7 4.0 2.0	28	TU	0424 1103 1658 2328	1.3 4.3 1.6 4.4
14	TU	0012 0622 1305 1852	3.9 1.8 4.0 2.0	29	W	0530 1212 1812	1.4 4.3 1.6
15	W	0133 0717 1402 1945	3.9 1.8 4.1 1.8	30	TH	0041 0645 1326 1932	4.4 1.4 4.5 1.4

JULY

Date	Day	Time	m	Date	Day	Time	m
1	F	0155 0801 1430 2037	4.5 1.3 4.8 1.2	16	SA	0231 0825 1452 2051	4.0 1.7 4.3 1.6
2	SA	0257 0900 1524 2130	4.8 1.1 5.0 0.9	17	SU	0319 0911 1535 2134	4.2 1.6 4.5 1.4
3	SU	0351 0949 1614 2217	5.0 0.9 5.2 0.7	18	M	0401 0953 1615 2215	4.4 1.4 4.8 1.2
4	M	0441 1034 1701 ● 2302	5.2 0.8 5.4 0.6	19	TU	0441 1030 1653 ○ 2252	4.6 1.2 4.9 0.9
5	TU	0529 1117 1746 2344	5.2 0.8 5.4 0.6	20	W	0520 1105 1731 2328	4.8 1.0 5.1 0.8
6	W	0614 1158 1830	5.2 0.9 5.3	21	TH	0559 1141 1810	4.9 0.9 5.2
7	TH	0026 0658 1239 1912	0.7 5.1 1.0 5.2	22	F	0005 0637 1221 1848	0.6 5.0 0.8 5.2
8	F	0107 0742 1321 1955	0.8 4.9 1.2 5.0	23	SA	0046 0717 1302 1930	0.6 5.0 0.9 5.1
9	SA	0150 0825 1405 2037	1.0 4.7 1.4 4.7	24	SU	0128 0759 1347 2015	0.6 4.9 1.0 5.0
10	SU	0235 0908 1453 2122	1.3 4.5 1.7 4.5	25	M	0214 0846 1436 2105	0.8 4.7 1.1 4.8
11	M	0326 0954 1551 2209	1.6 4.3 1.9 4.2	26	TU	0304 0938 1530 ◑ 2201	1.0 4.6 1.4 4.6
12	TU	0426 1043 1702 ◐ 2301	1.8 4.1 2.1 4.0	27	W	0359 1037 1633 2305	1.3 4.4 1.6 4.4
13	W	0534 1138 1810	1.9 4.0 2.1	28	TH	0503 1147 1746	1.5 4.3 1.7
14	TH	0000 0637 1246 1909	3.9 2.0 4.0 2.0	29	F	0023 0619 1309 1916	4.3 1.6 4.3 1.6
15	F	0122 0734 1359 2002	3.9 1.9 4.1 1.9	30	SA	0144 0748 1418 2034	4.3 1.5 4.6 1.3
				31	SU	0248 0854 1515 2128	4.5 1.3 4.8 1.1

AUGUST

Date	Day	Time	m	Date	Day	Time	m
1	M	0343 0944 1604 2214	4.8 1.1 5.1 0.8	16	TU	0336 0934 1549 2156	4.4 1.4 4.7 1.1
2	TU	0431 1026 1650 ● 2253	5.0 1.0 5.3 0.7	17	W	0416 1013 1628 2234	4.7 1.1 5.0 0.8
3	W	0516 1104 1733 2329	5.1 0.9 5.3 0.6	18	TH	0455 1048 1707 ○ 2310	4.9 0.8 5.2 0.5
4	TH	0558 1139 1813	5.2 0.9 5.3	19	F	0534 1124 1747 2346	5.1 0.6 5.4 0.4
5	F	0003 0638 1214 1851	0.7 5.1 0.9 5.2	20	SA	0614 1202 1828	5.2 0.5 5.5
6	SA	0038 0716 1250 1929	0.8 5.0 1.1 5.0	21	SU	0025 0654 1243 1911	0.3 5.2 0.5 5.4
7	SU	0115 0753 1328 2007	0.9 4.8 1.3 4.8	22	M	0107 0737 1327 1956	0.4 5.1 0.7 5.2
8	M	0153 0832 1406 2048	1.2 4.6 1.5 4.5	23	TU	0152 0823 1414 2045	0.6 4.9 0.9 4.9
9	TU	0232 0914 1447 2132	1.5 4.4 1.8 4.3	24	W	0240 0914 1507 2141	0.9 4.7 1.2 4.6
10	W	0315 1000 1535 ◐ 2220	1.7 4.2 2.0 4.0	25	TH	0335 1012 1611 ◑ 2247	1.3 4.4 1.5 4.3
11	TH	0406 1050 1716 2314	2.0 4.0 2.2 3.9	26	F	0442 1126 1730	1.6 4.2 1.7
12	F	0556 1146 1837	2.1 3.9 2.2	27	SA	0012 0606 1257 1915	4.1 1.8 4.2 1.7
13	SA	0014 0705 1251 1936	3.8 2.1 4.0 2.0	28	SU	0137 0745 1410 2033	4.1 1.7 4.4 1.4
14	SU	0133 0801 1409 2028	3.9 1.9 4.2 1.7	29	M	0242 0850 1506 2125	4.4 1.5 4.7 1.1
15	M	0249 0850 1506 2114	4.1 1.7 4.4 1.4	30	TU	0334 0937 1553 2206	4.7 1.2 4.9 0.9
				31	W	0418 1015 1636 2240	4.9 1.0 5.1 0.7

Chart Datum: 0·20 metres above Ordnance Datum (Dublin)
HAT is 5·9m above Chart Datum

TIME ZONE (UT)
For Summer Time add ONE hour in **non-shaded areas**

IRELAND – GALWAY

LAT 53°16′N LONG 9°03′W

TIMES AND HEIGHTS OF HIGH AND LOW WATERS

Dates in amber are **SPRINGS**
Dates in yellow are **NEAPS**

2016

SEPTEMBER

Date	Day	Moon	Time	m	Time	m	Time	m	Time	m
1	TH	●	0459	5.0	1047	0.9	1715	5.2	2308	0.6
2	F		0538	5.1	1116	0.8	1752	5.2	2335	0.6
3	SA		0614	5.1	1147	0.8	1828	5.1		
4	SU		0007	0.7	0648	5.0	1220	0.9	1902	5.0
5	M		0041	0.9	0722	4.9	1255	1.1	1937	4.8
6	TU		0115	1.1	0759	4.7	1330	1.3	2016	4.6
7	W		0151	1.3	0838	4.5	1407	1.6	2058	4.3
8	TH		0228	1.6	0922	4.3	1447	1.8	2145	4.1
9	F	◐	0310	1.9	1011	4.1	1536	2.1	2237	3.8
10	SA		0402	2.2	1105	3.9	1802	2.2	2336	3.7
11	SU		0637	2.2	1206	3.9	1911	2.1		
12	M		0043	3.8	0738	2.0	1316	4.0	2005	1.7
13	TU		0213	4.0	0829	1.7	1431	4.3	2052	1.3
14	W		0309	4.4	0913	1.3	1520	4.7	2134	0.9
15	TH		0350	4.7	0952	1.0	1601	5.1	2212	0.6
16	F	○	0428	5.0	1027	0.7	1642	5.4	2247	0.3
17	SA		0508	5.3	1103	0.4	1723	5.6	2323	0.2
18	SU		0549	5.4	1141	0.3	1807	5.6		
19	M		0002	0.1	0631	5.4	1222	0.3	1851	5.5
20	TU		0044	0.3	0715	5.3	1306	0.5	1938	5.3
21	W		0128	0.6	0801	5.1	1353	0.8	2028	4.9
22	TH		0217	1.0	0852	4.7	1448	1.2	2124	4.5
23	F	◑	0314	1.4	0950	4.4	1554	1.5	2232	4.2
24	SA		0426	1.8	1105	4.1	1721	1.7		
25	SU		0003	4.0	0557	1.9	1245	4.1	1903	1.7
26	M		0129	4.1	0730	1.8	1358	4.3	2020	1.4
27	TU		0231	4.3	0835	1.6	1452	4.6	2109	1.2
28	W		0319	4.6	0920	1.3	1537	4.8	2148	1.0
29	TH		0401	4.8	0956	1.1	1617	5.0	2218	0.8
30	F		0438	5.0	1024	1.0	1654	5.1	2241	0.7

OCTOBER

Date	Day	Moon	Time	m	Time	m	Time	m	Time	m
1	SA	●	0513	5.0	1050	0.9	1729	5.1	2306	0.7
2	SU		0547	5.1	1120	0.8	1802	5.0	2337	0.8
3	M		0620	5.0	1153	0.9	1836	4.9		
4	TU		0010	0.9	0653	4.9	1227	1.0	1911	4.8
5	W		0044	1.1	0728	4.8	1302	1.2	1947	4.6
6	TH		0119	1.3	0805	4.6	1338	1.4	2027	4.3
7	F		0156	1.6	0847	4.3	1418	1.7	2112	4.1
8	SA		0238	1.9	0934	4.1	1504	1.9	2204	3.9
9	SU	◐	0327	2.1	1028	4.0	1602	2.1	2302	3.8
10	M		0433	2.3	1128	3.9	1840	2.1		
11	TU		0007	3.8	0711	2.1	1234	4.0	1937	1.7
12	W		0123	4.0	0803	1.8	1346	4.3	2026	1.3
13	TH		0234	4.4	0847	1.4	1446	4.7	2108	0.9
14	F		0319	4.8	0926	0.9	1533	5.1	2146	0.5
15	SA		0400	5.2	1003	0.6	1616	5.5	2222	0.3
16	SU	○	0442	5.4	1040	0.3	1701	5.6	2259	0.1
17	M		0525	5.6	1119	0.2	1746	5.7	2339	0.2
18	TU		0609	5.6	1202	0.3	1833	5.6		
19	W		0022	0.4	0654	5.4	1247	0.5	1921	5.3
20	TH		0108	0.7	0742	5.2	1336	0.8	2012	4.9
21	F		0158	1.1	0833	4.8	1432	1.2	2109	4.5
22	SA	◑	0257	1.5	0930	4.5	1540	1.5	2216	4.2
23	SU		0412	1.9	1041	4.2	1705	1.7	2346	4.0
24	M		0538	2.0	1221	4.1	1829	1.7		
25	TU		0108	4.1	0656	1.9	1335	4.2	1945	1.5
26	W		0208	4.3	0803	1.7	1430	4.4	2038	1.3
27	TH		0256	4.5	0852	1.5	1515	4.6	2117	1.2
28	F		0337	4.7	0929	1.3	1554	4.8	2147	1.0
29	SA		0413	4.8	0958	1.1	1630	4.9	2212	1.0
30	SU	●	0447	4.9	1026	1.0	1704	4.9	2240	0.9
31	M		0520	5.0	1057	0.9	1738	4.9	2312	0.9

NOVEMBER

Date	Day	Moon	Time	m	Time	m	Time	m	Time	m
1	TU		0553	5.0	1130	0.9	1813	4.9	2344	1.0
2	W		0627	5.0	1204	1.0	1848	4.8		
3	TH		0018	1.1	0701	4.8	1239	1.1	1924	4.6
4	F		0054	1.3	0736	4.7	1316	1.3	2001	4.4
5	SA		0131	1.5	0814	4.5	1356	1.5	2043	4.2
6	SU		0214	1.8	0859	4.3	1442	1.7	2133	4.0
7	M	◐	0303	2.0	0953	4.1	1537	1.9	2231	3.9
8	TU		0405	2.2	1053	4.1	1650	2.0	2333	3.9
9	W		0549	2.2	1157	4.1	1857	1.8		
10	TH		0042	4.1	0728	1.9	1306	4.4	1952	1.4
11	F		0153	4.4	0816	1.5	1412	4.7	2037	1.0
12	SA		0248	4.8	0859	1.0	1506	5.1	2118	0.7
13	SU		0334	5.2	0939	0.7	1554	5.4	2157	0.4
14	M	○	0419	5.5	1019	0.4	1641	5.6	2238	0.3
15	TU		0504	5.6	1102	0.3	1729	5.6	2320	0.4
16	W		0550	5.7	1146	0.4	1817	5.5		
17	TH		0004	0.6	0636	5.5	1233	0.5	1906	5.3
18	F		0052	0.8	0724	5.3	1322	0.8	1957	5.0
19	SA		0142	1.2	0815	5.0	1417	1.1	2052	4.7
20	SU		0240	1.6	0909	4.7	1521	1.4	2153	4.4
21	M	◑	0350	1.9	1010	4.4	1635	1.6	2309	4.1
22	TU		0505	2.0	1136	4.2	1747	1.7		
23	W		0030	4.1	0614	2.0	1259	4.1	1852	1.7
24	TH		0135	4.2	0717	1.9	1359	4.2	1950	1.6
25	F		0226	4.4	0811	1.8	1447	4.4	2035	1.5
26	SA		0309	4.5	0854	1.6	1528	4.5	2112	1.4
27	SU		0346	4.7	0930	1.4	1604	4.7	2145	1.2
28	M		0420	4.8	1004	1.2	1639	4.8	2218	1.2
29	TU	●	0454	5.0	1038	1.1	1715	4.8	2251	1.1
30	W		0529	5.0	1112	1.1	1752	4.8	2325	1.1

DECEMBER

Date	Day	Moon	Time	m	Time	m	Time	m	Time	m
1	TH		0605	5.0	1146	1.1	1828	4.8	2359	1.2
2	F		0639	4.9	1221	1.1	1904	4.7		
3	SA		0035	1.3	0712	4.8	1259	1.2	1939	4.6
4	SU		0114	1.5	0748	4.7	1340	1.3	2019	4.4
5	M		0157	1.6	0831	4.6	1425	1.5	2105	4.3
6	TU		0245	1.8	0922	4.4	1516	1.6	2200	4.2
7	W	◐	0342	2.0	1020	4.3	1617	1.7	2300	4.1
8	TH		0451	2.0	1122	4.3	1729	1.7		
9	F		0005	4.2	0613	1.9	1231	4.4	1854	1.5
10	SA		0116	4.5	0735	1.6	1341	4.7	2001	1.3
11	SU		0219	4.8	0831	1.2	1443	5.0	2052	1.0
12	M		0312	5.1	0919	0.9	1536	5.3	2138	0.8
13	TU		0401	5.4	1004	0.7	1627	5.5	2223	0.6
14	W	○	0448	5.6	1050	0.5	1716	5.5	2307	0.6
15	TH		0536	5.6	1135	0.5	1804	5.5	2352	0.7
16	F		0623	5.6	1221	0.6	1853	5.4		
17	SA		0038	0.9	0709	5.4	1308	0.8	1941	5.1
18	SU		0125	1.2	0756	5.2	1357	1.0	2031	4.9
19	M		0216	1.5	0845	4.9	1451	1.3	2122	4.6
20	TU		0314	1.8	0936	4.6	1552	1.6	2218	4.3
21	W	◑	0421	2.0	1032	4.3	1659	1.8	2324	4.1
22	TH		0529	2.1	1145	4.1	1802	1.9		
23	F		0041	4.1	0631	2.1	1312	4.1	1900	1.9
24	SA		0145	4.2	0728	2.0	1412	4.1	1953	1.8
25	SU		0235	4.3	0819	1.8	1459	4.3	2040	1.7
26	M		0317	4.5	0903	1.6	1539	4.5	2121	1.5
27	TU		0354	4.7	0944	1.4	1617	4.6	2200	1.4
28	W		0431	4.9	1022	1.3	1654	4.7	2236	1.3
29	TH	●	0508	5.0	1058	1.1	1732	4.8	2311	1.2
30	F		0544	5.1	1132	1.1	1809	4.9	2345	1.2
31	SA		0620	5.1	1207	1.0	1845	4.9		

Chart Datum: 0·20 metres above Ordnance Datum (Dublin)
HAT is 5·9m above Chart Datum

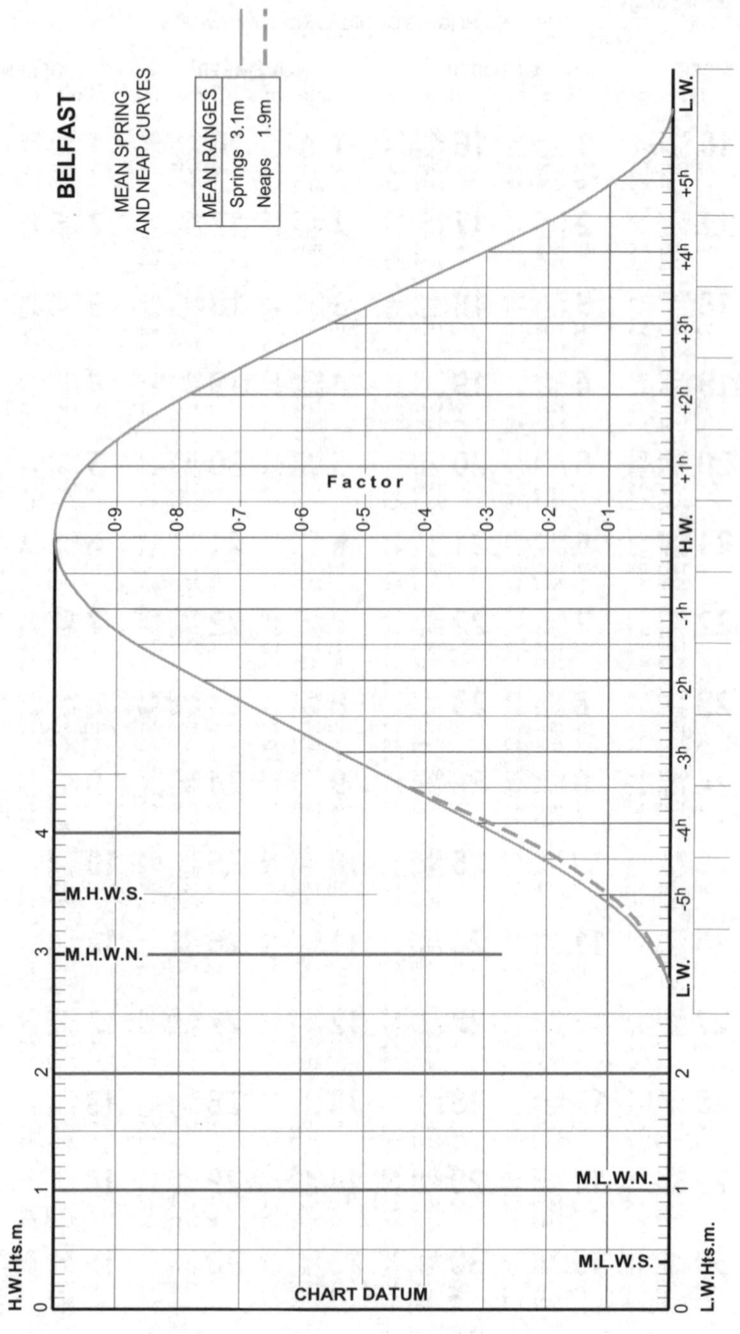
BELFAST
MEAN SPRING
AND NEAP CURVES
MEAN RANGES
Springs 3.1m
Neaps 1.9m
Factor
H.W.
L.W.
M.H.W.S.
M.H.W.N.
M.L.W.N.
M.L.W.S.
CHART DATUM
H.W.Hts.m.
L.W.Hts.m.

TIME ZONE (UT)
For Summer Time add ONE hour in **non-shaded areas**

NORTHERN IRELAND – BELFAST

LAT 54°36′N LONG 5°55′W

TIMES AND HEIGHTS OF HIGH AND LOW WATERS

Dates in amber are **SPRINGS**
Dates in yellow are **NEAPS**

2016

JANUARY

Date	Day	Time	m
1	F	0336 0925 1553 2150	3.1 1.1 3.4 0.9
2	SA	0426 1019 1644 ◑ 2248	3.0 1.2 3.3 1.0
3	SU	0519 1126 1738 2356	3.0 1.3 3.2 1.1
4	M	0616 1238 1836	3.0 1.3 3.1
5	TU	0101 0716 1340 1938	1.1 3.0 1.2 3.1
6	W	0158 0820 1434 2039	1.0 3.1 1.1 3.2
7	TH	0247 0915 1521 2131	0.9 3.2 0.9 3.3
8	F	0330 0959 1603 2214	0.8 3.4 0.8 3.4
9	SA	0411 1037 1643 2251	0.7 3.5 0.7 3.4
10	SU	0451 1108 1722 ● 2326	0.7 3.6 0.6 3.4
11	M	0530 1141 1802	0.6 3.6 0.5
12	TU	0004 0610 1220 1842	3.5 0.6 3.7 0.4
13	W	0047 0652 1304 1925	3.4 0.6 3.7 0.4
14	TH	0135 0737 1351 2011	3.4 0.6 3.7 0.4
15	F	0226 0825 1442 2102	3.4 0.7 3.7 0.5
16	SA	0320 0917 1536 ◐ 2159	3.3 0.7 3.6 0.6
17	SU	0420 1016 1637 2306	3.2 0.9 3.4 0.7
18	M	0526 1125 1749	3.2 0.9 3.3
19	TU	0021 0640 1244 1913	0.8 3.1 1.0 3.2
20	W	0130 0751 1356 2025	0.8 3.2 0.9 3.2
21	TH	0232 0853 1500 2125	0.7 3.3 0.8 3.3
22	F	0327 0947 1554 2216	0.7 3.5 0.6 3.4
23	SA	0416 1035 1641 2303	0.6 3.6 0.5 3.4
24	SU	0459 1119 1723 ○ 2346	0.6 3.7 0.5 3.3
25	M	0540 1200 1802	0.6 3.7 0.5
26	TU	0026 0617 1239 1837	3.3 0.7 3.7 0.5
27	W	0103 0652 1317 1911	3.2 0.7 3.7 0.6
28	TH	0139 0726 1355 1945	3.2 0.8 3.6 0.6
29	F	0218 0802 1435 2021	3.2 0.8 3.5 0.7
30	SA	0259 0842 1518 2103	3.1 0.9 3.4 0.8
31	SU	0345 0927 1604 2149	3.1 1.0 3.3 0.9

FEBRUARY

Date	Day	Time	m
1	M	0434 1020 1655 ◑ 2245	3.0 1.1 3.1 1.0
2	TU	0529 1131 1752	2.9 1.2 3.0
3	W	0001 0627 1258 1854	1.1 2.9 1.2 2.9
4	TH	0121 0731 1403 1958	1.1 2.9 1.1 3.0
5	F	0219 0835 1456 2100	1.0 3.1 0.9 3.1
6	SA	0309 0928 1542 2148	0.8 3.2 0.7 3.2
7	SU	0352 1008 1624 2228	0.7 3.4 0.5 3.3
8	M	0433 1044 1704 ● 2306	0.5 3.5 0.3 3.4
9	TU	0512 1121 1743 2346	0.5 3.6 0.3 3.4
10	W	0552 1203 1824	0.4 3.7 0.2
11	TH	0030 0633 1249 1906	3.4 0.4 3.7 0.2
12	F	0118 0718 1337 1951	3.4 0.4 3.7 0.3
13	SA	0208 0804 1427 2040	3.4 0.4 3.7 0.4
14	SU	0300 0855 1520 2134	3.3 0.5 3.5 0.5
15	M	0356 0952 1619 ◐ 2240	3.2 0.7 3.4 0.7
16	TU	0458 1102 1730 2359	3.1 0.8 3.2 0.9
17	W	0613 1226 1859	3.1 0.9 3.0
18	TH	0113 0733 1343 2015	0.9 3.1 0.8 3.0
19	F	0219 0839 1451 2115	0.8 3.2 0.7 3.1
20	SA	0318 0933 1547 2205	0.7 3.4 0.6 3.2
21	SU	0406 1020 1631 2249	0.7 3.5 0.5 3.2
22	M	0447 1103 1707 ○ 2330	0.6 3.6 0.4 3.2
23	TU	0522 1142 1740	0.6 3.6 0.4
24	W	0006 0555 1218 1811	3.2 0.6 3.6 0.5
25	TH	0039 0626 1252 1841	3.2 0.6 3.5 0.5
26	F	0110 0656 1326 1912	3.2 0.6 3.5 0.5
27	SA	0143 0729 1403 1946	3.2 0.6 3.4 0.6
28	SU	0220 0806 1440 2024	3.2 0.7 3.4 0.6
29	M	0258 0848 1521 2107	3.1 0.8 3.2 0.8

MARCH

Date	Day	Time	m
1	TU	0341 0935 1610 ◑ 2157	3.0 0.9 3.1 0.9
2	W	0435 1034 1710 2259	2.9 1.1 2.9 1.1
3	TH	0539 1213 1815	2.8 1.2 2.8
4	F	0039 0645 1333 1921	1.1 2.8 1.0 2.9
5	SA	0152 0751 1430 2025	1.0 2.9 0.8 3.0
6	SU	0245 0850 1518 2118	0.8 3.1 0.5 3.2
7	M	0331 0936 1601 2202	0.6 3.3 0.3 3.3
8	TU	0412 1018 1642 2243	0.5 3.5 0.2 3.4
9	W	0451 1100 1721 ● 2327	0.3 3.6 0.1 3.5
10	TH	0531 1145 1801	0.3 3.7 0.1
11	F	0012 0612 1233 1843	3.5 0.2 3.7 0.1
12	SA	0101 0657 1324 1929	3.5 0.2 3.7 0.2
13	SU	0151 0744 1415 2018	3.5 0.3 3.6 0.3
14	M	0242 0835 1509 2112	3.4 0.4 3.5 0.5
15	TU	0334 0932 1606 ◐ 2217	3.3 0.5 3.3 0.8
16	W	0433 1043 1716 2338	3.2 0.7 3.0 0.9
17	TH	0545 1210 1846	3.0 0.8 2.9
18	F	0053 0710 1327 2000	1.0 3.0 0.8 2.9
19	SA	0203 0818 1436 2058	0.9 3.1 0.7 3.0
20	SU	0303 0913 1532 2147	0.8 3.3 0.5 3.1
21	M	0352 0959 1613 2229	0.7 3.4 0.5 3.2
22	TU	0430 1041 1645 2307	0.6 3.5 0.4 3.2
23	W	0501 1119 1714 ○ 2342	0.6 3.5 0.5 3.2
24	TH	0531 1153 1743	0.6 3.4 0.5
25	F	0012 0600 1225 1811	3.2 0.6 3.4 0.5
26	SA	0039 0629 1256 1842	3.2 0.6 3.4 0.5
27	SU	0108 0701 1329 1915	3.2 0.6 3.4 0.6
28	M	0140 0737 1404 1952	3.2 0.6 3.3 0.6
29	TU	0214 0816 1443 2034	3.2 0.7 3.2 0.7
30	W	0253 0901 1531 2121	3.1 0.8 3.1 0.9
31	TH	0341 0955 1632 ◑ 2219	3.0 0.9 2.9 1.1

APRIL

Date	Day	Time	m
1	F	0447 1110 1741 2334	2.9 1.0 2.8 1.1
2	SA	0602 1259 1848	2.8 0.9 2.9
3	SU	0117 0711 1400 1952	1.1 2.9 0.7 3.0
4	M	0217 0813 1451 2048	0.9 3.1 0.4 3.2
5	TU	0305 0906 1535 2135	0.6 3.3 0.2 3.4
6	W	0348 0953 1616 2221	0.4 3.5 0.1 3.5
7	TH	0428 1039 1656 ● 2306	0.3 3.7 0.0 3.6
8	F	0509 1127 1738 2354	0.2 3.7 0.0 3.6
9	SA	0552 1217 1822	0.2 3.7 0.1
10	SU	0043 0637 1309 1908	3.6 0.2 3.7 0.2
11	M	0134 0726 1402 1958	3.6 0.2 3.6 0.4
12	TU	0224 0817 1455 2052	3.5 0.3 3.4 0.6
13	W	0315 0915 1552 2157	3.4 0.5 3.2 0.8
14	TH	0410 1026 1700 ◐ 2313	3.3 0.6 3.0 1.0
15	F	0515 1148 1826	3.1 0.7 2.9
16	SA	0026 0638 1301 1937	1.0 3.0 0.7 2.9
17	SU	0134 0749 1407 2034	1.0 3.1 0.7 3.0
18	M	0236 0845 1501 2121	0.9 3.2 0.6 3.1
19	TU	0326 0932 1542 2203	0.8 3.3 0.5 3.1
20	W	0405 1014 1614 2240	0.7 3.4 0.5 3.2
21	TH	0437 1051 1644 2314	0.6 3.4 0.5 3.2
22	F	0506 1125 1714 ○ 2344	0.6 3.4 0.6 3.2
23	SA	0536 1155 1744	0.6 3.3 0.6
24	SU	0010 0606 1225 1815	3.3 0.6 3.3 0.6
25	M	0038 0638 1257 1849	3.3 0.6 3.3 0.6
26	TU	0109 0713 1333 1927	3.3 0.6 3.3 0.7
27	W	0145 0752 1415 2009	3.3 0.6 3.2 0.7
28	TH	0225 0837 1504 2056	3.3 0.7 3.1 0.9
29	F	0312 0929 1603 2152	3.2 0.8 3.0 1.0
30	SA	0410 1036 1710 ◑ 2258	3.0 0.9 2.9 1.1

Chart Datum: 2·01 metres below Ordnance Datum (Belfast)
HAT is 3·9m above Chart Datum

TIME ZONE (UT)
For Summer Time add ONE hour in **non-shaded areas**

NORTHERN IRELAND – BELFAST

LAT 54°36′N LONG 5°55′W

TIMES AND HEIGHTS OF HIGH AND LOW WATERS

Dates in amber are **SPRING**
Dates in yellow are **NEAPS**

201

MAY

Date	Day	Time	m	Time	m	Time	m	Time	m
1	SU	0521	3.0	1213	0.8	1818	2.9		
2	M	0022	1.1	0634	3.0	1324	0.6	1921	3.1
3	TU	0138	0.9	0740	3.2	1419	0.4	2019	3.2
4	W	0233	0.7	0839	3.4	1506	0.2	2110	3.4
5	TH	0321	0.5	0931	3.5	1550	0.1	2159	3.5
6	F	0406	0.4	1020	3.7	1633	0.1	● 2247	3.6
7	SA	0450	0.3	1110	3.7	1717	0.1	2336	3.7
8	SU	0535	0.2	1201	3.7	1803	0.2		
9	M	0025	3.7	0622	0.2	1253	3.6	1851	0.4
10	TU	0116	3.7	0711	0.2	1346	3.5	1941	0.5
11	W	0205	3.6	0803	0.3	1439	3.3	2036	0.7
12	TH	0254	3.5	0859	0.5	1534	3.2	2136	0.9
13	F	0345	3.4	1005	0.6	1635	3.0	◐ 2244	1.0
14	SA	0442	3.2	1117	0.7	1750	2.9	2351	1.1
15	SU	0549	3.1	1224	0.7	1902	2.9		
16	M	0054	1.1	0706	3.1	1325	0.7	2000	2.9
17	TU	0154	1.0	0808	3.1	1419	0.7	2048	3.0
18	W	0248	0.9	0858	3.2	1503	0.7	2131	3.1
19	TH	0332	0.8	0942	3.3	1540	0.6	2209	3.2
20	F	0409	0.7	1020	3.3	1613	0.6	2243	3.3
21	SA	0441	0.7	1056	3.3	1646	0.6	○ 2316	3.3
22	SU	0513	0.7	1128	3.3	1719	0.6	2345	3.4
23	M	0547	0.6	1158	3.3	1754	0.7		
24	TU	0011	3.4	0621	0.6	1230	3.3	1829	0.7
25	W	0044	3.4	0657	0.6	1308	3.3	1908	0.7
26	TH	0122	3.4	0736	0.6	1352	3.2	1950	0.8
27	F	0204	3.4	0819	0.6	1441	3.2	2038	0.8
28	SA	0252	3.3	0911	0.7	1538	3.1	2131	0.9
29	SU	0346	3.2	1011	0.7	1641	3.0	◑ 2232	1.0
30	M	0448	3.2	1125	0.7	1748	3.0	2340	1.0
31	TU	0559	3.2	1243	0.6	1852	3.1		

JUNE

Date	Day	Time	m	Time	m	Time	m	Time	m
1	W	0054	0.9	0710	3.3	1345	0.5	1952	3.2
2	TH	0201	0.8	0815	3.4	1438	0.4	2048	3.4
3	F	0257	0.6	0912	3.5	1528	0.3	2140	3.5
4	SA	0349	0.4	1005	3.6	1615	0.3	2230	3.6
5	SU	0437	0.3	1056	3.6	1701	0.3	● 2319	3.7
6	M	0524	0.3	1146	3.6	1749	0.4		
7	TU	0008	3.7	0611	0.3	1237	3.5	1836	0.5
8	W	0057	3.7	0659	0.3	1328	3.4	1926	0.6
9	TH	0144	3.7	0747	0.4	1418	3.3	2017	0.7
10	F	0231	3.6	0838	0.5	1508	3.1	2110	0.9
11	SA	0319	3.5	0933	0.6	1600	3.0	2207	1.0
12	SU	0408	3.4	1036	0.7	1656	2.9	◐ 2308	1.1
13	M	0502	3.2	1139	0.8	1756	2.9		
14	TU	0009	1.1	0600	3.1	1239	0.8	1902	2.9
15	W	0108	1.1	0706	3.1	1334	0.8	2001	3.0
16	TH	0205	1.0	0811	3.1	1422	0.8	2051	3.1
17	F	0255	0.9	0904	3.1	1505	0.8	2134	3.2
18	SA	0339	0.8	0948	3.2	1544	0.7	2213	3.3
19	SU	0416	0.7	1028	3.3	1620	0.7	2249	3.3
20	M	0452	0.7	1103	3.3	1657	0.7	○ 2321	3.4
21	TU	0528	0.6	1134	3.3	1734	0.7	2347	3.4
22	W	0605	0.6	1206	3.3	1813	0.7		
23	TH	0020	3.5	0642	0.5	1245	3.3	1852	0.7
24	F	0101	3.5	0722	0.5	1330	3.3	1935	0.7
25	SA	0145	3.5	0805	0.5	1419	3.2	2021	0.7
26	SU	0232	3.5	0853	0.5	1513	3.2	2111	0.8
27	M	0324	3.4	0948	0.6	1612	3.1	◑ 2207	0.8
28	TU	0421	3.3	1053	0.6	1716	3.1	2310	0.9
29	W	0527	3.3	1206	0.6	1822	3.1		
30	TH	0021	0.9	0641	3.3	1316	0.6	1927	3.2

JULY

Date	Day	Time	m	Time	m	Time	m	Time	m
1	F	0135	0.8	0755	3.3	1417	0.5	2029	3.3
2	SA	0240	0.7	0859	3.4	1511	0.5	2125	3.5
3	SU	0337	0.5	0955	3.4	1602	0.4	2217	3.6
4	M	0428	0.4	1046	3.5	1650	0.5	● 2305	3.7
5	TU	0516	0.3	1134	3.4	1736	0.5	2352	3.7
6	W	0601	0.3	1221	3.4	1822	0.6		
7	TH	0038	3.7	0644	0.4	1308	3.3	1906	0.7
8	F	0122	3.7	0727	0.4	1353	3.2	1950	0.8
9	SA	0206	3.6	0808	0.5	1437	3.1	2034	0.8
10	SU	0250	3.5	0851	0.6	1523	3.1	2119	0.9
11	M	0335	3.4	0937	0.7	1610	3.0	2209	1.0
12	TU	0423	3.3	1032	0.9	1700	2.9	◐ 2310	1.1
13	W	0515	3.1	1138	0.9	1753	2.9		
14	TH	0017	1.1	0611	3.0	1244	1.0	1851	2.9
15	F	0121	1.1	0713	3.0	1341	1.0	1953	3.0
16	SA	0218	1.0	0819	3.0	1432	0.9	2054	3.1
17	SU	0308	0.9	0916	3.1	1516	0.8	2142	3.2
18	M	0351	0.8	1002	3.2	1557	0.7	2221	3.3
19	TU	0431	0.6	1039	3.3	1636	0.6	○ 2253	3.4
20	W	0509	0.5	1111	3.3	1715	0.6	2322	3.5
21	TH	0546	0.5	1144	3.3	1754	0.6	2357	3.5
22	F	0625	0.4	1223	3.3	1834	0.6		
23	SA	0038	3.6	0704	0.4	1308	3.3	1915	0.6
24	SU	0124	3.6	0746	0.4	1357	3.3	2000	0.6
25	M	0212	3.6	0832	0.4	1449	3.3	2049	0.6
26	TU	0303	3.5	0924	0.5	1546	3.2	◑ 2143	0.7
27	W	0359	3.4	1024	0.6	1647	3.2	2244	0.8
28	TH	0502	3.3	1137	0.7	1754	3.1	2358	0.9
29	F	0620	3.2	1255	0.7	1907	3.2		
30	SA	0119	0.9	0744	3.1	1401	0.7	2016	3.3
31	SU	0229	0.7	0853	3.2	1459	0.6	2115	3.4

AUGUST

Date	Day	Time	m	Time	m	Time	m	Time	m
1	M	0329	0.6	0949	3.3	1551	0.6	2206	3.5
2	TU	0420	0.5	1038	3.3	1638	0.6	● 2253	3.6
3	W	0505	0.4	1123	3.3	1722	0.6	2336	3.7
4	TH	0546	0.4	1205	3.3	1803	0.6		
5	F	0018	3.7	0624	0.4	1246	3.2	1840	0.7
6	SA	0058	3.6	0658	0.5	1324	3.2	1916	0.7
7	SU	0138	3.6	0732	0.5	1404	3.1	1952	0.8
8	M	0218	3.5	0807	0.6	1445	3.1	2030	0.8
9	TU	0300	3.4	0846	0.7	1529	3.1	2113	0.9
10	W	0345	3.3	0930	0.8	1617	3.0	◐ 2203	1.1
11	TH	0434	3.1	1023	1.0	1709	3.0	2309	1.2
12	F	0529	3.0	1134	1.1	1805	2.9		
13	SA	0037	1.2	0630	2.9	1300	1.1	1905	2.9
14	SU	0144	1.1	0735	2.9	1401	1.0	2009	3.0
15	M	0239	0.9	0842	3.0	1451	0.9	2106	3.2
16	TU	0326	0.7	0934	3.2	1534	0.7	2149	3.3
17	W	0408	0.5	1013	3.3	1614	0.6	2223	3.5
18	TH	0446	0.4	1047	3.4	1653	0.6	○ 2256	3.6
19	F	0524	0.3	1122	3.4	1731	0.5	2334	3.6
20	SA	0602	0.3	1202	3.4	1810	0.5		
21	SU	0017	3.7	0641	0.2	1248	3.4	1852	0.5
22	M	0104	3.7	0723	0.3	1336	3.4	1937	0.5
23	TU	0153	3.7	0808	0.4	1428	3.4	2026	0.6
24	W	0245	3.6	0859	0.5	1523	3.3	2120	0.7
25	TH	0341	3.4	0958	0.7	1623	3.2	◑ 2222	0.8
26	F	0446	3.2	1114	0.9	1731	3.1	2343	0.9
27	SA	0609	3.0	1239	0.9	1851	3.1		
28	SU	0109	0.9	0738	3.0	1349	0.9	2004	3.2
29	M	0221	0.8	0846	3.1	1450	0.8	2103	3.4
30	TU	0322	0.6	0940	3.2	1542	0.7	2153	3.5
31	W	0411	0.5	1026	3.3	1626	0.7	2238	3.6

Chart Datum: 2·01 metres below Ordnance Datum (Belfast)
HAT is 3·9m above Chart Datum

TIME ZONE (UT)
For Summer Time add ONE hour in **non-shaded areas**

NORTHERN IRELAND – BELFAST

LAT 54°36′N LONG 5°55′W

TIMES AND HEIGHTS OF HIGH AND LOW WATERS

Dates in amber are **SPRINGS**
Dates in yellow are **NEAPS**

2016

SEPTEMBER

Date	Time	m	Time	m	Time	m	Time	m
1 TH ●	0451	0.4	1108	3.3	1705	0.7	2318	3.6
2 F	0526	0.4	1146	3.2	1740	0.7	2356	3.6
3 SA	0557	0.5	1221	3.2	1812	0.7		
4 SU	0032	3.6	0626	0.6	1254	3.2	1842	0.7
5 M	0108	3.5	0656	0.6	1328	3.2	1914	0.8
6 TU	0145	3.5	0728	0.6	1406	3.2	1950	0.8
7 W	0224	3.4	0805	0.7	1447	3.2	2031	0.9
8 TH	0305	3.3	0847	0.8	1532	3.1	2117	1.0
9 F ◐	0352	3.1	0934	1.0	1623	3.0	2213	1.1
10 SA	0449	3.0	1033	1.2	1722	2.9	2342	1.2
11 SU	0552	2.9	1205	1.3	1824	2.9		
12 M	0111	1.1	0658	2.9	1330	1.2	1927	3.0
13 TU	0210	0.9	0804	3.0	1424	1.0	2026	3.2
14 W	0259	0.7	0900	3.2	1510	0.8	2113	3.4
15 TH	0342	0.5	0943	3.3	1550	0.6	2153	3.5
16 F ○	0421	0.3	1022	3.5	1628	0.5	2232	3.7
17 SA	0458	0.2	1101	3.5	1706	0.5	2314	3.7
18 SU	0536	0.2	1143	3.6	1746	0.4	2359	3.8
19 M	0616	0.2	1229	3.6	1829	0.4		
20 TU	0048	3.8	0659	0.3	1319	3.6	1915	0.4
21 W	0140	3.7	0746	0.4	1410	3.5	2005	0.5
22 TH	0233	3.6	0837	0.6	1504	3.4	2100	0.6
23 F ◑	0331	3.4	0936	0.8	1603	3.3	2205	0.8
24 SA	0437	3.2	1055	1.0	1711	3.2	2331	0.9
25 SU	0603	3.0	1222	1.1	1832	3.2		
26 M	0056	0.9	0728	3.0	1335	1.1	1946	3.3
27 TU	0209	0.8	0832	3.1	1438	1.0	2045	3.4
28 W	0310	0.6	0923	3.2	1530	0.8	2134	3.5
29 TH	0356	0.6	1007	3.3	1611	0.8	2217	3.6
30 F	0431	0.5	1047	3.3	1645	0.7	2257	3.6

OCTOBER

Date	Time	m	Time	m	Time	m	Time	m
1 SA ●	0459	0.6	1123	3.3	1715	0.7	2333	3.6
2 SU	0527	0.6	1155	3.3	1744	0.8		
3 M	0005	3.5	0554	0.7	1224	3.3	1812	0.8
4 TU	0037	3.5	0623	0.7	1254	3.4	1844	0.8
5 W	0111	3.5	0656	0.7	1328	3.4	1919	0.8
6 TH	0148	3.4	0732	0.8	1404	3.4	1958	0.9
7 F	0227	3.3	0813	0.9	1443	3.3	2043	1.0
8 SA	0312	3.2	0859	1.0	1530	3.2	2135	1.1
9 SU ◐	0410	3.0	0954	1.2	1633	3.0	2243	1.2
10 M	0517	2.9	1104	1.3	1742	3.0		
11 TU	0032	1.2	0624	2.9	1249	1.3	1847	3.0
12 W	0136	1.0	0729	3.0	1352	1.1	1948	3.2
13 TH	0228	0.7	0826	3.2	1441	0.9	2041	3.4
14 F	0312	0.5	0914	3.4	1523	0.7	2127	3.6
15 SA	0352	0.3	0957	3.6	1602	0.5	2211	3.7
16 SU ○	0431	0.2	1040	3.7	1641	0.4	2257	3.8
17 M	0510	0.2	1125	3.7	1723	0.4	2345	3.8
18 TU	0552	0.3	1213	3.7	1808	0.4		
19 W	0036	3.8	0637	0.4	1303	3.7	1856	0.4
20 TH	0130	3.7	0726	0.5	1355	3.7	1947	0.5
21 F	0224	3.6	0819	0.7	1448	3.6	2044	0.6
22 SA ◑	0322	3.4	0919	1.0	1544	3.5	2150	0.8
23 SU	0427	3.2	1035	1.1	1649	3.3	2314	0.9
24 M	0548	3.0	1158	1.2	1806	3.3		
25 TU	0033	0.9	0707	3.0	1309	1.2	1919	3.3
26 W	0143	0.8	0809	3.1	1413	1.1	2019	3.4
27 TH	0243	0.8	0859	3.2	1507	1.0	2109	3.5
28 F	0328	0.7	0943	3.3	1548	0.9	2153	3.5
29 SA	0401	0.7	1022	3.4	1622	0.8	2233	3.5
30 SU ●	0429	0.7	1058	3.4	1651	0.8	2308	3.5
31 M	0458	0.7	1129	3.4	1720	0.8	2340	3.5

NOVEMBER

Date	Time	m	Time	m	Time	m	Time	m
1 TU	0527	0.8	1157	3.5	1750	0.8		
2 W	0010	3.5	0557	0.8	1225	3.5	1821	0.8
3 TH	0043	3.5	0630	0.8	1257	3.5	1856	0.8
4 F	0118	3.4	0707	0.8	1331	3.5	1934	0.8
5 SA	0157	3.3	0747	0.9	1409	3.4	2017	0.9
6 SU	0242	3.2	0833	1.0	1453	3.3	2107	1.0
7 M ◐	0337	3.1	0926	1.2	1548	3.2	2208	1.1
8 TU	0443	3.0	1029	1.3	1656	3.1	2328	1.1
9 W	0551	3.0	1145	1.3	1807	3.2		
10 TH	0052	1.0	0655	3.1	1306	1.2	1912	3.3
11 F	0151	0.7	0754	3.3	1404	1.0	2011	3.5
12 SA	0239	0.6	0846	3.5	1453	0.8	2103	3.6
13 SU	0323	0.4	0934	3.6	1538	0.6	2153	3.8
14 M ○	0406	0.3	1021	3.8	1622	0.5	2242	3.8
15 TU	0449	0.3	1109	3.8	1707	0.4	2332	3.8
16 W	0534	0.4	1158	3.9	1754	0.4		
17 TH	0024	3.8	0621	0.5	1249	3.9	1842	0.4
18 F	0118	3.7	0711	0.7	1339	3.8	1934	0.5
19 SA	0212	3.5	0804	0.8	1431	3.7	2029	0.6
20 SU	0308	3.4	0902	1.0	1524	3.6	2132	0.7
21 M ◑	0408	3.2	1010	1.2	1621	3.5	2245	0.9
22 TU	0519	3.0	1123	1.2	1727	3.3	2357	0.9
23 W	0633	3.0	1230	1.2	1840	3.3		
24 TH	0101	0.9	0735	3.1	1333	1.2	1944	3.3
25 F	0159	0.9	0828	3.2	1429	1.1	2038	3.4
26 SA	0248	0.9	0914	3.3	1517	1.0	2125	3.4
27 SU	0326	0.8	0955	3.4	1555	0.9	2206	3.5
28 M	0400	0.8	1032	3.4	1628	0.9	2244	3.5
29 TU ●	0432	0.8	1106	3.5	1700	0.8	2318	3.5
30 W	0504	0.8	1137	3.5	1732	0.8	2349	3.4

DECEMBER

Date	Time	m	Time	m	Time	m	Time	m
1 TH	0538	0.8	1205	3.6	1806	0.8		
2 F	0019	3.4	0612	0.8	1233	3.6	1841	0.8
3 SA	0053	3.4	0649	0.9	1307	3.6	1918	0.8
4 SU	0132	3.4	0729	0.9	1346	3.5	2000	0.8
5 M	0217	3.3	0813	1.0	1430	3.5	2046	0.9
6 TU	0308	3.2	0903	1.1	1519	3.4	2141	0.9
7 W ◐	0407	3.1	1000	1.1	1617	3.3	2245	0.9
8 TH	0513	3.1	1104	1.2	1724	3.3	2359	0.9
9 F	0620	3.2	1215	1.1	1835	3.3		
10 SA	0109	0.8	0722	3.3	1326	1.0	1942	3.4
11 SU	0208	0.6	0821	3.4	1426	0.8	2043	3.6
12 M	0300	0.5	0914	3.6	1520	0.7	2138	3.7
13 TU	0348	0.5	1005	3.7	1609	0.5	2230	3.7
14 W ○	0435	0.5	1055	3.8	1657	0.4	2321	3.7
15 TH	0522	0.5	1144	3.9	1745	0.4		
16 F	0012	3.7	0609	0.6	1234	3.9	1833	0.4
17 SA	0104	3.6	0658	0.7	1323	3.9	1922	0.4
18 SU	0155	3.5	0748	0.8	1411	3.8	2013	0.5
19 M	0247	3.3	0840	0.9	1500	3.7	2107	0.7
20 TU	0340	3.2	0937	1.1	1550	3.6	2207	0.8
21 W ◑	0435	3.1	1040	1.2	1644	3.4	2311	0.9
22 TH	0536	3.0	1144	1.2	1742	3.3		
23 F	0014	1.0	0643	3.0	1246	1.2	1848	3.2
24 SA	0112	1.0	0747	3.0	1345	1.2	1956	3.2
25 SU	0205	1.0	0841	3.1	1440	1.1	2053	3.2
26 M	0252	0.9	0927	3.3	1526	1.0	2140	3.3
27 TU	0332	0.9	1008	3.4	1606	0.9	2221	3.4
28 W	0409	0.8	1045	3.5	1641	0.8	2259	3.4
29 TH ●	0445	0.8	1120	3.5	1716	0.7	2333	3.4
30 F	0521	0.8	1149	3.6	1751	0.7		
31 SA	0001	3.4	0557	0.8	1213	3.6	1827	0.7

Chart Datum: 2·01 metres below Ordnance Datum (Belfast)
HAT is 3·9m above Chart Datum

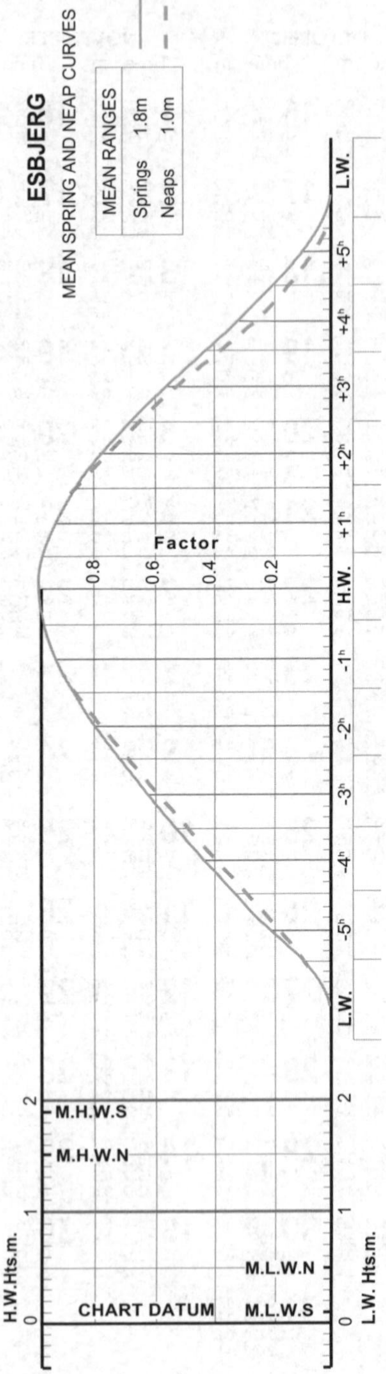
ESBJERG
MEAN SPRING AND NEAP CURVES
MEAN RANGES
Springs 1.8m
Neaps 1.0m
Factor
0.8
0.6
0.4
0.2
L.W.
-5h
-4h
-3h
-2h
-1h
H.W.
+1h
+2h
+3h
+4h
+5h
L.W.
H.W.Hts.m.
0
1
2
M.H.W.S
M.H.W.N
CHART DATUM
M.L.W.N
M.L.W.S
L.W. Hts.m.

TIME ZONE -0100
(Danish Standard Time)
Subtract 1 hour for UT
For Danish Summer Time add ONE hour in **non-shaded areas**

DENMARK – ESBJERG

LAT 55°28'N LONG 8°26'E

TIMES AND HEIGHTS OF HIGH AND LOW WATERS

Dates in amber are **SPRINGS**
Dates in yellow are **NEAPS**

2016

JANUARY

Date	Day	Moon	Time m	Time m	Time m	Time m
1	F		0038 0.4	0658 1.9	1313 0.4	1929 1.7
2	SA	◑	0121 0.5	0742 1.9	1359 0.5	2018 1.7
3	SU		0209 0.5	0835 1.9	1450 0.5	2115 1.7
4	M		0304 0.6	0936 1.8	1548 0.5	2220 1.7
5	TU		0409 0.6	1042 1.8	1654 0.5	2325 1.7
6	W		0520 0.6	1148 1.8	1757 0.5	
7	TH		0026 1.8	0624 0.5	1248 1.8	1851 0.4
8	F		0121 1.9	0718 0.4	1343 1.8	1938 0.4
9	SA		0209 1.9	0804 0.4	1433 1.9	2021 0.3
10	SU	●	0254 1.9	0848 0.3	1518 1.9	2102 0.3
11	M		0335 2.0	0929 0.2	1600 1.9	2142 0.2
12	TU		0414 2.0	1010 0.2	1641 1.9	2224 0.2
13	W		0452 2.0	1053 0.1	1721 1.8	2306 0.2
14	TH		0532 2.0	1136 0.1	1803 1.8	2350 0.2
15	F		0615 2.0	1222 0.1	1848 1.8	
16	SA		0037 0.2	0702 2.0	1312 0.2	1937 1.8
17	SU	◐	0127 0.2	0755 2.0	1405 0.2	2034 1.7
18	M		0223 0.3	0857 1.9	1504 0.3	2139 1.7
19	TU		0327 0.3	1009 1.9	1611 0.4	2250 1.7
20	W		0439 0.4	1123 1.8	1721 0.4	2358 1.8
21	TH		0551 0.3	1231 1.8	1827 0.3	
22	F		0100 1.8	0657 0.2	1333 1.8	1923 0.3
23	SA		0156 1.9	0754 0.2	1427 1.8	2013 0.2
24	SU	○	0246 2.0	0844 0.1	1515 1.8	2059 0.2
25	M		0331 2.0	0929 0.1	1558 1.8	2141 0.2
26	TU		0412 2.0	1011 0.1	1636 1.7	2219 0.2
27	W		0448 2.0	1049 0.2	1709 1.7	2256 0.2
28	TH		0520 1.9	1124 0.2	1740 1.7	2330 0.2
29	F		0551 1.9	1159 0.3	1810 1.7	
30	SA		0006 0.3	0622 1.9	1234 0.3	1843 1.7
31	SU		0043 0.3	0658 1.8	1312 0.3	1923 1.7

FEBRUARY

Date	Day	Moon	Time m	Time m	Time m	Time m
1	M	◑	0125 0.3	0742 1.8	1355 0.4	2012 1.7
2	TU		0212 0.4	0835 1.7	1445 0.4	2111 1.6
3	W		0309 0.4	0939 1.7	1545 0.5	2221 1.6
4	TH		0418 0.5	1054 1.7	1657 0.5	2335 1.7
5	F		0535 0.4	1208 1.7	1807 0.4	
6	SA		0041 1.7	0642 0.4	1312 1.7	1906 0.3
7	SU		0138 1.8	0738 0.3	1407 1.8	1956 0.2
8	M	●	0228 1.9	0825 0.1	1457 1.8	2041 0.2
9	TU		0313 1.9	0909 0.1	1542 1.8	2124 0.1
10	W		0356 2.0	0952 0.0	1624 1.8	2206 0.0
11	TH		0437 2.0	1035 0.0	1705 1.8	2248 0.0
12	F		0518 2.0	1118 0.0	1745 1.8	2332 0.0
13	SA		0600 2.0	1203 0.0	1828 1.7	
14	SU		0018 0.0	0647 1.9	1249 0.1	1915 1.7
15	M	◐	0106 0.1	0739 1.9	1339 0.2	2008 1.7
16	TU		0200 0.2	0839 1.8	1436 0.3	2111 1.6
17	W		0303 0.2	0951 1.7	1544 0.3	2224 1.6
18	TH		0419 0.3	1107 1.7	1700 0.4	2336 1.7
19	F		0538 0.2	1217 1.7	1809 0.3	
20	SA		0041 1.7	0645 0.2	1318 1.7	1908 0.2
21	SU		0139 1.8	0741 0.1	1412 1.7	1957 0.2
22	M	○	0229 1.9	0829 0.0	1459 1.7	2042 0.1
23	TU		0314 1.9	0912 0.0	1539 1.7	2122 0.1
24	W		0353 1.9	0951 0.1	1614 1.7	2159 0.1
25	TH		0427 1.9	1025 0.1	1645 1.7	2232 0.1
26	F		0456 1.8	1057 0.1	1712 1.6	2304 0.1
27	SA		0523 1.8	1127 0.2	1737 1.6	2336 0.1
28	SU		0550 1.8	1158 0.2	1805 1.7	
29	M		0010 0.1	0621 1.7	1233 0.2	1840 1.7

MARCH

Date	Day	Moon	Time m	Time m	Time m	Time m
1	TU		0049 0.2	0702 1.7	1313 0.2	1924 1.6
2	W	◑	0134 0.2	0751 1.7	1400 0.3	2017 1.6
3	TH		0227 0.3	0851 1.6	1456 0.3	2121 1.6
4	F		0331 0.3	1006 1.6	1606 0.4	2240 1.6
5	SA		0450 0.3	1130 1.6	1724 0.4	2359 1.6
6	SU		0608 0.3	1241 1.6	1833 0.3	
7	M		0104 1.7	0709 0.1	1340 1.7	1929 0.2
8	TU		0159 1.8	0800 0.0	1433 1.7	2017 0.1
9	W	●	0248 1.9	0847 -0.1	1519 1.8	2102 0.0
10	TH		0334 1.9	0930 -0.2	1603 1.8	2145 -0.1
11	F		0418 1.9	1013 -0.2	1644 1.8	2228 -0.2
12	SA		0500 1.9	1056 -0.2	1724 1.7	2312 -0.2
13	SU		0544 1.9	1140 -0.1	1806 1.7	2357 -0.1
14	M		0630 1.8	1225 0.0	1851 1.7	
15	TU	◐	0046 0.0	0721 1.7	1315 0.1	1942 1.6
16	W		0139 0.1	0821 1.6	1410 0.2	2045 1.6
17	TH		0243 0.2	0933 1.6	1518 0.3	2158 1.6
18	F		0402 0.2	1049 1.5	1637 0.3	2312 1.6
19	SA		0523 0.2	1157 1.6	1749 0.3	
20	SU		0018 1.7	0628 0.1	1257 1.6	1848 0.2
21	M		0116 1.8	0722 0.0	1350 1.7	1937 0.1
22	TU		0207 1.8	0809 0.0	1436 1.7	2021 0.0
23	W	○	0251 1.8	0850 0.0	1515 1.7	2100 0.0
24	TH		0330 1.8	0927 0.0	1550 1.7	2136 0.0
25	F		0403 1.8	0958 0.0	1619 1.6	2208 0.0
26	SA		0432 1.7	1027 0.1	1645 1.6	2238 0.0
27	SU		0457 1.7	1055 0.1	1709 1.6	2309 0.0
28	M		0522 1.7	1126 0.1	1735 1.6	2342 0.0
29	TU		0553 1.6	1200 0.1	1808 1.6	
30	W		0021 0.0	0631 1.6	1241 0.1	1849 1.6
31	TH	◑	0106 0.1	0719 1.6	1327 0.2	1939 1.6

APRIL

Date	Day	Moon	Time m	Time m	Time m	Time m
1	F		0157 0.1	0817 1.5	1421 0.2	2039 1.6
2	SA		0259 0.2	0929 1.5	1528 0.3	2153 1.6
3	SU		0415 0.2	1054 1.5	1646 0.3	2318 1.6
4	M		0534 0.1	1210 1.5	1800 0.2	
5	TU		0030 1.7	0639 0.0	1312 1.6	1859 0.1
6	W		0130 1.7	0733 -0.1	1406 1.7	1951 0.0
7	TH	●	0222 1.8	0821 -0.2	1454 1.7	2038 -0.1
8	F		0311 1.9	0906 -0.2	1539 1.7	2124 -0.2
9	SA		0357 1.9	0951 -0.2	1621 1.7	2208 -0.2
10	SU		0441 1.8	1033 -0.2	1702 1.7	2253 -0.2
11	M		0526 1.8	1117 -0.1	1743 1.7	2339 -0.2
12	TU		0612 1.7	1203 0.0	1828 1.7	
13	W		0027 -0.1	0703 1.6	1251 0.1	1918 1.6
14	TH	◐	0121 0.0	0803 1.5	1345 0.2	2018 1.6
15	F		0224 0.1	0912 1.5	1450 0.3	2130 1.6
16	SA		0342 0.2	1024 1.4	1608 0.3	2242 1.6
17	SU		0500 0.1	1130 1.5	1721 0.3	2348 1.6
18	M		0603 0.1	1229 1.5	1821 0.2	
19	TU		0046 1.7	0657 0.0	1321 1.6	1912 0.1
20	W		0138 1.7	0743 0.0	1407 1.6	1957 0.0
21	TH		0224 1.8	0824 -0.1	1448 1.7	2036 0.0
22	F	○	0303 1.7	0859 0.0	1524 1.7	2112 0.0
23	SA		0338 1.7	0930 0.0	1554 1.6	2143 0.0
24	SU		0408 1.6	0959 0.0	1621 1.6	2213 0.0
25	M		0434 1.6	1028 0.0	1646 1.6	2245 0.0
26	TU		0501 1.6	1100 0.0	1713 1.6	2320 0.0
27	W		0533 1.6	1136 0.0	1745 1.7	
28	TH		0000 0.0	0611 1.6	1216 0.1	1824 1.7
29	F		0045 0.0	0657 1.5	1303 0.1	1912 1.6
30	SA	◑	0136 0.0	0754 1.5	1357 0.2	2009 1.6

Chart Datum: 0·69 metres below Dansk Normal Null
HAT is 2·2 metres above Chart Datum

TIME ZONE -0100
(Danish Standard Time)
Subtract 1 hour for UT
For Danish Summer Time add
ONE hour in **non-shaded areas**

DENMARK – ESBJERG

LAT 55°28′N LONG 8°26′E

TIMES AND HEIGHTS OF HIGH AND LOW WATERS

Dates in amber are **SPRING**
Dates in yellow are **NEAPS**

201

MAY

Day	Time	m	Day	Time	m
1 SU	0236	0.1	16 M	0425	0.2
	0903	1.5		1052	1.4
	1500	0.2		1642	0.3
	2119	1.6		2309	1.6
2 M	0347	0.1	17 TU	0530	0.1
	1023	1.4		1151	1.5
	1613	0.2		1745	0.2
	2241	1.6			
3 TU	0502	0.1	18 W	0009	1.7
	1138	1.5		0624	0.1
	1725	0.2		1245	1.6
	2356	1.7		1840	0.1
4 W	0608	0.0	19 TH	0103	1.7
	1242	1.6		0712	0.0
	1829	0.1		1333	1.6
				1927	0.1
5 TH	0100	1.7	20 F	0151	1.7
	0705	-0.1		0754	0.0
	1338	1.6		1417	1.7
	1924	0.0		2009	0.1
6 F	0157	1.8	21 SA	0233	1.7
	0756	-0.2		0830	0.0
	1429	1.7		1456	1.7
	● 2015	-0.1		○ 2046	0.0
7 SA	0248	1.8	22 SU	0312	1.6
	0843	-0.2		0903	0.0
	1515	1.7		1530	1.7
	2103	-0.2		2120	0.1
8 SU	0336	1.8	23 M	0345	1.6
	0928	-0.2		0933	0.1
	1559	1.7		1601	1.7
	2149	-0.2		2152	0.0
9 M	0423	1.8	24 TU	0416	1.6
	1012	-0.1		1005	0.1
	1641	1.7		1629	1.7
	2235	-0.2		2226	0.0
10 TU	0509	1.7	25 W	0447	1.6
	1056	-0.1		1039	0.1
	1724	1.7		1658	1.7
	2322	-0.2		2303	0.0
11 W	0555	1.6	26 TH	0521	1.6
	1141	0.0		1117	0.0
	1808	1.7		1730	1.7
				2344	0.0
12 TH	0011	-0.1	27 F	0559	1.5
	0645	1.5		1158	0.1
	1228	0.1		1809	1.7
	1856	1.7			
13 F	0103	0.0	28 SA	0029	0.0
	0739	1.5		0644	1.5
	1319	0.2		1245	0.1
	◐ 1951	1.6		1855	1.7
14 SA	0203	0.1	29 SU	0120	0.0
	0841	1.4		0738	1.5
	1418	0.3		1337	0.1
	2056	1.6		◑ 1950	1.7
15 SU	0312	0.2	30 M	0217	0.0
	0948	1.4		0841	1.5
	1529	0.3		1436	0.2
	2204	1.6		2055	1.7
			31 TU	0321	0.1
				0953	1.5
				1543	0.2
				2210	1.7

JUNE

Day	Time	m	Day	Time	m
1 W	0430	0.1	16 TH	0541	0.2
	1106	1.5		1200	1.6
	1653	0.2		1800	0.3
	2326	1.7			
2 TH	0537	0.0	17 F	0021	1.6
	1212	1.6		0633	0.2
	1800	0.1		1254	1.6
				1853	0.2
3 F	0033	1.7	18 SA	0113	1.7
	0637	0.0		0719	0.2
	1312	1.6		1342	1.7
	1900	0.0		1939	0.2
4 SA	0134	1.8	19 SU	0201	1.7
	0732	-0.1		0800	0.1
	1405	1.7		1426	1.7
	1954	-0.1		2021	0.1
5 SU	0229	1.8	20 M	0245	1.7
	0821	-0.1		0836	0.1
	1454	1.7		1506	1.7
	● 2045	-0.1		○ 2057	0.1
6 M	0320	1.7	21 TU	0324	1.6
	0909	-0.1		0910	0.1
	1540	1.8		1542	1.7
	2133	-0.2		2133	0.1
7 TU	0408	1.7	22 W	0400	1.6
	0954	0.0		0945	0.1
	1624	1.8		1615	1.7
	2221	-0.1		2210	0.1
8 W	0454	1.6	23 TH	0436	1.6
	1037	0.0		1022	0.1
	1706	1.8		1647	1.8
	2307	-0.1		2249	0.0
9 TH	0538	1.6	24 F	0512	1.6
	1121	0.1		1101	0.1
	1749	1.8		1722	1.8
	2354	0.0		2330	0.0
10 F	0623	1.5	25 SA	0551	1.6
	1206	0.1		1143	0.1
	1833	1.7		1800	1.8
11 SA	0042	0.1	26 SU	0015	0.0
	0710	1.5		0634	1.6
	1253	0.2		1229	0.1
	1921	1.7		1845	1.8
12 SU	0134	0.1	27 M	0103	0.0
	0802	1.4		0723	1.6
	1344	0.2		1319	0.1
	◐ 2015	1.7		◑ 1936	1.8
13 M	0230	0.2	28 TU	0157	0.0
	0900	1.4		0819	1.6
	1442	0.3		1414	0.1
	2117	1.6		2036	1.8
14 TU	0334	0.2	29 W	0255	0.1
	1002	1.5		0924	1.5
	1548	0.3		1515	0.2
	2221	1.6		2145	1.7
15 W	0440	0.2	30 TH	0400	0.1
	1103	1.5		1035	1.5
	1657	0.3		1624	0.2
	2323	1.6		2300	1.7

JULY

Day	Time	m	Day	Time	m
1 F	0508	0.2	16 SA	0542	0.4
	1145	1.6		1208	1.6
	1734	0.2		1811	0.4
2 SA	0012	1.7	17 SU	0033	1.7
	0613	0.1		0639	0.3
	1248	1.7		1304	1.7
	1839	0.1		1906	0.3
3 SU	0116	1.7	18 M	0127	1.7
	0712	0.1		0727	0.3
	1345	1.7		1354	1.8
	1939	0.0		1953	0.3
4 M	0215	1.8	19 TU	0218	1.7
	0804	0.1		0809	0.2
	1438	1.8		1439	1.8
	● 2032	0.0		○ 2035	0.2
5 TU	0307	1.7	20 W	0303	1.7
	0852	0.1		0848	0.2
	1525	1.8		1520	1.8
	2121	0.0		2115	0.1
6 W	0355	1.7	21 TH	0344	1.7
	0937	0.1		0927	0.2
	1609	1.9		1558	1.9
	2207	0.0		2154	0.1
7 TH	0439	1.7	22 F	0423	1.7
	1021	0.1		1006	0.1
	1651	1.9		1634	1.9
	2251	0.0		2233	0.0
8 F	0519	1.6	23 SA	0500	1.7
	1102	0.1		1045	0.1
	1730	1.8		1711	1.9
	2334	0.1		2315	0.0
9 SA	0558	1.6	24 SU	0539	1.7
	1143	0.1		1127	0.1
	1809	1.8		1751	1.9
				2358	0.0
10 SU	0017	0.1	25 M	0621	1.7
	0637	1.6		1212	0.1
	1224	0.2		1833	1.9
	1849	1.8			
11 M	0100	0.2	26 TU	0044	0.0
	0718	1.5		0706	1.7
	1307	0.2		1300	0.1
	1933	1.8		1922	1.9
12 TU	0145	0.3	27 W	0134	0.1
	0805	1.5		0757	1.7
	1354	0.3		1351	0.2
	◐ 2022	1.7		◑ 2018	1.9
13 W	0234	0.3	28 TH	0229	0.2
	0859	1.5		0857	1.6
	1448	0.4		1450	0.2
	2120	1.7		2126	1.8
14 TH	0331	0.4	29 F	0331	0.3
	1001	1.5		1006	1.6
	1551	0.4		1558	0.3
	2226	1.6		2242	1.8
15 F	0436	0.4	30 SA	0442	0.3
	1106	1.6		1120	1.7
	1703	0.4		1713	0.3
	2331	1.6		2357	1.8
			31 SU	0552	0.3
				1228	1.7
				1825	0.2

AUGUST

Day	Time	m	Day	Time	m
1 M	0103	1.8	16 TU	0053	1.
	0655	0.3		0651	0.
	1329	1.8		1319	1.
	1927	0.2		1923	0.
2 TU	0203	1.8	17 W	0148	1.
	0749	0.2		0740	0.
	1423	1.9		1410	1.
	● 2020	0.1		2009	0.
3 W	0254	1.8	18 TH	0238	1.
	0838	0.2		0824	0.
	1511	1.9		1455	2.
	2109	0.1		○ 2052	0.
4 TH	0341	1.8	19 F	0323	1.
	0921	0.2		0906	0.
	1554	2.0		1537	2.
	2152	0.1		2133	0.
5 F	0421	1.8	20 SA	0404	1.
	1003	0.2		0946	0.
	1633	2.0		1617	2.
	2233	0.1		2214	0.
6 SA	0457	1.7	21 SU	0443	1.
	1042	0.2		1027	0.
	1709	1.9		1656	2.
	2311	0.2		2255	0.
7 SU	0530	1.7	22 M	0522	1.
	1118	0.2		1109	0.
	1742	1.9		1736	2.
	2347	0.2		2338	0.
8 M	0602	1.7	23 TU	0603	1.
	1154	0.2		1153	0.
	1815	1.9		1820	2.
9 TU	0023	0.3	24 W	0023	0.
	0635	1.7		0645	1.
	1232	0.3		1239	0.
	1850	1.8		1908	2.
10 W	0100	0.3	25 TH	0111	0.
	0712	1.7		0733	1.
	1312	0.3		1330	0.
	◐ 1931	1.8		◑ 2003	1.
11 TH	0140	0.4	26 F	0203	0.
	0756	1.7		0831	1.
	1357	0.4		1428	0.
	2020	1.8		2111	1.
12 F	0227	0.5	27 SA	0305	0.
	0851	1.7		0942	1.
	1450	0.5		1538	0.
	2121	1.7		2229	1.
13 SA	0324	0.5	28 SU	0418	0.
	0959	1.7		1059	1.
	1556	0.5		1700	0.
	2234	1.7		2344	1.
14 SU	0434	0.5	29 M	0535	0.
	1113	1.7		1209	1.
	1716	0.5		1814	0.
	2348	1.7			
15 M	0549	0.5	30 TU	0051	1.
	1221	1.7		0639	0.
	1827	0.5		1312	1.
				1915	0.
			31 W	0148	1.
				0733	0.
				1406	2.
				2006	0.

Chart Datum: 0·69 metres below Dansk Normal Null
HAT is 2·2 metres above Chart Datum

TIME ZONE -0100
(Danish Standard Time)
Subtract 1 hour for UT
For Danish Summer Time add ONE hour in **non-shaded areas**

DENMARK – ESBJERG

LAT 55°28′N LONG 8°26′E

TIMES AND HEIGHTS OF HIGH AND LOW WATERS

Dates in amber are **SPRINGS**
Dates in yellow are **NEAPS**

2016

SEPTEMBER

Date	Day	Time	m	Time	m	Time	m	Time	m
1	TH	0239	1.9	0821	0.3	1454	2.1	● 2052	0.1
2	F	0322	1.9	0904	0.2	1536	2.1	2133	0.2
3	SA	0400	1.9	0943	0.2	1614	2.1	2210	0.2
4	SU	0433	1.9	1019	0.2	1646	2.0	2245	0.3
5	M	0503	1.8	1053	0.3	1715	2.0	2316	0.3
6	TU	0530	1.8	1126	0.3	1743	1.9	2347	0.4
7	W	0557	1.8	1200	0.3	1812	1.9		
8	TH	0020	0.4	0628	1.8	1236	0.4	1849	1.9
9	F	0057	0.4	0708	1.8	1318	0.4	◐ 1934	1.8
10	SA	0141	0.5	0757	1.8	1406	0.5	2030	1.8
11	SU	0233	0.6	0857	1.8	1506	0.5	2139	1.7
12	M	0337	0.6	1012	1.8	1623	0.6	2303	1.7
13	TU	0457	0.6	1132	1.8	1745	0.5		
14	W	0017	1.8	0610	0.5	1240	1.9	1849	0.4
15	TH	0118	1.9	0708	0.4	1337	2.0	1940	0.3
16	F	0211	1.9	0757	0.3	1427	2.1	○ 2027	0.2
17	SA	0258	2.0	0842	0.2	1512	2.1	2109	0.1
18	SU	0341	2.0	0924	0.2	1556	2.2	2151	0.1
19	M	0422	2.0	1006	0.1	1638	2.2	2233	0.1
20	TU	0502	2.0	1050	0.1	1720	2.1	2316	0.1
21	W	0542	2.0	1134	0.1	1804	2.1		
22	TH	0000	0.2	0624	1.9	1221	0.2	1853	2.0
23	F	0048	0.3	0712	1.9	1312	0.3	◑ 1949	1.9
24	SA	0140	0.5	0809	1.9	1411	0.4	2057	1.8
25	SU	0242	0.6	0920	1.8	1523	0.5	2215	1.8
26	M	0357	0.6	1037	1.9	1646	0.5	2328	1.8
27	TU	0515	0.6	1148	1.9	1759	0.4		
28	W	0032	1.9	0620	0.5	1250	2.0	1857	0.3
29	TH	0127	1.9	0713	0.4	1345	2.1	1946	0.2
30	F	0216	2.0	0800	0.3	1432	2.1	2030	0.2

OCTOBER

Date	Day	Time	m	Time	m	Time	m	Time	m
1	SA	0259	2.0	0843	0.3	1515	2.1	● 2110	0.2
2	SU	0336	2.0	0921	0.3	1551	2.1	2145	0.3
3	M	0409	2.0	0956	0.3	1622	2.0	2216	0.4
4	TU	0436	1.9	1027	0.3	1650	2.0	2245	0.4
5	W	0501	1.9	1058	0.4	1715	2.0	2315	0.4
6	TH	0525	1.9	1131	0.4	1742	1.9	2347	0.4
7	F	0554	2.0	1206	0.4	1817	1.9		
8	SA	0024	0.5	0632	2.0	1248	0.4	1900	1.9
9	SU	0106	0.5	0718	1.9	1336	0.5	◐ 1954	1.8
10	M	0157	0.6	0814	1.9	1433	0.5	2100	1.8
11	TU	0258	0.6	0921	1.9	1544	0.6	2221	1.8
12	W	0413	0.7	1043	1.9	1703	0.5	2340	1.8
13	TH	0530	0.6	1159	2.0	1812	0.4		
14	F	0045	1.9	0633	0.5	1302	2.0	1909	0.3
15	SA	0141	2.0	0727	0.4	1357	2.1	1958	0.2
16	SU	0230	2.0	0815	0.3	1447	2.2	○ 2044	0.2
17	M	0316	2.1	0901	0.2	1533	2.2	2127	0.1
18	TU	0359	2.1	0945	0.1	1618	2.2	2211	0.2
19	W	0440	2.1	1030	0.1	1703	2.1	2254	0.2
20	TH	0521	2.1	1116	0.2	1749	2.1	2339	0.3
21	F	0605	2.0	1203	0.2	1839	2.0		
22	SA	0026	0.4	0653	2.0	1256	0.3	◑ 1935	1.9
23	SU	0118	0.5	0749	2.0	1355	0.4	2041	1.8
24	M	0218	0.6	0857	1.9	1506	0.5	2154	1.8
25	TU	0331	0.7	1012	2.0	1626	0.5	2303	1.8
26	W	0448	0.6	1121	2.0	1735	0.4		
27	TH	0005	1.9	0553	0.5	1222	2.1	1832	0.4
28	F	0100	2.0	0648	0.5	1316	2.1	1921	0.3
29	SA	0148	2.0	0736	0.4	1405	2.1	2006	0.3
30	SU	0232	2.0	0819	0.3	1448	2.1	● 2045	0.3
31	M	0310	2.0	0858	0.3	1526	2.1	2118	0.4

NOVEMBER

Date	Day	Time	m	Time	m	Time	m	Time	m
1	TU	0344	2.0	0933	0.4	1558	2.0	2149	0.4
2	W	0412	2.0	1004	0.4	1627	2.0	2218	0.4
3	TH	0438	2.0	1035	0.4	1652	1.9	2247	0.4
4	F	0503	2.0	1108	0.4	1721	1.9	2320	0.4
5	SA	0531	2.0	1144	0.4	1754	1.9	2358	0.5
6	SU	0607	2.0	1226	0.4	1836	1.9		
7	M	0042	0.5	0651	2.0	1314	0.4	◐ 1928	1.9
8	TU	0131	0.5	0743	2.0	1409	0.5	2030	1.8
9	W	0230	0.6	0846	2.0	1514	0.5	2145	1.8
10	TH	0338	0.6	1001	2.0	1627	0.5	2302	1.8
11	F	0451	0.6	1119	2.0	1736	0.4		
12	SA	0011	1.9	0558	0.5	1228	2.1	1836	0.3
13	SU	0110	2.0	0657	0.4	1327	2.1	1930	0.3
14	M	0203	2.0	0750	0.3	1422	2.1	○ 2018	0.2
15	TU	0251	2.1	0839	0.2	1512	2.1	2105	0.2
16	W	0336	2.1	0927	0.2	1600	2.1	2150	0.2
17	TH	0421	2.1	1013	0.2	1648	2.1	2234	0.3
18	F	0503	2.1	1100	0.2	1735	2.0	2320	0.3
19	SA	0548	2.1	1149	0.2	1824	1.9		
20	SU	0006	0.4	0635	2.0	1240	0.3	1917	1.8
21	M	0057	0.5	0729	2.0	1337	0.4	◑ 2017	1.8
22	TU	0153	0.6	0830	2.0	1442	0.5	2122	1.8
23	W	0258	0.6	0938	2.0	1554	0.5	2227	1.8
24	TH	0410	0.6	1045	2.0	1702	0.5	2328	1.8
25	F	0518	0.6	1146	2.0	1800	0.4		
26	SA	0024	1.9	0617	0.5	1242	2.0	1851	0.4
27	SU	0115	2.0	0709	0.4	1333	2.1	1937	0.4
28	M	0200	2.0	0754	0.4	1419	2.0	2017	0.4
29	TU	0242	2.0	0835	0.4	1500	2.0	● 2052	0.4
30	W	0319	2.0	0911	0.4	1535	2.0	2124	0.4

DECEMBER

Date	Day	Time	m	Time	m	Time	m	Time	m
1	TH	0351	2.0	0943	0.4	1607	1.9	2154	0.4
2	F	0420	2.0	1015	0.4	1636	1.9	2226	0.4
3	SA	0447	2.0	1049	0.4	1706	1.9	2300	0.4
4	SU	0516	2.0	1127	0.4	1741	1.9	2339	0.4
5	M	0551	2.0	1209	0.3	1821	1.9		
6	TU	0023	0.4	0633	2.1	1256	0.3	1910	1.8
7	W	0112	0.4	0722	2.0	1348	0.3	◐ 2006	1.8
8	TH	0206	0.5	0820	2.0	1448	0.4	2112	1.8
9	F	0308	0.5	0928	2.0	1553	0.4	2225	1.8
10	SA	0415	0.5	1045	2.0	1701	0.4	2336	1.8
11	SU	0525	0.5	1157	2.0	1806	0.3		
12	M	0039	1.9	0629	0.4	1303	2.0	1903	0.3
13	TU	0137	2.0	0727	0.3	1401	2.0	1956	0.3
14	W	0230	2.0	0821	0.2	1455	2.0	○ 2045	0.2
15	TH	0318	2.0	0911	0.2	1546	2.0	2132	0.2
16	F	0404	2.1	0959	0.2	1633	2.0	2217	0.3
17	SA	0448	2.1	1047	0.2	1720	1.9	2302	0.3
18	SU	0532	2.1	1134	0.2	1806	1.8	2347	0.4
19	M	0617	2.0	1223	0.3	1853	1.8		
20	TU	0034	0.4	0704	2.0	1313	0.3	1944	1.7
21	W	0124	0.5	0757	2.0	1408	0.4	◑ 2039	1.7
22	TH	0219	0.5	0856	1.9	1509	0.5	2139	1.7
23	F	0323	0.6	1000	1.9	1615	0.5	2241	1.8
24	SA	0432	0.6	1103	1.9	1719	0.5	2340	1.8
25	SU	0539	0.5	1202	1.9	1815	0.4		
26	M	0036	1.9	0636	0.5	1257	1.9	1905	0.4
27	TU	0126	1.9	0727	0.4	1347	1.9	1948	0.4
28	W	0212	1.9	0811	0.4	1432	1.9	2027	0.4
29	TH	0254	2.0	0849	0.4	1512	1.9	● 2100	0.4
30	F	0330	2.0	0924	0.4	1549	1.8	2133	0.4
31	SA	0403	2.0	0958	0.3	1623	1.8	2208	0.3

Chart Datum: 0·69 metres below Dansk Normal Null
HAT is 2·2 metres above Chart Datum

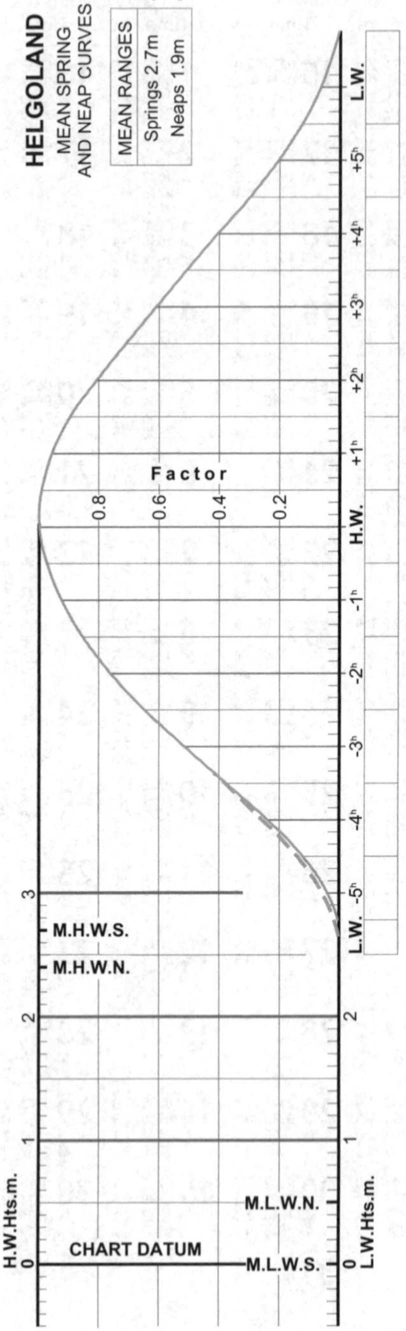
HELGOLAND
MEAN SPRING
AND NEAP CURVES
MEAN RANGES
Springs 2.7m
Neaps 1.9m
Factor
0.8
0.6
0.4
0.2
L.W.
+5h
+4h
+3h
+2h
+1h
H.W.
-1h
-2h
-3h
-4h
-5h
L.W.
H.W.Hts.m.
L.W.Hts.m.
M.H.W.S.
M.H.W.N.
CHART DATUM
M.L.W.N.
M.L.W.S.
0
1
2
3

TIME ZONE -0100
(German Standard Time)
Subtract 1 hour for UT
For German Summer Time add ONE hour in **non-shaded areas**

GERMANY – HELGOLAND

LAT 54°11'N LONG 7°53'E

TIMES AND HEIGHTS OF HIGH AND LOW WATERS

Dates in amber are **SPRINGS**
Dates in yellow are **NEAPS**

2016

JANUARY

Date	Time	m	Date	Time	m
1	0354	3.1	16	0353	3.2
	1041	0.8		1048	0.5
F	1624	2.8	SA	1624	2.9
	2249	0.9		2301	0.6
2	0434	3.0	17	0444	3.2
	1120	0.9		1137	0.6
SA	1707	2.7	SU	1716	2.9
◑	2333	0.9	◐	2353	0.7
3	0521	2.9	18	0540	3.1
	1206	0.9		1231	0.7
SU	1757	2.7	M	1815	2.8
4	0029	1.0	19	0057	0.8
	0620	2.9		0646	3.0
M	1306	0.9	TU	1337	0.7
	1900	2.7		1925	2.8
5	0139	1.0	20	0216	0.8
	0730	2.8		0803	2.9
TU	1417	0.9	W	1455	0.8
	2010	2.8		2043	2.9
6	0252	1.0	21	0337	0.7
	0840	2.9		0921	2.9
W	1526	0.9	TH	1611	0.7
	2114	2.9		2154	3.0
7	0359	0.9	22	0449	0.6
	0942	2.9		1028	2.9
TH	1625	0.8	F	1716	0.6
	2210	2.9		2254	3.0
8	0455	0.8	23	0547	0.5
	1035	3.0		1146	2.9
F	1715	0.7	SA	1807	0.5
	2258	3.0		2344	3.1
9	0543	0.7	24	0635	0.4
	1121	3.0		1210	3.0
SA	1800	0.7	SU	1850	0.5
	2341	3.1	○		
10	0627	0.6	25	0026	3.2
	1205	3.1		0717	0.4
SU	1843	0.6	M	1250	3.0
●				1928	0.5
11	0022	3.2	26	0106	3.3
	0710	0.6		0756	0.5
M	1248	3.1	TU	1329	3.0
	1927	0.6		2006	0.5
12	0103	3.2	27	0144	3.3
	0753	0.5		0833	0.6
TU	1331	3.1	W	1406	3.0
	2008	0.5		2041	0.6
13	0143	3.3	28	0220	3.2
	0834	0.4		0906	0.6
W	1411	3.0	TH	1440	3.0
	2048	0.5		2112	0.6
14	0222	3.3	29	0252	3.2
	0915	0.4		0938	0.6
TH	1450	3.0	F	1514	2.9
	2128	0.5		2144	0.6
15	0305	3.3	30	0324	3.1
	1000	0.4		1009	0.7
F	1535	2.9	SA	1548	2.9
	2213	0.5		2216	0.7
			31	0358	3.0
				1040	0.7
			SU	1622	2.8
				2249	0.8

FEBRUARY

Date	Time	m	Date	Time	m
1	0433	3.0	16	0518	3.0
	1111	0.8		1202	0.6
M	1659	2.7	TU	1744	2.8
◑	2330	0.8			
2	0518	2.8	17	0032	0.6
	1158	0.9		0620	2.8
TU	1751	2.7	W	1306	0.7
				1855	2.8
3	0031	0.9	18	0152	0.7
	0621	2.7		0741	2.8
W	1307	0.9	TH	1431	0.8
	1902	2.7		2020	2.8
4	0150	0.9	19	0321	0.7
	0741	2.7		0907	2.8
TH	1429	0.9	F	1556	0.7
	2021	2.7		2141	2.9
5	0312	0.9	20	0440	0.6
	0859	2.8		1020	2.8
F	1544	0.8	SA	1705	0.6
	2132	2.8		2244	3.0
6	0422	0.7	21	0537	0.4
	1004	2.8		1114	2.9
SA	1647	0.7	SU	1754	0.5
	2230	3.0		2331	3.1
7	0519	0.6	22	0621	0.4
	1059	2.9		1156	2.9
SU	1739	0.6	M	1835	0.5
	2318	3.1	○		
8	0608	0.5	23	0010	3.1
	1146	3.0		0700	0.4
M	1827	0.5	TU	1233	2.9
●				1912	0.5
9	0002	3.2	24	0046	3.2
	0654	0.4		0735	0.4
TU	1230	3.0	W	1307	3.0
	1912	0.5		1946	0.4
10	0044	3.2	25	0121	3.2
	0739	0.3		0808	0.5
W	1313	3.0	TH	1340	3.0
	1955	0.4		2018	0.4
11	0127	3.3	26	0154	3.1
	0822	0.2		0839	0.5
TH	1356	3.0	F	1412	3.0
	2037	0.3		2048	0.4
12	0209	3.3	27	0225	3.1
	0905	0.2		0909	0.5
F	1437	3.0	SA	1444	2.9
	2119	0.3		2119	0.5
13	0253	3.2	28	0257	3.1
	0949	0.3		0939	0.5
SA	1520	3.0	SU	1517	2.9
	2202	0.4		2150	0.5
14	0339	3.2	29	0328	3.0
	1033	0.4		1007	0.6
SU	1605	3.0	M	1547	2.9
	2247	0.5		2218	0.5
15	0427	3.1			
	1116	0.5			
M	1651	2.9			
◐	2333	0.5			

MARCH

Date	Time	m	Date	Time	m
1	0357	2.9	16	0457	2.9
	1031	0.6		1136	0.6
TU	1615	2.8	W	1719	2.9
	2248	0.6			
2	0430	2.8	17	0011	0.5
	1104	0.7		0559	2.7
W	1655	2.7	TH	1240	0.7
◑	2336	0.7		1830	2.8
3	0525	2.6	18	0130	0.6
	1206	0.8		0721	2.6
TH	1802	2.6	F	1407	0.8
				1958	2.8
4	0054	0.8	19	0304	0.6
	0645	2.6		0851	2.6
F	1333	0.9	SA	1538	0.7
	1928	2.6		2124	2.9
5	0225	0.8	20	0425	0.5
	0815	2.6		1006	2.7
SA	1503	0.8	SU	1649	0.6
	2052	2.8		2227	3.0
6	0348	0.6	21	0521	0.4
	0933	2.7		1057	2.8
SU	1617	0.6	M	1735	0.5
	2159	2.9		2309	3.0
7	0453	0.5	22	0559	0.3
	1033	2.9		1134	2.9
M	1716	0.5	TU	1812	0.4
	2252	3.0		2346	3.0
8	0546	0.3	23	0634	0.3
	1123	3.0		1208	2.9
TU	1806	0.4	W	1848	0.4
	2337	3.2	○		
9	0634	0.3	24	0022	3.1
	1207	3.0		0708	0.3
W	1852	0.3	TH	1241	2.9
●				1923	0.3
10	0021	3.2	25	0056	3.0
	0719	0.2		0741	0.4
TH	1251	3.0	F	1313	2.9
	1937	0.2		1955	0.3
11	0106	3.2	26	0128	3.0
	0804	0.1		0811	0.4
F	1336	3.0	SA	1345	2.9
	2021	0.2		2025	0.3
12	0152	3.2	27	0159	3.0
	0849	0.2		0841	0.4
SA	1419	3.0	SU	1416	2.9
	2105	0.2		2055	0.3
13	0237	3.2	28	0230	3.0
	0931	0.2		0911	0.4
SU	1502	3.0	M	1448	2.9
	2148	0.2		2126	0.4
14	0322	3.1	29	0301	2.9
	1012	0.3		0938	0.4
M	1544	3.0	TU	1517	2.9
	2230	0.3		2153	0.4
15	0408	3.0	30	0330	2.8
	1051	0.5		1001	0.5
TU	1627	3.0	W	1544	2.8
◐	2314	0.4		2220	0.5
			31	0401	2.7
				1030	0.6
			TH	1619	2.7
			◑	2302	0.6

APRIL

Date	Time	m	Date	Time	m
1	0448	2.6	16	0107	0.6
	1125	0.8		0658	2.5
F	1718	2.6	SA	1339	0.7
				1929	2.8
2	0012	0.7	17	0235	0.5
	0604	2.5		0823	2.5
SA	1249	0.8	SU	1507	0.7
	1843	2.7		2052	2.8
3	0144	0.7	18	0354	0.4
	0734	2.6		0936	2.6
SU	1423	0.8	M	1618	0.5
	2010	2.8		2155	2.9
4	0312	0.5	19	0449	0.3
	0858	2.7		1026	2.7
M	1543	0.6	TU	1704	0.4
	2123	2.9		2238	2.9
5	0422	0.4	20	0526	0.3
	1003	2.8		1102	2.8
TU	1646	0.4	W	1741	0.4
	2220	3.0		2315	3.0
6	0518	0.2	21	0600	0.3
	1056	2.9		1137	2.9
W	1740	0.3	TH	1819	0.4
	2310	3.1		2353	3.0
7	0609	0.2	22	0637	0.3
	1143	3.0		1213	2.9
TH	1829	0.2	F	1857	0.3
●	2357	3.2	○		
8	0657	0.1	23	0030	3.0
	1228	3.0		0712	0.3
F	1916	0.2	SA	1247	2.9
				1931	0.3
9	0044	3.2	24	0102	3.0
	0743	0.1		0744	0.3
SA	1313	3.0	SU	1319	2.9
	2002	0.1		2002	0.3
10	0132	3.2	25	0134	2.9
	0827	0.1		0814	0.3
SU	1357	3.1	M	1350	2.9
	2047	0.1		2033	0.3
11	0219	3.1	26	0206	2.9
	0910	0.2		0843	0.3
M	1441	3.1	TU	1421	2.9
	2131	0.2		2104	0.3
12	0304	3.0	27	0238	2.9
	0950	0.3		0912	0.4
TU	1523	3.0	W	1453	2.9
	2213	0.2		2134	0.3
13	0350	2.9	28	0311	2.8
	1029	0.4		0941	0.5
W	1607	3.0	TH	1524	2.9
	2258	0.4		2205	0.4
14	0441	2.8	29	0346	2.7
	1115	0.6		1015	0.6
TH	1659	2.9	F	1601	2.9
◐	2354	0.5		2246	0.5
15	0541	2.6	30	0432	2.7
	1217	0.7		1105	0.7
F	1807	2.8	SA	1655	2.8
			◑	2349	0.6

Chart Datum: 1·68 metres below Normal Null (German reference level)
HAT is 3·0 metres above Chart Datum

TIME ZONE -0100
(German Standard Time)
Subtract 1 hour for UT
For German Summer Time add ONE hour in **non-shaded areas**

GERMANY – HELGOLAND

LAT 54°11'N LONG 7°53'E

TIMES AND HEIGHTS OF HIGH AND LOW WATERS

Dates in amber are **SPRINGS**
Dates in yellow are **NEAPS**

2016

MAY

Date	Day	Time	m	Time	m	Time	m	Time	m
1	SU	0538	2.6	1219	0.7	1809	2.8		
2	M	0111	0.6	0700	2.6	1346	0.7	1931	2.8
3	TU	0235	0.5	0821	2.7	1506	0.6	2045	3.0
4	W	0346	0.3	0929	2.8	1612	0.5	2147	3.0
5	TH	0446	0.2	1027	2.9	1711	0.3	2243	3.1
6	F	0542	0.2	1119	3.0	1807	0.2	● 2335	3.2
7	SA	0634	0.1	1206	3.0	1856	0.2		
8	SU	0024	3.1	0720	0.1	1250	3.1	1943	0.1
9	M	0112	3.1	0804	0.2	1335	3.1	2029	0.1
10	TU	0200	3.0	0848	0.2	1421	3.1	2114	0.2
11	W	0249	3.0	0929	0.3	1506	3.1	2158	0.3
12	TH	0336	2.9	1011	0.4	1551	3.0	2244	0.4
13	F	0426	2.8	1057	0.6	1642	3.0	◐ 2336	0.5
14	SA	0522	2.7	1153	0.7	1740	2.9		
15	SU	0038	0.6	0626	2.6	1302	0.7	1849	2.8
16	M	0151	0.5	0738	2.5	1419	0.6	2003	2.8
17	TU	0303	0.5	0848	2.6	1528	0.5	2108	2.8
18	W	0401	0.4	0942	2.7	1622	0.5	2158	2.9
19	TH	0445	0.3	1024	2.8	1705	0.4	2241	2.9
20	F	0524	0.4	1103	2.9	1747	0.4	2322	2.9
21	SA	0604	0.4	1144	3.0	1828	0.4	○	
22	SU	0002	3.0	0643	0.4	1221	3.0	1905	0.3
23	M	0036	3.0	0716	0.3	1254	3.0	1939	0.3
24	TU	0110	2.9	0749	0.3	1326	3.0	2012	0.3
25	W	0145	2.9	0821	0.4	1400	3.0	2045	0.4
26	TH	0221	2.9	0853	0.4	1434	3.0	2119	0.4
27	F	0258	2.9	0928	0.5	1511	3.0	2157	0.4
28	SA	0339	2.8	1009	0.6	1554	3.0	2243	0.5
29	SU	0426	2.8	1058	0.6	1644	3.0	◑ 2339	0.5
30	M	0523	2.7	1200	0.7	1746	2.9		
31	TU	0047	0.5	0632	2.7	1314	0.7	1858	3.0

JUNE

Date	Day	Time	m	Time	m	Time	m	Time	m
1	W	0201	0.4	0746	2.7	1430	0.6	2011	3.0
2	TH	0311	0.4	0856	2.8	1540	0.5	2118	3.1
3	F	0416	0.3	0958	2.9	1645	0.4	2219	3.1
4	SA	0517	0.2	1055	3.0	1745	0.3	2317	3.1
5	SU	0613	0.2	1146	3.0	1838	0.2	●	
6	M	0008	3.1	0700	0.2	1231	3.1	1925	0.1
7	TU	0056	3.0	0744	0.2	1316	3.1	2012	0.2
8	W	0145	3.0	0829	0.3	1404	3.2	2059	0.3
9	TH	0234	3.0	0912	0.4	1450	3.2	2143	0.3
10	F	0321	2.9	0954	0.5	1534	3.1	2227	0.4
11	SA	0406	2.8	1036	0.6	1619	3.1	2312	0.6
12	SU	0454	2.7	1122	0.7	1707	3.0	◐	
13	M	0000	0.6	0545	2.7	1216	0.7	1801	2.9
14	TU	0055	0.6	0643	2.6	1318	0.7	1904	2.8
15	W	0158	0.6	0746	2.6	1426	0.6	2010	2.8
16	TH	0302	0.6	0848	2.7	1530	0.6	2112	2.9
17	F	0358	0.5	0942	2.8	1625	0.6	2204	2.9
18	SA	0447	0.5	1029	2.9	1713	0.5	2251	2.9
19	SU	0532	0.5	1113	3.0	1758	0.5	2334	3.0
20	M	0613	0.5	1153	3.1	1839	0.4	○	
21	TU	0013	3.0	0652	0.4	1230	3.1	1917	0.4
22	W	0051	3.0	0729	0.4	1307	3.1	1954	0.4
23	TH	0129	3.0	0805	0.5	1343	3.2	2031	0.4
24	F	0207	3.0	0841	0.5	1419	3.2	2108	0.4
25	SA	0245	2.9	0919	0.5	1459	3.2	2150	0.4
26	SU	0329	2.9	1003	0.5	1546	3.1	2239	0.4
27	M	0418	2.8	1053	0.6	1636	3.1	◑ 2330	0.5
28	TU	0511	2.8	1146	0.6	1730	3.1		
29	W	0026	0.5	0609	2.8	1248	0.6	1833	3.0
30	TH	0130	0.5	0715	2.8	1400	0.7	1943	3.0

JULY

Date	Day	Time	m	Time	m	Time	m	Time	m
1	F	0241	0.5	0825	2.9	1515	0.6	2055	3.0
2	SA	0352	0.5	0933	2.9	1625	0.5	2202	3.0
3	SU	0457	0.4	1035	3.0	1729	0.3	2303	3.0
4	M	0555	0.3	1130	3.0	1824	0.3	● 2357	3.0
5	TU	0644	0.3	1217	3.1	1912	0.2		
6	W	0045	3.0	0728	0.4	1302	3.2	1957	0.3
7	TH	0131	3.0	0812	0.4	1348	3.3	2042	0.4
8	F	0217	3.0	0854	0.5	1432	3.3	2124	0.5
9	SA	0259	3.0	0933	0.5	1511	3.2	2202	0.5
10	SU	0339	2.9	1009	0.6	1550	3.1	2240	0.6
11	M	0419	2.8	1047	0.7	1630	3.1	2318	0.7
12	TU	0501	2.8	1128	0.7	1713	3.0	◐ 2358	0.7
13	W	0546	2.7	1217	0.8	1804	2.9		
14	TH	0050	0.8	0641	2.7	1319	0.8	1908	2.8
15	F	0155	0.8	0747	2.7	1431	0.8	2018	2.8
16	SA	0305	0.7	0853	2.8	1541	0.7	2124	2.9
17	SU	0408	0.7	0952	2.9	1640	0.7	2220	2.9
18	M	0500	0.6	1043	3.0	1730	0.6	2308	3.0
19	TU	0547	0.6	1128	3.1	1814	0.5	○ 2352	3.0
20	W	0630	0.6	1209	3.2	1857	0.5		
21	TH	0033	3.1	0712	0.5	1248	3.2	1938	0.5
22	F	0113	3.1	0752	0.5	1326	3.3	2017	0.4
23	SA	0151	3.0	0829	0.5	1404	3.3	2056	0.4
24	SU	0230	3.0	0908	0.4	1446	3.2	2139	0.4
25	M	0315	2.9	0953	0.5	1533	3.2	2228	0.4
26	TU	0404	2.9	1041	0.5	1624	3.2	2316	0.5
27	W	0454	2.9	1130	0.6	1714	3.1	◑	
28	TH	0003	0.6	0545	2.9	1225	0.7	1811	3.0
29	F	0101	0.7	0647	2.9	1336	0.7	1922	3.0
30	SA	0214	0.7	0801	2.9	1457	0.7	2041	3.0
31	SU	0334	0.7	0917	3.0	1614	0.6	2154	3.0

AUGUST

Date	Day	Time	m	Time	m	Time	m	Time	m
1	M	0444	0.6	1024	3.0	1719	0.4	2256	3.0
2	TU	0542	0.5	1119	3.1	1812	0.4	● 2348	3.0
3	W	0630	0.5	1206	3.2	1859	0.4		
4	TH	0033	3.0	0713	0.5	1248	3.3	1941	0.4
5	F	0114	3.0	0754	0.5	1329	3.3	2021	0.5
6	SA	0154	3.1	0832	0.5	1408	3.3	2057	0.5
7	SU	0231	3.0	0906	0.6	1444	3.2	2131	0.6
8	M	0306	3.0	0939	0.6	1518	3.2	2204	0.6
9	TU	0342	2.9	1012	0.7	1554	3.1	2236	0.7
10	W	0418	2.9	1046	0.7	1630	3.0	◐ 2308	0.8
11	TH	0453	2.8	1123	0.8	1710	2.9	2347	0.9
12	F	0538	2.7	1216	0.9	1807	2.8		
13	SA	0048	0.9	0643	2.7	1330	0.9	1921	2.7
14	SU	0207	0.9	0801	2.8	1452	0.9	2041	2.8
15	M	0326	0.8	0914	2.9	1605	0.8	2149	2.8
16	TU	0430	0.7	1013	3.0	1702	0.7	2244	2.9
17	W	0522	0.7	1102	3.1	1750	0.6	2330	3.0
18	TH	0609	0.6	1145	3.2	1835	0.5	○	
19	F	0012	3.1	0653	0.5	1225	3.3	1918	0.4
20	SA	0053	3.1	0734	0.5	1306	3.3	2000	0.4
21	SU	0133	3.1	0814	0.4	1347	3.3	2041	0.4
22	M	0213	3.1	0854	0.4	1430	3.3	2124	0.4
23	TU	0256	3.0	0938	0.4	1516	3.2	2209	0.5
24	W	0342	3.0	1024	0.5	1605	3.2	2253	0.6
25	TH	0429	3.0	1110	0.6	1655	3.1	◑ 2337	0.7
26	F	0519	3.0	1203	0.7	1751	3.0		
27	SA	0034	0.8	0622	2.9	1316	0.8	1905	2.9
28	SU	0153	0.9	0744	2.9	1445	0.8	2032	2.9
29	M	0321	0.9	0909	3.0	1609	0.7	2151	2.9
30	TU	0437	0.7	1018	3.1	1713	0.5	2250	3.0
31	W	0531	0.6	1108	3.2	1800	0.5	2335	3.0

Chart Datum: 1·68 metres below Normal Null (German reference level)
HAT is 3·0 metres above Chart Datum

TIME ZONE -0100
(German Standard Time)
Subtract 1 hour for UT
For German Summer Time add ONE hour in **non-shaded areas**

GERMANY – HELGOLAND

LAT 54°11'N LONG 7°53'E

TIMES AND HEIGHTS OF HIGH AND LOW WATERS

Dates in amber are **SPRINGS**
Dates in yellow are **NEAPS**

2016

SEPTEMBER

Date	Time	m	Time	m	Time	m	Time	m
1 TH ●	0614	0.6	1150	3.2	1840	0.4		
2 F	0014	3.0	0653	0.6	1229	3.2	1919	0.5
3 SA	0052	3.1	0731	0.6	1306	3.2	1955	0.5
4 SU	0127	3.1	0806	0.5	1342	3.2	2027	0.6
5 M	0201	3.1	0838	0.6	1415	3.2	2058	0.6
6 TU	0233	3.0	0908	0.6	1447	3.1	2128	0.6
7 W	0306	3.0	0940	0.6	1519	3.1	2158	0.7
8 TH	0338	2.9	1010	0.7	1551	3.0	2224	0.8
9 F	0409	2.9	1039	0.8	1625	2.8	◐ 2255	0.9
10 SA	0446	2.8	1123	0.9	1714	2.7	2349	1.0
11 SU	0545	2.7	1233	1.0	1828	2.6		
12 M	0110	1.1	0708	2.7	1403	1.0	1956	2.7
13 TU	0241	1.0	0832	2.8	1527	0.9	2115	2.8
14 W	0357	0.9	0940	3.0	1633	0.7	2216	2.9
15 TH	0455	0.7	1032	3.1	1723	0.6	2305	3.0
16 F	0544	0.6	1117	3.2	1809	0.5	○ 2348	3.1
17 SA	0629	0.5	1159	3.3	1854	0.4		
18 SU	0030	3.1	0713	0.5	1242	3.3	1938	0.4
19 M	0112	3.1	0756	0.4	1327	3.3	2021	0.4
20 TU	0154	3.1	0838	0.4	1412	3.3	2104	0.5
21 W	0236	3.2	0921	0.4	1457	3.2	2145	0.6
22 TH	0318	3.1	1004	0.5	1544	3.1	2226	0.7
23 F	0403	3.1	1049	0.6	1634	3.0	◑ 2311	0.8
24 SA	0455	3.0	1144	0.7	1733	2.9		
25 SU	0010	1.0	0602	2.9	1258	0.8	1851	2.8
26 M	0133	1.0	0728	2.9	1431	0.8	2021	2.8
27 TU	0306	1.0	0856	3.0	1559	0.8	2142	2.9
28 W	0423	0.9	1005	3.1	1701	0.6	2238	2.9
29 TH	0515	0.7	1051	3.2	1740	0.5	2315	3.0
30 F	0552	0.6	1127	3.2	1814	0.5	2349	3.0

OCTOBER

Date	Time	m	Time	m	Time	m	Time	m
1 SA ●	0628	0.6	1204	3.2	1851	0.5		
2 SU	0025	3.0	0706	0.6	1242	3.2	1926	0.5
3 M	0100	3.1	0740	0.5	1316	3.1	1957	0.6
4 TU	0132	3.1	0811	0.5	1347	3.1	2027	0.6
5 W	0203	3.1	0840	0.6	1417	3.1	2055	0.6
6 TH	0233	3.0	0910	0.6	1447	3.0	2122	0.6
7 F	0303	3.0	0939	0.7	1518	2.9	2147	0.8
8 SA	0332	2.9	1007	0.8	1551	2.8	2217	0.9
9 SU	0407	2.9	1045	0.9	1636	2.7	◐ 2305	1.1
10 M	0501	2.8	1149	1.0	1744	2.6		
11 TU	0022	1.1	0619	2.8	1316	1.0	1911	2.7
12 W	0154	1.1	0747	2.9	1445	0.9	2035	2.8
13 TH	0317	0.9	0901	3.0	1556	0.7	2142	2.9
14 F	0421	0.8	0958	3.1	1652	0.6	2235	3.0
15 SA	0514	0.7	1047	3.2	1741	0.5	2322	3.1
16 SU ○	0603	0.6	1133	3.3	1828	0.4		
17 M	0006	3.1	0650	0.5	1219	3.3	1914	0.4
18 TU	0049	3.2	0735	0.4	1305	3.3	1958	0.4
19 W	0132	3.2	0820	0.4	1352	3.3	2041	0.5
20 TH	0215	3.2	0904	0.4	1439	3.2	2123	0.6
21 F	0257	3.2	0947	0.5	1525	3.0	2203	0.7
22 SA	0342	3.1	1033	0.6	1616	2.9	◑ 2249	0.9
23 SU	0435	3.1	1128	0.8	1717	2.8	2349	1.0
24 M	0541	3.0	1239	0.9	1831	2.7		
25 TU	0107	1.1	0702	2.9	1404	0.9	1956	2.7
26 W	0236	1.0	0827	3.0	1529	0.8	2114	2.8
27 TH	0354	0.9	0936	3.0	1632	0.7	2211	2.9
28 F	0447	0.8	1024	3.1	1711	0.6	2248	2.9
29 SA	0524	0.7	1100	3.1	1744	0.6	2321	3.0
30 SU	0600	0.6	1138	3.1	1820	0.6	● 2358	3.0
31 M	0639	0.6	1216	3.1	1856	0.6		

NOVEMBER

Date	Time	m	Time	m	Time	m	Time	m
1 TU	0033	3.1	0714	0.5	1250	3.1	1929	0.6
2 W	0105	3.1	0745	0.5	1320	3.1	1958	0.6
3 TH	0135	3.1	0815	0.5	1351	3.0	2026	0.6
4 F	0205	3.1	0845	0.6	1422	3.0	2053	0.6
5 SA	0235	3.0	0914	0.6	1454	2.9	2121	0.8
6 SU	0306	3.0	0945	0.7	1529	2.8	2154	0.9
7 M	0343	3.0	1023	0.9	1613	2.8	◐ 2240	1.0
8 TU	0432	2.9	1120	1.0	1712	2.7	2346	1.1
9 W	0539	2.9	1236	0.9	1829	2.7		
10 TH	0110	1.1	0700	2.9	1400	0.9	1951	2.7
11 F	0233	1.0	0818	3.0	1515	0.7	2103	2.9
12 SA	0343	0.8	0922	3.1	1617	0.6	2202	3.0
13 SU	0443	0.7	1018	3.2	1712	0.5	2255	3.1
14 M	0538	0.6	1110	3.2	1804	0.4	○ 2343	3.1
15 TU	0629	0.5	1158	3.3	1851	0.4		
16 W	0027	3.2	0715	0.4	1245	3.2	1936	0.4
17 TH	0111	3.2	0802	0.4	1334	3.2	2021	0.5
18 F	0157	3.2	0850	0.4	1424	3.1	2105	0.6
19 SA	0242	3.3	0935	0.5	1512	3.0	2147	0.7
20 SU	0327	3.2	1020	0.6	1602	2.9	2233	0.8
21 M	0417	3.1	1111	0.7	1657	2.8	◑ 2327	1.0
22 TU	0515	3.1	1211	0.8	1801	2.7		
23 W	0032	1.0	0623	3.0	1322	0.8	1912	2.6
24 TH	0148	1.0	0738	2.9	1436	0.8	2025	2.7
25 F	0302	0.9	0849	2.9	1542	0.7	2127	2.8
26 SA	0404	0.8	0946	3.0	1632	0.7	2213	2.9
27 SU	0450	0.8	1030	3.1	1712	0.7	2251	3.0
28 M	0532	0.7	1111	3.1	1751	0.7	2330	3.0
29 TU ●	0612	0.6	1150	3.0	1828	0.6		
30 W	0007	3.1	0649	0.6	1225	3.0	1902	0.6

DECEMBER

Date	Time	m	Time	m	Time	m	Time	m
1 TH	0040	3.1	0722	0.5	1258	3.0	1933	0.6
2 F	0112	3.1	0754	0.6	1331	3.0	2004	0.6
3 SA	0144	3.1	0826	0.6	1404	3.0	2034	0.7
4 SU	0215	3.1	0857	0.7	1438	3.0	2106	0.7
5 M	0249	3.1	0932	0.7	1515	2.9	2142	0.8
6 TU	0328	3.1	1013	0.8	1558	2.8	2227	0.9
7 W	0414	3.1	1103	0.8	1650	2.8	◐ 2322	1.0
8 TH	0510	3.0	1205	0.8	1754	2.7		
9 F	0031	1.0	0620	3.0	1317	0.8	1908	2.8
10 SA	0149	0.9	0735	3.0	1432	0.8	2022	2.9
11 SU	0304	0.9	0847	3.1	1542	0.7	2128	3.0
12 M	0413	0.7	0951	3.1	1645	0.6	2228	3.0
13 TU	0515	0.6	1050	3.1	1743	0.4	2321	3.1
14 W ○	0611	0.4	1142	3.1	1832	0.4		
15 TH	0008	3.2	0700	0.4	1231	3.1	1918	0.4
16 F	0054	3.2	0748	0.4	1321	3.1	2004	0.5
17 SA	0142	3.3	0837	0.4	1412	3.1	2051	0.6
18 SU	0230	3.3	0924	0.5	1500	3.0	2134	0.6
19 M	0313	3.3	1007	0.6	1545	2.9	2215	0.7
20 TU	0356	3.2	1050	0.7	1631	2.8	2300	0.8
21 W	0443	3.1	1136	0.8	1721	2.7	◑ 2350	0.9
22 TH	0536	3.0	1228	0.8	1817	2.7		
23 F	0049	0.9	0638	2.9	1329	0.8	1921	2.6
24 SA	0157	0.9	0747	2.9	1437	0.8	2028	2.7
25 SU	0307	0.9	0856	2.9	1542	0.8	2128	2.8
26 M	0410	0.8	0954	3.0	1636	0.8	2218	2.9
27 TU	0502	0.8	1042	3.0	1722	0.7	2303	3.0
28 W	0546	0.7	1125	3.0	1802	0.7	2343	3.1
29 TH ●	0625	0.6	1203	3.0	1839	0.6		
30 F	0019	3.1	0702	0.6	1239	3.0	1914	0.6
31 SA	0053	3.1	0737	0.6	1315	3.0	1949	0.6

Chart Datum: 1·68 metres below Normal Null (German reference level)
HAT is 3·0 metres above Chart Datum

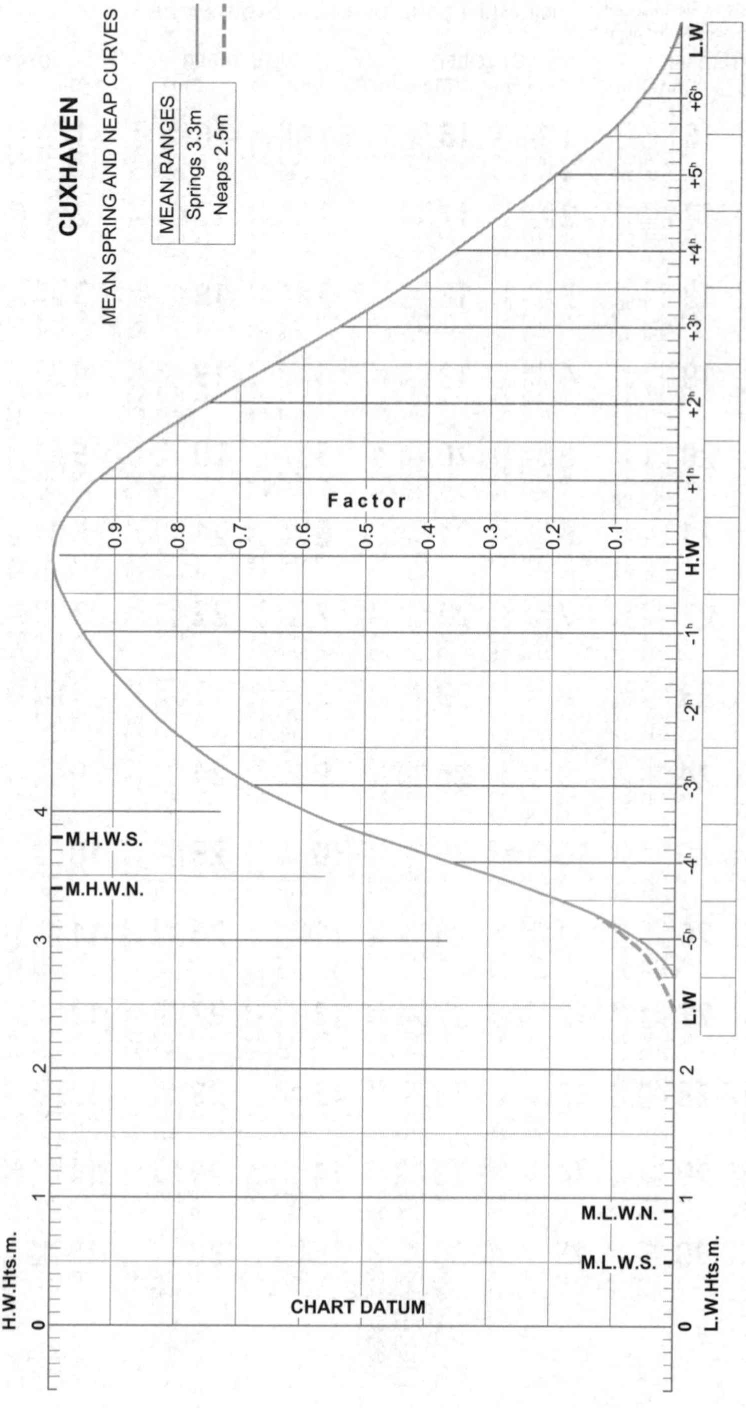
CUXHAVEN
MEAN SPRING AND NEAP CURVES
MEAN RANGES
Springs 3.3m
Neaps 2.5m
Factor
0.9
0.8
0.7
0.6
0.5
0.4
0.3
0.2
0.1
L.W
-5h
-4h
-3h
-2h
-1h
H.W
+1h
+2h
+3h
+4h
+5h
+6h
L.W
H.W.Hts.m.
0
1
2
3
4
M.H.W.S.
M.H.W.N.
CHART DATUM
L.W.Hts.m.
M.L.W.S.
M.L.W.N.

TIME ZONE -0100
(German Standard Time)
Subtract 1 hour for UT
For German Summer Time add ONE hour in **non-shaded areas**

GERMANY – CUXHAVEN

LAT 53°52'N LONG 8°43'E

TIMES AND HEIGHTS OF HIGH AND LOW WATERS

Dates in amber are **SPRINGS**
Dates in yellow are **NEAPS**

2016

JANUARY

Date	Day	Moon	Time	m	Time	m	Time	m	Time	m
1	F		0508	3.6	1202	0.7	1739	3.3		
2	SA	◑	0007	0.8	0547	3.5	1236	0.8	1821	3.2
3	SU		0048	0.9	0633	3.4	1320	0.8	1910	3.1
4	M		0140	0.9	0730	3.4	1419	0.9	2013	3.2
5	TU		0249	1.0	0840	3.4	1531	0.9	2123	3.3
6	W		0406	0.9	0950	3.4	1642	0.8	2228	3.4
7	TH		0516	0.9	1053	3.5	1743	0.7	2324	3.5
8	F		0616	0.7	1147	3.5	1836	0.7		
9	SA		0012	3.6	0706	0.6	1236	3.6	1923	0.6
10	SU	●	0055	3.7	0752	0.6	1321	3.6	2008	0.6
11	M		0137	3.7	0836	0.5	1405	3.6	2053	0.5
12	TU		0218	3.8	0920	0.5	1448	3.6	2135	0.5
13	W		0258	3.8	1002	0.4	1529	3.6	2212	0.5
14	TH		0336	3.8	1042	0.4	1609	3.5	2251	0.5
15	F		0418	3.8	1125	0.4	1653	3.5	2334	0.5
16	SA		0506	3.8	1211	0.5	1741	3.4		
17	SU	◐	0022	0.6	0557	3.7	1258	0.6	1832	3.4
18	M		0112	0.6	0652	3.6	1349	0.6	1930	3.3
19	TU		0214	0.7	0758	3.5	1454	0.7	2040	3.3
20	W		0331	0.8	0915	3.5	1613	0.7	2157	3.4
21	TH		0454	0.7	1033	3.5	1730	0.7	2308	3.5
22	F		0610	0.6	1141	3.5	1837	0.5		
23	SA		0009	3.6	0712	0.4	1239	3.5	1930	0.5
24	SU	○	0058	3.6	0801	0.4	1327	3.5	2013	0.5
25	M		0140	3.8	0842	0.4	1407	3.5	2051	0.5
26	TU		0219	3.8	0921	0.5	1445	3.5	2129	0.5
27	W		0257	3.9	0959	0.6	1521	3.5	2204	0.6
28	TH		0332	3.8	1032	0.6	1556	3.5	2235	0.6
29	F		0405	3.7	1102	0.6	1629	3.5	2305	0.6
30	SA		0438	3.7	1131	0.6	1703	3.4	2337	0.7
31	SU		0512	3.6	1159	0.7	1737	3.3		

FEBRUARY

Date	Day	Moon	Time	m	Time	m	Time	m	Time	m
1	M	◑	0007	0.7	0546	3.5	1227	0.7	1813	3.2
2	TU		0043	0.8	0629	3.4	1309	0.8	1904	3.2
3	W		0139	0.9	0731	3.3	1416	0.9	2014	3.2
4	TH		0258	0.9	0849	3.2	1538	0.9	2132	3.3
5	F		0424	0.8	1006	3.3	1658	0.7	2243	3.4
6	SA		0539	0.7	1114	3.4	1805	0.6	2342	3.5
7	SU		0640	0.6	1212	3.5	1902	0.6		
8	M	●	0031	3.7	0732	0.5	1302	3.6	1952	0.5
9	TU		0115	3.7	0819	0.4	1348	3.6	2038	0.4
10	W		0157	3.8	0905	0.3	1431	3.6	2121	0.3
11	TH		0239	3.9	0949	0.3	1513	3.6	2202	0.3
12	F		0321	3.9	1031	0.2	1555	3.6	2242	0.3
13	SA		0406	3.8	1113	0.3	1638	3.6	2325	0.4
14	SU		0453	3.8	1156	0.4	1723	3.5		
15	M	◐	0008	0.4	0540	3.7	1237	0.5	1808	3.5
16	TU		0051	0.5	0630	3.5	1320	0.6	1859	3.4
17	W		0146	0.6	0732	3.4	1420	0.7	2008	3.3
18	TH		0303	0.6	0852	3.3	1544	0.7	2132	3.3
19	F		0434	0.6	1019	3.3	1712	0.7	2252	3.4
20	SA		0557	0.5	1134	3.4	1824	0.6	2356	3.6
21	SU		0700	0.4	1230	3.4	1916	0.5		
22	M	○	0044	3.7	0746	0.4	1313	3.5	1956	0.5
23	TU		0123	3.7	0824	0.4	1349	3.5	2033	0.5
24	W		0159	3.8	0859	0.4	1422	3.5	2108	0.4
25	TH		0234	3.8	0932	0.4	1453	3.5	2140	0.4
26	F		0307	3.7	1003	0.5	1526	3.5	2210	0.4
27	SA		0338	3.7	1033	0.5	1558	3.5	2240	0.5
28	SU		0410	3.6	1102	0.5	1631	3.5	2311	0.5
29	M		0441	3.6	1127	0.5	1700	3.4	2337	0.5

MARCH

Date	Day	Moon	Time	m	Time	m	Time	m	Time	m
1	TU		0510	3.4	1147	0.6	1728	3.3		
2	W	◑	0002	0.6	0542	3.3	1215	0.7	1808	3.2
3	TH		0044	0.7	0635	3.1	1311	0.8	1913	3.1
4	F		0158	0.7	0753	3.1	1438	0.8	2038	3.2
5	SA		0333	0.7	0922	3.2	1612	0.7	2201	3.3
6	SU		0501	0.6	1041	3.3	1733	0.6	2310	3.5
7	M		0612	0.4	1146	3.4	1838	0.5		
8	TU		0004	3.6	0709	0.3	1239	3.5	1931	0.4
9	W	●	0051	3.7	0758	0.2	1326	3.6	2017	0.3
10	TH		0134	3.8	0844	0.2	1410	3.6	2101	0.2
11	F		0218	3.8	0929	0.1	1453	3.6	2145	0.2
12	SA		0304	3.8	1012	0.2	1536	3.6	2229	0.2
13	SU		0351	3.8	1054	0.2	1619	3.6	2311	0.2
14	M		0437	3.7	1135	0.3	1701	3.6	2352	0.3
15	TU	◐	0523	3.6	1212	0.4	1743	3.5		
16	W		0032	0.4	0611	3.4	1253	0.6	1833	3.4
17	TH		0122	0.5	0711	3.2	1351	0.7	1942	3.3
18	F		0238	0.6	0833	3.1	1516	0.7	2109	3.3
19	SA		0413	0.6	1003	3.2	1650	0.6	2234	3.4
20	SU		0540	0.5	1120	3.3	1805	0.5	2338	3.5
21	M		0640	0.3	1212	3.4	1855	0.4		
22	TU		0021	3.6	0721	0.3	1249	3.4	1932	0.4
23	W	○	0058	3.6	0756	0.3	1322	3.5	2008	0.4
24	TH		0134	3.6	0830	0.3	1354	3.5	2044	0.3
25	F		0208	3.6	0903	0.3	1426	3.5	2116	0.3
26	SA		0240	3.6	0934	0.3	1457	3.5	2146	0.3
27	SU		0312	3.6	1003	0.4	1529	3.5	2217	0.3
28	M		0343	3.5	1032	0.4	1601	3.5	2247	0.3
29	TU		0415	3.5	1057	0.4	1630	3.4	2313	0.3
30	W		0443	3.3	1118	0.4	1657	3.4	2336	0.4
31	TH	◑	0513	3.2	1142	0.6	1732	3.3		

APRIL

Date	Day	Moon	Time	m	Time	m	Time	m	Time	m
1	F		0012	0.5	0600	3.1	1231	0.7	1831	3.2
2	SA		0118	0.6	0714	3.0	1354	0.8	1953	3.2
3	SU		0251	0.6	0844	3.1	1531	0.7	2121	3.3
4	M		0424	0.5	1008	3.2	1657	0.5	2235	3.5
5	TU		0540	0.3	1116	3.3	1806	0.4	2333	3.6
6	W		0639	0.2	1212	3.5	1903	0.3		
7	TH	●	0024	3.7	0732	0.1	1302	3.5	1953	0.2
8	F		0111	3.8	0820	0.1	1346	3.6	2039	0.1
9	SA		0158	3.8	0905	0.1	1430	3.7	2125	0.1
10	SU		0246	3.8	0949	0.1	1514	3.7	2211	0.1
11	M		0334	3.7	1032	0.2	1557	3.7	2254	0.2
12	TU		0420	3.6	1111	0.3	1639	3.6	2335	0.2
13	W		0506	3.5	1149	0.4	1722	3.5		
14	TH	◐	0015	0.3	0555	3.3	1231	0.5	1813	3.5
15	F		0105	0.5	0655	3.2	1327	0.7	1918	3.4
16	SA		0215	0.5	0811	3.1	1446	0.7	2040	3.3
17	SU		0343	0.5	0936	3.1	1616	0.6	2202	3.4
18	M		0507	0.4	1050	3.2	1731	0.5	2306	3.5
19	TU		0606	0.3	1140	3.3	1822	0.4	2349	3.5
20	W		0645	0.2	1216	3.4	1859	0.3		
21	TH		0026	3.5	0720	0.3	1250	3.5	1938	0.3
22	F	○	0104	3.5	0758	0.3	1326	3.5	2017	0.3
23	SA		0141	3.5	0833	0.3	1400	3.5	2052	0.2
24	SU		0215	3.5	0905	0.3	1431	3.5	2123	0.2
25	M		0246	3.5	0934	0.3	1502	3.5	2154	0.2
26	TU		0319	3.4	1003	0.3	1534	3.5	2225	0.2
27	W		0352	3.4	1031	0.3	1605	3.5	2255	0.3
28	TH		0425	3.3	1058	0.4	1638	3.5	2324	0.4
29	F		0500	3.2	1129	0.5	1716	3.4		
30	SA	◑	0001	0.5	0546	3.2	1216	0.6	1809	3.3

Chart Datum: 2·06 metres below Normal Null (German reference level)
HAT is 4·1 metres above Chart Datum

TIME ZONE -0100
(German Standard Time)
Subtract 1 hour for UT
For German Summer Time add ONE hour in **non-shaded areas**

GERMANY – CUXHAVEN

LAT 53°52′N LONG 8°43′E

TIMES AND HEIGHTS OF HIGH AND LOW WATERS

Dates in amber are **SPRINGS**
Dates in yellow are **NEAPS**

2016

MAY

Date	Time	m	Date	Time	m
1 SU	0100 0651 1327 1922	0.5 3.1 0.7 3.3	16 M	0259 0852 1526 2115	0.5 3.0 0.6 3.3
2 M	0221 0814 1455 2044	0.5 3.1 0.6 3.4	17 TU	0414 1001 1639 2220	0.4 3.1 0.5 3.4
3 TU	0349 0935 1619 2159	0.4 3.2 0.5 3.5	18 W	0516 1056 1736 2310	0.3 3.2 0.4 3.4
4 W	0504 1044 1730 2301	0.3 3.3 0.4 3.6	19 TH	0601 1138 1821 2352	0.3 3.4 0.4 3.5
5 TH	0606 1143 1833 2357	0.2 3.4 0.3 3.7	20 F	0642 1217 1905	0.3 3.5 0.4
6 F ●	0703 1236 1929	0.1 3.5 0.2	21 SA ○	0034 0724 1257 1948	3.5 0.3 3.5 0.3
7 SA	0050 0756 1323 2019	3.7 0.1 3.6 0.1	22 SU	0114 0803 1334 2026	3.5 0.3 3.6 0.3
8 SU	0139 0842 1407 2105	3.7 0.1 3.7 0.1	23 M	0149 0837 1407 2100	3.5 0.3 3.6 0.3
9 M	0227 0925 1451 2151	3.7 0.1 3.7 0.1	24 TU	0224 0909 1439 2133	3.5 0.3 3.6 0.3
10 TU	0316 1008 1536 2237	3.6 0.2 3.7 0.2	25 W	0300 0941 1513 2207	3.4 0.3 3.6 0.3
11 W	0404 1050 1619 2320	3.5 0.3 3.7 0.3	26 TH	0336 1013 1547 2241	3.4 0.4 3.6 0.3
12 TH	0451 1130 1704	3.4 0.4 3.6	27 F	0413 1047 1625 2318	3.4 0.5 3.6 0.4
13 F ◐	0002 0540 1213 1754	0.4 3.3 0.5 3.5	28 SA	0454 1126 1708	3.3 0.6 3.6
14 SA	0050 0636 1304 1852	0.5 3.2 0.6 3.5	29 SU ◑	0001 0541 1214 1759	0.5 3.3 0.6 3.5
15 SU	0148 0740 1409 2001	0.5 3.1 0.7 3.4	30 M	0054 0639 1313 1901	0.5 3.2 0.6 3.5
			31 TU	0201 0749 1427 2013	0.5 3.2 0.6 3.5

JUNE

Date	Time	m	Date	Time	m
1 W	0315 0903 1544 2126	0.4 3.3 0.6 3.6	16 TH	0414 1002 1641 2224	0.5 3.2 0.6 3.4
2 TH	0428 1012 1657 2232	0.4 3.4 0.5 3.6	17 F	0512 1056 1739 2316	0.5 3.4 0.5 3.5
3 F	0534 1114 1804 2333	0.3 3.5 0.4 3.6	18 SA	0603 1143 1831	0.4 3.5 0.5
4 SA	0637 1211 1907	0.2 3.5 0.2	19 SU	0003 0649 1227 1918	3.5 0.4 3.6 0.4
5 SU ●	0031 0733 1302 2000	3.7 0.1 3.6 0.1	20 M ○	0046 0732 1307 2000	3.5 0.4 3.6 0.4
6 M	0123 0821 1347 2047	3.6 0.1 3.7 0.1	21 TU	0126 0811 1345 2038	3.5 0.4 3.7 0.4
7 TU	0212 0905 1432 2133	3.6 0.2 3.7 0.2	22 W	0205 0849 1421 2117	3.6 0.4 3.7 0.4
8 W	0301 0948 1518 2221	3.5 0.3 3.8 0.3	23 TH	0245 0926 1457 2154	3.5 0.4 3.8 0.4
9 TH	0350 1031 1602 2305	3.5 0.4 3.8 0.4	24 F	0324 1001 1533 2231	3.5 0.4 3.7 0.4
10 F	0436 1112 1646 2347	3.4 0.5 3.7 0.4	25 SA	0403 1038 1613 2313	3.5 0.5 3.7 0.4
11 SA	0522 1153 1731	3.4 0.5 3.6	26 SU	0446 1122 1659	3.4 0.5 3.7
12 SU ◐	0029 0609 1237 1820	0.5 3.3 0.6 3.5	27 M ◑	0000 0535 1211 1750	0.4 3.4 0.6 3.7
13 M	0113 0700 1326 1914	0.6 3.2 0.7 3.4	28 TU	0049 0628 1303 1845	0.5 3.3 0.6 3.7
14 TU	0206 0757 1426 2017	0.6 3.1 0.6 3.4	29 W	0143 0726 1403 1948	0.5 3.3 0.6 3.6
15 W	0308 0900 1534 2124	0.5 3.1 0.6 3.4	30 TH	0245 0833 1514 2059	0.5 3.4 0.6 3.6

JULY

Date	Time	m	Date	Time	m
1 F	0356 0943 1629 2209	0.5 3.4 0.6 3.6	16 SA	0416 1008 1652 2237	0.7 3.3 0.7 3.4
2 SA	0508 1050 1742 2316	0.4 3.5 0.4 3.6	17 SU	0521 1107 1755 2332	0.6 3.5 0.6 3.5
3 SU	0615 1151 1848	0.3 3.5 0.3	18 M	0616 1157 1848	0.5 3.6 0.5
4 M ●	0017 0715 1245 1945	3.6 0.2 3.6 0.2	19 TU ○	0021 0705 1242 1935	3.5 0.5 3.7 0.5
5 TU	0112 0805 1333 2034	3.6 0.2 3.7 0.2	20 W	0106 0750 1323 2019	3.6 0.5 3.8 0.5
6 W	0201 0849 1417 2119	3.5 0.3 3.8 0.3	21 TH	0149 0833 1402 2101	3.6 0.5 3.8 0.4
7 TH	0248 0932 1502 2204	3.6 0.4 3.9 0.4	22 F	0230 0914 1440 2141	3.6 0.4 3.9 0.4
8 F	0333 1014 1544 2246	3.6 0.5 3.9 0.5	23 SA	0310 0951 1517 2220	3.6 0.4 3.9 0.4
9 SA	0415 1052 1624 2324	3.5 0.5 3.8 0.5	24 SU	0349 1028 1558 2302	3.5 0.4 3.8 0.4
10 SU	0455 1128 1703 2359	3.4 0.6 3.7 0.6	25 M	0432 1112 1645 2349	3.5 0.5 3.8 0.4
11 M	0535 1205 1744	3.4 0.6 3.6	26 TU	0521 1201 1737	3.5 0.5 3.8
12 TU ◐	0034 0616 1243 1827	0.6 3.3 0.7 3.5	27 W ◑	0036 0610 1249 1829	0.5 3.5 0.6 3.7
13 W	0112 0701 1327 1918	0.7 3.2 0.8 3.4	28 TH	0122 0702 1342 1926	0.6 3.4 0.6 3.6
14 TH	0200 0756 1426 2022	0.7 3.2 0.8 3.4	29 F	0217 0804 1449 2037	0.6 3.4 0.7 3.5
15 F	0305 0901 1539 2132	0.7 3.2 0.8 3.4	30 SA	0329 0919 1610 2155	0.7 3.4 0.7 3.5
			31 SU	0449 1034 1730 2308	0.6 3.5 0.5 3.5

AUGUST

Date	Time	m	Date	Time	m
1 M	0602 1140 1838	0.5 3.6 0.4	16 TU	0544 1127 1820 2357	0.7 3.5 0.6 3.5
2 TU ●	0011 0702 1234 1934	3.5 0.4 3.7 0.3	17 W	0641 1216 1911	0.6 3.7 0.5
3 W	0104 0751 1321 2021	3.5 0.4 3.8 0.3	18 TH ○	0045 0730 1300 1958	3.6 0.6 3.8 0.5
4 TH	0150 0834 1403 2103	3.6 0.5 3.9 0.4	19 F	0130 0816 1340 2042	3.7 0.5 3.9 0.4
5 F	0232 0914 1443 2144	3.6 0.5 3.9 0.5	20 SA	0211 0857 1419 2124	3.7 0.4 3.9 0.4
6 SA	0310 0953 1522 2221	3.6 0.5 3.9 0.5	21 SU	0251 0936 1500 2204	3.6 0.4 3.9 0.3
7 SU	0347 1027 1557 2253	3.6 0.5 3.8 0.6	22 M	0331 1015 1542 2246	3.6 0.4 3.9 0.4
8 M	0422 1059 1632 2325	3.5 0.6 3.7 0.6	23 TU	0414 1058 1629 2330	3.6 0.4 3.8 0.5
9 TU	0458 1132 1707 2355	3.5 0.7 3.7 0.7	24 W	0500 1144 1718	3.6 0.5 3.8
10 W ◐	0533 1204 1743	3.4 0.7 3.6	25 TH ◑	0014 0546 1230 1808	0.6 3.6 0.6 3.7
11 TH	0023 0608 1236 1824	0.8 3.3 0.8 3.4	26 F	0057 0635 1320 1906	0.7 3.5 0.6 3.5
12 F	0058 0653 1324 1920	0.8 3.3 0.9 3.3	27 SA	0150 0738 1429 2020	0.8 3.4 0.7 3.4
13 SA	0156 0757 1436 2035	0.9 3.2 0.9 3.2	28 SU	0306 0859 1557 2147	0.8 3.4 0.7 3.4
14 SU	0315 0914 1600 2153	0.9 3.3 0.8 3.3	29 M	0436 1024 1725 2307	0.8 3.5 0.7 3.5
15 M	0435 1027 1718 2301	0.8 3.4 0.7 3.4	30 TU	0555 1133 1833	0.7 3.6 0.5
			31 W	0008 0652 1224 1922	3.5 0.6 3.7 0.4

Chart Datum: 2·06 metres below Normal Null (German reference level)
HAT is 4·1 metres above Chart Datum

TIME ZONE -0100
(German Standard Time)
Subtract 1 hour for UT
For German Summer Time add ONE hour in **non-shaded areas**

GERMANY – CUXHAVEN

LAT 53°52′N LONG 8°43′E

TIMES AND HEIGHTS OF HIGH AND LOW WATERS

Dates in amber are **SPRINGS**
Dates in yellow are **NEAPS**

2016

SEPTEMBER

Date	Day	Time	m	Time	m	Time	m	Time	m	Moon
1	TH	0053	3.6	0735	0.5	1305	3.8	2003	0.4	●
2	F	0132	3.6	0814	0.5	1344	3.8	2041	0.5	
3	SA	0209	3.6	0853	0.5	1421	3.8	2117	0.5	
4	SU	0243	3.6	0928	0.5	1456	3.8	2151	0.6	
5	M	0317	3.6	0959	0.5	1529	3.8	2221	0.6	
6	TU	0349	3.6	1029	0.6	1601	3.7	2250	0.6	
7	W	0422	3.5	1100	0.6	1632	3.6	2317	0.7	
8	TH	0453	3.5	1129	0.7	1704	3.5	2340	0.7	
9	F	0522	3.4	1156	0.8	1737	3.3			◐
10	SA	0007	0.8	0600	3.3	1233	0.9	1826	3.2	
11	SU	0056	1.0	0659	3.2	1339	0.9	1940	3.1	
12	M	0216	1.0	0820	3.2	1509	0.9	2108	3.2	
13	TU	0349	1.0	0944	3.4	1639	0.8	2227	3.3	
14	W	0511	0.8	1054	3.5	1750	0.6	2330	3.4	
15	TH	0615	0.6	1147	3.6	1845	0.5			
16	F	0022	3.6	0707	0.6	1232	3.7	1933	0.4	○
17	SA	0107	3.6	0753	0.5	1315	3.8	2019	0.4	
18	SU	0149	3.7	0837	0.4	1357	3.9	2102	0.4	
19	M	0230	3.7	0919	0.4	1441	3.9	2145	0.4	
20	TU	0311	3.7	1001	0.4	1526	3.9	2226	0.4	
21	W	0354	3.7	1043	0.4	1612	3.8	2308	0.5	
22	TH	0436	3.7	1126	0.5	1658	3.7	2348	0.6	
23	F	0521	3.6	1209	0.6	1748	3.5			◑
24	SA	0030	0.8	0610	3.5	1300	0.7	1847	3.4	
25	SU	0125	0.9	0715	3.5	1410	0.8	2005	3.3	
26	M	0244	1.0	0840	3.5	1543	0.8	2136	3.3	
27	TU	0419	0.9	1009	3.6	1714	0.7	2258	3.4	
28	W	0541	0.8	1119	3.7	1821	0.6	2356	3.5	
29	TH	0636	0.7	1206	3.7	1903	0.5			
30	F	0034	3.5	0713	0.6	1243	3.7	1937	0.5	

OCTOBER

Date	Day	Time	m	Time	m	Time	m	Time	m	Moon
1	SA	0107	3.6	0749	0.6	1319	3.7	2013	0.5	●
2	SU	0141	3.6	0827	0.5	1356	3.7	2049	0.5	
3	M	0215	3.6	0903	0.5	1430	3.7	2121	0.5	
4	TU	0247	3.6	0934	0.5	1501	3.7	2150	0.6	
5	W	0318	3.6	1003	0.5	1531	3.6	2216	0.6	
6	TH	0348	3.6	1032	0.6	1601	3.5	2241	0.6	
7	F	0417	3.5	1059	0.6	1631	3.4	2305	0.7	
8	SA	0445	3.5	1126	0.7	1703	3.3	2331	0.9	
9	SU	0521	3.4	1159	0.8	1747	3.2			◐
10	M	0015	1.0	0614	3.3	1258	0.9	1856	3.1	
11	TU	0130	1.1	0732	3.3	1425	0.9	2023	3.1	
12	W	0304	1.0	0859	3.4	1558	0.8	2149	3.3	
13	TH	0433	0.9	1015	3.5	1715	0.7	2258	3.4	
14	F	0542	0.7	1114	3.6	1814	0.5	2353	3.5	
15	SA	0639	0.6	1203	3.7	1905	0.4			
16	SU	0041	3.6	0729	0.5	1250	3.8	1954	0.4	○
17	M	0125	3.7	0815	0.5	1335	3.9	2039	0.4	
18	TU	0207	3.8	0900	0.4	1421	3.9	2123	0.4	
19	W	0249	3.8	0945	0.4	1509	3.9	2205	0.5	
20	TH	0332	3.8	1028	0.4	1555	3.7	2246	0.6	
21	F	0415	3.7	1110	0.5	1641	3.6	2326	0.7	
22	SA	0459	3.7	1153	0.6	1731	3.4			◑
23	SU	0009	0.8	0549	3.6	1244	0.7	1831	3.3	
24	M	0104	1.0	0653	3.5	1351	0.8	1945	3.2	
25	TU	0219	1.0	0812	3.5	1517	0.8	2110	3.2	
26	W	0348	1.0	0937	3.5	1645	0.7	2230	3.3	
27	TH	0510	0.9	1049	3.6	1752	0.6	2328	3.4	
28	F	0607	0.7	1138	3.6	1834	0.5			
29	SA	0005	3.5	0645	0.7	1215	3.7	1907	0.5	
30	SU	0037	3.5	0722	0.6	1252	3.7	1943	0.6	●
31	M	0113	3.6	0801	0.6	1330	3.6	2020	0.5	

NOVEMBER

Date	Day	Time	m	Time	m	Time	m	Time	m	Moon
1	TU	0148	3.6	0838	0.5	1404	3.6	2053	0.5	
2	W	0220	3.6	0910	0.5	1435	3.6	2121	0.5	
3	TH	0250	3.6	0939	0.5	1506	3.5	2148	0.5	
4	F	0319	3.6	1008	0.5	1536	3.4	2214	0.6	
5	SA	0349	3.6	1037	0.6	1608	3.4	2240	0.7	
6	SU	0420	3.6	1106	0.7	1642	3.3	2311	0.9	
7	M	0457	3.5	1142	0.8	1725	3.2	2353	1.0	◐
8	TU	0545	3.4	1235	0.9	1824	3.2			
9	W	0058	1.0	0653	3.4	1349	0.9	1943	3.2	
10	TH	0222	1.0	0814	3.4	1516	0.8	2107	3.2	
11	F	0349	0.9	0932	3.5	1634	0.7	2220	3.4	
12	SA	0504	0.8	1038	3.6	1739	0.6	2321	3.5	
13	SU	0608	0.6	1134	3.7	1836	0.5			
14	M	0014	3.6	0704	0.6	1226	3.8	1929	0.4	○
15	TU	0101	3.7	0755	0.5	1315	3.8	2017	0.4	
16	W	0144	3.8	0841	0.4	1402	3.8	2101	0.4	
17	TH	0227	3.8	0928	0.4	1451	3.7	2145	0.5	
18	F	0313	3.8	1015	0.4	1541	3.6	2228	0.6	
19	SA	0358	3.8	1059	0.5	1629	3.5	2310	0.7	
20	SU	0442	3.8	1142	0.6	1718	3.4	2353	0.8	
21	M	0531	3.7	1230	0.7	1812	3.3			◑
22	TU	0043	0.9	0627	3.6	1326	0.8	1915	3.2	
23	W	0145	1.0	0733	3.5	1435	0.8	2026	3.1	
24	TH	0259	0.9	0847	3.4	1551	0.7	2139	3.2	
25	F	0416	0.9	0959	3.5	1701	0.7	2241	3.3	
26	SA	0521	0.8	1057	3.5	1753	0.7	2328	3.4	
27	SU	0610	0.7	1143	3.6	1835	0.6			
28	M	0007	3.5	0654	0.7	1225	3.6	1914	0.6	
29	TU	0045	3.6	0736	0.6	1304	3.6	1952	0.6	●
30	W	0122	3.6	0814	0.5	1340	3.5	2026	0.5	

DECEMBER

Date	Day	Time	m	Time	m	Time	m	Time	m	Moon
1	TH	0155	3.6	0847	0.5	1413	3.5	2057	0.5	
2	F	0226	3.6	0919	0.5	1446	3.5	2128	0.6	
3	SA	0258	3.7	0951	0.6	1520	3.5	2157	0.6	
4	SU	0330	3.7	1023	0.6	1553	3.4	2227	0.7	
5	M	0403	3.7	1056	0.7	1629	3.4	2302	0.8	
6	TU	0442	3.6	1136	0.7	1712	3.3	2344	0.9	
7	W	0527	3.6	1223	0.8	1803	3.3			◐
8	TH	0038	0.9	0624	3.5	1323	0.8	1908	3.2	
9	F	0146	0.9	0733	3.5	1435	0.8	2023	3.3	
10	SA	0305	0.9	0849	3.6	1551	0.7	2138	3.4	
11	SU	0424	0.8	1001	3.6	1703	0.7	2245	3.5	
12	M	0536	0.7	1106	3.7	1808	0.5	2345	3.6	
13	TU	0641	0.5	1204	3.7	1907	0.4			
14	W	0038	3.6	0737	0.4	1258	3.7	1958	0.4	○
15	TH	0124	3.7	0826	0.3	1347	3.6	2043	0.4	
16	F	0209	3.8	0913	0.4	1437	3.6	2128	0.5	
17	SA	0256	3.9	1003	0.5	1528	3.6	2214	0.6	
18	SU	0343	3.9	1050	0.5	1616	3.5	2257	0.6	
19	M	0427	3.8	1132	0.6	1701	3.4	2337	0.7	
20	TU	0510	3.7	1212	0.6	1747	3.3			
21	W	0018	0.8	0556	3.6	1254	0.7	1836	3.2	◑
22	TH	0105	0.8	0648	3.5	1343	0.7	1931	3.1	
23	F	0200	0.9	0748	3.4	1443	0.8	2034	3.1	
24	SA	0307	0.9	0856	3.4	1553	0.8	2141	3.2	
25	SU	0420	0.9	1005	3.4	1700	0.8	2242	3.4	
26	M	0527	0.8	1105	3.5	1757	0.7	2333	3.5	
27	TU	0623	0.7	1155	3.5	1843	0.7			
28	W	0017	3.6	0710	0.6	1238	3.5	1924	0.6	
29	TH	0056	3.6	0750	0.6	1317	3.5	2002	0.6	●
30	F	0132	3.7	0826	0.6	1354	3.6	2038	0.6	
31	SA	0207	3.7	0903	0.5	1431	3.5	2114	0.6	

Chart Datum: 2·06 metres below Normal Null (German reference level)
HAT is 4·1 metres above Chart Datum

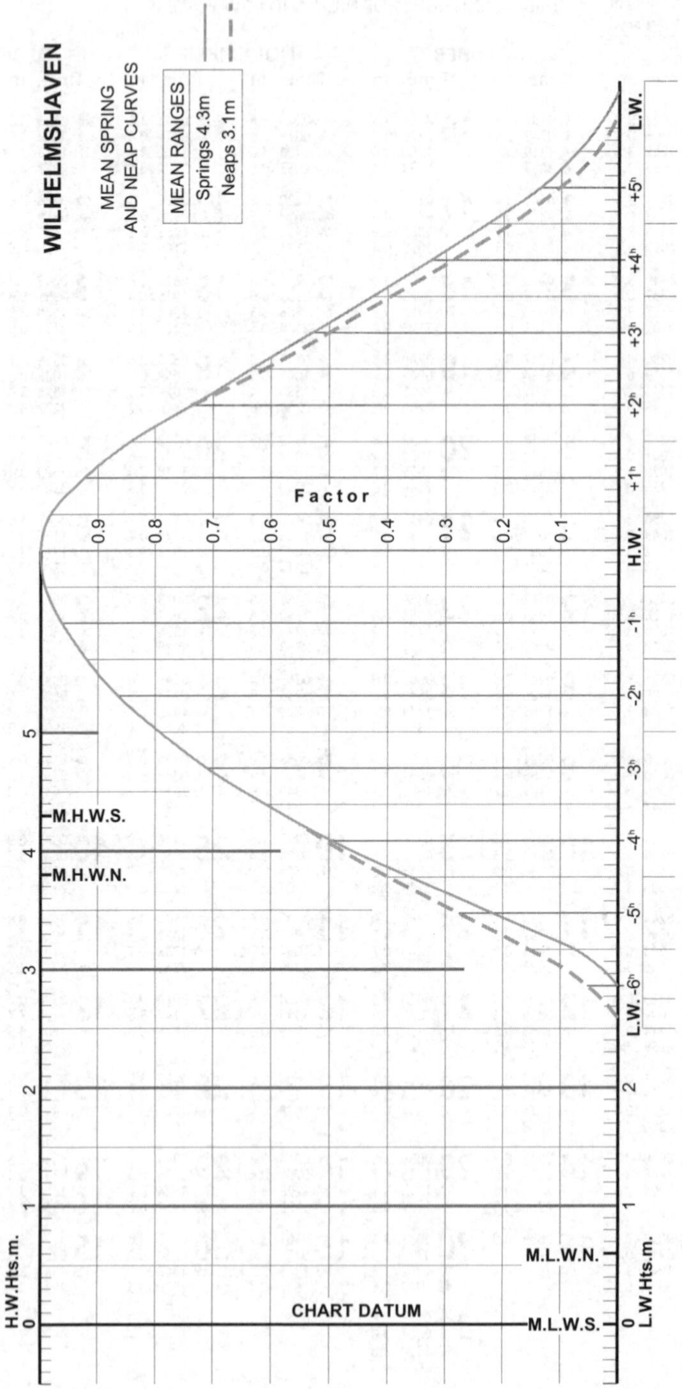
WILHELMSHAVEN
MEAN SPRING
AND NEAP CURVES
MEAN RANGES
Springs 4.3m
Neaps 3.1m
Factor
0.9
0.8
0.7
0.6
0.5
0.4
0.3
0.2
0.1
L.W. -6h -5h -4h -3h -2h -1h H.W. +1h +2h +3h +4h +5h L.W.
H.W.Hts.m.
0 1 2 3 4 5
M.H.W.S.
M.H.W.N.
CHART DATUM
M.L.W.N.
M.L.W.S.
L.W.Hts.m.
0 1 2

TIME ZONE -0100 (German Standard Time) **Subtract 1 hour for UT** For German Summer Time add ONE hour in **non-shaded areas**

GERMANY – WILHELMSHAVEN

LAT 53°31'N LONG 8°09'E

TIMES AND HEIGHTS OF HIGH AND LOW WATERS

Dates in amber are **SPRINGS** Dates in yellow are **NEAPS**

2016

JANUARY

Day	Time	m	Day	Time	m
1 F	0450 1108 1718 2314	4.7 0.9 4.3 1.1	16 SA	0454 1113 1727 2323	4.8 0.6 4.4 0.8
2 SA	0529 1143 1758 ◑ 2352	4.6 1.0 4.1 1.2	17 SU ◐	0544 1200 1816	4.8 0.7 4.4
3 SU	0614 1225 1848	4.4 1.1 4.1	18 M	0012 0637 1251 1912	0.8 4.6 0.8 4.3
4 M	0043 0712 1322 1951	1.3 4.3 1.2 4.1	19 TU	0112 0741 1354 2020	1.0 4.5 1.0 4.3
5 TU	0150 0821 1432 2102	1.3 4.3 1.2 4.2	20 W	0228 0858 1512 2137	1.0 4.5 1.0 4.4
6 W	0307 0931 1543 2208	1.3 4.4 1.1 4.4	21 TH	0350 1017 1630 2250	1.0 4.5 0.9 4.5
7 TH	0418 1034 1645 2305	1.2 4.4 1.0 4.5	22 F	0506 1127 1737 2353	0.8 4.5 0.8 4.6
8 F	0518 1128 1739 2355	1.0 4.5 0.9 4.6	23 SA	0609 1226 1832	0.6 4.5 0.6
9 SA	0609 1217 1829	0.8 4.5 0.8	24 SU	0044 0701 1314 ○ 1918	4.7 0.5 4.5 0.6
10 SU	0039 0656 1303 ● 1915	4.7 0.7 4.6 0.7	25 M	0127 0745 1355 1959	4.8 0.5 4.5 0.6
11 M	0121 0741 1348 2000	4.8 0.7 4.6 0.7	26 TU	0206 0825 1432 2037	4.9 0.6 4.5 0.7
12 TU	0203 0825 1433 2043	4.9 0.6 4.6 0.6	27 W	0244 0904 1508 2113	4.9 0.6 4.6 0.7
13 W	0243 0907 1514 2121	4.9 0.5 4.6 0.6	28 TH	0319 0938 1541 2144	4.9 0.7 4.5 0.7
14 TH	0323 0946 1555 2156	4.9 0.5 4.5 0.6	29 F	0351 1009 1613 2214	4.8 0.8 4.4 0.8
15 F	0406 1027 1640 2237	4.9 0.5 4.5 0.7	30 SA	0423 1039 1645 2244	4.7 0.8 4.4 0.9
			31 SU	0456 1108 1716 2313	4.6 0.9 4.3 1.0

FEBRUARY

Day	Time	m	Day	Time	m
1 M	0530 1136 1751 ◑ 2347	4.5 1.0 4.2 1.1	16 TU	0616 1223 1844	4.6 0.8 4.4
2 TU	0613 1215 1843	4.3 1.1 4.1	17 W	0043 0717 1322 1951	0.8 4.4 1.0 4.3
3 W	0042 0715 1318 1955	1.2 4.2 1.2 4.1	18 TH	0158 0837 1443 2115	0.9 4.3 1.0 4.3
4 TH	0200 0833 1438 2115	1.3 4.2 1.2 4.2	19 F	0330 1005 1611 2237	0.9 4.3 1.0 4.5
5 F	0324 0950 1557 2227	1.2 4.3 1.0 4.4	20 SA	0454 1121 1724 2343	0.8 4.4 0.8 4.6
6 SA	0438 1058 1705 2327	1.0 4.4 0.9 4.5	21 SU	0558 1217 1818	0.6 4.4 0.7
7 SU	0539 1155 1805	0.8 4.5 0.8	22 M	0032 0647 1301 ○ 1902	4.7 0.5 4.5 0.6
8 M	0017 0632 1246 ● 1857	4.7 0.7 4.6 0.7	23 TU	0113 0727 1338 1941	4.8 0.5 4.5 0.6
9 TU	0102 0721 1334 1944	4.8 0.5 4.6 0.6	24 W	0149 0804 1412 2016	4.8 0.5 4.5 0.6
10 W	0146 0808 1420 2028	4.9 0.4 4.6 0.5	25 TH	0224 0838 1444 2048	4.8 0.6 4.5 0.5
11 TH	0230 0851 1503 2108	4.9 0.3 4.6 0.4	26 F	0257 0910 1515 2118	4.8 0.6 4.5 0.5
12 F	0313 0933 1545 2146	4.9 0.3 4.6 0.4	27 SA	0328 0940 1545 2148	4.7 0.6 4.5 0.6
13 SA	0357 1016 1628 2226	4.9 0.4 4.5 0.4	28 SU	0359 1009 1615 2218	4.7 0.7 4.4 0.7
14 SU	0443 1059 1712 2309	4.8 0.5 4.5 0.6	29 M	0430 1036 1643 2243	4.6 0.7 4.4 0.7
15 M	0529 1140 1755 ◐ 2351	4.8 0.6 4.5 0.7			

MARCH

Day	Time	m	Day	Time	m
1 TU	0457 1057 1709 2307	4.5 0.8 4.3 0.8	16 W	0558 1158 1820	4.4 0.7 4.4
2 W	0529 1122 1749 ◑ 2347	4.3 0.9 4.1 1.0	17 TH	0021 0658 1254 1927	0.7 4.2 1.0 4.3
3 TH	0621 1214 1856	4.1 1.1 4.1	18 F	0135 0820 1417 2055	0.9 4.1 1.1 4.3
4 F	0059 0739 1337 2022	1.1 4.0 1.2 4.1	19 SA	0309 0951 1550 2222	0.9 4.1 1.0 4.4
5 SA	0231 0908 1510 2147	1.1 4.1 1.0 4.3	20 SU	0438 1108 1706 2328	0.7 4.3 0.8 4.6
6 SU	0358 1027 1631 2256	0.9 4.3 0.8 4.5	21 M	0540 1201 1757	0.5 4.4 0.6
7 M	0508 1133 1738 2353	0.7 4.4 0.7 4.6	22 TU	0013 0621 1239 1836	4.6 0.4 4.4 0.6
8 TU	0606 1228 1834	0.5 4.5 0.6	23 W	0050 0658 1314 ○ 1914	4.7 0.4 4.5 0.5
9 W	0041 0657 1316 ● 1922	4.8 0.4 4.6 0.4	24 TH	0126 0735 1348 1950	4.7 0.4 4.5 0.5
10 TH	0127 0745 1402 2007	4.9 0.2 4.6 0.3	25 F	0201 0809 1419 2023	4.7 0.5 4.5 0.4
11 F	0213 0830 1447 2051	4.9 0.2 4.6 0.2	26 SA	0234 0840 1449 2053	4.7 0.5 4.5 0.4
12 SA	0259 0915 1531 2133	4.9 0.2 4.6 0.2	27 SU	0305 0910 1519 2123	4.6 0.5 4.5 0.4
13 SU	0345 0959 1612 2213	4.9 0.3 4.6 0.3	28 M	0335 0939 1548 2152	4.6 0.5 4.5 0.5
14 M	0430 1040 1653 2252	4.8 0.4 4.6 0.4	29 TU	0405 1005 1615 2217	4.5 0.5 4.5 0.5
15 TU	0513 1117 1733 ◐ 2331	4.6 0.5 4.5 0.5	30 W	0432 1026 1641 2240	4.4 0.6 4.4 0.6
			31 TH	0501 1050 1715 ◑ 2314	4.2 0.8 4.2 0.8

APRIL

Day	Time	m	Day	Time	m
1 F	0546 1135 1815	4.1 1.0 4.1	16 SA	0114 0758 1348 2028	0.8 4.0 1.0 4.3
2 SA	0018 0700 1253 1939	0.9 4.0 1.1 4.1	17 SU	0241 0924 1516 2153	0.8 4.0 0.9 4.4
3 SU	0148 0831 1428 2108	0.9 4.1 1.0 4.3	18 M	0405 1039 1631 2258	0.6 4.2 0.7 4.5
4 M	0319 0956 1555 2223	0.8 4.2 0.8 4.5	19 TU	0505 1131 1722 2342	0.4 4.3 0.6 4.5
5 TU	0434 1106 1706 2324	0.5 4.4 0.6 4.6	20 W	0545 1207 1800	0.4 4.4 0.5
6 W	0535 1204 1805	0.4 4.5 0.5	21 TH	0019 0622 1243 1841	4.6 0.4 4.5 0.5
7 TH	0017 0630 1255 ● 1858	4.8 0.2 4.6 0.4	22 F	0058 0702 1319 ○ 1921	4.6 0.4 4.5 0.4
8 F	0107 0720 1342 1945	4.9 0.1 4.7 0.2	23 SA	0135 0739 1353 1957	4.6 0.4 4.6 0.4
9 SA	0154 0808 1427 2031	4.9 0.1 4.7 0.2	24 SU	0209 0811 1424 2028	4.6 0.4 4.6 0.3
10 SU	0242 0853 1511 2115	4.9 0.2 4.7 0.2	25 M	0241 0841 1454 2059	4.6 0.4 4.6 0.3
11 M	0329 0937 1553 2156	4.8 0.2 4.7 0.2	26 TU	0312 0910 1523 2129	4.5 0.4 4.5 0.4
12 TU	0414 1017 1633 2234	4.7 0.4 4.6 0.3	27 W	0343 0938 1553 2158	4.4 0.5 4.5 0.4
13 W	0457 1055 1713 2315	4.5 0.5 4.6 0.5	28 TH	0414 1006 1623 2227	4.4 0.5 4.5 0.5
14 TH ◐	0544 1136 1801	4.3 0.7 4.5	29 F	0447 1037 1700 2304	4.3 0.7 4.4 0.6
15 F	0005 0642 1232 1905	0.6 4.1 0.9 4.4	30 SA ◑	0531 1121 1753	4.1 0.9 4.3

Chart Datum: 2·7 metres below Normal Null (German reference level)
HAT is 5·1 metres above Chart Datum

TIME ZONE -0100
(German Standard Time)
Subtract 1 hour for UT
For German Summer Time add ONE hour in **non-shaded areas**

GERMANY – WILHELMSHAVEN

LAT 53°31'N LONG 8°09'E

TIMES AND HEIGHTS OF HIGH AND LOW WATERS

Dates in amber are **SPRINGS**
Dates in yellow are **NEAPS**

2016

MAY

Day	Time	m	Time	m	Time	m	Time	m
1 SU	0001	0.8	0637	4.1	1229	1.0	1908	4.3
2 M	0119	0.8	0800	4.1	1354	0.9	2033	4.4
3 TU	0244	0.6	0923	4.2	1519	0.8	2149	4.5
4 W	0359	0.5	1034	4.3	1631	0.6	2253	4.7
5 TH	0503	0.3	1135	4.5	1735	0.5	2352	4.8
6 F ●	0602	0.2	1231	4.6	1833	0.3		
7 SA	0046	4.8	0657	0.2	1320	4.7	1924	0.2
8 SU	0136	4.8	0746	0.1	1404	4.8	2009	0.1
9 M	0224	4.8	0830	0.2	1448	4.8	2054	0.1
10 TU	0312	4.7	0914	0.3	1532	4.7	2138	0.2
11 W	0359	4.6	0956	0.4	1614	4.7	2220	0.3
12 TH	0443	4.4	1036	0.5	1656	4.7	2302	0.4
13 F	0529	4.3	1119	0.7	1743	4.6	◐ 2351	0.6
14 SA	0622	4.2	1210	0.9	1840	4.5		
15 SU	0049	0.7	0726	4.0	1313	0.9	1949	4.4
16 M	0159	0.7	0839	4.0	1427	0.9	2104	4.4
17 TU	0313	0.6	0950	4.1	1538	0.7	2211	4.4
18 W	0416	0.5	1046	4.3	1635	0.6	2302	4.5
19 TH	0503	0.4	1128	4.4	1722	0.6	2344	4.5
20 F	0545	0.5	1208	4.5	1807	0.5		
21 SA	0026	4.6	0629	0.5	1249	4.6	○ 1853	0.5
22 SU	0106	4.6	0710	0.4	1326	4.6	1932	0.4
23 M	0142	4.6	0744	0.4	1400	4.7	2006	0.4
24 TU	0217	4.6	0816	0.4	1432	4.7	2039	0.4
25 W	0252	4.5	0849	0.4	1503	4.7	2112	0.4
26 TH	0326	4.4	0921	0.5	1536	4.6	2145	0.4
27 F	0401	4.4	0956	0.6	1612	4.6	2222	0.5
28 SA	0441	4.3	1035	0.7	1654	4.6	2305	0.6
29 SU	0527	4.3	1120	0.8	1745	4.5	◑ 2357	0.6
30 M	0625	4.2	1217	0.8	1848	4.5		
31 TU	0101	0.6	0735	4.2	1328	0.8	2002	4.5

JUNE

Day	Time	m	Time	m	Time	m	Time	m
1 W	0214	0.6	0850	4.3	1445	0.8	2115	4.6
2 TH	0327	0.5	1001	4.4	1558	0.7	2223	4.7
3 F	0434	0.4	1105	4.5	1706	0.6	2327	4.7
4 SA	0538	0.3	1205	4.6	1809	0.4		
5 SU	0027	4.8	0636	0.2	1258	4.7	● 1904	0.2
6 M	0120	4.7	0726	0.2	1343	4.8	1951	0.1
7 TU	0209	4.7	0811	0.2	1427	4.8	2036	0.2
8 W	0256	4.6	0856	0.3	1513	4.8	2124	0.3
9 TH	0343	4.5	0940	0.4	1556	4.8	2208	0.4
10 F	0427	4.5	1021	0.6	1638	4.8	2250	0.5
11 SA	0510	4.4	1101	0.7	1721	4.7	2333	0.6
12 SU ◐	0555	4.2	1144	0.8	1807	4.6		
13 M	0018	0.7	0644	4.1	1232	0.9	1901	4.5
14 TU	0110	0.8	0742	4.0	1329	0.9	2004	4.4
15 W	0211	0.8	0846	4.1	1435	0.9	2111	4.4
16 TH	0317	0.7	0949	4.3	1542	0.8	2213	4.4
17 F	0417	0.7	1044	4.4	1642	0.7	2306	4.5
18 SA	0509	0.6	1132	4.5	1735	0.7	2353	4.5
19 SU	0557	0.6	1217	4.6	1824	0.6		
20 M	0037	4.6	0641	0.5	1259	4.7	○ 1907	0.5
21 TU	0117	4.6	0721	0.5	1336	4.7	1946	0.5
22 W	0157	4.6	0759	0.5	1412	4.8	2025	0.5
23 TH	0236	4.6	0837	0.5	1447	4.8	2102	0.4
24 F	0314	4.5	0913	0.5	1523	4.8	2138	0.5
25 SA	0351	4.4	0948	0.6	1603	4.8	2218	0.5
26 SU	0435	4.4	1030	0.6	1649	4.7	2304	0.5
27 M	0523	4.4	1118	0.7	1739	4.7	◑ 2354	0.6
28 TU	0614	4.3	1208	0.7	1833	4.7		
29 W	0046	0.6	0712	4.3	1307	0.8	1935	4.6
30 TH	0148	0.6	0818	4.3	1417	0.8	2046	4.7

JULY

Day	Time	m	Time	m	Time	m	Time	m
1 F	0259	0.7	0929	4.4	1531	0.8	2159	4.7
2 SA	0411	0.6	1038	4.5	1644	0.6	2308	4.7
3 SU	0518	0.5	1143	4.6	1750	0.4		
4 M	0012	4.7	0619	0.3	1239	4.7	● 1849	0.3
5 TU	0108	4.6	0711	0.3	1327	4.8	1939	0.2
6 W	0156	4.6	0757	0.4	1411	4.9	2025	0.3
7 TH	0242	4.6	0842	0.5	1455	4.9	2111	0.4
8 F	0326	4.6	0924	0.5	1537	4.9	2154	0.5
9 SA	0406	4.5	1003	0.6	1615	4.9	2231	0.6
10 SU	0444	4.4	1038	0.7	1652	4.8	2307	0.7
11 M	0521	4.3	1114	0.8	1731	4.7	2344	0.8
12 TU ◐	0600	4.2	1151	0.9	1813	4.5		
13 W	0022	0.9	0643	4.2	1234	1.0	1903	4.4
14 TH	0109	0.9	0738	4.1	1332	1.0	2007	4.3
15 F	0213	1.0	0845	4.2	1445	1.0	2118	4.3
16 SA	0324	0.9	0954	4.3	1558	0.9	2223	4.4
17 SU	0428	0.8	1054	4.4	1702	0.8	2320	4.4
18 M	0524	0.7	1146	4.6	1755	0.7		
19 TU	0009	4.5	0615	0.6	1231	4.7	○ 1842	0.6
20 W	0055	4.6	0702	0.6	1313	4.8	1928	0.6
21 TH	0139	4.7	0746	0.6	1353	4.9	2011	0.5
22 F	0221	4.7	0827	0.5	1432	4.9	2050	0.4
23 SA	0301	4.6	0904	0.5	1510	4.9	2128	0.4
24 SU	0340	4.5	0939	0.5	1551	4.9	2209	0.4
25 M	0423	4.5	1020	0.5	1638	4.8	2255	0.5
26 TU	0511	4.5	1108	0.6	1727	4.8	2343	0.6
27 W ◑	0558	4.5	1156	0.7	1816	4.8		
28 TH	0029	0.7	0647	4.4	1246	0.8	1912	4.6
29 F	0123	0.8	0748	4.4	1352	0.9	2022	4.6
30 SA	0234	0.9	0902	4.4	1512	0.9	2142	4.5
31 SU	0354	0.8	1019	4.5	1632	0.7	2258	4.6

AUGUST

Day	Time	m	Time	m	Time	m	Time	m
1 M	0508	0.7	1128	4.6	1741	0.6		
2 TU	0003	4.6	0609	0.5	1225	4.7	● 1840	0.4
3 W	0057	4.6	0701	0.5	1313	4.8	1929	0.4
4 TH	0143	4.6	0746	0.5	1355	4.9	2013	0.4
5 F	0224	4.6	0827	0.6	1436	4.9	2054	0.5
6 SA	0303	4.6	0906	0.6	1514	4.9	2132	0.6
7 SU	0339	4.6	0940	0.6	1548	4.9	2205	0.7
8 M	0412	4.5	1011	0.7	1622	4.8	2236	0.8
9 TU	0444	4.4	1043	0.8	1656	4.7	2308	0.9
10 W	0516	4.4	1114	0.9	1730	4.6	◐ 2338	0.9
11 TH	0549	4.3	1146	1.0	1808	4.4		
12 F	0012	1.0	0633	4.2	1233	1.1	1904	4.3
13 SA	0106	1.2	0739	4.2	1343	1.2	2018	4.2
14 SU	0222	1.2	0858	4.2	1507	1.1	2137	4.2
15 M	0343	1.0	1013	4.4	1624	0.9	2246	4.4
16 TU	0452	0.9	1114	4.5	1726	0.8	2343	4.5
17 W	0550	0.8	1204	4.7	1818	0.7		
18 TH	0033	4.6	0642	0.7	1249	4.8	○ 1906	0.6
19 F	0119	4.7	0728	0.6	1331	4.9	1951	0.5
20 SA	0203	4.7	0811	0.5	1412	5.0	2033	0.4
21 SU	0244	4.7	0850	0.4	1454	5.0	2113	0.4
22 M	0325	4.6	0927	0.4	1537	4.9	2155	0.4
23 TU	0407	4.6	1007	0.5	1623	4.9	2239	0.5
24 W	0451	4.6	1052	0.6	1709	4.8	2323	0.7
25 TH ◑	0535	4.5	1136	0.7	1756	4.7		
26 F	0005	0.8	0620	4.5	1225	0.8	1850	4.5
27 SA	0058	1.0	0720	4.4	1331	1.0	2004	4.4
28 SU	0212	1.1	0841	4.4	1459	1.0	2132	4.4
29 M	0342	1.1	1007	4.5	1628	0.9	2254	4.4
30 TU	0502	0.9	1118	4.6	1738	0.7	2356	4.5
31 W	0601	0.7	1212	4.7	1830	0.6		

Chart Datum: 2·7 metres below Normal Null (German reference level)
HAT is 5·1 metres above Chart Datum

TIME ZONE -0100
(German Standard Time)
Subtract 1 hour for UT
For German Summer Time add ONE hour in **non-shaded areas**

GERMANY – WILHELMSHAVEN

LAT 53°31′N LONG 8°09′E

TIMES AND HEIGHTS OF HIGH AND LOW WATERS

Dates in amber are **SPRINGS**
Dates in yellow are **NEAPS**

2016

SEPTEMBER

Date	Day	Time	m	Time	m	Time	m	Time	m
1	TH	0043	4.6	0647	0.7	1255	4.8	● 1913	0.5
2	F	0124	4.6	0728	0.6	1335	4.8	1952	0.5
3	SA	0201	4.6	0807	0.6	1412	4.9	2029	0.6
4	SU	0236	4.6	0842	0.6	1447	4.8	2103	0.6
5	M	0308	4.6	0913	0.6	1520	4.8	2134	0.7
6	TU	0338	4.6	0943	0.7	1551	4.7	2203	0.8
7	W	0408	4.5	1013	0.8	1622	4.6	2231	0.8
8	TH	0436	4.5	1040	0.8	1652	4.5	2255	0.9
9	F	0504	4.4	1106	0.9	1722	4.3	◐ 2321	1.1
10	SA	0539	4.2	1142	1.1	1809	4.2		
11	SU	0006	1.2	0639	4.1	1246	1.2	1921	4.1
12	M	0123	1.3	0802	4.1	1415	1.2	2048	4.1
13	TU	0255	1.2	0927	4.3	1543	1.1	2209	4.3
14	W	0417	1.0	1038	4.5	1654	0.8	2314	4.4
15	TH	0522	0.9	1133	4.6	1749	0.7		
16	F	0007	4.5	0617	0.7	1221	4.8	○ 1839	0.5
17	SA	0055	4.6	0705	0.6	1305	4.9	1926	0.4
18	SU	0140	4.7	0749	0.5	1350	5.0	2011	0.4
19	M	0223	4.7	0832	0.5	1435	5.0	2054	0.4
20	TU	0305	4.7	0913	0.4	1520	5.0	2137	0.5
21	W	0346	4.7	0953	0.5	1604	4.8	2218	0.6
22	TH	0427	4.7	1032	0.6	1649	4.7	2258	0.7
23	F	0509	4.6	1114	0.7	1735	4.5	◑ 2339	0.9
24	SA	0555	4.5	1203	0.9	1832	4.3		
25	SU	0033	1.2	0657	4.4	1313	1.0	1948	4.2
26	M	0151	1.3	0821	4.4	1444	1.1	2119	4.2
27	TU	0325	1.3	0951	4.5	1618	1.0	2243	4.3
28	W	0448	1.0	1104	4.7	1727	0.8	2342	4.5
29	TH	0545	0.8	1153	4.7	1810	0.6		
30	F	0021	4.5	0623	0.7	1231	4.7	1845	0.6

OCTOBER

Date	Day	Time	m	Time	m	Time	m	Time	m
1	SA	0056	4.6	0701	0.7	1308	4.7	● 1922	0.6
2	SU	0132	4.6	0739	0.7	1345	4.7	1959	0.6
3	M	0206	4.6	0814	0.6	1420	4.7	2033	0.6
4	TU	0237	4.6	0846	0.6	1451	4.7	2103	0.7
5	W	0306	4.6	0915	0.6	1521	4.6	2129	0.7
6	TH	0334	4.6	0943	0.7	1550	4.6	2154	0.8
7	F	0401	4.5	1008	0.8	1618	4.4	2217	0.9
8	SA	0427	4.4	1033	0.9	1647	4.3	2243	1.1
9	SU	0500	4.3	1107	1.1	1728	4.1	◐ 2325	1.3
10	M	0553	4.2	1204	1.2	1835	4.0		
11	TU	0035	1.4	0711	4.2	1328	1.3	2001	4.1
12	W	0208	1.4	0840	4.3	1459	1.1	2128	4.2
13	TH	0336	1.2	0958	4.5	1616	0.9	2239	4.3
14	F	0447	0.9	1058	4.6	1715	0.7	2337	4.5
15	SA	0545	0.8	1150	4.8	1808	0.6		
16	SU	0028	4.6	0638	0.7	1239	4.9	○ 1859	0.5
17	M	0115	4.7	0726	0.6	1326	4.9	1946	0.4
18	TU	0159	4.8	0811	0.5	1413	5.0	2032	0.4
19	W	0242	4.8	0854	0.5	1501	4.9	2116	0.5
20	TH	0324	4.8	0936	0.5	1546	4.8	2157	0.6
21	F	0404	4.7	1014	0.5	1631	4.6	2235	0.8
22	SA	0446	4.7	1055	0.7	1718	4.4	◑ 2317	1.0
23	SU	0534	4.6	1146	0.9	1815	4.2		
24	M	0011	1.2	0635	4.5	1253	1.1	1927	4.1
25	TU	0125	1.4	0754	4.5	1417	1.1	2052	4.1
26	W	0252	1.3	0920	4.5	1546	1.0	2213	4.2
27	TH	0413	1.1	1032	4.6	1654	0.8	2311	4.4
28	F	0511	0.9	1122	4.7	1737	0.7	2350	4.5
29	SA	0551	0.8	1200	4.7	1812	0.7		
30	SU	0024	4.5	0629	0.8	1238	4.7	● 1850	0.7
31	M	0101	4.6	0710	0.7	1317	4.6	1929	0.7

NOVEMBER

Date	Day	Time	m	Time	m	Time	m	Time	m
1	TU	0136	4.6	0747	0.6	1351	4.6	2002	0.6
2	W	0207	4.6	0819	0.6	1423	4.6	2031	0.6
3	TH	0236	4.6	0848	0.6	1453	4.5	2058	0.7
4	F	0304	4.6	0916	0.7	1522	4.5	2124	0.7
5	SA	0332	4.6	0944	0.8	1552	4.4	2151	0.9
6	SU	0401	4.5	1013	0.9	1624	4.3	2222	1.1
7	M	0436	4.5	1048	1.0	1705	4.2	◐ 2302	1.2
8	TU	0524	4.4	1139	1.2	1803	4.1		
9	W	0003	1.4	0632	4.3	1251	1.2	1921	4.1
10	TH	0124	1.4	0754	4.4	1415	1.1	2044	4.2
11	F	0250	1.2	0914	4.5	1533	0.9	2159	4.3
12	SA	0406	1.1	1021	4.6	1639	0.8	2302	4.5
13	SU	0511	0.9	1119	4.7	1738	0.6	2359	4.6
14	M	0610	0.7	1214	4.8	1833	0.5	○	
15	TU	0049	4.7	0702	0.6	1304	4.9	1923	0.4
16	W	0134	4.8	0748	0.5	1353	4.8	2008	0.5
17	TH	0218	4.8	0833	0.5	1442	4.8	2054	0.5
18	F	0302	4.9	0919	0.5	1531	4.7	2137	0.6
19	SA	0346	4.8	1002	0.5	1617	4.5	2218	0.8
20	SU	0429	4.8	1044	0.7	1703	4.4	2300	1.0
21	M	0515	4.7	1131	0.9	1755	4.3	◑ 2349	1.2
22	TU	0610	4.6	1228	1.0	1856	4.1		
23	W	0050	1.3	0715	4.5	1335	1.1	2007	4.0
24	TH	0201	1.3	0830	4.4	1450	1.0	2120	4.1
25	F	0316	1.2	0942	4.5	1600	0.9	2223	4.3
26	SA	0421	1.0	1040	4.6	1655	0.8	2310	4.4
27	SU	0512	1.0	1126	4.6	1737	0.8	2350	4.5
28	M	0557	0.9	1208	4.6	1819	0.8		
29	TU	0030	4.6	0641	0.8	1248	4.6	● 1859	0.7
30	W	0107	4.6	0720	0.7	1324	4.6	1933	0.7

DECEMBER

Date	Day	Time	m	Time	m	Time	m	Time	m
1	TH	0140	4.6	0754	0.6	1357	4.5	2005	0.7
2	F	0212	4.7	0826	0.6	1431	4.5	2037	0.7
3	SA	0242	4.7	0858	0.7	1503	4.5	2107	0.8
4	SU	0312	4.7	0929	0.7	1535	4.4	2137	0.9
5	M	0345	4.7	1002	0.8	1611	4.4	2211	1.0
6	TU	0423	4.6	1040	0.9	1653	4.3	2252	1.1
7	W	0509	4.6	1126	1.0	1744	4.2	◐ 2342	1.2
8	TH	0605	4.5	1224	1.0	1848	4.2		
9	F	0047	1.2	0715	4.5	1334	1.0	2002	4.2
10	SA	0205	1.2	0830	4.6	1449	1.0	2117	4.3
11	SU	0323	1.1	0943	4.7	1602	0.9	2226	4.5
12	M	0436	0.9	1050	4.7	1708	0.7	2329	4.6
13	TU	0541	0.7	1152	4.7	1809	0.6		
14	W	0024	4.7	0639	0.6	1247	4.7	○ 1902	0.5
15	TH	0112	4.8	0728	0.5	1337	4.7	1949	0.5
16	F	0158	4.8	0816	0.5	1427	4.7	2036	0.6
17	SA	0244	4.9	0905	0.5	1517	4.6	2122	0.7
18	SU	0330	4.9	0952	0.6	1603	4.6	2205	0.7
19	M	0413	4.9	1033	0.6	1646	4.4	2244	0.8
20	TU	0455	4.8	1113	0.8	1730	4.3	2324	1.0
21	W	0540	4.7	1156	0.9	1817	4.2	◑	
22	TH	0009	1.1	0630	4.5	1245	1.0	1911	4.1
23	F	0102	1.2	0730	4.4	1344	1.0	2013	4.1
24	SA	0207	1.2	0839	4.4	1453	1.1	2121	4.2
25	SU	0320	1.2	0947	4.4	1601	1.1	2223	4.4
26	M	0427	1.1	1047	4.5	1659	1.0	2315	4.5
27	TU	0524	1.0	1137	4.5	1747	0.9		
28	W	0000	4.6	0612	0.9	1220	4.5	1830	0.8
29	TH	0040	4.6	0654	0.8	1259	4.5	● 1909	0.7
30	F	0117	4.7	0732	0.7	1337	4.6	1946	0.7
31	SA	0151	4.7	0810	0.7	1415	4.5	2023	0.7

Chart Datum: 2·7 metres below Normal Null (German reference level)
HAT is 5·1 metres above Chart Datum

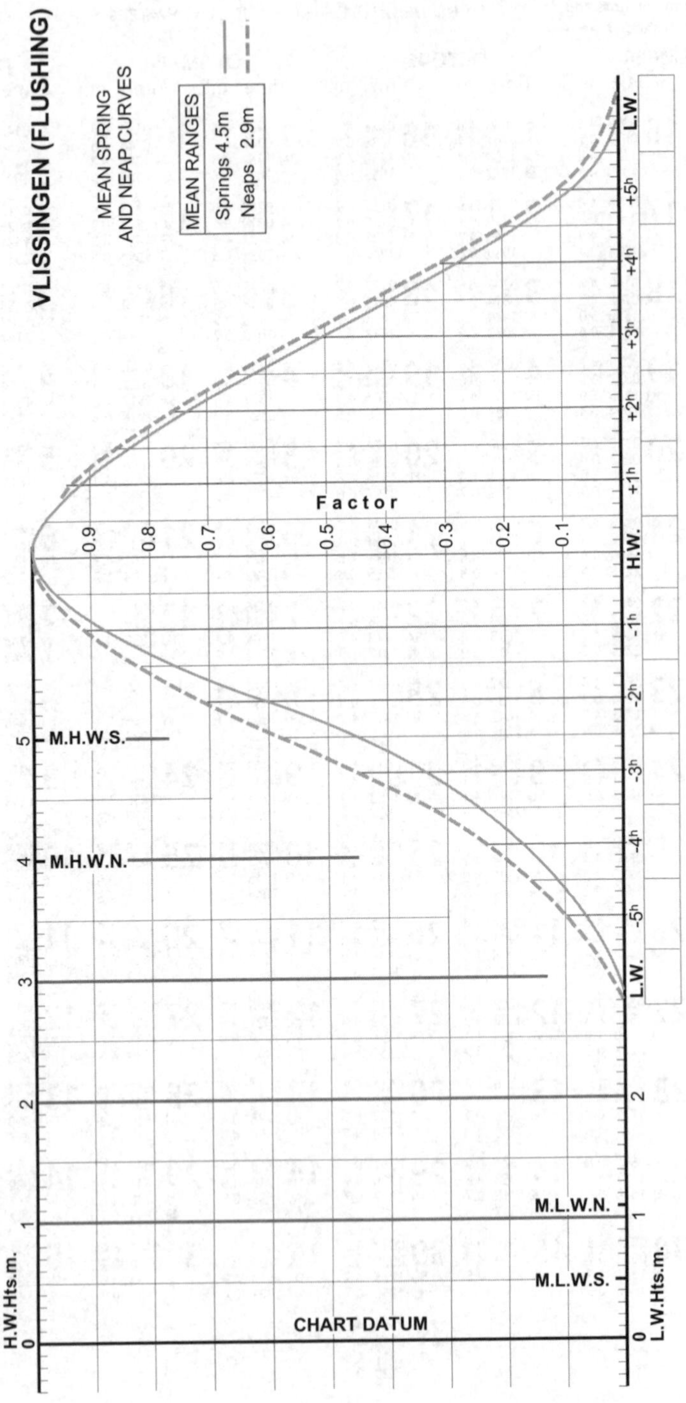
VLISSINGEN (FLUSHING)
MEAN SPRING AND NEAP CURVES
MEAN RANGES
Springs 4.5m
Neaps 2.9m
Factor
0.9
0.8
0.7
0.6
0.5
0.4
0.3
0.2
0.1
L.W.
-5h
-4h
-3h
-2h
-1h
H.W.
+1h
+2h
+3h
+4h
+5h
L.W.
H.W.Hts.m.
0
1
2
3
4
5
M.H.W.S.
M.H.W.N.
CHART DATUM
M.L.W.S.
M.L.W.N.
L.W.Hts.m.
0
1
2

TIME ZONE -0100
(Dutch Standard Time)
Subtract 1 hour for UT
For Dutch Summer Time add
ONE hour in **non-shaded areas**

NETHERLANDS – VLISSINGEN

LAT 51°27'N LONG 3°36'E

TIMES AND HEIGHTS OF HIGH AND LOW WATERS

Dates in amber are **SPRINGS**
Dates in yellow are **NEAPS**

2016

JANUARY

Date	Day	Time	m	Time	m	Time	m	Time	m
1	F	0010	1.1	0622	4.4	1256	0.9	1849	4.4
2	SA	0055	1.2	0708	4.2	1335	1.0	◑ 1939	4.2
3	SU	0200	1.3	0801	4.1	1446	1.1	2045	4.0
4	M	0316	1.4	0916	3.9	1540	1.2	2144	4.0
5	TU	0415	1.3	1025	4.0	1645	1.2	2259	4.1
6	W	0515	1.2	1125	4.2	1745	1.1	2356	4.4
7	TH	0611	1.1	1215	4.4	1830	1.0		
8	F	0035	4.6	0656	0.9	1256	4.6	1916	0.9
9	SA	0119	4.8	0738	0.8	1335	4.8	1956	0.8
10	SU	0157	4.9	0818	0.6	1413	5.0	● 2036	0.7
11	M	0235	5.0	0906	0.5	1453	5.1	2118	0.7
12	TU	0316	5.0	0945	0.4	1533	5.1	2200	0.7
13	W	0356	5.0	1036	0.4	1615	5.1	2246	0.7
14	TH	0436	4.9	1118	0.4	1659	5.0	2330	0.8
15	F	0525	4.8	1205	0.4	1749	4.9		
16	SA	0016	0.9	0616	4.7	1256	0.5	1850	4.7
17	SU	0106	1.0	0716	4.5	1346	0.6	◐ 1956	4.5
18	M	0206	1.1	0819	4.4	1445	0.8	2102	4.4
19	TU	0309	1.1	0930	4.3	1556	0.9	2216	4.4
20	W	0435	1.1	1039	4.4	1721	0.9	2325	4.4
21	TH	0556	1.0	1145	4.5	1820	0.8		
22	F	0026	4.6	0650	0.8	1245	4.7	1912	0.7
23	SA	0115	4.7	0740	0.6	1336	4.9	1955	0.7
24	SU	0201	4.9	0826	0.5	1418	5.0	○ 2035	0.7
25	M	0240	4.9	0905	0.5	1459	5.0	2116	0.8
26	TU	0317	4.9	0948	0.5	1537	5.0	2152	0.8
27	W	0357	4.9	1021	0.5	1615	4.9	2231	0.8
28	TH	0435	4.8	1106	0.6	1652	4.8	2306	0.9
29	F	0508	4.7	1135	0.7	1728	4.7	2338	1.0
30	SA	0545	4.6	1206	0.8	1808	4.5		
31	SU	0016	1.0	0626	4.4	1235	0.9	1849	4.3

FEBRUARY

Date	Day	Time	m	Time	m	Time	m	Time	m
1	M	0046	1.1	0716	4.2	1320	1.0	◑ 1946	4.1
2	TU	0135	1.2	0816	4.1	1414	1.2	2046	4.0
3	W	0305	1.3	0919	4.0	1556	1.2	2155	4.0
4	TH	0430	1.3	1035	4.0	1659	1.2	2316	4.1
5	F	0525	1.1	1145	4.2	1806	1.0		
6	SA	0016	4.4	0625	0.9	1236	4.5	1850	0.9
7	SU	0056	4.6	0715	0.7	1315	4.8	1936	0.8
8	M	0137	4.8	0759	0.6	1356	5.0	● 2015	0.7
9	TU	0215	5.0	0845	0.4	1435	5.2	2100	0.6
10	W	0256	5.1	0932	0.3	1515	5.2	2146	0.6
11	TH	0336	5.1	1015	0.2	1557	5.2	2228	0.6
12	F	0418	5.1	1102	0.2	1643	5.1	2316	0.6
13	SA	0505	5.0	1145	0.3	1728	5.0	2356	0.7
14	SU	0553	4.9	1229	0.4	1825	4.8		
15	M	0045	0.8	0649	4.7	1320	0.6	◐ 1925	4.5
16	TU	0140	0.9	0756	4.5	1416	0.8	2036	4.3
17	W	0245	1.1	0906	4.3	1524	1.0	2149	4.1
18	TH	0415	1.1	1025	4.2	1653	1.0	2309	4.2
19	F	0535	1.0	1139	4.4	1810	0.9		
20	SA	0015	4.4	0640	0.8	1245	4.6	1859	0.8
21	SU	0106	4.6	0729	0.6	1329	4.8	1946	0.8
22	M	0148	4.8	0812	0.5	1405	4.9	○ 2019	0.7
23	TU	0225	4.8	0849	0.5	1446	4.9	2058	0.7
24	W	0257	4.9	0928	0.5	1517	5.0	2129	0.7
25	TH	0336	4.9	1002	0.5	1550	4.9	2205	0.7
26	F	0407	4.9	1036	0.5	1625	4.9	2235	0.8
27	SA	0438	4.8	1106	0.6	1655	4.7	2306	0.8
28	SU	0511	4.7	1130	0.7	1727	4.6	2336	0.9
29	M	0541	4.6	1156	0.8	1759	4.5		

MARCH

Date	Day	Time	m	Time	m	Time	m	Time	m
1	TU	0006	0.9	0615	4.4	1229	0.9	1846	4.3
2	W	0050	1.0	0710	4.2	1326	1.0	◑ 1950	4.1
3	TH	0150	1.2	0824	4.0	1434	1.2	2110	3.9
4	F	0346	1.2	0952	4.0	1614	1.2	2236	4.0
5	SA	0506	1.1	1105	4.2	1736	1.1	2345	4.2
6	SU	0600	0.9	1208	4.5	1825	0.9		
7	M	0032	4.5	0656	0.7	1251	4.8	1909	0.8
8	TU	0115	4.8	0742	0.5	1332	5.0	1955	0.6
9	W	0155	5.0	0825	0.3	1413	5.2	● 2040	0.5
10	TH	0236	5.1	0910	0.2	1455	5.3	2126	0.5
11	F	0316	5.2	0955	0.1	1535	5.3	2208	0.5
12	SA	0358	5.2	1040	0.1	1621	5.2	2255	0.5
13	SU	0446	5.1	1126	0.2	1706	5.0	2338	0.6
14	M	0531	5.0	1208	0.4	1801	4.7		
15	TU	0026	0.7	0626	4.7	1251	0.6	◐ 1901	4.5
16	W	0115	0.8	0729	4.5	1356	0.8	2012	4.2
17	TH	0225	1.0	0846	4.2	1505	1.0	2135	4.0
18	F	0356	1.0	1009	4.2	1635	1.1	2255	4.1
19	SA	0526	0.9	1130	4.4	1755	0.9	2359	4.3
20	SU	0628	0.7	1225	4.6	1850	0.8		
21	M	0048	4.5	0715	0.6	1311	4.8	1925	0.8
22	TU	0131	4.7	0756	0.5	1349	4.8	1959	0.7
23	W	0208	4.8	0825	0.5	1426	4.9	○ 2035	0.7
24	TH	0237	4.8	0900	0.5	1455	4.9	2108	0.7
25	F	0307	4.9	0936	0.5	1526	4.9	2142	0.6
26	SA	0339	4.9	1006	0.5	1556	4.9	2216	0.7
27	SU	0408	4.8	1035	0.6	1627	4.8	2239	0.7
28	M	0439	4.8	1059	0.7	1656	4.7	2305	0.7
29	TU	0509	4.7	1128	0.8	1726	4.5	2341	0.8
30	W	0542	4.6	1202	0.8	1805	4.4		
31	TH	0020	0.8	0625	4.4	1250	1.0	◑ 1854	4.2

APRIL

Date	Day	Time	m	Time	m	Time	m	Time	m
1	F	0126	1.0	0746	4.1	1355	1.2	2031	4.0
2	SA	0250	1.1	0916	4.0	1534	1.2	2155	3.9
3	SU	0427	1.0	1036	4.2	1656	1.1	2305	4.2
4	M	0530	0.8	1135	4.5	1801	0.9		
5	TU	0002	4.5	0631	0.6	1225	4.8	1848	0.7
6	W	0045	4.8	0716	0.4	1306	5.1	1936	0.6
7	TH	0126	5.0	0806	0.3	1348	5.2	● 2021	0.5
8	F	0210	5.2	0847	0.2	1433	5.3	2103	0.4
9	SA	0254	5.2	0932	0.1	1515	5.3	2150	0.4
10	SU	0335	5.2	1017	0.2	1602	5.1	2233	0.4
11	M	0421	5.2	1100	0.3	1649	4.9	2321	0.5
12	TU	0511	5.0	1146	0.5	1741	4.7		
13	W	0005	0.6	0606	4.8	1230	0.7	1839	4.4
14	TH	0054	0.7	0716	4.5	1325	0.9	◐ 1945	4.2
15	F	0203	0.9	0825	4.3	1446	1.1	2110	4.0
16	SA	0330	0.9	0950	4.2	1620	1.1	2229	4.0
17	SU	0500	0.9	1106	4.3	1735	1.0	2335	4.2
18	M	0559	0.7	1201	4.6	1825	0.9		
19	TU	0025	4.4	0650	0.6	1248	4.7	1906	0.8
20	W	0106	4.6	0726	0.6	1326	4.8	1935	0.8
21	TH	0139	4.7	0800	0.6	1356	4.8	2008	0.7
22	F	0207	4.7	0832	0.5	1425	4.8	○ 2042	0.6
23	SA	0239	4.8	0905	0.5	1455	4.9	2115	0.6
24	SU	0311	4.9	0936	0.6	1527	4.9	2150	0.6
25	M	0342	4.8	1005	0.6	1559	4.8	2219	0.6
26	TU	0415	4.8	1041	0.7	1629	4.7	2249	0.7
27	W	0446	4.7	1111	0.8	1706	4.6	2326	0.7
28	TH	0521	4.6	1146	0.9	1742	4.5		
29	F	0006	0.7	0608	4.5	1229	1.0	1838	4.2
30	SA	0105	0.8	0716	4.2	1336	1.1	◑ 2001	4.1

Chart Datum: 2·56 metres below NAP Datum
HAT is 5·4 metres above Chart Datum

TIME ZONE -0100
(Dutch Standard Time)
Subtract 1 hour for UT
For Dutch Summer Time add ONE hour in **non-shaded areas**

NETHERLANDS – VLISSINGEN

LAT 51°27′N LONG 3°36′E

TIMES AND HEIGHTS OF HIGH AND LOW WATERS

Dates in amber are **SPRINGS**
Dates in yellow are **NEAPS**

2016

MAY

Date	Time	m	Date	Time	m
1 SU	0226 0842 1500 2116	0.9 4.2 1.1 4.0	16 M	0405 1030 1656 2258	0.9 4.3 1.1 4.1
2 M	0339 0955 1613 2226	0.8 4.3 1.1 4.2	17 TU	0519 1128 1746 2350	0.8 4.4 1.0 4.3
3 TU	0456 1101 1726 2328	0.7 4.6 0.9 4.5	18 W	0616 1216 1830	0.7 4.5 0.9
4 W	0601 1157 1826	0.6 4.8 0.7	19 TH	0031 0656 1255 1905	4.4 0.7 4.6 0.8
5 TH	0016 0652 1246 1909	4.7 0.4 5.0 0.6	20 F	0108 0726 1328 1940	4.5 0.7 4.7 0.7
6 F	0106 0740 1328 ● 1958	5.0 0.3 5.2 0.5	21 SA	0139 0800 1359 ○ 2016	4.7 0.6 4.8 0.6
7 SA	0147 0825 1415 2046	5.1 0.2 5.2 0.4	22 SU	0212 0831 1431 2049	4.8 0.6 4.8 0.6
8 SU	0233 0910 1458 2130	5.2 0.2 5.2 0.4	23 M	0247 0908 1505 2125	4.8 0.6 4.9 0.6
9 M	0318 0955 1545 2217	5.2 0.3 5.1 0.4	24 TU	0318 0946 1537 2205	4.8 0.7 4.8 0.6
10 TU	0405 1036 1632 2306	5.1 0.4 4.9 0.4	25 W	0352 1021 1610 2240	4.8 0.7 4.7 0.6
11 W	0456 1119 1726 2350	5.0 0.6 4.7 0.5	26 TH	0426 1056 1647 2314	4.7 0.8 4.6 0.6
12 TH	0549 1208 1819	4.8 0.7 4.5	27 F	0507 1136 1729 2359	4.7 0.9 4.5 0.6
13 F	0045 0649 1305 ◐ 1919	0.6 4.6 0.9 4.2	28 SA	0552 1225 1825	4.6 1.0 4.3
14 SA	0151 0800 1404 2035	0.7 4.4 1.1 4.0	29 SU	0055 0656 1320 ◑ 1936	0.7 4.4 1.0 4.2
15 SU	0255 0916 1524 2152	0.8 4.2 1.1 4.0	30 M	0154 0817 1423 2045	0.7 4.4 1.1 4.2
			31 TU	0304 0926 1534 2156	0.7 4.4 1.0 4.3

JUNE

Date	Time	m	Date	Time	m
1 W	0415 1030 1656 2255	0.7 4.6 0.9 4.5	16 TH	0519 1135 1734 2351	0.9 4.3 1.0 4.3
2 TH	0531 1127 1756 2352	0.6 4.8 0.8 4.7	17 F	0616 1218 1830	0.9 4.5 0.9
3 F	0626 1221 1850	0.5 5.0 0.6	18 SA	0036 0649 1255 1910	4.4 0.8 4.6 0.8
4 SA	0043 0718 1309 1940	4.9 0.4 5.1 0.5	19 SU	0116 0730 1331 1950	4.6 0.8 4.7 0.7
5 SU	0128 0806 1356 ● 2028	5.1 0.3 5.1 0.4	20 M	0147 0805 1406 ○ 2028	4.7 0.7 4.8 0.6
6 M	0216 0850 1443 2116	5.1 0.4 5.1 0.4	21 TU	0222 0839 1446 2106	4.8 0.7 4.8 0.5
7 TU	0301 0935 1530 2202	5.1 0.4 5.0 0.4	22 W	0259 0919 1518 2145	4.9 0.7 4.8 0.5
8 W	0350 1017 1617 2246	5.1 0.6 4.9 0.4	23 TH	0335 1002 1557 2230	4.9 0.7 4.8 0.5
9 TH	0437 1059 1706 2336	5.0 0.7 4.7 0.5	24 F	0415 1039 1635 2316	4.8 0.8 4.7 0.5
10 F	0528 1146 1756	4.8 0.8 4.6	25 SA	0455 1126 1717 2354	4.8 0.9 4.6 0.5
11 SA	0019 0625 1236 1848	0.5 4.6 1.0 4.4	26 SU	0541 1215 1806	4.7 0.9 4.5
12 SU	0111 0726 1330 ◐ 1945	0.7 4.4 1.1 4.2	27 M	0051 0636 1306 ◑ 1908	0.5 4.6 1.0 4.4
13 M	0209 0826 1436 2044	0.8 4.2 1.2 4.0	28 TU	0146 0746 1359 2016	0.6 4.5 1.0 4.4
14 TU	0316 0935 1545 2206	0.9 4.2 1.2 4.0	29 W	0246 0851 1506 2122	0.6 4.5 1.0 4.4
15 W	0420 1046 1645 2305	0.9 4.2 1.1 4.1	30 TH	0346 1000 1615 2227	0.7 4.6 1.0 4.5

JULY

Date	Time	m	Date	Time	m
1 F	0506 1105 1736 2327	0.7 4.6 0.9 4.6	16 SA	0536 1142 1749	1.0 4.3 1.0
2 SA	0606 1205 1832	0.6 4.8 0.7	17 SU	0002 0621 1230 1839	4.3 1.0 4.5 0.9
3 SU	0025 0701 1255 1926	4.8 0.5 4.9 0.6	18 M	0046 0700 1309 1925	4.5 0.9 4.6 0.8
4 M	0116 0745 1345 ● 2015	4.9 0.5 5.0 0.4	19 TU	0126 0740 1345 ○ 2005	4.7 0.8 4.8 0.6
5 TU	0205 0831 1432 2102	5.0 0.5 5.0 0.4	20 W	0206 0818 1422 2046	4.8 0.8 4.9 0.5
6 W	0250 0915 1515 2145	5.1 0.6 5.0 0.4	21 TH	0241 0900 1501 2130	5.0 0.7 4.9 0.4
7 TH	0336 0956 1559 2232	5.1 0.7 4.9 0.4	22 F	0316 0946 1536 2216	5.0 0.7 4.9 0.4
8 F	0420 1038 1645 2311	5.0 0.8 4.8 0.5	23 SA	0356 1025 1619 2259	5.0 0.7 4.9 0.4
9 SA	0508 1120 1728 2355	4.9 0.9 4.7 0.5	24 SU	0438 1109 1700 2346	5.0 0.8 4.8 0.4
10 SU	0551 1159 1809	4.7 1.0 4.6	25 M	0526 1155 1747	4.9 0.8 4.7
11 M	0035 0640 1245 1856	0.7 4.5 1.1 4.4	26 TU	0029 0618 1242 1841	0.5 4.8 0.9 4.6
12 TU	0126 0725 1346 ◐ 1945	0.8 4.3 1.2 4.2	27 W	0121 0720 1336 ◑ 1948	0.5 4.6 1.0 4.5
13 W	0220 0826 1443 2044	0.9 4.1 1.2 4.0	28 TH	0212 0826 1440 2055	0.6 4.5 1.0 4.4
14 TH	0314 0936 1549 2206	1.0 4.0 1.2 4.0	29 F	0321 0936 1550 2205	0.8 4.4 1.1 4.4
15 F	0436 1046 1655 2316	1.1 4.1 1.1 4.1	30 SA	0436 1045 1710 2312	0.8 4.4 1.0 4.5
			31 SU	0551 1151 1820	0.8 4.6 0.8

AUGUST

Date	Time	m	Date	Time	m
1 M	0016 0646 1247 1916	4.7 0.7 4.8 0.6	16 TU	0019 0635 1246 1859	4.5 1.0 4.6 0.8
2 TU	0108 0735 1335 ● 2003	4.9 0.7 4.9 0.5	17 W	0101 0718 1325 1946	4.7 0.9 4.8 0.7
3 W	0157 0818 1421 2048	5.0 0.7 5.0 0.4	18 TH	0141 0756 1401 ○ 2025	4.9 0.8 5.0 0.5
4 TH	0237 0858 1500 2129	5.1 0.7 5.0 0.4	19 F	0218 0838 1436 2108	5.1 0.7 5.1 0.4
5 F	0321 0938 1539 2210	5.1 0.8 5.0 0.4	20 SA	0256 0926 1517 2153	5.2 0.7 5.1 0.3
6 SA	0359 1015 1617 2248	5.0 0.8 4.9 0.5	21 SU	0336 1005 1557 2238	5.2 0.7 5.1 0.3
7 SU	0438 1049 1657 2325	4.9 0.9 4.8 0.6	22 M	0418 1052 1639 2326	5.2 0.7 5.1 0.4
8 M	0517 1131 1732	4.8 0.9 4.7	23 TU	0505 1132 1726	5.0 0.8 4.9
9 TU	0000 0556 1202 1811	0.7 4.6 1.0 4.5	24 W	0008 0555 1219 1816	0.4 4.9 0.8 4.8
10 W	0036 0640 1245 ◐ 1901	0.9 4.4 1.1 4.3	25 TH	0056 0652 1316 ◑ 1918	0.6 4.6 0.9 4.6
11 TH	0105 0731 1324 1956	1.0 4.2 1.2 4.1	26 F	0148 0800 1415 2032	0.8 4.4 1.1 4.4
12 F	0204 0826 1454 2100	1.2 4.0 1.3 4.0	27 SA	0244 0912 1535 2145	0.9 4.3 1.1 4.3
13 SA	0346 0935 1616 2226	1.3 4.0 1.3 4.0	28 SU	0425 1036 1706 2301	1.0 4.3 1.1 4.4
14 SU	0445 1100 1720 2330	1.2 4.1 1.2 4.2	29 M	0536 1145 1816	1.0 4.5 0.8
15 M	0546 1200 1816	1.1 4.3 1.0	30 TU	0008 0636 1238 1905	4.7 0.9 4.7 0.6
			31 W	0101 0722 1325 1952	4.9 0.8 4.8 0.5

Chart Datum: 2·56 metres below NAP Datum
HAT is 5·4 metres above Chart Datum

TIME ZONE -0100
(Dutch Standard Time)
Subtract 1 hour for UT
For Dutch Summer Time add ONE hour in **non-shaded areas**

NETHERLANDS – VLISSINGEN

LAT 51°27'N LONG 3°36'E

TIMES AND HEIGHTS OF HIGH AND LOW WATERS

Dates in amber are **SPRINGS**
Dates in yellow are **NEAPS**

2016

SEPTEMBER

Date	Day	Time	m	Time	m	Time	m	Time	m
1	TH	0146	5.0	0802	0.8	1406	4.9	● 2032	0.5
2	F	0226	5.1	0840	0.8	1440	5.0	2108	0.5
3	SA	0258	5.1	0916	0.8	1517	5.0	2146	0.5
4	SU	0335	5.1	0950	0.8	1551	5.0	2220	0.6
5	M	0412	5.0	1026	0.9	1625	4.9	2252	0.7
6	TU	0445	4.8	1056	0.9	1659	4.8	2326	0.8
7	W	0516	4.7	1126	1.0	1731	4.7	2345	0.9
8	TH	0549	4.5	1152	1.0	1805	4.5		
9	F	0015	1.0	0636	4.3	1229	1.1	◐ 1855	4.3
10	SA	0059	1.2	0725	4.1	1325	1.3	2016	4.0
11	SU	0204	1.4	0846	4.0	1530	1.4	2124	4.0
12	M	0416	1.4	1006	4.0	1640	1.2	2249	4.1
13	TU	0504	1.2	1122	4.2	1746	1.0	2356	4.5
14	W	0605	1.1	1216	4.5	1836	0.8		
15	TH	0035	4.8	0652	0.9	1257	4.8	1918	0.6
16	F	0115	5.0	0735	0.8	1335	5.0	○ 2002	0.5
17	SA	0153	5.2	0815	0.7	1413	5.2	2047	0.4
18	SU	0233	5.4	0903	0.6	1453	5.3	2130	0.3
19	M	0314	5.4	0946	0.6	1536	5.3	2215	0.3
20	TU	0357	5.3	1030	0.6	1615	5.2	2257	0.4
21	W	0442	5.1	1113	0.7	1703	5.1	2342	0.5
22	TH	0530	4.9	1201	0.8	1755	4.9		
23	F	0026	0.7	0627	4.6	1250	0.9	◑ 1855	4.6
24	SA	0119	0.9	0736	4.4	1356	1.1	2009	4.4
25	SU	0224	1.1	0852	4.2	1516	1.1	2129	4.3
26	M	0355	1.2	1020	4.2	1650	1.1	2256	4.4
27	TU	0531	1.1	1129	4.4	1800	0.8	2359	4.7
28	W	0625	1.0	1225	4.6	1849	0.7		
29	TH	0049	4.9	0706	0.9	1305	4.8	1931	0.6
30	F	0129	5.0	0746	0.8	1346	4.9	2010	0.6

OCTOBER

Date	Day	Time	m	Time	m	Time	m	Time	m
1	SA	0206	5.0	0818	0.8	1417	5.0	● 2041	0.6
2	SU	0235	5.0	0852	0.8	1451	5.0	2115	0.6
3	M	0308	5.0	0926	0.8	1526	5.0	2150	0.7
4	TU	0341	5.0	0958	0.8	1555	5.0	2219	0.8
5	W	0415	4.9	1030	0.9	1627	4.9	2245	0.9
6	TH	0442	4.7	1056	0.9	1657	4.7	2316	1.0
7	F	0515	4.6	1120	1.0	1727	4.6	2342	1.0
8	SA	0548	4.5	1155	1.0	1808	4.4		
9	SU	0026	1.2	0631	4.3	1250	1.2	◐ 1903	4.2
10	M	0126	1.4	0801	4.0	1404	1.3	2045	4.1
11	TU	0315	1.4	0920	4.0	1555	1.2	2206	4.2
12	W	0436	1.3	1035	4.2	1706	1.0	2311	4.5
13	TH	0535	1.1	1135	4.5	1759	0.8		
14	F	0006	4.8	0626	0.9	1223	4.8	1849	0.6
15	SA	0045	5.1	0708	0.8	1306	5.1	1938	0.5
16	SU	0126	5.3	0752	0.7	1345	5.3	○ 2021	0.4
17	M	0208	5.4	0838	0.6	1428	5.4	2106	0.3
18	TU	0252	5.4	0926	0.6	1512	5.4	2150	0.4
19	W	0336	5.3	1008	0.6	1556	5.3	2233	0.5
20	TH	0422	5.1	1056	0.6	1643	5.2	2318	0.6
21	F	0512	4.9	1139	0.7	1733	4.9		
22	SA	0005	0.8	0608	4.6	1232	0.8	◑ 1838	4.7
23	SU	0056	1.0	0715	4.4	1335	1.0	1956	4.5
24	M	0206	1.2	0830	4.2	1444	1.1	2116	4.3
25	TU	0334	1.3	0956	4.1	1626	1.0	2229	4.4
26	W	0506	1.2	1105	4.3	1735	0.9	2336	4.6
27	TH	0605	1.1	1159	4.5	1831	0.7		
28	F	0025	4.8	0645	1.0	1246	4.7	1905	0.7
29	SA	0107	4.9	0720	0.9	1318	4.8	1946	0.7
30	SU	0138	4.9	0752	0.9	1352	4.9	● 2016	0.7
31	M	0211	5.0	0826	0.8	1426	4.9	2048	0.7

NOVEMBER

Date	Day	Time	m	Time	m	Time	m	Time	m
1	TU	0242	5.0	0859	0.8	1457	5.0	2120	0.7
2	W	0316	5.0	0936	0.8	1527	5.0	2156	0.8
3	TH	0346	4.9	1006	0.8	1602	4.9	2220	0.9
4	F	0417	4.8	1035	0.9	1631	4.8	2245	1.0
5	SA	0447	4.7	1106	0.9	1702	4.7	2320	1.1
6	SU	0521	4.6	1140	0.9	1741	4.6		
7	M	0000	1.1	0610	4.4	1230	1.0	◐ 1835	4.4
8	TU	0100	1.3	0716	4.2	1333	1.1	2006	4.2
9	W	0215	1.4	0840	4.1	1516	1.1	2122	4.3
10	TH	0346	1.3	0955	4.2	1614	1.0	2232	4.5
11	F	0444	1.2	1056	4.5	1726	0.8	2329	4.8
12	SA	0545	1.0	1151	4.8	1822	0.6		
13	SU	0020	5.1	0646	0.8	1238	5.0	1912	0.5
14	M	0106	5.3	0729	0.7	1326	5.2	○ 1958	0.4
15	TU	0148	5.3	0818	0.6	1407	5.3	2046	0.4
16	W	0233	5.3	0906	0.5	1454	5.4	2128	0.4
17	TH	0319	5.2	0952	0.5	1538	5.3	2213	0.5
18	F	0405	5.1	1038	0.6	1626	5.2	2256	0.7
19	SA	0457	4.9	1126	0.6	1717	5.0	2342	0.9
20	SU	0549	4.7	1215	0.7	1819	4.8		
21	M	0036	1.0	0649	4.4	1316	0.9	◑ 1928	4.5
22	TU	0129	1.2	0756	4.2	1414	1.0	2035	4.4
23	W	0256	1.3	0909	4.1	1534	1.0	2156	4.3
24	TH	0405	1.3	1025	4.2	1700	1.0	2302	4.4
25	F	0525	1.2	1125	4.3	1755	0.9	2355	4.6
26	SA	0615	1.1	1211	4.5	1841	0.9		
27	SU	0038	4.7	0650	1.0	1251	4.6	1912	0.8
28	M	0112	4.8	0726	0.9	1327	4.7	1945	0.8
29	TU	0147	4.8	0759	0.8	1358	4.8	● 2021	0.8
30	W	0218	4.9	0838	0.8	1436	4.9	2056	0.8

DECEMBER

Date	Day	Time	m	Time	m	Time	m	Time	m
1	TH	0251	4.9	0916	0.7	1506	4.9	2125	0.8
2	F	0325	4.9	0945	0.7	1537	4.9	2158	0.9
3	SA	0357	4.8	1026	0.8	1612	4.8	2230	1.0
4	SU	0432	4.7	1056	0.8	1647	4.8	2308	1.0
5	M	0507	4.6	1136	0.8	1727	4.7	2345	1.1
6	TU	0551	4.5	1220	0.8	1815	4.6		
7	W	0040	1.2	0650	4.4	1326	0.9	◐ 1930	4.4
8	TH	0139	1.2	0806	4.3	1426	0.9	2046	4.4
9	F	0256	1.2	0916	4.3	1535	0.9	2152	4.5
10	SA	0406	1.2	1019	4.5	1646	0.8	2256	4.7
11	SU	0516	1.0	1119	4.7	1749	0.7	2352	4.9
12	M	0615	0.9	1216	4.9	1851	0.6		
13	TU	0046	5.1	0712	0.7	1303	5.1	1941	0.5
14	W	0132	5.1	0803	0.6	1350	5.2	○ 2026	0.5
15	TH	0219	5.2	0850	0.5	1438	5.3	2110	0.5
16	F	0305	5.1	0938	0.5	1525	5.3	2153	0.6
17	SA	0353	5.0	1022	0.5	1616	5.2	2237	0.7
18	SU	0441	4.9	1110	0.5	1702	5.0	2320	0.9
19	M	0528	4.8	1156	0.6	1755	4.8		
20	TU	0005	1.0	0622	4.6	1246	0.7	1849	4.6
21	W	0055	1.1	0716	4.4	1335	0.9	◑ 1952	4.4
22	TH	0155	1.3	0815	4.2	1440	1.0	2105	4.2
23	F	0305	1.3	0925	4.1	1550	1.1	2216	4.2
24	SA	0420	1.3	1040	4.1	1655	1.1	2315	4.3
25	SU	0525	1.2	1136	4.2	1755	1.0		
26	M	0005	4.4	0615	1.1	1221	4.4	1840	1.0
27	TU	0050	4.5	0654	1.0	1301	4.5	1918	0.9
28	W	0126	4.6	0741	0.9	1339	4.7	1956	0.9
29	TH	0155	4.7	0815	0.8	1415	4.8	● 2031	0.8
30	F	0236	4.8	0856	0.7	1447	4.9	2106	0.8
31	SA	0305	4.9	0932	0.6	1521	4.9	2146	0.8

Chart Datum: 2·56 metres below NAP Datum
HAT is 5·4 metres above Chart Datum

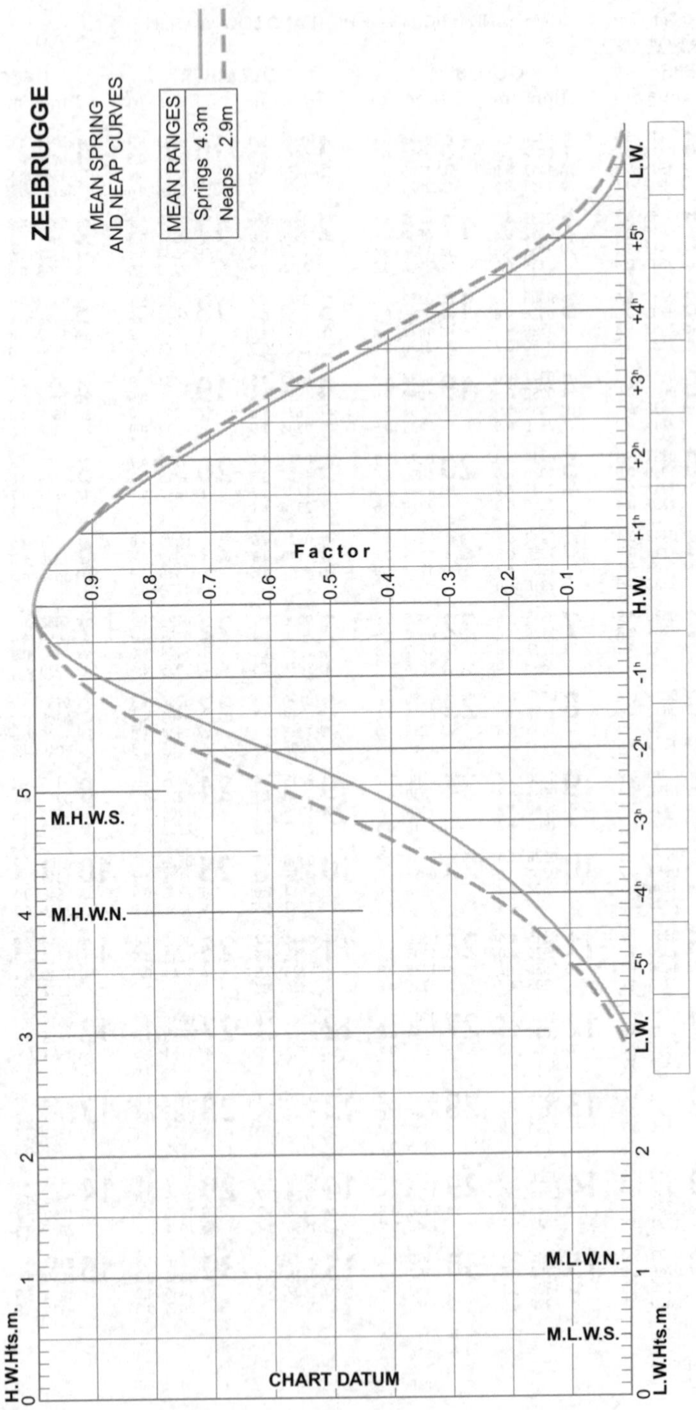
ZEEBRUGGE
MEAN SPRING AND NEAP CURVES
MEAN RANGES
Springs 4.3m
Neaps 2.9m
H.W.Hts.m.
M.H.W.S.
M.H.W.N.
CHART DATUM
Factor
M.L.W.N.
M.L.W.S.
L.W.Hts.m.
L.W.
-5h
-4h
-3h
-2h
-1h
H.W.
+1h
+2h
+3h
+4h
+5h
L.W.

TIME ZONE -0100
(Belgian Standard Time)
Subtract 1 hour for UT
For Belgian Summer Time add ONE hour in **non-shaded areas**

BELGIUM – ZEEBRUGGE

LAT 51°21′N LONG 3°12′E

TIMES AND HEIGHTS OF HIGH AND LOW WATERS

Dates in amber are **SPRINGS**
Dates in yellow are **NEAPS**

2016

JANUARY

Date	Day	Time	m	Time	m	Time	m	Time	m
1	F	0539	4.2	1149	0.9	1811	4.2		
2	SA ◑	0002	1.3	0630	4.0	1245	1.1	1908	4.0
3	SU	0106	1.5	0732	3.8	1412	1.2	2015	3.8
4	M	0252	1.6	0845	3.6	1532	1.3	2134	3.7
5	TU	0410	1.5	1006	3.6	1635	1.2	2248	3.8
6	W	0511	1.3	1113	3.8	1730	1.2	2343	4.0
7	TH	0603	1.2	1203	4.0	1816	1.1		
8	F	0026	4.2	0645	1.0	1242	4.2	1856	1.0
9	SA	0102	4.4	0723	0.9	1316	4.4	1933	0.9
10	SU ●	0134	4.6	0800	0.7	1350	4.7	2011	0.8
11	M	0207	4.7	0839	0.6	1425	4.8	2051	0.7
12	TU	0244	4.9	0920	0.5	1505	5.0	2134	0.6
13	W	0324	4.9	1004	0.4	1548	5.1	2220	0.6
14	TH	0409	5.0	1050	0.3	1635	5.1	2308	0.5
15	F	0457	4.9	1139	0.2	1727	5.0	2358	0.5
16	SA	0551	4.8	1230	0.2	1825	4.9		
17	SU ◐	0051	0.6	0651	4.7	1324	0.3	1928	4.7
18	M	0149	0.7	0756	4.5	1424	0.5	2034	4.5
19	TU	0254	0.8	0904	4.4	1533	0.6	2143	4.4
20	W	0413	0.8	1014	4.4	1648	0.7	2250	4.4
21	TH	0525	0.8	1119	4.5	1751	0.7	2349	4.5
22	F	0621	0.7	1214	4.6	1842	0.7		
23	SA	0038	4.6	0707	0.6	1300	4.7	1926	0.8
24	SU ○	0121	4.7	0749	0.6	1341	4.8	2004	0.8
25	M	0159	4.7	0826	0.6	1419	4.8	2039	0.9
26	TU	0236	4.7	0901	0.6	1457	4.8	2110	0.9
27	W	0313	4.7	0934	0.5	1535	4.8	2140	0.9
28	TH	0350	4.6	1006	0.5	1614	4.7	2213	0.9
29	F	0428	4.5	1041	0.6	1654	4.5	2250	0.9
30	SA	0507	4.4	1120	0.7	1735	4.3	2330	1.1
31	SU	0549	4.1	1203	0.9	1821	4.1		

FEBRUARY

Date	Day	Time	m	Time	m	Time	m	Time	m
1	M ◑	0017	1.3	0637	3.9	1302	1.2	1915	3.8
2	TU	0129	1.6	0739	3.6	1443	1.4	2028	3.5
3	W	0329	1.6	0904	3.4	1558	1.4	2201	3.5
4	TH	0437	1.5	1035	3.6	1657	1.3	2312	3.8
5	F	0534	1.3	1134	3.9	1748	1.1		
6	SA	0000	4.1	0621	1.0	1217	4.2	1830	1.0
7	SU	0037	4.4	0659	0.8	1253	4.5	1909	0.8
8	M ●	0110	4.6	0737	0.5	1328	4.8	1948	0.6
9	TU	0145	4.9	0817	0.3	1406	5.1	2030	0.4
10	W	0224	5.1	0859	0.1	1447	5.3	2115	0.3
11	TH	0306	5.2	0944	0.0	1530	5.3	2201	0.2
12	F	0350	5.3	1030	-0.1	1616	5.3	2247	0.2
13	SA	0437	5.2	1116	-0.1	1705	5.1	2335	0.3
14	SU	0527	5.0	1204	0.1	1758	4.9		
15	M ◐	0024	0.4	0622	4.8	1256	0.3	1857	4.6
16	TU	0118	0.6	0724	4.5	1354	0.6	2002	4.3
17	W	0225	0.9	0835	4.2	1507	0.8	2116	4.1
18	TH	0352	1.0	0952	4.1	1629	0.9	2232	4.1
19	F	0507	0.9	1105	4.2	1735	0.9	2335	4.2
20	SA	0605	0.8	1201	4.4	1828	0.9		
21	SU	0024	4.4	0652	0.7	1246	4.6	1910	0.9
22	M ○	0104	4.5	0733	0.6	1324	4.7	1947	0.9
23	TU	0140	4.6	0808	0.6	1400	4.7	2019	0.9
24	W	0215	4.6	0841	0.5	1436	4.8	2049	0.8
25	TH	0251	4.7	0912	0.5	1512	4.8	2119	0.8
26	F	0326	4.7	0944	0.5	1549	4.7	2152	0.8
27	SA	0401	4.6	1018	0.5	1625	4.6	2227	0.8
28	SU	0436	4.4	1053	0.7	1700	4.4	2302	1.0
29	M	0511	4.2	1128	0.9	1737	4.1	2338	1.2

MARCH

Date	Day	Time	m	Time	m	Time	m	Time	m
1	TU	0550	4.0	1207	1.1	1820	3.8		
2	W ◑	0021	1.5	0640	3.7	1312	1.4	1920	3.5
3	TH	0241	1.7	0756	3.5	1520	1.5	2100	3.4
4	F	0400	1.5	0945	3.5	1622	1.4	2231	3.6
5	SA	0459	1.3	1059	3.9	1716	1.2	2326	4.0
6	SU	0549	1.0	1146	4.3	1802	0.9		
7	M	0006	4.4	0631	0.6	1226	4.7	1843	0.7
8	TU	0044	4.8	0711	0.3	1304	5.0	1924	0.4
9	W ●	0122	5.1	0753	0.1	1344	5.3	2008	0.2
10	TH	0202	5.3	0836	-0.1	1425	5.4	2053	0.0
11	F	0244	5.5	0921	-0.2	1509	5.5	2139	0.0
12	SA	0329	5.5	1007	-0.2	1554	5.4	2225	0.0
13	SU	0415	5.4	1052	-0.1	1642	5.2	2311	0.1
14	M	0503	5.1	1139	0.1	1732	4.9	2358	0.4
15	TU ◐	0556	4.8	1227	0.4	1828	4.5		
16	W	0049	0.7	0655	4.5	1324	0.8	1932	4.2
17	TH	0156	1.0	0806	4.1	1442	1.1	2048	3.9
18	F	0327	1.1	0928	4.0	1606	1.2	2209	3.9
19	SA	0443	1.0	1045	4.1	1714	1.1	2315	4.0
20	SU	0543	0.9	1142	4.3	1808	1.0		
21	M	0004	4.2	0631	0.8	1226	4.4	1851	1.0
22	TU	0043	4.4	0712	0.7	1303	4.6	1926	0.9
23	W ○	0119	4.5	0746	0.6	1338	4.7	1958	0.8
24	TH	0153	4.6	0818	0.6	1413	4.7	2028	0.8
25	F	0228	4.6	0850	0.5	1449	4.7	2100	0.7
26	SA	0302	4.6	0923	0.5	1524	4.6	2134	0.7
27	SU	0335	4.5	0956	0.6	1556	4.5	2207	0.8
28	M	0407	4.4	1028	0.8	1627	4.3	2238	1.0
29	TU	0439	4.3	1057	1.0	1700	4.1	2307	1.2
30	W	0515	4.1	1128	1.2	1739	3.9	2342	1.3
31	TH ◑	0602	3.9	1213	1.4	1834	3.7		

APRIL

Date	Day	Time	m	Time	m	Time	m	Time	m
1	F	0047	1.5	0711	3.7	1432	1.5	2007	3.5
2	SA	0318	1.4	0859	3.7	1544	1.3	2146	3.7
3	SU	0418	1.1	1019	4.0	1639	1.1	2247	4.1
4	M	0511	0.8	1113	4.4	1729	0.8	2334	4.5
5	TU	0559	0.5	1157	4.8	1816	0.5		
6	W	0016	4.9	0643	0.2	1239	5.2	1900	0.3
7	TH ●	0057	5.2	0728	-0.1	1320	5.4	1945	0.1
8	F	0139	5.4	0813	-0.2	1403	5.5	2031	-0.1
9	SA	0223	5.5	0858	-0.3	1447	5.5	2117	-0.1
10	SU	0307	5.5	0943	-0.2	1533	5.3	2202	0.0
11	M	0353	5.4	1028	0.0	1619	5.1	2247	0.2
12	TU	0441	5.1	1113	0.3	1708	4.8	2333	0.4
13	W	0532	4.8	1200	0.6	1801	4.5		
14	TH ◐	0022	0.7	0629	4.5	1254	1.0	1901	4.1
15	F	0126	1.0	0737	4.1	1409	1.3	2014	3.8
16	SA	0255	1.2	0857	3.9	1535	1.4	2136	3.8
17	SU	0410	1.1	1016	4.0	1644	1.3	2246	3.9
18	M	0513	1.0	1116	4.2	1741	1.1	2338	4.1
19	TU	0604	0.8	1201	4.3	1826	1.0		
20	W	0019	4.3	0645	0.7	1240	4.5	1902	0.9
21	TH	0056	4.4	0721	0.7	1316	4.6	1935	0.8
22	F ○	0131	4.5	0754	0.6	1351	4.6	2008	0.8
23	SA	0206	4.5	0828	0.6	1426	4.6	2042	0.7
24	SU	0240	4.5	0902	0.7	1500	4.5	2117	0.8
25	M	0312	4.4	0936	0.8	1531	4.4	2150	0.9
26	TU	0342	4.4	1007	0.9	1600	4.3	2220	1.0
27	W	0414	4.3	1034	1.1	1633	4.2	2248	1.1
28	TH	0452	4.2	1105	1.2	1714	4.0	2325	1.2
29	F	0541	4.1	1154	1.3	1810	3.9		
30	SA ◑	0040	1.3	0650	4.0	1340	1.3	1936	3.8

Chart Datum: 0·23 metres below TAW Datum
HAT is 5·6 metres above Chart Datum

TIME ZONE -0100
(Belgian Standard Time)
Subtract 1 hour for UT
For Belgian Summer Time add ONE hour in **non-shaded areas**

BELGIUM – ZEEBRUGGE

LAT 51°21'N LONG 3°12'E

TIMES AND HEIGHTS OF HIGH AND LOW WATERS

Dates in amber are **SPRINGS**
Dates in yellow are **NEAPS**

2016

MAY

Day	Time	m	Day	Time	m
1 SU	0232 0824 1501 2104	1.1 4.0 1.2 3.9	16 M	0328 0934 1603 2207	1.1 3.9 1.4 3.8
2 M	0336 0940 1601 2209	0.9 4.2 0.9 4.2	17 TU	0433 1042 1705 2306	1.0 4.0 1.2 3.9
3 TU	0432 1039 1656 2302	0.6 4.6 0.7 4.6	18 W	0529 1133 1756 2352	0.9 4.2 1.1 4.1
4 W	0526 1128 1749 2349	0.3 4.9 0.4 4.9	19 TH	0615 1215 1838	0.8 4.3 0.9
5 TH	0617 1214 1838	0.1 5.1 0.2	20 F	0032 0654 1254 1914	4.2 0.8 4.4 0.9
6 F	0033 0704 1258 ● 1925	5.2 0.0 5.3 0.1	21 SA	0110 0730 1331 ○ 1950	4.3 0.8 4.5 0.8
7 SA	0118 0750 1343 2011	5.4 -0.1 5.4 0.0	22 SU	0146 0806 1406 2026	4.4 0.8 4.5 0.8
8 SU	0203 0836 1427 2056	5.4 -0.1 5.3 0.0	23 M	0219 0841 1439 2102	4.4 0.8 4.4 0.9
9 M	0248 0920 1513 2141	5.4 0.0 5.2 0.1	24 TU	0251 0916 1509 2137	4.3 0.9 4.3 0.9
10 TU	0334 1004 1559 2225	5.3 0.3 5.0 0.2	25 W	0323 0950 1540 2211	4.3 1.0 4.3 1.0
11 W	0422 1048 1646 2309	5.0 0.5 4.7 0.5	26 TH	0357 1022 1616 2246	4.4 1.1 4.2 1.0
12 TH	0511 1131 1735 2355	4.8 0.8 4.4 0.7	27 F	0439 1101 1700 2333	4.4 1.1 4.2 1.0
13 F	0604 1219 1830 ◐	4.5 1.1 4.1	28 SA	0530 1157 1757	4.3 1.1 4.1
14 SA	0052 0704 1323 1934	0.9 4.2 1.3 3.8	29 SU	0043 0636 1313 ◑ 1912	0.9 4.3 1.0 4.0
15 SU	0212 0815 1450 2050	1.1 3.9 1.4 3.7	30 M	0155 0755 1422 2028	0.8 4.3 0.9 4.1
			31 TU	0257 0905 1524 2133	0.6 4.4 0.7 4.3

JUNE

Day	Time	m	Day	Time	m
1 W	0356 1006 1625 2231	0.4 4.6 0.6 4.6	16 TH	0448 1100 1722 2324	1.0 3.9 1.2 3.8
2 TH	0456 1101 1725 2324	0.3 4.8 0.4 4.8	17 F	0542 1150 1813	1.0 4.1 1.0
3 F	0553 1152 1819	0.2 5.0 0.3	18 SA	0010 0627 1233 1854	4.0 0.9 4.2 0.9
4 SA	0013 0644 1240 1907	5.0 0.1 5.1 0.2	19 SU	0050 0707 1311 1933	4.1 0.9 4.3 0.9
5 SU	0100 0731 1326 ● 1953	5.2 0.1 5.1 0.2	20 M	0127 0744 1346 ○ 2009	4.2 0.9 4.3 0.8
6 M	0147 0816 1411 2038	5.2 0.2 5.1 0.2	21 TU	0200 0821 1418 2046	4.3 0.9 4.4 0.8
7 TU	0232 0859 1455 2121	5.2 0.3 5.0 0.2	22 W	0233 0857 1450 2124	4.4 0.9 4.4 0.8
8 W	0318 0942 1539 2204	5.1 0.5 4.8 0.3	23 TH	0307 0935 1524 2203	4.4 0.9 4.4 0.8
9 TH	0403 1022 1624 2245	4.9 0.7 4.6 0.5	24 F	0344 1014 1603 2246	4.5 0.9 4.4 0.7
10 F	0449 1102 1709 2327	4.7 0.9 4.4 0.6	25 SA	0428 1100 1649 2334	4.6 0.9 4.4 0.6
11 SA	0537 1142 1758	4.5 1.1 4.2	26 SU	0518 1151 1742	4.6 0.8 4.4
12 SU	0014 0629 1231 ◐ 1852	0.8 4.2 1.3 4.0	27 M	0027 0618 1249 ◑ 1846	0.5 4.5 0.7 4.4
13 M	0117 0729 1342 1956	1.0 4.0 1.4 3.7	28 TU	0124 0725 1348 1954	0.4 4.5 0.7 4.4
14 TU	0235 0839 1509 2112	1.1 3.8 1.4 3.6	29 W	0223 0832 1450 2059	0.4 4.5 0.6 4.4
15 W	0346 0956 1621 2226	1.1 3.8 1.3 3.7	30 TH	0325 0935 1557 2202	0.3 4.6 0.6 4.5

JULY

Day	Time	m	Day	Time	m
1 F	0431 1036 1705 2302	0.3 4.6 0.5 4.6	16 SA	0509 1124 1747 2346	1.2 3.8 1.2 3.8
2 SA	0534 1133 1804 2357	0.3 4.7 0.4 4.8	17 SU	0601 1211 1835	1.1 4.0 1.0
3 SU	0628 1225 1855	0.3 4.8 0.4	18 M	0029 0644 1251 1914	4.0 1.0 4.2 0.9
4 M	0047 0716 1312 ● 1940	4.9 0.4 4.8 0.3	19 TU	0106 0722 1324 ○ 1950	4.2 1.0 4.3 0.8
5 TU	0134 0759 1356 2022	5.0 0.5 4.8 0.3	20 W	0139 0758 1356 2026	4.4 0.9 4.5 0.7
6 W	0218 0841 1438 2103	5.0 0.6 4.8 0.4	21 TH	0213 0836 1430 2105	4.6 0.8 4.6 0.6
7 TH	0300 0919 1519 2143	5.0 0.7 4.7 0.4	22 F	0249 0917 1506 2147	4.7 0.7 4.7 0.4
8 F	0342 0956 1600 2221	4.9 0.8 4.6 0.4	23 SA	0329 1000 1547 2231	4.8 0.6 4.8 0.3
9 SA	0425 1031 1641 2258	4.7 0.9 4.5 0.5	24 SU	0412 1046 1632 2317	4.9 0.6 4.8 0.2
10 SU	0508 1107 1724 2338	4.5 1.0 4.3 0.6	25 M	0501 1134 1722	4.9 0.5 4.7
11 M	0553 1148 1811	4.3 1.1 4.1	26 TU	0005 0555 1224 1819	0.2 4.8 0.5 4.6
12 TU	0026 0643 1241 ◐ 1904	0.8 4.1 1.2 3.9	27 W	0057 0656 1319 ◑ 1922	0.2 4.7 0.6 4.5
13 W	0132 0743 1402 2010	1.0 3.8 1.4 3.6	28 TH	0153 0800 1420 2028	0.3 4.5 0.6 4.4
14 TH	0256 0858 1536 2134	1.2 3.6 1.4 3.5	29 F	0257 0906 1533 2137	0.4 4.4 0.7 4.4
15 F	0407 1021 1647 2251	1.2 3.7 1.3 3.6	30 SA	0410 1015 1649 2245	0.5 4.4 0.7 4.4
			31 SU	0519 1120 1751 2346	0.6 4.5 0.6 4.6

AUGUST

Day	Time	m	Day	Time	m
1 M	0615 1214 1843	0.6 4.6 0.5	16 TU	0004 0619 1225 1849	4.0 1.1 4.2 0.9
2 TU	0037 0702 1300 ● 1927	4.7 0.6 4.7 0.5	17 W	0041 0657 1258 1925	4.3 0.9 4.4 0.7
3 W	0121 0744 1341 2007	4.8 0.7 4.7 0.5	18 TH	0115 0734 1331 ○ 2002	4.6 0.8 4.7 0.5
4 TH	0202 0822 1419 2045	4.9 0.8 4.7 0.4	19 F	0150 0813 1406 2042	4.9 0.6 4.9 0.3
5 F	0241 0857 1457 2121	4.9 0.8 4.7 0.4	20 SA	0228 0855 1445 2124	5.1 0.4 5.1 0.1
6 SA	0319 0930 1535 2155	4.8 0.8 4.7 0.4	21 SU	0308 0939 1527 2208	5.2 0.3 5.1 0.0
7 SU	0358 1002 1613 2229	4.8 0.8 4.6 0.5	22 M	0352 1025 1612 2254	5.2 0.3 5.1 0.0
8 M	0438 1036 1652 2306	4.6 0.8 4.5 0.6	23 TU	0439 1111 1700 2340	5.1 0.3 5.0 0.1
9 TU	0518 1115 1732 2346	4.4 0.9 4.3 0.8	24 W	0530 1159 1753	5.0 0.4 4.9
10 W	0601 1158 1817 ◐	4.2 1.1 4.0	25 TH	0030 0627 1251 ◑ 1853	0.2 4.7 0.5 4.7
11 TH	0036 0650 1255 1911	1.0 3.9 1.4 3.7	26 F	0125 0731 1353 2001	0.4 4.5 0.7 4.4
12 F	0159 0755 1452 2029	1.3 3.6 1.6 3.4	27 SA	0233 0840 1513 2114	0.7 4.3 0.9 4.3
13 SA	0332 0932 1615 2213	1.4 3.4 1.5 3.4	28 SU	0352 0955 1632 2230	0.8 4.2 0.9 4.3
14 SU	0438 1053 1718 2319	1.4 3.6 1.3 3.7	29 M	0503 1105 1735 2334	0.8 4.3 0.7 4.5
15 M	0534 1145 1810	1.3 3.9 1.1	30 TU	0600 1200 1827	0.8 4.5 0.6
			31 W	0023 0647 1244 1911	4.7 0.8 4.6 0.6

Chart Datum: 0·23 metres below TAW Datum
HAT is 5·6 metres above Chart Datum

TIME ZONE -0100
(Belgian Standard Time)
Subtract 1 hour for UT
For Belgian Summer Time add ONE hour in **non-shaded areas**

BELGIUM – ZEEBRUGGE

LAT 51°21'N LONG 3°12'E

TIMES AND HEIGHTS OF HIGH AND LOW WATERS

Dates in amber are **SPRINGS**
Dates in yellow are **NEAPS**

2016

SEPTEMBER

Date	Day	Time	m	Time	m	Time	m	Time	m	Moon
1	TH	0105	4.8	0727	0.8	1322	4.7	1949	0.6	●
2	F	0142	4.8	0802	0.9	1358	4.7	2024	0.5	
3	SA	0219	4.9	0834	0.8	1434	4.8	2057	0.5	
4	SU	0255	4.9	0905	0.8	1510	4.8	2129	0.5	
5	M	0332	4.8	0937	0.8	1546	4.7	2202	0.5	
6	TU	0408	4.7	1011	0.8	1621	4.6	2236	0.7	
7	W	0444	4.5	1046	0.9	1657	4.4	2312	0.9	
8	TH	0521	4.2	1123	1.2	1734	4.1	2350	1.2	
9	F	0600	3.9	1204	1.4	1819	3.8			◐
10	SA	0043	1.5	0652	3.6	1327	1.7	1924	3.5	
11	SU	0256	1.6	0831	3.4	1542	1.6	2125	3.4	
12	M	0406	1.5	1014	3.5	1644	1.4	2243	3.7	
13	TU	0503	1.3	1111	3.9	1736	1.1	2333	4.1	
14	W	0549	1.1	1153	4.3	1818	0.8			
15	TH	0012	4.5	0629	0.9	1229	4.6	1855	0.5	
16	F	0048	4.9	0707	0.6	1304	5.0	1934	0.3	○
17	SA	0125	5.2	0748	0.4	1342	5.2	2016	0.1	
18	SU	0204	5.4	0832	0.2	1422	5.4	2059	-0.1	
19	M	0246	5.4	0917	0.1	1505	5.5	2144	-0.1	
20	TU	0330	5.4	1002	0.1	1550	5.4	2229	0.0	
21	W	0416	5.3	1048	0.2	1637	5.3	2315	0.1	
22	TH	0506	5.0	1135	0.4	1729	5.0			
23	F	0004	0.4	0600	4.7	1226	0.6	1828	4.7	◑
24	SA	0059	0.7	0703	4.4	1328	0.9	1935	4.4	
25	SU	0209	1.0	0814	4.2	1450	1.0	2052	4.2	
26	M	0331	1.1	0933	4.1	1609	1.0	2212	4.3	
27	TU	0442	1.1	1046	4.2	1713	0.9	2316	4.4	
28	W	0541	1.0	1141	4.4	1806	0.8			
29	TH	0004	4.6	0628	1.0	1224	4.5	1850	0.7	
30	F	0044	4.7	0707	0.9	1301	4.6	1928	0.7	

OCTOBER

Date	Day	Time	m	Time	m	Time	m	Time	m	Moon
1	SA	0121	4.8	0741	0.9	1336	4.7	2001	0.6	●
2	SU	0156	4.9	0812	0.8	1411	4.8	2033	0.6	
3	M	0232	4.9	0843	0.8	1446	4.8	2105	0.6	
4	TU	0307	4.8	0916	0.8	1520	4.7	2138	0.7	
5	W	0341	4.6	0949	0.9	1553	4.6	2210	0.9	
6	TH	0413	4.4	1022	1.0	1625	4.4	2241	1.1	
7	F	0445	4.2	1052	1.2	1700	4.2	2312	1.3	
8	SA	0521	4.0	1125	1.4	1741	4.0	2350	1.5	
9	SU	0607	3.7	1215	1.6	1840	3.7			◐
10	M	0156	1.7	0729	3.5	1502	1.6	2035	3.6	
11	TU	0330	1.6	0927	3.6	1604	1.4	2201	3.9	
12	W	0426	1.3	1031	4.0	1656	1.0	2256	4.3	
13	TH	0515	1.0	1117	4.4	1743	0.7	2340	4.7	
14	F	0559	0.8	1158	4.8	1825	0.4			
15	SA	0020	5.1	0641	0.5	1237	5.1	1907	0.2	
16	SU	0100	5.3	0724	0.3	1318	5.4	1950	0.0	○
17	M	0141	5.5	0809	0.1	1400	5.6	2035	-0.1	
18	TU	0224	5.6	0854	0.0	1444	5.6	2120	-0.1	
19	W	0309	5.5	0940	0.1	1529	5.5	2205	0.1	
20	TH	0355	5.3	1025	0.2	1617	5.3	2251	0.3	
21	F	0444	5.0	1112	0.4	1708	5.1	2338	0.6	
22	SA	0537	4.7	1202	0.7	1806	4.8			◑
23	SU	0032	0.9	0637	4.4	1302	0.9	1910	4.4	
24	M	0140	1.2	0745	4.1	1421	1.1	2024	4.2	
25	TU	0301	1.4	0902	4.0	1537	1.1	2144	4.2	
26	W	0412	1.3	1018	4.1	1643	1.0	2251	4.3	
27	TH	0514	1.2	1116	4.2	1739	0.9	2341	4.5	
28	F	0605	1.1	1200	4.4	1826	0.8			
29	SA	0022	4.6	0645	1.0	1239	4.5	1904	0.8	
30	SU	0059	4.7	0720	0.9	1315	4.6	1938	0.8	●
31	M	0135	4.8	0753	0.9	1350	4.7	2011	0.8	

NOVEMBER

Date	Day	Time	m	Time	m	Time	m	Time	m	Moon
1	TU	0210	4.8	0826	0.9	1424	4.7	2044	0.8	
2	W	0245	4.7	0900	0.9	1458	4.6	2117	0.9	
3	TH	0317	4.5	0933	1.0	1530	4.5	2149	1.1	
4	F	0347	4.4	1004	1.2	1601	4.4	2217	1.2	
5	SA	0418	4.2	1032	1.3	1635	4.3	2246	1.4	
6	SU	0454	4.1	1104	1.4	1718	4.2	2325	1.5	
7	M	0541	3.9	1158	1.5	1817	4.0			◐
8	TU	0045	1.6	0655	3.7	1409	1.4	1954	3.9	
9	W	0241	1.5	0838	3.8	1518	1.2	2117	4.1	
10	TH	0343	1.2	0947	4.1	1614	0.9	2217	4.5	
11	F	0438	1.0	1040	4.5	1706	0.6	2307	4.8	
12	SA	0529	0.7	1127	4.8	1755	0.3	2352	5.1	
13	SU	0616	0.4	1211	5.2	1842	0.1			
14	M	0036	5.3	0702	0.2	1255	5.4	1927	0.0	○
15	TU	0120	5.5	0748	0.1	1340	5.6	2012	0.0	
16	W	0205	5.5	0833	0.1	1425	5.6	2058	0.1	
17	TH	0250	5.4	0919	0.1	1512	5.5	2143	0.3	
18	F	0337	5.2	1004	0.2	1600	5.3	2228	0.5	
19	SA	0425	5.0	1050	0.4	1650	5.1	2313	0.8	
20	SU	0515	4.7	1138	0.6	1743	4.8			
21	M	0002	1.1	0609	4.4	1233	0.9	1841	4.5	◑
22	TU	0101	1.3	0709	4.1	1342	1.1	1946	4.2	
23	W	0216	1.5	0819	3.9	1456	1.1	2102	4.1	
24	TH	0331	1.5	0937	3.9	1604	1.1	2216	4.1	
25	F	0439	1.4	1044	4.0	1705	1.1	2313	4.3	
26	SA	0537	1.2	1135	4.2	1758	1.0	2358	4.4	
27	SU	0624	1.1	1217	4.3	1841	0.9			
28	M	0038	4.5	0702	1.0	1255	4.4	1917	0.9	
29	TU	0116	4.6	0738	0.9	1332	4.5	1952	0.9	●
30	W	0152	4.6	0812	0.9	1407	4.5	2026	1.0	

DECEMBER

Date	Day	Time	m	Time	m	Time	m	Time	m	Moon
1	TH	0226	4.5	0847	1.0	1440	4.5	2100	1.1	
2	F	0258	4.4	0922	1.0	1511	4.4	2133	1.2	
3	SA	0328	4.4	0955	1.1	1544	4.4	2204	1.3	
4	SU	0400	4.3	1028	1.2	1620	4.4	2237	1.3	
5	M	0438	4.2	1107	1.2	1705	4.3	2322	1.3	
6	TU	0527	4.1	1206	1.1	1802	4.3			
7	W	0031	1.3	0632	4.0	1322	1.0	1920	4.2	◐
8	TH	0150	1.2	0754	4.1	1430	0.9	2035	4.3	
9	F	0257	1.1	0904	4.2	1531	0.7	2138	4.5	
10	SA	0400	0.9	1003	4.5	1631	0.5	2235	4.8	
11	SU	0500	0.7	1058	4.8	1728	0.3	2327	5.0	
12	M	0555	0.5	1149	5.0	1820	0.2			
13	TU	0016	5.1	0644	0.3	1237	5.2	1907	0.2	
14	W	0103	5.2	0731	0.2	1324	5.4	1953	0.2	○
15	TH	0149	5.3	0816	0.2	1411	5.4	2038	0.3	
16	F	0234	5.2	0901	0.2	1457	5.4	2122	0.5	
17	SA	0320	5.1	0945	0.3	1543	5.2	2205	0.6	
18	SU	0405	4.9	1029	0.4	1630	5.0	2247	0.8	
19	M	0451	4.7	1113	0.6	1718	4.8	2329	1.0	
20	TU	0538	4.5	1159	0.7	1808	4.5			
21	W	0015	1.2	0629	4.2	1254	0.9	1902	4.2	◑
22	TH	0114	1.4	0727	4.0	1402	1.1	2007	4.0	
23	F	0232	1.5	0838	3.8	1515	1.2	2126	3.9	
24	SA	0352	1.5	1000	3.8	1624	1.2	2239	3.9	
25	SU	0503	1.4	1106	3.9	1726	1.1	2334	4.1	
26	M	0602	1.2	1156	4.0	1817	1.1			
27	TU	0019	4.2	0647	1.1	1238	4.2	1859	1.1	
28	W	0059	4.4	0725	1.0	1316	4.3	1935	1.0	
29	TH	0135	4.4	0801	0.9	1350	4.4	2009	1.1	●
30	F	0209	4.4	0836	0.9	1423	4.4	2044	1.1	
31	SA	0240	4.4	0911	0.9	1456	4.5	2119	1.1	

Chart Datum: 0·23 metres below TAW Datum
HAT is 5·6 metres above Chart Datum

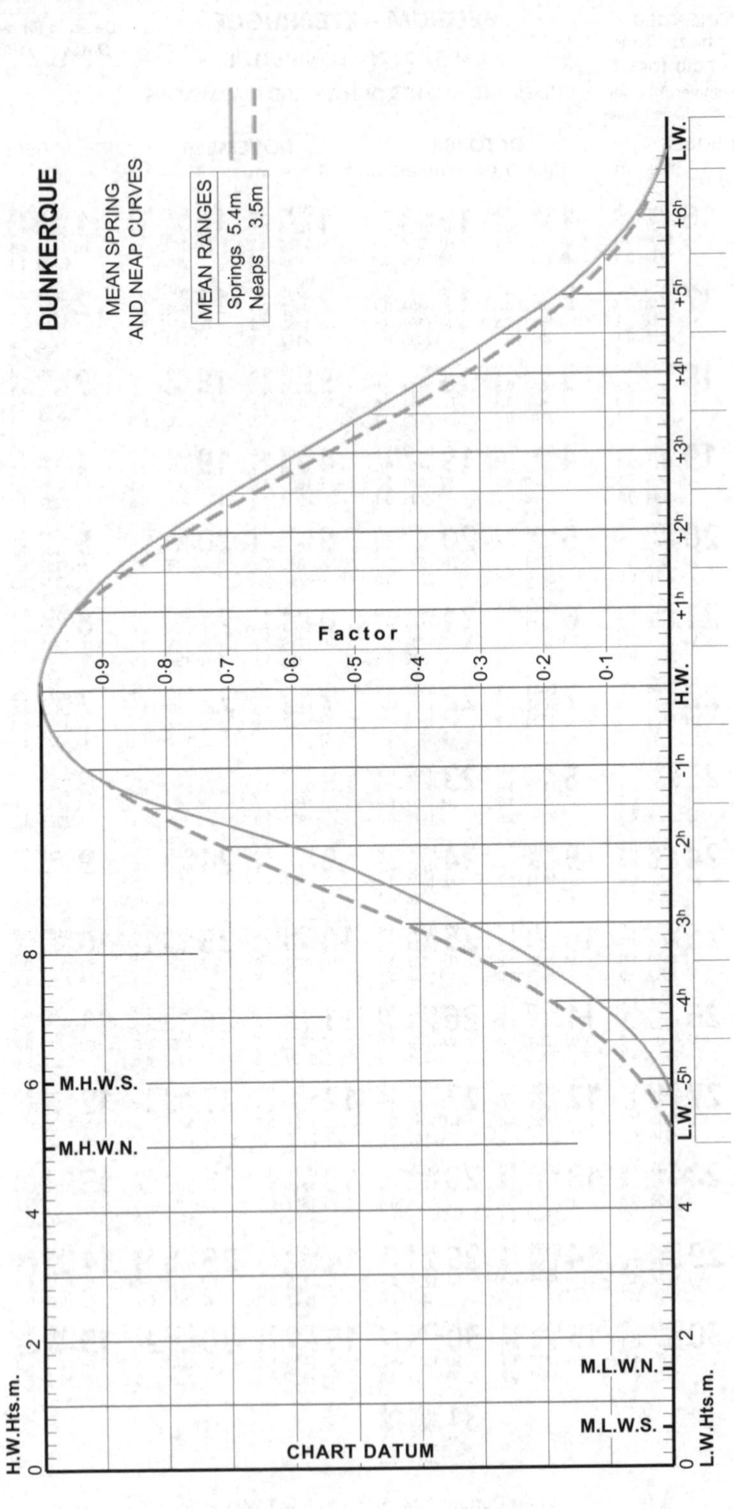
DUNKERQUE
MEAN SPRING AND NEAP CURVES
MEAN RANGES
Springs 5.4m
Neaps 3.5m
Factor
0·9
0·8
0·7
0·6
0·5
0·4
0·3
0·2
0·1
L.W.
-5h
-4h
-3h
-2h
-1h
H.W.
+1h
+2h
+3h
+4h
+5h
+6h
L.W.
H.W.Hts.m.
0
2
4
M.H.W.N.
6
M.H.W.S.
8
CHART DATUM
L.W.Hts.m.
0
M.L.W.S.
M.L.W.N.
2
4

TIME ZONE -0100
(French Standard Time)
Subtract 1 hour for UT
For French Summer Time add ONE hour in **non-shaded areas**

FRANCE – DUNKERQUE

LAT 51°03'N LONG 2°22'E

TIMES AND HEIGHTS OF HIGH AND LOW WATERS

Dates in amber are **SPRINGS**
Dates in yellow are **NEAPS**

2016

JANUARY

Date	Time	m	Time	m	Time	m	Time	m
1 F	0452	5.3	1149	1.2	1721	5.2		
2 SA ◑	0007	1.6	0541	5.1	1236	1.4	1814	5.0
3 SU	0100	1.7	0639	4.9	1337	1.6	1918	4.8
4 M	0210	1.8	0750	4.8	1448	1.6	2030	4.8
5 TU	0323	1.8	0903	4.8	1555	1.6	2136	4.9
6 W	0427	1.6	1005	5.0	1654	1.4	2232	5.1
7 TH	0523	1.4	1056	5.3	1745	1.2	2318	5.4
8 F	0610	1.2	1139	5.5	1829	1.0	2358	5.6
9 SA	0652	1.0	1217	5.7	1910	0.9		
10 SU ●	0034	5.8	0733	0.8	1254	5.9	1951	0.7
11 M	0111	5.9	0814	0.6	1333	6.1	2033	0.7
12 TU	0149	6.0	0857	0.5	1413	6.1	2115	0.6
13 W	0230	6.0	0939	0.5	1456	6.1	2157	0.7
14 TH	0312	6.0	1022	0.5	1540	6.0	2240	0.8
15 F	0356	5.9	1106	0.6	1629	5.8	2325	0.9
16 SA	0446	5.7	1155	0.8	1724	5.7		
17 SU ◐	0016	1.1	0544	5.6	1252	0.9	1826	5.4
18 M	0119	1.3	0650	5.4	1401	1.1	1939	5.3
19 TU	0232	1.4	0808	5.2	1515	1.2	2101	5.2
20 W	0347	1.4	0929	5.3	1630	1.1	2211	5.3
21 TH	0503	1.2	1035	5.5	1741	1.0	2310	5.5
22 F	0605	1.0	1130	5.7	1835	0.9	2359	5.7
23 SA	0655	0.8	1217	5.8	1920	0.8		
24 SU ○	0041	5.8	0739	0.6	1259	5.9	2000	0.8
25 M	0120	5.9	0819	0.5	1339	6.0	2038	0.8
26 TU	0157	5.9	0857	0.5	1418	6.0	2113	0.8
27 W	0234	5.9	0933	0.6	1454	5.9	2147	0.9
28 TH	0307	5.8	1007	0.7	1528	5.8	2220	1.0
29 F	0340	5.7	1039	0.8	1602	5.6	2252	1.1
30 SA	0416	5.5	1112	1.0	1639	5.4	2325	1.3
31 SU	0456	5.3	1148	1.2	1723	5.2		

FEBRUARY

Date	Time	m	Time	m	Time	m	Time	m
1 M ◑	0005	1.5	0544	5.1	1233	1.4	1818	4.9
2 TU	0056	1.7	0646	4.8	1335	1.6	1924	4.7
3 W	0210	1.9	0759	4.7	1455	1.7	2038	4.7
4 TH	0333	1.8	0916	4.8	1609	1.6	2150	4.9
5 F	0444	1.6	1022	5.1	1713	1.3	2249	5.2
6 SA	0542	1.2	1114	5.4	1805	1.1	2336	5.5
7 SU	0631	0.9	1158	5.7	1851	0.8		
8 M ●	0016	5.7	0715	0.6	1237	5.9	1934	0.6
9 TU	0054	6.0	0758	0.4	1316	6.1	2016	0.5
10 W	0132	6.1	0840	0.3	1356	6.2	2059	0.4
11 TH	0212	6.2	0923	0.2	1438	6.2	2141	0.4
12 F	0253	6.2	1007	0.2	1522	6.1	2224	0.5
13 SA	0337	6.1	1050	0.3	1609	6.0	2307	0.7
14 SU	0425	5.9	1136	0.6	1701	5.8	2355	0.9
15 M ◐	0520	5.7	1229	0.8	1800	5.4		
16 TU	0053	1.2	0624	5.4	1335	1.1	1913	5.1
17 W	0206	1.4	0745	5.1	1452	1.3	2040	5.0
18 TH	0327	1.4	0913	5.1	1617	1.3	2157	5.1
19 F	0450	1.3	1025	5.3	1728	1.1	2300	5.3
20 SA	0553	1.0	1122	5.5	1819	1.0	2350	5.5
21 SU	0642	0.8	1208	5.7	1904	0.8		
22 M ○	0029	5.7	0723	0.6	1246	5.8	1942	0.8
23 TU	0103	5.8	0801	0.5	1322	5.9	2017	0.7
24 W	0138	5.9	0836	0.5	1356	5.9	2049	0.7
25 TH	0210	5.9	0908	0.5	1428	5.9	2121	0.7
26 F	0240	5.9	0940	0.6	1458	5.8	2152	0.8
27 SA	0310	5.8	1010	0.7	1528	5.7	2221	0.9
28 SU	0341	5.7	1039	0.8	1601	5.5	2251	1.1
29 M	0415	5.5	1110	1.0	1636	5.3	2325	1.3

MARCH

Date	Time	m	Time	m	Time	m	Time	m
1 TU	0454	5.2	1149	1.3	1722	5.0		
2 W ◑	0008	1.5	0550	4.9	1240	1.5	1832	4.7
3 TH	0107	1.7	0709	4.7	1353	1.7	1949	4.6
4 F	0233	1.8	0830	4.7	1522	1.7	2108	4.7
5 SA	0402	1.6	0947	4.9	1638	1.4	2219	5.0
6 SU	0512	1.2	1048	5.3	1739	1.1	2312	5.4
7 M	0607	0.8	1135	5.7	1829	0.8	2354	5.7
8 TU	0653	0.5	1216	6.0	1913	0.5		
9 W ●	0032	6.0	0737	0.3	1255	6.2	1956	0.4
10 TH	0110	6.2	0820	0.1	1335	6.3	2038	0.3
11 F	0151	6.3	0903	0.1	1418	6.3	2121	0.3
12 SA	0233	6.3	0947	0.1	1502	6.2	2204	0.4
13 SU	0318	6.2	1031	0.2	1549	6.0	2248	0.5
14 M	0406	6.1	1117	0.5	1640	5.8	2335	0.8
15 TU ◐	0500	5.8	1208	0.9	1738	5.4		
16 W	0031	1.1	0604	5.4	1312	1.2	1849	5.0
17 TH	0142	1.4	0725	5.1	1431	1.5	2018	4.8
18 F	0307	1.4	0855	5.0	1559	1.5	2138	4.9
19 SA	0431	1.3	1009	5.1	1710	1.3	2241	5.2
20 SU	0534	1.0	1106	5.4	1801	1.0	2330	5.4
21 M	0622	0.8	1150	5.6	1842	0.9		
22 TU	0007	5.6	0702	0.7	1225	5.7	1920	0.8
23 W ○	0041	5.7	0737	0.6	1259	5.8	1951	0.7
24 TH	0114	5.8	0809	0.5	1331	5.9	2023	0.7
25 F	0144	5.9	0840	0.5	1401	5.9	2054	0.7
26 SA	0212	5.9	0911	0.6	1428	5.8	2125	0.7
27 SU	0241	5.8	0941	0.7	1458	5.8	2154	0.8
28 M	0312	5.7	1010	0.8	1528	5.6	2223	0.9
29 TU	0342	5.5	1040	1.0	1558	5.4	2256	1.1
30 W	0414	5.3	1117	1.2	1635	5.1	2337	1.3
31 TH ◑	0501	5.0	1205	1.4	1740	4.8		

APRIL

Date	Time	m	Time	m	Time	m	Time	m
1 F	0033	1.5	0628	4.8	1312	1.6	1909	4.7
2 SA	0149	1.6	0750	4.8	1438	1.6	2027	4.7
3 SU	0320	1.5	0910	5.0	1602	1.4	2144	5.0
4 M	0437	1.2	1017	5.4	1709	1.0	2242	5.4
5 TU	0538	0.8	1108	5.7	1802	0.7	2327	5.7
6 W	0628	0.5	1151	6.0	1849	0.5		
7 TH ●	0006	6.0	0714	0.2	1231	6.2	1933	0.4
8 F	0046	6.2	0758	0.1	1313	6.3	2016	0.3
9 SA	0129	6.3	0842	0.1	1356	6.3	2100	0.2
10 SU	0213	6.4	0926	0.1	1443	6.2	2145	0.3
11 M	0300	6.3	1011	0.3	1531	6.0	2230	0.4
12 TU	0350	6.1	1058	0.6	1622	5.7	2318	0.7
13 W	0444	5.8	1148	0.9	1718	5.4		
14 TH ◐	0012	1.0	0546	5.4	1249	1.3	1825	5.0
15 F	0120	1.3	0703	5.0	1405	1.5	1950	4.8
16 SA	0240	1.4	0829	4.9	1529	1.5	2108	4.9
17 SU	0400	1.3	0941	5.1	1639	1.4	2210	5.1
18 M	0505	1.1	1037	5.3	1733	1.1	2258	5.3
19 TU	0554	0.9	1121	5.5	1815	1.0	2339	5.5
20 W	0634	0.8	1159	5.6	1852	0.9		
21 TH	0014	5.7	0707	0.7	1233	5.7	1923	0.8
22 F ○	0048	5.7	0738	0.7	1304	5.8	1954	0.7
23 SA	0118	5.8	0810	0.6	1333	5.8	2027	0.7
24 SU	0146	5.8	0843	0.6	1401	5.8	2100	0.7
25 M	0216	5.8	0915	0.7	1432	5.8	2131	0.8
26 TU	0248	5.7	0946	0.8	1503	5.6	2203	0.9
27 W	0321	5.6	1019	0.9	1536	5.4	2237	1.0
28 TH	0355	5.4	1057	1.1	1614	5.2	2320	1.2
29 F	0444	5.2	1145	1.3	1715	5.0		
30 SA ◑	0013	1.3	0602	5.0	1246	1.5	1836	4.8

Chart Datum: 2·69 metres below IGN Datum
HAT is 6·4 metres above Chart Datum

TIME ZONE -0100
(French Standard Time)
Subtract 1 hour for UT
For French Summer Time add ONE hour in **non-shaded areas**

FRANCE – DUNKERQUE

LAT 51°03'N LONG 2°22'E

TIMES AND HEIGHTS OF HIGH AND LOW WATERS

Dates in amber are SPRINGS
Dates in yellow are NEAPS

2016

MAY

Date	Day	Time	m	Time	m	Time	m	Time	m
1	SU	0121	1.4	0716	5.0	1404	1.5	1949	4.9
2	M	0244	1.3	0832	5.1	1526	1.3	2104	5.1
3	TU	0402	1.0	0943	5.4	1635	1.0	2207	5.4
4	W	0506	0.7	1039	5.7	1733	0.8	2257	5.7
5	TH	0601	0.5	1125	6.0	1824	0.6	2341	6.0
6	F ●	0650	0.3	1208	6.2	1910	0.4		
7	SA	0024	6.2	0736	0.2	1251	6.3	1956	0.3
8	SU	0109	6.3	0821	0.2	1338	6.2	2042	0.3
9	M	0156	6.3	0907	0.3	1426	6.1	2127	0.3
10	TU	0245	6.2	0953	0.4	1516	6.0	2214	0.4
11	W	0337	6.0	1040	0.7	1606	5.7	2301	0.6
12	TH	0430	5.8	1128	1.0	1659	5.4	2353	0.9
13	F ◐	0527	5.4	1223	1.3	1758	5.1		
14	SA	0052	1.2	0633	5.1	1329	1.5	1911	4.9
15	SU	0202	1.3	0752	4.9	1443	1.6	2027	4.9
16	M	0315	1.3	0901	5.0	1555	1.5	2129	5.0
17	TU	0421	1.2	0958	5.1	1653	1.3	2220	5.2
18	W	0515	1.0	1046	5.3	1741	1.1	2305	5.4
19	TH	0559	0.9	1128	5.5	1820	1.0	2345	5.5
20	F	0635	0.9	1205	5.6	1853	0.9		
21	SA ○	0021	5.6	0708	0.8	1237	5.7	1927	0.8
22	SU	0053	5.7	0742	0.8	1307	5.7	2002	0.8
23	M	0123	5.7	0818	0.7	1338	5.8	2038	0.7
24	TU	0155	5.8	0853	0.8	1412	5.8	2113	0.7
25	W	0232	5.7	0929	0.8	1448	5.7	2149	0.8
26	TH	0310	5.6	1005	0.9	1526	5.5	2227	0.9
27	F	0351	5.5	1045	1.0	1609	5.3	2309	1.0
28	SA	0441	5.4	1131	1.2	1704	5.2	2359	1.1
29	SU ◑	0542	5.2	1227	1.3	1808	5.1		
30	M	0100	1.1	0646	5.2	1335	1.3	1914	5.1
31	TU	0214	1.1	0755	5.3	1452	1.2	2024	5.2

JUNE

Date	Day	Time	m	Time	m	Time	m	Time	m
1	W	0329	1.0	0908	5.4	1602	1.1	2133	5.4
2	TH	0435	0.7	1010	5.7	1705	0.8	2230	5.7
3	F	0535	0.6	1103	5.9	1801	0.7	2320	5.9
4	SA	0629	0.5	1150	6.0	1852	0.5		
5	SU ●	0008	6.1	0718	0.4	1236	6.1	1940	0.4
6	M	0055	6.2	0805	0.4	1324	6.1	2027	0.3
7	TU	0144	6.2	0851	0.5	1413	6.0	2113	0.3
8	W	0234	6.1	0937	0.6	1502	5.9	2159	0.4
9	TH	0324	6.0	1021	0.8	1549	5.7	2244	0.6
10	F	0413	5.8	1106	1.0	1636	5.5	2329	0.8
11	SA	0502	5.5	1152	1.2	1725	5.3		
12	SU ◐	0019	1.0	0555	5.2	1245	1.4	1822	5.1
13	M	0116	1.2	0659	5.0	1348	1.6	1930	4.9
14	TU	0220	1.3	0809	4.9	1455	1.6	2038	4.9
15	W	0325	1.3	0911	5.0	1559	1.5	2137	5.0
16	TH	0425	1.2	1006	5.1	1657	1.3	2229	5.2
17	F	0517	1.1	1053	5.3	1744	1.2	2314	5.3
18	SA	0601	1.0	1135	5.4	1825	1.0	2354	5.5
19	SU	0640	1.0	1212	5.5	1902	0.9		
20	M ○	0030	5.6	0717	0.9	1245	5.6	1940	0.8
21	TU	0103	5.7	0756	0.8	1319	5.7	2019	0.7
22	W	0139	5.8	0835	0.8	1355	5.8	2058	0.6
23	TH	0218	5.8	0914	0.8	1435	5.8	2137	0.6
24	F	0259	5.8	0954	0.8	1516	5.7	2217	0.7
25	SA	0342	5.7	1034	0.9	1558	5.6	2259	0.7
26	SU	0428	5.6	1118	1.0	1646	5.5	2346	0.8
27	M ◑	0521	5.5	1208	1.1	1742	5.4		
28	TU	0040	0.9	0619	5.4	1309	1.2	1843	5.3
29	W	0147	1.0	0724	5.4	1421	1.2	1951	5.3
30	TH	0259	1.0	0838	5.4	1533	1.1	2105	5.4

JULY

Date	Day	Time	m	Time	m	Time	m	Time	m
1	F	0408	0.9	0949	5.5	1641	1.0	2212	5.6
2	SA	0514	0.8	1049	5.7	1744	0.8	2309	5.8
3	SU	0614	0.7	1141	5.8	1839	0.6		
4	M ●	0000	5.9	0706	0.6	1229	5.9	1929	0.5
5	TU	0047	6.1	0753	0.6	1315	6.0	2015	0.4
6	W	0135	6.1	0837	0.6	1401	6.0	2059	0.4
7	TH	0222	6.1	0920	0.7	1445	5.9	2142	0.4
8	F	0306	6.0	1000	0.8	1527	5.8	2222	0.6
9	SA	0350	5.8	1040	1.0	1607	5.7	2302	0.7
10	SU	0431	5.6	1119	1.1	1648	5.5	2342	0.9
11	M	0513	5.4	1201	1.3	1732	5.3		
12	TU ◐	0027	1.1	0602	5.1	1250	1.5	1826	5.0
13	W	0121	1.3	0700	4.9	1353	1.6	1931	4.9
14	TH	0226	1.5	0808	4.8	1502	1.7	2043	4.8
15	F	0332	1.5	0916	4.9	1608	1.6	2147	5.0
16	SA	0434	1.4	1015	5.0	1707	1.4	2242	5.2
17	SU	0528	1.2	1105	5.2	1757	1.2	2329	5.4
18	M	0615	1.1	1148	5.4	1840	1.0		
19	TU ○	0008	5.6	0656	0.9	1225	5.6	1920	0.8
20	W	0045	5.7	0736	0.8	1301	5.8	2000	0.6
21	TH	0122	5.9	0817	0.7	1338	5.9	2041	0.5
22	F	0201	6.0	0858	0.7	1416	5.9	2122	0.5
23	SA	0241	6.0	0939	0.7	1456	5.9	2203	0.5
24	SU	0322	5.9	1020	0.7	1537	5.8	2245	0.5
25	M	0407	5.8	1102	0.8	1623	5.7	2329	0.6
26	TU	0457	5.7	1148	1.0	1716	5.6		
27	W ◑	0020	0.8	0553	5.6	1244	1.1	1816	5.5
28	TH	0122	1.0	0658	5.4	1354	1.3	1926	5.3
29	F	0234	1.1	0815	5.3	1509	1.3	2047	5.3
30	SA	0348	1.1	0935	5.3	1624	1.2	2202	5.5
31	SU	0503	1.0	1041	5.5	1734	0.9	2304	5.7

AUGUST

Date	Day	Time	m	Time	m	Time	m	Time	m
1	M	0606	0.9	1136	5.7	1830	0.7	2356	5.8
2	TU ●	0657	0.8	1223	5.8	1918	0.6		
3	W	0041	6.0	0740	0.7	1304	5.9	2001	0.5
4	TH	0122	6.0	0821	0.7	1344	6.0	2042	0.4
5	F	0203	6.0	0900	0.7	1422	6.0	2120	0.5
6	SA	0243	6.0	0936	0.8	1459	5.9	2157	0.6
7	SU	0320	5.9	1011	0.9	1534	5.8	2231	0.7
8	M	0355	5.7	1045	1.0	1609	5.6	2305	0.9
9	TU	0431	5.5	1119	1.2	1648	5.4	2341	1.1
10	W ◐	0512	5.3	1158	1.4	1734	5.2		
11	TH	0024	1.3	0603	5.0	1248	1.6	1833	4.9
12	F	0121	1.6	0705	4.8	1357	1.8	1943	4.7
13	SA	0236	1.7	0819	4.7	1518	1.8	2100	4.8
14	SU	0350	1.7	0933	4.8	1629	1.6	2208	5.0
15	M	0456	1.5	1035	5.1	1729	1.3	2302	5.3
16	TU	0550	1.2	1124	5.4	1817	1.0	2346	5.6
17	W	0635	1.0	1204	5.7	1859	0.8		
18	TH ○	0024	5.8	0716	0.8	1240	5.9	1940	0.5
19	F	0101	6.0	0757	0.7	1316	6.0	2021	0.4
20	SA	0138	6.1	0838	0.6	1353	6.1	2103	0.3
21	SU	0217	6.2	0919	0.5	1432	6.1	2144	0.3
22	M	0259	6.1	1001	0.6	1513	6.1	2226	0.4
23	TU	0343	6.0	1043	0.7	1559	6.0	2310	0.6
24	W	0433	5.8	1128	0.9	1652	5.8	2359	0.8
25	TH ◑	0529	5.6	1221	1.1	1753	5.6		
26	F	0059	1.1	0636	5.3	1331	1.3	1906	5.3
27	SA	0214	1.3	0758	5.1	1451	1.4	2035	5.2
28	SU	0336	1.4	0924	5.1	1614	1.3	2155	5.3
29	M	0457	1.2	1033	5.4	1725	1.0	2257	5.6
30	TU	0555	1.0	1127	5.6	1819	0.8	2347	5.8
31	W	0642	0.9	1211	5.8	1903	0.6		

Chart Datum: 2·69 metres below IGN Datum
HAT is 6·4 metres above Chart Datum

TIME ZONE -0100
(French Standard Time)
Subtract 1 hour for UT
For French Summer Time add ONE hour in **non-shaded areas**

FRANCE – DUNKERQUE

LAT 51°03′N LONG 2°22′E

TIMES AND HEIGHTS OF HIGH AND LOW WATERS

Dates in amber are **SPRINGS**
Dates in yellow are **NEAPS**

2016

SEPTEMBER

Date	Time	m	Time	m	Time	m	Time	m
1 TH ●	0028	5.9	0724	0.8	1247	5.9	1943	0.5
2 F	0105	6.0	0800	0.8	1321	6.0	2020	0.5
3 SA	0140	6.0	0835	0.8	1356	6.0	2055	0.5
4 SU	0215	6.0	0908	0.8	1428	6.0	2128	0.6
5 M	0247	5.9	0941	0.9	1500	5.9	2159	0.7
6 TU	0317	5.8	1012	1.0	1531	5.7	2229	0.9
7 W	0350	5.6	1042	1.2	1606	5.5	2301	1.1
8 TH	0426	5.4	1115	1.4	1646	5.3	2337	1.4
9 F ◐	0511	5.1	1156	1.6	1742	5.0		
10 SA	0025	1.6	0615	4.8	1253	1.9	1855	4.7
11 SU	0133	1.9	0730	4.6	1417	2.0	2013	4.7
12 M	0301	1.9	0848	4.7	1547	1.8	2131	4.9
13 TU	0421	1.6	1001	5.0	1657	1.4	2233	5.3
14 W	0522	1.3	1056	5.4	1750	1.0	2320	5.7
15 TH	0610	1.0	1138	5.7	1835	0.7		
16 F ○	0000	6.0	0653	0.8	1214	6.0	1917	0.5
17 SA	0036	6.2	0734	0.6	1249	6.2	1958	0.3
18 SU	0112	6.3	0815	0.5	1327	6.3	2040	0.2
19 M	0152	6.3	0857	0.5	1407	6.3	2122	0.3
20 TU	0235	6.3	0939	0.5	1451	6.3	2205	0.4
21 W	0320	6.1	1023	0.7	1538	6.1	2250	0.6
22 TH	0410	5.9	1109	0.9	1632	5.9	2339	0.9
23 F ◑	0508	5.6	1202	1.1	1735	5.6		
24 SA	0040	1.3	0615	5.3	1312	1.4	1850	5.3
25 SU	0157	1.5	0741	5.0	1435	1.5	2023	5.1
26 M	0325	1.6	0909	5.0	1601	1.4	2142	5.3
27 TU	0442	1.4	1017	5.3	1710	1.1	2244	5.5
28 W	0539	1.1	1110	5.5	1801	0.8	2331	5.7
29 TH	0622	1.0	1150	5.7	1844	0.7		
30 F	0009	5.9	0702	0.9	1224	5.9	1921	0.6

OCTOBER

Date	Time	m	Time	m	Time	m	Time	m
1 SA ●	0042	6.0	0736	0.9	1256	6.0	1954	0.6
2 SU	0115	6.0	0808	0.9	1328	6.0	2026	0.6
3 M	0145	6.0	0840	0.9	1358	6.0	2057	0.7
4 TU	0214	6.0	0911	0.9	1427	5.9	2128	0.8
5 W	0243	5.9	0942	1.0	1458	5.8	2157	1.0
6 TH	0314	5.7	1011	1.1	1530	5.6	2227	1.2
7 F	0346	5.5	1042	1.3	1604	5.4	2302	1.4
8 SA	0421	5.2	1121	1.5	1647	5.1	2346	1.6
9 SU ◐	0517	4.9	1212	1.8	1812	4.8		
10 M	0047	1.9	0647	4.7	1324	1.9	1931	4.7
11 TU	0209	1.9	0804	4.7	1457	1.8	2049	4.9
12 W	0339	1.7	0920	5.0	1618	1.4	2158	5.3
13 TH	0448	1.3	1022	5.4	1718	1.0	2250	5.7
14 F	0541	1.0	1107	5.7	1807	0.7	2331	6.0
15 SA	0626	0.8	1145	6.0	1851	0.5		
16 SU ○	0008	6.3	0709	0.6	1222	6.3	1934	0.3
17 M	0047	6.4	0752	0.5	1303	6.4	2017	0.3
18 TU	0129	6.4	0835	0.5	1345	6.5	2101	0.3
19 W	0213	6.4	0919	0.5	1431	6.4	2145	0.4
20 TH	0300	6.2	1004	0.6	1521	6.2	2231	0.7
21 F	0352	5.9	1052	0.8	1616	5.9	2322	1.0
22 SA ◑	0449	5.6	1146	1.1	1718	5.6		
23 SU	0021	1.4	0554	5.2	1253	1.4	1832	5.3
24 M	0136	1.6	0717	5.0	1413	1.5	2001	5.1
25 TU	0301	1.7	0842	5.0	1535	1.4	2118	5.2
26 W	0416	1.5	0949	5.2	1644	1.2	2218	5.4
27 TH	0514	1.3	1041	5.4	1737	0.9	2305	5.6
28 F	0558	1.1	1122	5.6	1819	0.8	2343	5.8
29 SA	0637	1.0	1157	5.8	1855	0.8		
30 SU ●	0016	5.9	0710	1.0	1231	5.9	1926	0.8
31 M	0049	5.9	0741	0.9	1303	5.9	1957	0.8

NOVEMBER

Date	Time	m	Time	m	Time	m	Time	m
1 TU	0118	5.9	0813	0.9	1331	5.9	2029	0.8
2 W	0145	5.9	0845	0.9	1400	5.9	2101	0.9
3 TH	0214	5.9	0917	1.0	1432	5.8	2131	1.0
4 F	0247	5.8	0947	1.1	1505	5.7	2202	1.2
5 SA	0319	5.6	1020	1.2	1539	5.5	2237	1.4
6 SU	0354	5.3	1058	1.4	1620	5.2	2321	1.6
7 M ◐	0440	5.1	1147	1.6	1732	5.0		
8 TU	0017	1.7	0604	4.9	1250	1.7	1851	4.9
9 W	0128	1.8	0720	4.8	1410	1.7	2003	5.0
10 TH	0252	1.7	0832	5.0	1534	1.4	2116	5.3
11 F	0407	1.4	0940	5.3	1641	1.0	2214	5.7
12 SA	0507	1.1	1032	5.7	1736	0.7	2301	6.0
13 SU	0559	0.8	1116	6.0	1825	0.5	2343	6.2
14 M ○	0645	0.6	1159	6.3	1911	0.4		
15 TU	0025	6.4	0731	0.5	1242	6.4	1956	0.4
16 W	0109	6.4	0816	0.5	1328	6.5	2042	0.4
17 TH	0156	6.3	0902	0.5	1417	6.4	2128	0.5
18 F	0245	6.2	0949	0.6	1508	6.2	2215	0.8
19 SA	0336	5.9	1038	0.8	1602	6.0	2304	1.1
20 SU	0429	5.6	1129	1.0	1700	5.6	2359	1.4
21 M ◑	0528	5.3	1228	1.3	1805	5.3		
22 TU	0103	1.6	0639	5.0	1338	1.4	1925	5.1
23 W	0217	1.8	0801	5.0	1453	1.5	2039	5.1
24 TH	0332	1.7	0908	5.1	1603	1.3	2139	5.2
25 F	0435	1.5	1002	5.2	1701	1.2	2229	5.4
26 SA	0526	1.3	1049	5.4	1748	1.1	2312	5.6
27 SU	0609	1.2	1130	5.6	1826	1.0	2350	5.7
28 M	0644	1.1	1207	5.7	1858	0.9		
29 TU ●	0024	5.8	0716	1.0	1240	5.8	1930	0.9
30 W	0054	5.8	0749	0.9	1310	5.8	2004	0.9

DECEMBER

Date	Time	m	Time	m	Time	m	Time	m
1 TH	0123	5.9	0823	0.9	1340	5.9	2039	0.9
2 F	0154	5.9	0858	0.9	1414	5.9	2113	1.0
3 SA	0229	5.8	0931	1.0	1450	5.8	2146	1.1
4 SU	0304	5.7	1006	1.1	1527	5.6	2223	1.2
5 M	0341	5.5	1045	1.2	1608	5.4	2304	1.4
6 TU	0424	5.3	1130	1.3	1704	5.3	2354	1.5
7 W ◐	0525	5.1	1225	1.4	1811	5.2		
8 TH	0055	1.6	0636	5.1	1332	1.4	1919	5.2
9 F	0209	1.6	0745	5.1	1451	1.3	2030	5.3
10 SA	0326	1.4	0855	5.3	1604	1.1	2138	5.6
11 SU	0433	1.2	0959	5.6	1706	0.8	2235	5.8
12 M	0532	0.9	1053	5.9	1802	0.6	2324	6.0
13 TU	0626	0.7	1142	6.1	1853	0.5		
14 W ○	0011	6.2	0715	0.6	1229	6.3	1941	0.5
15 TH	0058	6.2	0803	0.5	1317	6.4	2028	0.5
16 F	0145	6.2	0850	0.4	1407	6.3	2114	0.6
17 SA	0233	6.1	0937	0.5	1457	6.2	2200	0.8
18 SU	0321	5.9	1023	0.6	1547	6.0	2245	1.0
19 M	0408	5.7	1109	0.8	1636	5.7	2331	1.3
20 TU	0457	5.5	1158	1.1	1729	5.4		
21 W ◑	0021	1.5	0551	5.2	1252	1.3	1831	5.1
22 TH	0120	1.7	0659	5.0	1356	1.5	1944	5.0
23 F	0228	1.8	0813	4.9	1503	1.5	2051	4.9
24 SA	0336	1.7	0917	5.0	1608	1.4	2148	5.1
25 SU	0442	1.6	1012	5.1	1707	1.3	2239	5.2
26 M	0535	1.4	1100	5.3	1754	1.2	2323	5.4
27 TU	0618	1.2	1143	5.5	1833	1.1		
28 W	0002	5.5	0653	1.1	1220	5.6	1908	1.0
29 TH ●	0035	5.7	0729	1.0	1252	5.7	1944	0.9
30 F	0106	5.8	0805	0.9	1325	5.8	2020	0.9
31 SA	0139	5.8	0842	0.8	1400	5.9	2057	0.9

Chart Datum: 2·69 metres below IGN Datum
HAT is 6·4 metres above Chart Datum

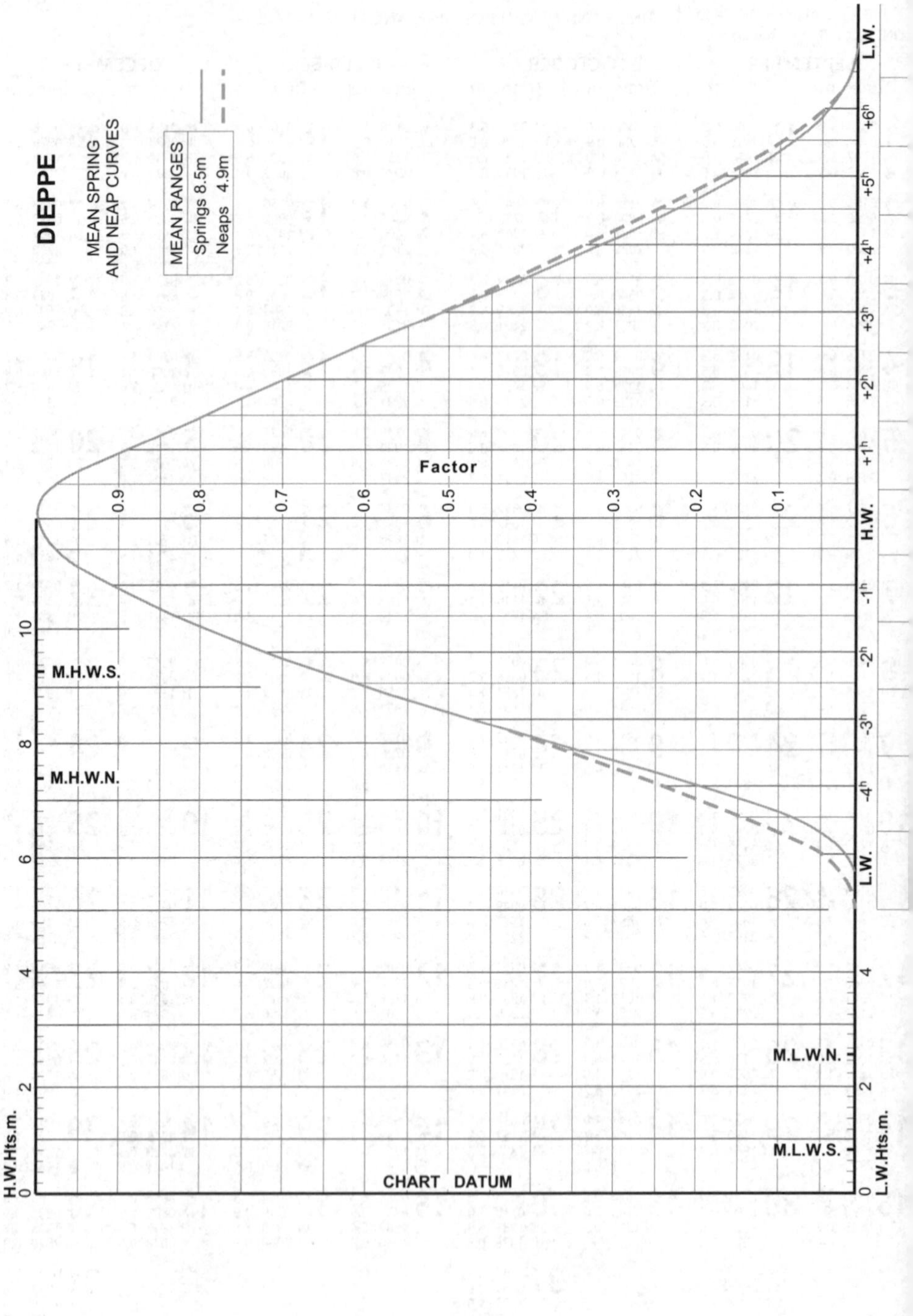
DIEPPE
MEAN SPRING
AND NEAP CURVES
MEAN RANGES
Springs 8.5m
Neaps 4.9m
Factor
0.9
0.8
0.7
0.6
0.5
0.4
0.3
0.2
0.1
L.W.
-4h
-3h
-2h
-1h
H.W.
+1h
+2h
+3h
+4h
+5h
+6h
L.W.
H.W.Hts.m.
0
2
4
6
8
10
M.H.W.S.
M.H.W.N.
CHART DATUM
L.W.Hts.m.
0
2
4
M.L.W.S.
M.L.W.N.

TIME ZONE -0100
(French Standard Time)
Subtract 1 hour for UT
For French Summer Time add ONE hour in **non-shaded areas**

FRANCE – DIEPPE

LAT 49°56′N LONG 1°05′E

TIMES AND HEIGHTS OF HIGH AND LOW WATERS

Dates in amber are **SPRINGS**
Dates in yellow are **NEAPS**

2016

JANUARY

Date	Day	Time	m	Time	m	Time	m	Time	m
1	F	0348	8.0	1030	2.3	1604	7.7	2250	2.3
2	SA	0431	7.6	1114	2.6	1651	7.3	◑ 2338	2.7
3	SU	0524	7.2	1209	2.9	1751	7.0		
4	M	0037	2.9	0633	7.1	1317	3.0	1907	6.9
5	TU	0150	2.9	0748	7.2	1432	2.8	2020	7.2
6	W	0304	2.6	0851	7.6	1538	2.4	2118	7.6
7	TH	0405	2.2	0942	8.1	1633	1.9	2207	8.1
8	F	0456	1.8	1028	8.5	1722	1.5	2251	8.5
9	SA	0542	1.5	1110	8.8	1807	1.2	2333	8.8
10	SU ●	0626	1.3	1150	9.1	1851	1.0		
11	M	0013	9.1	0709	1.1	1231	9.3	1934	0.8
12	TU	0055	9.3	0752	0.9	1313	9.4	2017	0.7
13	W	0136	9.3	0834	0.9	1355	9.4	2058	0.7
14	TH	0219	9.2	0916	1.0	1439	9.2	2138	0.9
15	F	0303	9.0	0958	1.2	1524	8.9	2220	1.2
16	SA	0349	8.7	1043	1.5	1613	8.5	2306	1.5
17	SU ◐	0441	8.3	1135	1.8	1712	8.1		
18	M	0001	1.9	0545	8.0	1239	2.1	1823	7.8
19	TU	0111	2.1	0701	7.8	1358	2.1	1941	7.8
20	W	0232	2.1	0818	8.0	1516	1.9	2056	8.0
21	TH	0346	1.9	0927	8.3	1625	1.6	2200	8.4
22	F	0451	1.6	1025	8.7	1724	1.3	2253	8.7
23	SA	0546	1.3	1114	9.0	1815	1.0	2339	9.0
24	SU ○	0633	1.1	1156	9.2	1859	0.9		
25	M	0020	9.2	0714	1.0	1235	9.3	1938	0.8
26	TU	0057	9.2	0751	1.0	1312	9.2	2013	0.9
27	W	0132	9.1	0826	1.1	1346	9.1	2045	1.0
28	TH	0206	9.0	0856	1.3	1420	8.9	2114	1.3
29	F	0239	8.7	0924	1.6	1452	8.5	2140	1.6
30	SA	0310	8.4	0952	1.9	1524	8.1	2210	1.9
31	SU	0343	7.9	1027	2.2	1559	7.7	2247	2.3

FEBRUARY

Date	Day	Time	m	Time	m	Time	m	Time	m
1	M	0422	7.5	1111	2.6	1644	7.2	◑ 2334	2.7
2	TU	0515	7.1	1208	2.9	1749	6.8		
3	W	0037	3.0	0634	6.9	1321	3.0	1921	6.8
4	TH	0159	3.0	0803	7.1	1446	2.7	2040	7.2
5	F	0321	2.6	0909	7.6	1557	2.2	2138	7.8
6	SA	0424	2.0	1001	8.2	1654	1.6	2228	8.4
7	SU	0518	1.5	1048	8.7	1746	1.2	2313	8.9
8	M	0608	1.1	1133	9.2	1835	0.8	● 2357	9.2
9	TU	0656	0.8	1216	9.5	1922	0.5		
10	W	0040	9.5	0742	0.6	1259	9.7	2006	0.3
11	TH	0122	9.7	0825	0.5	1342	9.8	2047	0.3
12	F	0205	9.7	0906	0.5	1425	9.6	2127	0.4
13	SA	0247	9.4	0946	0.8	1508	9.3	2205	0.8
14	SU	0330	9.1	1027	1.1	1554	8.8	2247	1.3
15	M	0417	8.5	1114	1.6	1647	8.2	◐ 2336	1.8
16	TU	0515	8.0	1212	2.1	1756	7.7		
17	W	0042	2.3	0632	7.6	1330	2.3	1920	7.4
18	TH	0207	2.5	0800	7.5	1457	2.2	2045	7.6
19	F	0331	2.2	0917	7.9	1613	1.8	2151	8.1
20	SA	0441	1.8	1015	8.4	1715	1.4	2242	8.6
21	SU	0536	1.5	1102	8.8	1803	1.1	2325	8.9
22	M ○	0620	1.2	1142	9.0	1843	0.9		
23	TU	0002	9.1	0657	1.0	1217	9.2	1918	0.8
24	W	0036	9.2	0730	1.0	1250	9.2	1950	0.8
25	TH	0108	9.2	0801	1.0	1322	9.2	2020	0.9
26	F	0139	9.1	0830	1.1	1353	9.0	2046	1.1
27	SA	0208	8.9	0856	1.3	1422	8.8	2111	1.3
28	SU	0236	8.6	0922	1.5	1450	8.4	2137	1.7
29	M	0305	8.3	0952	1.9	1521	8.0	2209	2.1

MARCH

Date	Day	Time	m	Time	m	Time	m	Time	m
1	TU	0338	7.8	1030	2.3	1600	7.5	2250	2.5
2	W	0423	7.3	1119	2.7	1654	7.0	◑ 2347	2.9
3	TH	0528	6.9	1226	2.9	1816	6.7		
4	F	0103	3.1	0706	6.8	1354	2.8	1957	7.0
5	SA	0235	2.8	0832	7.3	1519	2.3	2107	7.6
6	SU	0351	2.1	0933	8.0	1625	1.6	2202	8.3
7	M	0451	1.5	1025	8.7	1722	1.1	2251	8.9
8	TU	0546	1.0	1112	9.2	1815	0.6	2336	9.4
9	W ●	0638	0.6	1157	9.7	1904	0.2		
10	TH	0020	9.7	0726	0.3	1241	9.9	1950	0.1
11	F	0103	9.9	0810	0.2	1324	10.0	2031	0.0
12	SA	0145	9.9	0851	0.2	1407	9.9	2110	0.3
13	SU	0227	9.7	0931	0.5	1450	9.5	2148	0.7
14	M	0309	9.2	1010	0.9	1535	8.9	2227	1.2
15	TU	0355	8.6	1054	1.5	1626	8.2	◐ 2314	1.9
16	W	0450	7.9	1150	2.0	1732	7.5		
17	TH	0018	2.4	0605	7.3	1305	2.4	1859	7.2
18	F	0143	2.6	0739	7.2	1434	2.4	2028	7.4
19	SA	0311	2.4	0900	7.6	1554	2.0	2134	7.9
20	SU	0423	1.9	0957	8.1	1655	1.5	2223	8.4
21	M	0516	1.5	1042	8.6	1741	1.2	2303	8.8
22	TU	0558	1.3	1120	8.8	1819	1.0	2338	9.0
23	W ○	0632	1.1	1154	9.0	1852	0.9		
24	TH	0010	9.1	0704	1.0	1225	9.1	1922	0.9
25	F	0040	9.1	0734	1.0	1255	9.1	1952	0.9
26	SA	0110	9.1	0803	1.0	1325	9.0	2019	1.0
27	SU	0139	9.0	0830	1.1	1354	8.8	2044	1.3
28	M	0207	8.7	0856	1.4	1423	8.6	2111	1.6
29	TU	0236	8.4	0925	1.7	1455	8.2	2141	1.9
30	W	0309	8.0	1001	2.0	1532	7.7	2220	2.4
31	TH	0351	7.6	1047	2.4	1622	7.2	◑ 2313	2.7

APRIL

Date	Day	Time	m	Time	m	Time	m	Time	m
1	F	0449	7.1	1149	2.7	1734	6.9		
2	SA	0025	2.9	0617	6.9	1312	2.7	1914	7.0
3	SU	0155	2.7	0752	7.3	1441	2.3	2032	7.6
4	M	0316	2.1	0900	8.0	1552	1.6	2132	8.4
5	TU	0421	1.4	0956	8.7	1653	1.0	2224	9.0
6	W	0520	0.9	1047	9.3	1750	0.5	2312	9.5
7	TH	0615	0.5	1134	9.7	1841	0.2	● 2357	9.8
8	F	0705	0.2	1220	10.0	1928	0.1		
9	SA	0042	10.0	0751	0.1	1305	10.0	2011	0.1
10	SU	0125	9.9	0833	0.2	1348	9.9	2051	0.3
11	M	0207	9.7	0914	0.4	1432	9.5	2130	0.7
12	TU	0250	9.2	0953	0.9	1517	8.9	2209	1.3
13	W	0335	8.6	1037	1.4	1608	8.2	2256	1.9
14	TH	0429	7.9	1130	2.0	1710	7.6	◐ 2357	2.4
15	F	0538	7.3	1239	2.4	1829	7.2		
16	SA	0114	2.7	0705	7.1	1400	2.4	1956	7.3
17	SU	0235	2.5	0828	7.4	1517	2.2	2104	7.8
18	M	0346	2.1	0928	7.9	1619	1.8	2153	8.2
19	TU	0441	1.7	1013	8.3	1706	1.5	2233	8.6
20	W	0524	1.4	1051	8.6	1745	1.2	2308	8.8
21	TH	0601	1.3	1125	8.8	1820	1.1	2340	8.9
22	F ○	0634	1.1	1157	8.9	1852	1.1		
23	SA	0011	9.0	0707	1.1	1229	8.9	1923	1.1
24	SU	0042	9.0	0737	1.1	1300	8.9	1953	1.1
25	M	0112	8.9	0806	1.1	1330	8.8	2021	1.3
26	TU	0142	8.8	0836	1.3	1402	8.6	2050	1.5
27	W	0214	8.5	0908	1.5	1436	8.3	2123	1.8
28	TH	0250	8.2	0944	1.8	1515	7.9	2202	2.2
29	F	0332	7.8	1028	2.2	1604	7.5	2253	2.5
30	SA	0427	7.4	1127	2.4	1710	7.2	◑ 2359	2.6

Chart Datum: 4·43 metres below IGN Datum
HAT is 10·1 metres above Chart Datum

TIME ZONE -0100
(French Standard Time)
Subtract 1 hour for UT
For French Summer Time add
ONE hour in **non-shaded areas**

FRANCE – DIEPPE

LAT 49°56′N LONG 1°05′E

TIMES AND HEIGHTS OF HIGH AND LOW WATERS

Dates in amber are **SPRING**
Dates in yellow are **NEAP**

201

MAY

Day	Time	m	Time	m	Time	m	Time	m
1 SU	0544	7.2	1240	2.4	1836	7.3		
2 M	0120	2.5	0712	7.5	1404	2.1	1955	7.8
3 TU	0241	2.0	0825	8.0	1518	1.6	2059	8.4
4 W	0350	1.4	0926	8.6	1622	1.0	2155	9.0
5 TH	0451	0.9	1020	9.2	1721	0.7	2246	9.4
6 F	0549	0.6	1111	9.6	1815	0.4	● 2334	9.7
7 SA	0641	0.4	1159	9.8	1905	0.3		
8 SU	0020	9.8	0730	0.3	1245	9.8	1950	0.3
9 M	0104	9.8	0814	0.3	1330	9.7	2032	0.5
10 TU	0148	9.6	0857	0.5	1415	9.4	2113	0.9
11 W	0232	9.2	0938	0.9	1501	8.9	2153	1.4
12 TH	0318	8.6	1020	1.4	1549	8.3	2238	1.9
13 F	0408	8.0	1109	1.9	1645	7.8	◐ 2332	2.3
14 SA	0507	7.5	1207	2.3	1750	7.4		
15 SU	0037	2.6	0618	7.2	1314	2.4	1904	7.3
16 M	0147	2.6	0736	7.2	1423	2.3	2016	7.5
17 TU	0253	2.3	0843	7.5	1526	2.1	2111	7.9
18 W	0352	2.0	0935	7.9	1620	1.8	2156	8.2
19 TH	0441	1.7	1017	8.2	1705	1.5	2234	8.5
20 F	0524	1.5	1054	8.5	1745	1.4	2310	8.7
21 SA	0603	1.3	1129	8.6	1822	1.3	○ 2343	8.8
22 SU	0639	1.2	1203	8.7	1856	1.2		
23 M	0017	8.9	0713	1.2	1237	8.8	1929	1.2
24 TU	0049	8.9	0746	1.1	1311	8.8	2002	1.3
25 W	0123	8.8	0820	1.2	1346	8.7	2036	1.4
26 TH	0159	8.6	0856	1.3	1424	8.5	2112	1.6
27 F	0238	8.4	0934	1.6	1505	8.2	2153	1.9
28 SA	0322	8.1	1018	1.8	1553	7.9	2241	2.1
29 SU	0414	7.8	1111	2.0	1652	7.7	◑ 2340	2.3
30 M	0520	7.6	1215	2.1	1804	7.7		
31 TU	0051	2.2	0637	7.7	1330	1.9	1918	8.0

JUNE

Day	Time	m	Time	m	Time	m	Time	m
1 W	0208	1.9	0751	8.1	1444	1.6	2026	8.4
2 TH	0319	1.5	0856	8.5	1551	1.2	2126	8.8
3 F	0423	1.1	0956	8.9	1652	0.9	2221	9.2
4 SA	0523	0.8	1050	9.3	1749	0.7	2312	9.4
5 SU	0618	0.6	1140	9.5	1842	0.6	●	
6 M	0001	9.6	0709	0.5	1228	9.5	1930	0.6
7 TU	0047	9.6	0757	0.5	1315	9.5	2014	0.7
8 W	0132	9.4	0840	0.6	1359	9.3	2056	1.0
9 TH	0215	9.1	0922	0.9	1444	8.9	2136	1.3
10 F	0259	8.7	1002	1.3	1528	8.5	2216	1.7
11 SA	0344	8.2	1043	1.7	1615	8.0	2300	2.1
12 SU	0433	7.7	1129	2.1	1706	7.6	◐ 2352	2.4
13 M	0529	7.3	1223	2.4	1806	7.3		
14 TU	0052	2.6	0634	7.1	1325	2.5	1913	7.3
15 W	0156	2.5	0744	7.2	1429	2.4	2019	7.5
16 TH	0300	2.3	0847	7.5	1530	2.2	2113	7.8
17 F	0357	2.0	0939	7.8	1624	1.9	2159	8.1
18 SA	0447	1.8	1023	8.1	1711	1.7	2240	8.4
19 SU	0532	1.5	1103	8.4	1753	1.5	2318	8.6
20 M	0613	1.4	1141	8.6	1831	1.4	○ 2355	8.8
21 TU	0652	1.2	1218	8.7	1909	1.3		
22 W	0031	8.9	0730	1.1	1255	8.8	1946	1.2
23 TH	0109	8.9	0809	1.1	1334	8.9	2025	1.3
24 F	0148	8.9	0848	1.1	1414	8.8	2104	1.4
25 SA	0229	8.7	0928	1.2	1456	8.6	2145	1.5
26 SU	0313	8.5	1010	1.4	1541	8.4	2231	1.7
27 M	0401	8.2	1057	1.6	1633	8.2	◑ 2322	1.9
28 TU	0458	8.0	1152	1.8	1734	8.0		
29 W	0024	2.0	0607	7.9	1258	1.8	1845	8.0
30 TH	0137	1.9	0721	8.0	1413	1.7	1957	8.2

JULY

Day	Time	m	Time	m	Time	m	Time	m
1 F	0252	1.7	0832	8.3	1525	1.5	2103	8.5
2 SA	0400	1.4	0937	8.6	1629	1.3	2203	8.8
3 SU	0502	1.1	1035	8.9	1729	1.1	2257	9.1
4 M	0600	0.9	1127	9.2	1823	0.9	● 2347	9.3
5 TU	0653	0.7	1215	9.3	1913	0.9		
6 W	0033	9.4	0741	0.7	1300	9.3	1957	0.9
7 TH	0116	9.3	0823	0.7	1342	9.2	2038	1.0
8 F	0157	9.1	0902	0.9	1423	9.0	2115	1.2
9 SA	0237	8.8	0938	1.2	1502	8.7	2149	1.6
10 SU	0316	8.5	1011	1.6	1541	8.3	2224	1.9
11 M	0355	8.0	1046	1.9	1622	7.9	2303	2.3
12 TU	0439	7.6	1129	2.3	1709	7.5	◐ 2352	2.6
13 W	0532	7.2	1222	2.6	1808	7.2		
14 TH	0053	2.7	0640	7.0	1328	2.8	1920	7.1
15 F	0204	2.7	0756	7.0	1440	2.6	2028	7.4
16 SA	0313	2.4	0900	7.4	1545	2.3	2124	7.8
17 SU	0412	2.1	0953	7.8	1639	2.0	2212	8.2
18 M	0503	1.7	1038	8.2	1726	1.6	2255	8.5
19 TU	0549	1.4	1120	8.6	1810	1.4	○ 2335	8.8
20 W	0633	1.2	1200	8.8	1852	1.2		
21 TH	0015	9.0	0716	1.0	1240	9.0	1934	1.1
22 F	0055	9.2	0758	0.8	1320	9.1	2015	1.0
23 SA	0136	9.2	0839	0.8	1401	9.2	2056	1.0
24 SU	0217	9.1	0919	0.8	1442	9.1	2136	1.1
25 M	0300	8.9	0959	1.0	1526	8.8	2218	1.3
26 TU	0345	8.7	1041	1.3	1612	8.5	2305	1.6
27 W	0437	8.3	1130	1.6	1707	8.2	◑	
28 TH	0000	1.9	0540	8.0	1231	1.9	1816	7.9
29 F	0110	2.0	0657	7.8	1348	2.0	1934	7.9
30 SA	0231	1.9	0815	7.9	1506	1.9	2048	8.2
31 SU	0345	1.6	0927	8.3	1615	1.6	2153	8.5

AUGUST

Day	Time	m	Time	m	Time	m	Time	m
1 M	0451	1.3	1027	8.7	1717	1.3	2249	8.9
2 TU	0549	1.0	1118	9.0	1811	1.1	● 2336	9.1
3 W	0640	0.9	1203	9.2	1858	1.0		
4 TH	0019	9.3	0724	0.8	1244	9.3	1939	1.0
5 F	0058	9.3	0803	0.8	1322	9.3	2016	1.0
6 SA	0135	9.2	0838	0.9	1357	9.1	2049	1.2
7 SU	0210	9.0	0909	1.1	1432	8.9	2118	1.4
8 M	0244	8.7	0937	1.5	1505	8.5	2146	1.7
9 TU	0317	8.3	1005	1.8	1538	8.1	2218	2.1
10 W	0351	7.8	1038	2.2	1614	7.6	◐ 2258	2.5
11 TH	0432	7.3	1123	2.7	1702	7.2	2351	2.8
12 F	0531	6.9	1223	3.0	1812	6.9		
13 SA	0100	3.0	0657	6.7	1342	3.1	1941	7.0
14 SU	0225	2.8	0822	7.0	1504	2.7	2051	7.4
15 M	0337	2.4	0923	7.6	1607	2.2	2145	8.0
16 TU	0434	1.8	1013	8.2	1659	1.7	2232	8.5
17 W	0525	1.4	1058	8.6	1748	1.3	2315	8.9
18 TH	0613	1.6	1140	9.0	1834	1.0	○ 2357	9.2
19 F	0700	0.7	1221	9.3	1919	0.8		
20 SA	0038	9.5	0744	0.6	1302	9.5	2002	0.7
21 SU	0119	9.6	0825	0.5	1343	9.5	2043	0.7
22 M	0201	9.5	0905	0.6	1424	9.4	2123	0.8
23 TU	0243	9.3	0943	0.8	1506	9.2	2203	1.1
24 W	0327	8.9	1023	1.2	1551	8.7	2246	1.5
25 TH	0416	8.4	1109	1.7	1643	8.2	◑ 2339	1.9
26 F	0518	7.9	1209	2.1	1752	7.8		
27 SA	0050	2.2	0639	7.5	1329	2.4	1917	7.6
28 SU	0217	2.2	0806	7.6	1454	2.2	2040	7.9
29 M	0336	1.9	0922	8.1	1608	1.8	2147	8.3
30 TU	0444	1.5	1019	8.6	1709	1.5	2239	8.8
31 W	0540	1.1	1106	9.0	1759	1.2	2323	9.1

Chart Datum: 4·43 metres below IGN Datum
HAT is 10·1 metres above Chart Datum

TIME ZONE -0100
(French Standard Time)
Subtract 1 hour for UT
For French Summer Time add ONE hour in **non-shaded areas**

FRANCE – DIEPPE

LAT 49°56'N LONG 1°05'E

TIMES AND HEIGHTS OF HIGH AND LOW WATERS

Dates in amber are **SPRINGS**
Dates in yellow are **NEAPS**

2016

SEPTEMBER

Date	Day	Time	m	Time	m	Time	m	Time	m	Moon
1	TH	0625	0.9	1147	9.2	1841	1.1			●
2	F	0001	9.2	0704	0.9	1223	9.3	1917	1.0	
3	SA	0036	9.2	0738	0.9	1256	9.3	1950	1.0	
4	SU	0109	9.2	0809	1.0	1328	9.2	2020	1.1	
5	M	0141	9.0	0837	1.2	1359	9.0	2047	1.4	
6	TU	0212	8.8	0903	1.4	1429	8.7	2112	1.6	
7	W	0241	8.4	0927	1.8	1457	8.3	2140	2.0	
8	TH	0310	8.0	0957	2.2	1529	7.8	2215	2.4	
9	F	0346	7.5	1036	2.7	1609	7.3	2301	2.8	◐
10	SA	0436	7.0	1130	3.1	1710	6.9			
11	SU	0005	3.1	0553	6.6	1245	3.3	1844	6.7	
12	M	0132	3.1	0739	6.8	1419	3.0	2014	7.2	
13	TU	0259	2.6	0851	7.5	1534	2.4	2115	7.8	
14	W	0404	1.9	0945	8.2	1631	1.7	2205	8.5	
15	TH	0458	1.3	1032	8.8	1723	1.2	2251	9.0	
16	F	0550	0.9	1116	9.3	1813	0.9	2334	9.5	○
17	SA	0638	0.6	1159	9.6	1900	0.6			
18	SU	0017	9.7	0724	0.4	1240	9.8	1944	0.5	
19	M	0059	9.9	0807	0.3	1322	9.8	2026	0.5	
20	TU	0142	9.8	0846	0.4	1404	9.7	2106	0.6	
21	W	0224	9.5	0925	0.8	1446	9.3	2146	1.0	
22	TH	0308	9.0	1005	1.2	1530	8.8	2229	1.5	
23	F	0358	8.4	1051	1.8	1623	8.2	2322	2.0	◑
24	SA	0501	7.8	1152	2.4	1733	7.6			
25	SU	0033	2.4	0624	7.4	1315	2.6	1902	7.4	
26	M	0203	2.4	0755	7.5	1442	2.4	2028	7.7	
27	TU	0324	2.0	0908	8.0	1556	2.0	2132	8.2	
28	W	0429	1.6	1002	8.6	1654	1.5	2221	8.7	
29	TH	0521	1.2	1046	8.9	1740	1.3	2303	9.0	
30	F	0602	1.1	1123	9.1	1817	1.1	2338	9.1	

OCTOBER

Date	Day	Time	m	Time	m	Time	m	Time	m	Moon
1	SA	0637	1.0	1157	9.2	1850	1.1			●
2	SU	0011	9.2	0708	1.0	1228	9.2	1921	1.1	
3	M	0041	9.1	0738	1.1	1258	9.2	1950	1.2	
4	TU	0112	9.0	0806	1.2	1327	9.0	2018	1.3	
5	W	0141	8.8	0832	1.5	1356	8.8	2043	1.6	
6	TH	0210	8.5	0857	1.8	1424	8.4	2110	1.9	
7	F	0239	8.2	0926	2.2	1455	8.0	2143	2.3	
8	SA	0314	7.7	1002	2.6	1534	7.5	2226	2.7	
9	SU	0401	7.2	1053	3.0	1628	7.0	2325	3.0	◐
10	M	0508	6.8	1202	3.3	1751	6.8			
11	TU	0044	3.1	0649	6.9	1333	3.1	1930	7.1	
12	W	0216	2.7	0812	7.5	1457	2.5	2039	7.8	
13	TH	0329	2.0	0911	8.2	1600	1.8	2134	8.5	
14	F	0427	1.3	1001	8.9	1655	1.2	2223	9.1	
15	SA	0522	0.9	1048	9.4	1747	0.8	2309	9.6	
16	SU	0613	0.5	1133	9.7	1837	0.5	2354	9.9	○
17	M	0701	0.4	1217	9.9	1924	0.4			
18	TU	0038	10.0	0745	0.3	1300	10.0	2007	0.4	
19	W	0122	9.9	0827	0.5	1343	9.8	2049	0.6	
20	TH	0206	9.6	0907	0.8	1427	9.4	2130	1.0	
21	F	0252	9.1	0948	1.3	1513	8.8	2214	1.5	
22	SA	0343	8.4	1035	1.9	1606	8.2	2306	2.0	◑
23	SU	0444	7.8	1135	2.5	1713	7.6			
24	M	0014	2.5	0601	7.4	1253	2.7	1835	7.3	
25	TU	0137	2.5	0727	7.4	1416	2.6	2000	7.5	
26	W	0255	2.2	0840	7.9	1527	2.1	2105	8.0	
27	TH	0359	1.8	0934	8.4	1624	1.7	2155	8.4	
28	F	0449	1.5	1018	8.7	1709	1.5	2236	8.7	
29	SA	0530	1.3	1055	8.9	1747	1.3	2311	8.9	
30	SU	0605	1.2	1128	9.1	1820	1.2	2343	9.0	●
31	M	0637	1.2	1159	9.1	1852	1.2			

NOVEMBER

Date	Day	Time	m	Time	m	Time	m	Time	m	Moon
1	TU	0014	9.0	0709	1.2	1229	9.1	1924	1.2	
2	W	0045	8.9	0739	1.3	1259	9.0	1953	1.3	
3	TH	0115	8.8	0807	1.5	1329	8.8	2021	1.5	
4	F	0146	8.6	0834	1.8	1359	8.5	2050	1.8	
5	SA	0218	8.3	0905	2.1	1432	8.2	2123	2.1	
6	SU	0254	7.9	0941	2.4	1511	7.8	2204	2.4	
7	M	0339	7.5	1028	2.8	1602	7.3	2257	2.7	◐
8	TU	0439	7.2	1131	3.0	1713	7.1			
9	W	0007	2.8	0602	7.1	1250	2.9	1842	7.2	
10	TH	0131	2.6	0727	7.5	1415	2.5	1958	7.8	
11	F	0249	2.0	0833	8.2	1525	1.8	2059	8.4	
12	SA	0354	1.4	0929	8.8	1625	1.3	2153	9.0	
13	SU	0452	1.0	1020	9.4	1720	0.8	2244	9.5	
14	M	0546	0.7	1108	9.7	1813	0.6	2332	9.8	○
15	TU	0636	0.5	1155	9.9	1903	0.4			
16	W	0019	9.9	0724	0.5	1240	9.9	1949	0.4	
17	TH	0105	9.8	0809	0.6	1325	9.8	2034	0.6	
18	F	0151	9.6	0852	0.9	1411	9.4	2117	0.9	
19	SA	0238	9.1	0934	1.4	1458	8.9	2200	1.4	
20	SU	0327	8.6	1020	1.9	1548	8.3	2249	1.9	
21	M	0422	8.0	1114	2.3	1647	7.7	2346	2.3	◑
22	TU	0526	7.6	1219	2.6	1755	7.4			
23	W	0054	2.6	0639	7.4	1330	2.7	1911	7.3	
24	TH	0205	2.5	0754	7.6	1439	2.4	2023	7.5	
25	F	0311	2.3	0855	7.9	1540	2.1	2119	7.9	
26	SA	0406	2.0	0943	8.3	1630	1.8	2203	8.3	
27	SU	0452	1.7	1023	8.6	1713	1.6	2241	8.5	
28	M	0532	1.5	1058	8.8	1751	1.4	2316	8.7	
29	TU	0608	1.4	1132	8.9	1827	1.3	2350	8.8	●
30	W	0643	1.4	1204	8.9	1900	1.3			

DECEMBER

Date	Day	Time	m	Time	m	Time	m	Time	m	Moon
1	TH	0023	8.8	0715	1.4	1237	8.9	1933	1.3	
2	F	0055	8.8	0747	1.5	1309	8.9	2004	1.4	
3	SA	0128	8.7	0818	1.6	1342	8.7	2037	1.5	
4	SU	0203	8.5	0852	1.8	1418	8.4	2112	1.8	
5	M	0241	8.3	0929	2.1	1458	8.1	2152	2.0	
6	TU	0325	8.0	1014	2.4	1546	7.8	2239	2.2	
7	W	0417	7.7	1108	2.5	1645	7.5	2338	2.4	◐
8	TH	0523	7.5	1214	2.6	1758	7.5			
9	F	0048	2.4	0641	7.7	1331	2.4	1916	7.8	
10	SA	0207	2.1	0753	8.1	1447	1.9	2025	8.3	
11	SU	0319	1.6	0857	8.6	1555	1.4	2126	8.8	
12	M	0423	1.2	0954	9.1	1655	1.0	2221	9.2	
13	TU	0520	0.9	1046	9.5	1751	0.7	2313	9.5	
14	W	0615	0.7	1136	9.7	1844	0.5			○
15	TH	0003	9.7	0706	0.6	1224	9.8	1933	0.5	
16	F	0051	9.7	0753	0.7	1311	9.7	2020	0.6	
17	SA	0137	9.5	0838	0.9	1356	9.4	2103	0.8	
18	SU	0223	9.2	0920	1.2	1441	9.1	2145	1.2	
19	M	0308	8.8	1002	1.6	1527	8.6	2226	1.6	
20	TU	0355	8.3	1045	2.1	1615	8.0	2310	2.1	
21	W	0445	7.8	1134	2.4	1708	7.5			◑
22	TH	0001	2.5	0543	7.4	1232	2.7	1811	7.2	
23	F	0102	2.7	0650	7.3	1338	2.7	1923	7.1	
24	SA	0209	2.7	0801	7.4	1446	2.6	2031	7.3	
25	SU	0315	2.5	0901	7.7	1547	2.3	2126	7.7	
26	M	0412	2.2	0948	8.1	1639	1.9	2211	8.0	
27	TU	0500	1.9	1030	8.4	1723	1.6	2251	8.4	
28	W	0542	1.7	1108	8.6	1803	1.4	2328	8.6	
29	TH	0620	1.5	1144	8.8	1841	1.3			●
30	F	0004	8.7	0656	1.4	1219	8.9	1917	1.2	
31	SA	0040	8.9	0731	1.4	1254	9.0	1952	1.2	

Chart Datum: 4·43 metres below IGN Datum
HAT is 10·1 metres above Chart Datum

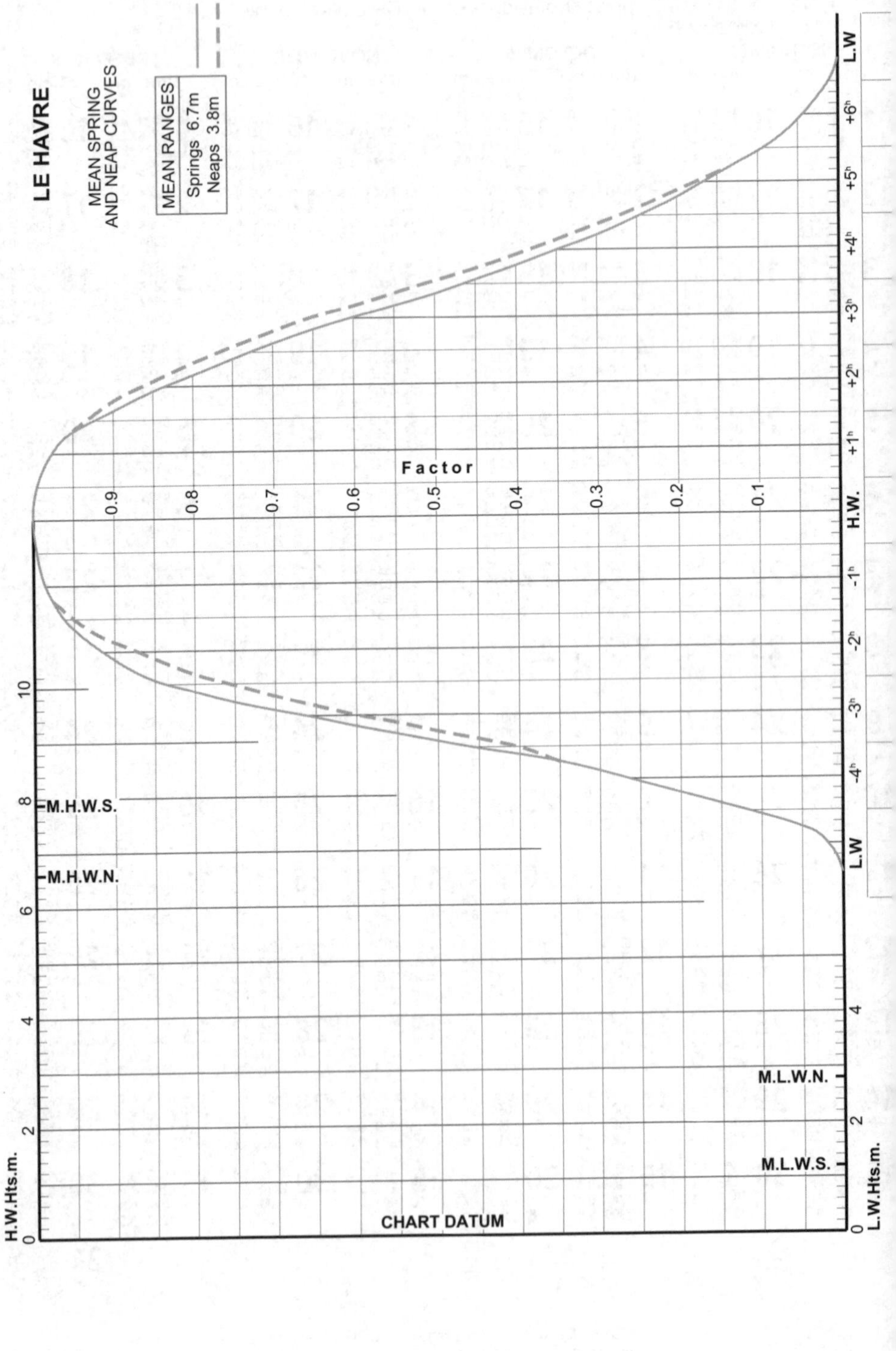
LE HAVRE
MEAN SPRING AND NEAP CURVES
MEAN RANGES
Springs 6.7m
Neaps 3.8m
Factor
0.9
0.8
0.7
0.6
0.5
0.4
0.3
0.2
0.1
L.W
-4h
-3h
-2h
-1h
H.W.
+1h
+2h
+3h
+4h
+5h
+6h
L.W
H.W.Hts.m.
0
2
4
6
8
10
M.H.W.S.
M.H.W.N.
CHART DATUM
L.W.Hts.m.
0
2
4
M.L.W.S.
M.L.W.N.

TIME ZONE -0100
(French Standard Time)
Subtract 1 hour for UT
For French Summer Time add ONE hour in **non-shaded areas**

FRANCE – LE HAVRE

LAT 49°29'N LONG 0°07'E

TIMES AND HEIGHTS OF HIGH AND LOW WATERS

Dates in amber are **SPRINGS**
Dates in yellow are **NEAPS**

2016

JANUARY

Date	Day	Time	m	Time	m	Time	m	Time	m
1	F	0256	7.0	0944	2.7	1504	6.9	2205	2.7
2	SA ◑	0344	6.8	1026	3.0	1557	6.6	2250	3.0
3	SU	0445	6.6	1117	3.3	1707	6.4	2344	3.2
4	M	0550	6.5	1218	3.3	1817	6.4		
5	TU	0051	3.2	0654	6.6	1334	3.2	1924	6.5
6	W	0212	3.0	0755	6.9	1452	2.8	2024	6.8
7	TH	0318	2.6	0847	7.2	1547	2.4	2114	7.1
8	F	0409	2.3	0931	7.4	1634	2.0	2157	7.4
9	SA	0454	1.9	1012	7.7	1718	1.7	2238	7.6
10	SU ●	0537	1.7	1052	7.9	1801	1.4	2318	7.8
11	M	0620	1.5	1132	8.0	1844	1.2	2359	7.9
12	TU	0703	1.4	1214	8.1	1926	1.1		
13	W	0042	8.0	0745	1.4	1257	8.1	2007	1.1
14	TH	0126	7.9	0826	1.5	1342	7.9	2047	1.3
15	F	0211	7.8	0907	1.7	1428	7.7	2127	1.6
16	SA	0258	7.5	0950	2.0	1517	7.5	2212	1.9
17	SU ◐	0350	7.3	1040	2.3	1615	7.2	2308	2.3
18	M	0455	7.1	1147	2.5	1730	7.0		
19	TU	0022	2.5	0614	7.0	1308	2.6	1852	7.0
20	W	0142	2.5	0728	7.2	1424	2.4	2003	7.2
21	TH	0254	2.3	0830	7.4	1534	2.0	2103	7.4
22	F	0401	2.0	0924	7.6	1638	1.7	2154	7.6
23	SA	0500	1.8	1011	7.7	1731	1.4	2239	7.7
24	SU ○	0549	1.6	1053	7.9	1815	1.3	2321	7.8
25	M	0628	1.5	1132	7.9	1852	1.2	2359	7.8
26	TU	0704	1.5	1208	7.9	1926	1.3		
27	W	0034	7.8	0738	1.5	1243	7.8	1958	1.4
28	TH	0109	7.7	0809	1.7	1317	7.6	2028	1.7
29	F	0142	7.5	0839	2.0	1349	7.4	2056	2.0
30	SA	0214	7.2	0907	2.3	1420	7.2	2124	2.4
31	SU	0246	7.0	0938	2.7	1455	6.8	2157	2.7

FEBRUARY

Date	Day	Time	m	Time	m	Time	m	Time	m
1	M ◑	0326	6.7	1019	3.0	1545	6.5	2244	3.1
2	TU	0428	6.5	1114	3.3	1701	6.3	2344	3.3
3	W	0550	6.4	1222	3.3	1828	6.3		
4	TH	0101	3.3	0707	6.5	1351	3.1	1947	6.5
5	F	0233	3.0	0815	6.9	1509	2.6	2048	6.9
6	SA	0338	2.5	0907	7.3	1606	2.1	2136	7.3
7	SU	0430	2.0	0952	7.6	1657	1.6	2220	7.7
8	M ●	0520	1.6	1035	7.9	1746	1.2	2301	7.9
9	TU	0607	1.2	1117	8.1	1833	0.9	2344	8.1
10	W	0653	1.0	1159	8.3	1917	0.7		
11	TH	0026	8.2	0736	0.9	1243	8.3	1958	0.7
12	F	0109	8.2	0817	1.0	1326	8.2	2037	0.9
13	SA	0152	8.0	0856	1.2	1410	8.0	2115	1.3
14	SU	0236	7.7	0935	1.6	1456	7.6	2154	1.7
15	M ◐	0323	7.4	1019	2.1	1549	7.2	2243	2.3
16	TU	0421	7.0	1118	2.5	1703	6.8	2352	2.7
17	W	0544	6.8	1239	2.7	1834	6.7		
18	TH	0116	2.8	0708	6.8	1403	2.6	1952	6.9
19	F	0237	2.6	0818	7.0	1524	2.3	2055	7.1
20	SA	0354	2.3	0913	7.3	1632	1.9	2144	7.4
21	SU	0454	1.9	0959	7.5	1721	1.5	2226	7.6
22	M ○	0537	1.7	1038	7.7	1759	1.4	2303	7.7
23	TU	0612	1.5	1113	7.8	1832	1.2	2336	7.8
24	W	0644	1.4	1146	7.9	1903	1.2		
25	TH	0008	7.8	0715	1.4	1218	7.8	1932	1.3
26	F	0039	7.7	0744	1.5	1249	7.7	2000	1.5
27	SA	0110	7.6	0810	1.7	1319	7.6	2026	1.8
28	SU	0138	7.4	0836	2.0	1348	7.3	2051	2.1
29	M	0206	7.2	0903	2.3	1420	7.0	2119	2.5

MARCH

Date	Day	Time	m	Time	m	Time	m	Time	m
1	TU	0241	6.9	0937	2.7	1501	6.7	2158	2.9
2	W ◑	0330	6.6	1025	3.1	1601	6.3	2255	3.3
3	TH	0443	6.3	1131	3.3	1731	6.2		
4	F	0009	3.4	0615	6.4	1256	3.2	1907	6.4
5	SA	0149	3.1	0738	6.7	1431	2.7	2020	6.8
6	SU	0306	2.5	0840	7.1	1536	2.1	2112	7.3
7	M	0405	1.9	0929	7.6	1633	1.5	2157	7.7
8	TU	0459	1.4	1013	7.9	1726	1.1	2240	8.0
9	W ●	0550	1.0	1057	8.2	1815	0.7	2323	8.2
10	TH	0637	0.7	1141	8.4	1901	0.5		
11	F	0006	8.4	0721	0.6	1225	8.5	1943	0.5
12	SA	0049	8.4	0802	0.6	1308	8.4	2022	0.7
13	SU	0132	8.2	0841	0.9	1352	8.1	2059	1.1
14	M	0214	7.8	0920	1.4	1437	7.6	2137	1.7
15	TU ◐	0258	7.4	1001	2.0	1529	7.2	2222	2.3
16	W	0353	7.0	1056	2.5	1643	6.7	2329	2.8
17	TH	0517	6.6	1213	2.8	1816	6.6		
18	F	0051	3.0	0646	6.6	1339	2.8	1937	6.7
19	SA	0217	2.8	0801	6.8	1507	2.4	2040	7.0
20	SU	0340	2.4	0857	7.1	1613	2.0	2126	7.3
21	M	0435	2.0	0940	7.4	1658	1.7	2205	7.5
22	TU	0515	1.7	1017	7.6	1734	1.5	2239	7.7
23	W ○	0547	1.5	1050	7.7	1805	1.3	2310	7.7
24	TH	0619	1.4	1121	7.8	1836	1.3	2340	7.8
25	F	0649	1.4	1152	7.7	1905	1.3		
26	SA	0010	7.7	0717	1.4	1223	7.7	1932	1.5
27	SU	0040	7.6	0743	1.6	1253	7.6	1958	1.7
28	M	0108	7.5	0809	1.8	1323	7.4	2024	2.0
29	TU	0138	7.3	0838	2.1	1356	7.1	2054	2.4
30	W	0214	7.0	0910	2.4	1437	6.8	2130	2.8
31	TH ◑	0259	6.7	0953	2.8	1532	6.5	2221	3.1

APRIL

Date	Day	Time	m	Time	m	Time	m	Time	m
1	F	0403	6.4	1053	3.1	1650	6.3	2331	3.3
2	SA	0529	6.4	1214	3.1	1827	6.4		
3	SU	0110	3.1	0658	6.6	1353	2.7	1946	6.9
4	M	0233	2.5	0807	7.1	1503	2.1	2043	7.4
5	TU	0335	1.9	0901	7.5	1603	1.5	2131	7.8
6	W	0432	1.3	0949	7.9	1700	1.0	2216	8.1
7	TH ●	0527	0.9	1035	8.2	1753	0.7	2300	8.3
8	F	0617	0.6	1120	8.4	1840	0.5	2344	8.4
9	SA	0702	0.5	1205	8.4	1924	0.5		
10	SU	0028	8.4	0745	0.6	1250	8.3	2004	0.7
11	M	0111	8.2	0826	0.9	1334	8.0	2043	1.2
12	TU	0153	7.8	0905	1.3	1420	7.6	2122	1.8
13	W	0237	7.4	0947	1.9	1512	7.1	2207	2.4
14	TH ◐	0330	7.0	1039	2.5	1623	6.7	2308	2.9
15	F	0448	6.6	1147	2.8	1749	6.6		
16	SA	0022	3.1	0614	6.5	1303	2.8	1907	6.7
17	SU	0140	2.9	0730	6.6	1423	2.6	2013	6.9
18	M	0257	2.6	0830	6.9	1531	2.3	2059	7.2
19	TU	0356	2.2	0914	7.2	1619	1.9	2137	7.4
20	W	0439	1.9	0951	7.4	1658	1.7	2210	7.6
21	TH	0516	1.7	1023	7.5	1733	1.6	2240	7.7
22	F ○	0550	1.5	1054	7.6	1806	1.5	2311	7.7
23	SA	0621	1.5	1126	7.6	1836	1.5	2342	7.7
24	SU	0650	1.5	1158	7.6	1904	1.6		
25	M	0013	7.6	0718	1.5	1230	7.5	1933	1.7
26	TU	0044	7.5	0747	1.7	1303	7.4	2003	2.0
27	W	0118	7.4	0819	1.9	1341	7.2	2036	2.3
28	TH	0156	7.1	0853	2.2	1424	6.9	2113	2.6
29	F	0242	6.8	0934	2.5	1516	6.7	2201	2.9
30	SA ◑	0340	6.6	1028	2.8	1624	6.5	2305	3.1

Chart Datum: 4·38 metres below IGN Datum
HAT is 8·4 metres above Chart Datum

TIME ZONE -0100
(French Standard Time)
Subtract 1 hour for UT
For French Summer Time add ONE hour in **non-shaded areas**

FRANCE – LE HAVRE

LAT 49°29'N LONG 0°07'E

TIMES AND HEIGHTS OF HIGH AND LOW WATERS

Dates in amber are **SPRINGS**
Dates in yellow are **NEAPS**

2016

MAY

Date	Day	Time	m	Time	m	Time	m	Time	m
1	SU	0455	6.5	1142	2.8	1749	6.6		
2	M	0034	2.9	0618	6.7	1316	2.5	1909	7.0
3	TU	0158	2.5	0731	7.1	1429	2.0	2011	7.4
4	W	0303	1.9	0831	7.5	1531	1.5	2103	7.8
5	TH	0403	1.4	0923	7.8	1631	1.1	2151	8.0
6	F	0500	1.0	1012	8.1	1727	0.8	● 2237	8.2
7	SA	0554	0.7	1059	8.2	1817	0.7	2322	8.3
8	SU	0643	0.6	1146	8.3	1903	0.7		
9	M	0007	8.2	0727	0.7	1232	8.2	1946	1.0
10	TU	0051	8.1	0809	0.9	1318	7.9	2027	1.4
11	W	0134	7.8	0851	1.3	1405	7.6	2107	1.9
12	TH	0219	7.4	0932	1.8	1455	7.2	2151	2.4
13	F	0309	7.0	1020	2.3	1557	6.8	◐ 2245	2.8
14	SA	0414	6.7	1116	2.7	1708	6.6	2347	3.0
15	SU	0529	6.5	1219	2.8	1818	6.6		
16	M	0053	3.0	0639	6.5	1326	2.8	1926	6.8
17	TU	0200	2.8	0746	6.7	1432	2.6	2020	7.0
18	W	0303	2.5	0838	6.9	1529	2.3	2102	7.2
19	TH	0355	2.2	0918	7.1	1617	2.0	2137	7.4
20	F	0439	1.9	0954	7.3	1659	1.9	2210	7.5
21	SA	0518	1.8	1028	7.4	1735	1.8	○ 2244	7.6
22	SU	0553	1.7	1103	7.5	1808	1.7	2317	7.6
23	M	0624	1.6	1137	7.5	1839	1.7	2350	7.6
24	TU	0656	1.6	1211	7.5	1912	1.8		
25	W	0024	7.6	0730	1.6	1248	7.4	1947	1.9
26	TH	0102	7.5	0805	1.8	1329	7.3	2023	2.1
27	F	0144	7.3	0842	2.0	1414	7.1	2102	2.4
28	SA	0230	7.1	0922	2.2	1504	7.0	2148	2.6
29	SU	0323	6.9	1012	2.4	1603	6.8	◑ 2246	2.7
30	M	0427	6.8	1116	2.5	1714	6.8		
31	TU	0002	2.7	0541	6.9	1239	2.4	1830	7.0

JUNE

Date	Day	Time	m	Time	m	Time	m	Time	m
1	W	0123	2.4	0656	7.1	1356	2.1	1937	7.4
2	TH	0232	2.0	0802	7.4	1501	1.7	2035	7.7
3	F	0334	1.6	0859	7.7	1602	1.4	2127	7.9
4	SA	0434	1.2	0952	7.9	1701	1.2	2215	8.0
5	SU	0531	1.0	1041	8.0	1755	1.1	● 2302	8.1
6	M	0623	0.9	1129	8.0	1844	1.1	2347	8.1
7	TU	0710	0.9	1216	8.0	1928	1.2		
8	W	0032	8.0	0753	1.1	1302	7.8	2010	1.5
9	TH	0115	7.8	0834	1.4	1347	7.6	2050	1.8
10	F	0158	7.5	0914	1.8	1433	7.3	2130	2.2
11	SA	0243	7.2	0954	2.2	1523	7.0	2214	2.6
12	SU	0335	6.8	1038	2.6	1620	6.7	◐ 2303	2.9
13	M	0437	6.6	1130	2.8	1721	6.6		
14	TU	0000	3.0	0542	6.5	1228	2.9	1823	6.6
15	W	0102	3.0	0645	6.5	1333	2.9	1924	6.8
16	TH	0210	2.8	0748	6.7	1439	2.7	2018	7.0
17	F	0311	2.5	0841	6.9	1536	2.4	2102	7.2
18	SA	0402	2.2	0925	7.1	1623	2.2	2141	7.4
19	SU	0445	2.0	1004	7.2	1704	2.0	2219	7.5
20	M	0525	1.8	1042	7.4	1742	1.9	○ 2255	7.6
21	TU	0601	1.7	1119	7.5	1819	1.8	2331	7.7
22	W	0638	1.6	1156	7.5	1856	1.7		
23	TH	0009	7.7	0716	1.5	1236	7.5	1934	1.8
24	F	0049	7.7	0755	1.5	1318	7.5	2014	1.8
25	SA	0132	7.6	0833	1.7	1402	7.4	2054	2.0
26	SU	0218	7.4	0913	1.9	1449	7.3	2137	2.2
27	M	0307	7.2	0958	2.1	1541	7.1	◑ 2227	2.4
28	TU	0402	7.1	1053	2.3	1642	7.0	2331	2.5
29	W	0508	7.0	1204	2.3	1754	7.1		
30	TH	0049	2.4	0625	7.0	1324	2.2	1907	7.2

JULY

Date	Day	Time	m	Time	m	Time	m	Time	m
1	F	0204	2.2	0738	7.2	1434	2.0	2011	7.5
2	SA	0310	1.8	0841	7.5	1538	1.8	2107	7.7
3	SU	0412	1.5	0937	7.6	1639	1.6	2158	7.8
4	M	0513	1.3	1027	7.8	1737	1.4	● 2245	7.9
5	TU	0607	1.2	1115	7.8	1828	1.4	2330	8.0
6	W	0655	1.1	1200	7.9	1911	1.4		
7	TH	0013	7.9	0736	1.2	1243	7.8	1951	1.5
8	F	0054	7.8	0813	1.4	1324	7.6	2027	1.8
9	SA	0134	7.6	0849	1.7	1404	7.4	2102	2.1
10	SU	0213	7.3	0922	2.0	1444	7.2	2137	2.4
11	M	0253	7.0	0956	2.4	1527	6.9	2215	2.7
12	TU	0339	6.7	1035	2.8	1619	6.7	◐ 2301	3.0
13	W	0439	6.4	1124	3.0	1721	6.5	2357	3.2
14	TH	0546	6.3	1225	3.2	1825	6.5		
15	F	0105	3.2	0653	6.4	1340	3.1	1928	6.7
16	SA	0222	2.9	0800	6.6	1454	2.8	2026	6.9
17	SU	0323	2.6	0856	6.9	1548	2.5	2114	7.2
18	M	0413	2.2	0941	7.2	1635	2.2	2156	7.4
19	TU	0458	1.9	1022	7.4	1719	1.9	○ 2235	7.6
20	W	0541	1.6	1101	7.5	1801	1.7	2314	7.8
21	TH	0623	1.4	1141	7.7	1843	1.6	2354	7.9
22	F	0705	1.3	1221	7.8	1924	1.5		
23	SA	0036	7.9	0746	1.2	1303	7.8	2004	1.5
24	SU	0118	7.9	0825	1.3	1347	7.7	2044	1.6
25	M	0202	7.7	0903	1.5	1431	7.6	2124	1.8
26	TU	0248	7.5	0943	1.8	1517	7.4	2208	2.1
27	W	0338	7.3	1030	2.1	1611	7.2	◑ 2303	2.4
28	TH	0440	7.0	1133	2.4	1721	7.0		
29	F	0019	2.5	0601	6.9	1256	2.5	1843	7.0
30	SA	0141	2.4	0722	7.0	1413	2.4	1954	7.2
31	SU	0251	2.1	0830	7.3	1520	2.1	2054	7.5

AUGUST

Date	Day	Time	m	Time	m	Time	m	Time	m
1	M	0357	1.8	0926	7.5	1625	1.9	2145	7.7
2	TU	0502	1.6	1016	7.6	1726	1.7	● 2231	7.8
3	W	0555	1.4	1100	7.8	1814	1.6	2313	7.9
4	TH	0638	1.3	1142	7.8	1853	1.5	2353	8.0
5	F	0715	1.3	1220	7.8	1928	1.5		
6	SA	0029	7.9	0747	1.4	1256	7.7	2000	1.7
7	SU	0105	7.7	0818	1.6	1330	7.5	2030	1.9
8	M	0139	7.5	0847	1.9	1404	7.3	2058	2.2
9	TU	0211	7.3	0913	2.3	1436	7.1	2127	2.6
10	W	0245	7.0	0942	2.7	1512	6.8	◐ 2202	2.9
11	TH	0328	6.6	1022	3.0	1604	6.6	2253	3.2
12	F	0434	6.3	1120	3.4	1721	6.4	2359	3.4
13	SA	0559	6.2	1235	3.4	1839	6.4		
14	SU	0124	3.2	0718	6.4	1408	3.2	1950	6.7
15	M	0245	2.8	0826	6.7	1516	2.7	2047	7.1
16	TU	0342	2.3	0917	7.1	1608	2.3	2132	7.4
17	W	0433	1.9	1000	7.5	1657	1.9	2214	7.7
18	TH	0521	1.5	1041	7.7	1743	1.6	○ 2255	8.0
19	F	0607	1.2	1121	7.9	1828	1.3	2336	8.1
20	SA	0651	1.0	1203	8.0	1910	1.2		
21	SU	0018	8.2	0732	0.9	1245	8.1	1951	1.1
22	M	0101	8.2	0811	1.0	1327	8.0	2030	1.3
23	TU	0144	8.0	0848	1.3	1410	7.8	2108	1.6
24	W	0229	7.7	0925	1.7	1454	7.6	2149	2.0
25	TH	0317	7.4	1008	2.1	1545	7.2	◑ 2240	2.4
26	F	0418	7.0	1108	2.6	1655	6.9	2356	2.7
27	SA	0546	6.8	1235	2.8	1825	6.9		
28	SU	0123	2.7	0712	6.9	1358	2.7	1942	7.0
29	M	0239	2.4	0821	7.1	1511	2.4	2043	7.3
30	TU	0352	2.0	0917	7.4	1621	2.1	2133	7.6
31	W	0454	1.7	1002	7.6	1716	1.8	2216	7.8

Chart Datum: 4·38 metres below IGN Datum
HAT is 8·4 metres above Chart Datum

TIME ZONE -0100 (French Standard Time)
Subtract 1 hour for UT
For French Summer Time add ONE hour in **non-shaded areas**

FRANCE – LE HAVRE

LAT 49°29′N LONG 0°07′E

TIMES AND HEIGHTS OF HIGH AND LOW WATERS

Dates in amber are **SPRINGS**
Dates in yellow are **NEAPS**

2016

SEPTEMBER

Date	Day	Moon	Time	m	Time	m	Time	m	Time	m
1	TH	●	0540	1.5	1042	7.7	1756	1.6	2254	7.9
2	F		0616	1.4	1118	7.8	1829	1.5	2329	8.0
3	SA		0648	1.3	1152	7.8	1901	1.5		
4	SU		0002	7.9	0718	1.4	1224	7.8	1930	1.6
5	M		0034	7.8	0746	1.6	1256	7.6	1958	1.8
6	TU		0106	7.6	0812	1.9	1325	7.5	2023	2.1
7	W		0135	7.4	0836	2.2	1353	7.3	2048	2.4
8	TH		0205	7.1	0901	2.6	1425	7.0	2118	2.8
9	F	◐	0244	6.8	0935	3.0	1509	6.7	2202	3.1
10	SA		0338	6.4	1028	3.4	1616	6.4	2306	3.4
11	SU		0502	6.2	1141	3.6	1748	6.3		
12	M		0029	3.4	0638	6.3	1320	3.4	1913	6.6
13	TU		0206	3.0	0755	6.7	1443	2.9	2017	7.0
14	W		0311	2.4	0849	7.2	1540	2.3	2106	7.5
15	TH		0405	1.8	0934	7.6	1632	1.7	2150	7.9
16	F	○	0456	1.4	1016	7.9	1721	1.4	2232	8.1
17	SA		0545	1.0	1058	8.1	1808	1.1	2315	8.3
18	SU		0631	0.8	1141	8.3	1853	0.9	2358	8.4
19	M		0714	0.7	1223	8.3	1934	0.9		
20	TU		0042	8.4	0754	0.9	1306	8.2	2014	1.1
21	W		0126	8.2	0831	1.2	1348	8.0	2052	1.4
22	TH		0210	7.8	0908	1.7	1432	7.6	2132	1.9
23	F	◑	0259	7.4	0950	2.3	1523	7.3	2223	2.4
24	SA		0403	7.0	1050	2.8	1635	6.9	2339	2.8
25	SU		0535	6.7	1219	3.1	1809	6.7		
26	M		0108	2.8	0700	6.8	1345	2.9	1927	6.9
27	TU		0228	2.5	0809	7.1	1503	2.5	2029	7.2
28	W		0339	2.1	0901	7.4	1607	2.1	2117	7.5
29	TH		0433	1.8	0943	7.6	1654	1.8	2156	7.7
30	F		0514	1.6	1019	7.8	1730	1.7	2231	7.9

OCTOBER

Date	Day	Moon	Time	m	Time	m	Time	m	Time	m
1	SA	●	0547	1.5	1052	7.9	1801	1.6	2303	7.9
2	SU		0617	1.4	1123	7.9	1832	1.5	2334	7.9
3	M		0648	1.5	1153	7.8	1901	1.6		
4	TU		0006	7.8	0716	1.6	1223	7.7	1928	1.7
5	W		0036	7.7	0742	1.9	1252	7.6	1954	2.0
6	TH		0106	7.5	0807	2.2	1320	7.4	2020	2.2
7	F		0137	7.2	0834	2.5	1354	7.1	2051	2.6
8	SA		0217	6.9	0907	2.9	1437	6.8	2130	3.0
9	SU	◐	0308	6.6	0955	3.3	1537	6.5	2227	3.3
10	M		0421	6.4	1101	3.5	1701	6.4	2344	3.3
11	TU		0557	6.4	1235	3.4	1832	6.6		
12	W		0124	3.0	0719	6.8	1408	2.9	1942	7.0
13	TH		0238	2.4	0817	7.3	1509	2.2	2036	7.5
14	F		0335	1.8	0906	7.7	1604	1.7	2124	7.9
15	SA		0429	1.3	0950	8.1	1656	1.2	2209	8.2
16	SU	○	0520	1.0	1034	8.3	1746	0.9	2253	8.4
17	M		0608	0.8	1117	8.4	1832	0.8	2338	8.5
18	TU		0653	0.7	1201	8.4	1916	0.8		
19	W		0023	8.4	0735	0.9	1245	8.3	1958	1.0
20	TH		0109	8.2	0816	1.2	1329	8.0	2039	1.4
21	F		0155	7.8	0855	1.8	1414	7.7	2121	1.9
22	SA	◑	0245	7.4	0939	2.3	1505	7.3	2212	2.4
23	SU		0350	7.0	1039	2.9	1616	6.9	2322	2.8
24	M		0516	6.8	1158	3.1	1744	6.7		
25	TU		0042	2.9	0635	6.8	1319	3.0	1900	6.8
26	W		0159	2.6	0743	7.0	1433	2.7	2005	7.0
27	TH		0305	2.3	0836	7.3	1534	2.3	2053	7.3
28	F		0357	2.0	0917	7.6	1619	2.0	2133	7.6
29	SA		0438	1.8	0952	7.7	1657	1.8	2207	7.7
30	SU	●	0514	1.7	1024	7.8	1732	1.6	2239	7.8
31	M		0547	1.6	1054	7.8	1804	1.6	2310	7.8

NOVEMBER

Date	Day	Moon	Time	m	Time	m	Time	m	Time	m
1	TU		0619	1.6	1125	7.8	1835	1.6	2341	7.7
2	W		0648	1.7	1155	7.8	1903	1.7		
3	TH		0013	7.7	0716	1.9	1225	7.7	1931	1.9
4	F		0045	7.5	0745	2.1	1257	7.5	2001	2.1
5	SA		0120	7.3	0816	2.4	1334	7.2	2034	2.4
6	SU		0201	7.0	0851	2.8	1418	7.0	2112	2.7
7	M	◐	0251	6.8	0935	3.1	1513	6.7	2202	3.0
8	TU		0355	6.6	1034	3.3	1625	6.6	2309	3.1
9	W		0516	6.6	1154	3.3	1748	6.7		
10	TH		0038	2.9	0638	6.9	1327	2.9	1903	7.0
11	F		0200	2.4	0742	7.3	1436	2.3	2004	7.5
12	SA		0303	1.8	0835	7.8	1534	1.7	2057	7.9
13	SU		0400	1.4	0924	8.1	1630	1.2	2146	8.2
14	M	○	0454	1.0	1010	8.3	1723	0.9	2233	8.4
15	TU		0546	0.9	1056	8.4	1813	0.8	2320	8.4
16	W		0634	0.8	1141	8.4	1900	0.8		
17	TH		0007	8.4	0719	1.0	1227	8.3	1944	0.9
18	F		0054	8.2	0802	1.3	1312	8.1	2028	1.3
19	SA		0142	7.9	0845	1.8	1358	7.7	2112	1.7
20	SU		0232	7.5	0930	2.3	1448	7.3	2200	2.2
21	M	◑	0332	7.1	1023	2.7	1550	6.9	2256	2.6
22	TU		0442	6.9	1126	3.0	1705	6.7		
23	W		0000	2.9	0552	6.8	1234	3.1	1817	6.7
24	TH		0109	2.8	0701	6.9	1344	2.9	1925	6.8
25	F		0215	2.6	0800	7.1	1447	2.6	2022	7.1
26	SA		0312	2.4	0846	7.4	1540	2.3	2106	7.3
27	SU		0400	2.1	0924	7.6	1624	2.0	2143	7.5
28	M		0442	1.9	0958	7.7	1704	1.8	2216	7.6
29	TU	●	0520	1.8	1030	7.7	1739	1.7	2250	7.6
30	W		0554	1.8	1102	7.8	1812	1.7	2323	7.6

DECEMBER

Date	Day	Moon	Time	m	Time	m	Time	m	Time	m
1	TH		0626	1.8	1134	7.8	1843	1.7	2356	7.6
2	F		0657	1.9	1207	7.7	1915	1.7		
3	SA		0030	7.5	0730	2.0	1242	7.6	1948	1.9
4	SU		0108	7.4	0804	2.2	1321	7.4	2024	2.1
5	M		0150	7.3	0841	2.5	1405	7.2	2102	2.3
6	TU		0237	7.1	0924	2.7	1455	7.0	2147	2.6
7	W	◐	0333	6.9	1015	2.9	1555	6.8	2243	2.7
8	TH		0439	6.8	1120	3.0	1706	6.8	2355	2.7
9	F		0554	7.0	1242	2.8	1823	7.0		
10	SA		0119	2.4	0705	7.3	1400	2.4	1932	7.3
11	SU		0231	2.0	0806	7.6	1506	1.9	2033	7.7
12	M		0333	1.6	0900	7.9	1606	1.4	2127	8.0
13	TU		0431	1.3	0950	8.2	1703	1.1	2217	8.2
14	W	○	0526	1.1	1038	8.3	1756	0.9	2306	8.3
15	TH		0618	1.0	1125	8.3	1846	0.8	2354	8.3
16	F		0705	1.1	1211	8.3	1933	0.9		
17	SA		0041	8.1	0750	1.3	1256	8.1	2016	1.2
18	SU		0127	7.9	0833	1.6	1341	7.8	2058	1.5
19	M		0214	7.6	0914	2.0	1427	7.5	2139	2.0
20	TU		0303	7.3	0957	2.5	1517	7.1	2222	2.4
21	W	◑	0358	7.0	1044	2.8	1616	6.8	2311	2.8
22	TH		0459	6.8	1139	3.1	1722	6.6		
23	F		0008	3.0	0603	6.7	1242	3.1	1829	6.6
24	SA		0114	3.0	0708	6.8	1355	3.0	1938	6.7
25	SU		0225	2.8	0808	7.0	1459	2.7	2035	6.9
26	M		0323	2.5	0854	7.2	1552	2.3	2119	7.2
27	TU		0412	2.3	0933	7.4	1637	2.1	2157	7.4
28	W		0454	2.0	1009	7.6	1716	1.8	2233	7.5
29	TH	●	0532	1.9	1044	7.7	1753	1.7	2308	7.6
30	F		0608	1.8	1119	7.8	1827	1.6	2343	7.6
31	SA		0643	1.8	1154	7.8	1903	1.5		

Chart Datum: 4·38 metres below IGN Datum
HAT is 8·4 metres above Chart Datum

TIME ZONE -0100
(French Standard Time)
Subtract 1 hour for UT
For French Summer Time add ONE hour in **non-shaded areas**

FRANCE – CHERBOURG

LAT 49°39′N LONG 1°38′W

TIMES AND HEIGHTS OF HIGH AND LOW WATERS

Dates in amber are **SPRINGS**
Dates in yellow are **NEAPS**

2016

JANUARY

Date	Day	Time	m	Time	m	Time	m	Time	m
1	F	0056	5.4	0735	2.4	1305	5.4	2000	2.3
2	SA	0138	5.2	0822	2.7	1352	5.1	◑ 2049	2.6
3	SU	0233	5.0	0920	2.9	1453	4.9	2152	2.8
4	M	0342	4.9	1034	2.9	1606	4.9	2307	2.8
5	TU	0457	5.0	1147	2.7	1724	5.0		
6	W	0014	2.6	0600	5.3	1246	2.5	1825	5.3
7	TH	0109	2.3	0650	5.6	1336	2.1	1915	5.6
8	F	0156	2.0	0735	5.9	1421	1.8	1959	5.8
9	SA	0239	1.8	0816	6.2	1504	1.5	2040	6.1
10	SU	0321	1.5	0855	6.4	1546	1.3	● 2120	6.2
11	M	0403	1.4	0936	6.5	1627	1.1	2200	6.3
12	TU	0445	1.3	1016	6.6	1709	1.0	2241	6.4
13	W	0527	1.3	1057	6.6	1751	1.0	2324	6.3
14	TH	0609	1.4	1140	6.5	1834	1.2		
15	F	0008	6.1	0654	1.6	1225	6.2	1919	1.4
16	SA	0054	5.9	0743	1.8	1314	5.9	2010	1.7
17	SU	0147	5.6	0839	2.1	1411	5.6	◐ 2110	2.0
18	M	0253	5.4	0948	2.3	1528	5.4	2222	2.2
19	TU	0414	5.4	1107	2.3	1651	5.4	2340	2.2
20	W	0528	5.5	1224	2.1	1803	5.5		
21	TH	0052	2.0	0632	5.7	1330	1.8	1907	5.7
22	F	0152	1.8	0728	6.0	1426	1.5	2002	6.0
23	SA	0245	1.6	0817	6.2	1515	1.3	2049	6.1
24	SU	0330	1.4	0900	6.4	1557	1.2	○ 2129	6.2
25	M	0410	1.3	0938	6.4	1635	1.1	2205	6.3
26	TU	0446	1.3	1014	6.4	1710	1.1	2240	6.2
27	W	0520	1.4	1049	6.3	1743	1.3	2314	6.1
28	TH	0553	1.6	1122	6.2	1814	1.5	2345	5.9
29	F	0624	1.8	1154	5.9	1845	1.8		
30	SA	0015	5.7	0657	2.1	1224	5.6	1918	2.1
31	SU	0049	5.4	0734	2.4	1259	5.3	1956	2.4

FEBRUARY

Date	Day	Time	m	Time	m	Time	m	Time	m
1	M	0129	5.1	0819	2.7	1346	5.0	◑ 2044	2.7
2	TU	0224	4.9	0919	2.9	1452	4.8	2152	2.9
3	W	0339	4.8	1040	2.9	1619	4.7	2318	2.8
4	TH	0511	5.0	1201	2.7	1747	5.0		
5	F	0031	2.6	0618	5.3	1303	2.3	1847	5.3
6	SA	0128	2.2	0709	5.7	1355	1.9	1936	5.7
7	SU	0218	1.8	0755	6.1	1443	1.4	2021	6.1
8	M	0304	1.4	0838	6.4	1529	1.1	● 2105	6.3
9	TU	0349	1.2	0921	6.6	1613	0.8	2148	6.5
10	W	0432	1.0	1004	6.8	1656	0.7	2230	6.6
11	TH	0514	0.9	1047	6.8	1737	0.7	2311	6.6
12	F	0557	0.9	1128	6.7	1819	0.8	2353	6.4
13	SA	0640	1.2	1210	6.4	1902	1.1		
14	SU	0035	6.1	0725	1.5	1253	6.1	1949	1.6
15	M	0120	5.8	0817	1.9	1344	5.6	◐ 2044	2.0
16	TU	0218	5.4	0920	2.2	1459	5.2	2154	2.4
17	W	0340	5.2	1042	2.4	1630	5.1	2320	2.5
18	TH	0506	5.2	1209	2.3	1753	5.2		
19	F	0039	2.3	0620	5.4	1319	2.0	1901	5.5
20	SA	0143	2.0	0718	5.7	1416	1.7	1953	5.8
21	SU	0234	1.7	0806	6.0	1501	1.4	2035	6.0
22	M	0316	1.5	0845	6.2	1540	1.2	○ 2111	6.2
23	TU	0352	1.4	0920	6.3	1614	1.1	2144	6.2
24	W	0425	1.3	0953	6.4	1646	1.1	2215	6.2
25	TH	0457	1.3	1025	6.3	1716	1.2	2245	6.2
26	F	0526	1.4	1055	6.2	1745	1.4	2313	6.0
27	SA	0555	1.6	1123	6.0	1813	1.6	2341	5.8
28	SU	0625	1.8	1151	5.8	1842	1.9		
29	M	0010	5.6	0656	2.1	1222	5.5	1914	2.2

MARCH

Date	Day	Time	m	Time	m	Time	m	Time	m
1	TU	0043	5.3	0734	2.4	1301	5.1	1955	2.6
2	W	0128	5.0	0825	2.7	1357	4.8	◑ 2054	2.8
3	TH	0236	4.8	0939	2.8	1522	4.7	2222	2.9
4	F	0413	4.8	1112	2.7	1707	4.8	2353	2.7
5	SA	0542	5.1	1228	2.3	1819	5.2		
6	SU	0100	2.3	0640	5.5	1327	1.8	1911	5.7
7	M	0154	1.8	0730	6.0	1419	1.4	1959	6.1
8	TU	0243	1.3	0817	6.4	1507	0.9	2045	6.4
9	W	0330	1.0	0903	6.7	1553	0.6	● 2129	6.7
10	TH	0415	0.7	0947	6.9	1637	0.4	2212	6.8
11	F	0458	0.6	1031	7.0	1720	0.5	2254	6.8
12	SA	0541	0.7	1114	6.8	1801	0.7	2334	6.6
13	SU	0623	0.9	1154	6.5	1844	1.1		
14	M	0014	6.3	0707	1.3	1237	6.1	1929	1.6
15	TU	0057	5.8	0757	1.8	1326	5.6	◐ 2021	2.1
16	W	0151	5.4	0857	2.2	1436	5.1	2130	2.5
17	TH	0308	5.1	1019	2.5	1611	4.9	2259	2.7
18	F	0441	5.0	1149	2.4	1740	5.1		
19	SA	0023	2.5	0601	5.2	1301	2.1	1846	5.4
20	SU	0126	2.1	0700	5.6	1355	1.8	1933	5.7
21	M	0215	1.8	0745	5.9	1438	1.5	2012	5.9
22	TU	0254	1.6	0823	6.1	1515	1.3	2046	6.1
23	W	0329	1.4	0857	6.2	1547	1.2	○ 2117	6.2
24	TH	0400	1.3	0929	6.3	1618	1.2	2147	6.2
25	F	0430	1.3	0959	6.3	1647	1.2	2216	6.2
26	SA	0459	1.3	1028	6.2	1715	1.4	2243	6.1
27	SU	0528	1.4	1056	6.0	1743	1.6	2311	6.0
28	M	0557	1.6	1125	5.8	1811	1.8	2340	5.8
29	TU	0628	1.9	1156	5.6	1843	2.1		
30	W	0013	5.5	0704	2.2	1233	5.3	1922	2.4
31	TH	0054	5.2	0751	2.5	1324	4.9	◑ 2017	2.7

APRIL

Date	Day	Time	m	Time	m	Time	m	Time	m
1	F	0154	4.9	0858	2.7	1442	4.7	2140	2.9
2	SA	0324	4.8	1027	2.6	1627	4.8	2315	2.7
3	SU	0501	5.0	1150	2.3	1747	5.2		
4	M	0028	2.3	0608	5.5	1255	1.8	1843	5.7
5	TU	0126	1.8	0701	6.0	1350	1.3	1932	6.1
6	W	0218	1.3	0751	6.4	1441	0.9	2020	6.5
7	TH	0307	0.9	0840	6.7	1530	0.6	● 2106	6.8
8	F	0354	0.6	0927	6.9	1616	0.4	2151	6.9
9	SA	0439	0.5	1013	6.9	1700	0.5	2234	6.8
10	SU	0523	0.6	1057	6.8	1743	0.7	2315	6.6
11	M	0607	0.8	1139	6.4	1826	1.1	2355	6.3
12	TU	0651	1.2	1222	6.0	1911	1.7		
13	W	0038	5.9	0739	1.7	1311	5.5	2002	2.2
14	TH	0129	5.4	0837	2.2	1417	5.1	◐ 2107	2.6
15	F	0239	5.1	0952	2.4	1543	4.9	2231	2.7
16	SA	0406	4.9	1117	2.4	1710	5.0	2351	2.6
17	SU	0527	5.1	1226	2.2	1814	5.3		
18	M	0054	2.3	0628	5.4	1321	1.9	1901	5.6
19	TU	0143	2.0	0714	5.6	1405	1.7	1940	5.8
20	W	0224	1.7	0753	5.9	1442	1.5	2015	6.0
21	TH	0259	1.6	0829	6.0	1516	1.4	2048	6.1
22	F	0332	1.4	0902	6.1	1548	1.4	○ 2119	6.2
23	SA	0403	1.4	0933	6.1	1618	1.4	2148	6.2
24	SU	0434	1.4	1002	6.1	1648	1.5	2216	6.1
25	M	0504	1.4	1032	6.0	1718	1.6	2246	6.0
26	TU	0535	1.6	1104	5.9	1748	1.8	2319	5.9
27	W	0607	1.7	1140	5.6	1822	2.1	2355	5.6
28	TH	0645	2.0	1219	5.4	1903	2.3		
29	F	0037	5.4	0731	2.2	1308	5.1	1958	2.6
30	SA	0133	5.1	0833	2.4	1417	4.9	◑ 2112	2.7

Chart Datum: 3·33 metres below IGN Datum
HAT is 7·0 metres above Chart Datum

TIME ZONE -0100
(French Standard Time)
Subtract 1 hour for UT
For French Summer Time add ONE hour in **non-shaded areas**

FRANCE – CHERBOURG

LAT 49°39′N LONG 1°38′W

TIMES AND HEIGHTS OF HIGH AND LOW WATERS

Dates in amber are **SPRINGS**
Dates in yellow are **NEAPS**

2016

MAY

Date	Day	Time	m	Time	m	Time	m	Time	m
1	SU	0249	5.0	0952	2.4	1549	5.0	2238	2.6
2	M	0423	5.1	1113	2.2	1711	5.3	2353	2.2
3	TU	0532	5.5	1221	1.8	1811	5.7		
4	W	0055	1.8	0630	5.9	1320	1.4	1903	6.1
5	TH	0150	1.3	0724	6.3	1414	1.0	1953	6.5
6	F	0243	1.0	0816	6.6	1505	0.8	● 2041	6.7
7	SA	0333	0.7	0906	6.8	1554	0.7	2128	6.8
8	SU	0420	0.6	0954	6.8	1640	0.7	2213	6.8
9	M	0506	0.7	1040	6.6	1725	0.9	2256	6.6
10	TU	0551	0.9	1125	6.3	1808	1.3	2338	6.3
11	W	0635	1.2	1209	6.0	1853	1.7		
12	TH	0021	5.9	0722	1.7	1257	5.5	1942	2.2
13	F	0109	5.5	0814	2.1	1353	5.2	◐ 2039	2.5
14	SA	0209	5.2	0916	2.4	1502	5.0	2150	2.7
15	SU	0321	5.0	1029	2.5	1618	5.0	2304	2.7
16	M	0436	5.0	1137	2.4	1726	5.1		
17	TU	0008	2.5	0541	5.2	1234	2.2	1818	5.4
18	W	0101	2.2	0634	5.4	1323	2.0	1902	5.6
19	TH	0146	2.0	0718	5.6	1405	1.8	1941	5.8
20	F	0226	1.8	0758	5.8	1443	1.7	2017	6.0
21	SA	0302	1.6	0835	5.9	1517	1.6	○ 2051	6.1
22	SU	0336	1.5	0908	6.0	1551	1.6	2123	6.1
23	M	0409	1.4	0940	6.0	1624	1.6	2153	6.1
24	TU	0443	1.4	1013	6.0	1657	1.7	2227	6.1
25	W	0518	1.5	1049	5.9	1732	1.8	2304	6.0
26	TH	0553	1.6	1127	5.8	1809	1.9	2343	5.8
27	F	0633	1.8	1209	5.6	1852	2.1		
28	SA	0027	5.6	0719	1.9	1258	5.4	1945	2.3
29	SU	0119	5.4	0815	2.1	1357	5.2	◑ 2050	2.5
30	M	0223	5.3	0923	2.2	1512	5.2	2204	2.4
31	TU	0341	5.3	1037	2.1	1632	5.4	2318	2.2

JUNE

Date	Day	Time	m	Time	m	Time	m	Time	m
1	W	0457	5.5	1147	1.8	1739	5.7		
2	TH	0024	1.9	0601	5.8	1251	1.5	1835	6.0
3	F	0124	1.5	0659	6.1	1349	1.3	1928	6.3
4	SA	0220	1.2	0755	6.3	1444	1.1	2019	6.5
5	SU	0314	1.0	0847	6.5	1535	1.0	● 2108	6.6
6	M	0404	0.8	0937	6.5	1623	1.0	2154	6.6
7	TU	0451	0.9	1025	6.4	1708	1.2	2238	6.5
8	W	0536	1.0	1109	6.2	1751	1.4	2320	6.3
9	TH	0619	1.2	1153	6.0	1834	1.7		
10	F	0003	6.0	0701	1.6	1236	5.7	1917	2.0
11	SA	0046	5.7	0745	1.9	1322	5.4	2005	2.4
12	SU	0134	5.3	0833	2.2	1415	5.1	◐ 2100	2.6
13	M	0230	5.1	0931	2.5	1516	5.0	2205	2.7
14	TU	0335	4.9	1037	2.5	1623	5.0	2313	2.7
15	W	0444	5.0	1141	2.5	1727	5.2		
16	TH	0014	2.5	0548	5.1	1238	2.3	1821	5.4
17	F	0106	2.3	0641	5.3	1327	2.1	1906	5.6
18	SA	0151	2.0	0727	5.5	1410	2.0	1947	5.8
19	SU	0232	1.8	0808	5.7	1449	1.8	2025	6.0
20	M	0310	1.6	0846	5.8	1526	1.7	○ 2100	6.1
21	TU	0348	1.5	0922	5.9	1604	1.6	2136	6.2
22	W	0425	1.4	0957	6.0	1641	1.6	2211	6.2
23	TH	0503	1.4	1035	6.0	1719	1.6	2250	6.2
24	F	0542	1.4	1116	5.9	1759	1.7	2332	6.1
25	SA	0622	1.5	1158	5.8	1842	1.9		
26	SU	0016	5.9	0707	1.6	1244	5.7	1931	2.0
27	M	0104	5.7	0757	1.8	1336	5.5	◑ 2028	2.2
28	TU	0159	5.6	0856	2.0	1438	5.4	2134	2.3
29	W	0306	5.4	1005	2.0	1554	5.4	2247	2.2
30	TH	0426	5.5	1118	2.0	1708	5.6	2358	2.0

JULY

Date	Day	Time	m	Time	m	Time	m	Time	m
1	F	0537	5.6	1226	1.8	1812	5.8		
2	SA	0103	1.7	0641	5.8	1329	1.6	1909	6.1
3	SU	0204	1.4	0740	6.1	1427	1.4	2002	6.3
4	M	0259	1.2	0834	6.2	1520	1.3	● 2052	6.4
5	TU	0350	1.0	0924	6.3	1608	1.2	2137	6.5
6	W	0436	1.0	1009	6.3	1651	1.3	2220	6.4
7	TH	0518	1.1	1051	6.2	1732	1.4	2300	6.3
8	F	0557	1.2	1130	6.0	1810	1.6	2339	6.1
9	SA	0634	1.5	1208	5.8	1848	1.9		
10	SU	0017	5.8	0711	1.8	1245	5.6	1926	2.2
11	M	0056	5.5	0749	2.1	1325	5.3	2009	2.5
12	TU	0138	5.2	0833	2.4	1411	5.1	◐ 2101	2.7
13	W	0230	5.0	0928	2.6	1510	4.9	2207	2.8
14	TH	0335	4.8	1037	2.7	1623	4.9	2320	2.7
15	F	0451	4.9	1149	2.7	1735	5.1		
16	SA	0024	2.5	0601	5.0	1248	2.5	1831	5.4
17	SU	0117	2.3	0656	5.3	1338	2.2	1918	5.6
18	M	0203	2.0	0742	5.6	1423	2.0	2000	5.9
19	TU	0246	1.7	0824	5.8	1505	1.8	○ 2040	6.1
20	W	0327	1.5	0904	6.0	1546	1.6	2118	6.3
21	TH	0408	1.3	0942	6.1	1626	1.5	2158	6.4
22	F	0449	1.2	1022	6.2	1706	1.4	2237	6.4
23	SA	0529	1.1	1102	6.2	1747	1.4	2319	6.4
24	SU	0609	1.2	1144	6.1	1829	1.5		
25	M	0001	6.3	0651	1.3	1227	6.0	1914	1.7
26	TU	0046	6.0	0738	1.6	1313	5.8	2005	1.9
27	W	0136	5.8	0831	1.9	1408	5.5	◑ 2106	2.2
28	TH	0237	5.5	0936	2.1	1520	5.4	2220	2.3
29	F	0401	5.3	1053	2.2	1643	5.4	2339	2.2
30	SA	0521	5.4	1210	2.1	1755	5.6		
31	SU	0051	1.9	0630	5.6	1317	1.9	1856	5.9

AUGUST

Date	Day	Time	m	Time	m	Time	m	Time	m
1	M	0153	1.6	0731	5.9	1416	1.7	1951	6.1
2	TU	0248	1.4	0825	6.1	1508	1.5	● 2039	6.3
3	W	0336	1.2	0911	6.2	1552	1.4	2121	6.4
4	TH	0418	1.1	0951	6.3	1632	1.3	2200	6.5
5	F	0456	1.1	1027	6.2	1709	1.4	2236	6.4
6	SA	0531	1.2	1102	6.1	1742	1.5	2311	6.2
7	SU	0603	1.4	1135	6.0	1815	1.7	2344	6.0
8	M	0634	1.7	1206	5.8	1847	2.0		
9	TU	0016	5.7	0706	2.0	1238	5.5	1922	2.3
10	W	0049	5.4	0741	2.3	1315	5.2	◐ 2004	2.6
11	TH	0131	5.1	0825	2.6	1403	5.0	2100	2.8
12	F	0229	4.8	0927	2.9	1510	4.8	2217	2.9
13	SA	0348	4.7	1052	2.9	1641	4.9	2340	2.8
14	SU	0520	4.9	1211	2.7	1756	5.2		
15	M	0043	2.4	0626	5.2	1309	2.4	1850	5.5
16	TU	0135	2.1	0716	5.5	1358	2.0	1935	5.9
17	W	0221	1.7	0801	5.9	1443	1.7	2018	6.2
18	TH	0306	1.3	0843	6.2	1526	1.4	○ 2059	6.5
19	F	0348	1.1	0924	6.4	1608	1.2	2140	6.7
20	SA	0430	0.9	1005	6.5	1650	1.1	2222	6.7
21	SU	0511	0.8	1046	6.5	1731	1.1	2302	6.7
22	M	0552	0.9	1126	6.4	1812	1.2	2344	6.5
23	TU	0633	1.1	1207	6.2	1856	1.5		
24	W	0027	6.2	0718	1.5	1251	6.0	1945	1.8
25	TH	0115	5.8	0809	1.9	1342	5.6	◑ 2044	2.2
26	F	0214	5.4	0913	2.3	1452	5.3	2200	2.4
27	SA	0344	5.2	1036	2.5	1623	5.2	2327	2.4
28	SU	0512	5.2	1200	2.4	1743	5.4		
29	M	0043	2.1	0625	5.5	1310	2.1	1847	5.7
30	TU	0145	1.8	0724	5.8	1407	1.8	1940	6.1
31	W	0235	1.5	0812	6.1	1453	1.6	2024	6.3

Chart Datum: 3·33 metres below IGN Datum
HAT is 7·0 metres above Chart Datum

TIME ZONE -0100
(French Standard Time)
Subtract 1 hour for UT
For French Summer Time add ONE hour in **non-shaded areas**

FRANCE – CHERBOURG

LAT 49°39'N LONG 1°38'W

TIMES AND HEIGHTS OF HIGH AND LOW WATERS

Dates in amber are **SPRINGS**
Dates in yellow are **NEAPS**

2016

SEPTEMBER

Date	Day	Time	m	Time	m	Time	m	Time	m
1	TH	0318	1.3	0852	6.2	1534	1.4	● 2102	6.4
2	F	0356	1.2	0927	6.3	1609	1.4	2136	6.5
3	SA	0430	1.2	0959	6.3	1642	1.4	2209	6.4
4	SU	0501	1.3	1030	6.3	1712	1.5	2241	6.3
5	M	0530	1.4	1100	6.1	1742	1.6	2310	6.1
6	TU	0559	1.7	1127	5.9	1811	1.9	2339	5.9
7	W	0627	2.0	1157	5.7	1842	2.2		
8	TH	0009	5.6	0658	2.3	1228	5.4	1918	2.5
9	F	0045	5.2	0736	2.6	1310	5.1	◐ 2006	2.8
10	SA	0138	4.9	0830	2.9	1413	4.9	2116	3.0
11	SU	0256	4.7	0954	3.1	1544	4.8	2250	2.9
12	M	0438	4.8	1131	2.9	1719	5.1		
13	TU	0008	2.6	0556	5.2	1239	2.5	1819	5.5
14	W	0105	2.1	0649	5.6	1332	2.1	1908	5.9
15	TH	0154	1.6	0735	6.0	1419	1.6	1953	6.3
16	F	0240	1.2	0818	6.4	1503	1.3	○ 2036	6.7
17	SA	0325	0.9	0901	6.6	1547	1.0	2119	6.9
18	SU	0408	0.7	0944	6.8	1630	0.9	2203	7.0
19	M	0451	0.7	1025	6.8	1712	0.9	2245	6.9
20	TU	0533	0.8	1106	6.7	1754	1.0	2327	6.7
21	W	0615	1.1	1147	6.4	1839	1.3		
22	TH	0009	6.3	0659	1.6	1230	6.1	1927	1.8
23	F	0055	5.8	0750	2.1	1320	5.7	◑ 2026	2.2
24	SA	0200	5.4	0855	2.5	1431	5.3	2144	2.5
25	SU	0331	5.1	1022	2.7	1604	5.2	2315	2.5
26	M	0502	5.2	1150	2.6	1729	5.3		
27	TU	0030	2.2	0614	5.5	1257	2.3	1833	5.7
28	W	0128	1.9	0707	5.8	1350	1.9	1922	6.0
29	TH	0215	1.6	0749	6.1	1433	1.7	2002	6.2
30	F	0254	1.4	0826	6.2	1510	1.5	2038	6.4

OCTOBER

Date	Day	Time	m	Time	m	Time	m	Time	m
1	SA	0328	1.3	0858	6.3	1543	1.4	● 2111	6.4
2	SU	0400	1.3	0929	6.4	1614	1.4	2142	6.4
3	M	0430	1.4	0959	6.3	1643	1.5	2211	6.3
4	TU	0459	1.5	1027	6.2	1712	1.6	2240	6.2
5	W	0527	1.7	1054	6.1	1741	1.8	2308	6.0
6	TH	0555	2.0	1123	5.9	1811	2.0	2339	5.7
7	F	0625	2.3	1155	5.6	1845	2.3		
8	SA	0015	5.4	0701	2.6	1234	5.3	1929	2.6
9	SU	0104	5.1	0751	2.9	1332	5.0	◐ 2032	2.9
10	M	0217	4.8	0909	3.1	1457	4.9	2201	2.9
11	TU	0357	4.9	1048	3.0	1636	5.1	2327	2.6
12	W	0522	5.2	1205	2.6	1745	5.5		
13	TH	0031	2.1	0618	5.7	1301	2.1	1837	6.0
14	F	0124	1.6	0705	6.1	1351	1.6	1925	6.4
15	SA	0213	1.2	0751	6.5	1438	1.2	2011	6.8
16	SU	0300	0.9	0836	6.8	1525	0.9	○ 2057	7.0
17	M	0345	0.7	0920	6.9	1610	0.8	2143	7.0
18	TU	0430	0.7	1004	6.9	1654	0.8	2227	6.9
19	W	0514	0.9	1046	6.8	1738	0.9	2311	6.7
20	TH	0558	1.2	1129	6.5	1824	1.3	2356	6.3
21	F	0643	1.6	1213	6.1	1913	1.7		
22	SA	0045	5.8	0735	2.2	1303	5.7	◑ 2010	2.2
23	SU	0148	5.4	0838	2.6	1411	5.3	2124	2.5
24	M	0311	5.1	1001	2.8	1537	5.2	2251	2.5
25	TU	0438	5.2	1126	2.7	1700	5.3		
26	W	0003	2.3	0547	5.4	1231	2.4	1804	5.5
27	TH	0059	2.0	0638	5.7	1322	2.1	1854	5.8
28	F	0144	1.8	0719	6.0	1405	1.8	1935	6.1
29	SA	0223	1.6	0756	6.2	1442	1.7	2011	6.2
30	SU	0258	1.5	0829	6.3	1515	1.6	● 2045	6.3
31	M	0330	1.5	0901	6.3	1547	1.5	2117	6.3

NOVEMBER

Date	Day	Time	m	Time	m	Time	m	Time	m
1	TU	0401	1.5	0931	6.3	1618	1.5	2146	6.3
2	W	0432	1.6	0959	6.3	1648	1.6	2215	6.2
3	TH	0501	1.8	1028	6.2	1719	1.7	2246	6.0
4	F	0531	2.0	1100	6.0	1750	1.9	2320	5.8
5	SA	0603	2.2	1134	5.8	1825	2.2	2358	5.5
6	SU	0640	2.5	1215	5.5	1908	2.4		
7	M	0045	5.2	0730	2.8	1307	5.2	◐ 2005	2.6
8	TU	0150	5.0	0839	2.9	1420	5.1	2120	2.7
9	W	0316	5.0	1005	2.9	1549	5.1	2243	2.5
10	TH	0441	5.3	1125	2.6	1705	5.5	2353	2.1
11	F	0544	5.7	1228	2.1	1804	5.9		
12	SA	0052	1.7	0635	6.1	1322	1.6	1857	6.3
13	SU	0145	1.3	0724	6.5	1414	1.2	1947	6.7
14	M	0235	1.0	0812	6.8	1503	0.9	○ 2037	6.9
15	TU	0324	0.8	0858	6.9	1552	0.8	2125	6.9
16	W	0411	0.8	0944	7.0	1639	0.8	2213	6.9
17	TH	0457	1.0	1029	6.8	1725	0.9	2259	6.6
18	F	0543	1.3	1114	6.6	1812	1.2	2346	6.3
19	SA	0629	1.7	1159	6.2	1900	1.6		
20	SU	0035	5.9	0719	2.1	1248	5.8	1952	2.0
21	M	0132	5.5	0816	2.5	1347	5.5	◑ 2054	2.4
22	TU	0238	5.2	0924	2.7	1458	5.2	2206	2.5
23	W	0352	5.1	1042	2.8	1613	5.2	2318	2.5
24	TH	0502	5.3	1150	2.6	1722	5.3		
25	F	0017	2.3	0559	5.5	1245	2.3	1818	5.5
26	SA	0107	2.1	0645	5.8	1332	2.1	1903	5.8
27	SU	0150	1.9	0725	6.0	1412	1.9	1944	5.9
28	M	0228	1.8	0802	6.1	1449	1.7	2021	6.1
29	TU	0303	1.7	0836	6.2	1523	1.6	● 2055	6.1
30	W	0337	1.7	0908	6.3	1556	1.6	2127	6.1

DECEMBER

Date	Day	Time	m	Time	m	Time	m	Time	m
1	TH	0409	1.7	0939	6.3	1629	1.6	2158	6.1
2	F	0442	1.8	1010	6.2	1703	1.6	2231	6.0
3	SA	0515	1.9	1044	6.1	1737	1.7	2307	5.9
4	SU	0550	2.0	1122	6.0	1813	1.9	2347	5.7
5	M	0629	2.2	1203	5.8	1855	2.1		
6	TU	0032	5.5	0716	2.5	1251	5.5	1946	2.3
7	W	0127	5.3	0815	2.6	1350	5.3	◐ 2048	2.4
8	TH	0235	5.2	0926	2.7	1503	5.3	2201	2.3
9	F	0355	5.3	1042	2.5	1625	5.4	2315	2.1
10	SA	0508	5.6	1153	2.2	1732	5.7		
11	SU	0021	1.8	0607	6.0	1255	1.8	1832	6.1
12	M	0120	1.5	0701	6.3	1352	1.4	1927	6.4
13	TU	0215	1.2	0752	6.6	1446	1.1	2021	6.6
14	W	0307	1.0	0841	6.8	1538	0.9	○ 2112	6.7
15	TH	0357	1.0	0929	6.8	1627	0.8	2201	6.7
16	F	0445	1.1	1016	6.8	1714	0.9	2249	6.5
17	SA	0530	1.3	1101	6.6	1759	1.1	2334	6.3
18	SU	0615	1.5	1145	6.3	1844	1.4		
19	M	0019	6.0	0659	1.9	1229	6.0	1928	1.8
20	TU	0105	5.6	0746	2.3	1317	5.6	2016	2.1
21	W	0156	5.3	0838	2.6	1411	5.3	◑ 2110	2.4
22	TH	0255	5.1	0941	2.8	1514	5.1	2216	2.6
23	F	0402	5.1	1053	2.8	1626	5.0	2324	2.6
24	SA	0510	5.2	1159	2.6	1734	5.1		
25	SU	0024	2.4	0608	5.4	1255	2.4	1831	5.4
26	M	0116	2.2	0655	5.6	1342	2.1	1917	5.6
27	TU	0200	2.0	0736	5.9	1424	1.9	1959	5.8
28	W	0240	1.9	0815	6.1	1502	1.7	2037	5.9
29	TH	0316	1.8	0850	6.2	1538	1.6	● 2112	6.0
30	F	0352	1.7	0924	6.3	1614	1.5	2145	6.1
31	SA	0428	1.6	0957	6.3	1650	1.4	2220	6.1

Chart Datum: 3·33 metres below IGN Datum
HAT is 7·0 metres above Chart Datum

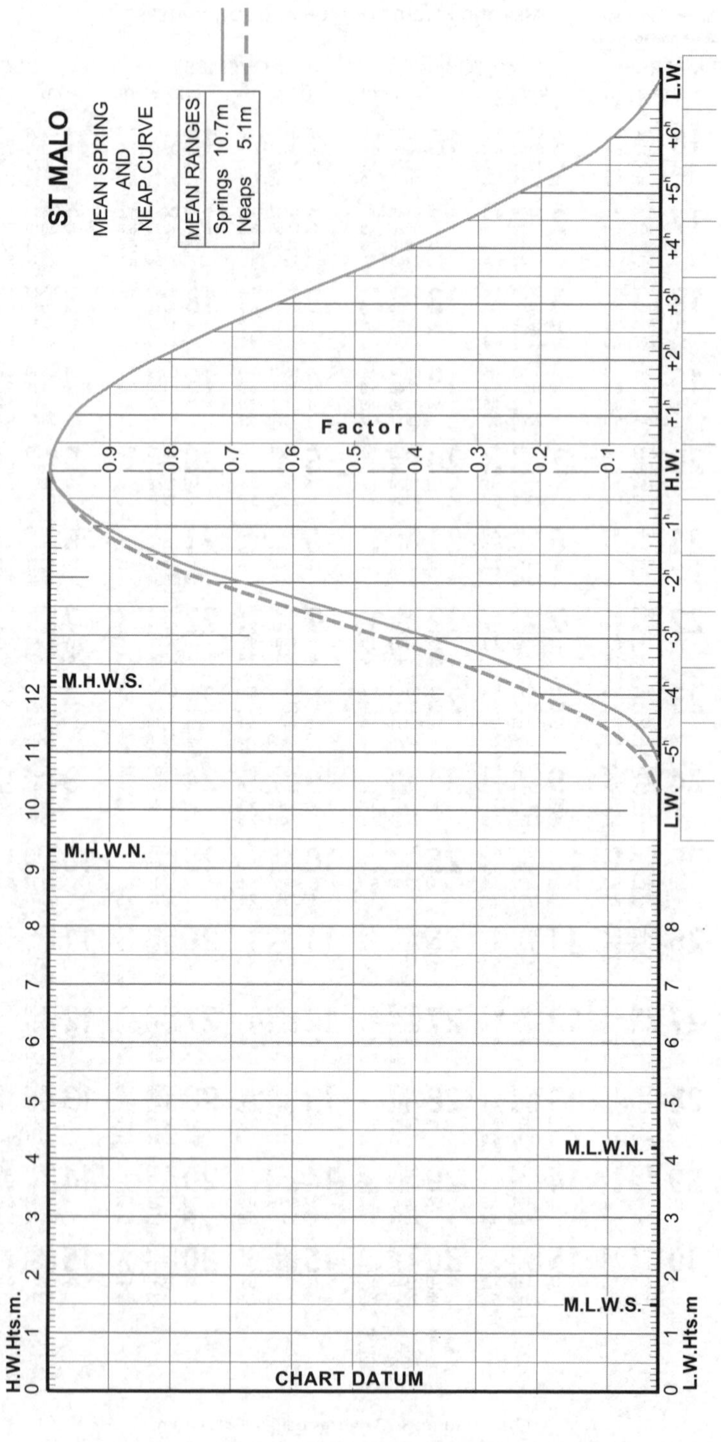
ST MALO
MEAN SPRING AND NEAP CURVE
MEAN RANGES
Springs 10.7m
Neaps 5.1m
Factor
0.9
0.8
0.7
0.6
0.5
0.4
0.3
0.2
0.1
L.W.
-5h
-4h
-3h
-2h
-1h
H.W.
+1h
+2h
+3h
+4h
+5h
+6h
L.W.
H.W.Hts.m.
M.H.W.S.
M.H.W.N.
M.L.W.N.
M.L.W.S.
CHART DATUM
L.W.Hts.m
0
1
2
3
4
5
6
7
8
9
10
11
12

TIME ZONE -0100
(French Standard Time)
Subtract 1 hour for UT
For French Summer Time add ONE hour in **non-shaded areas**

FRANCE – ST MALO

LAT 48°38′N LONG 2°02′W

TIMES AND HEIGHTS OF HIGH AND LOW WATERS

Dates in amber are **SPRINGS**
Dates in yellow are **NEAPS**

2016

JANUARY

Date	Day	Time	m	Time	m	Time	m	Time	m
1	F	0539	3.8	1109	9.9	1801	3.9	2337	9.5
2	SA ◑	0617	4.3	1153	9.3	1843	4.4		
3	SU	0028	9.0	0709	4.7	1253	8.9	1941	4.7
4	M	0141	8.7	0820	4.9	1411	8.8	2100	4.7
5	TU	0301	8.9	0939	4.6	1527	9.1	2215	4.3
6	W	0405	9.5	1045	4.0	1628	9.6	2315	3.7
7	TH	0457	10.1	1140	3.4	1719	10.2		
8	F	0007	3.1	0543	10.8	1231	2.8	1805	10.8
9	SA	0055	2.6	0627	11.3	1318	2.2	1848	11.3
10	SU ●	0141	2.1	0708	11.8	1405	1.8	1930	11.7
11	M	0225	1.8	0749	12.1	1450	1.5	2012	12.0
12	TU	0308	1.6	0830	12.3	1533	1.3	2053	12.1
13	W	0351	1.5	0911	12.4	1615	1.4	2135	12.0
14	TH	0431	1.7	0953	12.1	1656	1.6	2217	11.6
15	F	0512	2.1	1037	11.6	1738	2.1	2302	11.1
16	SA	0555	2.6	1124	11.0	1823	2.7	2351	10.5
17	SU ◐	0644	3.2	1219	10.3	1917	3.3		
18	M	0051	10.0	0746	3.7	1328	9.8	2024	3.6
19	TU	0207	9.7	0903	3.8	1451	9.7	2142	3.6
20	W	0329	9.9	1025	3.5	1609	10.0	2259	3.3
21	TH	0440	10.4	1138	3.0	1715	10.5		
22	F	0006	2.7	0539	11.0	1240	2.4	1810	11.1
23	SA	0102	2.3	0629	11.5	1332	2.0	1857	11.5
24	SU ○	0150	1.9	0713	11.9	1417	1.7	1940	11.8
25	M	0231	1.7	0752	12.1	1456	1.6	2018	11.9
26	TU	0308	1.7	0829	12.1	1531	1.6	2052	11.8
27	W	0341	1.8	0902	12.0	1603	1.9	2125	11.5
28	TH	0412	2.1	0934	11.6	1631	2.3	2155	11.1
29	F	0439	2.6	1004	11.1	1657	2.8	2224	10.6
30	SA	0505	3.2	1033	10.5	1722	3.4	2254	10.0
31	SU	0533	3.8	1105	9.8	1752	4.0	2328	9.4

FEBRUARY

Date	Day	Time	m	Time	m	Time	m	Time	m
1	M ◑	0610	4.3	1145	9.2	1834	4.5		
2	TU	0018	8.8	0705	4.8	1249	8.7	1938	4.9
3	W	0142	8.6	0825	4.9	1424	8.6	2110	4.8
4	TH	0315	8.8	0955	4.5	1548	9.0	2233	4.3
5	F	0424	9.5	1105	3.8	1651	9.8	2335	3.5
6	SA	0518	10.4	1204	3.0	1743	10.6		
7	SU	0031	2.7	0607	11.2	1258	2.2	1831	11.3
8	M ●	0123	2.0	0652	11.9	1350	1.5	1916	11.9
9	TU	0212	1.4	0736	12.5	1438	1.0	1959	12.4
10	W	0259	1.0	0818	12.9	1524	0.7	2042	12.7
11	TH	0342	0.8	0900	13.0	1606	0.6	2123	12.7
12	F	0423	0.9	0941	12.8	1645	1.0	2203	12.3
13	SA	0501	1.4	1022	12.2	1724	1.6	2243	11.7
14	SU	0540	2.1	1105	11.4	1803	2.4	2326	10.8
15	M ◐	0622	2.9	1153	10.5	1850	3.2		
16	TU	0019	10.0	0717	3.7	1257	9.6	1953	3.9
17	W	0133	9.4	0834	4.1	1427	9.2	2116	4.1
18	TH	0307	9.3	1006	4.0	1557	9.4	2243	3.8
19	F	0427	9.9	1126	3.4	1707	10.1	2353	3.1
20	SA	0526	10.6	1227	2.7	1758	10.8		
21	SU	0048	2.5	0614	11.3	1317	2.1	1842	11.3
22	M ○	0133	2.1	0656	11.7	1359	1.8	1921	11.7
23	TU	0212	1.8	0734	12.0	1436	1.6	1957	11.9
24	W	0247	1.6	0808	12.1	1508	1.6	2029	11.9
25	TH	0318	1.7	0839	12.1	1538	1.7	2058	11.8
26	F	0346	1.9	0908	11.8	1604	2.0	2126	11.5
27	SA	0411	2.2	0935	11.4	1627	2.5	2152	11.0
28	SU	0435	2.7	1002	10.9	1649	3.0	2218	10.5
29	M	0500	3.3	1028	10.2	1715	3.6	2245	9.9

MARCH

Date	Day	Time	m	Time	m	Time	m	Time	m
1	TU	0531	3.9	1100	9.5	1750	4.2	2322	9.2
2	W ◑	0616	4.5	1148	8.9	1842	4.8		
3	TH	0026	8.6	0723	4.9	1317	8.4	2005	5.0
4	F	0217	8.5	0902	4.7	1507	8.7	2148	4.6
5	SA	0348	9.2	1029	4.0	1622	9.5	2304	3.7
6	SU	0451	10.1	1135	3.0	1720	10.5		
7	M	0006	2.8	0544	11.1	1235	2.1	1810	11.4
8	TU	0102	1.9	0632	12.0	1330	1.3	1857	12.2
9	W ●	0155	1.1	0718	12.8	1421	0.6	1941	12.8
10	TH	0243	0.6	0802	13.2	1507	0.3	2024	13.1
11	F	0327	0.4	0844	13.4	1550	0.2	2105	13.1
12	SA	0408	0.5	0925	13.1	1629	0.6	2144	12.7
13	SU	0446	1.0	1005	12.5	1706	1.4	2223	12.0
14	M	0523	1.8	1045	11.5	1743	2.3	2304	11.0
15	TU ◐	0603	2.8	1131	10.4	1826	3.3	2353	10.0
16	W	0653	3.7	1232	9.4	1925	4.1		
17	TH	0104	9.2	0808	4.3	1405	8.9	2051	4.5
18	F	0244	9.0	0945	4.3	1542	9.2	2222	4.1
19	SA	0407	9.6	1107	3.6	1648	9.9	2332	3.4
20	SU	0506	10.3	1206	2.9	1737	10.6		
21	M	0025	2.7	0552	11.0	1253	2.3	1818	11.2
22	TU	0109	2.3	0632	11.5	1333	2.0	1856	11.6
23	W ○	0147	1.9	0709	11.8	1409	1.8	1930	11.8
24	TH	0221	1.8	0742	12.0	1440	1.7	2001	11.9
25	F	0251	1.7	0813	12.0	1509	1.8	2030	11.8
26	SA	0319	1.8	0841	11.8	1535	2.0	2057	11.7
27	SU	0345	2.1	0908	11.5	1559	2.3	2123	11.3
28	M	0410	2.5	0934	11.1	1622	2.8	2148	10.8
29	TU	0435	3.0	1001	10.5	1649	3.4	2216	10.2
30	W	0506	3.6	1033	9.8	1722	4.0	2251	9.6
31	TH ◑	0547	4.1	1117	9.2	1810	4.5	2346	9.0

APRIL

Date	Day	Time	m	Time	m	Time	m	Time	m
1	F	0648	4.6	1232	8.6	1923	4.9		
2	SA	0125	8.7	0818	4.6	1426	8.7	2106	4.6
3	SU	0308	9.1	0952	4.0	1549	9.5	2230	3.8
4	M	0419	10.1	1104	3.0	1651	10.5	2336	2.8
5	TU	0516	11.1	1208	2.0	1744	11.5		
6	W	0036	1.8	0607	12.1	1306	1.2	1833	12.3
7	TH ●	0132	1.0	0655	12.8	1358	0.6	1918	12.9
8	F	0222	0.5	0740	13.2	1446	0.2	2002	13.2
9	SA	0308	0.3	0824	13.3	1529	0.3	2044	13.2
10	SU	0350	0.5	0906	13.1	1609	0.7	2124	12.8
11	M	0429	1.0	0947	12.4	1646	1.4	2203	12.0
12	TU	0506	1.8	1028	11.5	1723	2.4	2244	11.1
13	W	0546	2.7	1113	10.4	1806	3.4	2332	10.1
14	TH ◐	0634	3.7	1211	9.4	1901	4.2		
15	F	0038	9.3	0742	4.3	1336	8.9	2021	4.6
16	SA	0210	9.0	0912	4.4	1509	9.0	2148	4.3
17	SU	0334	9.3	1031	3.9	1618	9.6	2257	3.7
18	M	0434	10.0	1130	3.3	1707	10.3	2350	3.1
19	TU	0521	10.6	1217	2.7	1748	10.9		
20	W	0035	2.6	0602	11.1	1258	2.4	1825	11.3
21	TH	0114	2.3	0639	11.4	1335	2.1	1900	11.6
22	F ○	0150	2.1	0713	11.6	1408	2.0	1932	11.7
23	SA	0222	2.0	0745	11.7	1439	2.0	2001	11.8
24	SU	0252	2.0	0814	11.6	1507	2.1	2029	11.7
25	M	0321	2.1	0843	11.5	1535	2.3	2057	11.4
26	TU	0349	2.3	0912	11.2	1602	2.7	2126	11.1
27	W	0418	2.7	0943	10.7	1631	3.1	2158	10.6
28	TH	0452	3.2	1019	10.1	1706	3.7	2237	10.0
29	F	0533	3.7	1105	9.5	1753	4.2	2331	9.4
30	SA ◑	0629	4.1	1213	9.0	1900	4.5		

Chart Datum: 6·29 metres below IGN Datum
HAT is 13·6 metres above Chart Datum

TIME ZONE -0100
(French Standard Time)
Subtract 1 hour for UT
For French Summer Time add ONE hour in **non-shaded areas**

FRANCE – ST MALO

LAT 48°38'N LONG 2°02'W

TIMES AND HEIGHTS OF HIGH AND LOW WATERS

Dates in amber are **SPRINGS**
Dates in yellow are **NEAPS**

2016

MAY

Date	Day	Time	m	Time	m	Time	m	Time	m
1	SU	0053	9.1	0748	4.2	1347	9.1	2031	4.4
2	M	0226	9.4	0915	3.8	1511	9.6	2154	3.7
3	TU	0341	10.1	1030	3.0	1617	10.5	2304	2.8
4	W	0443	11.0	1136	2.1	1714	11.4		
5	TH	0007	2.0	0539	11.9	1237	1.4	1805	12.2
6	F	0105	1.3	0630	12.5	1332	0.9	● 1853	12.7
7	SA	0158	0.8	0718	12.9	1422	0.6	1939	13.0
8	SU	0246	0.6	0804	12.9	1507	0.6	2022	13.0
9	M	0331	0.7	0848	12.7	1548	1.0	2104	12.6
10	TU	0411	1.1	0931	12.1	1627	1.6	2145	12.0
11	W	0451	1.8	1013	11.4	1705	2.4	2227	11.2
12	TH	0531	2.7	1057	10.5	1746	3.3	2313	10.3
13	F	0615	3.5	1149	9.7	1836	4.0	◐	
14	SA	0009	9.6	0711	4.1	1256	9.1	1941	4.5
15	SU	0124	9.1	0823	4.4	1418	9.0	2058	4.5
16	M	0244	9.1	0937	4.2	1530	9.3	2207	4.1
17	TU	0350	9.5	1040	3.8	1625	9.9	2304	3.6
18	W	0442	10.1	1132	3.3	1710	10.4	2353	3.1
19	TH	0526	10.5	1217	2.9	1751	10.9		
20	F	0036	2.7	0606	10.9	1258	2.6	1827	11.2
21	SA	0115	2.5	0643	11.2	1335	2.4	○ 1902	11.5
22	SU	0152	2.3	0718	11.3	1410	2.3	1934	11.6
23	M	0226	2.2	0750	11.4	1442	2.3	2006	11.6
24	TU	0300	2.1	0823	11.4	1515	2.3	2038	11.5
25	W	0333	2.2	0856	11.2	1547	2.5	2111	11.3
26	TH	0407	2.5	0932	10.9	1621	2.8	2148	11.0
27	F	0444	2.8	1012	10.5	1659	3.3	2231	10.5
28	SA	0527	3.2	1100	10.0	1746	3.7	2323	10.0
29	SU	0619	3.6	1159	9.6	1845	4.0	◑	
30	M	0030	9.7	0725	3.7	1313	9.5	2000	4.0
31	TU	0149	9.7	0841	3.5	1431	9.8	2119	3.6

JUNE

Date	Day	Time	m	Time	m	Time	m	Time	m
1	W	0304	10.2	0956	3.0	1541	10.4	2231	3.0
2	TH	0411	10.8	1105	2.4	1643	11.1	2337	2.3
3	F	0511	11.4	1209	1.9	1739	11.8		
4	SA	0039	1.7	0607	12.0	1307	1.4	1831	12.3
5	SU	0135	1.3	0658	12.3	1359	1.2	● 1919	12.5
6	M	0226	1.1	0747	12.4	1446	1.2	2004	12.6
7	TU	0313	1.1	0833	12.3	1529	1.4	2047	12.4
8	W	0355	1.4	0916	11.9	1609	1.8	2129	12.0
9	TH	0435	1.8	0957	11.4	1647	2.4	2209	11.4
10	F	0513	2.5	1038	10.7	1726	3.0	2251	10.7
11	SA	0552	3.2	1121	10.1	1806	3.7	2336	10.0
12	SU	0634	3.8	1211	9.5	1855	4.2	◐	
13	M	0030	9.4	0727	4.3	1312	9.1	1957	4.5
14	TU	0138	9.1	0832	4.4	1425	9.0	2106	4.5
15	W	0251	9.1	0940	4.3	1533	9.3	2212	4.2
16	TH	0355	9.4	1042	3.9	1628	9.8	2308	3.7
17	F	0447	9.9	1134	3.5	1714	10.3	2357	3.2
18	SA	0532	10.4	1221	3.1	1755	10.8		
19	SU	0042	2.8	0614	10.7	1304	2.8	1834	11.2
20	M	0124	2.5	0653	11.0	1344	2.5	○ 1911	11.4
21	TU	0204	2.3	0730	11.2	1422	2.3	1947	11.6
22	W	0243	2.1	0807	11.4	1500	2.2	2024	11.7
23	TH	0322	2.0	0845	11.4	1537	2.2	2101	11.7
24	F	0400	2.1	0925	11.3	1615	2.4	2141	11.5
25	SA	0440	2.3	1006	11.1	1655	2.7	2224	11.1
26	SU	0522	2.6	1051	10.7	1738	3.0	2312	10.7
27	M	0608	3.0	1142	10.3	1829	3.4	◑	
28	TU	0008	10.3	0703	3.3	1242	10.0	1931	3.7
29	W	0115	10.0	0810	3.4	1353	9.9	2045	3.6
30	TH	0230	10.1	0924	3.3	1507	10.2	2202	3.3

JULY

Date	Day	Time	m	Time	m	Time	m	Time	m
1	F	0343	10.4	1037	2.9	1617	10.7	2313	2.8
2	SA	0450	10.9	1145	2.5	1719	11.2		
3	SU	0019	2.2	0550	11.3	1246	2.0	1814	11.7
4	M	0118	1.8	0645	11.7	1341	1.7	● 1904	12.1
5	TU	0210	1.5	0734	11.9	1429	1.6	1949	12.3
6	W	0257	1.4	0818	12.0	1512	1.6	2032	12.3
7	TH	0338	1.5	0859	11.9	1551	1.8	2111	12.0
8	F	0416	1.8	0938	11.6	1627	2.2	2148	11.6
9	SA	0450	2.3	1014	11.1	1700	2.7	2224	11.0
10	SU	0523	2.9	1049	10.5	1732	3.4	2300	10.4
11	M	0554	3.5	1126	9.9	1807	4.0	2340	9.7
12	TU	0631	4.1	1210	9.3	1852	4.5	◐	
13	W	0030	9.1	0720	4.5	1309	8.9	1954	4.8
14	TH	0139	8.8	0829	4.7	1426	8.9	2111	4.7
15	F	0258	8.9	0947	4.6	1540	9.2	2222	4.3
16	SA	0406	9.3	1052	4.1	1637	9.8	2320	3.7
17	SU	0500	9.9	1146	3.5	1726	10.4		
18	M	0011	3.1	0548	10.4	1235	3.0	1810	11.0
19	TU	0058	2.6	0632	10.9	1321	2.6	○ 1851	11.4
20	W	0144	2.2	0713	11.3	1405	2.2	1931	11.8
21	TH	0228	1.9	0754	11.6	1447	2.0	2011	12.1
22	F	0311	1.7	0834	11.9	1529	1.8	2051	12.2
23	SA	0353	1.6	0914	11.9	1609	1.8	2131	12.1
24	SU	0433	1.7	0955	11.8	1648	2.0	2213	11.8
25	M	0512	2.0	1036	11.4	1727	2.5	2256	11.3
26	TU	0554	2.5	1121	10.8	1811	3.0	2345	10.7
27	W	0641	3.1	1213	10.3	1905	3.5	◑	
28	TH	0045	10.1	0741	3.5	1319	9.9	2016	3.8
29	F	0201	9.8	0855	3.7	1440	9.8	2139	3.7
30	SA	0324	9.9	1015	3.5	1559	10.2	2258	3.3
31	SU	0439	10.3	1129	3.0	1706	10.8		

AUGUST

Date	Day	Time	m	Time	m	Time	m	Time	m
1	M	0007	2.6	0541	10.9	1232	2.5	1802	11.4
2	TU	0105	2.1	0634	11.4	1327	2.1	● 1851	11.9
3	W	0156	1.8	0720	11.8	1414	1.8	1934	12.2
4	TH	0240	1.6	0801	11.9	1454	1.7	2013	12.3
5	F	0319	1.6	0839	11.9	1530	1.8	2049	12.2
6	SA	0353	1.8	0913	11.8	1602	2.0	2123	11.9
7	SU	0423	2.2	0945	11.4	1631	2.5	2154	11.4
8	M	0449	2.7	1015	10.9	1656	3.1	2224	10.7
9	TU	0513	3.3	1045	10.3	1722	3.7	2255	10.0
10	W	0540	3.9	1117	9.7	1755	4.3	◐ 2331	9.4
11	TH	0617	4.5	1201	9.1	1844	4.8		
12	F	0027	8.8	0713	4.9	1312	8.6	1958	5.1
13	SA	0156	8.5	0840	5.1	1448	8.7	2132	4.8
14	SU	0326	8.8	1010	4.6	1603	9.3	2245	4.1
15	M	0431	9.5	1114	3.9	1659	10.1	2342	3.4
16	TU	0524	10.3	1208	3.2	1747	10.9		
17	W	0034	2.6	0611	11.0	1259	2.5	1831	11.6
18	TH	0124	2.0	0655	11.6	1347	2.0	○ 1914	12.1
19	F	0213	1.5	0737	12.1	1433	1.5	1955	12.6
20	SA	0258	1.2	0818	12.4	1517	1.3	2036	12.8
21	SU	0340	1.0	0858	12.5	1557	1.3	2116	12.7
22	M	0420	1.2	0938	12.4	1635	1.5	2156	12.4
23	TU	0458	1.6	1018	11.9	1713	2.1	2237	11.7
24	W	0536	2.3	1059	11.2	1753	2.8	2322	10.8
25	TH	0619	3.1	1147	10.4	1842	3.5	◑	
26	F	0019	10.0	0715	3.8	1251	9.7	1952	4.1
27	SA	0140	9.4	0833	4.2	1420	9.4	2123	4.1
28	SU	0314	9.4	1002	4.0	1548	9.8	2250	3.6
29	M	0432	10.0	1119	3.4	1656	10.5	2357	2.8
30	TU	0531	10.7	1220	2.7	1749	11.3		
31	W	0052	2.2	0619	11.3	1311	2.2	1834	11.8

Chart Datum: 6·29 metres below IGN Datum
HAT is 13·6 metres above Chart Datum

TIME ZONE -0100
(French Standard Time)
Subtract 1 hour for UT
For French Summer Time add ONE hour in **non-shaded areas**

FRANCE – ST MALO

LAT 48°38′N LONG 2°02′W

TIMES AND HEIGHTS OF HIGH AND LOW WATERS

Dates in amber are **SPRINGS**
Dates in yellow are **NEAPS**

2016

SEPTEMBER

Date	Day	Time m	Time m	Time m	Time m	Moon
1	TH	0139 1.9	0701 11.8	1354 1.9	1915 12.1	●
2	F	0219 1.7	0739 12.0	1432 1.8	1951 12.3	
3	SA	0254 1.7	0813 12.0	1504 1.8	2024 12.2	
4	SU	0324 1.8	0844 11.9	1534 2.0	2054 12.0	
5	M	0351 2.1	0913 11.6	1559 2.3	2122 11.6	
6	TU	0415 2.6	0940 11.2	1623 2.8	2149 11.0	
7	W	0436 3.1	1006 10.6	1646 3.4	2215 10.3	
8	TH	0500 3.7	1032 10.0	1714 4.0	2245 9.6	
9	F	0531 4.3	1106 9.3	1755 4.6	2327 8.9	◐
10	SA	0618 4.9	1202 8.7	1857 5.1		
11	SU	0050 8.4	0735 5.3	1352 8.5	2035 5.1	
12	M	0246 8.6	0923 5.0	1527 9.0	2208 4.4	
13	TU	0402 9.3	1041 4.2	1630 9.9	2312 3.5	
14	W	0458 10.2	1140 3.2	1721 10.9		
15	TH	0008 2.5	0546 11.2	1234 2.4	1808 11.8	
16	F	0102 1.8	0632 11.9	1326 1.7	1852 12.5	○
17	SA	0152 1.2	0715 12.5	1414 1.2	1935 13.0	
18	SU	0239 0.8	0757 12.9	1500 0.9	2017 13.2	
19	M	0322 0.6	0838 13.0	1541 0.9	2058 13.1	
20	TU	0402 0.9	0918 12.8	1620 1.2	2138 12.6	
21	W	0440 1.4	0957 12.2	1657 1.8	2219 11.8	
22	TH	0517 2.2	1038 11.4	1737 2.7	2303 10.8	
23	F	0559 3.2	1125 10.4	1824 3.6	2359 9.8	◑
24	SA	0654 4.0	1229 9.6	1934 4.3		
25	SU	0124 9.1	0815 4.5	1403 9.2	2110 4.3	
26	M	0303 9.2	0948 4.3	1534 9.6	2237 3.8	
27	TU	0421 9.9	1104 3.6	1639 10.4	2340 3.0	
28	W	0513 10.6	1201 2.9	1729 11.1		
29	TH	0030 2.4	0557 11.3	1248 2.3	1812 11.7	
30	F	0113 2.0	0636 11.7	1328 2.0	1850 12.0	

OCTOBER

Date	Day	Time m	Time m	Time m	Time m	Moon
1	SA	0151 1.9	0712 11.9	1404 1.9	1925 12.1	●
2	SU	0224 1.8	0745 12.0	1435 1.9	1956 12.1	
3	M	0253 1.9	0814 11.9	1504 2.0	2025 11.9	
4	TU	0320 2.1	0841 11.7	1530 2.3	2052 11.6	
5	W	0344 2.5	0907 11.4	1554 2.7	2118 11.2	
6	TH	0407 3.0	0933 10.9	1619 3.2	2145 10.6	
7	F	0430 3.5	0959 10.3	1647 3.7	2214 9.9	
8	SA	0501 4.1	1031 9.7	1725 4.3	2253 9.2	
9	SU	0544 4.7	1119 9.0	1820 4.8		◐
10	M	0001 8.6	0652 5.1	1254 8.6	1946 5.0	
11	TU	0201 8.6	0834 5.0	1445 9.0	2125 4.4	
12	W	0327 9.3	1003 4.3	1555 9.8	2238 3.5	
13	TH	0427 10.3	1109 3.3	1650 10.9	2339 2.5	
14	F	0518 11.3	1206 2.3	1740 11.8		
15	SA	0035 1.6	0605 12.1	1300 1.5	1827 12.6	
16	SU	0128 1.0	0650 12.8	1352 1.0	1913 13.1	○
17	M	0216 0.6	0734 13.2	1439 0.7	1956 13.3	
18	TU	0301 0.5	0816 13.2	1523 0.7	2039 13.2	
19	W	0343 0.8	0857 13.0	1604 1.1	2121 12.7	
20	TH	0422 1.4	0938 12.3	1643 1.7	2203 11.8	
21	F	0501 2.3	1020 11.5	1724 2.6	2248 10.8	
22	SA	0543 3.2	1108 10.5	1811 3.5	2344 9.8	◑
23	SU	0637 4.1	1210 9.6	1916 4.2		
24	M	0103 9.1	0752 4.5	1337 9.2	2044 4.4	
25	TU	0237 9.1	0921 4.4	1506 9.4	2207 4.0	
26	W	0354 9.7	1034 3.8	1611 10.1	2309 3.3	
27	TH	0445 10.4	1130 3.2	1701 10.7	2358 2.8	
28	F	0528 11.0	1216 2.7	1743 11.3		
29	SA	0040 2.4	0607 11.5	1256 2.3	1822 11.6	
30	SU	0118 2.2	0643 11.7	1333 2.1	1857 11.8	●
31	M	0152 2.1	0715 11.8	1406 2.1	1929 11.8	

NOVEMBER

Date	Day	Time m	Time m	Time m	Time m	Moon
1	TU	0222 2.1	0745 11.8	1436 2.1	1959 11.7	
2	W	0251 2.2	0813 11.7	1505 2.3	2027 11.5	
3	TH	0318 2.5	0841 11.5	1533 2.5	2055 11.2	
4	F	0345 2.8	0909 11.1	1601 2.9	2125 10.8	
5	SA	0412 3.3	0939 10.6	1632 3.4	2157 10.2	
6	SU	0445 3.8	1014 10.1	1710 3.9	2238 9.6	
7	M	0527 4.3	1101 9.4	1801 4.3	2339 9.0	◐
8	TU	0627 4.7	1217 9.0	1912 4.5		
9	W	0113 8.9	0752 4.8	1356 9.1	2041 4.2	
10	TH	0243 9.4	0921 4.2	1514 9.8	2200 3.5	
11	F	0350 10.2	1033 3.3	1616 10.7	2305 2.6	
12	SA	0446 11.2	1135 2.4	1710 11.6		
13	SU	0005 1.8	0537 12.0	1233 1.6	1801 12.4	
14	M	0101 1.1	0625 12.7	1328 1.1	1850 12.9	○
15	TU	0153 0.8	0711 13.0	1418 0.8	1937 13.1	
16	W	0240 0.7	0756 13.1	1505 0.8	2022 12.9	
17	TH	0324 0.9	0840 12.9	1549 1.0	2107 12.5	
18	F	0406 1.4	0923 12.4	1631 1.6	2151 11.8	
19	SA	0447 2.2	1006 11.6	1713 2.4	2236 10.9	
20	SU	0529 3.0	1053 10.7	1758 3.2	2327 10.0	
21	M	0618 3.8	1147 9.9	1852 3.9		◑
22	TU	0030 9.4	0719 4.4	1257 9.3	2000 4.3	
23	W	0150 9.1	0834 4.5	1418 9.2	2116 4.2	
24	TH	0307 9.3	0946 4.2	1530 9.6	2222 3.9	
25	F	0407 9.9	1047 3.7	1625 10.1	2316 3.4	
26	SA	0454 10.4	1137 3.2	1711 10.6		
27	SU	0002 2.9	0536 10.9	1221 2.8	1753 11.0	
28	M	0043 2.6	0613 11.3	1301 2.5	1830 11.3	
29	TU	0121 2.4	0648 11.5	1338 2.3	1904 11.4	●
30	W	0155 2.3	0721 11.6	1412 2.2	1937 11.5	

DECEMBER

Date	Day	Time m	Time m	Time m	Time m	Moon
1	TH	0228 2.3	0752 11.6	1445 2.2	2008 11.4	
2	F	0300 2.4	0823 11.6	1518 2.3	2040 11.3	
3	SA	0331 2.6	0855 11.4	1551 2.6	2114 11.0	
4	SU	0403 2.9	0929 11.0	1625 2.9	2151 10.6	
5	M	0438 3.3	1007 10.6	1704 3.3	2232 10.1	
6	TU	0519 3.7	1053 10.1	1750 3.7	2325 9.7	
7	W	0612 4.1	1153 9.6	1849 3.9		◐
8	TH	0034 9.4	0719 4.3	1310 9.5	2002 3.9	
9	F	0154 9.5	0839 4.0	1429 9.8	2120 3.5	
10	SA	0308 10.1	0956 3.4	1540 10.4	2231 2.8	
11	SU	0413 10.8	1104 2.7	1642 11.2	2337 2.1	
12	M	0510 11.6	1208 2.0	1739 11.8		
13	TU	0037 1.6	0604 12.2	1306 1.4	1832 12.3	
14	W	0132 1.2	0654 12.6	1401 1.0	1923 12.6	○
15	TH	0223 1.0	0741 12.8	1450 0.9	2010 12.6	
16	F	0309 1.1	0827 12.7	1536 1.0	2056 12.3	
17	SA	0352 1.4	0910 12.4	1619 1.4	2139 11.9	
18	SU	0433 1.9	0953 11.8	1700 2.0	2221 11.2	
19	M	0513 2.6	1035 11.1	1740 2.8	2304 10.5	
20	TU	0553 3.3	1119 10.3	1821 3.5	2351 9.8	
21	W	0639 4.0	1210 9.6	1909 4.1		◑
22	TH	0048 9.2	0735 4.4	1314 9.2	2010 4.4	
23	F	0201 9.0	0843 4.6	1431 9.0	2120 4.4	
24	SA	0316 9.2	0953 4.3	1541 9.3	2226 4.1	
25	SU	0415 9.7	1054 3.9	1637 9.8	2322 3.6	
26	M	0504 10.2	1146 3.4	1723 10.3		
27	TU	0010 3.2	0546 10.7	1232 2.9	1805 10.7	
28	W	0053 2.8	0625 11.1	1313 2.6	1844 11.0	
29	TH	0132 2.5	0701 11.4	1352 2.3	1920 11.3	●
30	F	0210 2.3	0736 11.6	1430 2.1	1955 11.4	
31	SA	0246 2.2	0811 11.7	1507 2.1	2031 11.4	

Chart Datum: 6·29 metres below IGN Datum
HAT is 13·6 metres above Chart Datum

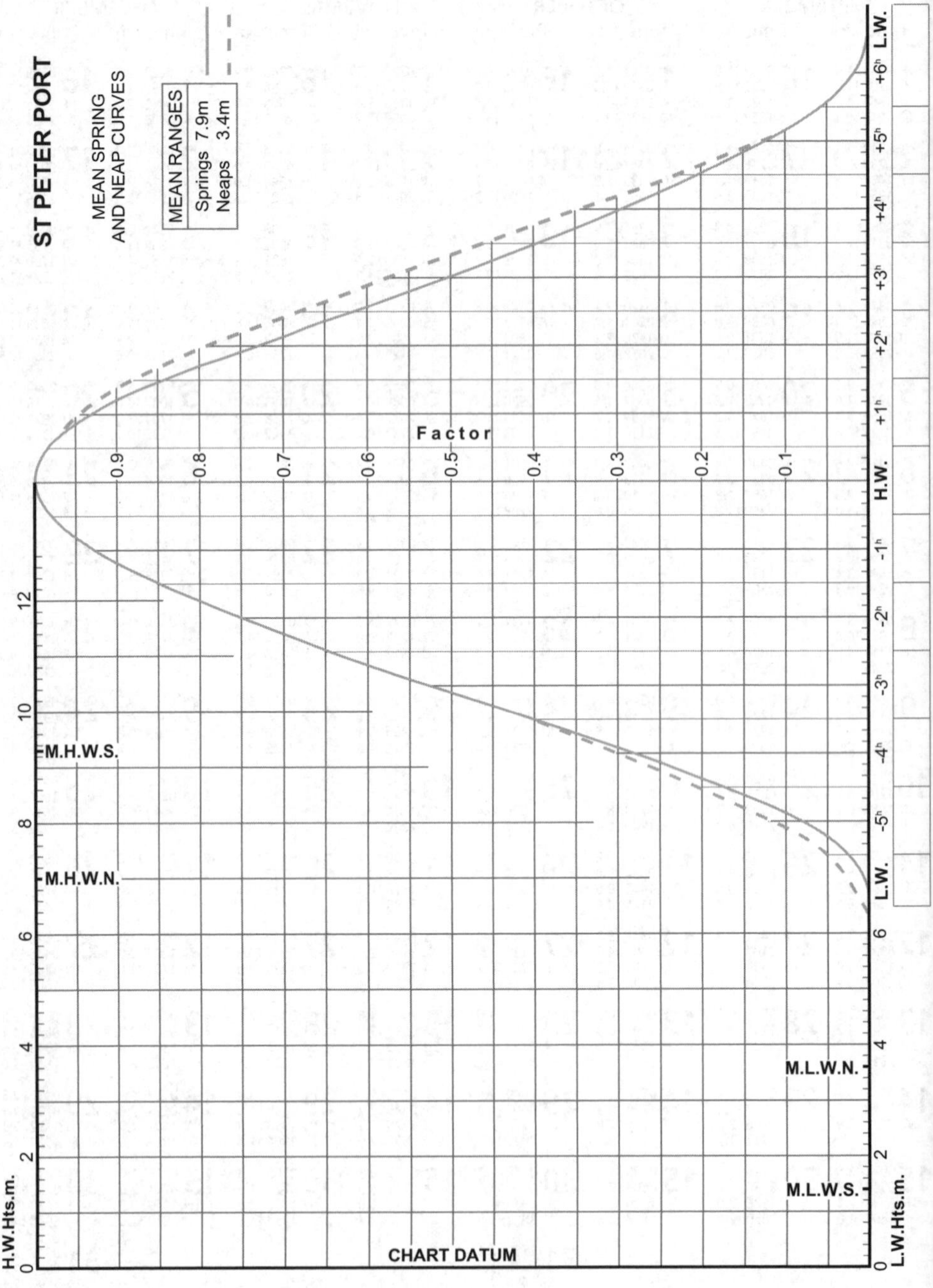
ST PETER PORT
MEAN SPRING AND NEAP CURVES
MEAN RANGES
Springs 7.9m
Neaps 3.4m
Factor
0.9
0.8
0.7
0.6
0.5
0.4
0.3
0.2
0.1
H.W.Hts.m.
0
2
4
6
8
10
12
M.H.W.S.
M.H.W.N.
CHART DATUM
L.W.Hts.m.
0
2
4
6
M.L.W.S.
M.L.W.N.
L.W.
-5h
-4h
-3h
-2h
-1h
H.W.
+1h
+2h
+3h
+4h
+5h
+6h
L.W.

TIME ZONE (UT)
For Summer Time add ONE hour in **non-shaded areas**

CHANNEL ISLES – ST PETER PORT

LAT 49°27′N LONG 2°31′W

TIMES AND HEIGHTS OF HIGH AND LOW WATERS

Dates in amber are **SPRINGS**
Dates in yellow are **NEAPS**

2016

JANUARY

Date	Day	Time	m	Time	m	Time	m	Time	m
1	F	0440	3.2	1039	7.7	1708	3.2	2306	7.3
2	SA	0524	3.6	1125	7.2	1755	3.6	◑ 2359	7.0
3	SU	0622	3.9	1224	6.9	1856	3.8		
4	M	0109	6.8	0732	4.0	1338	6.9	2006	3.8
5	TU	0224	7.0	0843	3.8	1450	7.0	2113	3.5
6	W	0329	7.3	0946	3.4	1551	7.4	2212	3.1
7	TH	0421	7.8	1040	2.9	1642	7.8	2303	2.7
8	F	0508	8.3	1129	2.4	1730	8.3	2349	2.2
9	SA	0552	8.7	1214	1.9	1814	8.6		
10	SU	0033	1.9	0634	9.1	1259	1.6	● 1857	8.9
11	M	0116	1.6	0715	9.3	1342	1.3	1938	9.1
12	TU	0158	1.4	0756	9.4	1423	1.2	2019	9.2
13	W	0238	1.4	0837	9.4	1504	1.3	2100	9.1
14	TH	0318	1.6	0919	9.2	1545	1.5	2142	8.9
15	F	0400	1.9	1003	8.9	1629	1.8	2227	8.5
16	SA	0446	2.3	1051	8.4	1717	2.3	◐ 2318	8.0
17	SU	0540	2.7	1148	8.0	1815	2.7		
18	M	0021	7.6	0649	3.1	1300	7.6	1928	3.0
19	TU	0140	7.4	0815	3.2	1424	7.5	2052	3.1
20	W	0303	7.6	0938	3.0	1540	7.7	2206	2.8
21	TH	0411	8.0	1043	2.5	1643	8.1	2306	2.4
22	F	0506	8.5	1138	2.0	1735	8.5	2358	1.9
23	SA	0555	8.9	1226	1.6	1822	8.8		
24	SU	0043	1.6	0638	9.2	1311	1.4	○ 1905	9.0
25	M	0126	1.4	0719	9.4	1351	1.3	1944	9.1
26	TU	0203	1.4	0756	9.3	1427	1.3	2019	9.0
27	W	0237	1.5	0830	9.2	1500	1.6	2052	8.8
28	TH	0308	1.8	0902	8.9	1529	1.9	2122	8.5
29	F	0336	2.2	0932	8.5	1556	2.3	2151	8.1
30	SA	0404	2.6	1003	8.0	1624	2.8	2223	7.7
31	SU	0436	3.1	1038	7.5	1657	3.2	2300	7.3

FEBRUARY

Date	Day	Time	m	Time	m	Time	m	Time	m
1	M	0516	3.5	1121	7.1	1742	3.6	◑ 2350	6.9
2	TU	0618	3.9	1222	6.8	1853	3.9		
3	W	0106	6.7	0742	3.9	1348	6.7	2017	3.8
4	TH	0236	6.9	0901	3.6	1509	7.0	2132	3.5
5	F	0346	7.4	1008	3.1	1614	7.5	2234	2.9
6	SA	0442	7.9	1104	2.5	1708	8.0	2328	2.3
7	SU	0531	8.5	1156	1.9	1757	8.6		
8	M	0017	1.7	0617	9.1	1244	1.3	● 1842	9.1
9	TU	0103	1.3	0701	9.5	1329	0.9	1925	9.4
10	W	0146	0.9	0743	9.8	1411	0.6	2006	9.6
11	TH	0228	0.8	0825	9.9	1452	0.6	2047	9.6
12	F	0308	0.9	0906	9.7	1531	0.9	2127	9.3
13	SA	0347	1.2	0947	9.3	1611	1.3	2208	8.9
14	SU	0429	1.8	1031	8.7	1655	2.0	2253	8.3
15	M	0516	2.4	1122	8.0	1746	2.7	◐ 2348	7.6
16	TU	0618	3.1	1229	7.3	1854	3.2		
17	W	0106	7.2	0745	3.4	1402	7.0	2027	3.4
18	TH	0242	7.2	0923	3.3	1529	7.2	2153	3.2
19	F	0358	7.6	1033	2.8	1632	7.7	2254	2.7
20	SA	0453	8.1	1126	2.3	1722	8.2	2344	2.2
21	SU	0540	8.6	1211	1.8	1806	8.6		
22	M	0027	1.7	0621	9.0	1252	1.4	○ 1846	8.9
23	TU	0107	1.4	0659	9.2	1330	1.3	1922	9.1
24	W	0142	1.3	0735	9.3	1403	1.2	1955	9.1
25	TH	0214	1.3	0807	9.2	1433	1.4	2026	9.0
26	F	0242	1.5	0836	9.0	1500	1.7	2053	8.7
27	SA	0308	1.8	0904	8.7	1524	2.0	2120	8.4
28	SU	0333	2.2	0932	8.2	1548	2.5	2147	8.0
29	M	0400	2.7	1001	7.8	1616	2.9	2217	7.5

MARCH

Date	Day	Time	m	Time	m	Time	m	Time	m
1	TU	0433	3.2	1037	7.3	1652	3.4	◑ 2258	7.1
2	W	0519	3.6	1128	6.9	1748	3.8	2359	6.8
3	TH	0637	3.9	1245	6.6	1919	4.0		
4	F	0132	6.7	0817	3.7	1426	6.8	2053	3.7
5	SA	0308	7.1	0936	3.2	1545	7.3	2206	3.1
6	SU	0414	7.8	1039	2.5	1644	7.9	2305	2.3
7	M	0508	8.5	1134	1.7	1736	8.6	2357	1.6
8	TU	0557	9.2	1223	1.1	1822	9.2		
9	W	0044	1.0	0642	9.7	1309	0.5	● 1906	9.7
10	TH	0129	0.5	0726	10.1	1353	0.3	1948	9.9
11	F	0212	0.3	0808	10.2	1434	0.2	2029	9.9
12	SA	0252	0.4	0849	10.0	1513	0.5	2108	9.6
13	SU	0331	0.8	0930	9.5	1552	1.1	2148	9.1
14	M	0411	1.5	1012	8.8	1633	1.9	2230	8.4
15	TU	0456	2.3	1100	7.9	1721	2.7	◐ 2321	7.6
16	W	0554	3.0	1204	7.2	1826	3.4		
17	TH	0035	7.0	0719	3.5	1341	6.8	2002	3.7
18	F	0219	6.9	0905	3.4	1512	7.0	2134	3.4
19	SA	0338	7.3	1014	2.9	1614	7.5	2235	2.9
20	SU	0433	7.8	1105	2.4	1701	8.0	2322	2.3
21	M	0518	8.4	1147	1.9	1743	8.5		
22	TU	0003	1.9	0557	8.8	1227	1.6	1820	8.8
23	W	0041	1.5	0634	9.1	1303	1.4	○ 1855	9.1
24	TH	0116	1.4	0708	9.2	1335	1.3	1928	9.1
25	F	0147	1.3	0740	9.2	1404	1.4	1958	9.1
26	SA	0215	1.4	0810	9.0	1430	1.6	2025	8.8
27	SU	0241	1.7	0838	8.7	1454	1.9	2051	8.5
28	M	0306	2.0	0905	8.3	1519	2.3	2118	8.2
29	TU	0333	2.5	0933	7.9	1546	2.8	2147	7.8
30	W	0404	2.9	1009	7.5	1621	3.2	2226	7.4
31	TH	0447	3.3	1057	7.1	1712	3.6	◑ 2323	7.0

APRIL

Date	Day	Time	m	Time	m	Time	m	Time	m
1	F	0555	3.6	1208	6.8	1831	3.9		
2	SA	0045	6.8	0735	3.6	1343	6.8	2014	3.7
3	SU	0224	7.1	0902	3.1	1511	7.3	2135	3.1
4	M	0341	7.7	1010	2.4	1616	8.0	2238	2.3
5	TU	0440	8.5	1107	1.7	1709	8.7	2332	1.5
6	W	0532	9.2	1158	1.0	1758	9.3		
7	TH	0021	0.9	0619	9.7	1246	0.5	● 1843	9.8
8	F	0108	0.4	0705	10.1	1331	0.2	1927	10.1
9	SA	0152	0.2	0749	10.2	1413	0.2	2008	10.0
10	SU	0234	0.3	0831	9.9	1454	0.5	2049	9.7
11	M	0314	0.7	0912	9.4	1534	1.1	2129	9.2
12	TU	0355	1.4	0955	8.7	1615	1.9	2211	8.5
13	W	0440	2.2	1043	7.9	1702	2.7	2300	7.7
14	TH ◐	0536	2.9	1143	7.2	1803	3.4		
15	F	0007	7.1	0653	3.5	1311	6.8	1929	3.8
16	SA	0142	6.9	0830	3.5	1440	6.9	2101	3.6
17	SU	0304	7.1	0941	3.1	1543	7.3	2203	3.1
18	M	0401	7.6	1033	2.7	1631	7.8	2251	2.6
19	TU	0447	8.1	1116	2.2	1712	8.3	2332	2.2
20	W	0527	8.5	1154	1.9	1749	8.6		
21	TH	0010	1.8	0604	8.8	1230	1.6	1824	8.9
22	F	0045	1.6	0639	8.9	1303	1.5	○ 1858	9.0
23	SA	0117	1.5	0712	9.0	1333	1.6	1929	9.0
24	SU	0147	1.5	0744	8.9	1401	1.7	1959	8.8
25	M	0216	1.7	0813	8.7	1428	1.9	2026	8.6
26	TU	0244	2.0	0842	8.4	1456	2.3	2055	8.3
27	W	0313	2.3	0914	8.0	1526	2.6	2128	8.0
28	TH	0347	2.7	0951	7.7	1603	3.0	2209	7.6
29	F	0431	3.0	1041	7.3	1653	3.4	2304	7.3
30	SA ◑	0534	3.3	1146	7.0	1805	3.6		

Chart Datum: 5·06 metres below Ordnance Datum (Local)
HAT is 10·3 metres above Chart Datum

TIME ZONE (UT)
For Summer Time add ONE hour in **non-shaded areas**

CHANNEL ISLES – ST PETER PORT

LAT 49°27′N LONG 2°31′W

TIMES AND HEIGHTS OF HIGH AND LOW WATERS

Dates in amber are **SPRINGS**
Dates in yellow are **NEAPS**

2016

MAY

Date	Day	Time	m	Time	m	Time	m	Time	m
1	SU	0017	7.2	0700	3.3	1309	7.1	1937	3.5
2	M	0144	7.3	0826	3.0	1433	7.4	2100	3.0
3	TU	0304	7.8	0937	2.4	1542	8.0	2207	2.3
4	W	0408	8.4	1037	1.7	1639	8.7	2304	1.6
5	TH	0504	9.0	1131	1.1	1731	9.3	2357	1.0
6	F ●	0555	9.5	1221	0.7	1819	9.7		
7	SA	0045	0.6	0643	9.8	1308	0.5	1905	9.9
8	SU	0132	0.4	0730	9.9	1353	0.5	1949	9.9
9	M	0217	0.5	0814	9.7	1436	0.8	2031	9.7
10	TU	0259	0.9	0857	9.3	1518	1.3	2112	9.2
11	W	0342	1.4	0941	8.7	1600	1.9	2155	8.5
12	TH	0427	2.1	1027	8.0	1645	2.7	2241	7.9
13	F	0518	2.8	1121	7.4	1739	3.3	◐ 2338	7.3
14	SA	0621	3.3	1230	7.0	1847	3.7		
15	SU	0051	7.0	0737	3.5	1349	6.9	2007	3.7
16	M	0212	7.0	0851	3.3	1457	7.1	2116	3.4
17	TU	0316	7.3	0948	3.0	1549	7.5	2209	3.0
18	W	0407	7.7	1035	2.7	1634	7.9	2254	2.6
19	TH	0450	8.0	1116	2.3	1714	8.3	2333	2.2
20	F	0530	8.3	1154	2.1	1751	8.6		
21	SA	0010	2.0	0608	8.6	1230	1.9	○ 1827	8.8
22	SU	0046	1.8	0644	8.7	1303	1.8	1902	8.8
23	M	0121	1.7	0719	8.7	1336	1.8	1935	8.8
24	TU	0154	1.8	0752	8.6	1408	2.0	2006	8.7
25	W	0227	1.9	0826	8.4	1440	2.2	2039	8.5
26	TH	0301	2.1	0901	8.2	1515	2.4	2116	8.3
27	F	0339	2.4	0942	7.9	1555	2.7	2159	8.0
28	SA	0424	2.7	1030	7.7	1644	3.0	2252	7.7
29	SU	0521	2.9	1129	7.5	1746	3.2	◑ 2357	7.6
30	M	0632	3.0	1239	7.4	1904	3.2		
31	TU	0111	7.6	0750	2.8	1356	7.6	2025	2.9

JUNE

Date	Day	Time	m	Time	m	Time	m	Time	m
1	W	0228	7.9	0903	2.4	1508	8.0	2136	2.4
2	TH	0338	8.3	1008	2.0	1610	8.5	2238	1.9
3	F	0438	8.7	1105	1.5	1706	9.0	2334	1.4
4	SA	0534	9.1	1159	1.2	1758	9.4		
5	SU	0026	1.0	0625	9.4	1249	0.9	● 1846	9.6
6	M	0115	0.8	0713	9.5	1336	0.9	1932	9.7
7	TU	0202	0.8	0800	9.4	1421	1.1	2015	9.5
8	W	0246	1.0	0844	9.1	1503	1.4	2057	9.2
9	TH	0329	1.4	0926	8.7	1544	1.9	2138	8.7
10	F	0411	2.0	1009	8.2	1626	2.5	2220	8.1
11	SA	0455	2.5	1053	7.7	1710	3.0	2305	7.6
12	SU	0544	3.0	1144	7.2	1802	3.4	◐ 2359	7.2
13	M	0640	3.4	1245	7.0	1903	3.7		
14	TU	0104	7.0	0743	3.5	1352	7.0	2010	3.6
15	W	0214	7.0	0847	3.4	1456	7.2	2113	3.4
16	TH	0316	7.2	0944	3.2	1549	7.5	2207	3.0
17	F	0409	7.6	1033	2.8	1636	7.9	2254	2.7
18	SA	0455	7.9	1117	2.5	1719	8.2	2337	2.3
19	SU	0538	8.2	1157	2.2	1759	8.5		
20	M	0018	2.0	0619	8.4	1237	2.0	○ 1838	8.7
21	TU	0058	1.8	0658	8.6	1316	1.9	1915	8.8
22	W	0137	1.7	0736	8.6	1353	1.9	1951	8.8
23	TH	0215	1.7	0814	8.6	1430	1.9	2028	8.8
24	F	0253	1.8	0852	8.5	1508	2.1	2108	8.7
25	SA	0332	1.9	0933	8.4	1548	2.3	2151	8.5
26	SU	0416	2.2	1019	8.1	1634	2.5	2239	8.2
27	M	0506	2.4	1111	7.9	1728	2.8	◑ 2336	7.9
28	TU	0606	2.6	1212	7.7	1835	3.0		
29	W	0042	7.8	0716	2.7	1323	7.7	1952	2.9
30	TH	0158	7.8	0832	2.6	1438	7.9	2109	2.7

JULY

Date	Day	Time	m	Time	m	Time	m	Time	m
1	F	0313	8.0	0943	2.4	1547	8.2	2217	2.3
2	SA	0419	8.3	1046	2.0	1647	8.6	2317	1.8
3	SU	0518	8.7	1142	1.7	1741	9.0		
4	M	0012	1.4	0611	9.0	1235	1.4	● 1831	9.3
5	TU	0102	1.1	0700	9.2	1322	1.2	1917	9.5
6	W	0149	1.0	0746	9.2	1407	1.2	2000	9.4
7	TH	0232	1.1	0828	9.1	1447	1.4	2040	9.2
8	F	0312	1.4	0908	8.8	1525	1.8	2118	8.9
9	SA	0349	1.8	0944	8.4	1601	2.2	2153	8.4
10	SU	0425	2.3	1020	8.0	1636	2.7	2230	7.9
11	M	0502	2.8	1059	7.5	1715	3.2	2311	7.4
12	TU ◐	0544	3.3	1145	7.2	1804	3.5		
13	W	0001	7.1	0637	3.6	1244	6.9	1904	3.8
14	TH	0107	6.8	0741	3.7	1353	6.9	2013	3.7
15	F	0220	6.9	0848	3.6	1501	7.1	2118	3.5
16	SA	0326	7.2	0949	3.3	1559	7.5	2216	3.0
17	SU	0422	7.5	1042	2.9	1649	7.9	2307	2.6
18	M	0511	7.9	1130	2.5	1734	8.3	2354	2.2
19	TU ○	0557	8.3	1215	2.1	1817	8.7		
20	W	0038	1.8	0640	8.6	1259	1.8	1858	9.0
21	TH	0122	1.5	0721	8.9	1340	1.6	1938	9.2
22	F	0203	1.3	0802	9.0	1420	1.5	2017	9.2
23	SA	0243	1.3	0841	9.0	1459	1.6	2057	9.2
24	SU	0323	1.4	0921	8.9	1539	1.7	2139	9.0
25	M	0403	1.7	1004	8.6	1621	2.1	2223	8.6
26	TU	0448	2.1	1050	8.2	1708	2.5	◑ 2314	8.2
27	W	0541	2.5	1145	7.9	1807	2.8		
28	TH	0016	7.8	0646	2.9	1254	7.6	1923	3.1
29	F	0134	7.5	0806	3.0	1415	7.5	2050	3.0
30	SA	0258	7.6	0927	2.8	1532	7.8	2207	2.7
31	SU	0410	7.9	1035	2.5	1636	8.3	2308	2.2

AUGUST

Date	Day	Time	m	Time	m	Time	m	Time	m
1	M	0509	8.4	1132	2.0	1730	8.7		
2	TU	0001	1.7	0600	8.8	1222	1.6	● 1817	9.1
3	W	0050	1.3	0646	9.0	1308	1.4	1901	9.4
4	TH	0133	1.2	0729	9.2	1350	1.3	1942	9.4
5	F	0213	1.2	0808	9.2	1427	1.4	2019	9.3
6	SA	0249	1.3	0843	9.0	1501	1.6	2052	9.0
7	SU	0321	1.7	0915	8.7	1532	2.0	2123	8.6
8	M	0350	2.1	0945	8.3	1600	2.4	2154	8.2
9	TU	0418	2.6	1016	7.8	1630	2.9	2227	7.7
10	W	0448	3.1	1052	7.4	1706	3.4	◐ 2306	7.2
11	TH	0530	3.6	1137	7.0	1759	3.8		
12	F	0000	6.8	0635	3.9	1245	6.7	1916	4.0
13	SA	0120	6.7	0756	3.9	1411	6.8	2035	3.8
14	SU	0245	6.8	0910	3.7	1524	7.2	2144	3.3
15	M	0353	7.3	1013	3.2	1622	7.7	2242	2.8
16	TU	0448	7.8	1107	2.6	1711	8.3	2333	2.2
17	W	0536	8.3	1155	2.1	1757	8.8		
18	TH	0020	1.6	0621	8.8	1242	1.6	○ 1840	9.3
19	F	0105	1.2	0704	9.2	1325	1.2	1922	9.6
20	SA	0147	0.9	0745	9.4	1406	1.0	2002	9.7
21	SU	0228	0.8	0825	9.5	1446	1.0	2042	9.7
22	M	0307	1.0	0904	9.3	1524	1.3	2122	9.4
23	TU	0346	1.3	0945	9.0	1604	1.7	2205	8.9
24	W	0428	1.9	1028	8.5	1648	2.3	2252	8.3
25	TH	0517	2.5	1120	7.9	1744	2.9	◑ 2352	7.6
26	F	0621	3.1	1229	7.4	1901	3.3		
27	SA	0116	7.2	0748	3.4	1400	7.2	2041	3.4
28	SU	0252	7.3	0919	3.2	1524	7.6	2201	2.9
29	M	0404	7.7	1027	2.8	1626	8.1	2300	2.4
30	TU	0459	8.2	1120	2.2	1717	8.6	2348	1.9
31	W	0546	8.7	1207	1.8	1801	9.0		

Chart Datum: 5·06 metres below Ordnance Datum (Local)
HAT is 10·3 metres above Chart Datum

TIME ZONE (UT)
For Summer Time add ONE hour in **non-shaded areas**

CHANNEL ISLES – ST PETER PORT

LAT 49°27′N LONG 2°31′W

TIMES AND HEIGHTS OF HIGH AND LOW WATERS

Dates in amber are **SPRINGS**
Dates in yellow are **NEAPS**

2016

SEPTEMBER

Day		Time	m	Time	m	Time	m	Time	m	Moon
1	TH	0032	1.5	0627	9.0	1249	1.5	1841	9.3	●
2	F	0112	1.3	0706	9.2	1327	1.3	1919	9.4	
3	SA	0148	1.2	0741	9.3	1402	1.3	1953	9.4	
4	SU	0221	1.4	0814	9.1	1433	1.5	2024	9.1	
5	M	0249	1.7	0843	8.9	1500	1.9	2052	8.8	
6	TU	0314	2.1	0910	8.5	1525	2.3	2120	8.4	
7	W	0337	2.5	0937	8.1	1550	2.8	2148	7.9	
8	TH	0402	3.0	1007	7.6	1620	3.3	2221	7.4	
9	F	0435	3.5	1045	7.1	1702	3.7	2307	6.9	◐
10	SA	0527	4.0	1142	6.8	1813	4.0			
11	SU	0019	6.6	0701	4.2	1314	6.7	1953	4.0	
12	M	0203	6.7	0834	3.9	1448	7.0	2113	3.5	
13	TU	0325	7.2	0945	3.4	1554	7.6	2216	2.9	
14	W	0423	7.8	1043	2.7	1646	8.3	2309	2.1	
15	TH	0513	8.5	1133	2.0	1734	9.0	2358	1.5	
16	F	0559	9.1	1220	1.4	1818	9.5			○
17	SA	0043	1.0	0642	9.5	1305	1.0	1901	9.9	
18	SU	0127	0.6	0724	9.8	1347	0.7	1943	10.1	
19	M	0208	0.5	0805	9.9	1428	0.7	2024	10.0	
20	TU	0248	0.7	0844	9.7	1507	1.0	2104	9.6	
21	W	0327	1.2	0925	9.3	1547	1.5	2146	9.0	
22	TH	0408	1.8	1007	8.6	1631	2.2	2233	8.3	
23	F	0456	2.6	1058	7.9	1726	3.0	2333	7.5	◑
24	SA	0600	3.3	1208	7.3	1846	3.5			
25	SU	0104	7.0	0733	3.7	1346	7.1	2032	3.5	
26	M	0244	7.1	0908	3.5	1511	7.4	2149	3.1	
27	TU	0351	7.6	1012	3.0	1610	8.0	2243	2.5	
28	W	0441	8.1	1102	2.4	1657	8.5	2328	2.0	
29	TH	0524	8.6	1145	2.0	1738	8.9			
30	F	0008	1.7	0602	9.0	1224	1.6	1816	9.2	

OCTOBER

Day		Time	m	Time	m	Time	m	Time	m	Moon
1	SA	0045	1.5	0638	9.2	1301	1.5	1852	9.3	●
2	SU	0119	1.4	0712	9.3	1333	1.5	1925	9.3	
3	M	0149	1.5	0743	9.2	1403	1.6	1955	9.1	
4	TU	0216	1.7	0811	9.0	1429	1.9	2023	8.9	
5	W	0240	2.1	0838	8.6	1455	2.2	2050	8.5	
6	TH	0304	2.5	0904	8.2	1520	2.7	2117	8.0	
7	F	0330	3.0	0933	7.8	1549	3.1	2149	7.6	
8	SA	0401	3.4	1008	7.4	1628	3.6	2232	7.1	
9	SU	0447	3.9	1102	7.0	1728	3.9	2339	6.8	◐
10	M	0605	4.2	1222	6.8	1909	4.0			
11	TU	0116	6.7	0754	4.1	1404	7.0	2038	3.6	
12	W	0250	7.2	0913	3.5	1519	7.6	2146	2.9	
13	TH	0353	7.9	1015	2.7	1616	8.3	2242	2.1	
14	F	0445	8.6	1107	2.0	1706	9.0	2332	1.5	
15	SA	0532	9.2	1156	1.4	1754	9.6			
16	SU	0019	0.9	0617	9.7	1243	0.9	1839	10.0	○
17	M	0104	0.6	0701	10.0	1327	0.6	1923	10.2	
18	TU	0147	0.5	0743	10.1	1410	0.6	2005	10.1	
19	W	0229	0.7	0825	9.9	1451	0.9	2048	9.7	
20	TH	0310	1.2	0906	9.4	1533	1.4	2131	9.0	
21	F	0352	1.9	0950	8.8	1618	2.2	2218	8.2	
22	SA	0440	2.7	1040	8.0	1713	2.9	2317	7.5	◑
23	SU	0542	3.4	1147	7.4	1828	3.5			
24	M	0043	7.0	0708	3.8	1319	7.1	2005	3.6	
25	TU	0218	7.1	0841	3.7	1443	7.3	2121	3.3	
26	W	0325	7.5	0946	3.2	1542	7.8	2215	2.8	
27	TH	0414	8.0	1035	2.7	1629	8.2	2259	2.4	
28	F	0456	8.4	1117	2.3	1710	8.6	2338	2.0	
29	SA	0533	8.8	1155	2.0	1748	8.9			
30	SU	0014	1.8	0608	9.1	1231	1.8	1823	9.1	●
31	M	0048	1.7	0642	9.2	1304	1.7	1856	9.1	

NOVEMBER

Day		Time	m	Time	m	Time	m	Time	m	Moon
1	TU	0118	1.7	0713	9.2	1334	1.7	1928	9.0	
2	W	0146	1.9	0743	9.0	1402	1.9	1957	8.8	
3	TH	0213	2.1	0811	8.7	1430	2.2	2026	8.5	
4	F	0240	2.5	0839	8.4	1459	2.6	2056	8.2	
5	SA	0308	2.9	0910	8.1	1530	2.9	2130	7.8	
6	SU	0342	3.3	0947	7.7	1610	3.3	2213	7.4	
7	M	0427	3.7	1038	7.3	1705	3.6	2313	7.0	◐
8	TU	0533	4.0	1149	7.1	1826	3.7			
9	W	0034	7.0	0708	3.9	1317	7.2	1956	3.5	
10	TH	0205	7.3	0835	3.5	1438	7.7	2110	2.9	
11	F	0316	7.9	0942	2.8	1542	8.3	2210	2.2	
12	SA	0414	8.6	1039	2.1	1637	8.9	2304	1.6	
13	SU	0505	9.2	1131	1.5	1729	9.4	2354	1.1	
14	M	0553	9.7	1220	1.0	1817	9.8			○
15	TU	0042	0.8	0639	10.0	1308	0.7	1904	10.0	
16	W	0128	0.7	0724	10.1	1353	0.7	1949	9.9	
17	TH	0212	0.9	0808	9.9	1438	0.9	2034	9.6	
18	F	0255	1.3	0851	9.5	1522	1.4	2118	9.0	
19	SA	0339	1.9	0936	8.9	1608	2.0	2205	8.4	
20	SU	0425	2.6	1024	8.2	1659	2.7	2258	7.7	
21	M	0520	3.2	1121	7.6	1800	3.3			◑
22	TU	0006	7.2	0629	3.7	1234	7.2	1915	3.6	
23	W	0129	7.0	0751	3.8	1355	7.2	2033	3.5	
24	TH	0242	7.2	0903	3.6	1501	7.4	2134	3.2	
25	F	0337	7.6	0958	3.2	1553	7.8	2223	2.9	
26	SA	0422	8.0	1043	2.8	1637	8.1	2304	2.5	
27	SU	0501	8.4	1123	2.4	1717	8.4	2342	2.3	
28	M	0538	8.7	1200	2.2	1754	8.7			
29	TU	0017	2.1	0613	8.9	1235	2.0	1830	8.8	●
30	W	0050	2.0	0648	9.0	1309	1.9	1904	8.8	

DECEMBER

Day		Time	m	Time	m	Time	m	Time	m	Moon
1	TH	0121	2.0	0720	9.0	1341	2.0	1938	8.7	
2	F	0153	2.1	0752	8.8	1414	2.1	2010	8.5	
3	SA	0224	2.3	0823	8.6	1446	2.3	2042	8.3	
4	SU	0256	2.6	0857	8.3	1521	2.6	2119	8.0	
5	M	0332	2.9	0936	8.0	1601	2.9	2202	7.7	
6	TU	0415	3.2	1024	7.8	1650	3.1	2255	7.5	
7	W	0511	3.5	1124	7.5	1753	3.3			◐
8	TH	0001	7.3	0624	3.6	1236	7.5	1910	3.2	
9	F	0119	7.4	0750	3.4	1355	7.7	2028	2.9	
10	SA	0237	7.8	0906	2.9	1508	8.1	2137	2.5	
11	SU	0343	8.3	1011	2.4	1611	8.6	2238	2.0	
12	M	0440	8.9	1108	1.8	1707	9.0	2333	1.5	
13	TU	0532	9.4	1202	1.3	1800	9.4			
14	W	0024	1.1	0621	9.7	1253	1.0	1849	9.6	○
15	TH	0113	1.0	0709	9.9	1341	0.8	1937	9.6	
16	F	0159	1.0	0755	9.8	1427	0.9	2022	9.5	
17	SA	0243	1.3	0838	9.6	1511	1.2	2106	9.1	
18	SU	0326	1.7	0921	9.1	1554	1.7	2149	8.6	
19	M	0408	2.3	1004	8.6	1638	2.3	2233	8.0	
20	TU	0453	2.8	1050	8.0	1725	2.9	2322	7.5	
21	W	0543	3.4	1142	7.4	1818	3.4			◑
22	TH	0021	7.1	0643	3.7	1246	7.1	1921	3.6	
23	F	0133	7.0	0754	3.8	1359	7.0	2030	3.7	
24	SA	0244	7.1	0904	3.7	1505	7.2	2134	3.4	
25	SU	0341	7.5	1001	3.3	1559	7.5	2225	3.1	
26	M	0427	7.9	1048	2.9	1645	7.9	2309	2.7	
27	TU	0509	8.3	1130	2.5	1728	8.2	2348	2.4	
28	W	0549	8.6	1210	2.2	1808	8.5			
29	TH	0026	2.2	0626	8.8	1248	2.0	1846	8.6	●
30	F	0103	2.0	0703	8.9	1325	1.9	1923	8.7	
31	SA	0138	2.0	0738	8.9	1402	1.8	1958	8.7	

Chart Datum: 5·06 metres below Ordnance Datum (Local)
HAT is 10·3 metres above Chart Datum

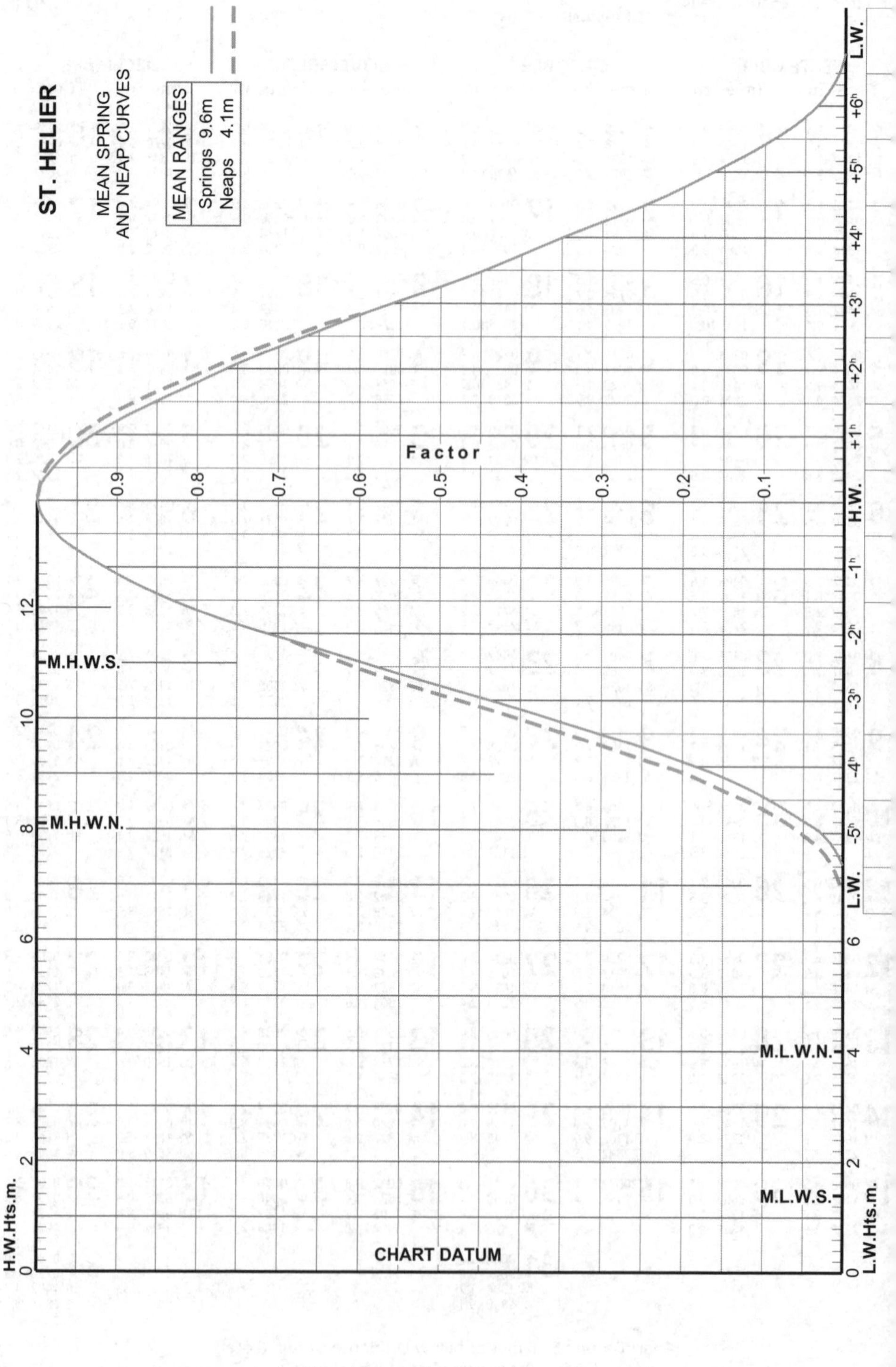
ST. HELIER
MEAN SPRING
AND NEAP CURVES
MEAN RANGES
Springs 9.6m
Neaps 4.1m
Factor
0.9
0.8
0.7
0.6
0.5
0.4
0.3
0.2
0.1
L.W.
-5h
-4h
-3h
-2h
-1h
H.W.
+1h
+2h
+3h
+4h
+5h
+6h
L.W.
H.W.Hts.m.
0
2
4
6
8
10
12
M.H.W.S.
M.H.W.N.
CHART DATUM
L.W.Hts.m.
M.L.W.S.
M.L.W.N.

TIME ZONE (UT)
For Summer Time add ONE hour in **non-shaded areas**

CHANNEL ISLES – ST HELIER

LAT 49°11'N LONG 2°07'W

TIMES AND HEIGHTS OF HIGH AND LOW WATERS

Dates in amber are **SPRINGS**
Dates in yellow are **NEAPS**

2016

JANUARY

Date	Day	Time	m	Time	m	Time	m	Time	m
1	F	0443	3.4	1025	9.0	1707	3.6	2255	8.5
2	SA	0525	3.9	1111	8.4	1753	4.0	◑ 2350	8.1
3	SU	0620	4.3	1213	8.0	1855	4.3		
4	M	0105	7.9	0732	4.4	1334	7.9	2012	4.3
5	TU	0223	8.1	0850	4.2	1447	8.2	2124	3.9
6	W	0324	8.5	0955	3.7	1545	8.6	2223	3.4
7	TH	0414	9.1	1049	3.1	1634	9.2	2313	2.8
8	F	0458	9.7	1138	2.5	1719	9.8		
9	SA	0000	2.3	0541	10.2	1224	2.0	1802	10.2
10	SU	0045	2.0	0623	10.7	1309	1.6	● 1845	10.6
11	M	0127	1.7	0705	11.0	1351	1.4	1928	10.9
12	TU	0208	1.5	0747	11.2	1432	1.2	2010	10.9
13	W	0248	1.5	0829	11.2	1513	1.2	2052	10.8
14	TH	0329	1.6	0911	11.0	1554	1.5	2135	10.5
15	F	0411	1.9	0955	10.5	1637	1.9	2219	10.0
16	SA	0455	2.4	1041	10.0	1724	2.4	◐ 2308	9.5
17	SU	0547	2.9	1135	9.3	1819	2.9		
18	M	0006	9.0	0650	3.3	1243	8.8	1928	3.3
19	TU	0121	8.7	0809	3.5	1405	8.7	2048	3.3
20	W	0243	8.8	0930	3.2	1525	8.9	2203	3.0
21	TH	0356	9.3	1042	2.7	1632	9.4	2309	2.5
22	F	0456	9.9	1143	2.2	1727	10.0		
23	SA	0005	2.0	0545	10.4	1236	1.8	1814	10.4
24	SU	0053	1.7	0629	10.8	1321	1.5	○ 1856	10.6
25	M	0135	1.6	0709	10.9	1400	1.5	1934	10.7
26	TU	0212	1.6	0745	10.9	1434	1.5	2008	10.6
27	W	0244	1.7	0819	10.8	1504	1.8	2040	10.4
28	TH	0313	2.0	0850	10.4	1532	2.1	2110	10.0
29	F	0341	2.4	0919	10.0	1559	2.5	2139	9.5
30	SA	0409	2.8	0949	9.4	1627	3.0	2210	9.0
31	SU	0441	3.4	1022	8.8	1700	3.6	2246	8.4

FEBRUARY

Date	Day	Time	m	Time	m	Time	m	Time	m
1	M	0521	3.9	1103	8.2	1745	4.1	◑ 2337	7.9
2	TU	0619	4.3	1206	7.8	1852	4.4		
3	W	0058	7.7	0739	4.5	1337	7.7	2021	4.4
4	TH	0230	7.9	0905	4.1	1501	8.1	2141	3.9
5	F	0337	8.6	1014	3.4	1603	8.8	2243	3.1
6	SA	0431	9.3	1111	2.6	1656	9.5	2337	2.4
7	SU	0520	10.1	1203	1.9	1745	10.2		
8	M	0027	1.8	0606	10.7	1253	1.4	● 1830	10.8
9	TU	0114	1.3	0651	11.3	1339	0.9	1915	11.2
10	W	0158	1.0	0735	11.6	1422	0.7	1958	11.5
11	TH	0239	0.8	0817	11.7	1503	0.6	2039	11.4
12	F	0319	0.9	0859	11.5	1542	0.8	2120	11.1
13	SA	0359	1.2	0940	11.0	1622	1.3	2200	10.5
14	SU	0439	1.8	1022	10.3	1703	2.1	2243	9.8
15	M	0524	2.6	1109	9.4	1751	2.9	◐ 2335	9.0
16	TU	0621	3.3	1211	8.6	1856	3.5		
17	W	0046	8.4	0740	3.7	1339	8.2	2022	3.8
18	TH	0219	8.3	0912	3.6	1512	8.4	2149	3.4
19	F	0342	8.8	1032	3.0	1622	9.0	2258	2.8
20	SA	0443	9.5	1133	2.4	1715	9.7	2352	2.2
21	SU	0532	10.1	1222	1.9	1759	10.2		
22	M	0038	1.8	0613	10.5	1304	1.6	○ 1838	10.5
23	TU	0117	1.6	0650	10.8	1340	1.5	1913	10.7
24	W	0151	1.5	0724	10.9	1411	1.5	1945	10.7
25	TH	0220	1.5	0755	10.8	1438	1.6	2014	10.6
26	F	0247	1.7	0824	10.6	1504	1.8	2041	10.3
27	SA	0314	1.9	0851	10.3	1529	2.1	2107	9.9
28	SU	0341	2.4	0917	9.8	1555	2.6	2132	9.4
29	M	0409	2.9	0944	9.2	1623	3.2	2200	8.8

MARCH

Date	Day	Time	m	Time	m	Time	m	Time	m
1	TU	0441	3.5	1016	8.5	1657	3.8	◑ 2237	8.2
2	W	0526	4.1	1104	8.0	1750	4.3	2341	7.7
3	TH	0637	4.4	1228	7.6	1918	4.5		
4	F	0126	7.7	0812	4.3	1415	7.8	2057	4.1
5	SA	0259	8.2	0937	3.6	1533	8.6	2212	3.3
6	SU	0403	9.1	1043	2.7	1632	9.5	2312	2.4
7	M	0457	10.0	1140	1.8	1724	10.3		
8	TU	0005	1.6	0546	10.9	1232	1.1	1812	11.0
9	W	0055	1.0	0633	11.5	1320	0.6	● 1857	11.5
10	TH	0141	0.6	0718	11.9	1405	0.3	1940	11.8
11	F	0224	0.4	0801	12.0	1447	0.2	2021	11.8
12	SA	0305	0.5	0842	11.8	1526	0.5	2101	11.4
13	SU	0344	0.9	0923	11.2	1604	1.2	2140	10.7
14	M	0423	1.6	1003	10.3	1643	2.0	2220	9.9
15	TU	0505	2.5	1048	9.3	1728	3.0	◐ 2308	9.0
16	W	0558	3.3	1147	8.4	1829	3.7		
17	TH	0017	8.2	0717	3.9	1318	7.9	1959	4.0
18	F	0156	8.1	0854	3.8	1455	8.2	2130	3.7
19	SA	0323	8.5	1013	3.2	1604	8.8	2239	3.0
20	SU	0423	9.3	1112	2.5	1655	9.5	2331	2.4
21	M	0511	9.9	1159	2.0	1737	10.1		
22	TU	0015	2.0	0551	10.3	1239	1.7	1814	10.4
23	W	0052	1.7	0626	10.6	1313	1.6	○ 1847	10.6
24	TH	0124	1.6	0659	10.7	1343	1.5	1918	10.7
25	F	0153	1.5	0729	10.8	1410	1.6	1946	10.7
26	SA	0221	1.6	0757	10.6	1436	1.7	2013	10.5
27	SU	0248	1.8	0824	10.4	1502	2.0	2038	10.2
28	M	0316	2.1	0850	9.9	1528	2.4	2103	9.7
29	TU	0344	2.6	0916	9.4	1556	3.0	2129	9.2
30	W	0415	3.2	0947	8.8	1628	3.6	2204	8.6
31	TH	0455	3.7	1032	8.2	1715	4.1	◑ 2300	8.0

APRIL

Date	Day	Time	m	Time	m	Time	m	Time	m
1	F	0558	4.1	1147	7.8	1833	4.4		
2	SA	0036	7.8	0728	4.1	1333	7.9	2014	4.1
3	SU	0219	8.2	0859	3.5	1500	8.6	2137	3.4
4	M	0332	9.1	1010	2.7	1604	9.5	2242	2.4
5	TU	0430	10.1	1111	1.8	1659	10.4	2339	1.6
6	W	0522	10.9	1206	1.1	1748	11.1		
7	TH	0031	0.9	0611	11.6	1257	0.5	● 1835	11.7
8	F	0120	0.5	0657	11.9	1343	0.3	1919	11.9
9	SA	0205	0.3	0741	12.0	1427	0.3	2001	11.9
10	SU	0247	0.4	0824	11.7	1507	0.6	2041	11.5
11	M	0328	0.8	0905	11.1	1546	1.3	2121	10.8
12	TU	0408	1.6	0947	10.2	1626	2.1	2201	9.9
13	W	0450	2.4	1032	9.2	1710	3.0	2248	9.0
14	TH	0541	3.3	1129	8.4	1808	3.8	◐ 2353	8.3
15	F	0654	3.8	1252	7.9	1931	4.1		
16	SA	0124	8.0	0823	3.9	1424	8.1	2058	3.9
17	SU	0250	8.4	0940	3.4	1532	8.7	2206	3.3
18	M	0352	9.0	1038	2.8	1624	9.3	2258	2.7
19	TU	0440	9.6	1124	2.4	1706	9.8	2342	2.3
20	W	0521	10.0	1204	2.1	1744	10.2		
21	TH	0019	2.0	0557	10.3	1240	1.9	1817	10.4
22	F	0054	1.8	0630	10.4	1311	1.8	○ 1848	10.6
23	SA	0125	1.7	0701	10.5	1341	1.7	1917	10.6
24	SU	0155	1.7	0730	10.5	1410	1.8	1946	10.5
25	M	0225	1.8	0759	10.3	1438	2.0	2013	10.3
26	TU	0255	2.0	0828	10.0	1507	2.3	2042	9.9
27	W	0325	2.4	0859	9.6	1537	2.8	2112	9.5
28	TH	0359	2.9	0933	9.1	1612	3.3	2150	8.9
29	F	0440	3.3	1020	8.5	1659	3.8	2245	8.4
30	SA	0538	3.7	1129	8.2	1808	4.0	◑	

Chart Datum: 5·88 metres below Ordnance Datum (Local)
HAT is 12·2 metres above Chart Datum

TIME ZONE (UT)
For Summer Time add ONE hour in **non-shaded areas**

CHANNEL ISLES – ST HELIER

LAT 49°11′N LONG 2°07′W

TIMES AND HEIGHTS OF HIGH AND LOW WATERS

Dates in amber are **SPRINGS**
Dates in yellow are **NEAPS**

2016

MAY

Date	Day	Time	m	Time	m	Time	m	Time	m
1	SU	0007	8.2	0656	3.7	1259	8.2	1937	3.9
2	M	0141	8.5	0821	3.3	1424	8.7	2101	3.3
3	TU	0257	9.2	0935	2.6	1532	9.5	2209	2.5
4	W	0400	10.0	1039	1.9	1630	10.3	2309	1.7
5	TH	0456	10.7	1136	1.2	1722	11.0		
6	F	0004	1.1	0547	11.3	1230	0.8	● 1810	11.5
7	SA	0056	0.7	0635	11.6	1320	0.6	1857	11.7
8	SU	0144	0.5	0722	11.7	1406	0.6	1941	11.7
9	M	0229	0.6	0806	11.4	1449	0.9	2023	11.3
10	TU	0312	1.0	0849	10.9	1530	1.5	2104	10.7
11	W	0354	1.6	0932	10.1	1611	2.2	2145	10.0
12	TH	0437	2.4	1016	9.3	1654	3.0	2230	9.2
13	F	0524	3.1	1108	8.6	1745	3.6	◐ 2326	8.5
14	SA	0623	3.7	1216	8.1	1852	4.0		
15	SU	0041	8.2	0736	3.9	1336	8.1	2009	4.0
16	M	0201	8.3	0849	3.7	1446	8.5	2118	3.6
17	TU	0307	8.7	0950	3.3	1542	9.0	2214	3.2
18	W	0400	9.1	1040	2.9	1628	9.4	2301	2.8
19	TH	0445	9.5	1123	2.5	1709	9.8	2342	2.4
20	F	0524	9.8	1202	2.3	1745	10.1		
21	SA	0020	2.1	0559	10.1	1239	2.1	○ 1818	10.3
22	SU	0056	1.9	0633	10.2	1314	2.0	1850	10.4
23	M	0131	1.8	0706	10.3	1347	2.0	1922	10.5
24	TU	0205	1.8	0739	10.3	1419	2.0	1955	10.4
25	W	0238	1.9	0813	10.1	1451	2.2	2029	10.2
26	TH	0312	2.2	0849	9.8	1526	2.5	2105	9.8
27	F	0350	2.5	0929	9.4	1605	2.9	2147	9.4
28	SA	0433	2.8	1017	9.0	1652	3.3	2240	9.0
29	SU	0526	3.1	1116	8.7	1752	3.5	◑ 2347	8.7
30	M	0632	3.3	1229	8.6	1906	3.5		
31	TU	0105	8.8	0747	3.1	1347	8.9	2025	3.2

JUNE

Date	Day	Time	m	Time	m	Time	m	Time	m
1	W	0221	9.2	0901	2.7	1458	9.4	2136	2.6
2	TH	0329	9.8	1007	2.1	1600	10.0	2239	2.0
3	F	0429	10.3	1108	1.7	1657	10.6	2339	1.5
4	SA	0525	10.8	1205	1.3	1749	11.1		
5	SU	0034	1.1	0616	11.1	1259	1.1	● 1837	11.3
6	M	0126	0.9	0705	11.2	1347	1.0	1923	11.4
7	TU	0214	1.0	0751	11.1	1433	1.2	2006	11.2
8	W	0259	1.2	0834	10.7	1515	1.6	2048	10.7
9	TH	0340	1.7	0916	10.2	1555	2.1	2128	10.1
10	F	0420	2.3	0957	9.5	1634	2.8	2208	9.5
11	SA	0500	2.9	1040	8.9	1715	3.3	2254	8.9
12	SU	0544	3.4	1131	8.4	1804	3.8	◐ 2350	8.4
13	M	0638	3.8	1236	8.2	1906	4.0		
14	TU	0100	8.2	0742	3.9	1347	8.2	2015	4.0
15	W	0212	8.3	0850	3.8	1452	8.5	2120	3.7
16	TH	0313	8.6	0949	3.4	1545	8.9	2215	3.3
17	F	0405	9.0	1040	3.1	1631	9.3	2303	2.8
18	SA	0449	9.4	1126	2.7	1712	9.7	2348	2.5
19	SU	0530	9.7	1208	2.4	1750	10.1		
20	M	0029	2.1	0608	10.0	1249	2.2	○ 1827	10.3
21	TU	0110	1.9	0646	10.2	1327	2.0	1904	10.5
22	W	0148	1.8	0724	10.3	1404	2.0	1941	10.6
23	TH	0226	1.7	0803	10.3	1440	2.0	2020	10.5
24	F	0304	1.8	0843	10.2	1518	2.1	2100	10.3
25	SA	0343	2.0	0925	10.0	1559	2.3	2143	10.0
26	SU	0426	2.2	1010	9.6	1644	2.7	2231	9.6
27	M	0514	2.6	1101	9.3	1736	3.0	◑ 2326	9.3
28	TU	0609	2.8	1201	9.0	1839	3.2		
29	W	0033	9.0	0715	3.0	1311	8.9	1952	3.2
30	TH	0148	9.0	0829	2.9	1425	9.2	2107	2.9

JULY

Date	Day	Time	m	Time	m	Time	m	Time	m
1	F	0302	9.3	0940	2.6	1535	9.6	2216	2.5
2	SA	0409	9.8	1046	2.2	1637	10.1	2320	2.0
3	SU	0509	10.2	1147	1.8	1732	10.6		
4	M	0019	1.6	0602	10.6	1243	1.5	● 1821	10.9
5	TU	0113	1.3	0651	10.8	1332	1.4	1907	11.1
6	W	0201	1.2	0736	10.9	1417	1.4	1950	11.1
7	TH	0244	1.3	0817	10.7	1458	1.6	2030	10.8
8	F	0322	1.6	0856	10.3	1534	2.0	2106	10.4
9	SA	0357	2.0	0932	9.9	1607	2.5	2142	9.9
10	SU	0429	2.6	1007	9.3	1640	3.0	2218	9.3
11	M	0502	3.1	1046	8.8	1717	3.5	2259	8.7
12	TU	0541	3.6	1133	8.3	1804	3.9	◐ 2353	8.2
13	W	0632	4.0	1237	8.0	1905	4.2		
14	TH	0104	8.0	0740	4.2	1353	8.0	2019	4.1
15	F	0221	8.0	0854	4.0	1500	8.4	2129	3.8
16	SA	0324	8.4	0958	3.6	1555	8.8	2227	3.3
17	SU	0417	8.9	1052	3.1	1642	9.4	2318	2.7
18	M	0503	9.4	1141	2.6	1725	9.9		
19	TU	0005	2.2	0546	9.9	1227	2.2	○ 1806	10.3
20	W	0051	1.9	0628	10.3	1310	1.9	1847	10.7
21	TH	0134	1.6	0710	10.6	1351	1.7	1928	10.9
22	F	0215	1.4	0751	10.7	1431	1.6	2009	11.0
23	SA	0254	1.3	0832	10.8	1510	1.6	2051	10.9
24	SU	0334	1.4	0914	10.6	1550	1.7	2133	10.6
25	M	0415	1.7	0956	10.2	1632	2.1	2216	10.2
26	TU	0458	2.1	1041	9.7	1719	2.6	◑ 2305	9.6
27	W	0547	2.6	1133	9.2	1814	3.1		
28	TH	0004	9.0	0647	3.1	1239	8.8	1924	3.4
29	F	0120	8.7	0802	3.3	1358	8.8	2045	3.3
30	SA	0243	8.8	0921	3.1	1518	9.1	2203	2.9
31	SU	0358	9.2	1033	2.7	1625	9.7	2311	2.3

AUGUST

Date	Day	Time	m	Time	m	Time	m	Time	m
1	M	0500	9.8	1136	2.2	1720	10.3		
2	TU	0010	1.8	0551	10.3	1231	1.8	● 1808	10.7
3	W	0101	1.5	0637	10.6	1318	1.5	1852	11.0
4	TH	0146	1.3	0718	10.8	1400	1.5	1931	11.0
5	F	0224	1.4	0756	10.8	1436	1.6	2007	10.9
6	SA	0258	1.5	0830	10.5	1507	1.8	2040	10.6
7	SU	0327	1.9	0902	10.2	1536	2.2	2111	10.2
8	M	0354	2.3	0931	9.7	1604	2.7	2141	9.6
9	TU	0421	2.9	1002	9.2	1635	3.2	2213	9.0
10	W	0452	3.4	1036	8.6	1712	3.8	◐ 2252	8.4
11	TH	0533	4.0	1123	8.1	1803	4.2	2349	7.8
12	F	0632	4.4	1238	7.7	1916	4.5		
13	SA	0117	7.6	0755	4.5	1411	7.9	2041	4.2
14	SU	0244	7.9	0918	4.1	1521	8.4	2153	3.6
15	M	0347	8.6	1022	3.4	1614	9.1	2250	2.9
16	TU	0439	9.3	1116	2.7	1702	9.8	2342	2.2
17	W	0526	10.0	1205	2.1	1747	10.5		
18	TH	0030	1.7	0610	10.5	1252	1.7	○ 1830	11.0
19	F	0117	1.3	0653	11.0	1336	1.3	1912	11.4
20	SA	0200	1.0	0735	11.2	1417	1.1	1954	11.6
21	SU	0241	0.8	0816	11.3	1457	1.1	2036	11.5
22	M	0320	0.9	0857	11.1	1537	1.3	2117	11.1
23	TU	0359	1.3	0937	10.7	1617	1.7	2158	10.5
24	W	0440	1.9	1019	10.0	1700	2.4	2243	9.7
25	TH	0525	2.7	1107	9.3	1752	3.1	◑ 2339	8.9
26	F	0623	3.4	1210	8.6	1904	3.6		
27	SA	0058	8.3	0743	3.7	1339	8.4	2033	3.7
28	SU	0235	8.4	0911	3.5	1509	8.8	2157	3.2
29	M	0353	8.9	1026	3.0	1616	9.4	2303	2.5
30	TU	0451	9.6	1126	2.3	1709	10.1	2358	1.9
31	W	0538	10.2	1216	1.9	1754	10.6		

Chart Datum: 5·88 metres below Ordnance Datum (Local)
HAT is 12·2 metres above Chart Datum

TIME ZONE (UT)
For Summer Time add ONE hour in **non-shaded areas**

CHANNEL ISLES – ST HELIER

LAT 49°11′N LONG 2°07′W

TIMES AND HEIGHTS OF HIGH AND LOW WATERS

Dates in amber are **SPRINGS**
Dates in yellow are **NEAPS**

2016

SEPTEMBER

Date	Day	Time	m	Time	m	Time	m	Time	m
1	TH ●	0044	1.6	0619	10.6	1259	1.6	1833	10.9
2	F	0125	1.4	0657	10.8	1337	1.5	1909	11.0
3	SA	0159	1.4	0730	10.8	1409	1.6	1941	11.0
4	SU	0228	1.6	0801	10.7	1437	1.7	2012	10.8
5	M	0254	1.8	0830	10.5	1504	2.0	2040	10.4
6	TU	0319	2.2	0856	10.1	1530	2.4	2106	9.9
7	W	0345	2.7	0922	9.5	1558	3.0	2133	9.3
8	TH	0412	3.3	0949	8.9	1630	3.6	2203	8.6
9	F ◐	0445	3.9	1024	8.3	1713	4.2	2247	8.0
10	SA	0536	4.5	1122	7.7	1821	4.6		
11	SU	0008	7.5	0658	4.7	1310	7.6	1953	4.5
12	M	0201	7.7	0836	4.4	1445	8.1	2117	3.9
13	TU	0318	8.4	0951	3.7	1546	9.0	2221	3.0
14	W	0413	9.3	1049	2.8	1637	9.9	2316	2.2
15	TH	0502	10.1	1140	2.0	1724	10.7		
16	F ○	0006	1.5	0548	10.8	1230	1.4	1809	11.3
17	SA	0055	1.0	0632	11.3	1316	1.0	1853	11.7
18	SU	0140	0.7	0715	11.7	1359	0.8	1935	11.9
19	M	0222	0.5	0756	11.7	1440	0.7	2017	11.8
20	TU	0302	0.7	0837	11.5	1520	1.0	2058	11.3
21	W	0341	1.2	0917	10.9	1600	1.6	2140	10.6
22	TH	0421	2.0	0957	10.1	1643	2.4	2224	9.6
23	F ◑	0506	2.8	1044	9.3	1735	3.2	2320	8.7
24	SA	0604	3.6	1148	8.5	1849	3.8		
25	SU	0044	8.1	0728	4.1	1323	8.2	2023	3.9
26	M	0226	8.2	0900	3.8	1457	8.6	2145	3.3
27	TU	0340	8.8	1012	3.2	1601	9.3	2247	2.6
28	W	0434	9.6	1108	2.5	1650	10.0	2337	2.1
29	TH	0518	10.2	1154	2.0	1732	10.5		
30	F	0020	1.8	0556	10.6	1234	1.8	1809	10.8

OCTOBER

Date	Day	Time	m	Time	m	Time	m	Time	m
1	SA ●	0057	1.6	0631	10.8	1308	1.7	1843	10.9
2	SU	0128	1.6	0702	10.8	1338	1.7	1914	10.9
3	M	0155	1.7	0731	10.8	1406	1.8	1942	10.8
4	TU	0221	1.9	0759	10.6	1433	2.0	2010	10.5
5	W	0247	2.2	0824	10.3	1501	2.3	2036	10.0
6	TH	0314	2.6	0849	9.8	1529	2.8	2102	9.5
7	F	0341	3.2	0915	9.2	1600	3.4	2131	8.8
8	SA	0412	3.8	0946	8.6	1639	4.0	2210	8.2
9	SU ◐	0457	4.4	1034	8.0	1739	4.4	2319	7.7
10	M	0611	4.7	1209	7.7	1907	4.5		
11	TU	0111	7.7	0751	4.5	1401	8.0	2038	4.0
12	W	0242	8.3	0915	3.8	1513	8.9	2148	3.1
13	TH	0343	9.2	1018	2.9	1608	9.8	2246	2.2
14	F	0435	10.2	1112	2.0	1658	10.7	2338	1.5
15	SA	0523	10.9	1203	1.4	1745	11.4		
16	SU ○	0028	0.9	0608	11.5	1251	0.9	1830	11.8
17	M	0116	0.6	0652	11.9	1337	0.7	1915	12.0
18	TU	0200	0.5	0735	11.9	1421	0.7	1958	11.8
19	W	0242	0.8	0817	11.6	1503	1.0	2041	11.3
20	TH	0323	1.3	0858	11.0	1545	1.6	2124	10.5
21	F	0405	2.1	0940	10.2	1630	2.4	2209	9.6
22	SA ◑	0450	3.0	1026	9.3	1722	3.2	2305	8.7
23	SU	0548	3.7	1127	8.6	1832	3.8		
24	M	0024	8.1	0707	4.2	1257	8.2	2000	3.9
25	TU	0200	8.2	0835	4.0	1428	8.5	2118	3.5
26	W	0313	8.7	0945	3.4	1533	9.1	2218	2.9
27	TH	0406	9.4	1039	2.8	1623	9.7	2307	2.4
28	F	0450	10.0	1124	2.4	1705	10.2	2348	2.1
29	SA	0528	10.3	1203	2.1	1742	10.5		
30	SU ●	0023	2.0	0602	10.6	1237	1.9	1815	10.6
31	M	0055	1.9	0633	10.7	1308	1.9	1846	10.7

NOVEMBER

Date	Day	Time	m	Time	m	Time	m	Time	m
1	TU	0124	1.9	0703	10.7	1338	1.9	1916	10.6
2	W	0153	2.0	0731	10.6	1408	2.0	1944	10.4
3	TH	0221	2.2	0758	10.4	1437	2.2	2013	10.1
4	F	0250	2.5	0826	10.0	1508	2.6	2042	9.7
5	SA	0319	3.0	0854	9.5	1540	3.1	2114	9.1
6	SU	0352	3.5	0928	9.0	1619	3.6	2154	8.6
7	M ◐	0435	4.0	1015	8.5	1712	4.0	2255	8.1
8	TU	0538	4.4	1131	8.1	1827	4.2		
9	W	0024	8.0	0706	4.4	1309	8.2	1954	3.9
10	TH	0156	8.4	0833	3.8	1431	8.8	2109	3.2
11	F	0306	9.2	0942	3.0	1534	9.7	2212	2.4
12	SA	0403	10.0	1041	2.2	1629	10.5	2308	1.7
13	SU	0455	10.8	1135	1.5	1720	11.2		
14	M ○	0001	1.1	0544	11.4	1227	1.0	1808	11.6
15	TU	0051	0.8	0630	11.7	1316	0.8	1856	11.8
16	W	0139	0.8	0716	11.8	1403	0.8	1942	11.6
17	TH	0224	1.0	0759	11.6	1449	1.0	2026	11.2
18	F	0308	1.4	0842	11.1	1533	1.6	2111	10.5
19	SA	0351	2.1	0925	10.4	1618	2.3	2156	9.7
20	SU	0436	2.8	1010	9.6	1707	3.0	2247	8.9
21	M ◑	0527	3.6	1104	8.8	1806	3.6	2350	8.3
22	TU	0633	4.0	1214	8.4	1918	3.9		
23	W	0110	8.2	0749	4.1	1337	8.3	2031	3.8
24	TH	0226	8.4	0900	3.8	1449	8.7	2135	3.4
25	F	0326	8.9	0959	3.3	1545	9.1	2227	3.0
26	SA	0415	9.4	1047	2.9	1631	9.6	2311	2.7
27	SU	0456	9.9	1129	2.6	1711	9.9	2349	2.4
28	M	0532	10.2	1206	2.3	1748	10.1		
29	TU ●	0024	2.2	0606	10.4	1242	2.1	1821	10.3
30	W	0058	2.1	0638	10.5	1315	2.0	1853	10.4

DECEMBER

Date	Day	Time	m	Time	m	Time	m	Time	m
1	TH	0131	2.1	0709	10.5	1348	2.0	1925	10.3
2	F	0202	2.2	0740	10.5	1421	2.1	1957	10.2
3	SA	0233	2.4	0812	10.2	1454	2.4	2031	9.9
4	SU	0306	2.7	0845	9.9	1528	2.7	2107	9.5
5	M	0341	3.1	0922	9.5	1608	3.0	2148	9.1
6	TU	0423	3.5	1007	9.1	1655	3.4	2240	8.7
7	W ◐	0516	3.8	1107	8.7	1756	3.6	2348	8.5
8	TH	0627	3.9	1223	8.6	1910	3.6		
9	F	0107	8.6	0748	3.7	1344	8.8	2027	3.2
10	SA	0224	9.0	0904	3.2	1457	9.4	2137	2.7
11	SU	0330	9.7	1010	2.5	1600	10.0	2239	2.1
12	M	0429	10.4	1110	1.9	1657	10.7	2337	1.5
13	TU	0522	11.0	1206	1.4	1751	11.1		
14	W ○	0031	1.2	0612	11.4	1300	1.0	1841	11.4
15	TH	0122	1.0	0700	11.6	1350	0.9	1928	11.4
16	F	0210	1.1	0746	11.5	1437	1.0	2014	11.1
17	SA	0255	1.4	0829	11.2	1522	1.4	2057	10.6
18	SU	0337	1.9	0911	10.6	1604	2.0	2139	10.0
19	M	0419	2.5	0952	10.0	1646	2.6	2222	9.3
20	TU	0500	3.1	1035	9.3	1729	3.3	2309	8.7
21	W ◑	0547	3.7	1126	8.7	1820	3.8		
22	TH	0008	8.3	0645	4.1	1232	8.3	1924	4.0
23	F	0121	8.1	0756	4.2	1348	8.2	2034	4.0
24	SA	0233	8.3	0905	4.0	1458	8.4	2137	3.7
25	SU	0333	8.8	1004	3.5	1554	8.8	2231	3.3
26	M	0422	9.2	1054	3.1	1641	9.3	2316	2.9
27	TU	0504	9.7	1137	2.7	1722	9.6	2357	2.6
28	W	0542	10.0	1218	2.3	1759	9.9		
29	TH ●	0036	2.3	0617	10.3	1257	2.1	1835	10.2
30	F	0113	2.1	0652	10.5	1334	1.9	1910	10.3
31	SA	0149	2.1	0727	10.6	1409	1.9	1946	10.3

Chart Datum: 5·88 metres below Ordnance Datum (Local)
HAT is 12·2 metres above Chart Datum

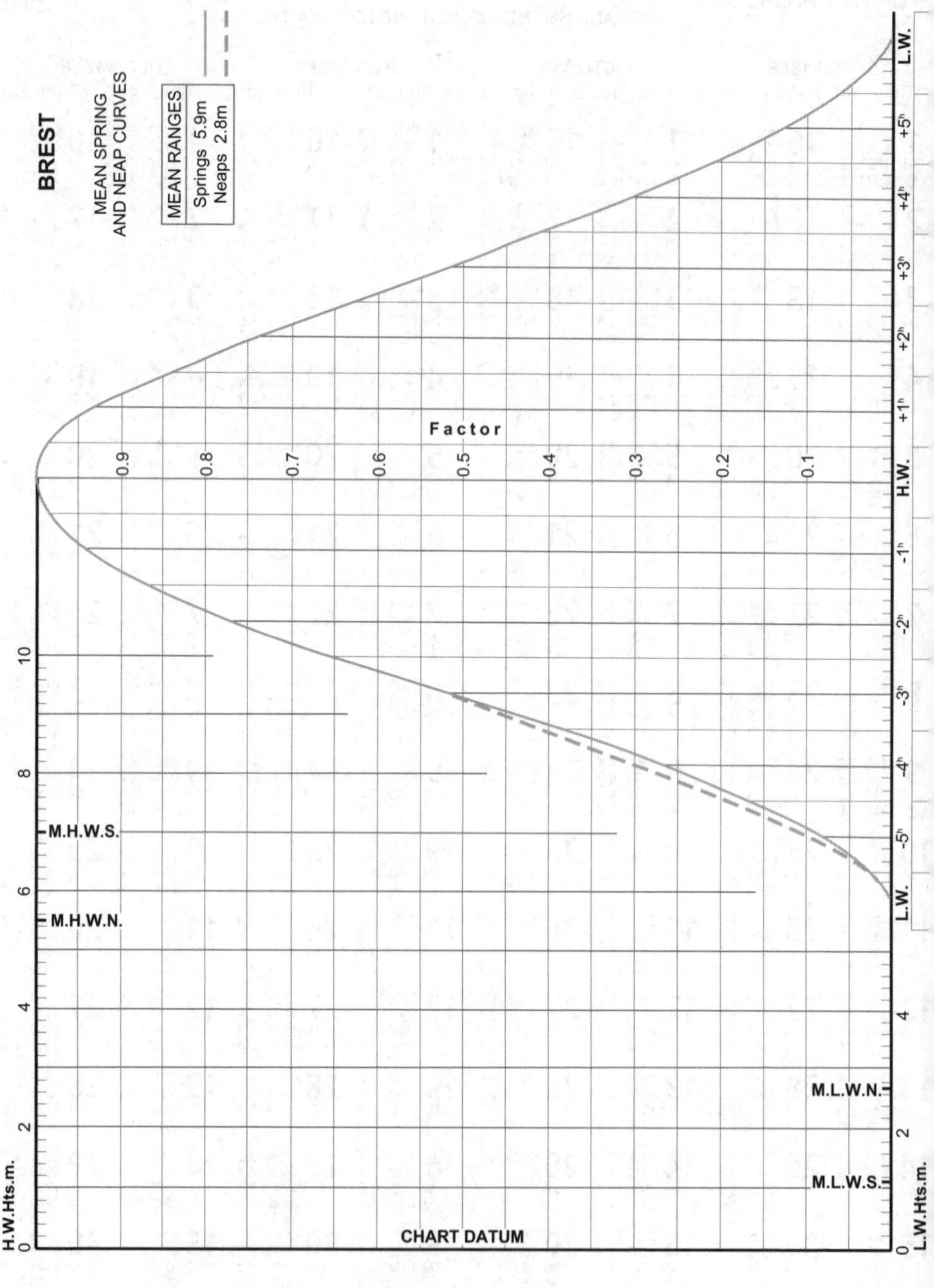
BREST
MEAN SPRING AND NEAP CURVES
MEAN RANGES
Springs 5.9m
Neaps 2.8m
Factor
0.9
0.8
0.7
0.6
0.5
0.4
0.3
0.2
0.1
L.W.
-5h
-4h
-3h
-2h
-1h
H.W.
+1h
+2h
+3h
+4h
+5h
L.W.
H.W.Hts.m.
0
2
4
6
8
10
M.H.W.S.
M.H.W.N.
CHART DATUM
L.W.Hts.m.
M.L.W.S.
M.L.W.N.

TIME ZONE -0100
(French Standard Time)
Subtract 1 hour for UT
For French Summer Time add ONE hour in **non-shaded areas**

FRANCE – BREST

LAT 48°23'N LONG 4°30'W

TIMES AND HEIGHTS OF HIGH AND LOW WATERS

Dates in amber are **SPRINGS**
Dates in yellow are **NEAPS**

2016

JANUARY

Date	Day	Time	m	Time	m	Time	m	Time	m
1	F	0321	2.5	0916	5.8	1551	2.6	2148	5.6
2	SA ◑	0408	2.8	1007	5.5	1644	2.8	2246	5.3
3	SU	0506	3.0	1112	5.3	1746	2.9	2354	5.3
4	M	0614	3.0	1224	5.3	1853	2.9		
5	TU	0102	5.4	0723	2.9	1331	5.5	1956	2.7
6	W	0203	5.7	0823	2.6	1428	5.8	2049	2.4
7	TH	0254	6.0	0914	2.3	1517	6.1	2136	2.1
8	F	0339	6.4	0959	1.9	1600	6.4	2219	1.8
9	SA	0421	6.7	1041	1.6	1641	6.6	2300	1.5
10	SU ●	0502	6.9	1122	1.3	1721	6.8	2341	1.3
11	M	0542	7.1	1203	1.1	1801	7.0		
12	TU	0022	1.2	0623	7.2	1244	1.0	1843	7.0
13	W	0104	1.2	0705	7.2	1327	1.1	1926	6.9
14	TH	0148	1.3	0749	7.1	1411	1.2	2011	6.7
15	F	0234	1.5	0835	6.8	1459	1.5	2101	6.4
16	SA	0324	1.8	0927	6.5	1553	1.8	2156	6.1
17	SU ◐	0421	2.1	1026	6.2	1653	2.1	2301	5.9
18	M	0527	2.3	1136	5.9	1803	2.3		
19	TU	0016	5.8	0642	2.4	1254	5.9	1918	2.3
20	W	0132	6.0	0757	2.2	1408	6.1	2028	2.1
21	TH	0239	6.2	0903	1.9	1510	6.3	2127	1.8
22	F	0335	6.6	0959	1.6	1601	6.6	2218	1.6
23	SA	0423	6.8	1047	1.3	1647	6.8	2303	1.4
24	SU ○	0506	7.0	1130	1.2	1727	6.9	2344	1.3
25	M	0545	7.1	1209	1.2	1805	6.9		
26	TU	0022	1.3	0621	7.1	1246	1.2	1839	6.8
27	W	0057	1.4	0654	6.9	1320	1.4	1912	6.6
28	TH	0132	1.6	0727	6.7	1354	1.7	1945	6.4
29	F	0206	1.8	0759	6.4	1428	2.0	2019	6.1
30	SA	0241	2.2	0833	6.1	1504	2.3	2056	5.8
31	SU	0320	2.5	0912	5.7	1545	2.6	2142	5.5

FEBRUARY

Date	Day	Time	m	Time	m	Time	m	Time	m
1	M ◑	0406	2.8	1002	5.4	1637	2.9	2243	5.3
2	TU	0505	3.0	1111	5.2	1745	3.0	2358	5.2
3	W	0620	3.0	1233	5.2	1902	3.0		
4	TH	0114	5.4	0736	2.8	1348	5.4	2011	2.7
5	F	0219	5.7	0841	2.4	1448	5.8	2107	2.3
6	SA	0313	6.2	0933	2.0	1537	6.2	2155	1.8
7	SU	0359	6.6	1019	1.5	1622	6.6	2240	1.4
8	M ●	0443	7.0	1103	1.1	1704	7.0	2323	1.1
9	TU	0526	7.3	1146	0.8	1746	7.2		
10	W	0006	0.9	0608	7.5	1228	0.6	1828	7.3
11	TH	0049	0.8	0650	7.6	1311	0.6	1910	7.3
12	F	0132	0.8	0733	7.5	1354	0.8	1953	7.1
13	SA	0217	1.1	0817	7.1	1440	1.2	2039	6.7
14	SU	0305	1.4	0905	6.7	1530	1.7	2131	6.3
15	M ◐	0359	1.9	1000	6.2	1628	2.1	2232	5.9
16	TU	0502	2.3	1109	5.8	1737	2.5	2349	5.7
17	W	0618	2.5	1234	5.6	1857	2.6		
18	TH	0114	5.7	0742	2.4	1356	5.7	2014	2.4
19	F	0227	6.0	0853	2.1	1500	6.1	2115	2.0
20	SA	0323	6.3	0948	1.8	1550	6.4	2205	1.7
21	SU	0410	6.6	1034	1.5	1632	6.6	2248	1.5
22	M ○	0450	6.8	1114	1.3	1709	6.8	2325	1.3
23	TU	0526	7.0	1149	1.2	1743	6.9		
24	W	0000	1.3	0558	7.0	1221	1.2	1814	6.9
25	TH	0032	1.3	0628	6.9	1252	1.3	1843	6.8
26	F	0104	1.4	0658	6.8	1323	1.5	1913	6.6
27	SA	0135	1.6	0728	6.6	1353	1.8	1944	6.3
28	SU	0207	1.9	0758	6.3	1425	2.1	2016	6.0
29	M	0242	2.2	0832	5.9	1500	2.4	2054	5.7

MARCH

Date	Day	Time	m	Time	m	Time	m	Time	m
1	TU	0322	2.5	0913	5.6	1544	2.8	2145	5.4
2	W ◑	0414	2.8	1011	5.3	1644	3.0	2258	5.2
3	TH	0522	3.0	1135	5.1	1805	3.1		
4	F	0024	5.3	0646	2.9	1304	5.3	1929	2.8
5	SA	0141	5.6	0803	2.5	1416	5.7	2036	2.4
6	SU	0243	6.1	0903	2.0	1512	6.2	2129	1.8
7	M	0334	6.6	0954	1.4	1559	6.7	2217	1.3
8	TU	0421	7.1	1041	0.9	1644	7.2	2302	0.9
9	W ●	0505	7.5	1125	0.6	1727	7.5	2346	0.6
10	TH	0548	7.8	1209	0.4	1809	7.6		
11	F	0030	0.5	0631	7.8	1252	0.4	1851	7.5
12	SA	0114	0.5	0714	7.6	1335	0.7	1933	7.3
13	SU	0159	0.8	0758	7.2	1421	1.1	2018	6.9
14	M	0246	1.3	0845	6.7	1509	1.6	2108	6.4
15	TU ◐	0339	1.8	0939	6.1	1605	2.2	2208	5.9
16	W	0440	2.3	1047	5.6	1713	2.6	2325	5.6
17	TH	0557	2.6	1213	5.4	1836	2.7		
18	F	0053	5.5	0723	2.6	1339	5.5	1956	2.5
19	SA	0208	5.8	0835	2.3	1443	5.9	2057	2.2
20	SU	0304	6.1	0929	1.9	1531	6.2	2146	1.9
21	M	0349	6.4	1013	1.6	1611	6.5	2226	1.6
22	TU	0428	6.7	1050	1.4	1646	6.7	2302	1.4
23	W ○	0501	6.8	1124	1.3	1717	6.8	2334	1.4
24	TH	0532	6.9	1154	1.3	1746	6.9		
25	F	0005	1.3	0601	6.9	1224	1.3	1815	6.8
26	SA	0036	1.4	0630	6.8	1253	1.5	1844	6.7
27	SU	0107	1.5	0659	6.6	1323	1.7	1914	6.5
28	M	0138	1.8	0729	6.4	1353	2.0	1945	6.2
29	TU	0212	2.0	0802	6.1	1428	2.3	2022	5.9
30	W	0252	2.3	0842	5.7	1510	2.6	2110	5.6
31	TH ◑	0341	2.6	0936	5.4	1606	2.9	2217	5.3

APRIL

Date	Day	Time	m	Time	m	Time	m	Time	m
1	F	0444	2.8	1053	5.2	1721	3.0	2341	5.3
2	SA	0603	2.8	1222	5.3	1848	2.8		
3	SU	0102	5.6	0724	2.5	1341	5.7	2002	2.4
4	M	0209	6.1	0831	2.0	1442	6.2	2100	1.8
5	TU	0305	6.6	0926	1.4	1533	6.8	2151	1.2
6	W	0355	7.1	1015	0.9	1620	7.2	2239	0.8
7	TH ●	0442	7.5	1102	0.5	1704	7.5	2325	0.5
8	F	0527	7.8	1147	0.4	1748	7.7		
9	SA	0010	0.4	0611	7.8	1232	0.4	1831	7.6
10	SU	0055	0.5	0655	7.6	1316	0.7	1914	7.3
11	M	0141	0.8	0740	7.2	1401	1.1	1959	6.9
12	TU	0229	1.3	0828	6.6	1449	1.7	2048	6.4
13	W	0321	1.8	0921	6.1	1544	2.2	2146	5.9
14	TH ◐	0421	2.3	1026	5.6	1649	2.6	2259	5.6
15	F	0533	2.6	1146	5.4	1807	2.8		
16	SA	0022	5.5	0653	2.6	1307	5.4	1925	2.7
17	SU	0137	5.7	0804	2.4	1412	5.7	2028	2.4
18	M	0234	5.9	0859	2.1	1501	6.1	2117	2.1
19	TU	0320	6.2	0943	1.8	1542	6.3	2158	1.8
20	W	0358	6.4	1020	1.7	1617	6.5	2234	1.6
21	TH	0432	6.6	1054	1.5	1649	6.7	2307	1.5
22	F ○	0504	6.7	1125	1.5	1719	6.8	2338	1.5
23	SA	0534	6.7	1156	1.5	1749	6.8		
24	SU	0010	1.5	0605	6.7	1226	1.6	1819	6.7
25	M	0042	1.6	0635	6.6	1257	1.7	1850	6.6
26	TU	0115	1.7	0707	6.4	1329	1.9	1923	6.4
27	W	0151	1.9	0742	6.1	1406	2.2	2002	6.1
28	TH	0231	2.1	0823	5.8	1449	2.4	2050	5.8
29	F	0320	2.4	0917	5.6	1543	2.7	2152	5.6
30	SA ◑	0419	2.6	1027	5.4	1652	2.8	2308	5.5

Chart Datum: 3·64 metres below IGN Datum
HAT is 7·9 metres above Chart Datum

TIME ZONE -0100
(French Standard Time)
Subtract 1 hour for UT
For French Summer Time add ONE hour in **non-shaded areas**

FRANCE – BREST

LAT 48°23'N LONG 4°30'W

TIMES AND HEIGHTS OF HIGH AND LOW WATERS

Dates in amber are **SPRINGS**
Dates in yellow are **NEAPS**

2016

MAY

Date	Day	Time	m	Time	m	Time	m	Time	m
1	SU	0531	2.6	1147	5.4	1812	2.7		
2	M	0025	5.7	0648	2.3	1305	5.7	1927	2.3
3	TU	0134	6.1	0757	1.9	1410	6.2	2029	1.8
4	W	0234	6.6	0856	1.4	1505	6.7	2124	1.3
5	TH	0328	7.0	0949	1.0	1555	7.1	2215	0.9
6	F	0418	7.4	1039	0.7	1642	7.4	● 2303	0.6
7	SA	0506	7.6	1126	0.6	1727	7.6	2351	0.5
8	SU	0552	7.5	1212	0.6	1812	7.5		
9	M	0037	0.6	0638	7.3	1258	0.9	1857	7.3
10	TU	0124	0.9	0724	7.0	1343	1.2	1942	6.9
11	W	0212	1.3	0811	6.5	1431	1.7	2030	6.4
12	TH	0303	1.8	0902	6.1	1522	2.2	2124	6.0
13	F	0358	2.2	1000	5.7	1620	2.5	◐ 2228	5.7
14	SA	0501	2.5	1108	5.4	1728	2.8	2339	5.5
15	SU	0611	2.6	1220	5.4	1840	2.7		
16	M	0050	5.5	0718	2.5	1327	5.5	1945	2.6
17	TU	0151	5.7	0817	2.3	1421	5.8	2039	2.3
18	W	0241	5.9	0904	2.1	1506	6.1	2123	2.1
19	TH	0323	6.1	0945	1.9	1544	6.3	2202	1.9
20	F	0400	6.3	1022	1.8	1619	6.5	2238	1.7
21	SA	0435	6.4	1056	1.7	1653	6.6	○ 2313	1.6
22	SU	0509	6.5	1130	1.6	1726	6.7	2347	1.6
23	M	0542	6.5	1203	1.6	1759	6.7		
24	TU	0021	1.6	0615	6.5	1236	1.7	1832	6.6
25	W	0056	1.6	0650	6.4	1312	1.8	1909	6.5
26	TH	0134	1.7	0728	6.2	1351	2.0	1949	6.3
27	F	0216	1.9	0812	6.0	1435	2.2	2037	6.1
28	SA	0304	2.1	0903	5.8	1527	2.4	2134	5.9
29	SU	0400	2.2	1006	5.7	1629	2.5	◑ 2241	5.8
30	M	0504	2.3	1116	5.6	1740	2.5	2351	5.9
31	TU	0615	2.2	1229	5.8	1853	2.2		

JUNE

Date	Day	Time	m	Time	m	Time	m	Time	m
1	W	0101	6.1	0724	1.9	1337	6.2	1959	1.9
2	TH	0205	6.4	0828	1.6	1437	6.6	2059	1.5
3	F	0304	6.8	0925	1.2	1532	6.9	2153	1.1
4	SA	0357	7.1	1018	1.0	1622	7.2	2245	0.9
5	SU	0448	7.2	1107	0.9	1710	7.3	● 2334	0.8
6	M	0536	7.2	1155	0.9	1756	7.3		
7	TU	0022	0.8	0623	7.1	1241	1.1	1841	7.1
8	W	0108	1.0	0708	6.8	1326	1.3	1925	6.9
9	TH	0154	1.3	0753	6.5	1410	1.7	2009	6.5
10	F	0241	1.7	0838	6.1	1457	2.0	2056	6.1
11	SA	0329	2.1	0927	5.8	1547	2.4	2148	5.8
12	SU	0422	2.4	1022	5.5	1642	2.6	◐ 2247	5.5
13	M	0520	2.6	1124	5.4	1745	2.8	2352	5.4
14	TU	0622	2.7	1229	5.4	1850	2.8		
15	W	0057	5.4	0724	2.6	1330	5.5	1951	2.6
16	TH	0155	5.6	0820	2.4	1424	5.8	2044	2.4
17	F	0245	5.8	0907	2.2	1510	6.0	2129	2.1
18	SA	0329	6.0	0950	2.0	1550	6.2	2210	1.9
19	SU	0408	6.2	1029	1.9	1628	6.4	2248	1.7
20	M	0446	6.4	1106	1.7	1705	6.6	○ 2326	1.6
21	TU	0522	6.5	1143	1.6	1741	6.7		
22	W	0003	1.5	0559	6.5	1219	1.6	1818	6.7
23	TH	0041	1.5	0637	6.5	1258	1.6	1857	6.7
24	F	0120	1.5	0717	6.4	1338	1.7	1939	6.6
25	SA	0203	1.6	0800	6.3	1423	1.8	2024	6.4
26	SU	0249	1.7	0849	6.1	1512	2.0	2116	6.2
27	M	0341	1.9	0944	5.9	1608	2.2	◑ 2215	6.1
28	TU	0439	2.1	1048	5.8	1712	2.3	2320	6.0
29	W	0546	2.1	1157	5.9	1822	2.2		
30	TH	0031	6.0	0656	2.0	1308	6.0	1933	2.0

JULY

Date	Day	Time	m	Time	m	Time	m	Time	m
1	F	0141	6.2	0803	1.8	1415	6.3	2038	1.7
2	SA	0245	6.4	0905	1.6	1514	6.6	2138	1.4
3	SU	0343	6.7	1001	1.4	1607	6.9	2231	1.2
4	M	0434	6.9	1052	1.2	1656	7.1	● 2321	1.0
5	TU	0522	6.9	1139	1.1	1742	7.1		
6	W	0007	1.0	0607	6.9	1224	1.2	1825	7.1
7	TH	0051	1.1	0649	6.8	1306	1.3	1905	6.9
8	F	0133	1.3	0729	6.6	1347	1.6	1944	6.6
9	SA	0214	1.6	0808	6.3	1427	1.9	2023	6.3
10	SU	0254	1.9	0848	6.0	1509	2.2	2104	6.0
11	M	0337	2.3	0932	5.7	1554	2.5	2151	5.6
12	TU	0425	2.6	1024	5.4	1647	2.8	◐ 2249	5.4
13	W	0522	2.8	1127	5.3	1750	2.9	2355	5.2
14	TH	0625	2.8	1234	5.3	1857	2.9		
15	F	0104	5.3	0730	2.8	1339	5.5	2001	2.7
16	SA	0205	5.5	0829	2.5	1434	5.7	2055	2.4
17	SU	0258	5.8	0918	2.3	1522	6.0	2142	2.1
18	M	0343	6.0	1002	2.0	1604	6.3	2225	1.8
19	TU	0424	6.3	1043	1.8	1645	6.6	○ 2305	1.5
20	W	0504	6.5	1123	1.5	1724	6.8	2344	1.3
21	TH	0543	6.7	1203	1.4	1803	7.0		
22	F	0024	1.2	0622	6.8	1243	1.3	1843	7.0
23	SA	0105	1.1	0703	6.8	1324	1.3	1924	7.0
24	SU	0147	1.2	0745	6.6	1407	1.4	2008	6.8
25	M	0231	1.4	0831	6.5	1454	1.7	2056	6.5
26	TU	0320	1.7	0922	6.2	1547	1.9	2150	6.2
27	W	0416	2.0	1020	6.0	1647	2.2	◑ 2253	6.0
28	TH	0520	2.2	1129	5.8	1757	2.3		
29	F	0006	5.8	0632	2.3	1246	5.8	1913	2.2
30	SA	0125	5.9	0746	2.2	1400	6.1	2026	2.0
31	SU	0235	6.1	0853	1.9	1503	6.4	2128	1.7

AUGUST

Date	Day	Time	m	Time	m	Time	m	Time	m
1	M	0333	6.4	0950	1.6	1557	6.7	2221	1.4
2	TU	0423	6.7	1039	1.4	1644	6.9	● 2309	1.2
3	W	0508	6.8	1124	1.3	1727	7.0	2351	1.1
4	TH	0549	6.9	1205	1.2	1805	7.0		
5	F	0031	1.1	0626	6.8	1243	1.3	1841	6.9
6	SA	0107	1.3	0700	6.7	1319	1.5	1914	6.7
7	SU	0142	1.5	0733	6.4	1354	1.7	1947	6.5
8	M	0217	1.8	0807	6.2	1430	2.0	2021	6.1
9	TU	0252	2.2	0843	5.9	1508	2.4	2059	5.8
10	W	0332	2.5	0926	5.5	1552	2.7	◐ 2146	5.4
11	TH	0420	2.8	1022	5.3	1649	3.0	2250	5.2
12	F	0523	3.0	1135	5.2	1800	3.0		
13	SA	0008	5.1	0638	3.0	1252	5.3	1915	2.9
14	SU	0125	5.3	0750	2.8	1359	5.6	2021	2.6
15	M	0228	5.6	0848	2.5	1453	5.9	2114	2.2
16	TU	0318	6.0	0936	2.1	1540	6.4	2200	1.8
17	W	0402	6.4	1020	1.7	1623	6.7	2243	1.4
18	TH	0444	6.7	1102	1.4	1704	7.1	○ 2324	1.1
19	F	0524	6.9	1143	1.1	1744	7.3		
20	SA	0005	0.9	0604	7.1	1224	1.0	1825	7.4
21	SU	0046	0.8	0645	7.1	1306	1.0	1906	7.3
22	M	0128	0.9	0726	7.0	1350	1.1	1949	7.1
23	TU	0212	1.2	0810	6.8	1436	1.4	2035	6.8
24	W	0300	1.5	0859	6.4	1527	1.8	2128	6.3
25	TH	0354	2.0	0956	6.0	1626	2.2	◑ 2231	5.9
26	F	0458	2.4	1107	5.7	1738	2.4	2350	5.6
27	SA	0615	2.5	1231	5.7	1901	2.5		
28	SU	0116	5.7	0735	2.4	1351	5.9	2018	2.2
29	M	0228	6.0	0844	2.1	1454	6.3	2119	1.8
30	TU	0323	6.3	0939	1.8	1545	6.6	2209	1.5
31	W	0410	6.6	1025	1.5	1629	6.9	2253	1.3

Chart Datum: 3·64 metres below IGN Datum
HAT is 7·9 metres above Chart Datum

TIME ZONE -0100
(French Standard Time)
Subtract 1 hour for UT
For French Summer Time add
ONE hour in **non-shaded areas**

FRANCE – BREST

LAT 48°23′N LONG 4°30′W

TIMES AND HEIGHTS OF HIGH AND LOW WATERS

Dates in amber are **SPRINGS**
Dates in yellow are **NEAPS**

2016

SEPTEMBER

Date	Day	Time	m	Time	m	Time	m	Time	m
1	TH ●	0450	6.8	1106	1.4	1707	7.0	2331	1.2
2	F	0526	6.9	1143	1.3	1742	7.0		
3	SA	0006	1.2	0559	6.9	1217	1.3	1813	7.0
4	SU	0038	1.3	0630	6.8	1249	1.5	1843	6.8
5	M	0110	1.5	0700	6.6	1321	1.7	1913	6.6
6	TU	0140	1.8	0730	6.4	1354	1.9	1944	6.3
7	W	0212	2.1	0802	6.1	1428	2.3	2017	5.9
8	TH	0246	2.4	0839	5.7	1507	2.6	2056	5.6
9	F ◐	0328	2.8	0927	5.4	1557	2.9	2152	5.2
10	SA	0424	3.1	1037	5.2	1704	3.1	2313	5.1
11	SU	0543	3.2	1204	5.2	1827	3.0		
12	M	0043	5.2	0708	3.0	1322	5.5	1944	2.7
13	TU	0156	5.5	0816	2.6	1422	5.9	2043	2.2
14	W	0251	6.0	0908	2.1	1512	6.4	2133	1.7
15	TH	0337	6.5	0955	1.6	1557	6.9	2218	1.2
16	F ○	0420	6.9	1039	1.2	1640	7.3	2301	0.9
17	SA	0502	7.3	1121	0.9	1722	7.6	2343	0.6
18	SU	0543	7.4	1204	0.7	1804	7.7		
19	M	0026	0.6	0624	7.5	1247	0.7	1846	7.6
20	TU	0109	0.7	0706	7.3	1331	0.9	1930	7.3
21	W	0153	1.1	0750	7.0	1418	1.3	2017	6.8
22	TH	0241	1.5	0839	6.5	1509	1.8	2110	6.3
23	F ◑	0334	2.1	0937	6.1	1610	2.2	2215	5.8
24	SA	0439	2.5	1050	5.7	1724	2.6	2338	5.5
25	SU	0559	2.7	1219	5.6	1850	2.6		
26	M	0105	5.6	0722	2.6	1338	5.9	2005	2.3
27	TU	0214	5.9	0829	2.3	1439	6.2	2103	1.9
28	W	0307	6.3	0922	1.9	1527	6.6	2150	1.6
29	TH	0350	6.6	1006	1.6	1608	6.8	2231	1.4
30	F	0427	6.8	1044	1.5	1643	6.9	2306	1.3

OCTOBER

Date	Day	Time	m	Time	m	Time	m	Time	m
1	SA ●	0501	6.9	1118	1.4	1715	7.0	2339	1.3
2	SU	0531	6.9	1150	1.4	1745	6.9		
3	M	0009	1.4	0600	6.9	1221	1.5	1814	6.8
4	TU	0039	1.6	0630	6.7	1252	1.7	1844	6.6
5	W	0109	1.8	0659	6.5	1324	1.9	1913	6.4
6	TH	0139	2.1	0730	6.3	1357	2.2	1945	6.1
7	F	0212	2.4	0805	5.9	1435	2.5	2023	5.7
8	SA	0252	2.7	0849	5.6	1522	2.8	2114	5.4
9	SU ◐	0344	3.0	0953	5.4	1623	3.0	2229	5.2
10	M	0456	3.2	1119	5.3	1742	3.0		
11	TU	0000	5.2	0624	3.0	1241	5.5	1903	2.7
12	W	0119	5.6	0740	2.6	1347	6.0	2009	2.2
13	TH	0219	6.1	0837	2.1	1442	6.5	2102	1.7
14	F	0309	6.6	0927	1.5	1530	7.0	2150	1.2
15	SA	0355	7.1	1013	1.1	1615	7.4	2236	0.8
16	SU ○	0439	7.4	1059	0.7	1700	7.7	2321	0.6
17	M	0522	7.6	1143	0.6	1744	7.8		
18	TU	0005	0.5	0604	7.7	1228	0.6	1828	7.7
19	W	0050	0.7	0648	7.5	1314	0.8	1914	7.3
20	TH	0135	1.1	0733	7.1	1402	1.2	2002	6.8
21	F	0224	1.6	0823	6.6	1454	1.7	2055	6.3
22	SA ◑	0317	2.1	0920	6.2	1554	2.2	2200	5.8
23	SU	0421	2.6	1032	5.8	1706	2.6	2318	5.5
24	M	0537	2.8	1155	5.7	1827	2.6		
25	TU	0040	5.6	0657	2.7	1312	5.8	1939	2.4
26	W	0148	5.8	0804	2.4	1413	6.1	2037	2.1
27	TH	0240	6.2	0856	2.1	1501	6.4	2123	1.8
28	F	0323	6.4	0940	1.8	1541	6.6	2203	1.7
29	SA	0401	6.7	1018	1.7	1616	6.7	2238	1.5
30	SU ●	0434	6.8	1052	1.6	1648	6.8	2311	1.5
31	M	0505	6.9	1124	1.5	1719	6.8	2342	1.5

NOVEMBER

Date	Day	Time	m	Time	m	Time	m	Time	m
1	TU	0535	6.9	1156	1.6	1749	6.8		
2	W	0012	1.6	0606	6.8	1228	1.7	1820	6.6
3	TH	0043	1.8	0636	6.6	1300	1.8	1851	6.4
4	F	0115	2.0	0708	6.4	1334	2.1	1924	6.2
5	SA	0149	2.3	0743	6.2	1413	2.3	2002	5.9
6	SU	0229	2.6	0827	5.9	1458	2.6	2052	5.6
7	M ◐	0319	2.8	0925	5.6	1555	2.8	2159	5.4
8	TU	0423	3.0	1040	5.5	1704	2.8	2320	5.4
9	W	0542	2.9	1159	5.6	1821	2.6		
10	TH	0038	5.6	0659	2.6	1309	6.0	1931	2.2
11	F	0143	6.1	0803	2.1	1409	6.5	2030	1.7
12	SA	0239	6.6	0858	1.6	1502	7.0	2123	1.2
13	SU	0329	7.1	0949	1.1	1552	7.4	2212	0.9
14	M ○	0416	7.4	1037	0.8	1639	7.6	2300	0.7
15	TU	0502	7.6	1125	0.6	1726	7.7	2347	0.6
16	W	0548	7.7	1212	0.6	1813	7.6		
17	TH	0033	0.8	0633	7.5	1259	0.8	1900	7.3
18	F	0120	1.1	0719	7.2	1348	1.2	1948	6.8
19	SA	0208	1.6	0808	6.8	1439	1.7	2040	6.4
20	SU	0300	2.0	0902	6.3	1535	2.1	2139	5.9
21	M ◑	0357	2.5	1004	5.9	1639	2.5	2246	5.6
22	TU	0504	2.7	1117	5.7	1749	2.6	2358	5.5
23	W	0616	2.8	1230	5.7	1858	2.6		
24	TH	0106	5.7	0725	2.6	1334	5.8	1959	2.4
25	F	0204	5.9	0822	2.4	1427	6.1	2049	2.2
26	SA	0251	6.2	0909	2.1	1511	6.3	2132	2.0
27	SU	0331	6.4	0950	1.9	1549	6.5	2210	1.8
28	M	0408	6.6	1027	1.8	1623	6.6	2244	1.7
29	TU ●	0441	6.7	1101	1.7	1657	6.6	2318	1.7
30	W	0514	6.8	1135	1.6	1729	6.7	2351	1.7

DECEMBER

Date	Day	Time	m	Time	m	Time	m	Time	m
1	TH	0547	6.8	1209	1.7	1802	6.6		
2	F	0024	1.8	0620	6.7	1243	1.7	1835	6.5
3	SA	0058	1.9	0654	6.6	1318	1.9	1910	6.3
4	SU	0134	2.1	0731	6.4	1357	2.0	1950	6.1
5	M	0215	2.3	0814	6.2	1441	2.2	2037	5.9
6	TU	0302	2.5	0905	6.0	1532	2.4	2134	5.7
7	W ◐	0358	2.6	1007	5.8	1632	2.5	2243	5.6
8	TH	0505	2.7	1118	5.8	1742	2.5	2356	5.7
9	F	0618	2.5	1229	6.0	1853	2.2		
10	SA	0106	6.0	0728	2.2	1336	6.3	1959	1.9
11	SU	0209	6.4	0830	1.8	1436	6.7	2057	1.5
12	M	0305	6.9	0927	1.3	1532	7.1	2151	1.1
13	TU	0357	7.2	1020	1.0	1623	7.3	2242	0.9
14	W ○	0447	7.5	1110	0.8	1713	7.4	2331	0.8
15	TH	0534	7.6	1159	0.7	1800	7.4		
16	F	0019	0.9	0621	7.5	1247	0.8	1847	7.2
17	SA	0105	1.1	0706	7.3	1334	1.1	1933	6.9
18	SU	0151	1.4	0752	6.9	1421	1.5	2020	6.5
19	M	0238	1.8	0838	6.5	1510	1.9	2108	6.1
20	TU	0327	2.2	0929	6.1	1602	2.3	2202	5.7
21	W ◑	0422	2.6	1026	5.8	1700	2.6	2304	5.5
22	TH	0523	2.8	1132	5.5	1804	2.7		
23	F	0010	5.5	0630	2.8	1240	5.5	1909	2.7
24	SA	0115	5.6	0736	2.7	1344	5.6	2008	2.6
25	SU	0213	5.8	0833	2.5	1437	5.9	2058	2.3
26	M	0301	6.1	0921	2.3	1521	6.1	2141	2.1
27	TU	0342	6.3	1002	2.0	1601	6.3	2220	1.9
28	W	0420	6.5	1040	1.8	1637	6.5	2257	1.8
29	TH ●	0456	6.7	1116	1.7	1712	6.6	2333	1.7
30	F	0531	6.8	1152	1.6	1747	6.6		
31	SA	0008	1.6	0607	6.8	1227	1.5	1823	6.6

Chart Datum: 3·64 metres below IGN Datum
HAT is 7·9 metres above Chart Datum

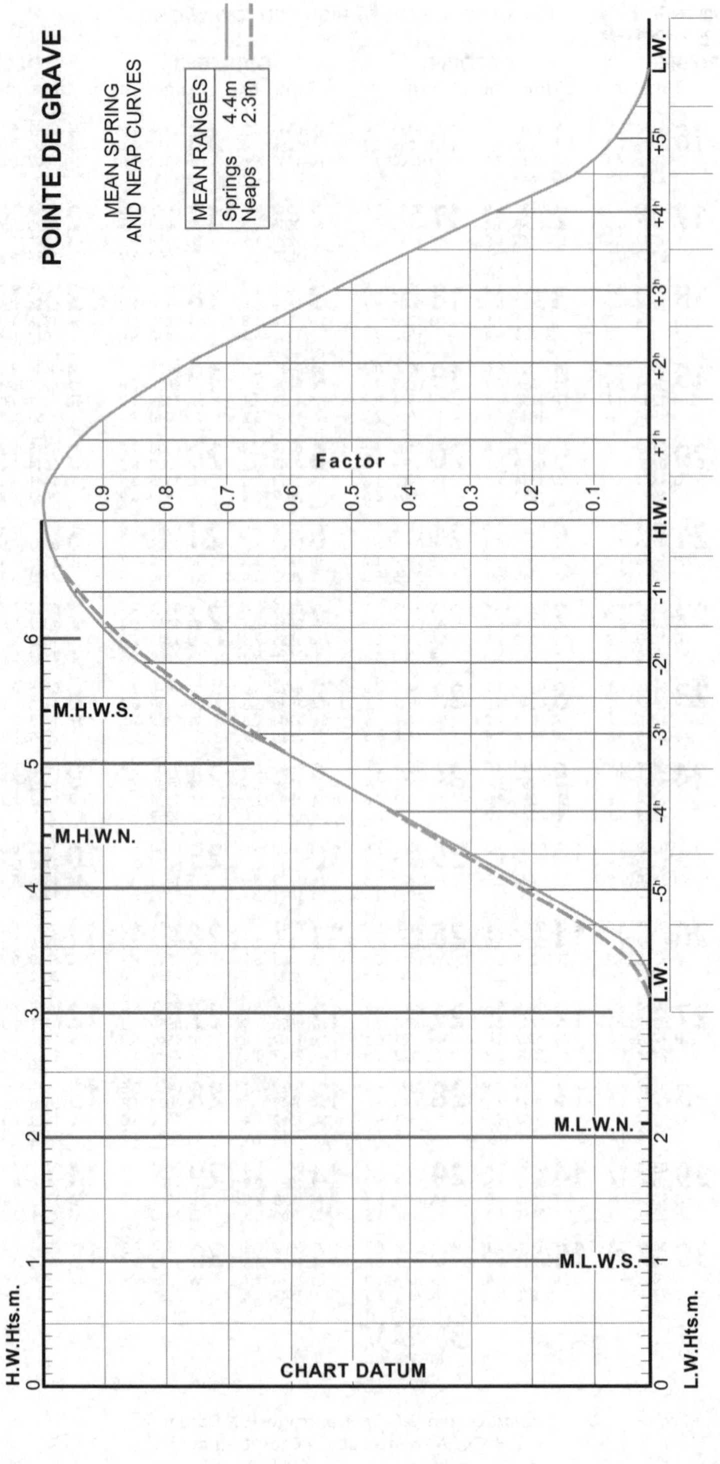
POINTE DE GRAVE
MEAN SPRING AND NEAP CURVES
MEAN RANGES
Springs 4.4m
Neaps 2.3m
Factor
0.9
0.8
0.7
0.6
0.5
0.4
0.3
0.2
0.1
H.W.Hts.m.
L.W.Hts.m.
CHART DATUM
M.H.W.S.
M.H.W.N.
M.L.W.N.
M.L.W.S.
L.W.
-5h
-4h
-3h
-2h
-1h
H.W.
+1h
+2h
+3h
+4h
+5h
L.W.

TIME ZONE -0100
(French Standard Time)
Subtract 1 hour for UT
For French Summer Time add ONE hour in **non-shaded areas**

FRANCE – POINTE DE GRAVE

LAT 45°34'N LONG 1°04'W

TIMES AND HEIGHTS OF HIGH AND LOW WATERS

Dates in amber are **SPRINGS**
Dates in yellow are **NEAPS**

2016

JANUARY

Date	Day	Time	m	Time	m	Time	m	Time	m
1	F	0308	1.9	0935	4.5	1541	2.0	2208	4.3
2	SA	0359	2.2	1033	4.3	1637	2.2	◑ 2313	4.2
3	SU	0501	2.3	1141	4.2	1742	2.3		
4	M	0023	4.2	0609	2.3	1253	4.2	1848	2.2
5	TU	0129	4.3	0713	2.2	1358	4.3	1948	2.1
6	W	0224	4.5	0810	2.1	1451	4.5	2039	1.9
7	TH	0310	4.7	0900	1.8	1535	4.7	2124	1.7
8	F	0351	4.9	0945	1.6	1615	4.9	2206	1.5
9	SA	0431	5.1	1028	1.4	1655	5.1	2247	1.4
10	SU	0511	5.3	1110	1.2	1734	5.2	● 2329	1.2
11	M	0551	5.4	1152	1.1	1814	5.2		
12	TU	0010	1.2	0633	5.5	1234	1.1	1856	5.2
13	W	0052	1.2	0716	5.5	1316	1.1	1940	5.1
14	TH	0135	1.2	0802	5.4	1359	1.2	2027	5.0
15	F	0220	1.3	0851	5.2	1445	1.3	2120	4.8
16	SA	0309	1.5	0947	5.0	1537	1.5	2223	4.7
17	SU	0407	1.7	1053	4.8	1639	1.7	◐ 2337	4.6
18	M	0514	1.8	1209	4.7	1750	1.8		
19	TU	0053	4.6	0629	1.8	1325	4.7	1905	1.8
20	W	0201	4.7	0743	1.7	1432	4.8	2015	1.7
21	TH	0300	4.9	0849	1.6	1530	4.9	2114	1.5
22	F	0352	5.1	0945	1.4	1619	5.0	2204	1.3
23	SA	0437	5.2	1034	1.2	1702	5.1	2249	1.2
24	SU	0518	5.3	1118	1.1	1741	5.2	○ 2330	1.2
25	M	0557	5.3	1158	1.1	1818	5.2		
26	TU	0009	1.2	0632	5.3	1235	1.2	1851	5.1
27	W	0044	1.2	0705	5.2	1310	1.3	1922	5.0
28	TH	0119	1.4	0736	5.0	1343	1.4	1953	4.8
29	F	0153	1.5	0809	4.9	1417	1.6	2028	4.6
30	SA	0229	1.7	0846	4.6	1454	1.8	2109	4.4
31	SU	0309	2.0	0931	4.4	1536	2.1	2203	4.2

FEBRUARY

Date	Day	Time	m	Time	m	Time	m	Time	m
1	M	0358	2.2	1030	4.2	1632	2.3	◑ 2312	4.1
2	TU	0504	2.3	1145	4.1	1747	2.4		
3	W	0031	4.1	0621	2.3	1308	4.1	1901	2.3
4	TH	0143	4.3	0730	2.2	1416	4.3	2004	2.1
5	F	0240	4.6	0829	1.9	1509	4.6	2057	1.8
6	SA	0327	4.8	0921	1.6	1554	4.8	2145	1.5
7	SU	0410	5.1	1008	1.4	1637	5.1	2229	1.3
8	M	0453	5.4	1053	1.1	1718	5.3	● 2313	1.1
9	TU	0535	5.6	1136	0.9	1759	5.4	2356	0.9
10	W	0617	5.7	1219	0.8	1841	5.4		
11	TH	0038	0.9	0701	5.7	1301	0.8	1924	5.4
12	F	0120	0.9	0746	5.6	1343	0.9	2009	5.2
13	SA	0203	1.0	0833	5.3	1426	1.1	2057	5.0
14	SU	0250	1.3	0925	5.0	1515	1.4	2154	4.7
15	M	0343	1.5	1028	4.7	1613	1.7	◐ 2307	4.5
16	TU	0449	1.8	1148	4.5	1724	1.9		
17	W	0032	4.4	0609	1.9	1312	4.4	1846	2.0
18	TH	0149	4.5	0731	1.9	1425	4.5	2002	1.9
19	F	0252	4.7	0840	1.7	1522	4.7	2102	1.7
20	SA	0343	4.9	0935	1.4	1608	4.9	2152	1.4
21	SU	0425	5.1	1020	1.3	1647	5.0	2234	1.3
22	M	0502	5.2	1101	1.2	1721	5.1	○ 2313	1.2
23	TU	0536	5.3	1138	1.1	1753	5.1	2348	1.2
24	W	0607	5.3	1211	1.1	1822	5.1		
25	TH	0021	1.2	0636	5.2	1243	1.2	1850	5.1
26	F	0052	1.3	0705	5.1	1313	1.3	1919	5.0
27	SA	0122	1.4	0734	4.9	1342	1.5	1951	4.8
28	SU	0153	1.6	0807	4.7	1413	1.7	2026	4.6
29	M	0227	1.8	0844	4.5	1448	1.9	2108	4.4

MARCH

Date	Day	Time	m	Time	m	Time	m	Time	m
1	TU	0308	2.0	0932	4.3	1532	2.2	2207	4.2
2	W	0402	2.2	1041	4.1	1636	2.4	◑ 2328	4.1
3	TH	0522	2.3	1212	4.0	1807	2.4		
4	F	0055	4.2	0645	2.2	1338	4.2	1925	2.2
5	SA	0204	4.5	0755	2.0	1439	4.5	2027	1.9
6	SU	0258	4.8	0853	1.6	1529	4.8	2120	1.6
7	M	0346	5.1	0944	1.3	1614	5.1	2207	1.2
8	TU	0431	5.4	1031	1.0	1657	5.4	2253	0.9
9	W	0514	5.7	1116	0.8	1740	5.5	● 2337	0.7
10	TH	0558	5.8	1159	0.7	1822	5.6		
11	F	0020	0.7	0642	5.8	1241	0.7	1905	5.5
12	SA	0102	0.7	0727	5.6	1323	0.8	1949	5.4
13	SU	0145	0.9	0814	5.4	1406	1.1	2036	5.1
14	M	0230	1.1	0905	5.0	1453	1.4	2129	4.8
15	TU	0322	1.5	1007	4.6	1548	1.7	◐ 2239	4.5
16	W	0426	1.8	1129	4.3	1659	2.0		
17	TH	0009	4.3	0548	2.0	1257	4.3	1823	2.1
18	F	0131	4.4	0714	1.9	1410	4.4	1942	2.0
19	SA	0237	4.6	0822	1.7	1506	4.6	2043	1.8
20	SU	0327	4.8	0915	1.5	1549	4.8	2131	1.5
21	M	0406	5.0	0958	1.4	1624	4.9	2213	1.4
22	TU	0440	5.1	1037	1.2	1655	5.0	2250	1.3
23	W	0510	5.2	1112	1.2	1724	5.1	○ 2323	1.2
24	TH	0539	5.2	1143	1.2	1753	5.1	2354	1.2
25	F	0607	5.2	1213	1.2	1821	5.1		
26	SA	0024	1.3	0636	5.1	1241	1.3	1850	5.0
27	SU	0053	1.3	0705	5.0	1310	1.5	1920	4.9
28	M	0123	1.5	0736	4.8	1339	1.6	1954	4.8
29	TU	0156	1.6	0811	4.6	1413	1.8	2034	4.6
30	W	0235	1.8	0856	4.4	1455	2.0	2127	4.4
31	TH	0324	2.0	0959	4.2	1552	2.2	◑ 2240	4.2

APRIL

Date	Day	Time	m	Time	m	Time	m	Time	m
1	F	0434	2.2	1126	4.1	1716	2.3		
2	SA	0006	4.3	0600	2.2	1257	4.2	1842	2.2
3	SU	0124	4.5	0716	1.9	1406	4.5	1950	1.9
4	M	0225	4.8	0819	1.6	1500	4.9	2048	1.5
5	TU	0317	5.2	0915	1.3	1548	5.2	2140	1.2
6	W	0406	5.5	1005	0.9	1633	5.4	2229	0.9
7	TH	0452	5.7	1052	0.7	1717	5.6	● 2315	0.7
8	F	0538	5.8	1137	0.6	1801	5.7	2359	0.6
9	SA	0623	5.8	1220	0.7	1845	5.6		
10	SU	0043	0.6	0709	5.6	1302	0.8	1930	5.4
11	M	0126	0.8	0757	5.3	1345	1.1	2016	5.1
12	TU	0211	1.1	0847	4.9	1431	1.4	2108	4.8
13	W	0302	1.4	0948	4.6	1525	1.7	2214	4.5
14	TH	0403	1.8	1106	4.3	1632	2.0	◐ 2338	4.3
15	F	0521	2.0	1230	4.2	1752	2.1		
16	SA	0100	4.3	0643	2.0	1341	4.3	1910	2.1
17	SU	0207	4.5	0752	1.8	1437	4.5	2013	1.9
18	M	0258	4.6	0845	1.6	1519	4.7	2102	1.7
19	TU	0337	4.8	0929	1.5	1554	4.8	2144	1.5
20	W	0411	4.9	1007	1.4	1625	4.9	2221	1.4
21	TH	0441	5.0	1041	1.3	1654	5.0	2254	1.3
22	F	0511	5.1	1112	1.3	1724	5.1	○ 2326	1.3
23	SA	0541	5.1	1142	1.3	1755	5.1	2357	1.3
24	SU	0611	5.0	1212	1.3	1826	5.1		
25	M	0028	1.3	0641	4.9	1242	1.4	1857	5.0
26	TU	0100	1.4	0713	4.8	1314	1.6	1932	4.9
27	W	0134	1.5	0750	4.6	1350	1.7	2014	4.7
28	TH	0214	1.7	0836	4.5	1433	1.9	2106	4.5
29	F	0302	1.8	0936	4.3	1527	2.1	2211	4.4
30	SA	0404	2.0	1054	4.2	1641	2.2	◑ 2328	4.4

Chart Datum: 2·83 metres below IGN Datum
HAT is 6·1 metres above Chart Datum

TIME ZONE -0100
(French Standard Time)
Subtract 1 hour for UT
For French Summer Time add ONE hour in **non-shaded areas**

FRANCE – POINTE DE GRAVE

LAT 45°34'N LONG 1°04'W

TIMES AND HEIGHTS OF HIGH AND LOW WATERS

Dates in amber are **SPRING**
Dates in yellow are **NEAPS**

201

MAY

Day	Time	m	Day	Time	m
1 SU	0521 1219 1801	2.0 4.3 2.1	16 M	0118 0707 1352 1930	4.3 1.9 4.3 2.0
2 M	0044 0636 1330 1911	4.6 1.8 4.6 1.8	17 TU	0215 0805 1439 2024	4.4 1.8 4.5 1.8
3 TU	0151 0743 1429 2014	4.8 1.5 4.9 1.5	18 W	0259 0852 1517 2109	4.6 1.7 4.7 1.7
4 W	0248 0843 1520 2111	5.1 1.3 5.2 1.2	19 TH	0337 0932 1552 2148	4.7 1.5 4.8 1.6
5 TH	0340 0937 1608 2203	5.4 1.0 5.4 0.9	20 F	0411 1008 1625 2224	4.8 1.5 4.9 1.5
6 F	0430 1027 1655 ● 2252	5.6 0.8 5.5 0.7	21 SA	0445 1041 1659 ○ 2258	4.9 1.4 5.0 1.4
7 SA	0518 1114 1741 2339	5.7 0.7 5.6 0.7	22 SU	0518 1114 1732 2332	4.9 1.4 5.1 1.3
8 SU	0606 1158 1827	5.6 0.8 5.5	23 M	0551 1147 1806	4.9 1.4 5.1
9 M	0024 0653 1242 1913	0.7 5.5 0.9 5.4	24 TU	0007 0624 1221 1841	1.3 4.9 1.4 5.0
10 TU	0109 0741 1326 2000	0.9 5.2 1.1 5.1	25 W	0042 0659 1257 1919	1.3 4.8 1.5 4.9
11 W	0154 0830 1411 2049	1.1 4.9 1.4 4.9	26 TH	0119 0738 1335 2002	1.4 4.7 1.6 4.8
12 TH	0243 0925 1502 2147	1.4 4.6 1.7 4.6	27 F	0200 0824 1419 2052	1.5 4.6 1.7 4.7
13 F	0338 1031 1601 ◐ 2256	1.7 4.3 1.9 4.4	28 SA	0247 0920 1511 2151	1.6 4.4 1.8 4.6
14 SA	0445 1143 1712	1.9 4.2 2.1	29 SU	0343 1028 1615 ◑ 2258	1.7 4.4 1.9 4.6
15 SU	0010 0558 1253 1825	4.3 2.0 4.2 2.1	30 M	0450 1144 1727	1.8 4.4 1.9
			31 TU	0010 0601 1257 1836	4.7 1.7 4.6 1.7

JUNE

Day	Time	m	Day	Time	m
1 W	0119 0709 1359 1942	4.8 1.5 4.8 1.5	16 TH	0214 0808 1438 2029	4.3 1.9 4.5 1.9
2 TH	0221 0813 1454 2043	5.0 1.3 5.0 1.3	17 F	0301 0854 1520 2114	4.5 1.7 4.6 1.7
3 F	0318 0911 1546 2139	5.2 1.1 5.2 1.0	18 SA	0342 0935 1559 2154	4.6 1.6 4.8 1.6
4 SA	0411 1004 1635 2232	5.3 1.0 5.4 0.9	19 SU	0420 1014 1636 2233	4.7 1.5 4.9 1.4
5 SU	0502 1053 1723 ● 2321	5.4 0.9 5.5 0.8	20 M	0457 1051 1712 ○ 2311	4.8 1.4 5.0 1.3
6 M	0550 1140 1810	5.4 0.9 5.4	21 TU	0533 1128 1749 2350	4.9 1.3 5.1 1.2
7 TU	0008 0638 1224 1856	0.8 5.3 1.0 5.3	22 W	0609 1206 1827	4.9 1.3 5.1
8 W	0053 0724 1307 1942	0.9 5.1 1.1 5.1	23 TH	0028 0647 1244 1907	1.2 4.9 1.3 5.1
9 TH	0137 0809 1351 2027	1.1 4.8 1.3 4.9	24 F	0108 0728 1324 1950	1.2 4.8 1.4 5.0
10 F	0222 0855 1437 2114	1.3 4.6 1.6 4.7	25 SA	0149 0812 1408 2038	1.3 4.7 1.5 4.9
11 SA	0310 0945 1528 2207	1.6 4.4 1.8 4.5	26 SU	0233 0904 1456 2131	1.4 4.6 1.6 4.8
12 SU	0404 1043 1626 ◐ 2308	1.8 4.2 2.0 4.3	27 M	0324 1003 1552 ◑ 2232	1.5 4.5 1.7 4.7
13 M	0505 1148 1732	2.0 4.1 2.1	28 TU	0423 1113 1657 2341	1.6 4.5 1.7 4.7
14 TU	0013 0611 1252 1837	4.2 2.0 4.2 2.1	29 W	0530 1226 1807	1.6 4.5 1.7
15 W	0117 0714 1350 1937	4.2 2.0 4.3 2.0	30 TH	0053 0640 1334 1916	4.7 1.6 4.7 1.6

JULY

Day	Time	m	Day	Time	m
1 F	0201 0748 1435 2022	4.8 1.5 4.9 1.4	16 SA	0225 0818 1450 2041	4.3 1.9 4.5 1.8
2 SA	0302 0851 1529 2122	5.0 1.3 5.1 1.2	17 SU	0314 0906 1533 2127	4.5 1.7 4.7 1.6
3 SU	0358 0947 1620 2217	5.1 1.1 5.2 1.0	18 M	0357 0949 1613 2211	4.6 1.6 4.9 1.4
4 M	0449 1038 1708 ● 2308	5.2 1.0 5.3 0.9	19 TU	0437 1030 1652 ○ 2252	4.8 1.4 5.1 1.3
5 TU	0536 1124 1755 2354	5.2 1.0 5.3 0.9	20 W	0516 1111 1731 2333	4.9 1.3 5.2 1.1
6 W	0621 1208 1838	5.1 1.0 5.3	21 TH	0554 1151 1811	5.0 1.2 5.3
7 TH	0038 0703 1249 1920	1.0 5.0 1.1 5.1	22 F	0014 0633 1231 1852	1.0 5.0 1.1 5.3
8 F	0119 0742 1329 1958	1.1 4.9 1.3 5.0	23 SA	0054 0714 1312 1935	1.0 5.0 1.1 5.2
9 SA	0158 0819 1410 2036	1.3 4.7 1.4 4.7	24 SU	0135 0757 1354 2021	1.1 4.9 1.2 5.1
10 SU	0239 0857 1452 2118	1.5 4.5 1.7 4.5	25 M	0217 0845 1439 2111	1.2 4.8 1.3 5.0
11 M	0322 0943 1540 2208	1.7 4.3 1.9 4.3	26 TU	0304 0939 1530 2209	1.3 4.7 1.5 4.8
12 TU	0412 1041 1637 ◐ 2308	1.9 4.2 2.1 4.2	27 W	0359 1045 1632 ◑ 2318	1.5 4.5 1.6 4.6
13 W	0512 1148 1742	2.1 4.1 2.2	28 TH	0504 1202 1743	1.7 4.5 1.7
14 TH	0016 0618 1258 1848	4.1 2.1 4.1 2.1	29 F	0035 0617 1318 1859	4.6 1.7 4.5 1.7
15 F	0125 0722 1359 1948	4.1 2.1 4.3 2.0	30 SA	0149 0731 1423 2011	4.6 1.7 4.7 1.5
			31 SU	0253 0839 1520 2114	4.7 1.5 4.9 1.3

AUGUST

Day	Time	m	Day	Time	m
1 M	0349 0936 1610 2208	4.9 1.3 5.1 1.2	16 TU	0333 0926 1550 2148	4.6 1.6 4.9 1.4
2 TU	0437 1026 1655 ● 2256	5.0 1.2 5.2 1.0	17 W	0415 1010 1630 2232	4.8 1.4 5.2 1.2
3 W	0521 1110 1737 2339	5.1 1.1 5.3 1.0	18 TH	0455 1052 1711 ○ 2314	5.0 1.2 5.4 1.0
4 TH	0601 1151 1816	5.1 1.1 5.2	19 F	0535 1133 1752 2356	5.2 1.0 5.5 0.9
5 F	0019 0637 1229 1851	1.0 5.0 1.1 5.2	20 SA	0615 1215 1833	5.3 0.9 5.5
6 SA	0056 0709 1305 1924	1.1 4.9 1.2 5.0	21 SU	0037 0657 1255 1917	0.9 5.3 0.9 5.5
7 SU	0131 0740 1340 1956	1.2 4.8 1.4 4.8	22 M	0117 0739 1337 2002	0.9 5.2 1.0 5.3
8 M	0205 0813 1416 2032	1.4 4.6 1.6 4.6	23 TU	0159 0825 1421 2052	1.1 5.0 1.2 5.1
9 TU	0241 0851 1455 2114	1.6 4.4 1.8 4.4	24 W	0244 0917 1510 2150	1.3 4.8 1.4 4.8
10 W	0321 0940 1541 ◐ 2208	1.9 4.2 2.0 4.2	25 TH	0337 1021 1611 ◑ 2302	1.5 4.5 1.7 4.5
11 TH	0410 1045 1642 2318	2.1 4.1 2.2 4.0	26 F	0441 1145 1726	1.8 4.4 1.8
12 F	0519 1204 1758	2.3 4.0 2.3	27 SA	0027 0600 1308 1850	4.4 1.9 4.5 1.8
13 SA	0037 0635 1320 1909	4.0 2.3 4.2 2.2	28 SU	0144 0721 1417 2005	4.5 1.9 4.7 1.7
14 SU	0150 0742 1419 2010	4.1 2.1 4.4 2.0	29 M	0248 0830 1513 2106	4.6 1.7 4.9 1.4
15 M	0247 0838 1507 2102	4.4 1.9 4.7 1.7	30 TU	0340 0925 1600 2156	4.8 1.4 5.1 1.2
			31 W	0423 1012 1640 2240	5.0 1.3 5.2 1.1

Chart Datum: 2·83 metres below IGN Datum
HAT is 6·1 metres above Chart Datum

TIME ZONE -0100
(French Standard Time)
Subtract 1 hour for UT
For French Summer Time add ONE hour in **non-shaded areas**

FRANCE – POINTE DE GRAVE

LAT 45°34′N LONG 1°04′W

TIMES AND HEIGHTS OF HIGH AND LOW WATERS

Dates in amber are **SPRINGS**
Dates in yellow are **NEAPS**

2016

SEPTEMBER

Date	Day	Time	m	Time	m	Time	m	Time	m
1	TH	0501	5.1	1053	1.2	1717	5.2	● 2319	1.1
2	F	0535	5.1	1131	1.1	1750	5.2	2355	1.1
3	SA	0606	5.1	1206	1.2	1820	5.2		
4	SU	0029	1.2	0635	5.0	1238	1.2	1849	5.1
5	M	0100	1.3	0704	4.9	1309	1.4	1919	4.9
6	TU	0130	1.5	0735	4.8	1341	1.6	1951	4.7
7	W	0201	1.7	0809	4.6	1414	1.8	2028	4.5
8	TH	0235	1.9	0851	4.4	1453	2.0	2115	4.2
9	F	0316	2.1	0947	4.2	1544	2.2	◐ 2221	4.0
10	SA	0414	2.3	1107	4.1	1701	2.4	2350	4.0
11	SU	0543	2.4	1235	4.1	1828	2.3		
12	M	0115	4.1	0704	2.3	1344	4.4	1936	2.1
13	TU	0217	4.4	0806	2.0	1437	4.7	2032	1.7
14	W	0306	4.7	0858	1.7	1523	5.0	2122	1.4
15	TH	0350	5.0	0945	1.4	1606	5.3	2207	1.1
16	F	0432	5.2	1029	1.1	1648	5.5	○ 2251	0.9
17	SA	0513	5.4	1112	0.9	1730	5.7	2334	0.8
18	SU	0554	5.5	1155	0.8	1814	5.7		
19	M	0016	0.8	0637	5.5	1236	0.8	1858	5.6
20	TU	0058	0.9	0720	5.4	1319	0.9	1945	5.4
21	W	0140	1.1	0806	5.1	1403	1.1	2035	5.1
22	TH	0225	1.3	0858	4.9	1452	1.4	2135	4.7
23	F	0317	1.6	1003	4.6	1553	1.7	◑ 2252	4.5
24	SA	0422	1.9	1132	4.4	1711	2.0		
25	SU	0021	4.4	0544	2.1	1258	4.5	1839	1.9
26	M	0136	4.5	0707	2.0	1407	4.7	1953	1.8
27	TU	0237	4.6	0814	1.8	1502	4.9	2050	1.5
28	W	0325	4.8	0907	1.6	1544	5.0	2136	1.3
29	TH	0403	5.0	0952	1.4	1620	5.1	2217	1.2
30	F	0436	5.1	1031	1.3	1652	5.2	2254	1.2

OCTOBER

Date	Day	Time	m	Time	m	Time	m	Time	m
1	SA	0507	5.1	1107	1.2	1722	5.2	● 2327	1.2
2	SU	0536	5.1	1140	1.3	1751	5.2	2358	1.3
3	M	0605	5.1	1210	1.3	1819	5.1		
4	TU	0028	1.4	0634	5.0	1240	1.4	1848	5.0
5	W	0057	1.5	0704	4.9	1310	1.6	1919	4.8
6	TH	0127	1.7	0737	4.7	1342	1.7	1954	4.6
7	F	0159	1.9	0816	4.5	1419	1.9	2036	4.3
8	SA	0238	2.1	0906	4.3	1505	2.2	2138	4.1
9	SU	0331	2.3	1018	4.2	1611	2.3	◐ 2306	4.0
10	M	0450	2.5	1146	4.2	1741	2.3		
11	TU	0036	4.2	0620	2.4	1303	4.4	1857	2.1
12	W	0143	4.4	0728	2.1	1403	4.8	1957	1.8
13	TH	0236	4.8	0824	1.7	1453	5.1	2050	1.4
14	F	0322	5.1	0915	1.4	1540	5.4	2139	1.1
15	SA	0406	5.4	1002	1.1	1625	5.6	2226	0.9
16	SU	0450	5.6	1048	0.9	1710	5.8	○ 2310	0.8
17	M	0533	5.6	1133	0.8	1755	5.8	2354	0.8
18	TU	0617	5.6	1217	0.8	1841	5.7		
19	W	0037	0.9	0703	5.5	1301	0.9	1930	5.4
20	TH	0121	1.1	0750	5.3	1347	1.1	2022	5.1
21	F	0207	1.4	0843	5.0	1437	1.4	2122	4.7
22	SA	0259	1.7	0949	4.7	1536	1.8	◑ 2240	4.5
23	SU	0402	2.0	1114	4.5	1651	2.0		
24	M	0003	4.4	0520	2.2	1237	4.5	1815	2.0
25	TU	0116	4.4	0641	2.1	1345	4.6	1927	1.9
26	W	0214	4.6	0748	1.9	1439	4.8	2024	1.7
27	TH	0300	4.8	0842	1.7	1521	4.9	2110	1.5
28	F	0337	4.9	0926	1.6	1556	5.0	2150	1.4
29	SA	0409	5.0	1005	1.5	1627	5.1	2225	1.4
30	SU	0439	5.1	1040	1.4	1656	5.2	● 2258	1.3
31	M	0509	5.2	1112	1.4	1726	5.2	2329	1.4

NOVEMBER

Date	Day	Time	m	Time	m	Time	m	Time	m
1	TU	0540	5.2	1144	1.4	1756	5.1	2359	1.4
2	W	0611	5.1	1215	1.5	1826	5.0		
3	TH	0029	1.6	0642	5.0	1246	1.5	1857	4.8
4	F	0101	1.7	0716	4.9	1320	1.7	1932	4.7
5	SA	0135	1.9	0755	4.7	1357	1.8	2015	4.5
6	SU	0215	2.0	0844	4.6	1442	2.0	2112	4.3
7	M	0305	2.2	0947	4.4	1540	2.2	◐ 2229	4.2
8	TU	0413	2.3	1103	4.4	1656	2.2	2354	4.3
9	W	0534	2.3	1220	4.5	1812	2.1		
10	TH	0106	4.5	0645	2.1	1327	4.8	1918	1.8
11	F	0203	4.8	0747	1.8	1423	5.1	2017	1.5
12	SA	0254	5.1	0843	1.4	1515	5.4	2110	1.2
13	SU	0342	5.4	0935	1.2	1604	5.6	2200	1.0
14	M	0428	5.6	1025	0.9	1652	5.7	○ 2248	0.8
15	TU	0514	5.7	1113	0.8	1739	5.7	2334	0.8
16	W	0601	5.7	1200	0.8	1828	5.6		
17	TH	0019	0.9	0648	5.6	1246	0.9	1917	5.4
18	F	0104	1.1	0737	5.4	1333	1.1	2009	5.1
19	SA	0150	1.4	0830	5.1	1422	1.4	2106	4.8
20	SU	0240	1.7	0930	4.8	1517	1.7	2213	4.5
21	M	0338	1.9	1041	4.6	1622	1.9	◑ 2326	4.4
22	TU	0446	2.1	1156	4.5	1735	2.0		
23	W	0037	4.4	0600	2.2	1306	4.5	1847	2.0
24	TH	0138	4.5	0710	2.1	1405	4.6	1948	1.9
25	F	0227	4.6	0808	1.9	1450	4.7	2037	1.7
26	SA	0307	4.8	0855	1.8	1528	4.8	2119	1.6
27	SU	0341	4.9	0936	1.7	1602	4.9	2156	1.5
28	M	0414	5.0	1013	1.6	1635	5.0	2230	1.5
29	TU	0447	5.1	1047	1.5	1707	5.1	● 2303	1.5
30	W	0520	5.2	1121	1.5	1739	5.0	2336	1.5

DECEMBER

Date	Day	Time	m	Time	m	Time	m	Time	m
1	TH	0554	5.2	1154	1.4	1811	5.0		
2	F	0009	1.5	0627	5.1	1229	1.5	1844	4.9
3	SA	0043	1.6	0703	5.0	1304	1.6	1920	4.8
4	SU	0120	1.7	0742	4.9	1343	1.7	2002	4.6
5	M	0200	1.9	0828	4.8	1426	1.8	2054	4.5
6	TU	0248	2.0	0923	4.7	1517	1.9	2158	4.4
7	W	0346	2.1	1028	4.6	1620	2.0	◐ 2313	4.4
8	TH	0454	2.1	1140	4.6	1731	2.0		
9	F	0027	4.5	0605	2.0	1251	4.8	1840	1.8
10	SA	0132	4.8	0711	1.8	1355	5.0	1944	1.6
11	SU	0229	5.0	0813	1.5	1453	5.2	2043	1.3
12	M	0321	5.3	0912	1.3	1547	5.4	2138	1.1
13	TU	0411	5.5	1006	1.0	1638	5.6	2229	1.0
14	W	0459	5.6	1058	0.9	1727	5.6	○ 2317	0.9
15	TH	0548	5.6	1146	0.8	1816	5.5		
16	F	0004	1.0	0636	5.6	1233	0.9	1904	5.4
17	SA	0049	1.1	0724	5.4	1319	1.1	1952	5.1
18	SU	0134	1.3	0812	5.2	1405	1.3	2041	4.9
19	M	0220	1.5	0902	4.9	1453	1.5	2133	4.6
20	TU	0310	1.8	0956	4.7	1546	1.8	2231	4.4
21	W	0406	2.0	1057	4.5	1646	2.0	◑ 2336	4.3
22	TH	0511	2.2	1205	4.4	1753	2.1		
23	F	0043	4.3	0619	2.2	1313	4.4	1900	2.1
24	SA	0144	4.4	0724	2.1	1412	4.4	1958	2.0
25	SU	0233	4.6	0820	2.0	1459	4.6	2047	1.9
26	M	0315	4.7	0907	1.8	1539	4.7	2128	1.7
27	TU	0353	4.9	0947	1.7	1616	4.8	2206	1.6
28	W	0429	5.0	1025	1.6	1651	4.9	2242	1.5
29	TH	0504	5.1	1102	1.5	1725	5.0	● 2318	1.5
30	F	0539	5.2	1138	1.4	1759	5.0	2354	1.4
31	SA	0614	5.2	1215	1.4	1834	5.0		

Chart Datum: 2·83 metres below IGN Datum
HAT is 6·1 metres above Chart Datum

Great books, now available as apps!

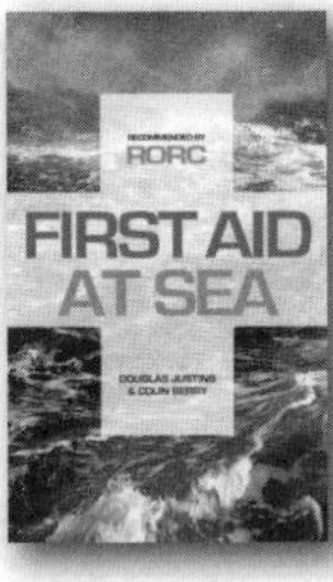

First Aid At Sea
Covering all the medical emergencies likely to occur at sea, this app is designed to be clear and concise about the right treatments, and also features instant access to Basic Life Support techniques.

VHF/DSC Handbook
An invaluable app to have to hand, it covers everything you need to know about radio functions, and features a quiz covering both theory and practice, along with a quick-reference guide to emergency procedure.

Illustrated Boat Dictionary
A unique visual reference, this app features annotated illustrations covering all the topics and terms boaters will need to refer to when abroad, with translations in nine languages, including French, Spanish, Italian, Portuguese and Greek.

International Certificate Of Competence
The ideal reference for any of the 8,000 boaters who take the ICC course every year, this app covers everything within the syllabus and includes a quiz to help students prepare for the exam.

Visit **www.adlardcoles.com** to buy at discount